PROCEEDINGS OF

SIGIR 2·0·0·2

the Twenty-Fifth Annual International ACM SIGIR Conference

on Research and Development in Information Retrieval

August 11 - 15, 2002

Tampere, Finland

UNIVERSITY OF TAMPERE

acm PRESS

Edited by Micheline Beaulieu, Ricardo Baeza-Yates,
Sung Hyon Myaeng and Kalervo Järvelin

Special Issue of the SIGIR Forum

The Association for Computing Machinery
1515 Broadway
New York, New York 10036

ACM ISBN: 1-58113-561-0

Additional copies may be ordered prepaid from:

ACM Order Department
PO Box 11405
New York, NY 10286-1405

Phone: 1-800-342-6626
(US and Canada)
+1-212-626-0500
(all other countries)
Fax: +1-212-944-1318
E-mail: acmhelp@acm.org

ACM Order Number 606020
Printed in the USA

Preface from the Conference Chair

Welcome to the 25th Anniversary of SIGIR, the Conference of Research and Development in Information Retrieval! Welcome, too, to the city of Tampere. SIGIR was last held in Northern Europe ten years ago, 1992, and the Finnish IR community is happy to host SIGIR for the first time in Finland in its silver anniversary year. During its 25 years, SIGIR has established and held its role as the key information retrieval conference, which presents the state of the art and latest developments to the entire community and beyond. This is also reflected in the record-breaking number of papers, 219, submitted to the conference. The Conference Program Co-Chairs, Micheline Beaulieu, Ricardo Baeza-Yates and Sung Hyon Myaeng therefore had both the pleasure of putting together an excellent program and the challenge of selecting the best among the many excellent contributions.

You are cordially invited to participate fully in this conference, to take advantage of all that the technical program has to offer. There are tutorials, keynote addresses, technical paper sessions, poster and demonstration sessions, and workshops that will advance the state of the art of information retrieval and its applications, and discuss their key issues.

The Program Committee, along with the Workshops Committee (Pia Borlund and Jaana Kekäläinen, Co-Chairs), the Tutorials Committee (Efthimis Efthimiadis, Chair), the Posters Committee (James Allan, Chair), the Mentoring Committee (Peter Anick, Chair), the Best Paper Awards Committee (Donna Harman, Chair), and the Demonstrations Committee (Eija Airio and Mark Sanderson, Co-Chairs), have organized an excellent series of sessions for anyone interested in advancing information retrieval. The Organizing Committee has done its best to ensure a pleasing combination of well-organized logistics and a pleasant social program for the conference.

I want to thank all of the volunteers who have worked hard on these committees to make the conference a success. Particular thanks go to Organizing Committee Chairs, Leena Lahti (Treasurer), Jaana Kekäläinen (Exhibits Chair), Leena Sulonen and Mirja Björk (Registration & Local Arrangements Co-Chairs), Eero Sormunen (Publicity Chair), and Pasi Kytöharju (Information Architect), who have generously expended time and effort to implement the conference program.

This conference is co-sponsored by the ACM SIGIR and the University of Tampere. The joint organization took place in excellent cooperation, therefore thanks to both co-sponsors. We would also like to thank our corporate donors, Alma Media, Nokia, eTampere, Microsoft Research, and TietoEnator, for their generous support for the conference. This support has been essential for the work of the Program Committee (including a program meeting in Sheffield, UK) and conference logistics, while keeping the conference fees moderate. We also thank the Academy of Finland for providing financial security for the conference.

Hoping that every day at our conference has a wonderful silver lining!

Kal Järvelin
Conference Chair
May 2002

Preface from the Program Committee Chairs

It is pleasing to report that on this 25th Anniversary of SIGIR, the Conference of Research and Development on Information Retrieval has attracted a record-breaking number of papers. There were 219 paper submissions with 44 (20%) being accepted, representing the different geographic areas as follows: 25 from the Americas, 12 from Africa and Europe and 7 from Asia and Australasia. In addition out of the 70 posters submitted, 48 have been selected together with 8 tutorials, 6 workshops as well as 13 demonstrations. The contributions in these proceedings represent a diverse and comprehensive coverage of IR research including theoretical models, techniques related to specific tasks (e.g. filtering, summarization, text categorization, clustering), system performance, approaches to query formulation, retrieval in different environments, (e.g. the Web, Arabic language, cross-language and multimedia) as well as evaluative and user based studies.

The selection of quality contributions for the SIGIR conference is dependent on a robust and equitable two tier reviewing process. The PC Chairs and 22 meta reviewers, 2 for each of the 11 topic areas in the call for papers, nominated over 90 first tier reviewers. Each reviewer was manually assigned between 6 and 8 papers by the PC chairs in accordance to reviewers' stated subject expertise and each paper was allocated three reviewers. The role of the meta reviewers was to oversee the process for each of their topic area, by resolving disagreements between reviewers and producing a meta review for each paper drawn from the first tier reviews. The meta review then served as the basis of discussion at the Programme Committee meeting. Meta reviewers were selected for their subject expertise in the different topic areas and attention was also paid to geographic representation and PC Committee experience. All the reviewing was blind with the identification of authors being released only after the selection of papers was completed.

We are indebted to all our colleagues who agreed to act as reviewers and meta reviewers and for their cooperation in meeting the very tight deadlines. We are also grateful to all the authors who submitted papers and in spite of the keen competition continue to do so. We particularly welcomed submissions from related research communities and from novices in the field. Our thanks to Peter Anick and his team who volunteered to act as mentors for authors who needed help and advise on submissions. It is worth noting that out of the 44 papers accepted, half are student papers (at least the first author is a student), an encouraging sign for this growing field of research.

In addition to papers the PC Committee also confirmed the selection of posters, tutorials and workshops. We are grateful to James Allan, Efthimis Eftimiadis and Jaana Kekäläinen and Pia Borlund who were the respective chairs for each of these and to Donna Harman who chaired the best paper awards committee. We also wish to thank Mark Sanderson who took on board the submission software and ensured the smooth running of the reviewing process and Kalervo Jarvelin the conference chair who kept us on our toes.

Finally special thanks to our keynote speakers Keith van Rijsbergen and Kimmo Koskenniemi for agreeing to participate in the celebration of this 25th anniversary conference of SIGIR.

Micheline Beaulieu (Africa and Europe)
Ricardo Baeza-Yates (Americas)
Sung Hyon Myaeng (Asia and Australasia)

May 2002

Table of Contents

SIGIR'02 Conference Organization xii

SIGIR'02 Members of the Program Committee xiv

SIGIR'02 Area Coordinators xvi

SIGIR'02 Tutorials & Workshops xvii

Keynote

- **Landmarks in Information Retrieval: the message out of the bottle** 1
  Keith Van Rijsbergen *(University of Glasgow)*

Session I: Web Information Retrieval

Chair: David Hawking *(Australian National University, Australia)*

- **Impact Transformation: Effective and Efficient Web Retrieval** 3
  V. N. Anh, A. Moffat *(The University of Melbourne)*
- **Analysis of Lexical Signatures for Finding Lost or Related Documents** 11
  S.-T. Park *(The Pennsylvania State University),* D. M. Pennock *(NEC Research Institute),*
  C. L. Giles *(The Pennsylvania State University, NEC Research Institute),*
  R. Krovetz *(The Pennsylvania State University)*
- **Using Sampled Data and Regression to Merge Search Engine Results** 19
  L. Si, J. Callan *(Carnegie Mellon University)*
- **The Importance of Prior Probabilities for Entry Page Search** 27
  W. Kraaij *(TNO TPD),* T. Westerveld, D. Hiemstra *(University of Twente)*

Session II: Information Retrieval Theory

Chair: Bruce Croft *(University of Massachusetts, USA)*

- **Term-Specific Smoothing for the Language Modeling Approach to Information Retrieval: The Importance of a Query Term** 35
  D. Hiemstra *(University of Twente)*
- **Title Language Model for Information Retrieval** 42
  R. Jin, A. G. Hauptmann, C. Zhai *(Carnegie Mellon University)*
- **Two-Stage Language Models for Information Retrieval** 49
  C. Zhai, J. Lafferty *(Carnegie Mellon University)*

Session III: User Studies

Chair: Peter Ingwersen *(Royal School of Library and Information Science, Denmark)*

- **Finding Relevant Documents using Top Ranking Sentences: An Evaluation of Two Alternative Schemes** 57
  R. W. White *(University of Glasgow),* I. Ruthven *(University of Strathclyde),*
  J. M. Jose *(University of Glasgow)*
- **Predicting Category Accesses for a User in a Structured Information Space** 65
  M. Chen, A. S. LaPaugh, J. P. Singh *(Princeton University)*
- **Detecting and Browsing Events in Unstructured Text** 73
  D. A. Smith *(Tufts University)*

Session IVa: Filtering
Chair: Stephen Robertson *(Microsoft Cambridge, UK)*

- **Novelty and Redundancy Detection in Adaptive Filtering** 81
  Y. Zhang, J. Callan, T. Minka *(Carnegie Mellon University)*
- **Improving Realism of Topic Tracking Evaluation** 89
  A. Leuski, J. Allan *(University of Massachusetts)*
- **Bayesian Online Classifiers for Text Classification and Filtering** 97
  K. M. A. Chai *(DSO National Laboratories),* H. T. Ng *(National University of Singapore),*
  H. L. Chieu *(DSO National Laboratories)*

Session IVb: Summarization
Chair: John Tait *(University of Sunderland, UK)*

- **The Use of Unlabeled Data to Improve Supervised Learning for Text Summarization** .. 105
  M.-R. Amini, P. Gallinari *(University of Pierre and Marie Curie)*
- **Generic Summarization and Keyphrase Extraction Using Mutual Reinforcement Principle and Sentence Clustering** 113
  H. Zha *(Pennsylvania State University)*
- **Cross-Document Summarization by Concept Classification** 121
  H. Hardy, N. Shimizu, T. Strzalkowski, L. Ting *(University of Albany, SUNY)*,
  G. B. Wise *(GE Global Research Center),* X. Zhang *(University of Albany, SUNY)*

Session Va: Text Categorization
Chair: David Lewis *(Consultant, USA)*

- **Unsupervised Document Classification using Sequential Information Maximization** ... 129
  N. Slonim, N. Friedman, N. Tishby *(The Hebrew University)*
- **Topic Difference Factor Extraction between Two Document Sets and its Application to Text Categorization** 137
  T. Kawatani *(Hewlett-Packard Laboratories, Japan)*
- **Text Genre Classification with Genre-Revealing and Subject-Revealing Features** 145
  Y.-B. Lee, S. H. Myaeng *(Chugnam National University)*
- **A New Family of Online Algorithms for Category Ranking** 151
  K. Crammer, Y. Singer *(The Hebrew University)*

Session Vb: Cross-language Information Retrieval
Chair: Doug Oard *(University of Maryland, USA)*

- **Comparing Cross-Language Query Expansion Techniques by Degrading Translation Resources** 159
  P. McNamee, J. Mayfield *(The Johns Hopkins University Applied Physics Laboratory)*
- **Statistical Cross-Language Information Retrieval using N-Best Query Translations** 167
  M. Federico, N. Bertoldi *(ITC-irst Centro per la Ricerca Scientifica e Tecnologica)*
- **Cross-Lingual Relevance Models** 175
  V. Lavrenko, M. Choquette, W. B. Croft *(University of Massachusetts)*
- **Resolving Query Translation Ambiguity using a Decaying Co-occurrence Model and Syntactic Dependence Relations** 183
  J. Gao *(Microsoft Research),* J.-Y. Nie *(Université de Montréal),* H. He *(Tianjin University),*
  W. Chen *(Tsinghua University),* M. Zhou *(Microsoft Research)*

Session VIa: Clustering

Chair: Sung Hyon Myeang *(Chungnam National University, Korea)*

- **Document Clustering with Cluster Refinement and Model Selection Capabilities** 191
  X. Liu, Y. Gong, W. Xu *(NEC USA, Inc.)*, S. Zhu *(University of Rochester)*,
- **Document Clustering with Committees** 199
  P. Pantel, D. Lin *(University of Alberta)*
- **Probabilistic Combination of Text Classifiers Using Reliability Indicators: Models and Results** 207
  P. N. Bennett *(Carnegie Mellon University)*, S. T. Dumais, E. Horvitz *(Microsoft Research)*

Session VIb: Efficiency

Chair: Ricardo Baeza-Yates *(University of Chile, Chile)*

- **Efficient Phrase Querying with an Auxiliary Index** 215
  D. Bahle, H. E. Williams, J. Zobel *(RMIT University)*
- **Compression of Inverted Indexes For Fast Query Evaluation** 222
  F. Scholer, H. E. Williams, J. Yiannis, J. Zobel *(RMIT University)*
- **Set-Based Model: A New Approach for Information Retrieval** 230
  B. Pôssas, N. Ziviani, W. Meira Jr., B. Ribeiro-Neto *(Universidade Federal de Minas Gerais)*

Session VIIa: Collaborative Filtering

Chair: Jamie Callan *(Carnegie Mellon University, USA)*

- **Collaborative Filtering with Privacy via Factor Analysis** 238
  J. Canny *(University of California, Berkeley)*
- **Inverted File Search Algorithms for Collaborative Filtering** 246
  R. Cöster *(Stockholm University)*, M. Svensson *(Swedish Institute of Computer Science)*
- **Methods and Metrics for Cold-Start Recommendations** 253
  A. I. Schein, A. Popescul, L. H. Ungar *(University of Pennsylvania)*, D. M. Pennock *(NEC Research Institute)*

Session VIIb: Arabic Information Retrieval

Chair: Carol Peters *(Italian National Research Council, Italy)*

- **Term Selection for Searching Printed Arabic** 261
  K. Darwish, D. W. Oard *(University of Maryland)*
- **Empirical Studies in Strategies for Arabic Retrieval** 269
  J. Xu *(BBN Technologies)*, A. Fraser *(USC/ISI)*, R. Weischedel *(BBN Technologies)*,
- **Improving Stemming for Arabic Information Retrieval: Light Stemming and Co-Occurrence Analysis** 275
  L. S. Larkey *(University of Massachusetts)*, L. Ballesteros *(Mt. Holyoke College)*, M. E. Connell *(University of Massachusetts)*

Session VIII: Queries

Chair: *Amit Singhal (Google, USA)*

- **Automatic Query Refinement using Lexical Affinities with Maximal Information Gain** 283
  D. Carmel, E. Farchi, Y. Petruschka, A. Soffer *(Haifa University)*
- **Web Question Answering: Is More Always Better?** 291
  S. Dumais, M. Banko, E. Brill, J. Lin, A. Ng *(Microsoft Research)*

- **Predicting Query Performance** 299
  S. Cronen-Townsend, Y. Zhou, W. B. Croft *(University of Massachusetts)*
- **Using Part-of-speech Patterns to Reduce Query Ambiguity** 307
  J. Allan, H. Raghavan *(University of Massachusetts)*

Keynote

- **Are human languages an inconvenience or an opportunity for IR?** 315
  K Koskenniemi *(University of Helsinki)*

Session IX: Evaluation

Chair: Karen Sparck Jones *(Cambridge University, UK)*

- **The Effect of Topic Set Size on Retrieval Experiment Error** 316
  E. M. Voorhees *(National Institute of Standards and Technology),* C. Buckley *(Sabir Research, Inc.)*
- **Liberal Relevance Criteria of TREC — Counting on Negligible Documents?** 324
  E. Sormunen *(University of Tampere)*

Session X: Multimedia

Chair: Alan Smeaton *(Dublin City University, Ireland)*

- **Robust Temporal and Spectral Modeling for Query By Melody** 331
  S. Shalev-Shwartz *(Hebrew University),* S. Dubnov *(Ben-Gurion University),*
  N. Friedman, Y. Singer *(The Hebrew University)*
- **Video Retrieval using an MPEG-7 Based Inference Network** 339
  A. Graves, M. Lalmas *(University of London)*

Posters

Using Self-Supervised Word Segmentation in Chinese Information Retrieval 349
F. Peng, X. Huang, D. Schuurmans, N. Cercone *(University of Waterloo),*
S. E. Robertson *(Microsoft Research and City University)*

Automatic Classification in Product Catalogs 351
B. Wolin *(Commerce One Laboratories)*

PageRank, HITS and a Unified Framework for Link Analysis 353
C. Ding, X. He, P. Husbands *(Lawrence Berkeley National Laboratory),*
H. Zha *(Pennslyvania State University),* H. D. Simon *(Lawrence Berkeley National Laboratory)*

Task Orientation in Question Answering 355
V. Murdock, W. B. Croft *(University of Massachusetts)*

Experiments in High-Dimensional Text Categorization 357
F. J. Damerau, T. Zhang, S. M. Weiss, N. Indurkhya *(IBM T.J. Watson Research Center)*

The Relationship Betweem ASK and Relevance Criteria 359
X.-J. Yuan, N. J. Belkin, J.-Y. Kim *(Rutgers University)*

ICA and SOM in Text Document Analysis 361
E. Bingham, J. Kuusisto, K. Lagus *(Helsinki University of Technology)*

Improving Hierarchical Text Classification Using Unlabeled Data 363
V. Boyapati *(Whizbang! Laboratories-Research)*

Do Thumbnail Previews Help Users Make Better Relevance Decisions about Web Search Results? 365
S. Dziadosz, R. Chandrasekar *(Microsoft Corporation)*

Amilcare: Adaptive Information Extraction for Document Annotation 367
F. Ciravegna, A. Dingli, Y. Wilks, D. Petrelli *(University of Sheffield)*

The Impact of Corpus Size on Question Answering Performance 369
C. L. A. Clarke, G. V. Cormack, M. Laszlo, T. R. Lynam, E. L. Terra *(University of Waterloo)*

Effective Collection Metasearch in a Hierarchical Environment: Global vs. Localized Retrieval Performance 371
J. G. Conrad *(TLR Research & Development),* C. Yang *(Oracle Corporation),* J. S. Claussen *(West Group)*

Experimenting with Graphical User Interfaces for Structured Document Retrieval 373
F. Crestani *(University of Strathclyde),* P. de la Fuente, J. Vegas *(Universidad de Valladolid)*

The Web Retrieval Task and its Evaluation in the Third NTCIR Workshop 375
K. Eguchi, K. Oyama, E. Ishida, K. Kuriyama, N. Kando *(National Institute of Informatics)*

How Many Bits are Needed to Store Term Frequencies? 377
M. Franz, J. S. McCarley *(IBM T.J. Watson Research Center)*

Non-Linear Reading for a Structured Web Indexation 379
M. Géry *(MRIM Group)*

Document Normalization Revisited 381
A. Chowdhury *(America Online),* M. C. McCabe *(U.S. Government),*
D. Grossman, O. Frieder *(Illinois Institute of Technology)*

User-Centered Interface Design for Cross-Language Information Retrieval 383
P. Hansen *(Swedish Institute of Computer Science),* D. Petrelli *(University of Sheffield),*
J. Karlgren *(Swedish Institute of Computer Science),* M. Beaulieu, M. Sanderson *(University of Sheffield)*

Implementation of Relevance Feedback for Content-based Music Retrieval Based on User Preferences 385
K. Hoashi *(KDDI R&D Laboratories, Inc.),* E. Zeitler *(Uppsala University),*
N. Inoue *(KDDI R&D Laboratories, Inc.)*

Spatial Information Retrieval and Geographical Ontologies—An Overview of the SPIRIT Project 387
C. B. Jones *(Cardiff University),* R. Purves *(University of Zurich),* A. Ruas *(IGN Paris),*
M. Sanderson *(University of Sheffield),* M. Sester *(University of Hannover),*
M. van Kreveld *(Utrecht University),* R. Weibel *(University of Zurich)*

A Visualisation Tool for Topic Tracking Analysis and Development 389
G. J. F. Jones, S. M. Gabb *(University of Exeter)*

A New Method of Parameter Estimation for Multinomial Naive Bayes Text Classifiers 391
S.-B. Kim, H.-C. Rim *(Korea University),* H.-S. Lim *(Chonan University)*

Study of Category Score Algorithms for k-NN Classifier 393
H. Kou *(University of Versailles),* G. Gardarin *(e-XMLMedia)*

Higher Precision for Two-Word Queries 395
K. L. Kwok *(Queens College, CUNY)*

The Boomerang Effect: Retrieving Scientific Documents via the Network of References and Citations 397
B. Larsen, P. Ingwersen *(Royal School of Library and Information Science)*

A Logistic Regression Approach to Distributed IR 399
R. R. Larson *(University of California, Berkeley)*

Automatic Metadata Generation & Evaluation 401
E. D. Liddy, E. Allen, S. Harwell, S. Corieri, O. Yilmazel, N. E. Ozgencil, A. Diekema, N. McCracken, J. Silverstein *(Syracuse University)*, S. Sutton *(University of Washington)*

A Critical Examination of TDT's Cost Function 403
R. Manmatha, A. Feng, J. Allan *(University of Massachusetts)*

Converting On-Line Bilingual Dictionaries from Human-Readable to Machine-Readable Form 405
J. Mayfield, P. McNamee *(The Johns Hopkins University Applied Physics Laboratory)*

Modeling (In)Variability of Human Judgments for Text Summarization 407
T. Nomoto *(National Institute of Japanese Literature)*,
Y. Matsumoto *(Nara Institute of Science and Technology)*

Content-based Music Indexing and Organization 409
A. Rauber *(Vienna University of Technology)*,
E. Pampalk *(Austrian Research Institute for Artificial Intelligence)*,
D. Merkl *(Vienna University of Technology)*

Relative and Absolute Term Selection Criteria: A Comparative Study for English and Japanese IR 411
T. Sakai *(Toshiba Corporate R & D Center)*, S. E. Robertson *(Microsoft Research Ltd. and City University)*

Experiments on Data Fusion Using Headline Information 413
X. M. Shou, M. Sanderson *(University of Sheffield)*,

Building Thematic Lexical Resources by Term Categorization 415
A. Lavelli, B. Magnini *(ITC-irst)*, F. Sebastiani *(Istituto di Elaborazione dell'Informazione)*

Topic Structure Modeling 417
D. A. Evans, J. G. Shanahan, V. Sheftel *(Clairvoyance Corporation)*

Language Model for IR Using Collection Information 419
R. Jin, L. Si, A. G. Hauptmann, J. Callan *(Carnegie Mellon University)*

Automatic Evaluation of World Wide Web Search Services 421
A. Chowdhury *(America Online Inc.)*, I. Soboroff *(National Institute of Standards and Technology)*

Does WT10g Look Like the Web? 423
I. Soboroff *(National Institute of Standards and Technology)*

Biterm Language Models for Document Retrieval 425
M. Srikanth, R. Srihari *(State University of New York at Buffalo)*

Selecting Indexing Strings using Adaptation 427
Y. Takeda, K. Umemura *(Toyohashi University of Technology)*

Error Correction in a Chinese OCR Test Collection 429
Y.-H. Tseng *(Fu Jen Catholic University)*

User Interface Effects in Past Batch Versus User Experiments 431
A. Turpin *(Curtin University of Technology)*, W. Hersh *(Oregon Health & Sciences University)*

K-tree/forest: Efficient Indexes for Boolean Queries 433
R. M. Verma, S. Behl *(University of Houston)*

Example-Based Phrase Translation in Chinese-English CLIR 435
B. Wang, X. Cheng, S. Bai *(Chinese Academy of Sciences)*

Probabilistic Multimedia Retrieval 437
T. Westerveld *(University of Twente)*

Chinese Keyword Extraction Based on Max-duplicated Strings of the Documents 439
W. Yang, X. Li *(Tsinghua University)*

A Hierarchical Approach: Query Large Music Database by Acoustic Input 441
Y. Feng, Y. Zhuang, Y. Pan *(Zhejiang University)*

Correlating Multilingual Documents via Bipartite Graph Modeling 443
H. Zha, X. Ji *(The Pennsylvania State University)*

Demos

A System Using Implicit Feedback and Top Ranking Sentences to Help Users Find Relevant Web Documents 446
R. W. White, J. M. Jose *(University of Glasgow)*, I. Ruthven *(University of Strathclyde)*

Indexing, Searching, and Retrieving of Recorded Live Presentations with the AOF (Authoring on the Fly) Search Engine 447
W. Hürst *(Universität Freiburg)*

UTACLIR -- General Query Translation Framework for Several Language Pairs 448
H. Keskustalo, T. Hedlund, E. Airio *(University of Tampere)*

HyREX: Hyper-media Retrieval Engine for XML 449
N. Fuhr, N. Gövert, K. Großjohann *(University of Dortmund)*

Query Performance Analyser — a Web-Based Tool for IR Research and Instruction 450
E. Sormunen, S. Hokkanen, P. Kangaslampi, P. Pyy, B. Sepponen *(University of Tampere)*

Adaptive Information Extraction for Document Annotation in Amilcare 451
F. Ciravegna, A. Dingli, Y. Wilks, D. Petrelli *(University of Sheffield)*

ExWrap: Semi-Automatic Wrapper Generation by Example 452
B. Schmitt, M. Christoffel, J. Schneider *(University of Karlsruhe)*

Souvenir: Flexible Note-Taking Tool to Pinpoint and Share Media Highlights 453
A. Spoerri *(Rutgers University)*

Hierarchical Approach to Term Suggestion Device 454
H. Joho, M. Sanderson, M. Beaulieu *(University of Sheffield)*

Translingual Vocabulary Mappings for Multilingual Information Access 455
F. C. Gey, A. Chen, M. Buckland, R. Larson *(University of California, Berkeley)*

GS Textplorer — Adaptive Framework for Information Retrieval 456
J. Honkela, V. H. Tuulos *(Gurusoft, Inc.)*

CuTeX: A System for Extracting Data from Text Tables 457
H. Davulcu, S. Mukherjee, A. Seth, I. V. Ramakrishnan *(SUNY Stony Brook)*

YellowPager: A Tool for Ontology-based Mining of Service Directories from Web Sources 458
P. Choudhari, H. Davulcu, A. Joglekar, A. More, S. Mukherjee, S. Patil,
I. V. Ramakrishnan *(SUNY Stony Brook)*

Author Index 459

Conference Organization

Organizing Committee

General Chair: Kalervo Järvelin, University of Tampere, Finland

Treasurer: Leena Lahti, University of Tampere, Finland

Exhibits Chair: Jaana Kekäläinen, University of Tampere, Finland

Corporate Sponsors Chair: Kalervo Järvelin, University of Tampere, Finland

Registration & Local Arrangements Chairs: Leena Sulonen, Tampere Conference Service Ltd, Finland
Mirja Björk, University of Tampere, Finland

Publicity Chair: Eero Sormunen, University of Tampere, Finland

Information Architect: Pasi Kytöharju, University of Tampere, Finland

Program Committee

Program Chairs: Micheline Beaulieu, University of Sheffield, UK (Africa/Europe)
Ricardo Baeza-Yates, University of Chile, Chile (Americas)
Sung Hyon Myaeng, Chungnam National University, Korea (Asia/Oceania)

Posters Chair: James Allan, University of Massachusetts, USA

Tutorials Chair: Efthimis N. Efthimiadis, University of Washington, USA

Workshops Co-Chairs: Jaana Kekäläinen, University of Tampere, Finland
Pia Borlund, Royal School of Library and Information Science, Denmark

Demonstrations Co-Chairs: Eija Airio, University of Tampere, Finland
Mark Sanderson, University of Sheffield, UK

Mentoring Chair: Peter Anick, AltaVista, USA

Tutorials Committee

Chair: Efthimis N. Efthimiadis, University of Washington, USA
Giorgio Brajnik, University of Udine, Italy
Susan Dumais, Microsoft Research, USA
Susan Gauch, University of Kansas, USA
Donna Harman, NIST, USA
Elizabeth Liddy, Syracuse University, USA
Noriko Kando, National Institute of Informatics, Japan
Edie Rasmussen, University of Pittsburgh, USA
Alan Smeaton, Dublin City University, Ireland
Emmanuel Yannakoudakis, Athens University of Economics and Business, Greece

Awards Committee

Chair: Donna Harman, National Institute of Standards and Technology, USA
Gordon Cormack, University of Waterloo, Canada
David Hull, Clairvoyance Corp., USA
Wessel Kraaij, TNO TPD, The Netherlans
Kui Lam Kwok, Queens College, City University of New York, USA
Mehran Sahami, Stanford University, USA
Hinrich Schuetze, Novation Biosciences, USA
Howard Turtle, Cogitech, USA

Mentors

Chair: Peter Anick, AltaVista,USA
James Allan, University of Massachusetts, USA
Andrei Broder, AltaVista, USA
Eric Brown, IBM T. J. Watson Research Center, USA
David Eichmann, University of Iowa, USA
James French, University of Virginia, USA
Norbert Fuhr, Dortmund University, Germany
Susan Gauch, University of Kansas, USA
Warren Greiff, MITRE Corporation, USA
Marti Hearst, UC Berkeley, USA
William Hersh, Oregon Health & Science University, USA
Mun-Kew Leong, Laboratories for Information Technology, Singapore
Vibhu Mittal, Google/Carnegie-Mellon University, USA
Paul Over, NIST, USA
Jay Ponte, The MITRE Corporation, USA
Amanda Spink, Pennsylvania State University, USA
Ross Wilkinson, CSIRO, Australia
Jinxi Xu, BBN Technologies, USA

Members of Regional Program Committees
(Reviewers)

Helena Ahonen-Myka, University of Helsinki, Finland
James Allan, University of Massachusetts, USA
Peter Anick, AltaVista, USA
Javed Aslam, Dartmouth College, USA
Peter Bailey, The Australian National University, Australia
Roberto Basili, University of Roma, Italy
Branimir Boguraev, IBM Research Watson, USA
Gloria Bordogna, ITIM-CNR, Italy
Pia Borlund, Royal School of Library and Information Science, Denmark
Mohand Boughanem, IRIT Toulouse, France
Martin Braschler, Eurospider Information Technology AG, Switzerland
Andrei Broder, AltaVista, USA
Eric Brown, IBM Research Watson, USA
Jack Bryar, NewsEdge, USA
Chris Buckley, Sabir Research, Inc, USA
Jamie Carbonell, Carnegie Mellon University, USA
Soumen Chakrabarti, IIT Bombay, India
Kuang-hua Chen, National Taiwan University, Taiwan
Lee-Feng Chien, Academia Sinica, Taiwan
Gordon Cormack, University of Waterloo, Canada
Nick Craswell, CSIRO, Australia
Fabio Crestani, University of Strathclyde, UK
Tamas Doszkocs, National Library of Medicine, USA
Susan Dumais, Microsoft Research, USA
John Eakins, University of Northumbria, UK
Efthimis N. Efthimiadis, University of Washington, USA
David Eichmann, University of Iowa, USA
Charles Elkan, CSE, UCSD, USA
Jim French, University of Virginia, USA
Ayse Goker, Robert Gordon University, UK
Julio Gonzalo, UNED, Spain
Sanda Harabagiu, University of Texas, USA
Marti Hearst, University of California, Berkeley, USA
Monika Henzinger, Google Inc, USA
Mark Hepple, University of Sheffield, UK
Djoerd Hiemstra, University of Twente, Netherlands
Christian Jacquemin, LIMSI-CNRS, France
Thorsten Joachims, Cornell University, USA
Gareth Jones, University of Exeter, UK
Michael Jordan, University of California, Berkeley, USA
Noriko Kando, National Institute of Informatics, Japan
Martin Kaszkiel, Google Inc., USA
Christopher Khoo, Nanyang Technological Univ., Singapore
Mounia Lalmas, Queen Mary University of London, UK
Joon Ho Lee, Soongsil University, Korea
Liz Liddy, Syracuse University, USA
Xia Lin, Drexel University, USA
Robert Luk, Hong Kong Polytechnic University, Hong Kong
Yoelle Maarek, IBM Research Lab in Haifa, Israel
David Madigan, Rutgers University, USA
Stephane Marchand-Maillet, Univ. of Geneva, Switzerland
James Mayfield, The Johns Hopkins University Applied Physics Laboratory, USA
Scott McCarley, IBM TJ Watson Research Center, USA
Sharon McDonald, University of Sunderland, UK
Bernard Merialdo, Institut EURECOM, France
Mandar Mitra, Indian Statistical Institute, Kolkata (Calcutta), India
Alistair Moffat, University of Melbourne, Australia
Thomas Montgomery, Ford Motor Company, USA
Josiane Mothe, IRIT - Institut de Recherche en Informatique de Toulouse, France
Craig Nevill-Manning, Google, Inc, USA
Hwee Tou Ng, DSO National Laboratories, Singapore
Jian-Yun Nie, University of Montreal, Canada
Kamal Nigam, WhizBang Labs, USA
Chris Paice, Lancaster University
Gabriella Pasi, ITIM – CNR, Italy
Ari Pirkola, University of Tampere, Finland
Berthier Ribeiro-Neto, Federal Univ. of Minas Gerais, Brazil
John Riedl, University of Minnesota , USA
Ellen Riloff, University of Utah, USA
Knut Magne Risvik, Fast Search & Transfer ASA
Airi Salminen, University of Jyväskylä, Finland
Mark Sanderson, University of Sheffield, UK
Jacques Savoy, University of Neuchatel, Switzerland
John Smith, IBM Research Watson, USA
Barry Smyth, University College Dublin, Ireland
Ian Soboroff, NIST, USA
Eero Sormunen, University of Tampere, Finland
Padmini Srinivasan, University of Iowa, USA
Ulrich Thiel, Fraunhofer IPSI, Germany
Takenobu Tokunaga, Tokyo Institute of Technology, Japan
Hans Uzkoreit, DFKI Saarbruecken & Saarland Univ., Germany
Arjen de Vries, CWI, The Netherlands
Ross Wilkinson, CSIRO, Australia
Hugh Williams, RMIT University, Australia
Jinxi Xu, BBN Technologies/Verizon, USA
Yiming Yang, Carnegie Mellon University, USA
Byoung-Tak Zhang, Seoul National University, Korea
Andrew Zisserman, University of Oxford, UK
Nivio Ziviani, Federal University of Minas Gerais, Brazil

Additional Reviewers

Einat Amitay, IBM Research Lab, Haifa, Israel
Vo Ngoc Anh, University of Melbourne, Australia
Claudine Badue, Federal Univ. of Minas Gerais, Brazil
Pavel Calado, Federal University Minas Gerais, Brazil
David Carmel, IBM Research Lab, Haifa, Israel
Jonathan Edwards, University of Northumbria at Newcastle, UK
Rodrigo Fonseca, Federal Univ. of Minas Gerais, Brazil
Tim Gollins, Government Communication Headquarters, Cheltenham, UK
Carlos Goncalves, Federal Univ. of Minas Gerais, Brazil
David Harper, Robert Gordon University, UK
Fang Huang, University of Sheffield, UK
Hideo Hojo, University of Sheffield, UK
Giles Hubert, IRIT, Toulouse, France
Gabriella Kazai, Queen Mary University of London, UK
Owen de Kretser, University of Melbourne, Australia
Victor Lavrenko, University of Massachusetts, USA
Anton Leuski, University of Massachusetts, USA
Paul McNamee, Johns Hopkins University, USA
Wagner Meira Jr., Federal Univ. of Minas Gerais, Brazil
Alessandro Moschitti, University of Rome 2, Italy
Edleno Moura, Akwan Information Technologies, Brazil
Apostol Natsev, IBM, USA
Rani Nelken, IBM Research Lab, Haifa, Israel
Daniella Petrelli, University of Sheffield, UK
Jeremy Pickens, University of Massachusetts, USA
Bruno Possas, Federal University of Minas Gerais, Brazil
Falk Scholer, RMIT, Australia
Vaughan Shanks, RMIT, Australia
Aya Soffer, IBM Research Lab, Haifa, Israel
Andy Song, RMIT, Australia
Saied Tahaghoghi, RMIT, Australia
Belle Tseng, IBM, USA
Theodora Tsikrika, Queen Mary University of London, UK
Ricardo Ueda, University of Sao Paulo, Brazil
Sandra Uitdenbogerd, RMIT, Australia
Phil Vines, RMIT, Australia
Peter Willett, University of Sheffield, UK
Bianca Zadrozny, UCSD, USA
Fabio Zanzotto, University of Rome 2, Italy

Poster Reviewers

James Allan (chair), University of Massachusetts, USA
Jay Aslam, Dartmouth College, USA
Nick Belkin, Rutgers University, USA
Peter Bruza, Distributed Systems Technology Centre, Australia
Nick Craswell, CSIRO, Australia
Anne Diekema, Syracuse University, USA
Martin Franz, IBM, USA
Susan Gauch, University of Kansas, USA
Lee Giles, Pennsylvania State University, USA
Donna Harman, NIST, USA
Jim Jansen, Pennsylvania State University, USA
Hongyan Jing, Lucent Technologies, USA
Leah Larkey, University of Massachusetts, USA
Victor Lavrenko, University of Massachusetts, USA
Anton Leuski, University of Massachusetts, USA
Gina-Anne Levow, University of Chicago, USA
Elizabeth D. Liddy, Syracuse University, USA
Robert Luk, Hong Kong Polytechnic University, Hong Kong
R Manmatha, University of Massachusetts, USA
Filippo Menczer, University of Iowa, USA
Mark Montague, Dartmouth College, USA
Gonzalo Navarro, Universidad de Chile, Chile
Gautam Pant, University of Iowa, USA
Jeremy Pickens, University of Massachusetts, USA
Jay Ponte, The MITRE Corporation, USA
Dragomir Radev, University of Michigan, USA
Dawei Song, Distributed Systems Technology Centre, Australia
Amanda Spink, Pennsylvania State University, USA
Ross Wilkinson, CSIRO, Australia
Jinxi Xu, BBN Technologies, USA

Area Coordinators
(Metareviewers)

Formal Models, Language Models, Search Strategies, Fusion/Combination	Keith van Rijsbergen, University of Glasgow, UK Bruce Croft, University of Massachusetts, USA
Machine Learning for IR, Text Data Mining, Clustering, Text Categorization	William Cohen, WhizBang Labs, USA David Lewis, Independent Consultant, USA David Hull, Clairvoyance Corporation, USA
Cross-lingual Retrieval, Multilingual Retrieval, Machine Translation for IR	Doug Oard, University of Maryland, USA Carol Peters, CNR Pisa, Italy
Topic Detection and Tracking, Content-Based Filtering, Collaborative Filtering, Agents	Stephen Robertson, Microsoft Cambridge, UK Jamie Callan, Carnegie Mellon University, USA
Web IR, Citation and Link Analysis, XML and Metadata, Digital Libraries	David Hawking, Australian National University, Australia Amit Singhal, Google, USA
Video and Image Access, Audio and Speech Retrieval, Music Retrieval	Alan Smeaton, Dublin City University, Ireland Mark Maybury, MITRE, USA
Text Representation and Indexing, Information Extraction, Lexical Acquisition, Natural Language Processing for IR	Tomek Strzalkowski, SUNY University at Albany, USA Rob Gaizauskas, University of Sheffield, UK
Performance, Compression, Scalability, Architectures, Distributed Search, Mobile Applications	Justin Zobel, RMIT University, Australia Charlie Clarke, University of Waterloo, Canada
Interfaces, Visualization, Interactive IR, User Models, User Studies	Peter Ingwersen, Royal School of Library and Information Science, Denmark Gary Marchionini, University of North Carolina - Chapel Hill, USA
Summarization, Question Answering	John Tait, University of Sunderland, UK Jussi Karlgren, Swedish Institute of Computer Science, Sweden
Evaluation, Building Test Collections, Experimental Design and Metrics	Ellen Voorhees, NIST, USA Karen Sparck Jones, Cambridge University, UK

Pre-Conference Tutorials

- **Search from the Web to the Enterprise: Issues, Solutions, Evaluation**
  By K. Bharat, A. Broder, D. Hawking & V. Raghavan (Google, IBM, CSIRO, Verity)

- **Machine Learning for Text Classification Applications**
  By David D. Lewis, (Independent Consultant, Chicago)

- **Genomic Information Retrieval**
  By Hugh E. Williams & Peter M. Smooker (RMIT University, Melbourne)

- **Designing Information Architectures for Search**
  By Marti A. Hearst (University of California, Berkeley)

- **Support Vector and Kernel Methods**
  By Thorsten Joachims (Cornell University)

- **Practical Guidelines for Multimedia Information Retrieval**
  By Dulce B. Ponceleon & Savitha Srinivasan (IBM Almaden Research Center)

Post-Conference Workshops

- **Cross-language Information Retrieval: A Research Roadmap**
  Organizers: F. Gey, N. Kando, C. Peters

- **Information Retrieval and OCR: From Converting Content to Grasping Meaning**
  Organizers: J. Callan, D. Grossman, A. Hauptmann, P. Kantor

- **Mathematical/Formal Methods in information Retrieval**
  Organizers: S. Dominich, M. Lalmas, K. van Rijsbergen

- **Mobile Personal Information Retrieval**
  Organizers: M.-K. Leong, G. Loudon

- **Operational Text Classification Systems**
  Organizers: S. Dumais, D. Lewis, T. Montgomery, I. Moulinier, F. Sebastiani

- **XML and Information Retrieval**
  Organizers: R. Baeza-Yates, N. Fuhr, Y. Maarek

SIGIR 2002 WAS SUPPORTED BY

Main Corporate Donor:

ALMA | MEDIA

Major Corporate Donor:

NOKIA

Connecting People

Corporate Donors:

Microsoft Research

TietoEnator
Building the Information Society

eTampere

Academy of Finland

Opening Keynote Address

Landmarks in Information Retrieval: The message out of the bottle

C.J. 'Keith' van Rijsbergen
University of Glasgow

For many years I have wanted to give a talk like this: look back on our subject, identify the high (and perhaps low) points, consider what worked, what did not work, and speculate a little about the future. Now that I at last have the opportunity to give such a talk the realisation has dawned just how difficult it is to do justice to the topic. The only way out of this difficulty for me is to emphasise that this is a personal account, based on my involvement with the field since 1968, and that errors of omission and commission are not deliberate but simply due to lack of knowledge and time on my part.

To talk of landmarks is easy but to say what they are in IR is not. They come in various shapes and sizes: events, publications, experiment, ideas, etc. In the course of this presentation I shall be judiciously mixing all of these. However, the emphasis will be on ideas and their subsequent modelling and testing through experimentation. The interaction between theory and experiment will be a recurring theme. I will try and associate these developments with key individuals, thereby running the risk of ignoring some; I apologise for this in advance.

The pre-history of our subject can be traced back to the work in the 19th century, perhaps even further, but I will pick it up at the middle of the last century (20th) starting with the work of Robert Fairthorne and Vannevar Bush. This early work emphasised the possibility of using mechanical devices to store and retrieve information. Of course the foundations of modern information retrieval were properly laid after 1945 with the pioneering work of Cleverdon, Salton, Sparck Jones, and others. This work gave rise to a strong experimental methodology for the evaluation of theoretical ideas, which has been sustained to this day. It has been a hallmark of IR research that theory is developed in the context of experimentation. There is no doubt that many disciplines are jealous of the success of TREC.

IR research has thrown up a number of successful models. These models have been based on some, often unstated, assumptions (or hypotheses). I will attempt to identify some of the underlying ideas, giving credit where is due, that led to the fruitful exploration of retrieval models. This will include system-oriented as well as user-oriented ideas, especially those concerned with the measurement of retrieval performance.

IR has been fortunate in that the subject has grown through the active collaboration between computer scientists and information scientists. This has meant that traditional approaches to the storage and retrieval of information emanating from the library world, for example, have always strongly influenced new developments. This tension between manual (human) processes and automatic computer-based processes in IR has always been fruitful. Even now with the evolution of ideas about meta-data and ontologies needed to enhance web retrieval, the debate about controlled vocabularies versus automatic indexing is relevant. Issues of scalability are particularly important here.

One of the strengths that have emerged in our subject is that many of our models can be deployed independently of medium or modality. For example, retrieving images or audio sequences can be handled in ways similar to those used to retrieve text data. This has proved to be great boon to IR. The development of web retrieval through the deployment of various kinds of search engines has been based on the considerable early work in IR although detailing the specific influences is not easy. It is clear that the underlying mathematical and statistical models in IR have been ubiquitous in application. The extreme difficulty encountered in making NLP work for IR forced researchers to develop powerful statistical, probabilistic, geometrical, and logical techniques to complement linguistic ones. This is now paying off because of the similar difficulties encountered in other media.

Having given some account of how we got here I will spend a little time talking about where we go from here, how *do* we extract the message from the bottle?

SIGIR'02, August 11-15, 2002, Tampere, Finland.
ACM 1-58113-561-0/02/0008.

Impact Transformation: Effective and Efficient Web Retrieval

Vo Ngoc Anh Alistair Moffat
Department of Computer Science and Software Engineering
The University of Melbourne
Victoria 3010, Australia
www.cs.mu.oz.au/~{vo,alistair}

ABSTRACT

We extend the applicability of impact transformation, which is a technique for adjusting the term weights assigned to documents so as to boost the effectiveness of retrieval when short queries are applied to large document collections. In conjunction with techniques called quantization and thresholding, impact transformation allows improved query execution rates compared to traditional vector-space similarity computations, as the number of arithmetic operations can be reduced. The transformation also facilitates a new dynamic query pruning heuristic. We give results based upon the *TREC* web data that show the combination of these various techniques to yield highly competitive retrieval, in terms of both effectiveness and efficiency, for both short and long queries.

Categories and Subject Descriptors

E.5 [**Files**]: Organization/structure; H.3.1 [**Information Storage and Retrieval**]: Content Analysis and Indexing–*indexing methods*; H.3.2 [**Information Storage and Retrieval**]: Information Storage–*file organization*; H.3.3 [**Information Storage and Retrieval**]: Information Search and Retrieval–*search process*; H.3.4 [**Information Storage and Retrieval**]: Systems and Software–*performance evaluation (efficiency and effectiveness)*

General Terms

Algorithms, performance, experimentation

Keywords

Web searching, dynamic pruning, index compression

1. INTRODUCTION

The *vector space model* is widely used in information retrieval systems [Salton, 1989], and is usually evaluated via a pre-computed *index*. In the index, each distinct term t that appears in the document collection has an associated *document frequency*, denoted f_t, which indicates the number of documents it appears in. In addition, each term is associated with an *inverted list* of *pointers* $\langle d, f_{d,t}\rangle$ recording that term t appears in document d a total of $f_{d,t}$ times. Finally, each document d has a corresponding value W_d associated with it, its *document length*, which is calculated as a function of f_t and $f_{d,t}$ for the terms t in that document. Generally speaking, W_d is greater when a document becomes physically longer, but W_d might depend also upon the relative scarcity of the terms.

To evaluate a query q against a database, the vector space model calculates a score $S_{q,d}$ between q and each document d of the database, and presents the r documents with the highest scores. For our purposes here, $S_{q,d}$ is best described as

$$S_{q,d} = \sum_{t\in q\cap d} w_{d,t} \cdot w_{q,t} \tag{1}$$

where the values of $w_{d,t}$ and $w_{q,t}$, called *term impacts* or simply *impacts*, represent the degree of "importance" of term t in document d and query q respectively. The *document impacts* and *query impacts* are both derived from the original statistical values f_t, $f_{d,t}$, $f_{q,t}$, W_d, and W_q, where $f_{q,t}$ is the frequency of the term in the query, and W_q the length of the query.

There is a large number of different ways in which $w_{d,t}$ and $w_{q,t}$ might be calculated. Nevertheless, in the notation of Equation 1, $w_{d,t}$ is usually a product of functions monotonic in three factors: the document-term frequency $f_{d,t}$; the *inverse document frequency* $1/f_t$; and the *inverse document length* $1/W_d$. Mechanisms which combine the first two factors have historically been referred to as being "*TF · IDF*" [Salton, 1989]. The third factor comprising $w_{d,t}$, which we similarly denote by *IDL*, acts to penalize long documents, which tend to have large values for $\sum$ *TF · IDF*. Four possible cosine measures, labelled *Cos.1* to *Cos.4* for later reference, are detailed in Table 1.

In this paper we extend the applicability of *impact transformation*, a technique for adjusting the quantities $w_{d,t}$ and $w_{q,t}$ used in the computation of $S_{q,d}$, and show that it significantly boosts retrieval effectiveness when short queries are applied to large document collections. In conjunction with two other techniques we call *quantization* and *thresholding*, impact normalization also allows improved query execution rates compared to traditional implementations of Equation 1. These claims are based upon experiments carried out using the *TREC* web data.

2. SHORT QUERIES

Generally speaking, a short query cannot be expected to result in better effectiveness than a longer one with the same meaning. But given the preponderance of short queries to most web search engines, it is important to discover any techniques that might improve effectiveness for web-style retrieval.

To explore short queries, we employ the subcollection *Web1* of

Metrics	Factors of $w_{d,t}$			Factors of $w_{q,t}$		
Label	*TF*	*IDF*	*IDL*	*TF*	*IDF*	*IQL*
Cos.1	$f_{d,t}$	$\log_e(1+N/f_t)$	$1/W_d$	$f_{q,t}$	$\log_e(1+N/f_t)$	$1/W_q$
Cos.2	$f_{d,t}$	1	$1/W_d$	$f_{q,t}$	$\log_e(1+f^m/f_t)$	$1/W_q$
Cos.3	$1+\log_e f_{d,t}$	1	$1/W_d$	$1+\log_e f_{q,t}$	$\log_e(1+f^m/f_t)$	$1/W_q$
Cos.4	$1+\log_e f_{d,t}$	1	$1/((1-s)+s\cdot W_d/W^a)$	$1+\log_e f_{q,t}$	$\log_e(1+f^m/f_t)$	1

Table 1: Elements of some similarity heuristics based upon the cosine rule. Here W_x (x can be either d or q) is the document or query length, calculated as $\sqrt{(\sum_{t\in d}(TF \cdot IDF)^2)}$; W^a is the average value of W_d over the documents in the collection; f^m is the greatest value of f_t in the collection; and s is a constant with typical value of 0.7 [Singhal et al., 1996]. Each of the four listed similarity computations is calculated as the summation over the terms common to the query and the document of the product of the six listed factors.

Impact value, % of maximum	Impact rank, % of maximum
0.1	2.49
1.0	25.12
10.0	93.65

Table 2: Distribution of impacts of *Cos.1* in *Web1*. In *Web1* there are approximately 101 million document impact values, varying between $L = 4.6 \times 10^{-6}$ and $U = 1.0$.

the *wt10g* collection, distributed as Disk One by *NIST* as part of the *TREC-9* process [Hawking, 2001]. The collection consists of 383,429 documents, and has a total size of 2,458 MB. For this collection we have 50 *TREC-9* topics labelled 451–500, with, on average, 14.2 identified relevant documents per topic.

Four sets of queries from these topics are used throughout our presentation: *Real*, *Short*, *Long*, and *Manual*, of average length 3.5, 3.5, 17.3, and 3.2 terms respectively. Each of the *Real* queries is taken directly from the "title" field of the corresponding *TREC* topic. This set contains a non-trivial number of spelling mistakes, and the *Short* queries are derived from the corresponding *Real* by correcting all spelling errors. Each of the *Long* queries is produced by concatenating the "title" and the "description" fields of the corresponding topic, with no further editing. The final set of queries, *Manual*, was compiled manually from all three fields of the *TREC* topics (that is, "title", "description", and "narrative"). These queries should be regarded as representing a good statement of information need compiled by an experienced querier.

We started with an investigation of cosine measure *Cos.1*, and analyzed the distribution of document impacts of the collection *Web1* as follows. First, the maximal value, U, of the impacts was calculated, and a series of breakpoints whose value represent a portion of U introduced. Then, for each breakpoint, the number of impacts that are smaller was counted. Some values extracted from the cumulative distribution are listed in Table 2.

Table 2 shows that the majority of the impacts have low values. For example, half of the impact values are smaller than 2.07% of the maximum impact value U recorded for this collection.

The skewed impact distribution does not create any particular problems for long queries. The score for a document is given by the sum of the impacts of the query terms, and with many query terms, it is unlikely that any single term dominates the scoring. Indeed, some retrieval systems even discard low (or potentially low) impacts to improve retrieval efficiency, without loss on effectiveness. For example, Persin et al. [1996] set a lower-bound threshold for the product $TF \cdot IDF$ and discard all values below that threshold. In earlier work, Harman and Candela [1990] explored a similar pruning strategy that discarded whole terms, based upon their

Number of terms in query	Number of queries in set	Number of matching terms	Prob. of retrieval %	Prob. of relevance %
2	16	2	25.6	75.3
		1	74.4	24.7
3	12	3	15.0	37.2
		2	44.2	43.9
		1	40.8	18.9
4	12	4	5.8	19.7
		3	16.7	39.8
		2	25.0	32.1
		1	52.5	8.4

Table 3: Probability of a document being retrieved compared with its probability of being relevant, categorized as a function of the number of terms in the query. The number in the column "Prob. of retrieval" shows the distribution of query terms in the documents retrieved from *Web1* using *Cos.1* and query set *Manual*, while the number in the column "Prob. of relevance" shows the distribution of the query terms in the documents judged to be relevant by the *TREC* assessors.

weight. Moffat and Zobel [1996] subsequently found that pruning based upon *IDF* alone did adversely impact retrieval effectiveness, and that terms with low *IDF* values should be allowed to permute the selected documents, even if they did not select any.

The skew distribution of impact values does create problems for short queries. In a query of only two terms we would normally suppose that both are reasonably important to the person who posed the query, and that they would prefer answer documents that contain both to answer documents that contain only one. But most vector-space mechanisms allow a single occurrence of a term in a short document to have the same impact as multiple occurrences of both (or either) terms in a longer document.

To draw out this effect, we analyzed the *TREC* relevance judgments supplied for *Web1*, and compared them to the documents selected by *Cos.1* for those queries. First, the queries were partitioned into sets determined by the number of terms in each, with the single query containing only one term and nine other queries containing five or more terms excluded from further consideration. The remaining 40 queries were then classified by their length, ranging from two terms (16 queries) to four terms (12 queries). For the queries in each group the relevance judgments were used to determine the set of relevant documents from the collection, and those documents examined to determine the distribution of query terms in them. From this data it was then possible to calculate the probability that an "average" relevant document has a certain number of terms in common with its corresponding query.

We also separately processed the queries using *Cos.1*, retrieving the top 10 ranked documents for each query. These top 10 documents were then examined in the same way, to calculate the probability that an "average" returned document matches its query in a certain number of terms.

Table 3 summarizes the outcomes. Function *Cos.1* consistently over-emphasizes documents containing only a subset of the query terms. It is clear that the shorter the query, the more important it is that all query terms be present in answer documents if retrieval effectiveness is to be maximized.

3. NORMALIZATION

Table 3 suggests that some kind of impact normalization may be beneficial. As we noted in our earlier work [Anh and Moffat, 2002], normalization is not a new technique in information retrieval, and there have been several successful attempts to normalize individual factors of the impacts. The employment of *IDL* mentioned in Section 1 is one example, and there are many others. For example, the `Smart` system normalizes the *TF* factor to $(0.5 + 0.5 \cdot \mathit{TF}/\max(\mathit{TF}))$ as a replacement for both *TF* and *IDL* factors. A similar approach is employed by the `INQUERY` system with a slightly different formula of $(0.4 + 0.6 \cdot \mathit{TF}/\max(\mathit{TF}))$ [Callan et al., 1992, Salton and Buckley, 1988]. These normalizations turn out to be in favor of long documents [Broglio et al., 1994]. The `Okapi` system uses another kind of normalization, based on the length in bytes of documents [Robertson et al., 1994].

In a similar vein, Singhal et al. [1996] exploit the fact that the cosine measure tends to be biased in favor of short documents. In an experiment similar to that reported in Table 3, they compare the probability of documents being relevant with the probability of them being retrieved, for different groups of documents parameterized by document length W_d, and conclude that it would be better to normalize W_d by boosting low values. They then introduce *pivoted document length normalization* - a technique in which the document length W_d is normalized to $(1 - s) + s \cdot W_d/W^a$. This is the technique listed as *Cos.4* in Table 1. The constant s is the *slope*, with the typical value of 0.7, largely independent of the collection; and so a document of raw length close to zero will have pivoted length of $1 - s$; a document of length W^a will have a pivoted length of 1; and a document of length $2W^a$ has pivoted length $1 + s$. It is interesting to note that the normalizations of the `Smart` and the `INQUERY` systems can also be classified as pivoted, with the pivot point taken as the maximum value f^m.

What remains is to normalize the product of the three factors - to generate impact values that meet our needs. We seek to reduce the dominance of large impact values, and allow modest ones to exert a greater influence over the outcome of a similarity computation. A pivoted impact normalization scheme was thus an obvious candidate for experiments [Anh and Moffat, 2002]. All the impacts, except the maximum value, are promoted to (relatively) higher values. The smaller the impact, the greater the relative gain. But a weakness of this direct approach is that even the smallest impact values also get promoted, in contravention of the usual expectation that very small impacts have no value in retrieval.

An alternative normalization scheme preserves the highest and lowest impacts, but adjusts the values between them to "smooth" the distribution. We thus examine normalization schemes that have two (or more) fixpoints: one at the minimum impact value L, and the other at the maximum impact value U. Based on our conjecture as to why the cosine measure performs relatively poorly on short queries, the criteria for choosing a normalization scheme can be described as:

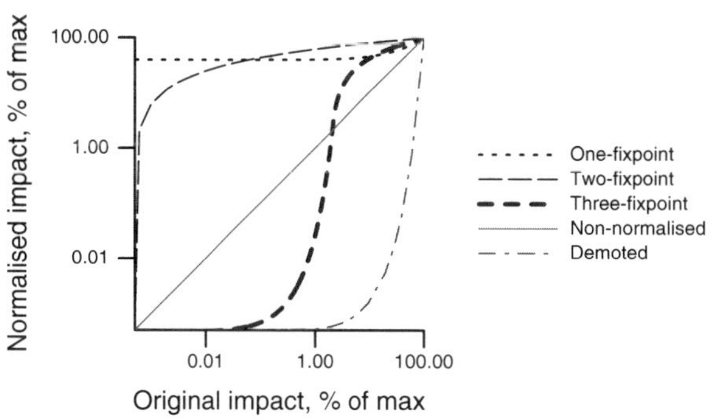

Figure 1: Behavior of different normalization methods in comparison with original impacts. The graph shows the transformations used for *Web1* and the cosine measure *Cos.1*.

1. *Major criterion*: For the bulk of the impact curve, the scheme needs to allocate large relative increase to the small values, and small relative increases to large impacts.

2. *Minor criterion*: The very small impacts have no value in deciding the similarity score, and the normalization scheme should not make them important. That is, the normalization mapping must not boost very small values by large relative amounts. One way of attaining this objective is to simply exclude very small impact values from the set adjusted by the mapping.

There are a number of candidate normalization schemes that satisfy one or both of these criteria. Our experiments examine the following four mappings:

1. *One-fixpoint promotion*: Based upon the precedent set by pivoting [Singhal et al., 1996], this mapping fixes the maximum impact U as the only invariant. It satisfies the major criterion, but does not satisfy the minor one. Instead, the smallest value gets the greatest relative increase. For this method a slope value s must be chosen.

2. *Two-fixpoint promotion*: All impacts are increased, with higher relative increments for small values, but with the minimum and maximum values unchanged. The function we have chosen for this mapping takes an impact of w to a normalized impact of $L + L \cdot \log_B(w/L)$, where $B = (U/L)^{L/(U-L)}$. This scheme satisfies the major criterion and is better than the one-fixpoint scheme with regard to the minor criterion.

3. *Two-fixpoint demotion*: For completeness, we also experimented with this counter-intuitive approach. Impact value w is mapped to $L \cdot B^{(w-L)/L}$, where all constants are as defined earlier. This mechanism flagrantly violates the major criterion, but sits well the minor criterion.

4. *Three-fixpoint adjustment*: The minimum, maximum, and median are all kept invariant. Values to the left of the median value are demoted, and values to the right are promoted. The intention with this proposal is to better balance the two criteria - especially since the median impact is (Table 2) close to the minimum value L. However, since the concept of "very small" in the minor criterion is somewhat vague, the choice of the median as the transition point is rather arbitrary.

Method	*Recp.Rank*	*Prec.10*	*Av.Prec*
Standard	100	100	100
Demoted	82	89	91
One-fixpoint	109	112	106
Two-fixpoint	**115**	**124**	114
Three-fixpoint	114	118	**116**

Table 4: Relative effectiveness of normalized impacts, as a percentage of the unnormalized score for each of three underlying effectiveness metrics, using *Cos.4* on *Web1* with query set *Manual*. The raw *Recp.Rank*, *Prec.10* and *Av.Prec* (over 1,000 retrieved documents) values are 0.4491, 0.2106 and 0.1978 respectively.

The behavior of these four normalization methods is illustrated in Figure 1 for the *Web1* collection and *Cos.1*. In this graph, one-fixpoint promotion has been plotted with a slope of $s = 0.6$.

To see the effect of normalization upon retrieval effectiveness, experiments were conducted for *Cos.1* over database *Web1* with *Manual* queries, measured using three standard metrics: the average reciprocal rank of the first relevant document; the average precision at 10 documents retrieved; and the average value of the number calculated by averaging the precision at each relevant document in the collection with $r = 1{,}000$ documents retrieved (with precision assumed to be zero for relevant documents not retrieved). The one-fixpoint normalization was done with slope $s = 0.6$ - the value which gave the best performance in preliminary experiments.

The results, standardized to a score of 100% for unnormalized retrieval, are shown in Table 4. In general, they confirm our hypothesis. The two-fixpoint and three-fixpoint methods outperform the one-fixed point method in all of the three evaluation metrics. However, in contrast to our expectation, the three-fixpoint was not superior to the two-fixpoint mechanism. It is possible that the three-fixpoint adjustment might give better performance with a different choice of transition point. But whether a general rule can be devised for determining the transition point is a non-trivial question, and we prefer to avoid such data-driven tuning. The important point to note is that all three positive normalizations are markedly better than the unnormalized computation, while the *demotion* adjustment degrades retrieval effectiveness.

In the remaining experiments below we make use of two-fixpoint promotion. This choice frees us from choosing the slope for pivoted normalization, and from calculating the median (or other value) for the three-fixpoint adjustment.

4. QUANTIZATION

One obvious way to implement normalization is to pre-calculate all impacts, map them to their normalized equivalent, and store the mapped values in the inverted lists instead of the within-document frequencies $f_{d,t}$. While superficially attractive, this adds considerably to the cost of storing the inverted file, as each impact value will require rather more storage space than the few bits required by each $f_{d,t}$ value in a conventional inverted file [Witten et al., 1999].

On the other hand, there is no basis for requiring that the normalized impact values be stored exactly - indeed, they have already been substantially modified - and the use of approximate values is plausible. Anh et al. [2001] represent the impact values by b-bit integers, for some small value b. Anh et al. further *impact sort* each of the index lists, so that the terms of greatest impact appear first. When b-bit quantities are used, sorting partitions each index list into 2^b segments. Within each segment the pointers are all of equal approximate impact value, and are sorted by document number. This structure allows query processing to proceed from the most to least important pointers in each list; furthermore, processing of the index lists corresponding to different query terms can be interleaved so that processing proceeds from the most to the least important pointers across all query lists. During querying, as index list segments are selected for processing, the inverse transformation is applied, and (approximate) inverse impact scores accumulated as similarity contributions. The availability of this pointer ordering means that pruning techniques of the type described by Persin et al. [1996] can be applied.

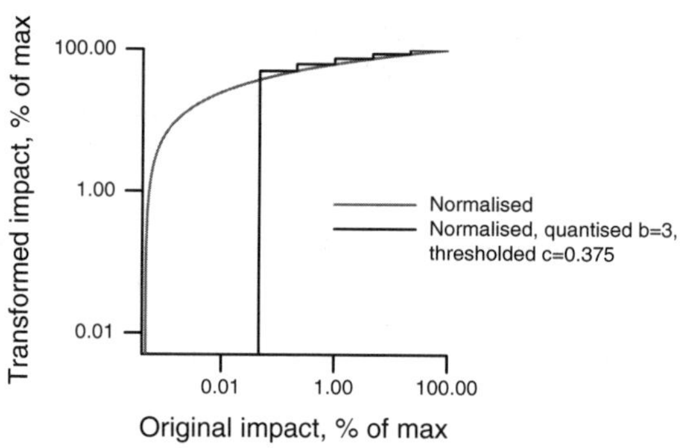

Figure 2: Final end-to-end transformation of document impacts, showing normalization using two-fixpoint promotion, quantization using $b = 3$, and then thresholding with $c = 0.375$, for the *Web1* collection and *Cos.1*.

A useful consequence of normalization followed by quantization is that the quantized integer values can be used to represent the impacts themselves without referring back to either the original or normalized impacts [Anh and Moffat, 2002]. That is, the b-bit integer (in raw terms, a value x between 0 and $2^b - 1$) associated with each index pointer can be directly used in the similarity computation (by using $x+1$ as a value between 1 and 2^b), avoiding the need for an inverse mapping to be calculated during query evaluation.

In our earlier work [Anh and Moffat, 2002] we also experimented with an alternative inverse quantization in which the values in the range 0 to $2^b - 1$ were used directly, without adding one. When the quantized value is $x = 0$, direct use of the quantized impact value is tantamount to not including that $w_{d,t}$ in the similarity computation. While this may seem somewhat counter-intuitive in comparison to the $x + 1$ scheme, there is negligible difference in retrieval effectiveness between the two [Anh and Moffat, 2002]. And if the index is only going to be used for ranked queries and not Boolean queries, then the low-weight entries for which the quantized normalized impact is zero can be eliminated from the index, a definite point in favor of the use of x rather than $x + 1$. Soffer et al. [2001] have similarly observed that low-impact entries need not be stored in an index that is required to support only ranked queries.

Here we extend our previous development, and, as a further component in the chain of impact conversions, *threshold* the quantized values, discarding any that fall below a cutoff fraction c. For example, when $c = 0.25$, any quantized impact values less than or equal to 0.25×2^b are discarded, and deemed to be irrelevant. A threshold of $c = 0$ includes all pointers in the index and in the similarity scores calculated using the index. Figure 2 shows the combined effect of normalization, quantization with $b = 3$, and thresholding with $c = 0.375$. Of the eight impact buckets created when $b = 3$, three of them (0.375×8) are considered to be of no subsequent value.

c	Pointers %	Space %
0.000	100	100
0.125	98	97
0.250	95	92
0.375	78	71
0.500	36	31
0.625	7	6

Table 5: Index (inverted file only) savings arising from thresholding of quantized impact values with $b = 5$, for the *Web1* collection, and *Cos.4*. The baseline of 100% corresponds to an index containing 100,997,559 pointers and occupying 128 MB. A "standard" document-sorted index containing the same number of $\langle d, f_{d,t} \rangle$ pointers requires 87% of the space of that baseline.

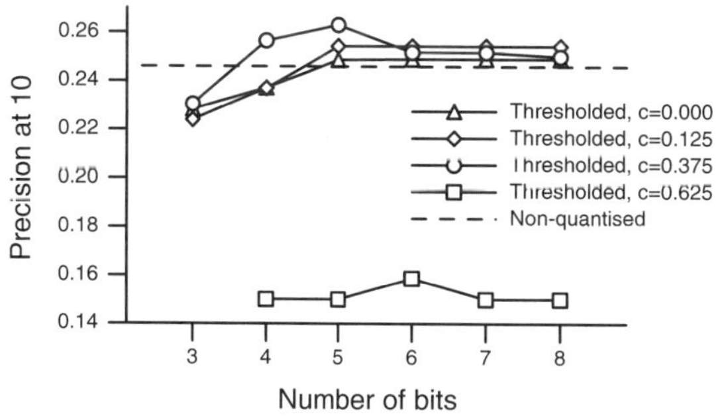

Figure 3: Impact of two-fixpoint promotion, quantization, and thresholding, *Cos.4* applied to *Web1* and using the *Manual* query set. The lines show the *Prec.10* for different values of the threshold c, at different values of the quantization parameter b.

Thresholding serves a number of purposes. First, if the pointers whose thresholded impact scores are zero are not stored in the index, then index space can be saved. Second, it makes the two-fixpoint normalization closer to the three-fixpoint method, by better meeting the minor criterion listed earlier. And finally, the use of these thresholded and quantized values automatically provides pruning during query processing, increasing the throughput of the underlying retrieval engine.

Before examining retrieval effectiveness, a comment on index organization is appropriate. The transformed (that is, normalized, then quantized, then thresholded) impacts are topologically similar to the approximate impacts used by Anh et al. [2001], and we adopt their suggestions with regard to index organization and query processing. The inverted lists are impact-sorted, so each inverted list consists of (as many as) 2^b blocks, all of the pointers in each block having the same transformed impact. Within each block, the pointers are ordered by document number d, and represented using codes based upon document differences [Witten et al., 1999].

Anh et al. [2001] also describe a fast ranking algorithm for use in conjunction with impact-sorted indexes, and that process can be applied here. But now we do not need their table-driven inverse quantization technique, as the quantized impacts are used directly as surrogates for the normalized values. The result of adding normalization is that greatly improved retrieval effectiveness is possible. In particular, Anh et al. were unable to obtain retrieval effectiveness better than the formulations described in Table 1, and introduced quantization solely to obtain faster execution.

Table 5 shows the extent of the index space savings if zero-impact pointers are not stored in an impact-sorted index. The baseline, of 100%, refers to a complete impact-sorted index in which all pointers are stored, index lists have (as many as) 2^b segments, and the usual compression regimes are used.

Retrieval effectiveness (precision at 10 documents, *Prec.10*) as a function of b, the number of bits used for the quantization, and c, the threshold value, is plotted in Figure 3. In these experiments we use *Cos.4* applied to *Web1* and the *Manual* query set. The dotted horizontal line indicates the retrieval effectiveness attained by an implementation of *Cos.4*, with impact normalization, but no quantization, and no thresholding.

The other lines correspond to different values of threshold c, and are plotted as a function of the quantization parameter b. The normalized impacts are quantized into linear buckets over the interval $(1, 2^b)$ by division and truncation. That is, a normalized impact w is quantized to the value $1 + \lfloor 2^b \cdot w/(U + \epsilon) \rfloor$, where ϵ is used to force the value U to map to 2^b.

As can be seen in Figure 3, use of an over-aggressive threshold adversely affects retrieval effectiveness, irrespective of the fidelity of the quantization approximation. But a modest amount of thresholding is fine, and the best retrieval (in this particular experiment) is achieved when normalized impacts less than $c = 0.375$ are discarded. This evidence supports the comment made earlier about the possibility of the three-fixpoint normalization scheme being able to give better effectiveness performance if a good transition point can be determined.

Also pleasing is that good effectiveness can be obtained even with relatively small values of b. Use of $b = 4$ appears to be sufficient - which, in conjunction with $c = 0.375$, means that just 10 non-zero impact levels are actually influencing the similarity computation. However, for safety, in all subsequent experiments we err on the side of caution and use $b = 5$ and $c = 0.375$, and thus carry 20 different non-zero impact values. As was shown in Table 5, quantization and thresholding decrease rather than increase the cost of storing the index.

A further comment in connection with Figure 3 is warranted: while effectiveness appears somewhat volatile in terms of both b and c, the volatility shown is the usual variance associated with *Prec.10* as an effectiveness metric [Buckley and Voorhees, 2000], and not a fundamental instability caused by our transformations. If we plot average precision (*Av.Prec*) instead, the curves converge to horizontal lines quickly from around $b = 4$.

5. LONG QUERIES AND PRUNING

The techniques presented so far in this paper were developed specifically for short queries, and might lead to problems on long queries, since a relatively modest number of originally small impacts might dominate over a smaller number of originally high impacts. That is, we expected the combined transformation to reduce retrieval effectiveness for long queries.

Hybrid schemes, in which the amount of transformation applied is governed by the length of the query, or schemes which moderate the aggressiveness of the transformation during query evaluation, are thus a possible compromise. When dealing with long queries we must also verify that pruning techniques - under which some or all of the pointers in all or some of the index lists are not processed - can be applied without loss of retrieval effectiveness, since it is the use of pruning that allows long queries to be executed quickly.

A range of pruning techniques have been described [Buckley and Lewit, 1985, Harman and Candela, 1990, Moffat and Zobel, 1996, Persin et al., 1996, Turtle and Flood, 1995, Wong and Lee,

1993]. Care is needed when applying these techniques to impacts, as it might be inappropriate to only apply pruning to low impact pointers. For example, in the database *Web1*, with the quantization $b = 5$, we observed that even very common words like "the" and "a" can result in transformed impact scores of 32 in some documents, while other rarer words do not.

The following approaches were explored during our investigation into pruning strategies for long queries.

1. *None*: The long queries are processed in exactly the same way as employed for the short queries, using all components of the transformation.

2. *Quit*: We process only the three most important terms of the queries where three is the integer approximation of the average length of the short queries experimented with in the previous two sections, and importance is assessed via *IDF*. The motivation is clear: the transformation works well with short queries, so a policy of turning long queries into short queries by selecting just a few important terms might be possible. This strategy is similar to the *Quit* approach of Moffat and Zobel [1996], but the rationale for considering it quite different. Moffat and Zobel focus on saving memory, and are willing to accept some loss of effectiveness to do so. The strategy proposed here results from a desire to improve effectiveness.

3. *Continue*: The *Quit* method might be too greedy, as it ignores a non-trivial number of query terms. To ameliorate this, we continue to process query terms after the stopping condition is met. The strategy is similar to *Quit*, but after fully processing three terms, the pointers in the remaining inverted lists are used to update the existing non-zero accumulators, with no new accumulators being generated. This policy is closely related to the *Continue* mechanism of Moffat and Zobel [1996].

4. *BlockFine*: We apply a penalty to each amount added to an accumulator, that is, to the product of transformed document and query impacts. The penalty *TakeAway* is initially zero, and is increased by one after each equi-impact block from one of the inverted lists is processed. As each block is processed, the value *TakeAway* is subtracted from each score contribution - which is a product of the b-bit value and the integer-quantized $w_{q,t}$ value - before it is added to the accumulator for that document. Since the blocks of all inverted lists are processed in decreasing order of the impact products, this strategy partially reverses the normalization process - normalization shortens the relative gaps between moderately-high impacts values, whereas the *BlockFine* heuristic increases it. The *BlockFine* scheme also provides automatic query pruning, since at some point in the computation the score contributions will become zero and processing can be stopped.

5. *TermFine*: A penalty is again levied against score contributions, but is now incremented for each term, rather than for each block. That is, for a particular inverted list, the *TakeAway* is a constant, determined by the *IDF* for that term, and used whenever an equi-impact block from that term's inverted list is being processed. This strategy is a hybrid between *Quit* and *BlockFine*.

Table 6 shows the effect of pruning on effectiveness for *Cos.4* and three of the query sets. In the table, the figures shown for *Short* and *Manual* (which are both short queries) allow a check to be made that the pruning methods do not now harm the effectiveness on short queries.

Pruning	Average precision (*Av.Prec*)			
	Standard	Transformed impacts		
method	*Long*	*Long*	*Short*	*Manual*
None	0.2133	0.1743	0.2014	0.2413
Quit (Q)	0.1696	0.2055	0.2137	0.2288
Continue (C)	**0.2168**	0.1994	0.2158	0.2431
TermFine (T)	N/A	0.2349	0.2231	**0.2586**
BlockFine (B)	N/A	0.2237	0.2155	0.2442
T&B	N/A	0.2421	**0.2239**	0.2565
C&T&B	N/A	**0.2467**	**0.2239**	0.2567

Table 6: Effectiveness of different pruning strategies for *Long* queries, for collection *Web1* and heuristic *Cos.4*. The "Standard" column shows the effect of pruning on untransformed impacts, calculated using a document-sorted index. Other columns show the effectiveness obtained by two-fixpoint promoted normalization, quantization with $b = 5$, and thresholding with $c = 0.375$, calculated using an impact-sorted index. The last line of the heading shows the query set used to obtain the results in that column. The *Quit* and *Continue* strategies alway select three terms for full processing. The "Standard" mechanism, with no pruning, and no impact transformation, obtains average precision of 0.1951 and 0.2106 respectively on query sets *Short* and *Manual*.

A number of interesting comparisons can be made in the table. First, consider the *Long* queries. As was expected, the direct application of impact transformation to these queries reduces the effectiveness markedly, with *Av.Prec* dropping from 0.2133 to 0.1743. The *Quit* and *Continue* strategies work well, but they still cannot raise *Av.Prec* back to the baseline. Changing to the *TermFine* and *BlockFine* strategies (and especially *TermFine*) succeeds in doing that; with the combination of *Continue*, *TermFine* and *BlockFine* (C&T&B) doing the best job. In this latter combination, blocks are processed in decreasing order of effect upon the similarity score. Three terms are identified at the beginning of the query, and blocks from those three terms still have the penalty arising from the block ordering applied, but no additional penalty for the term ordering. The block ordering is calculated taking into account the term penalty. Blocks from any remaining terms have both penalties applied. Processing stops when it becomes impossible for any further positive score contributions to arise; and finally, only blocks from the three terms with the highest *IDF* factors are permitted to create accumulators.

Second, consider the two columns showing the performance of the transformed impact, plus pruning, on the short queries. Pruning using the C&T&B strategy again performs well, with further gains in retrieval effectiveness achieved. Note that the *Manual* queries consistently generate better retrieval results than do the other two formulations, and that clever index processing is not yet a substitute for the use of human intelligence in selecting terms. Nevertheless, compared to the untransformed standard evaluation on the same queries, a considerable gain in retrieval effectiveness is again achieved through the use of impact transformation.

Third, comparing the effect of *Quit* and *Continue* for the original and transformed impacts, it is clear that if very fast processing is required, then impact transformation greatly improves the effectiveness of the *Quit* strategy, which is the fastest to evaluate.

Finally, the table shows that the best compromise between effectiveness and efficiency is probably the combined C&T&B mechanism, that is, the combination of *Continue*, *TermFine* and *BlockFine* strategies. It not only offers the highest improvement in effectiveness for both long and short queries, but also promises a high level of pruning.

6. LARGE COLLECTIONS

The results of the previous sections - experiments on the database *Web1* using *Cos.4* - have made it clear that impact transformation is a powerful technique, and achieves a good improvement in retrieval effectiveness. One obvious question to address is the extent to which this improved performance applies to other vector space formulations and other databases.

To compare our technique with other recent mechanisms, we use the collection *wt10g*, which was generated for the 2001 *TREC-9* experiments [Hawking, 2001]. It contains about 10 GB of data, with approximately 1.69 million documents, and is accompanied by 50 *TREC* topics (451-500), with on average 47.2 identified relevant documents per topic. We continue to employ the same query formulations already discussed: *Short*, *Real* and *Long*.

This collection is large, and to process it we distribute it across a number of computers, with a separate index built for each subcollection. There are many different paradigms for distributed querying (see, for example, Badue et al. [2001]). In our experiments the documents of the collection are randomly distributed to create approximately equal-sized homogeneous subcollections, one subcollection for each machine. Each query is processed separately against each subcollection using the local index, and then a global result listing compiled using the local scores. By assigning documents randomly to collections, we expect minimal degradation of retrieval effectiveness compared to a monolithic system.

In the experiments described below, we employ a Beowulf-style cluster of 16 computers, each an 800 MHz Intel Pentium III with 256 MB RAM, local hard disk of 40 GB, running Debian GNU Linux. The cluster is served by a 933 MHz Intel Pentium III with 1 GB RAM, a 9 GB SCSI disk for system needs, and four 36 GB SCSI disks in a RAID-5 configuration for data..

Figure 4 dispels any concern as to the applicability of the transformation and pruning heuristics described in this paper. For the four different vector space formulations given in Table 1, the graph shows the "before" and "after" effect of impact normalization, quantization, thresholding, and pruning. There is a marked improvement in all four mechanisms, no matter how effectiveness is measured.

Of particular interest is that impact transformation works especially well for the measures with originally low effectiveness capturing the gains of pivoting, plus more. Furthermore, even for *Cos.4*, the gain is still considerable, with an improvement in *Recp.Rank*, *Prec.10* and *Av.Prec* of approximately 26%, 23% and 43% respectively when "before" and "after" are compared.

Figure 5 shows a further before and after comparison for short queries, compared to the best values scored by the groups that participated in *TREC-9*. In *TREC-9* the participants were permitted to submit results from a number of different runs. To plot the graphs, the best run in terms of *Av.Prec* for each group was isolated; and then the best run for each group in terms of *Prec.10*. (For most groups these were not the same run.) After ordering these runs, the "before" and "after" effectiveness scores for our implementation of *Cos.4* were inserted, where "after" corresponds to the full gamut of improvements we have devised, as reported for the smaller collection in the last line of Table 6. The *TREC-9* results are nominally based upon use of the raw queries, the set we denote as *Real*, but that some participating groups undertook an automatic spell-correction process [Hawking, 2001], which equates (subject to the foibles of the automatic correction process) to our manually-corrected set *Short*. Spelling correction clearly makes a difference to retrieval effectiveness, and when the *Short* queries are used, our results rank highly. Note also that the majority of the *TREC 9* systems rely on additional techniques like relevance feedback and multiple term indexing, heuristics that we are yet to implement or consider.

On the *Long* queries we obtain a similar improvement. Our *Av.Prec* score of 0.2683 for the *wt10g* collection is highly competitive, and again involves no techniques apart from those described in this paper.

As a last comment, we acknowledge that we have made use of the *TREC-9* results after the event, and that this is subtly different from participating "blind". We have avoided any iterative training, and have eschewed tunable parameters, but even so, some feedback effect from the known relevance judgments seems inevitable. We hope to remedy this deficiency in the 2002 *TREC* round.

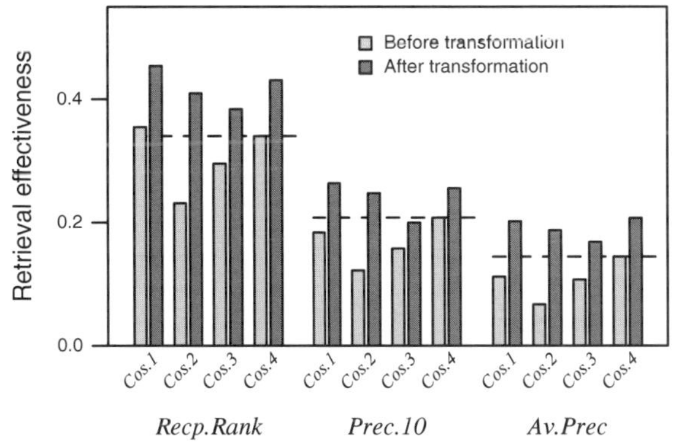

Figure 4: Effect of transformation on different cosine measures for the collection *wt10g* and *Real* queries. The collection is distributed on 16 computers with local indexes. The dotted horizontal lines show the "before transformation" effectiveness attained by *Cos.4* for that metric. The "after" results refer to two-fixpoint impact normalization using $b = 5$ and $c = 0.375$, and execution-time query pruning using the combined C&T&B mechanism. No pruning is applied in the "before" computation.

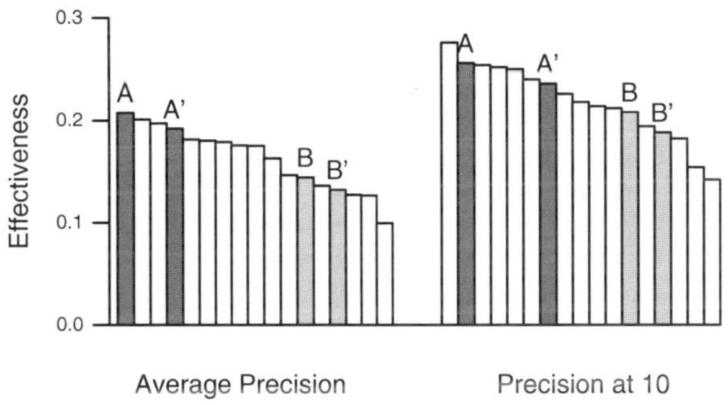

Figure 5: Relative performance of before and after transformation in comparison with scores of the top 13 *TREC-9* groups. The bars labelled B and B′ represent the "before", or no-transformation situation, for the queries *Short* and *Real* respectively; the bars labelled A and A′ show the "after" situation, using transformation and pruning. The *TREC-9* figures are taken from Hawking [2001].

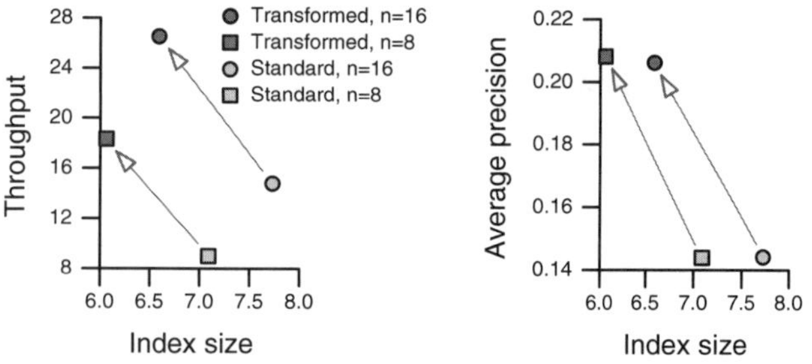

Figure 6: Effectiveness and efficiency of "before" and "after" retrieval systems, using *Cos.4*, for the database *wt10g*, distributed over $n = 8$ and $n = 16$ computers. The horizontal axis in each graph measures index size, as a percentage of the source data size. Here, the index includes all inverted files and all vocabularies and the like. The left-hand graph shows the throughput of the systems, in queries per second, based on the elapsed time to process a set of $10{,}000$ randomly generated queries (average length 3.3 terms, with no stopwords chosen as query terms) on otherwise idle machines. The right-hand graph shows *Av.Prec*, using the *Short* queries. In this assessment each subcollection returns $r_i = 1{,}000$ document identifiers from its subcollection. The n lists are then merged by the server to identify the top $r = 1{,}000$ documents overall.

7. SPEED

Figure 6 summarizes the effectiveness and efficiency of our implementation. Space limits preclude a full description of the distributed structures used, and we must of necessity be terse. To quantify effectiveness, we make use of "before" and "after" results using *Cos.4* and *wt10g*. To quantify index space, we measure the combined size of all index-related files, as a fraction of the original source text. And to quantify retrieval speed, we measured the elapsed time on our distributed system to identify the top $r = 1{,}000$ documents (but not fetch or present those documents) for a synthetic query load containing $10{,}000$ non-stopword queries, averaging 3.3 terms each. The conclusion is very clear - compared to our previous best results for impact-based retrieval computation [Anh et al., 2001], impact transformation and query-time pruning allow improved query throughput at reduced index cost, and also improved precision at reduced index cost. That is, we have increased both effectiveness and efficiency.

Acknowledgment. This work was supported by the Victorian Partnership for Advanced Computing. The query set *Manual* was created by Owen de Kretser (University of Melbourne).

References

V. N. Anh, O. de Kretser, and A. Moffat. Vector-space ranking with effective early termination. In W. B. Croft, D. J. Harper, D. H. Kraft, and J. Zobel, editors, *Proc. 24th Annual International ACM SIGIR Conference on Research and Development in Information Retrieval*, pages 35-42, New Orleans, LA, September 2001. ACM Press, New York.

V. N. Anh and A. Moffat. Improved retrieval effectiveness through impact transformation. In X. Zhou, editor, *Proc. 13th Australasian Database Conference*, pages 41-48, Melbourne, Australia, January 2002.

C. Badue, R. Baeza-Yates, B. Ribeiro-Neto, and N. Ziviani. Distributed query processing using partitioned inverted files. In G. Navarro, editor, *Proc. Symp. String Processing and Information Retrieval*, pages 10-20, Laguna de San Rafael, Chile, November 2001.

J. Broglio, J. P. Callan, W. B. Croft, and D. W. Nachbar. Document retrieval and routing using the INQUERY system. In D. K. Harman, editor, *Proc. Third Text REtrieval Conference (TREC-3)*, pages 29-38, Gaithersburg, MD, April 1994. NIST Special Publication 500-225.

C. Buckley and A. F. Lewit. Optimization of inverted vector searches. In *Proc. 8th Annual International ACM SIGIR Conference on Research and Development in Information Retrieval*, pages 97-110, Montreal, Canada, June 1985. ACM Press, New York.

C. Buckley and E. M. Voorhees. Evaluating evaluation measure stability. In N. J. Belkin, P. Ingwersen, and M.-K. Leong, editors, *Proc. 23rd Annual International ACM SIGIR Conference on Research and Development in Information Retrieval*, pages 33-40, Athens, Greece, September 2000. ACM Press, New York.

J. P. Callan, W. B. Croft, and S. M. Harding. The INQUERY retrieval system. In *Proc. Int. Conf. Database and Expert Systems Applications*, pages 78-83, Dublin, Ireland, 1992. Boole Press.

D. K. Harman and G. Candela. Retrieving records from a gigabyte of text on a minicomputer using statistical ranking. *Journal of the American Society for Information Science*, 41(8):581-589, August 1990.

D. Hawking. Overview of the TREC-9 Web Track. In E. M. Voorhees and D. K. Harman, editors, *The Ninth Text REtrieval Conference (TREC-9)*, pages 87-102, Gaithersburg, MD, November 2001. NIST Special Publication 500-249.

A. Moffat and J. Zobel. Self-indexing inverted files for fast text retrieval. *ACM Transactions on Information Systems*, 14(4):349-379, October 1996.

M. Persin, J. Zobel, and R. Sacks-Davis. Filtered document retrieval with frequency-sorted indexes. *Journal of the American Society for Information Science*, 47(10):749-764, October 1996.

S. E. Robertson, S. Walker, S. Jones, M. M. Hancock-Beaulieu, and M. Gatford. Okapi at TREC-3. In D. K. Harman, editor, *Proc. Third Text REtrieval Conference (TREC-3)*, Gaithersburg, MD, November 1994. NIST Special Publication 500-225.

G. Salton. *Automatic Text Processing: The Transformation, Analysis, and Retrieval of Information by Computer*. Addison-Wesley, Reading, Massachusetts, 1989.

G. Salton and C. Buckley. Term-weighting approaches in automatic text retrieval. *Information Processing & Management*, 24(5):513-523, 1988.

A. Singhal, C. Buckley, and M. Mitra. Pivoted document length normalization. In H.-P. Frei, D. Harman, P. Schäuble, and R. Wilkinson, editors, *Proc. 19th Annual International ACM SIGIR Conference on Research and Development in Information Retrieval*, pages 21-29. ACM Press, New York, August 1996.

A. Soffer, D. Carmel, and D. Cohen. Static index pruning for information retrieval systems. In W. B. Croft, D. J. Harper, D. H. Kraft, and J. Zobel, editors, *Proc. 24th Annual International ACM SIGIR Conference on Research and Development in Information Retrieval*, pages 43-50, New Orleans, LA, September 2001. ACM Press, New York.

H. Turtle and J. Flood. Query evaluation: strategies and optimizations. *Information Processing & Management*, 31(1):831-850, November 1995.

I. H. Witten, A. Moffat, and T. C. Bell. *Managing Gigabytes: Compressing and Indexing Documents and Images*. Morgan Kaufmann, San Francisco, second edition, 1999.

W. Y. P. Wong and D. K. Lee. Implementations of partial document ranking using inverted files. *Information Processing & Management*, 29(5):647-669, September 1993.

Analysis of Lexical Signatures for Finding Lost or Related Documents

Seung-Taek Park[1] David M. Pennock[2] C. Lee Giles[1,2,3] Robert Krovetz[2]

[1]Department of Computer Science and Engineering
[3]School of Information Sciences and Technology
The Pennsylvania State University
University Park, PA 16802 USA
{separk@cse, giles@ist}.psu.edu

[2]NEC Research Institute
4 Independence Way
Princeton, NJ 08540 USA
{dpennock, krovetz}@research.nj.nec.com

ABSTRACT

A *lexical signature* of a web page is often sufficient for finding the page, even if its URL has changed. We conduct a large-scale empirical study of eight methods for generating lexical signatures, including Phelps and Wilensky's [14] original proposal (PW) and seven of our own variations. We examine their performance on the web and on a TREC data set, evaluating their ability both to uniquely identify the original document and to locate other relevant documents if the original is lost. Lexical signatures chosen to minimize document frequency (DF) are good at unique identification but poor at finding relevant documents. PW works well on the relatively small TREC data set, but acts almost identically to DF on the web, which contains billions of documents. Term-frequency-based lexical signatures (TF) are very easy to compute and often perform well, but are highly dependent on the ranking system of the search engine used. In general, TFIDF-based method and hybrid methods (which combine DF with TF or TFIDF) seem to be the most promising candidates for generating effective lexical signatures.

Categories and Subject Descriptors

H.3.3 [**Information Systems**]: Information Storage and Retrieval—*Information Search and Retrieval*; E.2 [**Data**]: Data Storage Representations; H.3.7 [**Information Systems**]: Information Storage and Retrieval—*Digital Libraries*; H.3.2 [**Information Systems**]: Information Storage and Retrieval—*Information Storage*

General Terms

Algorithms, Measurement, Performance, Reliability, Experimentation, Verification.

Keywords

lexical signatures, robust hyperlinks, dead links, broken URLs, information retrieval, World Wide Web, search engines, indexing, digital libraries, TREC, term frequency, inverse document frequency

1. INTRODUCTION

The World Wide Web is a dynamic information resource: web pages and hyperlinks are constantly being added, modified, moved, and deleted by independent entities around the world. Pitkow [15, 16] reports that around five to eight percent of requested hyperlinks on the web are broken (i.e., return an error); Lawrence et al. [12] find that many URL citations in research papers become invalid as early as a year or two after publication. Because of the web's scale, dynamics, distributed control, and lack of facilities for maintaining persistence of information, finding desired information remains a challenging problem. General-purpose search engines only cover a limited portion of the web, and most take several months to update new information [9, 10]. One solution is to build a greater variety of special-purpose search engines that can react more quickly to changes within their particular domain. For example, Lawrence, Giles, and Bollacker [11] developed ResearchIndex to collect and maintain a searchable index of computer science research papers. However, these efforts require considerable start-up and maintenance costs, and so may not be feasible for every domain.

Several initiatives address the problem of broken links by proposing mechanisms for assigning location independent names to documents in addition to URLs [3, 6, 7, 17, 18]. None of these approaches have been widely adopted because they require users either to acquire new software or to explicitly maintain the validity of name dereferencing. Other different approaches are addressed in [1, 2, 4, 5, 13]. Phelps and Wilensky [14] propose a less burdensome solution: compute a *lexical signature* for each document, or a string of about five key identifying words in the document. If the document cannot be found by URL, then it can often be located by feeding its signature words into a search engine. Phelps and Wilensky propose that lexical signature words be chosen by maximizing a modified term-frequency inverse-document-frequency (TFIDF) measure, capping term frequency (TF) at five, among other modifications. They also propose methods for embedding lexical signatures into hyperlinks and instrumenting browsers to automatically perform content-based dereferencing (i.e., query a search engine and process the results) when standard URL dereferencing fails. Phelps and Wilensky report that, in most cases, a search engine returns the desired document and only that document. If the search engine returns no documents (because the desired document no longer exists or is not indexed), then the authors suggest removing one or more words from the lexical signature and using this reduced signature to search for substitute documents. Thus, a secondary purpose for lexical signatures is to discover relevant or similar documents when the desired document is truly lost.

We find that, because Phelps and Wilensky's method (PW) caps TF at five, it places too much emphasis on document rarity and, on huge document collections like the web, acts almost identically to the method that choose lexical signatures by minimizing DF (document frequency). Both DF and PW are good at uniquely identifying a document when it exists and is indexed by the search engine, but neither is good at finding relevant documents when the target document is not in the search engine's database. Moreover, we believe that unique identification is often unnecessary: as long as the search engine returns the desired document as the first-ranked document (even among many documents), then the lexical signature is effective.

In this paper, we study the relative efficacy of eight different methods for generating lexical signatures, including PW. We conducted tests both on actual web documents, where search engine coverage and ranking algorithms are limited, and on a TREC data set, where search coverage is complete. PW performs well on the latter data set, but more like DF on the web. Lexical signatures based on maximizing term frequency (TF) are easy to compute and maintain, since they do not depend on measuring statistics across the database. TF often performs well, but depends to a large extent on how the search engine ranks documents. TFIDF-based method and hybrid methods that use one or two minimum-DF words along with maximum-TF or maximum-TFIDF words perform well both on real web data and on the idealized TREC data, in terms of both finding the desired document and finding alternate relevant documents.

2. TERMINOLOGY

2.1 Lexical Signature

Phelps and Wilensky's [14] main motivation was to associate lexical signatures with documents, so that when the lexical signature is fed to a search engine, the desired document—and only that document—is returned. Then, when URLs change and links to documents become invalid, new locations for documents can be easily found via search engines. To achieve this goal, Phelps and Wilensky argued that lexical signatures should have following characteristics:

1. Lexical signatures should extract the desired document and only that document.
2. Lexical signatures should be robust enough to find documents that have been slightly modified.
3. New lexical signatures should have minimal overlap with existing lexical signatures.
4. Lexical signatures should have minimal search engine dependency.

We prefer a slightly weaker notion of unique identification: as long as the desired document is the top-ranked document returned by the search engine, we are satisfied. We also pay closer attention to the other potential benefit of lexical signatures: to help the user find relevant documents when the desired documents is truly lost. We therefore modify the first desired characteristic of lexical signatures as follows:

- 1a Lexical signatures should easily extract the desired document. When a search engine returns more than one document, the desired document should be the top-ranked document.
- 1b Lexical signatures should be useful enough to find relevant information when the precise documents being searched for are lost.

2.2 What is a Term?

Lexical signatures are composed of a small number of *terms*. Phelps and Wilensky [14] used individual words as terms, where words are case-insensitive, contained in the context of the document (not in meta-tags), contain at least four letters, and do not include any numbers. In our experiments, these rules of thumb for defining terms proved to be fairly effective. Number queries caused many problems with document retrieval: for example, if the query '2,000' is given to search engines, some return documents that contain only '2 000', '2;000', '2:000', or '2,000', but not '2000'. Also, many words that have less than four letters are stop words (e.g., 'the', 'of', or 'in'). In our experiments, filtering out these short words for the most part slightly improved the efficacy of the lexical signatures.

2.3 Basic and Hybrid Methods for Generating Lexical Signatures

In our experiments, we explore lexical signatures containing five terms. We generate eight kinds of lexical signatures for each document: four *basic* lexical signatures and four *hybrid* lexical signatures. Basic lexical signatures are generated using a single metric. For example, TF-based signatures are generated based on the term frequency values of words in the given document. Hybrid signatures combine terms generated from two different basic methods. For example, TF3DF2 uses three TF-based words and two DF-based words. A detailed explanation of the basic lexical signature methods follows.

Basic Lexical Signature Methods

1. **TF**: Select terms in decreasing term frequency (TF) order. If there is a tie, then pick words based on increasing document frequency (DF). If tied again, randomly select the words.
2. **DF**: Select words in increasing DF order. If there is a tie, then pick words based on decreasing TF order. If tied again, randomly select the words.
3. **TFIDF**: Select words in decreasing term-frequency inverse-document-frequency (TFIDF) order. If there is a tie, then pick words based on increasing DF order. If tied again, randomly select the words.

4. **PW**: Select words based on Phelps and Wilensky's [14] method, or decreasing TFIDF order where the TF term is capped at five. If there is a tie, then pick words based on increasing DF order. If tied again, randomly select the words.

Since we are also interested in the ability of lexical signatures to extract relevant documents when they fail to find missing documents, we find it useful to divide a lexical signature into two parts. The first part is useful for finding relevant documents and the second for uniquely identifying the desired document. If the desired document is not extracted because a search engine has not indexed it or the document is lost or gone, the second part of the lexical signature is removed and we attempt to find relevant documents using only the first part. Since we want to use the first part of lexical signatures to find relevant documents, we filter out in that part all words that have the document frequency one. This leads us to propose the following hybrid lexical signature methods:

Hybrid Lexical Signature Methods

1. **TF3DF2**: Select two words in increasing DF order. Then filter out all words which have DF value one. Select three words maximizing TF.
2. **TF4DF1**: Select one word based on increasing DF order first. Then filter out all words which have DF value one. Select four words maximizing TF.
3. **TFIDF3DF2**: Select two words based on increasing DF order first. Then filter out all words which have DF value one. Select three words maximizing TFIDF.
4. **TFIDF4DF1**: Select one word based on increasing DF order first. Then filter out all words which have DF value one. Select four words maximizing TFIDF.

2.4 Similarity Method: Cosine Measure

To measure the similarity between returned documents and the desired document, we use the cosine measure within the vector-space model [20]. For n unique words in our corpus, each document can be represented as an n-dimension vector. For example document A can be represented as

$$A = (a_1, .., a_n),$$

where if the ith word in the corpus appears in document A, then a_i is either the word's TF value, or the word's TFIDF value. Otherwise, $a_i = 0$. There is no easy way to extract the exact DF value of each word for all documents on the World Wide Web. Also, even though we could extract the DF value of each word for documents indexed by a search engine, the heavy search query burden for a search engine would not be tolerated. Thus, we use TF values with the cosine measure on actual web pages (which gives a slight bias to TF-based lexical signatures in our experiments), and use TFIDF values on TREC data (which gives a slight bias to TFIDF-based method). Using the vector space model, the cosine similarity measure between documents A and B is:

$$\cos\theta = \frac{A \cdot B}{|A||B|} = \frac{\sum_{i=1}^{n} a_i b_i}{\sqrt{\sum_{i=1}^{n} a_i^2 \sum_{i=1}^{n} b_i^2}}$$

In practice, documents on the web are regularly updated or modified. We would like to consider extremely similar documents that result from minor modifications to be the same document. Therefore, if the cosine value of two documents is greater than 0.9, we consider them to be the same document.

3. EMPIRICAL RESULTS FROM WEB DATA

Phelps and Wilensky [14] report that their lexical signatures extract only in most cases one or two documents, one of which is the desired document. However, *most cases* is not defined. What percentage of lexical signatures will extract the single desired document? If a list of documents is returned, is the desired document in that list? We postulate that if the desired document appears in the top ten of the list, especially at the first place, such lexical signatures are effective.

3.1 Web Data Set

For this experiment, we extracted the first 1500 URLs from pre-crawled data[1] (containing 1.5 million documents and their URLs) and downloaded each corresponding document. Several web documents do not have any words or have only a few words in their content, e.g. some documents only contain Java scripts or flash links. We excluded all documents and corresponding URLs that contained less than fifty words. The URLs that could not be downloaded because of server failures or corresponding document removals were also excluded. After removing stop words from word tokens, we again removed any URLs and corresponding documents that contained less than five unique words. Our original data set now reduces to 980 documents and their corresponding lexical signatures.

3.2 Experimental Method

Since there is no obvious way to get the document frequency (DF) of each word for the entire web, we used a search engine to generate a DF list for all words in our document set. In this experiment, we assumed that the DF value of each word from the search engine *Google*[2] is proportional to the actual DF value for the entire Web. Based on document frequency list and term frequency list of each document, we examine eight different lexical signatures per document.

After generating lexical signatures for all methods, we used them as queries for three search engines: *YahooGoogle*,[3] which uses *Google*'s searching algorithm, *AltaVista*,[4] and *MSN*.[5] Unlike *MSN* and *YahooGoogle*, *Altavista* returns all documents that contain any words in the lexical signature. To solve this problem, we used the advanced search option for *Altavista* (Using this option, *Altavista* only returns documents that contain all words in query). If a search engine did not return any documents, we removed a word from the

[1]The data used in this experiment was created by crawling all of dmoz.org and tnen retrieving all links external to the dmoz.org domain (i.e., all websites listed in Open Directory) .From these URLS any href tag was extracted eliminating any files with a file name extension that indicated that it was not html (e.g., pdf, ps, doc, etc). Thus the data set consists of all sites listed in DMOZ plus all sites two forward links away from DMOZ.

[2]http://www.google.com/

[3]http://google.yahoo.com/

[4]http://www.altavista.com/

[5]http://www.msn.com/

given lexical signature based on its lowest DF order and requeried the search engine. This procedure was continued until the search engine returned documents or all of words in the given lexical signature were removed. After the search engine returned the list of documents, those documents were downloaded and the similarity between returned documents and the target document was calculated using the cosine measure. If the search engine returned more than ten documents, we analyzed only the top ten ranked documents and ignored the rest. For all queries to *YahooGoogle*, all but two queries to *MSN*, and all but four queries to *Altavista*, at least some documents were returned.

3.3 Retrieval Performance

Our concern is not only with whether or not the desired document is returned but with its location in a possible list of returned documents. We define retrieval performance of lexical signatures as the percentage of times the desired document is returned based on how and when the document is returned. Since we already have a signature for the desired document, our performance measure is similar to recall.

We define the following disjoint classes. *Unique* represents the percentage of lexical signatures that successfully extract and return the single desired document. (This is the class discussed by Phelps and Wilensky.) *Top* represents the percentage of lexical signatures that extract a list of documents with the desired document first ranked. *High* is the percentage of lexical signatures that successfully returned a list with the desired document but not first ranked, but one of top ten. *Other* represents the percentage of lexical signatures that failed to extract the desired document. Because these classes are disjoint, the above added together represent 100% of all cases. Figures 1, 2, and 3 show the retrieval performance of each lexical signatures in extracting the desired documents for three different search engines averaged over 980 unique lexical signatures.

Figures 1, 2, and 3 show that considering only the *unique* extraction property of lexical signatures is not the only important factor in extracting the desired document. Note that DF and PW are most efficient for the *unique* property. However, if we focus on just retrieving the desired document, i.e. the case where *unique*, *top*, and *high* are combined, then hybrid methods are most consistent over three different search engines and efficient. Using this definition of retrieval performance, PW and DF methods performed worse than others for *YahooGoogle*. Phelps and Wilensky argued that the original TFIDF did not sufficiently emphasize the contribution of rarity; that is, if lexical signatures are chosen to minimize DF, it would be more helpful to filter out other documents and extract only the single desired document. However, since they limit the words in the lexical signature to a TF of 5, we argue that rarity is actually overemphasized and, as the number of documents on the Web increases, the PW and DF lexical signature methods become similar which is indicated by their retrieval performances shown in Figures 1, 2, and 3.

3.4 Finding Relevant Documents

Suppose the desired document cannot be extracted; can the lexical signature find a related one? If so, which method works best? Figure 4, shows the percentage of all 980 documents not found in each search engines using all lexical signature methods; specifically 194, 172, and 232 documents

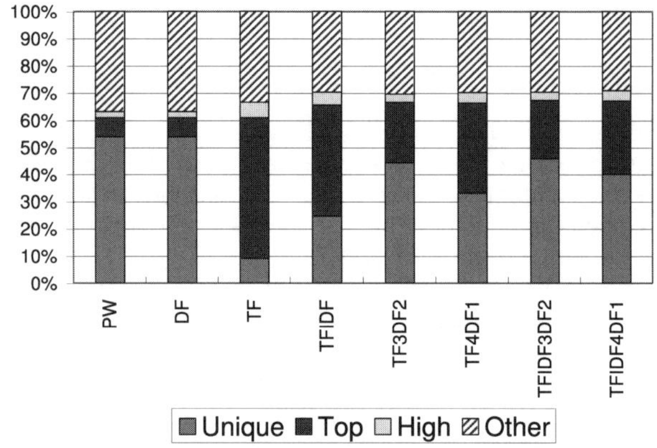

Figure 1: Retrieval performance of lexical signature methods for *YahooGoogle*

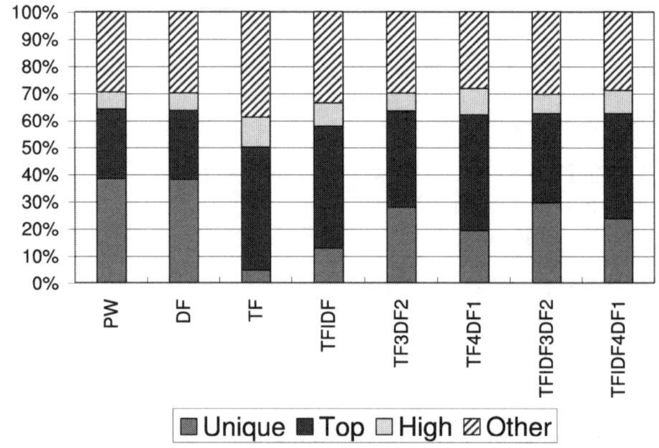

Figure 2: Retrieval performance of lexical signature methods for *MSN*

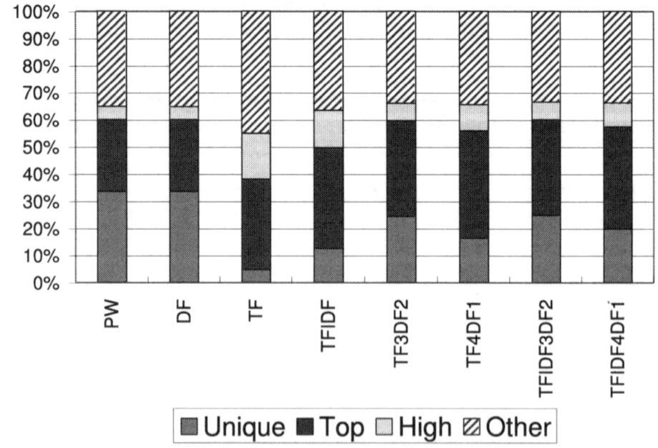

Figure 3: Retrieval performance of lexical signature methods for *AltaVista*

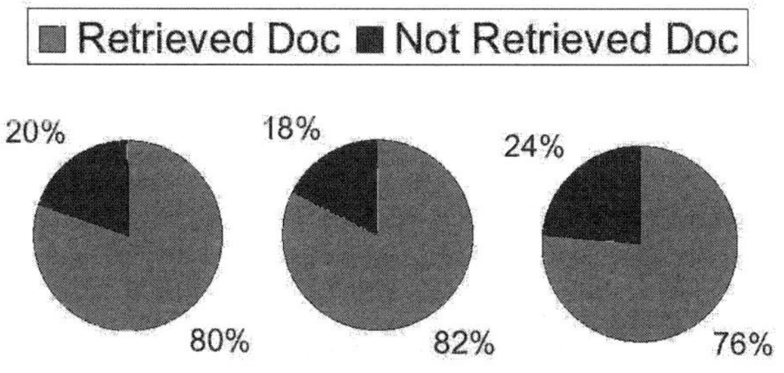

(a) YahooGoogle (b)MSN (c) AltaVista

Figure 4: Coverage of each search engine

(*Not Retrieved Doc*) could not be retrieved from *YahooGoogle*, *MSN*, and *Altavista*, respectively. There could be many reasons for this. The desired documents are not yet indexed by the search engines; they are moved to another server; they are deleted; they are modified or updated; they consist of very few unique words; their names are changed; the words in the lexical signature are not indexed; etc.

In those situations, lexical signatures should be expected to extract highly relevant documents. Also, if the search engine returns a list of relevant documents, then it would be useful if first ranked document be one of the most relevant ones.

We now only consider the effect of lexical signatures on retrieving related documents to the *Not Retrieved Documents* class. We analyze the cosine similarity of the documents retrieved in the *Not Retrieved Document* class to the desired document. Figure 5 gives the average cosine values of the first ranked documents and Figure 6 shows average cosine values of the top ten documents. Here, DF and PW have the worst average cosine values for both first ranked documents and top ten documents.

Figure 7 shows the average cosine values of the first ranked document for all 980 documents. In general PW, DF (because of their better retrieval performance) and hybrid methods yield better average similarity for first ranked documents than TF and TFIDF, and TF and TFIDF show more variation between search engines.

3.5 Observations

Two characteristics which are important for a successful search engine are document coverage and ranking. The efficiency of lexical signatures is highly dependent on these characteristics. Since DF and PW lexical signatures extract only one or few documents in most cases, they would appear more dependent on document coverage rather than ranking. However lexical signatures such as TF which return a list of documents rely on both document coverage and ranking of search engines.

We have shown that the *unique* property of lexical signatures is not the only important factor in desired document retrieval. If we focus only on retrieving the desired documents, hybrid methods show better performance than DF and PW with *YahooGoogle*. Furthermore, DF's and PW's poor performance in extracting relevant documents when

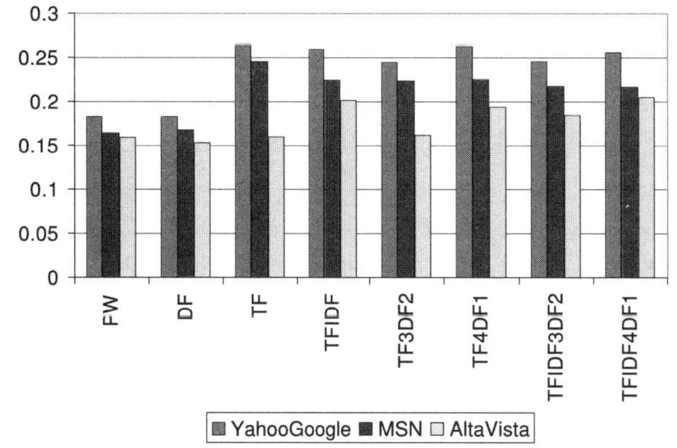

Figure 5: Average cosine value of the first ranked for *Not Retrieved Documents*

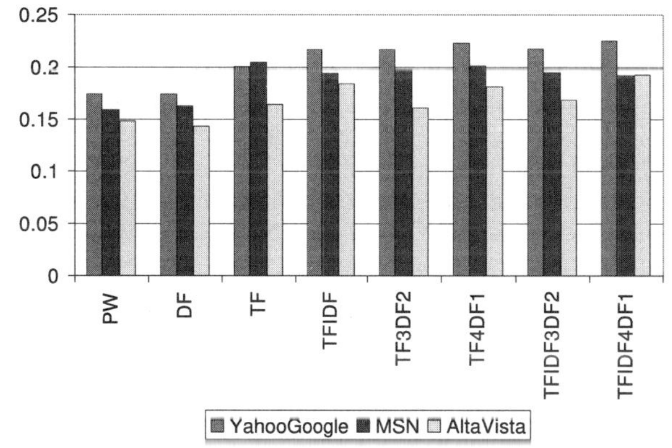

Figure 6: Average cosine value of top ten documents for *Not Retrieved Documents*

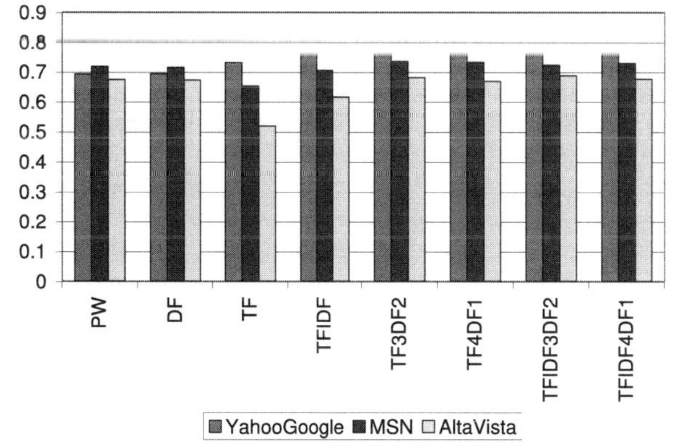

Figure 7: Average cosine value of the first ranked documents for all 980 documents

the desired one is missing make its usage for lexical signatures questionable. Unlike DF, TF is easy to compute and does not need to be updated unless the documents are modified. Also, TF extracts more relevant documents than PW and DF in the case where search engines cannot extract the desired documents. TFIDF is another good candidate for lexical signatures. Its retrieval performance on desired documents is better than TF. And when the desired document cannot be extracted, extracted documents by TFIDF are more relevant than those of DF and PW. Hybrid methods appear to be the best candidates for lexical signatures. They show excellent performance for retrieving both the desired documents and relevant documents when the desired one is missing. Also, their performance overall are more consistent than those of basic methods.

4. EMPIRICAL RESULTS FROM TREC DATA

Let's review some of the limitations of the previous experiment. First, document frequency (DF) of each word from a search engine is not the actual DF on the entire Web. Moreover, different search engines may have different document frequencies. For many reasons search engines are not easy to use for this experiment. Our data size in previous experiments is too small if we consider number of documents on the World Wide Web. Using search engines to increase our data size is prohibitive for many reasons, including search engine query policies and the changing nature of web documents.

One solution to these problems is to use TREC data for lexical signature experiments. We extracted 100,000 documents from the TREC 3, 4 and 5 data resources and did similar experiments.

4.1 Data Set and Experimental Environment

We extracted 100,000 articles from the TREC, 20,000 articles from Ziff-Davis (most articles are computer related), 40,000 articles from AP Newswire, and 20,000 articles from the Wall Street Journal and 20,000 articles from the San Jose Mercury News. We removed all tags, serial numbers that can identify the articles, dates, and names of newspapers and magazine such as *AP Newswires* in all articles. After removing stop words, we generated a term frequency list for each article and document frequency list for all articles. Our corpus contained 404,657 unique words and 219,930 words had document frequency one. Most articles were around 200 words length; Figure 8 shows the distribution of length of all articles.

We built a simple search engine for the experiment which has its own index file for all unique words, except stop words. The engine has two inputs, pageID (name of the page) and its lexical signature. When we feed a pageID and its lexical signature to the engine, it returns all pages that contain all words of the lexical signature except the target page of the given pageID. If our routine does not return any pages, the lexical signature is unique. Unlike real search engines, coverage of the search engine is complete for all documents. Since it does not have any ranking algorithm, we analyzed all returned documents by the search engine.

4.2 *Unique* Property

First, we studied the *unique* class of lexical signature methods. If a search engine does not have a ranking algorithm, this property should be the most important factor for lexical signatures. Figure 9 demonstrates the retrieval performance *unique* class for different lexical signature methods. As we expect, DF shows the best performance for this property and all hybrid methods have a better performance than any basic methods except DF. Since the number of documents in TREC data is much smaller than the actual web, the PW lexical signatures are more similar to the TFIDF ones. Note that hybrid methods outperform even the PW on this *unique* class.

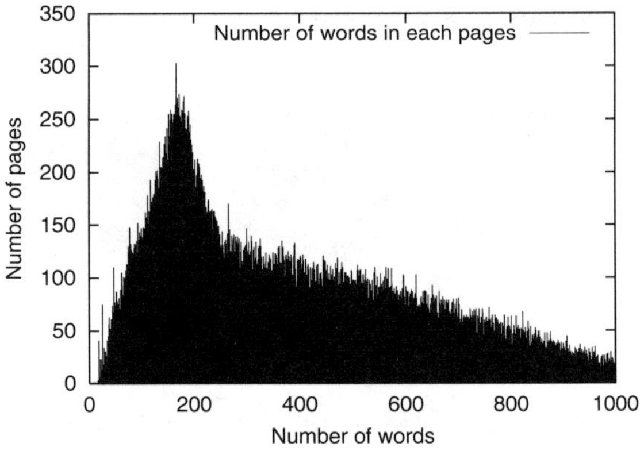

Figure 8: Distribution of number of words in each article

4.3 Finding Relevant Documents

If the desired document is not returned, the best scenario is extracting the most similar document. One of properties that lexical signatures should have is robustness to minor modifications of the desired document. We assume that even though two documents are not identical, one is a modified version of the other if their similarity measure is greater than 0.9.

In Figure 10, we denote *Similar* numbers of lexical signatures that successfully found our definition of modified versions of documents. The poor performance of DF can be explained by the *uniqueness-robustness trade-off*, as Phelps and Wilensky said, i.e. if a lexical signature is chosen to minimize DF, then it would be most appropriate to extract the single desired document but its robustness for minor modification will be significantly impaired. TF3DF2 and TFIDF3DF2 show the best performance and other methods show similar results. *Fail* measures the number of lexical signatures that failed to return any documents after all words are removed. Because about half of unique words in our corpus have document frequency one, it is possible that all words in a DF lexical signature are document frequency one words. If so, no documents will be returned when the desired document is missing. For all other methods except DF, some documents are returned using lexical signatures.

Figure 11 shows the average cosine value of the best cases (most relevant returned documents) and average cases (average cosine value of all returned document) when the desired document is missing. In general, hybrid methods extract more relevant documents than basic methods and their average cosine values, except TF4DF1, are higher than those of basic methods.

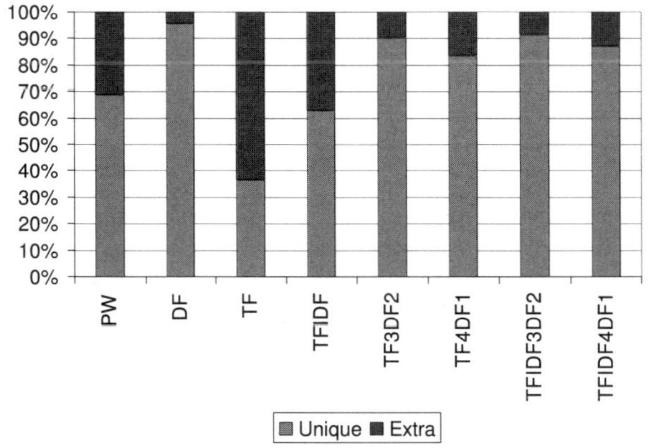

Figure 9: Retrieval performance for the unique class on TREC data.

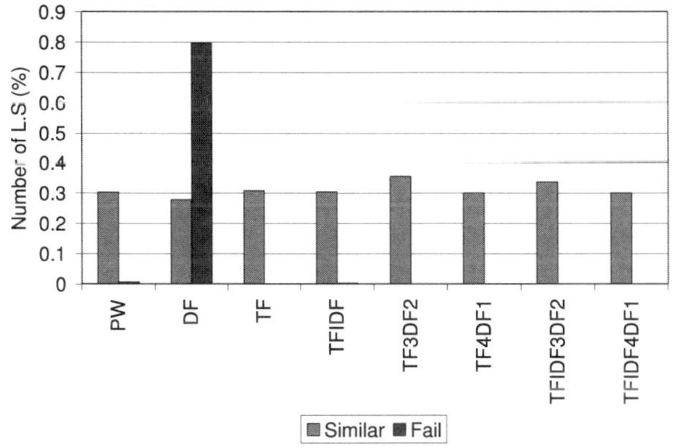

Figure 10: Number of lexical signatures that found the modified versions of documents or found no documents

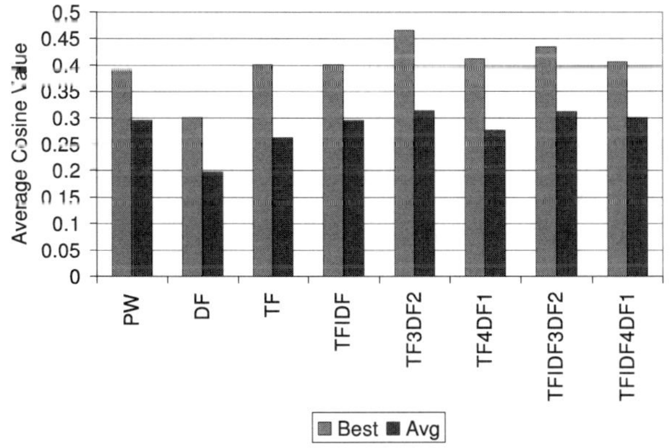

Figure 11: Average cosine value of best cases and average cases when the desired document is not extracted.

4.4 Observations

When the coverage of a search engine is complete and number of documents is relatively small (100,000 documents), hybrid methods show better performance for the *unique* extraction property than basic methods except DF. Because these methods are also excellent for retrieving relevant documents when the desired page is missing, they constitute the most promising candidates for lexical signatures. This result demonstrates that only one or two words minimizing the DF are enough for unique identification of the original document. Even though DF has the best performance for this property, it is not robust enough for minor document modifications and has poor performance for retrieving relevant documents. TF shows good performance for retrieving relevant documents when the desired document is missing but worst for the *unique* property. TFIDF and PW methods work well for both *unique* property and its *relevance*. When the number of documents in database is relatively small, PW acts similar to TFIDF.

5. CONCLUSIONS AND FUTURE WORK

5.1 Summary

Because the web does not have a well-adopted standard for maintaining persistence of information [12], the act of moving and deleting documents creates a large number of broken links throughout the web. Such broken links pose a significant problem for the growing number of people that rely on the web as a universal database. Phelps and Wilensky [14] show that even a small number of words can often uniquely identify each document on the web. In this paper, we studied eight methods for generating lexical signatures, including Phelps and Wilensky's original proposal and seven of our own. We argue that the *unique* extraction property is not the only important property for lexical signatures. As long as the desired document appears first in a returned document list, the lexical signature is effective. Also, since the coverage of search engines is limited, and documents are added, moved, modified, and deleted frequently, the ability to retrieve highly relevant documents when the desired document cannot be extracted is another important property for lexical signatures. Moreover, since different search engines have different coverages and ranking systems, the consistency of lexical signatures across search engines should be considered.

We find that DF-based lexical signatures are best at uniquely identifying documents, on both web data and TREC data. However, DF is worst at retrieving relevant documents when the desired document is missing. PW acts almost identically to DF when number of document is large, as is the case on the web. However, when the number of documents is relatively small (e.g., around 100,000 documents), PW acts like TFIDF and its relevance performance improves. TF is worst at uniquely retrieving documents, but works well for finding relevant documents. Even though TF is easy to compute and maintain, its performance variability across different search engines could outweigh its benefits. TFIDF is the best candidate for lexical signatures among the basic methods, due to its effectiveness at extracting both the desired document and relevant ones. But hybrid methods seem even better candidates for generating lexical signatures. They show good retrieval of unique documents on both web and TREC data—even better than PW on TREC data. Hybrid methods return the desired document within the top few returned documents more often than even DF and PW. In addition, they show excellent performance in retrieving relevant documents when the desired page is missing. Finally, their ability to extract both desired and relevant documents is relatively stable over different search engines.

5.2 Performance Evaluation Methods for Search Engines

It is widely argued that search engines should be evaluated by their ability to retrieve highly relevant documents rather than all possible pages [8, 19]. Lexical signatures are good query terms that can extract relevant documents when the desired document cannot be retrieved. One limitation of lexical signatures mentioned by Phelps and Wilensky is that their performance can depend on particular search engines. However, this limitation can be exploited to evaluate search engine performance. Because a document's TF values are independent of other documents in the database, and because TF-based lexical signatures usually extract more than ten documents, the ability of TF-based signatures to extract relevant documents is highly dependent on the search engine's ranking system. By measuring similarities of returned documents with the targeted one, by using a similarity measure or human responses, we can evaluate the search engine's ability to retrieve and rank relevant documents. In our experiments, *YahooGoogle* shows the best performance (among the engines tested) for retrieving both desired documents and relevant documents, in almost all cases.

6. ACKNOWLEDGMENTS

The authors gratefully thank Dr. Gary Flake for providing valuable experimental data, and the referees and Dr. Steve Lawrence for useful comments. We gratefully acknowledge partial support from Ford Motor Co.

7. REFERENCES

[1] A. Aimar, I. Hannell, A. Khodabandeh, P. Palazzi, B. Rousseau, M. Ruggier, J. Casey, and N. Drakos. Weblinker, A Tool for Managing WWW cross-references. *Computer Networks and ISDN Systems*, 28(1&2), December 1995.

[2] K. Andrews, F. Kappe, and H. Maurer. The Hyper-G Network Information Systems. *Journal of Universal Computer Science*, 1(4):206–220, April 1995.

[3] W. Arms, C. Blanchi, and E. Overly. An Architecture for Information in Digital Libraries. *D-Lib Magazine*, February 1997.

[4] R. T. Fielding. Maintaining distributed hypertext infostructures: Welcome to MOMspider's Web. *Computer Networks and ISDN Systems*, 27(2):193–204, 1994.

[5] A. Goldberg and P. N. Yianilos. Towards an Archival Intermemory. In *Proceedings of IEEE Advances in Digital Libraries, ADL 98*, pages 147–156, Santa Barbara, CA, 1998. IEEE Computer Society.

[6] D. Ingham, S. Caughey, and M. Little. Fixing the 'Broken-Link' Problem: The W3Objects Approach. In *Computer Networks and ISDN System*, pages 1255–1268. 5th International World Wide Web Conference, May 1996.

[7] D. Ingham, M. Little, S. Caughey, and S. Shrivastava. W3Objects: Bringing Object-Oriented Technology to the Web. In *The Web Journal*, pages 89–105. 4th International World Wide Web Conference, December 1995.

[8] K. Jarvelin and J. Kekalainen. IR Evaluation Methods for Retrieving highly Relevant Documents. In *SIGIR 2000*, pages 41–48, July 2000.

[9] S. Lawrence and C. L. Giles. Searching the World Wide Web. *Science*, 280(5360):98–100, April 1998.

[10] S. Lawrence and C. L. Giles. Accessibility of information on the Web. *Nature*, 400:107–109, July 1999.

[11] S. Lawrence, C. L. Giles, and K. Bollacker. Digital Libraries and Autonomous Citation Indexing. *IEEE Computer*, 32(6):67–71, 1999.

[12] S. Lawrence, D. M. Pennock, G. Flake, R. Krovetz, F. M. Coetzee, E. Glover, F. A. Nielsen, A. Kruger, and C. L. Giles. Persistence of Web References in Scientific Research. *IEEE Computer*, 34(2):26–31, February 2001.

[13] G. Oberholzer and E. Wilde. Extended Link Visualization with DHTML: The Web as an open hypermedia system. Technical Report TIK-Report No. 125, Computer Engineering and Networks Laboratory (TIK), ETH Zrich, January 2002.

[14] T. A. Phelps and R. Wilensky. Robust Hyperlinks: Cheap, Everywhere, Now. In *Proceedings of Digital Documents and Electronic Publishing 2000 (DDEP00)*, September 2000.

[15] J. Pitkow. Web Characterization Activity Answers to the W3C HTTP-NGs Protocol Design Group's Questions. World Wide Web Consortium, 1998. http://www.w3.org/WCA/Reports/1998-01-PDG-answers.htm.

[16] J. E. Pitkow. Summary of WWW characterizations. *Computer Networks and ISDN Systems*, 30(1–7):551–558, 1998.

[17] K. Shafer, S. Weibel, E. Jul, and J. Fausey. Introduction to Persistent Uniform Resource Locators. In *INET 96*. Internet Society, Reston, Va., 1996.

[18] K. Sollins and L. Masinter. Functional Requirements for Uniform Resource Names. Internet Request for Comments, Dec 1994. http://ietf.org/rfc/rfc1737.txt.

[19] E. M. Voorhees. Evaluation by Highly Relevant Documents. In *SIGIR 2001*, pages 74–80, September 2001.

[20] I. H. Witten, A. Moffat, and T. C. Bell. *Managing Gigabytes 2nd Edition.* A Harcourt Science and Technology Company, 525 B Street, Suite 1990, San Diego, CA 92101 - 4495, USA, 1999.

Using Sampled Data and Regression to Merge Search Engine Results

Luo Si and Jamie Callan
School of Computer Science
Carnegie Mellon University
Pittsburgh, PA 15213
lsi@cs.cmu.edu, callan@cs.cmu.edu

ABSTRACT

This paper addresses the problem of merging results obtained from different databases and search engines in a distributed information retrieval environment. The prior research on this problem either assumed the exchange of statistics necessary for normalizing scores (*cooperative* solutions) or is heuristic. Both approaches have disadvantages.

We show that the problem in uncooperative environments is simpler when viewed as a component of a distributed IR system that uses query-based sampling to create resource descriptions. Documents sampled for creating resource descriptions can also be used to create a sample centralized index, and this index is a source of training data for adaptive results merging algorithms. A variety of experiments demonstrate that this new approach is more effective than a well-known alternative, and that it allows query-by-query tuning of the results merging function.

Categories & Subject Descriptors:

H.3.3 **[Information Search and Retrieval]:** Distributed Information Retrieval, Results Merging

General Terms: Algorithms

Keywords:

Distributed Information Retrieval, Results Merging, Regression

1. INTRODUCTION

The proliferation of online searchable databases on local area networks and the Internet creates a problem of finding information that may be distributed among many text databases (*distributed information retrieval*) [1]. Distributed information retrieval includes three sub-problems. First, information about the contents of each individual database must be acquired. This task is called *resource description* [2,3,4]. Second, a set of text databases must be selected for search [5,8,9]. This task is called *resource selection* or *collection selection*. Third, after results are returned from selected databases, they must be merged into a single ranked list. This task is called *results merging* [1,7,8,10, 11,12,15]. All three tasks are important and interrelated.

Environmental characteristics can simplify or complicate the solution of these problems. In a small local area network the individual search engines might all be of the same type; we call this the *single engine type* case. In a large organization there may be a small number of search engine types, and it may be known which databases use which types of search engine. This knowledge can simplify resource description and results merging. In a very large network or on the Internet there may be many search engine types, and it may not be known which type of engine is associated with each database.

There is also variation in the extent to which search engines *cooperate* in distributed information retrieval. Varying degrees of cooperation have been assumed in prior research, for example assuming that search engines would provide complete and partial resource descriptions [3,10], normalizing statistics [11], normalized document scores [20], or training data [23].

In this paper, we focus on environments containing multiple types of independent, uncooperative search engines. We assume that search engines will run queries and return documents, but they do not provide other information about themselves or their databases. Our goal is solutions that can be applied on wide-area, multi-party, multi-vendor networks where resource providers may not cooperate or may have an incentive to cheat.

The state of the art in distributed IR research is that reasonably good solutions exist for acquiring resource descriptions and for selecting which databases to search, but only weak solutions exist for merging results. Most of the prior research on data fusion and meta-search does not apply, because it assumes considerable overlap in the contents of the databases searched, and hence considerable overlap in the documents returned. But in distributed IR environments, it is more likely that different databases contain, and return, different documents.

The results merging problem is difficult because each engine may use a different ranking algorithm, and may base its ranking on corpus statistics (e.g., idf, average document length) that vary widely. Merging based upon unnormalized ("raw") document scores or document ranks works well when search engines and corpora are very similar, but can be very inaccurate when they differ. Merging based upon weighted document scores [1,2] or ranks [8] has been the state-of-the-art for merging quickly, but is heuristic and prone to unexpected failure. The alternative solution is to download the contents of the retrieved documents and then to re-rank them at the search client [11,12], which produces a consistent ranking but can be very time-consuming.

In this paper we present a fast and effective new solution to the results merging problem. Our new solution uses three different types of information to normalize the document scores produced by individual databases: Information about the database contents (from the *resource description*), information about how well the database is thought to satisfy the query (the *database score*), and the document score returned by the database. No cooperation is assumed, and there are no assumptions about the type(s) of search engines used. That information is used to build functions that transform document scores from different search engines into a normalized form suitable for merging.

We also present experiments comparing the new approach to the results merging algorithm usually used with the well-known CORI resource selection algorithm [1]. We demonstrate that the new approach is more effective on two distributed IR testbeds, particularly a subject-oriented testbed with skewed vocabulary patterns [20]. We demonstrate its effectiveness in both *single search engine type* and multiple *engine types* environments.

The next section discusses related work. Section 3 describes our new approach to merging results. Section 4 explains our experimental methodology. Sections 5, 6, and 7 present our experimental results for the single search engine type and multiple search engine type cases. Section 8 concludes.

2. PRIOR RESEARCH

There has been considerable research on acquiring resource descriptions, ranking resources, and merging results. We survey related work in this section to provide an overview of the state of the art, focusing on the research that is the most relevant or most closely related to the new research presented in this paper.

The STARTS protocol is one solution for acquiring resource descriptions [3]. It requires every resource provider to provide accurate resource descriptions to a resource ranking algorithm upon request. It is a cooperative protocol, because it only works when every resource provider supplies accurate vocabulary, frequency, and corpus information. STARTS is a good solution in environments where cooperation can be guaranteed. However, in multi-party environments some resource providers may choose not to cooperate; when they do cooperate, it is impossible to know whether they provide accurate information.

Query-based sampling [4] is an alternative approach to acquiring resource descriptions that does not require explicit cooperation from resource providers. The database selection service constructs its own resource descriptions by sampling individual databases contents via the normal process of running queries and retrieving documents. This solution has been shown to acquire rather accurate resource descriptions using a relatively small number of randomly-generated queries (e.g., 75) to retrieve a relatively small number of documents (e.g., 300).

There are many resource ranking algorithms; we cannot survey all of them here. gGlOSS [6], CORI [4,1] and CVV [8] are three of the best-known resource ranking algorithms. gGlOSS, is based on the vector space model. It represents a database by the document frequency of each word in the database, and the sum of the term weights in each document in the database. The CVV resource ranking algorithm uses a combination of document frequency and cue validity variance information. The variability of the fraction of documents in a database that contains a specific word is characterized by the cue validity variance. The CORI resource ranking algorithm represents each database by its terms, their document frequencies, and summary corpus statistics such as total word count.

Different researchers using different datasets have shown the CORI algorithm to be the most stable and effective of the three algorithms [9,13]. CVV is often nearly as effective as CORI, but can fail dramatically when its underlying assumptions are violated. CORI and gGlOSS are compatible with resource descriptions acquired by query-based sampling; CVV is not.

We use the CORI algorithm in the research reported here, so we sketch it briefly. The belief $p(r_k \mid db_i)$ in database db_i according to the query term r_k is determined [1,2] by:

$$T = \frac{df}{df + 50 + 150 * cw / avg\_cw} \qquad (1)$$

$$I = \frac{\log(\frac{|DB| + 0.5}{cf})}{\log(|DB| + 1.0)} \qquad (2)$$

$$p(r_k \mid c_i) = b + (1 - b) * T * I \qquad (3)$$

where:
df is the number of documents in db_i that contains the r_k
cf is the number of databases that contain r_k
|DB| is the number of databases to be ranked
cw is the number of words in db_i
avg_cw is the average cw of the databases to be ranked
b is the default belief, usually 0.4.

The combination of belief values depends on the query structure. In the simple case relevant to our research, it is the average of the beliefs of the query terms. Generally the 5 or 10 databases with highest belief are selected [1,4,9].

In general, the results merging task is difficult because different databases may have different types of search engines and different corpus statistics. The most accurate solution is to normalize the scores of documents retrieved from different databases, either by using global corpus statistics [10,7], which requires cooperation, or by recomputing document scores at the search client [11], which has high communications costs. A less costly solution is to download only parts of documents [12].

A related approach used for meta-search is to heuristically combine the outputs of search engines, for example, Lee's COMBSUM and COMBMNZ algorithms [14]. The main drawback of these techniques is that they rely on a lot of overlap among the results from different search engines. Javed's Bayesian model is theoretically solid, but it also relies on overlap among the results and also needs relevance information about some queries [21]. Manmatha proposed that a score modeling method might also work well for results merging in distributed IR [15], but our experience is that the modeling technique assumes the presence of many relevant documents in each database, which is often not satisfied in our experiments.

The CORI merging algorithm is a linear combination of the score of the database and the score of the document. It makes no assumption about the number of overlap documents or the number of relevant documents in each database. The intuition is to favor documents from databases with high scores and to enable high-scoring documents from low-scoring databases to be ranked highly. This algorithm has been very effective, but it has not been applied to search engines other than INQUERY.

The CORI results merging algorithm serves as a baseline later in this paper, so we provide its algorithm here. A "normalized" score suitable for merging is calculated as shown below.

$$C_i' = \frac{(R_i - R_{min})}{(R_{max} - R_{min})} \quad (4)$$

$$D' = \frac{(D - D_{min})}{(D_{max} - D_{min})} \quad (5)$$

$$D'' = \frac{D' + 0.4 * D' * C_i'}{1.4} \quad (6)$$

If T in Equation 1 is set to 1.0 for each query term, a score R_{max} can be computed for each query. If T is set to 0.0 for each query term, a score R_{min} can be computed for each query. These are the highest and lowest scores that the resource ranking algorithm could potentially assign to a database. So Equation 4 is the normalized database weighting score that can be calculated only from information in the resource selection index. Equation 5 tries to normalize document score from individual search engines to the range between 0 and 1. It needs the individual search engines to cooperate by providing D_{max} and D_{min}. In the absence of cooperation, D_{max} is set to the maximum document score returned by the search engine and D_{min} is set to the minimum. Equation 6 calculates the final document scores that can be compared directly.

The research most similar to what we propose in the following sections is based on building logistic regression models for results merging [16]. A key difference is that in the prior research relevance information from additional queries was used to train the models, whereas our new method does not need relevance information. Another is that the same regression model was used for all queries to a given database, but we build different regression models for each query to each database.

3. REGRESSION MODEL

Distributed IR algorithms are often evaluated by comparing them to *centralized* solutions, in which all documents are stored in a single search engine. Indeed, solutions that rely upon exchanging corpus statistics are in effect replacing engine-specific document scores with the scores those documents would have gotten if they had been in a single, centralized database.

Results merging is a difficult problem when viewed in isolation, because little information is available for estimating centralized document scores. The CORI results merging algorithm views the problem in the context of the database ranking algorithm, producing "normalized" document scores as a linear combination of database-specific document scores and the scores of the databases they were retrieved from. It is effective, but it is not a general solution because the weighting of database scores and document scores is determined by a constant tuned to produce good average case performance for the CORI database ranking algorithm and the INQUERY search engine.

We can enlarge our view of the distributed IR environment further still, by defining how resource descriptions are obtained. Query-based sampling is a technique in which resource descriptions are created by submitting queries to a search engine and observing the contents of the documents that are returned. Several studies have shown that query-based sampling produces accurate resource descriptions [1,4], but that is not our concern here. The central insight in the research presented here is that results merging is an easier problem if we assume that resource descriptions are created by query-based sampling.

Ordinarily the documents obtained by query-based sampling are discarded after resource descriptions are created, but that need not be the case. Instead, the documents sampled from the various databases can be combined into a single, centralized sample database. This centralized sample database is a subset, perhaps a very small subset, of the complete centralized database often used as a baseline in distributed IR experiments. However, it provides an important source of additional information for results merging.

After the query is sent to the N best databases and different ranked lists are returned, the same query can be used to search the centralized sample database. The result is a set of database-specific document rankings, and a single centralized sample document ranking. Our first hypothesis is that some documents will appear in a database-specific ranking *and* the centralized sample document ranking. This hypothesis might seem unlikely, but recall that resource descriptions are created from the documents in the centralized sample database; a database is only selected for search when its resource description (and hence some documents in the centralized database) matches the query closely. Our second hypothesis is that the scores of documents that appear in both lists can be used to find a function that will map *all* database-specific document scores into their corresponding centralized document scores.

Regression is an efficient and effective mathematical tool for this kind of problem. First we assume the kind of function that is suitable for this problem. Then we try to find the parameter values that can best fit the training data under some criterion. It can be formalized as follows:

$$\lambda = \arg\max_{\lambda} \sum_i (f(\lambda, x_i) - y_i)^2 \quad (7)$$

Here, λ is the parameter set, $f(\lambda, x_i)$ is some kind of function, and (x_i, y_i) is the ith training data point.

What form of merging function should we choose? Linear functions are simple, can be fit with a small amount of data, and can be solved efficiently. Because we may have only a limited amount of training data for each database, and because the CORI algorithm is evidence that a linear function can be successful, we chose simple linear models for our experiments.

If it is known that all search engines are of the same type (*single engine type* case), then one regression model can be calculated with all the training data. If the search engine types differ or are not known (*multiple engine types* case), different regression models must be learned for each database. Our interest is primarily in the second case, so we describe it first.

3.1 Multiple Search Engine Types

The training data for linear regression are pairs of "overlap" document scores (Dd_{ij}, Dc_{ij}) obtained from the distributed and centralized sample databases. We assume that a simple linear model $Dd_{ij}' = a_i * Dd_{ij} + b_i$ relates the scores, where Dd_{ij}' is an approximation of Dc_{ij}. Regression over all training data from a given database i is expressed in matrix representation as:

$$\begin{bmatrix} Dd_{i,1} & 1 \\ Dd_{i,2} & 1 \\ \ldots & 1 \\ Dd_{i,n} & 1 \end{bmatrix} * [a_i \quad b_i] = \begin{bmatrix} Dc_{i,1} \\ Dc_{i,2} \\ \ldots \\ Dc_{i,n} \end{bmatrix} \quad (8)$$

where a_i and b_i are the parameters in the linear formula. Call these matrices X (database-specific scores and constants), W (parameters) and Y (centralized sample scores). Simple algebraic manipulation allows this problem to be expressed as:

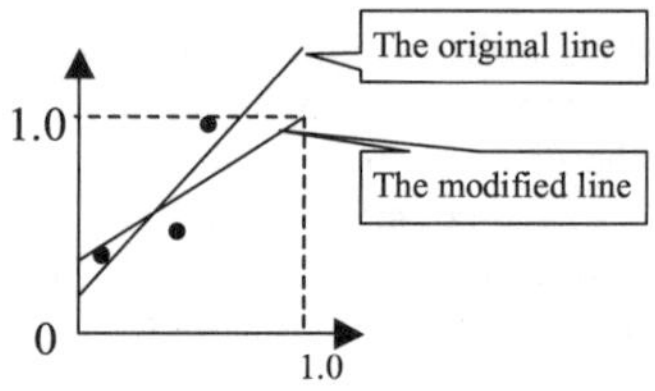

Figure 1. The linear model adjustment.

$$W = (X^T X)^{-1}(Y^T X) \quad (9)$$

Equation 9 is the solution with a Minimum Square Error (MSE) criterion. The result is a set of constants (a_i, b_i) for each database i that allow *all* database-specific document scores to be mapped to close approximations of their corresponding scores in the centralized sample database. These approximations of centralized scores are comparable across databases, and can be used for merging ranked lists returned by different databases.

3.1.1 Model Adjustment

Data sparseness can cause an anomaly in the linear models learned. The model learned from "overlap" training data might produce a document score greater than 1 for unseen documents. A score above 1 is not itself a problem, but it signals that the model is biased high, i.e., has too large a slope, which gives an advantage to documents returned by that database (Figure 1).

We address this case by finding the nearest line that intersects (1,1). If the original line is expressed as y=ax+b and the adjusted line is y=a'x+b', then the problem can be expressed as:

$$(a',b') = \arg\min_{a',b'} \int_0^1 [(a'-a)*x + (b'-b)]^2 dx \quad (10)$$

By simple mathematical modification, we get:

$$a' = \frac{3-a-3b}{2} \cdot \quad b' = 1-a' \quad (11)$$

This modification gives slightly better accuracy.

3.1.2 Training Data Requirements

For the multiple search engine types case, as different kinds of search engines have different searching algorithms, a regression model should be calculated for each different database. At least two training data per database are required to fit a linear model, but more data produces a more accurate model. We call a database "bad" if it has less than 3 overlap documents, because we assume that a database with many relevant documents should also have a pretty large number of overlap documents.

If the number of bad databases is less than a threshold, the results from those databases are just discarded. The threshold is assigned empirically as 3. If the number of bad databases exceeds the threshold, there is insufficient data to train the models, so the CORI results merging algorithm is used.

We also must choose how many data points to use in learning the linear regression model for each database. We believe that it is more important to be precise at the top of the merged ranking, so our solution is to limit training to the top 10 "overlap" documents from each database. If a database has fewer than 10 "overlap" documents, all are used. This value was set empirically. Preliminary experiments suggested that it is a reasonable choice.

3.2 Single Search Engine Type

In some environments it is known that a single engine is used for all databases. In this environment it might be possible to combine training data from different databases, which might be sufficient to learn a slightly more complex model.

The CORI results merging algorithm is a relatively successful single-engine heuristic that combines the database score C_i and the database-specific document score Dd_{ij} via the model:

$$Dd_{ij}' = \frac{Dd_{ij} + 0.4 Dd_{ij} C_i}{1.4} \quad (12)$$

This model uses one parameter to control the impact of the database score. Our hypothesis is that training data and linear regression will allow this parameter to be adjusted on a query-by-query basis, which will improve results merging accuracy.

As with the multi-engine type solution, training data are based on pairs of "overlap" document scores (Dd_{ij}, Dc_{ij}) obtained from the distributed and centralized sample databases. The database score C_i is also included, as shown above. Regression over the training data from all databases is expressed as:

$$\begin{bmatrix} Dd_{11} & C_1 Dd_{11} \\ Dd_{12} & C_1 Dd_{12} \\ \ldots & \ldots \\ Dd_{nn_l} & C_n Dd_{nn_l} \end{bmatrix} * [a \quad b] = \begin{bmatrix} Dc_{11} \\ Dc_{12} \\ \ldots \\ Dc_{nn_l} \end{bmatrix} \quad (13)$$

We call these matrices, X, W, and Y, as in the multi-engine type case (Section 3, Equation 8), and solve as described in Equation 9. The result is a pair of constants (a, b) that allow *all* database-specific document scores to be mapped to close approximations of their corresponding scores in the centralized sample database.

$$D'' = a * D' + b * C' * D' \quad (14)$$

These approximations of centralized scores are comparable across databases, and can be used for merging ranked lists returned by different databases.

The model adjustment required for the multi-engine type case (Section 3.1.1) is not required for the single-engine type case. Even if the learned model is biased, there is only one model (as opposed to one per database), so it affects all documents equally.

3.2.1 Training Data Requirements

In the single search engine type case only one regression model is built because all the databases use the same search algorithm. Because the training data from different databases are merged, it is more likely that there will be sufficient training data. One can back off to the CORI results merging algorithm if there is not sufficient training data, as in the multi-engine type case, but that was never necessary in our experiments.

For the single search engine type case, we use only the 20 top documents to build the regression model for all the databases. This value was determined empirically.

4. Experimental Methodology

4.1 Testbeds

Testbed characteristics have been shown to highly influence the performance of distributed retrieval systems. Two different testbeds were used in our experiments (Tables 1 and 2). Our goal

Table1: Testbed statistics.

Testbed	Size (GB)	Number of documents			Size (MB)		
		Min	Avg	Max	Min	Avg	Max
Trec123	3.2	752	10782	39713	28	32	42
Trec4	2.0	301	5675	82727	4	20	249

was to test our solutions with testbeds that have different degrees of heterogeneity and different types of queries.

Trec123-100col-bysource: 100 databases created from TREC CDs 1, 2 and 3. They are organized by source and publication date [1, 4, 17], and are somewhat heterogeneous. 50 queries were created from the Title fields of TREC topics 51-100.

Trec4-kmeans: 100 databases created from TREC 4 data. A k-means clustering algorithm was used to organize the databases by topic [18], so the databases are homogenous and the word distributions are very skewed. 50 queries were created from the Description fields of TREC topics 201-250.

4.2 Search Engines

We used three different search engines in our experiments: INQUERY, the Lemur toolkit unigram language model [22], and an in-house version of SMART using "ltc" weighting [19]. These three search engines were selected because they are each effective, but based on very different retrieval models. INQUERY and SMART are each well-known and have been described many times in the research literature, so we do not describe them in detail. Language models are a somewhat newer approach to retrieval, so we sketch the details briefly and refer the reader elsewhere for more information.

The basic idea is to estimate a language model for each document and to rank documents by the likelihood of the query according to the language model:

$$P(Q \mid d) = \prod_{i=1}^{m} P(t_i \mid d) \qquad (15)$$

where Q is the query, d is a specific document, and t_i $t_i$is i'th word in the query. Jelinek-Mercer smoothing was used to generate the document language model. It is just a linear combination of the maximum likelihood ($p_{ml}(w|d)$) and collection ($p_c(w|c)$) language models. A coefficient λ controls the influence of each model

$$P(w \mid d) = (1-\lambda)p_{ml}(w \mid d) + \lambda p_c(w \mid c) \qquad (16)$$

In our experiments, λ is set to 0.5.

5. Results: "Overlap" Documents

Our first hypothesis was that a sufficient number of documents would appear in both the centralized and database-specific rankings. These "overlap" documents are crucial to our second hypothesis, because the pairs of centralized and database-specific document scores (Ds_{ij}, Cs_{ij}) are training data. We know that some minimum amount of training data is required to calculate the regression model accurately. Are there enough?

Many factors influence the number of data points, such as the number of documents obtained by query-based sampling and the characteristics of the query and the databases. Generally, the number of overlap documents increases based on i) the number of documents sampled from each database; ii) the length of the query; and iii) the degree of topic homogeneity in each database.

Table2: Query set statistics.

Name	TREC Topic Set	TREC Topic Field	Average Length (Words)
Trec123	51-100	Title	3
Trec4	201-250	Description	7.2

A set of experiments with two testbeds investigated the average number of "overlap" documents. Experiments were conducted with two 100-database testbeds: trec123 (organized by source and date) and trec4_kmeans (organized by topic). In each testbed databases were assigned randomly to INQUERY, SMART, and Language Modeling search engines. Database resource descriptions were obtained as described in [4], by repeatedly submitting one-word random queries to a database and examining the top 4 documents returned until 300 unique documents were seen. During overlap evaluation, the CORI resource-ranking algorithm ranked databases, and the top 10 were considered selected for search. 1000 documents were retrieved from each selected database. The INQUERY search engine was also used to search the centralized sample database, and all retrieved documents from this database were used.

Figures 2 and 3 show the average number of overlap documents per query in each testbed. For most queries on the trec123 testbed there are more than 50 overlap documents. All of the queries for the trec4-kmeans testbed have more than 200 overlap documents. The different numbers of overlap documents in the two testbeds is not surprising, because the trec4-kmeans testbed has longer queries and homogenous databases.

Three out of fifty queries on the trec123 testbed backed off to the default CORI results merging algorithm because there were too many (4 or more) databases that had too few (less than 4) overlap documents to be confident of learning accurate models. None of the trec4_kmeans queries backed off to the CORI results merging algorithm, i.e., all had sufficient training data.

These results suggest that there are usually enough overlap documents for training a linear regression model.

6. Results: Multiple Engines

A series of multi-engine type experiments was conducted to test the effectiveness of the new approach to results merging. Two 100-database testbeds with different document distribution patterns were used (Section 4.1), and three different types of search engines were used (Section 4.2) in several different combinations. Our goal was to determine whether the new approach is robust under a variety of different conditions.

One test examined an environment in which 100 databases were randomly assigned to one of three search engines ("three-engine" test). A second set of tests examined an environment in which 100 databases were randomly assigned to one of two search engines ("two-engine" tests"). "Two-engine" tests were conducted with each pair of engines, so there are three "two-engine" tests. In each experiment the CORI algorithm ranked databases, and the top 10 were considered selected for search

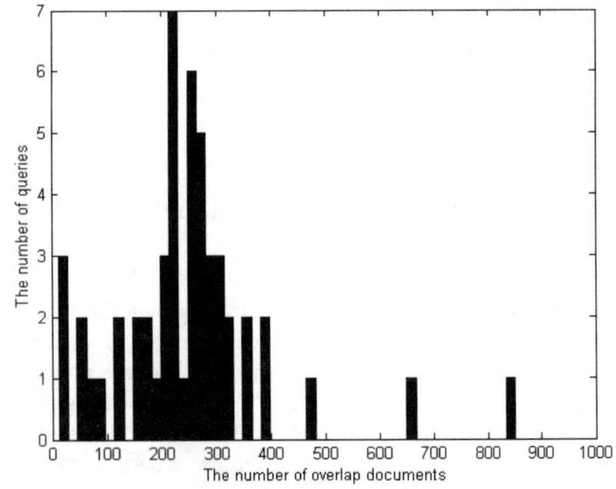

Figure 2. The distribution of overlap documents for 50 "Title" queries on the trec123 testbed.

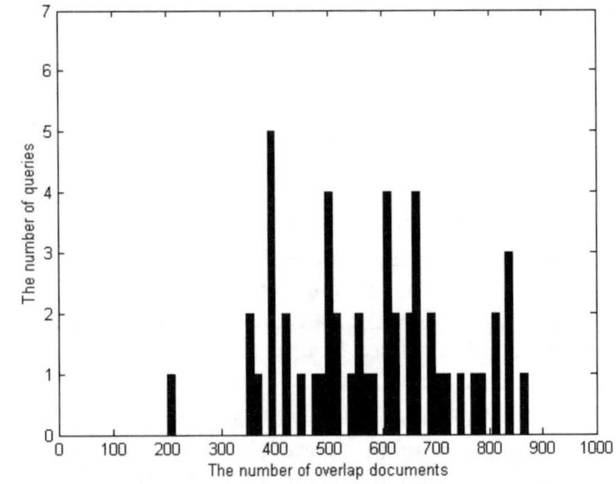

Figure 3. The distribution of overlap documents for 50 "Description" queries on the trec4 testbed.

Tests were also conducted with the CORI results merging algorithm, which we consider representative of the state-of-the-art in this area, and it is used as a baseline for comparison in the results below. Note that the CORI results merging algorithm is tuned to work well with the INQUERY search engine but would not necessarily be expected to work well with other search engines, or when the search engine is not known.

The "two engine" results are summarized in Table 3 (INQUERY and language model engines), Table 4 (INQUERY and SMART), and Table 5 (SMART and language model engine). Each table contains results averaged over 50 queries. Regression results shown in bold typeface are significantly better than the corresponding CORI performance (paired Wilcoxon test at p=0.05).

The trec123 testbed was the easiest for the results merging algorithms, because it has a relatively even distribution of vocabulary across databases. The regression algorithm was always as good as or better than the CORI results merging algorithm, but the largest difference was about 10%, for the INQUERY and SMART combination. The trec4_kmeans data was more difficult, because it has a very skewed vocabulary distribution. The regression algorithm handled this testbed far more effectively than the CORI results merging algorithm.

Table 3. Precision in "two search-engine type" environment (INQUERY and language model). Bold typeface indicates Regression significantly better than CORI.

Docs	**Trec123**		**Trec4_kmeans**	
Rank	**CORI**	**Regression**	**CORI**	**Regression**
5	0.3600	*0.4080* (+13.3%)	0.2640	**0.4040** (+53.0%)
10	0.3460	*0.3820* (+10.4%)	0.1900	**0.3780** (+98.9%)
15	0.3480	*0.3560* (+2.3%)	0.1840	**0.3400** (+84.8%)
20	0.3400	*0.3440* (+1.2%)	0.1800	**0.3130** (+73.9%)
30	0.3247	0.3200 (-1.4%)	0.1647	**0.2740** (+66.4%)

Table 4. Precision in "two search-engine type" environment (INQUERY and SMART). Bold typeface indicates Regression significantly better than CORI.

Docs	**Trec123**		**Trec4_kmeans**	
Rank	**CORI**	**Regression**	**CORI**	**Regression**
5	0.2840	*0.3280* (+15.5%)	0.2280	**0.3360** (+47.3%)
10	0.2700	*0.3040* (+12.6%)	0.1660	**0.3080** (+85.5%)
15	0.2640	*0.2947* (+11.6%)	0.1613	**0.2760** (+71.1%)
20	0.2610	*0.2820* (+8.0%)	0.1610	**0.2620** (+62.7%)
30	0.2487	**0.2867** (+15.3%)	0.1487	**0.2240** (+50.6%)

Table 5. Precision in "two search-engine type" environment (language model and SMART). Bold typeface indicates Regression significantly better than CORI.

Docs	**Trec123**		**Trec4_kmeans**	
Rank	**CORI**	**Regression**	**CORI**	**Regression**
5	0.2880	*0.2960* (+2.8%)	0.2120	**0.3400** (+60.4%)
10	0.2680	*0.2860* (+6.7%)	0.1800	**0.3120** (+73.3%)
15	0.2693	*0.2840* (+5.5%)	0.1680	**0.2720** (+61.9%)
20	0.2680	0.2750 (+2.6%)	0.1620	**0.2530** (+56.2%)
30	0.2620	*0.2687* (+1.6%)	0.1507	**0.2333** (+51.4%)

The "three engine" results are summarized in Table 6. As in the "two engine" experiments, the regression model has a clear advantage over the CORI results merging algorithm, and that advantage is more pronounced on the trec4_kmeans testbed.

6.1 Tuning the CORI Parameter

There are two factors in the merging problem: document score and database weight. The CORI results merging algorithm used as a baseline assigns a constant value for the database weight for all the queries. The power of our regression model is that it can automatically adjust the database weight, and the weight can be different for different queries.

It is an open question how well the CORI baseline could do if it had a better database weight parameter in the merging formula. The formula can be expressed as shown below:

$$D'' = \frac{D' + k * D' * C_i'}{1 + k} \qquad (17)$$

Table 6. Precision in "three search-engine type" environment (INQUERY, language model and SMART). Bold typeface indicates Regression significantly better than CORI.

Docs Rank	Trec123		Trec4_kmeans	
	CORI	Regression	CORI	Regression
5	0.3240	*0.3520* (+8.6%)	0.2560	**0.3640** (+42.2%)
10	0.3020	*0.3400* (+12.6%)	0.1920	**0.2940** (+54.4%)
15	0.3013	*0.3280* (+8.9%)	0.1787	**0.2760** (+43.5%)
20	0.2960	**0.3290** (+11.1%)	0.1770	**0.2540** (+47.4%)
30	0.2947	*0.3200* (+7.0%)	0.1560	**0.2300** (+46.0%)

Table 7. Precision in "one search-engine type" environment (INQUERY). Bold typeface indicates Regression significantly better than CORI.

Docs Rank	Trec123		Trec4_kmeans	
	CORI	Regression	CORI	Regression
5	0.4480	*0.4680* (+4.5%)	0.4240	*0.4520* (+6.6%)
10	0.4220	*0.4360* (+3.3%)	0.3860	*0.4060* (+5.2%)
15	0.4053	*0.4107* (+1.3%)	0.3400	*0.3573* (+4.6%)
20	0.3820	*0.3840* (+0.5%)	0.3140	*0.3230* (+2.9%)
30	0.3627	*0.3647* (+0.6%)	0.2753	**0.2913** (+5.8%)

The parameter *k* controls the effect of the database score in the results merging formula. A series of experiments using two testbeds was conducted to examine the effects of varying *k*.

When *k* was set to a constant value, average precision at rank r remained relatively constant over a range *k* values (Figures 4 and 5). However, the regression results show that setting k on a query-by-query basis for different databases provided a large improvement over any constant value of k. The ability to tune the results-merging formula on a query-by-query basis is the real power of the regression approach.

7. Results: Single Engine

A series of single-engine type experiments was conducted to test the effectiveness of the new approach to results merging. In each case the search engine was INQUERY, chosen in part because it is well-tuned for use with the baseline CORI results merging algorithm. The combination of CORI and INQUERY has been the state-of-the-art in this research area. Two 100-database testbeds with different document distribution patterns were used (Section 4.1). As in the multi-engine experiments, the CORI algorithm was used to rank databases for each query, and the top 10 were considered selected for search.

The experimental results are summarized in Table 7. They show that the regression model performs about the same as the CORI results merging algorithm when the vocabulary is distributed relatively evenly across the testbed (trec123), but that it has a small advantage when the vocabulary distribution is skewed (trec4_kmeans). The CORI results merging algorithm is clearly well-tuned for the INQUERY search engine, but even in a "best case" scenario for the CORI results merging algorithm, the new regression approach to results merging has a small advantage.

8. Conclusion

This paper presents a new solution for merging retrieval results returned by different databases in a distributed information retrieval

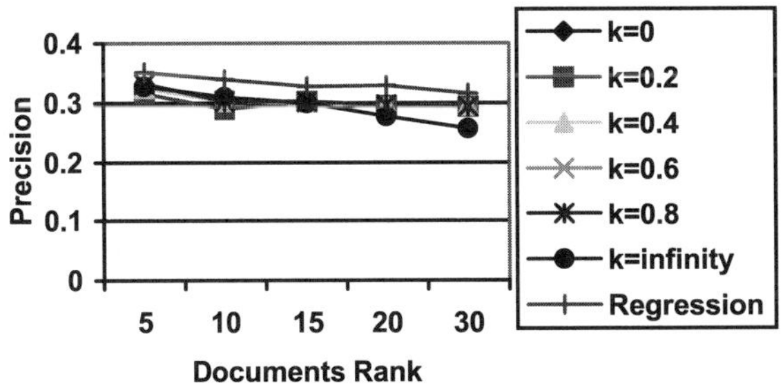

Figure 4. How varying the k parameter in the CORI results merging algorithm affects Precision. trec123 testbed.

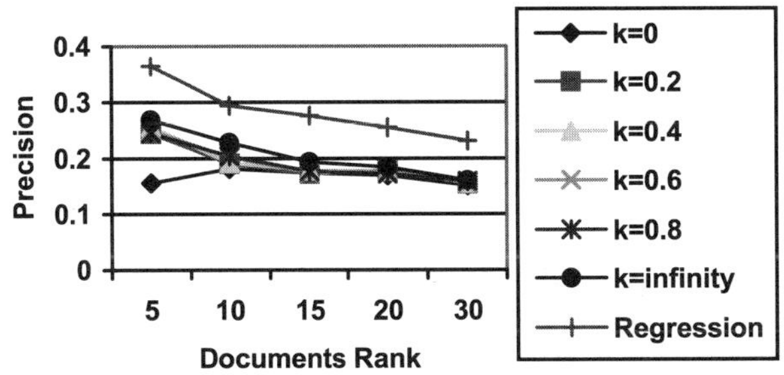

Figure 5. How varying the k parameter in the CORI results merging algorithm affects Precision. trec4_kmeans testbed.

environment. A common approach is to view results-merging in isolation from the rest of the distributed retrieval system, which conveniently bounds the problem, but which also limits the information available for solving the problem. By viewing it in the context of a complete distributed retrieval solution, other options become available. In particular, when resource descriptions for database selection are constructed by query-based sampling, a set of documents becomes available that can serve as training data for adaptive merging methods.

In this paper we present a particular adaptive solution based on linear regression and simple models for transforming database-specific scores into approximations of scores that would be obtained if all of the documents were in a single, centralized database. This is a more principled approach to normalizing document scores returned from different databases and different search engines than most of the prior research on this problem. Experiments with two rather different 100-database testbeds and in single-engine type and multiple-engine type configurations demonstrate that this approach is more effective than a well-known and relatively effective heuristic solution.

Our experiments demonstrate that our particular adaptive solution is effective in large part because it can tune the transformation on a query-by-query basis for different databases. There is no single parameter setting of the models we explored that provides similar effectiveness. Although one might expect that query-by-query tuning would be effective, we are not aware of any prior solutions that enable such tuning automatically.

We make no claims that the particular models and approach to regression presented here are the best. They are effective, but one can imagine other models and methods. Exploration of other models, features, and learning methods is an important topic for future research. The problem is challenging, because the amount of training data (the number of "overlap" documents) is often very small for a single query. However some queries produce large amounts of training data, so it may make sense to use different algorithms depending on the amount of training data available for a particular query.

We began this paper by arguing that in many interesting distributed retrieval environments one cannot rely upon any kind of cooperation from search engines beyond their traditional service of accepting queries and returning documents. Our experiments show that a results merging algorithm that assumes no cooperation has better performance than a well-known heuristic algorithm. Solutions designed for completely cooperative environments will always have an advantage, but our results suggest that the performance difference will begin to shrink, and that partially cooperative solutions such as the CORI results merging algorithm may find limited applicability.

Results-merging in uncooperative environments has been a major open problem in distributed IR research for seven or eight years. It is not yet a solved problem, but the research reported here represents an important step forward in the state-of-the-art.

ACKNOWLEDGMENTS

This research was supported by NSF grants EIA-9983253 and IIS-0118767. Any opinions, findings, conclusions, or recommendations expressed in this paper are the authors', and do not necessarily reflect those of the sponsor.

REFERENCES

[1] J. Callan. Distributed information retrieval. In W.B. Croft, editor, *Advances in information retrieval.* pp. 127-150. Kluwer Academic Publishers, 2000.

[2] J. Callan, W.B. Croft, and J. Broglio, TREC and TIPSTER experiments with INQUERY. *Information Processing and Management, 31(3):327-343,* 1995.

[3] L. Gravano, C. Chang, H. Garcia-Molina, and A. Paepcke. STARTS: Stanford Proposal for Internet Meta-Searching. *In Proc. of the ACM-SIGMOD Int'l Conference on Management of Data,* 1997.

[4] J. Callan and M. Connell. Query-based sampling of text databases. *ACM Transactions on Information Systems, 19(2):97-130,* 2001.

[5] N. Fuhr. A decision-theoretic approach to database selection in networked IR. *ACM Transactions on Information Systems, 17(3):229--249,* 1999.

[6] L. Gravano and H. Garcia-Molina. Generalizing GloSS to Vector-Space Databases and Broker Hierarchies. *In Proceedings of the 21st International Conference on Very Large Databases (VLDB),* 1995.

[7] J. Xu and J. Callan. Effective Retrieval with Distributed Collections. In *Proc. of the 21st Annual Int'l ACM SIGIR Conference on Research and Development in Information Retrieval,* 1998.

[8] B. Yuwono and D. Lee. Server Ranking for Distributed Text Retrieval Systems on Internet. *In Proc. of the Int. Conf. on Database Systems for Adv. Applications, pages 41-49,* 1997.

[9] N. Craswell, P.Bailey, and D.Hawking. Server selection on the World Wide Web. *In Proc. of the Fifth ACM Conference on Digital Libraries, pp. 37-46.* ACM, 2000.

[10] C. L. Viles and J. C. French. Dissemination of Collection Wide Information in a Distributed Information Retrieval System. In *Proc. of the 18th Annual Int'l ACM SIGIR Conference on Research and Development in Information Retrieval,* 1995.

[11] S. T. Kirsch. Document retrieval over networks wherein ranking and relevance scores are computed at the client for multiple database documents. U.S. Patent 5,659,732.

[12] N. Craswell, D. Hawking, and P. Thistlewaite. Merging Results from Isolated Search Engines. *In Proc. of the Tenth Australasian Database Conf., pages 189--200,* 1999

[13] J.C. French, A.L. Powell, J. Callan, C.L. Viles, T. Emmitt, K.J. Prey, and Y. Mou. Comparing the performance of database selection algorithms. In *Proc. of the 22nd Annual Int'l ACM SIGIR Conference on Research and Development in Information Retrieval,* 1999.

[14] J. H. Lee. Analyses of multiple evidence combination. In *Proc. of the 20th Annual Int'l ACM SIGIR Conference on Research and Development in Information Retrieval,* 1997.

[15] R. Manmatha, T. Rath, and F. Feng. Modeling score distributions for combining the outputs of search engines. In *Proc. of the 24th Annual Int'l ACM SIGIR Conference on Research and Development in Information Retrieval,* 2001.

[16] A. Le Calv , J. Savoy. Database Merging Strategy Based on Logistic Regression. *Information Processing & Management, 36(3),* 2000.

[17] A.L. Powell, J.C. French, J. Callan, M. Connell, and C.L. Viles, The impact of database selection on distributed searching. In *Proc. of the 23rd Annual Int'l ACM SIGIR Conference on Research and Development in Information Retrieval,* 2000.

[18] J. Xu and W.B. Croft, Cluster-based language models for distributed retrieval. In *Proc. of the 22nd Annual Int'l ACM SIGIR Conference on Research and Development in Information Retrieval,* 1999.

[19] C. Buckley, A. Singhal, M. Mitra, and G. Salton, New retrieval approaches using SMART. *In Proceedings of 1995 Text REtrieval Conference (TREC-3).* National Institute of Standards and Technology, special publication.

[20] L. Larkey, M. Connell, and J. Callan. Collection selection and results merging with topically organized U.S. patents and TREC data. *In Proceedings of Conference of Information and Knowledge Management,* 2000.

[21] J. A. Aslam, M. Montague. Models for Metasearch. In *Proc. of the 23rd Annual Int'l ACM SIGIR Conference on Research and Development in Information Retrieval,* 2001.

[22] P. Ogilvie, J. Callan. Experiments using the Lemur toolkit. *In Proc of 2001 Text REtrieval Conference (TREC 2001).* National Institute of Standards and Technology, special publication.

[23] Ellen Voorhees, Narendra K. Gupta, and Ben Johnson-Laird. Learning Collection Fusion Strategies. In *Proc. of the 18th Annual International ACM SIGIR Conference on Research and Development in Information Retrieval,* 1995.

The Importance of Prior Probabilities for Entry Page Search

Wessel Kraaij
TNO TPD
PO BOX 155
2600 AD Delft
The Netherlands
kraaijw@acm.org

Thijs Westerveld
University of Twente
PO BOX 217
7500 AE Enschede
The Netherlands
westerve@cs.utwente.nl

Djoerd Hiemstra
University of Twente
PO BOX 217
7500 AE Enschede
The Netherlands
hiemstra@cs.utwente.nl

ABSTRACT

An important class of searches on the world-wide-web has the goal to find an entry page (homepage) of an organisation. Entry page search is quite different from Ad Hoc search. Indeed a plain Ad Hoc system performs disappointingly. We explored three non-content features of web pages: page length, number of incoming links and URL form. Especially the URL form proved to be a good predictor. Using URL form priors we found over 70% of all entry pages at rank 1, and up to 89% in the top 10. Non-content features can easily be embedded in a language model framework as a prior probability.

Categories and Subject Descriptors

H.3.3 [**Information Storage and Retrieval**]: Information Search and Retrieval

General Terms

Experimentation

Keywords

Entry Page Search, Prior Probabilities, Links, URLs, Language Models, Parameter Estimation

1. INTRODUCTION

Entry page searching is different from general information searching, not only because entry pages differ from other web documents, but also because the goals of the tasks are different. In a general, Ad Hoc search task as defined for TREC [35, 36, 37], the goal is to find as many relevant documents as possible. The entry page (EP) task is concerned with finding the central page of an organisation, which functions as a portal for the information[1]. Since EP search has the goal to retrieve just one document, an IR system should probably be more optimised for high precision than for high recall. Search engine users typically prefer to find an EP in the first screen of results. Since queries are usually very short, finding an EP with a high initial precision is quite difficult. This paper explores ways to enhance IR systems designed for the Ad Hoc task by taking advantage of document features, which are usually ignored for the Ad Hoc task, since they were not effective. Our experiments for the EP task at TREC-2001 have shown that link structure, URLs and anchor texts are useful sources of information for locating entry pages[38].

Experiments of other groups confirmed the effectiveness of these features [6, 14, 7, 27, 32, 39]. In this paper we show how knowledge about the relationship between the non-content features of a webpage an its likelihood of being an EP can easily be incorporated in a retrieval model based on statistical language models. In Section 2 we discuss related work on tuning retrieval models to a specific task and other work on the use of information sources other than the document content. Section 3 discusses the basic language modelling approach and how priors can be used in this model. In Section 4 we discuss different sources of prior knowledge that can be used in an EP searching task. We describe our evaluation methodology in Section 5 and discuss our experiments and present results in Section 6. We conclude with a discussion of these results and a summary of our main conclusions.

[1] Entry pages for individual persons are usually referred to as homepages.

SIGIR'02, August 11-15, 2002, Tampere, Finland.

2. CONTEXT AND RELATED WORK

In this section we will give argue that it is common practice to tailor IR methods to a specific search task, or even to a certain test collection, to optimize performance. It is important though, to use principled methods instead of ad hoc solutions.

2.1 Tuning IR systems

The use of proper term statistics is of the utmost importance for the quality of retrieval results on the Ad Hoc search task. All main IR models based on relevance ranking exploit these statistics and are based on at least two ingredients: the frequency of a term in a document and the distribution of a term in the document collection. IR models typically have evolved in close relationship with the availability of test collections. The older test collections were based on abstracts, so it was safe to assume that documents had about the same length. Since test collections are based on full text, this assumption does not hold anymore, and IR models have been refined to include a component which models the document length influence. Early attempts to combine the three main ingredients of an IR system were rather ad hoc and were not based on formal models. For example, Salton and Buckley [30] evaluated many combinations of term frequency statistics, document frequency statistics and document length normalisation without an explicit model for the relationship between these factors. The combine and test strategy was pursued further by Zobel and Moffat [40]. They tested 720 different term weighting strategies based on different similarity functions, length normalisation strategies, document term weighting etc. on 6 different query collections. They concluded that their exhaustive test strategy (4 weeks of computation time) had not resulted in any conclusive results that held across test collections. Instead of trying many ad hoc algorithms, Robertson and Walker [29] experimented with simple approximations of the 2-Poisson model[2]. The OKAPI formula is an approximation of a theoretically justified model, integrating the three components. The OKAPI formula includes tuning parameters that determine e.g. the influence of the term frequency or the influence of the document length normalisation. The parameters can be used to tune a system to the retrieval task and test collection at hand.

Based on the success of Robertson and Walker, Singhal et al. [33] showed that for the Ad Hoc search task, there is a correlation between the document length and the a-priori probability of relevance. The document length is a good example of information about a document that is not directly related to its contents, but might still be related to the possible relevance of the document: If we build a rather silly system that returns the longest document for any user query, then we actually might do better than returning a random document from the collection.

2.2 Non-content features of WEB pages

An important source of prior knowledge for web based information retrieval is the hyperlink structure. The idea behind most link structure analysis is that if there exists a link from document A to document B, this probably means that document A and B are on the same topic (*topic locality* assumption) and that the author of document A recommends document B (*recommendation* assumption). Two of the most widely known and used algorithms for link structure analysis are PageRank [4] and HITS [18]. Both methods base there calculations on the assumption that a page to which many documents link is highly recommended and therefore an authority. The authoritativeness of a document is even higher if the documents that link to it are some sort of authorities themselves. HITS and PageRank (or variants of those) are reported to be successful in numerous studies of retrieval quality [18, 3, 1, 25, 5], however when measuring relevance only, without taking quality or authoritativeness into account, HITS and PageRank based methods have not been able to improve retrieval effectiveness for Ad Hoc search tasks [15, 13, 20, 31, 8].

Davison [11] shows that the topic locality assumption holds: when pages are linked, they are likely to contain related content. This means that documents that are linked to relevant documents are potentially relevant themselves. However, exploitation of this idea by spreading retrieval scores over links has not proven successful in a general information retrieval task yet [20, 12]. On the other hand, the TREC-2001 evaluation showed that link structure analysis *does* improve content only results in an entry page search task [14, 38].

Another source of prior knowledge in web based retrieval is the URL. We are not aware of any studies in which URL knowledge was used for an Ad Hoc search. However, the TREC-2001 evaluation showed that the fact that entry pages tend to have shorter URLs than other documents can be successfully exploited by a ranking algorithm.[14, 38, 27, 32, 39].

2.3 Priors in LM based IR

Prior knowledge can be used in a standard way in the language modelling approach to information retrieval. The language modelling approach uses simple document-based unigram language models for document ranking [26]. Early TREC Ad Hoc experiments by Hiemstra and Kraaij [17] show that indeed the document length serves as a helpful prior for the Ad Hoc task, especially for short queries. Miller et al. [23] combined information in their document priors, including document length, source and average word length. In this paper we adapt the standard language modelling approach to the entry page search by including the prior probabilities in the estimation process. We show that proper use of prior probabilities results improvements of more than 100 % over the base-line language modelling system on the entry page task. Although we mainly address entry page searching here, we follow a generic approach. By following the suggested language modelling approach we can quickly adapt our standard retrieval system to other tasks or domains, e.g. automatic summarisation [19].

[2]However, the motivation to extend the original probabilistic model [28] with within-document term frequency and document length normalisation was probably based on empirical observations.

3. LANGUAGE MODELLING AND PRIOR PROBABILITIES

For all our experiments we used an information retrieval system based on a simple statistical language model [16]. We are interested in the probability that a document D is relevant given a query Q, which can be reformulated as follows using Bayes' rule:

$$P(D|Q) \;=\; \frac{P(D)\,P(Q|D)}{P(Q)}$$

The main motivation for applying Bayes' rule is that the probabilities on the right-hand side can be estimated more accurately than the probabilities on the left-hand side. For the purpose of document ranking, we can simply ignore $P(Q)$ since it does not depend on the documents. The probability $P(Q|D)$ can be represented by a document-based unigram language model. The standard language modelling approach would model the query Q as a sequence of n query terms $T_1, \cdots, T_n$, and use a linear combination of a unigram document model $P(T_i|D)$ and a collection model $P(T_i|C)$ for smoothing[3] as follows:

$$P(D|T_1, \cdots, T_n) \propto P(D) \prod_{i=1}^{n} (1-\lambda) P(T_i|C) + \lambda P(T_i|D) \tag{1}$$

The probability measure $P(T_i|C)$ defines the probability of drawing a term at random from the collection, $P(T_i|D)$ defines the probability of drawing a term at random from the document and λ is the interpolation parameter, which is assumed to be some fixed constant. This leaves us with the definition of the prior probability of relevance of a document $P(D)$[4].

3.1 Estimating Priors

We distinguish two approaches to estimating the prior: direct estimation of the prior on some training data, and definition of the prior based on some general modelling assumptions.

As an example, let's have a look at the assumption that the prior probability of relevance is correlated with the document length on the Ad Hoc task. Figure 1 shows a plot of the probability of relevance against the document length for the Ad Hoc task of the TREC-2001 web track. To smooth the estimates, we divided the document

[3]This smoothing technique is also known as Jelinek-Mercer smoothing

[4]Relevance is not explicitly encoded in formula (1). Cf. [21] for a variant formulation of the model that includes relevance as a variable in the model. Both models lead to an equivalent term weighting function

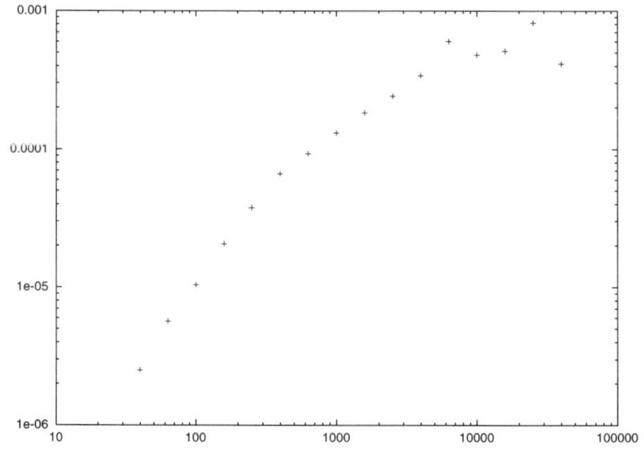

Figure 1: Prior probability of relevance given document length on the Ad Hoc task

length, which varies from documents containing only one or two words to documents containing over 10,000 words, into 16 bins on a logscale. Each point on the plot marks the probability of relevance of the documents in one of these bins. The 16 bins and the corresponding probabilities define a discrete probability measure $P(D)$ which takes one of 16 different values based on the bin in which D falls. As such, it can be used directly in Equation 1. Alternatively, looking at the plot, one could make the general modelling assumption that the a-priori probability of relevance is taken to be a linear function of the document length, so:

$$P_{doclen}(D) = P(R|D) = C \cdot doclen(D) \quad (2)$$

where R is a binary random variable 'relevance', $doclen(D)$ is the total number of words in document D, and C is a constant that can be ignored in the ranking formula. The intuition behind this assumption is that longer documents tend to cover more topics and thus have a higher probability of relevance. Indeed, the linear relationship between document length and probability of relevance is a reasonable model for different Ad Hoc test collections [20]. Including the prior especially can improve m.a.p. with up to 0.03 on an absolute scale, depending on the query length.

3.2 Combining Priors

What if we have different sources of information that might influence the a-priori probability of relevance, e.g. the length of a web page or its top level domain? The problem can be formalised as follows, we want to estimate:

$$P(R|D) = P(R|\bar{\mathbf{x}}) = P(R|x_1, x_2, \ldots, x_n) \quad (3)$$

In formula (3), R is a binary random variable 'relevance', $\bar{\mathbf{x}}$ is a shorthand for $(\bar{\mathbf{D}} = \bar{\mathbf{x}})$, i.e. $\bar{\mathbf{D}}$ is a random variable 'document' with as value a vector of document features $\bar{\mathbf{x}} = (x_1, x_2, ..., x_k)$. The problem is that we do not have a closed form solution for the prior $P(R|\bar{\mathbf{x}})$ and there is a very limited set of training data to estimate the prior for different feature values, so we have to find a smart way to estimate our prior. A possible approach is to apply the Naive Bayes assumption. Consider the Naive Bayes approach [24, 22] to classification:

$$C' = \text{argmax}_{C_k} P(C_k|\bar{\mathbf{x}}) = \frac{P(\bar{\mathbf{x}}|C_k)P(C_k)}{P(\bar{\mathbf{x}})} \quad (4)$$

Here, C' represents the class of an instance which is chosen among the set of mutually disjoint classes C_k. The decision rule chooses the C_k for which the numerator $P(\bar{\mathbf{x}}|C_k)P(C_k)$ is maximal given a certain vector of attributes $\bar{\mathbf{x}}$. Especially when there are many features, it is difficult to estimate the probabilities. A common strategy is to assume that the features are conditionally independent: $P(\bar{\mathbf{x}}|C_k) = \prod_i P(x_i|C_k)$, this is the well known *naive* Bayes assumption. This assumption results in a smaller number of probabilities that have to be estimated. The same estimation problem holds for the denominator, but this term can be ignored for classification tasks, since it is constant across the classes. In our case, there are only 2 different classes, namely relevant documents and irrelevant documents (or entry pages vs. non-entry pages). In addition, we're not only interested in the class with the highest probability, but we want to estimate the exact probability that a document is relevant given several attributes, since we want to use it for ranking. Therefore we cannot ignore the denominator since it is different for each attribute vector. So, Formula 5 should be used to estimate the priors.

$$P(C_k|\bar{\mathbf{x}}) = \frac{\prod_{j=1}^{n} P(x_j|C_k)P(C_k)}{\sum_k(\prod_{j=1}^{n} P(x_j|C_k)P(C_k))} \quad (5)$$

Indeed, the parameters in this formula are much easier to estimate. As an example, suppose we have three features, with five values each. Direct estimation of the probability of relevance would require the estimation of 125 conditional probabilities. In the Naive Bayes approach, only 30 relative frequencies would have to be computed. An alternative approach could be to reduce the number of parameters in our model, e.g. reducing the number of classes per feature to three, yielding $3^3 = 27$ parameters in order to reduce variance.

For our experiment with combined priors, we combined two features (URL form and #inlinks) each with 4 different feature values. As a simple baseline, we assumed conditional independence of the features given relevance, and approximated Formula 5 by replacing the denominator by $\prod_j^n P(x_j)$, obviating the need to build a training set for non Entry Pages. The approximated formula can be further reduced to:

$$P(C_k|\bar{\mathbf{x}}) = \frac{\prod_{j=1}^{n} P(C_k|x_j)P(C_k)}{\prod_{j=1}^{n} P(C_k)} = K \prod_{j=1}^{n} P(C_k|x_j) \quad (6)$$

which is equivalent to the product of the individual priors and a constant.

We contrasted this approximated Naive Bayes run, with a run where we directly estimated (3), but based on a reduced number of classes. We defined seven disjoint classes in such a way that there were at least 4 positive training examples in each class. This was done by merging several attribute vectors into one class. Section 6.2 describes the procedure in more detail.

3.3 Combining Content Models

Just as we might have different sources of information to estimate prior probabilities, we might as well have different sources of information to estimate content models. As an example, consider the possibility to estimate a document language model on the anchor texts of all hyperlinks pointing to the document. Note that the score provided by a query on the anchor texts is not a document prior. The anchor texts and the body texts ('content-only') provide two very different textual representations of the documents. The IR language models can accommodate several document representations in a straightforward manner, by defining a mixture model. Our preferred way of combining two representations would be by the following, revised ranking formula.

$$P(D|T_1, \cdots, T_n) \propto P(D) \prod_{i=1}^{n} ((1-\lambda-\mu)P(T_t|C) + \lambda P_{\text{content}}(T_i|D) + \mu P_{\text{anchor}}(T_i|D)) \quad (7)$$

So, the combination of the anchor run with the content run would be done on a 'query term by query term' basis, whereas the combination with the document prior is done separately. Unfortunately, the current implementation of our retrieval system does not support combining document representations like this. Instead, the anchor experiments described in the next sections were done separately from the content runs, their document scores being combined afterwards. In a document summarisation setting we showed the potential of similar mixture models for ranking [19].

4. PRIOR PROBABILITIES IN ENTRY PAGE SEARCH

In an entry page search task, a user is searching for the main entry page of a specific organisation or group within an organisation. This is the main entry point for information about that group on the WWW. From here, one can usually navigate to the other web pages of the same group. For example the main entry page of SIGIR 2002 is `http://www.sigir2002.org`.

A query in an entry page search task consists of nothing more than the name of the organisation or group whose entry page we're after. In general there are only a few correct answers: the URL of the entry page of the requested organisation and perhaps some alternate URLs pointing to the same page and a few mirror sites.

Entry page searching is similar to known item searching. In both types of searches, a user is looking for one specific piece of information. However, in known item search the user has already seen the information needed, whereas in entry page search this is not necessarily the case.

Since entry page search is a different task than Ad Hoc search, different prior probabilities might be needed. We investigated which sources of information are useful priors for entry page searching and whether priors are needed at all for such a task.

We looked at three different sources of information: i) The length of a document ; ii) The number of links pointing to a document (inlinks) ; iii) The depth of a document's URL.

Features we didn't investigate, but which might be useful for estimating whether a page is an entry page include: the number of occurrences of certain cue words (e.g. 'Welcome', 'home'), the number of links in a document (outlinks) and the number of times a page is visited.

4.1 Document Length

Section 3.1 showed that document length priors are useful in an Ad Hoc search task. Here we investigate whether the length of a document is also a useful indicator of the probability that a document is an entry page. Figure 2 shows a plot of the probability of relevance versus page length, calculated on the training data provided for the entry page search task of TREC-2001's web track.

Indeed document length can predict the relevance of a page, since the distribution is not uniform. Pages with a medium length (60-1000 words) have a higher probability, with a maximum around 100-200 words. However, the differences are much less marked as for Ad Hoc search. Although it is clear that the dependence of the probability of relevance on document length is quite different from the Ad Hoc task, we ran an experiment where we used our best performing IR model for the Ad Hoc task (language model plus

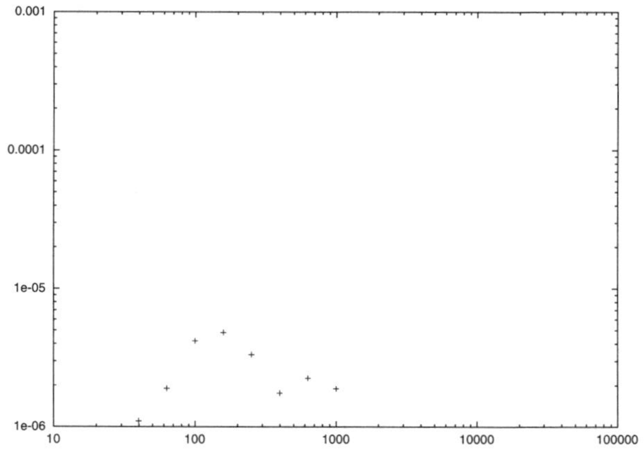

Figure 2: Prior probability of relevance given document length on the Entry Page task ($P(entry\ page|doclen)$)

document length prior as defined in (2)) on the EP task, to show that models that perform well on Ad Hoc do not necessarily perform well on the Entry Page task.

4.2 Number of InLinks

In a hypertext collection like the WWW, documents are connected through hyperlinks. A hyperlink is a connection between a source and a target document. Our inlinks based prior is based on the observation that entry pages tend to have a higher number of inlinks than other documents (i.e. they are referenced more often). The plot of the probability of being an entry page against the number of inlinks in Figure 3 shows this correlation for the training data for the entry page task of TREC-2001's web track. Since the

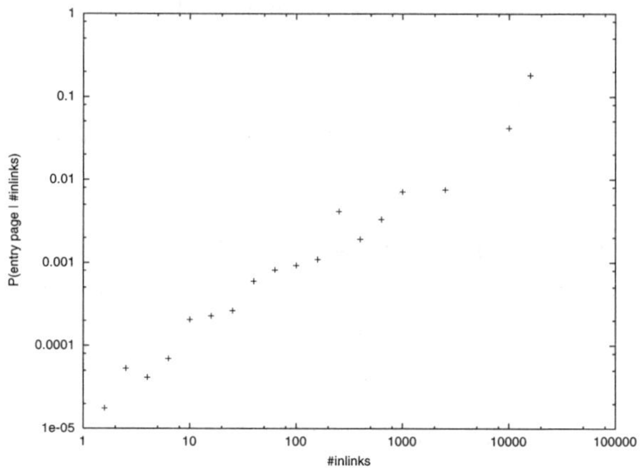

Figure 3: Prior probability of relevance given number of inlinks on the Entry Page task ($P(entry\ page|inlinkCount)$)

plot suggests a linear relationship, we define the inlink prior as:

$$P_{inlink}(D) = P(R|D) = C \cdot inlinkCount(D) \quad (8)$$

where R is a binary random variable 'relevance', $inlinkcount(D)$ is the count of the number of inlinks in document D and C is a constant.

Note that, although we didn't differentiate between links from the same host and links from other hosts, doing so might be interesting. These different types of links have different functions. Links from other hosts often imply a form of recommendation, whereas links from the same host mainly serve navigational purposes. However, both types of links probably point more often to entry pages than to other pages. Recommendation links usually point to the main entry point of a site and sites are often organised in such a way that each page links to the entry page.

4.3 URL Depth

A third source of prior information is the URL of a document. A URL defines the unique location of a document on the WWW. It consists of the name of the server, a directory path and a filename. A first observation is that documents that are right at the top level of a specific server (i.e. the documents of which the URL is no more than a server name) are often entry pages. Also, as we descend deeper into the directory tree, the relative amount of entry pages decreases. Thus the probability of being an entry page seems to be inversely related to the depth of the path in the corresponding URL.

We define four types of URLs:

root: a domain name, optionally followed by 'index.html' (e.g. `http://www.sigir.org`)

subroot: a domain name, followed by a single directory, optionally followed by 'index.html' name (e.g. `http://www.sigir.org/sigirlist/`)

path: a domain name, followed by an arbitrarily deep path, but not ending in a file name other than 'index.html' (e.g. `http://www.sigir.org/sigirlist/issues/`)

file: anything ending in a filename other than 'index.html' (e.g. `http://www.sigir.org/resources.html`)

Analysis of both WT10g, the collection used in TREC-2001's web track, and the correct answers to the training topics for the track's entry page task (i.e. the correct entry pages), shows that entry pages have a very different distribution over the four URL-types (cf. Table 1). As suspected, entry pages seem to be mainly of type

URL type	Entry pages		WT10g	
root	79	(73.1%)	12258	(0.7%)
subroot	15	(13.9%)	37959	(2.2%)
path	8	(7.4%)	83734	(4.9%)
file	6	(5.6%)	1557719	(92.1%)

Table 1: Distributions of entry pages and WT10g over URL-types

root while most documents in the collection are of type file. For inlinks, we were able to define a model for the prior probability of relevance given the number of inlinks, which is a good approximation of the real data. For the URL prior it is less straightforward to define such an analytical model. Therefore, we estimated the URL based prior directly on the training collection:

$$P_{URL}(D) = P(EP|URLtype(D) = t_i) = \frac{c(EP, t_i)}{c(t_i)}, \quad (9)$$

where $URLtype(D)$ is the type of the URL of document D, $c(EP, t_i)$ is the number of documents that is both an entry page and of type t_i and $c(t_i)$ is the number of documents of type t_i. The resulting probabilities for the different URL-types are listed in Table 2. Note that the prior probabilities differ several orders of magnitude; a root page has an almost 2000 times larger probability of being an entry page than any other page.

$P(Entry\,page \mid root)$	$6.44 \cdot 10^{-03}$
$P(Entry\,page \mid subroot)$	$3.95 \cdot 10^{-04}$
$P(Entry\,page \mid path)$	$9.55 \cdot 10^{-05}$
$P(Entry\,page \mid file)$	$3.85 \cdot 10^{-06}$

Table 2: Prior probabilities for different URL-types, estimated on the training data

5. EVALUATION

We compared the different priors discussed in the previous section using collections and relevance judgements from the entry page finding task of TREC-2001's web track. The Text Retrieval Conferences (TREC) [35, 36, 37], are a series of workshops aimed at large-scale testing of retrieval technology. The entry page finding task was designed to evaluate methods for locating entry pages. In this task a search topic consists of a single phrase stating the name of a specific group or organisation, for some examples cf. Table 3. A

Worldnet Africa
Hunt Memorial Library
Haas Business School
University of Wisconsin Lidar Group

Table 3: Example topics for entry page search task

system should retrieve the entry page for the group or organisation described in the topic. E.g. when a topic is *University of Wisconsin Lidar Group*, the entry page for this specific group should be retrieved. Retrieving the homepage for the whole University or for a subgroup of the Lidar group would be counted incorrect. Topics for the entry page finding task were created by randomly selecting a document from the document collection and following links from there until they got to a document they considered to be the homepage of a site that contained the document they started with. This way, 145 topics were constructed for this task. In addition a set of 100 topics was provided for training purposes. We used the latter set for making the plots in sections 4.1 and 4.2 from which we inferred the document length and inlink priors. The same set was used for estimating the URL priors as described in section 4.3. The experiments reported in the next section are all conducted using the set of 145 test topics.

The collection to be searched for this task is the WT10g collection [2], a 10 gigabytes subset of the VLC2 collection which in turn is a subset of a 1997 crawl of the WWW done by the Internet Archive [5]. WT10g is designed to have a relatively high density of inter-server hyperlinks.

For each combination of document prior and language model, we ranked our document collection and returned the top 100 results. Runs were evaluated by the mean reciprocal rank (MRR) measure. For each topic the reciprocal value ($1/n$) of the rank (n) of the highest ranked correct entry page is computed, subsequently these values are averaged. If no correct entry page was found for a specific topic the reciprocal of the rank for this topic is defined 0.

6. EXPERIMENTS

For our experiments we used the IR model described in section 3. The prior probability in our model, $P(D)$ was instantiated by one of the priors defined in section 4 or left out (i.e. uniform priors). The language models ($P(Q|D)$) were either estimated on

[5] `http://www.archive.org`

the document collection (WT10g) or on the collection of anchor based pseudo documents. This anchor-based collection was generated from the original WT10g data by gathering all anchor texts from links pointing to the same document in one pseudo document. This pseudo document was then used as a description of the original document.[6]. Again, we didn't differentiate between links from the same server and links from other servers. Documents were preprocessed as follows

1. remove HTML comment and script document fragments
2. remove HTML markup tags
3. map HTML entities to ISO-Latin1 characters
4. stop terms
5. stem terms using the Porter algorithm

Table 4 shows the mean reciprocal rank (MRR) for runs on both the web page and the anchor text collection in combination with different priors. Both inlinks and URL form help to increase search effectiveness, especially the URL prior is highly effective. Further discussion is deferred until Section 7.

Ranking method	Content ($\lambda = 0.9$)	Anchors($\lambda = 0.9$)
$P(Q\|D)$	0.3375	0.4188
$P(Q\|D)P_{doclen}(D)$	0.2634	0.5600
$P(Q\|D)P_{URL}(D)$	**0.7705**	0.6301
$P(Q\|D)P_{inlink}(D)$	0.4974	0.5365

Table 4: Results for different priors

6.1 Combining content models

We combined page content and anchor runs by a linear interpolation of the result files: $RSV' = \alpha RSV_{page} + (1 - \alpha)RSV_{anchor}$ Table 5 shows that although the combination strategy is not optimal

α	MRR
0.5	0.3978
0.7	0.4703
0.8	**0.4920**
0.9	0.4797

Table 5: Combining web page text and anchor text

(cf. Section 3.3), combining both content representation is useful. Best result is achieved for $\alpha = 0.8$: MRR=0.4920 (anchor text only run: MRR = 0.4188). We also investigated the effect of priors on these combined runs (Table 6).

Ranking method	Content+Anchors ($\alpha = 0.8$)
$P(Q\|D)$	0.4920
$P(Q\|D)P_{URL}(D)$	**0.7748**
$P(Q\|D)P_{inlink}(D)$	0.5963

Table 6: Results for different priors(content+anchor)

6.2 Combining Priors

In section 4 we saw that both the number of inlinks and the URL can give important information about whether a page is an entry page or not. The results in Table 4 confirm this. A combination of these two sources of information might also be useful. In section 3.2 we discussed different approaches for combining priors. Table 8 shows the results for both combination approaches. All runs are based on the web page corpus and do not regard anchor text. We have argued that the main problem of combining features is that it is difficult to estimate $P(EP|\bar{\mathbf{x}})$ directly, since the training collection is small. A simple approach is to multiply the individual priors, which is an approximation of a model based on the conditional independence assumption. This baseline combination run yielded an MMR value of 0.7504, which is lower than a run based on just the URL prior.

We conjecture that this disappointing result is due to the fact that there is conditional dependence between the features or that the approximation of the denominator is too crude. We investigated a variant run, without indepence assumptions, where we directly estimated $P(EP|\bar{\mathbf{x}})$, but based on a model with a reduced number of parameters.

For this approach we could not work with Formula (8), instead we disretized the #inlinks feature space in four bins on a logscale. Subsequently, we defined seven disjoint document classes. Table 7 shows their statistics. Since there are just a few entry pages in the training set of category non-root, we only divided the root class in four separate bins based on the number of inlinks. From these

Document type t_i	#entry pages		#WT10g	
root with 1-10 inlinks	39	(36.1%)	8938	(0.5%)
root with 11-100 inlinks	25	(23.1%)	2905	(0.2%)
root with 101-1000 inlinks	11	(10.2%)	377	(0.0%)
root with 1000+ inlinks	4	(3.7%)	38	(0.0%)
subroot	15	(13.9%)	37959	(2.2%)
path	8	(7.4%)	83734	(4.9%)
file	6	(5.6%)	1557719	(92%)

Table 7: Distribution entry pages and WT10g over different document types

statistics we computed a combined inlink-URL prior, using:

$$P_{inlink-URL}(EP|dt(D) = t_i) = \frac{c(EP, t_i)}{c(t_i)}, \qquad (10)$$

where $dt(D)$ is the document type of D and $c(.)$ is as defined in equation 9.

Table 8 summarises results for the combination experiments. In addition to the already tabulated single prior results, it shows the result for a run where the inlink prior was estimated on the training data instead of being modeled by Formula (2). The MRR of this run is lower than the run based on the analytical inlink prior, which probably means that the number of bins is too small. The combination runs show a marked difference: the run based on a naive multiplication of priors scores scores worse then the run based on the URL prior. However, the combination run which directly estimates $P(EP|\bar{\mathbf{x}})$, based on seven disjoint classes does improves upon the individual prior runs, so combination of priors performs better than a single prior.

7. DISCUSSION

The entry page task is significantly different from the Ad Hoc task. The main difference is that just one page is relevant, so recall enhancement techniques do not play a role, on the contrary, the goal is to boost initial precision. We experimented with content-only runs, based on either the web page content or its related anchor

[6]The experiments in this paper are based on the CSIRO anchor collection [6, 7], whereas the experiments reported in [38] are based on an anchor collection we built ourselves

Ranking method	Content	description
$P(Q\|D)P_{URL}(D)$	0.7705	
$P(Q\|D)P_{inlink}(D)$	0.4974	analytical prior
$P(Q\|D)P_{inlink}(D)$	0.4752	4 bins
$P(Q\|D)P_{URL+inlink}(D)$	0.7504	baseline: product of priors (analytical inlink prior)
$P(Q\|D)P_{URL+inlink}(D)$	**0.7749**	direct estimation (7 disjoint classes)

Table 8: Combining priors

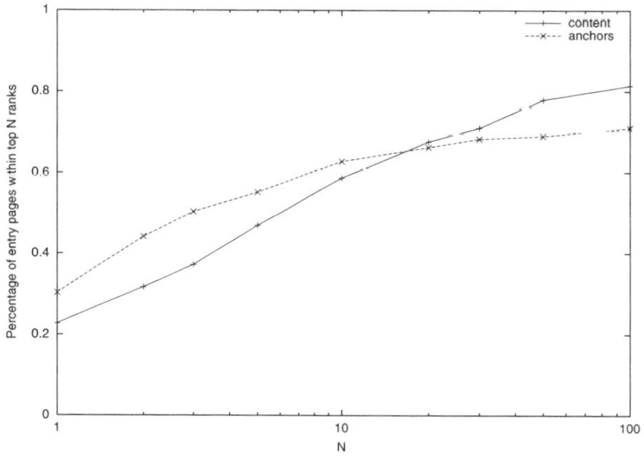

Figure 4: Succes at N for content and anchor runs

text, and with runs which also exploited other page characteristics, like number of links and URL form.

Interestingly, a run based on just the anchor text outperformed the basic content run by far, indicating that anchor text linking to entry pages often contains the name of the organisation's entry page. Combining both textual representations by simple interpolation proved effective: MRR = 0.4920 (+17%).

For content runs, an (exact) match of the query is not sufficiently discriminating to find entry pages, since a lot of web pages will have exact matches. Therefore, other features have to be used. We tested three different features: document length, number of inlinks and the URL form. A linear document length prior did significantly decrease MRR for the content run, which we had expected, since such a prior did not fit the training data at all. Nevertheless it is interesting to see that choosing a wrong prior can harm results. The linear document length prior seems to help the anchor run though, but that is an illusion. The length of an anchor text document consists of a concatenation of the anchor texts of the links pointing to a particular web page. Thus, the length of an anchor text 'document' is linearly related to the number of inlinks. Indeed, the anchor runs based on an inlinks prior or a document length prior have rather equivalent performance gains. There seems to be an additional gain of the document length prior though; apparently more verbose anchor texts are correlated with entry pages. The best results are achieved by the runs with a URL form based prior (the content run with a URL prior found over 70% of the entrypages at rank 1, and 87% in the top 10[7]). Surprisingly, the better result was achieved by the URL prior run based on the web page text. This can be explained by the fact that this run has a larger recall than the anchor text run. The URL prior is a powerful precision enhancing device which combines well with the web page content run, which has good recall. Figure 4 illustrates this: while the anchor run has a high initial success rate (30.3% of entry pages were found at rank 1; 22.8% for content), the content run in the end finds more homepages(81.4% found in top 100; 71.0% for anchors).

We also investigated whether we could combine URL and inlink features. A simple multiplication of priors (assuming conditional and statistical independence) deteriorated results. Another strategy, bases on a reduced number of classes, but without any independence assumptions yielded a small gain w.r.t. the URL prior run. We think that we could improve upon these results. With more training data we might be able to estimate the joint conditional probabilities of the two features in a more accurate way. The fact that the training data based inlink prior performed worse than the analytical prior (8) indicated that the number of bins is probably too small. The small number of bins might also have contributed to the disappointing results of the combination runs that use the inlink binning approach. We tested the latter hypothesis, by a further refinement of the URL root category in 9 bins (based on #inlinks classes) instead of 4 bins. This resulted in a further improvement (MRR= 0.7832; 72% at 1; 89% in top 10), confirming our hypothesis. We also reran the inlink run based on 9 bins instead of 4 bins: MRR 0.5064, which is even better than the analytical inlink prior. It is thus safe to conclude that the number of classes is critical for the performance of the training data based priors.

[7]The corresponding content only run only returned 22% of the entry pages at rank 1, and 59% in the top 10.

8. CONCLUSIONS

There are several web page features which can help to improve the effectiveness of an entry page retrieval system, i.e. the number of inlinks and the form of the URL. We have shown that an IR system based on unigram language models can accommodate these types of information in an almost trivial way, by estimating the posterior probability of a page given its features and using this probability as a prior in the model. The URL form feature proved to have the strongest predictive power, yielding over 70% of entry pages at rank 1, and up to 89% in the top 10. Initial experiments with combining both features showed a further improvement. The performance of the combined prior model is highly sensitive to the number of model parameters since the training collection was very small (100 topics).

Acknowledgements

This research was funded by the DRUID project of the Telematics Institute, The Netherlands. We would like to thank David Hawking and Nick Craswell of CSIRO, for making their collection of anchor text available.

9. REFERENCES

[1] B. Amento, L. Terveen, and W. Hill. Does "authority" mean quality? Predicting expert quality ratings of web documents. In Croft et al. [9], pages 296-303.

[2] P. Bailey, N. Craswell, and D. Hawking. Engineering a multi-purpose test collection for web retrieval experiments. *Information Processing and Management*, In press.

[3] K. Bharat and M. R. Henzinger. Improved algorithms for topic distillation in a hyperlinked environment. In Croft et al. [10], pages 104-111.

[4] S. Brin and L. Page. The anatomy of a large-scale hypertextual Web search engine. *Computer Networks and ISDN Systems*, 30(1-7):107-117, 1998.

[5] D. Cohn and H. Chang. Learning to probabilistically identify authoritative documents. In *Proceedings of the 17th International Conference on Machine Learning*, 2000.

[6] N. Craswell, D. Hawking, and S. Robertson. Effective site finding using link anchor information. In Croft et al. [9], pages 250-7.

[7] N. Craswell, D. Hawking, R. Wilkinson, and M. Wu. TREC10 web and interactive tracks at CSIRO. In Voorhees and Harman [37], pages 261-268.

[8] F. Crivellari and M. Melucci. Web document retrieval using passage retrieval, connectivity information, and automatic link weighting - TREC-9 report. In Voorhees and Harman [36], pages 611-620.

[9] W. B. Croft, D. J. Harper, D. H. Kraft, and J. Zobel, editors. *Proceedings of the 23rd Annual International Conference on Research and Development in Information Retrieval*, 2000.

[10] W. B. Croft, A. Moffat, C. van Rijsbergen, R. Wilkinson, and J. Zobel, editors. *Proceedings of the 21st Annual International Conference on Research and Development in Information Retrieval*, 1998.

[11] B. D. Davison. Topical locality in the web. In Croft et al. [9], pages 272-9.

[12] C. Gurrin and A. F. Smeaton. Dublin city university experiments in connectivity analysis for TREC-9. In Voorhees and Harman [36], pages 179-188.

[13] D. Hawking. Overview of the TREC-9 web track. In Voorhees and Harman [36], pages 87-102.

[14] D. Hawking and N. Craswell. Overview of the TREC-2001 web track. In Voorhees and Harman [37], pages 25-31.

[15] D. Hawking, E. voorhees, N. Craswell, and P. Bailey. Overview of the TREC-8 web track. In Voorhees and Harman [35], pages 131-148.

[16] D. Hiemstra. *Using language models for information retrieval*. PhD thesis, Centre for Telematics and Information Technology, University of Twente, 2001.

[17] D. Hiemstra and W. Kraaij. Twenty-One at TREC-7: Ad-hoc and cross-language track. In Voorhees and Harman [34], pages 227-238.

[18] J. M. Kleinberg. Authoritative sources in a hyperlinked environment. *Journal of the ACM*, 46(5):604-632, 1999.

[19] W. Kraaij, M. Spitters, and M. van der Heijden. Combining a mixture language model and naive bayes for multi-document summarisation. In *Working notes of the DUC2001 workshop (SIGIR2001), New Orleans*, 2001.

[20] W. Kraaij and T. Westerveld. TNO/UT at TREC-9: How different are web documents? In Voorhees and Harman [36], pages 665-671.

[21] J. Lafferty and C. Zhai. Probabilistic IR models based on document and query generation. In J. Callan, B. Croft, and J. Lafferty, editors, *Proceedings of the workshop on Language Modeling and Informati on Retrieval*, 2001.

[22] D. D. Lewis. Naive (Bayes) at forty: The independence assumption in information retrieval. In C. Nédellec and C. Rouveirol, editors, *Proceedings of ECML-98, 10th European Conference on Machine Learning*, number 1398 in Lecture Notes in Computer Science, pages 4-15, Chemnitz, DE, 1998. Springer Verlag, Heidelberg, DE.

[23] D. R. H. Miller, T. Leek, and R. M. Schwartz. BBN at TREC-7: using hidden markov models for information retrieval. In Voorhees and Harman [34], pages 133-142.

[24] T. Mitchell. *Machine Learning*. McGraw Hill, 1997.

[25] A. Y. Ng, A. X. Zheng, and M. I. Jordan. Stable algorithms for link analysis. In Croft et al. [9], pages 258-266.

[26] J. M. Ponte and W. B. Croft. A language modeling approach to information retrieval. In Croft et al. [10], pages 275-281.

[27] D.-Y. Ra, E.-K. Park, and J.-S. Jang. Yonsei/etri at TREC-10: Utilizing web document properties. In Voorhees and Harman [37], pages 643-650.

[28] S. Robertson and K. Sparck Jones. Relevance weighting of search terms. *Journal of the American Society for Information Science*, 27(3):129-146, 1976.

[29] S. E. Robertson and S. Walker. Some simple effective approximations to the 2-poisson model for probabilistic weighted retrieval. In *Proceedings of the 17th ACM Conference on Research and Development in Information Retrieval (SIGIR'94)*, pages 232-241, 1994.

[30] G. Salton and C. Buckley. Term-weighting approaches in automatic text retrieval. *Information Processing & Management*, 24(5):513-523, 1988.

[31] J. Savoy and Y. Rasolofo. Report on the TREC-9 experiment: Link-based retrieval and distributed collections. In Voorhees and Harman [36], pages 579-588.

[32] J. Savoy and Y. Rasolofo. Report on the TREC-10 experiment: Distributed collections and entrypage searching. In Voorhees and Harman [37], pages 578-590.

[33] A. Singhal, C. Buckley, and M. Mitra. Pivoted document length normalization. In *Proceedings of the 19th ACM Conference on Research and Development in Information Retrieval (SIGIR'96)*, pages 21-29, 1996.

[34] E. M. Voorhees and D. K. Harman, editors. *The Seventh Text Retrieval Conference (TREC7)*, volume 7. National Institute of Standards and Technology, NIST, 1999.

[35] E. M. Voorhees and D. K. Harman, editors. *The Eighth Text Retrieval Conference (TREC8)*, volume 8. National Institute of Standards and Technology, NIST, 2000.

[36] E. M. Voorhees and D. K. Harman, editors. *The Ninth Text Retrieval Conference (TREC9)*, volume 9. National Institute of Standards and Technology, NIST, 2001.

[37] E. M. Voorhees and D. K. Harman, editors. *The Tenth Text Retrieval Conference (TREC-2001)*, volume 10. National Institute of Standards and Technology, NIST, 2002.

[38] T. Westerveld, W. Kraaij, and D. Hiemstra. Retrieving web pages using content, links, URL's and anchors. In Voorhees and Harman [37], pages 52-61.

[39] W. Xi and E. A. Fox. Machine learning approaches for homepage finding tasks at TREC-10. In Voorhees and Harman [37], pages 633-642.

[40] J. Zobel and A. Moffat. Exploring the similarity space. *SIGIR FORUM*, 32(1):18-34, 1998.

Term-Specific Smoothing for the Language Modeling Approach to Information Retrieval: The Importance of a Query Term

Djoerd Hiemstra
University of Twente,
Centre for Telematics and Information Technology
P.O. Box 217, 7500 AE Enschede, The Netherlands
hiemstra@cs.utwente.nl

ABSTRACT

This paper follows a formal approach to information retrieval based on statistical language models. By introducing some simple reformulations of the basic language modeling approach we introduce the notion of *importance* of a query term. The importance of a query term is an unknown parameter that explicitly models which of the query terms are generated from the relevant documents (the important terms), and which are not (the unimportant terms). The new language modeling approach is shown to explain a number of practical facts of today's information retrieval systems that are not very well explained by the current state of information retrieval theory, including stop words, mandatory terms, coordination level ranking and retrieval using phrases.

Categories and Subject Descriptors

H.3.3 [**Information Storage and Retrieval**]: Information Search and Retrieval

General Terms

Theory

Keywords

Information Retrieval, Formal Models, Language Models, Search Strategies

1. INTRODUCTION

Information retrieval research has a long tradition of experimental work; most of today's information retrieval research is firmly based on the scientific method. Over 80 % of the papers presented at SIGIR 2001 [6] report some experimental results.

In their SIGIR paper on the Okapi weighting algorithms, Robertson and Walker [25] distinguish two forms of approaches to information retrieval research: Firstly, approaches based on formal models, where the model specifies an exact formula to be tried empirically; and secondly ad-hoc approaches, where formulae are empirically tried because they seem to be plausible. In this paper we follow a third form of approaches to information retrieval research, suggested by Bruza and Huibers [3]: Approaches based on formal models, where the model specifies an exact formula that is used to proof some simple mathematical properties of the model. Such properties do not have to be tried or verified empirically on some test collection, because their truth can be shown to hold by some simple mathematics.[1]

1.1 Information Retrieval in Practice

User surveys show that about 85 % of the users of the internet use web search engines to locate information [16]. Let's have a look at some practical situations in which millions of people find themselves on a daily basis, those of web search engines.

Web search engines like Google or AltaVista provide their users with a simple text field to enter some words. They respond by providing a ranked list of references to web pages that are hopefully relevant to the user. The way this ranking is produced can be modeled reasonably well with a language modeling approach to information retrieval, including for instance Google's page ranking approach using statistics on hyperlinks [14]. But the quality of the ranking is not the main issue here. The main issue is that successful retrieval engines give the user a sense of control over the system, i.e. they provide a mechanism that gives users the possibility to override the basic ranking mechanism. This will be illustrated below by two simple web search engine examples.[2]

If we for instance enter the query `IT magazines` in Google, then the system will only retrieve documents containing the word "magazines", stating that "IT" is a very common word

[1] Note that we do not argue in any way that we do not believe in experimental work. On the contrary, experimentation is of the utmost importance in information retrieval research!
[2] Similar mechanisms exist in commercial online services as provided by e.g. Dialog and LexisNexis.

that is not included in the search.[3] It makes perfect sense to ignore the word "IT" because it matches virtually every (English) document on the internet. In this case however, it is clearly wrong. But there is no harm done: The proper response of the user is now to search for `+IT magazines`. By using the '+' operator, the user indicates that "IT" is an important word for this search that should not be ignored, even if the search engine would have decided otherwise on the basis of the word's statistics.

As a second example, consider e.g. entering the query `compassioned extrovert computers` in AltaVista. None of the web pages indexed by the system matches all three words, but the system will retrieve lots of documents that match two words out of three. The top ranked documents however, are documents that match the two words "compassioned" and "extrovert", i.e., many documents about people that possess these qualities, but no computers. This makes perfect sense because the word "computers" is much more frequent than "compassioned" or "extrovert", and it is standard practice to rank documents containing words that occur very frequently in the collection below documents containing infrequent words (see e.g. [30]). From the user's point of view however, it is wrong if it is computers he/she is looking for. But again there is no harm done if we enter the query `compassioned extrovert +computers`. As in the example above, the '+' operator indicates that the word "computers" is an important word, that should not be ignored on the basis of its statistics. The system will respond by retrieving only documents that match the words "compassioned" and "computers", or documents that match "extrovert" and "computers".

1.2 The Limitations of Statistics in Document Ranking

What's the point to all this? The examples show that there are limitations to the performance that can be achieved by ranking on the basis of word statistics. Often, the importance of a word for the final document ranking is reflected by its frequency distribution in the collection. Sometimes however, the statistics and the rules-of-the-thumb are wrong; as in the first example where "IT" is erroneously ignored based on its frequency; and as in the second example where "computers" is erroneously considered as less important than the other two words based on the fact that it is much more frequent on the world wide web.

Note that the solution to such problems is not developing even better statistical ranking algorithms. Statistics work *most* of the time: That's the beauty and the curse of statistics! In cases where statistical ranking is clearly wrong, the user (or perhaps the system) should be able to override the system's default behaviour by explicitly stating which words are the important words in the query. As shown in the examples, this is standard practice in the popular commercial retrieval systems already, but it is not reflected in any mathematical model of information retrieval.

In the following sections, we extend recent advances on the use of language models for information retrieval. In Section 2 we extend the language modeling approach to information retrieval by introducing the concept of importance of a query term. Our objective is to develop mathematical models that provide the mechanisms described in the examples above. In Section 3 we show the implications of query term importance by concentrating on mathematical properties of the language modeling approach that hold in any empirical setting. In Section 4, we will further generalize query term importance to a situation in which there may be different combinations of multiple models for each term.

[3]Note that most retrieval systems do not distinguish upper case from lower case, and confuse the acronym "IT" with the word "it".

2. LANGUAGE MODELING AND TERM IMPORTANCE

The language modeling approach to information retrieval defines a simple unigram language model for each document in a collection [21]. For each document D the language model defines the probability $P(T_1, \cdots, T_n|D)$ of a sequence of n query terms $T_1, \cdots, T_n$ and the documents are ranked by that probability. Essential in this approach is *smoothing* of the probabilities. Smoothing is the task of reevaluating the probabilities, in order to assign some non-zero probability to query terms that do not occur in a document. As such, smoothed probability estimation is an alternative for maximum likelihood estimation. The standard language modeling approach to information retrieval uses a linear interpolation smoothing of the document model $P(T_i|D)$ with a general collection model $P(T_i|C)$ [1, 10, 15, 17, 19, 29]. Linear interpolation smoothing needs a parameter λ which is set empirically on some test collection, or alternatively estimated by the EM-algorithm on a test collection [17, 19].

$$P(T_1, \cdots, T_n|D) = \prod_{i=1}^{n} ((1-\lambda)P(T_i|C) + \lambda P(T_i|D)) \quad (1)$$

There are many other approaches to smoothing language models (see e.g. [12]), some of which have been suggested for information retrieval as well, for instance smoothing using the geometric mean and backing-off by Ponte and Croft [21]; and Dirichlet smoothing and absolute discounting suggested in a recent study by Zhai and Lafferty [32]. Zhai and Lafferty evaluated a number of approaches to smoothing on several large and small TREC collections. They find that different situations call for different approaches to smoothing. Interestingly, they explain their empirical results by suggesting that there is more to smoothing than just the reevaluation of probabilities, which they call the *estimation* role of smoothing. A second role of smoothing, which they call the *query modeling* role, is to "explain" the common and non-informative words in a query. All smoothing approaches have this dual role, but linear interpolation smoothing defines a fixed smoothing parameter across – and independent of – all documents, which is necessary for query modeling.

The linear interpolation smoothing as defined by Equation 1 can be explicitly modeled as a two-state hidden Markov model [17]. So, instead of looking at smoothing as an alternative to maximum likelihood estimation of probabilities (the estimation role), we can look at smoothing as a model with some hidden events in which all probabilities are maximum likelihood estimates (the query modeling role). In this paper we will take the query modeling role somewhat further, by explicitly defining a hidden event for each query term. Such a *term-specific* smoothing approach can derived as follows.

First we assume independence between query terms:

$$P(T_1,\cdots,T_n|D) \;=\; \prod_{i=1}^{n} P(T_i|D)$$

Then we introduce for each query term T_i a binary random variable I_i denoting the *importance* of a query term. Thus, $I_i = 1$ if the query term is important and $I_i = 0$ if the query term is unimportant. The importance of a query term is a hidden variable, so we have to marginalize it by summing over its possible values: 0 and 1.

$$= \prod_{i=1}^{n} \Big(\sum_{i_i \in \{0,1\}} P(T_i, I_i = i_i|D) \Big)$$

Furthermore, let's assume that the importance of a query term does not depend on the document model. This is motivated by the fact that the importance of a query term will be used to encode the information (and only the information) about a term that cannot be derived from the document statistics or the collection statistics.

$$= \prod_{i=1}^{n} \Big(\sum_{i_i \in \{0,1\}} P(I_i = i_i) P(T_i|I_i = i_i, D) \Big)$$

If we write the full sum over the importance values we get:

$$= \prod_{i=1}^{n} \big(P(I_i = 0)P(T_i|I_i = 0, D) + P(I_i = 1)P(T_i|I_i = 1, D)\big)$$

How does this equation relate to Equation 1? We use λ_i to denote the unknown probability of term importance, so $\lambda_i = P(I_i = 1)$ and therefore $(1 - \lambda_i) = P(I_i = 0)$; We make the assumption that the probability of an important query term is determined by the document language model, so we use $P(T_i|D)$ as a short-hand of $P(T_i|I_i = 1, D)$; and we make the assumption that the probability of an unimportant term is determined by the collection model, using $P(T_i|C)$ as a short-hand of $P(T_i|I_i = 0, D)$. This gives us:

$$P(T_1,\cdots,T_n|D) \;=\; \prod_{i=1}^{n} \big((1-\lambda_i)P(T_i|C) + \lambda_i P(T_i|D)\big) \quad (2)$$

Equation 2 differs from Equation 1 by the fact that we have a separate smoothing parameter λ_i for each query term i. But maybe the correct view is that we did not use any smoothing of probabilities at all. We just formulated a bit more complex model, and all of the model's probabilities are defined by maximum likelihood estimates. This is visualized in Figure 1.

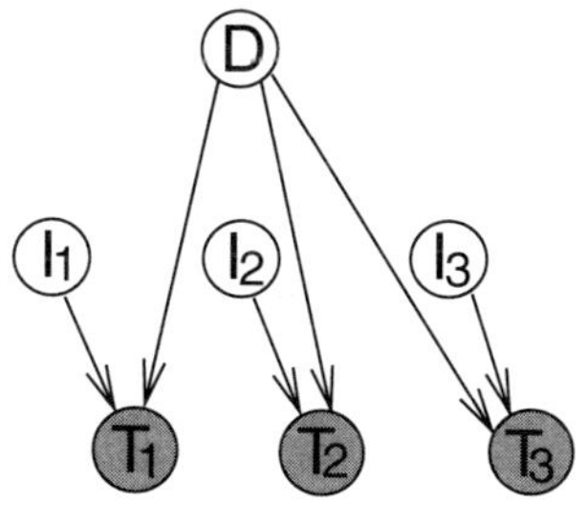

Figure 1: The language modeling approach as a Bayesian network

Figure 1 shows a graphical illustration of the model as a Bayesian network. In a Bayesian network, random variables are represented as nodes, and the arcs represent the model's conditional dependencies. Following the convention in [13], clear nodes represent unknown, hidden variables, and shaded nodes represent the observed variables; in this case the query terms.

3. MATHEMATICAL PROPERTIES OF TERM-SPECIFIC SMOOTHING

Term-specific smoothing provides the means to explain the examples described in Section 1. We will do so by first looking at the extreme values of the probability of term importance.

3.1 Stop words

The probability of term importance $\lambda_i = 0$ implies that we are absolutely certain that the query term is not important. It is easy to verify that any query term for which $\lambda_i = 0$, the document model $P(T_i|D)$ can be dropped from the calculation of the document score (because $\lambda_i P(T_i|D)$ will be zero whatever the value of $P(T_i|D)$). Therefore, we can simply ignore the query term all together, as is done with the word "IT" in the first example described in Section 1.

Words from the query that are ignored during the search are usually referred to as *stop words*. Words might be ignored because they occur very frequently in the collection. Frequent words might not contribute significantly to the final document score, but they do require a lot of processing power. The motivation for stopping is in this case based on a trade-off between speed and quality: the quality of the search results might be somewhat worse, but the processing speed will be much better [2, 4, 20].

Note however that words might be ignored for different reasons, that is, stop words are not always words that occur in many documents. Often, words are stopped if they occur in a list that enumerates words that usually carry little meaning, like for instance "the", "it" and "a". These words do also have a high frequency in English, but most publicly available stop lists contain some words which are not frequently used at all. For instance the stop list in [22], contains words like "hereupon" and "whereafter", which occur respectively two and four times in the TREC-8 ad hoc collection.

3.2 Mandatory terms

A query term for which the probability of term importance $\lambda_i = 1$ results in the following. For this query term, the collection model can be dropped from the calculation of the document score, because $(1-\lambda_i)P(T_i|C)$ will be zero whatever the value of $P(T_i|C)$. As a result, the probabilities of the document model are no longer smoothed with the probabilities of the collection model: Documents that do not match the query term are assigned zero probability, and since any multiplication with zero will be zero, the final document score will be zero as well no matter how well it matches the other query terms.

Assigning $\lambda_i = 1$ implies that we are absolutely certain that the relevant documents contain the term. A document will only get a non-zero probability if it matches the important term: Any document that does not contain the important term will not be retrieved. We will call a query term that should occur in every document retrieved a *mandatory* term. Usually, it is the user who decides which terms in his/her query are mandatory terms, for instance by using the '+' operator as described in the examples of Section 1.

3.3 Coordination level ranking

So, $\lambda_i = 1$ ensures that all retrieved documents contain the ith query term. This makes us suspect that for values close to 1, the ranking will be a *coordination level* ranking. Coordination level ranking is a partial ranking of the documents such that documents containing n query terms are always ranked above documents containing $n-1$ query terms.

According to studies of user preferences, users like systems that obey the conditions of coordination level ranking. Users have their own mental models of how search engines work or should work [18]. They may start to question the integrity of a search engine that ranks a document that matches one query term above documents that match two query terms; even if this seems reasonable from the query's semantics. For instance, it seems reasonable that for the query `big brown bear`, documents containing only "bear" are more likely to be relevant than documents about big brown 'whatevers'. However, users (read: customers) might consider the former result an error because it does not fit their mental model of how a search engine should work [27]. Obviously, users become particularly aware of such rankings if short queries are used. In a lot of practical situations short queries are the rule rather than the exception, especially in situations where there is no or little user training like with web search engines.

For systems that use some form of *tf.idf*-like term weighting, it is certainly not uncommon that documents containing k query terms are ranked below documents containing $k-1$ query terms. For some research groups, this is the main motivation for developing ranking methods that are based on other statistics, e.g. on the lexical distance of search terms in documents [5, 8]. As pointed out by experiments of Wilkinson et al. [31], some *tf.idf* measures behave more "like" coordination level ranking than others. For instance, the Okapi BM25 algorithm [25] behaves more like coordination level ranking than the Smart tfc.nfc algorithm [28]. They showed that weighting measures that are more like coordination level ranking perform better on TREC experiments, especially if short queries are used. Following their results, it might be useful to investigate what exactly makes a weighting algorithm behave like coordination level ranking.

A proof of coordination level ranking if λ approaches 1

As said, we suspect that high values of λ_i lead to coordination level ranking. Let us go back for a moment to the standard language modeling approach with one fixed λ for all query terms. This would be the system of our choice if no information on stop words, on mandatory terms, or on relevant documents (see Section 3.5) is available. First, let's have a look again at Equation 1:

$$P(T_1, \cdots, T_n|D) \;=\; \prod_{i=1}^{n}((1-\lambda)P(T_i|C) + \lambda P(T_i|D))$$

Dividing the formula by $\prod_{i=1}^{n}((1-\lambda)P(T_i|C))$ will not affect the ranking because λ and $P(T_i|C)$ have the same value for each document.

$$P(T_1, \cdots, T_n|D) \;\propto\; \prod_{i=1}^{n}(1 + \frac{\lambda P(T_i|D)}{(1-\lambda)P(T_i|C)})$$

Any monotonic transformation of the document ranking function will produce the same ranking of the documents. Instead of using the product of weights, the formula can as well rank documents by the sum of logarithmic weights.

$$P(T_1, \cdots, T_n|D) \;\propto\; \sum_{i=1}^{n}\log(1 + \frac{\lambda P(T_i|D)}{(1-\lambda)P(T_i|C)})$$

The right-hand side of the equation defines a sum of log-likelihood ratios. Terms that do not match a document do not contribute to the sum [9, 32]. This gives us an easy way to formulate the requirement of coordination level ranking in terms of k matching terms, that is, a document that matches k terms should always have a higher score than a document that matches $k-1$ terms:

$$k \log\left(1 + m\tfrac{\lambda}{1-\lambda}\right) \;>\; (k-1)\log\left(1 + n\tfrac{\lambda}{1-\lambda}\right)$$

The left-hand side of the inequality is the matching score of a document that contains k query terms. The right-hand side of the inequality is the matching score of a document that contains $k-1$ query terms. In the inequality, m and n $(n, m > 0)$ replace the $P(T_i|D)/P(T_i|C)$ ratios of the matching terms. Note that the $P(T_i|D)/P(T_i|C)$ ratio is proportional to the frequency of occurrence of the term in a document and inversely proportional to the frequency of occurrence of the term in the collection, just as a *tf.idf* weight [9, 32]. For the simplicity of the proof, m is taken as the minumum of the $P(T_i|D)/P(T_i|C)$ ratios of the k matching terms of the document on the left-hand side, and n is taken as the maximum of the $P(T_i|D)/P(T_i|C)$ ratios of the $k-1$ matching terms of the document on the right-hand side. Proofing coordination level ranking for the extreme values of m and n will proof coordination level ranking for practical cases in which the ratio's values differ per matching term. Note that coordination level ranking might not be fulfilled if $n \gg m$.

It is easy to verify that the inequality holds if $k = 1$. For $k = 1$, the right-hand side is zero, and the inequality is true if $\lambda > 0$, no matter what the values of m and n are.

If $k > 1$, the k's might be moved to the left-hand side of the inequality and the rest to the right-hand side, resulting in:

$$\frac{k}{k-1} \;>\; \frac{\log\left(1 + n\frac{\lambda}{1-\lambda}\right)}{\log\left(1 + m\frac{\lambda}{1-\lambda}\right)}$$

In the following, we will proof that right-hand side of the inequality goes to 1 if λ approaches 1. So in the limiting case, the inequality will be true, because $k\,/\,(k-1) > 1$ for any bounded $k > 1$. So, we only have to show that for any fixed m and n:

$$\lim_{\lambda \to 1} \frac{\log\left(1 + n\frac{\lambda}{1-\lambda}\right)}{\log\left(1 + m\frac{\lambda}{1-\lambda}\right)} \;=\; 1$$

This can be shown as follows.

$$\frac{\log\left(1+n\frac{\lambda}{1-\lambda}\right)}{\log\left(1+m\frac{\lambda}{1-\lambda}\right)} = \frac{\log\left(\frac{1-\lambda+n\lambda}{1-\lambda}\right)}{\log\left(\frac{1-\lambda+m\lambda}{1-\lambda}\right)}$$

$$= \frac{\log(1-\lambda+n\lambda)-\log(1-\lambda)}{\log(1-\lambda+m\lambda)-\log(1-\lambda)}$$

Divding the numerator and the denominator by $-\log(1-\lambda)$ results in:

$$= \frac{1-\dfrac{\log(1-\lambda+n\lambda)}{\log(1-\lambda)}}{1-\dfrac{\log(1-\lambda+m\lambda)}{\log(1-\lambda)}}$$

which will in fact approach 1 if λ approaches 1, because $\lim_{\lambda\to 1}\log(1-\lambda+n\lambda)=\log n$, $\lim_{\lambda\to 1}\log(1-\lambda+m\lambda)=\log m$, and $\lim_{\lambda\to 1}\log(1-\lambda)=\infty$.

A value of λ close to 1 results in coordination level rankings. A high value implies that we are pretty confident that all query terms are important terms, which in general would be the case with short queries. For longer queries, it might no longer be justified to assume that all query terms are important, and a lower value of λ might be a better choice. In fact, this is supported by the experimental results of Zhai and Lafferty [32]: A high value of λ is a good choice for short queries, whereas a lower value is more appropriate for longer, verbose queries.

3.4 Discussion

The probability of term importance λ_i provides a mathematical model (or explanation) of a number of simple facts of information retrieval, if we consider its extreme values $\lambda_i=0$, $\lambda_i=1$ and $\lambda_i\to 1$ for all i:

- Sometimes systems ignore words, and the reasons to ignore them cannot always be explained by statistics.
- Often users/customers may want to restrict the retrieved list of documents to documents that match one or more specific terms, regardless of the frequency distributions of these terms.
- Users/customers may want to enforce a coordination level ranking of the documents, regardless of the frequency distribution of the terms.

We showed that it is possible to reason about these facts in terms of a language modeling approach to information retrieval. Note that we do not have to show empirically on a test collection that our language modeling system supports stop words, mandatory words and coordination level ranking: We are able to show by using some simple mathematics that this will be the case in any empirical setting.

3.5 Relevance feedback

As shown above, there are two extremes to explicitly modeling the importance of a term. At one end of the spectrum terms might be completely ignored if we assume that they are unimportant. At the other end of the spectrum terms are mandatory in the retrieved list of documents if we assume that they are important. However, in general we might expect the optimal values of λ_i to be somewhere between the extremes.

Finding optimal values for some unknown parameters in information retrieval is often addressed from the viewpoint of relevance feedback [24, 26]. Given some examples of relevant documents, what would be the probability of term importance for each term that maximizes retrieval performance? A standard approach to optimization in the language modeling field is the use of the Expectation Maximization (EM) algorithm [7]. The EM-algorithm will maximize the probability of the observed data given some training data. The EM-algorithm that maximizes the probability of the query given some relevant documents would be defined as follows.

$$\text{E-step:}\quad m_i = \sum_{j=1}^{r} \frac{\lambda_i^{(p)}\cdot P(T_i|D_j)}{(1-\lambda_i^{(p)})P(T_i|C)+\lambda_i^{(p)}P(T_i|D_j)}$$

$$\text{M-step:}\quad \lambda_i^{(p+1)} = \frac{m_i}{r}$$

The algorithm iteratively maximizes the probability of the query $T_1,\cdots,T_n$ given r relevant documents $D_1,\cdots,D_r$. Before the iteration process starts, the unknown parameters λ_i are initialized to their default values $\lambda_i^{(0)}$. Each iteration p estimates a new value $\lambda_i^{(p+1)}$ by first doing the E-step and then the M-step until the value of $\lambda_i^{(p+1)}$ is not significantly different from the value of $\lambda_i^{(p)}$ anymore.

Experimental results on a retrospective relevance weighting task show that this algorithm provides a relative performance gain that is as good as relevance feedback via the traditional probabilistic model [11]. In this study, the performance of the language modeling approach – with and without relevance feedback – is about 60 % higher than the performance of the probabilistic model.

4. A GENERALIZATION OF TERM IMPORTANCE

A simple but powerful generalization of the model presented so far is allowing the random variable I_i to have more than two realizations. Such an approach defines a linear combination of more than one document model and the background model; combining the standard document model with e.g. a model of the title words, or e.g. a model of anchor texts of hyperlinks pointing to the document.

Interesting from this perspective is the combination of the unigram document model with a bigram document model to explicitly include the search for phrases, as suggested by Miller et al. [17] and Song and Croft [29]. The model might be defined as a multi-state hidden Markov model [17]. Equation 3 defines such a higher order model.

$$P(T_1,\cdots,T_n|D) = \big((1-\lambda_1)P(T_1|C)+\lambda_1 P(T_1|D)\big) \prod_{i=2}^{n}\big((1-\lambda_i-\mu_i)P(T_i|C)+\lambda_i P(T_i|D)+\mu_i P(T_i|T_{i-1},D)\big) \qquad (3)$$

In this case, the importance of a term T_i might be 0 (unimportant as before), 1 (important as before) and 2 (the query term T_i is generated from the bigram model). Similar to Equation 2, μ_i is used instead of $P(I_i=2)$ and $P(T_i|T_{i-1},D)$ instead of $P(T_i|T_{i-1},I_i=2,D)$. The conditional dependencies now include dependencies between query terms. This is visualized in the Bayesian network of Figure 2.

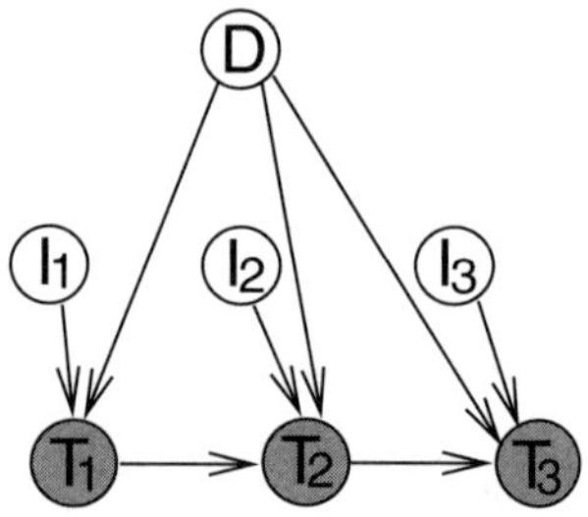

Figure 2: Graphical model of dependence relations between query terms

In such a generalized model, we have both stop words and stop bigrams. Consider for example the query `last will of Alfred Nobel`. It does not make sense to search for all possible bigrams in the document collection, because this might take to much system resources. Based on the term statistics, the system might e.g. decide that the bigrams "last will"[4], "will of" and "of Alfred" are all 'stop bigrams', that is, $\mu_i = 0$ for these bigrams. The system might decide that "of" is a stop word as well, that is, $\lambda_i = 0$ and $\mu_i = 0$ for this word.

Similarly, users might override the system's decisions if they are not satisfied with the search results. For instance, the query `"last will" of Alfred Nobel` indicates that "last will" should not be a stop bigram ($\mu_i > 0$); and the query `+"last will" of Alfred Nobel` indicates that "last will" is a mandatory bigram, that is, $\mu_i = 1$ and $\lambda_i = 0$ for this bigram.

Note that the use of single or double quotes to mark phrases is standard practice in many information retrieval systems, for instance web search engines like Google and AltaVista, and for instance commercial online services like those provided by Dialog and LexisNexis.

5. CONCLUSION

In this paper we extended the language modeling approach to information retrieval by explicitly modeling the importance of a term. By doing so, we are able to define complex models in which we might decide on a rather ad-hoc basis that some words are stop words, others are mandatory words, some pairs of words should be considered as phrases, some phrases might be mandatory, etc. Any such ad-hoc decision would override the default ranking algorithm.

Decisions on stop words and stop phrases (bigrams) are typically taken by the system, based on a trade-off between search quality and search speed. Including all document representations in each search would take too much of the system's resources, so only a few representations will be considered in practice by default, including maybe one or two bigrams.

Decisions on mandatory words and phrases are typically taken by the user. A user that is not satisfied with the system's default behaviour, or a user that has some experience with the system, will be able to mark the words and phrases he/she thinks are important. In such cases it is important that the user has some idea of how the system works. The system's default behaviour should be rather transparent, e.g. by always providing coordination level rankings.

Today's statistical ranking algorithms perform quite well in empirical settings, especially algorithms motivated by the language modeling approach. However, there will always be a few exceptions to the good performance: Some queries for which the statistics are clearly wrong. There might be only one or two of those examples in test collection with 50 topics. Whether or not the user's ad hoc decisions on mandatory words and phrases will actually result in significantly better system performance in terms of precision and recall might therefore be hard to measure. Such cases are addressed by this paper.

What about the statistical ranking algorithms of the future? Now that we have identified ways to model ad hoc decisions on multiple levels of language models in order to construct complex query representations, the next step might be trying to automate these ad hoc decisions. Such an automatic ad hoc decision (which would then of course no longer be 'ad hoc') might be based on the fact that it describes the data more *parsimoniously* [23]. For instance, in a multiple level language model, some levels might be defined as models of specific topics. As such, a unigram model of general language, modified by a small number of topic-specific unigram models, each of which has parameters for only a small number of topic-specific specialist terms and phrases, would be a very parsimonious, and possibly quite powerful, model for a collection of documents...

[4]Note that "will" is a very frequent word in English.

6. REFERENCES

[1] A. Berger and J. Lafferty. Information retrieval as statistical translation. In *Proceedings of the 22nd ACM Conference on Research and Development in Information Retrieval (SIGIR'99)*, pages 222–229, 1999.

[2] H.E. Blok, D. Hiemstra, S. Choenni, F.M.G. de Jong, H.M. Blanken, and P.M.G. Apers. Predicting the cost-quality trade-off for information retrieval queries: Facilitating database design and query optimisation. In *Proceedings of the 10th International Conference on Information and Knowledge Management (CIKM'01)*, pages 207–214, 2001.

[3] P.D. Bruza and T.W.C. Huibers. Investigating aboutness axioms using information fields. In *Proceedings of the 17th ACM Conference on Research and Development in Information Retrieval (SIGIR'94)*, pages 112–121, 1994.

[4] C. Buckley and A.F. Lewit. Optimization of inverted vector searches. In *Proceedings of the 8th ACM Conference on Research and Development in Information Retrieval (SIGIR'85)*, pages 97–110, 1985.

[5] C.L.A. Clarke, G.V. Cormack, and E.A. Tudhope. Relevance ranking for one to three term queries. In *Proceedings of RIAO'97*, pages 388–400, 1997.

[6] W.B. Croft, D.J. Harper, D.H. Kraft, and J. Zobel, editors. *Proceedings of the 24th ACM Conference on Research and Development in Information Retrieval (SIGIR'01)*. ACM Press, 2001.

[7] A.P. Dempster, N.M. Laird, and D.B. Rubin. Maximum likelihood from incomplete data via the

em-algorithm plus discussions on the paper. *Journal of the Royal Statistical Society*, 39(B):1–38, 1977.

[8] D. Hawking and P. Thistlewaite. Relevance weighting using distance between term occurrences. Technical Report TR-CS-96-08, The Australian National University, 1996. (http://cs.anu.edu.au/techreports/)

[9] D. Hiemstra. A probabilistic justification for using *tf.idf* term weighting in information retrieval. *International Journal on Digital Libraries*, 3(2):131–139, 2000.

[10] D. Hiemstra and W. Kraaij. Twenty-One at TREC-7: Ad-hoc and cross-language track. In *Proceedings of the seventh Text Retrieval Conference TREC-7*, pages 227–238. NIST Special Publication 500-242, 1998.

[11] D. Hiemstra and A.P. de Vries. Relating the new language models of information retrieval to the traditional retrieval models. Technical Report TR-CTIT-00-09, Centre for Telematics and Information Technology, 2000. (http://www.ctit.utwente.nl)

[12] F. Jelinek. *Statistical Methods for Speech Recognition*. MIT Press, 1997.

[13] M.I. Jordan, editor. *Learning in Graphical Models*. Kluwer Academic Press, 1998.

[14] W. Kraaij, T. Westerveld, and D. Hiemstra. The importance of prior probabilities for entry page search. In *Proceedings of the 25th ACM Conference on Research and Development in Information Retrieval (SIGIR'02)*, 2002. (in this volume)

[15] J. Lafferty and C. Zhai. Document language models, query models, and risk minimization. In *Proceedings of the 24th ACM Conference on Research and Development in Information Retrieval (SIGIR'01)*, pages 111–119, 2001.

[16] S. Lawrence and C.L. Giles. Accessibility of information on the web. *Nature*, 400:107–109, 1999.

[17] D.R.H. Miller, T. Leek, and R.M. Schwartz. A hidden Markov model information retrieval system. In *Proceedings of the 22nd ACM Conference on Research and Development in Information Retrieval (SIGIR'99)*, pages 214–221, 1999.

[18] J. Muramatsu and W. Pratt. Transparent queries: Investigating users' mental models of search engines. In In *Proceedings of the 24th ACM Conference on Research and Development in Information Retrieval (SIGIR'01)*, pages 217–224, 2001.

[19] K. Ng. A maximum likelihood ratio information retrieval model. In *Proceedings of the eighth Text Retrieval Conference, TREC-8*. NIST Special Publications, 1999.

[20] M. Persin. Document filtering for fast ranking. In *Proceedings of the 7th ACM Conference on Research and Development in Information Retrieval (SIGIR'84)*, pages 339–349, 1984.

[21] J.M. Ponte and W.B. Croft. A language modeling approach to information retrieval. In *Proceedings of the 21st ACM Conference on Research and Development in Information Retrieval (SIGIR'98)*, pages 275–281, 1998.

[22] C.J. van Rijsbergen. *Information Retrieval, second edition*. Butterworths, 1979. (http://www.dcs.gla.ac.uk/Keith/Preface.html)

[23] S.E. Robertson and D. Hiemstra. Language models and probability of relevance, In *Proceedings of the Workshop on Language Modeling and Information Retrieval*, pages 21–25, 2001.

[24] S.E. Robertson and K. Sparck-Jones. Relevance weighting of search terms. *Journal of the American Society for Information Science*, 27:129–146, 1976.

[25] S.E. Robertson and S. Walker. Some simple effective approximations to the 2-Poisson model for probabilistic weighted retrieval. In *Proceedings of the 17th ACM Conference on Research and Development in Information Retrieval (SIGIR'94)*, pages 232–241, 1994.

[26] J.J. Rocchio. Relevance feedback in information retrieval. In G. Salton, editor, *The Smart Retrieval System: Experiments in Automatic Document Processing*, pages 313–323. Prentice Hall, 1971.

[27] D.E. Rose and C. Stevens. V-twin: A lightweight engine for interactive use. In E.M. Voorhees and D.K. Harman, editors, *Proceedings of the 5th Text Retrieval Conference TREC-5*, pages 279–290. NIST Special Publication 500-238, 1996.

[28] G. Salton and C. Buckley. Term-weighting approaches in automatic text retrieval. *Information Processing & Management*, 24(5):513–523, 1988.

[29] F. Song and W.B. Croft. A general language model for information retrieval. In *Proceedings of the 8th International Conference on Information and Knowledge Management (CIKM'99)*, pages 316–321, 1999.

[30] K. Sparck-Jones. A statistical interpretation of term specifity and its application in retrieval. *Journal of Documentation*, 28(1):11–20, 1972.

[31] R. Wilkinson, J. Zobel, and R. Sacks-Davis. Similarity measures for short queries. In D.K. Harman, editor, *Proceedings of the 4th Text Retrieval Conference TREC-4*, pages 277–286. NIST Special Publication 500-236, 1995.

[32] C. Zhai and J. Lafferty. A study of smoothing methods for language models applied to ad hoc information retrieval. In *Proceedings of the 24th ACM Conference on Research and Development in Information Retrieval (SIGIR'01)*, pages 334–342, 2001.

Title Language Model for Information Retrieval

Rong Jin
Language Technologies Institute
School of Computer Science
Carnegie Mellon University

Alex G. Hauptmann
Computer Science Department
School of Computer Science
Carnegie Mellon University

ChengXiang Zhai
Language Technologies Institute
School of Computer Science
Carnegie Mellon University

ABSTRACT

In this paper, we propose a new language model, namely, a title language model, for information retrieval. Different from the traditional language model used for retrieval, we define the conditional probability *P(Q|D)* as the probability of using query *Q* as the title for document *D*. We adopted the statistical translation model learned from the title and document pairs in the collection to compute the probability *P(Q|D)*. To avoid the sparse data problem, we propose two new smoothing methods. In the experiments with four different TREC document collections, the title language model for information retrieval with the new smoothing method outperforms both the traditional language model and the vector space model for IR significantly.

Categories and Subject Descriptors

H.3.3 [**Information Search and Retrieval**]: Retrieval Models — *language model; machine learning for IR*

General Terms

Algorithms

Keywords

title language model, statistical translation model, smoothing, machine learning

1. INTRODUCTION

Using language models for information retrieval has been studied extensively recently [1,3,7,8,10]. The basic idea is to compute the conditional probability *P(Q|D)*, i.e. the probability of generating a query *Q* given the observation of a document *D*. Several different methods have been applied to compute this conditional probability. In most approaches, the computation is conceptually decomposed into two distinct steps: (1) Estimating a document language model; (2) Computing the query likelihood using the estimated document model based on some query model. For example, Ponte and Croft [8] emphasized the first step, and used several heuristics to smooth the Maximum Likelihood Estimate (MLE) of the document language model, and assumed that the query is generated under a multivariate Bernoulli model. The BBN method [7] emphasized the second step and used a two-state hidden Markov model as the basis for generating queries, which, in effect, is to smooth the MLE with linear interpolation, a strategy also adopted in Hiemstra and Kraaij [3]. In Zhai and Lafferty [11], it has been found that the retrieval performance is affected by both the estimation accuracy of document language models and the appropriate modeling of the query, and a two-stage smoothing method was suggested to explicitly address these two distinct steps.

SIGIR '02, August 11-15, 2002, Tempere, Finland.

A common deficiency in these approaches is that they all apply an estimated document language model directly to generating queries, but presumably queries and documents should be generated through different stochastic processes, since they have quite different characteristics. Therefore, there exists a "gap" between a document language model and a query language model. Indeed, such a gap has been well-recognized in [4], where separate models are proposed to model queries and documents respectively. The gap has also been recognized in [6], where a document model is estimated based on a query through averaging over document models based on how well they explain the query. In most existing approaches using query likelihood for scoring, this gap has been implicitly addressed through smoothing. Indeed, in [11] it has been found that the optimal setting of smoothing parameters is actually query-dependent , which suggests that smoothing may have helped bridge this gap.

Although filling the gap by simple smoothing has been shown to be empirically effective, ideally we should estimate a *query language model* directly based on the observation of a *document,* and apply the estimated query language model, instead of the document language model, to generate queries. The question then is, "What evidence do we have for estimating a query language model given a document?". This is a very challenging question, since the information available to us in a typical ad hoc retrieval setting includes no more than a database of documents and queries.

In this paper, we propose to use the titles of documents as the evidence for estimating a query language model for a given document -- essentially to approximate the query language model given a document by the title language model for that document, which is easier to estimate. The motivation of this work is based on the observation that queries are more like titles than documents in many aspects. For example, both titles and queries tend to be very short and concise description of information. The reasoning process in author's mind when making up the title for a document is similar to what is in a user's mind when formulating a query based on some "ideal document" -- both would be trying to capture what the document is *about*. Therefore, it is reasonable to assume that the titles and queries are created through a similar generation process. The title information has been exploited previously for improving information retrieval, but, so far, only heuristic methods, such as increasing the weight of title words have been tried (e.g., [5,10]). Here we use the title information in a more principled way by treating a title as an observation from a document-title statistical translation model.

Technically, the title language model approach falls into the general source-channel framework proposed in Berger and Lafferty [1], where the difference between a query and a document is explicitly addressed by treating query formulation as a "corruption" of the "ideal document" in the information theoretic sense. Conceptually, however, the title language model is different from the synthetic query translation model explored in [1]. The use of synthesized queries provides an interesting way to train a statistical translation model that can address important issues such as synonymy and polysemy, whereas the title language model is meant to directly approximate queries with titles. Moreover, training with the titles poses special difficulties due to data sparseness, which we discuss below.

A document can potentially have many different titles, but the author only provides one title for each document. Thus, if we estimate title language models only based on the observation of the author-given titles, it will suffer severely from the problem of sparse data. The use of a statistical translation model can alleviate this problem. The basic idea is to treat the document-title pairs as 'translation' pairs observed from some translation model that captures the intrinsic document to query translation patterns. This means, we would train the statistical 'translation' model based on the document-title pairs in the whole collection. Once we have this general translation model in hand, we can estimate the title language model for a particular document by applying the learned translation model to the document.

Even if we pool all the document-title pairs together, the training data is still quite sparse given the large number of parameters involved. Since titles are typically much shorter than documents, we would expect that most words in a document would never occur in any of the titles in the collection. To address this problem, we extend the standard learning algorithms of the translation models by adding special parameters to model the "self-translation" probabilities of words. We propose two such techniques: One assumes that all words have the same self-translation probability and the other assumes that each title has an extra unobserved null word slot that can only be filled by a word generated through self-translation.

The proposed title language model and the two self-translation smoothing methods are evaluated with four different TREC databases. The results show that the title language model approach consistently performs better than both the simple language modeling approach and the Okapi retrieval function. We also observe that the smoothing of self-translation probabilities has a significant impact on the retrieval performance. Both smoothing methods improve the performance significantly over the non-smoothed version of the title language model. The null word based smoothing method consistently performs better than the method of tying self-translation probabilities. The rest of the paper is organized as follows: We first present the title language model approach in Section 2, describing the two self-translation smoothing methods. We then present the experiments and results in Section 3. Section 4 gives the conclusions and future work.

2. A TITLE LANGUAGE MODEL FOR IR

The basic idea of the title language model approach is to estimate the title language model for a document and then to compute the likelihood that the query would have been generated from the estimated model. Therefore, the key issue is how to estimate the title language model for a document based on the observation of a collection of documents.

A simple approach would be to estimate the title language model for a document using only the title of that document. However, because of the flexibility in choosing different titles and the fact that each document has only one title given by the author(s), it would be almost impossible to obtain a good estimation of title language model directly from the titles.

Our approach is to exploit statistical translation models to find the title language model based on the observation of a document. More specifically, we use a statistical translation model to "convert" the language model of a document to the title language model for that document. To accomplish this conversion process, we need to answer two questions:

1. How to estimate such a statistical translation model?
2. How to apply the estimated statistical translation model to convert a document language model to a title language model and use the estimated title language model to score documents with respect to a query?

Sections 2.1 and 2.2 address these two questions respectively.

2.1 Learning a Statistical Title Translation Model

The key component in a statistical title translation model is the word translation probability $P(tw|dw)$, i.e. the probability of using word tw in the title, given that word dw appears in the document. Once we have the set of word translation probabilities $P(tw|dw)$, we can easily calculate the title language model for a document based on the observation of that document.

To learn the set of word translation probabilities, we can take advantage of the document-title pairs in the collection. By viewing documents as samples of a 'verbose' language and titles as samples of a 'concise' language, we can treat each document-title pair as a translation pair, i.e. a pair of texts written in the 'verbose' language and the 'concise' language respectively.

Formally, let $\{<t_i, d_i>, i = 1, 2, \ldots, N\}$ be the title-document pairs in the collection. According to the standard statistical translation model [2], we can find the optimal model M^* by maximizing the probability of generating titles from documents, or

$$M^* = \arg\max_{M} \prod_{i=1}^{N} P(t_i \mid d_i, M) \quad (1)$$

Based on the model 1 for the statistical translation model [2], Equation (1) can be expanded as

$$
\begin{aligned}
M^* &= \underset{M}{\operatorname{argmax}} \prod_{i=1}^{N} P(t_i \mid d_i, M) \\
&\approx \underset{M}{\operatorname{argmax}} \prod_{i=1}^{N} \prod_{tw \in t_i} \left\{ \frac{\varepsilon}{|d_i|+1} \left(P(tw \mid \phi, M) + \sum_{dw \in d_i} P(tw \mid dw, M) c(dw, d_i) \right) \right\} \\
&\approx \underset{M}{\operatorname{argmax}} \prod_{i=1}^{N} \prod_{tw \in t_i} \left\{ \frac{P(tw \mid \phi, M)}{|d_i|+1} + \sum_{dw \in d_i} P(tw \mid dw, M) P(dw \mid d_i) \right\}
\end{aligned}
\quad (2)
$$

where ε is a constant, ϕ stands for the null word, $|d_i|$ is the length of document d_i, $c(dw, d_i)$ is the number of times that word dw appears in document d. In the last step of Equation (2), we throw out the constant ε and use the approximation that $P(dw \mid d) \approx c(dw, d)/(|d|+1)$. To find the optimal word translation probabilities $P(tw|dw, M^*)$, we can use the EM algorithm. The details of the algorithm can be found in the literature for statistical translation models, such as [2]. We call this model "model 1" for easy reference.

2.1.1 The problem of under-estimating self-translation probabilities

There is a serious problem with using model 1 described above directly to learn the correlation between the words in documents and titles. In particular, the self-translation probability of a word (i.e., $P(w'=w|w)$) will be under-estimated significantly. A document can potentially have many different titles, but authors generally only give one title for every document. Because titles are usually much shorter than documents, only an extremely small portion of the words in a document can be expected to actually appear in the title. We measured the vocabulary overlapping between titles and documents on three different TREC collections: AP(1988), WSJ(1990-1992) and SJM(1991), and found that, on average, only 5% of the words in a document also appear in its title. This means that, most of the document words would never appear in any title, which will result in a zero self-translation probability for most of the words. Therefore, if we follow the learning algorithm for the statistical translation model directly, the following scenario may occur: For some documents, even though they contain every single query word, the probability $P(Q|D)$ can still be very low due to the zero self-translation probability. In the following subsections, we propose two different learning algorithms that can address this problem. As will be shown later, both algorithms improve the retrieval performance significantly over the model 1, indicating that the proposed methods for modeling the self-translation probabilities are effective.

2.1.2 Tying self-translation probabilities (Model 2)

One way to avoid the problem of zero self translation probability is to tie all the self translation probabilities $P(w'=w|w)$ with a single parameter P_{self}. Essentially, we assume that all the self-translation probabilities have approximately the same value, and so can be replace with a single parameter. Since there are always some title words actually coming from the body of documents, the unified self-translation probability P_{self} will not be zero. We call the corresponding model Model 2.

We can also apply the EM algorithm to estimate all the word translation probabilities, including the smoothing parameter P_{self}. The updating Equations are as follows:

Let $P(w'|w)$ and P_{self} stand for the parameters obtained from the previous iteration, $P'(w|w)$ and P'_{self} stand for the updated values of the parameters in the current iteration. According to the EM algorithm, the updating equation for the self-translation probability P'_{self}, will be

$$
P'_{self} = \frac{1}{Z_{self}} \sum_i \sum_w \frac{P_{self} C(w, d_i) C(w, t_i)}{P_{self} C(w, d_i) + \sum_{w' \in d_i \wedge w \neq w'} P(w \mid w') C(w', d_i)} \quad (3)
$$

where variable Z_{self} is the normalization constant and is defined as

$$
Z_{self} = \sum_i \left(\begin{array}{l} \displaystyle\sum_w \sum_{w' \neq w} \frac{P(w \mid w') C(w, t_i) C(w', d_i)}{P_{self} C(w, d_i) + \sum_{w'' \in d_i \wedge w'' \neq w} P(w \mid w'') C(w'', d_i)} + \\ \displaystyle\sum_w \frac{P_{self} C(w, d_i) C(w, t_i)}{P_{self} C(w, d_i) + \sum_{w' \in d_i \wedge w \neq w'} P(w \mid w') C(w', d_i)} \end{array} \right) \quad (4)
$$

For those non-self-translation probabilities, i.e. $P(w' \neq w|w)$, the EM updating equations are identical to the ones used for the standard learning algorithm of a statistical translation model except that in the normalization equations, the self-translation probability should be replaced with P_{self}, or

$$
\forall w \quad \sum_{w' \neq w} P'(w' \mid w) = 1 - P'_{self} \quad (5)
$$

2.1.3 Adding a Null Title Word Slot (Model 3)

One problem with tying all the self-translation probabilities for different words with a single unified self-translation probability is that we lose some information about the relative importance of words. Specifically, those words with a higher probability in the titles should have a higher self-translation probability than those with a lower probability in the titles. Tying them would cause under-estimation of the former and over-estimation of the latter. As a result, the self-translation probability may be less than the translation probability for other words, which is not desirable.

In this subsection, we propose a better smoothing model that is able to discriminate the self-translation probabilities for different document words. It is based on the idea of introducing an extra NULL word slot in the title. An interesting property of this model is that the self-translation probability is guaranteed to be no less than the translation probability for any other word, i.e. $P(w|w) \geq P(w' \neq w|w)$. We call this model Model 3.

Titles are typically very short and therefore only provide us with very limited data. Now, suppose we had sampled more title words from the title language model of a given document, what kinds of words would we expect to have seen? Given no other information, it would be reasonable to assume that we will more likely observe a word that occurs in the document. To capture this intuition, we assume that there is an extra NULL, unobserved, word slot in each title, that can only be filled in by self-translating any word in the body of the document. Use e_t to stand for the extra word slot in the title t. With the count of this extra word slot, the standard statistical translation model between the document d and title t will be modified as

$$P(t \mid d,M) \approx P(c_t \mid d,M)\prod_{tw\in t} P(tw \mid d,M)$$
$$\approx \left(\sum_{dw\in d} P(dw \mid dw,M)P(dw \mid d)\right)\times \qquad (6)$$
$$\prod_{tw\in t}\left(\frac{P(tw \mid \phi,M)}{\mid d\mid +1} + \sum_{dw\in d} P(tw \mid dw,M)P(dw \mid d)\right)$$

To find the optimal statistical translation model, we will still maximize the translation probability from documents to titles. Substituting the document-title translation probability $P(t|d,M)$ with equation (6), the optimization goal (Equation (1)) can be written as

$$M^* = \underset{M}{\operatorname{argmax}}\prod_{i=1}^{N}\left\{\begin{array}{l}\sum_{dw\in d_i} P(dw\mid dw,M)P(dw\mid d_i)\times \\ \prod_{tw\in t_i}\left(\frac{P(tw\mid \phi,M)}{\mid d_i\mid +1}+\sum_{dw\in d_i}P(tw\mid dw,M)P(dw\mid d_i)\right)\end{array}\right\} \qquad (7)$$

Because the extra word slot in every title provides a chance for any word in the document to appear in the title through the self-translation process, it is not difficult to prove that, this model will ensure that the self-translation probability $P(w|w)$ will be no less than $P(w'\neq w|w)$ for any word w. The EM algorithm can again be applied to maximize Equation (7) and learn the word translation probabilities. The updating equations for the word translation probabilities are essentially the same as what are used for the standard learning algorithm for statistical translation models, except for the inclusion of the extra counts due to the null word slot.

2.2 Computing Document Query Similarity

In this section, we discuss how to apply the learned statistical translation model to find the title language model for a document and use the estimated title language model to compute the relevance value of a document with respect to a query. To accomplish this, we define the conditional probability $P(Q|D)$ as the probability of using query Q as the title for document D, or, the probability of translating document D into query Q using the statistical title translation model, which is given below.

$$P(Q \mid D,M) = \prod_{qw\in Q}\left\{\frac{\varepsilon}{\mid d\mid +1}\left(P(qw\mid \phi,M)+\sum_{dw\in d}P(qw\mid dw,M)c(dw,D)\right)\right\} \qquad (8)$$
$$\approx \varepsilon\prod_{qw\in Q}\left\{\frac{P(qw\mid \phi,M)}{\mid D\mid +1}+\sum_{dw\in D}P(qw\mid dw,M)P(dw\mid D)\right\}$$

As can be seen from Equation (8), the document language model $P(dw|D)$ is not directly used to compute the probability of a query term. Instead, it is "converted" into a title language model through using word translation probabilities $P(qw|dw)$. Such conversion also happens in the model proposed in [1], but there the translation model is meant to capture synonym and polysemy relations, and is trained with synthetic queries. Similar to the traditional language modeling approach, to deal with the query words that can't be generated from title language model, we need to do further smoothing, i.e.

$$P(Q \mid D,M) = \prod_{qw\in Q}\left\{\begin{array}{l}\frac{\lambda\varepsilon}{\mid d\mid +1}\left(P(qw\mid \phi,M)+\sum_{dw\in d}P(qw\mid dw,M)c(dw,D)\right)+ \\ (1-\lambda)P(qw\mid GE)\end{array}\right\} \qquad (8')$$
$$\approx \varepsilon\prod_{qw\in Q}\left\{\begin{array}{l}\lambda\left(\frac{P(qw\mid \phi,M)}{\mid D\mid +1}+\sum_{dw\in D}P(qw\mid dw,M)P(dw\mid D)\right)+ \\ (1-\lambda)P(qw\mid GE)\end{array}\right\}$$

where constant λ is the smoothing constant and $P(qw|GE)$ is the general English language model which can be easily estimated from the collection [1]. In our experiment, we set the smoothing constant λ to be 0.5 for all different models and all different collections.

Equation (8') is the general formula that can be used to score a document with respect to a query with any specific translation model. A different translation model would thus result in a different retrieval formula. In the next section, we will compare the retrieval performance using different statistical title translation models, including Model 1, Model 2 and Model 3.

3. EXPERIMENT

3.1 Experiment Design

The goal of our experiments is to answer the following three questions:

1. *Will the title language model be effective for information retrieval?* To answer this question, we will compare the performance of title language model with that of the state-of-art information retrieval methods, including the Okapi method and the traditional language model for information retrieval.

2. *How general is the trained statistical title translation model?* Can a model estimated on one collection be applied to another? To answer this question, we conduct an experiment that applies the statistical title translation model learned from one collection to other collections. We then compare the performance of using a "foreign" translation model with that of using no translation model.

3. *How important is the smoothing of self-translation in the title language model approach for information retrieval?* To answer this question, we can compare the results for title language model 1 with model 2 and model 3.

We used three different TREC testing collections for evaluation: AP88 (Associated Press, 1988), WSJ90-92 (wall street journal from 1990 to 1992) and SJM (San Jose Mercury News, 1991). We used TREC4 queries (201-250) and their relevance judgments for evaluation. The average length of the titles in these collections is four to five words. The different characteristics of the three databases allow us to check the robustness of our models.

3.2 Baseline Methods

The two baseline methods are the Okapi method[9] and the traditional language modeling approach. The exact formula for the Okapi method is shown in Equation (9)

$$Sim(Q,D)=\sum_{qw\in Q}\left\{\frac{tf(qw,D)\log(\frac{N-df(qw)+0.5}{df(qw)+0.5})}{0.5+1.5\frac{|D|}{avg\_dl}+tf(qw,D)}\right\} \qquad (9)$$

where $tf(qw,D)$ is the term frequency of word qw in document D, $df(qw)$ is the document frequency for the word qw and avg_dl is the average document length for all the documents in the collection. The exact equation used for the traditional language modeling approach is shown in Equation (10).

$$P(Q\,|\,D)=\prod_{qw\in Q}((1-\lambda)P(qw\,|\,GE)+\lambda P(dw\,|\,D)) \qquad (10)$$

The constant λ is the smoothing constant (similar to the λ in Equation (8')), and $P(qw|GE)$ is the general English language model estimated from the collection. To make the comparison fair, the smoothing constant for the traditional language model is set to be 0.5, which is same as for the title language model.

3.3 Experiment Results

The results on AP88, WSJ and SJM are shown in Table 1, Table 2, and Table 3, respectively. In each table, we include the precisions at different recall points and the average precision. Several interesting observations can be made on these results:

Table 1: Results for AP88 Collection 'LM' stands for traditional language model, 'Okapi' stands for Okapi formula and model-1, model-2 and model-3 stand for title language model 1, model 2 and model 3.

Collection	LM	Okapi	Model 1	Model 2	Model 3
Recall 0.1	0.4398	0.4798	0.2061	0.4885	0.5062
Recall 0.2	0.3490	0.3789	0.1409	0.4082	0.4024
Recall 0.3	0.3035	0.3286	0.1154	0.3417	0.3572
Recall 0.4	0.2492	0.2889	0.0680	0.2830	0.3133
Recall 0.5	0.2114	0.2352	0.0525	0.2399	0.2668
Recall 0.6	0.1689	0.2011	0.0277	0.1856	0.2107
Recall 0.7	0.1369	0.1596	0.0174	0.1460	0.1742
Recall 0.8	0.0811	0.0833	0.0174	0.0897	0.1184
Recall 0.9	0.0617	0.0611	0.0115	0.0651	0.0738
Recall 1.0	0.0580	0.0582	0.0115	0.0618	0.0639
Avg. Prec.	**0.2238**	**0.2463**	**0.2108**	**0.2516**	**0.2677**

First, let us compare the results between different title language models, namely model 1, model 2 and model 3. As seen from Table 1, 2 and 3, for all the three collections, model 1 is inferior to model 2, which is inferior to model 3, in terms of both average precision and precisions at different recall points. In particular, on the WSJ collection, title language model 1 performs extremely poorly compared with the other two methods. This result indicates that title language model 1 may fail to find relevant documents in some cases due to the problem of zero self-translation probability, as we discussed in Section 2. Indeed, we computed the percentage of title words that cannot be found in their documents. This number is 25% for AP88 collection, 34% for SJM collection and 45% for WSJ collection. This high percentage of "missing" title words strongly suggests that the smoothing of self-translation probability will be critical. Indeed, for the WSJ collection, which has the highest percentage of missing title words, title language model 1, without any smoothing of self-translation probability, degrades the performance more dramatically than for collections AP88 and SJM, where more title words can be found in the documents, and the smoothing of self-translation probability is not as critical.

Table 2: Results for WSJ collection. 'LM' stands for traditional language model, 'Okapi' stands for Okapi formula and model-1, model-2 and model-3 stand for title language model 1, model 2 and model 3.

Collection	LM	Okapi	Model 1	Model 2	Model 3
Recall 0.1	0.4308	0.4539	0.2061	0.4055	0.4271
Recall 0.2	0.3587	0.3546	0.1409	0.3449	0.3681
Recall 0.3	0.2721	0.2724	0.1154	0.2674	0.2878
Recall 0.4	0.2272	0.1817	0.0680	0.2305	0.2432
Recall 0.5	0.1812	0.1265	0.0525	0.1723	0.1874
Recall 0.6	0.1133	0.0840	0.0277	0.1172	0.1369
Recall 0.7	0.0525	0.0308	0.0174	0.0764	0.0652
Recall 0.8	0.0328	0.0218	0.0174	0.0528	0.0465
Recall 0.9	0.0153	0.0106	0.0115	0.0350	0.0204
Recall 1.0	0.0153	0.0106	0.0115	0.0321	0.0204
Avg. Prec.	**0.1844**	**0.1719**	**0.0761**	**0.1851**	**0.1950**

Table 3: Results for SJM Collection. 'LM' stands for traditional language model, 'Okapi' stands for Okapi formula and model-1, model-2 and model-3 stand for title language model 1, model 2 and model 3.

Collection	LM	Okapi	Model 1	Model 2	Model 3
Recall 0.1	0.4009	0.4054	0.4226	0.4249	0.4339
Recall 0.2	0.3345	0.3232	0.3281	0.3650	0.3638
Recall 0.3	0.2813	0.2348	0.2712	0.2890	0.3019
Recall 0.4	0.2076	0.1692	0.1991	0.2236	0.2296
Recall 0.5	0.1815	0.1378	0.1670	0.1874	0.1919
Recall 0.6	0.1046	0.0986	0.1095	0.1393	0.1431
Recall 0.7	0.0816	0.0571	0.0782	0.0862	0.0974
Recall 0.8	0.0460	0.0312	0.0688	0.0591	0.0788
Recall 0.9	0.0375	0.0312	0.0524	0.0386	0.0456
Recall 1.0	0.0375	0.0312	0.0524	0.0386	0.0456
Avg. Prec.	**0.1845**	**0.1727**	**0.1910**	**0.1983**	**0.2081**

The second dimension of comparison is to compare title language models with traditional language model. As already pointed out by Berger and Lafferty [1], the traditional language model can be viewed as a special case of translation language model, i.e. all the translation probability $P(w'|w)$ become delta functions $\delta(w,w')$. Therefore, the comparison along this dimension can indicate if the translation probabilities learned from the correlation between titles and documents are effective in improving retrieval accuracy. As seen from Table 1, Table 2, and Table 3, title language model 3 performances significantly better than the traditional language model over all the three collections in terms of all the performance measures. Thus, we can conclude that the translation probability learned from title-document pairs appears to be helpful for finding relevant documents.

Lastly, we can also compare the performance of the title language model approach with the Okapi method [8]. For all the three collections the title language model 3 outperforms Okapi significantly in terms of all the performance measures, except in one case -- The precision at 0.1 recall on the WSJ collection is slightly worse than both the traditional language model approach and Okapi.

To test the generality of the estimated translation model, we applied the statistical title translation model leaned from the AP88 collection to the AP90 collection. We hypothesize that, if two collections are 'similar', the statistical title translation model learned from one collection should be able to give a good approximation of the correlation between documents and titles of the other collection. Therefore, it would make sense to apply the translation model learned from one collection to another 'similar' collection.

Table 4: Results for AP90. 'LM' stands for traditional language model, 'Okapi' stands for Okapi formula and model-3 stand for title language model 3. Different from the previous experiments in which the translation model is learned from the retrieved collection itself, this experiment applies the translation model learned from AP88 to retrieve relevant document in AP90 collection.

Collection	LM	Okapi	Model3
Recall 0.1	0.4775	0.4951	0.5137
Recall 0.2	0.4118	0.4308	0.4454
Recall 0.3	0.3124	0.3374	0.3628
Recall 0.4	0.2700	0.2894	0.3248
Recall 0.5	0.2280	0.2567	0.2665
Recall 0.6	0.1733	0.2123	0.2222
Recall 0.7	0.1294	0.1230	0.1372
Recall 0.8	0.0991	0.0969	0.1136
Recall 0.9	0.0782	0.0659	0.0963
Recall 1.0	0.0614	0.0550	0.0733
Avg. Prec.	**0.2411**	**0.2511**	**0.2771**

Table 4 gives the results of applying the translation model learned from AP88 to AP90. Since title language model 3 already demonstrated its superiority to model 1 and model 2, we only considered model 3 in this experiment. From Table 3, we see that title generation model 3 outperforms the traditional language model and Okapi method significantly in terms of all measures. We also applied the statistical title translation model learned from AP88 to WSJ to further examine the generality of the model and our learning method. This time, the performance of title language model 3 with the statistical title translation model learned from AP88 is only about the same as the traditional language model and Okapi method for the collection WSJ. Since the statistical title translation model learned from AP88 can be expected to be a much better approximation of the correlation between documents and titles for AP90 than for WSJ, these results suggest that applying the translation model learned from a "foreign" database is helpful only when the "foreign" database is similar to the "native" one. But, it is interesting to note that it has never resulted in any degradation of performance.

4. CONCLUSIONS

Bridging the "gap" between a query language model and document language model is an important issue when applying language models to information retrieval. In this paper, we propose bridging this gap by exploiting document titles to estimate a title language model, which can be regarded as an approximate query language model. The essence of our work is to approximate the query language model for a document with the title language model for the document. Operationally, we first estimate such a translation model by using all the document-title pairs in a collection. The translation model can then be used to "convert" a regular document language model to a title language model. Finally, the title language model estimated for each document is used to compute the query likelihood. Intuitively, the scoring is based on the likelihood that the query could have been a title for a document.

Based on the experiment results, we can draw the following conclusions:

- Based on the comparison between the title language models and the traditional language model and the Okapi method, we can conclude that the title language model for information retrieval is an effective retrieval method. In all our experiments, the title language model gives a better performance than both the traditional language model and the Okapi method.
- Based on the comparison between three different title language models for information retrieval, we can conclude that title generation model 2 and 3 are superior to model 1, and model 3 is superior to model 2. Since the difference between the three different title language models is on how to handle the self-translation probability, we can conclude that, first, it is crucial to smooth the self-translation probability to avoid the zero self-translation probability. Second, a better smoothing method for self-translation probability can improve the performance. Results show that adding an extra null word slot to the title is a reasonable smoothing method for the self-translation probabilities.

- The success of applying the title language model learned from AP88 to AP90 appears to indicate that, in the case when the two collections are similar, the correlation between documents and titles in one collection also tend to be similar to that in the other. Therefore, it would seem to be appropriate to apply the statistical title translation model learned from one collection to the retrieval task of another similar collection. Even if the collections are not similar, applying a learned statistical title translation model from a foreign database does not seem to degrade the performance either. Thus, the statistical title translation model learned from title-document pairs may be used as a "general" resource that can be applied to retrieval task for different collections.

There are several directions for the future work. First, it would be interesting to see how the style or quality of titles would affect the effectiveness of our model. One possibility is to use the collections where the quality of titles has high variances (e.g., the Web data). Second, we have assumed that queries and titles are similar, but there may be queries (e.g., long and verbose queries) that are quite different from titles. So, it would be interesting to further evaluate the robustness of our model by using many different types of queries. Finally, using title information is only one way to bridge the query-document gap; it would be very interesting to further explore other effective methods that can generate an appropriate query language model for a document.

5. ACKNOWLEDGEMENTS

We thank Jamie Callan, Yiming Yang, Luo Si, and the anonymous reviewers for their helpful comments on this work. This material is based in part on work supported by National Science Foundation under Cooperative Agreement No. IRI-9817496. Partial support for this work was provided by the National Science Foundation's National Science, Mathematics, Engineering, and Technology Education Digital Library Program under grant DUE-0085834. This work was also supported in part by the Advanced Research and Development Activity (ARDA) under contract number MDA908-00-C-0037. Any opinions, findings, and conclusions or recommendations expressed in this material are those of the authors and do not necessarily reflect the views of the National Science Foundation or ARDA.

6. REFERENCES

[1] A. Berger and J. Laffety (1999). Information retrieval as statistical translation. In *Proceedings of SIGIR '99.* pp. 222-229.

[2] P. Brown, S. Della Pietra, V. Della Pietra, and R. Mercer (1993). The mathematics of statistical machine translation: Parameter estimation. *Computational Linguistics*, 19(2), pp. 263--311.

[3] D. Hiemstra and W. Kraaij (1999), Twenty-One at TREC-7: ad-hoc and cross-language track, In *Proceedings of the seventh Text Retrieval Conference TREC-7*, NIST Special Publication 500-242, pages 227-238, 1999.

[4] J. Lafferty and C. Zhai (2001), Document language models, query models, and risk minimization for information retrieval, In *Proceedings of SIGIR 2001*, pp. 111-119.

[5] A. M. Lam-Adesina, G. J. F. Jones, Applying summarization techniques for term selection in relevance feedback , In *Proceedings of SIGIR 2001*, pp. 1-9.

[6] V. Lavrenko and W. B. Croft (2001), Relevance-based Language Models, In *Proceedings of SIGIR 2001*, pp. 120-127.

[7] D. Miller, T. Leek and R. M. Schwartz (1999). A hidden Markov model information retrieval system. Proceedings of SIGIR'1999, pp. 214-222. .

[8] J. Ponte and W. B. Croft (1998). A language modeling approach to information retrieval. In *Proceedings of SIGIR' 1998*, pp. 275-281.

[9] S.E. Robertson et al.(1993). Okapi at TREC-4. In *The Fourth Text Retrieval Conference (TREC-4)*. 1993

[10] E. Voorhees and D. Harman (ed.) (1996), The Fifth Text REtrieval Conference (TREC-5), NIST Special Publication 500-238.

[11] C. Zhai and J. Lafferty (2001). A study of smoothing methods for language models applied to ad hoc information retrieval. In *Proceeding of SIGIR'01*, 2001, pp. 334-342.

Two-Stage Language Models for Information Retrieval

ChengXiang Zhai
School of Computer Science
Carnegie Mellon University
Pittsburgh, PA 15213

John Lafferty
School of Computer Science
Carnegie Mellon University
Pittsburgh, PA 15213

ABSTRACT

The optimal settings of retrieval parameters often depend on both the document collection and the query, and are usually found through empirical tuning. In this paper, we propose a family of *two-stage* language models for information retrieval that explicitly captures the different influences of the query and document collection on the optimal settings of retrieval parameters. As a special case, we present a two-stage smoothing method that allows us to estimate the smoothing parameters completely automatically. In the first stage, the document language model is smoothed using a Dirichlet prior with the collection language model as the reference model. In the second stage, the smoothed document language model is further interpolated with a query background language model. We propose a leave-one-out method for estimating the Dirichlet parameter of the first stage, and the use of document mixture models for estimating the interpolation parameter of the second stage. Evaluation on five different databases and four types of queries indicates that the two-stage smoothing method with the proposed parameter estimation methods consistently gives retrieval performance that is close to—or better than—the best results achieved using a single smoothing method and exhaustive parameter search on the test data.

Categories and Subject Descriptors

H.3.3 [**Information Search and Retrieval**]: Retrieval Models—*language models, parameter setting*

General Terms

Algorithms

Keywords

risk minimization, two-stage language models, two-stage smoothing, Dirichlet prior, interpolation, parameter estimation, leave-one-out, mixture model

1. INTRODUCTION

It is well-known that the optimal settings of retrieval parameters generally depend on both the document collection and the query. For example, specialized term weighting for short queries was studied in [3]. Salton and Buckley studied many different term weighting methods used in the vector-space retrieval model; their recommended methods strongly depend on the type of the query and the characteristics of the document collection [13]. It has been a great challenge to find the optimal settings of retrieval parameters automatically and adaptively accordingly to the characteristics of the collection and queries, and empirical parameter tuning seems to be inevitable in order to achieve good retrieval performance. This is evident in the large number of parameter-tuning experiments reported in virtually every paper published in the TREC proceedings [15].

The need for empirical parameter tuning is due in part from the fact that most existing retrieval models are based on certain *preassumed* representation of queries and documents, rather than on a direct modeling of the queries and documents. As a result, the "adaptability" of the model is restricted by the particular representation assumed, and reserving free parameters for tuning becomes a way to accommodate any difference among queries and documents that has not been captured well in the representation. In order to be able to set parameters automatically, it is necessary to model queries and documents directly. This goal has been explored recently in the language modeling approach to information retrieval, which has attracted significant attention since it was first proposed in [9].

The first uses of the language modeling approach focused on its empirical effectiveness using simple models [9, 7, 2, 1]. Recent work has begun to develop more sophisticated models and a systematic framework for this new family of retrieval methods. In [4], a risk minimization retrieval framework is proposed that incorporates language modeling as natural components, and that unifies several existing retrieval models in a framework based on Bayesian decision theory. One important advantage of the risk minimization retrieval framework over the traditional models is its capability of modeling both queries and documents directly through statistical language models, which provides a basis for exploiting statistical estimation methods to set retrieval parameters automatically. Several special language models are explored in [6, 4, 16], and in all uses of language modeling in IR, smoothing plays a crucial role. The empirical study in [17] reveals that not only is retrieval performance generally sensitive to the setting of smoothing parameters, but also that this sensitivity depends on the type of queries that are input to the system.

In this paper, we propose a family of language models for information retrieval that we refer to as *two-stage models*. The first stage involves the estimation of a *document* language model independent of the query, while the second stage involves the computation of the likelihood of the query according to a *query* language model, which is based on the estimated document language model. Thus, the two-stage strategy explicitly captures the different influences of the query and document collection on the optimal settings of retrieval parameters.

We derive the two-stage models within the general risk minimization retrieval framework, and present a special case that leads to a two-stage *smoothing* method. In the first stage of smoothing, the document language model is smoothed using a Dirichlet prior with the collection language model as the reference model. In the second stage, the smoothed document language model is further interpolated with a query background language model. we propose a leave-one-out method for estimating the first-stage Dirichlet parameter and make use of a mixture model for estimating the second-stage interpolation parameter. Evaluation on five different databases and four types of queries indicates that the two-stage smoothing method with the proposed parameter estimation method—which is fully automatic—consistently gives retrieval performance that is close to, or better than, the result of using a single smoothing method and exhaustive parameter search on the test data.

The proposed two-stage smoothing method represents a step toward the goal of setting database-specific and query-specific retrieval parameters fully automatically, without the need for tedious experimentation. The effectiveness and robustness of the approach, along with the fact that there is no ad hoc parameter tuning involved, make it very useful as a solid baseline method for the evaluation of retrieval models.

The rest of the paper is organized as follows. We first derive the two-stage language models in Section 2, and present the two-stage smoothing method as a special case in Section 3. We then describe, in Section 4, methods for estimating the two parameters involved in the two-stage smoothing method. We report our experimental results in Section 5. Section 6 presents conclusions and suggestions for future work.

2. TWO-STAGE LANGUAGE MODELS

2.1 The risk minimization framework

The risk minimization retrieval framework is a general probabilistic retrieval framework based on Bayesian decision theory [4]. In this framework, queries and documents are modeled using statistical language models, user preferences are modeled through loss functions, and retrieval is cast as a risk minimization problem. The framework unifies several existing retrieval models within one general probabilistic framework, and facilitates the development of new principled approaches to text retrieval.

In traditional retrieval models, such as the vector-space model [12] and the BM25 retrieval model [11], the retrieval parameters have almost always been introduced heuristically. The lack of a direct modeling of queries and documents makes it hard for these models to incorporate, in a principled way, parameters that adequately address special characteristics of queries and documents. For example, the vector-space model *assumes* that a query and a document are both represented by a term vector. However, the mapping from a query or a document to such a vector can be somehow arbitrary. Thus, because the model "sees" a document through its vector representation, there is no principled way to model the length of a document. As a result, heuristic parameters must be used (see, e.g., the pivot length normalization method [14]). Similarly, in the BM25 retrieval formula, there is no direct modeling of queries, making it necessary to introduce heuristic parameters to incorporate query term frequencies [11].

One important advantage of the risk minimization retrieval framework [4] over these traditional models is its capability of modeling both queries and documents directly through statistical language modeling. Although a query and a document are similar in the sense that they are both text, they do have important differences. For example, queries are much shorter and often contain just a few keywords. Thus, from the viewpoint of language modeling, a query and a document require different language models. Practically, separating a query model from a document model has the important advantage of being able to introduce *different* retrieval parameters for queries and documents when appropriate. In general, using statistical language models allows us to introduce all parameters in a probabilistic way, and also makes it possible to set the parameters automatically through statistical estimation methods.

2.2 Derivation of two-stage language models

The original language modeling approach as proposed in [9] involves a two-step scoring procedure: (1) Estimate a document language model for each document; (2) Compute the query likelihood using the estimated document language model (directly). The two-stage language modeling approach is a generalization of this two-step procedure, in which a query language model is introduced so that the query likelihood is computed using a query model that is based on the estimated document model, instead of using the estimated document model directly. The use of an explicit and separate query model makes it possible to factor out any influence of queries on the smoothing parameters for document language models.

We now derive the family of two-stage language models for information retrieval formally using the risk minimization framework.

In the risk minimization framework presented in [4], documents are ranked based on the following risk function:

$$R(\mathbf{d}_i;\mathbf{q}) = \sum_{R\in\{0,1\}} \int_{\Theta_Q}\int_{\Theta_D} L(\theta_Q,\theta_D,R) \times p(\theta_Q\,|\,\mathbf{q},\mathcal{U})\, p(\theta_D\,|\,d_i,\mathcal{S})\, p(R\,|\,\theta_Q,\theta_D)\, d\theta_D\, d\theta_Q$$

Let us now consider the following special loss function, indexed by a small constant ϵ,

$$L_\epsilon(\theta_Q,\theta_D,R) = \begin{cases} 0 & \text{if } \Delta(\theta_Q,\theta_D)\le\epsilon \\ c & \text{otherwise} \end{cases}$$

where $\Delta : \Theta_Q \times \Theta_D \rightarrow \mathbb{R}$ is a model distance function, and c is a constant positive cost. Thus, the loss is zero when the query model and the document model are close to each other, and is c otherwise. Using this loss function, we obtain the following risk:

$$R(\mathbf{d};\mathbf{q}) = c - \int_{\Theta_D}\int_{\theta_Q\in S_\epsilon(\theta_D)} p(\theta_Q\,|\,\mathbf{q},\mathcal{U})\, p(\theta_D\,|\,\mathbf{d},\mathcal{S})\, d\theta_Q\, d\theta_D$$

where $S_\epsilon(\theta_D)$ is the sphere of radius ϵ centered at θ_D in the parameter space.

Now, assuming that $p(\theta_D\,|\,\mathbf{d},\mathcal{S})$ is concentrated on an estimated value $\hat{\theta}_D$, we can approximate the value of the integral over Θ_D by the integrand's value at $\hat{\theta}_D$. Note that the constant c can be ignored for the purpose of ranking. Thus, using $A \sim B$ to mean that A and B have the same effect for ranking, we have that

$$R(\mathbf{d};\mathbf{q}) \sim -\int_{\theta_Q\in S_\epsilon(\hat{\theta}_D)} p(\theta_Q\,|\,\mathbf{q},\mathcal{U})\, d\theta_Q$$

When θ_Q and θ_D belong to the same parameter space (i.e., $\Theta_Q = \Theta_D$) and ϵ is very small, the value of the integral can be approximated by the value of the function at $\hat{\theta}_D$ times a constant (the volume of $S_\epsilon(\hat{\theta}_D)$), and the constant can again be ignored for the purpose of ranking. That is,

$$R(\mathbf{d};\mathbf{q}) \sim -p(\hat{\theta}_D\,|\,\mathbf{q},\mathcal{U})$$

Therefore, using this risk we will be actually ranking documents according to $p(\hat{\theta}_D \mid \mathbf{q}, \mathcal{U})$, i.e., the posterior probability that the user used the estimated document model as the query model. Applying Bayes' formula, we can rewrite this as

$$p(\hat{\theta}_D \mid \mathbf{q}, \mathcal{U}) \propto p(\mathbf{q} \mid \hat{\theta}_D, \mathcal{U}) p(\hat{\theta}_D \mid \mathcal{U}) \quad (1)$$

Equation 1 is our basic two-stage language model retrieval formula. Similar to the model discussed in [1], this formula has the following interpretation: $p(\mathbf{q} \mid \hat{\theta}_D, \mathcal{U})$ captures how well the estimated document model $\hat{\theta}_D$ explains the query, whereas $p(\hat{\theta}_D \mid \mathcal{U})$ encodes our prior belief that the user would use $\hat{\theta}_D$ as the query model. While this prior could be exploited to model different document sources or other document characteristics, in this paper we assume a uniform prior.

The generic two-stage language model can be refined by specifying a concrete model $p(\mathbf{d} \mid \theta_D, \mathcal{S})$ for generating documents and a concrete model $p(\mathbf{q} \mid \theta_Q, \mathcal{U})$ for generating queries; different specifications lead to different retrieval formulas. If the query generation model is the simplest unigram language model, we have the scoring procedure of the original language modeling approach proposed in [9]; that is, we first estimate a document language model and then compute the query likelihood using the estimated model. In the next section, we present the generative models that lead to the two-stage smoothing method suggested in [17].

3. THE TWO-STAGE SMOOTHING METHOD

Let $\mathbf{d} = d_1 d_2 ... d_n$ denote a document, $\mathbf{q} = q_1 q_2 ... q_m$ denote a query, and $V = \{w_1, ..., w_{|V|}\}$ denote the words in the vocabulary. We consider the case where both θ_Q and θ_D are parameters of unigram language models, i.e., multinomial distributions over words in V.

The simplest generative model of a document is just the unigram language model θ_D, a multinomial. That is, a document would be generated by sampling words independently according to $p(\cdot \mid \theta_D)$, or

$$p(\mathbf{d} \mid \theta_D, \mathcal{S}) = \prod_{i=1}^{n} p(d_i \mid \theta_D)$$

Each document is assumed to be generated from a potentially different model as assumed in the general risk minimization framework. Given a particular document $\mathbf{d}$, we want to estimate θ_D. We use a Dirichlet prior on θ_D with parameters $\alpha = (\alpha_1, \alpha_2, \ldots, \alpha_{|V|})$, given by

$$\text{Dir}(\theta \mid \alpha) = \frac{\Gamma(\sum_{i=1}^{|V|} \alpha_i)}{\prod_{i=1}^{|V|} \Gamma(\alpha_i)} \prod_{i=1}^{|V|} \theta_i^{\alpha_i - 1} \quad (2)$$

The parameters α_i are chosen to be $\alpha_i = \mu\, p(w_i \mid \mathcal{S})$ where μ is a parameter and $p(\cdot \mid \mathcal{S})$ is the "collection language model," which can be estimated based on a set of documents from a source $\mathcal{S}$. The posterior distribution of θ_D is given by

$$p(\theta_D \mid \mathbf{d}, \mathcal{S}) \propto \prod_{w \in V} p(w \mid \theta_D)^{c(w,\mathbf{d}) + \mu p(w \mid \mathcal{S}) - 1}$$

and so is also Dirichlet, with parameters $\alpha_i = c(w_i, \mathbf{d}) + \mu p(w_i \mid \mathcal{S})$. Using the fact that the Dirichlet mean is $\alpha_j / \sum_k \alpha_k$, we have that

$$\begin{aligned} p_\mu(w \mid \hat{\theta}_D) &= \int_{\theta_D} p(w \mid \theta_D) p(\theta_D \mid \mathbf{d}, \mathcal{S}) d\theta_D \\ &= \frac{c(w, d) + \mu\, p(w \mid \mathcal{S})}{|d| + \mu} \end{aligned}$$

where $|\mathbf{d}| = \sum_{w \in V} c(w, \mathbf{d})$ is the length of $\mathbf{d}$. This is the Dirichlet prior smoothing method described in [17].

We now consider the query generation model. The simplest model is again the unigram language model θ_Q, which will result in a retrieval model with the Dirichlet prior as the single smoothing method. However, as observed in [17], such a model will not be able to explain the interactions between smoothing and the type of queries. In order to capture the common and non-discriminative words in a query, we assume that a query is generated by sampling words from a two-component mixture of multinomials, with one component being θ_Q and the other some query background language model $p(\cdot \mid \mathcal{U})$. That is,

$$p(\mathbf{q} \mid \theta_Q, \lambda, \mathcal{U}) = \prod_{i=1}^{m} ((1 - \lambda) p(q_i \mid \theta_Q) + \lambda p(q_i \mid \mathcal{U}))$$

where λ is a parameter, roughly indicating the amount of "noise" in $\mathbf{q}$.

Combining our estimate of θ_D with this query model, we have the following retrieval scoring formula for document $\mathbf{d}$ and query $\mathbf{q}$.

$$\begin{aligned} p(\mathbf{q} \mid \hat{\theta}_D, \lambda, \mathcal{U}) &= \\ &= \prod_{i=1}^{m} \left((1 - \lambda) p(q_i \mid \hat{\theta}_D) + \lambda\, p(q_i \mid \mathcal{U}) \right) \\ &= \prod_{i=1}^{m} \left((1 - \lambda) \frac{c(q_i, d) + \mu\, p(q_i \mid \mathcal{S})}{|\mathbf{d}| + \mu} + \lambda\, p(q_i \mid \mathcal{U}) \right) \end{aligned}$$

In this formula, the document language model is effectively smoothed in two steps. First, it is smoothed with a Dirichlet prior, and second, it is interpolated with a query background model. Thus, we refer to this as *two-stage smoothing*.

The above model has been empirically motivated by the observation that smoothing plays two different roles in the query likelihood retrieval method. One role is to improve the maximum likelihood estimate of the document language model, at the very least assigning non-zero probabilities to words that are not observed in the document. The other role is to "explain away" the common/non discriminative words in the query, so that the documents will be discriminated primarily based on their predictions of the "topical" words in the query. The two-stage smoothing method explicitly decouples these two roles. The first stage uses Dirichlet prior smoothing method to improve the estimate of a document language model; this method normalizes documents of different lengths appropriately with a prior sample size parameter, and performs well empirically [17]. The second stage is intended to bring in a query background language model to explicitly accommodate the generation of common words in queries.

The query background model $p(\cdot \mid \mathcal{U})$ is in general different from the collection language model $p(\cdot \mid \mathcal{S})$. With insufficient data to estimate $p(\cdot \mid \mathcal{U})$, however, we can assume that $p(\cdot \mid \mathcal{S})$ would be a reasonable approximation of $p(\cdot \mid \mathcal{U})$. In this form, the two-stage smoothing method is essentially a combination of Dirichlet prior smoothing with Jelinek-Mercer smoothing [17]. Indeed, it is very easy to verify that when $\lambda = 0$, we end up with just the Dirichlet prior smoothing, whereas when $\mu = 0$, we will have Jelinek-Mercer smoothing. Since the combined smoothing formula still follows the general smoothing scheme discussed in [17], it can be implemented very efficiently. In the next section, we present methods for estimating μ and λ from data.

Collection	avg. doc length	max. doc length	vocab. size	$\hat{\mu}$
AP88-89	446	2678	254872	640.643
WSJ87-92	435	8980	260259	792.001
ZF1-2	455	53753	447066	719.637

Table 1: Estimated values of μ along with database characteristics.

4. PARAMETER ESTIMATION

4.1 Estimating μ

The purpose of the Dirichlet prior smoothing at the first stage is to address the estimation bias due to the fact that a document is an extremely small amount of data with which to estimate a unigram language model. More specifically, it is to discount the maximum likelihood estimate appropriately and assign non-zero probabilities to words not observed in a document; this is the usual role of language model smoothing. A useful objective function for estimating smoothing parameters is the "leave-one-out" likelihood, that is, the sum of the log-likelihoods of each word in the observed data computed in terms of a model constructed based on the data with the target word excluded ("left out"). This criterion is essentially based on cross-validation, and has been used to derive several well-known smoothing methods including the Good-Turing method [8].

Formally, let $\mathcal{C} = \{d_1, d_2, ..., d_N\}$ be the collection of documents. Using our Dirichlet smoothing formula, the leave-one-out log-likelihood can be written as

$$\ell_{-1}(\mu \,|\, \mathcal{C}) = \sum_{i=1}^{N} \sum_{w \in V} c(w, d_i) \log \left(\frac{c(w, d_i) - 1 + \mu p(w|\mathcal{C})}{|d_i| - 1 + \mu} \right)$$

Thus, our estimate of μ is

$$\hat{\mu} = \arg\max_{\mu} \ell_{-1}(\mu|\mathcal{C})$$

which can be easily computed using Newton's method. The update formula is

$$\mu^{(k+1)} = \mu^{(k)} - g(\mu^{(k)})/g'(\mu^{(k)})$$

where the first and second derivatives of ℓ_{-1} are given by

$$g(\mu) = \ell'_{-1}(\mu) = \sum_{i=1}^{N} \sum_{w \in V} \frac{c(w, d_i)((|d_i| - 1)p(w \,|\, \mathcal{C}) - c(w, d_i) + 1)}{(|d_i| - 1 + \mu)(c(w, d_i) - 1 + \mu p(w \,|\, \mathcal{C}))}$$

and

$$g'(\mu) = \ell''_{-1}(\mu) = -\sum_{i=1}^{N} \sum_{w \in V} \frac{c(w, d_i)((|d_i| - 1)p(w \,|\, \mathcal{C}) - c(w, d_i) + 1)^2}{(|d_i| - 1 + \mu)^2 (c(w, d_i) - 1 + \mu p(w \,|\, \mathcal{C}))^2}$$

Since $g' \leq 0$, as long as $g' \neq 0$, the solution will be a global maximum. In our experiments, starting from value 1.0 the algorithm always converges.

The estimated values of μ for three databases are shown in Table 1. There is no clear correlation between the database characteristics shown in the table and the estimated value of μ.

4.2 Estimating λ

With the query model hidden, the query likelihood is

$$p(\mathbf{q} \,|\, \lambda, \mathcal{U}) = \int_{\Theta_Q} \prod_{i=1}^{m} ((1 - \lambda)p(q_i \,|\, \theta_Q) + \lambda p(q_i \,|\, \mathcal{U}))\, p(\theta_Q \,|\, \mathcal{U})\, d\theta_Q$$

In order to estimate λ, we approximate the query model space by the set of all N estimated document language models in our collection. That is, we will approximate the integral with a sum over all the possible document language models estimated on the collection, or

$$p(\mathbf{q} \,|\, \lambda, \mathcal{U}) = \sum_{i=1}^{N} \pi_i \prod_{j=1}^{m} ((1 - \lambda)p(q_j \,|\, \hat{\theta}_{d_i}) + \lambda p(q_j \,|\, \mathcal{U}))$$

where $\pi_i = p(\hat{\theta}_{d_i} \,|\, \mathcal{U})$, and $p(\cdot \,|\, \hat{\theta}_{d_i})$ is the smoothed unigram language model estimated based on document d_i using the Dirichlet prior approach.

Thus, we assume that the query is generated from a mixture of N document models with unknown mixing weights $\{\pi_i\}_{i=1}^N$. Leaving $\{\pi_i\}_{i=1}^N$ free is important, because what we really want is not to maximize the likelihood of generating the query from *every* document in the collection, instead, we want to find a λ that can maximize the likelihood of the query given *relevant* documents. With $\{\pi_i\}_{i=1}^N$ free to estimate, we would indeed allocate higher weights on documents that predict the query well in our likelihood function; presumably, these documents are also more likely to be relevant.

With this likelihood function, the parameters λ and $\{\pi_i\}_{i=1}^N$ can be estimated using the EM algorithm. The update formulas are

$$\pi_i^{(k+1)} = \frac{\pi_i^{(k)} \prod_{j=1}^{m} ((1 - \lambda^{(k)})\, p(q_j \,|\, \hat{\theta}_{d_i}) + \lambda^{(k)} p(q_j \,|\, \mathcal{U}))}{\sum_{i'=1}^{N} \pi_{i'}^{(k)} \prod_{j=1}^{m} ((1 - \lambda^{(k)}) p(q_j \,|\, \hat{\theta}_{d_{i'}}) + \lambda^{(k)} p(q_j \,|\, \mathcal{U}))}$$

and

$$\lambda^{(k+1)} = \frac{1}{m} \sum_{i=1}^{N} \pi_i^{(k+1)} \sum_{j=1}^{m} \frac{\lambda^{(k)} p(q_j \,|\, \mathcal{U})}{(1 - \lambda^{(k)}) p(q_j \,|\, \hat{\theta}_{d_i}) + \lambda^{(k)} p(q_j \,|\, \mathcal{U})}$$

5. EXPERIMENTS

In this section we first present experimental results that confirm the dual-role of smoothing, which provides an empirical justification for using the two-stage smoothing method for retrieval. We then present results of the two-stage smoothing method using the estimated parameters, comparing it to the optimal performance from using single smoothing methods and an exhaustive parameter search.

5.1 Influence of Query Length and Verbosity on Smoothing

In [17], strong interactions between smoothing and the type of queries have been observed. However, it is unclear whether the high sensitivity observed on long queries is due to a higher density of common words in such queries, or to just the length. The two-stage smoothing method assumes that it is the former. In order to clarify this, we design experiments to examine two query factors—length and "verbosity." Specifically, we consider four different types of queries, i.e., short keyword, long keyword, short verbose, and long verbose queries, and compare how they each behave with respect to smoothing. As we will show, the high sensitivity is indeed caused by the presence of common words in the query, and this provides an empirical justification for the two-stage smoothing method.

We generate the four types of queries from TREC topics 1-150. These 150 topics are special because, unlike other TREC topics, they all have a "concept" field, which contains a list of keywords related to the topic; these keywords serve well as the "long keyword" version of our queries. Figure 1 shows an example of such a topic (topic 52).

```
Title:  South African Sanctions
Description: Document discusses sanctions against
             South Africa.
Narrative:
  A relevant document will discuss any aspect of
South African sanctions, such as: sanctions
declared/proposed by a country against the South
African government in response to its apartheid
policy, or in response to pressure by an individual,
organization or another country; international
sanctions against Pretoria imposed by the United
Nations; the effects of sanctions against S. Africa;
opposition to sanctions; or, compliance with
sanctions by a company.  The document will identify
the sanctions instituted or being considered, e.g.,
corporate disinvestment, trade ban, academic boycott,
arms embargo.

Concepts:

1. sanctions, international sanctions,
   economic sanctions
2. corporate exodus, corporate disinvestment, stock
   divestiture, ban on new investment, trade ban,
   import ban on South African diamonds, U.N. arms
   embargo, curtailment of defense contracts,
   cutoff of nonmilitary goods, academic boycott,
   reduction of cultural ties
3. apartheid, white domination, racism
4. antiapartheid, black majority rule
5. Pretoria
```

Figure 1: Example topic, number 52. The keywords are used as the "long keyword" version of our queries.

We use all of the 150 topics, and generate the four versions of queries in the following way:

1. short keyword: Using only the title of the topic description (usually a noun phrase)[1]

2. short verbose: Using only the description field (usually one sentence).

3. long keyword: Using the concept field (about 28 keywords on average).

4. long verbose: Using the title, description and the narrative field (more than 50 words on average).

[1]Occasionally, a few function words were manually excluded, in order to make the queries purely keyword-based.

The relevance judgments available for these 150 topics are mostly on the documents in TREC disk 1 and disk 2. In order to observe any possible difference in smoothing caused by the types of documents, we partition the documents in disks 1 and 2 and use the three largest subsets of documents, accounting for a majority of the relevant documents for our queries. The three databases are AP88-89, WSJ87-92, and ZIFF1-2, each about 400MB–500MB in size. The queries without relevance judgments for a particular database were ignored for all of the experiments on that database. Four queries do not have judgments on AP88-89, and 49 queries do not have judgments on ZIFF1-2. Preprocessing of the documents is minimized; only a Porter stemmer is used, and no stop words are removed. Combining the four types of queries with the three databases gives us a total of 12 different testing collections.

To understand the interaction between different query factors and smoothing, we examine the sensitivity of retrieval performance to smoothing on each of the four different types of queries. For both Jelinek-Mercer and Dirichlet smoothing, on each of our 12 testing collections we vary the value of the smoothing parameter and record the retrieval performance at each parameter value. The results are plotted in Figure 2. In each case, we show how the average precision varies according to different values of the smoothing parameter.

From these figures, we see that the two types of keyword queries behave similarly, as do the two types of verbose queries. The retrieval performance is generally much less sensitive to smoothing in the case of the keyword queries than for the verbose queries, whether long or short. Therefore, the sensitivity is much more correlated with the verbosity of the query than with the length of the query. Indeed, the short verbose queries are clearly more sensitive than the long keyword queries. In all cases, insufficient smoothing is much more harmful for verbose queries than for keyword queries. This confirms that smoothing is indeed responsible for "explaining" the common words in a query, and provides an empirical justification for the two-stage smoothing approach.

We also see a consistent order of performance among the four types of queries. As expected, long keyword queries are the best and short verbose queries are the worst. Long verbose queries are worse than long keyword queries, but better than short keyword queries, which are better than the short verbose queries. This appears to suggest that queries with only (presumably good) keywords tend to perform better than more verbose queries. Also, longer queries are generally better than short queries.

5.2 Effectiveness of the Two-stage Smoothing Method

To evaluate the two-stage smoothing method, we first test it on the same 12 testing collections as described earlier. These collections represent a very good diversity in the types of queries, but the databases are all homogeneous and relatively small. In order to further test the robustness of the two-stage smoothing method, we then test it on three much bigger and more heterogeneous TREC collections. These are the official ad hoc retrieval collections used in TREC-7, TREC-8, and the TREC-8 small web track. The official TREC-7 and TREC-8 ad hoc tasks have used the same document database (i.e., TREC disk4 and disk5 excluding the Congressional Record data), but different topics (topics 351-400 for TREC-7 and 401-450 for TREC-8). The TREC-8 web track and the TREC-8 official ad hoc task share the same 50 topics. Since these topics do not have a concept field, we have only three types of queries: short-keyword, short-verbose, and long-verbose. The size of these large collections is about 2GB in the original source. Again, we perform minimum pre-processing - only a Porter stemmer was used, and no

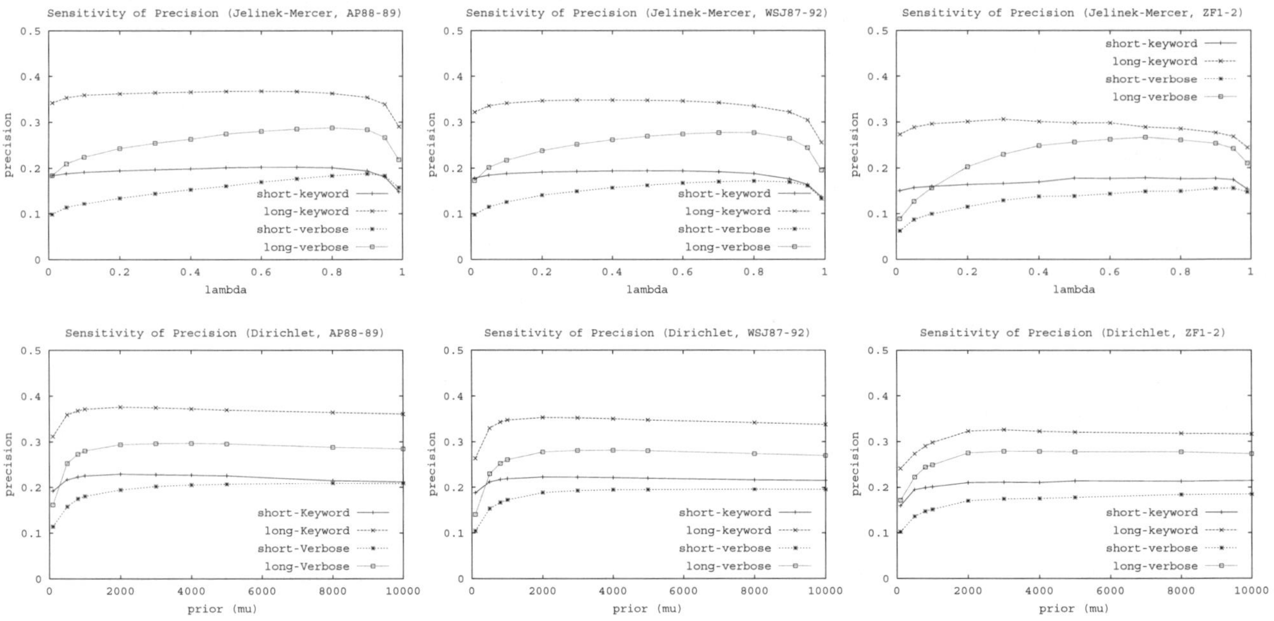

Figure 2: Sensitivity of Precision for Jelinek-Mercer smoothing (top) and Dirichlet prior smoothing (bottom) on AP88-89 (left), WSJ87-92 (center), and Ziff1-2 (right).

stop words were removed.

For each testing collection, we compare the retrieval performance of the estimated two-stage smoothing parameters with the best results achievable using a single smoothing method. The best results of a single smoothing method are obtained through an exhaustive search on its parameter space, so are the ideal performance of the smoothing method. In all our experiments, we use the collection language model to approximate the query background model.

The results are shown in Table 2. The four types of queries are abbreviated with the two initial letters (e.g., SK for Short-Keyword). The standard TREC evaluation procedure for ad hoc retrieval is followed, and we have considered three performance measures - non-interpolated average precision, initial precision (i.e., precision at 0.0 recall), and precision at five documents. In all the results, we see that, the performance of two-stage smoothing with the estimated parameter values is consistently very close to, or better than the best performance of a single method by all the three measures. Only in a few cases, the difference is statistically significant (indicated with a star).

To quantify the sensitivity of the retrieval performance to the smoothing parameter for single smoothing methods, we also show (in parentheses) the median average precision at all the parameter values that are tried[2]. We see that, for Jelinek-Mercer, the sensitivity is clearly higher on verbose queries than on keyword queries; the median is usually much lower than the best performance for verbose queries. This means that, it is much harder to tune the λ in Jelinek-Mercer for verbose queries than for keyword queries. Interestingly, for Dirichlet prior, the median is often just slightly below the best, even when the queries are verbose. (The worst cases are significantly lower, though.) From the sensitivity curves in Figure 2, we see that as long as we set a relatively large value for μ in Dirichlet prior, the performance will not be much worse than the best performance, and there is a great chance that the median is at a large value for μ. This immediately suggests that we can expect to perform reasonably well if we simply set μ to some "safe" large value. However, it is clear, from the results in Table 2, that such a simple approach would not perform so well as our parameter estimation methods. Indeed, the two-stage performance is always better than the median, except for three cases of short-keyword queries when it is slightly worse. Since the Dirichlet prior smoothing dominates the two-stage smoothing effect for these short-keyword queries (due to "little noise"), this somehow suggests that the leave-one-out method might have under-estimated μ.

Note that, in general, Jelinek-Mercer has not performed as well as Dirichlet prior in all our experiments. But, in two cases of verbose queries (Trec8-SV and Trec8-LV on the Trec7/8 database), it does outperform Dirichlet prior. In these two cases, the two-stage smoothing method performs either as well as or better than the Jelinek-Mercer. Thus, the two-stage smoothing performance appears to always track the *best performing* single method at its optimal parameter setting.

The performance of two-stage smoothing does not reflect the performance of a "full-fledged" language modeling approach, which would involve more sophisticated feedback models [4, 6, 16]. Thus, it is really not comparable with the performance of other TREC systems. Yet some of the performance figures shown here are actually competitive when compared with the performance of the official TREC submissions (e.g., the performance on the TREC-8 ad hoc task and the TREC-8 web track).

These results of the two-stage smoothing method are very encouraging, especially because there is no ad hoc parameter tuning involved in the retrieval process with the approach. Both μ and λ are automatically estimated based on a specific database and query; μ is completely determined by the given database, and λ is deter-

[2]For Jelinek-Mercer, we tried 13 values {0.01, 0.05, 0.1, 0.2, 0.3, 0.4, 0.5, 0.6,0.7,0.8,0.9,0.95, 0.99}; for Dirichlet prior, we tried 10 values {100, 500, 800, 1000, 2000, 3000, 4000, 5000, 8000, 10000}.

Database	*Query*	*Best Jelinek-Mercer*				*Best Dirichlet*				*Two-Stage*		
		AvgPr	(med)	InitPr	Pr@5d	AvgPr	(med)	InitPr	Pr@5d	AvgPr	Initpr	Pr@5d
AP88-89	SK	0.203	(0.194)	0.573	0.341	**0.230**	(0.224)	**0.623**	**0.381**	0.222*	0.611	0.375
	LK	0.368	(0.362)	**0.767**	0.530	**0.376**	(0.368)	0.755	**0.533**	0.374	0.754	**0.533**
	SV	0.188	(0.158)	0.569	0.342	**0.209**	(0.195)	**0.609**	**0.379**	0.204	0.598	0.368
	LV	0.288	(0.263)	**0.711**	0.463	**0.298**	(0.285)	0.704	**0.490**	0.292	0.689	0.473
WSJ87-92	SK	0.194	(0.188)	0.629	0.392	**0.223**	(0.218)	0.660	0.438	0.218*	**0.662**	**0.450**
	LK	0.348	(0.341)	0.814	0.597	0.353	(0.343)	0.834	**0.608**	**0.358**	**0.850***	0.607
	SV	0.172	(0.158)	0.615	0.377	0.196	(0.188)	0.638	0.413	**0.199**	**0.660**	**0.425**
	LV	0.277	(0.252)	**0.768**	**0.533**	0.282	(0.270)	0.750	0.504	**0.288***	0.762	0.520
ZF1-2	SK	0.179	(0.170)	0.455	0.248	**0.215**	(0.210)	**0.514**	**0.301**	0.200	0.494	0.299
	LK	0.306	(0.290)	0.675	0.404	**0.326**	(0.316)	0.681	**0.438**	0.322	**0.696**	0.434
	SV	0.156	(0.139)	0.450	0.224	**0.185**	(0.170)	0.456	0.255	0.181	**0.487**	**0.271***
	LV	0.267	(0.242)	0.593	0.339	**0.279**	(0.273)	0.606	0.378	**0.279***	**0.618**	**0.384**

Database	*Query*	*Best Jelinek-Mercer*				*Best Dirichlet*				*Two-Stage*		
		AvgPr	(med)	InitPr	Pr@5d	AvgPr	(med)	InitPr	Pr@5d	AvgPr	Initpr	Pr@5d
Trec7/8	Trec7-SK	0.167	(0.165)	0.632	0.400	**0.186**	(0.182)	**0.688**	**0.432**	0.182	0.673	0.420
	Trec7-SV	0.173	(0.138)	0.646	0.416	**0.182**	(0.168)	**0.656**	**0.436**	0.181	0.655	0.416
	Trec7-LV	0.222	(0.195)	0.723	0.496	0.224	(0.212)	**0.763**	**0.524**	**0.230**	0.760	0.516
	Trec8-SK	0.239	(0.237)	0.621	0.44	0.256	(0.244)	0.717	0.488	**0.257**	**0.719**	**0.496**
	Trec8-SV	**0.231**	(0.192)	0.687	0.456	0.228	(0.222)	0.670	0.432	**0.231**	**0.719**	**0.484**
	Trec8-LV	0.265	(0.234)	**0.789**	**0.556**	0.260	(0.252)	0.753	0.492	**0.268**	0.787	0.524
Web	Trec8-SK	0.243	(0.212)	0.607	0.368	**0.294**	(0.281)	**0.756**	0.484	0.278*	0.730	**0.488**
	Trec8-SV	0.203	(0.191)	0.611	0.392	**0.267**	(0.249)	**0.699**	**0.492**	0.253	0.680	0.436
	Trec8-LV	0.259	(0.234)	**0.790**	0.464	0.275	(0.248)	0.752	**0.508**	**0.284**	0.781	**0.508**

Table 2: Comparison of the estimated two-stage smoothing with the best single stage smoothing methods on small collections (top) and large collections (bottom). The best number for each measure is shown in boldface. An asterisk (*) indicates that the difference between the two-stage smoothing performance and the best single smoothing performance is statistically significant according to the Wilcoxin signed rank test at the level of 0.05.

mined by the database and the query together. The method appears to be quite robust according to our experiments with all the different types of queries and different databases.

6. CONCLUSIONS

In this paper we derive general two-stage language models for information retrieval using the risk minimization retrieval framework, and present a concrete two-stage smoothing method as a special case. The two-stage smoothing strategy explicitly captures the different influences of the query and document collection on the optimal settings of smoothing parameters. In the first stage, the document language model is smoothed using a Dirichlet prior with the collection model as the reference model. In the second stage, the smoothed document language model is further interpolated with a query background model.

We propose a leave-one-out method for estimating the first-stage Dirichlet prior parameter and a mixture model for estimating the second-stage interpolation parameter. These methods allow us to set the retrieval parameters automatically, yet adaptively according to different databases and queries. Evaluation on five different databases and four types of queries indicates that the two-stage smoothing method with the proposed parameter estimation scheme consistently gives retrieval performance that is close to, or better than, the best results attainable using a single smoothing method, achievable only through an exhaustive parameter search. The effectiveness and robustness of the two-stage smoothing approach, along with the fact that there is no ad hoc parameter tuning involved, make it a solid baseline approach for evaluating retrieval models.

While we have shown that the automatic two-stage smoothing gives retrieval performance close to the best results attainable using a single smoothing method, we have not yet analyzed the optimality of the estimated parameter values in the two-stage parameter space. For example, it would be important to see the relative optimality of the estimated μ and λ when fixing one of them. It would also be interesting to explore other estimation methods. For example, μ might be regarded as a hyperparameter in a hierarchical Bayesian approach. For the estimation of the query model parameter λ, it would be interesting to try different query background models. One possibility is to estimate the background model based on resources such as past queries, in addition to the collection of documents. Another interesting future direction is to exploit the query background model to address the issue of redundancy in the retrieval results. Specifically, a biased query background model may be used to represent/explain the sub-topics that a user has already encountered (e.g., through reading previously retrieved results), in order to focus ranking on the *new* sub-topics in a relevant set of documents.

ACKNOWLEDGEMENTS

We thank Rong Jin, Jamie Callan, and the anonymous reviewers for helpful comments on this work. This research was sponsored in full by the Advanced Research and Development Activity in Information Technology (ARDA) under its Statistical Language Modeling for Information Retrieval Research Program, contract MDA904-00-C-2106.

REFERENCES

[1] Berger, A. and Lafferty, J. (1999). Information retrieval as statistical translation. In *Proceedings of the 1999 ACM SIGIR Conference on Research and Development in Information Retrieval*, pages 222-229.

[2] Hiemstra, D. and Kraaij, W. (1998). Twenty-one at TREC-7: Ad-hoc and cross-language track. In *Proc. of Seventh Text REtrieval Conference (TREC-7)*.

[3] Kwok, K. and Chan, M. (98). Improving two-stage ad-hoc retrieval for short queries. In *Proceedings of SIGIR'98*, pages 250-256.

[4] Lafferty, J. and Zhai, C. (2001a). Document language models, query models, and risk minimization for information retrieval. In *Proceedings of SIGIR'2001*.

[5] Lafferty, J. and Zhai, C. (2001b). Probabilistic IR models based on query and document generation. In *Proceedings of the Language Modeling and IR workshop*. Extended abstract.

[6] Lavrenko, V. and Croft, B. (2001). Relevance-based language models. In *Proceedings of SIGIR'2001*.

[7] Miller, D. H., Leek, T., and Schwartz, R. (1999). A hidden Markov model information retrieval system. In *Proceedings of the 1999 ACM SIGIR Conference on Research and Development in Information Retrieval*, pages 214-221.

[8] Ney, H., Essen, U., and Kneser, R. (1995). On the estimation of 'small' probabilities by leaving-one-out. *IEEE Transactions on Pattern Analysis and Machine Intelligence*, (12):1202-1212.

[9] Ponte, J. and Croft, W. B. (1998). A language modeling approach to information retrieval. In *Proceedings of the ACM SIGIR*, pages 275-281.

[10] Robertson, S. and Sparck Jones, K. (1976). Relevance weighting of search terms. *Journal of the American Society for Information Science*, 27:129-146.

[11] Robertson, S. E., Walker, S., Jones, S., M.Hancock-Beaulieu, M., and Gatford, M. (1995). Okapi at TREC-3. In Harman, D. K., editor, *The Third Text REtrieval Conference (TREC-3)*.

[12] Salton, G., Wong, A., and Yang, C. S. (1975a). A vector space model for automatic indexing. *Communications of the ACM*, (11):613-620.

[13] Salton, G. and Buckley, C. (1988). Term-weighting approaches in automatic text retrieval. *Information Processing and Management*, 24:513-523.

[14] Singhal, A., Buckley, C., and Mitra, M. (1996). Pivoted document length normalization. In *Proceedings of the 1996 ACM SIGIR Conference on Research and Development in Information Retrieval*, pages 21-29.

[15] Voorhees, E. and Harman, D., editors (2001). *Proceedings of Text REtrieval Conference (TREC1-9)*. NIST Special Publications. http://trec.nist.gov/pubs.html.

[16] Zhai, C. and Lafferty, J. (2001a). Model-based feedback in the KL-divergence retrieval model. In *Tenth International Conference on Information and Knowledge Management (CIKM 2001)*.

[17] Zhai, C. and Lafferty, J. (2001b). A study of smoothing methods for language models applied to ad hoc information retrieval. In *Proceedings of SIGIR'2001*.

Finding Relevant Documents using Top Ranking Sentences: An Evaluation of Two Alternative Schemes

Ryen W. White
Department of Computing Science
University of Glasgow
Glasgow. G12 8QQ
whiter@dcs.gla.ac.uk

Ian Ruthven
Department of Computer and Information Sciences
University of Strathclyde
Glasgow. G1 1XH
ir@cis.strath.ac.uk

Joemon M. Jose
Department of Computing Science
University of Glasgow
Glasgow. G12 8QQ
jj@dcs.gla.ac.uk

ABSTRACT
In this paper we present an evaluation of techniques that are designed to encourage web searchers to interact more with the results of a web search. Two specific techniques are examined: the presentation of sentences that highly match the searcher's query and the use of implicit evidence. Implicit evidence is evidence captured from the searcher's interaction with the retrieval results and is used to automatically update the display. Our evaluation concentrates on the effectiveness and subject perception of these techniques. The results show, with statistical significance, that the techniques are effective and efficient for information seeking.

Categories and Subject Descriptors
H.3.3 [Information Search and Retrieval]: - search process, relevance feedback.

General Terms
Experimentation, Human Factors

Keywords
WWW, user studies, sentence extraction

1. INTRODUCTION
Web search engines are an essential tool for finding useful resources on the Internet. However, even though these tools are intended to *facilitate* access to the web, user studies such as [5] demonstrate that searchers display very limited interaction with search engine interfaces. For example, searchers typically input very short queries, around 1 or 2 search terms and typically do not use advanced search facilities to generate more complex queries.

One main conclusion from such user studies is that users are reluctant to view result lists beyond the first page of results, preferring instead to opt for query reformulation and resubmission. For this reason many web page designers place much importance on the creation of web documents that consistently appear in first page of popular web search engines. However, the reluctance of searchers to look beyond the first page of results means that they may miss out on useful documents and will have to generate new search terms for future searches. This type of search behaviour is one in which searchers run many searches, but with limited interaction with the retrieved set of documents. This is not only computationally expensive – many searches have to be run – but it is also cognitively expensive for the searcher to provide additional search terms. Previous research has indicated that reduced querying and increased interaction with the results of web searches can increase search effectiveness, e.g. [9].

In this paper we propose techniques for encouraging searchers to more fully examine the results of a web search, thus reducing the computational and cognitive loads. This research is based on two related research issues. Firstly we propose techniques that *recommend* retrieved pages to searchers. In particular we use sentences from retrieved web pages that highly match the searcher's query as a means of showing the searcher what kind of information has been retrieved. This system is intended to present the searcher with information on the *whole* retrieval result rather than just the top ten pages.

A second system uses a form of relevance feedback, [8], to automatically update the information that the interface displays to the searcher. In this case the system uses *implicit* information – information captured from the searcher's interaction with the interface – to estimate what information may be of use to the searcher. This system is intended to make the search interface less *passive*. That is, the system is intended to make a stronger connection between the searcher's interaction and the information presented.

Both systems are used to encourage searchers to interact more fully with the retrieval results of a web search. Our experiments compare these systems with each other and with an advanced web summarization system. The choice of this type of system as our baseline system is motivated by evidence, e.g. [10], that summarization techniques can also increase the searchers' interaction with search results.

SIGIR'02, August 11-15, 2002, Tampere, Finland.

The remainder of the paper is structured as follows. In section 2 we discuss the motivation behind our investigation and related work. In sections 3-5 we describe the systems we developed and in section 6 we present our experiments. In section 7 we highlight the main results from the experiments and we conclude with a discussion in section 8.

2. MOTIVATION

Most web search interfaces present the user with little information with which to decide whether or not to view a retrieved page. Typically the only information shown is the page title, URL and short (1-2 line) text fragments from the retrieved pages. These text fragments normally contain at least one instance of the query terms and are intended to give the user some notion of the context in which the query terms are used in the web page.

This minimal approach to describing the retrieved set of pages suffers from two flaws: the page descriptions generally do not contain sufficient information to help the user decide whether or not to view the page, [10] and the descriptions only relate to the titles displayed on the current page; there is no indication to the searcher of what other information has been retrieved.

The former problem – insufficient descriptions of the retrieved pages – is typically handled by summarization techniques that give fuller descriptions of the retrieved pages [10, 2]. In this paper we examine the second problem, that of helping the searchers perform more complete analyses of the retrieved pages.

Our intention behind these systems and the experiments we describe is to move away from the web pages themselves and to present the searchers with *indications* of the type of information to be found in the retrieved pages. In both our experimental systems, sections 4 and 5, this takes the form of presenting the searchers with those sentences, from the top thirty ranked pages, that highly match the searcher's query.

By presenting whole sentences to the searcher, we are presenting the query terms in the local context in which they are used within retrieved pages. The use of sentences allow the searcher to see representative samples of a page's text before s/he accesses the full-text of the retrieved page and hence to make better decisions as to what pages to view.

The use of sentences as a context device has been investigated elsewhere, e.g. Magennis and Van Rijsbergen, [6], used sentences to show users the context of expansion terms in relevance feedback. In Magennis and Van Rijsbergen's experiments the sentences came from documents already viewed by the user. In our experiments the sentences come from web pages that have *not* already been viewed by searchers. Sentences have also been the basis of many successful summarization systems. In these systems, sentences from a document which highly matches the searcher's query are used to compose a summary of the page. Our baseline system, section 3, against which we compare our experimental systems is a summarization system built on these principles.

In our experiments we use three search systems. Each system consists of an interface, with underlying functionality, which connects to existing web search engines. In all our experiments the underlying search engine is AltaVista[1]. We chose this search engine because it allows connections from external interfaces[2] and is one of the most-used publicly available search engines.

The first system – our baseline system – is a system which offers the searcher the opportunity to view short summaries of retrieved documents, section 3. The second system, section 4, extends the interface to display top-ranking sentences. The third system, section 5, automatically updates the list of top-ranking sentences in light of the searcher's interaction with the search results.

3. SYSTEM 1 – SUMMARIZATION

Our first system, System 1, is a summarization system. Once the underlying web search engine has performed a retrieval, System 1 downloads and summarises the top thirty ranked web pages.

The summaries are created through a sentence extraction model, presented in [10], in which the web pages are broken up into their component sentences and scored according to factors such as their position (initial introductory sentences are preferred), the words they contain (words that are emphasised by the web page author, e.g. emboldened terms are treated as important), and the proportion of query terms they contain. The latter component – scoring by query terms – biases the summaries towards the query. A number of the highest-scoring sentences are then chosen as the summary.

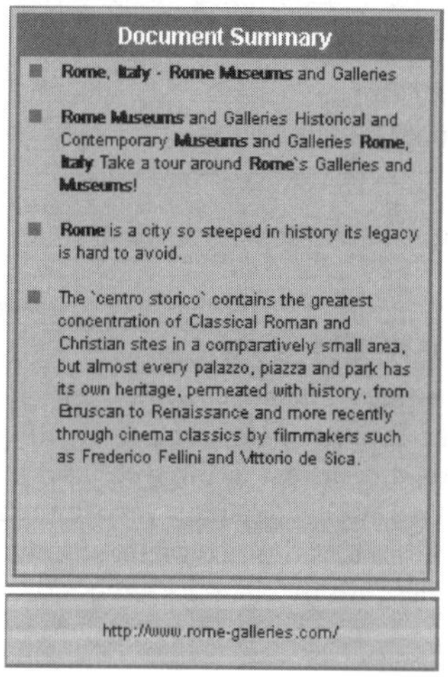

Figure 1: Web page summary

The system displays the titles of the retrieved pages in groups of ten titles. If the searcher passes the mouse over a retrieved title, a summary window appears next to the title. The summary window displays the document title, the top four highest-ranking sentences and the URL of the page, Figure 1.

---

1 *http://www.altavista.com*

2 Unlike some other search engines at system-build/experiment time, e.g. Google.

This form of web page summarization has previously been shown to increase searchers' satisfaction and search task success over conventional search engine interfaces, [10]. Consequently we use this system as it forms a stricter baseline system rather than a more standard web search interface.

4. SYSTEM 2 – TOP RANKING SENTENCES

The second system, System 2 is an extension of System 1. In a similar way, the System 2 interface displays the titles of web pages in groups of ten, and presents summaries on request. However, the System 2 interface also displays a list of *top-ranking* sentences. In this system the same sentence extraction method that is applied to *individual* documents in System 1 is applied to the top thirty documents as a *set*. That is, we split the top thirty documents into component sentences and rank the sentences according to the words they contain and the query words they contain. This allows a ranking of the sentences from the top thirty documents – the top ranking sentences. More than one sentence per document can appear in the list of top-ranking sentences. The sentences themselves are displayed to the searcher as shown in Figure 2.

Figure 2: Top-ranking sentences

If the searcher moves to a subsequent page of results, the system will use the next thirty pages to create the top-ranking sentences, e.g. if the searcher moved to the second page of results, then the sentences from pages in rank positions 11-40 would be used to create the top-ranking sentences.

The intention behind the top-ranking sentences is to encourage searchers to target useful information rather than simply assess the ranked list of titles themselves. That is we are attempting to get the user to make assessments on the content of pages rather than the more usual representations of titles and text fragments.

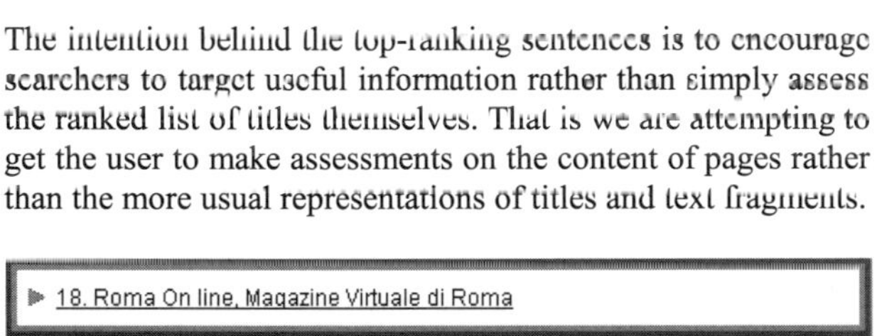

Figure 3: Document title window

If the searcher passes the mouse over a sentence the system will indicate which page contains this sentence. If the page is in the ten results currently being displayed, the system will simply highlight the title of the page. If the page is outwith this group of ten results, the title of the page containing the sentence will be shown in a small window below the main result list, Figure 3. Passing the mouse over this title will show a summary of the document.

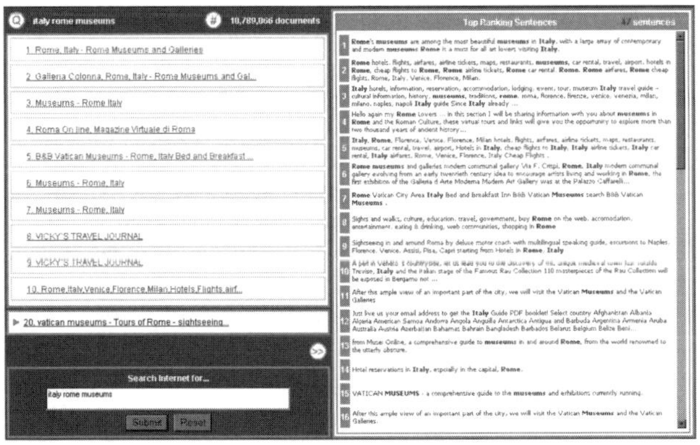

Figure 4: Top ranking sentences interface (Systems 2/3)

The system, thus, encourages searchers to view pages that appear later in the ranking, i.e. pages that have a lower retrieval score than the pages that are currently being listed. The aforementioned components are combined to form the interface of the system, as shown in Figure 4.

5. SYSTEM 3 – IMPLICIT FEEDBACK

The previous system, System 2, presents the searchers with indications of potentially relevant material – the top-ranking sentences. The query terms are shown in the *context* of the sentence in which they appear and the sentences are selected by their similarity to the query.

This notion of context in System 2 is static – the composition of a sentence does not change over time and the query is assumed to be constant within an individual search iteration. Our third system, System 3, uses the context of the search itself to improve the ranking of the sentences displayed to the searcher. The context in this case is the *implicit* information given by a searcher whilst interacting with the search system interface. As will be discussed below, implicit information is the evidence the searcher gives by viewing a page summary. This information is regarded as being implicit as the searcher does not give the information with the explicit purpose of changing the search results.

The context information is used to update the system's representation of the searcher's query, which in turn is used to re-rank the list of top-ranking sentences. Specifically, our notion of context is based on the assumption that searchers will spend a longer time reading interesting (potentially relevant) material and less time reading irrelevant material.

Several studies, e.g. [7], have found a correlation between the positive relevance of a document and viewing time. These studies, focusing on static corpora and full-text documents, have found that if a document is subjected to a lot of 'read wear' [4] it is likely to be relevant. In this study, we assume that these findings will hold for document summaries. That is we assume that summaries which searchers view for longer than expected are those that contain information similar to that desired by users. We discuss how we decide upon a searcher's expected summary reading time in section 6.2. We use summaries as we can detect which summaries a searcher has assessed and for how long (unlike titles) and searchers tend to view more summaries than web pages leading to more evidence. Any summary that the system believes contains relevant information is used for query modification.

The previous system, System 2, ranks sentences based on the searcher's query. System 3 ranks sentences based on the searcher's query *and* terms taken from the content of the *assumed* relevant summaries. Each time the system believes the searcher has identified a useful summary the content of all useful summaries is used to generate a list of possible query expansion terms. The function we used for this purpose is Robertson's *wpq* formula [8], equation 1.

The top 6 terms, from the *wpq* ranking of terms, are added to the original query, and the new query is used to re-rank the list of top-ranking sentences. This system, then, dynamically updates the list of top-ranking sentences each time the system assumes that the searcher has found a relevant summary.

$$wpq_t = \log\left(\frac{(r_t + 0.5)(N - n_t - R + 0.5)}{(n_t - r_t + 0.5)(R - r_t + 0.5)}\right) \times \left(\frac{r_t}{R} - \frac{n_t - r_t}{N - R}\right)$$

Equation 1: *wpq* formula, where r_t is the number of relevant summaries which contain term t, n_t is the number of summaries which contain term t, R is the number of relevant summaries, N is the number of summaries.

The automatic updating of the top-ranking sentences is intended to reflect the searcher's interaction with the system. That is, we are relating the searcher's search *actions* with the information displayed by the interface. Previous research, [9], has shown that this form of implicit relevance feedback can act as an effective substitute for explicit relevance feedback in which the searcher must *explicitly* indicate, e.g. by checkboxes, what pages or summaries are relevant. Explicit feedback gives more accurate information on what a user finds relevant but searchers are often reluctant to make these assessments, e.g. [3]. Implicit feedback, on the other hand, exploits the searchers' existing interaction with the system.

We use these systems to investigate two main research questions. Firstly, we investigate whether the use of top-ranking sentences encourages searchers to interact more fully with the retrieval results, and whether this leads to more effective searching. This is effectively a comparison between System 1 and Systems 2. Secondly, we investigate the effect implicit relevance feedback on the results obtained from the first research question. That is, does implicit relevance feedback improve searchers' perceptions of the system and does it lead to more effective interaction with the system. This is a comparison between System 2 (no feedback) and System 3 (implicit feedback). In both cases we shall consider measures of both search task success and searchers' perceptions of the systems. In the following section we present the experiments we carried out using these systems.

6. EXPERIMENTS

In this section we discuss the experimental methodology we used in our experiments, the search tasks used, and the experimental subjects who participated.

6.1 Experimental methodology

In our experiments 24 experimental subjects, section 6.4, each completed 3 search tasks, section 6.3, one search task was completed on each of the three systems. The presentation of tasks to subjects was held constant: each subject performed the search tasks in the same order, however the order of presentation of systems was rotated across subjects. Each subject was given 10 minutes to complete each task, although the subjects could terminate the search early if they felt they had completed the task.

The subjects were welcomed and given a short tutorial on the features that were incorporated into the three systems being tested. We also collected background data on aspects such as the subjects' experience and training in online searching. After this, subjects were introduced to tasks and systems according to the experimental design.

Once they had completed a search, the subject was asked to complete questionnaires regarding various aspects of the search. We used Semantic differentials, Likert scales and open-ended questions to collect this data. After the third experiment a final questionnaire was completed that asked searchers to rank the three systems based on their personal preference. In addition, we conducted semi-structured interviews after each search and after the experiment as a whole. Background logging was also used to record user interaction with the systems.

6.2 Timing tasks

Information was also collected on the time taken by subjects to view summaries for use by System 3. This system uses implicit evidence to update the list of top-ranking sentences. As described in section 5 this system assumes that subjects will spend longer viewing summaries that are interesting, or potentially relevant, than summaries that do not appear useful. To allow us to decide when a summary should be counted as useful we need a measure of how long a searcher will take to assess a summary's content. In particular we need to measure how long on average an individual searcher will take to decide whether a summary is relevant and how long the searcher will take to decide the summary is not relevant. To do this consistently we used a timing task before each search task.

We gave each subject a search description and presented them with a prepared list of thirty document titles[3]. We then asked them to view the summary for each document and mark, by clicking the document title, if the summary appears to be relevant to the search description. The time from the appearance of the summary until the subject clicked the document title was recorded for each relevant summary. For the non-relevant summaries, the time taken from when the

[3] These search descriptions and retrieved titles are unrelated to the actual search tasks we use in the main experiment.

summary appeared until the summary disappeared was recorded, i.e. the time from the searcher requesting a summary until moving to the next title. The times measured for the summaries was normalized by the summary length as we expect searchers to take a longer time to read a longer summary. Finally the times are averaged to give a measure of how long an *individual* searcher takes on average to read a *character* in a relevant and non-relevant summary.

The value of time taken for an individual subject to read a character in a relevant summary was used in System 3 to decide when to judge a summary as useful or not. Although the timing information was only used in System 3, this process was repeated, using different search descriptions and titles, before each experimental system was presented. This was to avoid undue attention being paid to System 3 by the experimental subjects.

6.3 Experimental tasks

In our experiments each subject was asked to complete three search tasks. These tasks were chosen to investigate the effectiveness of the three systems for different types of search task: *fact* search, *decision* search and *background* search. The fact search asked subjects to find a single item of information (a named person's *current* email address), the background search asked subjects to find as much information as possible on a given topic and the decision search, Figure 5, forced subjects to make a qualitative decision on the information they retrieved (which Rome museum is the *best* for impressionist painting).

Context
You are about to depart on a short tour along the west coast of Italy. The agenda includes a visit to the country's capital, Rome, during which you hope to find time to pursue your interest in impressionist paintings. Your time in the city is limited to only two (2) hours and as such you would like to look for possible places to visit prior to your departure.

Task
Bearing in mind this context, your task is to find information about the city's best impressionist art museum.

Figure 5: Simulated work task situation (decision search)

Each search task was placed within a simulated work task situation, [1], (example Figure 5). This technique asserts that subjects should be given search scenarios that reflect real-life search situations and should allow the searcher to make personal assessments on what constitutes relevant material.

6.4 Experimental subjects

We recruited 24 subjects for our experiments. Our recruitment was specifically aimed at targeting two groups of users: experienced and inexperienced searchers.

The experienced searchers were those who used computers and searched the web on a regular, often daily basis. Inexperienced searchers were those who both searched the web and used computers and the Internet infrequently. Per week, inexperienced searchers spent on average 5.1 hours online and experts an average of 29.8 hours online. Overall our subjects had an average age of 24.73 with a range of 33 years (youngest 16 years: oldest 49 years).

The classification between experienced and inexperienced searchers was made on the basis of the subjects' responses to questions about the level of their computing, Internet and web searching experience and their own opinion of their skill level.

7. RESULTS

In this section we present the results from our evaluation of the systems. In presenting these results we are primarily looking for results that relate to our two research questions: the utility of presenting top-ranking sentences (System 1 vs. System 2) and the effectiveness of implicit evidence (System 2 vs. System 3). Our results will concentrate on these comparisons, although fuller comparison between the systems is possible. Tests for statistical significance will be given where appropriate using a Mann-Whitney test, $p \leq 0.05$, unless otherwise stated.

We examine the results in a number of ways. Firstly we analyse the timing task results, section 7.1, then center our discussion around measures that assess the interaction (such as task completion and queries submitted), section 7.2, measures that assess the new interface features, section 7.3 and user preference, section 7.4.

7.1 Timing tasks

The difference between times taken to read a character for relevant and non-relevant summaries allows us to check the hypothesis that searchers spend longer reading relevant summaries. In Table 1, we show the average of these results. This shows that *on average* our experimental subjects spent more time, per character, in assessing a relevant than non-relevant summary. These averaged results are statistically significant using a Mann-Whitney test at $p \leq 0.05$ ($p = 0.01733$). This shows that the basic hypothesis is valid; the time taken to assess a summary can be used to indicate a searcher's interest in the contents of the summary. However, the values reported in Table 1 are averaged results – the results calculated for individual subjects may show a greater or smaller range in times. Although these results have been specifically calculated for our web searching experiments using summaries, this approach is generalisable to other search scenarios and systems.

Table 1: Time in seconds to read a character in a summary

	Relevant summary	Non-relevant summary
Time	0.02620	0.01937

7.2 Interactive measures

In this section we consider the interactive aspects of the search. These aspects relate specifically to differences in how the searchers interact with the different systems and the degree to which this affected their search effectiveness. We start by considering task completion.

Task completion: After each search task the subjects were asked to rate (on a Likert Scale) to what degree they felt they had completed the search task. The responses were on a scale of 1-5, with a value of 1 reflecting greater task completion. The averaged values are shown in Table 2. As can be seen, System 2 was judged by both experienced and inexperienced subjects as leading to a greater sense of task completion than System 1.

Table 2: Subject responses regarding task completion

	System 1	System 2	System 3
All subjects	3.54	1.63	2.38
Inexperienced	3.58	1.67	2.17
Experienced	3.50	1.59	2.58

The difference between the results given for System 1 and System 2 are statistically significant for all subject groups (all, experienced and inexperienced). The presentation of top-ranking sentences, therefore, does lead to a greater *perception* of task completion for the subjects. We next compare whether the top-ranking sentences leads to *faster* task completion.

In Table 3 we use data collected from background logging and present the average time taken to complete a task, as measured by when the searcher decided they had completed the task. Uncompleted tasks were given a search time of 600 seconds (the maximum 10 minutes allocated per search task) but are *not* used in the computation of the results reported in the Table 3. The table also shows (in brackets) the number of tasks completed on each system.

The difference between search completion time for System 1 and System 2 is statistically significant for all subject groups. The use of top-ranking sentences therefore also leads to faster task completion.

Table 3: Task completion times in seconds

	System 1	System 2	System 3
All subjects	549.40 (15)	496.67 (19)	508.71 (16)
Inexperienced	578.32 (6)	512.43 (9)	520.96 (7)
Experienced	522.74 (9)	486.21 (10)	503.15 (9)

System 3 also gives higher task completion figures compared to System 1. However, the use of implicit evidence to re-rank the top-ranking sentences was less conclusive. From Table 2, System 2 was shown to give a greater sense of task completion than System 3 which used implicit evidence. This result was statistically significant for the inexperienced subjects but not for the experienced searcher, however the results are consistent across the subject groups. The difference between task completion times was not statistically significant but System 2, with no re-ranking, lead to faster task completion, Table 3.

The use of implicit evidence, then, appears to degrade performance. One reason for this, as will be discussed in section 7.3, is that System 3 *removes* sentences from the list of top-ranking sentences. This was an unpopular and distracting feature.

Query iterations: One of the reasons that the subjects completed tasks more quickly with Systems 2 and 3 was that they submitted fewer queries to these systems. In Table 4 we present the average number of queries submitted to each system. This table shows that subjects submitted around 30% more queries to System 1 than either System 2 or System 3. Furthermore, all subject groups submitted significantly more queries to System 1 than System 2 demonstrating that the top-ranking sentences do lead to fewer query iterations.

On all systems, the inexperienced subjects submitted significantly more queries to *any* system than the experienced subjects. This finding points to the fact that less experienced searchers spend more time developing good queries and consequently require more support at the interface.

Table 4: Average queries submitted per subject

	System 1	System 2	System 3
All subjects	8.00	5.21	4.58
Inexperienced	9.33	5.67	6.25
Experienced	7.50	4.75	2.92

Experienced users, on the other hand, tend to submit fewer queries to any system. The difference between the number of queries submitted to System 3 was significantly less than the number submitted to System 2. This means that although experienced subjects tended to take slightly longer to complete their tasks on System 3 and had a lower perception of task completeness, they were interacting differently with the results of the search when using System 3. Experienced users noticed the removal of sentences and re-ranking more than inexperienced users. They felt that the removal hindered rather than helped their interaction, especially on occasions when the system's implicit impression of what was relevant did not match their own. In light of this finding, further research on the use of implicit evidence may be necessary.

Page views: One of the main aims of our work is to encourage subjects to view results that occur after the first page of 10 results. In Table 5 we present the average number of retrieved pages which appear in rank position 11 onwards in the result lists that were viewed by the searcher. This measures the degree to which subjects are accessing pages that appear after the first 10 results.

Table 5: Pages viewed after initial 10 results

	System 1	System 2	System 3
All subjects	4.63	8.21	8.13
Inexperienced	3.08	7.42	8.08
Experienced	6.17	9.00	8.17

From Table 5, it can be seen that subjects view more of these documents when using the systems with top-ranking sentences. The difference between the pages viewed when using System 2 is statistically greater than when using System 1. A similar result is obtained when comparing System 3 with System 1, which is also statistically significant. This indicates that the top-ranking sentences are serving their intended function in recommending potentially relevant documents encouraging greater interaction by the searcher.

Summary: The top-ranking function of Systems 2 and 3 appear to work well: they help searchers complete tasks more quickly and with a greater sense of task completion. They do this by encouraging searchers to interact more with the results of the search: running less queries but viewing more of the retrieved pages. The implicit feedback in System 3, on the other hand, does not appear to work well. However as we have shown above, may provide useful support for the inexperienced searchers.

7.3 Interface features

In this section we discuss the two novel features of our system: the top-ranking sentences, and the sentence re-ranking through implicit evidence.

Overall the subjects were in favour of the top-ranking sentences component of Systems 2 and 3. In Table 6, we present the averaged results obtained from asking the subjects how effective they found the top-ranking sentences and the degree to which re-ranking helped them find relevant documents. The responses were on a scale of 1-5, with a value of 1 reflecting greater satisfaction. The results are low indicating approval of the top-ranking sentences as an interactive technique.

Comparing the two systems, the results are not significant, i.e. the subjects did not prefer one system over the other. However for both aspects the inexperienced subjects gave better scores to System 3 than the experienced subjects. This suggests that the updating was of more use to the less experienced searchers.

Table 6: Subject responses regarding top-ranking sentences

		Inexperienced	Experienced
Effective	System 2	2.00	2.17
	System 3	1.92	2.33
Helped to find relevant documents	System 2	1.75	1.67
	System 3	1.25	1.75

This finding is reinforced if we examine the degree to which the subjects found the re-ranking process useful itself. In Table 7, we present the averaged results obtained from asking the subjects the same questions regarding the re-ranking of the top-ranking sentences. On both aspects, the inexperienced subjects gave higher ratings (closer to 1) than the experienced subjects. Both differences are statistically significant. The inexperienced subjects therefore may have obtained more use from the re-ranking than the experienced subjects as it provides more support for query creation. However we would need to investigate this more fully before we would make such a strong assertion.

Table 7: Subject responses regarding re-ranking

	Inexperienced	Experienced
Effective	2.25	2.67
Helped to find relevant documents	2.33	2.67

We also compared the subjects' response to the question (using Semantic differentials) of how *useful* was each of the three interface components: summary, top-ranking sentences and re-ranking of sentences. These results are shown in Table 8. This analysis is intended to compare the subjects' perceptions of the usefulness of the various components of the interface. The results show a positive response (less than 3) by all subject groups to the system components used. There were no statistically significant differences between any of the components (i.e. summary vs. top-ranking) or any user groups (inexperienced vs. experienced).

Table 8: Summarised subject responses

	All subjects	Inexperienced	Experienced
Summary	2.17	2.17	2.17
Top-ranking	1.95	2.08	1.8
Re-ranking	2.08	2.08	2.08

After each search and after the entire experiment we asked the subjects for their view on the systems used. Subjects found the top-ranking sentences helpful and easy to use. Though using the sentences, subjects felt that they were made more aware of potentially relevant documents (especially those that lay outside the first result page) than with the baseline, System 1. Sentence re-ranking did not receive as positive a reaction however.

The subjects had two reservations regarding the re-ranking of sentences in System 3. Firstly, as the re-ranking occurred at the same time as a summary appeared the subjects did not always notice the effect of the re-ranking. The presentation of the updating therefore needs improving in future systems.

Secondly, the top-ranking sentences in System 3 only contained sentences from web pages for which the searcher had not already viewed a summary. If the searcher viewed the summary for a page, then all sentences from a page were removed from the list of top-ranking sentences. We decided on this to increase the degree to which the list of top-ranking sentences would update. However, many searchers stated that they would prefer less updating and no removal of sentences.

Summary: The top-ranking sentences were popular in both systems but rather more popular with inexperienced searchers. The dynamic re-ranking of top-ranking sentences was given better ratings by inexperienced searchers.

7.4 User preference

In this section we will analyse the results obtained when, after the third task, users were asked to rank the three systems in order of preference. Table 9 shows the average ranking given to each of the three systems *by all users* based on two criteria; which systems users felt helped them to find relevant documents, and which they liked best.

All 24 subjects placed one of the systems that used top ranking sentences (System 2 or System 3) in first place. 19 participants (8 inexperienced and 11 experienced) placed the baseline system in third place, the last ranking position. We applied a Kruskal-Wallis Test, at $p \leq 0.05$, to the results obtained and found that the Systems 2 and 3 obtained rankings significantly better (closer to 1) than System 1. This result holds for both measures and across all user groups (all, inexperienced and experienced). Table 9 also shows that subjects gave System 2, on average, a higher ranking than System 3. This difference is again significant using a Kruskal-Wallis Test at $p \leq 0.05$.

Table 9: Average ranking (range 1-3, lower = better)

	System 1	System 2	System 3
Helped to find relevant documents	2.79	1.5	1.71
Preference	2.75	1.54	1.71
All measures	2.77	1.52	1.71

Summary: All subjects felt systems using top-ranking sentences were more helpful in finding relevant documents, and were preferred to the baseline system. Of those systems with top-ranking sentences, subjects felt the system *without* sentence re-ranking helped locate relevant documents better, and was preferred to, the system *with* sentence re-ranking.

8. CONCLUSIONS

In this paper we present an investigation into techniques for encouraging web searchers to more fully assess a retrieved set of web pages. We presented two techniques: the use of top-ranking sentences and the use of implicit evidence.

We conducted an experiment, based on a sound experimental methodology, in which we used both experienced and inexperienced users. Our experiment used simulated work tasks to generate information needs, and questionnaires using Likert scales, Semantic differentials and open-ended questions to collect data. The results of the experiment have shown, with statistical significance, that presenting searchers with indications of retrieved pages' content – top-ranking sentences – not only leads to greater task completion but is also a popular addition to the interface.

The most encouraging feature of our experiments is that they show that it is possible to get searchers to interact with more than a few search results, thus reducing cognitive and computational loads. In addition, the approach moves away from simply presenting titles to presenting alternative access methods for assessing and targeting potentially relevant information.

We also experimented with implicit evidence to gather more information about a searcher's information need and use this information to suggest unseen documents. This is preferred to our baseline system, however, was not as effective as top-ranking sentences without this additional feature. This may in part be due to some of the design decisions we made in implementing this technique. However, it did appear to be successful in helping inexperienced searchers who may submit poorer initial queries and require greater interface support.

We also investigated the assumption that searchers spend more time reading relevant document summaries than with non-relevant summaries. Our results show that users spend significantly longer viewing relevant document summaries than viewing non-relevant ones.

9. ACKNOWLEDGEMENTS

The work reported in this paper is funded by the UK Engineering and Physical Sciences Research Council grant number GR/R74642/01.

10. REFERENCES

[1] P. Borlund. Experimental components for the evaluation of interactive information retrieval systems. Journal of Documentation. **56**. 1. pp 71-90. 2000.

[2] A.L. Berger and V.O. Mittal. *OCELOT: A System for Summarizing Web Pages*. Proceedings of 23rd Annual International ACM SIGIR Conference on Research and Development in Information Retrieval. pp 144-151. Athens 2000.

[3] H. Fowkes and M. Beaulieu. *Interactive searching behaviour: Okapi experiment for TREC-8*. Proceedings of 22nd BCS-IRSG European Colloquium on IR Research. Electronic Workshops in Computing. Cambridge. 2000.

[4] W. C. Hill, J. D. Hollan, D. Wroblewski, and Tim McCandless. *Edit Wear and Read Wear*. Proceedings of ACM SIGCHI'92. pp 3-9. 1992.

[5] B. J. Jansen, A. Spink, and T. Saracevic. *Real life, real users, and real needs: a study and analysis of user queries on the web*. Information Processing and Management. **36**. 2. pp 207-227. 2000.

[6] M. Magennis and C. J. van Rijsbergen. *The potential and actual effectiveness of interactive query expansion*. Proceedings of the 20th International ACM SIGIR Conference on Research and Development in Information Retrieval pp 324-332. Philadelphia. 1997.

[7] D. Oard and J. Kim. *Implicit feedback for recommender systems*. Proceedings of the AAAI Workshop on Recommender System. Madison, Wisconsin. 1998.

[8] S. Robertson. *On term selection for query expansion*. Journal of Documentation. **46**. pp 359-364. 1990.

[9] R. W. White, I. Ruthven and J. M. Jose. *The use of implicit evidence for relevance feedback in web retrieval*. Proceedings of 24th BCS-IRSG European Colloquium on IR Research. Lecture notes in Computer Science 2291. pp 93-109. Glasgow. 2002.

[10] R. W. White, J. M. Jose and I. Ruthven. *A task-oriented study on the influencing effects of query-biased summarisation in web searching*. Information Processing and Management. 2002. *in press*.

Predicting Category Accesses for a User in a Structured Information Space*

Mao Chen
Department of Computer Science
Princeton University
Princeton, NJ 08544
maoch@cs.princeton.edu

Andrea S. LaPaugh
Department of Computer Science
Princeton University
Princeton, NJ 08544
aslp@cs.princeton.edu

Jaswinder Pal Singh
Department of Computer Science
Princeton University
Princeton, NJ 08544
jps@cs.princeton.edu

ABSTRACT

In a categorized information space, predicting users' information needs at the category level can facilitate personalization, caching and other topic-oriented services. This paper presents a two-phase model to predict the category of a user's next access based on previous accesses. Phase 1 generates a snapshot of a user's preferences among categories based on a temporal and frequency analysis of the user's access history. Phase 2 uses the computed preferences to make predictions at different category granularities. Several alternatives for each phase are evaluated, using the rating behaviors of on-line raters as the form of access considered. The results show that a method based on re-access pattern and frequency analysis of a user's whole history has the best prediction quality, even over a path-based method (Markov model) that uses the combined history of all users.

Categories and Subject Descriptors

H.3.5 [**Information Storage and Retrieval**]: Online Information Services – *data sharing, web-based services.*

General Terms: Algorithms

Keywords: Category access, prediction, access history, category structure, temporal analysis, Markov model

1. INTRODUCTION

A large amount of information available on the Internet is categorized in some way. The categorization can be done by any component in the information propagation chain: content providers at the server side, personal browsing agents at the user side, intermediary service providers such as search engines, etc. A user's navigation in a structured information space can be summarized as a traversal through a set of categories. There are many research projects and commercial products [5, 18, 19] for categorizing information, but to our knowledge very few take advantage of categorization to analyze users' access patterns at the category level. This paper presents a model to predict the category of a user's next access in a structured information space.

Our prediction model is based on analysis of a user's access history, possibly across many browsing sessions. A feature of our approach is that the only history used is that of the user whose behavior is being predicted. Therefore, the approach can be readily used in client-side applications. The model consists of two phases. Phase 1 computes a user's current preferred categories from the user's access history up to the current prediction. Our methods for computing category preferences incorporate temporal analysis while considering the possibility that a user's interest may shift over time. We propose two new approaches to this first phase problem. Using the preferences computed in phase 1, phase 2 predicts the categories of the user's next access at different category levels in the category topology of the information space. Phase 2 is based on the assumption that the category space is stable over time. This is often true even when the number and content of the items in each category changes dramatically.

Because of the difficulty of obtaining meaningful commercial data, we use a single data set to evaluate our prediction model. This data set records the rating behavior of on-line raters on a shopping site called Epinions [8]. This is an interesting data set because the rating of an item by a user is a strong indication of the user's interest in the item. We use two metrics, *precision* and *coverage*, to measure prediction quality. In our experiments, a method based on re-access pattern and frequency analysis of a user's whole history is shown to have the best prediction quality, even over a path-based method (Markov model) that uses the combined history of all users. In our experiments, an "access" is a rating explicitly given by a user and it does not include other user page accesses or click-throughs. This leaves open the question of whether the methods and the results can be generalized to other kinds of user accesses such as reading web pages, assuming goal-motivated traversals can be distinguished from random clicks.

The main contributions of this work are:

1. Proposing a framework to predict a user's accesses at the category-level in a structured information space;
2. Presenting new prediction mechanisms using temporal-frequency analysis on a single user's access pattern, and comparing them with path-based approaches;
3. Investigating user access patterns at the category-level.

The presented model is useful for many topic-oriented services. For example, content providers can push content associated with topics predicted to be of current interest to a user; a user-side

---

* This research was supported in part by NSF grant EIA 9806751

SIGIR'02, August 11-15, 2002, Tampere, Finland.

agent powered by the prediction mechanism can automatically send requests to single or multiple sites to get information that is possibly needed next by a user. Also, phase 1 can be used independently as a tool to adaptively generate a user preference profile or a personalized view based on the analysis. Many other interesting applications can be built by extending the proposed model. For example, if an uncategorized item is accessed by a set of users, the categories of the item can be estimated by aggregating the predicted categories of individual user's access to that item. This is an area of our ongoing research.

The next section presents different approaches to estimating a user's current preference level for each category. Section 3 discusses generating next-access predictions for multiple category levels. Experimental results are analyzed in section 4. Section 5 discusses related work. Section 6 draws some conclusions and indicates possible directions for future work.

2. PHASE 1: SCORING CATEGORIES BY USER'S CURRENT PREFERENCES

The key idea of our prediction model is to infer a user's preference for a category from the user's accesses of that category. In this paper user accesses refer to those accesses that show a user's interest (e.g. giving a rating to an item) rather than more casual click-throughs. We make two hypotheses about user behavior. The fundamental one is that a user's access history reflects a user's current preference, as long as the user's access history is long enough. In other words, a user is very likely to revisit a category that the user has visited. We also hypothesize that a user's interest may shift over time. Both hypotheses are shown to be reasonable by experiments in section 4.

To derive a user's preference from the user's accesses, one must determine *which* set of previous accesses should be used in the analysis, and *how* the user's current preference may be determined from these accesses. We call the former task *Episode Formation* and the latter *Episode Analysis.*

2.1 Episode Formation

In this paper, an *episode* is a set of consecutive accesses that may be considered as being performed toward a task [20]. Consider the case that a user wants to buy a desktop computer. The user visits the category "Desktops" several times to learn about products, then checks the category "Laptop" for comparison, after that the user accesses "Desktops" again to make a purchase. This process may span as long as or more than a couple of weeks, but it forms one single episode whose task is "Desktop". An episode may contain more than one task interleaved in time. In this paper, we assume that the *task structure* is same as the *category structure* of items. This assumption is reasonable for online traversals where the category structure is designed to facilitate browsing. A more complex scenario in which the task structure is distinct from the item structure is beyond the scope of this paper.

As many prediction models [3, 9, 13, 17] suggest, we assume that recent accesses are more related than distant accesses. Therefore, the episode that reflects the user's current preference is always a backward window starting from the user's latest access. In the following discussion, *episode* only refers to the most recent episode among a user's accesses. Inspired by He and Goker's argument that related accesses are also close in time [10], we group recent accesses using temporal analysis.

2.1.1 Static Approach

One way to define an *episode* is to include all the accesses a user has made up to the prediction time. This assumes that a user always has only one long-term goal. Alternatively, one can partition the access history. A simple static approach is to define a fixed window size, either by number of accesses or time period.

2.1.2 Adaptive Approach

The limitation of static approaches is that they assume similar behavior for all users and situations. One adaptive approach to defining the boundary between episodes is to set a threshold, or *timeout*, on the time interval between two consecutive accesses in an episode. However, the temporal pattern of episodes for different users may be distinct. For example, the *timeout* for an active user should be smaller than that for an inactive user. The suitable *timeout* may also vary with type of task and with time. A fixed *timeout* cannot capture the above factors adaptively.

We have designed a flat-clustering-based algorithm to determine the episode. The interval to separate an episode *E* from earlier accesses is based on the "age" of accesses relative to the current time. Specifically, an access is thought **not** to belong to *E* if the *age* of that access is two times older than the average *age* of accesses in *E,* with *age* being the interval between an access and the current time. We call this episode formation algorithm "*Adaptive-Time-Out*". The factor of "2" is chosen as the threshold for *age* based on preliminary experiments on the threshold.

Algorithm *Adaptive-Time-Out*

1. E = {L}, L is the last access by the user
2. G = the average interval in days between accesses in E and the current time
3. I = the interval in days between the access just before the earliest access in E and the current time
4. If I > 2G
    Then
  Return E
    Else
      E = E + {the access just before the earliest access in E}
      Go to 2

2.2 Episode Analysis

Once an episode is identified, the goal of episode analysis is to determine a user's preference in each category from accesses in the *episode.* An episode can be analyzed from several viewpoints.

- In *Existence* analysis, all categories accessed in an *episode* are given equal preference score regardless of when and how often they are accessed.
- *Frequency* analysis counts the number of accesses to every category in an *episode* as the category's preference score.
- *Recency* analysis gives each access in an *episode* a weight according to the *age* of the access as defined earlier.
- *Sequential* analysis assumes that a user repeats similar traversal paths from time to time. Under this assumption, a user's access after a sequence of accesses can be inferred from the old known paths that include the sequence.

Existence and frequency analyses are quite intuitive. A prediction model based on sequential analysis is usually known as a Markov model (refer to [6, 16] for details). Markov models are thought to be suitable to model users' navigation patterns among documents. However, some researchers point out that Markov models usually suffer from low applicability [refer to 6, 21], a problem that we might expect to be more serious in analyzing a single user's accesses, since many proposed Markov prediction models use traversals of a whole user community [13, 21, 23].

Because of the low applicability of Markov models we develop as an alternative a mechanism based purely on frequency and recency analysis. We define a function of access age to weigh each access in an episode. This function adapts to a particular user's re-access pattern. Specifically, the weight of an access at the time d units before the prediction time is the probability that a user re-accesses a category that was visited d units ago. This probability P_d is learned from that user's previous accesses using Equation 1. When a user has never re-accessed any category at a given interval d units, P_d cannot be learned for the user. In this case, P_d can be interpolated from probabilities for intervals adjacent to d.

$$P_d = \frac{N_d}{\sum_{i=1}^{m} N_i} \qquad \text{- Equation 1}$$

Where

N_d *: the frequency that the user reaccesses a category that is accessed by the user d units ago*

N_i *: the frequency that the user reaccesses a category that is accessed by the user i units ago.*

m : the largest interval between two consecutive accesses of a same category in the user's whole access history

Pitkow and Pirolli [17] used a similar idea to analyze the correlation between the desirability of a document and the interval between accesses of that document by users.

2.3 Scoring Categories

Given the above discussion of episode formation and episode analysis methods, we select a set of combinations of episode formation and analysis methods to constitute the category-level prediction methods we use in this paper. These methods compute preference scores for all categories at all category levels.

Personal-N^th-Order-Markov (*PN*): a transition matrix records the access frequency to each category immediately following sequences in the user's access history. For a given *episode E*, the preference score of a category is the access frequency to that category immediately following a sequence of *N* accesses in *E*.

Last-N-Accesses (*LN*): any category accessed by the user in the last *N* accesses is counted, with equal weight. For example, Amazon [1] uses this approach in listing the last *N* items browsed by a user in a personalized page for the user. Both *LN* and *PN* form the *episode* using a fixed window size in terms of the number of accesses.

Fixed-Episode-Interval (*FEI*): the boundary between episodes is set by a fixed interval, an approach popularly used to determine sessions from server logs. Each category is scored by the access frequency during the last episode.

Whole-History (WH): the preference score of a category is the total number of accesses the user has ever made to the category. That is, this is a pure frequency-based method in which the episode used is a user's entire history.

Past-Days (PD): the categories that are accessed by the user in the past *N* days are scored by the access frequency during the period. Different from *LN*, this method incorporates access frequency.

While not used in prediction directly, *Whole-History* and *Past-Days* are used by some E-Commerce sites to summarize a user's behavior. For example, eBay [7] stratifies a user's reputation as that in the past 7 days, in the past month and in the past 6 months. We use this idea to analyze a user's activity for prediction.

Adaptive-Episode-Interval (*AEI*): the boundary between episodes is set using the algorithm *Adaptive-Time-Out* proposed in section 2.1.2. Each category is scored by the access frequency during the last episode.

Time-Weighted (*TW*): every access is weighted by the function of access age built using equation 1. The preference score of a category is the sum of weights of all accesses to that category in the user's whole access history.

The methods presented so far use a single user's history. However, many prediction systems for page-level accesses use Markov models built from multiple users' accesses [15, 21, 23]. For comparison with this approach, we implemented an *All-N^th-Order-Markov* model [16] and use the "most-confident" rule proposed by Li et. al. [13] (in our preliminary experiments, this model has better prediction quality than an alternative model using the "longest match" rule proposed by Li et. al.).

Collaborative-N^th-Order-Markov (*CN*): a transition matrix is built from the traversals of the whole user community. The score of every category is the access frequency to that category immediately following the sequence of accesses matching the last *N* accesses made by the given user.

Table 1 summarizes the above methods along two dimensions, *episode formation* and *episode analysis*. Note that all methods that do not use a user's whole history as the *episode* consider recency as part of episode formation, which is not indicated explicitly in the table.

Table 1. Classification of methods in phase 1

			Episode Analysis			
			Exis.	Freq.	Freq. & Recen.	Seq.
Episode Formation	Static	All		*WH*	*TW*	
		Fixed size	*LN*	*PD*		*PN* *CN*
	Adp.	Fixed Interval		*FEI*		
		Adp. Interval		*AEI*		

3. PHASE 2:GENERATING PREDICTIONS

Our prediction generation method chooses the categories with the highest preference score computed in phase 1. When there is a tie, more than one prediction result is given by the prediction model. The main problem in this phase is to determine candidate categories for each prediction; in particular, whether all categories at a same category level should be considered candidates or only a subset of them. Clearly, this problem is strongly affected by the category topology of the information space.

In a flat category structure, all categories are at the same level and hence all categories are candidates for each prediction.

In contrast, a hierarchical structure, as shown in Figure 1, provides two kinds of topology information: layer or granularity, and containment of categories. Each page belongs to a set of categories, defined by the path from the leaf category to the root (containment path). Assuming accesses are only made to the pages, an access of a page can also be viewed as accesses of all categories in any containment path including the page. We define a prediction of a user's next access to consist of predictions for each category level. The information about layer and containment can be used to determine candidates at each category level.

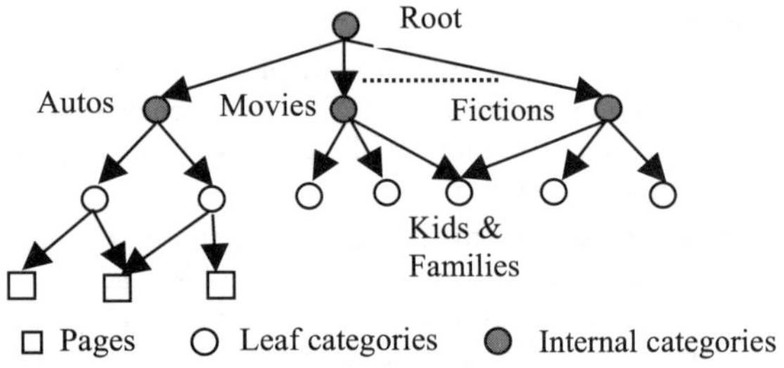

Figure 1. A hierarchical organization of a shopping site

3.1 Independent Approach

To predict the category of a user's next access at a given category level, a straightforward approach is to take all the categories at that level as candidates. This method uses the layer information in the structure. A problem with this approach is that since the predictions at different levels are done independently from each other, inconsistencies may result between the prediction results at different levels. For example, for the category hierarchy in Figure 1, a prediction for the next access at the category level 2 may be the "Kids and Families" category while the prediction at level 1 for the same access may be "Autos".

3.2 Top-down Approach

To keep the predictions for an access consistent with the hierarchy, the candidates for prediction at level l should be only children of the predicted categories for level $l-1$. This approach generates predictions for multiple category levels sequentially, in a *top-down* order. However, when the prediction for the coarser category level is wrong, this approach discards correct predictions that would have been generated by the independent approach at fine-grained levels. Our experimental results show that the prediction accuracy of the *top-down* approach is lower than that of the *independent* approach. Therefore for the bulk of our experiment we use the *independent* approach.

4. EXPERIMENTS

4.1 Experimental Setup

4.1.1 Data Collection

We use actual users' behaviors to evaluate the methods. Our data set records the rating behaviors of on-line raters at a shopping site called Epinions. Recall that we treat only actual ratings given as accesses, and not any other downloads, click-throughs or actions; this means that we are using past ratings given by the user as a predictor of which categories that user will give a rating in next.

For each rating by a given user, we only need to know the time that the rating is given and the category to which the rated object belongs. From the data we collected (in the summer of 2000), we extracted 356,899 ratings given by 38,010 users to 53,756 items spanning the period from July 1999 to August 2000.

We also extracted the category structure of Epinions, which is a hierarchy. Table 2 shows the distribution of all categories by level. The *category level* is the depth at which a category is located in the hierarchy as shown in Figure 1: coarse-grained categories have smaller category levels than finer-grained ones.

Table 2. Distribution of categories at Epinions.com

Level	1	2	3	4	5	6	7
# of categories	14	92	428	1747	516	30 4	32

4.1.2 Experimental Design and Metrics

This work aims to provide high quality predictions about a user's accesses. For a given prediction for one access, the *coverage* of that prediction is either 1 if the prediction is correct or 0 if it is incorrect. The *precision* of a prediction is defined as the fraction of a prediction (possibly with more than one result) that matches the user's next access, and the *precision* is either 0 (for a miss) or 1 divided by the number of categories in a prediction (for a hit). For each individual prediction, the *precision* is a value in [0, 1].

We measure the *prediction quality* of a method by the *average precision* and the *average coverage* of predictions for all users that make more than 10 accesses. Pairs of methods are compared using the *relative improvement* (*RI*) defined by equation 2. Of course, under this metric an absolute difference yields a smaller relative improvement when the performance of the base-line method is higher.

$$RI_{A,B} = \frac{Q_A - Q_B}{Q_B} \times 100\% \qquad \text{- Equation 2}$$

Where

$RI_{A,B}$: *the relative improvement in prediction quality of method A over method B*

Q_A : *the prediction quality of A, in precision or coverage*

Q_B : *the prediction quality of B, in precision or coverage*

All methods discussed in section 2 are self-learning. A prediction model built using any of the methods can generate predictions as early as the user's second access. In an experiment for a given user, each rating except the first one is predicted and the prediction quality is scored. The rating is then added to the training set for later predictions. Since the category structure of Epinions is hierarchical, the methods discussed in section 2 are compared using the *independent* approach in section 3. We split the predictions of a user's next rating by category level, and evaluate them at different category granularity independently.

4.2 Raw Data Analysis

The goal of this section is to investigate whether users re-access categories, and if so, to what degree. Algorithm *Base* simply uses all categories that a user has accessed as the multi-valued prediction for the user's next rating, and all the accessed categories have equal probability. Unlike *Whole-History*, *Base* uses existence analysis rather than frequency analysis on a user's whole history. Thus, the *coverage* of *Base* represents the probability that a user's next rating access is a *re-access* of some category. For a hit, *precision* of *Base* reflects the number of different categories that a user has accessed.

Figure 2 shows the evolution of *precision* and *coverage* of a prediction with the amount of information the prediction model has about a user in *Base*, stratified by category level. The x-axis of the curves in this figure is the number of ratings already given by a user when the prediction is generated. The y axis value of every point on the curves is the average of the corresponding values for all users. Users do not have equally long histories, so the curves for different users may have different lengths. Every average value shown in the figure results from at least 30 users.

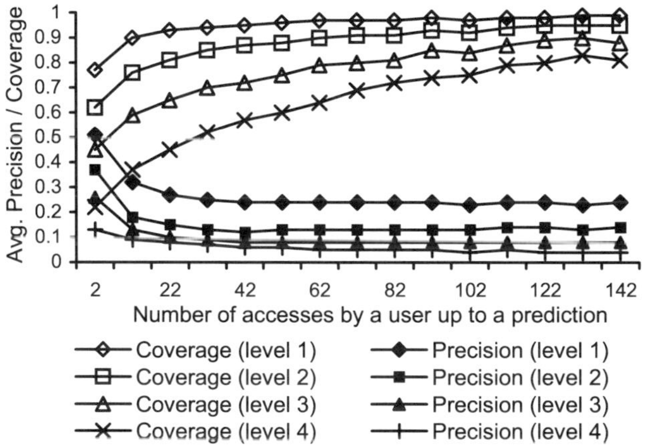

Figure 2. Precision and Coverage of a prediction in Base vs. the length of a user's access history

The curves referring to *coverage* in Figure 2 show that users tend to access categories that they have previously accessed, as expected, since our definition of coverage here is cumulative, this tendency becomes stronger with rating history. Especially at levels 1 and 2, the probability of re-access converges to a high value quickly. This tendency also increases from fine-grained levels to coarse-grained levels, which is due to the exponential increase of the total number of different categories with the category level.

However, the *precision* of *Base* is poor, especially at lower levels where there are more categories, since the categories included in a prediction accumulate. When a user's rating history is shorter than 20 ratings, the *precision* drops with a user's accesses quickly. Interestingly, the *precision* is stable after a user gives about 40 ratings. Recall that, for the *Base* algorithm, the *precision* is the ratio of *coverage* to *N*, where *N* denotes the number of different categories already rated by a user. The stability of *precision* can be explained by the similar growth rates of *coverage* and *N*. The poor precision clearly shows the intuitive result that *Base* is not a good prediction method.

4.3 Comparing Episode Formation Methods

As discussed in section 2, the *Whole-History* (*WH*), *Past-Days (PD)*, *Fixed-Episode-Interval* (*FEI*), and *Adaptive-Episode-Interval* (*AEI*) methods differ only in the episode formation method they use. Experiments showed 30 days to be the best threshold for *Past-Days*. For *FEI*, 1 day is a good "timeout" to split episodes. The four methods are compared using *relative improvement* as defined by equation 2, using *Whole-History* as the baseline method. Table 3 shows the results.

Table 3. Relative improvements of Past-Days, Fixed-Episode-Interval and Adaptive-Episode-Interval over Whole-History

Category Level		Level 1	Level 2	Level 3	Level 4
RI of Precision	*PD*	- 1.9	0.0	3.7	6.3
	FEI	7.4	18.2	14.8	0.0
	AEI	11.1	27.3	22.2	12.5
RI of Coverage	*PD*	- 1.6	0.0	0.0	0.0
	FEI	3.3	12.5	5.9	- 12.5
	AEI	8.2	20.0	11.8	-8.3

Past-Days (*PD*), which uses a fixed-size window, has no obvious advantage over *Whole-History*, which does not use temporal limitations at all. Except for category level 4, where the *absolute coverage* is quite low (*coverage* = 0.24 for *Whole-History*), the two adaptive episode formation approaches have higher *precision* and *coverage* than static approaches. We conclude that adaptive methods are better for episode definition. Furthermore, the magnitude of improvements using *Adaptive-Episode-Interval* (*AEI*) is always higher than using *Fixed-Episode-Interval* (*FEI*), which indicates that our most sophisticated method to form episodes is the best among the four approaches. The results exhibit the importance of incorporating temporal analysis in delineating episodes.

4.4 Comparing Episode Analysis Methods

4.4.1 Recency vs. No Recency

If a user's area of interest is stable over time, *Whole-History* should work well. Another prediction method that also takes a user's whole access history into consideration is *Time-Weighted*. The only difference between the two approaches is that *Time-Weighted* considers recency of accesses. Table 4 shows the *relative improvement* using *Time-Weighted* over *Whole-History*.

Table 4. Relative improvements of Time-Weighted over Whole-History

Category Level	*RI* of *Precision*	*RI* of *Coverage*
Level 1	13.0	11.5
Level 2	30.3	25.0
Level 3	25.9	20.6
Level 4	12.5	8.3

All values in Table 4 are positive, which means that weighing accesses by recency results in higher *precision* and *coverage*. This result supports our hypothesis that user's interest may shift over time and hence it is important to incorporate temporal factors in analyzing user accesses.

4.4.2 Sequential vs. Non-Sequential

Time-Weighted explicitly uses recency to analyze accesses in an *episode*, and *Adaptive-Episode-Interval* intrinsically incorporates recency analysis into episode formation. However, neither method uses sequential analysis.

For comparison, we implemented two Markov models. One uses only the accesses by the user under prediction, and the other uses the access history of the whole user community. According to preliminary experimental results, the first-order Markov model provides a better prediction quality than higher-order models when using a single user's history. For "Collaborative Markov model", we choose 3-gram [21] because we found in preliminary experiments that higher-order models bring much higher computational cost without correspondingly higher accuracy, and lower-order models do not give sufficient prediction quality.

Table 5 compares the two Markov models to *Adaptive-Episode-Interval* (*AEI*) and *Time-Weighted*, using *AEI* as baseline.

Table 5. Relative improvements using Personal-First-Order-Markov (*P1*), Collaborative-Third-Order-Markov (*C3*), and Time-Weighted (*TW*), over Adaptive-Episode-Interval (*AEI*)

Category Level		Level 1	Level 2	Level 3	Level 4
RI of Precision	*TW*	1.7	2.4	3.0	0.0
	P1	- 11.7	- 23.8	- 36.4	- 61.1
	C3	- 1.7	0.0	3.0	- 5.6
RI of Coverage	*TW*	3.0	4.2	7.9	18.2
	P1	- 12.1	- 25.0	- 36.8	- 59.1
	C3	- 9.1	- 10.4	- 5.3	0.0

Time-Weighted (*TW*) has better prediction quality than *Adaptive-Episode-Interval* (*AEI*) at all levels, especially in *coverage* at fine-grained category levels, while the two Markov models have lower *precision* and *coverage* than *AEI* in most cases.

Personal-First-Order-Markov (*P1*) is worse than the other three models. *Collaborative-Third-Order-Markov* (*C3*) has much better prediction quality than *P1*, but is still worse than the two methods that do not use sequential analysis, especially in terms of *coverage*. Since sequential analysis relies on dependence between accesses, we conjecture that this dependence at the category level is lower than that at the document level.

4.4.3 Recency vs. Existence

The last method in this discussion is *Last-N-Accesses*, which uses only *existence* in the episode analysis. In our experiments, we use two values for *N*. One value is 1, which means only the last access by a user is counted. The second value is 3, which means any category accessed by a user in the last 3 accesses is used in the prediction for the user's next access. Our preliminary experiments show that *Last-N* where *N* is bigger than 3 has similar advantage and disadvantage as *Last-3*.

Table 6. Relative improvements using Last-1, Last-3, and Time-Weighted over Collaborative-Third-Order-Markov

Category Level		Level 1	Level 2	Level 3	Level 4
RI of Precision	*L1*	0.0	- 2.4	- 11.8	- 17.7
	L3	- 13.6	- 21.4	- 20.6	- 5.9
	TW	3.4	2.4	0.0	5.9
RI of Coverage	*L1*	- 1.7	- 4.7	- 16.7	- 36.4
	L3	25.0	30.2	19.4	4.5
	TW	13.3	16.3	13.9	18.2

Table 6 compares *Last-1* (*L1*), *Last-3* (*L3*), and *Time-Weighted* (*TW*), using *Collaborative-Third-Order-Markov* (*C3*) as baseline. *L1* has worse *precision* and *coverage* than *C3*. *L3* improves *coverage* dramatically, but at the expense of *precision*. *TW* improves the coverage over *C3* at all levels, and also achieves smaller improvements in *precision*.

From the experiments in section 4.3 and 4.4, we conclude that:

(1) For methods that use only information about the user under prediction, the two methods based on recency-frequency analysis, *Adaptive-Episode-Interval* and *Time-Weighted*, have better *prediction quality* than other approaches.

(2) *Time-Weighted* has similar *precision* as *Adaptive-Episode-Interval*, but it is superior to the latter in *coverage* at fine-grained category levels.

(3) The Markov model that uses only personal navigation information has poor *precision* and *coverage*. The one that uses all users' accesses has much better quality. However, this *Collaborative-Third-Order-Markov* method is still less accurate than the two methods that do not use sequential analysis, especially in *coverage*.

4.5 Prediction Quality vs. User Access History

One desirable property of a prediction system is that the system's prediction ability evolves with information about a user. Figure 3 shows the trend of *precision* and *coverage* of *Time-Weighted* and *Personal-First-Order-Markov* with a user's rating history measured by the number of ratings.

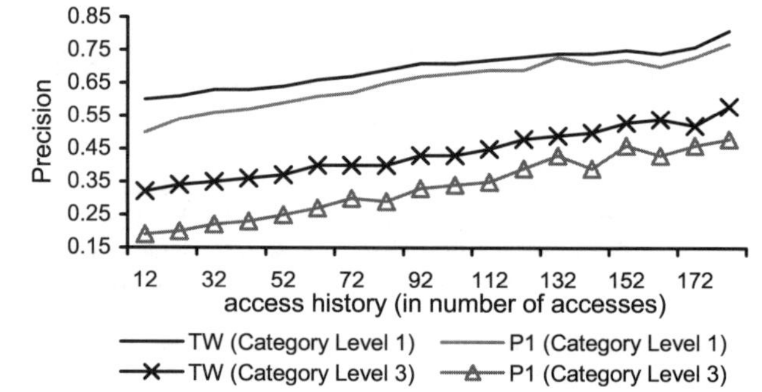

(a) Precision vs. access history of *Time-Weighted* and *Personal-First-Order-Markov*

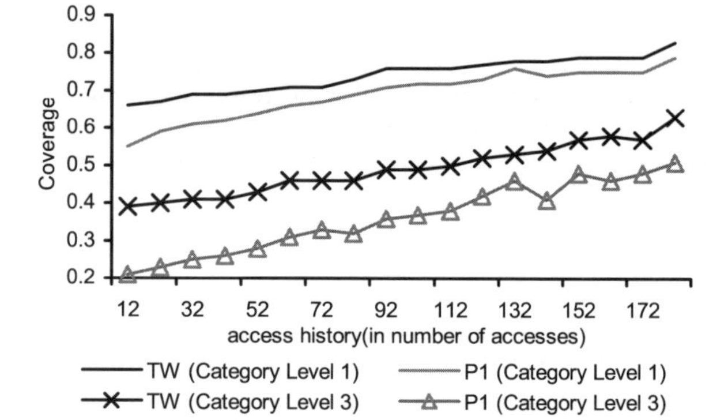

(b) Coverage vs. access history of *Time-Weighted* and *Personal-First-Order-Markov*

Figure 3. Prediction quality vs. length of access history

The *prediction quality* increases with a user's rating history using either metric for both methods. This characteristic is also observed for other methods discussed in this paper. The difference between the two methods at the finer-grained level is larger. The prediction quality for coarse-grained categories is always higher than that for fine-grained categories, so it is meaningful to give higher confidences to prediction results at coarser granularities.

4.6 Effect of Category Structure

Without hierarchy information, no prediction can be generated for coarse-grained categories. We conjectured that unless all leaf categories are at the same level of the category tree, using level information yields better prediction quality even when one is predicting only the accesses of leaf categories. This occurs because level information limits the candidates for each prediction. To test this hypothesis, we simulate the prediction for leaf categories using a flat approach with our methods, and compare the results with those given by algorithms that take advantage of category hierarchy. To simulate a flat structure, we consider all leaf categories from the original structure (keeping track, however, of the levels at which those leaf categories occurred in the hierarchy) and ignore all internal categories.

Because our results for the hierarchical structure are computed by level, we examine the prediction quality for the approach by separating out the leaf categories according to their levels in the original hierarchical structure of the data. Figure 4 shows the relative improvements in prediction quality for leaves that were at level 3 and at level 4 when the hierarchy based prediction methods are used on the original hierarchy, compared to when prediction is based on a flat structure. Prediction based on both the hierarchical and flat structures is done using the *Time-Weighted* method.

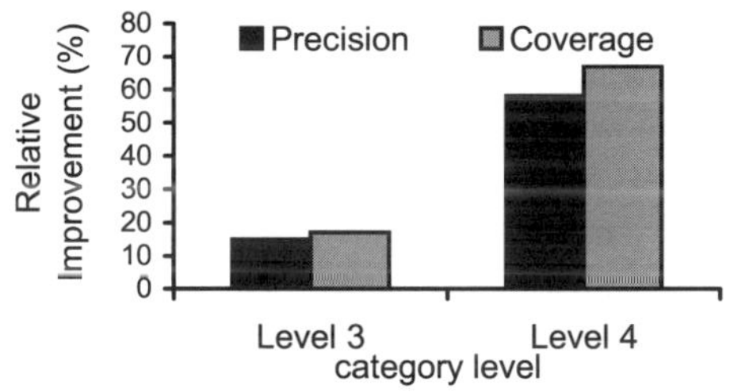

Figure 4. Relative improvements in *Precision* and *Coverage* of predictions at leaf-category levels after using hierarchy

Figure 4 shows that the hierarchy information helps to improve prediction quality for leaf categories. This improvement supports the hypothesis that level information helps to refine prediction quality by grouping leaf categories by level and thus reducing the number of candidates in each prediction.

The improvement at level 4 is bigger than that at level 3. This difference can be explained by the access pattern shown in Figure 5. Figure 5 shows the distribution of leaf categories and the distribution of accesses of leaf categories by all users. The distribution of leaf categories in the category topology is different from that of accessed leaf categories. For example, although the number of leaf categories at level 3 is only about 10% of all leaf categories, more than 40% of accesses of leaf categories are at level 3. In contrast, less than 30% of accesses are to leaf categories at level 4. Hence, distinguishing accesses of level 4 from those of other category levels is more helpful than distinguishing accesses for level 3.

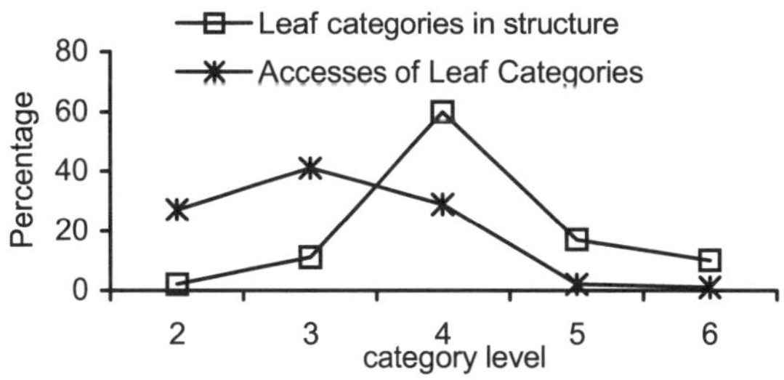

Figure 5. Distribution of leaf categories in category structure and of accesses of categories

5. RELATED WORK

5.1 Predicting User Document Accesses

There are many studies of user access predictions. Letizia [14] is a personal navigation agent that infers a user's interest by observing the user's browsing behavior, and recommends documents based on content analysis and link structure associated with the page that the user is browsing. Chi et. al. [3] infer a user's information need from the user's traversal path using content and linkage analysis. Our work focuses on temporal and frequency analysis of a user's access pattern.

Many usage mining based prediction techniques use Markov models and variants [6, 13, 15, 16, 21, 23]. Nanopoulos et. al. [15] consider noise in accesses and use ordered non-consecutive accesses in a transaction to do path mining. Pitkow and Pirolli [16] use longest repeated paths to build an All-k^{th}-Markov model. Zukerman et. al. [23] propose a hybrid model combing linkage analysis with transition analysis. We found that Markov models do not work so well for our purposes as compared to some of the methods we have proposed.

5.2 Episode Formation

In preprocessing, many prediction systems divide a user's accesses into sessions using a fixed "timeout" according to the features of the server logs. For example, Su et. al. [21] use 24 hours and 2 hours as timeout values for two data sets. He and Goker [10] propose a set of criteria to decide a suitable static interval when a web log is given. Chen et. al. [2] convert an access sequence into chunks of maximal forward references, using backward references as boundaries. Cooley et. al. [4] model user browsing behavior with two modes, "navigation purpose" and "information content purposes". The former is a sequence of navigational pages leading to one content page, while the latter is a sequence of "content pages". In contrast, our episode formation approach *Adaptive Episode Interval* uses temporal clustering with no limitation on episode pattern, and hence is more general.

5.3 Collaborative Recommendation

Traditional collaborative recommendation systems such as GroupLens [11] correlate users by explicit ratings given to objects by those users. Yan et. al. [22] cluster users by preferences inferred from users' accesses in each session. Fu et. al. [9] cluster sessions rather than users, considering that different sessions of a user may have different information needs. Our prediction model needs only the access information of the user under prediction, so it is able to work as a personal agent on the user side.

5.4 Interest Shift Detection

While detecting a user's interest shift is not our goal in this work, our methods are designed to be adaptive to such a shift by taking advantage of temporal analysis. Lam and Mostafa [12] propose a Bayesian approach to track user interest shift. However, they rely on a set of assumptions, including when shifts occur and the degree of shifts. Our methods do not rely on assumptions about the specific pattern of interest shift.

6. CONCLUSIONS

We have presented a model to predict a user's next access by category level in a structured information space. Our prediction methods are based on temporal and frequency analysis of a user's access history. Two new methods are presented in this paper: *Adaptive-Episode-Interval*, which incorporates recency analysis in episode formation, and *Time-Weighted*, which applies re-access pattern analysis in episode analysis. These two methods have better prediction quality, especially in *coverage*, than the other prediction methods discussed in this paper. In particular, these two approaches have higher prediction quality than either a Markov model using only the access history of the user under prediction, or a Markov model that combines multiple users' traversals.

Taking advantage of hierarchical category structure, we can not only generate predictions for user's accesses at multiple category levels, but also improve prediction quality for leaf categories. The basic model presented in this paper can also be applied to flat structures.

Future work includes modeling more complicated access patterns and further investigation of the relationship between category structure, task structure, and prediction quality.

7. REFERENCES

[1] Amazon.com. http://www.amazon.com

[2] Chen, M. S., Park, J. S., and Yu, P. S. Efficient Data Mining for Path Traversal Patterns. IEEE Trans. on Knowledge and Data Engineering, 10(2): 209-221, 1998.

[3] Chi. E. H., Pirolli, P., Chen, K., and Pitkow, J. Using Information Scent to Model User Information Needs and Actions on the Web. CHI 2001, Vol. 3, Issue 1, 490-497.

[4] Cooley, R., Mobasher, B., and Srivastava, J. Data Preparation for Mining World Wide Web Browsing Patterns. Knowledge and Information Systems, 1(1), 1999.

[5] Cutting, D. R., Karger, D. R., Pedersen, J. O., and Tukey, J. W. Scatter/gather: A cluster-based approach to browsing large document collections. In Proc. of SIGIR'92, 1992.

[6] Deshpande, M. and Karypis, G. Selective Markov Models for Predicting Web-Page Accesses. First SIAM International Conference on Data Mining (SDM'2001), 2001.

[7] eBay.com. http://www.ebay.com

[8] Epinions.com. http://www.epinions.com

[9] Fu,Y., Sandhu, K., and Shih, M. Fast Clustering of Web Users Based on Navigation Patterns. World Multiconference on Systemics, Cybernetics and Informatics (SCI/ISAS'99), Vol. 5, 560-567, 1999.

[10] He, D and Goker, A. Detecting Session Boundaries from Web User Logs. In Proceedings of the IRSG 22nd Annual Colloquium on Information Retrieval Research, 2000.

[11] Konstan, J. A., Miller, B. N., Maltz, D., Herlocker, J. L., Gordon, L. R., and Riedl, J. GroupLens: Applying Collaborative Filtering to Usenet News. Communications of ACM, Vol. 40, No. 3, 77-87, 1997.

[12] Lam, W. and Mostafa, J. Modeling User Interest Shift Using a Bayesian Approach. Journal of the American Society For Information Science and Technology, 52(5): 416-429, 2001.

[13] Li, T. Y., Yang, Q. and Wang K. Classification Pruning for Web-request Prediction. In Proceedings of WWW 10, 2001.

[14] Lieberman, H. Letizia: An Agent That Assists Web Browsing. Proceedings of the 1995 International Joint Conference on Artificial Intelligent, 1995.

[15] Nanopoulos, A., Katsaros, D., and Manolopoulos, Y. Effective Prediction of Web-user Accesses: A Data Mining Approach. WEBKDD'01, 2001.

[16] Pitkow, J. and Pirolli, P. Mining Longest Repeating Subsequences to Predict World Wide Web Surfing. In Proceedings of USITS'99: The 2nd USENIX Symposium on Internet Technologies & Systems, 1999.

[17] Pitkow, J and Pirolli, P. Life, Death, and Lawfulness on the Electronic Frontier. In Proceedings of CHI'97, 1997.

[18] Pirolli, P., Pitkow, J., and Rao, R. Silk from a Sow's Ear: Extracting Useable Structures from the Web. In Proceedings of CHI '96, 1996.

[19] Stratify Company. (2002) http://www.stratify.com/

[20] Srivastava, J., Cooley, R., Deshpande, M., and Tan, P. N. Web Usage Mining: Discovery and Applications of Usage Patterns from Web Data. SIGKDD Explorations 1(2), 12-23, 2000.

[21] Su, Z., Yang, Q. and Zhang, H. J. A prediction system for multimedia pre-fetching in Internet. In Proceedings of the ACM Multimedia Conference 2000, 2000.

[22] Yan, T. W., Jacobsen, M., Garcia-Molina, H. and Dayal, U. From User Access Patterns to Dynamic Hypertext Linking. In Proceedings of WWW5, 1996.

[23] Zukerman, I., Albrecht, D. W., and Nicholson, A. E. Predicting Users' Request on the WWW. In Proceedings of the International Conference on User Modeling (UM99).

Detecting and Browsing Events in Unstructured Text

David A. Smith
Perseus Project, Tufts University
Medford, MA 02155, U.S.A.
dasmith@perseus.tufts.edu

ABSTRACT

Previews and overviews of large, heterogeneous information resources help users comprehend the scope of collections and focus on particular subsets of interest. For narrative documents, questions of "what happened? where? and when?" are natural points of entry. Building on our earlier work at the Perseus Project with detecting terms, place names, and dates, we have exploited co-occurrences of dates and place names to detect and describe likely events in document collections. We compare statistical measures for determining the relative significance of various events. We have built interfaces that help users preview likely regions of interest for a given range of space and time by plotting the distribution and relevance of various collocations. Users can also control the amount of collocation information in each view. Once particular collocations are selected, the system can identify key phrases associated with each possible event to organize browsing of the documents themselves.

Categories and Subject Descriptors

H.3.1 [**Information Storage and Retrieval**]: Content Analysis and Indexing; H.5.2 [**Information Interfaces and Presentation**]: User Interfaces—*Graphical user interfaces*

General Terms

Design

Keywords

visualization, interactive IR, information extraction

1. INTRODUCTION

As digital libraries and the Internet grow in size and complexity, users have a greater need to get a sense of the scope and contents of information resources. In the terms of Greene et al. [7], we need *previews* to help us quickly grasp the overall relevance of documents and collections and *overviews* to exhibit their structure and highlight possible subsets of interest.

Historical documents provide a wealth of information about past events in an unstructured form. Natural questions about particular periods and places are "What happened then?" and "What happened there?", but they may not be best answered by ad hoc queries. Simply by restricting our question to a certain time or place, of course, we exclude many events, but questions of relevance, in a broad sense, remain. What events will different users find relevant when browsing four thousand years of history, or the nineteenth century, or 1862? What events are significant, in some sense, at global, national, and local scales? If these problems can be addressed, however, users will be able to browse document collections by the common and well-understood dimensions of time and space.

The Perseus Digital Library Project (`http://www.perseus.tufts.edu`) has focused on developing automatic methods for structuring large document collections from many genres, subjects, and historical periods [3, 4]. We have previously worked on named-entity, term, and date identification and on place name disambiguation [15]. Especially in the United States, where there are a Springfield and several Middletowns in every state, place names have to be disambiguated before they can be plotted on maps.

Building on our work with individual terms, names, and dates, we have exploited co-occurrences of dates and place names in our testbeds to detect and describe likely events in a digital library. We compare statistical measures for determining the relative significance of various events. We have built interfaces that help users preview likely regions of interest for a given range of space and time by plotting the distribution and relevance of various collocations. Users can also control the amount of collocation information in each view. Once particular collocations are selected, the system can identify key phrases associated with each possible event to facilitate browsing the documents themselves.

2. PRIOR WORK

Although our testbeds contain primarily unstructured historical texts, it is useful to compare our approach with the Topic Detection and Tracking (TDT) study. TDT aims at developing techniques for "discovering and threading together topically related material from streams of data such as newswire and broadcast news" [18]. Topics are defined as specific events, "something (non-trivial) happening in a certain place at a certain time" [19] although some researchers use *event* to mean a single happening within a larger *topic* story [10]. Due to its focus on news data, TDT possesses "an explicitly time-tagged corpus". TDT systems, by design, will aggregate stories over a span of several days, even with some gaps, into single event topics. Despite the definition of an event, however, as occurring in a certain place, most TDT systems do not directly take geographical location into account. Geographical names, rather, are treated just like other named entities, such as personal and company names, or even as single words. Although some TDT systems perform retrospective event detection across an entire corpus, many are designed to handle the more difficult task of classifying stories into topics in the order in which they come in. Applications to historical documents should be able to take advantage of less error-prone retrospective methods.

The most significant problem in adapting TDT methods to historical texts is the difficulty of handling long-running topics. For the mid-1990s events in the second TDT study, systems had trouble treating the O. J. Simpson case or the investigation of the Oklahoma city bombing as a single event [17, 19]. Many historical documents discuss long-running events — e.g., wars in addition to battles —, and many users will wish to browse digital libraries at a scale larger than events of a few days' length.

3. DOMAIN DEPENDENCIES

Since a precise dateline heads each story, modern news texts are of course explicitly time-tagged. Indexing schemes can associate every term — be it a word, phrase, or named entity — with that date. Most historical texts do not fit this model for three reasons: *discursiveness*, *digression*, and *scale*. First, historical texts tend to be discursive, not broken into discrete date units. While some genres, such as chronicles and diaries, do fit this format, they do not make up a very sizable portion of most digital library collections. Domain-specific formatting cues, such as the title and dateline in news stories, can be used to segment such texts, but a scalable solution would automatically discover which documents should be so segmented. Dividing documents into passages about a single time period would be a special case of such automatic topic partitioning systems as TextTiling [9] and automatic theme generation [14].

Most documents, however, although not neatly divisible into time-stamped chunks, still contain a large amount of date information, but the association of each date in a text and the terms around is not one of simple "aboutness". Second, historical documents tend to be more digressive than news stories. Even if there is a main linear narrative, a historian will often digress about events from before or after the main period, or taking place in another region. Finally, many historical documents are simply on a larger scale than news stories. Not only are books, and even chapters, often orders of magnitude longer than newspaper articles, but the ranges of time and space covered are often much larger.

In addition to problems of interpretation, historical documents present obstacles merely to identifying relevant dates. First of all, many scholarly works are strewn with bibliographic citations. Bibliographic dates can be useful in their own right; one could see, for example, that a work published in the 1990s cited works mostly from the 1960s. Bibliography is not, however, directly related to historical narrative and distracts from most information needs. News stories seldom make citations and current academic practice relegates much bibliography to a separate section, but older works often mix citations with narrative. In general, accurately identifying bibliographic references has been an active area of research with varying success [1]; nevertheless, as McKay and Cunningham point out [13], identifying bibliographic dates is easier than identifying (and linking) entire citations. Distinctions between the document creator's context and the context of the subject are not limited to date information. A place name associated with an author, such as an address, may have very little to do with the setting or topic of a document [12].

Further problems arise when older documents use dating schemes other than the modern, Western Gregorian calendar. Simultaneous events may have different dates on different calendars, as when the Russian revolution in Orthodox, Julian October took place in Western, Gregorian November. Even more involved are the problems with ancient systems that dated by the years in which various magistrates — such as Athenian archons or Roman consuls — served. At present, we often avoid these problems by acquiring texts already annotated, in footnotes or headings, with modern date equivalents. Also, older texts with more involved and uncertain dating systems tend, unfortunately for historians, to contain many fewer dates.

4. RANKING COLLOCATIONS

Once dates and other features have been identified and, if necessary, disambiguated, they can be used to detect events in documents. Our initial experiments have focused on associations of dates and places. To cite one precedent, Swan and Allan report better event detection when associating named entities, rather than simple phrases, with dates using χ^2 statistics [16]. Unlike other projects, we have privileged place names over other named entities since we can identify multiple names referring to a single place and distinguish uses of the same name for different places.

Since we cannot depend on our source documents having marked or easily detectable story divisions, we must define some sort of window of association. Given the discursive and digressive properties of our documents, mentioned above, we have chosen sentences and paragraphs. We count, for example, the number of sentences that contain each date or place and the number of times each date-place pair occurs in the same sentence. For each date-place pair, we can thus build a contingency table where a is the number of times date D and place P occur in the same sentence, b the number of times D occurs without P, c the number of times P occurs without D, and d the number of sentences in which neither D nor P occur.

These counts can be used to calculate several different measures of association between the date and place. Widely used measures are mutual information (MI) [2], chi-squared (χ^2), and phi-squared (ϕ^2), which is χ^2 normalized on the number of association windows. Dunning argued that the assumption that text tokens are normally distributed overestimated the significance of rare statistical events and proposed the log-likelihood test ($-2 \log \lambda$) based on the binomial or multinomial distributions [5].

We have experimented with these statistics to test their effectiveness at ranking possible events. We have concentrated on relative ordering of events by significance rather than deciding on absolute relevance or irrelevance. As described below, users can select the amount of event infor-

Collection	Docs.	Words (millions)
London	53	13.0
California	186	12.8
Upper Midwest	140	16.2
Chesapeake	142	6.9
South	908	35.4
Civil War	237	56.4

Table 1: Collections on 19th c. history

Place	Date	Count	$-2 \log \lambda$
Corinth, Mississippi	1862	320	2745.31
Gettysburg, Pennsylvania	July 3 1863	164	2076.08
Mobile Bay, Alabama	August 5 1864	110	1870.14
Mobile Bay, Alabama	August 6 1864	80	1375.46
California, United States	1849	227	1219.85
Malvern Hill, Virginia	July 1 1862	76	1113.22
Knoxville, Tennessee	1862	170	1078.49
Waterloo, Belgium	1815	82	995.16
Spotsylvania, Virginia	May 12 1864	66	994.90
Virginia, United States	1860	264	963.19
Pittsburg Landing, Tennessee	1862	124	881.62
Walcheren, Netherlands	1809	53	860.89
Gettysburg, Pennsylvania	1863	154	749.54
Chancellorsville, Virginia	May 3 1863	49	618.33
Crimea, Ukraine	1854	65	608.43
Atlanta, Georgia	1864	138	568.38
Huntsville, Alabama	1862	88	561.24
Great Britain, United Kingdom	1812	86	536.69
California, United States	1850	131	521.70
United States	1861	245	503.16

Table 2: 19th c. events: Ranked by log-likelihood

mation they want to see, and we hope this will effectively take them from short, highly precise lists, to total recall of all candidate events in the corpus.

4.1 Example Rankings

As an example, we compare the twenty top-ranked events by each test from a corpus of nineteenth-century historical documents (tables 2–4). The ϕ^2 measure would produce the same ranking as χ^2 and is not listed. We have also included place-date pairs ranked by raw association counts (table 5). Using a common rule of thumb in contingency table analysis, we exclude date-place pairs with fewer than five occurrences. Our collections for this period focus on British and U.S. history: a collection on the history and topography of London; one each on California, the Upper Midwest, and the Chesapeake region from the Library of Congress' American Memory project; a collection on the American South from ibiblio; and a collection of memoirs and official records of the U.S. Civil War (table 1). As one can infer from the table, many of these documents are quite long books; the London collection has an average of 245,000 words per document.

Place	Date	Count	χ^2
Wakulla county, Florida	January 7 1859	9	2193820
Mobile Bay, Alabama	August 5 1864	110	935482
Mobile Bay, Alabama	August 6 1864	80	736456
Queretaro, Mexico	May 1848	10	576247
Dooly, Georgia	December 17 1860	7	498001
Crisfield, Maryland	September 1874	5	491228
Broad Creek, Massachusetts	September 1874	5	439518
Walcheren, Netherlands	1809	53	290660
Spotsylvania, Virginia	May 12 1864	66	262641
Waynesboro, Georgia	December 4 1864	16	255647
Jeffersonville, Ohio	March 13 1862	5	255635
Mayo, Cape Verde	March 12 1835	5	246335
Malvern Hill, Virginia	July 1 1862	76	232525
Puerto Cabello, Venezuela	July 26 1861	6	191783
Gettysburg, Pennsylvania	July 3 1863	164	152491
Mobile Bay, Alabama	August 8 1864	20	141363
Pocomoke, North Carolina	September 1874	7	139885
Five Forks, Maryland	April 1 1865	5	138559
Appomattox county, Virginia	January 31 1863	6	137580
Greenwich, Connecticut	May 30 1848	7	125128

Table 3: Ranked by chi-squared

Place	Date	Count	MI
Wakulla county, Florida	January 7 1859	9	17.8951
Crisfield, Maryland	September 1874	5	16.5841
Broad Creek, Massachusetts	September 1874	5	16.4237
Dooly, Georgia	December 17 1860	7	16.1185
Queretaro, Mexico	May 1848	10	15.8144
Jeffersonville, Ohio	March 13 1862	5	15.6418
Mayo, Cape Verde	March 12 1835	5	15.5884
Puerto Cabello, Venezuela	July 26 1861	6	14.9042
Five Forks, Maryland	April 1 1865	5	14.7583
Appomattox county, Virginia	January 31 1863	6	14.4851
Greenbrier county, West Virginia	March 1858	5	14.3862
Abingdon, United Kingdom	March 22 1860	6	14.3106
Pocomoke, North Carolina	September 1874	7	14.2867
Greenwich, Connecticut	May 30 1848	7	14.1258
Ashley River, South Carolina	December 7 1864	5	14.0987
Waynesboro, Georgia	December 4 1864	16	13.9639
Pocotaligo, South Carolina	December 20 1864	7	13.7488
Washington, Georgia	May 4 1865	8	13.7094
Drummond Island, Michigan	March 1816	7	13.6673
Nantucket, Massachusetts	August 1841	5	13.6232

Table 4: Ranked by mutual information

Place	Date	Count
Corinth, Mississippi	1862	320
Virginia, United States	1860	264
United States	1861	245
California, United States	1849	227
Richmond, Virginia	1862	171
Knoxville, Tennessee	1862	170
Gettysburg, Pennsylvania	July 3 1863	164
Gettysburg, Pennsylvania	1863	154
United States	1812	152
United States	1860	146
Atlanta, Georgia	1864	138
Georgia, United States	1864	136
United States	1862	134
California, United States	1850	131
Virginia, United States	1861	131
Virginia, United States	1862	128
United States	1864	128
Pittsburg Landing, Tennessee	1862	124
Washington, United States	1862	124
United States	1848	122

Table 5: Ranked by raw association count

The log-likelihood measure achieves a balance between events at a very specific place and time — such as the battles of Gettysburg (specifically the third day, July 3, 1863), Mobile Bay, Malvern Hill, Spotsylvania, and Waterloo — and larger regions of concentration — such as the California Gold Rush of 1849 and 1850 or the Crimean War. Civil War battles are well represented, probably because several different memoirs, diaries, and official histories will discuss the same event, while events in other corpora are less likely to receive repeat coverage. The chi-squared and mutual information scores highlight associations of rarer dates and places; for example, January 7, 1859 in Wakulla county, Florida, is singled out as the day that the offices of Tax Assessor and Collector and Sheriff were combined. Since this particular day and place are not mentioned except when together, the chi-squared and mutual information scores overestimate the significance of these nine occurrences. Interestingly, all of the χ^2 scores in these top twenty are far above the significance threshold of 10.83 for 99.9% confidence; while the statistic may be useful for determining absolute significance, it may not be as useful for establishing rank among significant collocations.

On the whole, mutual information shows a greater bias for rare events: in the top twenty ranked by MI, no event is represented by more than 16 passages. Log-likelihood and χ^2 exhibit a greater range in the number of passages supporting each event. Although ranking by raw counts privileges whole years and larger regions such as states and countries, such a result may also be appropriate at scales of the whole world and a century.

Finally, note that the raw count list contains only one event with a month and day — the heavily covered battle of Gettysburg. All events in the mutual information

Place	Date	Count	$-2\log\lambda$
Aegospotami, Turkey	405 BC	24	467.124
Plataea	479 BC	17	241.044
Salamis, Greece	480 BC	20	211.093
Delium, Greece	424 BC	11	203.543
Lade, United Kingdom	494 BC	9	174.566
Athens, Greece	431 BC	18	160.520
Samos, Greece	440 BC	14	151.662
Olynthus	432 BC	9	146.786
Tanagra, Greece	457 BC	8	136.139
Sybaris	510 BC	9	129.891
Greece	480 BC	20	128.819
Athens, Greece	480 BC	22	125.905
Mantinea, Greece	418 BC	7	116.546
Athens, Greece	404 BC	14	114.052
Syracuse, Italy	485 BC	8	106.041
Amphipolis, Greece	422 BC	6	101.548
Sparta, Greece	404 BC	10	99.4967
Sardes, Turkey	481 BC	6	96.6489
Thurii	443 BC	5	96.5052
Sicily, Italy	415 BC	9	91.6774

Table 6: Events in the 6th and 5th centuries BC, ranked by log-likelihood

list contain a month, and χ^2 only shows one event without a month or day: the half-hearted Walcheren expedition of 1809 that is mentioned in many British officers' biographies. The log-likelihood measure, again, shows a balance of specific and more general dates. Similarly, neither mutual information nor χ^2 highlight any collocations with places larger than individual towns or cities. All but seven events in the raw count list involve an entire state or nation. The log-likelihood list contains mostly specific towns or cities as well as six larger areas: three states (California twice and Virginia), two geographical regions (Great Britain and the Crimea), and one nation (the United States).

Even outside the scope of precise dates, log-likelihood ranking can perform well. Beyond the nineteenth century, there are fewer dates precise to the day. Tables 6 and 7 show events in the sixth and fifth centuries BC, and the thirteenth and fourteenth centuries AD. The digital library contains substantial material on the ancient period. As noted above, however, there are fewer dates to exploit in older documents, and the lower counts bear this out. The low numbers show their effect by including the incorrect disambiguation of "Lade" for the United Kingdom instead of Greece. Still, decisive moments in Greek history are clear with the end of the Peloponnesian war at Aegispotami and of the Persian wars at Plataea. Our testbed does not contain any resources specifically for medieval history, but enough allusions are made in the London collection to detect some significant events in medieval England. The battles of Poitiers, Lewes, Crecy, and Bannockburn, at the top of the list, are decisive events in the Hundred Years War, the unrest in the reign of Henry III, and the Scottish struggle with the English. At these lower frequencies, the χ^2 measure seems to detect more spurious events (table 8).

4.2 Evaluating Rankings

Having some intuition about the characteristics of these ranking schemes, we can now try to quantify the differences among them. For the U.S. Civil War, Dyer's *Compendium of the War of the Rebellion* [6] includes a complete tabulation of all "battles, engagements, actions, skirmishes, etc." in that conflict. Each entry consists of a date range, a geographic name, an indicator of severity (e.g. "battle", "skirmish", "affair"), information on units engaged, and casualties. For this evaluation, we identified and disambiguated the toponyms in Dyer's list. Removing those places, such as "Bole's Farm", that could not be readily identified, we were left with 7602 distinct events.

Place	Date	Count	$-2\log\lambda$
Poitiers, France	1356	19	357.045
Lewes, United Kingdom	1264	19	314.943
Crecy, France	1346	16	309.233
Bannockburn, United Kingdom	1314	15	305.789
Neville's Cross, United Kingdom	1346	11	235.198
Gascony, France	1264	14	233.708
Lewes, United Kingdom	1265	13	222.948
Sluys, Netherlands	1340	11	217.536
Lewes, United Kingdom	1263	12	208.978
Montfort, France	1264	11	201.241
Flanders, Belgium	1297	14	193.794
Gascony, France	1265	11	193.198
Gascony, France	1297	11	190.275
Epsom, United Kingdom	1265	11	183.179
Lewes, United Kingdom	1258	11	182.392
Halidon Hill, United Kingdom	1333	8	177.775
Montfort, France	1263	9	176.772
Gascony, France	1253	10	176.184
Montfort, France	1265	9	172.843
Bannockburn, United Kingdom	1313	9	172.033

Table 7: Events in the 13th and 14th centuries

Place	Date	Count	χ^2
Neville's Cross, United Kingdom	1346	11	821941
Halidon Hill, United Kingdom	1333	8	821624
Bannockburn, United Kingdom	1314	15	786028
Boroughbridge, United Kingdom	1322	8	626645
Bretigny, France	1360	6	593667
Crecy, France	1346	16	530521
Poitiers, France	1356	19	483353
Sluys, Netherlands	1340	11	449818
Codnor, United Kingdom	1241	5	430686
Montfort, France	1263	9	363850
Montfort, France	1265	9	296822
Bannockburn, United Kingdom	1313	9	287064
Bannockburn, United Kingdom	1306	9	275102
Poitou, France	1214	7	267580
Crecy, France	1342	9	264700
Neville's Cross, United Kingdom	1341	5	262741
Neville's Cross, United Kingdom	1338	5	236020
Sluys, Netherlands	1344	6	228297
Montfort, France	1264	11	227686
Crecy, France	1356	9	215066

Table 8: Events in the 13th and 14th centuries ranked by chi-squared

Although the primary goal of our system is visualizing the content of digital collections, any evaluation of various methods against such an *a priori* list risks saying more about the corpus than about the methods themselves. Our test documents simply have more to say about the battle of Shiloh than the battle of Springfield, Missouri. By contrast, the TDT list of topics only contains events that are represented in the corpus of news stories. Even so, events of greater significance had a greater chance of being included in the collection: 68% of all events listed by Dyer as "battles" were detected by our system, against 10% of all other events.

Using the mean reciprocal rank method employed by TREC evaluations, we compared the collocation-ranking systems. For each day of each event in Dyer, we checked whether Dyer's geographic location matched any of our detected date-place collocations for that day. If there was a match, we then recorded how far down the list of collocations for that date the match fell. The reciprocals of the ranks for each ranking scheme were then averaged.

Table 9 shows that log likelihood reliably fell at the top of the list; its advantage is especially marked for low-frequency

Excl. < 5	$-2\log\lambda$	MI	χ^2	Count	α
Battles	0.780	0.724	0.751	0.757	0.50
All events	0.751	0.716	0.733	0.722	0.05
Incl. < 5					
Battles	0.542	0.174	0.327	0.507	0.03
All events	0.326	0.240	0.273	0.259	0.00

Table 9: Mean reciprocal rank in detecting Civil War events

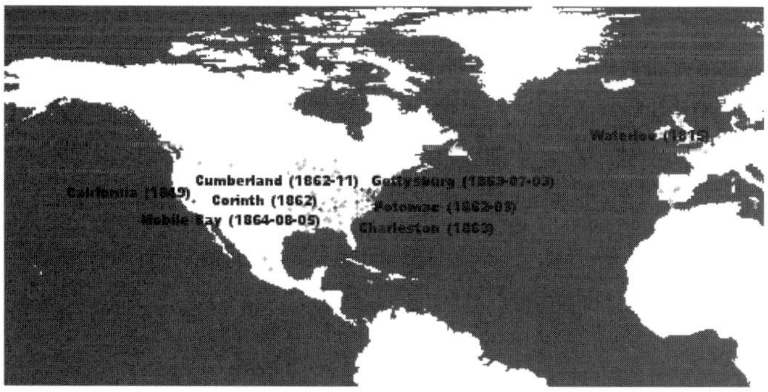

Figure 1: Significant collocations in the 19th c. Highlighted, labeled items include the battle of Waterloo, the eastern U.S. in the 1860s, and California in 1849.

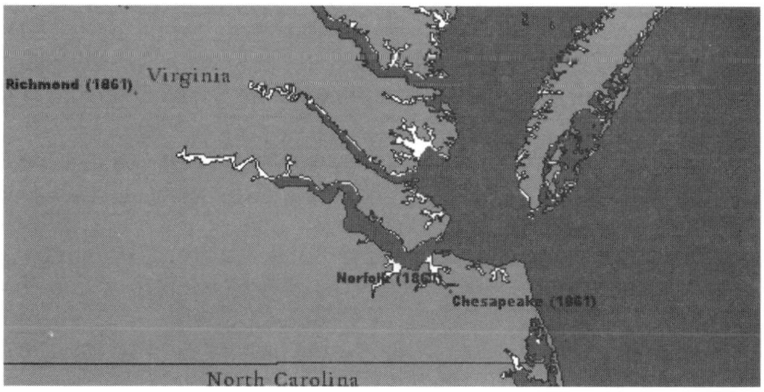

Figure 2: The Virginia Tidewater in 1861.

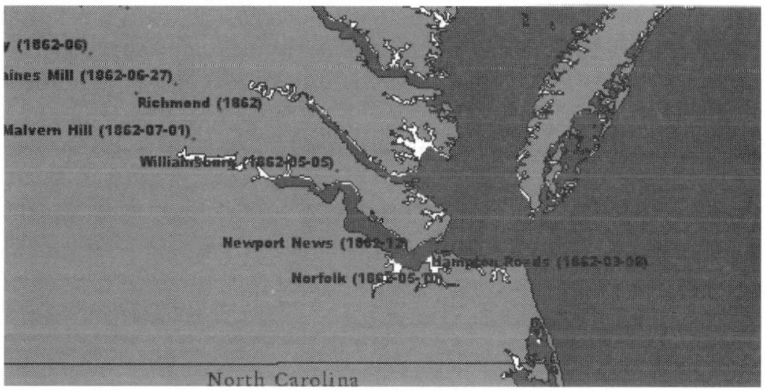

Figure 3: The Virginia Tidewater in 1862, showing action in the Peninsular Campaign.

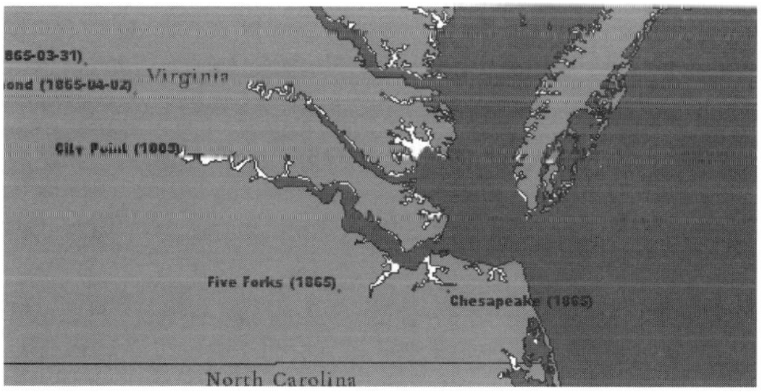

Figure 4: The Virginia Tidewater in 1865. Richmond fell on April 2. The map is empty for the remainder of the 1860s.

collocations. The relative performance of raw counts, chi-squared, and mutual information also confirms our intuition. The table also shows that events of high importance — the major battles — tend to rank higher than all events in general. Although raw counts performed quite well, sign test statistics show that log-likelihood held a significant advantage over counts in all tests except the small number of battles with five collocations for each day. The sign test was computed by counting the number of cases where log-likelihood outranked raw counts and then calculating the probability that this was due to chance. As shown in the last column, significance (α) for higher frequency battles was inconclusive: there was merely a 50% chance that log-likelihood was the better ranking. In all other cases, log-likelihood outperformed counts with small probabilities of error.

5. BROWSING EVENTS

5.1 Map Browsing

We have developed an interface to explore these associations with a combination of graphical and tabular display. In addition to lists or timelines of significant events, we also generate global or regional maps. When the user selects a particular range of space or time — whether a century, decade, or year — the map is updated to show the sites of significant events in that range. The locations of top-scoring events in any given space-time range are brighter in color and labeled on the map; lower-scoring events are lighter in color. The top-ranked events are also listed, with date, place, and the number of times they co-occur in the digital library. The user can adjust the number of events that are listed and labeled on the map.

A high-level view, such as figure 1, can serve as a preview, informing the user of the geographic and temporal range of a collection or document. It can also be seen as an overview that guides the user to particular concentrations of data — in this case, for instance, to the California Gold Rush and the Civil War. Figures 2–4 cover a more restricted geographic area and only one year each. By sequentially browsing the time dimension, the user can gain a sense of the ebb and flow of information about this part of the world. Users could further analyze event data in a temporally-aware GIS such as TimeMap (`htt://www.timemap.net`).

5.2 Phrase Browsing

If a user wishes to explore a candidate event more closely, he can click on the date-place collocation and call up a display of the individual passages from the digital library. Since our system disambiguates toponyms in texts, these searches are for the unique geographic identifiers, not string searches for the names themselves.

When searching for a combination of date and place, the default results display organizes retrieved passages by phrases common to two or more sentences. This display, first of all, takes advantage of the cluster hypothesis: result documents in one cluster are more likely to be relevant to the same topic [11, 8]. Thus, if more than one event has occurred in the given time and place, clustering can help to separate the documents pertaining to different events. The phrases that head each cluster can also provide a useful description of the event(s) contained in the retrieved documents. The retrieved passages could also be organized in other ways: by the document from which each passage comes or by personal names that co-occur with the event.

We produce the clusters at run time using a suffix-tree algorithm. As in [20], we can use this data structure to create a polythetic classification of search result passages as they are returned. For each sentence in the search results, we level case, remove punctuation, divide each sentence into words, and then strip off each suffix of a sentence: the first through last words, the second through last words, and so on. Once all these suffixes are inserted into a tree (specifically, a trie data structure), we can then easily determine all of the sentences that contain a given subsequence of words. These phrases are ranked by a score s that combines the number of words w in the phrase with the number of passages p in the cluster, using a cluster-constant c, usually set to 0.5 (equation 1; e is Euler's constant).

$$s = p \cdot \frac{1 - e^{-cw}}{1 + e^{-cw}} \qquad (1)$$

When cluster sizes are small, this formula favors longer common phrases, but for clusters with more documents, the cluster size will outweigh the phrase length. In normal display, we suppress clusters whose documents are a subset of a higher-ranked cluster. The examples show clusters for London, 1666, the date of the Great Fire (table 10); for California, 1849, the Gold Rush (table 11); for Atlanta, 1864, when a Union army captured the city (table 12); and, from the TDT3 corpus, for Libya, 1998, during the trial for the Pan Am bombing over Lockerbie, Scotland (table 13). Phrases containing dates are removed since they mostly show variations like "fire in 1666" and "fire in the year 1666".

These phrases can characterize events by listing associated people or places, such as the opposing generals Sherman and Johnston; Kofi Annan and Moammar Gadhafi; San Francisco; or Cape Horn, around which many sailed to California. Phrase clusters may also be more descriptive: "rebuilding of the city", "gold fever", "march to the sea", or "pan am bombing". The example from news texts also shows the extent to which multiple accounts of the same event can duplicate phrases such as "panel of scottish judges in the netherlands" (10 documents) or "libya has confirmed its seriousness and readiness to find a solution to the lockerbie problem" (7 documents, this from a quote by Kofi Annan). The user can also group passages by the book or collection

Phrase	Count	Score
fire of london	21	13.34
great fire	21	9.70
city of london	8	5.08
charles ii	6	2.77
act of parliament	4	2.54
duke of york	4	2.54
christ church oxford	3	1.91
house of commons	3	1.91
dreadful fire	3	1.39
rebuilding of the city	2	1.52
college oxford	3	1.39
privy council	3	1.39
view of london	2	1.27
burning of london	2	1.27
church of st	2	1.27

Table 10: Clusters for London, 1666

Phrase	Count	Score
san francisco	19	8.78
discovery of gold in california	8	6.79
discovery of gold	10	6.35
gold rush	9	4.16
united states	9	4.16
gold fields	7	3.23
trip to california	5	3.18
gold fever	6	2.77
cape horn	6	2.77
california gold	6	2.77
california during the years	3	2.28
early in the year	3	2.28

Table 11: Clusters for California, 1849

Phrase	Count	Score
military division of the mississippi	13	11.03
atlanta ga	19	8.78
atlanta georgia	18	8.32
atlanta campaign	14	6.47
march to the sea	5	3.81
major general	8	3.70
general sherman	7	3.23
sherman's army	5	2.31
effective strength of the army	3	2.54
advance on atlanta	4	2.54
battle of atlanta	4	2.54
capture of atlanta	4	2.54
general joseph e johnston	3	2.28
maj gen	4	1.85
kenesaw mountain	4	1.85

Table 12: Clusters for Atlanta, 1864

Phrase	Count	Score
secretary general kofi annan	31	23.61
secretary general	43	19.87
kofi annan	32	14.79
united states	29	13.40
lockerbie scotland	29	13.40
trial in the netherlands	13	9.90
panel of scottish judges in the netherlands	10	9.41
trial in a third country	11	9.33
moammar gadhafi	20	9.24
libyan leader	20	9.24
libya s foreign minister	12	9.14
foreign minister	19	8.78
hand over the two suspects	10	8.48
security council	18	8.32
pan am bombing	12	7.62
libya s official news agency jana	8	7.24
libya has confirmed its seriousness and readiness to find a solution to the lockerbie problem	7	7.00
travel to libya	11	6.99
libyan suspects	15	6.93
news agency	14	6.47
united nations	14	6.47

Table 13: Clusters for Libya, 1998

from which they come. The number of distinct documents recording a date-place collocation could be useful in deciding an event's significance.

6. CONCLUSIONS

Although historical documents do not often exhibit the tight topic focus and reliable structure of news or scholarly articles, their broad scope and lack of structure can provide a useful testbed for building more scalable architectures for event detection and information extraction systems. Once detected and ranked, date-place collocations can provide a useful generic interface to information systems through maps, timelines, and tabular displays.

Evaluating these and other methods of event detection requires attention to varying information needs. Does the user wish to gain a broad overview of a particular corpus or subcorpus or to focus on events that stand out from the rest of the corpus? Since the user can choose the amount of information to browse, we have concentrated on ranking events using statistical measures and have found evidence that the log-likelihood measure achieves a balance among spatial and temporal scope and frequency of occurrence. These ranking methods may also be useful for interpreting other kinds of collocations in text, such as co-occurrences of technical terms. We have built a browsing interface so that users can see regions of concentration within a document corpus and explore names and phrases associated with a given event. In future work, we hope to incorporate other document features into the event detection system. Since the distance between two places or dates is measurable, and not arbitrary as in some term models, we can work on grouping the data to minimize the aggregation effects of using individual days, years, or places as terms of association.

7. ACKNOWLEDGMENTS

The work presented in this paper has been supported by a grant from the Digital Library Initiative Phase 2 (NSF IIS-9817484), with particular backing from the National Endowment for the Humanities and the National Science Foundation. I would also like to thank Greg Crane, Jim French, Anne Mahoney, and the anonymous reviewers for their comments.

8. REFERENCES

[1] Donna Bergmark and Carl Lagoze. An architecture for automatic reference linking. In *Proceedings of ECDL 2001*, pages 115–126, Darmstadt, 4-9 September 2001.

[2] Kenneth Church and Patrick Hanks. Word association norms, mutual information, and lexicography. *Computational Linguistics*, 16(1):22–29, 1990.

[3] Gregory Crane, David A. Smith, and Clifford E. Wulfman. Building a hypertextual digital library in the humanities: A case study on London. In *Proceedings of the First ACM+IEEE Joint Conference on Digital Libraries*, pages 426–434, Roanoke, VA, 24-28 June 2001.

[4] Gregory R. Crane, Robert F. Chavez, Anne Mahoney, Thomas L. Milbank, Jeffrey A. Rydberg-Cox, David A. Smith, and Clifford E. Wulfman. Drudgery and deep thought: Designing a digital library for the humanities. *Communications of the Association for Computing Machinery*, 44(5):35–40, 2001.

[5] Ted Dunning. Accurate methods for the statistics of surprise and coincidence. *Computational Linguistics*, 19(1):61–74, 1993.

[6] Frederick H. Dyer. *A Compendium of the War of the Rebellion*. Thomas Yoseloff, New York, repr. of 1908 edition, 1959.

[7] Stephan Greene, Gary Marchionini, Catherine Plaisant, and Ben Shneiderman. Previews and overviews in digital libraries: Designing surrogates to support visual information seeking. *Journal of the American Society for Information Science*, 51(4):380–393, 2000.

[8] Marti Hearst and Jan O. Pedersen. Reexamining the cluster hypothesis: Scatter/gather on retrieval results. In *Proceedings of the 19th Annual ACM SIGIR Conference*, pages 76–84, Zurich, 1996. ACM Press.

[9] Marti A. Hearst and Christian Plaunt. Subtopic structuring for full-length document access. In *Proceedings of the 16th Annual ACM SIGIR Conference*, pages 59–68, Pittsburgh, PA, June 1993.

[10] Vikash Khandelwal, Rahul Gupta, and James Allan. An evaluation corpus for temporal summarization. In James Allan, editor, *Proceedings of HLT 2001, First International Conference on Human Language Technology Research*, San Francisco, 2001. Morgan Kaufmann.

[11] Anton Leuski. Evaluating document clustering for interactive information retrieval. In *Proceedings of the 2001 ACM CIKM*, pages 33–40, Atlanta, GA, 5–10 November 2001.

[12] Kevin S. McCurley. Geospatial mapping and navigation of the web. In *Proceedings of the Tenth International WWW Conference*, pages 221–229, Hong Kong, 1–5 May 2001.

[13] Dana McKay and Sally Jo Cunningham. Mining dates from historical documents. Technical report, Department of Computer Science, University of Waikato, 2000.

[14] Gerard Salton, Amit Sighal, Mandar Mitra, and Chris Buckley. Automatic text structuring and summarization. *Information Processing & Management*, 33(2):193–207, 1997.

[15] David A. Smith and Gregory Crane. Disambiguating geographic names in a historical digital library. In *Proceedings of ECDL*, pages 127–136, Darmstadt, 4-9 September 2001.

[16] Russell Swan and James Allan. Extracting significant time varying features from text. In *Proceedings of the Eighth International Conference on Information Knowledge Management (CIKM '99)*, pages 38–45, Kansas City, MO, November 1999.

[17] Russell Swan and James Allan. Automatic generation of overview timelines. In *Proceedings of the 23rd Annual International ACM SIGIR Conference on Research and Development in Information Retrieval*, pages 49–56, Athens, Greece, July 2000.

[18] Charles L. Wayne. Multilingual topic detection and tracking: Successful research enabled by corpora and evaluation. In *LREC 2000: 2nd International Conference on Language Resources and Evaluation*, Athens, Greece, June 2000.

[19] Yiming Yang, Tom Pierce, and Jaime Carbonell. A study on retrospective and on-line event detection. In *Proceedings of the 21st Annual International ACM SIGIR Conference on Research and Development in Information Retrieval*, pages 28–36, Melbourne, Australia, August 1998.

[20] Oren Zamir, Oren Etzioni, Omid Madani, and Richard M. Karp. Fast and intuitive clustering of web documents. In *Proceedings of the 3rd ACM SIGKDD Conference*, 1997.

Novelty and Redundancy Detection in Adaptive Filtering

Yi Zhang, Jamie Callan
School of Computer Science
Carnegie Mellon University
Pittsburgh, PA 15232, USA
{yiz,callan}@cs.cmu.edu

Thomas Minka
Department of Statistics
Carnegie Mellon University
Pittsburgh, PA 15232, USA
minka@cs.cmu.edu

ABSTRACT

This paper addresses the problem of extending an adaptive information filtering system to make decisions about the novelty and redundancy of relevant documents. It argues that relevance and redundance should each be modelled explicitly and separately. A set of five redundancy measures are proposed and evaluated in experiments with and without redundancy thresholds. The experimental results demonstrate that the cosine similarity metric and a redundancy measure based on a mixture of language models are both effective for identifying redundant documents.

Categories and Subject Descriptors

H.4.m [**Information Systems**]: Miscellaneous; D.2 [**Software**]: Software Engineering

General Terms

Algorithm, Design, Experimentation

1. INTRODUCTION

Information filtering systems monitor document streams to find documents that match information needs specified by user profiles. Most recent research on information filtering focuses on learning to become more accurate at identifying relevant documents, for example, based on long-term observations of the document stream and periodic feedback from the user. This research area is called *adaptive* information filtering, and system performance is typically evaluated using relevancy based recall, precision, and utility metrics [12].

A common complaint about information filtering systems is that they do not distinguish between documents that contain new relevant information and documents that contain information that is relevant but already known. An information filtering system would provide better service to its users if it identified three categories of documents for each user profile: i) not relevant, ii) relevant but contains no new information, and iii) relevant and contains new information.

SIGIR'02, August 11-15, 2002, Tampere, Finland.

Users could then decide for themselves how to treat relevant documents that contain no new information.

The decision about whether a document contains new information depends on whether the relevant information in the document is covered by information in documents delivered previously. This complicates the filtering problem. The relevance of a document is traditionally a stateless Boolean value. A document is or is not relevant, without regard to where the document appears in the stream of documents. Decisions about redundancy and novelty depend very much on where in the stream a document appears.

For this study we defined a task and created an evaluation dataset that contains known redundant documents. We model relevance and redundancy separately, and use different similarity measures for relevancy and redundancy. We also developed and tested a variety of redundancy measures.

The following sections describe our efforts towards evaluating and developing algorithms for redundancy/novelty detection while filtering. We begin with a description of the problem and a review of related work. Section 4 describes algorithms for measuring redundancy. Section 5 introduces a simple thresholding algorithm for deciding how much redundancy is "too much". Sections 6 and 7 describe our experimental methodology and results. Section 8 concludes.

2. REDUNDANCY/NOVELTY DETECTION

We want our filtering system to distinguish among relevant documents that contain *new (novel) relevant* information and relevant documents that don't. When a document arrives, the system must determine whether it is on topic (relevancy detection), and if it is on topic, whether it is redundant (redundancy detection). We define "Redundant" to mean that all of the relevant information in the document is covered by relevant documents delivered previously.[1]

The task of identifying novel and redundant documents has not been addressed by prior work, because of the lack of a clear definition of redundancy, and a lack of evaluation data. In the research reported here, novelty and redundancy are defined i) over the set of relevant documents, ii) with respect to previously seen documents, and iii) as opposite endpoints of a scale. The latter point is particularly important. When we treat novelty and redundancy as Boolean values, we imply a thresholding process that maps a value on a continuous redundancy/novelty scale to a Boolean value. We tested our approach to novelty and redundancy by creating

[1]This definition of redundancy includes "duplicate" and "near duplicate" documents as well as documents that are redundant in content but very different in presentation.

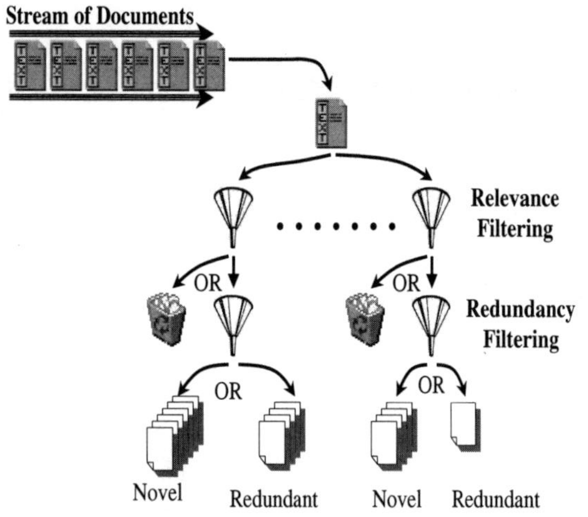

Figure 1: A system that includes traditional document filtering (for relevance) as well as second stage novelty/redundancy detection.

an evaluation dataset judged by undergraduate assessors

A system that delivers documents that are novel and relevant must identify documents that are similar to previously delivered relevant documents in the sense of having the same topic, but also dissimilar to the previously delivered documents in the sense of containing new information. These two goals are contradictory, and it may be unrealistic to expect a single component to satisfy them both.

This observation suggests a two stage approach to the problem, as shown in Figure 1. Traditional adaptive information filtering solutions can be used for relevancy filtering. It is less clear what type of algorithm should be used for redundancy filtering, and we defer discussion of solutions to Section 4; for now, we simply observe that a two-stage architecture is likely to simplify the problem.

We use the following notation throughout the paper. All notation is defined with respect to a particular user profile.

- A, B: sets of documents
- d_t: a document that arrives at time t and that is being evaluated for redundancy.
- $D(t)$: the set of all documents delivered for the profile by the time d_t arrives, not including d_t.
- $DR(t)$: the set of all relevant documents delivered for the profile. $DR(t) \subseteq D(t)$.
- $R(d_t)$: the measure of redundancy for document d_t
- d_i: usually refers to a relevant document that was delivered before d_t arrived.

We formulate the task based on the following assumptions, and they are basis for our research when acquiring redundancy judgements and developing algorithms.

Assumption 1 The redundancy of a new document d_t depends on $D(t)$, the documents the user saw before d_t arrived. We use $R(d_t) = R(d_t|D(t))$ to measure this.

Assumption 2 $R(d_t|D(t))$ depends on all the *relevant* documents $DR(t)$ the user has seen when d_t arrives, so $R(d_t|D(t)) = R(d_t|DR(t))$.

Assumption 3 For two documents set A, and B, if $B \subseteq A$ and B makes d_t redundant, then A also makes d_t redundant. To make it a softer assumption: $B \subseteq A \Rightarrow R(d_t|A) \geqslant R(d_t|B)$

Information filtering systems based on statistical retrieval models usually compute a score indicating how well each document matches a profile; documents with scores above a profile-specific dissemination threshold are delivered. Similarly, the task of identifying redundant documents can be divided into two subtasks: calculate a score to measure how redundant each document is for a profile, then identify documents with scores above a profile-specific redundancy threshold. In our architecture (Figure 1), the second stage redundancy filter consists of two elements: i) redundancy score calculation, and ii) redundancy threshold learning.

In an adaptive filtering system, each of these architectural components defines a different research agenda. The scoring mechanism requires profile-specific "anytime" updating of redundancy measures. The threshold mechanism requires a threshold updating module. The former is the focus of the research described in this paper. Although thresholding is not the focus of this paper, we did implement a simple threshold setting algorithm to make the system more complete, and to enable evaluation of redundancy measures in the context of an operational filtering system.

3. RELATED WORK

The research most closely related to novelty or redundancy detection in adaptive information filtering is perhaps the First Story Detection task associated with Topic Detection and Tracking (TDT) research [1]. A TDT system monitors a stream of chronologically-ordered documents, usually news stories. The First Story Detection (FSD) task is defined as detecting the first story that discusses a previously-unknown event. An *event* is defined as "something that happens at some specific time and place" [14].

Online clustering approaches have been a common solution to the FSD task [10, 3, 2, 5, 4, 13, 15, 1, 14]. New stories are compared to clusters of stories about previously-known events. If the new story matches an existing cluster, it describes a known event, otherwise it describes a new event.

One might argue that the concepts "event" and "novelty" are related, or that solutions defined to detect events also work for novelty. However, we think this unlikely. FSD is an event-based task, and TDT researchers have developed a distinct set of methods for topic tracking. Events have certain structures and occurrence patterns in the media. Information filtering profiles, in contrast, tend to be more subject-oriented and are often intended to follow a subject area over a relatively long period of time. Distinct events might or might not occur in the stream of relevant documents. We would also expect the two tasks to be sensitive to different vocabulary patterns. Indeed, because the user profile and a stream of relevant documents define a far smaller universe of documents than encountered in the TDT task, we might expect novelty/redundancy detection in a filtering environment to be an easier task than FSD in TDT.

FSD is a difficult problem, far from solved. The predicted and actual error rates are unacceptably high for all but a few applications [2, 5]. However, the similarities of the two tasks are worth exploring, and several of the redundancy measures we investigated are motivated by work on FSD.

4. REDUNDANCY MEASURES

We assume that traditional information filtering techniques are used to identify relevant documents; we recognize that the filtering system will make mistakes, i.e., it will deliver some documents that are not relevant and discard some documents that are actually relevant. However, for simplicity we assume that novelty/redundancy detection is performed on a stream of documents that are presumed to be relevant. We frame this problem as finding a measure $R(d_t|DR(t))$, based on Assumption 2 in Section 2.

One approach to novelty/redundancy detection is to cluster all previously delivered documents, and then to measure the redundancy of the current document by its distance to each cluster. This approach is similar to solutions for the TDT First Story Detection problem. Our concerns about this approach are that it is sensitive to clustering accuracy, and is based on strong assumptions about the nature of redundancy, which we think is user dependant.

Another approach is to measure redundancy based on the distance between the new document and each previously delivered document (document-document distance). This approach may be more robust than clustering, and may be a better match to how users view redundancy. When we asked assessors to annotate an evaluation dataset, we found that it was easiest for them to identify a new document as being redundant with a specific previously seen document, and harder to identify it as being redundant with *a set* of previously seen documents. This observation allows us to simplify the calculation of $R(d_t|DR(t))$ by setting it equal to the value of the maximally similar value in all $R(d_t|d_i)$.

$$R(d_t|DR(t)) = argmax_{d_i \in DR(t)} R(d_t|d_i)$$

Although duplicate detection is not our goal, it is an instructive case because it is simple. If d_t and d_i are exact duplicates ($d_t = d_i$) then $R(d_t|d_i)$ should have a high value because a duplicate document is maximally redundant. One natural way to measure $R(d_t|d_i)$ is using measures of similarity/distance/difference between d_t and d_i.

Document timestamps are also an important source of evidence, because documents are more likely to be redundant with other recently delivered documents. During redundancy decisions truncating the delivery history to the most recent N documents delivered for a profile also reduces the number of documents that must be considered, which reduces computational costs. N is set to 10 in all experiments reported in this paper.

Redundancy is not a symmetric metric. d_j may cause d_k to be viewed as redundant, but if the presentation order is reversed, d_k and d_j may both be viewed as containing novel information. A simple example is a document d_k that is a subset (e.g., a paragraph) of a longer document d_j. This problem characteristic motivates exploration of asymmetric forms of traditional similarity/distance/difference measures.

Below we present several different approaches to redundancy detection. The simple set distance measure is designed for a Boolean, set-oriented document representation. The geometric distance (cosine similarity) measure is a simple metric designed for "bag of words" document representations. Several variations of KL divergence and related smoothing algorithms are more complex metrics designed to measure differences in word distributions.

4.1 Set Difference

The set difference measure represents each document as a set of words. The novelty of a new document d_t is measured by the number of new words in the smoothed set representation of d_t. If a word w_i occurred frequently in document d_t but less frequently in an old document d_i, it is likely that new information not covered by d_i is covered by d_t.

Some words are expected to be frequent in a new document because they tend to be frequent in the corpus, or because they tend to be frequent in all relevant documents. There may also be topic-related stopwords, which are words that behave like stopwords in relevant documents, even if they are not stopwords in the corpus as a whole. An effective measure must compensate for both types of words.

Our set difference measure compensates for corpus stopwords by smoothing a new document's word frequencies with word counts from *all* previously seen documents. It compensates for topic stopwords by smoothing a new document's word frequencies with word counts from *all delivered* (presumed relevant) documents.

Thus we have the following measure for the redundancy of current document d_t with respect to old document d_i.

$$R(d_t|d_i) = \|Set(d_t) \bigcap \overline{Set(d_i)}\| \tag{1}$$

Where:
$w_j \in Set(d)$ iff $Count(w_j, d) > k$
$Count(w_j, d) = \alpha_1 * tf_{w_j,d} + \alpha_2 * df_{w_j} + \alpha_3 * rdf_{w_j}$
$tf_{w_j,d}$: the frequency of word w_j in document d
df_{w_j} : the number of filtered documents that contain w_j
rdf_{w_j} : the number of delivered relevant documents that contain word w_j
(α_1, α_2, α_3, k) are set to (0.8, 0.2, 0.0, 2) in our experiments; they could also be learned from training data.

We are not using the true difference between two sets

$$\|Set(d_t) \bigcap \overline{Set(d_i)}\| + \|\overline{Set(d_t)} \bigcap Set(d_i)\|$$

here because the words in

$$\|\overline{Set(d_t)} \bigcap Set(d_i)\|$$

shouldn't contribute to the novelty of d_t and the optimal novelty measure should be asymmetric.

4.2 Geometric Distance

There are several different geometric distance measure, such as Manhattan distance and Cosine distance [8]. Since Manhattan distance is very sensitive to document length, Cosine distance maybe more appropriate for our task. Prior research showed that a Cosine distance based measure was useful for the TDT FSD task [4].

Cosine distance is a symmetric measure related to the angle between two vectors [6]. If we represent document d as a vector $d = (w_1(d), w_2(d), .., w_n(d))^T$, then:

$$R(d_t|d_i) = \cos d_t, d_i \tag{2}$$

$$= \frac{\sum_{k=1}^{n} w_k(d_t) w_k(d_t)}{\| d_t \| \ \| d_i \|} \tag{3}$$

In our study, we used each unique word as one dimension, and set the tf.idf score as the weight of each dimension.

4.3 Distributional Similarity

Probabilistic language models have shown promise for identifying relevant documents in ad-hoc IR tasks (e.g., [10, 7,

16]). In the language model approach, a document d is represented by a unigram word distribution θ_d. Kullback-Leibler divergence, a distributional similarity measure, is one way to measure the redundancy of one document given another.

$$R(d_t|d_i) = -KL(\theta_{d_t}, \theta_{d_i}) \quad (4)$$
$$= -\sum_{w_i} P(w_i|\theta_{d_t}) log(\frac{P(w_i|\theta_{d_i})}{P(w_i|\theta_{d_t})}) \quad (5)$$

where θ_d is the language model for document d, and is a multinomial distribution.

θ_d can be found by maximum likelihood estimation (MLE):

$$P(w_i|d) = \frac{tf(w_i, d)}{\sum_{w_j} tf(w_j, d)}$$

The problem with using MLE is that if a word never occurs in document d, it will get a zero probability ($P(w_i|d) = 0$). Thus a word in d_t but not in d_i will make $KL(\theta_{d_t}, \theta_{d_i}) = \infty$.

Smoothing techniques are necessary to adjust the maximum likelihood estimation so that the KL-based measure is more appropriate. Prior research shows that retrieval performance is highly sensitive to smoothing parameters. Several smoothing methods have been applied to ad-hoc information retrieval and text classification (e.g., [17, 9]). Based on this prior research, we selected two methods: Bayesian smoothing using Dirichlet priors, and shrinkage.

4.3.1 Bayesian Smoothing Using Dirichlet Priors

This approach to smoothing uses the conjugate prior for a multinomial distribution, which is the Dirichlet distribution [17]. For a Dirichlet distribution with parameters

$$(\lambda p(w_1), \lambda p(w_2), ..., \lambda p(w_n))$$

the posterior distribution using Bayesian analysis for θ_d is

$$P_\lambda(w_i|d) = \frac{tf(w_i, d) + \lambda p(w_i)}{\sum_{w_j}(tf(w_j, d) + \lambda p(w_j))} \quad (6)$$

In our experiments, if w_j is in d_t, we set $\lambda p(w_j) = 0.5$, otherwise $\lambda p(w_j) = 0$.

4.3.2 Smoothing Using Shrinkage

This approach smooths by "shrinking" parameter estimates in sparse data towards the estimates in rich data [9]. This is a special case of the more general Jelinek-Mercer smoothing method, which involves deleted-interpolation estimation of linearly interpolated n-gram models [17]. For estimating the language model of document d, we can shrink its MLE estimator θ_{d_MLE} with the MLE estimator of a language model for general English θ_{E_MLE} and the MLE estimator of a language model for the topic θ_{T_MLE}:

$$\theta_d = \lambda_d \theta_{d\_MLE} + \lambda_T \theta_{T\_MLE} + \lambda_E \theta_{E\_MLE} \quad (7)$$

where $\lambda_d + \lambda_T + \lambda_E = 1$.

λ_E can be estimated from the documents the filtering system has processed, and λ_T can be estimated from the documents the filtering system has delivered (presumed relevant documents). We can derive empirical optimal values for λ_d, λ_T, and λ_E using "leave-one-out" cross validation as described in [9]. In our experiment, we used "leave-0.5-out".

4.4 A Mixture Model

In this section we introduce a new algorithm based on a generative model of document creation. This approach uses probabilistic language models and KL distance as described in Section 4.3. However, this new mixture model measure is based on a novel view of how relevant documents are generated. We can also view it as a language model with a smoothing algorithm designed specifically for our task.

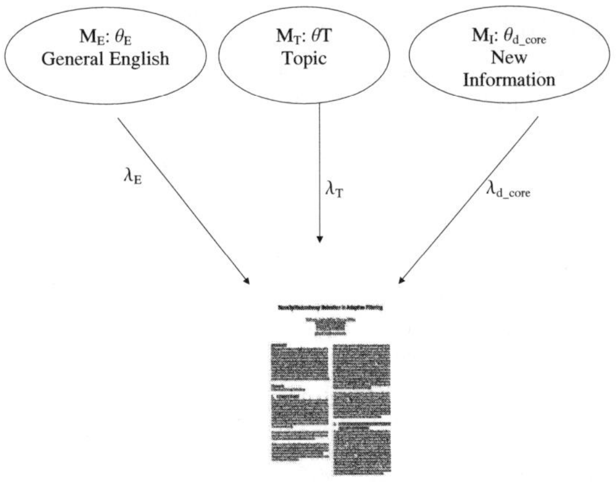

Figure 2: A mixture model for generating relevant documents.

As shown in Figure 2, we assume each relevant document is generated by the mixture of three language models: A General English language model θ_E, a user-specific Topic Model θ_T, and a document-specific Information Model θ_{d_core}. Each word w_i in the document is generated by each of the three language models with probability λ_E, λ_T and λ_{d_core} respectively:

$$P(w_i|\theta_E, \theta_T, \theta_{d\_core}, \lambda_E, \lambda_T, \lambda_{d\_core}) = \quad (8)$$
$$\lambda_E P(w_i|\theta_E) + \lambda_T P(w_i|\theta_T) + \lambda_{d\_core} P(w_i|\theta_{d\_core})$$

where $\lambda_E + \lambda_T + \lambda_{d\_core} = 1$.

For example, if information need is "Star Wars", in a relevant document words such as "is" and "the" probably come from the general English model θ_E. Words such as "star" and "wars" probably come from the Topic Model θ_T. For a document with the title "Martin Marietta Is Given Contract For Star Wars Site", the words "Martin" and "Marietta" are more likely to be generated from the new information model θ_{d_core}. θ_T is the core information of a topic, while θ_{d_core} is the core information of a particular relevant document.

$$R(d_t|d_i) = KL(\theta_{d_t\_core}, \theta_{d_i\_core}) \quad (9)$$

If we fix λ_E, λ_T, and λ_{d_core} then there exists a unique optimal value for the document core model $\theta^*_{d\_core}$ that maximizes the likelihood of the document.

$$\theta^*_{d\_core} = argmax_{\theta_{d\_core}} P(d|\theta_E, \theta_T, \theta_{d\_core}, \lambda_E, \lambda_T, \lambda_{d\_core}) \quad (10)$$

Three points are worth noting about the mixture model.

- Although Equations 7 and 8 look similar, the computations performed, and the final model acquired and used to calculate KL divergence, are quite different. Equation 7 uses shrinkage to increase the probability of words that occur frequently in the topic or in general English if they occur less frequently in document d. Equation 8 uses a mixture model to decrease the probability of these words. By shrinking with θ_{E_MLE} and θ_{T_MLE}, shrinkage smoothing reduces the distance between two documents due to those words, thus reducing their effect on the redundancy measure. With the mixture model, we directly decrease the probability of those words to reduce their effect.

- We must fix the values of λ_E, λ_T, and λ_{d_core}. If we train λ's and θ_{d_core} together, we get $\lambda_{d\_core} = 1$ and $\theta_{d\_core} = \theta_{d\_MLE}$, which is the unsmoothed language model for document d; the benefit of smoothing is lost.

- This model intentionally focus on *"what's new"* in a document, thus it avoids the contradiction between identifying relevance and novelty. If the task is to deliver relevant documents, the learning algorithm will try to recognize documents similar to already delivered relevant documents (training data). If the task is to deliver only documents containing novel information, the learning algorithm must avoid documents that are similar to those already delivered. This model introduces θ_T and θ_{d_core}, which means the measure of relevancy and redundancy are focused on different parts of a document. For relevancy, the system would like to focus on θ_T, while for redundancy it should focus on θ_{d_core}. Thus the two tasks are no longer contradictory

We can train $\theta_T, \theta_{d\_score}$, and θ_E using the EM algorithm, which has been used by others to find a language model for similar problems (e.g., [7], [16]).

5. REDUNDANCY THRESHOLDS

When we observed human assessors making redundancy decisions, we found that two annotators working on the same topics sometimes disagreed. Sometimes the disagreement was due to differences in the assessors' internal definition of redundancy. More often one assessor might feel that a document d_t should be considered redundant if a previously seen document d_i covered 80% of d_t; the other assessor might not consider it redundant unless the coverage exceeded 95%.

A person's tolerance for redundancy can be modeled with a user-dependent threshold that converts a redundancy score into a redundancy decision. User feedback about which documents are redundant serves as training data. Over time the system can learn to estimate the probability that a new document with a given redundancy score would be considered redundant : $P(\text{user j thinks } d_t \text{ is redundant} | R(d_t|DR(t)))$.

This two step process first maps the document d_t into a 1-dimensional space $R(d_t|DR(t)$ using a redundancy measure, and then learns from training data the probability of redundancy given the value on this dimension. This approach is similar in spirit to how many adaptive filtering systems identify relevant documents (e.g., [11, 18]).

Ideally, an optimization goal should be set before deciding what kind of threshold setting algorithm to use. However, our first step is a very simple algorithm for setting thresholds. Our solution is intentionally simple, in part because of the lack of adequate test collection labelled with redundant information for a given profile, and in part because this problem is not (yet) our research focus.

The algorithm for learning redundancy thresholds is:

- Initialize redundancy threshold RThreshold to a value that is so high that only very redundant documents (e.g., near duplicates) are considered redundant; and

- For each document d_t delivered (which means $R(d_t) < RThreshold$ when d_t arrives), ask the user if the document is redundant. If the document is redundant and if $R(d_t) > R(d_i)$ for all $d_i \in DR(t)$
  then $RThreshold = R(d_t)$
  else $RThreshold = RThreshold - \frac{RThreshold - R(d_t)}{10}$.

This is clearly a weak algorithm, because it only decreases the threshold. If the threshold becomes too low there is no method of increasing it again. The effectiveness of this algorithm is explored in Section 7.

6. EXPERIMENTAL METHODOLOGY

6.1 AP News & Wall Street Journal Dataset

We created a one gigabyte dataset by combining AP News and Wall Street Journal data from TREC CDs 1, 2, and 3. We chose these corpora because they are widely available, because information needs and relevance judgements are available from NIST, and because the two newswire corpora cover the same time period (1988 to 1990) and many of the same topics, guaranteeing some redundancy in the document stream. Documents were ordered chronologically. 50 TREC topics (101 to 150) simulated user profiles.

The decision about how to collect redundancy assessments depends in part upon how we view the task. If we viewed redundancy as a relationship between document d_t and a set of documents, for example a subset of the documents delivered for a particular profile, it would be impossible to collect redundancy assessments. We would need to enumerate all of the possible subsets of documents delivered at time t and then ask assessors to judge whether d_t is redundant with respect to each set. The number of possible subsets is 2^{t-1}, which is impractical for all but very small values of t. Although we know that in the "real world" redundancy *is* based on the set of documents delivered previously, we can only model it as a relationship among pairs of documents. This is the approach we adopted when developing algorithms, but that decision was based in part on how we intended to collect redundancy judgements.

We hired undergraduate students, who were otherwise unaffiliated with our research, to read the relevant documents for a profile in chronological order and to provide redundancy judgments. The decision to restrict their attention to relevant documents is based on assumption 2 in Section 2, and is consistent with a filtering system where another component makes decisions about relevance.

Assessors judged one topic at a time. They were instructed to make a decision for each document about whether the information it contained was redundant with document(s) seen previously for that topic, and to identify the prior document(s). Each topic was judged by two assessors and then differences were resolved by the assessors themselves.

We believe that in operational environments different people will have different definitions of redundancy and different redundancy thresholds. We modelled this environment by not giving assessors a precise definition of redundance. We provided two degrees of redundancy, *absolutely redundant* and *somewhat redundant*; assessors could apply them based on their expectations about how a good system should behave. If the assessor thought a person would definitely not want to read d_t because it absolutely contained no new information, d_t was marked as *absolutely redundant*. If the asses-

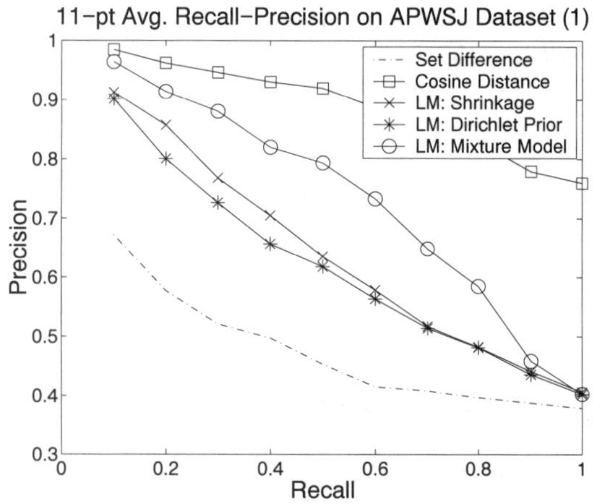

Figure 3: Comparing redundancy measures on AP News & Wall Street Journal data. Documents are considered *redundant* if an assessor marked it *absolutely redundant* or *somewhat redundant.*

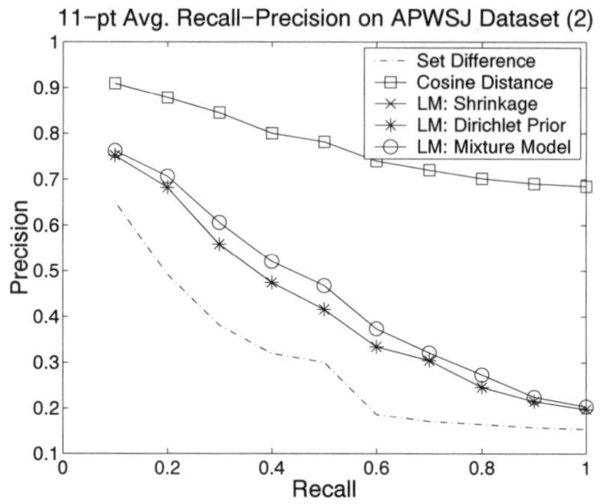

Figure 4: Comparing redundancy measures on AP News & Wall Street Journal data. Documents are considered *redundant* only if an assessor marked it as *absolutely redundant.* The Language Model (LM) measures using Shrinkage and Dirichlet Prior smoothing perform equally, thus overlap.

sor thought that a new document had some new information that a person might want to read, even though much of the document was redundant with a prior document, the document could be marked as *somewhat redundant.* Documents that were not *completely redundant* or *somewhat redundant* were marked as *novel.*

An example of the redundancy assessments is shown below. The first field is a profile id. The second field is the document id of a redundant document. Subsequent document ids are the documents that preceded it in the stream and that made it redundant. A '?' indicates that a document is only partially redundant.

q121 AP880214-0049 ? AP880214-0002 if user q121 read document AP880214-0002, then AP880214-0049 is somewhat redundant.

q121 AP880217-0031 AP880216-0137 if user q121 read document AP880216-0137, then AP880217-0031 is absolutely redundant.

q128 AP880218-0137 AP880218-0113 AP880218-0112 if user q128 read AP880218-0113 and AP880218-0112, then AP880218-0137 is absolutely redundant.

On average there are about 66.5 records per TREC topic (note that a single record may relate a document to several prior documents). About 19.2 records per profile are *absolutely redundant*; the rest represent partial redundance.

Students reported that the choice of corpus ("old") and topics made this a dull task, so we were unable to collect assessments for all 50 topics. The results in this paper are based on a set of adjudicated assessments for 33 profiles.

6.2 TREC Interactive Dataset

We combined the dataset used by the TREC-6, TREC-7, and TREC-8 Interactive Tracks to create a test dataset containing 210,158 documents from the 1991-1994 Financial Times of London. There are 20 TREC topics; each one defines a user profile. For each topic, TREC assessors have identified several instances. Different instances are about different aspects of the topic. A document on a topic could be mapped to multiple instances of that topic. The mapping from the relevant documents to instances is provided by NIST. In our evaluation, we treated each instance as one aspect of the topic and assumed that a user only wants to see one document on each aspect. Thus a document is redundant if the user has already seen at least one document for each instance this new document belongs to.

Since this dataset was not created explicitly for redundancy detection, it maybe not be as well-matched to the task as the AP News/Wall Street Journal dataset described above. However, we felt that a second dataset, even one that isn't perfect, would be a useful source of information.

6.3 Evaluation Methodology

We believe that it is important to evaluate a particular component of a system with a metric that is not affected by strengths and weaknesses in other parts of system. In this case, we would like to factor out how well the filtering system identifies relevant documents and sets redundancy thresholds. In our experiments we assume that the filtering system identifies relevant documents with 100% precision and recall by evaluating redundancy filtering only on a stream of documents marked relevant by NIST assessors. In some tests we also evaluate the effectiveness of redundancy-scoring algorithms, and factor out the effect of the redundancy threshold algorithm, by reporting average Precision and Recall figures *for redundant documents.* Precision and recall are well-known metrics in IR community. We adapt them to the redundancy detection task as shown below.

$$Redundancy - Precision = \frac{R^-}{R^- + N^-} \quad (11)$$

$$Redundancy - Recall = \frac{R^-}{R^- + R^+} \quad (12)$$

$$Redundancy - Mistake = \frac{R^+ + N^-}{R^+ + N^- + R^- + N^+} \quad (13)$$

R^-, R^+, N^-, N^+ correspond to the number of documents

Measure	Recall	Precision	Mistake
Set Distance	0.52	0.44	43.5%
Cosine Distance	0.62	0.63	28.1%
LM: Shrinkage	0.80	0.45	44.3%
LM: Dirichlet Prior	0.76	0.47	42.4%
LM: Mixture Model	0.56	0.67	27.4%

Table 1: Average performance of different redundancy measures with a simple thresholding algorithm, measured on 33 topics with the AP News & Wall Street Journal dataset. Both *absolutely redundant* and *somewhat redundant* documents are treated as *redundant*.

that fall into the following categories:

	Redundant	Non-Redundant
Delivered	R^+	N^+
Not Delivered	R^-	N^-

For simplicity, we will use *Precision* and *Recall* to refer to *Redundancy-Precision* and *Redundancy-Recall* in the rest of this paper.

7. EXPERIMENTAL RESULTS

The five redundancy measures described in Section 4 were compared on the two datasets described in Sections 6.1 and 6.2. A redundancy score was calculated for each relevant document d_t, based on the relevant documents d_i that preceded it in the document stream. The results are shown in Figures 3, 4 and 5 in the form of average Recall-Precision graphs over the set of redundant documents.

On both datasets the Set Difference measure is the least accurate. Representing a document as a set of Boolean word features, even with smoothing to add or delete additional words, was very ineffective.

The traditional cosine-similarity metric (a geometric distance measure) was very effective. This result was a small surprise, because cosine similarity is less well justified theoretically than the language modelling approaches. The cosine similarity metric is also symmetric; we expected asymmetric measures to be a better model of this task. However, cosine similarity has been demonstrated many times and over many tasks to be a robust similarity metric. Our results add redundancy detection to the long list of tasks for which it is effective.

The results for the three Language Modelling algorithms confirm prior research showing the importance of selecting a good smoothing algorithm. The mixture model approach was consistently more accurate than the other two smoothing algorithms on both corpora. It was also about as effective as the cosine similarity measure on the TREC Interactive Track dataset. This approach to mixing information from corpus, topic, and a document language models provides a new point of view about how to model documents, and it does deliver improved effectiveness compared to other language modelling approaches. This result is not completely surprising, because the algorithm explicitly models *what's new* in a document. However, these results suggest that it is not as robust as the cosine similarity measure.

We also implemented a simple threshold-setting algorithm (Section 5). The threshold-setting algorithm is simple and weak, in part because we did not set an optimization goal specifying the relative rewards and penalties for delivering novel and redundant documents. However, even a simple algorithm can be used to analyze the different redundancy measures. In particular, it provides a more accurate indication of what a user might see in an operational environment.

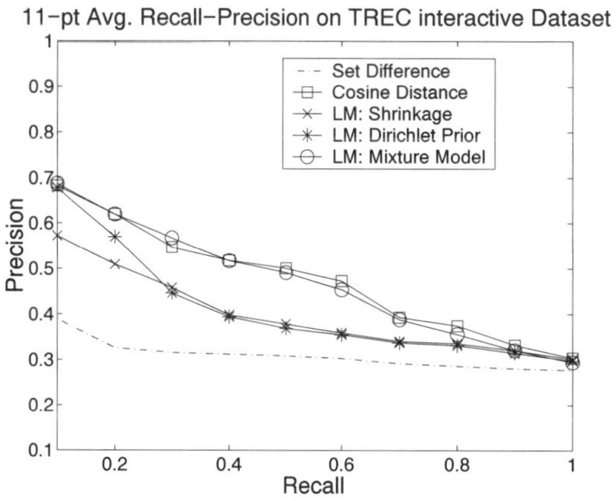

Figure 5: Comparing redundancy measure on TREC Interactive Track data. A document about aspect(s) already covered by previously delivered documents is considered redundant.

Measure	Recall	Precision	Mistake
Set Distance	0.36	0.29	28.1%
Cosine Distance	0.48	0.33	18.7%
LM: Shrinkage	0.375	0.45	21%
LM: Dirichlet Prior	0.375	0.45	21%
LM: Mixture Model	0.46	0.40	16.7%

Table 2: Average performance of different redundancy measures with a simple thresholding algorithm, measured on 33 topics with the AP News & Wall Street Journal dataset. Only *absolutely redundant* documents are treated as *redundant*.

Tables 1, 2, and 3 summarize the effectiveness of the five redundancy measures when used with the simple redundancy threshold algorithm. Results are reported for both datasets. (The metrics are described in Section 6.3).

If we evaluate the redundancy measures by the percentage of mistakes they make, the Cosine Similarity and Mixture Model redundancy measures are much better than the rest. These two measures yields a reasonably low percentage of mistakes when a strict definition of redundancy is used (Table 2), but a less satisfying percentage when *somewhat redundant* documents are treated as redundant (Table 1). This result implies that our simple redundancy threshold algorithm models the user by treating *somewhat redundant* as novel. We know that a good threshold setting algorithm is important to system accuracy, and we hypothesize that threshold setting should depends on each user. Table 2 shows that reasonably good accuracy is possible when the thresholding algorithm is well-matched to the task.

8. CONCLUSION

The research reported here is a first step towards adaptive information filtering systems that learn to identify documents that are novel and redundant in addition to relevant and nonrelevant. It defines a task, an evaluation methodol-

Measure	Recall	Precision	Mistake
Set Distance	0.43	0.28	46.8%
Cosine Distance	0.45	0.44	34.5%
LM: Shrinkage	0.79	0.33	53.3%
LM: Dirichlet Prior	0.73	0.34	49.0%
LM: Mixture Model	0.18	0.51	28.4%

Table 3: Average performance of different redundancy measures with a simple thresholding algorithm, measured on 20 topics with the TREC Interactive dataset.

ogy, and a set of novelty/redundancy measures. A reusable corpus was created from generally available documents, a set of adjudicated redundancy judgements was created, and an existing corpus was adapted to our task.

The experimental results demonstrate that it is possible to identify redundant documents with reasonable accuracy. They also demonstrate the importance of a suitable redundancy-threshold algorithm, analogous to the relevance-threshold algorithm found in many information filtering systems. Our results also suggest that the algorithm itself should depend on the user model of redundancy. The extremely small amount of training data (less than what is available for relevance-based adaptive filtering) makes it a challenging problem.

We proposed five measures for assessing the redundance of a new document with respect to a previously seen stream of documents. Our experimental results demonstrate that the well-known cosine similarity metric is effective on this new task. They also demonstrate that a new metric based on a mixture of language models can be as effective as the cosine similarity metric in some cases.

We believe that the metric based on a mixture of language models is an important contribution, whether or not it was the most effective algorithm for this task. We believe that viewing documents as a mix of information covered by corpus, topic, and "new information" models is an appropriate model of an information filtering task. The results reported here are a first attempt to apply this approach to a realistic task; we expect to see other attempts in the future.

This research is only a first attempt at redundancy/novelty detection in an adaptive filtering environment, so there are many open problems for future research. Our research on profile-specific "anytime" updating of redundancy measures just scratches the surface. Although cosine similarity worked well in our experiments, we believe that the underlying redundancy relationship is asymmetric, and that asymmetric measures will eventually be more accurate. It is also likely that other features, such as timestamp, document source, phrases, and proper names will be important sources of evidence for novelty decisions.

Our research measured redundancy based on document-document pairs, which is easy to assess and easy to model, but the underlying task is probably better modelled by comparing clusters of delivered documents to the new document. The best choice may be problem-specific, e.g., depending upon corpus or profile characteristics.

9. ACKNOWLEDGMENTS

We thank John Lafferty, Chengxiang Zhai, Yiming Yang, Chun Jin, and Wei Xu for their very helpful discussions and recommendations. This material is based on work supported by Air Force Research Laboratory contract F30602-98-C-0110. Any opinions, findings, conclusions or recommendations expressed in this paper are the authors', and do not necessarily reflect those of the sponsors.

10. REFERENCES

[1] J. Allan, J. Carbonell, G. Doddington, J. Yamron, and Y. Yang. Topic detection and tracking pilot study. In *Topic Detection and Tracking Workshop Report*. 2001.

[2] J. Allan, V. Lavrenko, and H. Jin. First story detetion in TDT is hard. In *Proc. of the 9th International Conference on Information and Knowledge Management*, 2000.

[3] J. Allan, R. Papka, and V. Lavrenko. On-line new event detection and tracking. In *Proc. of 21st Annual International ACM SIGIR Conference on Research and Development in Information Retrieval*, 1998.

[4] J. Carbonell, Y. Yang, R. Brown, C. Jin, and J. Zhang. CMU TDT report 13-14 Nov 2001. In *Topic Detection and Tracking Workshop Report*. 2001.

[5] M. Franz, A. Ittycheriah, J. S. McCarley, and T. Ward. First story detection: Combining similarity and novelty based approaches. In *Topic Detection and Tracking Workshop Report*, 2001.

[6] W. P. Jones and G. W. Furnas. Pictures of relevance. *Journal of the American Society for Information Science*, 1987.

[7] W. Kraaij, R. Pohlmann, and D. Hiemstra. Twenty-one at TREC-8: using language technology for information retrieval. In *Proceedings of the Eighth Text REtrieval Conference (TREC-8)*, 1999.

[8] L. Lee. Measures of distributional similarity. In *Proceedings of the 37th ACL*, 1999.

[9] A. McCallum, R. Rosenfeld, T. Mitchell, and A. Y. Ng. Improving text classification by shrinkage in a hierarchy of classes. In *Proceedings of The Eighteenth International Conference on Machine Learning*, 1998.

[10] D. R. H. Miller, T. Leek, and R. Schwartz. A hidden markov model information retrieval system. In *Proceedings of the 22th Annual International ACM SIGIR Conferenc eon Research and Development in Information Retrieval*, pages 214–221, 2001.

[11] S. Robertson. Threshold setting in adaptive filtering. *Journal of Documentation*, 2000.

[12] S. Robertson and D. Hull. The TREC-9 Filtering track report. In *The Ninth Text REtrieval Conference (TREC-9)*, 2001.

[13] M. Spitters and W. Kraaij. TNO at TDT2001: Language model-based topic detection. In *Topic Detection and Tracking Workshop Report*. 2001.

[14] N. Stokes and J. Carthy. Combining semantic and syntactic document classifiers to improve first story detection. In *Proceedings of the 24th Annual International ACM SIGIR Conferenc eon Research and Development in Information Retrieval*, 2001.

[15] J. Yamron, S. Knecht, and P. van Mulbregt. Dragon's tracking and detection systems for the TDT2000 evaluation. In *Proceedings of the Broadcast News Transcription and Understanding Workshop*, 1998.

[16] C. Zhai and J. Lafferty. Model-based feedback in the language modeling approach to information retrieval. In *Proceedings of Tenth International Conference on Information and Knowledge Management*, 2001.

[17] C. Zhai and J. Lafferty. A study of smoothing methods for language models applied to ad hoc information retrieval. In *Proc. of the 24th Annual Int'l ACM SIGIR Conferenc eon Research and Development in Information Retrieval*, pages 334–342, 2001.

[18] Y. Zhang and J. Callan. Maximum likelihood estimation for filteirng thresholds. In *Proc. of the 24th Annual Int'l ACM SIGIR Conferenc eon Research and Development in Information Retrieval*, 2001.

Improving Realism of Topic Tracking Evaluation

Anton Leuski and James Allan
Center for Intelligent Information Retrieval
Department of Computer Science
University of Massachusetts
Amherst, MA 01003
{leuski,allan}@cs.umass.edu

ABSTRACT

Topic tracking and information filtering are models of interactive tasks, but their evaluations are generally done in a way that does not reflect likely usage. The models either force frequent judgments or disallow any at all, assume the user is always available to make a judgment, and do not allow for user fatigue. In this study we extend the evaluation framework for topic tracking to incorporate those more realistic issues. We demonstrate that tracking can be done in a realistic interactive setting with minimal impact on tracking cost and with substantial reduction in required interaction.

Categories and Subject Descriptors

H.3.3 [**Information storage and Retrieval**]: Information Search and Retrieval—*information filtering, relevance feedback*

Keywords

Filtering, interactive tracking, topic detection and tracking

1. INTRODUCTION

The tasks of information filtering and topic tracking require monitoring a continuous stream of information to select only those items that are of interest to the user. There is an underlying message in discussion of the tasks that as they mature in capability, they can be deployed in an operational system with little change. However, in the laboratory evaluations that are used to measure system quality, both tasks make necessary simplifying assumptions that move them away from a realistic model of users.

Information filtering, as evaluated in the TREC workshops, is the task of monitoring a stream of documents to find those that are on a particular topic of interest (e.g., documents about the effects of osteoporosis). The system is given a brief description of the topic (that has ranged in size from several sentences to a few words) and then proceeds to look for stories on that topic. The system is permitted to adapt its representation of the topic by asking an oracle whether or not a particular document is relevant (it can, of course, adapt without asking the oracle, too). The oracle simulates a user who would judge whether the document is relevant.

Topic tracking, part of the Topic Detection and Tracking evaluation program [2], is similar in that it requires a system to monitor a stream of news stories for additional stories on the same topic. Here, all stories are news articles.[1] A topic is derived out of the events that are discussed in news, and generally incorporates all related events that grow out of some seminal happening (e.g., an earthquake might trigger a topic which would include reporting on the earthquake, rescue efforts, and so on).[2] For the tracking task, a system is presented with a small number of stories (one to four) that are known to be on the same topic. At that point, active "user" interaction ends. The system is required to determine the topic from those sample stories and then to select stories from the rest of the stream without user interaction. If the system finds a story that might be a match, it cannot ask the user for confirmation—i.e., it must make a *yes* or *no* decision about every story on its own.

In that way, TDT's tracking evaluation is less user-oriented than TREC's filtering evaluation. Filtering simulates interacting with the user to supervise the process, whereas tracking operates as if the user were not there. In this study, we are interested in bringing simulated user interaction from filtering to tracking, and then moving beyond that to make the interaction even more realistic, giving a better sense of the effectiveness of these technologies in a real world setting. We will model users interacting with the system during the tracking process itself to explore what is plausible and what is effective in that area. There are obviously other ways a user could be involved (e.g., highlighting specific relevant text, adding outside news stories for clarification, editing the internal representation of a topic, etc.). We will defer exploration of those interactions for later research.

In the next section we outline some related work in the area of interactive tracking. In Section 3 we describe a model of our interactive tracking system and show how TREC fil-

[1]TREC filtering evaluations have generally used news articles, too, though there is not a strong emphasis on that point.

[2]Note the difference between a tracking topic and a filtering topic. The latter is subject-based whereas the former is event-based. All event-based topics are also subject-based, but the reverse is not true. It would be reasonable to filter for stories about the effects of osteoporosis, but there is no corresponding event.

SIGIR'02, August 11-15, 2002, Tampere, Finland.

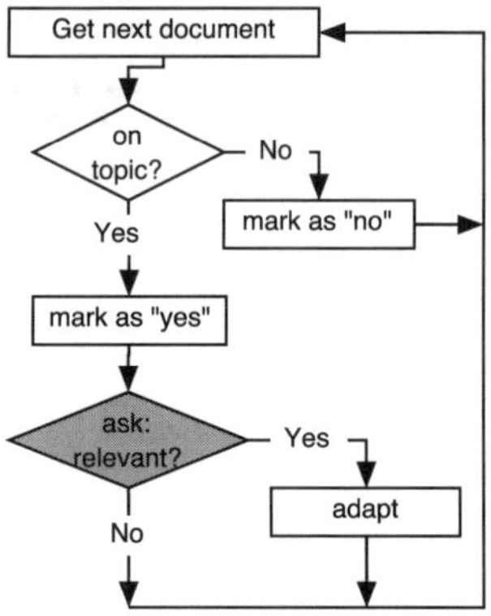

Figure 1: Shows the flow of control in TREC filtering task.

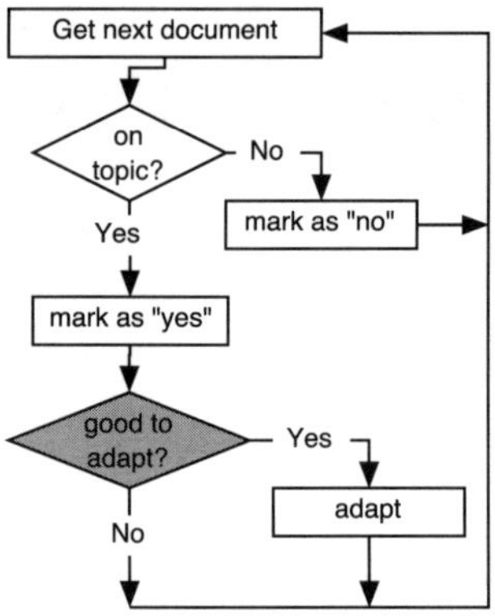

Figure 2: Shows the flow of control in TDT tracking task.

tering and TDT tracking fit into that model. We also present several more realistic variations of the task. Section 4 describes how we adjust the TDT tracking evaluation to incorporate interaction and Section 5 describes our experimental setup, including the system and evaluation corpora used. We present our results in Section 6, showing that TREC-style filtering interaction requires large numbers of user judgments and that nearly equivalent effectiveness can be realized with a more realistic usage model and substantially less user interaction. We conclude in Section 7 and describe the direction we are taking this work.

2. RELATED WORK

This work builds on the sequence of Topic Detection and Tracking evaluations that have run from 1998 through 2001 [2, 16]. The baseline system that we are using was adapted from the University of Massachusetts' TDT 2000 tracking system [3], a system that performed well in the evaluation.

This work is also strongly related to the TREC evaluations of information filtering [13]. We are considering interactive tracking, but there is no relationship between this work and the TREC interactive track [6] that focuses on user studies and the process of information retrieval.

One of the goals of the work discussed below is to reduce the amount of interaction that a user is required to perform, but to keep the effectiveness of the system unchanged. This is similar in spirit to earlier results that showed that TREC routing[3] results could be remain similar even if substantially fewer documents were judged [1]. Other approaches to reducing the user's workload include presenting summaries of single documents [11] or multiple documents [12]. Our focus is on extending the classic document at-a-time approach used in tracking and filtering, so we do not consider here how summarization would perform in these condition.

The "oracle" approach to evaluation, where a user's judgment is made by looking at a truth file, is common in information retrieval research. The adaptive tracking task uses such a technique [13] as has some work evaluating interaction strategies in the context of classic ranked retrieval [8, 9].

[3]TREC's routing task was a batch-oriented approximation of what eventually became filtering. It permitted massive amounts of relevance information for query adaption.

3. MODELING INTERACTIVE TRACKING

Figures 1 and 2 summarize the control flow in both TREC filtering and TDT tracking systems. Each system begins by extracting the next document from the stream of incoming documents. Then it decides whether the document is on-topic. The documents deemed off-topic are labeled as non-relevant and the system returns to the stream for the next document. If the document passes the test, it is marked as relevant and the system has to decide whether the document is good enough to adapt the topic representation. This last test is the main difference between the TREC filtering and TDT tracking approaches. The corresponding test block is highlighted in gray on both figures. A TREC filtering system asks the oracle (or the user in the real settings) to confirm that the document is relevant and adapts the topic representation upon receiving the confirmation. A TDT system makes its decision without any external input. A TREC system could also decide to adapt without user confirmation, but the evaluation model of TREC filtering does not encourage that: both cases are treated the same. Note that in this paper we consider only positive judgments while adapting the topic representation. A negative judgment made by either the user or the system may also be used to adapt the topic representation, however we defer this question for future study.

Both approaches make two unrealistic assumptions about the user's behavior. First, a traditional system either forces the user to judge *every* document it labels relevant as in TREC filtering or it avoids any dialog with the user as in TDT tracking. We are interested in an intermediate scenario where the system may request the user's judgments for some of the returned documents but it does not ask her to judge all of them. In her turn, the user may decide to ignore and not judge some of the documents requested by the system. For example, consider a situation when the system constantly keeps requesting judgments for documents and at some point in time the user grows tired and loses interest in the judging task. We expand the control flow for filtering and tracking to represent our model of interactive tracking (or filtering) and show it in Figure 3. The extended decision block just discussed is in gray. Here the system decides whether to involve the user and checks if the user is interested in making the judgment. If both conditions are satisfied it asks the user for the relevance judgment, otherwise it proceeds to decide

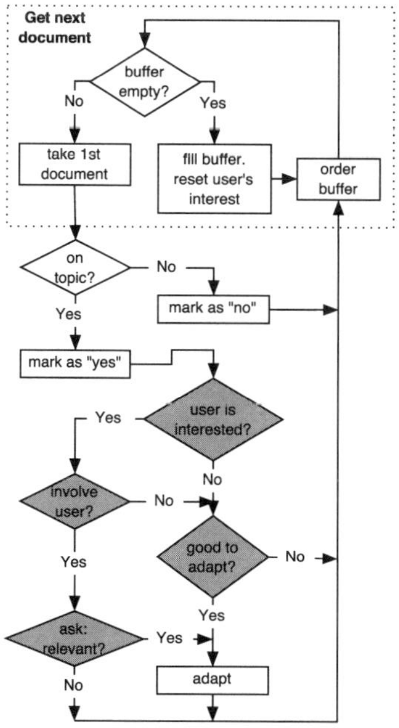

Figure 3: Shows the flow of control in the Interactive Tracking task.

whether the document can be used for adapting the topic representation on its own.

The second assumption, most apparent in the TREC filtering task, has two parts: (1) the system has to label each document before it can look at any other documents that follow and (2) the user is readily available at any time to make the judgments. An alternative to having the user at hand would be to suspend processing until she returns, but the delay may be inappropriate in many settings.

In contrast to this assumption, we consider a situation where the user interacts with the system at discrete time intervals. The system may defer its decisions until the next user's session. This can be viewed as the system collecting the incoming documents into an intermediate session buffer. At the beginning of each session the system lists the documents in the buffer for the user. If we can assume by analogy with the ranked list that the user will start at the top of the list and follow it down, examining one document after another, then the order of the documents in the session buffer is very important. For example, the system may elect to place the documents that it requests to be judged at the top of the list. After it receives the user's feedback it adapts the topic representation and possibly re-orders the rest of the list. Figure 3 shows this extended control block surrounded by a dotted line.

The complete flow of control in this extended tracking scenario is shown on Figure 3. We call this model the *Interactive Tracking* task. In the following sections we discuss how we evaluate an Interactive Tracking system.

4. EVALUATING INTERACTIVE TRACKING

In the TDT evaluation program [5] tracking is viewed as a detection task and its performance is characterized in terms of the probability of miss and false alarm errors. These error probabilities are then combined into a single cost, K, by assigning costs to miss and false alarm errors:

$$K = K_{miss} \cdot P_{miss} \cdot P_{target} + K_{fa} \cdot P_{fa} \cdot (1 - P_{target})$$

where K_{miss} and K_{fa} are the costs of a miss and false alarm, respectively, P_{miss} is the conditional probability of a miss or the proportion of relevant documents that were labeled as non-relevant by the system, P_{fa} is the conditional probability of a false alarm or the proportion of the non-relevant documents that were labeled as relevant by the system, and P_{target} is the *a priori* target probability. In this paper we compute the normalized version of the cost measure $Cost = K/K_{min}$, where

$$K_{min} = min(K_{miss} \cdot P_{target}, K_{fa} \cdot (1 - P_{target}))$$

The values for normalized costs of a miss ($C_{miss} = K_{miss} \cdot \frac{P_{target}}{K_{min}}$) and false alarm ($C_{fa} = K_{fa} \cdot \frac{(1-P_{target})}{K_{min}}$) are set to 1 and 4.9 as per conditions of the TDT tracking experiments [5] ($K_{miss} = 1$, $K_{fa} = 10$, and $P_{target} = 0.02$).

This evaluation accounts for the simple model of the user-system interaction assumed in the TDT tracking task: the user views all documents labeled relevant by the system and she does so in the order the documents were received. This interaction is *passive* as the system receives no feedback from the user.

In TREC filtering the interaction is *active* – the user is required to judge all documents returned by the system and the system is not expected to proceed without receiving the feedback, since the judgment is needed to adapt the query.

In Interactive Tracking we want to balance the system's tracking errors against the active interaction with the user. Here we differentiate among the notions of documents *presented*, *examined*, and *judged*. The documents *presented* to the user are the document labeled as relevant by the tracking system. We also consider the documents the user reads through or the *examined* documents and the *judged* documents – the documents that user labeled as relevant or non-relevant for the system. In TREC filtering these are all the same document sets. In TDT tracking it is assumed that the user will read all documents returned by the system, so the set of presented documents is the same as the set of examined documents, while the set of judged documents is empty. The Interactive Tracking model does not expect the user to read every document, so the set of examined documents might be smaller than the set of presented ones. For example, consider a situation when the user is reading the documents in the session buffer and sees too much non-relevant material. The user grows irritated and decides to stop reading – "There is nothing interesting in the news today!". We measure the user's involvement in the tracking process, or the user's *activity*, as the proportion of documents that were judged by the user among all documents examined by the user. We want to minimize the user's activity without a significant drop in the tracking cost:

$$Activity = \frac{\#\ of\ judged}{\#\ of\ examined}$$

An Interactive Tracking system buffers the incoming documents and may defer its labeling decisions until the next user's session. When the user begins the session, the system orders the documents in the buffer and presents them to the user. We assume that the user's goal is to locate the relevant material in the news stream as quickly as possible. To achieve this goal the user would prefer to have the relevant documents at the top of the list. At the same time we want to get the most improvement from our interaction with the user. If we want to request the user's feedback about some documents, we want to do it as early as possible and therefore we want to place these documents close to the top of the list. To measure the quality of the document ordering we compute the average precision of the document buffer ranked in the order it is examined.

To summarize, our goal is to keep the TDT cost value as low as possible while simultaneously reducing the measure of activity. We will in Section 6 that this is possible.

5. EXPERIMENTAL SETUP

For our study we created an Interactive Tracking system and conducted a number of simulation experiments. We simulated a user interacting with the tracking system with the help of the topic and relevance judgment information available for the TDT evaluation. In this section we describe our tracking system and the experimental data set.

5.1 System design

Our Interactive Tracking system uses the vector-space approach where each document is represented by a vector of term weights V. The weight of the ith term in the vocabulary, v_i is computed using the Inquery weighting formula, which uses Okapi's *tf* score [14] and Inquery's normalized *idf* score:

$$v_i = \frac{tf}{tf + 0.5 + 1.5\frac{doclen}{avgdoclen}} \cdot \frac{\log(\frac{colsize+0.5}{docf})}{\log(colsize+1)}$$

where *tf* is the number of times the term occurs in the document, *docf* is the number of documents the term occurs in, *doclen* is the number of terms in the document, *avgdoclen* is the average number of terms per document in the collection, and *colsize* is the number of documents in the collection. The document frequency and the collection statistics were determined from a training data set. The similarity between a pair of documents is measured by the cosine of the angle between the corresponding vectors [15].

The topic being tracked by the system is represented as a cluster of documents. At the beginning of the tracking process the cluster consists of the one single training document provided by the TDT experimental conditions (this is the condition called "$N_t = 1$"). While the system examines the incoming documents and receives judgments, it may adapt the topic representation by extending the cluster with new documents. The similarity between the cluster and an incoming document is the average similarity between the incoming document and every document in the cluster. This approach is based on the system used by the University of Massachusetts at Amherst at the latest TDT workshop [3].

We have conducted an extensive study comparing different clustering algorithms for building the topic representation. Specifically, we compared the centroid, complete-link, group average, single-link, weighted centroid, and Ward methods [7]. We considered an "ideal" tracking system to be one that discriminates between relevant and non-relevant documents using a fixed threshold on the similarity between the document and the topic representation. If a document-topic similarity is above that threshold the system labels the document as on-topic, otherwise it labels the document as off-topic. The topic representation was updated using only relevant documents in the incoming stream even if they were labeled as off-topic. The system built around the group average algorithm showed the smallest tracking cost numbers.

For each document the Interactive Tracking system selects one of the following four actions: (1) it silently labels the document as non-relevant, (2) it marks it as relevant, (3) it marks it as relevant and uses the document to adapt the topic representation, and (4) it questions the user to judge the document and if the document is relevant, the system adapts the topic representation. Note that in the last case the document is labeled as relevant for evaluation purposes. In the discussion that follows we use n, y, $y+$, and q to designate these actions, respectively.

The exact choice of the action is a function of the document-topic similarity $a(x)$. The goal of the system is to minimize the expected cost of all actions:

$$\begin{aligned} E[Cost] &= \sum_i (C_{a_i,R}P(a_i|R) + C_{a_i,N}P(a_i|N)) \\ &= \sum_i \sum_{x \in A_i} (C_{a_i,R}P(x|R) + C_{a_i,N}P(x|N)) \\ &= \sum_x (C_{a(x),R}P(x|R) + C_{a(x),N}P(x|N)) \end{aligned}$$

where $C_{a_i,R}$ and $C_{a_i,N}$ are the costs of taking the ith action a_i when the corresponding document is relevant and non-relevant, respectively, $P(a_i|R)$ and $P(a_i|N)$ are the probabilities of taking the action a_i conditioned on the document's relevance, x is the document-topic similarity as observed during the tracking process, $A_i = \{x|a_i = a(x)\}$ is the set of values for x for which we take the action a_i, and $P(x|R)$ and $P(x|N)$ are the probabilities of observing x conditioned on the document's relevance.

Note that for the case of two actions – labeling the documents as either relevant or non-relevant – the expected cost is the TDT tracking cost [5]:

$$\begin{aligned} E[Cost] &= C_{y,R}P(y|R) + C_{y,N}P(y|N) \\ &\quad + C_{n,R}P(n|R) + C_{n,N}P(n|N) \\ &= C_{fa}P(y|N) + C_{miss}P(n|R) \end{aligned}$$

where $C_{y,R} = C_{n,N} = 0$, $C_{y,N} = C_{fa}$, and $C_{n,R} = C_{miss}$.

Assuming that all costs $C_{a,r}$ are non-negative, to minimize the expected cost we want to minimize the individual components of the $E[Cost]$. This way for each observed document-topic similarity we select action a_{best} such that

$$a_{best} = \arg\min_a C_{a,R}P(x|R) + C_{a,N}P(x|N)$$

The costs $C_{a,r}$ serve as parameters for our system and they are defined in Table 1. Here C_1 is the cost of asking the user about a relevant document, C_2 is the cost of adapting the topic representation with a non-relevant document, C_3 is the cost of asking the user about a non-relevant document, and C_4 is the cost of not adapting the topic representation with a relevant document.

The values for the cost parameters C_i, $i = 1 \ldots 4$ were selected by optimizing the tracking system on a training data set.

The distributions for the conditional probabilities $P(x|R)$ and $P(x|N)$ are represented as parametric Beta distribu-

Table 1: Tracking costs $C_{a,r}$.

relevance	action			
	n	y	$y+$	q
R	$C_{miss} + C_4$	C_4	0	C_1
N	0	C_{fa}	$C_{fa} + C_2$	$C_{fa} + C_3$

tions with probability functions $p(x|\alpha_R, \beta_R)$ and $p(x|\alpha_N, \beta_N)$ defined as

$$p(x|\alpha, \beta) = \frac{\Gamma(\alpha + \beta)}{\Gamma(\alpha)\Gamma(\beta)} x^{\alpha-1}(1-x)^{\beta-1}$$

The corresponding parameters α_R, β_R, α_N, and β_N were determined by running the "ideal" tracking system on a training data set.

5.2 Experimental data sets

We used two different corpora for our experiments. The corpora were provided by Linguistic Data Consortium (LDC) for TDT experiments [4]. They contain stories from a variety of news sources including AP, CNN, New York Times, Voice of America, Xinhua, and Zaobao newswire. Our first corpus consists of manually transcribed English news stories from the TDT2 LDC corpus (January-June 1998). LDC also provides definitions and relevance judgments for 100 topics on that corpus. Out of those 100 topics we selected 84 topics that had more then one relevant document on the English part of the corpus. In this paper we call this data set TDT2.

The second corpus consisted of manually transcribed English and Mandarin news stories from the TDT3 LDC corpus (October-December 1998)[4]. There are two sets of 60 topics each defined on that corpus by LDC used in TDT'00 and TDT'01 evaluations [4]. In this paper we refer to this corpus and the corresponding topic sets as TDT3/1 and TDT3/2.

We report two sets of results. The first set was obtained on TDT3/1 by the tracking system trained on TDT2. The second set of numbers was produced on TDT3/2 by the system trained on TDT3/1. The latter is dangerously close to testing on the training data (the topics are different) but mirrors the official TDT'01 evaluation settings [16].

6. RESULTS

In this section we consider four different experimental questions. First we study four tracking systems that differ in the control flow in their interaction model. Then we investigate the effects of buffering and ordering of the document in the buffer on the overall system performance. Finally, we compare different users' strategies for interacting with the system.

6.1 Document at a time

The first experimental question in this paper is to compare four different tracking systems that process one document at a time and involve different amount of user interaction and adapting. The first system, *simple tracking* is the traditional TDT tracking system that discriminates stories into relevant and non-relevant categories and does not do any adapting of the topic representation (only actions n and y are allowed). The second approach, *tracking with adapting*, extends that system by allowing adaptation of the topic representation without involving the user (actions n, y, and $y+$ are allowed). The *filtering* system asks the user about every document it marks as relevant and adapts the topic representation if the user confirms the system's decision (only actions n and q are allowed). The *Interactive Tracking* system decides when to involve the user in the tracking process and when to adapt the topic on its own (i.e., it allows all four actions).

Table 2 shows the performance of these systems on both TDT3/1 and TDT3/2. The table shows the TDT tracking cost, conditional probabilities of a miss and false alarm, the number of documents that were labeled as non-relevant and are in fact non-relevant ("#n&non"), the number of documents labeled as non-relevant but are in truth relevant ("#n&rel"), and the same statistics for documents that the system marked as relevant but did not question the user about ("$yy+$") and the documents the system did question the user about ("q"). All the numbers shown are averaged across all topics in the corresponding data set.

The Interactive Tracking system ("n, y, q, $y+$") shows 48.5% and 45.0% improvement in the tracking cost over the simple tracking system ("n, y") on TDT3/1 and TDT3/2 respectively. It requires 25.9% and 25.6% fewer feedback requests to the user than the most successful filtering system ("n, q") in exchange for a small increase in the tracking cost: 6.9% and 3.4% on TDT3/1 and TDT3/2 respectively.

6.2 Ordering of documents

In the second experimental question we consider a scenario when the user interacts with the system at discrete time intervals. Specifically, she examines the documents twice a day at 9 AM and 4 PM each weekday. We simulated this setup by using the time stamps assigned to the documents in the corpus. The system buffers the documents that arrived between the sessions and opens the session by ordering and listing out the buffer. The documents labeled as non relevant are excluded from the list (even if they are in truth relevant, since the system does not know that). It is assumed that the user will start at the top of the list and follow it down. We compare three different sorting criteria: the action label, document time, and document-topic similarity or the score assigned by the system.

There are three possible orderings based on the action: (1) the system may first request the user's feedback for some of the documents, then it lists the rest of the documents labeled relevant ("q, $y+$, y"); (2) the system first lists all the documents it does not require the feedback on and then questions the user about the rest ("y+, y, q"); and (3) the system starts by listing documents that it believes to be relevant and uses for adapting without asking for the user's judgment, then presents the documents that the system needs the user's feedback, followed by the rest of the documents ("$y+$, q, y"). Inside each group the documents are sorted either by time (in increasing order) or by score, i.e., in decreasing order of document-topic similarity. These document orderings are dynamic – user feedback may affect the topic adaptation, which in turn will adjust the document scores, potentially relabeling the documents. Sampling by uncertainty [10] is another ordering approach that might work but we have not yet investigated that method.

Table 3 shows the performance of the Interactive Tracking system for these combinations of orderings. Addition-

[4]The official evaluation corpus for TDT'01 prepends this corpus with news stories from the July-September period

Table 2: Average performance of four tracking systems that differ in the amount of user involvement and topic adaption. All systems process one document at a time.

System	Data set	Actions	Cost	P_{miss}	P_{fa}	#n& non	#n& rel	#yy+& non	#yy+& rel	#q& non	#q& rel
simple tracking	TDT3/1	n, y	0.1948	10.16	1.90	34312.3	18.2	665.1	95.7	0.0	0.0
track. w/ adapting		n, y, $y+$	0.1728	8.63	1.76	34372.5	13.7	605.0	100.2	0.0	0.0
filtering		n, q	0.0935	2.08	1.48	34476.6	3.8	0.0	0.0	500.8	110.1
interactive track.		n, y, q, $y+$	0.1000	2.55	1.52	34460.3	4.1	144.5	30.0	372.7	79.8
simple tracking	TDT3/2	n, y	0.1475	10.65	0.84	31911.3	4.8	253.9	24.1	0.0	0.0
track. w/ adapting		n, y, $y+$	0.1269	8.57	0.84	31898.3	3.9	266.9	25.0	0.0	0.0
filtering		n, q	0.0785	3.82	0.82	31912.0	1.3	0.0	0.0	253.3	27.6
interactive track.		n, y, q, $y+$	0.0812	3.97	0.85	31900.1	1.3	75.1	8.5	190.0	19.1

ally, the first two rows present the system performance for orderings that ignore the action assignments and sort the documents based on time or score only. Note that the former is equivalent to presenting the documents in the order they arrive into the system (i.e., the results for the Interactive Tracking system in Table 2).

We observe a small variation in the tracking cost due to the document ordering. The earlier the system requests the user feedback, the smaller the cost. The variations in the cost are small as all system requests are answered in any scenario. The user's activity is also constant. There are large differences in the buffer precision depending on the sorting order. It is not surprising that ordering the documents by their similarity to the topic increases the precision. However, some improvement in the tracking cost comes at the expense of the precision: the document ordering scenario that has the smallest cost – documents ordered by action with the document the system requests user's judgments going first and then by score ("q, $y+$, y; score") – shows a significant drop in precision (16.0% and 15.4% on TDT3/1 and TDT3/2 respectively) when compared to the second best scenario where the documents are ordered by score.

6.3 Buffering schedule

The third experimental question is how the frequency of the user-system interaction affects the Interactive Tracking performance. We considered four different schedules for the interaction: the user examines the documents (1) twice every weekday at 9 AM and 4 PM; (2) once every weekday at 9 AM; (3) once every Monday, Wednesday, and Friday at 9 AM; and (4) once every Monday at 9 AM. Countless other schedules are possible, but we will show that it does not matter much. The documents are ordered using the best-cost ordering scenario – documents ordered by action with the document the system requests user's judgments going first and then by score. It is assumed that the user answers all system requests for relevance judgments.

Table 4 shows that the buffering schedule has no effect on the tracking cost. The tracking cost does not degrade if the user is not present to judge the documents all the time as required in TREC filtering. However, it still requires the user to answer all system requests for relevance judgments – at the end of Section 6.4 we show that the buffering schedule has a more pronounced effect on the system's performance if this condition is not met. The user's activity goes up slightly as the number of interactions decreases – there is a higher proportion of the system requests for judgments among all documents examined by the user. The average precision of the document buffer decreases significantly. As the user works less often with the system, she has to wade through more non-relevant material before finding relevant information at each session.

Table 5: Performance of the Interactive Tracking system with the user limiting the number of her answers to the system's requests to a fixed number N. The results were obtained on TDT3/1 data set.

N	Cost	P_{miss}	P_{fa}	Activity (%)	Precision (%)	number examined
all	0.0992	2.48	1.52	72.29	88.28	625.9
10	0.1027	2.52	1.58	49.80	87.36	651.2
5	0.1107	3.14	1.62	34.88	86.70	666.0
3	0.1160	3.43	1.67	24.49	85.54	678.5
2	0.1168	3.66	1.64	18.22	84.49	665.8
1	0.1391	5.56	1.71	9.80	81.49	686.1

6.4 Interaction strategies

Our previous experiments assumed that the user is willing to examine all the documents labeled as relevant by the system and she is also willing to answer all system requests for relevance judgments. In this section we investigate the question of the user limiting her activity to more realistic scenarios. We consider a user that interacts with the system twice every weekday at 9 AM and 4 PM. The system lists the documents in the buffer in the order of decreasing document-topic similarity. Recall from Section 6.2 that such an ordering results in the best average precision with the second best tracking cost.

The first strategy we consider is when the user limits her active interaction with the system (or the number of judged documents is less than the number of examined documents). Table 5 shows how the Interactive Tracking system performance changes when the user restricts her answers on the system requests for relevance judgments to a fixed number per session. For example, from the fourth row in the table we see that if the user makes at most 3 relevance judgments per session, the tracking cost increases by 16.9%, while the activity goes down by 66.1%, the precision decreases by 3.1%, and the number of examined documents grows by 8.4%.

This strategy assumes that the user, while limiting her active interaction, still examines all documents labeled as relevant by the system (the number of examined documents equals to the number of presented documents). That requires the user to wade through the whole document set returned by the system, which may contain a lot of non-

Table 3: The effect of document ordering in the session buffer for the Interactive Tracking system.

Data set	order of documents		Cost	P_{miss}	P_{fa}	Activity (%)	Precision (%)
TDT3/1		time	0.1000	2.55	1.52	72.18	58.24
		score	0.0992	2.48	1.52	72.29	88.28
	q, $y+$, y	time	0.0995	2.55	1.51	72.76	58.23
		score	0.0986	2.47	1.51	72.97	74.14
	$y+$, y, q	time	0.1014	2.60	1.54	71.09	64.24
		score	0.1008	2.54	1.54	71.26	71.72
	$y+$, q, y	time	0.1000	2.56	1.52	72.12	73.36
		score	0.0992	2.48	1.52	72.29	88.28
TDT3/2		time	0.0812	3.97	0.85	71.43	57.61
		score	0.0811	3.97	0.84	71.45	80.13
	q, $y+$, y	time	0.0802	3.87	0.85	71.73	57.37
		score	0.0802	3.87	0.85	71.82	67.76
	$y+$, y, q	time	0.0813	3.97	0.85	70.63	64.52
		score	0.0815	3.99	0.85	70.71	68.75
	$y+$, q, y	time	0.0812	3.97	0.85	71.34	71.00
		score	0.0811	3.97	0.84	71.45	80.13

Table 4: The effect of the buffering schedule on the Interactive Tracking performance.

Data set	schedule	number of batches	Cost	P_{miss}	P_{fa}	Activity (%)	Precision (%)
TDT3/1	9am, 4pm, every weekday	90.4	0.0986	2.47	1.51	72.97	74.14
	9am, every weekday	45.6	0.0986	2.47	1.51	73.17	68.75
	9am, Mon, Wed, Fri	18.6	0.0980	2.39	1.51	73.66	63.05
	9am, Mon	9.9	0.0978	2.38	1.51	74.36	58.18
TDT3/2	9am, 4pm, every weekday	83.0	0.0802	3.87	0.85	71.82	67.76
	9am, every weekday	41.9	0.0802	3.87	0.85	72.04	63.13
	9am, Mon, Wed, Fri	17.1	0.0808	3.94	0.84	72.83	55.74
	9am, Mon	9.1	0.0810	3.96	0.84	72.71	52.31

relevant material. The process is long and very tedious. What if the user stops reading the stories and "gives up" on the system after seeing too many non-relevant documents? In this case the number of examined documents is lower than the number of presented documents. The documents presented but not examined are evaluated as marked non-relevant and may generate additional misses.

Table 6 shows the performance of the Interactive Tracking system if the user stops after seeing a fixed number of non-relevant documents in the session buffer and *declares* the rest of the document in the buffer to be non-relevant. We observe a small (3.6%) improvement in tracking cost if the user gives up after at most 30 non-relevant documents. There is no change in both the activity and precision.

As the last strategy in this paper we consider a scenario where the user gives up when she sees N times more non-relevant documents than the relevant ones. If there are no relevant documents at the top of the session buffer, she stops after 5 non-relevant documents. Table 7 shows 13.1% improvement in tracking cost and 31.2% reduction in the number of examined documents for $N = 20$ versus the case when the user examines all document labeled relevant by the system (Table 3, the second row).

Finally, we take a look on how the buffering schedule affects the effectiveness of the user's strategy. Table 8 shows the same data as presented in Table 7 with the only difference being that the user interacts with the system once a week instead of twice a day. We observe a significant increase in cost and precision. If the user is answering every request for relevance judgments posed by the system and she is not reading through all the material presented by the system, she must be willing to adjust her interaction strategy based on her viewing schedule.

Table 6: Performance of the Interactive Tracking system when the user stops examining the documents after seeing a fixed number N of non-relevant stories.

N	Cost	P_{miss}	P_{fa}	Activity (%)	Precision (%)	number examined
all	0.0992	2.48	1.52	72.29	88.28	625.9
50	0.0973	2.63	1.45	72.62	88.30	606.7
40	0.0959	2.67	1.41	72.90	88.30	594.4
30	0.0957	2.88	1.37	72.94	88.37	577.9
20	0.0968	3.42	1.28	72.98	88.66	546.7
10	0.1009	5.03	1.03	73.52	89.81	460.7
3	0.1653	14.05	0.51	72.84	93.05	270.3
1	0.3102	30.59	0.21	66.88	100.00	146.9

7. CONCLUSION AND FUTURE WORK

We have compared the TREC filtering and TDT tracking models and highlighted the simplifications that were made for evaluation purposes. We have extended the model of interaction that they use to a more realistic one—viz., by allowing user interaction at intervals, by reducing the amount of input required from the user, and by allowing for user fatigue.

We showed that we can decrease the amount of necessary

Table 7: Performance of the Interactive Tracking system when the user stops examining the retrieved documents after she sees N times more non-relevant documents than the relevant ones. The user interacts with the system twice every weekday.

N	Cost	P_{miss}	P_{fa}	Activity (%)	Precision (%)	number examined
1	0.1463	11.32	0.67	74.60	91.53	327.7
2	0.1099	7.20	0.77	74.71	90.91	364.9
3	0.0987	5.81	0.83	74.51	90.57	382.9
5	0.0912	4.80	0.88	74.31	90.80	401.5
10	0.0874	4.15	0.94	73.88	90.63	420.7
20	0.0863	3.90	0.97	73.89	90.42	430.7

Table 8: Performance of the Interactive Tracking system when the user stops examining the retrieved documents after she sees N times more non-relevant documents than the relevant ones. The user interacts with the system once a week.

N	Cost	P_{miss}	P_{fa}	Activity (%)	Precision (%)	number examined
1	0.2613	24.87	0.26	71.59	86.08	169.8
2	0.2233	20.56	0.36	71.37	84.96	210.9
3	0.1812	15.97	0.44	71.74	82.30	236.5
5	0.1492	12.31	0.53	72.36	81.49	270.8
10	0.1386	10.70	0.65	71.49	80.88	308.3
20	0.1380	10.28	0.72	71.76	80.42	332.4

judgments from a user with only a small cost penalty. We next showed that arriving documents can be "batched up" with no significant impact on cost, although the precision of the batch improves when the batches are smaller (i.e., less time elapses). We also demonstrated that the documents in a batch are best presented to the user in order by their similarity to the topic (by score). In that case, one can optimize for cost by putting documents needing judgments first, or for precision by putting first those that the system is positive are relevant (i.e., no judgment requested) . Finally, we demonstrated that if the user gives up (stops providing necessary judgments) early, the cost of the final output is noticeably higher. However, if the user examines enough of the batch to be confident that the remainder is non-relevant, the cost stays low.

In sum, there are reasonable interactive strategies that do not grossly harm the cost of tracking. An interactive tracking system should be built with these results in mind.

The tracking system discussed in this paper uses fixed models of score distributions for relevant and non-relevant documents. These distributions are determined during the training phase of the experiments. We are currently investigating approaches that would allow to adjust the distributions on topic-by-topic basis using the user feedback.

In this paper we assumed that the documents are presented to the user in the form of the ranked list. There are alternative document set presentations that were proved to be more effective in directing the user towards relevant document such as different form of clustering [8]. We are interested in examining those approaches in the context of the Interactive Tracking system.

Acknowledgments

This material is based on work supported in part by the CIIR and in part by SPAWARSYSCEN-SD grant number N66001-99-8912. Any opinions, findings and conclusions or recommendations expressed in this material are the authors' and do not necessarily reflect those of the sponsors.

8. REFERENCES

[1] J. Allan. Relevance feedback with too much data. In *Proceedings of ACM SIGIR*, pages 337–343, 1995.

[2] J. Allan, editor. *Topic Detection and Tracking: Event-based Information Organization.* Kluwer Academic Publishers, Boston, 2002.

[3] J. Allan, V. Lavrenko, D. Frey, and V. Khandelwal. UMass at TDT 2000. Notebook publication for participants only, Nov. 2001.

[4] C. Cieri, S. Strassel, D. Graff, N. Martey, K. Rennert, and M. Liberman. Corpora for topic detection and tracking. In J. Allan, editor, *Topic Detection and Tracking: Event-based Information Organization*, pages 33–66. Kluwer Academic Publishers, 2002.

[5] J. G. Fiscus and G. R. Doddington. Topic detection and tracking evaluation overview. In J. Allan, editor, *Topic Detection and Tracking: Event-based Information Organization*, pages 17–31. Kluwer Academic Publishers, Boston, 2002.

[6] W. Hersh and P. Over. The TREC-9 interactive track report. In *Proceedings of the Text Retrieval Conference (TREC-9)*, pages 41–50, 2001.

[7] G. N. Lance and W. T. Williams. A general theory of classificatory sorting strategies: 1. hierarchical systems. *Computer Journal*, 9:373–380, 1967.

[8] A. Leuski. *Interactive Information Organization: Techniques and Evaluation.* PhD thesis, University of Massachusetts at Amherst, May 2001.

[9] A. Leuski and J. Allan. Evaluating a visual navigation system for a digital library. *International Journal on Digital Libraries*, 3(2):170–184, 2000.

[10] D. D. Lewis and W. A. Gale. A sequential algorithm for training text classifiers. In *Proceedings of ACM SIGIR*, pages 385–404, 1994.

[11] I. Mani, T. Firmin, D. House, G. Klein, B. Sundheim, and L. Hirschman. The TIPSTER SUMMAC text summarization evaluation. In *Proc. of EACL'99*, 1999.

[12] K. McKeown and D. Radev. Generating summaries of multiple news articles. In I. Mani and M. Maybury, editors, *Advances in Automatic Text Summarization.* MIT Press, Cambridge, Massachusetts, 1999.

[13] S. Robertson and D. A. Hull. The TREC-9 filtering track final report. In *Proceedings of the Text Retrieval Conference (TREC-9)*, pages 25–40, 2001.

[14] S. E. Robertson, S. Walker, S. Jones, M. M. Hancock-Beaulieu, and M. Gatford. Okapi at TREC-3. In D. Harman and E. Voorhees, editors, *Third Text REtrieval Conference (TREC-3).* NIST, 1995.

[15] G. Salton. *Automatic Text Processing.* Addison-Wesley, 1989.

[16] Proceedings of the TDT 2001 workshop. Notebook publication for participants only, 2001.

Bayesian Online Classifiers for Text Classification and Filtering

Kian Ming Adam Chai
DSO National Laboratories
20 Science Park Drive
Singapore 118230
ckianmin@dso.org.sg

Hwee Tou Ng
Department of Computer Science
National University of Singapore
3 Science Drive 2
Singapore 117543
nght@comp.nus.edu.sg

Hai Leong Chieu
DSO National Laboratories
20 Science Park Drive
Singapore 118230
chaileon@dso.org.sg

ABSTRACT

This paper explores the use of Bayesian online classifiers to classify text documents. Empirical results indicate that these classifiers are comparable with the best text classification systems. Furthermore, the online approach offers the advantage of continuous learning in the batch-adaptive text filtering task.

Categories and Subject Descriptors

H.3.3 [**Information Systems**]: Information Search and Retrieval—*Information filtering*

General Terms

Algorithms, Experimentation

Keywords

Text Classification, Text Filtering, Bayesian, Online, Machine Learning

1. INTRODUCTION

Faced with massive information everyday, we need automated means for classifying text documents. Since handcrafting text classifiers is a tedious process, machine learning methods can assist in solving this problem[15, 7, 27].

Yang & Liu[27] provides a comprehensive comparison of supervised machine learning methods for text classification. In this paper we will show that certain Bayesian classifiers are comparable with *Support Vector Machines*[23], one of the best methods reported in [27]. In particular, we will evaluate the *Bayesian online perceptron*[17, 20] and the *Bayesian online Gaussian process*[3].

For text classification and filtering, where the initial training set is large, online approaches are useful because they allow continuous learning without storing all the previously seen data. This continuous learning allows the utilization of information obtained from subsequent data after the initial training. Bayes' rule allows online learning to be performed in a principled way[16, 20, 17]. We will evaluate the Bayesian online perceptron, together with information gain considerations, on the batch-adaptive filtering task[18].

SIGIR'02, August 11-15, 2002, Tampere, Finland.

2. CLASSIFICATION AND FILTERING

For the text classification task defined by Lewis[9], we have a set of predefined categories and a set of documents. For each category, the document set is partitioned into two mutually exclusive sets of relevant and irrelevant documents. The goal of a text classification system is to determine whether a given document belongs to any of the predefined categories. Since the document can belong to zero, one, or more categories, the system can be a collection of binary classifiers, in which one classifier classifies for one category.

In *Text REtrieval Conference* (TREC), the above task is known as batch filtering. We will consider a variant of batch filtering called the batch-adaptive filtering[18]. In this task, during testing, if a document is retrieved by the classifier, the relevance judgement is fed back to the classifier. This feedback can be used to improve the classifier.

2.1 Corpora and Data

For text classification, we use the ModApte version of the Reuters-21578 corpus[1], where unlabelled documents are removed. This version has 9,603 training documents and 3,299 test documents. Following [7, 27], only categories that have at least one document in the training and test set are retained. This reduces the number of categories to 90.

For batch adaptive filtering, we attempt the task of TREC-9[18], where the OHSUMED collection[6] is used. We will evaluate on the OHSU topic-set, which consists of 63 topics. The training and test material consist of 54,710 and 293,856 documents respectively. In addition, there is a topic statement for each topic. For our purpose, this is treated as an additional training document for that topic. We will only use the title, abstract, author, and source sections of the documents for training and testing.

2.2 Representation

There are various ways to transform a document into a representation convenient for classification. We will use the

[1]Available via `http://www.daviddlewis.com/resources/testcollections/reuters21578`.

bag-of-words approach, where we only retain frequencies of words after tokenisation, stemming, and stop-words removal. These frequencies can be normalized using various schemes[19, 6]; we use the *ltc* normalization:

$$\begin{aligned} l_{i,d} &= 1 + \log_2 TF_{i,d} \\ t_i &= \log_2 \frac{N}{n_i} \\ ltc_{i,d} &= \frac{l_{i,d} \cdot t_i}{\sqrt{\sum_{j \in \{\text{terms in } d\}} (l_{j,d} \cdot t_j)^2}}, \end{aligned}$$

where the subscripts i and d denote the ith term and the dth document respectively, $TF_{i,d}$ is the frequency of the ith term in the dth document, n_i is the document-frequency of the ith term, and N is the total number of documents.

2.3 Feature Selection Metric

Given a set of candidate terms, we select features from the set using the *likelihood ratio* for *binomial distribution* advocated by Dunning[5]:

$$\lambda = \frac{\left(\frac{R_t+R_{\bar{t}}}{N}\right)^{R_t+R_{\bar{t}}} \left(\frac{N_t+N_{\bar{t}}}{N}\right)^{N_t+N_{\bar{t}}}}{\left(\frac{R_t}{R_t+N_t}\right)^{R_t} \left(\frac{N_t}{R_t+N_t}\right)^{N_t} \left(\frac{R_{\bar{t}}}{R_{\bar{t}}+N_{\bar{t}}}\right)^{R_{\bar{t}}} \left(\frac{N_{\bar{t}}}{R_{\bar{t}}+N_{\bar{t}}}\right)^{N_{\bar{t}}}},$$

where R_t (N_t) is the number of relevant (non-relevant) training documents which contain the term, $R_{\bar{t}}$ ($N_{\bar{t}}$) is the number of relevant (non-relevant) training documents which do not, and N is the total number of training documents.

Asymptotically, $-2 \ln \lambda$ is χ^2 distributed with 1 degree of freedom. We choose terms with $-2 \ln \lambda$ more than 12.13, i.e. at 0.05% significance level. More details on the feature selection procedures will be given in section 4.

2.4 Performance Measures

To evaluate a text classification system, we use the F_1 measure introduced by van Rijsbergen[22]. This measure combines recall and precision in the following way:

$$\begin{aligned} \text{Recall} &= \frac{\text{number of correct positive predictions}}{\text{number of positive examples}} \\ \text{Precision} &= \frac{\text{number of correct positive predictions}}{\text{number of positive predictions}} \\ F_1 &= \frac{2 \times \text{Recall} \times \text{Precision}}{\text{Recall} + \text{Precision}}. \end{aligned}$$

For ease of comparison, we summarize the F_1 scores over the different categories using the micro- and macro-averages of F_1 scores[11, 27]:

$$\begin{aligned} \text{Micro-avg } F_1 &= F_1 \text{ over categories and documents} \\ \text{Macro-avg } F_1 &= \text{average of within-category } F_1 \text{ values.} \end{aligned}$$

The micro- and macro-average F_1 emphasize the performance of the system on common and rare categories respectively. Using these averages, we can observe the effect of different kinds of data on a text classification system.

In addition, for comparing two text classification systems, we use the *micro sign-test* (s-test) and the *macro sign-test* (S-test), which are two significance tests first used for comparing text classification systems in [27]. The s-test compares all the binary decisions made by the systems, while the S-test compares the within-category F_1 values. Similar to the F_1 averages, the s-test and S-test compare the performance of two systems on common and rare categories respectively.

To evaluate a batch-adaptive filtering system, we use the `T9P` measure of TREC-9[18]:

$$\texttt{T9P} = \frac{\text{number of correct positive predictions}}{\text{Max}(50, \text{number of positive predictions})},$$

which is precision, with a penalty for not retrieving 50 documents.

3. BAYESIAN ONLINE LEARNING

Most of this section is based on work by Opper[17], Solla & Winther[20], and Csató & Opper[3].

Suppose that each document is described by a vector $\mathbf{x}$, and that the relevance indicator of $\mathbf{x}$ for a category is given by label $y \in \{-1, 1\}$, where -1 and 1 indicates irrelevant and relevant respectively. Given m instances of past data $\mathcal{D}_m = \{(y_t, \mathbf{x}_t), t = 1...m\}$, the *predictive probability* of the relevance of a document described by $\mathbf{x}$ is

$$p(y|\mathbf{x}, \mathcal{D}_m) = \int d\mathbf{a}\; p(y|\mathbf{x}, \mathbf{a}) p(\mathbf{a}|\mathcal{D}_m),$$

where we have introduced the classifier $\mathbf{a}$ to assist us in the prediction. In the Bayesian approach, $\mathbf{a}$ is a random variable with probability density $p(\mathbf{a}|\mathcal{D}_m)$, and we integrate over all the possible values of $\mathbf{a}$ to obtain the prediction.

Our aim is to obtain a reasonable description of $\mathbf{a}$. In the Bayesian online learning framework[16, 20, 17], we begin with a *prior* $p(\mathbf{a}|\mathcal{D}_0)$, and perform incremental Bayes' updates to obtain the *posterior* as data arrives:

$$p(\mathbf{a}|\mathcal{D}_{t+1}) = \frac{p(y_{t+1}|\mathbf{x}_{t+1}, \mathbf{a}) p(\mathbf{a}|D_t)}{\int d\mathbf{a}\; p(y_{t+1}|\mathbf{x}_{t+1}, \mathbf{a}) p(\mathbf{a}|D_t)}.$$

To make the learning online, the explicit dependence of the posterior $p(\mathbf{a}|\mathcal{D}_{t+1})$ on the past data is removed by approximating it with a distribution $p(\mathbf{a}|A_{t+1})$, where A_{t+1} characterizes the distribution of $\mathbf{a}$ at time $t+1$. For example, if $p(\mathbf{a}|A_{t+1})$ is a Gaussian, then A_{t+1} refers to its mean and covariance.

Hence, starting from the *prior* $p_0(\mathbf{a}) = p(\mathbf{a}|A_0)$, learning from a new example $(y_{t+1}, \mathbf{x}_{t+1})$ comprises two steps:

Update the posterior using Bayes rule

$$p(\mathbf{a}|A_t, (y_{t+1}, \mathbf{x}_{t+1})) \propto p(y_{t+1}|\mathbf{x}_{t+1}, \mathbf{a})\; p(\mathbf{a}|A_t)$$

Approximate the updated posterior by parameterisation

$$p(\mathbf{a}|A_t, (y_{t+1}, \mathbf{x}_{t+1})) \rightarrow p(\mathbf{a}|A_{t+1}),$$

where the approximation step is done by minimizing the *Kullback-Leibler distance* between the the approximating and approximated distributions.

The amount of information gained about $\mathbf{a}$ after learning from a new example can be expressed as the Kullback-Leibler distance between the posterior and prior distributions[25]:

$$\begin{aligned} IG(y_{t+1}, \mathbf{x}_{t+1}|\mathcal{D}_t) &= \int d\mathbf{a}\; p(\mathbf{a}|\mathcal{D}_{t+1}) \log_2 \frac{p(\mathbf{a}|\mathcal{D}_{t+1})}{p(\mathbf{a}|\mathcal{D}_t)} \\ &\approx \int d\mathbf{a}\; p(\mathbf{a}|A_{t+1}) \log_2 \frac{p(\mathbf{a}|A_{t+1})}{p(\mathbf{a}|A_t)}, \end{aligned}$$

where instances of the data $\mathcal{D}$ are replaced by the summaries A in the approximation.

To simplify notation henceforth, we use $p_t(\mathbf{a})$ and $\langle \ldots \rangle_t$ to denote $p(\mathbf{a}|A_t)$ and averages taken over $p(\mathbf{a}|A_t)$ respectively. For example, the predictive probability can be rewritten as

$$p(y|\mathbf{x}, \mathcal{D}_t) \approx p(y|\mathbf{x}, A_t) = \int d\mathbf{a}\, p(y|\mathbf{x}, \mathbf{a}) p_t(\mathbf{a}) = \langle p(y|\mathbf{x}, \mathbf{a}) \rangle_t .$$

In the following sections, the scalar field $h = \mathbf{a} \cdot \mathbf{x}$ will also be used to simplify notation and calculation.

3.1 Bayesian Online Perceptron

Consider the case where $\mathbf{a}$ describes a *perceptron.* We then define the *likelihood* as a *probit* model

$$p(y|\mathbf{x}, \mathbf{a}) = \Phi\left(\frac{y\mathbf{a} \cdot \mathbf{x}}{\sigma_0}\right),$$

where σ_0^2 is a fixed noise variance, and Φ is the cumulative Gaussian distribution

$$\Phi(u) = \frac{1}{\sqrt{2\pi}} \int_{-\infty}^{u} d\xi\ e^{-\xi^2/2}.$$

If $p_0(\mathbf{a})$ is the spherical unit Gaussian, and $p_t(\mathbf{a})$ is the Gaussian approximation, Opper[16, 17] and Solla & Winther[20] obtain the following updates by equating the means and covariances of $p(\mathbf{a}|A_{t+1})$ and $p(\mathbf{a}|A_t, (y_{t+1}, \mathbf{x}_{t+1}))$:

$$\begin{aligned} \langle \mathbf{a} \rangle_{t+1} &= \langle \mathbf{a} \rangle_t + \mathbf{s}_{t+1} \frac{\partial}{\partial \langle h \rangle_t} \ln \langle p(y_{t+1}|h) \rangle_t \\ \mathbf{C}_{t+1} &= \mathbf{C}_t + \mathbf{s}_{t+1}\mathbf{s}_{t+1}^{\mathrm{T}} \frac{\partial^2}{\partial \langle h \rangle_t^2} \ln \langle p(y_{t+1}|h) \rangle_t , \end{aligned}$$

where

$$\begin{aligned} \mathbf{s}_{t+1} &= \mathbf{C}_t \mathbf{x}_{t+1}, \\ \langle p(y_{t+1}|h) \rangle_t &= \Phi\left(\frac{y_{t+1}\langle h \rangle_t}{\sigma_{t+1}}\right), \\ \sigma_{t+1}^2 &= \sigma_0^2 + \mathbf{x}_{t+1}^T \mathbf{C}_t \mathbf{x}_{t+1} \quad \text{and} \\ \langle h \rangle_t &= \langle \mathbf{a} \rangle_t^{\mathrm{T}} \mathbf{x}_{t+1}. \end{aligned}$$

3.1.1 *Algorithm*

Training the Bayesian online perceptron on m data involves successive calculation of the means $\langle \mathbf{a} \rangle_t$ and covariances $\mathbf{C}_t$ of the posteriors, for $t \in \{1, ..., m\}$:

1. Initialize $\langle \mathbf{a} \rangle_0$ to be $\mathbf{0}$ and $\mathbf{C}_0$ to be $\mathbf{1}$ (identity matrix), i.e. a spherical unit Gaussian centred at origin.
2. For $t = 0, 1, ..., m-1$
3. y_{t+1} is the relevance indicator for document $\mathbf{x}_{t+1}$
4. Calculate $\mathbf{s}_{t+1}$, σ_{t+1}, $\langle h \rangle_t$ and $\langle p(y_{t+1}|h) \rangle_t$
5. Calculate $u = \frac{y_{t+1}\langle h \rangle_t}{\sigma_{t+1}}$ and $\square = \frac{1}{\sqrt{2\pi}} \exp(-\frac{1}{2}u^2)$
6. Calculate $\frac{\partial}{\partial \langle h \rangle_t} \ln \langle p(y_{t+1}|h) \rangle_t = \frac{y_{t+1}}{\sigma_{t+1}} \cdot \frac{1}{\langle p(y_{t+1}|h) \rangle_t} \cdot \square$
7. Calculate $\frac{\partial^2}{\partial \langle h \rangle_t^2} \ln \langle p(y_{t+1}|h) \rangle_t =$
$$-\frac{1}{\sigma_{t+1}^2}\left[\frac{u \cdot \square}{\langle p(y_{t+1}|h) \rangle_t} + \left(\frac{\square}{\langle p(y_{t+1}|h) \rangle_t}\right)^2\right]$$
8. Calculate $\langle \mathbf{a} \rangle_{t+1}$ and $\mathbf{C}_{t+1}$

The prediction for datum $(y, \mathbf{x})$ simply involves the calculation of $\langle p(y|\mathbf{x}, \mathbf{a}) \rangle_m = \langle p(y|h) \rangle_m$.

3.2 Bayesian Online Gaussian Process

Gaussian process (GP) has been constrained to problems with small data sets until recently when Csató & Opper[3] and Williams & Seeger[24] introduced efficient and effective approximations to the full GP formulation. This section will outline the approach in [3].

In the GP framework, $\mathbf{a}$ describes a function consisting of function values $\{a(\mathbf{x})\}$. Using the probit model, the likelihood can be expressed as

$$p(y|\mathbf{x}, \mathbf{a}) = \Phi\left(\frac{ya(\mathbf{x})}{\sigma_0}\right),$$

where σ_0 and Φ are described in section 3.1.

In addition, $p_0(\mathbf{a})$ is a GP prior which specifies a Gaussian distribution with zero mean function and *covariance/kernel* function $K_0(\mathbf{x}, \mathbf{x}')$ over a function space. If $p_t(\mathbf{a})$ is also a Gaussian process, then Csató & Opper obtain the following updates by equating the means and covariances of $p(\mathbf{a}|A_{t+1})$ and $p(\mathbf{a}|A_t, (y_{t+1}, \mathbf{x}_{t+1}))$:

$$\begin{aligned} \langle \mathbf{a} \rangle_{t+1} &= \langle \mathbf{a} \rangle_t + \mathbf{s}_{t+1} \frac{\partial}{\partial \langle h \rangle_t} \ln \langle p(y_{t+1}|h) \rangle_t \\ \mathbf{C}_{t+1} &= \mathbf{C}_t + \mathbf{s}_{t+1}\mathbf{s}_{t+1}^{\mathrm{T}} \frac{\partial^2}{\partial \langle h \rangle_t^2} \ln \langle p(y_{t+1}|h) \rangle_t , \end{aligned}$$

where

$$\begin{aligned} \mathbf{s}_{t+1} &= \mathbf{C}_t \mathbf{k}_{t+1} + \mathbf{e}_{t+1}, \\ \langle p(y_{t+1}|h) \rangle_t &= \Phi\left(\frac{y_{t+1}\langle h \rangle_t}{\sigma_{t+1}}\right), \\ \sigma_{t+1}^2 &= \sigma_0^2 + k_{t+1}^* + \mathbf{k}_{t+1}^T \mathbf{C}_t \mathbf{k}_{t+1} \quad \text{and} \\ \langle h \rangle_t &= \langle a(\mathbf{x}_{t+1}) \rangle_t = \langle \mathbf{a} \rangle_t^{\mathrm{T}} \mathbf{k}_{t+1} \end{aligned}$$

Notice the similarities to the updates in section 3.1. The main difference is the 'kernel trick' introduced into the equations through

$$\begin{aligned} k_{t+1}^* &= K_0(\mathbf{x}_{t+1}, \mathbf{x}_{t+1}) \quad \text{and} \\ \mathbf{k}_{t+1} &= (K_0(\mathbf{x}_1, \mathbf{x}_{t+1}), \ldots, K_0(\mathbf{x}_t, \mathbf{x}_{t+1}))^T \end{aligned}$$

New inputs $\mathbf{x}_{t+1}$ are added sequentially to the system via the $(t+1)$th unit vector $\mathbf{e}_{t+1}$. This results in a quadratic increase in matrix size, and is a drawback for large data sets, such as those for text classification. Csató & Opper overcome this by introducing sparseness into the GP. The idea is to replace $\mathbf{e}_{t+1}$ by the projection

$$\hat{\mathbf{e}}_{t+1} = \mathbf{K}_t^{-1}\mathbf{k}_{t+1},$$

where

$$\mathbf{K}_t = \{K_0(\mathbf{x}_i, \mathbf{x}_j), i, j = 1 \ldots t\}.$$

This approximation introduces an error

$$\epsilon_{t+1} = (k_{t+1}^* - \mathbf{k}_{t+1}^{\mathrm{T}}\mathbf{K}_t^{-1}\mathbf{k}_{t+1}) \frac{\partial}{\partial \langle h \rangle_t} \ln \langle p(y_{t+1}|h) \rangle_t ,$$

which is used to decide when to employ the approximation.

Hence, at any time the algorithm holds a set of *basis vectors.* It is usually desirable to limit the size of this set. To accommodate this, Csató & Opper describe a procedure for removing a basis vector from the set by reversing the process of adding new inputs.

For lack of space, the algorithm for the Bayesian Online Gaussian Process will not be given here. The reader is referred to [3] for more information.

4. EVALUATION

4.1 Classification on Reuters-21578

In this evaluation, we will compare Bayesian online perceptron, Bayesian online Gaussian process, and Support Vector Machines (SVM)[23]. SVM is one of the best performing learning algorithms on the Reuters-21578 corpus[7, 27].

The Bayesian methods are as described in section 3, while for SVM we will use the SVM^{light} package by Joachims[8]. Since SVM is a batch method, to have a fair comparison, the online methods are iterated through the training data 3 times before testing.[2]

4.1.1 Feature Selection

For the Reuters-21578 corpus, we select as features for each category the set of all words for which $-2\ln\lambda > 12.13$. We further prune these by using only the top 300 features. This reduces the computation time required for the calculation of the covariances of the Bayesian classifiers.

Since SVM is known to perform well for many features, for the SVM classifiers we also use the set of words which occur in at least 3 training documents[7]. This gives us 8,362 words. Note that these words are non-category specific.

4.1.2 Thresholding

The probabilistic outputs from the Bayesian classifiers can be used in various ways. The most direct way is to use the *Bayes decision rule*, $p(y = 1|\mathbf{x}, \mathcal{D}_m) > 0.5$, to determine the relevance of the document described by $\mathbf{x}$.[3] However, as discussed in [10, 26], this is not optimal for the chosen evaluation measure.

Therefore, in addition to 0.5 thresholding, we also empirically optimise the threshold for each category for the F_1 measure on the training documents. This scheme, which we shall call `MaxF1`, has also been employed in [27] for thresholding kNN and LLSF classifiers. The difference from our approach is that the threshold in [27] is calculated over a validation set. We do not use a validation set because we feel that, for very rare categories, it is hard to obtain a reasonable validation set from the training documents.

For the Bayesian classifiers, we also perform an analytical threshold optimisation suggested by Lewis[10]. In this scheme, which we shall call `ExpectedF1`, the threshold for each category is selected to optimise the expected F_1:

$$\mathrm{E}\left[F_1\right]_\theta \approx \begin{cases} \prod_{i\in\mathcal{D}}(1-p_i) & \text{if } |\mathcal{D}_+| = 0 \\ \frac{2\sum_{i\in\mathcal{D}_+} p_i}{|\mathcal{D}_+|+\sum_{i\in\mathcal{D}} p_i} & \text{otherwise,} \end{cases}$$

where θ is the threshold, p_i is the probability assigned to document i by the classifier, $\mathcal{D}$ is the set of all test documents, and $\mathcal{D}_+$ is the set of test documents with probabilities higher than the threshold θ.

Note that `ExpectedF1` can only be applied after the probabilities for all the test documents are assigned. Hence the classification can only be done in batch. This is unlike the first two schemes, where classification can be done online.

4.1.3 Results and Discussion

Table 1: Description of Methods

	Description[4]
SVM-1	$K_0 = \mathbf{x}_i \cdot \mathbf{x}_j + 1$
SVM-2	$K_0 = (\mathbf{x}_i \cdot \mathbf{x}_j + 1)^2$
SVM-R1	$K_0 = \exp(-\frac{1}{2}\lvert\mathbf{x}_i - \mathbf{x}_j\rvert^2)$
Perceptron	$\sigma_0 = 0.5$, one fixed feature (for bias)
GP-1	$\sigma_0 = 0.5$, $K_0 = \mathbf{x}_i \cdot \mathbf{x}_j + 1 + 10^{-4}\delta_{ij}$
GP-2	$\sigma_0 = 0.5$, $K_0 = (\mathbf{x}_i \cdot \mathbf{x}_j + 1)^2 + 10^{-4}\delta_{ij}$
GP-R1	$\sigma_0 = 0.5$, $K_0 = \exp(-\frac{1}{2}\lvert\mathbf{x}_i - \mathbf{x}_j\rvert^2) + 10^{-4}\delta_{ij}$

Table 2: Micro-/Macro-average F_1

	`0.5`	`MaxF1`	`ExpectedF1`
SVM_a-1	86.15 / 42.63	86.35 / 56.92	
SVM_a-2	85.44 / 40.13	86.19 / 56.42	
SVM_a-R1	84.99 / 37.61	86.63 / 53.14	
SVM_b-1	85.60 / 52.03	85.05 / 52.43	
SVM_b-2	85.60 / 50.53	84.50 / 50.49	
SVM_b-R1	85.75 / 50.52	84.65 / 51.27	
Perceptron	85.12 / 45.23	86.69 / 52.16	86.44 / 53.08
GP-1	85.08 / 45.20	86.73 / 52.12	86.54 / 53.12
GP-2	85.58 / 47.90	86.60 / 52.19	86.77 / 55.04
GP-R1	85.18 / 44.88	86.76 / 52.61	86.93 / 53.35

Table 1 lists the parameters for the algorithms used in our evaluation, while Table 2 and 3 tabulate the results. There are two sets of results for SVM, and they are labeled SVM_a and SVM_b. The latter uses the same set of features as the Bayesian classifiers (i.e. using the $-2\ln\lambda$ measure), while the former uses the set of 8,362 words as features.

Table 2 summarizes the results using F_1 averages. Table 3 compares the classifiers using s-test and S-test. Here, the `MaxF1` thresholds are used for the classification decisions. Each row in these tables compares the method listed in the first column with the other methods. The significance levels from [27] are used.

Several observations can be made:

- Generally, `MaxF1` thresholding increases the performance of all the systems, especially for rare categories.
- For the Bayesian classifiers, `ExpectedF1` thresholding improves the performance of the systems on rare categories.
- Perceptron implicitly implements the kernel used by GP-1, hence their similar results.
- With `MaxF1` thresholding, feature selection impedes the performance of SVM.
- In Table 2, SVM with 8,362 features have slightly lower micro-average F_1 to the Bayesian classifiers. However, the s-tests in Table 3 show that Bayesian classifiers outperform SVM for significantly many common categories. Hence, in addition to computing average F_1 measures, it is useful to perform sign tests.
- As shown in Table 3, for limited features, Bayesian classifiers outperform SVM for both common and rare categories.
- Based on the sign tests, the Bayesian classifiers outperform SVM (using 8,362 words) for common categories, and vice versa for rare categories.

[2]See section A.2 for discussion on the number of passes.

[3]For SVM, to minimise structural risks, we would classify the document as relevant if $\mathbf{w}\cdot\mathbf{x} + b > 0$, where $\mathbf{w}$ is the hyperplane, and b is the bias.

[4]See section A.3 for discussion on the jitter terms δ_{ij}.

Table 3: s-test/S-test using `MaxF1` thresholding

	SVM_a-1	SVM_a-2	SVM_a-R1	SVM_b-1	SVM_b-2	SVM_b-R1	Pptron	GP-1	GP-2	GP-R1
SVM_a-1		$\sim / \sim$	$< / \sim$	$\gg / \gg$	$\gg / \gg$	$\gg / \gg$	$\ll / \gg$	$\ll / \gg$	$\ll / \gg$	$\ll / \gg$
SVM_a-2	$\sim / \sim$		$\ll / \sim$	$> / \gg$	$\gg / \gg$	$\gg / \gg$	$\ll / \gg$	$\ll / \gg$	$\ll / \sim$	$\ll / >$
SVM_a-R1	$> / \sim$	$\gg / \sim$		$\gg / \sim$	$\gg / \gg$	$\gg / \gg$	$< / >$	$< / >$	$\sim / \sim$	$< / \sim$
SVM_b-1	$\ll / \ll$	$< / \ll$	$\ll / \sim$		$\gg / \sim$	$> / >$	$\ll / <$	$\ll / \sim$	$\ll / <$	$\ll / <$
SVM_b-2	$\ll / \ll$	$\ll / \ll$	$\ll / \ll$	$\ll / \sim$		$\sim / \sim$	$\ll / <$	$\ll / <$	$\ll / \ll$	$\ll / \ll$
SVM_b-R1	$\ll / \ll$	$\ll / \ll$	$\ll / \ll$	$< / <$	$\sim / \sim$		$\ll / <$	$\ll / \ll$	$\ll / \ll$	$\ll / \ll$
Perceptron	$\gg / \ll$	$\gg / \ll$	$> / <$	$\gg / >$	$\gg / >$	$\gg / >$		$\sim / \sim$	$\sim / \sim$	$\sim / \sim$
GP-1	$\gg / \ll$	$\gg / \ll$	$> / <$	$\gg / \sim$	$\gg / >$	$\gg / \gg$	$\sim / \sim$		$\sim / \sim$	$\sim / \sim$
GP-2	$\gg / \ll$	$\gg / \sim$	$\sim / \sim$	$\gg / >$	$\gg / \gg$	$\gg / \gg$	$\sim / \sim$	$\sim / \sim$		$\sim / \sim$
GP-R1	$\gg / \ll$	$\gg / <$	$> / \sim$	$\gg / >$	$\gg / \gg$	$\gg / \gg$	$\sim / \sim$	$\sim / \sim$	$\sim / \sim$	

"$\gg$" or "$\ll$" means P-value ≤ 0.01; "$>$" or "$<$" means $0.01 <$ P-value ≤ 0.05; "$\sim$" means P-value > 0.05.

The last observation suggests that one can use Bayesian classifiers for common categories, and SVM for rare ones.

4.2 Filtering on OHSUMED

In this section, only the Bayesian online perceptron will be considered. In order to avoid numerical integration of the information gain measure, instead of the probit model of section 3.1, here we use a simpler likelihood model in which the outputs are flipped with fixed probability κ:

$$p(y|\mathbf{x}, \mathbf{a}) = \kappa + (1 - 2\kappa)\Theta\left(y\mathbf{a} \cdot \mathbf{x}\right),$$

where

$$\Theta(x) = \begin{cases} 1 & x > 0 \\ 0 & \text{otherwise.} \end{cases}$$

The update equations will also change accordingly, e.g.

$$\begin{aligned} \langle p(y_{t+1}|h)\rangle_t &= \kappa + (1 - 2\kappa)\Phi\left(\frac{y_{t+1}\langle h\rangle_t}{\sigma_{t+1}}\right), \\ \sigma_{t+1}^2 &= \mathbf{x}_{t+1}^T \mathbf{C}_t \mathbf{x}_{t+1} \quad \text{and} \\ \langle h\rangle_t &= \langle \mathbf{a}\rangle_t^{\mathrm{T}} \mathbf{x}_{t+1}. \end{aligned}$$

Using this likelihood measure, we can express the information gained from datum $(y_{t+1}, \mathbf{x}_{t+1})$ as

$$IG(y_{t+1}, \mathbf{x}_{t+1}|\mathcal{D}_t) \approx$$

$$\log_2 \kappa + \Phi\left(\frac{y_{t+1}\widehat{\langle h\rangle}_{t+1}}{\widehat{\sigma}_{t+1}}\right) \log_2\left(\frac{1-\kappa}{\kappa}\right) - \log_2 \langle p(y_{t+1}|h)\rangle_t,$$

where

$$\begin{aligned} \widehat{\sigma}_{t+1}^2 &= \mathbf{x}_{t+1}^T \mathbf{C}_{t+1} \mathbf{x}_{t+1} \quad \text{and} \\ \widehat{\langle h\rangle}_{t+1} &= \langle \mathbf{a}\rangle_{t+1}^{\mathrm{T}} \mathbf{x}_{t+1}. \end{aligned}$$

We use $\kappa = 0.1$ in this evaluation. The following sections will describe the algorithm in detail. To simplify presentation, we will divide the batch-adaptive filtering task into batch and adaptive phases.

4.2.1 *Feature Selection and Adaptation*

During the batch phase, words for which $-2 \ln \lambda > 12.13$ are selected as features.

During the adaptive phase, when we obtain a feedback, we update the features by adding any new words with $-2 \ln \lambda > 12.13$. When a feature is added, the distribution of the perceptron $\mathbf{a}$ is extended by one dimension:

$$\langle \mathbf{a}\rangle \to \begin{pmatrix} \langle \mathbf{a}\rangle \\ \hdashline 0 \end{pmatrix} \qquad \mathbf{C} \to \left(\begin{array}{c:c} \mathbf{C} & 0 \\ \hdashline 0 & 1 \end{array}\right).$$

4.2.2 *Training the classifier*

During the batch phase, the classifier is iterated through the training documents 3 times. In addition, the relevant documents are collected for use during the adaptive phase.

During the adaptive phase, retrieved relevant documents are added to this collection. When a document is retrieved, the classifier is trained on that document and its given relevance judgement.

The classifier will be trained on irrelevant documents most of the time. To prevent it from "forgetting" relevant documents due to its limited capacity, whenever we train on an irrelevant document, we would also train on a past relevant document. This past relevant document is chosen successively from the collection of relevant documents.

This is needed also because new features might have been added since a relevant document was last trained on. Hence the classifier would be able to gather new information from the same document again due to the additional features

Note that the past relevant document does not need to be chosen in successive order. Instead, it can be chosen using a probability distribution over the collection. This will be desirable when handling topic-drifts.

We will evaluate the effectiveness of this strategy of retraining on past retrieved relevant documents, and denote its use by `+rel`. Though its use means that the algorithm is no longer online, asymptotic efficiency is unaffected, since only one past document is used for training at any instance.

4.2.3 *Information Gain*

During testing, there are two reasons why we retrieve a document. The first is that it is relevant, i.e. $p(y = 1|\mathbf{x}, \mathcal{D}_t) > 0.5$, where $\mathbf{x}$ represents the document. The second is that, although the document is deemed irrelevant by the classifier, the classifier would gain useful information from the document. Using the measure $IG(y, \mathbf{x}|\mathcal{D}_t)$, we calculate the expected information gain

$$\langle IG(\mathbf{x}|\mathcal{D}_t)\rangle = \sum_{v \in \{-1,1\}} p(y = v|\mathbf{x}, \mathcal{D}_t) \cdot IG(y = v, \mathbf{x}|\mathcal{D}_t).$$

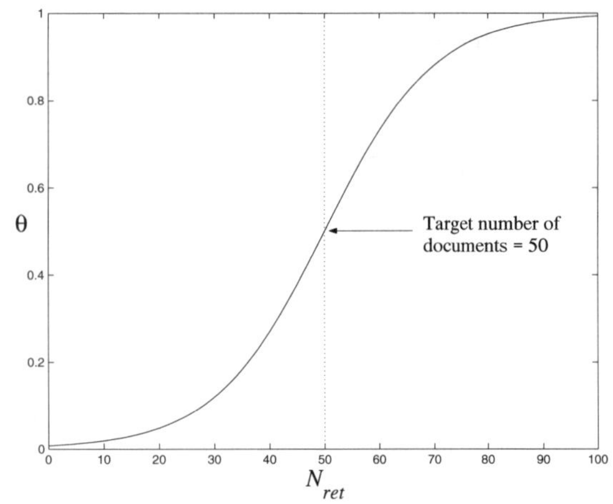

Figure 1: θ versus N_{ret} tuned for T9P

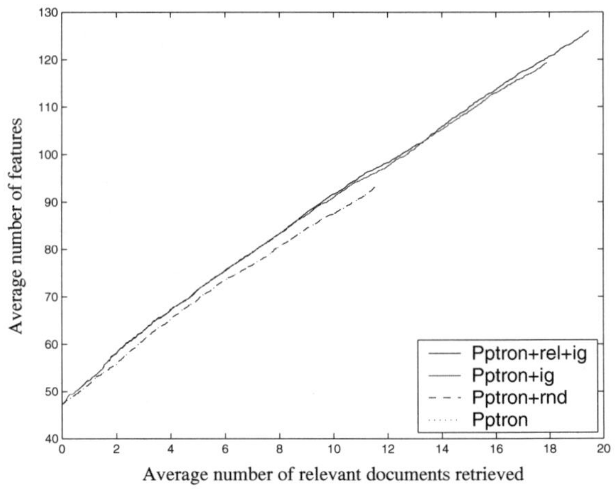

Figure 2: Variation of the number of features as relevant documents are retrieved. The plots for `Pptron+rel+ig` and `Pptron+ig` are very close. So are the plots for `Pptron+rnd` and `Pptron`.

A document is then deemed useful if its expected information gain is at least θ. Optimizing for the `T9P` measure (i.e. targeting 50 documents), we choose θ to be

$$\theta = 0.999\left(1 + \exp\left(-\frac{N_{\mathrm{ret}} - 50.0}{10}\right)\right)^{-1} + 0.001,$$

where N_{ret} is the total number of documents that the system has retrieved. Figure 1 plots θ against N_{ret}. Note that this is a kind of *active learning*, where the willingness to tradeoff precision for learning decreases with N_{ret}. The use of this information gain criteria will be denoted by `+ig`.

We will test the effectiveness of the information gain strategy, against an alternative one. The alternative, denoted by `+rnd`, will randomly select documents to retrieve based on the probability

$$U = \begin{cases} 0 & \text{if } N_{\mathrm{ret}} >= 50 \\ \frac{50 - N_{\mathrm{ret}}}{293856} & \text{otherwise,} \end{cases}$$

where 293,856 is the number of test documents.

4.2.4 Results and Discussion

Table 4 lists the results of seven systems. The first two are of Microsoft Research Cambridge and Fudan University respectively. These are the only runs in TREC-9 for the task. The third is of the system as described in full, i.e. Bayesian online perceptron, with retraining on past retrieved relevant documents, and with the use of information gain. The rest are of the Bayesian online perceptron with different combinations of strategies.

Besides the `T9P` measure, for the sake of completeness, Table 4 also lists the other measures used in TREC-9. Taken together, the measures show that Bayesian online perceptron, together with the consideration for information gain, is a very competitive method.

For the systems with `+rel`, the collection of past known relevant documents is kept. Although Microsoft uses this same collection for its query reformulation, another collection of all previously seen documents is used for threshold adaptation. Fudan maintains a collection of past retrieved documents and uses this collection for query adaptation.

In a typical operational system, retrieved relevant documents are usually retained, while irrelevant documents are usually discarded. Therefore `+rel` is a practical strategy to adopt.

Figure 2 plots the average number of features during the adaptive phase. We can see that features are constantly added as relevant documents are seen. When the classifier is retrained on past documents, the new features enable the classifier to gain new information from these documents. If we compare the results for `Pptron+rel` and `Pptron` in Table 4, we find that not training on past documents causes the number of relevant documents retrieved to drop by 5%. Similarly, for `Pptron+rel+ig` and `Pptron+ig`, the drop is 8%.

Table 5 breaks down the retrieved documents into those that the classifier deems relevant and those that the classifier is actually *querying* for information, for `Pptron+ig` and `Pptron+rnd`. The table shows that none of the documents randomly queried are relevant documents. This is not surprising, since only an average of 0.017% of the test documents are relevant. In contrast, the information gain strategy is able to retrieve 313 relevant documents, which is 26.1% of the documents queried. This is a significant result.

Consider `Pptron+ig`. Table 4 shows that for `Pptron`, when the information gain strategy is removed, only 731 relevant documents will be retrieved. Hence, although most of the documents queried are irrelevant, information gained from these queries helps recall by the classifier (i.e. 815 documents versus 731 documents), which is important for reaching the target of 50 documents.

MacKay[13] has noted the phenomenon of querying for irrelevant documents which are at the edges of the input space, and suggested maximizing information in a defined region of interest instead. Finding this region for batch-adaptive filtering remains a subject for further research.

Comparing the four plots in Figure 2, we find that, on average, the information gain strategy causes about 3% more features to be discovered for the same number of relevant documents retrieved. A consequence of this is better recall.

[5] [18] reports results from run ok9bfr2po, while we report results from the slightly better run ok9bf2po.

Table 4: Results for Batch-adaptive filtering optimized for T9P measure.

	Microsoft[5]	Fudan	Pptron+rel+ig	Pptron+ig	Pptron+rnd	Pptron+rel	Pptron
Total retrieved	3562	3251	2716	2391	2533	1157	1057
Relevant retrieved	1095	1061	1227	1128	732	772	731
Macro-average recall	39.5	37.9	36.2	33.3	20.0	20.8	20.0
Macro-average precision	30.5	32.2	35.8	35.8	21.6	61.9	62.3
Mean T9P	**30.5**	**31.7**	**31.3**	**29.8**	**19.2**	**21.5**	**20.8**
Mean Utility	-4.397	-1.079	15.318	15.762	-5.349	18.397	17.730
Mean T9U	-4.397	-1.079	15.318	15.762	-5.349	18.397	17.730
Mean scaled utility	-0.596	-0.461	-0.025	0.016	-0.397	0.141	0.138
Zero returns	0	0	0	0	0	8	0

Table 5: Breakdown of documents retrieved for Pptron+ig and Pptron+rnd. The numbers for the latter are in brackets.

	Relevant		Not Relevant		Total	
# docs retrieved by perceptron classifier proper	815	(732)	378	(345)	1193	(1077)
# docs retrieved by information gain (or random strategy)	313	(0)	885	(1456)	1198	(1456)
Total	1128	(732)	1263	(1801)	2391	(2533)

5. CONCLUSIONS AND FURTHER WORK

We have implemented and tested Bayesian online perceptron and Gaussian processes on the text classification problem, and have shown that their performance is comparable to that of SVM, one of the best learning algorithms on text classification in the published literature. We have also demonstrated the effectiveness of online learning with information gain on the TREC-9 batch-adaptive filtering task.

Our results on text classification suggest that one can use Bayesian classifiers for common categories, and maximum margin classifiers for rare categories. The partitioning of the categories into common and rare ones in an optimal way is an interesting problem.

SVM has been employed to use relevance feedback by Drucker *et al*[4], where the retrieval is in groups of 10 documents. In essence, this is a form of adaptive routing. It would be instructive to see how Bayesian classifiers perform here, without storing too many previously seen documents.

It would also be interesting to compare the merits of incremental SVM[21, 1] with the Bayesian online classifiers.

Acknowledgments

We would like to thank Lehel Csató for providing details on the implementation of the Gaussian process, Wee Meng Soon for assisting in the data preparation, Yiming Yang for clarifying the representation used in [27], and Loo Nin Teow for proof-reading the manuscript. We would also like to thank the reviewers for their many helpful comments in improving the paper.

6. REFERENCES

[1] G. Cauwenberghs and T. Poggio. Incremental and decremental support vector machine learning. In T. K. Leen, T. G. Dietterich, and V. Tresp, editors, *NIPS 2000*, volume 13. The MIT Press, 2001.

[2] D. Cox and E. Snell. *Analysis of Binary Data.* Chapman & Hall, London, 2nd edition, 1989.

[3] L. Csató and M. Opper. Sparse representation for Gaussian process models. In T. K. Leen, T. G. Dietterich, and V. Tresp, editors, *NIPS 2000*, volume 13. The MIT Press, 2001.

[4] H. Drucker, B. Shahrary, and D. C. Gibbon. Relevance feedback using support vector machines. In *Proceedings of the 2001 International Conference on Machine Learning*, 2001.

[5] T. E. Dunning. Accurate methods for the statistics of surprise and coincidence. *Computational Linguistics*, 19(1):61–74, 1993.

[6] W. Hersh, C. Buckley, T. Leone, and D. Hickam. OHSUMED: An interactive retrieval evaluation and new large test collection for research. In *Proceedings of the 17th Annual International ACM SIGIR Conference on Research and Development in Information Retrieval*, pages 192–201, 1994.

[7] T. Joachims. Text categorization with support vector machines: Learning with many relevant features. In *Proceedings of the European Conference on Machine Learning (ECML)*, pages 137–142, 1998.

[8] T. Joachims. Making large-scale SVM learning practical. In B. Schólkopf, C. Burges, and A. Smola, editors, *Advances in Kernel Methods — Support Vector Learning*, chapter 11. The MIT Press, 1999.

[9] D. D. Lewis. *Representation and Learning in Information Retrieval.* PhD thesis, Department of Computer and Information Science, University of Massachusetts at Amherst, 1992.

[10] D. D. Lewis. Evaluating and optimizing automomous text classification systems. In *Proceedings of the 18th Annual International ACM SIGIR Conference on Research and Development in Information Retrieval*, pages 246–254, 1995.

[11] D. D. Lewis, R. E. Schapire, J. P. Callan, and R. Papka. Training algorithms for linear text classifiers. In *Proceedings of the 19th Annual International ACM SIGIR Conference on Research and Development in Information Retrieval*, pages 298–306, 1996.

[12] D. J. Mackay. Bayesian interpolation. *Neural Computation*, 4(3):415–447, 1991.

[13] D. J. Mackay. Information-based objective functions for active data selection. *Neural Computation*, 4(4):590–604, 1992.

[14] R. M. Neal. Monte Carlo implementation of Gaussian process models for Bayesian regression and classification. Technical Report CRG-TR-97-2, Department of Computer Science, University of Toronto, January 1997.

[15] H. T. Ng, W. B. Goh, and K. L. Low. Feature selection, perceptron learning, and a usability case study for text categorization. In *Proceedings of the 20th Annual International ACM SIGIR Conference on Research and Development in Information Retrieval*, pages 67–73, 1997.

[16] M. Opper. Online versus offline learning from random examples: General results. *Physical Review Letters*, 77:4671–4674, 1996.

[17] M. Opper. A Bayesian approach to online learning. In D. Saad, editor, *On-Line Learning in Neural Networks*. Combridge University Press, 1998.

[18] S. Robertson and D. A. Hull. The TREC-9 filtering track final report. In *Proceedings of the 9th Text REtrieval Conference (TREC-9)*, pages 25–40, 2001.

[19] G. Salton and C. Buckley. Term-weighting approaches in automatic text retrieval. *Information Processing and Management*, 24(5):513–523, 1988.

[20] S. A. Solla and O. Winther. Optimal perceptron learning: an online Bayesian approach. In D. Saad, editor, *On-Line Learning in Neural Networks*. Combridge University Press, 1998.

[21] N. A. Syed, H. Liu, and K. K. Sung. Incremental learning with support vector machines. In *Proceedings of the Workshop on Support Vector Machines at the International Joint Conference on Artificial Intelligence (IJCAI-99)*, 1999.

[22] C. van Rijsbergen. *Information Retrieval*. Butterworths, London, 1979.

[23] V. N. Vapnik. *The Nature of Statistical Learning Theory*. Springer, New York, 1995.

[24] C. K. Williams and M. Seeger. Using the Nyström method to speed up kernel machines. In T. K. Leen, T. G. Dietterich, and V. Tresp, editors, *NIPS 2000*, volume 13. The MIT Press, 2001.

[25] O. Winther. *Bayesian Mean Field Algorithms for Neural Networks and Gaussian Processes*. PhD thesis, University of Copenhagen, CONNECT, The Niels Bohr Institute, 1998.

[26] Y. Yang. A study on thresholding strategies for text categorization. In *Proceedings of the 24th Annual International ACM SIGIR Conference on Research and Development in Information Retrieval*, pages 137–145, 2001.

[27] Y. Yang and X. Liu. A re-examination of text categorization methods. In *Proceedings of the 22nd Annual International ACM SIGIR Conference on Research and Development in Information Retrieval*, pages 42–49, 1999.

APPENDIX

A. ON THE CHOICE OF PARAMETERS

A.1 Likelihood model

MacKay[12] has suggested the evidence framework for model selection. Here, we calculate the evidence on the training data using the final posterior for $\mathbf{a}$:

$$p(\mathcal{D}_m) = \prod_{t=1}^{m} \langle p(y_t|\mathbf{x}_t, \mathbf{a}) \rangle_m .$$

Table 6: Micro-/Macro-avg F_1 (MaxF1 thresholds) and Avg log-evidence on Reuters-21578 for different likelihood models, using Bayesian online perceptron.

	Micro-/Macro-avg F_1	Avg log-evidence
Logit	86.48 / 52.75	-45.02
Probit	86.69 / 52.16	-34.32
Flip	85.94 / 53.00	-368.8

Table 6 illustrates this for selecting the likelihood measure for the text classification task, using the Bayesian online perceptron. In the table, the probit model follows the formulation in section 3.1 with $\sigma_0 = 0.5$, logit model is estimated by the probit model with $\sigma_0 = 1.6474$[2], and the flip noise model is as described in section 4.2. Although their F_1 averages are similar, the evidences show that the probit model with $\sigma_0 = 0.5$ is a more likely model. The small evidence for the flip noise model is because much information is lost through the threshold function Θ.

A.2 Effects of multiple passes over data

Using the evidence measure defined in section A.1, Table 7 illustrates the effects of different number of passes over training data for Bayesian online perceptron. Treating the number of passes as a parameter for the algorithm, we see that having 3 passes over the data gives the highest average evidence, although there is no significant difference between 2, 3, or 4 passes. Similar results hold for the Gaussian process for the 3 different kernels. Hence, in section 4.1, we choose to use 3 passes for all the Bayesian algorithms.

Table 7: Micro-/Macro-avg F_1 (MaxF1 thresholds) and Avg log-evidence on Reuters-21578 for different passes over the training data, using Bayesian online perceptron.

Passes	Micro-/Macro-avg F_1	Avg log-evidence
1	87.08 / 52.87	-35.56
2	86.92 / 52.63	-34.36
3	86.69 / 52.16	-34.32
4	86.62 / 52.75	-34.54
5	85.22 / 46.93	-34.69

A.3 Jitter term

The addition of the jitter term $10^{-4}\delta_{ij}$ (where $\delta_{ij} = 1$ if $i = j$, and 0 otherwise) for Gaussian process for classification is recommended by Neal[14]. This term improves the conditioning of the matrix computations while having a small effect on the model. From our preliminary experiments, without the jitter term, the matrix operations in Bayesian online Gaussian process become ill-conditioned.

A.4 Sizes of the basis vectors sets

The sizes of the sets of basis vectors for GP in section 4.1 are limited to less than or equal to the number of features selected. This is because, as noted by Csató & Opper[3], for a feature space of finite dimension M, no more than M basis vectors are needed, due to linear dependence.

The Use of Unlabeled Data to Improve Supervised Learning for Text Summarization

Massih-Reza Amini and Patrick Gallinari
Computer Science Laboratory of Paris 6 (LIP6)
University of Pierre and Marie Curie
4, place de jussieu, case 169
75252 Paris cedex 05, France
{amini, gallinari}@poleia.lip6.fr

ABSTRACT

With the huge amount of information available electronically, there is an increasing demand for automatic text summarization systems. The use of machine learning techniques for this task allows one to adapt summaries to the user needs and to the corpus characteristics. These desirable properties have motivated an increasing amount of work in this field over the last few years. Most approaches attempt to generate summaries by extracting sentence segments and adopt the supervised learning paradigm which requires to label documents at the text span level. This is a costly process, which puts strong limitations on the applicability of these methods. We investigate here the use of semi-supervised algorithms for summarization. These techniques make use of few labeled data together with a larger amount of unlabeled data. We propose new semi-supervised algorithms for training classification models for text summarization. We analyze their performances on two data sets - the Reuters news-wire corpus and the Computation and Language (cmp_lg) collection of TIPSTER SUMMAC. We perform comparisons with a baseline – non learning – system, and a reference trainable summarizer system.

Categories & Subject Descriptors: I.5.4 *text processing*, B.2.4 *Algorithms*, G.3. *Stochastic processes*.

General Terms: Algorithms, performance, design.

Keywords: text summarization, machine learning, semi-supervised learning, text-span extraction.

1. INTRODUCTION

With the continuing growth of online text resources, it is becoming more and more important to help users to access information and to develop easy to use information research tools. Text summarization can be used together with conventional information research engines, and help users to quickly evaluate the relevance of documents or to navigate through a corpus.

Automated summarization dates back to the fifties [16]. The different attempts in this field have shown that human-quality text summarization was very complex since it encompasses discourse understanding, abstraction, and language generation [30]. Simpler approaches were then explored which consist in extracting representative text-spans, using statistical techniques and/or techniques based on surface domain-independent linguistic analyses.

SIGIR'02, August 11-15, 2002, Tampere, Finland.

Within this context, summarization can be defined as the selection of a subset of the document sentences which is representative of its content. This is typically done by ranking document sentences and selecting those with higher score and minimum overlap [6, 25]. Most of the recent work in summarization uses this paradigm. Usually, sentences are used as text-span units but paragraphs have also been considered [21, 31]. The latter may sometimes appear more appealing since they contain more contextual information. The quality of an *extract summary* might not be as good as an *abstract summary*, but it is considered good enough for a reader to understand the main ideas of a document.

Our work takes the text-span extraction paradigm and explores a machine learning approach for improving automatic summarization methods. The proposed model could be used both for generic and query-based summaries. However for evaluation purposes we will present results only on a generic summarization task. Previous work on the application of machine learning techniques for summarization [4, 8, 15, 17, 33] rely on the supervised learning paradigm. This requires a training set of documents and associated extract summaries. Learning systems are first trained to label document sentences as relevant when they are in the summary, or irrelevant otherwise. After training, they operate on unlabeled text by ranking the sentences of a new document. Labeling large amount of text spans for training summarization systems is time consuming and unrealistic for many applications. We consider here the use of semi-supervised techniques, which allow to train a system with only a few labeled documents together with large amounts of unlabeled documents. The latter being widely available and cheap, this could considerably help the development of trainable text summarizers.

For this, we introduce a new semi-supervised algorithm. Its originality is that it relies on a discriminative approach to semi-supervised learning rather than a generative approach, as it is usually the case. The advantage is that the algorithm is generic and can be used with many discriminant classifier, it leads to cheap and efficient implementations and shows better performances than generative systems. The algorithm is described in the framework of the Classification Expectation Maximization algorithm (CEM) [7, 19] and detailed for the case of a logistic classifier.

The paper is organized as follows, we first make a brief review of recent work in machine learning for text summarization and semi-supervised techniques (section 2). In section 3, we introduce two baseline text summarizers, a non trainable system and the Kupiec et al.'s trainable model [15], which are later used for comparison. We then describe our semi-supervised approach to text summarization based on sentence extraction and present the formal framework of the model and its interpretation as a CEM instance (section 4). Finally we present a series of experiments on Reuters news-wire and on the Computation and Language (cmp_lg) of TIPSTER SUMMAC collections in section 6, and carry on a set of comparisons.

2. RELATED WORK

Recently, several innovative methods for automated document summarization have been explored, they exploit statistical approaches [6, 25, 31, 35], linguistic approaches [13, 18, 26] and combinations of both [3, 10].

We will focus here on a statistical approach to the problem and more precisely on the use of machine learning techniques, which has recently motivated an increasing amount of interest in the field. Trainable text summarizers allow one to adapt to the specific user needs and to corpus characteristics, they may also help to improve the quality of summaries.

Text extracting for summarization has been cast in the framework of supervised learning for the first time in the seminal work of [15]. The authors propose a generic summarization model, which is based on a naive Bayes classifier operating on a synthetic representation of sentences. This method is described in more detail in section 3.2. Different authors built on this idea, e.g. [33] apply the same technique for other training and evaluation settings. [17] have used several machine learning techniques in order to select features indicating the salience of a sentence. They considered three types of features (locational, thematic and cohesion) and addressed the production of generic and user-focused summaries. [8] compare three supervised learning algorithms: C4.5, naive Bayes and neural networks. Their conclusion is that all three methods successfully completed the task by generating reasonable summaries. [4] adopt supervised learning methods to make synthetic summaries of web pages in the Ocelot system.

All these approaches rely on the supervised learning paradigm and require the labeling of text spans as relevant or not relevant which is either performed manually or by aligning an abstract with document sentences. Manual tagging or abstracting is a tedious task, it is unrealistic for large corpora, for query based summaries or for adapting summaries to different user needs or corpora.

The semi-supervised learning paradigm has emerged as a solution to this type of problem when large corpora of unlabeled data are available together with a much smaller amount of labeled data. In our case, for a given document collection, labeling a few documents at the text span level, or producing a few abstracts is usually affordable and does not take much time.

From a machine learning perspective, automatic summarization by extracting is typically a task for which semi-supervised learning seems appropriate. This learning paradigm has been first explored in statistics, a review of the work done prior to 92 in the context of discriminant analysis may be found in [19]. Most approaches propose to adapt the Expectation Maximization (EM) algorithm for handling both labeled and unlabeled data and perform maximum likelihood estimation. Theoretical work mostly focuses on gaussian mixtures, but practical algorithms may be used for more general settings, as soon as the different statistics needed for EM may be estimated. Recently this paradigm has been rediscovered by the machine learning community and is subject to a growing interest. For example [20] adapt EM to a mixture of experts model, [23] propose an algorithm which is a particular case of the general semi-supervised EM described in [19], they extend it to multiple mixtures and present an empirical evaluation for text classification. [28] propose a Kernel Discriminant Analysis which can be used for semi-supervised classification.

Other ideas bear some similarity with semi-supervised learning. This is the case of the co-training paradigm [5] which has been proposed independently for training classifiers when data may be described with two modalities. The algorithm we propose here is related to the decision directed paradigm [9], which has been used under different settings in the field of adaptive signal processing.

On the machine learning side, the originality of our work lies in the design of a discriminative approach to semi-supervised learning whereas others mainly rely on generative classifiers. The main benefits are the following: the approach is fully generic in the sense that most discriminant classifiers could be used within this framework, it does not rely on any parametric assumption about the data, discriminative training allows to have better performances than generative methods especially when there are few training data, it leads to very simple and fast implementations.

3. AUTOMATIC SUMMARIZERS

In this section, we present two baseline systems for sentence extraction. The first system is a non-trainable statistical model (section 3.1) and the second is Kupiec et al.'s naive Bayes trainable system [15] (section 3.2).

3.1 A baseline non-trainable system

Many systems for sentence extraction rely on the use of similarity measures between text spans (sentences or paragraphs) and queries, e.g. [10, 17]. Representative sentences are then selected by comparing the sentence score for a given document to a preset threshold. These systems differ in the representation of textual information and in the similarity measures they use. Usually, statistical and/or linguistic characteristics are used in order to encode the text (sentences and queries) into a fixed size vector and simple similarities (e.g. cosine) are then computed.

We build here on the work of [14] who used such a technique for the extraction of sentences relevant to a given query. They use a *tf-idf* representation and compute the similarity between sentence s_k and query q as:

$$Sim_1(q,s_k) = \sum_{w_i \in s_k, q} tf(w_i,q).tf(w_i,s_k).\left(1-\frac{\log(df(w_i)+1)}{\log(n+1)}\right)^2$$

Where, $tf(w,x)$ is the frequency of term w in x (q or s_k), $df(w)$ is the document frequency of term w and n is the total number of documents in the collection. Sentence s_k and query q are pre-processed by removing stop-words and performing Porter-reduction on the remaining words. For each document a threshold is then estimated from data for selecting the most relevant sentences.

In our experiments we have considered a generic query, where the query is enriched before computing the similarity. Since queries and sentences may be very short, this allows to compute more meaningful scores. Query expansion proceeds in two steps: first the query is expanded via a similarity thesaurus - WordNet in our experiments - second, highly ranked sentences, according to the generic query, are extracted from the document and the most frequent words in these sentences are included into the query. This process can be iterated. We also take into account the sentence length when computing the similarity $tf(w,s)$. The use of the document length has been shown to improve performance in Information Retrieval [27]. This leads to the following similarity:

$$Sim_2(q,s_k) = \sum_{w_i \in s_k,q} \bar{tf}(w_i,q).\bar{tf}(w_i,s_k).\left(1 - \frac{\log(df(w_i)+1)}{\log(n+1)}\right)^2$$

Where, $\bar{tf}(w,q)$ is the number of terms within the "semantic" class of w_i in the query q, and

$$\bar{tf}(w_i,s_k) = \frac{tf(w_i,s_k)}{tf(w_i,s_k) + \frac{\psi.l(s_k)}{\sum_s l(s)}}$$

Where ψ is the number of sentences in the current document, $l(s_k)$ is the length of s_k and $\sum_s l(s)$ is the summation over all sentence length.

Similar systems have been shown to perform well for sentence extraction based text summarization. For example [35] uses such an approach, which operates only on word frequencies for sentence extraction in the context of generic summaries, and shows that it compares well with human based sentence extraction.

3.2 Naive Bayes Model

Our baseline trainable summarizer is the model proposed by Kupiec et al. [15]. Sentences are encoded into five discrete features $\{F_j\}_{j=1,..,5}$. Four of them are binary: a sentence length cut-of feature indicates whether or not the sentence length is below a specified threshold, a fixed-phrase feature is set to 1 if the sentence contains occurrences of cue words, thematic word feature indexes sentences whose similarity with a generic query is above a preset threshold (we have used the Sim_2 measure in our implementation), upper case word feature indicates the occurrence of acronyms, excluding common abbreviations. Finally a paragraph feature is set to 1, 2 or 3 depending on the position of the sentence in the text. The computation of the posterior probability that sentence s will be included in summary S is achieved assuming statistical independence of the features and using a naive Bayes classifier:

$$p(s \in S / F_1,..,F_5) = \frac{\prod_{j=1}^{5} p(F_j / s \in S).p(s \in S)}{\prod_{j=1}^{5} p(F_j)}$$

where $p(s \in S)$ is a constant, $p(F_j / s \in S)$ and $p(F_j)$ are estimated directly from the training set by counting occurrence. For computing $p(F_j / s \in S)$ and $p(F_j)$, we have used a smoothing scheme (where counts in both the numerator and denominator are augmented by one for each feature) to prevent zero probabilities for infrequently occurring features. The use of this type of prior is sometimes referred to as *Laplace smoothing*. In the paper we refer to this system as the naive Bayes classifier.

4. A Semi-supervised algorithm for text-span classification

We now introduce an iterative discriminant algorithm for semi-supervised learning applied to text-span extraction. This algorithm is generic in the sense that it can be used with any discriminant classifier provided its output can be interpreted as a posterior class probability. We describe our algorithm in the general framework of the Classification EM (CEM) algorithm [7, 19]. This ensures that all nice properties of CEM (e.g. convergence) hold for our method. For text summarization, we are interested in two-class classification (relevant or irrelevant for the summary), we thus restrict our presentation and analysis to this case. For simplifying further the presentation, we consider here only the case of logistic classifiers, which have been used in our experiments. These two hypotheses are not restrictive since the algorithm and analysis can be easily extended for any discriminant classifier and for multi-class problems.

We first introduce the CEM unsupervised algorithm and propose a semi-supervised version of this method. We then describe our algorithm in the particular case of logistic regression.

4.1 Framework

We consider a binary decision problem and suppose available a set of m unlabeled data D_u and a set of n labeled data D_l. We will denote, $D_u=\{x_i \mid i=n+1,\dots,n+m\}$ and $D_l=\{(x_i, t_i) \mid i=1,\dots,n\}$ where $x_i \in \mathbb{R}^d$, $t_i=(t_{1i}, t_{2i})$ is the class indicator vector for x_i – here (t_{1i}, t_{2i}) = (1,0) when sentence i is relevant and (0,1) otherwise. Data in D_u are assumed drawn from a mixture of densities with two components C_1, C_2 in some unknown proportions π_1 and π_2. We will consider that unlabeled data have an associated missing indicator vector $t_i = (t_{1i}, t_{2i})$ for ($i=n+1, \dots, n+m$) which is a class or cluster indicator vector. The algorithms we consider attempt to iteratively partition the data into the two components C_1 and C_2. We also denote $(P_1^{(j)}, P_2^{(j)})$ the partition into two clusters computed by an algorithm at iteration j.

4.2 Classification Maximum Likelihood approach

The classification maximum likelihood (CML) approach [32] is a general framework which encompasses many clustering algorithms [7, 29]. It is only concerned with unsupervised learning, but we will see later that it can be easily adapted to semi-supervised learning.

In the two component case considered here, samples are supposed to be generated via a mixture density.

$$f(x,\Theta) = \pi_1.f_1(x,\theta_1) + \pi_2.f_2(x,\theta_2)$$

Where the f_k are parametric densities with unknown parameters θ_k and π_k is the mixture proportion. The goal here is to cluster the samples into 2 components P_1 and P_2. Under the mixture sampling scheme, samples x_i are taken from the mixture density f and the CML criterion is [7, 19]:

$$\log L_{CML}(P,\pi,\theta) = \sum_{k=1}^{2} \sum_{x_i \in D_u} t_{ki} \log\{\pi_k.f_k(x_i,\theta_k)\}$$

Where, $\sum_{x_i \in D_u}$ is a summation over all unlabeled samples which belong to D_u. This is different from the classical mixture maximum likelihood (MML) criterion. MML measures how well a model fits a data distribution, whereas CML measures the quality of the clustering performed with the model. For CML the mixture indicator t_{ki} associated to x_i is treated as an unknown parameter and corresponds to a hard decision about the membership of x_i to the kth mixture component. It has to be learned together with the density parameters. Such a parameter is not explicitly present in the MML criterion.

The classification EM algorithm (CEM) [7, 19] is an iterative technique, which has been proposed for maximizing L_{CML}, it is similar to the classical EM except for an additional ***C***-step where each x_i is assigned to one and only one component of the mixture. The algorithm is briefly described below.

CEM

Initialization: start from an initial partition $P^{(0)}$

j^{th} iteration, $j \geq 0$:

E –step. Estimate the posterior probability that x_i belongs to P_k (For all x_i in D_u and $k \in \{1,2\}$):

$$E[t_{ki}^{(j)} / x_i; P^{(j)}, \pi^{(j)}, \theta^{(j)}] = \frac{\pi_k^{(j)}.f_k(x_i;\theta_k^{(j)})}{\sum_{k=1}^{2} \pi_k^{(j)}.f_k(x_i;\theta_k^{(j)})}$$

C – step. Assign each x_i to the cluster $P_k^{(j+1)}$ with maximal posterior probability according to $E[t/x]$

M–step. Estimate the new parameters ($\pi^{(j+1)}$, $\theta^{(j+1)}$) which maximize $\log L_{CML}(P^{(j+1)}, \pi^{(j)}, \theta^{(j)})$.

4.3 Semi-supervised generative-CEM

CML criterion can be easily extended for semi-supervised learning. Since the t_{ki} for labeled data are known, this parameter is either 0 or 1 for data in D_l. The new criterion – denoted here L_C - becomes:

$$\log L_C = \sum_{k=1}^{2} \left\{ \sum_{x_i \in P_k} \log\{\pi_k.f_k(x_i,\theta_k)\} + \sum_{i=n+1}^{n+m} t_{ki} \log\{\pi_k.f_k(x_i,\theta_k)\} \right\}$$

The first summation inside the brackets is over the labeled samples, and the second one over unlabeled samples.

CEM can then be easily adapted for semi-supervised learning so as to maximize L_C instead of L_{CML}: for unlabeled data the t_{ki} are estimated as in the classical CEM (E and C steps), for labeled data, they are fixed to their known value. This is a *generative* approach to semi-supervised learning since it relies on the estimation of the f_k which model the data generation process. In this context, different models could be used depending on the distributional assumption about the input data. For our experiments the $\{f_k\}_{k=1,2}$ are assumed to be normal distributions.

After convergence, the model can be used for classification on new data using Bayes decision rule, i.e. x is assigned to the class with maximum a posteriori according to $p(P_k/x) = E[t_k/x]$.

4.4 Semi-supervised logistic-CEM

Because density estimation could be problematic especially for high dimensions or when only few data are labeled – this is what we are interested in - and since we are dealing with a classification problem, a more natural approach is to directly estimate the posteriors $p(P_k/x)$. This is known as the discriminant approach to classification.

For simplifying, we will consider here only the case of logistic classification [1]. In this case, the only distributional assumption is that the log likelihood ratio of class distributions is linear in the observations (see equation below), this is the case for a large family of distributions such as the exponential density family, (e.g. normal, beta, gamma, etc), and there is no explicit assumption on the nature of the densities.

$$\log\left(\frac{f_1(x)}{f_2(x)}\right) = \beta_0 + \beta^t.x, \text{where } \beta = (\beta_1, ..., \beta_d)$$

With this model, posterior probabilities have the simple form of a logistic function:

$$p(P_1/x) = \frac{1}{1+\exp(-(\beta_0 + \beta^t.x))} \quad \text{and} \quad p(P_2/x) = 1 - p(P_1/x)$$

Let us now express $\log L_C$ as a function of the posteriors $p(P_k/x)$:

$$\log L_C = \sum_{k=1}^{2} \left\{ \sum_{x_i \in P_k} \log\{p(P_k/x_i)\} + \sum_{i=n+1}^{n+m} t_{ki} \log\{p(P_k/x_i)\} \right\} + \sum_{i=1}^{n+m} \log\{f(x_i)\}$$

For discriminant classifiers, no assumption is made about the functional form of the marginal distribution $f(x)$, therefore, maximizing L_C is equivalent to maximizing $\tilde{L}_C$ [1]:

$$\log \tilde{L}_C(P, \beta_0, \beta) = \sum_{k=1}^{2} \left\{ \sum_{x_i \in P_k} \log\{p(P_k/x_i)\} + \sum_{i=n+1}^{n+m} t_{ki} \log\{p(P_k/x_i)\} \right\}$$

Any discriminant classifier which estimates the posteriors $p(P_k/x)$ can be trained to optimize $\tilde{L}_C$. With the logistic regression model, one uses a simple logistic unit G whose parameters are (β_0, β), i.e. $G(x) = \frac{1}{1+\exp(-(\beta_0 + \beta^t.x))}$, $G(x)$ is used as an estimate of $p(P_1/x)$ and $1 - G(x)$ as an estimate of $p(P_2/x)$. The estimation of β's can be performed using the logistic-CEM algorithm described below:

Logistic-CEM

Initialization: Train a discriminant logistic model $G^{(0)}(x)$ over D_l, let $P^{(0)}$ be the initial partition obtained from this model on $D_l \cup D_u$.

j^{th} iteration, $j \geq 0$:

E –step. Estimate the posterior probability that x_i belongs to P_k on D_u (i=n+1,…, n+m; k=1,2) using the output of the logistic classifier $G^{(j)}(x)$:

$$p(P_1^{(j)}/x) = \frac{1}{1+\exp(-(\beta_0^{(j)} + \beta^{t(j)}.x))} \quad \text{and} \quad p(P_2^{(j)}/x) = 1 - p(P_1^{(j)}/x)$$

C – step. Assign each $x_i \in D_u$ to the cluster $P_k^{(j+1)}$ with maximal posterior probability according to $p(P_k^{(j)}/x_i)$:

$$\forall x_i \in D_u, \forall k \in \{1,2\}, t_{ki}^{(j+1)} = sgn(p(P_k^{(j)} / x_i; \beta^{(j)}) - 0.5)$$

M–step. Find new parameters ($\beta_0^{(j+1)}$, $\beta^{(j+1)}$) which maximize $\log \tilde{L}_C$ ($P^{(j+1)}$, $\beta_0^{(j)}$, $\beta^{(j)}$).

The algorithm is guaranteed to converge. In order to maximize $\tilde{L}_C$ in step M, we have used a quasi-Newton gradient procedure. The advantage of this method is that at each iteration it requires to compute only the first derivatives of $\log \tilde{L}_C$ with regard to the parameters β.

The main difference here with the generative method is that no assumption is made on the conditional densities f_1 and f_2 except that their log ratio is linear in x. The algorithm directly attempts to estimate the $p(P_k/x)$ - the quantity we are interested in - instead of the conditional densities. It will be shown later to outperform

[1] A similar argument has been developed for supervised learning in the case of logistic classifiers [1, 19].

significantly the generative approach, especially when there are few labeled data available. It does so by using fewer parameters than the generative approach and is faster to run.

The above algorithm can be used with any other discriminant classifiers which also estimate the posteriors. We have performed experiments using neural networks and support vector machines but they did not show any improvement over the simple logistic regression method described here, which in turn performed slightly better than a pure linear classifier.

5. DATA SETS

A corpus of documents with the corresponding summaries is required for the evaluation. We have used *a*) the Reuters data set consisting of news-wire summaries [11], this corpus is composed of 1000 documents and their associated extracted sentence summaries and b) the Computation and Language (cmp_lg) collection of TIPSTER SUMMAC [12]. This corpus is composed of 183 scientific articles. For the latter, we have used the text-span alignment method described by [2] to generate extract-based summaries from the abstract of each article in the collection. In this method, extractive summaries required for training are automatically generated as follows: the relevance of each document sentence with respect to the human summary is computed, and highest score sentences are retained for the reference extract.

In both cases, the data set was split into a training and a test set whose size was respectively 1/3 and 2/3 of the available data. The evaluation is performed for a generic summarization task, a query was generated by collecting the most frequent words in the training set.

6. EXPERIMENTS

6.1 Compression ratio

A compression ratio must be specified or computed for extractive summaries. Empirical tests on the Reuters data set show that the compression ratio (summary size / document size) decreases with the size of the document. Figure 1 plots this ratio as a function of the document length. The graph is roughly hyperbolic, this suggests that the summary length, which is the product of the compression and the document length, is approximately constant. This is in agreement with [10] who found that summary length is independent of document length on similar databases. For each document in the Reuters data set, it was then decided to extract the same number of sentences than in its corresponding news-wire summary.

For the cmp_lg collection we followed the SUMMAC evaluation by using 10% compression ratio [34].

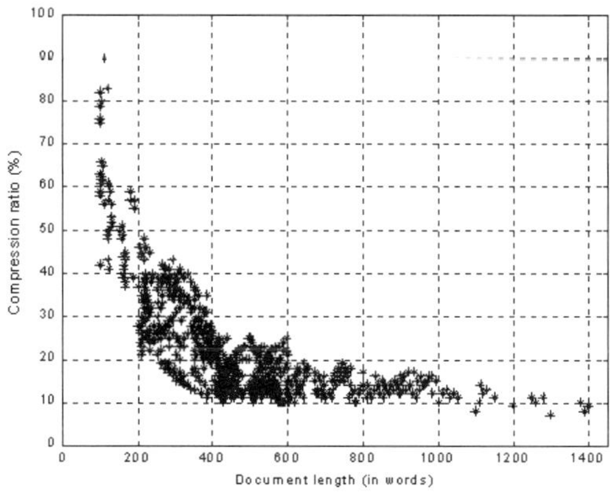

Figure 1. Compression as a percentage of document length on Reuters data set.

6.2 Sentence representation

We consider here the same set of features than those proposed by Kupiec et al. to represent sentences (section 3.2). The main difference here is that we do not use discrete feature values as they do and use both continuous and discrete features. This has been found more efficient and mixed continuous-categorical features are easily handled by our model. Each sentence *i* is then represented by a 5 feature vector, $\vec{x}_i$:

$$\vec{x}_i = (\varphi_1, \varphi_2, \varphi_3, \varphi_4, \varphi_5)$$

φ_1 is the normalized sentence length: $\frac{l(i)}{\sum_j l(j)}$, φ_2 is the normalized frequency of cue words in sentence *i*: $\frac{frequency\,of\,cue\,words}{l(i)}$, φ_3 = $Sim_2(i, q)$ where Sim_2 is the similarity introduced in section 3.1 for the baseline non trainable system, φ_4 is the normalized frequency of acronyms in *i*: $\frac{frequency\,of\,acronyms}{l(i)}$ and φ_5 is the same paragraph feature as in [15].

6.3 Results

Evaluation issues of summarization systems have been the object of several attempts, many of them being carried within the tipster program [24] and the Summac competition. This is a complex issue and many different aspects have to be considered simultaneously in order to evaluate and compare different summarizers [22]. For the extraction task we are dealing with, things are a bit easier. We compared the extract of a system with the desired summary and used the following Precision and Recall measures:

$$\text{Precision} = \frac{\#\text{of sentences extracted by the system which are in the target summaries}}{\text{total }\#\text{ of sentences extracted by the system}}$$

$$\text{Recall} = \frac{\#\text{of sentences extracted by the system which are in the target summaries}}{\text{total }\#\text{ of sentences in the target summaries}}$$

We first compare the systems trained in a fully supervised way. This gives an upper bound of their performances and provides a first ranking of the different algorithms. Results are in table 1.

Table 1. Comparison between the baseline system and different learning classifiers on Reuters and cmp_lg test sets. All trainable systems are trained in a fully supervised way, using an expanded query. Accuracy is the ratio of correct classification for both relevant and irrelevant sentences.

	Reuters data set		Cmp_lg collection	
System	**Average Precision (%)**	**Accuracy (%)**	**Average Precision (%)**	**Accuracy (%)**
Baseline	53,23	55,13	54,53	56,16
Naive Bayes	61,02	63,03	61,83	63,48
Generative-CEM	72,86	73,06	74,12	74,79
Logistic-CEM	73,84	74,22	75,26	76,92

For both collections, naive Bayes is approximately 8% better in precision and accuracy than the non-trainable baseline and the CEM algorithms are about 11% better than naive Bayes. The logistic classifier being slightly better than the generative gaussian. Precision-Recall curves (figure 2 top) confirm this ranking. From bottom to top, the curves correspond respectively to a random sentence selection, to the first sentences of a document, to the baseline system, to naive Bayes fully supervised, to the logistic-CEM trained using 10% of the labels in the training set to generative and logistic fully supervised algorithms. The baseline system improves the break-even point performances respectively compared to random selection and first sentences by 15% and 6% on the Reuters data set and by 17% and 5,5% on the cmp_lg collection. Trainable systems clearly outperform the baseline system for all recall values and the two CEMs are clearly above the naive Bayes classifier. Obtaining similar results for both collections with training sets of respectively 330 and 60 documents suggests that the task is slightly easier for cmp_lg than for Reuters. This is confirmed by further experiments.

Another interesting result is that both logistic and generative-CEM trained with semi-supervised, using 10% of labeled documents together with 90% of unlabeled documents on the training set give similar performances than the naive Bayes classifier trained with all labeled documents on the training set. This suggests that our classifiers are sound enough to take advantage of a small a priori information, and that unlabeled data do indeed contain relevant information for this task.

Figures 2-bottom shows the average precision on both sets for semi-supervised learning at different ratio of labeled-unlabeled documents in the training set, for the generative and logistic semi-supervised algorithms. 10% on the *x*-axis, means that 10% of the labeled documents in the training sets were used for training, the 90% remaining being used as unlabeled training documents. For comparison, we have also performed test with a logistic classifier trained only on the labeled sentences without using the unlabeled sentences in the training set (logistic-supervised in fig. 2 bottom). Logistic-CEM uniformly outperforms all other systems. This is particularly clear for SUMMAC cmp-lg, which is a small document set. In this case, the discriminant approach is clearly superior to the generative approach. With only 10% of labeled documents in the training set, the logistic-CEM approach is over the baseline non trainable system and using about 15% of labeled documents allows to reach half the performance increase we can get with fully supervised training with regard to the baseline non trainable system. Using unlabeled sentences do increase the performances (compare e.g. logistic-CEM and logistic-supervised curves in figure 2-bottom at 10%), this confirms the soundness of semi-supervised learning for this task.

As for the complexity, logistic-CEM system uses only 6 β coefficients, one for each characteristic and one bias. Once trained, it is only needed to compute a weighted sum of the characteristics to rank sentences. The generative-CEM has 60 parameters since we used full gaussians (lower performances were obtained with diagonal covariance matrices here). Naive Bayes is approximately the same order of complexity than logistic. Logistic-CEM is then particularly cheap and fast to operate.

The algorithms described here are generic, and different versions using different classifiers may be implemented (any conditional density model can be used for the generative system and any discriminant classifier whose score approximates the posterior class probabilities can be used for the discriminant CEM). They can operate on any categorical and/or numerical representation of sentences or more generally of text spans, so that richer representations may lead to better performances. They can also be extended to handle directly *word sequences* instead of fixed size representations as it is described here. We have performed tests on simple numerical sequential representations of sentences. The performances were roughly the same as above, using only automatically computed frequential information. This opens the way to the selection of arbitrary text spans not corresponding to sentences or paragraphs. Such text spans could be used in more sophisticated abstracting systems. The system can also be used in a fully unsupervised way: a non-trainable baseline system is used to provide an initial labeling of the sentences, and the classifiers then learn to improve this labeling using a variant of the algorithms presented here. This *fully unsupervised* scheme provided results similar to the semi-supervised methods trained with 10 % labeled data and to the Kupiec et al. fully supervised naive Bayes method. However, the two datasets we have been using are clean and documents are well structured. The algorithms should be evaluated on more noisy data and the scaling of this system on larger collections with heterogeneous documents has still to be investigated. Since our methods are fully automatic and learn from the data, and also because different machine learning techniques can be used within this general framework, there is hope that the system degrades gracefully for more complex tasks, but this remains to explore.

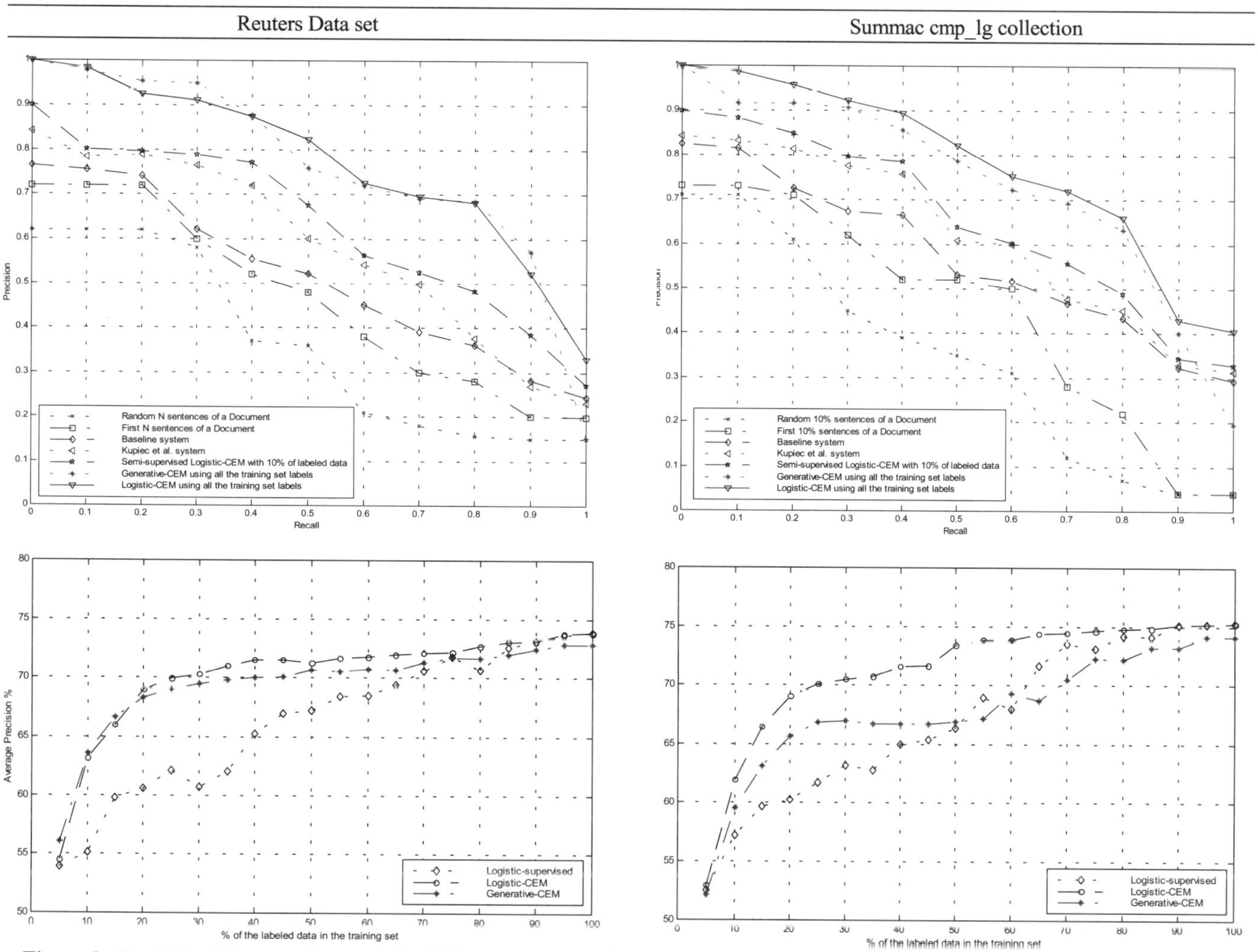

Figure 2. (Top) Precision recall curves for different systems. From bottom to top, the curves correspond respectively to a random selection of N first sentences, to the selection of N first sentences, to the baseline system, to Kupiec et al.'s system, to the CEM-logistic with 10% of labeled data and to generative and logistic fully supervised algorithms. (Bottom) Average precision of 3 trainable summarizers with respect to the ratio of labeled documents in the training set. The summarizers are the logistic and generative CEM algorithms and a logistic classifier trained only on x% labeled data.

7. Conclusion and future work

We have proposed a new general semi supervised approach for training text summarizers based on sentence segment extraction and performed an evaluation on two data sets, the news-wire summaries of Reuters data and the cmp_lg collection of TIPSTER SUMMAC. Our method has been compared to a non-trainable baseline system and to the Kupiec et al.'s fully supervised learning classifier. With only 10% labeled documents, our algorithm reaches the performances of these systems and outperform them using more labeled data. Experiments show that using only 10 to 20% of labeled sentences in the training set allows to reach half of the performance increase provided by a fully supervised approach.

We have also compared discriminant and generative approaches to semi-supervised learning and the former has been found clearly superior to the latter for small collections.

Finally we have briefly mentioned extensions of this system to sequential text representations and to unsupervised learning, which shows that this system is really flexible.

In future work, we plan to evaluate our systems on large and heterogeneous data sets.

Acknowledgements

Many thanks to Vibu O. Mittal who helped us a lot to improve this work and proposed further directions to investigate.

8. REFERENCES

[1] Anderson J.A., Richardson S.C. Logistic Discrimination and Bias correction in maximum likelihood estimation. *Technometrics*, 21 (1979) 71-78.

[2] Banko, M.; Mittal, V.; Kantrowitz, M.; and Goldstein, J. Generating Extraction-Based Summaries from Hand-Written One by Text Alignment. Pac. Rim Conf. on Comp. (1999)

[3] Barzilay R., Elhadad M. Using lexical chains for text summarization. Proceedings of the ACL'97/EACL'97 Workshop on Intelligent Scalable Text Summarization, (1997) 10-17.

[4] Berger A.L., Mittal V.O., OCELOT: A system for summarizing web pages. Research and Development in Information Retrieval (2000).

[5] Blum A., Mitchell T. Combining Labeled and Unlabeled Data with Co-Training. Proceedings of the 1998 Conference on Computational Learning Theory. (1998).

[6] Carbonell J.G., Goldstein J. The use of MMR, diversity-based reranking for reordering documents and producing summaries. Proceedings of the 21st ACM SIGIR, (1998) 335-336.

[7] Celeux G., Govaert G. A classification EM algorithm for clustering and two stochastic versions. Computational Statistics & Data Analysis. 14 (1992) 315-332.

[8] Chuang W.T., Yang J. Extracting sentence segments for text summarization: a machine learning approach. Proceedings of the 23rd ACM SIGIR. (2000) 152-159.

[9] Duda R. O., Hart P. T. Pattern Recognition and Scene Analysis. Edn. Wiley (1973).

[10] Goldstein J., Kantrowitz M., Mittal V., Carbonell J. Summarizing Text Documents: Sentence Selection and Evaluation Metrics. Proceedings of the 22nd ACM SIGIR (1999) 121-127.

[11] http://boardwatch.internet .com/mag/95/oct/bwm9.html

[12] http://www.itl.nist.gov/iaui/894.02/related_projects/tipster_summac/cmp_lg.html

[13] Klavans J.L., Shaw J. Lexical semantics in summarization. Proceedings of the First Annual Workshop of the IFIP working Group for NLP and KR. (1995).

[14] Knaus D., Mittendorf E., Schauble P., Sheridan P. Highlighting Relevant Passages for Users of the Interactive SPIDER Retrieval System. in TREC-4 proceedings. (1994).

[15] Kupiec J., Pedersen J., Chen F. A. Trainable Document Summarizer. Proceedings of the 18th ACM SIGIR. (1995) 68-73.

[16] Luhn P.H. Automatic creation of literature abstracts. IBM Journal (1958) 159-165.

[17] Mani I., Bloedorn E. Machine Learning of Generic and User-Focused Summarization. Proceedings of the Fifteenth National Conference on AI. (1998) 821-826.

[18] Marcu D. From discourse structures to text summaries. Proceedings of the ACL'97/EACL'97 Workshop on Intelligent Scalable Text Summarization. (1997) 82-88.

[19] McLachlan G.J. Discriminant Analysis and Statistical Pattern Recognition. Edn. John Wiley & Sons, New-York (1992).

[20] Miller D., Uyar H. A Mixture of Experts classifier with learning based on both labeled and unlabeled data. Advances in Neural Information Processing Systems. 9 (1996) 571-577.

[21] Mitra M., Singhal A., Buckley C. Automatic Text Summarization by Paragraph Extraction. Proceedings of the ACL'97/EACL'97 Workshop on Intelligent Scalable Text Summarization. (1997) 31-36.

[22] Mittal V., Kantrowitz M., Goldstein J., Carbonell J. Selecting Text Spans for Document Summaries: Heuristics and Metrics. Proceedings of the 6th National Conference on AI. (1999).

[23] Nigam K., McCallum A., Thrun A., Mitchell T. Text Classification from labeled and unlabeled documents using EM. In proceedings of National Conference on Artificial Intelligence. (1998).

[24] NIST. TIPSTER Information-Retrieval Text Research Collection on CD-ROM. National Institute of Standards and Technology, Gaithersburg, Maryland. (1993).

[25] Nomoto T., Matsumoto Y., A new Approach to Unsupervised Text Summarization. Proceedings of the 24th ACM SIGIR (2001) 26-34.

[26] Radev D., McKeown K. Generating natural language summaries from multiple online sources. Computational Linguistics. (1998).

[27] Robertson S., Sparck-Jones K., Relevance weighting of search terms. Journal of the American Society for Information Science, 27 3, (1976) 129-146.

[28] Roth V., Steinhage V. Nonlinear Discriminant Analysis using Kernel Functions. Advances in Neural Information Processing Systems. 12 (1999).

[29] Scott A.J., Symons M.J. Clustering Methods based on Likelihood Ratio Criteria. Biometrics. 27 (1991) 387-397.

[30] Sparck Jones K.: Discourse modeling for automatic summarizing. Technical Report 29D, Computer laboratory, university of Cambridge. (1993).

[31] Strzalkowski T., Wang J., Wise B. A robust practical text summarization system. Proceedings of the Fifteenth National Conference on AI. (1998) 26-30.

[32] Symons M.J. Clustering Criteria and Multivariate Normal Mixture. Biometrics. 37 (1981) 35-43.

[33] Teufel S., Moens M. Sentence Extraction as a Classification Task. Proceedings of the ACL'97/EACL'97 Workshop on Intelligent Scalable Text Summarization. (1997) 58-65.

[34] Tipster text phase III 18-month workshop notes, May 1998. FairFax, VA.

[35] Zechner K.: Fast Generation of Abstracts from General Domain Text Corpora by Extracting Relevant Sentences. COLING. (1996) 986-989.

Generic Summarization and Keyphrase Extraction Using Mutual Reinforcement Principle and Sentence Clustering

Hongyuan Zha
Department of Computer Science & Engineering
Pennsylvania State University
University Park, PA 16802
zha@cse.psu.edu

ABSTRACT

A novel method for *simultaneous* keyphrase extraction and generic text summarization is proposed by modeling text documents as weighted undirected and weighted bipartite graphs. Spectral graph clustering algorithms are used for partitioning sentences of the documents into topical groups with sentence link priors being exploited to enhance clustering quality. Within each topical group, saliency scores for keyphrases and sentences are generated based on a mutual reinforcement principle. The keyphrases and sentences are then ranked according to their saliency scores and selected for inclusion in the top keyphrase list and summaries of the document. The idea of building a hierarchy of summaries for documents capturing different levels of granularity is also briefly discussed. Our method is illustrated using several examples from news articles, news broadcast transcripts and web documents.

Categories and Subject Descriptors

H.3.3 [**Information Systems**]: Information Search and Retrieval—*Clustering*; H.4.m [**Information Systems**]: Miscellaneous—*Text Summarization*; G.1.3 [**Numerical Analysis**]: Numerical Linear Algebra—*Singular value decomposition*; G.2.2 [**Discrete Mathematics**]: Graph Theory—*Graph algorithms*

General Terms

Algorithms, Experimentation, Theory

Keywords

text summarization, keyphrase extraction, mutual reinforcement principle, bipartite graph, graph partitioning, singular value decomposition

SIGIR'02, August 11-15, 2002, Tampere, Finland.

1. INTRODUCTION

Text summarization is an increasingly pressing practical problem due to the explosion of the amount of textual information available. For example, web search engines have exploited the use of text summarization from the very beginning: starting with the extraction of certain number of bytes from the beginning of each document to the more sophisticated query-focused summaries typified by Google's snippets (see also the recent work in [1]). Query-focused summaries provide the users with the useful information for initial relevance judgement so that they can quickly zero in on documents deserving further inspection. In contrast, a generic summary in general distills the most important overall information from a document (or a set of documents), it can be especially useful when the documents are relatively long and contain a variety of topics. With many search engines starting to index documents in postscript and pdf formats, we will see increased availability of long and multi-part documents and the pressing needs for efficiently generating effective generic summaries for those documents. In addition, there is also a great amount of news articles and broadcast transcripts generated daily from various news agencies needing effective summarization.

Automatic text summarization is an extremely active research field making connections with many other research areas such as information retrieval, natural language processing and machine learning [5]. Informally, the goal of text summarization is *to take a textual document, extract content from it and present the most important content to the user in a condensed form and in a manner sensitive to the user's or application's needs* [13]. In this paper we concentrate on the shallow approach of text summarization using sentence and keyphrase extractions. Abstract generation utilizing materials not present in the documents to be summarized is a more challenging problem and will not be addressed here [1, 13, 14]. Two basic approaches to sentence extraction can be distinguished on whether they are supervised or unsupervised in nature. Supervised approaches need human-generated summary extracts for feature extraction and parameter estimation as is typified by the methods in [10, 3] where sentence classifiers are trained using human-generated sentence-summary pairs as training examples. Possible drawbacks of the supervised approaches are domain-dependency and the problems caused by the potential inconsistency of human-generated summaries. In this paper we adopt the unsupervised approach, we *explicitly* model both keyphrases and the sentences that contain them using weighted undirected and weighted bipartite graphs and generate sentence extracts on the fly without extensive training. Our method can also be viewed as representing a more sophisticated and effective approach to exploiting the term co-occurrence relationship in textual documents.

Many text summarization methods are surveyed in [5, 13, 14]. We mention here several recent approaches that are closest in spirit to our approach. In [18], documents are modeled using undirected graphs with the vertices representing paragraphs, and edge weights representing similarity between two paragraphs. Salient paragraphs are those connected to many other paragraphs with similarity above certain thresholds. In [6], Latent semantic indexing was used as the bases for sentence selection of a given textual document, exploiting the components of multiple singular vectors. However, the singular vectors other than the one corresponding to the largest singular value can have both positive and negative components, making ranking sentences by singular vector component values less meaningful. In [4], QR decomposition with column pivoting applied to term-sentence matrices was used for sentence selection, providing another example of unsupervised summarization methods. To emphasize diversity of topic coverage in a generic summary, in [15] it was proposed to use a variation of the K-means method to cluster the sentences of a document into different topical groups, and then apply a sentence weighting model within each topical group for sentence selection.

The basic idea of our summarization method is to first cluster sentences of a document (or a set of documents) into topical groups and then, within each topical group, to select the keyphrases and sentences by their saliency scores. Our major contributions are 1) proposing the use of sentence link priors resulted from the linear ordering of the sentences in a document to enhance sentence clustering quality; and 2) developing the mutual reinforcement principle for simultaneous keyphrase and sentence saliency score computation. We also alluded to the possibility of building a summary hierarchy based on a hierarchical clustering of the sentences of a document. The rest of the paper is organized as follows: in section 2, we develop the mutual reinforcement principle and its connection to computing the largest singular value triplet of the weight matrix of the term-sentence bipartite graph. In section 3, we introduce the sentence link prior and show how we can incorporate it into the sum-of-squares sentence clustering objective function using spectral clustering techniques. We also discuss link strength selection using generalized cross-validation. In section 4, we describe some experimental results using documents from the newswires, broadcasting transcripts and the World Wide Web. We conclude the paper in section 5 with pointers to future research.

2. THE MUTUAL REINFORCEMENT PRINCIPLE

For each document, we generate two sets of objects: one the set of terms $T = \{t_1, \ldots, t_n\}$ and the other the set of sentences $S = \{s_1, \ldots, s_m\}$ in the document. [1] We build a weighted *bipartite* graph from T and S in the following way: if the term t_i appears in sentence s_j, we then create an edge between t_i and s_j. We can also specify *nonnegative* weights on the edges of the weighted bipartite graph with w_{ij} indicating the weight on the edge (t_i, s_j). For example, we can simply choose w_{ij} to be the number of times t_i appears in s_j. More sophisticated weighting schemes will be discussed later. We denote the weighted bipartite graph by $G(T, S, W)$ where $W = [w_{ij}]$ is the m-by-n weight matrix containing all the pairwise edge weights. For each term t_i and each sentence s_j we wish to compute their saliency scores $u(t_i)$ and $v(s_j)$, respectively. To this end, we state the following *mutual reinforcement principle*:[2]

> A term should have a high saliency score if it appears in many sentences with high saliency scores while a sentence should have a high saliency score if it contains many terms with high saliency scores.

In essence the principle dictates that the saliency score of a term is determined by the saliency scores of the sentences it appears in, and the saliency score of a sentence is determined by the saliency scores of the terms it contains. Mathematically, the above statement is rendered as

$$u(t_i) \propto \textstyle\sum_{v(s_j)\sim u(t_i)} w_{ij} v(s_j),$$
$$v(s_j) \propto \textstyle\sum_{u(t_i)\sim u(t_i)} w_{ij} u(t_i),$$

where the summations are over the neighbors of the vertices in question, and $a \sim b$ indicates there is an edge between vertices a and b, i.e., when computing a term score, the summation is over all sentences that contain the term and when computing a sentence score, the summation is over all terms that appear in the sentence. The symbol $\propto$ stands for "proportional to". Now we collect the saliency scores for terms and sentences into two vectors u and v, respectively, the above equation can then be written in the following matrix format

$$u = \frac{1}{\sigma} W v, \quad v = \frac{1}{\sigma} W^T u,$$

where W is the weight matrix of the bipartite graph of the document in question, W^T stands for the matrix transpose of W, and $1/\sigma$ is the proportionality constant. It is easy to see that u and v are the left and right singular vectors of W corresponding to the singular value σ. If we choose σ to be the largest singular value of W, then its is guaranteed that both u and v have *nonnegative* components. The corresponding component values of u and v give the term and sentence saliency scores, respectively. We can rank terms and sentences in decreasing order of their saliency scores, and select the top t terms (with the highest saliency scores) to add to the top term list and the top s sentences (with the highest saliency scores) to add to the summary. Here t and s are some user-defined values, and s can be estimated from the compression rate of the desired summary.

REMARK. For numerical computation of the largest singular value triplet $\{u, \sigma, v\}$, we can use a variation of the power method adapted to the case of singular value triplets: choose an initial value for v to be the vector of all ones. Alternate between the following two steps until convergence,

1. Compute and normalize

$$u = Wv, \quad u = u/\|u\|,$$

[1]The choice is flexible, for example, terms can be words or phrases and sentences can be replaced by paragraphs or other text units.

[2]Similar ideas have also been used to find the hub and authority web pages in a link graph [9].

2. Compute and normalize

$$v = W^T u, \quad v = v/\|v\|,$$

where the vector norm $\|\cdot\|$ can be chosen to the Euclidean norm, and σ can be computed as $\sigma = u^T W v$ upon convergence. For a detailed analysis of the singular value decomposition for related types of matrices, the reader is referred to [19].

REMARK. The above general weighted bipartite graph model can be extended further by adding vertex weights to the terms and/or sentences. Both types of weights can incorporate certain kind of prior information, for example, the weight of a sentence vertex can be increased if it contains certain bonus words; we can also modify the weight of a sentence vertex based on its position in the document. In general, let D_T and D_S be two diagonal matrices the diagonal elements of which represent the weights of the term vertices and sentence vertices, respectively. Then instead of finding the largest singular value triplet of the edge weight matrix W, we compute the largest singular value triplet $\{u, \sigma, v\}$ of the scaled matrix $D_T W D_S$. A specific sentence vertex weighting scheme will be discussed later.

3. CLUSTERING SENTENCES INTO TOPICAL GROUPS

The saliency score computation discussed in Section 2 can be more effective if it is applied within each topical group of a document (or a set of documents). To this end we discuss effective algorithms for sentence clustering with the purpose to reveal the latent topical structure of textual documents. The idea of using sentences clustering has also been recently used in [18, 15]. For sentence clustering we first build an *undirected weighted* graph with vertices representing the sentences of a document and two sentences s_i and s_j are linked by an edge if there are terms shared by the two sentences, we also specify an edge weight w_{ij} for the edge (s_i, s_j), in general w_{ij} indicates the similarity between the two sentences s_i and s_j, and there are many different ways for their specification. We denote the resulting graph as $G(S, W_S)$, where S is the set of sentences and $W_S = [w_{ij}]$ gives the edge weights. It is quite easy to verify that W_S has the same *sparsity pattern* as $W^T W$, where W is the weight matrix for the bipartite graph introduced in Section 2.

3.1 Incorporating sentence link priors

Documents consist of sentences arranged in a *linear* order, and near-by sentences in terms of this intrinsic linear order tend to be about the same topic. The fact that topical groups within a document are usually made of sections of consecutive sentences is a strong prior that needs to be fully exploited during the sentence clustering process. The prior which we call sentence link prior will be especially helpful when dealing with broadcasting transcripts where there are no syntactic cues such as paragraph heading/ending to indicate topic boundaries. To ease discussion, we call s_i and s_j are *near-by* to each other if s_i is followed by s_j in the linear order of the document (or s_j is followed by s_i, since the graph we consider is undirected anyway).

The weighted undirected graph framework we are using for sentence clustering naturally lends itself to incorporating the sentence link prior. In general, pairs of vertices (sentences) with large similarity weight tend to be clustered into the same group. A simple approach to taking advantage of this goes as follows: we strengthen the similarity weight between near-by sentences, i.e., we modify the weights for all the near-by sentence pairs,

$$\hat{w}_{ij} = \begin{cases} w_{ij} + \alpha & \text{if } s_i \text{ and } s_j \text{ are near-by} \\ w_{ij} & \text{otherwise} \end{cases}$$

We call α the sentence link strength, and the modified weight matrix is denoted by $W_S(\alpha)$. There are $n-1$ modifications in total for a document with n sentences. There is also the possibility of strengthen the similarity of pairs of sentences that are two (or more) edges away from each other. Notice that incorporating sentence link prior is different from the requirement in text segmentation: we do allow several sections of consecutive sentences to form a single topical group.

The parameter α can be considered as a regularization parameter, and we use the idea of generalized cross-validation (GCV) for choosing a good α [12]. For a fixed α, we apply the spectral clustering technique discussed in the next section to $W(\alpha)$ to obtain a set of sentence clusters $\Pi^*(\alpha)$. For any sentence clustering Π we define $\gamma(\Pi)$ to be the number of consecutive sentence segments it generates which is then used as a measure of model complexity for the clustering Π. The idea is to simultaneously minimize the clustering cost function and the model complexity. To this end, we compute a function of α defined as

$$\text{GCV}(\alpha) = (n - k - J(W, \Pi^*(\alpha)))\,/\gamma(\Pi^*(\alpha)), \qquad (1)$$

where k is the desirable number of sentence clusters, W is the weight matrix for the term-sentence bipartite graph and $\Pi^*(\alpha)$ is the set of clusters obtained by applying spectral clustering to the modified weight matrix $W(\alpha)$. We then select the α that maximizes the above function as the *estimated* optimal α value.

3.2 Building a summary hierarchy

Summaries can actually capture the essential information of textual documents at different levels of granularity. This issue is closely related to the compression rate and coverage/diversity of summaries [13]. However, the point of view of *hierarchical* sentence clustering seems to provide a rather natural and fruitful way of tackling the issue. We start with a sentence cluster hierarchy with the lower-level clusters (nodes) representing finer structures of the document. Summarization is then done at each node of the hierarchy using all the sentences that belong to this node. Two basic variations exist when carry out summarization at a non-root node of the hierarchy.

- The terms used in summarization remain the same for all the nodes;
- The terms used in summarization at a particular node do not include the top terms (i.e., those terms having high saliency scores) from the summarization of its parent nodes.

The idea for the second approach is that we only retain terms that can distinguish finer structures of the document. Another possibility is to use the first approach in the above for all the *leave* nodes of the hierarchy, and at the next higher level carry out a summary of summaries until the root-node is reached. Currently, we have only limited experiences with the ideas proposed above, and we will not elaborate on the issues further.

3.3 Sum-of-squares cost function for sentence clustering and spectral relaxation

We start with the weight matrix W for the bipartite graph $G(T, S, W)$. Here each sentence is represented by a column of $W = [w_1, \ldots, w_n]$ which we will call the sentence vector. A partition Π of the sentence vectors can be written in the following form

$$WE = [W_1, \ldots, W_k], \quad W_i = [w_1^{(i)}, \ldots, w_{n_i}^{(i)}], \qquad (2)$$

where E is a permutation matrix, and W_i is m-by-n_i, i.e., the ith sentence cluster contains the sentence vectors in W_i. For a given partition Π, the associated sum-of-squares cost function is defined as [7]

$$J(W, \Pi) = \sum_{i=1}^{k} \sum_{s=1}^{n_i} \|w_s^{(i)} - m_i\|^2, \quad m_i = \sum_{s=1}^{n_i} w_s^{(i)}/n_i, \qquad (3)$$

i.e., m_i is the centroid of the sentence vectors in cluster i, and n_i is the number of sentences in cluster i.

The traditional K-means algorithm is iterative in nature and in each iteration, the following is performed [7]:

1) For each sentence vector w, find the center m_i that is closest to w, and associate w with this center.

2) Compute a new set of centers by taking, for each center, the center of mass of sentence vectors associated with this center.

It can be proved that the above algorithm is equivalent to finding a local minimum of $J(W, \Pi)$ with respect to Π using coordinate descent. Despite the popularity of K-means clustering algorithm, one of its major drawbacks is that the coordinate descent search method is prone to local minima giving rise to some clusters with very few data points. Moreover, it is also not easy to incorporate the sentence link prior into the above sum-of-squares cost function in order to improve sentence clustering quality. Much research has been done on computing refined initial centroids and adding explicit constraints to the sum-of-squares cost function for K-means clustering so that the search can converge to a better local minimum [2]. It was shown, however, that an equivalent formulation of the sum-of-squares minimization can be derived as a matrix trace maximization problem with special constraints; relaxing the constraints leads to a trace maximization problem that possesses optimal *global* solutions [20]. This formulation also makes K-means method easily adaptable to utilizing the sentence link priors discused in the above subsection.

Here we give a brief presentation of the spectral relaxation approach for K-means clustering. Let e be a vector of appropriate dimension with all elements equal to one, it is easy to see that the centroids can be written as

$$m_i = W_i e / n_i.$$

Now let

$$X = \mathrm{diag}(e/\sqrt{n_1}, \ldots, e/\sqrt{n_k}).$$

It was shown in [20] that the sum-of-squares cost function can be written as

$$J(W, \Pi) = \mathrm{trace}(W^T W) - \mathrm{trace}(X^T W^T W X),$$

and its minimization is equivalent to

$$\max\{\ \mathrm{trace}(X^T W^T W X) \mid X = \mathrm{diag}(e/\sqrt{n_1}, \ldots, e/\sqrt{n_k})\}.$$

Ignoring the special structure of X and let it be an arbitrary orthonormal matrix, we obtain a *relaxed* matrix trace maximization problem

$$\max_{X^T X = I_k} \mathrm{trace}(X^T W^T W X). \qquad (4)$$

An extension of the Rayleigh-Ritz characterization of eigenvalues of symmetric matrices shows that the above maximum is achieved by the first k largest eigenvectors of the Gram matrix $W^T W$ [8, Section 4.3.18]. As a by-product, we also have the following inequality

$$\min_{\Pi} J(W, \Pi) \geq \mathrm{trace}(W^T W) - \max_{X^T X = I_k} \mathrm{trace}(X^T W^T W X)$$

$$= \sum_{i=k+1}^{\min\{m,n\}} \sigma_i^2(W),$$

where $\sigma_i(W)$ is the i largest singular value of W. This gives a *lower bound* for the minimum of the sum-of-squares cost function. The spectral relaxation formulation of the K-means algorithm also makes it easy to consider more general kernel functions: instead of using $w_i^T w_j$ we can compute the Gram matrix using any Mercer kernel $K(x, x')$ to obtain $[K(w_i, w_j)]_{i,j=1}^n$. In particular, we can replace $W^T W$ by $W_S(\alpha)$ after incorporating the link strength α. The assignment of the cluster labels to each sentence is done by using QR decomposition with pivoting (see below).

The sentence clustering algorithm based on the modified weight matrix $W_S(\alpha)$ is now summarized as follows:

- Compute the k eigenvectors $V_k = [v_1, \ldots, v_k]$ of $W_S(\alpha)$ corresponding to the largest k eigenvalues.

- Compute the pivoted QR decomposition of V_k^T as

  $$(V_k)^T P = QR = Q[R_{11}, R_{12}],$$

  where Q is a k-by-k orthogonal matrix, R_{11} is a k-by-k upper triangular matrix, and P is a permutation matrix.

- Compute

  $$\hat{R} = R_{11}^{-1}[R_{11}, R_{12}]P^T = [I_k, R_{11}^{-1} R_{12}]P^T.$$

  Then the cluster membership of each sentence is determined by the row index of the largest element *in absolute value* of the corresponding column of $\hat{R}$. This gives rise to the clustering $\Pi^*(\alpha)$ used in (1).

4. EXPERIMENTAL RESULTS

Evaluation for generic text summarization is a very challenging task: although it can be done against a set of documents with manual summarizations, human-generated sentence extracts do, however, tend to differ significantly especially for longer documents [6, 13]. Another approach is to evaluate extrinsically the summarization algorithms based on, for example, their performance on document retrieval or text categorization. Here we will provide some preliminary quantitative and qualitative assessment of our summarization algorithm. We collected a set of ten documents consisting of news articles, news broadcast transcripts and web pages.

- News articles

Document	optimal α	accuracy	estimated α	accuracy	sentence #	cluster #
sf	7.94	82.17%	7.94	82.17%	157	7
pge	63	69.23%	12.59	57.95 %	195	6
flg	19.95	68.07%	125.89	66.87 %	166	7
heart	7.94	87.23%	7.97	87.23%	47	3
enron	39.8	75.86%	14.59	74.71%	87	6
cnn	31.62	71.79%	79.43	64.69%	507	16
cnn1	2.2	73.96%	50.11	69.81%	265	10
cnn2	25.1	64.89%	125.89	60.11 %	544	12
cnn3	1.99	72.52%	12.59	65.32%	223	10
dna	3.16	74.68%	7.94	70.89%	79	8

Table 1: Clustering accuracy with optimal and estimated α

sf: story.news.yahoo.com/news?tmpl=story&u=/nyt/20020121/ts_nyt/conduct_of_war_is_redefined_by_success_of_special_forces

pge: www0.mercurycenter.com/local/center/dereg1201.htm

flg: www0.mercurycenter.com/local/center/fal122301.htm

enron: story.news.yahoo.com/news?tmpl=story&cid=68&u=/nyt/20020120/ts_nyt/multiple_safeguards_failed_to_detect_problems_at_enron

- CNN broadcast transcripts

cnn : monoyline
cnn1: newsroom
cnn2: Wolf Blitzer repots
cnn3: science and technology week

- Web pages

dna:
www.pbs.org/wgbh/nova/neanderthals/mtdna.html
heart:
www.pbs.org/wgbh/nova/heart/treating.html

We manually divide each document into topical groups: for web pages and news articles we rely on the section structure of the documents, and for news broadcast transcripts we rely on the contents of the documents. We notice that the clustering is usually not unique, some clusters can be merged into a bigger cluster and some clusters can be split into several smaller ones to capture the finer structure of the documents. The number of sentences and the number of clusters for each document are listed in the Table 1. (Other items of the table will be discussed later.)

We first illustrate *quantitatively* the difference in sentence clustering resulting from using the sentence link prior. In processing the documents, we deleted words appearing in a stop word list and applied Porter's stemming [16]. We used the following sentence similarity measure to construct the weight matrix W_S: each sentence is represented by a sentence vector using the weight matrix W of the term-sentence bipartite graph introduced in section 2, i.e., columns of W correspond to the sentences of the document in question. The weight matrix $W_S = (w_{ij})$ for the sentence graph is computed with w_{ij} equal to the dot-product between the sentence vectors of sentences s_i and s_j. The sentence vectors are weighted with **tf.idf** weighting and normalized to have Euclidean length one.

To measure the quality of sentence clustering, we use a variation of the confusion matrix which is frequently used for measuring classifier accuracy. We assume the manually generated section number gives the *true* cluster label of each sentence. We then compute the accuracy of our clustering algorithm against the section labels. In particular, for a k cluster case, we compute a k-by-k confusion matrix $C = [c_{ij}]$ with c_{ij} the number of sentences in cluster i that belong to section j. It is actually quite subtle to compute the accuracy using the confusion matrix because we do not know which cluster matches which section. An optimal way is to solve the following maximization problem

$$\max\{\ \mathrm{trace}(CP)\ \mid P \text{ is a permutation matrix}\},$$

and divide the maximum by the total number of sentences to obtain the clustering accuracy. This is equivalent to finding a perfect matching of a complete weighted bipartite graph which can be solved using Kuhn-Munkres algorithm [11]. In our computation, we used a greedy algorithm to compute a sub-optimal solution.

As an illustration, for a sequence of α values, we applied the spectral clustering algorithm to the weight matrix $W_S(\alpha)$ of the document **dna**, and in Figure 1 we plot the clustering accuracy against α. In the same figure, we also contrast the results of sentence clustering with and without link priors, the one without link priors tend to be more fragmented. Based on the results for the ten documents, a general conclusion seems to be that the clustering algorithm matches the section structure of the document poorly when there is no near-by sentence constraints (i.e., $\alpha = 0$). With too large an α value, sentence similarities are overwhelmed by link strength, the results are also poor. Our generalized cross-validation method seems to be quite effective at selecting a good α that produces clustering quality close to that given by the optimal α. In Table 1, we list the optimal α and the corresponding sentence clustering accuracy for each document. We also list the estimated α using GCV(α) discussed in section 3.1 and the corresponding sentence clustering accuracy. In general, clustering accuracy is a relatively flat function of α, and the estimated α even though may differ considerably from the optimal α still produces clustering accuracy that matchs well the best clustering accuracy, as

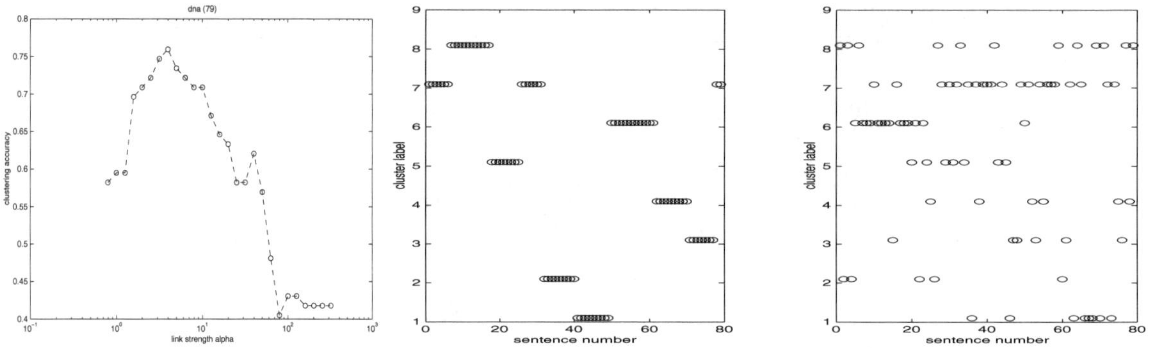

Figure 1: (Left) sentence clustering accuracy versus sentence link strength α. Sentence cluster distribution with link prior (middle) and without link prior (right)

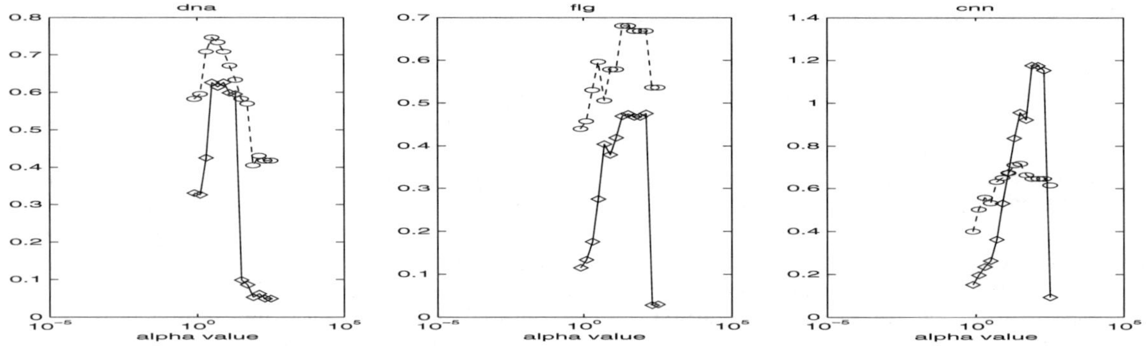

Figure 2: Clustering accuracy vs. α (circles); GCV(α) vs. α (diamonds)

can be seen from Figure 2.

For the computation of keyphrase and sentence saliency scores, we considered sentence vertex weights when applying the mutual reinforcement principle. Specifically, for the i-th sentence we apply the weight

$$\frac{\log_2(\text{number of terms in sentence} + 1)}{\log_2(i + \text{total number of sentences})}.$$

The idea is to mitigate the influence of long sentences by scaling each sentence by a factor proportional to the length of the sentence in terms of number of words; at the same time sentences close to the beginning of the document get a small boost based on their positions in the document.

For a detailed illustration we use document `dna` which consists of a story lead plus seven sections with sections headings given below

1. Tracing Ancestry with MtDNA (title) (1–6)
2. Nuclear DNA vs mitochondrial DNA (7–15)
3. Inheriting mtDNA (16–25)
4. Defining mitochondrial ancestors (26–37)
5. Finding mitochondrial ancestors (38–52)
6. Dating mitochondrial ancestors (53–63)
7. Neanderthals and mtDNA (63–70)
8. Final note (71–79)

There are 79 sentences in total, and we number the sentences consecutively starting from 1. The numbers in parentheses in the above indicate sentence sequence range in each section.

In Table 2, for $\alpha = 3.5$, we look at the clusters generated by listing the top five terms and the top one sentence in each topical groups. We also list the sentence numbers in the each topical group in parentheses.

The clustering result matches the section structure quite well except for cluster 8 which actually consists of two sentence sequences. Taking a closer look at the sentences in cluster 8, we found that sentences 1 to 4 discuss issues related the common ancestor "Eve", and section 4 with section heading *Defining mitochondrial ancestors* is about the same topic. So here sentence similarities win over sentence link strength. We have also applied the mutual reinforcement principle to all the sentences in the document `dna`, and the first few keywords and sentences extracted are related to the main topic of document. Similar analysis has also been applied to the other nine documents with quite similar results, the details of which will not be reported here due to the lack of space (see `http://www.cse.psu.edu/ zha/sum.html`).

5. CONCLUSIONS

In this paper we presented a novel method for simultaneous extraction of keyphrases and sentences from textual documents. We explore the sentence link priors embedded in the linear ordering of a document to enhance the quality of clustering sentences of documents into topical groups. We also develop the mutual reinforcement principle to compute

Cluster 1 (71–79) mtdna matern recent recombin alter In fact, recent studies show that paternal mtDNA can on rare occasions enter an egg during fertilization and alter the maternal mtDNA through recombination.	Cluster 2 (47–52) group tree similar famili comput Later, with the help of a computer program, they put together a sort of family tree, grouping those with the most similar DNA together, then grouping the groups, and then grouping the groups of groups.
Cluster 3 (53–61) ancestor mutat mtdna rate live For instance, if they took the mutation rate to be one in every 1,000 years and knew that there was a difference of 10 mutations between the mtDNA of people living today and the mtDNA of an ancestor who lived long ago, then they could infer that the ancestor lived 10,000 years ago.	Cluster 4 (62–70) modern neanderth mtdna european anthropologist This was an unwelcome finding for anthropologists who believe that there was some interbreeding between Neanderthals and early modern humans living in Europe (which might have helped to explain why modern Europeans possess some Neanderthal-like features);
Cluster 5 (36–46) mtdna live mutat inherit long Even though everyone on Earth living today has inherited his or her mtDNA from one person who lived long ago, our mtDNA is not exactly alike.	Cluster 6 (16–24) egg nuclear cell mtdna mothers Whenever an egg cell is fertilized, nuclear chromosomes from a sperm cell enter the egg and combine with the egg's nuclear DNA, producing a mixture of both parents' genetic code.
Cluster 7 (16–24) human mtdna live scientist includ In recent years, scientists have used mtDNA to trace the evolution and migration of human species,including when the common ancestor to modern humans and Neanderthals lived -- though there has been considerable debate over the validity and value of the findings.	Cluster 8 (1–4, 26–35) ancestor live common ev mtdna It also does not mean that the mtDNA originated with this "Eve"; she and her contemporaries also had their own "most recent common ancestor though matrilineal descent," a woman who lived even further into the past who passed on her mtDNA to everyone living during "Eve's" time.

Table 2: Clustering and sentence extract results for document dna. For each cluster we list five top words and one sentence.

keyphrase and sentence saliency scores within each topical groups. We have also illustrated our method using a variety of documents with different characteristics. Many issues need further investigation: 1) more research needs to be done for the determination of optimal link strength α; 2) other possible ways for sentence clustering. One promising approach is to use a two-stage method: first segment the sentences and then cluster the segments into topical groups; 3) the issues of replacing the use of simple terms by noun phrases, this will impact how the weight matrix W and W_S will be constructed, and in general the construction of sentence similarity using various resources beyond lexical match. We have experimented with using Ramshaw and Marcus noun phrase chuncker for extracting noun phrases [17]; 4) more extensive and systematic experimentation of the method for both single and multiple documents [5]; and 5) extension to translingual summarization [21].

Acknowledgement. The research was supported in part by NSF grant CCR-9901986. The author also wants to thank the referees for many constructive comments and suggestions.

6. REFERENCES

[1] A. L. Berger and V. O. Mittal. OCELOT: a system for summarizing Web pages. Proceedings of the 23rd International Conference on Research in Information Retrieval (SIGIR '00), pp. 144 - 151, 2000.

[2] P. S. Bradley and Usama M. Fayyad. *Refining Initial Points for K-Means Clustering.* Proc. 15th International Conf. on Machine Learning, 91–99, 1998.

[3] W. T. Chuang and J. Yang. Extracting sentence segments for text summarization: a machine learning approach Proceedings of the 23rd International Conference on Research in Information Retrieval (SIGIR '00), pp. 152–159, 2000.

[4] J. Conroy and D. P. O'Leary. Text Summarization via Hidden Markov Models and Pivoted QR Matrix Decomposition. Technical Report, Dept. Comp. Sci., CS-TR-4221, Univ. Maryland, 2001.

[5] Document Understanding Conference. `http://www-nlpir.nist.gov/projects/duc/`.

[6] Y. Gong and X. Liu. Generic text summarization using relevance measure and latent semantic analysis. Proceedings of the 24th International Conference on Research in Information Retrieval (SIGIR '01), pp. 19–25, 2001.

[7] J.A. Hartigan and M.A. Wong. (1979). *A K-means Clustering Algorithm.* Applied Statistics, 28:100–108.

[8] R. Horn and C. Johnson. *Matrix Analysis.* Cambridge University Press, 1985.

[9] J. Kleinberg. Authoritative Sources in a Hyperlinked Environment. Proc. ACM-SIAM SODA, 1998.

[10] J. Kupiec, J. Pedersen and F. Chen. A Trainable Document Summarizer. Proceedings of the 18th International Conference on Research in Information Retrieval (SIGIR '95), pp. 55-60, 1995.

[11] L. Lovasz and M.D. Plummer. (1986) *Matching Theory.* Amsterdam: North Holland.

[12] Z. Luo. Clustering under Spatial Contiguity Constraint: A penalized K-means method. Technical Report, Department of Statistics, Penn State University, 2001.

[13] I. Mani. *Automatic Summarization.* John Benjamins Pub Co., 2001.

[14] I. Mani and M. Maybury. *Advances in automatic text summarization.* MIT Press, 1999.

[15] T. Nomoto and Y. Matsumoto. A new approach to unsupervised text summarization. Proceedings of the 24th International Conference on Research in Information Retrieval (SIGIR '01), pp. 26–34, 2001.

[16] M. Porter. The Porter Stemming Algorithm. `www.tartarus.org/ martin/PorterStemmer`

[17] L. A. Ramshaw and M. P. Marcus. Text Chunking Using Transformation-Based Learning. *Proceedings of the Third ACL Workshop on Very Large Corpora",* Cambridge MA, USA, 1995.

[18] G. Salton, A. Singhal, M. Mitra and C. Buckley. Automatic text structuring and summarization. 341–355, *Advances in Automatic Text Summarization,* edited by I. Mani and M. Maybury, 1999.

[19] H. Zha and Z. Zhang. On Matrices with Low-rank-plus-shift Structures: Partial SVD and Latent Semantic Indexing,. *SIAM Journal of Matrix Analysis and Applications,* 21:522-536, 1999.

[20] H. Zha, M. Gu, X. He, C. Ding, and H. Simon. Spectral Relaxation for K-means Clustering. Advances in Neural Information Processing Systems, 14, eds. T. Dietterich, S. Becker, Z. Ghahramani, MIT Press, 2002.

[21] H. Zha and X. Ji. Correlating Multilingual Documents via Bipartite Graph Modeling. To appear in Proceedings of the 25th International Conference on Research in Information Retrieval (SIGIR '02), 2002.

Cross-Document Summarization by Concept Classification

Hilda Hardy†, Nobuyuki Shimizu†, Tomek Strzalkowski†, Liu Ting†, G. Bowden Wise‡, and Xinyang Zhang†

†NLIP Laboratory, University at Albany, SUNY
1400 Washington Avenue
Albany, NY 12222

hardyh@cs.albany.edu

‡GE Global Research Center
1 Research Circle
Niskayuna, NY 12309

ABSTRACT
In this paper we describe a Cross Document Summarizer XDoX designed specifically to summarize large document sets (50-500 documents and more). Such sets of documents are typically obtained from routing or filtering systems run against a continuous stream of data, such as a newswire. XDoX works by identifying the most salient themes within the set (at the granularity level that is regulated by the user) and composing an extraction summary, which reflects these main themes. In the current version, XDoX is not optimized to produce a summary based on a few unrelated documents; indeed, such summaries are best obtained simply by concatenating summaries of individual documents. We show examples of summaries obtained in our tests as well as from our participation in the first Document Understanding Conference (DUC).

Categories and Subject Descriptors
I.2.7 [**Artificial Intelligence**]: Natural Language Processing – *text analysis.*

General Terms: Algorithms, Measurement, Performance.

Keywords: Summary, clustering, n-grams, multi-document summarization, passage similarity, term weights.

1. INTRODUCTION
An automated multi-document summarization system requires techniques different from those necessary to summarize a single document. Many newswire articles on the same topic, for example, are likely to contain redundant material. Articles may also reveal new developments of events over time, or they may include various information and opinions on an issue or a person. Most current automated systems work by identifying the most important sentences or paragraphs in the set of documents and building a summary with these passages. Several systems use Carbonell and Goldstein's Maximal Marginal Relevance measure [1], which selects passages based on a combination of relevance and anti-redundancy. Columbia's SIMFINDER [4] uses several varieties of word overlap in addition to other features to determine similarity values between passages in order to form clusters, followed by sentence extraction (CENTRIFUSER) or reformulation (MULTIGEN, FUF/SURGE). Radev et al's WebInEssence [13] clusters documents according to keyword overlap and performs centroid-based sentence extraction. Marcu [8] selects important sentences based on the discourse structure of the text. Lin and Hovy's NEATS system [7] creates a query based on single terms, bigrams and trigrams most characteristic of each document set, finally producing a ranked list of sentences. TNO's system [6] scores sentences by combining a unigram language model approach with a Bayesian classifier based on surface features. Our XDoX system clusters passages based on our unique *n*-gram scoring methods, and builds an extraction summary by selecting a representative passage from each cluster.

SIGIR'02, August 11-15, 2002, Tampere, Finland.

2. XDOX OVERVIEW
The XDoX system (Cross Document Summarizer) is designed to summarize sets of 50-500 documents that have been retrieved or routed from a text database, the Internet, or a news source, according to a query or a user-defined profile. Built for information analysts, the system uses clustering techniques to subdivide the documents into meaningful topics and themes, and to separate unrelated material. XDoX presents the user with two kinds of overall summary, one with more detail related to the complexity of the document set, and one with fewer details and limited length. In addition, a summary of each topical cluster is available via a Graphical User Interface. The GUI also allows the user to view individual passages or full documents. Thus the system answers both the indicative and the exploratory needs of our customers.

XDoX has been developed over the last 2 years with several intermediate designs considered. An earlier version of the system [16] produced clusters of documents according to their mutual similarity, which was based primarily on straightforward term overlap between documents. In addition, WordNet lexical database [2] [10] was used to facilitate the matching of synonyms and other related terms. This early work focused on evaluation of various document clustering techniques, but we found that most known clustering methods could not alone support an effective summarizer. Whether or not WordNet is used, the resulting clusters were often of poor quality, formed around common but semantically unimportant terms.

Our new approach improves the quality of the clusters and the summaries chiefly by implementing concept-based clustering and summarization. Instead of clustering entire documents, we cluster passages [11], or sequences of text, which usually correspond to the natural paragraphs designed by the author or editor, or that may be obtained automatically [5]. Our similarity metric is based on *n*-gram matching rather than just single-term overlap. For example, a word in a sequence of six words (or a 6-gram) receives proportionately more weight than the same word occurring in two distinct three-word sequences (or trigrams), which in turn is weighted more than if it were found in three bigrams, and so on. Individual term weights are computed at document level using a variant of pivoted document length normalization metric [15] and added to *n*-gram weights.

We have found that our new approach produces excellent summaries in most cases. The summaries are based on high-quality clusters that form around significant common concepts or themes that occur repeatedly across the set of documents. The paragraph is a useful semantic unit for conceptual clustering, because most writers view a paragraph as a topical unit, and organize their thoughts accordingly. A few examples of themes detected in large document sets are: "lie detector test" (a theme occurring in a set of documents on labor relations), "South Georgia and South Sandwich Islands" (a theme found in a set of documents on Falkland oil exploration), and "blood alcohol levels" (a theme detected in a set on automobile accidents).

3. OUTLINE OF XDOX ARCHITECTURE

The XDoX system is written in Java, except for our single document summarizer, which is written in C++. The system has several distinct modules. Their basic tasks, inputs and outputs are shown in Figure 1.

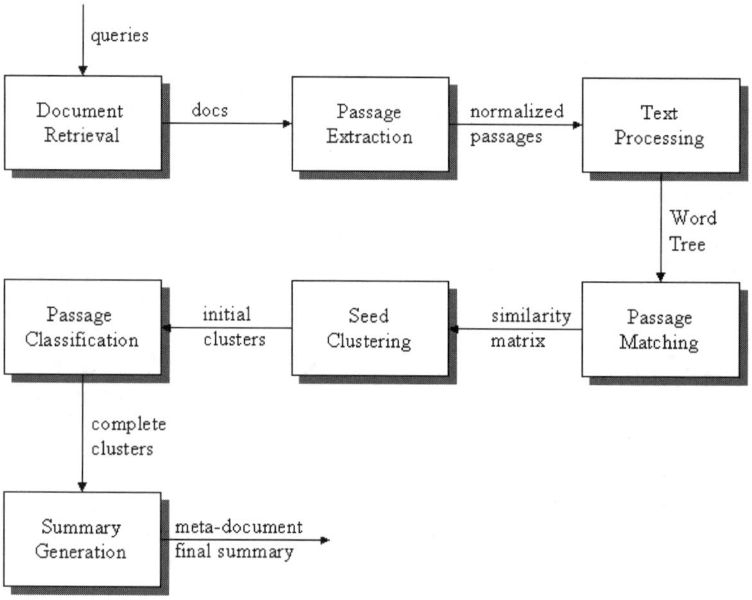

Figure 1. XDoX System Architecture

4. TEXT PROCESSING

As shown above, documents are first chunked into paragraphs, according to existing paragraph boundaries. SGML tags, lists of keywords, author by-lines, news sources, locations, etc., are all removed. Subtitles and one-line paragraphs are merged with the following text. Titles of articles are eligible to be clustered, except when they have fewer than three terms.

In preparation for comparing *n*-grams in passages, stopwords are removed and the remaining words are stemmed, using the Porter algorithm. Each stem is mapped to a unique integer code. All the stemmed words are placed into a simple binary `Word Tree` structure, using Java's red-black `TreeMap` class. The tree contains a node for each stem. The value for each node is an ordered list of occurrences of the stem, including positional information (document, paragraph, location in the paragraph) as well as the code of the following stem. The `Word Tree` can be constructed in linear time.

4.1 Document-level Term Weighting

We chose a term weighting scheme that uses average term frequency in a document as the normalization factor. In the function

$$\frac{1+\log(tf)}{1+\log(average(tf))},$$

tf(t) is the actual frequency of term *t* in document *D*. This normalization method has been shown to perform 5.7% better than maximum term frequency based normalization for 200 TREC queries on the entire TREC collection [15]. Combining this *tf* factor with the pivoted normalization used in the SMART system, we arrive at the weighting strategy:

$$\frac{\dfrac{1+\log(tf)}{1+\log(average(tf))}}{(1-c)average(L)+c\times L},$$

where L is the number of unique terms in document D and c is a constant between 0 and 1. This weighting scheme is related to BM25 used in the Okapi system [15], which has been reported to perform consistently better than standard cosine normalization in document retrieval applications.

5. PASSAGE SIMILARITY METRIC BASED ON *N*-GRAMS

After the text processing module has built the `Word Tree` and computed term weights, the passage matching module compares passages and assigns similarity scores to every pair of passages in the document set (not including pairs from the same document). The output is a table of paragraph pairs and their similarity values, represented as a matrix.

5.1 A Fast Algorithm for Matching *N*-grams

In order to compare large numbers of documents efficiently using *n*-gram matching, we chose to work with a very small subset of all possible substrings in the documents: we look only at *n*-grams, where *n* is 1 to 6, that are actually matched somewhere among the passages in the document set. Our goal was to minimize the number of comparisons made, and so we construct *n*-grams on the fly, in a bottom-up manner, from the `Word Tree` data structure. The algorithm is as follows:

For each document D_i (D_1 to D_{n-1}):

a. Get the first word *w* in the first paragraph.
b. From the Word Tree, get a list *a* of all instances of *w* occurring in documents D_{i+1} to D_n. These are matching unigrams. List *a* becomes the start of a "live *n*-grams" list that grows and shrinks as matching *n*-grams are built and removed from the list when completed. (Java's ArrayList class is handy for this purpose.)
c. For each word *v* which follows *w* in D_i:
    1) From the Word Tree, get a list *b* of all instances of *v* in documents D_{i+1} to D_n. Each *v* either continues an *n*-gram, *wv*, or begins a new unigram.
    2) Taking advantage of the sequential order of both lists, add or insert each *v* from list *b* in the proper place in list *a*. If an *n*-gram in list *a* cannot be extended by an occurrence in list *b*, or if it would create a sequence longer than *n*, then the *n*-gram is removed from the list and stored in a matrix structure.

Invariants: 1) The list of live *n*-grams, as well as each new list of word occurrences, remains in sequential order, 2) the final word of each *n*-gram in the list is the same, and 3) each finished *n*-gram is the longest possible *n*-gram.

For example, the list of live *n*-grams for the passage excerpt P1 below would progress as follows when matched with passages P2-P4: (The numbered words correspond to the intermediate steps in the process. Final *n*-grams are underlined.)

1 2 3 4 5
P1 ... *Federal Reserve Chairman Alan Greenspan said...*
P2 ... *Federal Reserve Board ...Greenspan remarked ...*
P3 ... *United States Federal Reserve Chairman Alan Greenspan is ...*
P4 ... *Chairman Alan Greenspan announced today ...*

1 *Federal (P2); Federal (P3)*
2 *<u>Federal Reserve (P2)</u>; Federal Reserve (P3)*
3 *Federal Reserve Chairman (P3); Chairman (P4)*
4 *Federal Reserve Chairman Alan (P3); Chairman Alan (P4)*
5 *<u>Greenspan (P2)</u>; <u>Federal Reserve Chairman Alan Greenspan (P3)</u>; <u>Chairman Alan Greenspan (P4)</u>*

The goal is to find the best matches between any two paragraphs, where "best" is defined as maximum length. For example, the phrase *bovine spongiform encephalopathy (BSE)*, when found in two passages, is counted as a 4-gram and not four unigrams, or two bigrams, or any of the other possible combinations for this phrase. Sometimes overlaps must be eliminated, as in this example:

P1 *Terrorist attacks (on) American targets...American targets.*
P2 *Terrorist attacks...Terrorist attacks (on) American targets...American targets... attacks.*

These two sample passages produce only two *n*-gram matches: a 4-gram: *Terrorist attacks (on) American targets* and a bigram: *American targets.*

The above algorithm may easily be modified for other-size passage matching, sentence matching, or even phrase matching tasks, such as may be required in clustering of dynamic or streaming data, or in question answering. The running time depends on both the total number of terms and the number of distinct terms in the document set. With a smaller ratio of total terms to distinct terms, fewer operations must be performed. The average number of times each term appears in the document set is $a = n/m$, where n = *total number of terms* and m = *number of distinct terms.* The number of operations required is approximately:

$$m(\frac{a(a-1)}{2}),$$

which gives us a best case running time of $O(n)$, when all terms are distinct, and a worst-case running time of $O(n^2)$, when all terms are the same. The actual number of operations also depends on factors such as the variation in the number of occurrences of each distinct term, as well as the distribution of terms across the documents.

The result of the *n*-gram matching stage is a matrix structure that contains all the common *n*-grams shared between each pair of paragraphs.

5.2 Passage Similarity Scores

For computing the similarity between any two passages, we use a cosine coefficient function, modified according to *n*-gram weights. Because it would be cumbersome to assign a weight to every *n*-gram we find, we weight individual terms instead, dividing the *n*-gram weight among all the terms in the *n*-gram. The weight of term T_i in passage X_i is the weight of T_i in document X (as described above) plus the *n*-gram weight. The *n*-gram weight is given as $(n_i)/n^2$, where n_i is the length of the *n*-gram of which term T_i is an element, and n is the length of the maximum *n*-gram. When n is 6, for example, a term that is part of a bigram receives a weight premium of 0.056 in addition to its document term weight. Every term in a matching 6-gram gets an additional 0.167 weight. The final passage similarity function is as follows:

$$sim(X_i, Y_i) = \frac{\sum_{j=1}^{t} x_{ij} \times y_{ij}}{\sqrt{\sum_{j=1}^{t} (x_{ij})^2 \times \sum_{j=1}^{t} (y_{ij})^2}},$$

where x_{ij} is the weight of term T_j in paragraph X_i and y_{ij} is the weight of term T_j in paragraph Y_i. When the scoring is finished, we have a similarity matrix whose $(i,j)^{th}$ entry gives the similarity between the ith and j^{th} passages.

6. SEED-CLUSTERING ALGORITHM

In order to form seed clusters we apply the well-known complete-link algorithm to our similarity matrix [18]. This algorithm becomes computationally expensive when used over large numbers of documents, each of which may have many passages to score. We have found it both practical and effective to run the complete-link only to the point at which we reach a target number of candidate seed clusters. We want a target that will allow the clusters to illustrate a good distribution of sub-themes or concepts in the document set, one that avoids over-generalization on the one hand and too much detail on the other. For most sets of documents, a good target is $\log_2 N$, where N is the number of documents. Initially, each passage is a cluster. We run the algorithm as follows:

1. Merge the most similar two clusters (clusters *i* and *j*).
2. Update the similarity matrix to reflect the pairwise similarity between the new cluster *(ij)* and the original clusters. We remove all the entries for *i* and *j* and replace them with new *ij* entries.
3. Repeat steps 1 and 2 until the target number of seed clusters is reached.

We add the restrictions that a seed cluster must contain three or more passages, and that there must be at least two common terms among the first three passages in the cluster. Clusters with larger common stem sets are preferred, as well as clusters whose common stem sets do not overlap much with another cluster. After the target is reached, some candidate seed clusters may be weeded out for failing to meet these criteria.

By having the system stop after reaching a specified number of clusters, we remove another difficulty inherent in the complete-link algorithm: choosing a proper threshold. When this choice is left up to the user, he or she must often make several tries before reaching a reasonable number of clusters. If the threshold is high, too many small clusters are formed around narrow or incidental concepts. If the threshold is too low, the clusters are fewer and larger, and the topics become fuzzy or obscured.

However, if the system is set to aim for a target number of candidate seed clusters, it will adapt its performance to the specific makeup of the document set at hand: it will adjust for document sets that happen not to have many subtopics; and it will likewise adjust for document sets that cover a wider range of themes or concepts.

7. CLASSIFICATION ALGORITHM

All remaining passages are classified as satellites around the seed clusters. For this stage we perform *M*-bin classification, where *M* is the number of seeds. If a passage has no similarity to any of the seeds, it is placed into a miscellaneous "trash cluster". Passages in a cluster are presented in descending order: seed passages come first, in the order in which they were added to the cluster, so that those with the tightest similarity to one another are shown first. Next come the satellite passages, ordered according to their degree of similarity with the seed cluster.

8. GENERATING 2 KINDS OF SUMMARY

After the clusters are formed, we create a "meta-document", selecting one of the highest-scoring, or most characteristic, passages from each cluster, and concatenating them together. In order to improve the summary's readability and help to resolve dangling references, the system searches for a lead paragraph among the first few passages in the top clusters. If such a paragraph is found, we use it to begin the summary. Next, our single-document summarizer creates a summary of this meta-document, using the query terms, if any, as the "title".

Like our multi-document summarizer, the single-document system segments text into passages or equal-sized chunks. Adjacent passages that are strongly linked to one another are reconnected. All passages are scored with respect to a query derived from the title, topic description, and terms occurring frequently in the text. Scores are then normalized by the length of the passage. Passages are combined into groups of two or more and re-scored, until a clear winning passage or passage group emerges to form the summary. Our techniques have been shown to achieve an excellent balance between text compression and content preservation [17].

The user, then, has two types of summary to view. The meta-document is more suitable for groups of documents that describe similar but isolated events, such as alcohol-related traffic accidents, or different people who have something in common, such as winners of the Nobel Peace Prize. The summary of the meta-document is more appropriate for groups of documents which are all related to the same topic or event, such as oil exploration in the Falkland Islands, or the U.S. Presidential election in the year 2000.

9. DUC PARTICIPATION AND EVALUATION

The Albany/GE team participated in both the single-document and the multi-document tracks in DUC 2001. For cross-document summarization, the XDoX system works best on large document sets that have multiple themes. For sets that have fewer than 20 documents, as in the DUC data, our system works well with some parameter adjustments, as long as the documents contain sufficient common concepts around which to form clusters. We have seen excellent results from document sets pertaining to a single event, topic, or person, such as gun control, the eruption of Mt. Pinatubo, the Charles Keating scandal, or the Rodney King beating. XDoX has difficulty generating a longer, more detailed summary when there are 10 or fewer documents concerning isolated incidents, such as gas explosions or earthquakes, or when there is little repetition (see examples below). We are considering augmenting the system with selective use of our single-document summarizer [17].

In August 2001 NIST completed the evaluation of single- and multiple-document summaries submitted by DUC participants. For the multiple-document summarization track, 60 sets of 10 documents were used; 30 for training and 30 for testing. Participants were required to submit fixed-length summaries of 50, 100, 200, and 400 words. Of the 25 groups who signed up, 12 submitted multi-document summaries. Ten information analysts from NIST compared human-written model summaries with peer summaries (system-created, baseline, or human). The analysts formed intrinsic judgments based on peer grammaticality, cohesion, and organization; coverage of each model unit by the peer; and other characteristics of peer material. In Figures 2 through 5, "R" represents our XDoX system.

On grammaticality, our system ranked 6th of 12. Because we used only text extraction, no language generation, any grammatical errors must have come from the documents themselves. We chose to group subtitles and one-line text units, such as dates standing alone, with the following text, so these may have been interpreted as sentence fragments. On cohesion and organization our system ranked 3rd and 2nd, respectively. We attribute these high numbers to our method of extracting paragraphs as a whole, rather than extracting individual sentences.

On per-unit content, assessors marked peer units which expressed at least some of the same facts as the current model unit. For this evaluation, precision scores (number of peer units matched with model units divided by total number of peer units) were considered problematic. Lengths of peer summaries were fixed, and the precision metric was insensitive to duplicate information and partially unused peer units [12]. Recall scores were considered a better indication of coverage. When recall is defined as dividing the number of model units matched with peer units by the total number of units in the model summary, 5 other systems performed better than ours for the 50-word and 100-word summaries. For the 200-word summaries, 6 other systems generated better results, and for the 400-word summaries our system came in last. We think that our relatively poor performance for the longer summaries is due to our methods of creating clusters and selecting a representative paragraph from each cluster to form the summary.

These methods were designed to produce representative summaries for large document sets (50-200 documents and more). When the document set is very small, as is the case for all the DUC sets, and when the system finds few subtopics among the passages, too few clusters are created and the resulting summary is much shorter than 400 words.

Assessors classified unmarked peer units into one of three categories: 1) should be in the model in place of something already there; 2) relevant to the model's subject; and 3) not related to the model. Unfortunately, the precision and recall measures defined above do not take into account the first category ("Needed'' in Figure 5). For this category our system performed better than all others except one. In both the second and third categories ("Related'' and "1 – Unrelated'' in Figure 5), our system ranked in the middle, with 6 others performing better for the relevant peer units, and 5 others receiving a higher score for peer units not related to the model. To emphasize the similarity in results among the systems, we also show the average of these three fields in Figure 5.

On the whole, we are pleased with our performance in the 2001 Document Understanding Conference. We consider our summaries readable, coherent, and excellent at capturing the main points of the document sets. We think the DUC assessors did well given the program guidelines and the difficulties inherent in judging summaries. We look forward to extrinsic methods of evaluation being incorporated into future DUC conferences.

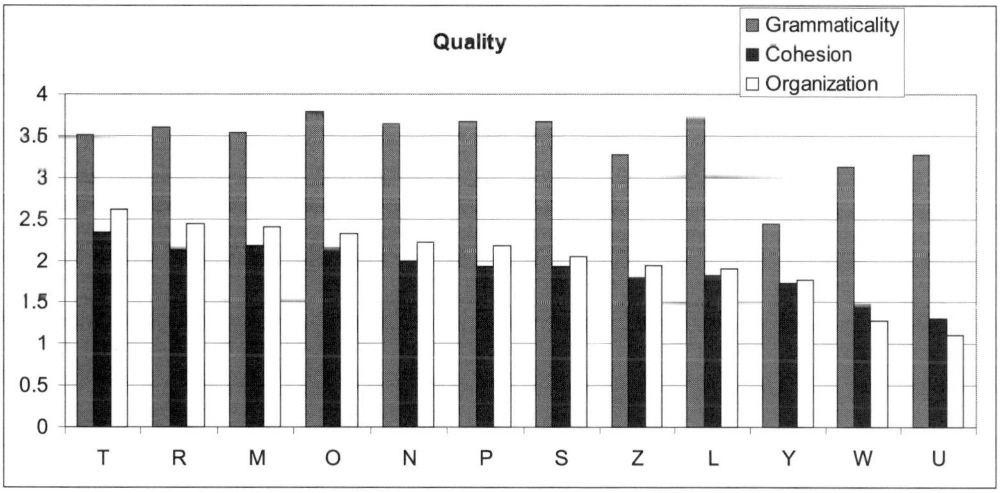

Figure 2. NIST intrinsic quality assessments for multi-document summarization systems.

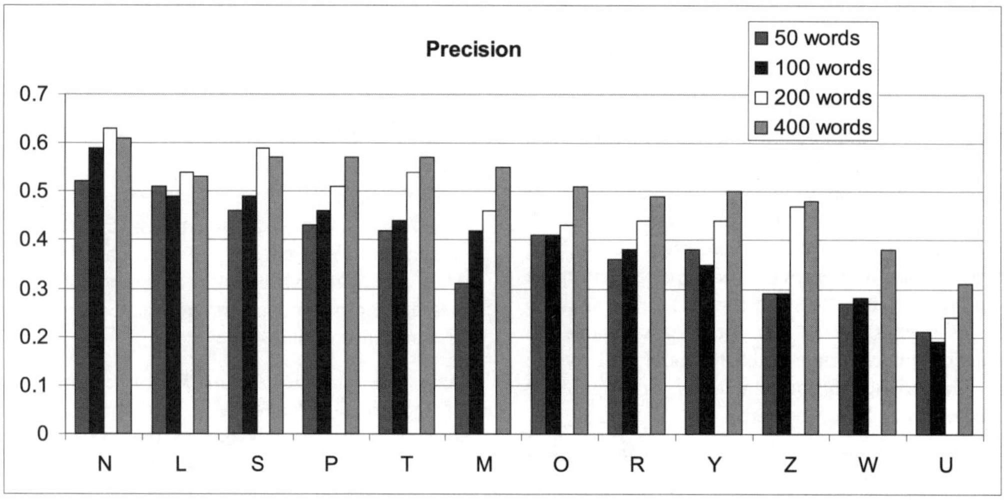

Figure 3. Average precision for multi-document summarization systems.

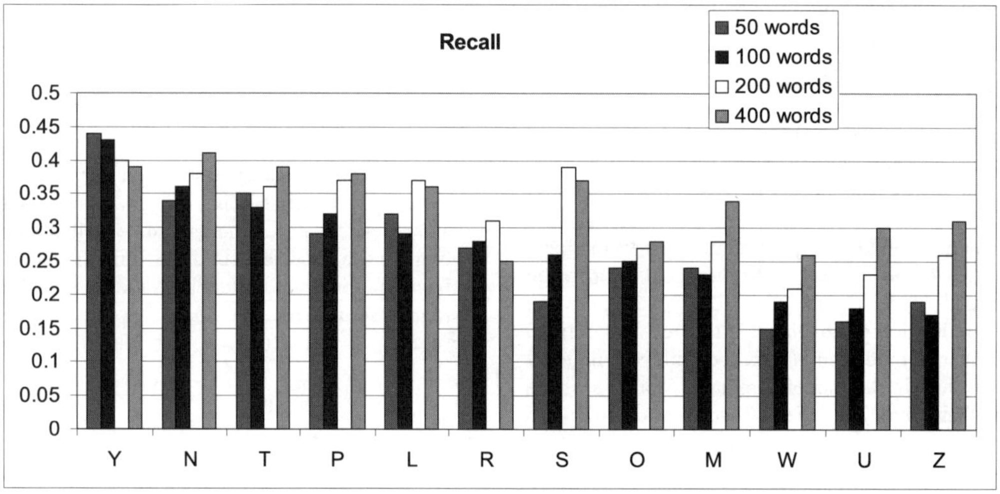

Figure 4. Average recall for multi-document summarization systems.

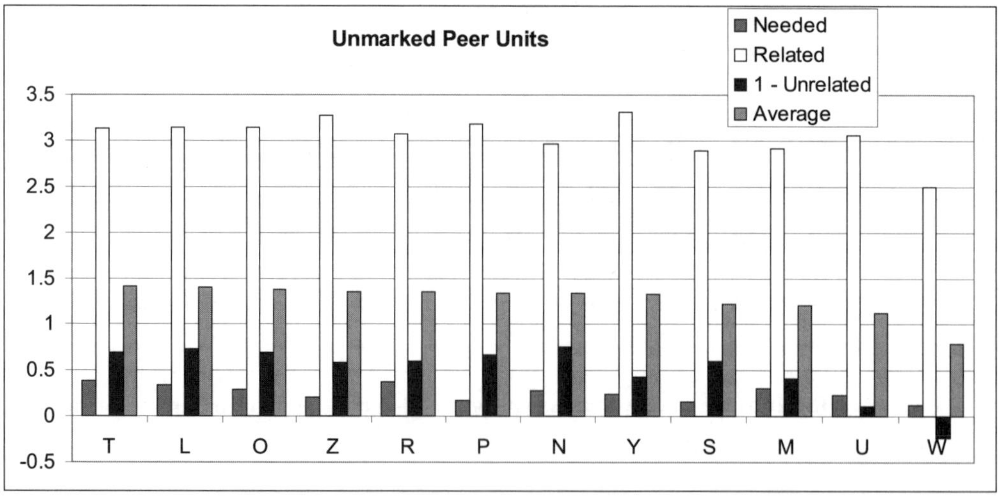

Figure 5. Results for unmatched peer units in multi-document summarization systems.

10. EXAMPLES

The following examples were generated by the XDoX system from the DUC 2001 data.

```
<multi size="50" docset="d06a">
```

A panel that investigated the Los Angeles Police Department after officers were videotaped beating a motorist has decided not to seek Chief Daryl Gates' resignation and neither blamed nor cleared him.

In mid-June, a lawsuit against the Los Angeles Police Department was settled when police agreed to stop using a martial-arts weapon, nunchakus, while arresting anti-abortion advocates.

```
</multi>
```

```
<multi size="50" docset="d13c">
```

President Bush on Monday nominated Clarence Thomas, a conservative Republican with a controversial record on civil rights, to replace retiring Justice Thurgood Marshall on the Supreme Court.

CLARENCE THOMAS; Born: June 23, 1948, in Pinpoint, Ga. Education: B.A. from Holy Cross College, 1971; J.D. from Yale Law School, 1974.

```
</multi>
```

```
<multi size="100" docset="d22d">
```

Firefighters in California, Michigan, Montana, Wyoming and Utah battled holiday weekend fires, which blackened more than 6,000 acres of forest and wilderness areas.

Elsewhere in Utah, the Uinta Canyon fire had burned 3,850 acres 20 miles north of Roosevelt in the Ashley National Forest. Forest Service spokeswoman Cece Stewart said three helicopters scattered incendiary bombs made of chemically treated plastic balls on an unburned 200-acre area between fire lines and the main fire in an effort to stop the fire's advance.

```
</multi>
```

```
<multi size="100" docset="d39g">
```

Officials estimate the tunnel trains may carry 28 million passengers in the first year of operation. Eurotunnel doesn't expect a profit until the end of the century.

In London, the conservative Daily Express newspaper noted today that Britons will be able to walk to France for the first time since the Ice Age.

The tunnel's cost has soared from an initial estimate of $9.4 billion to $16.7 billion, including an extra $1.97 billion in case of unforeseen cost overruns.

Eurotunnel PLC announced Oct. 8 that it had reached an agreement with its banks on $3.5 billion in new credit. More than 200 banks are involved in financing the world's costliest tunnel.

```
</multi>
```

```
<multi size="400" docset="d16c">
```

A major earthquake rumbled through the jungles of southern Sudan on Sunday near the war-torn region's largest city, but officials said there appeared to be no casualties and little damage.

The Richter scale is a measure of ground motion as recorded on seismographs. Every increase of one number means a tenfold increase in magnitude. Thus a reading of 7.5 reflects an earthquake 10 times stronger than one of 6.5.

An earthquake of 3.5 on the Richter scale can cause slight damage in the local area, 4 moderate damage, 5 considerable damage, 6 severe damage. A 7 reading is a "major" earthquake, capable of widespread heavy damage; 8 is a "great" quake, capable of tremendous damage.

In the past 35 years there have been two major earthquakes in Hokkaido. In 1968, the Tokachi-Oki earthquake measuring a 7.9 on the Richter scale killed 52 people.

The agency said the quake had a magnitude of 7.1 on the Richter scale, the same as the Oct. 17 earthquake that devastated the San Francisco Bay area. In Washington, the U.S. Geological Survey said the quake measured 7.3 on the Richter scale.

```
</multi>
```

The following summary was obtained from the set of top 100 documents retrieved from the TREC data collection with Topic 358 on the subject of alcohol related driving fatalities.

```
<multi size="400" docset="TRECtopic358">
```

Drinkers beware. When the New Year begins at midnight, a tough new law will take effect making it all the more risky to drink and drive.

Under the new law that takes effect Jan 1, a driver with 0.08% or higher is presumed to be drunk; however, those with lower levels could also be cited for drunk driving.

According to court records, Giunta's blood-alcohol content was 0.29%, more than three times the level at which a motorist is considered legally drunk.

The Department clearly and specifically limited the NPRM to consideration of whether blood testing should be used for situations in which breath testing was not readily available for reasonable suspicion and post-accident tests, or in shy lung situations. For this reason, the issue raised by some commenters of whether employers should have the flexibility or discretion to use blood testing as an alternative to breath testing, even when breath testing is readily available in reasonable suspicion and post-accident testing or even in random or pre-employment testing, is outside the scope of the rulemaking.

The author, Sen. Bill Leonard (R-Big Bear), predicted that the measure will win legislative approval and be sent to Gov. George Deukmejian, whose Administration supports it.

```
</multi>
```

11. CONCLUSION

Our latest version of the XDoX system, using our new passage-clustering techniques, implements a reasonable approximation of conceptual clustering. The overall quality is significantly better than that of our previous version, and compares favorably with the other DUC participants. The summaries are readable, coherent and well organized. In most cases the system successfully presents main points, skips over minor details, and avoids redundancy. Because our scoring methods emphasize longer common *n*-grams containing significant terms, we avoid "false" clusters based on common but unimportant single terms. XDoX will create summaries based on the concepts repeated across the document set, regardless of any pre-specified query, topic, or named entities. Thus it is robust, topic-independent, and may easily be extended to applications in other domains and other languages. For small document sets, however, our clustering techniques are sometimes less effective. If it is necessary to generate longer, more detailed summaries for small groups of documents that have little repetition, such as documents having to do with unrelated examples of one type of event, different strategies should be employed.

12. ACKNOWLEDGMENTS

This paper is based on work supported in part by the Defense Advanced Research Projects Agency (DARPA) and by the Advanced Research and Development Activity (ARDA). Any opinions, findings, and conclusions or recommendations expressed in this material are those of the authors and do not necessarily reflect the views of the U.S. Government.

13. REFERENCES

[1] Carbonell, J., and Goldstein, J. The use of MMR, diversity-based reranking for reordering documents and producing summaries. In Proceedings of SIGIR (1998), 335-336.

[2] Fellbaum, C. (ed.). WordNet – An Electronic Lexical Database. MIT Press, 1998.

[3] Firmin, T., and Chrzanowski, M. J. An Evaluation of Automatic Text Summarization Systems. In I. Mani and M. Maybury (eds.), Advances in Automatic Text Summarization. MIT Press, 1999.

[4] Hatzivassiloglou, V., Klavans, J. L., Holcombe, M. L., Barzilay, R., Kan, M., and McKeown, K. R. SIMFINDER: A Flexible Clustering Tool for Summarization. In NAACL 2001 Workshop on Automatic Summarization (Pittsburgh, PA), 41-49.

[5] Hearst, M. Multi-paragraph segmentation of expository text. In Proceedings of the 32nd Annual Meeting of the Association for Computational Linguistics (Las Cruces, NM, 1994), Association for Computational Linguistics, 9-16.

[6] Kraaij, W., Spitters, M., and van der Heijden, M. Combining a mixture language model and Naïve Bayes for multi-document summarization. In SIGIR 2001 Workshop on Text Summarization (New Orleans, LA), 95-103.

[7] Lin, C. and Hovy, E. NEATS: A Multidocument Summarizer. In SIGIR 2001 Workshop on Text Summarization (New Orleans, LA), 131-134.

[8] Marcu, D. Discourse-Based Summarization in DUC–2001. In SIGIR 2001 Workshop on Text Summarization (New Orleans, LA), 109-116.

[9] McKeown, K. and Radev, D. Generating summaries of multiple news articles. In Proceedings, 18th Annual International ACM SIGIR Conference on Research and Development in Information Retrieval (Seattle, WA, 1995), 74-82.

[10] Miller, G.A. WordNet: A Lexical Database. Communication of the ACM 38, 11(1995), 39-41.

[11] Mitra, M., Singhal, A., and Buckley, C. Automatic text summarization by paragraph extraction. In Proceedings of the ACL'97/EACL'97 Workshop on Intelligent Scalable Text Summarization (Madrid, Spain, 1997).

[12] Over, P. Introduction to DUC-2001: an Intrinsic Evaluation of Generic News Text Summarization Systems. http://www.itl.nist.gov/iaui/894.02/projects/duc/duc2001/pauls_slides/index.htm.

[13] Radev, D. R., Fan, W., and Zhang, Z. WebInEssence: A Personalized Web-Based Multi-Document Summarization and Recommendation System. In NAACL 2001 Workshop on Automatic Summarization (Pittsburgh, PA), 79-88.

[14] Robertson, S. E., Walker, S., Jones, S., Hancock-Beaulieu, M. M., and Gatford, M. Okapi at TREC-3. In Harman, D. (ed.), The Third Text Retrieval Conference (TREC-3). National Institute of Standards and Technology Special Publication 500-225, 1995, 219-230.

[15] Singhal, A., Buckley, C., and Mitra, M. Pivoted Document Length Normalization. SIGIR 1996, 21-29.

[16] Stein, G., Strzalkowski, T., and Wise, B. Interactive, Text-Based Summarization of Multiple Documents. Computational Intelligence 16, 4 (2000), 606-613.

[17] Strzalkowski, T., Stein, G., Wang, J., and Wise, B. A Robust, Practical Text Summarizer. In I. Mani and M. Maybury (eds.), Advances in Automatic Text Summarization. MIT Press, 1999, 137-154.

[18] Willett, P. Recent trends in hierarchical document clustering: A critical review. Information Processing and Management, 24, 5 (1988).

Unsupervised Document Classification using Sequential Information Maximization

Noam Slonim[1,2] Nir Friedman[1] Naftali Tishby[1,2]

[1]School of Computer Science and Engineering
[2]The Interdisciplinary Center for Neural Computation
The Hebrew University, Jerusalem 91904, Israel
email: {noamm,nir,tishby}@cs.huji.ac.il

ABSTRACT

We present a novel sequential clustering algorithm which is motivated by the *Information Bottleneck (IB)* method. In contrast to the agglomerative *IB* algorithm, the new sequential (*sIB*) approach is guaranteed to converge to a local maximum of the information, as required by the original IB principle. Moreover, the time and space complexity are significantly improved. We apply this algorithm to unsupervised document classification. In our evaluation, on small and medium size corpora, the *sIB* is found to be consistently superior to all the other clustering methods we examine, typically by a significant margin. Moreover, the *sIB* results are comparable to those obtained by a *supervised* Naive Bayes classifier. Finally, we propose a simple procedure for trading cluster's recall to gain higher precision, and show how this approach can extract clusters which match the existing topics of the corpus almost perfectly.

Categories and Subject Descriptors

I.5.3 [**Pattern Recognition**]: Clustering—*Algorithms*; I.5.4 [**Pattern Recognition**]: Applications—*Text processing*; E.4 [**Data**]: Coding and Information Theory—*Data compaction and compression*

General Terms

Algorithms, Theory, Performance, Experimentation

1. MOTIVATION

Unsupervised document clustering is a central problem in information retrieval. Possible applications includes use of clustering for improving retrieval [18], and for navigating and browsing large document collections [3, 5, 19]. Several recent works suggest using clustering techniques for *unsupervised* document classification [4, 14, 16]. In this task, we are given a collection of unlabeled documents and attempt to find clusters that are highly correlated with the true topics of the documents. This practical situation is especially difficult since no labeled examples are provided for the topics, hence unsupervised methods must be employed.

The results of [4, 14] show that agglomerative clustering methods that are motivated by the *Information Bottleneck* (IB) method [17] perform well in this task. Agglomerative procedures, however, suffer from two main obstacles. First, in general there is no guarantee to find a solution which is a local maximum of the target function. Second, an agglomerative procedure is typically computationally expensive, and in fact infeasible for relatively large data sets.

In this paper, we suggest a simple framework for casting any given agglomerative procedure into a sequential clustering algorithm. The resulting sequential algorithm is guaranteed to find a local maximum of the target function (under very mild conditions). Moreover, it has time and space complexity which are significantly better than those of the agglomerative procedure. In particular we use this framework to suggest a new algorithm—the *sequential Information Bottleneck (sIB)* algorithm.

We provide theoretical justification as to why this sequential algorithm might find clusters that have high accuracy, and evaluate the algorithm on real life corpora. Our results demonstrate the superiority of *sIB* over a range of clustering methods (agglomerative, K-means, and other sequential procedures) typically by a significant margin. Moreover, *sIB* performance was comparable to that of a standard *supervised* Naive Bayes classifier trained over a significant number of labeled documents.

SIGIR'02, August 11-15, 2002, Tampere, Finland.

2. THE INFORMATION BOTTLENECK METHOD

Most clustering algorithms start either from pairwise 'distances' between points (pairwise clustering) or with a distortion measure between a data point and a class centroid (vector quantization). Too often the choice of the distance or distortion function is arbitrary, sensitive to the specific representation, which may not accurately reflect the relevant structure of the high dimensional data.

In the context of document clustering, a natural measure of similarity of two documents is the similarity between their word conditional distributions. Specifically, for every document we can define

$$p(y|x) = \frac{n(y|x)}{\sum_{y' \in Y} n(y'|x)}, \quad (1)$$

where $n(y|x)$ is the number of occurrences of the word y in the document x. To avoid an undesirable bias due to different document lengths we also require a uniform prior distribution, $p(x) = \frac{1}{|X|}$, where $|X|$ is the number of documents in the corpus. Roughly speaking, one would like documents with similar conditional word distributions to belong to the same cluster. This formulation of finding a cluster hierarchy of the members of one set (e.g., documents), based on the similarity of their conditional distributions with respect to the members of another set (e.g., words), was first introduced in [10] and was termed "distributional clustering".

The issue of selecting and justifying the 'right' distance measure between distributions remains, however, unresolved in that earlier work. Recently, Tishby, Pereira, and Bialek [17] proposed a principled approach to this problem, which avoids the arbitrary choice of a distortion measure. In this approach, given the joint distribution $p(X, Y)$, one looks for a compact representation of X, which preserves as much information as possible about the relevant variable Y. The mutual information, $I(X;Y)$, between the random variables X and Y is given by (e.g., [2])

$$I(X;Y) = \sum_{x \in X, y \in Y} p(x)p(y|x) \log \frac{p(y|x)}{p(y)} \quad (2)$$

and is the natural statistical measure of the information that variable X contains about variable Y. In [17] it is argued that both the compactness of the representation and the preserved relevant information are naturally measured by mutual information, hence the above principle can be formulated as a trade-off between these quantities. More formally stated, we introduce a compressed representation T of X, by defining $P(T \mid X)$. The compactness of the representation is now determined by $I(T;X)$, while the quality of the clusters, T, is measured by the fraction of the information they capture about Y, namely, $I(T;Y)/I(X;Y)$. This general problem has an exact optimal formal solution without any assumption about the origin of the joint distribution $p(X, Y)$ [17]. This solution is given in terms of the three distributions that characterize every cluster $t \in T$: the prior probability for this cluster, $p(t)$, its membership probabilities $p(t|x)$, and its distribution over the relevance variable, $p(y|t)$. In general, the membership probabilities, $p(t|x)$, are 'soft', i.e., every $x \in X$ can be assigned to every $t \in T$ with some (normalized) probability. The information bottleneck principle determines the distortion measure between the points x and t to be the $D_{KL}(p(y|x)\|p(y|t)) = \sum_y p(y|x) \log \frac{p(y|x)}{p(y|t)}$, the Kullback-Leibler divergence [2] between the conditional distributions $p(y|x)$ and $p(y|t)$. Specifically, the formal solution is given by the following equations which must be solved self-consistently,

$$\begin{cases} p(t|x) = \frac{p(t)}{Z(\beta,x)} \exp\left(-\beta D_{KL}(p(y|x)\|p(y|t))\right) \\ p(y|t) = \frac{1}{p(t)} \sum_x p(t|x)p(x)p(y|x) \\ p(t) = \sum_x p(t|x)p(x) , \end{cases} \quad (3)$$

where $Z(\beta, x)$ is a normalization factor, and the single positive (Lagrange multiplier) parameter β determines the trade-off between compression and precision and the "softness" of the classification. Intuitively, in this procedure the information contained in X about Y is 'squeezed' through a compact 'bottleneck' of clusters T, that is forced to represent the 'relevant' part in X with respect to Y.

3. SEQUENTIAL CLUSTERING

Consider the following general scenario. We are given a set of objects X and we would like to find a partition $T(X)$ which maximize some score function $\mathcal{F}(T)$. There is a variety of score functions that we might consider, for each we may derive specialized algorithms. One algorithm that can be applied to almost any score function is agglomerative clustering. In this approach we start with a partition of X into singletons, and at each step we greedily choose the merger of two clusters that maximizes the score. We repeat such greedy agglomeration steps until we get the desired number of clusters, which we will denote by K. Agglomerative clustering is particularly attractive when the score function $\mathcal{F}$ is *decomposable*, i.e., if $T = \{t_1, \ldots, t_K\}$, then $\mathcal{F}(T) = \sum_i \mathcal{F}(\{t_i\})$. In this case, the change in the total score by merging two clusters is simply $d_{\mathcal{F}}(t_i, t_j) = \mathcal{F}(\{t_i\} \cup \{t_j\}) - \mathcal{F}(\{t_i\}) - \mathcal{F}(\{t_j\})$.

There are two main obstacles to agglomerative clustering. First, this greedy approach is not guaranteed to find the optimal partition of X into K clusters. In fact, it is not even guaranteed to find a stable solution, in the sense that each object belongs to the cluster it is most similar to. Second, an agglomeration procedure have the time complexity of $O(|X|^3|Y|)$ (where $|Y|$ is the dimension of the representation of every x) and a memory consumption of $O(|X|^2)$ which makes it infeasible for large data sets.

We describe a simple idea for solving these two problems by casting an agglomerative (known) algorithm into a new sequential clustering procedure. Unlike agglomerative clustering, this procedure maintains a partition with exactly K clusters. We start from an initial random partition $T = \{t_1, t_2, ..., t_K\}$ of X. At each step, we "draw" some $x \in X$ out of its current cluster $t(x)$ and represent it as a new singleton cluster. Using a greedy agglomeration step we can now merge x into t^{new} such that $t^{new} = \arg\min_{t \in T} d_{\mathcal{F}}(\{x\}, t)$, to obtain a new partition T^{new} (with the appropriate cardinality). Assuming that $t_{new} \neq t$ it is easy to verify that $\mathcal{F}(T^{new}) > \mathcal{F}(T)$. Therefore, each such step either improves the score, or leaves the current partition unchanged. If $\mathcal{F}(T)$ is known to be upper bounded we are guaranteed to converge to a local maximum in the sense that no more assignment changes can be performed.

Since this algorithm can get trapped in a local optima, we repeat the above procedure for random initializations of T to obtain n different solutions, from which we choose the one which maximize $\mathcal{F}(T)$. Finally, to avoid too slow convergence we define two "convergence" parameters denoted by ε and $maxL$. Specifically we declare that the algorithm converged if we already performed $maxL$ loops over X or if in the last loop we got less than $\varepsilon \cdot |X|$ assignment changes. A Pseudo-code for the algorithm is given in Figure 1.

What is the complexity of this sequential approach? In each "drawing" step we should calculate $d_{\mathcal{F}}(\{x\}, t)$ for every $t \in T$ which is an order of $O(K|Y|)$. Our time complexity is thus bounded by $O(nLK|X||Y|)$ where L is the number of loops we should perform (over X) until convergence is attained. Since typically $nLK \ll |X|^2$ we get a significant

Input:
$|X|$ objects to be clustered
Parameters: K, n, $maxL$, ε

Output:
A partition T of X into K clusters

Main Loop:
```
For i = 1, ..., n
    T_i ← random partition of X.
    c ← 0, C ← 0, done = FALSE
    While not done
        For j = 1, ..., |X|
            draw x_j out of t(x_j)
            t^new(x_j) = argmin_t' d_F({x_j}, t')
            If t^new(x_j) ≠ t(x_j) then c ← c + 1
            Merge x_j into t^new(x_j)
        C ← C + 1
        if C ≥ maxL or c ≤ ε·|X| then
            done ← TRUE
T ← argmax_{T_i} F(T_i)
```

Figure 1: Pseudo-code for the sequential clustering algorithm.

run time improvement. Additionally, we dramatically improve our memory consumption toward an order of $O(K^2)$. One clear disadvantage of this approach is in loosing the tree structure output of the agglomeration procedure.

Our sequential clustering algorithm is reminiscent of the standard K-means algorithm. The main difference, is that K-means perform *parallel updates*, in which first we choose for each x its new cluster, and then we move *all* the elements to their new clusters in one step. As a consequence, the definition of the clusters (i.e., their centroids in K-means) changes only after all the elements move to their preferred clusters. To show that such a step is justified, we have to require more structure of the target function $\mathcal{F}$. We also note here that our sequential framework has some relations to the *incremental* variant of the EM algorithm for maximum likelihood [9], which still needs to be explored.

4. SEQUENTIAL IB CLUSTERING

The application of the above discussion in the context of the *Information Bottleneck* method is straightforward. We define $\mathcal{F}(T) = I(T;Y)$ and represent each x by $p(x,y)$. The greedy merging criterion is known from the *Agglomerative Information Bottleneck (AIB)* algorithm [13, 16]. Specifically, in this context we get

$$d(x,t) = (p(x)+p(t)) \cdot JS(p(y|x), p(y|t)) \ , \quad (4)$$

where $JS(p,q)$ is the *Jensen-Shannon* divergence [8, 12] defined as

$$JS(p,q) = \pi_1 D_{KL}(p\|\bar{p}) + \pi_2 D_{KL}(q\|\bar{p}) \ ,$$

where in our context

$$\{p,q\} \equiv \{p(y|x), p(y|t)\}$$
$$\{\pi_1,\pi_2\} \equiv \{\tfrac{p(x)}{p(x)+p(t)}, \tfrac{p(t)}{p(x)+p(t)}\} \quad (5)$$
$$\bar{p} = \pi_1 p(y|x) + \pi_2 p(y|t) \ .$$

Notice that any given partition T defines some membership ("hard") probability $p(t|x)$, which in turn defines $p(y|t)$ and $p(t)$ for every $t \in T$ through Eqs.(3). Additionally since $I(T;Y)$ is indeed upper bounded we are guaranteed to converge to a local maximum of the information.

The JS divergence is non-negative and is equal to zero if and only if both its arguments are identical. It is upper bounded and symmetric, though it is not a metric. One interpretation of the JS-divergence relates it to the (logarithmic) measure of the likelihood that the two sample distributions originate by the most likely common source, denoted here by $\bar{p}$ [12]. Using this interpretation we can interpret the new algorithm as follows. At each step we draw some x and merge it back into its most probable source. We refer to this algorithm as the *'sIB'* algorithm.

5. OTHER CLUSTERING METHODS

We can use the same sequential framework with other similarity criteria to construct other algorithms for purposes of comparison. In each of these algorithms we used exactly the same procedure described in figure 1. The only difference was in the choice of $d_{\mathcal{F}}(x,t)$.

A common divergence measure among probability distributions is the KL-divergence. An interesting question is how well the sequential clustering algorithm will perform while using this measure instead of the JS-divergence. More specifically, we define $d(x,t) = (p(x)+p(t)) \cdot D_{KL}(p(y|x)\|p(y|t))$. We refer to this algorithm as the *'sKL'* algorithm.

Another common divergence measure among probability distributions is the $L1$ norm defined as $\|(p(y) - q(y)\|_1 = \sum_y |p(y) - q(y)|$. Unlike the JS (and the KL) divergence the $L1$ norm satisfies all the metric properties. Therefore we defined the *'sL1'* algorithm by setting $d(x,t) = (p(x)+p(t)) \cdot \|p(y|x) - p(y|t)\|_1$.

In the third comparison algorithm we use the standard cosine measure under the vector space model. Specifically we define $d(x,t) = \langle \bar{x}, \bar{t} \rangle$ where $\bar{x}$ is the counts vector of x normalized such that $\|\bar{x}\|_2 = 1$. The centroid $\bar{t}$ is defined as the average of all the (normalized) count vectors representing the documents assigned into t (again, normalized to 1 under the L_2 norm). Due to this normalization $\langle \bar{x}, \bar{t} \rangle$ is simply the cosine of the angle between these two vectors (and is proportional to $\|\bar{x} - \bar{t}\|_2^2$). Notice that in this case we update assignments by merging x into $t^{new}(x) = \arg\max_{t'} d(x,t')$. We will term this algorithm *'sK-means'*. We also implemented a standard parallel version of this algorithm which we will term *'K-means'*.

Lastly, we also compare our results to the original *AIB* algorithm [13] and to the recent Iterative Double Clustering *(IDC)* procedure suggested by El-Yaniv and Souroujon [4]. This method, which is a natural extension of the previous work in [14], uses an iterative double-clustering procedure over documents and words. It was shown in [4] to work surprisingly well on relatively small data sets, and even to be competitive with a *supervised* SVM classifier trained with a small training set.

6. THE EXPERIMENTAL DESIGN

6.1 The datasets

Following [4, 14] we used several standard *labeled* data sets to evaluate the different clustering methods described above. As our first data set we used the 20Newsgroup corpus collected by Lang [7]. This corpus contains about 20,000 articles evenly distributed among 20 UseNet discussion groups, some of which are of very similar topics. After removing all file headers[1] our pre-processing included lowering upper case characters, uniting all digits into one symbol and ignoring non alpha-numeric characters. We also removed stop words and words that occurred only once, ending up with a vocabulary of 74,000 unique words. We further included a standard feature selection procedure (e.g., [14]), where we selected the 2000 words with the highest contribution to the mutual information about the documents. Specifically, we sorted all words by $I(y; X) \equiv p(y) \sum_{x \in X} p(x|y) \log \frac{p(x|y)}{p(x)}$ and selected the top 2000.

For a medium-scale experiment we used the whole corpus except for documents with less than 10 words occurrences, ending up with a counts matrix of 17,446 documents versus 2,000 words. We constructed two different tests over this data. First we measured our performance with respect to all the 20 different classes. Additionally we applied an easier test where we measured our performance with respect to 10 meta-categories in this corpus.[2] We will term these two tests *NG20* and *NG10* respectively. For small-scale experiments we used the 9 subsets of this corpus already used in [4, 14]. Each of these subsets consist of 500 documents randomly chosen from several discussion groups.

As a third medium scale test we used the 10,789 documents of the 10 most frequent categories in the Reuters-21578 corpus (http://www.daviddlewis.com/resources/testcollections/reuters21578/) under the ModApte split. After the same pre-processing we got a counts matrix of 8,796 documents versus 2,000 words.

As the last medium scale test we used a subset of the new release of Reuters-2000 corpus. Specifically we used the 22,498 documents of the 10 most frequent categories in the 10 first days of this corpus (last 10 days in August 1996). After the same pre-processing (except for not uniting digits due to a technical reason), we ended up with a counts matrix of 22,463 documents versus 2,000 words. Notice that these two last corpora are multi labeled.

One issue is how to evaluate different restarts of the algorithms. For the *sIB* we naturally choose the run that found the most informative clusters and report results for it. For other algorithms, we can use their respective scoring function. However, to ensure that this does not lead to poor performance, we choose to present for each of these algorithms the *best* result, in terms of the correlation to the true classification, among all n iterations. This choice provides an overestimate of the performance of these algorithms, and thus penalizes the sequential IB algorithm in the comparisons below.

[1]Unfortunately there is no clear standard about what should be referred as a file header in this corpus. In particular, the results reported in [14, 15] stripped of the header including the subject line (as instructed in http://www.cs.cmu.edu/~mccallum/bow). On the other hand, the results reported in [1, 4] does make use of the subject line which in many cases contain useful information. To make our results comparable with [4] we decided to use the subject line in this paper.

[2]Specifically we united the 5 "comp" categories, the 3 "religion" categories, the 3 "politics" categories, the two "sport" categories and the two "transportation" categories into 5 big meta-categories.

6.2 The evaluation method

As our evaluation measures we used micro-averaged precision and recall. To estimate these measures we first assign all the documents in some cluster $t \in T$ with the most dominant label in that cluster.[3] Given these uni-labeled assignments we can estimate for each category $c \in C$ the following quantities: $\alpha(c, T)$ defines the number of documents correctly assigned to c (i.e., their true label sets include c), $\beta(c, T)$ defines the number of documents incorrectly assigned to c and $\gamma(c, T)$ defines the number of documents incorrectly not assigned to c. The micro-averaged precision is now defined by

$$P(T) = \frac{\sum_c \alpha(c, T)}{\sum_c \alpha(c, T) + \beta(c, T)} \tag{6}$$

and the micro-averaged recall is defined by

$$R(T) = \frac{\sum_c \alpha(c, T)}{\sum_c \alpha(c, T) + \gamma(c, T)} . \tag{7}$$

It is easy to verify that if the corpus and the algorithm are both uni-labeled then $P(T) = R(T)$, thus for our uni-labeled data sets we will report only $P(T)$.

As a simplifying assumption we assume that the user is (approximately) aware of the correct number of categories in the corpus. Therefore, for all the unsupervised techniques we measure $P(T)$ and $R(T)$ for $|T| = |C|$. Choosing the appropriate number of clusters is in general a question of model selection which is beyond the scope of this work.

7. EXPERIMENTAL RESULTS

7.1 Maximizing information and clusters precision

A first natural question to ask is what are the performance of the new *sIB* algorithm versus the *AIB* algorithm in terms of maximizing $I(T; Y)$. Comparing the results over the 9 small data sets (for which running *AIB* is feasible) we found that *sIB* (with n=15) always extract solutions that preserve significantly more information than *AIB* (the improvement is of 17% on the average). Moreover, even if we do not choose for *sIB* the iteration which maximized $I(T; Y)$ but compare *all* the 15 random restarts (for every data set) with the *AIB* results, we found that more than 90% of these runs preserve more information than *AIB*.

The next question we address is whether clustering solutions that preserve more information are better correlated with the real statistical sources (i.e., the categories). In Figure 2(a) we present the progress of the information and precision for a specific restart of *sIB* over the *NG10* data set. We clearly see that while the information is increasing for every assignment update (as guaranteed by the algorithm), $P(T)$ is increasing in parallel. In fact, less than 5% of the updates reduced $P(T)$. Similar results obtained for all the other data sets.

[3]The underlying assumption here is that if the cluster is relatively homogeneous the user will be able to correctly identify its most dominant topic.

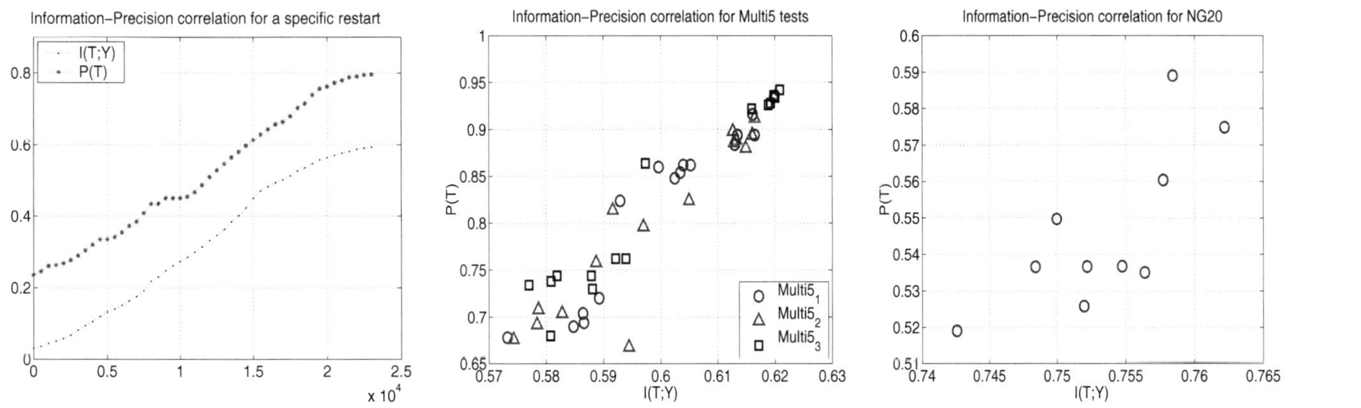

(a) (b) (c)

Figure 2: (a) Progress of $I(T;Y)$ and $P(T)$ during the assignment updates of *sIB* over the *NG10* data set. Correlation of *final values* of $I(T;Y)$ and $P(T)$ for all random restarts of *sIB* over (b) the three $Multi5$ tests and (c) the *NG20* test.

Lastly, we would like to check whether choosing the iteration which maximized $I(T;Y)$ is a reasonable unsupervised criterion for identifying solutions with high precision. In Figure 2(b,c) we see the *final values* of $I(T;Y)$ versus $P(T)$ for all the n random restarts of *sIB* over the three $Multi5$ tests and the *NG20* test. Clearly these final values are correlated. In fact, in 9 out of our 13 tests the iteration which maximized $I(T;Y)$ also maximized $P(T)$, and when it did not the gap was relatively small.

7.2 Results for small-scale experiments

In Table 1 we present the results for the small-scale 9 subsets of the 20Newsgroups corpus. The results for the *IDC* algorithm are taken from [4]. For all the unsupervised algorithms we set $n = 15$, $\varepsilon = 0$ and $maxL = 30$. However, all algorithms except for *sL1* attained full convergence in all 15 restarts and over all datasets after less than 30 loops.

To gain some perspective about how hard is the classification task we also present results of a *supervised* Naive Bayes (*NB*) classifier (see [15] for the details of the implementation). The test set for this classifier consisted of the same 500 documents in each data set while the training set consisted of different 500 documents randomly chosen from the appropriate categories. We repeated this process 10 times and averaged the results.

Several results should be noted specifically.

- *sIB* outperformed all the other unsupervised techniques in all data sets, typically with an impressive gap. Taking into account that for the other techniques we present an "unfair" choice of the *best* result (among all 15 restarts) we see these results as especially encouraging.
- In particular *sIB* was clearly superior to *IDC* and *AIB* which are both also motivated by the *Information Bottleneck* method. Nonetheless, in contrast to *sIB*, the specific implementation of *IDC* in [4] is not guaranteed to maximize $I(T;Y)$ which might explain its inferior performance. We believe that the same explanation holds for the inferiority of *AIB*.
- *sIB* was also competitive with the *supervised NB* classifier. A significant difference between these two was evident only for the three *Multi10* subsets, i.e., only when the number of real categories was relatively high.
- The poor performance of the *sKL* algorithm was due to a typical fast convergence into one huge cluster which consisted of almost all documents. This tendency is due to the over sensitivity of this algorithms to "zero" probabilities in the centroid representations and it was clearly less dominant in the medium scale experiments.
- The *AIB* results are significantly better than those reported in [14] (P(T)=45.8) although the algorithm is the same. The difference is probably due to the inclusion of the subject lines of the messages, in contrast to these previous results.

7.3 Results for medium scale experiments

In Table 2 we present the results for the medium-scale data sets. To the best of our knowledge our results are the first reported results (using direct evaluation measures as precision and recall) for unsupervised methods over corpora in that scale (order of 10^4 documents).

For all the unsupervised algorithms we set $n = 10$, $\varepsilon = 10^{-2}|X|$ (where $|X|$ is the number of documents in the corpus) and $maxL = 10$. We note here that this last choice of $maxL = 10$ was in fact probably too low for some of the algorithms (see below). For these tests as well we applied the supervised *NB* classifier. For each test, the training set consisted of $1,000$ documents, randomly chosen out of the dataset, while the test set consisted of the remaining documents. Again, we repeated this process 10 times and averaged the results.

Notice that the two Reuters tests are multi-labeled while all our classification schemes are uni-labeled. Therefore the recall of these schemes is inherently limited. This is especially evident for the *new-Reuters* test in which the average number of labels per document was 1.78 and hence the maximum attained (micro-averaged) recall was limited to 56%.

Our main findings are listed in the following.

- Similar to the small-scale experiments, *sIB* outperforms all the other unsupervised techniques, typically

Table 1: Micro-averaged precision results over the small data sets. In all unsupervised algorithms the number of clusters was taken to be identical with the number of real categories (indicated in parenthesis). For *K-means*, *sK-means*, *sL1* and *sKL* the results are the best results among all 15 restarts. For *sIB* the results are for the restart which maximized $I(T;Y)$;. The test set for the *NB* classifier consisted of the same 500 documents in each data set while the training set consisted of different 500 documents randomly chosen from the appropriate categories. We repeated this process 10 times and averaged the results.

$P(T)$	*sIB*	*IDC*	*sK-means*	*K-means*	*AIB*	*sL1*	*sKL*	*NB*
$Binary_1$ *(2)*	91.4	85	62.4	65.6	84.0	74.4	50.4	87.8
$Binary_2$ *(2)*	89.2	83	54.6	61.8	59.8	58.0	50.2	85.4
$Binary_3$ *(2)*	93.0	80	63.2	64.0	85.0	76.6	51.8	88.1
$Multi5_1$ *(5)*	89.4	86	47.0	47.4	56.6	51.6	20.6	92.8
$Multi5_2$ *(5)*	91.2	88	47.0	46.0	63.8	45.2	20.6	92.6
$Multi5_3$ *(5)*	94.2	86	57.0	50.4	76.8	52.4	20.6	93.2
$Multi10_1$ *(10)*	70.2	56	31.0	30.8	42.4	34.2	10.4	73.5
$Multi10_2$ *(10)*	63.8	49	32.8	31.0	34.0	31.2	10.0	74.6
$Multi10_3$ *(10)*	67.0	55	33.8	31.4	38.8	31.4	10.2	74.6
Average	**83.3**	**74.0**	**47.6**	**47.6**	**60.1**	**50.6**	**27.2**	**84.7**

Table 2: Micro-averaged precision results over the medium scale data sets. In all the unsupervised algorithms the number of clusters was taken to be identical with the number of real categories (indicated in parenthesis). The *NB* classifier was trained over 1,000 randomly chosen documents and tested over the remaining. We repeated this process 10 times and averaged the results.

$P(T)$	*sIB*	*sK-means*	*K-means*	*sL1*	*sKL*	*NB*
NG10 (10)	79.5	76.3	70.3	27.7	58.8	80.8
NG20 (20)	57.5	54.1	53.4	15.3	28.8	65.0
Reuters (10)	85.8	64.9	66.4	70.1	59.4	90.8
new-Reuters (10)	83.5	66.9	67.3	73.0	81.0	85.8
Average	**76.6**	**65.6**	**64.4**	**46.5**	**57.0**	**80.6**

with a significant margin and in spite of the "unfair" comparison.

- Interestingly, *sIB* was almost competitive with the supervised *NB* classifier which was trained over 1,000 labeled documents.
- Both our sequential and parallel *K-means* implementations performed surprisingly well, especially over the uni-labeled *NG10* and *NG20* tests. As in the small data sets, the differences between the parallel and the sequential implementation were minor.
- The convergence rate of the *sIB* and the *sK-means* algorithms were typically better than those of the other algorithms. In particular, *sIB* and *sK-means* converged in most of their iterations while, for example, *sL1* did not converged in any iteration.

7.4 Improving clusters precision

In supervised text classification one is able to trade precision versus recall by defining some thresholding strategy. In the following we suggest a similar idea for the *unsupervised* classification scenario. Notice that once a partition T is obtained we are able to estimate $d(x, t(x))$ $\forall x \in X$. Clearly this provide us with an estimate of how "typical" is x in $t(x)$. Specifically in the context of *sIB*, $d(x, t(x))$ is related to the loss of information by *not* holding x as a singleton cluster.

By sorting the documents in each cluster $t \in T$ with respect to $d(x, t)$ and "labeling" only the top $r\%$ of the documents in that cluster we can now reduce the recall while (hopefully) improving the precision. More specifically while defining the "label" for every cluster we use only documents that were sorted among the top $r\%$ for that cluster (and refer to the remaining as "unlabeled"). Notice that this procedure is independent of the specific definition of $d(x, t)$ and thus could be applied for all the sequential algorithms we tested.

In Figure 3 we present the Precision-Recall curves for some of our medium scale tests. Again, we find *sIB* to be clearly superior to all the other unsupervised methods examined. In particular for $r = 10\%$ *sIB* attains very high precision in a totally unsupervised manner for our real world corpora. These results raise the possibility of a new approach for combining unsupervised and supervised classification methods. Specifically we could use these high precision "labeled" clusters as a training set for a *supervised* classifier. Assuming that the precision of our "labels" is indeed relatively high and that the supervised classifier is not too sensitive for a small amount of "noise" in its training set, we predict that we can now label the remaining "unlabeled" documents (and new ones) with a reasonable performance. This issue, however, is left for future research.

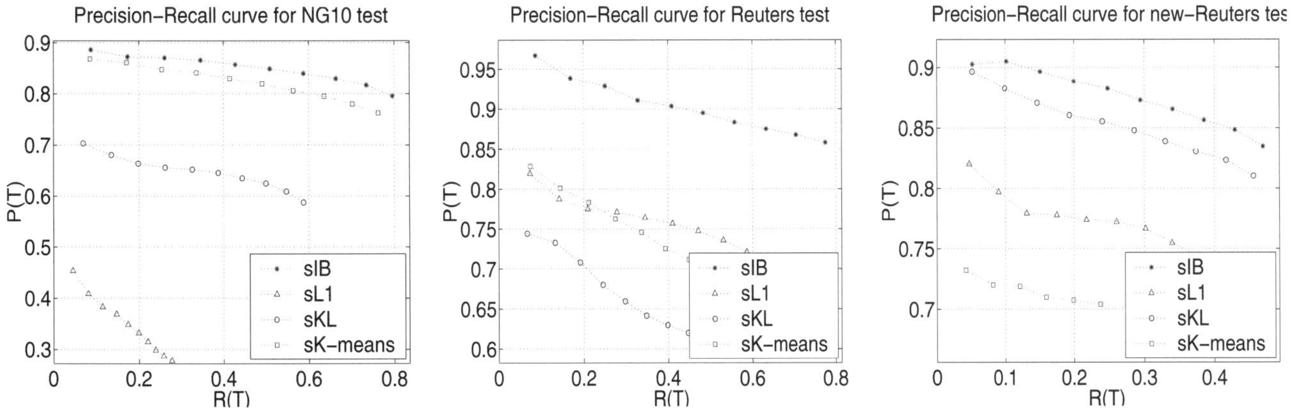

Figure 3: Precision-Recall curves for some of our medium scale tests. For the other tests the results were similar. Notice that the results for *sIB* are for the specific restart which maximized $I(T;Y)$ while for the other methods we present the best result over all 10 restarts.

7.5 Using other representations

It is well known that a word-counts representation of documents is typically noisy and different techniques can provide more sophisticated representations. In this work we concentrated on comparing different algorithms for a *fixed* (counts) representation. Nonetheless, it is interesting to ask what are the performance using different representations. Although this is not the focus of this work we performed additional experiments regarding this issue. A well known approach in the context of text classification is the *tf-idf* representation [11]. Specifically, each word count is multiplied by the inverse-document-frequency of the word, defined by $idf(y) = log(\frac{|X|}{|X(y)|})$ where $|X(y)|$ is the number of documents in which y occurred. Rich empirical evidence support the benefits of using this representation for text processing applications.

Therefore we applied the *sK-means* and the parallel *K-means* for all our tests, using the *tf-idf* representation. The results presented in Table 3 indeed verify that this representation could significantly improve *K-means* performance. The improvement is especially impressive for the small (and more noisy) data sets and for the multi-labeled *Reuters* data sets. Interestingly, under this representation we see that the sequential implementation yield superior performance to the parallel one, which implies better robustness to local optima using a sequential approach.

Comparing *sIB* with these results we still see that *sIB* attained superior performance in almost all our tests (although the gap in some cases was minor). Recall that this comparison is with the *best* result obtained using the *tf-idf* representation over all n restarts. Comparing *sIB* with the averaged *tf-idf* performance we obviously see a more significant margin in favor of *sIB*.

These results are of special interest taking into account that the *tf-idf* representation is specifically "tailored" for the context of text classification while *sIB* is a general approach using the naive counts representation. Moreover, there is strong empirical evidence suggesting that *sIB* might improve its performance using more robust representations such as word-clusters [4, 14, 16].

8. CONCLUDING REMARKS

In this paper we introduced the *sIB* algorithm. We showed that it has several important advantages over the agglomerative *IB* algorithm, both in terms of complexity and quality of clusters it finds. The reduced complexity allows us to use this algorithm on larger datasets. Moreover, the performance of *sIB* are superior to all the other unsupervised methods we examined, including methods which are especially designed for text classification. Additionally, our unsupervised results are even competitive with a standard supervised Naive Bayes classifier. In the appendix below, we provide preliminary theoretical analysis to motivate these empirical observations.

An interesting question is comparing *sIB* with the parallel versions of *IB* algorithms [17]. Our preliminary results showed, rather surprisingly, that using *sIB* we seem to obtain solutions that preserve more information than by solving the self-consistent equations directly. However, this issue calls for a more thorough investigation and theoretical understanding.

Lastly, we note here that extending the *sIB* algorithm to solve multi-variate variations of the *Information Bottleneck* principle [6] is straightforward, using the recent extension of the *AIB* algorithm into the multi-variate case [16].

Acknowledgments

We thank Yoram Singer, Leo Kontorovich, Benjy Weinberger, and in particular Koby Crammer for useful discussions and comments on previous drafts of this paper. This work was supported in part by the Israel Science Foundation (ISF) and by the US-Israel Bi-national Science Foundation (BSF). N. Friedman was also supported by an Alon fellowship and the Harry & Abe Sherman Senior Lectureship in Computer Science.

9. REFERENCES

[1] R. Bekkerman, R. El-Yaniv, Y. Winter, and N. Tishby. On Feature Distributional Clustering for Text Categorization. In *ACM SIGIR 2001*, 2001.

[2] T. M. Cover and J. A. Thomas. *Elements of Information Theory*. John Wiley & Sons, New York, 1991.

Table 3: Micro-averaged precision results using *tf-idf* representation. The first row present the average performance over the small 9 tests. The results for *sIB*, *sK-means* and *K-means* are repeated for convenience. For all algorithms except for *sIB* we present the best result among all restarts. For the *tf-idf* representation we also present in parenthesis the averaged results over all restarts.

$P(T)$	*sIB*	*sK-means*	*tf-idf:sK-means*	*K-means*	*tf-idf:K-means*
Small	83.3	47.6	81.4 (67.7)	47.6	61.9 (51.3)
10NG	79.5	76.3	76.1 (70.8)	70.3	71.9 (67.8)
20NG	57.5	54.1	58.4 (54.9)	53.4	54.1 (51.6)
Reuters	85.8	64.9	85.4 (81.8)	66.4	82.8 (76.6)
new − Reuters	83.5	66.9	81.5 (77.7)	67.3	79.5 (77.7)
Average	**77.9**	**62.0**	**76.6 (70.6)**	**61.0**	**70.0 (65.0)**

[3] K. Eguchi. Adaptive Cluster-based Browsing Using Incrementally Expanded Queries and Its Effects. In *ACM SIGIR 99*, 1999.

[4] R. El-Yaniv and O. Souroujon. Iterative Double Clustering for Unsupervised and Semi-supervised Learning. In *Proc. of Neural Information Processing Systems (NIPS-14)*, 2002, to appear.

[5] M. A. Hearst and J. O. Pedersen. Reexamining the Cluster Hypothesis: Scatter/Gather on Retrieval Results. In *ACM SIGIR 96*, 1996.

[6] N. Friedman, O. Mosenzon, N. Slonim, and N. Tishby. Multivariate Information Bottleneck. In *Proc. of the 17th conf. on Uncertainty in artificial Intelligence (UAI-17)*, 2001.

[7] K. Lang. Learning to filter netnews. In *Proc. of the 12th Int. Conf. on Machine Learning*, 1995.

[8] J. Lin. Divergence Measures Based on the Shannon Entropy. *IEEE Transactions on Information theory*, 37(1), 1991.

[9] R. M. Neal and G. E. Hinton. A view of the EM algorithm that justifies incremental, sparse, and other variants. In M. I. Jordan (editor), *Learning in Graphical Models*, pp. 355-368, 1998.

[10] F. C. Pereira, N. Tishby, and L. Lee. Distributional clustering of English words. In *30th Annual Meeting of the Association for Computational Linguistics, Columbus, Ohio*, 1993.

[11] G. Salton. Developments in Automatic Text Retrieval. *Science, Vol. 253*, pages 974–980, 1990.

[12] A. Schriebman, R. El-Yaniv, S. Fine and N. Tishby. On the two-sample problem and the Jensen-Shannon divergence for Markov sources. In preparation.

[13] N. Slonim and N. Tishby. Agglomerative Information Bottleneck. In *Proc. of Neural Information Processing Systems (NIPS-12)*, 1999.

[14] N. Slonim and N. Tishby. Document Clustering using Word Clusters via the Information Bottleneck Method. In *ACM SIGIR 2000*, 2000.

[15] N. Slonim and N. Tishby. The power of word clusters for text classification. In *23rd European Colloquium on Information Retrieval Research (ECIR), 2001.*

[16] N. Slonim, N. Friedman and N. Tishby. Multivariate Agglomerative Information Bottleneck. In *Proc. of Neural Information Processing Systems (NIPS-14)*, 2002, to appear.

[17] N. Tishby, F. Pereira, and W. Bialek. The Information Bottleneck method. In *Proc. 37th Allerton Conference on Communication and Computation.* 1999.

[18] C. J. van Rijsbergen. *Information Retrieval.* London: Butterworths; 1979.

[19] O. Zamir and O. Etzioni. Web Document Clustering: A Feasibility Demonstration. In *ACM SIGIR 98*, 1998.

APPENDIX

A. CLUSTERS ACCURACY AND MUTUAL INFORMATION

In the following we give some preliminary theoretical analysis which relates information maximization clustering with supervised classification. We assume the following setting. We are given a set of objects $x \in X$ which are represented as conditional distributions $p(y|x)$. The *true* (unknown) classification of these objects induces a partition of X into K disjoint classes where each class is characterized through a distribution $p(y|c_k)$, $c_k \in C$. Denoting the class of some specific $x \in X$ by $c(x)$ we assume the following (strong) asymptotic assumption: $p(y|x) = p(y|c(x))\ \forall x \in X$.

In the context of document classification $p(y|x)$ is typically the relative frequencies of the words $y \in Y$ in some document x while $p(y|c(x))$ represent the relative frequencies of the words over all the documents that belong to the class $c(x)$. Therefore, the violation of this assumption becomes less severe as the sample size for $p(y|x)$ (i.e., the length of the document x) is increased.

Using the labeling scheme described in section 6.2, for any given partition the micro-averaged precision $P(T)$ is well defined. In particular, if we denote by T^* the partition which is perfectly correlated with the true classes, then clearly $P(T^*) = 1$.

Notice that every partition T defines a set of "hard" membership probabilities $p(t|x)$. These probabilities in turn, defines through Eqs.(3) (using the Markov independence assumption between T and Y given X) the set of centroid distributions $p(y|t)$ and prior distribution $p(t)$. Therefore, for any partition T, $I(T;Y)$ is well defined. Under the above assumption we get:

Proposition A.1. *$I(T^*;Y) > I(T;Y)$ for any partition $T \neq T^*$ such that $|T| = K$.*

Thus, the "true" partition T^*, maximizes the information, and by definition the precision.

Nonetheless, this proposition refers only to the perfect partition and does not provide insight about the information preserved by other partitions. We define the distortion of some partition T with respect to the true classification by $D(T) \equiv E_{P(x)}[D_{KL}(P(Y \mid c(x))\|P(Y \mid t(x)))]$. Based on our asymptotic assumption, we then get:

Proposition A.2. $D(T^{(1)}) \leq D(T^{(2)}) \iff I(T^{(1)};Y) \geq I(T^{(2)};Y)$

Hence, roughly speaking, seeking partitions which are more similar to the true classification is equivalent to seeking partitions that are more informative about the feature space Y.

Topic Difference Factor Extraction between Two Document Sets and its Application to Text Categorization

Takahiko Kawatani
Hewlett-Packard Labs Japan
3-8-13, Takaido-Higashi, Suginami-Ku, Tokyo, 168-0072 Japan
takahiko_kawatani@hp.com

ABSTRACT

To improve performance in text categorization, it is important to extract distinctive features for each class. This paper proposes topic difference factor analysis (TDFA) as a method to extract projection axes that reflect topic differences between two document sets. Suppose all sentence vectors that compose each document are projected onto projection axes. TDFA obtains the axes that maximize the ratio between the document sets as to the sum of squared projections by solving a generalized eigenvalue problem. The axes are called topic difference factors (TDF's). By applying TDFA to the document set that belongs to a given class and a set of documents that is misclassified as belonging to that class by an existent classifier, we can obtain features that take large values in the given class but small ones in other classes, as well as features that take large values in other classes but small ones in the given class. A classifier was constructed applying the above features to complement the kNN classifier. As the results, the micro-averaged F_1 measure for Reuters-21578 improved from 83.69 to 87.27%.

Categories & Subject Descriptors: H.3.m [**Miscellaneous**].

General Terms: Algorithms, Experimentation, Performance.

1. INTRODUCTION

Recently text categorization research has become more and more popular. According to Yang's comparative study of classifiers [1], k nearest neighbors (kNN)[1,2,3], support vector machines (SVM)[1,4], and Linear Least Squares Fit (LLSF)[5] outperform other methods proposed so far. Adaboost also achieves high performance [6]. However, because these methods have been studied in depth, increasing performance by improving individual methods seems difficult. A new approach is necessary.

Every classifier has information about document classes, and compares it with an input document. We call this information the class model. The class model is the average vector of documents belonging to the same class in Rocchio's model [7], the set of documents belonging to the same class in kNN, and a set of simple hypotheses in Adaboost. The class model needs to be precise to enable high performance. However, many classifiers, even precise class models, do not consider class-model overlapping. In most classifiers the class model of a certain class shares information with other classes. If an overlap exits in class models, unnecessary likelihood can be generated for classes an input document does not belong to. Therefore, class-model overlapping may cause misclassification. To prevent misclassification, a class model should be described using each class's distinctive information so that class model overlapping is reduced.

This paper focuses on this issue. To clarify each class's distinctive information, it is essential to extract features that reflect differences between a document set of a given class and a document set that belongs to other classes.

First, this paper proposes a method to extract projection axes that reflect topic differences between two document sets. Suppose that each document is represented as a set of sentence vectors, whose components represent frequency related values of corresponding terms, and that all sentence vectors are projected onto projection axes. The projection axes are obtained so that the ratio between the document sets as to the sum of the squared projections is maximized. By projecting the sentence vectors onto the projection axes, we can obtain the features that take large values in one document set but small ones in the other. Here, a feature denotes a linear combination of terms. Since the projection axis reflects the topic difference between the document sets, we call it a topic difference factor (TDF), and the method topic-difference-factor analysis (TDFA). By applying TDFA to text categorization, we can obtain features that take large values in a given class but small ones in other classes, and features take small values in the given class but large ones in other classes. This paper proposes a classification scheme that applies the features in a complementary classifier to an existent one. The proposed complementary classifier corrects the likelihood scores of an input document that are assigned to each class by an existent classifier.

The rest of this paper is organized as follows. Section 2 describes how TDF's are obtained and how TDFA is interpreted. What TDF's are obtained is also illustrated for simple examples of sentence vectors. Section 3 shows how TDF's are obtained for the complementary classifier and how likelihood scores are corrected. Section 4 presents experimental results using Reuters-21578. They show that the micro averaged F_1 measure was significantly improved. Section 5 summarizes the paper.

2. TOPIC DIFFERENCE FACTOR (TDF)

2.1 Approach

We consider two document sets, $D=\{D_1,..,D_M\}$ and $T=\{T_1,.., T_N\}$. Let the k-th sentence vector in document D_m and T_n be $\boldsymbol{d}_{mk}$ $(k=1,..,K_D(m))$ and $\boldsymbol{t}_{nk}(k=1,..,K_T(n))$, respectively. Here, let $\boldsymbol{\alpha}$ be the projection axis to be obtained. We assume $\|\boldsymbol{\alpha}\|=1$. Let P_D and P_T be the sums of squared projections of all sentence vectors in document sets D and T onto $\boldsymbol{\alpha}$, respectively. They are obtained as follows. That is,

$$P_D = \sum_{m=1}^{M}\sum_{k=1}^{K_D(m)}(\boldsymbol{d}_{mk}{}^T\boldsymbol{\alpha})^2 = \boldsymbol{\alpha}^T\boldsymbol{S}_D\boldsymbol{\alpha}\,, \qquad (1)$$

$$P_T = \sum_{n=1}^{N}\sum_{k=1}^{K_T(n)}(\boldsymbol{t}_{nk}{}^T\boldsymbol{\alpha})^2 = \boldsymbol{\alpha}^T\boldsymbol{S}_T\boldsymbol{\alpha}\,, \qquad (2)$$

where T denotes transpose, and $\boldsymbol{S}_D$ and $\boldsymbol{S}_T$ are the matrices defined by

$$S_D = \sum_{m=1}^{M}\sum_{k=1}^{K_D(m)}\boldsymbol{d}_{mk}\boldsymbol{d}_{mk}{}^T\,, \qquad (3)$$

$$S_T = \sum_{n=1}^{N}\sum_{k=1}^{K_T(n)}\boldsymbol{t}_{nk}\boldsymbol{t}_{nk}{}^T\,. \qquad (4)$$

We call these matrices square sum matrices. The matrix divided by the number of sentences is the so-called autocorrelation matrix. Let $J(\boldsymbol{\alpha})$ be a criterion function which represents how strongly the differences between the document sets D and T are reflected on $\boldsymbol{\alpha}$. We define $J(\boldsymbol{\alpha})$ as

$$J(\boldsymbol{\alpha}) = \frac{P_D}{P_T} = \frac{\boldsymbol{\alpha}^T\boldsymbol{S}_D\boldsymbol{\alpha}}{\boldsymbol{\alpha}^T\boldsymbol{S}_T\boldsymbol{\alpha}}\,. \qquad (5)$$

Since the sum of squared projections of all sentence vectors onto the $\boldsymbol{\alpha}$ that maximizes $J(\boldsymbol{\alpha})$ should be large for document set D and small for T, the $\boldsymbol{\alpha}$ reflects information that appears frequently in document set D but rarely in T. In other words, it reflects distinctive information that should exist in document set D. Therefore, we call such an $\boldsymbol{\alpha}$ the positive topic difference factor (P-TDF) of document set D. Criterion function $J(\boldsymbol{\alpha})$ has the same form as that in linear discriminant analysis[8,10]. As in linear discriminant analysis, plural $\boldsymbol{\alpha}$'s are obtained as the eigenvectors of the following generalized eigenvalue problem.

$$\boldsymbol{S}_D\boldsymbol{\alpha} = \lambda\boldsymbol{S}_T\boldsymbol{\alpha}\,. \qquad (6)$$

Alternatively, $\boldsymbol{\alpha}$'s can be expressed as the eigenvectors of $\boldsymbol{S}_T^{-1}\boldsymbol{S}_D$.

Let $\boldsymbol{\beta}$ be another projection axis to be obtained. When $J(\boldsymbol{\beta})$ is defined as

$$J(\boldsymbol{\beta}) = \frac{P_T}{P_D} = \frac{\boldsymbol{\beta}^T\boldsymbol{S}_T\boldsymbol{\beta}}{\boldsymbol{\beta}^T\boldsymbol{S}_D\boldsymbol{\beta}}\,, \qquad (7)$$

information that appears frequently in document set T but rarely in D is reflected on the $\boldsymbol{\beta}$ that maximizes $J(\boldsymbol{\beta})$. The $\boldsymbol{\beta}$ becomes the P-TDF of document set T. We also call the $\boldsymbol{\beta}$ the negative topic difference factor (N-TDF) of document set D. In this case, plural $\boldsymbol{\beta}$'s are obtained as the eigenvectors of the following generalized eigenvalue problem.

$$\boldsymbol{S}_T\boldsymbol{\beta} = \lambda\boldsymbol{S}_D\boldsymbol{\beta}\,. \qquad (8)$$

In Eqs.(1) and (2), $\boldsymbol{d}_{mk}$ and $\boldsymbol{t}_{nk}$ might be replaced by their normalized forms, $\hat{\boldsymbol{d}}_{mk} = \boldsymbol{d}_{mk}/\|\boldsymbol{d}_{mk}\|$ and $\hat{\boldsymbol{t}}_{nk} = \boldsymbol{t}_{nk}/\|\boldsymbol{t}_{nk}\|$, respectively, to prevent influence from sentence-length variance. In this case, criterion $J(\boldsymbol{\alpha})$ or $J(\boldsymbol{\beta})$ represents the ratio between the document sets as to the sum of the squared cosine similarities of $\boldsymbol{\alpha}$ or $\boldsymbol{\beta}$ with all sentence vectors.

2.2 Interpretation

We consider the case of Eq.(6). Let λ_i and $\boldsymbol{\alpha}_i$ be the i-th eigenvalue and eigenvector, respectively. Since $\lambda_i=\boldsymbol{\alpha}_i^T\boldsymbol{S}_D\boldsymbol{\alpha}_i/\boldsymbol{\alpha}_i^T\boldsymbol{S}_T\boldsymbol{\alpha}_i$, λ_i represents the value of $J(\boldsymbol{\alpha}_i)$. It is known that the eigenvectors of Eq.(6) can be acquired in a two-stage procedure, and that the matrices $\boldsymbol{S}_D$ and $\boldsymbol{S}_T$ are diagonalized simultaneously[9].

Let ρ_j and $\boldsymbol{\phi}_j$ be the j-th eigenvalue and eigenvector of $\boldsymbol{S}_T$, respectively. The sum of the squared projections of all sentence vectors in document set T onto $\boldsymbol{\phi}_1$ is greater than that onto any other vector, and λ_1 represents the sum of the squared projections onto $\boldsymbol{\phi}_1$. The $\boldsymbol{\phi}_2$ gives the largest sum of the squared projections of all sentence vectors under the constraint that $\boldsymbol{\phi}_2$ is orthogonal to $\boldsymbol{\phi}_1$, and λ_2 represents the sum of the squared projections onto $\boldsymbol{\phi}_2$. The same relationship holds for the higher order eigenvectors. Suppose a sentence vector $\boldsymbol{d}_{mk}$ in document set D be mapped into vector $\boldsymbol{y}_{mk}$ in space Y. The j-th component of $\boldsymbol{y}_{mk}$ is given by

$$y_{mkj} = \boldsymbol{\phi}_j{}^T\boldsymbol{d}_{mk}/\sqrt{\rho_j}\,. \qquad (9)$$

The eigenvectors of the squared sum matrix of document set D in space Y correspond to α's in the original space. That is, the principal components of document set D in space Y correspond to α's.

On mapping to space Y, the inner product between ϕ_j and d_{mk} is divided by the square root of ρ_j as shown in Eq.(9). This means that document set D in space Y is compressed in the directions of the ϕ_j's with large eigenvalues, and expanded in those with small eigenvalues. For the principal components of the scaled document set D in space Y, consequently, the directions of the principal components of document set T become less dominant, and the sum of squared projections of all sentence vectors on α becomes large for document set D and small for T. If d_{mk} describes the content that document set T does not include but D does, $\sum_{i=1}^{L}(d_{mk}{}^T\alpha_i)^2$ takes a large value. The value of L should be determined experimentally.

2.3 Regularization

We consider the case of Eq.(6) again. For eigenvectors to be obtained in Eq.(6), matrix S_T must be regular. When the number of sample sentence vectors is less than the dimension of the vectors, or when a certain pair of terms always co-occurs, matrix S_T is actually not regular. In these cases, matrix S_T must be regularized. Regularization can be achieved by biasing diagonal components as follows [10,12].

$$\hat{S}_T = S_T + \sigma^2 I, \qquad (10)$$

where σ^2 and I are a bias parameter and the identity matrix, respectively.

The meaning of Eq. (10) is as follows. Suppose that every term has a vector with the same dimension as the sentence vector and that value σ is given only to the component that corresponds to each term. Let u_l *be* the l-th term vector. Since $\sum_l u_l u_l^T = \sigma^2 I$, adding σ^2 to all diagonal components is equivalent to adding all term vectors to document set T. As mentioned above, the eigenvectors of S_T are the projection axes that maximize the sum of the squared projections of all sentence vectors in document set T, and the eigenvalues are the sums. Since the sum of the squared projections of all term vectors onto any normalized vector is always σ^2, in this case, the eigenvectors of S_T do not change by adding all term vectors to document set T. Since the sum of squared projections of all term vectors is added to that of all sentence vectors, however, the eigenvalues of S_T get biased by σ^2 and the criterion function also changes to

$$J(\alpha) = P_D / (P_T + \sigma^2). \qquad (11)$$

Higher order eigenvalues of S_T usually take very small values, nearly 0. Very small eigenvalues are easily affected by noises in document set T. Since the scaling factors for document set D in space Y become very large along the directions of higher order eigenvectors, the principal component of document set D easily suffer from noises in T. Thanks to eigenvalue biasing, those scaling factors become smaller and noise influence can be reduced.

2.4 Example

This section illustrates what TDF's are obtained for simple examples. Suppose that four 5-dimensional sentence vectors are given in document set D and T as shown in Table 1. The n-th component in the vectors is supposed to represent the existence of term n. Let D-m or T-m represent the m-th sentence vector in document set D or T. The differences and similarities between the document sets D and T are as follows.

- Term 5 does not occur in document set T, but it occurs in D-1.
- In document set D, term 2 co-occurs with term 3 in D-3, and term 1 with term 4 in D-4.
- In document set T, term 1 co-occurs with term 3 in T-3 and term 2 with term 4 in T-4.
- In both document sets, term 1 co-occurs with term 2 in D-1 and T-1, and term 3 with term 4 in D-2 and T-2.

The TDF's were obtained by setting σ^2 at 0.1. Table 2 shows eigenvalue λ_n (n=1,..5) and eigenvector $\alpha_n=(\alpha_{n1},.., \alpha_{n5})$ (n=1,..5) of Eq.(6) as P-TDF's of document set D. Table 3 shows eigenvalues μ_n (n=1,..5) and eigenvector $\beta_n=(\beta_{n1},.., \beta_{n5})$ (n=1,..5) of Eq.(8) as N-TDF's of document set D. In Table 2 and 3, α_n or β_n is normalized so that $\alpha_n^T S_D \alpha_n=\lambda_n$ or $\beta_n^T S_T \beta_n=\mu_n$. Consequently, the dynamic range of the squared inner products between sentence vectors and TDF get larger for lower order PDF. This normalization means weighting according to the degree of topic differences reflected on each eigenvector. This normalization was applied in the experiments. Table 4 shows the projections of each sentence vector onto both the first and the second eigenvector.

From these results the following can be noted.

(1) For the first eigenvector, α_1, shown in Table 2, both α_{11} and α_{14} take negative values, and both α_{12} and α_{13} positive values. This shows that α_1 reflects the term co-occurrence between 1 and 4 and the one between 2 and 3 in document set D, so the projections of D-3 and D-4 onto α_1 have large absolute values with different signs, and the projections of any other sentence vectors take zero, as shown in Table 4 .

Table 1. Sentence vectors comprising document set D and T.

#	D	T
1	11001	11000
2	00110	00110
3	01100	10100
4	10010	01010

Table 2. P-TDF's of document set D.

n	λ_n	α_{n1}	α_{n2}	α_{n3}	α_{n4}	α_{n5}
1	20.00	-1.58	1.58	1.58	-1.58	0.00
2	10.74	0.11	0.11	-0.04	-0.04	3.05
3	0.97	-0.01	-0.01	-0.40	-0.40	0.01
4	0.22	-0.41	-0.41	0.14	0.14	0.84
5	0.00	0.35	-0.35	0.35	-0.35	0.00

Table 3. N-TDF's of document set D.

n	μ_n	β_{n1}	β_{n2}	β_{n3}	β_{n4}	β_{n5}
1	20.00	1.58	-1.58	1.58	-1.58	0.00
2	2.78	-0.72	-0.72	0.23	0.23	1.31
3	0.97	0.01	0.01	-0.40	-0.40	-0.01
4	0.00	-0.25	0.25	0.25	-0.25	0.65
5	0.00	0.24	-0.24	-0.24	0.24	0.70

Table 4. Projections of each document.

text	α_1	α_2	β_1	β_2
D-1	0.00	3.27	0.00	-0.13
D-2	0.00	-0.07	0.00	0.46
D-3	3.16	0.08	0.00	-0.49
D-4	-3.16	0.08	0.00	-0.49
T-1	0.00	0.22	0.00	-1.44
T-2	0.00	-0.07	0.00	0.46
T-3	0.00	0.08	3.16	-0.49
T-4	0.00	0.08	-3.16	-0.49

(2) For the second eigenvector $\boldsymbol{\alpha}_2$ shown in Table 2, only α_{25} takes a large value. This shows that $\boldsymbol{\alpha}_2$ reflects the occurrence of term 5 in document set D , so only D-1 takes a large projection value as shown in Table 4.

(3) Similarly, the term co-occurrence between 1 and 3 and that between 2 and 4 in document set T are reflected on $\boldsymbol{\beta}_1$ shown in Table 3. Only projections of T-3 and T-4 take non-zero values.

(4) The difference between D-1 and T-1 is reflected on $\boldsymbol{\beta}_2$, as shown in Table 3. The projection of T-1 takes a large absolute value.

(5) In Table 2 and 3, the eigenvectors of the 3rd order or higher are not effective as TDF's because the eigenvalues of those orders are small.

These observations confirm that not only the term occurrence difference between the document sets but also the term co-occurrence differences are reflected on TDF's. In this paper, a document is represented as a set of sentence vectors so that the term co-occurrence difference is reflected precisely on the TDF's.

3. APPLICATION TO TEXT CATEGORIZATION

3.1 Approach

As described in section 1, this paper does not aim at developing a classifier that only uses TDF's, but at a classification scheme that combines an existent classifier with its complementary one which uses TDF's. The reasons are as follows.

(1) We define a set of documents belonging to class l as document set D and a set of documents belonging to classes other than l as document set T. If we construct a classifier that only uses TDF's, we have to apply TDFA to the document sets. In this case, document set T must include all documents that are not included in D. As a result the number of documents in document set T would probably be much larger than that in D, and document set T would probably include many documents irrelevant to class l. In such a case, it is doubtful whether subtle differences between class l and documents easily confused with those in class l can be reflected exactly on the TDF's. To reflect such subtleties , only the documents that are easily confused should be included in document set T. Those documents can be obtained by using the results of an existent classifier.

(2) It is considered easier to achieve high performance by combining TDF-based classifier with an existent high performance classifier than by constructing a classifier using TDF's only.

Based on these considerations, a classification scheme was constructed such that the complementary classifier corrects likelihood scores obtained by an existent classifier. The existent classifier acts as the main classifier. If an input document has features that should appear in a given class, a gain is added to the likelihood score of the class in the complementary classifier, and if an input document has features that should not appear in a given class, a penalty is imposed.

3.2 Complementary Classifier

The TDF's of class l is obtained as follows. First, all training documents are classified by the main classifier and the likelihood scores of each class are obtained. Let γ be a threshold given for each class. The training documents that have a likelihood score of class l larger than γ are selected. Among the selected documents, the documents belonging to class l are added to document set D and the documents belonging to other classes to T. Every document in document set T is the one that has been misclassified or nearly misclassified as belonging to class l. We call such a document a competing document of class l. Document sets D and T are thus defined and used for solving Eq.(6) and (8). The P-TDF's of class l are given by eigenvector $\{\boldsymbol{\alpha}_n\}(n=1,..,L_G)$ of Eq.(6) and N-TDF's by eigenvector $\{\boldsymbol{\beta}_n\}(n=1,..,L_P)$ of Eq.(8).

Let $g(X)$ and $p(X)$ be a gain and a penalty of input document X for class l, respectively. Suppose document X is composed of a sentence vector set $\{\boldsymbol{x}_1,.., \boldsymbol{x}_K\}$. $g(X)$ and $p(X)$ can be obtained as follows.

$$g(X) = \Sigma_{i=1}^{L_G} \Sigma_{k=1}^{K} (\boldsymbol{x}_k{}^T \boldsymbol{\alpha}_i)^2 , \qquad (12)$$

$$p(X) = \Sigma_{i=1}^{L_P} \Sigma_{k=1}^{K} (\boldsymbol{x}_k{}^T \boldsymbol{\beta}_i)^2 , \qquad (13)$$

where L_G and L_P are parameters whose values should optimally be determined by experiments. Let $Lik(X)$ be the likelihood score of document X for class l in the main classifier and $Lik_C(X)$ the corrected likelihood score. $Lik_C(X)$ can be given as follows.

$$Lik_C(X) = Lik(X) + a\, g(X) - b\, p(X), \qquad (14)$$

where a and b are positive parameters, which should be determined by experiments. $Lik_C(X)$ is computed for documents that have $Lik(X)$ larger than γ. A document with $Lik(X)$ smaller than or equal to γ is not judged as belonging to class l under any conditions. If $Lik_C(X)$ exceeds another threshold δ, the input document X is judged as belonging to class l.

When Eqs.(12) or (13) are used as a gain or a penalty, $g(X)$ or $p(X)$ tend to take a large value for long documents. To reduce the influence of document-length variance, normalizing $g(X)$ or $p(X)$ by the number of sentences in document X might be effective. When sentence vectors are normalized to reduce influence from sentence-length variance in the TDF calculation, the normalized sentence vectors in document X should be used in Eqs.(12) and (13).

4. EXPERIMENTS

4.1 Experimental Conditions

The experimental conditions in this paper follow Yang's experiments [1] and Reuters-21578 was used. According to ModApte Split, the documents were selected which belong to classes that have at least one document in the training set and the test set. This resulted in 87 classes, a training set of 7770 documents, and a test set of 3019 documents.

For the training and the test data, sentence segmentation, lemmatization, replacement of uppercases by lowercases, replacement of all digits by "0", removal of "-", "/" and all punctuation, stop-word removal, and term selection were conducted as a preprocess. Sentence segmentation was needed since a document is represented as a set of sentence vectors in this paper. Ordinary documents were segmented by finding periods. In the corpus, however, there are many table-like documents where terms are spaced by the same interval without any punctuation. For such documents one line was regarded as one sentence. For the term selection, 2500 terms were selected based on χ^2 statistics[11].

To represent sentences as vectors, each term was weighted based on *tf-idf*. The weight of the i-th term, w_i, was determined as follows.

$$w_i = (1 + \log f_i)\log(N_D / n_i) , \qquad (15)$$

where f_i, n_i, and N_D represent the frequency of an i-th term in a given sentence, the number of documents including an i-th term and the total number of documents, respectively.

4.2 Experimental Methods

As the main classifier, kNN classifier [1] was used ,which enables high performance by using a simple algorithm. For a given input document, the classifier calculates similarity scores with each training document and then, finds k nearest neighbors out of the training documents. As the similarity measure, the cosine similarity was adopted, as it is commonly done. The value of k was set at 45 in accordance with Yang's experiment [1]. The similarity scores with the documents belonging to the same class out of all k documents are summed up as the likelihood score of that class. Thus, the likelihood scores are obtained for the classes that the documents of k nearest neighbors belong to. The input document is judged as belonging to a class if the likelihood score of that class is larger than a threshold. The threshold is determined in advance for each class so that it maximizes the evaluation score.

To evaluate the proposed method, the standard recall, precision, and F_1 measure were used. Recall (r) is defined as the ratio of correct assignments by the classifier divided

Table 5. Performance comparison for Reuters-21578.

classifier	*Recall*	*Precision*	F_1
SVM	81.20	91.37	85.99
kNN	83.39	88.07	85.67
LSF	85.07	84.89	84.98
Nnet	78.42	87.85	82.87
NB	76.88	82.45	79.56
kNN(this paper)	81.57	85.93	83.69

by the total number of correct assignments. Precision (p) is defined as the ratio of correct assignments by the classifier divided by the total number of classifier's assignments. The F_1 measure is defined as F_1=2rp/(r+p). Table 5 shows the micro-averaged evaluation scores reported by Yang [1] for several well-known methods including the kNN classifier and those of the kNN classifier in this paper. In Table 5, Nnet and NB stand for neural network and naive Bayes, respectively. The F_1 measure of the kNN result in this paper is 83.69%, which is inferior to that in Yang's report by 2%.

When L_G and L_P in Eqs.(12) and (13), and a and b in Eq.(14) were determined, the following problem occurred. Although these parameters should be determined using training data, TDF's obtained by using training data were tuned to the training data. If the parameters are determined by using such TDF's, the parameters would be doubly tuned to the training data. Evaluating test data using the parameters obtained in such a way is obviously inappropriate. To remedy this problem, cross validation was also conducted. The test data were divided into N blocks, and the parameters were determined by using N-1 blocks as the secondary training data and the remaining block was used as true test data. After running experiments N times by rotating the blocks, the results for each true test data were summed up as the results of total test data. Since the summed up results were not tuned to the test data, the results can be compared with other method's results.

The parameters were obtained as follows. The a and b in Eq.(14) were obtained by applying linear discriminant analysis. Threshold δ was obtained for each class to maximize the F_1 measure. The linear discriminant analysis and threshold determination were conducted for every combination of L_G with L_P, each of which was restricted to be lower than 15. The L_G and L_P were determined by selecting the combination which gave the best results. The linear discriminant analysis was conducted between a document set and a competing document set of each class. The competing documents were selected by using threshold γ that was used in the TDF-calculation stage. For the analysis, a 3-dimensional vector, whose components were given by $Lik(X)$, $g(X)$ and $p(X)$, was generated for each document. As a result of the linear discriminant analysis, the weights of $Lik(X)$, $g(X)$, and $p(X)$, which optimally separate a document set from a competing document set of each class, were obtained. By dividing the weights of $g(X)$ and $p(X)$ by that of $Lik(X)$, a and b in Eq.(14) were determined.

Furthermore, the experiments confirmed that combining sentence vector normalization with normalizing Eqs.(12) and (13) by the number of sentences in an input document was effective. The experimental results shown in the next paragraph are the best ones obtained by varying the parameters including γ and σ^2.

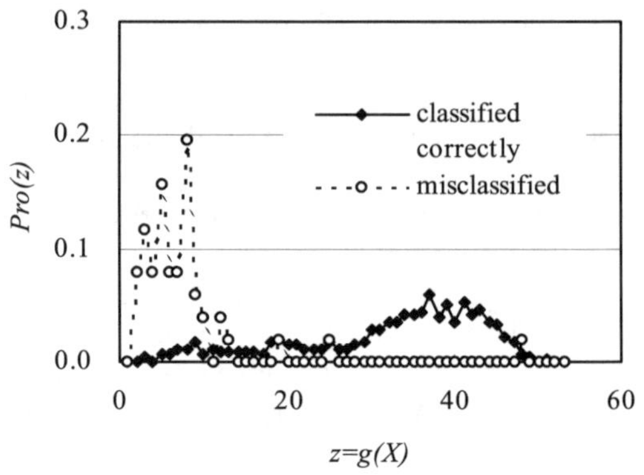

Figure 1. Probability density distribution of $g(x)$ for correctly classified and misclassified documents by kNN as belonging to class "earn".

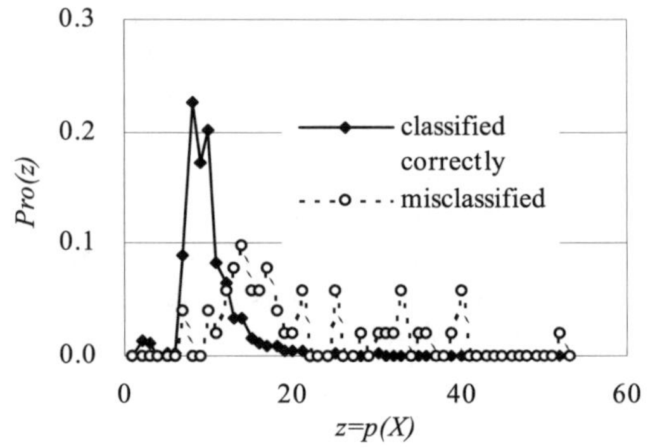

Figure 2. Probability density distribution of $p(x)$ for correctly classified and misclassified documents by kNN as belonging to class "earn".

4.3 Experimental Results

Figure 1 shows the probability density distributions of gain $g(X)$ for test documents correctly classified and misclassified by kNN as belonging to class "earn". In Fig.1, the horizontal axis shows $z=g(X)$ and the vertical axis the probability density $Prob(z_k)$, which is derived as follows.

$$Prob(z_k) = n(z_k) / \sum_k n(z_k) \qquad (16)$$

where $n(z_k)$ represents the number of documents whose $g(X)$ take value z_k. Similarly, Fig. 2 shows the probability density distributions of penalty $p(X)$. The number of documents correctly classified as belonging to class "earn" is 1077 and the number of the misclassified documents 51. Both L_G and L_P in Eqs.(12) and (13) were set at 5. Out of all documents, the misclassified documents are the most difficult ones to separate from the documents belonging to class "earn". As shown in Figs.1 and 2, however, the misclassified documents are well separated though slight overlaps occurred.

The effectiveness of introducing σ^2 in Eq.(11) was investigated when cross validation was conducted. The σ^2 was set at the average of the diagonal components of $\boldsymbol{S}_T$ multiplied by τ. Figure 3 shows the relationship between τ and the F_1 measure when a likelihood score was corrected only by $g(X)$. The N was set at 20. As the figure shows, the F_1 measure peaks at τ=2.0. As mentioned in **2.3**, $\boldsymbol{\alpha}$ tends to be easily affected by noises in document set T if σ^2 is small. This is the reason why the F_1 measure is small for τ<2.0. If σ^2 is too large, on the other hand, P_T in Eq.(11) is not necessarily small because σ^2 becomes dominant in the denominator. Therefore, P_D / P_T may be small. This is the reason why the F_1 measure is small for τ>2.0.

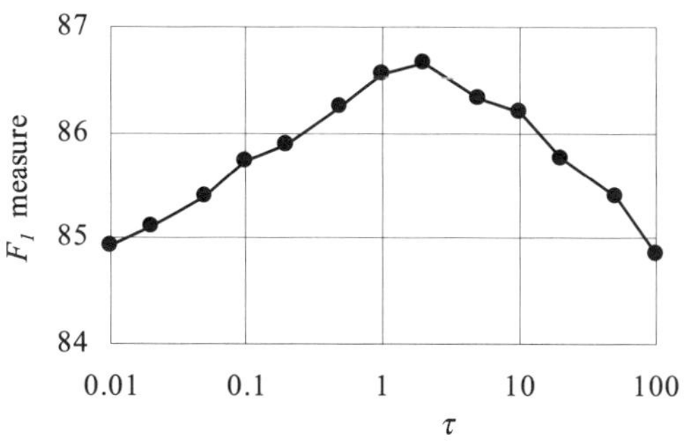

Figure 3. Relationship between F_1 measure and regularization parameter.

Table 6 shows the classification results for training data and test data before the likelihood correction. Table 7 illustrates the classification results after the likelihood correction without cross validation. It shows the following three cases: (a) evaluate trainig data using parameters trained by training data, (b) evaluate all test data using parameters trained by all test data, (c) evaluate all test data using parameters trained by training data. When parameters were trained using training data, the F_1 measure of training data significantly increased. The F_1 measure, nevertheless, remains less than 95%. This implies that class boundaries are not clear between many classes. The F_1 measures of all test data using parameters trained by all test data, 89.33%, is quite different from that by training data, 85.87%. The former seems to be due to overtuning to test data, and the latter due to overtuning to training data. These F_1 measures do not represent true performance for test data.

Table 6. Performance before liklihood correction.

evaluation data	*Recall*	*Precision*	F_1
training data	90.69	89.02	89.85
test data	81.57	85.93	83.69

Table 7. Performance after liklihood correction without cross validation.

	evaluation data	parameter training dsta	*Recall*	*Precision*	F_1
a	training data	training data	94.15	95.06	94.60
b	test data	test data	85.44	93.59	89.33
c	test data	training data	84.74	87.02	85.87

Table 8 shows the classification results based on cross validation for N=2, 5, 10, and 20. Table 8 shows the F_1 measures when the likelihood was corrected by either only $g(X)$ or $p(X)$, and the F_1 measures, precision, and recall when the likelihood was corrected by both $g(X)$ and $p(X)$. These measures are micro-averaged ones. From this table, the following can be noted.

Table8. Performance after liklihood correction with cross validation .

		N			
Lik$_C$(X)	measure	2	5	10	20
Lik(X)+ag(X)	F_1	86.44	86.70	86.67	86.66
Lik(X)-bp(X)	F_1	84.55	85.04	85.09	85.18
Lik(X)+ag(X) -bp(X)	F_1	86.64	86.95	87.10	87.27
	Precision	90.03	90.59	91.03	91.28
	Recall	83.49	83.60	83.49	83.60

- Likelihood correction by $g(X)$ or $p(X)$ effectively improves performance.
- Likelihood correction by $g(X)$ is more effective than that by $p(X)$. This fact shows that, in each class, it is easier to extract features that should occur than features that should not occur. This is because a competing document set of each class is composed of documents belonging to various classes and because P-TDF's of each competing document set(N-TDF's of each class) are not clear in comparison with P-TDF's of each class.
- The F_1 measure improved from 83.69% obtained by kNN classifier alone to 87.27% when the likelihood was corrected by both $g(X)$ and $p(X)$. The score is significantly better than the scores of the other classifiers shown in Table 5.

The averages of L_G and L_P were 3.0 and 1.7, respectively, when N was set at 20. When the dimension of sentence vectors was individually determined for each class by assigning only terms appearing in each class and its competing document set to the vector components, the processing time to obtain 15 eigenvectors of Eqs.(6) or (8) for all classes was about 60 minutes using a workstation with a 120-Mhz clock. Thus, the computational cost of the proposed method is not high.

5. Summary

The objective of this paper is to extract distinctive features for each document class and to apply them to text categorization. This paper proposes Topic Difference Factor Analysis as a method to extract difference factors between two document sets by obtaining projection axes which maximize the ratio between the document sets as to the sum of squared projections of all sentence vectors. Tests confirmed that not only term occurrence difference between document sets but also term co-occurrence difference are reflected on the topic difference factors. By applying this method to document classification, we can obtain the features that should occur in a given class and the features that should not occur in the class. This paper proposes a classification scheme that uses the features in a complementary classifier to correct the likelihood of an input to each class of an existent classifier. By applying the kNN classifier as the existent one, improved the micro-averaged F_1 measure for Reuters-21578 from 83.69 to 87.27%.

These experimental results prove that topic difference factors have been successfully extracted. This paper, however, has not shown what the topic difference factors are for each class. Interpreting topic difference factors is an important remaining problem. TDFA has many possible applications, and the interpretation will be important for new applications.

REFERENCES

[1] Y. Yang and X. Liu. Re-examination of Text Categorization. In *Proceedings of the 22nd Annual International ACM SIGIR Conference on Research and Development in Information Retrieval (SIGIR'99)*, pp. 43-49, 1999.

[2] B. Masand, G. Linoff and D. Walts. Classifying News Stories Using Memory Based Reasoning. In *Proceedings of the 15th Annual International ACM SIGIR Conference on Research and Development in Information Retrieval (SIGIR'92)*, pp. 59-64, 1992.

[3] Y. Yang. Expert network: Effective and Efficient Learning from Human Decisions in Text Categorization and Retrieval. In *Proceedings of the 17th Annual International ACM SIGIR Conference on Research and Development in Information Retrieval (SIGIR'94)*, pp. 13-22, 1994.

[4] T. Joachims. Text Categorization with Support Vector Machines: Learning with Many Relevant Features. In *European Conference on Machine Learning (ECML)*, 1998.

[5] Y. Yang and C.G. Chute. An Example-based Mapping method for Text Categorization. *ACM Transaction on Information Systems (TOIS)*, 12(3), pp. 252-277, 1994.

[6] R. E. Schapire and Y. Singer. BoosTexter: A Boosting-based System for Text Categorization. *Machine Learning*, 39, pp. 135-168, 2000.

[7] J. Rocchio. Relevance feedback in information retrieval. In G. Salton, editor, *The Smart Retrieval System-Experiments in Automatic Document Processing*, pp. 313-323, Prentice-Hall, 1971.

[8] R. O. Duda and P. E. Hart. *Pattern Classification and Scene Analysis*, John Wiley & Sons Inc., 1973.

[9] K. Fukunaga. *Introduction to Statistical Pattern Recognition (Second Edition)*, Academic Press Inc., 1990.

[10] G. J. McLachlan. *Discriminant Analysis and Statistical Pattern Recognition*, John Wiley & Sons, Inc., 1992.

[11] Y. Yang and J. P. Pederson. Feature Selection in Statistical Learning for Text Categorization. In *The Fourteenth International Conference on Machine Learning*, pp. 412-420, 1997.

[12] J. H. Friedman. Regularized Discriminant Analysis. *J. Amer. Statist. Assoc.* **84**, pp.165-175, 1989..

Text Genre Classification with Genre-Revealing and Subject-Revealing Features

Yong-Bae Lee & Sung Hyon Myaeng
Dept. of Computer Science, Chungnam National University
Daejon,Korea
+82-42-821-5446
{yblee, shmyaeng}@cs.cnu.ac.kr

ABSTRACT

Subject or prepositional content has been the focus of most classification research. Genre or style, on the other hand, is a different and important property of text, and automatic text genre classification is becoming important for classification and retrieval purposes as well as for some natural language processing research. In this paper, we present a method for automatic genre classification that is based on statistically selected features obtained from both subject-classified and genre-classified training data. The experimental results show that the proposed method outperforms a direct application of a statistical learner often used for subject classification. We also observe that the deviation formula and discrimination formula using document frequency ratios also work as expected. We conjecture that this dual feature set approach can be generalized to improve the performance of subject classification as well.

Categories and Subject Descriptors

H.3.4 [**Information Storage and Retrieval**]: System and Software – *Current awareness systems, efficiency and effectiveness.*

General Terms: Performance, Experimentation, Verification.

Keywords: text genre, classification, statistical method, tf, idf, subject categories.

1. INTRODUCTION

Text classification research has been mostly focused on subject or prepositional content of text. As text-based applications have become more diverse and the amount of information has increased tremendously, however, different aspects of text can be useful for various purposes including classification. We focus on text genre or the style of text that often characterizes the purpose for which the text has been written. Examples for genre are: research article, novel, poem, news article, editorial, homepage, advertisement, manual, court decision etc.

Genre classes are clearly different from subject classes that most classification research has dealt with. From an information retrieval point of view, a retrieval query about a certain topic such as "IBM" would get many documents related to the company IBM from an Internet search engine, but they may be of different genre such as a company homepage, product specification, product advertisement, or critical review of a certain product. As such, classifying documents based on genre would result in a totally different outcome than that from ordinary subject-based classification.

Automatic genre classification has been studied in the recent past. Karlgren and Cutting [6] explored the use of structural cues and rather simple cues such as counts of third person pronouns in text with discriminant analysis. In subsequent work[4, 5], she investigated the relationship between the genre of retrieved vs un-retrieved documents and relevant vs non-relevant documents. Used features are simple statistics, such as sentence length and word length, and syntactic complexity such as average depth of a parse tree.

Identifying text genre would be beneficial to many text-based applications. For instance, if the genre of every document is known a priori, information retrieval results could be better presented to the user, depending on the preference the user has. As pointed out by Kessler *et al.* [7], the performance of many natural language processing tools, such as part-of-speech tagging, parsing, and word sense disambiguation, could be enhanced since some language usages embedded in grammatical constructions and word senses are related to the genre of text. In Web applications, genre detection would help wrappers that attempt to extract specified information from semi-structured.

Kessler *et al.* [7] identified cues in four categories: structural cues (e.g. counts of POS tags), lexical cues (e.g. words used in expressing dates), character-level cues (e.g. punctuation marks), and derivative cues (e.g. average sentence length as a ration and standard deviation in sentence length as a variation). They decided not to use the structural cues because of the high computational cost. Their computational methods were logistic regression and neural networks (a simple perceptron and multi-layer perceptron) that combine 55 cues.

More recently, Stamatatos *et al.* [10] reported on their work for genre detection using word frequencies and punctuation marks. Instead of using sophisticated linguistic cues, they attempted to develop a method that works for unrestricted text in any domain and language with minimal computational cost in extracting cues.

In this paper, we take the stance more related to traditional information retrieval and text classification approaches than to natural language processing. Instead of focusing on sophisticated linguistic cues and their values as to how they are related to individual genre classes, we attempt to improve upon a direct application of a well-studied text classification method to genre classification by using the *tf* and *idf* statistics. Our hypothesis is that the use of the features selected and the weights calculated for one type of classification (e.g. genre) can be complemented with the use of features and weights obtained for other type (e.g. subject). By using both genre class and subject class training data for a statistical classifier, we can achieve a better performance than simply using the same classifier with genre class training data alone.

2. THE GENRE CLASSIFIER

2.1 Method

The main thrust of the genre classifier we developed is the use of the statistics from two different class sets, genre classes and subject classes, in the training data. The goodness value of a term for a genre depends on three factors:

- how many documents belonging to the genre contain the term
- how evenly the term is distributed among the subject classes that divide the genre class, and
- how discriminating the term is among different genre classes.

The main idea for the first two factors is to find terms that are found in as many genre documents as possible and distributed as evenly as possible among all subject classes. Our assumption is that a good genre-revealing term would show up across different subject classes while appearing in many documents in the genre. In other words, even if a term appears in many documents belonging to a particular genre, we don't wan it to be specific to a particular subject area that happens to be discussed heavily in the subset. Therefore it would be helpful to eliminate the terms that are too specific to a certain subject area by looking at their distributions. Furthermore, the third factor ensures terms that are good indicators for many genre classes are downgraded since they are not good discriminators.

The table in Appendix illustrates the point made above. Among the genre classes, we chose the 'personal homepage' genre that has been identified as a truly digital genre as opposed to those borrowed from the paper world [3]. In our preliminary analysis, 533 documents belonging to the 'personal homepage' genre class are sub-divided into four subject categories. The numbers in parentheses represent the number of documents in each genre or subject class. The term 'home' appearing in many of the 288 genre class documents also has high document frequencies for all the subject classes. It should be considered a good genre-revealing term. On the other hand, the term 'play' having a high document frequency (154) for the genre class but appearing only in the 'celerity' subject class is not a good representative for the genre.

2.2 Computation

For each term in the training document set, we compute its goodness value in two ways. The first is to use a term's document frequency ratios for genre and subject classes, i.e. in how many documents belonging to a genre class or to a subject class within the genre class the term appears. More specifically, $DFR_m\ (t_k)$ for a term t_k 's document frequency ratio for genre m, is:

$$DFR_m(t_k) = \frac{df_{m,k}}{df_m}$$

Likewise, $DFR_m(t_k^i)$ for the term appearing in the subject class i is defined to be:

$$DFR_m(t_k^i) = \frac{df_{m,k}^i}{df_m^i}$$

The goodness value for a term in a genre class can now be computed as:

$$V_{m,k} = DFR_m\ (t_k) * (1 - \sigma) \quad (1)$$

where deviation σ is defined to be:

$$\sigma = \sqrt{\frac{\sum_{i=1}^{n_c}(DFR_m(t_k) - DFR_m(t_k^i))^2}{n_c}}$$

Here n_c is the number of subject categories. The formula in the square root computes the degree to which the term is distributed among various groups of documents corresponding to subject classes, or variance of term distributions among the subject classes. $DFR_m(t_k)$ serves as the mean document frequency ratio for all the subject classes, and $DFR_m(t_k^i)$ is the document frequency ratio for t_k in the subject class i within the genre class m. The smaller deviation in the subject classes, the better the term is. The sum of the document frequencies for all the subject classes is equal to the document frequency for the genre class.

Alternatively we can compute the goodness values using term frequencies as follows:

$$V_{m,k} = \frac{tf_{m,k}}{\max\limits_{1 \le i \le n}[tf_{m,i}]} * (1 - \sigma) \quad (2)$$

where the first part is the normalized term frequency, and σ is newly defined as:

$$\sigma = \sqrt{\frac{1}{n_c}} \times \sqrt{\left(\frac{\sum_{i=1}^{n_c} tf_{m,k}^i}{n_c \cdot tf_m} - \frac{tf_{m,k}^i}{tf_m^i}\right)^2}$$

where the $tf_{m,k}$ and $tf_{m,k}^i$ represent the total frequency of t_k in the genre class m and in the subject class i within the genre class, respectively. The first part of the formula is a normalizing factor.

Accommodating the discrimination factor above, the final term weight for t_k in the genre m becomes:

$$W_{m,k} = \sqrt{\frac{\sum_{i=1}^{n_g}(V_{m,k} - V_{i,k})^2}{n_g}} \quad (3)$$

where n_g is the number of genre classes and $V_{i,k}$ is the goodness value for the term in the i-th genre class only.

Given the term weights above a threshold for each of the genre classes, calculated in the training stage, we can form a vector for each genre class G_m. The genre decision for a new document D is computed as follows:

$$\max_m[sim(G_m, D)] \quad (4)$$

where the cosine similarity is used for $sim\ (G_m, D)$.

This method for computing the term weight for a genre class can be used for other kinds of classifiers. In our study, the naïve Bayesian classifier approach (see, for example [8]) was considered[1]. By applying the approach directly to genre classification, we can compute the probability of a document belonging to a genre class g_i as follows:

$$P(d \mid g_i) = P(g_i)\prod_{k=1}^{T} P(t_k \mid g_i) \quad (5)$$

where $P(t_k \mid g_i)$ is the probability of a term appearing in the genre class g_i, which can be computed from a training document set.

Given this framework, we were interested in understanding the role of our term selection method, i.e., the method of using both genre and subject classes in the training document set. It is quite natural to consider the weight $W_{m,k}$ in (3) as an estimate for the probability of a term k representing the genre class m, so that we get:

$$P(t_k \mid g_i) = P(g_i) \prod W_{i,k}$$

Here $P(g_i)$ can be estimated with the ratio of the number of documents in the genre i to the total number of documents in the training set. This is compared against the case where the term frequency observed in the documents belonging to the genre class i are used to estimate the probability $P(t_k \mid g_i)$.

3. EXPERIMENTS

3.1 Testing Ground

We collected Web documents to test the genre classification method proposed in this paper. While Brown Corpus has been used for some previous genre-related research, it doesn't have subject classes assigned to individual documents, which are critical to our study. Also, our primary interest lies in Web applications.

For practical purposes, we considered seven genre classes: reportage, editorial, technical paper, critical review, personal homepage, Q&A, and product specification. These genre classes would help Web search engine users distinguish what they want from the rest of the documents retrieved, all of which contain subject-bearing query terms.

The total numbers of Korean and English documents collected are 7,828 and 7,615, respectively. The Korean documents were collected by a linguist and a computer scientist and the English documents by three people who majored in English literature and by one linguist. More than twenty portal sites were used in the collection building process to eliminate possible bias toward particular document types. Each document was examined by at least two people for inclusion in the collection as well as in the designated genre and subject classes. A half of the collected documents in each sub-collection, Korean and English, was used for training and the other half for testing. Fig. 1 shows the numbers of Korean and English documents in each genre class, together with possible category classes they can belong to.

[1] While the naïve Bayesian classifier approach is known to be inferior to other approaches like support vector machines and k-nearest neighbors [11], we chose it because of its simplicity and extensibility to Web documents with links as in [9].

At the beginning, we were most interested in the general performance level of the proposed genre classification method. It wasn't clear how effective it would be to use the idea of selecting terms based on the notion of document frequency and term frequency ratios, not other more linguistically oriented features, from genre-specified training documents. We had two approaches to be tested: one based on document frequency ratios and the other based on term frequency ratios.

Genre classes and subject classes within each genre		Korean	English
Reportage	robbery, fraud, violence, suicide, murder, fire, …	929	815
Editorial	economy, education, sports, international, politics,…	750	849
Research articles	engineering, arts, basic science, biomedical, …	1,051	1,200
Reviews	education, finance, foods, culture, sports, cosmetics, students, teachers, professors, celebrity, …	2,362	1,490
Homepage	laws, customers, cuisine, medicine, computer, …,	906	1,067
Q&A	computer, cosmetics, sports, video	960	1,020
Spec		870	1,174
Total		7,828	7,615

Fig. 1. Document counts in each genre and subject classes

Immediately after finding out the performance was reasonable, we launched other experiments to see the value of using both genre-revealing and subject-revealing terms for genre classification. In particular, we wanted to compare the following cases:

- Case 1: the use of term frequency values in the genre-specified training documents only,
- Case 2: the use of document frequency (or term frequency) ratios to compute the deviation between two distributions of terms: one from the genre-specified and the other from the subject-specified training documents (using the formula (1) or (2))
- Case 3: Case 2 (using both document and term frequency ratios) together with the use of inter-genre discrimination power of terms (using the formula (1) or (2) together with (3))

The Naïve Bayesian approach as in (5) and the similarity approach as in (4) were both used as the genre determination method for testing documents. In the experiments, we used both English and Korean document collections to confirm whatever trend we see in one language is also the case in the other.

Effectiveness was measured with micro-average recall/precision scores [11] when different cases were compared. Since no duplicate classes are assigned to each document, precision and recall values are the same in our experiments.

3.2 Results and Discussions

3.2.1 Overall Comparisons

Table 1 shows the summary of the results indicating the differences among the three cases, using *tf* (ordinary method) only, using deviation values, and using the combination of deviation values and the discrimination values but with *df* or *tf* ratios. They were applied to the Naïve Bayesian approach and the similarity approach using the English collection. The numbers are micro-average precision/recall values.

Table 1. Overall comparisons among different approaches

approaches / cases		Similarity-Based	Naïve Bayesian Approach
Case 1	df	0.75	-
	tf	0.63	0.83 (0.75)
Case 2	df	0.81 (0.87)	0.80 (0.74)
	tf	0.79	-
Case 3	df	0.87 (0.90)	0.79 (0.70)
	tf	0.80	-

Case 1: with ordinary tf values
Case 2: with deviation values using df ratios or tf ratios
Case 3: with deviation values using df or tf ratios and discrimination values

First of all, the result shows that in the similarity-based approach, the use of *df* ratios gives significantly better performance than *tf* ratios across all the cases. This is in line with our initial hypothesis that *df* ratios would be a better factor than *tf* ratios in this context. The other promising result is that the use of the deviation formula and the discrimination formula used in Case 2 and Case 3, respectively, actually improves the performance, again confirming our initial hypothesis. In other words, the deviation formula helps selecting terms that are more genre-related than subject-related, and the discrimination formula also helps increasing the weight of a term that appears in a smaller number of genre classes.

It is interesting to see that the overall performance orders in the cases are quite different when the naïve Bayesian approach is used. The best result was obtained when the ordinary *tf* values were only used. The use of the *df* ratios and the new formulas gave slightly worse results. We suspect that in order to get an optimal result, it is important to stick to the literal interpretation of the Naïve Bayesian approach, especially in computing the probability of a term occurring in a genre class, instead of estimating with *df* ratios and the deviation and discrimination formulas.

We were able to repeat many of the performance comparison results using the Korean collection. The micro-average precision/recall values for the three cases under the naïve Bayesian approach were 0.75, 0.74, and 0.70, respectively, and the same for Cases 2 and 3 under the similarity-based approach were 0.87 and 0.90. Again the superiority of using *tf* values was observed when the Naïve Bayesian approach was used. In the similarity-based approach, we only confirmed the superiority of the Case 3 against the Case 2. The performance difference between the new method and the best Naïve Bayesian approach was greater in the Korean collection than in the English collection.

3.2.2 Inter-genre variations

Table 2 is an example of a detailed result for the proposed method (Case 3) using *df* ratios with performance numbers for individual genre classes in the English collection.

Table 2. Documents assigned to the seven genre classes

Guess / Actual	A	B	C	D	E	F	G
A (425)	351	67	3	0	1	3	0
B (408)	26	381	1	0	0	0	0
C (745)	35	11	655	1	6	27	10
D (600)	1	3	1	586	7	2	0
E (534)	25	4	32	10	435	26	2
F (510)	16	11	61	4	45	372	1
G (587)	0	1	46	2	2	9	527
P/R (%)	77/ 83	80/ 93	82/ 88	97/ 98	88/ 81	85/ 73	98/ 90

A: Editorial B: Reportage C: Review D: Research Paper
E: Homepage F: Q&A G: Product Spec

Looking at the first row, we can see that among the 425 documents in the 'editorial' genre (A), 351 documents are correctly assigned and 67 are incorrectly assigned to the 'reportage' genre (B). The first column, on the other hand, indicates that among all the documents assigned to the 'editorial' genre (A) by the classifier, 351 are correct where as 26 were incorrectly assigned to the 'reportage' genre.

By browsing through the numbers in the cells, we can easily identify the genre classes that confuse the classifier. For instance, confusion between the 'reportage' and 'editorial' genre classes is the greatest. On the other hand, there was no confusion at all between the 'editorial' and 'product spec' genre classes. The confusion case is understandable because documents in the two genre classes are both from newspapers, perhaps sharing some subject-bearing terms. This indicates that our use of terms alone, as opposed to other more linguistically oriented features in sentences, has a limitation in some genre classification.

Table 3. Documents assigned to six genre classes

Guess / Actual	A+B	C	D	E	F	G
A+B (833)	812	12	0	2	7	0
C (745)	25	673	0	6	31	10
D (600)	3	1	583	11	2	0
E (534)	12	39	8	441	32	2
F (510)	14	67	4	48	377	0
G (587)	1	48	0	1	11	526
P/R (%)	94/ 97	80/ 90	98/ 97	87/ 83	82/ 74	98/ 90

A+ B: Newspaper C: Review D: Research Paper
E: Homepage F: Q&A G: Product Spec

Table 3 is the case where two of the genre classes that confused the classifier most, 'reportage' and 'editorial', are merged into 'newspaper'. Overall, it clearly gives a better precision/recall values (micro-average being 90% vs 87%) than the seven-genre case. The precision/recall values for the newly formed genre class are much higher than either in the seven-genre case

3.2.3 *Tuning the threshold*

In order to obtain the best possible results for each case, so that the comparisons are made among them, we had to adjust the cutoff levels for *tf* and *df* ratio values in selecting the terms to represent each genre class that are used in subsequent computation. That is, we modulated the number of genre-revealing terms to be considered by adjusting the thresholds for *tf* and *df* ratios manually. The number of terms selected for the seven genre classes are in table 4.

Table 4. Selected term numbers for each genre class

Genre	A	B	C	D	E	F	G
# terms	89	86	131	130	166	117	128

The adjustments were based on the observations of correlations between the threshold and the performance values. This can be done when a result as in Table 2 is obtained. The general strategy is to increase the threshold (i.e. to select a smaller number of terms) when precision for the particular genre class is low, and to lower the threshold (i.e. to select a larger number of terms) when recall for the particular genre class is low. Using a larger number of terms for the genre class means that more documents would be classified into the genre, resulting in higher recall for the genre. On the other hand, a smaller number of terms for the genre class would reduce the number of documents assigned to it, increasing precision.

4. CONCLUSION

In this paper we presented a new methodology for genre classification using word statistics. In particular, we introduced the *df* ratio, *df* ratio deviation formula, and discrimination formula that are combined to select genre-revealing terms from the training document set. The deviation formula makes use of both genre-classified documents and subject-classified documents to eliminate terms that more subject related than genre related.

We constructed our own Web document collections in English and Korean, and tested effectiveness of the proposed method against other possibilities using some of the formulas as well as *tf* and the *tf* ratios within the same similarity-based framework. It turned out that the *df* ratio always gave a better result than *tf* itself or *tf* ratios, although the ordinary *tf* values gave the best result when the Naïve Bayesian framework was employed. The proposed method outperformed the best case of the Naïve Bayesian results.

Analyzing the results in detail, we realized that some genre classes are significantly confusing to the classifier because they tend to share some subject-specific terms, although we attempted to eliminate subject-related terms using the deviation formula. We probably need to explore other ways to obtain the same effect. In addition, we need to consider other more linguistically oriented features and expressions in our future study so that the mutually confusing genre classes are separated more easily.

Another avenue we need to explore further is the method for determining the number of genre-revealing terms as well as the effects of different numbers in more detail. The number of terms we used for each genre is much larger than the number (around 30) found in other study [10]. The heuristic method we used to decide on the term numbers for individual genre classes need to be modeled into an automatic method.

Finally, further studies are needed to compare the proposed method against other frameworks that can be applied to genre classification. We are in the process of devising a method for using both *tf* and *idf* and applying the current method to other classification theories such as k-nearest neighbor and support vector machine.

5. ACKNOWLEDGMENTS

Our thanks go to Enquest Technology, Inc. for allowing us to use the English and Korean genre collections.

REFERENCES

[1] Ivan Bretan, John Dewe, Anders Hallberg, Niklas Wolkert, Jussi Karlgren, “Web-Specific Genre Visualization”, Proc. of the 30th Hawaii International Conference on System Science, Jan 1997.

[2] Johan Dewe, Jussi Karlgren, Ivan Bretan, “Assembling a Balanced Corpus from the Internet”, 11th Nordic Conference of Computational Linguistics, pages 100-107, Copenhagen, 1998.

[3] Andrew Dillon, Barbara A. Gushrowski, “Genre and the Web: Is the Personal Home Page the First Uniquely Digital Genre?”, JASIS, 51(2):202-205, 2000.

[4] Jussi Karlgren, “Stylistic Variation in an Information Retrieval Experiment”, Proc. of the 2nd International Conference on New Methods in Language Processing-NeMLaP, 1996.

[5] Jussi Karlgren, Ivan Brettan, Johan Dewe, Anders Hallberg, Niklas Wolkert, “Iterative Information Retrieval Using Fast Clustering and Usage-Specific Genres”, 8th DELOS Workshop on User Interfaces in Digital Libraries, pages 85-92, 1998.

[6] Jussi Karlgren, Douglass Cutting, “Recognizing Text Genres with Simple Metrics Using Discriminant Analysis”, Proc. of COLING94, Kyoto, 1994.

[7] Brett Kessler, Geoffrey Nunberg, Hinrich Schütze, “Automatic Detection of Text Genre”, ACL’97, pages 32-38, July 1997.

[8] D. Lewis and M. Ringuette, “Compariosn of two learning algorithms for text categorization,” Proc. of the 3rd Annual Symposium on Document Analysis and Information Retrieval, 1994.

[9] H. J. Oh, S. H. Myaeng, and M. Lee, “A practical hypertext categorization method using links and incrementally available class information”, Proc. of the 23rd ACM SIGIR Conference, pages 264-271, Athenes, Greece, 2000.

[10] E.Stamatatos, N.Fakotakis, G. Kokkinakis, “Text Genre Detection Using Common Word Frequencies”, Proc. of the 18th International Conference on COLING2000, 2000.

[11] Y. Yang and X. Liu, “A re-examination of text categorization methods,” Proc. Of the 22nd ACM SIGIR Conference, 1999.

Appendix

Genre		Subject							
Personal Homepage (533)		Student (149)		Teacher/ Professor (144)		Company Employee (128)		Celebrity (112)	
University	397	school	106	university	133	university	103	the	100
the	354	university	102	professor	101	school	83	play	99
school	329	html	94	the	98	home	76	film	89
home	288	the	84	teach	94	the	72	act	77
page	262	page	77	education	94	education	72	actor	70
html	245	student	75	science	93	association	70	television	65
education	239	computer	73	research	90	office	62	role	65
college	216	charset	73	state	87	law	62	home	64
text	203	text	72	page	82	com	62	star	60
state	203	home	70	school	80	experience	58	school	60
include	203	time	66	home	78	computer	58	new	60
science	202	web	64	department	77	include	57	theatre	54
time	201	college	58	student	74	state	56	time	53
charset	201	name	57	publication	74	practice	56	page	53
student	193	education	57	college	74	personal	56	eye	53
computer	187	friend	55	study	67	html	55	production	52
new	184	iso	53	graduate	67	mail	54	include	51
graduate	184	graduate	52	faculty	66	service	52	love	50
study	173	experience	51	national	64	college	52	hair	49
experience	173	edu	51	technology	63	bar	52	angel	49
this	172	science	50	new	63	attorney	52	height	47
mail	172	this	49	edu	63	page	50	award	46
web	167	major	49	professional	62	business	48	stage	45
research	167	high	49	american	62	legal	47	series	45
information	165	music	48	association	61	system	46	movie	44
american	163	live	48	institute	61	science	46	commercial	44
play	154	people	47	assistant	61	lawyer	46	train	43
com	152	email	47	mail	60	information	46	life	43
site	151	site	46	information	60	court	45	career	43
office	151	play	46	associate	59	text	44	brown	43
name	150	don	46	society	57	site	44	born	43
national	148	born	46	international	57	professional	44	html	42
association	139	life	45	course	55	county	43	com	42
system	136	study	44	text	54	charset	43	university	41

A New Family of Online Algorithms for Category Ranking

Koby Crammer
School of Computer Science & Engineering
The Hebrew University, Jerusalem 91904, Israel
kobics@cs.huji.ac.il

Yoram Singer
School of Computer Science & Engineering
The Hebrew University, Jerusalem 91904, Israel
singer@cs.huji.ac.il

ABSTRACT

We describe a new family of topic-ranking algorithms for multi-labeled documents. The motivation for the algorithms stems from recent advances in online learning algorithms. The algorithms we present are simple to implement and are time and memory efficient. We evaluate the algorithms on the Reuters-21578 corpus and the new corpus released by Reuters in 2000. On both corpora the algorithms we present outperform adaptations to topic-ranking of Rocchio's algorithm and the Perceptron algorithm. We also outline the formal analysis of the algorithm in the mistake bound model. To our knowledge, this work is the first to report performance results with the entire new Reuters corpus.

Categories and Subject Descriptors

H.3.3 [**Information Storage and Retrieval**]: Information Search and Retrieval; I.2.6 [**Artificial Intelegence**]: Learning—*Concept Learning, Connectionism and neural nets*

General Terms

Algorithms, Experimentation,Theory.

Keywords

Category ranking, Online learning, Perceptrons.

1. INTRODUCTION

The focus of this paper is the problem of topic ranking for text documents. We use the Reuters corpus (release 2000) as our running example. In this corpus there are about a hundred different topics. Each document in the corpus is tagged with a set of topics that are relevant to its content. For instance, a document from late August 1996, discusses a bill by Bill Clinton to increase the minimum wage by a whole 90 cents. This document is associated with 9 topics; four of them are `labour`, `economics`, `unemployment`, and `retail sales`. This example shows that there is a semantic overlap between the topics. Given a feed of documents, such as the Reuters newswire, the task of topic ranking is concerned with ordering the topics according to their relevance for each document independently. The framework that we use in this paper is that of *supervised learning*. In this framework we receive a training set of documents each of which is provided with its set of relevant topics. Given the labeled corpus, the goal is to learn a topic-ranking function that gets a document and outputs a ranking of the topics.

In the machine learning community this setting is often referred to as a *multilabel* classification problem. The motivation of most, if not all, of the machine learning algorithms for this problem stem from a decision theoretic view. Namely, the output of the algorithms is a predicted set of relevant topics and the quality of the predictions is measures by how successful we are in identifying the set of relevant topics. In this paper we combine techniques from statistical learning theory with the more natural goals of information retrieval tasks. We do so by adopting and generalizing techniques from online prediction algorithms to the particular task of topic ranking. Our starting point is the Perceptron algorithm [8]. Despite (or because of) its age and simplicity the Perceptron algorithm and its variants have proved to be surprisingly effective in a broad range of applications in machine learning and information retrieval (see for instance [3, 6] and the references therein). The original Perceptron algorithm has been designed for binary classification problems. Our family of algorithms borrows the core motivation of the Perceptron algorithm and largely generalizes it to the more complex problem of topic ranking. Since the family of algorithms uses Multiclass Multilabel feedback we refer to the various variants as the MMP algorithm.

A few learning algorithms for multi-labeled data have been devised in the machine learning community. Two notable examples are a multilabel version of AdaBoost called AdaBoost.MH [10] and a multilabel generalization of Vapnik's Support Vector Machines by Elisseeff and Weston [2]. These two multilabel algorithms take the same general approach by reducing a multilabel problem into multiple binary problems by comparing all pairs of labels. Our starting point is similar as we use an implicit reduction into pairs. Yet, using a simple pre-computation, MMP is much simpler to implement and use than both SVM and AdaBoost.MH. Note, however, that in contrast to AdaBoost.MH and SVM which were designed for batch settings, in which all the examples are given in advance, MMP , like the Perceptron, is used in online settings in which the examples are presented one at a time.

Our experiments with the two corpora by Reuters sug-

SIGIR'02, August 11-15, 2002, Tampere, Finland.

gest that MMP can offer a viable alternative to existing algorithms and can be used for processing massive datasets.

2. PROBLEM SETTING

As discussed above, the text processing task in this paper is concerned with is category or topic ranking. In this problem we are given access to a stream of documents. Each document is associated with *zero* or more categories from a predefined set of topics. We denote the set of possible categories by $\mathcal{Y}$ and the number of different topics by k, ($k = |\mathcal{Y}|$). In the new distribution of the Reuters corpus (which we refer to as Reuters-2000) there are 102 different topics while Reuters-21578 consists of 91 different topics. Since there is semantic overlap between the topics a document is typically associated with more than one topic. More formally, a document is labeled with a set $y \subset \mathcal{Y}$ of relevant topics. In the Reuters-2000 corpus the average size of y is 3.2 while in Reuters-21578 the average size is 1.24. We say that a topic r (also referred to as a class or category) is *relevant* for a given document if r is in the set of relevant topics, $r \in y$.

In the machine learning community this setting is also often referred to as a multilabel classification problem. There are numerous different information filtering and routing tasks that are of practical use for multilabel problems. The focus of this paper is the design, analysis, and implementation of *category-ranking* algorithms. That is, given a document, the algorithms we consider return a list of topics ranked according to their relevance. However, as discussed above, the feedback for each document is the set y and thus the topics for each document in the training corpus are not ranked but rather marked as relevant or non-relevant.

Each document is represented using the vector space model [9] as vectors in $\mathbb{R}^n$. We denote a document by its vector representation $\bar{x} \in \mathbb{R}^n$. All the topic-ranking algorithms we discuss in this paper use the same mechanism: each algorithm maintains a set of k prototypes, $\bar{w}_1, \bar{w}_2, \ldots, \bar{w}_k$. Analogous to the representation of documents, each prototype is a vector, $\bar{w}_r \in \mathbb{R}^n$. The specific vector-space representation we used is based on the pivoted length normalization of Singhal et. al. [12]. Its description is deferred to the Sec. 4.2. The focus of the paper is a new family of algorithms that builds the prototype from examples, i.e., a corpus S of m documents each of which is assigned a set of relevant topics, $\{(\bar{x}_i, y_i)\}_{i=1}^m$.

The set of prototypes induce a ranking on the topics according to their similarity with the vector representation of the document. That is, given a document $\bar{x}$ the inner-products $\bar{w}_1 \cdot \bar{x}, \bar{w}_2 \cdot \bar{x}, \ldots, \bar{w}_k \cdot \bar{x}$ induce an ordering of the relevance level for each topic. We say that topic r is ranked higher than topic s if $\bar{w}_r \cdot \bar{x} > \bar{w}_s \cdot \bar{x}$. Given a feedback, i.e. the set of relevant topics y of a document $\bar{x}$, we say that the ranking induced by the prototypes is *perfect* if all the relevant topics are ranked higher than the non-relevant topics. In a perfect ranking any pair of topics $r \in y$ and $s \notin y$ ($s \in \mathcal{Y} - y$) the scores induced by $\bar{w}_r$ is higher than that the one induced by $\bar{w}_s$, $\bar{w}_r \cdot \bar{x} > \bar{w}_s \cdot \bar{x}$. We can measure the quality of a perfect topic-ranking by the size of the gap between the lowest score among the relevant topics to the highest score among the non-relevant topics,

$$\min_{r \in y}\{\bar{w}_r \cdot \bar{x}\} - \max_{s \notin y}\{\bar{w}_s \cdot \bar{x}\} \ . \qquad (1)$$

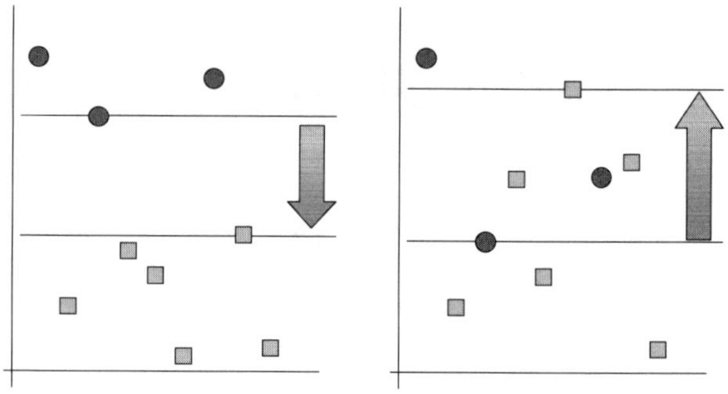

Figure 1: Illustration of the notion of the margin for a perfect ranking (left) and a non-perfect ranking.

Adopting the terminology used in learning theory we refer to the above quantity as the *margin* of a document $\bar{x}$ with respect to a set of relevant topics y and prototypes $\bar{w}_1, \ldots, \bar{w}_k$. Clearly, a perfect ranking of a document implies that its margin is positive. The margin can also be computed when the prototypes do not induce a perfect ranking. In this case the margin is negative. An illustration of the margin is given in Fig. 1. The illustration show the margin in case of a perfect ranking (left) and a non-perfect one (right). In both cases there are 9 different topics. The relevant topics are marked with circles and the non-relevant with squares. The value of the margin is the length of arrow where a positive values is denoted by an arrow pointing down and a negative margin by an arrow pointing up. The notion of margin is rather implicit in the algorithms we discuss in the paper. However, it plays an important role in the formal analysis of the algorithms.

3. CATEGORY-RANKING ALGORITHMS

MMP, being a descendant of the Perceptron algorithm, is an *online* algorithm: it gets an example, outputs a ranking, and updates the hypothesis it maintains – the set of prototypes $\bar{w}_1, \ldots, \bar{w}_k$. The update of the prototypes takes place *only* if the predicted ranking is *not* prefect. Online algorithms become especially handy when the training corpus is very large since they require minimal amounts of memory. In the case of batch training (i.e. when the training corpus is provided in advance and not example by example) we need to augment the online algorithm with a wrapper. Several approaches have been proposed for adapting online algorithms for batch settings. A detailed discussion is given in [3]. The approach we take in this paper is the simplest to implement. We run the algorithm in an online fashion on the provided training corpus and use the *final* set of topic prototypes, obtained after a single pass through the data, as the topic-ranking hypothesis. We leave more sophisticated schemes to future research. In the description below, we omit the index of the document and its set of relevant topics and denote them as $\bar{x}$ and y, respectively.

Given a document $\bar{x}$ we define the error-set of the induced ranking $\bar{w}_1, \ldots, \bar{w}_k$ with respect to the relevance (of topics) as the set of categories that are inconsistent with the predicted ranking. Formally, the error-set is defined as

$$E = \{(r, s) \ : \ r \in y, s \notin y, \bar{w}_r \cdot \bar{x} < \bar{w}_s \cdot \bar{x}\} \ .$$

Clearly, the predicted ranking is not perfect if and only if

Initialize: Set $\bar{w}_1 =, \ldots, = \bar{w}_k = \bar{0}$.
Loop: For $i = 1, 2, \ldots, m$

- Obtain a new document $\bar{x}_i \in \mathbb{R}^n$
- Rank the topics according to:
$$\bar{w}_1 \cdot \bar{x}_i, \ldots, \bar{w}_k \cdot \bar{x}_i$$
- Obtain the set of relevant topics y_i
- If the ranking of $\bar{x}_i$ is not perfect do:
  1. For $r \in y_i$ set:
  $$n_r = |\{s \notin y_i \,|\, \bar{w}_s \cdot \bar{x}_i \geq \bar{w}_r \cdot \bar{x}_i\}|$$
  2. For $r \notin y_i$ set:
  $$n_r = |\{s \in y_i \,|\, \bar{w}_s \cdot \bar{x}_i \leq \bar{w}_r \cdot \bar{x}_i\}|$$
  3. Set normalization factor:
  $$\begin{array}{ll} c = \sum_r n_r & (\ loss_1\ ) \\ c = \frac{1}{2} & (\ loss_2\ ) \\ c = \frac{1}{2}|y_i||\mathcal{Y} - y_i| & (\ loss_3\ ) \end{array}$$
  4. Update for $r \in y_i$:
  $$\bar{w}_r \leftarrow \bar{w}_r + \frac{n_r}{c}\bar{x}_i$$
  5. Update for $r \notin y_i$:
  $$\bar{w}_r \leftarrow \bar{w}_r - \frac{n_r}{c}\bar{x}_i$$

Return: $\bar{w}_1, \bar{w}_2, \ldots, \bar{w}_k$

Figure 2: The topic-ranking algorithm.

E is not empty. The size of E can be as large as $\left(\frac{k}{2}\right)^2$. A natural question that arises is what type of loss one should try to minimize whenever E is not empty. We now describe three different losses that yield a simple and efficient algorithms. These loss functions stem from learning theoretic insights and also exhibit good performance with respect to the common information retrieval performance measures. A nice property of the three losses is that they can be encapsulated into a single update scheme of the prototypes.

The first loss is the indicator function, that is, equals 1 if $|E| > 0$ and 0 otherwise. Put another way, this loss simply counts the number of times the topic-ranking was not perfect. The second loss is the size of E. Therefore, examples which were ranked perfectly suffer a zero loss while the rest of the examples suffer losses in proportion to how poorly the predicted rankings perform in terms of number of disordered topics. The third loss is a normalized version of the second loss, namely, it is $|E|/(|\mathcal{Y} - y||y|)$. Since maximal size of the error set is $|\mathcal{Y} - y||y|$, the third loss is bounded from above by one. On each document with rank prediction error MMP moves the prototypes whose indices constitute the error-set. The prototypes that correspond the set of relevant topics are moved toward $\bar{x}$ and those which correspond to non-relevant topics are moved away from $\bar{x}$. The motivation of this prototype-update stems from the Perceptron algorithm: it is straightforward to verify that this form of update will increase the value of inner-products between $\bar{x}$ and each of the prototypes in the subset of relevant categories and similarly decrease the rest of the inner-products. Put another way, this update of the prototypes is geared towards increasing the ranking-margin associated with the example and thus reducing the ranking losses above. The amount by which we move each prototype depends on its ranking and the type of loss we employ. We define n_r to be the number topics wrongly ranked with respect to topic r. If r is the index of a relevant topic $r \in y$, then n_r is the number of non-relevant topics ranked above r. Analogously, if r is the index of a non-relevant topic n_r is the number of relevant topics below r. Each prototype $\bar{w}_r$ is moved in the direction of $\bar{x}$ and in proportion to n_r. Once the values $n_1, \ldots, n_k$ are computed, we normalize each on of them by a scaling factor, denoted c. The value of c depends on the version of the loss that is used. This scaling factor c ensures that the sum over n_r equals the loss we are trying to make small, that is, $\sum_r n_r/c = 1$ for the first loss, $\sum_r n_r/c = |E|$ for the second loss, and $\sum_r n_r/c = |E|/(|\mathcal{Y}||\mathcal{Y} - y|)$ for the third loss. To summarize, if the topic ranking is not perfect each of prototype $\bar{w}_r$ corresponding to a wrongly ranked relevant topic is changed to $\bar{w}_r + (n_r/c)\bar{x}$ and an analogous modification is made to the wrongly ranked prototypes from the set of non-relevant topics. The pseudo code describing the algorithm is given in Fig. 2.

To analyze the performance of the algorithm we again need to use the notion of margin. Generalizing the notion of margin from one document to an entire corpus, we define the margin, denoted γ, of a set of prototypes $\bar{w}_1, \ldots, \bar{w}_k$ on a corpus S as the minimal margin attained on the documents in S,

$$\gamma_S = \min_{(\bar{x},y)\in S} \left\{ \min_{r\in y}\{\bar{w}_r \cdot \bar{x}\} - \max_{s\in\mathcal{Y}-y}\{\bar{w}_s \cdot \bar{x}\} \right\} . \quad (2)$$

For the purpose of the analysis we assume that the total norm of the prototypes is 1 ($\sum_r \|\bar{w}_r\|^2 = 1$). This assumption can be satisfied by global normalization of the prototypes that does not change the induced ranking. We are now ready to state the main theorem which shows that MMP make a bounded number of mistakes compared to a set of prototypes that is constructed with hindsight (after obtaining all the examples) and achieves a perfect ranking on the entire corpus.

THEOREM 1. **[Mistake bound]** *Let $(\bar{x}_1, y_1) \ldots (\bar{x}_m, y_m)$ be an input sequence for MMP where $\bar{x}_i \in \mathbb{R}^n$ and $y_i \in \{1 \ldots k\}$. Denote by $R = \max_i \|\bar{x}_i\|$. Assume that there exists a set of prototypes $\bar{w}_1^*, \ldots, \bar{w}_k^*$ of unit norm that achieves a perfect ranking on the entire sequence with margin γ_S. Then, MMP obtains the following bounds,*

$$\begin{aligned} \sum_i \text{loss}_1(\bar{x}_i, y_i) &\leq 2\frac{R^2}{\gamma^2} \\ \sum_i \text{loss}_2(\bar{x}_i, y_i) &\leq 2(k-1)\frac{R^2}{\gamma^2} \\ \sum_i \text{loss}_3(\bar{x}_i, y_i) &\leq 2\frac{R^2}{\gamma^2} . \end{aligned}$$

Due to the space restrictions the proof is omitted from the manuscript.

4. EXPERIMENTS

In this section we describe the experiments we performed that compare the three variants of MMP with a simple extension of the Perceptron algorithms and Rocchio's algorithm [7]. We start with a description of the datasets we used in our experiments.

4.1 Datasets

We evaluated the algorithms on two text corpora. Both corpora were provided by Reuters.

Reuters-21578: The documents in this corpus were collected from the Reuters newswire during 1987. The data set is available from *http://www.daviddlewis.com/resources.* We used the ModApte version of the corpus and pre-processed the documents as follows. All words were converted to lowercase, digits were mapped to a single token designating it is a digit, and non alpha-numeric characters were discarded. We also used a stop-list to remove very frequent words. The number of different words left after pre-processing is 27,747. After the pre-processing the corpus contains 10,789 documents each of which is associated with *one* or more topics. The number of different topics in the ModApte version of Reuters-21578 is 91. Since this corpus is of relatively small size, we used 5-fold cross validation in our experiments and did not use the original partition into training and test sets. While each document in the Reuters-21578 corpus can be multilabeled, in practice the number of such documents is relatively small. Over 80% of the documents are associated with a single topic. On the left hand side of Fig. 3 we show the distribution of the number of relevant topics. The average number of relevant topics per document is 1.24.

Reuters-2000: This corpus contains 809, 383 documents collected from the Reuters newswire in a year period (1996-08-20 to 1997-08-19). Since this corpus is large we used the first two thirds of the corpus for training and the remaining third for evaluation. The training set consisted of all documents that were posted from 1996-08-20 through 1997-04-10, resulting in 521, 439 training documents. The size of the corpus which was used for evaluation is 287, 944. We pre-processed as follows. We converted all upper-case characters to lower-case, replaced all non alpha-numeric characters with white-spaces, and discarded all the words that appeared only once in the training set. The number of different words that remained after this pre-processing is 225, 329. Each document in the collection is associated with *zero* or more topics. There are 103 different topics in the entire corpus, however, only 102 of them appear in the training set. The remaining category marked GMIL, for millennium issues, tags only 5 documents in the test set. We therefore discarded this category. Unlike the Reuters-21578 corpus, each document in the corpus is tagged by multiple topics: about 70% of the documents are associated with at least three different topics. The average number of topics associated with each document is 3.20. The distribution of the number of relevant topics per document appears on the right hand-side of Fig. 3.

4.2 Document representation

All the algorithms we evaluated use the same document representation. We implemented the pivoted length normalization of Singhal et. al. [12] as our term-weighting algorithm. This algorithm is considered to be one of the most

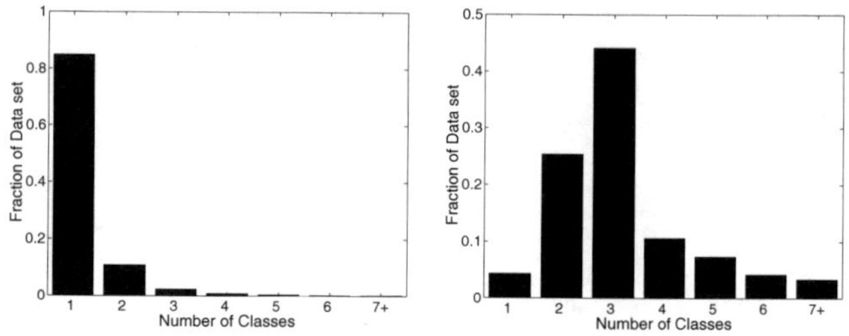

Figure 3: The distribution of the number of relevant topics in Reuters-21578 (left) and Reuters-2000.

effective algorithms for *document* ranking and retrieval. We now briefly outline the pivoted length normalization. Let d_i^l denote the number of times a word (or term) indexed l appears in the document indexed i. Let m_i denote the number of unique words appear in in the document indexed i by $m_i = |\{l \ : \ d_i^l > 0\}|$. Let u_l be the number of documents in which the term indexed l appears. As before, the total number of documents in the corpus is denoted by m. Using these definitions the *idf* weight of a word indexed l is $\log(m/u_l)$. The average frequency of the terms appearing in document t is,

$$\text{avg}[d_i^l] = \frac{\sum_l d_i^l}{m_i} ,$$

and the average frequency of number of unique terms in the documents is,

$$\text{avg}[m_i] = \frac{1}{m} \sum_{i=1}^{m} m_i .$$

Using these definitions the *tf* weight of a word indexed l appears in the document indexed t is,

$$\left(\frac{1 + \log(d_i^l)}{1 + \log(\text{avg}[d_i^l])} \right) \Big/ \left(1.0 - \textit{slope} + \textit{slope} \times \frac{m_i}{\text{avg}[m_i]} \right) .$$

Here *slope* is a parameter among 0 and 1. We set $\textit{slope} = 0.3$ which leads to the best performance at the experiments reported in [12].

4.3 Algorithms for comparison

In addition to the three variants of MMP we also implemented two more algorithms: Rocchio's algorithm [7] and the Perceptron algorithm. As with MMP these algorithms use the same pivoted length normalization as their vector space representation and employ the same form of category-ranking by using a set of prototypes $\bar{w}_1, \ldots, \bar{w}_k$.

Rocchio: We implemented an adaptation of Rocchio's method as adapted by Ittner et .al [5] to text categorization. In this variant of Rocchio the set of prototypes vectors $\bar{w}_1, \ldots, \bar{w}_k$ are set as follows,

$$w_r^l \stackrel{\text{def}}{=} \max \left\{ 0, \frac{\beta}{|R_r|} \sum_{i \in R_r} x_i^l - \frac{\gamma}{|R_r^c|} \sum_{i \in R_r^c} x_i^l \right\} ,$$

where R_r is the set of documents which contain the topic r as one of their relevant topics and R_r^c is its complement, i.e., all the documents for which r is not one of their relevant topics. Following the parameterization in [5], we set $\beta = 16$ and $\gamma = 4$. Last, as suggested by Amit Singhal in a private

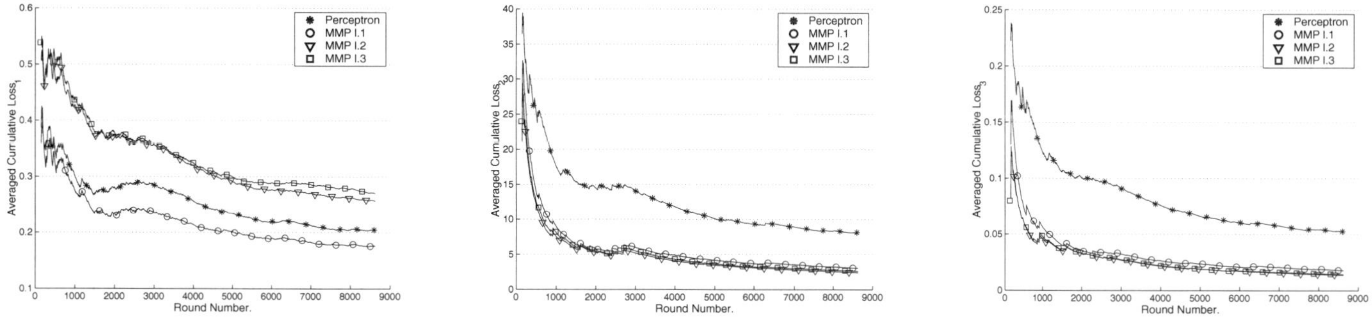

Figure 4: The round-averaged performance measures as a function of the number of training documents that were processed for Reuters-21578 : loss_1 (left), loss_2 (middle) and loss_3 (right).

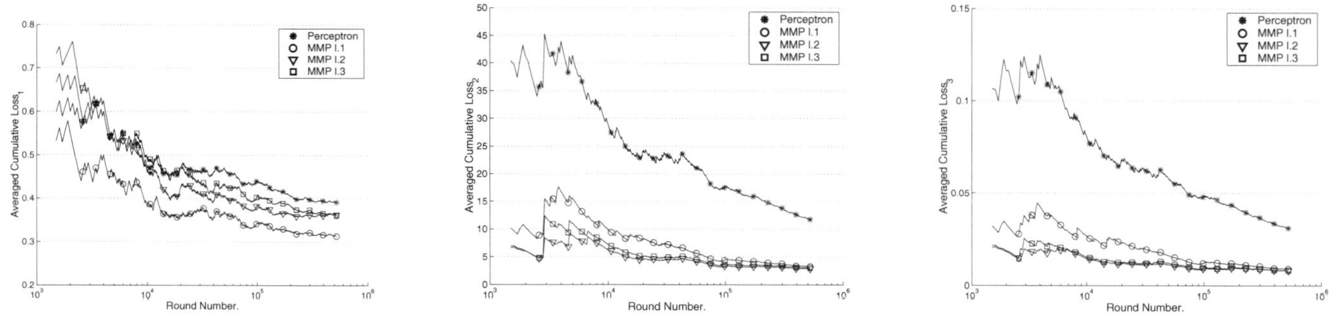

Figure 5: The round-averaged performance measures as a function of the number of training documents that were processed for Reuters-2000 : loss_1 (left), loss_2 (middle) and loss_3 (right). A log-scale was used for the x-axis.

communication, we normalize all of the prototypes to a unit norm.

Perceptron: We also implemented the Perceptron algorithm. Since the Perceptron algorithm is designed for binary classification problems, we decomposed the multilabel problem into multiple binary classification problems. For each topic r, the set of positive examples constitute the documents' indices from R_r, and R_r^c is the set of negative examples. We then ran the Perceptron algorithm on each of the binary problems separately and independently. We therefore obtained again a set of prototypes $\bar{w}_1, \ldots, \bar{w}_k$ each of which is an output of the corresponding output of Perceptron algorithm.

4.4 Feature Selection

For both datasets the number of unique terms after the pre-processing stage described above was still large: $27,747$ words in the Reuters-21578 and $225,339$ words in Reuters-2000. Since we used cross-validation for Reuters-21578 the actual number of unique terms was slightly lower, $25,061$ on the average. Yet, it was still relatively large and therefore employed feature selection for both corpora. We used weights of the prototypes generated by the adaptation of Rocchio's algorithm described above as our mean for feature selection. For each topic we sorted the terms according to their weights assigned by Rocchio. We then took for each topic the maximum between a hundred terms and the top portion of 2.5% from the sorted lists. This ensures that for each topic we have at least 100 terms.

The combined set of selected terms is used as the feature set for the various algorithms and is of size $3,468$ of Reuters-21578 and $9,325$ for Reuters-2000. The average number of unique words per document in the cross-validated training sets was reduced from 49 to 37 for Reuters-21578 and from 137 to 121 for Reuters-2000. After this feature selection stage we applied all the algorithms on the same representation of documents which are now restricted to the selected terms.

4.5 Evaluation Measures

Since the paper is concerned with both classical IR methods and more recent statistical learning algorithms we used two sets of performance measures to compare the effectiveness of the algorithms. First, we evaluated each of the algorithm with respect to the three losses employed by the variants of MMP. The second set of performance measures is based on measures used in evaluating document retrieval systems. Specifically, the performance measure we used in the evaluation are: *recall* at r, *precision* at r, *one-error*, *coverage*, *average-precision*, and $maxF_1$. We also provide precision-recall graphs. We now give formal descriptions of the evaluation measures used in our experiments.

For describing the evaluation measures used in the experiments we need the following definition. Given a set of prototypes and fixing the example to $(\bar{x}, y)$, we define $rank(\bar{x}, r)$ as the ranking of the topic indexed r in list of topics sorted according to the prototypes. Thus, the rank-value of the top-ranked topic is 1 and of the bottom-ranked topic is k. The performance measure for the test set is the average value of each measure over the documents in the set.

Algorithm	$\text{loss}_1 \times 100$	loss_2	$\text{loss}_3 \times 100$
Rocciho	18.82	1.17	1.00
Perceptron	15.71	4.87	3.13
MMP l. 1	**13.07**	1.33	0.91
MMP l. 2	17.99	**0.78**	**0.54**
MMP l. 3	19.13	0.92	0.60

Table 1: A comparison of the performance of the various algorithms on the test-set for different learning-theoretic performance measures on Reuters-21578.

Algorithm	OneErr × 100	Coverage	AvgP	maxF_1
Rocciho	14.48	1.29	0.90	0.85
Perceptron	9.59	4.27	0.91	0.89
MMP l. 1	**8.65**	1.42	**0.94**	**0.90**
MMP l. 2	13.42	**0.87**	0.91	0.86
MMP l. 3	14.51	0.96	0.90	0.84

Table 2: A comparison of the performance of the various algorithms on the test-set for different retrieval performance measures on Reuters-21578.

Recall The recall value at r is the ratio between the number of the topics from the set of relevant topics y whose rank is at most r and the size of the relevant topics y.

$$\text{Recall}(r) = \frac{|\{r \in y \ : \ rank(\bar{x}, r) \leq r\}|}{|y|} .$$

Precision The precision value at r is the ratio between the number of the topics from the set of relevant topics y whose rank is at most r and the position r.

$$\text{Precision}(r) = \frac{|\{r \in y \ : \ rank(\bar{x}, r) \leq r\}|}{r} .$$

OneErr The one-error (abbreviated OneErr) takes the values 0 or 1. It indicated whether the top-ranked element belongs to the set of relevant topics y (zero error) or not (error of 1),

$$\text{OneErr} = \begin{cases} 0 & r \in y \\ 1 & r \notin y \end{cases} .$$

Therefore, the average OneErr over a test corpus reflects the fraction of documents for which the top-ranked topic was not from the list of relevant topics.

Coverage The coverage value reflects how far we need to go down the ranked-list of topics in order to retrieve all the relevant topics,

$$\text{Coverage} = \max_{r \in y} rank(\bar{x}, r) - 1 .$$

For convenience this definition implies that for documents with a single relevant topic a perfect ranking achieves a coverage of zero.

AvgP The average precision (abbreviated AvgP), as the name implies, is the average precision taken at the positions of the relevant topics,

$$\text{AvgP} = \frac{1}{|y|} \sum_{r \in y} \frac{|\{r' \in y \ : \ rank(\bar{x}, r') \leq rank(\bar{x}, r)\}|}{rank(\bar{x}, r)} .$$

Algorithm	$\text{loss}_1 \times 100$	loss_2	$\text{loss}_3 \times 100$
Rocciho	70.71	12.42	3.33
Perceptron	38.86	10.43	2.64
MMP l. 1	**30.68**	2.87	**0.74**
MMP l. 2	34.59	**2.84**	0.75
MMP l. 3	34.57	2.90	0.75

Table 3: A comparison of the performance of the various algorithms on the test-set for different learning-theoretic performance measures on Reuters-2000.

Algorithm	OneErr × 100	Coverage	AvgP	maxF_1
Rocciho	24.42	9.89	0.73	0.63
Perceptron	6.04	9.45	0.87	0.86
MMP l. 1	**4.73**	4.08	**0.92**	**0.90**
MMP l. 2	5.81	4.01	0.91	0.88
MMP l. 3	6.49	**3.98**	0.91	0.87

Table 4: A comparison of the performance of the various algorithms on the test-set for different retrieval performance measures on Reuters-2000.

The average precision is perhaps the most common performance measure in document retrieval.

maxF_1 The F_1 value at r is defined as,

$$F_1(r) = \frac{2\,\text{Recall}(r)\,\text{Precision}(r)}{\text{Recall}(r) + \text{Precision}(r)} .$$

The maxF_1 is the maximal F_1 value that can be obtained. For further information on the F_1 performance measure see [13].

We would like to note that the there are natural relations between the learning theoretic losses, $\text{loss}_1 - \text{loss}_3$, and the retrieval-based performance measures. For instance, whenever OneErr is 1 then also $\text{loss}_1 = 1$, since if the top-ranked topic is not one of the relevant topics then clearly the ranking is not perfect and thus OneErr $\leq \text{loss}_1$. Also, if $|y| = 1$ then the Coverage and loss_2 coincide.

4.6 Results

Let us first discuss the performance of the online algorithms (the variants of MMP and Perceptron) on the training sets. In Fig. 4 and Fig. 5 we show the performance with respect to loss_1, loss_2 and loss_3 for Reuters-21578 and Reuters-2000 respectively. For each round (new document) we compute the cumulative loss of of the algorithms divided by the number of documents processes, i.e., the round number M: $(\sum_i^M \text{loss}_{\bar{x}_i, y_i}(i))/M$. Note that we used log-scale for the x-axis. As expected, we can see from the figures that each version of MMP performs well with respect to the loss measure it was trained on. In addition, the Perceptron performs well with respect to loss_1, especially on Reuters-21578. The relatively good performance of the Perceptron with respect to loss_1 might be attributed to the fact that the Reuters-21578 corpus is practically single-labeled and thus loss_1 and the classification error used by the Perceptron are practically synonymous. As we discuss in the sequel, the performance after most of the documents have been processed also is highly correlated with the performance of the algorithms on unseen test data. This type of behavior indeed agrees with the formal analysis of online algorithms [4].

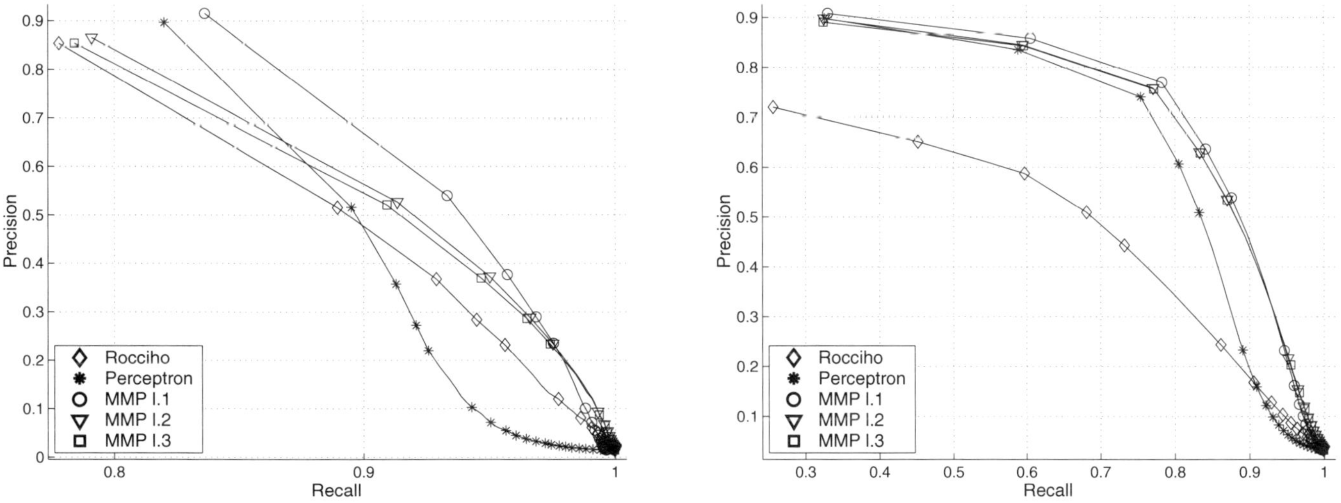

Figure 6: Precision (y-axis) versus recall (x-axis) graphs for the various algorithms on Reuters-21578 (left) and Reuters-2000 (right).

The performance of the algorithms on the test sets is summarized in four tables. A summary of the performances with respect to the learning-theoretic and information retrieval measures on Reuters-21578 are given in Table 1 and Table 2, respectively. An analogous summary for Reuters-2000 is given in Table 3 and Table 4. In addition we also provide in Fig. 6 precision-recall graphs for both corpora.

The performance of MMP and the Perceptron algorithm with respect to the learning-theoretic losses is consistent with their behavior on the test data: each variant of MMP performs well with respect to the loss it employs in training. Moving on to retrieval performance measures, we see that with respect to all performance measures, with the exception of Coverage, the best performing topic-ranking algorithm is MMP with $loss_1$. For coverage MMP trained with either $loss_2$ or $loss_3$ achieve the best performance. We also see strong correlations between $loss_1$ and OneErr and between $loss_2$ and Coverage. One possible explanation to the improved performance of $loss_1$ compared to $loss_2$ and $loss_3$ is that it gives each document the same weight in the update while the other losses prefer documents with large number of relevant topics. We plan to investigate this conjecture, both theoretically and empirically, in future work.

The Perceptron algorithm performs surprisingly well on both datasets with respect to most of the performance measures. The main deficiency of the algorithms is its relatively poor performance in terms of Coverage. It achieves the worst Coverage value in all cases. This behavior can also be observed in the precision-recall graphs. While the precision the Perceptron algorithm for low recall values is competitive with all the variants of MMP and even better than the variants that employ $loss_2$ and $loss_3$ on Reuters-21578, as long as recall is below 0.9. Alas, as the recall increases the precision of the Perceptron algorithm drops sharply and for high recall values it exhibits the worst precision. One possible explanation for this behavior is that the Perceptron is a tailored for classification and thus the implicit classification loss (the "hinge" loss) it employs is insensitive to the induced ranking.

Despite our attempts to implement a state-of-the-art version of Rocchio that takes into account phenomena like the length of the documents, Rocchio's performance was the worst. This is especially surprising since in a head-to-head comparison of Rocchio with recent variants of AdaBoost [11] the results of the two algorithms were practically indistinguishable, despite the fact that it took two orders of magnitude more to train the latter. Amit Singhal from Google offered one possible explanation for this relatively poor performance. Rocchio was originally designed for *document* retrieval. Furthermore, the recent improvements that employ length normalization were tuned on TREC's document retrieval tasks. Despite its similarity in nature to document ranking, the topic ranking problem seems to exhibit different statistical characteristics and might require new adaptations for topic ranking problems.

5. SUMMARY

In this paper we presented a new family of algorithms called MMP for topic-ranking which are simple to implement. The algorithmic approach suggested in this paper attempts to combine the formal properties of statistical learning techniques with the effectiveness of practical information retrieval algorithms. The online framework that we used to derive MMP makes the algorithm practical for massive datasets such as the new release of Reuters. We believe that our experiments show that MMP indeed makes a non-trivial step toward provably correct and practically effective methods for IR.

There are quite a few possible extensions and modifications to MMP that might further improve its effectiveness. One possible extension we are currently exploring a better fusion of IR-motivated losses such as the average precision into the core of the algorithm. We have preliminary results that indicate that such an improvement is plausible. A few more straightforward, yet powerful, extensions were not discussed in this paper. In particular, MMP can be incorporated with kernel-techniques [14, 1]. Other, more robust, methods for converting MMP to a batch algorithm (see for instance [3] and the references therein) are also possible and will be evaluated in future work.

Acknowledgments

Thanks to Amit Singhal for clarifications and suggestions on pivoted-length normalization. Thanks also to Noam Slonim for discussions, to Ofer Dekel and Benjy Weinberger for their help in pre-processing the corpora, and to Leo Kontorovich for comments on the manuscript. We also would like to acknowledge the financial support of EU project KerMIT No. IST-2000-25341 and the KerMIT group members for useful discussions.

6. REFERENCES

[1] N. Cristianini and J. Shawe-Taylor. *An Introduction to Support Vector Machines.* Cambridge University Press, 2000.

[2] A. Elisseeff and J. Weston. A kernel method for multi-labeled classification. In *Advances in Neural Information Processing Systems 14*, 2001.

[3] Y. Freund and R. E. Schapire. Large margin classification using the perceptron algorithm. In *Proceedings of the Eleventh Annual Conference on Computational Learning Theory*, 1998. To appear, *Machine Learning.*

[4] D. P. Helmbold and M. K. Warmuth. On weak learning. *Journal of Computer and System Sciences*, 50:551–573, 1995.

[5] D. J. Ittner, D. D. Lewis, and D. D. Ahn. Text categorization of low quality images. In *Symposium on Document Analysis and Information Retrieval*, pages 301–315, Las Vegas, NV, 1995. ISRI; Univ. of Nevada, Las Vegas.

[6] H. T. Ng, W. B. Goh, and K. L. Low. Feature selection, perceptron learning, and a usability case study for text categorization. In *Proceedings of the 20th Annual International ACM SIGIR Conference on Research and Development in Information Retrieval*, pages 67–73, 1997.

[7] J. Rocchio. Relevance feedback information retrieval. In Gerard Salton, editor, *The Smart retrieval system—experiments in automatic document processing*, pages 313–323. Prentice-Hall, Englewood Cliffs, NJ, 1971.

[8] F. Rosenblatt. The perceptron: A probabilistic model for information storage and organization in the brain. *Psychological Review*, 65:386–407, 1958. (Reprinted in *Neurocomputing* (MIT Press, 1988).).

[9] G. Salton. Developments in automatic text retrieval. *Science*, 253:974–980, 1991.

[10] R. E. Schapire and Y. Singer. Improved boosting algorithms using confidence-rated predictions. *Machine Learning*, 37(3):1–40, 1999.

[11] R. E. Schapire, Y. Singer, and A. Singhal. Boosting and Rocchio applied to text filtering. In *SIGIR '98: Proceedings of the 21st Annual International Conference on Research and Development in Information Retrieval*, 1998.

[12] A. Singhal, C. Buckley, and M. Mitra. Pivoted document length normalization. In *Research and Development in Information Retrieval*, pages 21–29, 1996.

[13] C. J. van Rijsbergen. *Information Retrieval.* Butterworths, London, 1979.

[14] V. N. Vapnik. *Statistical Learning Theory.* Wiley, 1998.

Comparing Cross-Language Query Expansion Techniques by Degrading Translation Resources

Paul McNamee and James Mayfield
The Johns Hopkins University Applied Physics Laboratory
11100 Johns Hopkins Road, Laurel, MD 20723-6099 USA
+1-443-778-3816
{mcnamee, mayfield}@jhuapl.edu

ABSTRACT

The quality of translation resources is arguably the most important factor affecting the performance of a cross-language information retrieval system. While many investigations have explored the use of query expansion techniques to combat errors induced by translation, no study has yet examined the effectiveness of these techniques across resources of varying quality. This paper presents results using parallel corpora and bilingual wordlists that have been deliberately degraded prior to query translation. Across different languages, translingual resources, and degrees of resource degradation, pre-translation query expansion is tremendously effective. In several instances, pre-translation expansion results in better performance when no translations are available, than when an uncompromised resource is used without pre-translation expansion. We also demonstrate that post-translation expansion using relevance feedback can confer modest performance gains. Measuring the efficacy of these techniques with resources of different quality suggests an explanation for the conflicting reports that have appeared in the literature.

Categories and Subject Descriptors: H.3.3 [**Information Systems**]: Information Search and Retrieval – *query formulation, relevance feedback*

General Terms: Experimentation

Keywords: cross-language information retrieval, translation resources, query expansion, query translation

1. INTRODUCTION

Cross-Language Information Retrieval (CLIR) systems seek to identify pertinent information in a collection of documents containing material in languages other than the one in which the user articulated her query. Intrinsic to the problem is a need to transform the query, document, or both, into a common terminological representation, using available translation resources. Thus, system performance is necessarily limited by the caliber of translations; clearly resources with broader coverage are preferable. High quality linguistic resources are typically difficult to obtain and exploit, or expensive to purchase. Participants in the major international CLIR evaluations such as CLEF, NTCIR, and TREC ([29], [30], [31]) frequently express a desire for better, and preferably low-cost, translation resources. The large multilingual collections available on the Internet have motivated researchers to attempt mining unstructured sources of linguistic data (e.g., Resnik [24]), fueled by the natural expectation that the use of more comprehensive resources will yield improvements in cross-language performance. It has even been suggested that CLIR evaluations may be measuring resource quality foremost (or equivalently, financial status) [7]. Scanning the papers of CLIR Track participants in TREC-9 and TREC-2001, we observe a trend toward the fusion of multiple resources in an attempt to improve lexical coverage. Clearly a need for enhanced resources is felt.

Typically, three types of resources are exploited for translingual mappings: bilingual wordlists (or machine readable dictionaries); parallel texts; and machine translation systems. The favorite appears to be bilingual wordlists, which are widely available, can be easy to use (especially if only word-by-word translation is attempted), and which preserve information such as alternate translations. Techniques using aligned parallel texts to produce statistical translation equivalents have become widely used since the publication of a method using Latent Semantic Indexing by Landauer and Littman [16]; however, these corpora are difficult to obtain and must first be aligned and indexed. Machine translation (MT) systems are perhaps the easiest approach for query translation, but may be computationally prohibitive for document translation. MT systems typically produce only a single candidate translation, thus some information of potential use to a retrieval system is lost. For an overview of translation methods in CLIR, see Oard and Diekema [19].

Regardless of the type of resource(s) used, several problems remain. Pirkola et al. [21] outline the major issues from a dictionary-based perspective; however, many of these same concerns arise when corpora or MT systems are used. They list difficulties with untranslatable terms, variations in inflectional forms, problems with phrase identification and translation, and translation ambiguity between the source and target languages as the main problems.

To cope with the paucity of translation resources and their inherent limitations, various techniques have been proposed. Query expansion is routinely used in monolingual retrieval, either by global methods such as thesauri, by local methods such as pseudo relevance feedback (PRF), or by local context analysis

(LCA) [26]. In a multilingual setting, expansion can take place prior to translation, afterwards, or at both times.

The effect of resource quality on retrieval efficacy has received little attention in the literature. This study explores the relationship between the quality of a translation resource and CLIR performance. The effectiveness of both corpus and dictionary-based resources was artificially lowered by randomly translating different proportions of query terms, simulating variability in the coverage of resources. We first discuss prior related work and then present our experimental design which explores multiple query expansion techniques. The remainder of the paper is devoted to an analysis of the empirical results.

2. PREVIOUS WORK

Regarding translation resources for CLIR, we believe that two points are widely agreed upon:

- resources are scarce and difficult to use; and
- resources with greater lexical coverage are preferable.

Because of the first point, the rarity of electronic sources for translation, investigators may be drawn to use the resources most readily available to them, rather than those best suited for bilingual retrieval. The second point is widely held, but to our knowledge, in only two cases has the benefit of increased lexical coverage been quantified [8], [27]; however, many different resources have been pair-wise compared extrinsically based on performance in bilingual retrieval tasks (e.g., [14], [18], [28]).

Degradation of documents and queries has been examined in two of the TREC evaluations, but only in a monolingual setting. Retrieval of garbled text documents was investigated to simulate a task where documents might contain numerous errors, such as if documents were created by optical character recognition [12]. And in TREC-9, short query forms containing realistic spelling errors were provided to test the ability of systems to cope with such mistakes. Also in TREC-9, the Query track examined the effects of query variability on system performance, but queries were re-stated, rather than purposefully weakened [5].

Query expansion based upon an entire query rather than on a candidate term's similarity to individual query search terms has been shown to be effective in monolingual settings [23]. Similarly, blind relevance feedback has been shown to be remarkably effective, especially when an initial query formulation lacks terms present in many relevant documents [25]. This might be the case when a query is very short, or when specific domain terminology (e.g., medicine, engineering) is used.

In a multilingual setting it seems plausible that pre-translation expansion would indeed be helpful. If a resource contains a restricted number of translatable search terms, then the degradation arising out of the translation process will cause many important query words to be unavailable for document ranking. But, if many words (or word forms) related to the query are translated, then the ultimate number of terms available for searching the target language is greater. This method presumes that the set of translated terms still represents the query semantics (i.e., the user's information request is not significantly altered by expansion *and* translation). If query translation does not produce a query with many coordinate terms, additional expansion through relevance feedback can likely improve precision as well as recall.

Many positive reports regarding the benefits of query expansion for CLIR have been reported; however, negative reports have been made frequently as well. We believe that differences in test collections, retrieval systems, language pairs, and translation resources obfuscate the conclusions of prior studies.

Ballesteros and Croft explored query expansion methods for CLIR and reported "combining pre- and post-translation expansion is most effective and improves precision and recall." [1] The use of both techniques led to an improvement from 42% to 68% of monolingual performance in mean average precision. The improvement from application of both methods was appreciably greater than the use of only pre- or post-translation expansion. Their work only examined a single language pair (English to Spanish), and relied on the Collins's English-Spanish electronic dictionary.

In a subsequent study [2], Ballesteros and Croft examined the use of co-occurrence statistics in parallel corpora to select translations from a machine-readable dictionary. Application of this technique was very effective and boosted bilingual performance from 68% to 88% of a monolingual baseline. Here they suggested that post-translation expansion helps remove errors due to incorrect translations.

More recently, Gey and Chen wrote an overview of the TREC-9 CLIR track, which focused on using English queries to search a Chinese news collection [9]. Their summaries of work by several top-scoring track participants reveal a disconcerting lack of consistency as to the merits of query expansion methods:

- 10% improvement in average precision with either pre-translation or post-translation expansion, but only short queries benefited from the use of both
- "Pre-translation query expansion did not help"
- "The best cross-language run did not use post-translation expansion"
- "Pre-translation expansion yielded an improvement of 42% over an unexpanded base run"
- "The best run used both pre- and post-translation expansion"
- "Post-translation query expansion yielded little improvement"

With inconsistent results like these, it is impossible to ascertain what techniques do and do not work. Each of the six systems referred to above used different translation resources, and we believe this amplifies the confusion. Until the effects of poor lexical coverage are better understood, shadows may hang over many research results unless the quality of translation resources employed is first ascertained. In an analysis of language resources used in the CLEF 2000 campaign [10], Gonzolo suggested measurement of resources and retrieval strategies in isolation, a recommendation we endorse.

In the TREC-2001 cross-language evaluation, which focused on English to Arabic retrieval, the system with the highest bilingual performance made use of several unique translation resources, which seems to agree with the notion that greater lexical coverage is helpful. However, it is impossible to discriminate between the benefits of the retrieval system that was employed and the resources utilized. Interestingly, the authors reported that pre-translation expansion was detrimental when post-translation relevance feedback was also applied, contradicting the results reported by Ballesteros and Croft [28].

A few investigations have examined the effect of resource size on CLIR performance. Two reports have measured retrieval performance as a function of resources for English-Chinese retrieval. Xu and Weischedel plotted performance on the TREC-5,6 Chinese tasks using a lexicon mined from parallel texts [27]. They used lexicons of a fixed size, where a lexicon of size *n* contained mappings for the *n* most frequent English words; bilingual performance was not improved for sizes greater than 20,000 terms. Franz et al. examined three parallel collections for use on the TREC-9 Chinese topics [8]. Using short queries, they found that out-of-vocabulary rate was more important than domain, dialect, or style in predicting system performance.

For the CLEF-2001 workshop, Kraaij examined the relative merits of an MT system, a lexical database, and a parallel corpus, and emphasized the benefits that can be obtained from combining such disparate translation resources [14]. With the use of all three resources he observed bilingual performance 98% of a monolingual baseline for English to French retrieval. Separate use of a dictionary, a corpus, and an MT system yielded performance only 73%, 90%, and 92% of a monolingual baseline. He offered the opinion that "the mean average precision of a run is proportional to the lexical coverage [of the translation resources]", but this statement appears to be based only on a qualitative examination of why performance on certain topics differed depending on the resources and language pairs used.

The results reported in the present paper confirm Kraaij's conjecture and quantify the degree to which inferior resource quality affects CLIR performance and under which circumstances query expansion techniques can mitigate translation errors due to poor lexical coverage.

3. EXPERIMENTS

3.1 Test Collection

The CLEF-2001 test collection was used for all of our experiments (see [20] for a description). The collection contains roughly 1 million newspaper articles published in 1994 or 1995 (see Table 1).

Table 1. CLEF-2001 Document Collection

	Documents	Unique words
Dutch	190,604	692,745
English	110,282	235,710
French	87,191	479,682
German	225,371	1,670,316
Italian	108,578	1,323,283
Spanish	215,737	382,664

The Bilingual Track in the CLEF-2001 evaluation permitted a variety of query languages to be used to search either the Dutch or English collections. Here we only explored the five language pairs Dutch, French, German, Italian, and Spanish, to English. The test suite contains fifty topic statements, but only forty-seven of the topics contain a relevant English article. A mixture of topics including local, national, and international subjects was selected. In each language topic statements were crafted by native speakers and significant effort was expended to ensure that the intended topic semantics were preserved in the respective languages.

3.2 Document and Query Processing

Document processing was designed to require minimal use of language specific resources such as stopword lists, lexicons, decompounders, stemmers, lists of phrases, or manually-built thesauri, so each language's sub-collection was handled much the same. Punctuation was eliminated, letters were down-cased, and diacritical marks were preserved. Thus documents and queries are represented as bags of unnormalized word forms. Queries were tokenized in the same fashion as documents, but obvious query structure (e.g., 'find documents that' or 'relevant documents must contain') was removed. We used a retrieval system developed in-house for all of our experiments. The system uses a statistical language model of retrieval with Jelinek-Mercer smoothing of document term frequencies. See [3], [13], and [22] for more details on these models.

To perform pre-translation expansion, we relied solely on local methods based on an initial retrieval from the appropriate source language sub-collection of the CLEF-2001 documents. For example, to investigate pre-translation expansion for Italian to English retrieval, we would first do a monolingual retrieval in the Italian collection (i.e., La Stampa and SDA-IT). Using the top ranked 25 retrieved documents as positive exemplars and presuming the lowest 75 ranked out of 1000 were irrelevant, we produced a set of 60 weighted terms for each query that included the original query terms; this is analogous to both query expansion and query term re-weighting as described in Harman [11]. It should be pointed out that the sub-collections in each language of the CLEF-2001 evaluation are contemporaneous, so this set of expansion terms might be somewhat better than an arbitrary monolingual collection. We did not investigate global methods for query expansion in the source language because this would have required a thesaurus in each source language that we wished to investigate.

When a query was expanded after translation, we again relied on pseudo relevance feedback based on terms extracted from retrieved target language documents. As with pre-translation expansion, we identified 60 weighted terms for use as an expanded query and searched the target language (English) collection for a second time.

3.3 Translation Resources

For reasons of convenience we only examined corpus- and dictionary based translation – it was not clear to us how to best degrade commercial translation software since many packages are optimized for grammatically correct sentences rather than word-by-word translation. Both the parallel corpus and the multilingual wordlist were extracted from the Web. These resources were not validated and may contain numerous errors.

We collected a variety of bilingual wordlists where English was one of the languages involved. Translation equivalents for over ninety thousand English words are available in at least one of forty or so languages. We did not attempt to utilize or reverse engineer web-based interfaces to dictionaries, but rather only sought wordlists in the public domain, or whose use appeared unrestricted; the Ergane dictionaries [32] and files from the Internet Dictionary Project [34] are the largest sources. We used the ABET extraction tool to convert these disparate wordlists to machine-readable form [17].

When translating a word using a bilingual wordlist we simply use all of the alternative mappings for the word, and each mapping is weighted using the same query term frequency as the original word. In our wordlist the mean number of entries per term by language is: 3.01 for Dutch; 2.08 for French; 1.58 for German; 1.52 for Italian; and 1.57 for Spanish.

We also built a set of aligned corpora using text mined from the Europa site [33]; specifically, we downloaded eight months of the Official Journal of the European Union (December 2000 through August 2001). The Journal is published in eleven languages in PDF format. We converted the PDF formatted documents to text encoded in ISO-8859-1, aligned the documents using simple rules for whitespace and punctuation with Church's char_align program [6], and then indexed the data. It was easiest to construct a separate aligned corpus for each non-English language, rather than to build a single, multiply aligned collection. The resulting collection contains roughly 100MB of text in each language. The number of words with at least one English translation produced by the two resources is shown in Table 2. It should be noted that many of the terms extracted from the aligned corpus are names or numbers that would not normally be contained in a dictionary, so the number of entries reported here is not a clear indication of a superior resource.

Table 2. Bilingual Resource Size (in terms)

	Wordlist	Corpus
Dutch	15,591	184,506
French	23,322	135,454
German	94,901	224,961
Italian	18,461	138,890
Spanish	25,028	146,938

When translating a word using an aligned corpus, we select the single best candidate translation.

3.4 Experimental Design

We now describe the experiments we undertook. We focused only on word-by-word query translation because of its simplicity. Our goal is to compare four methods of query expansion or augmentation under a spectrum of conditions corresponding to differing quality translation resources. The four methods examined are no use of expansion, pre-translation expansion only, post-translation only, and the use of both pre- and post-translation expansion. Figure 1 illustrates the procedure we followed.

Previously we mentioned that only 47 of the CLEF-2001 topics contain a relevant English article; however, 12 additional topics contain only one or two relevant documents. This may be attributable to the design goals of the evaluation: a certain number topics were sought that focused on local subjects, and the American-based LA Times is less likely to report on these issues. Since relevance feedback is only expected to enhance retrieval performance when a reasonable number of germane documents are present in the target language collection, we chose to evaluate our runs using the 35 topics with three or more relevant documents. Topics 44, 52, 54, 57, 59, 60, 62, 63, 67, 73, 74, 75, 78, 79, and 88 were discarded. Kwok and Chan [15] developed a technique designed to provide for good query expansion in this situation (where a target collection only has a small number of relevant documents), but we did not attempt it here. Their idea is based on searching a larger collection that is expected to contain

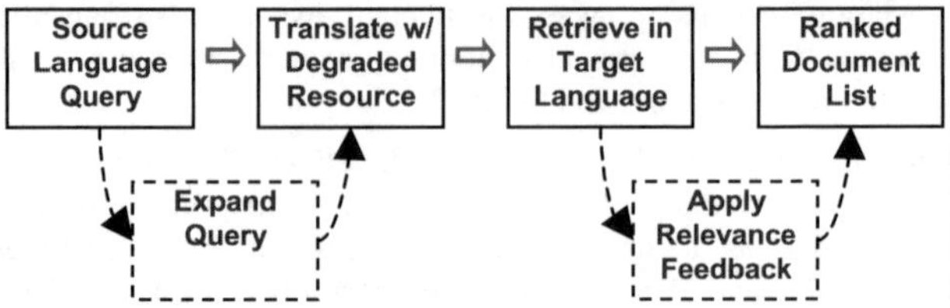

Title, Title + Desc, and Title + Desc + Narr query forms were considered in each of five source languages: Dutch, French, German, Italian, and Spanish. Source language expansion or no expansion was used, followed by translation. There were two methods for translation: use of a bilingual dictionary using all available translations; and statistical translation using an aligned parallel corpus. Eleven versions of each resource were simulated corresponding to different measures of lexical coverage. After translation, retrieval was performed on the target language collection, which was English, and optionally, pseudo relevance feedback was applied. A total of 1320 runs were created.

Figure 1. Overview of Experiments Performed

many more documents about that domain; they termed the technique 'collection enrichment'.

We considered two methods for impairing our translation resources. The first method was the simple idea of physically creating new wordlists or corpora with missing lexical entries. This seemed laborious, so instead we opted for simulating weaker resources by randomly declining to translate a given percentage of query terms. In other words, for each term, we would generate a random number between 0 and 1, and only if the value was greater than the degree of degradation did we attempt to find a target language mapping. We could have removed a percentage of all lexical entries from the resource, but since only a small percentage of the terms occur in the CLEF queries, this would be counterproductive. The same random seeds were used for both corpus or wordlist translations. In practice a language resource would likely have more mappings for common terms and fewer entries for proper nouns or obscure terms. We did not attempt to model this, but dropping low frequency words is probably a better idea than randomly omitting query terms.

Starting with no degradation, we removed terms in increments of 10%, up to complete degradation. When a decision was made not to translate a given term, the untranslated form was left in the query as a potential translation. This is a common practice, and is motivated by the observation that in related languages, many morphological cognates exist. Thus, even when a resource is 100% degraded, corresponding to a state in which no translation resource is available, it is still possible to retrieve relevant documents.

Different terms will be omitted from a query for a particular random seed; this is expected to increase the variance in our evaluation measures. Averaging over a number of trials, each using a different seed, would provide a clear solution to this problem. We decided against this for reasons of expediency; otherwise the number of runs would have been unmanageable. We chose to focus primarily on mean average precision to evaluate our results, but we collected statistics for precision at low recall levels as well.

In Table 3 a monolingual baseline is compared to bilingual queries at four levels of resource impairment and the effect of pre-translation expansion is shown. Italian is used as the source language and the parallel corpus is used to map terms into English for the short version of query 66, "Russian Withdrawal from Latvia" (Italian: "Ritiro delle truppe russe dalla Lettonia "). At 0% degradation pre-translation expansion is dramatically better due to several poor translations; at 40%, these translations are dropped because of the random resource degradation, so performance actually rises; however, at 80% only the term 'withdrawal' is correctly translated without expansion, so expansion is critical here. We note that at 100% degradation we still obtain a reasonable degree of performance, but only when expansion is used. This is due to cognates (like "estonia" and "russia") that were extracted from Italian articles during source language query expansion, but which require no translation into English.

Table 3. Illustration of the effects of pre-translation expansion and resource degradation

Degradation / Query	Recall at 1000 docs	Average Precision	Precision at 10 docs
English Monolingual	11	0.6923	0.8
{latvia=1, russian=1, withdrawal=1}			
0% Degradation	11	0.1176	0.1
{communities=1, directive=1, latvia=1, russian=1, troops=1, withdrawal=1}			
With Expansion	11	0.4791	0.7
{1517#-80, 31-119, agency=80, agreement=83, agreements=103, armed=74, august=134, baltic=177, countries=112, estonia=144, foreign=95, incubators=73, latvia=76, latvian=135, line=215, lithuania=135, living=82, maintain=92, military=112, minorities=77, moscow=199, near=71, negotiations=78, news=109, north=76, pension=73, pensioners=71, press=85, radar=94, reported=76, rights=86, russia=212, russian=74, service=84, soldiers=108, station=84, suspended=76, tallinn=77, troops=926, unit=70, voltage=75, warsaw=101, withdrawal=958, within=135}			
40% Degradation	11	0.6982	0.8
{delle=1, latvia=1, russian=1, troops=1, withdrawal=1}			
With Expansion	11	0.4400	0.5
{31=119, agosto=134, agreement=83, baltic=177, estonia=144, incubators=73, latvia=76, latvian=135, line=215, maintain=92, military=112, moscow=199, near=71, negotiations=78, news=109, north=76, pension=73, radar=94, reported=76, rights=86, russia=212, russian=74, service=84, soldiers=108, stampa=85, station=84, suspended=76, tallinn=77, troops=926, unit=70, voltage=75, warsaw=101, withdrawal=958, within-135}			
80% Degradation	11	0.0069	0.0
{delle=1, directive=1, russe=1, withdrawal=1}			
With Expansion	11	0.5077	0.6
{31=119, agosto=134, baltic=177, dislocate=73, estone=144, estonia=238, near=71, negotiations=78, news=109, pensione=73, radar=94, reported=76, riga=215, russe=1019, russia=212, russian=74, russo=118, service=84, stampa=85, station=84, tallinn=77, troops=926, unit=70, withdrawal=958}			
100% Degradation	0	0.0000	0.0
{dalla=1, delle=1, russe=1}			
With Expansion	11	0.2401	0.2
{31=119, agosto=134, baltic=148, dislocate=73, estone=144, estonia=238, news=109, pensione=73, radar=94, riga=215, russa=74, russe=1019, russi=193, russia=212, russo=118, service=84, stampa=85, stazione=84, tallinn=77}			

4. RESULTS

The resources used for translation in our experiments are uncurated resources derived from the Web. Because the adequacy of these resources for cross-language retrieval has not previously been demonstrated, we first assessed the performance of the uncompromised resources. Only if a sufficient level of performance was seen would our experiments be meaningful; otherwise concern about whether these conclusions hold for superior resources would arise.

A baseline of English monolingual performance is shown in Table 4, for the three query forms (title-only (or T), title+description (or TD), and title+description+narrative (or TDN)) with and without the application of pseudo relevance feedback.

Table 4. Mean Average Precision of a Monolingual Baseline

	T	T w/RF	TD	TD w/RF	TDN	TDN w/RF
English	0.3578	0.4067	0.4383	0.4284	0.4825	0.4780

In Table 5 we report the percentage of mean average precision achieved by each bilingual run performed with intact translation resources when pre-translation expansion was not used. For our English baselines, relevance feedback improved the title-only queries, but did not appreciably change when longer topic statements were used. Each column in the table (below) is compared to the corresponding English run. We observe that when the parallel corpus is used for translation, an average of between 68% and 75% relative performance is obtained, depending on the run condition; with our dictionary, only 35% to 59% is seen on average. The dictionary appears to be an inferior resource, but the lower performance could also be attributable to our failure to normalize word forms. Longer topic statements fare better, and relevance feedback is somewhat helpful. We point out that pre-translation query expansion was not used in the table below. Given the lower performance when using the dictionary for translation, we must be cautious in drawing conclusions from those data.

Table 5. Bilingual Performance with Uncompromised Resources (percentage of monolingual performance)

		T	T w/RF	TD	TD w/RF	TDN	TDN w/RF
Dutch	Corp.	66.6	67.4	63.0	71.6	59.7	61.5
	Dict.	43.9	55.2	26.3	35.3	24.5	41.4
French	Corp.	59.9	67.5	73.0	80.9	73.8	86.9
	Dict.	57.2	57.4	48.7	60.7	61.3	78.9
German	Corp.	70.9	69.6	65.4	72.3	67.0	69.0
	Dict.	42.3	37.5	26.1	33.3	38.7	43.0
Italian	Corp.	70.5	70.6	72.5	80.5	75.4	78.2
	Dict.	35.5	51.0	33.4	48.2	39.6	61.2
Spanish	Corp.	72.4	69.7	72.2	75.9	75.6	81.4
	Dict.	51.2	51.8	41.2	54.2	57.6	71.6
Mean	Corp.	68.1	69.0	69.2	72.2	70.3	75.4
	Dict.	46.0	50.6	35.1	46.3	44.3	59.2

Now we get to the heart of the matter – addressing the question of how performance worsens as a translation resource is degraded. Figure 2 shows the performance in an agglutinative language, Dutch; and retrieval in Spanish is illustrated in Figure 3. For each language, six conditions are shown corresponding to the use of T, TD, or TDN topic statements with either corpus- or dictionary-based translation.

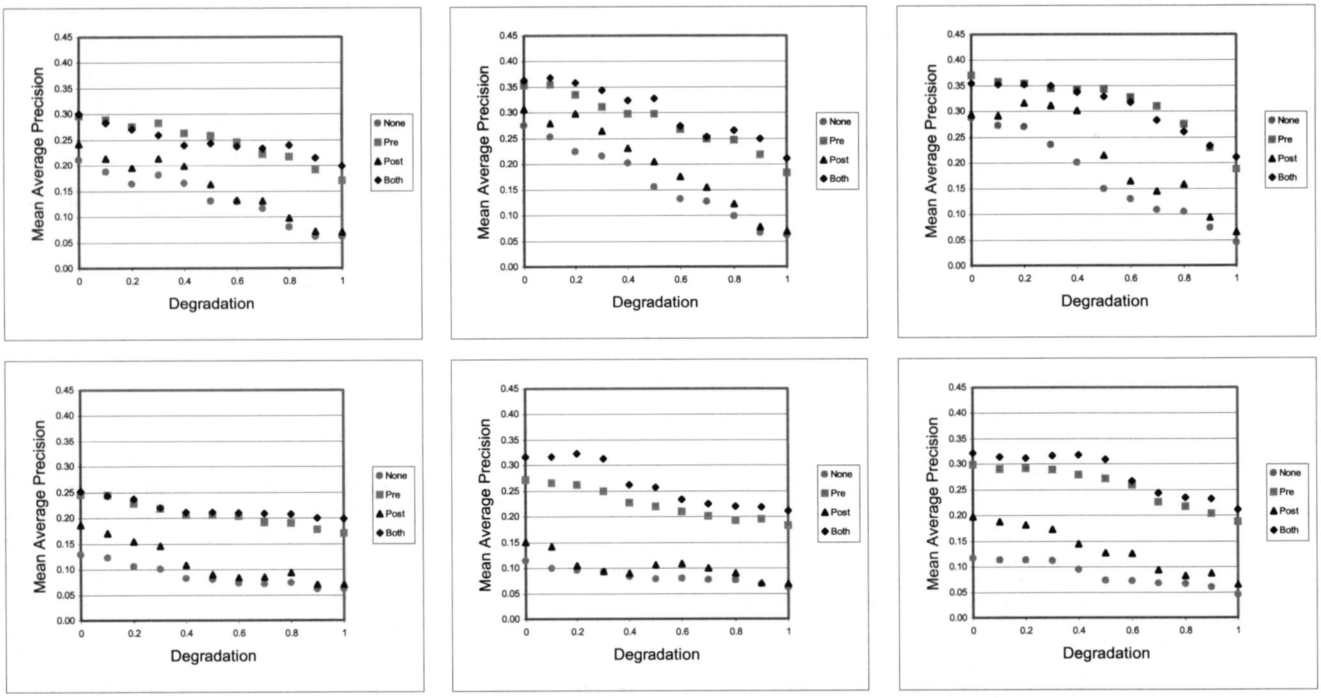

Figure 2. Effectiveness of expansion techniques as a function of resource degradation for the Dutch topics. Going from left to right, the three plots on the top row used the title-only, title+description, and title+description+narrative topic statements, respectively, and the parallel corpus for translation. Dictionary-based translation was used for the plots on the second row. Each plot shows the performance under four conditions: no expansion; only pre-translation expansion; only post-translation expansion; and both pre- and post-translation expansion.

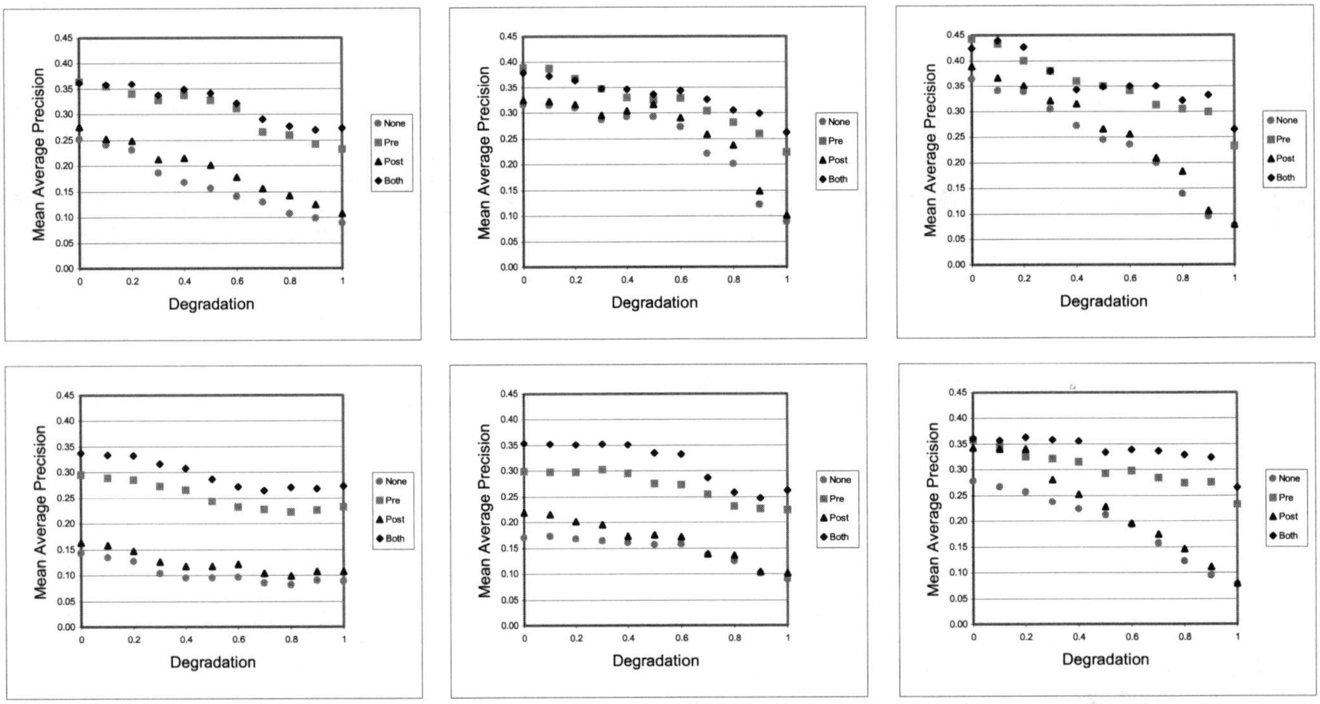

Figure 3. Effectiveness of expansion techniques as a function of resource degradation for the Spanish topics. The plots are arranged as in the previous figure.

4.1 No Expansion

Looking at Figures 2 and 3, we first note that retrieval performance drops linearly with decreased lexical coverage when no expansion is performed, confirming Kraaij's conjecture. The decrease depends on the caliber of the resource (the dictionary plots are noticeably worse), and on the length of the query. Unsurprisingly, longer queries perform better: they have further to fall when a weaker resource is used.

4.2 Post-Translation Expansion Alone

We find that the use of blind relevance feedback consistently increases the mean average precision by a modest amount. This occurs in each of the five language pairs and across variations in the lexical coverage of the different translation resources.

4.3 Pre-Translation Expansion Alone

Pre-translation expansion is tremendously useful across all levels of degradation. At higher levels of degradation, gains between 200 and 300% are realized. Only when a comprehensive translation resource is used, or when no comparable expansion collection is available, would we expect to see no benefit from expansion. Therefore, we recommend that this technique be applied whenever gains in precision justify the computational and procedural complexity of automated query expansion.

Amazingly, with no resource at all (i.e., the situation when a resource is 100% degraded), pre-translation expansion alone can result in better performance than when an uncompromised resource is used without expansion. This follows earlier work by Buckley et al. [4] that viewed English as "misspelled French" and attempted bilingual retrieval using rules for spelling correction and reliance on cognate matches. Pre-translation expansion appears to multiply the number of cognates useful for retrieval in related languages.

4.4 Pre- and Post-Translation Expansion

Finally, in agreement with the work cited earlier by Ballesteros and Croft, we confirm that a combination of pre- and post-translation expansion often yields the greatest performance. However, pre-translation expansion is responsible for the greatest gains. We see an improvement of approximately 10% - 15% when relevance feedback is also applied. This occurs either when the inferior resource, the wordlist, is used, or at high levels of degradation when the parallel corpus is used for translation.

4.5 Results in Other Languages

Figures 2 and 3 illustrated the detriment that occurs when a weaker translation resource is used, along with the ability of query expansion to ameliorate the losses due to poor lexical coverage, in Dutch and Spanish. The same trends hold in French, German, and Italian. A comparison of expansion techniques at four levels of lexical coverage is shown in Table 6.

The table shows the mean average precision experienced with corpus-based translation and TD topics. The highlighted cells indicate when an increase in performance using an expansion technique was statistically significant at the 95% confidence level (Wilcoxon test). The use of both pre-translation and post-translation expansion is almost always better, but at low levels of degradation, pre-translation expansion alone sometimes outperforms the combination. With high quality resources, many of the expansion terms will be correctly translated, and so gains that normally would occur by finding words related to, but not present in the initial query, using relevance feedback, are found instead by the initial feedback from the source language.

Table 6. Effects of Corpus Degradation on Expansion Utility

		0%	30%	70%	100%
Dutch	None	0.2759	0.2168	0.1274	0.0623
	Pre	0.3537	0.3121	0.2502	0.1832
	Post	0.3067	0.2643	0.1548	0.0697
	Both	0.3640	0.3439	0.2529	0.2113
French	None	0.3199	0.2502	0.2028	0.1091
	Pre	0.3603	0.3264	0.2618	0.1927
	Post	0.3467	0.2964	0.2907	0.1451
	Both	0.3698	0.3368	0.3060	0.2362
German	None	0.2784	0.2352	0.1409	0.0727
	Pre	0.3290	0.2903	0.2628	0.1944
	Post	0.3009	0.2566	0.1717	0.1135
	Both	0.3448	0.2974	0.3043	0.2440
Italian	None	0.3178	0.2482	0.2061	0.0823
	Pre	0.4209	0.3754	0.2552	0.2012
	Post	0.3449	0.3005	0.2310	0.0899
	Both	0.3989	0.3528	0.2643	0.2292
Spanish	None	0.3164	0.2863	0.2219	0.0887
	Pre	0.3890	0.3478	0.3040	0.2233
	Post	0.3253	0.2950	0.2583	0.1018
	Both	0.3799	0.3479	0.3262	0.2620

4.6 Limitations

To consider a breadth of source languages, query lengths, and expansion methods, some compromises were made; these should be considered in evaluating our results. Such factors include using a simple method for query term translation (unbalanced translation without translation of multiword units), reliance on contemporaneous newsprint collections for expansion, and use of a single random seed when selecting query terms not to translate.

5. CONCLUSIONS

In this paper we have demonstrated empirically the intuitive notion that bilingual retrieval performance drops off as the lexical coverage of translation resources decreases, and we confirmed that the relationship is approximately linear. Moreover, by using degraded translation resources we presented a framework to discover under which circumstances traditional query expansion techniques prove most beneficial.

We strongly recommend the use of pre-translation expansion when dictionary- or corpus-based query translation is performed; in some instances this expansion can treble performance. However, the computational expense and availability of comparable expansion collections should be considered. Additional relevance feedback in the target language is often useful, and can provide an additional 10-15% benefit. However, when high quality (i.e., comprehensive) resources are available, little gain is likely to occur. Differences in resource quality may account for disagreeing reports on the effectiveness of query expansion in cross-language retrieval.

We also demonstrated that even with very poor cross-language resources, good performance is still feasible when pre-translation expansion is used. This result is particularly important because it suggests that translingual retrieval in low-density languages will benefit significantly from such expansion.

6. REFERENCES

[1] L. Ballesteros and W. B. Croft, 'Phrasal Translation and Query Expansion Techniques for Cross-Language Information Retrieval.' In the *Proceedings of the 20th International ACM SIGIR Conference on Research and Development in Information Retrieval (SIGIR-97),* pp. 84-91, 1997.

[2] L. Ballesteros and W. B. Croft, 'Resolving Ambiguity for Cross-language Retrieval.' In the *Proceedings of the 21st International ACM SIGIR Conference on Research and Development in Information Retrieval (SIGIR-98)*, pp. 64-71, 1998.

[3] A. Berger and J. Lafferty, 'Information Retrieval as Statistical Translation.' In *Proceedings of the 22nd International ACM SIGIR Conference on Research and Development in Information Retrieval (SIGIR-99)*, pp. 222-229, 1999.

[4] C. Buckley, M. Mitra, J. Walz, and C. Cardie, 'Using Clustering and Super Concepts within SMART: TREC-6.' In E. Voorhees and D. Harman (eds.), *Proceedings of the Sixth Text REtrieval Conference (TREC-6)*, NIST Special Publication 500-240, 1998.

[5] C. Buckley, 'The TREC-9 Query Track.' In E. M. Voorhees and D. K. Harman, eds., *Proceedings of the Ninth Text REtrieval Conference (TREC-9),* pp. 81-85, 2001.

[6] K. W. Church, 'Char_align: A program for aligning parallel texts at the character level.' In the *Proceedings of the 31st Annual Meeting of the Association for Computational Linguistics*, pp. 1-8, 1993.

[7] A. Diekema, '*May the Best Team Win: Language Resources in CLIR.*' Position paper at the CLEF-2000 workshop. Available online at: http://clef.iei.pi.cnr.it:2002/DELOS/CLEF/diekema.pdf

[8] M. Franz, J. S. McCarley, T. Ward, and W. Zhu, 'Quantifying the Utility of Parallel Corpora.' *Proceedings of the 24th International ACM SIGIR Conference on Research and Development in Information Retrieval (SIGIR-01)*, pp. 398-399, 2001.

[9] F. Gey and A. Chen, 'TREC-9 Cross-Language Information Retrieval (English – Chinese) Overview.' In E. M. Voorhees and D. K. Harman, eds., *Proceedings of the Ninth Text REtrieval Conference (TREC-9),* pp. 15-23, 2001.

[10] J. Gonzolo, 'Language Resources in Cross-Language Text Retrieval: A CLEF Perspective.' In Carol Peters (ed.) *Cross-Language Information Retrieval and Evaluation: Proceedings of the CLEF-2000 Workshop*, Lisbon, Portugal, Lecture Notes in Computer Science 2069, Springer, pp. 36-47, 2001.

[11] D. Harman, 'Relevance Feedback Revisited.' In the *Proceedings of the 15th International ACM SIGIR Conference on Research and Development in Information Retrieval (SIGIR-92)*, pp. 1-10, 1992.

[12] D. Harman, 'Overview of the Fourth Text REtrieval Conference (TREC-4).' In D. K. Harman, ed., *Proceedings of the Fourth Text REtrieval Conference (TREC-4),* NIST Special Publication 500-236, pp. 1-24, 1995.

[13] D. Hiemstra, '*Using Language Models for Information Retrieval.*' Ph. D. Thesis, Center for Telematics and Information Technology, The Netherlands, 2000.

[14] W. Kraaij, 'TNO at CLEF-2001: Comparing Translation Resources.' To appear in Carol Peters (ed.), *Proceedings of the CLEF-2001 Workshop.*

[15] K. L. Kwok and M. Chan, 'Improving Two-Stage Ad-Hoc Retrieval for Short Queries.' In the *Proceedings of the 21st International ACM SIGIR Conference on Research and Development in Information Retrieval (SIGIR-98)*, pp. 250-256, 1998.

[16] T. K. Landauer and M. L. Littman, 'Fully automated cross-language document retrieval using latent semantic indexing.' In the *Proceedings of the 6th Annual Conference of the UW Centre for the New Oxford English Dictionary and Text Research.* 31-38, 1990.

[17] J. Mayfield and P. McNamee, 'Converting On-Line Bilingual Dictionaries from Human-Readable to Machine-Readable Form.' In these proceedings.

[18] P. McNamee and J. Mayfield, 'JHU/APL Experiments at CLEF: Translation Resources and Score Normalization.' To appear in Carol Peters (ed.), *Proceedings of the CLEF-2001 Workshop.*

[19] D. Oard and A. Diekema, 'Cross-Language Information Retrieval.' In M. Williams (ed.), *Annual Review of Information Science*, pp. 223-256, 1998.

[20] C. Peters, 'Foreward to the *Proceedings of the CLEF-2001 Workshop*', to appear in 2002.

[21] A. Pirkola, T. Hedlund, H. Keskusalo, and K. Järvelin, 'Dictionary-Based Cross-Language Information Retrieval: Problems, Methods, and Research Findings.' In *Information Retrieval*, vol. 4, pp. 209-230, 2001.

[22] J. M. Ponte and W. B. Croft, 'A Language Modeling Approach to Information Retrieval.' In the *Proceedings of the 21st International ACM SIGIR Conference on Research and Development in Information Retrieval (SIGIR-98)*, pp. 275-281, 1998.

[23] Y. Qiu and H. P. Frie, 'Concept Based Query Expansion.' In the *Proceedings of the 16th International ACM SIGIR Conference on Research and Development in Information Retrieval (SIGIR-93),* 1993.

[24] P. Resnik, 'Mining the Web for Bilingual Text.' *Proceedings of the 37th Annual Meeting of the Association for Computational Linguistics (ACL-99)*, 1999.

[25] G. Salton and C. Buckley, 'Improving Retrieval Performance by Relevance Feedback.' In the *Journal of the American Society for Information Science*, 41(4), pp. 288-297, 1990.

[26] J. Xu and W. B. Croft, 'Query Expansion Using Local and Global Document Analysis.' In the *Proceedings of the 19th International ACM SIGIR Conference on Research and Development in Information Retrieval (SIGIR-96)*, pp. 4-11, 1996.

[27] J. Xu and R. Weischedel, 'Cross-lingual Information Retrieval Using Hidden Markov Models.' In the *Proceedings of the Joint SIGDAT Conference on Empirical Methods in Natural Language Processing and Very Large Corpora (EMNLP/VLC-2000),* 2000.

[28] J. Xu, A. Fraser, and R. Weischedel, 'TREC 2001 Cross-lingual Retrieval at BBN.' In *TREC-2001 Notebook Papers*, pp. 122-131, 2001.

[29] Cross-Language Evaluation Forum, http://www.clef-campaign.org/

[30] NTCIR Project, http://research.nii.ac.jp/ntcir/

[31] Text REtrieval Conference, http://trec.nist.gov/

[32] http://dictionaries.travlang.com/

[33] http://europa.eu.int/

[34] http://www.june29.com/IDP/

Statistical Cross-Language Information Retrieval using N-Best Query Translations

Marcello Federico Nicola Bertoldi

ITC-irst Centro per la Ricerca Scientifica e Tecnologica
38050 Povo - Trento, Italy
{federico,bertoldi}@itc.it

ABSTRACT

This paper presents a novel statistical model for cross-language information retrieval. Given a written query in the source language, documents in the target language are ranked by integrating probabilities computed by two statistical models: a query-translation model, which generates most probable term-by-term translations of the query, and a query-document model, which evaluates the likelihood of each document and translation. Integration of the two scores is performed over the set of N most probable translations of the query. Experimental results with values $N = 1, 5, 10$ are presented on the Italian-English bilingual track data used in the CLEF 2000 and 2001 evaluation campaigns.

Categories and Subject Descriptors

H.3.3 [**Information Systems**]: Information Search and Retrieval.

General Terms

Algorithms, Theory

Keywords

CLIR, Query translation, Statistical model.

1. INTRODUCTION

The problem of Cross-Language Information Retrieval (CLIR) extends the information retrieval framework by assuming that queries and documents are not in the same language. In this paper, we look at CLIR from a statistical modelling perspective, similarly to how the problems of part-of-speech tagging, speech recognition, and machine translation have been, successfully, approached. Even if this point of view is not original, neither for IR [1] nor for CLIR [8], it is still open to new formulations. In fact, the resulting statistical models may significantly differ in terms of structure, captured dependencies, number of parameters, and quality and quantity of training data needed for parameter estimation.

In this work, a statistical model is presented which combines two basic components: an Hidden Markov Model (HMM) based query-translation model, and a Language Model (LM) based query-document model. The first permits to compute term-by-term translations of the source query, the latter to compute the likelihood of a translated query and a document. Remarkably, training of both components just requires a bilingual dictionary and the target document collection. Moreover, a retrieval algorithm is presented which integrates probabilities from both models over a set of N-best translations.

Experimental results of the CLIR algorithm are given on the Italian-English bilingual tracks used for the Cross Language Evaluation Forum [1] (CLEF) campaigns of 2000 and 2001 [13, 14].

The paper is arranged as follows. Section 2 introduces the statistical approach to CLIR. Sections 3 to 5 describe, respectively, the query document model, the query translation model, and the CLIR algorithm. Section 6 presents experimental results and Section 7 compares the presented CLIR method to other statistical approaches found in the literature. Finally, Section 8 states some conclusions.

2. STATISTICAL CLIR APPROACH

From a statistical perspective, the CLIR problem can be formulated as follows. Given a query $\mathbf{i}$ in the source language, e.g. Italian, one would like to find relevant documents d in the target language, e.g. English, within a collection $\mathcal{D}$. More formally, documents should be ranked according to the posterior probability:

$$\Pr(d \mid \mathbf{i}) \propto \Pr(\mathbf{i}, d) \qquad (1)$$

where the right term of formula (1) follows from the application of Bayes formula and from the constancy of $\Pr(\mathbf{i})$ with respect to the ranking of documents. To fill the language difference between query and documents, the hidden variable $\mathbf{e}$ is introduced, which represents an English (term-by-term) translation of $\mathbf{i}$. Hence, the following decomposition is derived:

[1] http://www.clef-campaign.org

Table 1: List of often used symbols.

$\mathbf{q}, \mathbf{i}, \mathbf{e}$	generic query, Italian query, and English query
q, i, e	generic term, Italian term, English term
$d, \mathcal{D}$	single document and document collection
$\mathcal{V}, \mathcal{V}(d)$	set of terms occurring in $\mathcal{D}$, and in d
$N, N(d)$	number of terms occurring in $\mathcal{D}$, and in d
$N(q), N(d, q), N(\mathbf{q}, w)$	frequency of term q in $\mathcal{D}$, in d, and in $\mathbf{q}$
N_q	number of documents in $\mathcal{D}$ which contain term q
$\lvert \cdot \rvert$	size of a set
$\mathcal{E}(i)$	set of possible English translations of Italian term i
$\mathcal{T}_N(\mathbf{i})$	set of N-best English translations of $\mathbf{i}$
$\mathcal{I}(\mathbf{e})$	subset of documents in $\mathcal{D}$ that contain at least one term of $\mathbf{e}$

$$\Pr(\mathbf{i}, d) = \sum_{\mathbf{e}} \Pr(\mathbf{i}, \mathbf{e}, d) \quad (2)$$

$$\approx \sum_{\mathbf{e}} \Pr(\mathbf{i}, \mathbf{e}) \Pr(d \mid \mathbf{e}) \quad (3)$$

$$= \sum_{\mathbf{e}} \Pr(\mathbf{i}, \mathbf{e}) \frac{\Pr(\mathbf{e}, d)}{\sum_{d'} \Pr(\mathbf{e}, d')} \quad (4)$$

In deriving formula (3), one makes the assumption (or approximation) that the probability of document d given query $\mathbf{i}$ and translation $\mathbf{e}$, does not depend on $\mathbf{i}$. Moreover, the main summation in (4) is taken over the set of possible translations of $\mathbf{i}$. As terms of $\mathbf{i}$ may typically admit more than one translation, the size of this set can grow exponentially with the length of $\mathbf{i}$. For instance, the here used bilingual Italian-English dictionary returns on average 1.84 English words for each Italian entry. Hence, the number of possible translations for a query of 40 terms is in the order of 10^{10}! Finally, the denominator in formula (4) requires summing over all document in $\mathcal{D}$ and should be computed for every possible translation $\mathbf{e}$.

In the following, statistical models will be described which, through suitable approximations, permit to efficiently compute formula (4). In particular, we will show how:

- probability $\Pr(\mathbf{e}, d)$ is computed by the query-document model,
- probability $\Pr(\mathbf{i}, \mathbf{e})$ is computed by the query-translation model,
- formula (4) is computed and documents are ranked by the CLIR algorithm.

A schematic view of the proposed CLIR approach is depicted in Figure 2. In particular, training data required by the statistical models are indicated.

3. QUERY-DOCUMENT MODEL

The query-document model computes the joint probability of a query $\mathbf{q}$ and a document d, written in the same language. This is accomplished through the product:

$$\Pr(\mathbf{q}, d) = \Pr(\mathbf{q} \mid d) \Pr(d) \quad (5)$$

where $\Pr(\mathbf{q} \mid d)$ represents the likelihood of $\mathbf{q}$ being generated by d, and $\Pr(d)$ the a-priori probability of d. In the following, no a-priori knowledge about the documents will be assumed, hence a uniform *a-priori* distribution is taken[2]. For what concerns the probability of $\mathbf{q}$ given d, an order-free multinomial (bag-of-word) model is assumed. Hence, assuming $\mathbf{q} = q_1, \ldots, q_n$, we have:

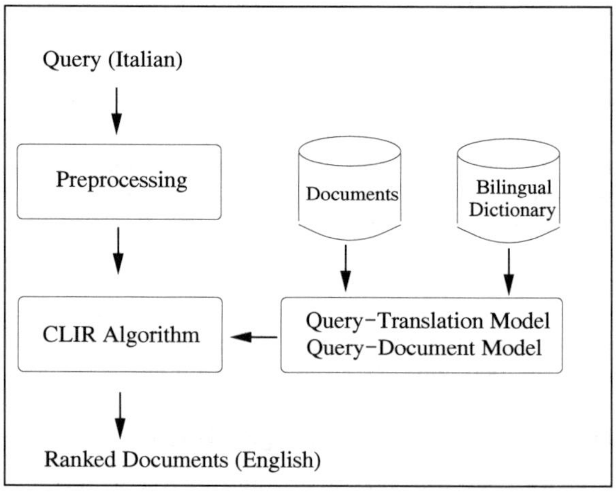

Figure 1: Statistical approach for CLIR.

$$\Pr(\mathbf{q} = q_1, \ldots, q_n \mid d) = \prod_{k=1}^{n} \Pr(q_k \mid d) \quad (6)$$

The probability of term q being generated by document d is estimated by a statistical LM. Previous work on IR [9, 11] have proposed to compute this probability by interpolating the relative frequency of q given d with the relative frequency of q over the whole collection. Moreover, interpolation weights are empirically estimated from the data. (See [19] for an extensive analysis of smoothing methods.)

This work combines the interpolation scheme with the smoothing method described in [17], which explicitly provides interpolation weights. More specifically, term frequencies of a document are smoothed linearly and the amount of probability assigned to never observed terms is assigned

[2]However, this model permits to apply any available prior distribution on documents.

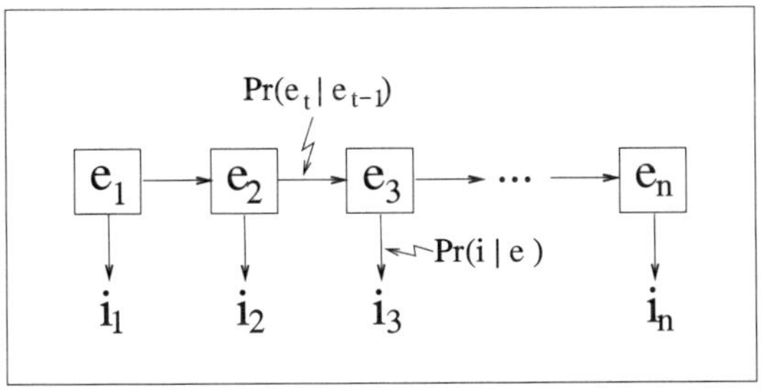

Figure 2: Dependency relations within the query-translation model.

proportionally to the size of the document vocabulary, i.e.:

$$\Pr(q \mid d) = \frac{N(d,q)}{N(d) + |\mathcal{V}(d)|} + \frac{|\mathcal{V}(d)|}{N(d) + |\mathcal{V}(d)|} \Pr(q) \qquad (7)$$

where $\Pr(q)$, the word probability over $\mathcal{D}$, is estimated by interpolating the smoothed relative frequency with the uniform distribution over the vocabulary $\mathcal{V}$ of $\mathcal{D}$:

$$\Pr(q) = \frac{N(q)}{N + |\mathcal{V}|} + \frac{|\mathcal{V}|}{N + |\mathcal{V}|}\frac{1}{|\mathcal{V}|} \qquad (8)$$

Of course, the resulting query-document model can be also applied to monolingual IR [2].

4. QUERY-TRANSLATION MODEL

The query-translation model computes the probability of any query-translation pair. This probability is modelled by an HMM [15] in which the observable variable is the Italian query $\mathbf{i}$, and the hidden variable is its English translation $\mathbf{e}$. According to the HMM, the joint probability of a pair $(\mathbf{i}, \mathbf{e})$ is decomposed as follows:

$$\Pr(\mathbf{i} = i_1, \ldots, i_n, \mathbf{e} = e_1, \ldots, e_n) =$$
$$\Pr(e_1)\Pr(i_1 \mid e_1) \prod_{k=2}^{n} \Pr(e_k \mid e_{k-1}) \Pr(i_k \mid e_k) \qquad (9)$$

Formula (9) puts in evidence two different conditional probabilities: the term translation probabilities $\Pr(i \mid e)$ and the target LM probabilities $\Pr(e \mid e')$. The role of these two probabilities can be appreciated in Figure 2, which shows the dependency relations between the terms in formula (9). Before considering at the way these probabilities are estimated, it is important to see how translations can be efficiently computed through the HMM.
Given a query-document model and a query $\mathbf{i}$, the most probable translation $\mathbf{e}^*$ can be computed through the well known Viterbi search algorithm (see [15]). Moreover, intermediate results of the Viterbi algorithm can be used by an A^* search algorithm [12] to efficiently compute the N most probable, or N-best, translations of $\mathbf{i}$. This procedure, which is a simplified version of the so called tree-trellis based algorithm [16], is described in the Appendix.

Probabilities $\Pr(i \mid e)$ are estimated from a bilingual dictionary as follows:

$$\Pr(i \mid e) = \frac{\delta(i,e)}{\sum_{i'} \delta(i',e)} \qquad (10)$$

where $\delta(i,e) = 1$ if the English term e is one of the translations of Italian term i and $\delta(i,e) = 0$ otherwise. In Section 6, it will be explained how out-of-dictionary words are processed.
Probabilities $\Pr(e \mid e')$ are estimated on the target document collection, through an order-free bigram LM, which tries to compensate for different word positions induced by the source and target languages. Let

$$\Pr(e \mid e') = \frac{\Pr(e,e')}{\sum_{e''} \Pr(e'',e')} \qquad (11)$$

where $\Pr(e,e')$ is the probability of e co-occurring with e', regardless of the order, within a text window of fixed size. Smoothing of this probability is performed through absolute discounting and interpolation as follows:

$$\Pr(e,e') = \max\left\{\frac{C(e,e') - \beta}{N}, 0\right\} + \beta \Pr(e)\Pr(e') \qquad (12)$$

where $C(e,e')$ is the number of co-occurrences appearing in the corpus, $\Pr(e)$ is estimated according to equation (8), and the absolute discounting term β is equal to the estimate proposed in [10]:

$$\beta = \frac{n_1}{n_1 + 2n_2} \qquad (13)$$

with n_k representing the number of term pairs occurring exactly k times in the corpus. Absolute discounting was chosen for its good performance and its suitability to the order-free case.

5. CLIR ALGORITHM

The CLIR algorithm is in charge of computing formula (4) and sorting documents according to the posterior probability (1). An algorithm is presented that relies on two approximations in order to limit the set of possible translations and documents to be taken into account.

The first approximation redefines the query-translation probability by limiting its support set to just the N-best translations of $\mathbf{i}$, indicated by $\mathcal{T}_N(\mathbf{i})$.

Approximation 1.

$$\Pr'(\mathbf{i},\mathbf{e}) = \begin{cases} \dfrac{\Pr(\mathbf{i},\mathbf{e})}{K_1(\mathbf{i})} & \text{if } \mathbf{e} \in \mathcal{T}_N(\mathbf{i}) \\ 0 & \text{otherwise} \end{cases} \qquad (14)$$

where $K_1(\mathbf{i})$ is a normalization term which can be disregarded in formula (1) for the sake of the document ordering, as it is constant with respect to the maximisation variable d.

The second approximation is to reduce the computational burden of the denominator in equation (4). Hence, the support set of the query-document model is limited to only documents which contain at least one term of the query. Given a translation $\mathbf{e}$, let $\mathcal{I}(\mathbf{e})$ indicate the set of documents containing terms of $\mathbf{e}$. This set is easy to compute when the collection is accessed through an inverted file index [4].

Approximation 2.

$$\Pr'(\mathbf{e}, d) = \begin{cases} \dfrac{\Pr(\mathbf{e}, d)}{K_2(\mathbf{e})} & \text{if } d \in \mathcal{I}(\mathbf{e}) \\ 0 & \text{otherwise} \end{cases} \quad (15)$$

where $K_2(\mathbf{e})$ is a normalization term that occurs both in the numerator and denominator of the fraction in (4), and can be therefore deleted. Thanks to this approximation, computation of the denominator in formula (4) can be performed by summing up the scores of just the documents accessed through the inverted file index.

Table 2: CLIR algorithm.

1.	Input $\mathbf{i}$
2.	Compute $\mathcal{T}_N(\mathbf{i})$ and scores $P[\mathbf{i}, \mathbf{e}]$
3.	For each $\mathbf{e} \in \mathcal{T}_N(\mathbf{i})$
4.	$N = 0$
5.	For each $d \in \mathcal{I}(\mathbf{e})$
6.	Compute $P[\mathbf{e}, d]$
7.	Update $N = N + P[\mathbf{e}, d]$
8.	For each $d \in \mathcal{I}(\mathbf{e})$
9.	Update $P[d] = P[d] + P[\mathbf{e}, d] * P[\mathbf{i}, \mathbf{e}]/N$
10.	Order documents according to $P[d]$

The CLIR algorithm applying the two approximations is shown in Table 2. Briefly, given an input query $\mathbf{i}$, the N-best translations $\mathcal{T}_N(\mathbf{i})$ and their probabilities $P[\mathbf{i}, \mathbf{e}]$ are computed first (cf. Appendix). Then, for each translation $\mathbf{e}$, the addenda in formula (4) are computed only for documents containing at least one term of $\mathbf{e}$. This requires one additional loop over the documents in order to compute the normalization term.

Let us denote by n the length of the query, by N the number of generated translations, by $\bar{\mathcal{E}}$ the average number of translations of a term, and by $\bar{\mathcal{I}}$ the average number of documents spanned by each entry of the inverted file index. Hence, the complexity of the algorithm can be estimated as follows:

- $\mathcal{O}(n\ \bar{\mathcal{E}}^2 + n\ N^2\ \bar{\mathcal{E}})$ for step 2 in the average case (see Appendix)
- $\mathcal{O}(n\ N\ \bar{\mathcal{I}})$ for steps 3-9 in the average case
- $\mathcal{O}(n\ \bar{\mathcal{E}}\ \bar{\mathcal{I}} \log(n\ \bar{\mathcal{E}}\ \bar{\mathcal{I}}))$ for step 10, in the worst case, i.e. N-best translations include all the available terms,

By the way, the number $\bar{\mathcal{I}}$ is somehow controlled by the stop-term removal phase applied during document indexing. Generally, terms occurring in many documents are not considered significant for IR and are removed from the index. For instance, in the performed experiments we had $\bar{\mathcal{I}} \approx 110$ with $|\mathcal{D}| = 110,282$, and $\bar{\mathcal{E}}$=1.84.

Remark. It is worth noticing that a simpler algorithm results in the 1-best translation case, see Table 3. In fact, in this condition it is possible to decouple the translation and retrieval phases, and to eliminate the normalization term in equation (4).

Table 3: CLIR algorithm in the 1-best case.

1.	Input $\mathbf{i}$
2.	Compute best translation $\mathbf{e}^*$
3.	For each $d \in \mathcal{I}(\mathbf{e}^*)$
4.	Compute $P[\mathbf{e}^*, d]$
5.	Order documents according to $P[\mathbf{e}^*, d]$

6. EXPERIMENTAL EVALUATION

Experimental evaluation of the CLIR model were performed on the Italian-to-English bilingual track data used in the CLEF 2000 (C0) and CLEF 2001 (C1) evaluations. The tracks consist of 33 and 47 topics, respectively, which are provided both in extended (Title+Description+Narrative) and synthetic (Title+Description) forms. The target collection consists of 110,282 newspaper articles from the *Los Angeles Times*. The number of relevant documents to be retrieved are 579 for C0 and 856 for C1.

Table 4: Statistics about the Italian to English bilingual tracks.

Track	Year	#Topics	#Relev. Docs
C0	2000	33	579
C1	2001	47	856

6.1 Preprocessing

Text preprocessing is applied on the target documents before indexing, and on the queries before retrieval. More specifically, the following preprocessing steps are carried out:

- *Tokenization* is performed on documents and queries to isolate words from punctuation marks, to recognize abbreviations and acronyms, correct possible word splits across lines, and discriminate between accents and quotation marks.
- *Base forms* are computed for Italian words by means of morphological analysis and POS tagging.
- *Stemming* is performed on English words by using the Porter's algorithm [4].
- *Stop-terms removal* is applied on the documents by removing terms with a low inverted document frequency [4].
- *Multi-word recognition* is applied for query-translation only. After translation, multi-words in the translated query are split into single words.
- *Proper names and numbers* in the query are recognized in order to improve coverage of the dictionary (see following subsection).
- *Out-of-dictionary terms* which have not been recognized as proper names or numbers are removed from the query.

6.2 Out-of-dictionary Words

The query-translation model relies on an Italian-English Collins dictionary of about 31K entries. On the average, each Italian entry is translated by the dictionary into 1.84 English words. The coverage of the dictionary with respect to the query base forms is about 89.7%, including numbers which are translated verbatim. Translation coverage was improved by applying proper name recognition on the Italian query and by forcing verbatim translation of proper names (with English version stemmed) not in the dictionary. Addition of this back-up list of proper names rises coverage to 94.6%. However, for these words there is no guarantee about the correctness of the translation. Finally, it is worth specifying that proper names and numbers are excluded from the computation of the N-best translations, but are just added to them afterwards.

6.3 Blind Relevance Feedback

After document ranking, Blind Relevance Feedback (BRF) can be applied. BRF is a well known technique that allows to improve retrieval performance. The basic idea is to perform retrieval in two steps. First, the documents matching the source query $\mathbf{q}$ are ranked, then the B best ranked documents are taken and the R most relevant terms in them are added to the query, and the retrieval phase is repeated. In the CLIR framework, R terms are added to each single translation of the N-best list and the retrieval algorithms is repeated once again.
In this work, new search terms are selected from the top B documents according to [7]:

$$r_w \frac{(r_w + 0.5)(N - N_w - B + r_w + 0.5)}{(N_w - r_w + 0.5)(B - r_w + 0.5)} \quad (16)$$

where r_w is the number of documents, among the B top documents, which contain term w. In all the performed experiments the values $B = 5$ and $R = 15$ were used [2].

6.4 Intra system experiments

A number of experiments were performed to investigate different settings of the proposed CLIR algorithm:

- N-best translation with $N = 1$, $N = 5$, and $N = 10$
- Query translation using a 2-gram LM vs. a 1-gram LM
- Retrieval with and without BRF

A first set of experiments was performed with the CLIR algorithm using 1-best, 5-best, and 10-best translations. For each condition, translations were generated by means of a 1-gram and a 2-gram LM. Results in terms of mean average precision (`mAvPr`) are reported in Table 5. By inspecting the table column-wise one can notice that 2-gram based translation performs significantly better than 1-gram based translation. As concerns the use of N-best translations, experiments indicate that using more than one translation slightly improves performance just for long topics (TDN).

Further experiments were carried out to evaluate the effect of BRF versus different N-best configurations, by using a 2-gram LM. Results of this set of experiments are reported in Table 6. On the average, higher relative improvements are observed with short topics (TD) especially with the 1-best modality, e.g. 13% on C0-1 (from .3859 to .4379). On the opposite, with long topics (TDN) the 5-best modality provided the highest improvements, e.g. 7.6% on C0-1 (from .4400 to .4736). These configurations also achieved the best absolute `mAvPr` (see figures in bold).

Table 5: Mean average precision results with different N-best and n-gram settings for query translation.

Task	Topics	N-best	1-gram	2-gram
C0	TDN	1-best	.3268	.3694
C0	TDN	5-best	.3274	.3734
C0	TDN	10-best	.3237	.3757
C0	TD	1-best	.2884	.3033
C0	TD	5-best	.2733	.2999
C0	TD	10-best	.2755	.3026
C1	TDN	1-best	.4375	.4811
C1	TDN	5-best	.4470	.4867
C1	TDN	10-best	.4502	.4849
C1	TD	1-best	.3813	.4440
C1	TD	5-best	.3903	.4405
C1	TD	10-best	.3961	.4366
C0-1	TDN	1-best	.3989	.4350
C0-1	TDN	5-best	.3977	.4400
C0-1	TDN	10-best	.3980	.4399
C0-1	TD	1-best	.3430	.3859
C0-1	TD	5-best	.3420	.3825
C0-1	TD	10-best	.3464	.3795

Table 6: Mean average precision results without/with BRF by using 2-gram based translations.

	Topics	1-best	+brf	5-best	+brf	10-best	+brf
C0	TDN	.3694	.3948	.3734	**.4109**	.3757	.4061
C0	TD	.3033	**.3327**	.2999	3189	.3026	.3205
C1	TDN	.4811	.5080	.4867	**.5177**	.4849	.5117
C1	TD	.4440	**.5117**	.4405	.5012	.4366	.4943
C0-1	TDN	.4350	.4613	.4400	**.4736**	.4399	.4682
C0-1	TD	.3859	**.4379**	.3825	.4260	.3795	.4226

6.5 Inter system experiments

Some results are now given which can help in evaluating the proposed method versus other approaches.

First comparative experiments only focused on the query-translation model. Hence, CLIR experiments were performed with different translations: i.e. computed by the Viterbi search algorithm, by a commercial text translation system, or by a human. In the second case, the Babelfish translation service, powered by Systran, was used which is available on the Internet[3]. In the third case, English versions of the queries as provided by CLEF were used. As Babelfish is supposed to works with fluent text, the preprocessing and

[3]http://world.altavista.com

Table 7: Mean average precision results with different query translations.

	Topics	Translation		+BRF
C0-1	TDN	Babelfish	.4034	.4409
C0-1	TDN	1-best	.4350	.4613
C0-1	TDN	Manual	.5202	.5585
C0-1	TD	Babelfish	.3418	.3908
C0-1	TD	1-best	.3859	.4379
C0-1	TD	Manual	.4765	.5290

Table 8: CLIR comparison with best performing systems at CLEF.

	Topics	System	Language	mAvPr
C0	TDN	APL/JHU	French	.4070
	TDN	5-best	Italian	.4109
C1	TD	U. Exeter	French	.4783
	TD	1-best	Italian	.5117

translation steps were inverted in the second case.

Given all the translations, the CLIR algorithm for the 1-best case was applied. Results for the whole topics (C0-1) are reported in Table 7 and can be summarized as follows. The statistical query-translation method outperforms the Babelfish translation system, especially on the shorter queries. By applying the paired mean test [6], significant differences in `mAvPr` were found, at level $\alpha = 0.001$, between the manual translation condition and, respectively, the Babelfish and 1-best translation conditions; at level $\alpha = 0.16$, between the Babelfish and 1-best conditions, but only for TD queries. On TDN queries, a significant difference, at level $\alpha = 0.17$, results when the 5-best CLIR method (`mAvPr` .4736, cf. Table 6) is compared against the 1-best method using Babelfish translations (`mAvPr` .4409).

By looking at the degradation in `mAvPr`, when moving from TDN to TD topics (see Table 7), it results that the 1-best translations give a relative decrease of 5.1%, which is close to the 5.3% relative decrease of the manual translations, and much better than the 11.4% relative decrease measured with the Babelfish translations.

Finally, a comparison with the best performing systems at CLEF 2000 and 2001 is reported in Table 8. For obvious reasons this comparison cannot be considered very informative, anyway it can be indicative about the achieved level of performance. It can be seen that the proposed CLIR model favourably compares with competitors on both evaluation sets, even if score differences are not statistically significant. Interestingly, both systems obtained best results by using French as source language [4].

7. DISCUSSION

This section tries to point out similarities and differences of the presented approach with respect to other statistical IR models presented in the literature.

For what concerns the query-document model, this is often referred to as language model approach and has been already applied for monolingual IR (see the extensive review in [19]) and CLIR [5]. A major difference with previous work is in the applied linear smoothing method, which uses for the estimation of the zero-frequency event probability simple and reliable statistics, i.e. the document size and the number of different words contained in it.

More significant differences can be observed between the query-translation model and other apparently similar approaches in the literature. In particular, the models proposed in [5, 18, 1] are considered.

The CLIR model described in [5] is based on the following decomposition:

$$\Pr(\mathbf{i} \mid d) \approx \prod_{k=1}^{n} \Pr(i_k \mid d)$$

$$= \prod_{k=1}^{n} \sum_{e_k} \Pr(i_k, e_k \mid d) \quad (17)$$

$$\approx \prod_{k=1}^{n} \sum_{e_k} \Pr(i_k \mid e_k) \Pr(e_k \mid d) \quad (18)$$

which makes use of two assumptions (or approximations): (i) terms of $\mathbf{i}$ are independent given d (eq. (17)); (ii) the probability of term i, given e and d only depends on e (eq. (18)). The most relevant difference with the model described by equation (4) is in the independence assumption between the query terms. The comparison with formula (4) becomes more clear after applying some term reordering.

$$(18) = \sum_{\mathbf{e}} \prod_{k=1}^{n} \Pr(i_k \mid e_k) \Pr(e_k \mid d) \quad (19)$$

$$\approx \sum_{\mathbf{e}} \Pr(\mathbf{i} \mid \mathbf{e}) \Pr(\mathbf{e} \mid d) \quad (20)$$

$$= \sum_{\mathbf{e}} \Pr(\mathbf{i}, \mathbf{e}, d) \quad (21)$$

Hence, the model by [5] can be derived from (4) by using a different decomposition of probability $\Pr(\mathbf{i}, \mathbf{e}, d)$ and by assuming a simpler translation model, i.e. almost equivalent to the 1-gram translation LM.

In [18], CLIR is performed with the following model:

$$\Pr(\mathbf{i} \mid d) \approx \prod_{k=1}^{n} \left[a \Pr(i_k) + (1-a) \sum_{e} \Pr(i_k e \mid d) \right] \quad (22)$$

which assumes independence among the query terms, and interpolates the $\Pr(i_k e \mid d)$, marginalized over possible translations e of i_k, with the probability of i_k in the source language. This approach uses an even more different decomposition of $\Pr(\mathbf{i} \mid d)$, and does not use Markovian assumptions in the translation process.

Finally, our query-translation model also shows similarities with the statistical machine translation models presented in [3] and applied to IR by [1]. In particular, it can be seen as a very simplification of the basic Model IBM-1, in which the alignment is taken equal to the identity function.

8. CONCLUSION

This work presented a novel statistical approach for cross-language information retrieval. Its most prominent features can be summarized as follows:

[4]In the bilingual track at CLEF, participants were, in fact, left free to choose the source language among a list of European languages.

- the posterior probability of documents is expressed as the expectation, over possible translations of the input query, of the probability of the document itself and a query translation;
- query translations are computed by an hidden Markov model, which couples a translation lexicon with a bigram language model in the target language;
- training of the query-translation model just needs a bilingual lexicon and the target document collection;
- computation of the posterior probability is efficiently carried out by limiting the expectation to the N-best translations.

An experimental evaluation of the CLIR model was carried out on the bilingual track data used in the CLEF 2000 and 2001 evaluations. Results show that the method is effective and improves over several alternative systems.

9. ACKNOWLEDGEMENTS

The authors would like to thank their colleagues at ITC-irst Bernardo Magnini and Emanuele Pianta for putting at disposal the electronic Italian-English dictionary. This work was partially funded by the *Fondo Unico della Provincia di Trento*, under the project WebFAQ.

10. REFERENCES

[1] A. Berger and J. D. Lafferty. Information retrieval as statistical translation. In *Proceedings of the 22nd Annual International ACM SIGIR Conference on Research and Development in Information Retrieval*, pages 222–229, 1999.

[2] N. Bertoldi and M. Federico. ITC-irst at CLEF 2000: Italian monolingual track. In C. Peters, editor, *Cross-Language Information Retrieval and Evaluation*, volume 2069 of *Lecture Notes in Computer Science*, pages 261–272, Heidelberg, Germany, 2001. Springer Verlag.

[3] P. F. Brown, V. S. A. Della Pietra, V. J. Della Pietra, and R. L. Mercer. The mathematics of statistical machine translation: Parameter estimation. *Computational Linguistics*, 19(2):263–312, 1993.

[4] W. B. Frakes and R. Baeza-Yates, editors. *Information Retrieval: Data Structures and Algorithms*. Prentice Hall, Englewood Cliffs, NJ, 1992.

[5] D. Hiemstra and F. de Jong. Disambiguation strategies for cross-language information retrieval. In *Proceedings of the 3rd European Conference on Research and Advanced Technology for Digital Libraries*, pages 274–293, 1999.

[6] D. Hull. Using statistical testing in the evaluation of retrieval experiments. In *Proceedings of the 16th Annual International ACM SIGIR Conference on Research and Development in Information Retrieval*, 1993.

[7] S. Johnson, P. Jourlin, K. S. Jones, and P. Woodland. Spoken document retrieval for TREC-8 at Cambridge University. In *Proceedings of the 8th Text REtrieval Conference*, Gaithersburg, MD, 1999.

[8] W. Kraaij, R. Pohlmann, and D. Hiemstra. Twenty-One at TREC-8: using Language Technology for Information Retrieval. In *Proceedings of the 8th Text Retrieval Conference TREC-8*, pages 285–300, 2000.

[9] D. R. H. Miller, T. Leek, and R. M. Schwartz. BBN at TREC-7: Using hidden Markov models for information retrieval. In *Proceedings of the 7th Text REtrieval Conference*, pages 133–142, Gaithersburg, MD, 1998.

[10] H. Ney, U. Essen, and R. Kneser. On structuring probabilistic dependences in stochastic language modelling. *Computer Speech and Language*, 8:1–38, 1994.

[11] K. Ng. A maximum likelihood ratio information retrieval model. In *Proceedings of the 8th Text REtrieval Conference*, Gaithersburg, MD, 1999.

[12] N. J. Nilsson. *Principles of Artificial Intelligence.* Springer Verlag, Berlin, Germany, 1982.

[13] C. Peters, editor. *Cross-Language Information Retrieval and Evaluation. Workshop of CLEF 2000, Lisbon, Portugal, Sept. 2000.* Springer, Berlin, Germany, 2001.

[14] C. Peters, editor. *Working notes for the CLEF 2001 Workshop.* Darmstatd, Germany, 2001.

[15] L. R. Rabiner. A tutorial on hidden Markov models and selected applications in speech recognition. In A. Weibel and K. Lee, editors, *Readings in Speech Recognition*, pages 267–296. Morgan Kaufmann, Los Altos, CA, 1990.

[16] F. K. Soong and E. F. Huang. A tree-trellis based fast search for finding the n-best sentence hypotheses in continuous speech recognition. In *Proceedings of the IEEE International Conference on Acoustics, Speech and Signal Processing*, volume 1, pages 705–708, Toronto, Canada, 1991.

[17] I. H. Witten and T. C. Bell. The zero-frequency problem: Estimating the probabilities of novel events in adaptive text compression. *IEEE Trans. Inform. Theory*, IT-37(4):1085–1094, 1991.

[18] J. Xu, R. Weischedel, and C. Nguyen. Evaluating a probabilistic model for cross-lingual information retrieval. In *Proceedings of the 24h Annual International ACM SIGIR Conference on Research and Development in Information Retrieval*, pages 105–110, 2001.

[19] C. Zhai and J. Lafferty. A study of smoothing methods for language models applied to ad hoc information retrieval. In *Proceedings of the 24th Annual International ACM SIGIR Conference on Research and Development in Information Retrieval*, pages 334–342, 2001.

APPENDIX
N-BEST TRANSLATION ALGORITHM

Generation of N-best translations with the proposed model can be efficiently performed with a simplified version of the tree-trellis based search algorithm by [16]. Briefly, the algorithm is based on two steps: a Viterbi search (cf. [15]) proceeding forward along the source query, and an A^* search algorithm [12] proceeding backward.

The Viterbi search algorithm, see Table 9, computes the optimal translation of an input query $\mathbf{i} = i_1, \ldots, i_n$. The algorithm uses a dynamic programming decomposition to compute, for each position t, along $\mathbf{i}$, and possible translation e of i_t, the best translation up to t and ending in e. This is carried out by finding the optimal continuation of all (optimal) translations computed at time $t-1$ (step 6). At each stage t, a backward link to the best incoming translation is also set (step 7) Finally, the optimal complete translation is obtained by following the backward chain starting from to the best translation at time n. It is easy to see that the complexity of this algorithm is, in the average case, $\mathcal{O}(n\bar{\mathcal{E}}^2)$, assuming $\bar{\mathcal{E}}$ is the average number of translations for a term.

The complete tree-trellis algorithm is shown in Table 10.

After a call to the Viterbi search, an A^* search is performed backward along the source query $\mathbf{i}$. At each iteration (step 8), the algorithm pops and examines the best partial theory (translation) from the stack *OpenSet*. If the translation covers the whole input query, then the reverted word sequence and its probability are added to the N-best list (steps 9-11). Otherwise, all possible one-word expansions of it are computed. Scores are assigned to each expansion by combining the backward score g, computed by the translation model from the end to the current position of $\mathbf{i}$, and the forward score h computed by the Viterbi search from the initial to the current position of $\mathbf{i}$. Each theory expansion is then inserted into *OpenSet* so that it results ordered according to $g \cdot h$.

The complexity of the A^* search algorithm is determined by the number of iterations times the cost of theory insertions (steps 6 and 16) performed at each step. As a theory at position k in the stack cannot expand into theories with a better score, each insertion operation just involves examination of the top N positions in *OpenSet*. Hence, at each iteration, the complexity of the insertion operations is $\mathcal{O}(\bar{\mathcal{E}}N)$. The number of iterations is n to find the best translation and $O(n)$ to find the second best, third best, etc. Hence, the total complexity of the A^* search is $\mathcal{O}(n\ N^2\ \bar{\mathcal{E}})$.

Table 9: Viterbi search algorithm.

1.	Input $\mathbf{i} = i_1, \ldots, i_n$
2.	Initialize for all $e \in \mathcal{E}(i_1)$ $Q[1,e] = P[i_1 \mid e]P[e]$
3.	Initialize for all $e \in \mathcal{E}(i_1)$ $B[1,e] = \epsilon$
4.	For $t = 1, \ldots, n-1$
5.	for all $e \in \mathcal{E}(i_{t+1})$
6.	$Q[t+1,e] = P[i_{t+1} \mid e] \max_{e' \in \mathcal{E}(i_t)} Q[t,e']P[e \mid e']$
7.	$B[t+1,e] = \arg\max_{e' \in \mathcal{E}(i_t)} Q[t,e']P[e \mid e']$
8.	Backtrack solution $\mathbf{e}^*$:
9.	$e_n^* = \arg\max_{e \in \mathcal{E}(i_n)} Q[n,e]$
10.	$e_t^* = B[e_{t+1}^*]$ for $t = n-1, n-2, \ldots, 1$

Table 10: Tree-trellis algorithm.

1.	Perform Viterbi algorithm steps 1-7
2.	Initialize OpenSet=[],BestList=[], NB=0
3.	for all $e \in \mathcal{E}(i_n)$
4.	path=[e]; time=n
5.	h=$Q[n,e]$; g=1
6.	insert (path,time,g,h) in OpenSet
7.	while OpenSet is not empty and $NB < N$
8.	$([e_n, \ldots, e_t], t, h, g)$ = pop OpenSet
9.	if $t = 1$
10.	append $(\mathbf{e} = [e_1, \ldots, e_n], P[\mathbf{i}, \mathbf{e}] = g \cdot h)$ to BestList
11.	$NB = NB + 1$
12.	else
13.	for all $e \in \mathcal{E}(i_{t-1})$
14.	path=$[e_n, \ldots, e_t, e]$; time=$t-1$
15.	$h = Q[t-1,e]$; $g' = g \cdot P[e_t \mid e]P[i_{t-1} \mid e])$
16.	insert (path,time,h,g') in OpenSet

Cross-Lingual Relevance Models

Victor Lavrenko, Martin Choquette and W. Bruce Croft
Center for Intelligent Information Retrieval
Department of Computer Science
University of Massachusetts, Amherst, MA 01003
{lavrenko,choquett,croft}@cs.umass.edu

ABSTRACT

We propose a formal model of Cross-Language Information Retrieval that does not rely on either query translation or document translation. Our approach leverages recent advances in language modeling to directly estimate an accurate topic model in the target language, starting with a query in the source language. The model integrates popular techniques of disambiguation and query expansion in a unified formal framework. We describe how the topic model can be estimated with either a parallel corpus or a dictionary. We test the framework by constructing Chinese topic models from English queries and using them in the CLIR task of TREC9. The model achieves performance around 95% of the strong mono-lingual baseline in terms of average precision. In initial precision, our model outperforms the mono-lingual baseline by 20%. The main contribution of this work is the unified formal model which integrates techniques that are essential for effective Cross-Language Retrieval.

Categories and Subject Descriptors

H.3.3 [**Information storage and Retrieval**]: Information Search and Retrieval—*Retrieval Models*

General Terms

Experimentation

Keywords

Cross-Language Information Retrieval, Language Models

1. INTRODUCTION

The task of Cross-Language Information Retrieval (CLIR) addresses a situation when a query is posed in one language but the system is expected to return the documents written in another language. The scenario could have been considered unlikely a mere decade ago, but the explosive growth of the World Wide Web has blurred national boundaries to the point where a casual user may find an interest in retrieving documents in a foreign language. Once a user obtains a set of relevant documents in a foreign language, she can use automatic machine translation software to get a sense of the content. What remains is the problem of retrieving that set of documents, starting with a query in the user's native language.

In recent years, the problem of Cross-Language Retrieval has enjoyed significant interest from the research community, and a number of techniques were proposed to solve the problem [2, 9, 19]. Most of these techniques center around a common idea: they attempt to *translate* the query from the user's language to the language of the documents. In most cases, the translation is done in a word-by-word fashion, using a dictionary, a machine translation system, or a similar resource. Typically, any given word may have multiple possible translations, so significant effort has been devoted to disambiguating the resulting translations, either through the use of context [19], statistical co-occurrence [3, 19], triangulated translation [8], or a number of similar techniques. In addition, researchers found that in many cases it is helpful to include words that are not direct translations of any query word, but are closely related to the meaning of the query. This observation led to the common use of heuristic *query expansion* techniques [2, 19].

In this paper, we propose a model of Cross-Language Retrieval that does not rely on a word-by-word translation of the query. Instead, we attempt to construct an accurate relevance model in the target language, and use that model to rank the documents in the collection. Following the work of Lavrenko and Croft [12], we use the term **relevance model** to refer to a probability distribution, which specifies how often we expect to see any given word in the documents relevant to the query. To estimate relevance models in a cross-lingual setting we extend the methods proposed by [12], and show how the estimation can be done with either a parallel corpus or a dictionary. The main contribution of this work is the unified formal framework for integrating techniques that are essential for effective Cross-Language Retrieval, such as query expansion for dealing with synonymy, and translation disambiguation for handling polysemy.

The remainder of the paper is structured as follows. Section 2 briefly surveys recent developments in the fields of Cross-Language Retrieval and statistical Language Modeling. Section 3 describes how relevance models can be estimated in a cross-lingual environment, and how we can use them for retrieving documents. Section 4 addresses specific implementation issues that arose in working with Chinese. In Section 5 we test the performance of our model on the cross-language retrieval task of TREC9, and compare our performance with results reported by other researchers.

2. RELATED WORK

Previous applications of language modeling to cross-language retrieval have been reported by Hiemstra and de Jong [9] and Xu *et al.* [18, 19]. Although the model proposed by Berger and Lafferty [4] applies to the "translation" of a document into a query in a monolingual environment, it can readily accommodate a bilingual environment. The three approaches above all make use of translation probabilities attached to pairs of words. The pairs of words and their corresponding probabilities are often obtained from a bilingual dictionary by assigning the same probability to all the translations of a word. When a parallel corpus or a pseudo-parallel corpus (where parallel documents are produced by an MT system) is available, the required translations and probabilities can be obtained by applying Brown *et al.*'s approach to machine translation [5] (or some related technique [10]). Xu *et al.* [18] showed that combining statistics from various lexical resources can help correct problems of coverage and lead to significant improvements.

When no parallel corpus is available, our model uses the same estimation techniques as the other language modeling approaches. Unlike those approaches, however, our model does not rely on word-by-word translation when a comparable corpus or, *a fortiori*, a parallel corpus is available. [1] In such a case, our approach is closer in spirit to that of Sheridan and Ballerini [15] where the retrieval process consists of two retrieval steps. First, the best matching documents in the source language are retrieved. A query is then built by selecting words occurring frequently in the documents in the target language that are comparable to the ones retrieved. Finally, the new query is used to retrieve documents in the target language. Our approach does not select new query terms though. Instead, it uses the set of comparable documents to estimate, for each word in the target vocabulary, the probability of observing the word in the set of relevant documents.

The use of additional disambiguation techniques such as those based on phrases and co-occurrence measures (e.g., mutual information) still have to be explored within our framework. These techniques have been put to good use in approaches that do not rely on language models (e.g., [3, 7]).

3. MATHEMATICAL FRAMEWORK

Let $Q = e_1 \dots e_k$ be the query in the source language and let R_Q be the set of target documents that are relevant to that query. Lavrenko and Croft [12] suggest that effective ranking of target documents could be achieved if we had a way of estimating the *relevance model* of Q, i.e. the set of probabilities $P(w|R_Q)$ for every word w in the target vocabulary. $P(w|R_Q)$ denotes the probability that a word sampled at random from a relevant document would be the word w. If we knew what documents comprised R_Q, estimation of these probabilities would be straightforward, but in a typical retrieval environment we are not given any examples of relevant documents. Lavrenko and Croft [12] argue that in the absence of training data, a reasonable way to approximate $P(w|R_Q)$ is by a joint probability of observing the word w together with query words $e_1 \dots e_k$:

$$P(w|R_Q) \approx P(w|Q) = \frac{P(w, e_1 \dots e_k)}{P(e_1 \dots e_k)} \quad (1)$$

3.1 Mono-lingual estimation

Lavrenko and Croft [12] describe two methods for estimating the joint probability $P(w, e_1 \dots e_k)$ for the mono-lingual case, where w and $e_1 \dots e_k$ are words from the same vocabulary. Both methods assume there exists a set $\mathcal{M}$ of underlying source distributions from which w and $e_1 \dots e_k$ could have been sampled. The two methods differ in the kinds of independence assumptions they make. In this paper we will consider only *Method 1* because of its relative simplicity, and its decomposability, which will be leveraged in section 4.1. *Method 1* assumes w and $e_1 \dots e_k$ to be mutually independent once we pick a source distribution from $\mathcal{M}$, leading to the following estimate:

$$P(w, e_1 \dots e_k) = \sum_{M \in \mathcal{M}} P(M) \left(P(w|M) \prod_{i=1}^{k} P(e_i|M) \right) \quad (2)$$

Here $P(M)$ denotes some prior distribution over the set $\mathcal{M}$ (usually taken to be uniform), while $P(w|M)$ specifies the probability of observing w if we sampled a random word from M (and similarly for $P(e_i|M)$). We can take the universe $\mathcal{M}$ to be the set of documents in the database, and assume that w and all e_i are identically distributed with probabilities estimated using a simple smoothing of the relative frequency:

$$P(w|M_D) = \lambda \left(\frac{tf_{w,D}}{\sum_v tf_{v,D}} \right) + (1 - \lambda) P(w) \quad (3)$$

Here λ is a tunable parameter which determines the degree of smoothing. $tf_{w,D}$ is the number of times the word w occurs in document D. $P(w)$ is the background probability of observing the word w, obtained from a large corpus. Equation (3) is used to estimate $P(e_i|M_D)$ in the same way as $P(w|M_D)$.

3.2 Cross-lingual estimation

In the remainder of this section we describe how to extend the estimation to the cross-lingual case, when, for example, w is a Chinese word, and $e_1 \dots e_k$ are English words. In this case we obviously cannot assume that w and e_i are identically distributed. We discuss two estimation strategies, one based on a parallel corpus of documents, and one based on a bilingual lexicon.

3.2.1 Estimation with a parallel corpus

Suppose we have at our disposal a parallel corpus, a set of document pairs $\{E, C\}$, where E is an English document, and C is a Chinese document discussing the same topic. We let $\mathcal{M}$ be the set of corresponding distribution pairs

[1] Generally, comparable corpora are sets of topically related documents written in different languages. We use a more restricted definition, which mandates links between topically-related documents. Linked documents may not be exact translations of each other.

$\{M_E, M_C\}$, and estimate the joint probability of observing together w and $e_1 \dots e_k$ as:

$$P(w, e_1 \dots e_k) = \sum_{\{M_E, M_C\} \in \mathcal{M}} P(\{M_E, M_C\}) \left(P(w|M_C) \prod_{i=1}^{k} P(e_i|M_E) \right) \quad (4)$$

Here $P(\{M_E, M_C\})$ can be kept uniform, and $P(w|M_C)$ and $P(e_i|M_E)$ are calculated according to equation (3), but each in its own language.

3.2.2 *Estimation with a bilingual lexicon*

If no parallel corpus is available, it is still possible to estimate the joint probability $P(w, e_1 \dots e_k)$ if we have a statistical lexicon, which gives the translation probability $P(e_i|w)$ for every English word e_i and every Chinese word w. Note that any bilingual dictionary can be turned into a statistical lexicon by simply assigning uniform translation probabilities to all English translations of a given Chinese word. While the quality of this lexicon may be inferior, it will still serve the purpose. In this case we let $\mathcal{M}$ be the set of documents in Chinese. $P(w|M_C)$ can be computed directly from equation (3). In order to compute $P(e_i|M_C)$ for an English word e_i in a Chinese document C, we can use the translation model, advocated by Berger and Lafferty [4] and recently used in cross-lingual setting by [9, 19]. According to [19]:

$$P(e_i|M_C) = (1 - \lambda)P(e_i) + \lambda \sum_{v} P(e_i|v) P_{ml}(v|M_C) \quad (5)$$

Here the summation goes over all the Chinese words v in the vocabulary, $P(e_i|v)$ is the translation probability from the statistical lexicon, and $P_{ml}(v|M_C)$ is simply the number of times v occurs in C, divided by the length of C. $P(e_i)$ is the background probability of e_i, computed over a large corpus.

3.3 Ranking with a Relevance Model

In the previous section we proposed a technique for estimating a Chinese relevance model, starting with an English query. What remains is to specify a document ranking method, which will allow us to use the constructed relevance model to retrieve Chinese documents. Lavrenko and Croft [12] advocate using the Probability Ranking Principle [14], where documents are ranked by the probability ratio: $P(D|R)/P(D|N)$. In our experiments we found that a more stable metric is the relative entropy (also known as Kullback-Leibler divergence), suggested by Lafferty and Zhai in [11]. They formulate the retrieval problem as that of a risk minimization, and provide justification for using relative entropy as a risk metric between two distributions. Lafferty and Zhai [11] used KL divergence with their own technique for estimating query (relevance) models, which is Markov chains on inverted indices. We found that relative entropy works well with estimation suggested by Lavrenko and Croft [12], as well as with our extension of that work. The relative entropy between a relevance model R and a document model D is defined as:

$$KL(R||D) = \sum_{w} P(w|R) \log \frac{P(w|R)}{P(w|D)} \quad (6)$$

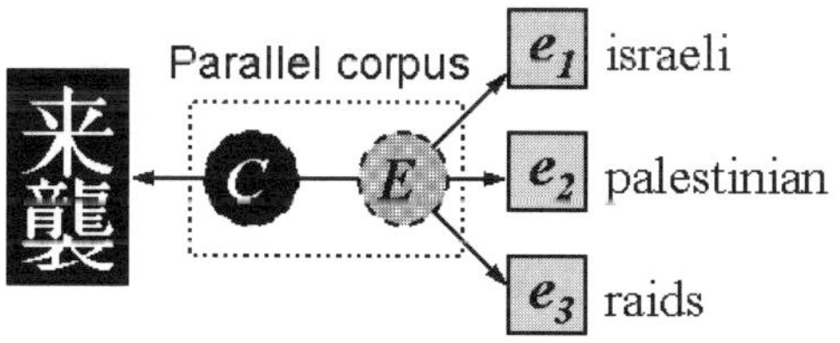

Figure 1: Graphical representation of cross-lingual relevance models. The model consists of a set of paired Chinese / English distributions. English queries are random samples from some English distribution from the paired set. Relevant Chinese documents are random samples from the corresponding Chinese distribution. Paired distributions could be estimated from a parallel corpus.

Documents are ranked in the order of increasing divergence, i.e. documents that have a smaller divergence with the Relevance Model are considered more relevant. In equation (6) $P(w|R)$ is computed from equation (1), as described above. $P(w|D)$ is calculated according to equation 3.

3.4 A Brief Summary of the Model

In this section we outlined a formal method for constructing a topic model in the target language, starting with a query in the source language. We also suggested using KL divergence with the topic model as a document ranking function. Massive query expansion is an integral part of the technique, since we compute the probability $P(w|R)$ for *every* word in the target language. Translation disambiguation is achieved automatically, because we compute co-occurrence (joint probability) between any word w and all the query words. Figure 1 shows a graphical representation of the underlying generative model.

4. IMPLEMENTATION

In the previous section we introduced cross-lingual relevance models, described how they can be estimated using either a parallel corpus or a bilingual lexicon, and described how the models could be used for retrieval purposes. In this section we describe how the system was implemented in practice, as well as specific processing steps that were performed on each language, and the resources that were used.

4.1 Making the Model Tractable

As specified, our model of estimation involves computing equation (2) or equation (4) over every document (or document pair) in the dataset. That computation has to be repeated for every word w in the Chinese vocabulary, which makes the estimation extremely expensive. In reality, it is possible to re-write equations (1) and (2) in a form that makes estimation feasible. If we expand the probability of the query as $P(e_1 \dots e_k) = \sum_w P(w, e_1 \dots e_k)$, and substitute equation (2) for the joint probability $P(w, e_1 \dots e_k)$, it becomes possible to estimate the probability of observing w in the set of relevant documents R_Q as:

$$P(w|R_Q) = \sum_{M \in \mathcal{M}} P(w|M) P(M|e_1 \dots e_k) \quad (7)$$

	LDC	CETA	HK News	Combined
English terms	86,000	35,000	21,000	104,997
Chinese terms	137,000	202,000	75,000	305,103

Table 1: Composition of the BBN bilingual lexicon

	HK News	TDT	HK News + TDT
Document pairs	18,147	46,692	64,839
English terms	28,806	67,542	83,152
Chinese terms	49,218	111,547	132,453

Table 2: Composition of the parallel corpus used in our experiments.

When expressed like this, it becomes obvious that a relevance model (under estimation method 1) is a linear mixture of distributions from $\mathcal{M}$, where each distribution M is "weighted" by its posterior probability of generating the query: $P(M|e_1 \dots e_k)$. In our model, the posterior probability is expressed as:

$$P(M|e_1 \dots e_k) = \frac{P(M)\prod_i P(e_i|M)}{\sum_M P(M)\prod_i P(e_i|M)} \quad (8)$$

In practice, because of the product in the numerator, this posterior has near-zero values for all but a few models M in a given collection $\mathcal{M}$. These models are precisely the models that rank highest when the query $e_1 \dots e_k$ is issued against the collection $\mathcal{M}$. Therefore, instead of computing equation (2) over the entire collection, we can compute equation (7) over some number n of top-ranked models retrieved by $e_1 \dots e_k$.

Expressing the relevance model in terms of equation (7) has another advantage. We could relax the strict probabilistic interpretation of the posterior $P(M|e_1 \dots e_k)$ and substitute any heuristic estimate, as long as it is non-negative and sums to 1. In this way, relevance models could be constructed from any ranked list of documents.

4.2 Resources

All of our experiments were performed on the dataset used in the TREC9 cross-lingual evaluation. The dataset consists of 127,938 Chinese documents, totaling around 100 million characters. We used the official set of 25 queries. We used two query representations: *short* queries used only the title field, while *long* queries used title, description and narrative fields.

Experiments involving a bilingual dictionary used the statistical lexicon created by Xu et.al [19]. The lexicon was assembled from three parts: the LDC dictionary, the CETA dictionary, and the statistical dictionary, learned from the Hong-Kong News corpus by applying the GIZA machine translation toolkit. Table 1 provides a summary of the dictionary components.

In the experiments that made use of the parallel corpus, we used the Hong-Kong News parallel dataset, which contains 18,147 news stories in English and Chinese. Because it is so small, the Hong-Kong parallel corpus has a significant word coverage problem. In order to alleviate the problem, we augmented the corpus with the TDT2 and TDT3 [?] pseudo-parallel datasets. These corpora contain 46,692 Chinese news stories along with their SYSTRAN translations into English. Since the documents are translated by software, we do not expect the quality of the TDT corpus to be as high as Hong-Kong News. We discuss the impact of adding the TDT corpus in section 5. The composition of the parallel corpus is detailed in Table 2.

4.3 English processing

The English portions of the dataset were pre-processed as follows. Both the documents and the queries were tokenized on whitespace and punctuation. Tokens with fewer than two characters were discarded. A total of 400 stopwords from the InQuery [1] stoplist were removed. We used the *kstem* stemmer, developed by Krovetz, to normalize the word forms in all documents and queries. As an exception, we used the *Porter* stemmer [13] on experiments that used the bilingual dictionary, due to the fact that the BBN statistical lexicon [19] was Porter-stemmed. No other form of processing was used on either the queries or the documents.

4.4 Chinese processing

The pre-processing performed on the Chinese part of the corpus was very crude, due to our limited knowledge of the language. The entire dataset, along with the Chinese queries was converted into the simplified encoding (GB). We carried out separate experiments with three forms of tokenization: (i) single Chinese characters (unigrams), (ii) half-overlapping adjacent pairs of Chinese characters (bigrams), and (iii) Chinese "words", obtained by running a simple dictionary-based segmenter, developed by F. F. Feng at the University of Massachusetts. In section 5 we report separate figures for all three forms of tokenization, as well as a linear combination of them. We did not remove any stopwords, or any punctuation characters from either Chinese documents or queries. This results in some spurious matches and also in these characters figuring prominently in the relevance models we constructed.

4.5 Example

Figure 2 provides an example of the relevance model estimated from query number 58: *"environmental protection laws"*. We show 20 tokens with highest probability under the model. It is evident that many stopwords and punctuation characters are assigned high probabilities. This is not surprising, since these characters were not removed during pre-processing, and we naturally expect these characters to occur frequently in the documents that discuss any topic. However, the model also assigns high probabilities to words that one would consider highly relevant to the topic of environmental protection.

5. EXPERIMENTAL RESULTS

In this section we carry out an evaluation of the proposed model of cross-language retrieval on the TREC9 dataset. We compare the performance of the following models:

1. **Mono-lingual baseline.** We use the basic language modeling system, which was reported as a baseline in a number of recent publications [19, 17]. The Chinese documents D are ranked according to the probability that a Chinese query $c_1 \dots c_k$ was generated from the document model M_D. Word probabilities are estimated according to equation (3).
2. **Mono-lingual Relevance Model.** This system is included as an alternative mono-lingual baseline, and

Q = "environmental protection laws" 环境保护法		
P(word|Q)	word	meaning
0.061	，	[punctuation]
0.036	的	[possessive suffix]
0.027	。	[punctuation]
0.017	和	and
0.016	、	[punctuation]
0.009	环境	environment
0.009	了	[end of sentence]
0.008	海洋	sea
0.008	法	law
0.008	资源	resource
0.007	全国	whole country
0.007	在	in
0.006	保护	protect
0.006	污染	pollution
0.006	胶	rubber
0.006	发泡	defects in plastic
0.005	与	and
0.005	中国	china
0.005	产品	product
0.005	法律	law

Figure 2: Example of a cross-lingual relevance model, estimated from query number 58. Shown are the 20 tokens with highest probabilities under the model.

to demonstrate the degree to which Relevance Models degrade, when estimated in a cross-lingual setting. Given a Chinese query $c_1 \dots c_k$, we estimate a Relevance Model as suggested by Lavrenko and Croft [12]. We used estimation method 1 (equation 2). We used relative entropy (equation 6) as the document ranking function.

3. **Probabilistic Translation Model.** As a cross-lingual baseline, we report the performance of our implementation of the system used by Xu et.al. [19]. The translation model was originally proposed by Berger and Lafferty [4] and Hiemstra and de Jong [9]. We used the formulation advocated by Xu et al. [19]. We used the same statistical lexicon and the same system parameters that were reported in [19].

4. **Cross-lingual Relevance Model (parallel).** Given an English query $e_1 \dots e_k$, we estimate a Relevance Model in Chinese using equations (1) and (4). We use the combined parallel corpus for estimating equation (4). The Chinese documents are then ranked by their Kullback-Leibler divergence from the Relevance model (equation 6).

5. **Cross-lingual Relevance Model (dictionary).** We estimate the cross-lingual relevance model using equations (1) and (2). Equation (5) is used to compute the probability of an English word e_i given a Chinese document C. We use the lexicon reported in [19] for translation probabilities $P(e_i|v)$. The documents are ranked by KL divergence from the Relevance Model (equation 6).

In all cases we performed separate experiments on the three representations of Chinese: unigrams, bigrams and "words". Refer to section 4.4 for details. The smoothing parameter λ was tuned separately for each representation as we found that smoothing affects unigrams and bigrams very differently. The results from the three representations were then linearly combined. The weights attached to each representation were set separately for every model, in order to show best results. As an exception, the Probabilistic Translation Model was evaluated on the same representation that was used by Xu et.al.[19]. Due to the absence of the training corpus, the tuning of all parameters was performed on the testing data using a brute-force hill-climbing approach. The small number of queries in the testing dataset precluded the use of any statistical significance tests.

5.1 Baseline Results

Table 3 shows the retrieval performance, of the described models on the TREC9 cross-language retrieval task. We use non-interpolated average precision as a performance measure. Percentage numbers indicate the difference from the mono-lingual baseline. We show results for both short and long versions of the queries. Our monolingual results form a strong baseline, competitive with the results reported by [17, 19]. This is somewhat surprising, since our processing of Chinese queries was very simplistic, and a lot of spurious matches were caused by punctuation and stopwords in the queries. We attribute the strong performance to the careful selection of smoothing parameters and combination of multiple representations.

Monolingual Relevance Model provides an even higher baseline for both short and long queries. The difference is highlighted in Figure 3. Relevance Models show good performance at higher recall, which is expected, since they can be interpreted as theoretically grounded query expansion techniques.

The Probabilistic Translation Model achieves around 85% - 90% percent of the mono-lingual baseline. Xu et.al. in [19] report the performance of the same model to be somewhat higher than our implementation (0.3100 for long queries). We attribute the differences to the different form of pre-processing used by Xu et.al, since we used the same bilingual lexicon and the same model parameters as [19].

5.2 Cross-lingual Relevance Model Results

Table 3 shows that Cross-lingual Relevance Models perform very well, achieving 93% - 98% of the mono-lingual baseline on the combined representation. This performance is better than most previously-reported results [17, 19], which is somewhat surprising, given our poor pre-processing of Chinese. Our model noticeably outperforms the Probabilistic Translation Model on both long and short queries (see figure 4). It is also encouraging to see that Cross-lingual Relevance Models perform very well on different representations of Chinese, even though they do not gain as much from the combination as the baselines.

Note that Relevance Models estimated using a bilingual lexicon perform better than the models estimated from the parallel corpus. We believe this is due to the fact that our parallel corpus has an acute coverage problem. The bilingual dictionary we used [19] covers a significantly larger number of both English and Chinese words. In addition, two thirds of our parallel corpus was obtained using automatic machine translation software, which uses a limited vocabulary. It is also worth noting that the remaining part of our parallel corpus, Hong-Kong News, was also used by Xu et al. [19] in the construction of their bilingual dictionary.

Average Precision	HK News	HK News + TDT	
Unigrams	0.1070	0.2258	+111%
Bigrams	0.1130	0.2519	+123%
"Words"	0.1210	0.2493	+106%

Table 5: Parallel corpus size has a very significant effect on the quality of Cross-lingual Relevance Models.

Table 5 illustrates just how serious the coverage problem is. We show performance of Relevance Models estimated using just the Hong-Kong News portion of the corpus, versus performance with the full corpus. We observe tremendous improvements of 100% to 200% percent, by adding the TDT data, even though this data was automatically generated using SYSTRAN.

5.2.1 High-precision performance

Average precision is one of the most frequently reported metrics in cross-language retrieval. This metric is excellent for research purposes, but it is also important to consider user-oriented metrics. Table 4 shows precision at different ranks in the ranked list of documents. Precision at 5 or 10 documents is what affects a typical user in the web-search setting. We observe that Cross-lingual Relevance Models exhibit exceptionally good performance in this high-precision area. Models estimated using the parallel corpus are particularly impressive, outperforming the mono-lingual baseline by 20% at 5 retrieved documents. Models estimated from the bilingual dictionary perform somewhat worse, though still outperforming mono-lingual performance at 5 documents. Both estimation methods outperform the Probabilistic Translation Model. We consider these results to be extremely encouraging, since they suggest that Cross-lingual Relevance Models perform very well in the important high-precision area.

6. CONCLUSION

We proposed a formal probabilistic model of Cross-Language Information Retrieval. The model is significantly different from other recently proposed models in that it does not attempt to translate either the query or the documents. The model starts with a query in the source language and directly estimates the model of relevant documents in the target language. Massive query expansion is an integral part of the model, rather than a heuristic addition. Our experiments demonstrate that performance of the model is as good as or better than that of previously reported models. The model performs around 90% - 95% of the strong mono-lingual baseline in terms of average precision. In terms of initial precision, the model outperforms the mono-lingual baseline by 20%. We discussed how Cross-Lingual Relevance Models can be estimated using either a parallel/comparable corpus, or a bilingual lexicon. Our experiments show that coverage is an extremely important aspect of the resources. We have been able to use a commercial MT system to increase the coverage of our corpus.

A number of questions remain open and need to be addressed in the future work. We would like to explore the use of unlabeled data to improve the coverage of the parallel corpus without performing expensive machine translation. We also plan to carry out additional experiments with sentence-aligned parallel corpora. Finally, we would like to explore applications of our model in other tasks, such as Topic Detection and Tracking, and in other languages.

7. ACKNOWLEDGMENTS

We would like to thank Jinxi Xu for providing us with the bilingual dictionary and Fang-Fang Feng for providing the Chinese segmenter and other resources. Many thanks to the reviewers, whose feedback proved to be very valuable. This work was supported in part by the Center for Intelligent Information Retrieval, and in part by SPAWARSYSCEN-SD grant number N66001-99-1-8912. Any opinions, findings and conclusions or recommendations expressed in this material are the author(s) and do not necessarily reflect those of the sponsor.

8. REFERENCES

[1] J. Allan, J. Callan, W. B. Croft, L. A. Ballesteros, D. Byrd, R. Swan, and J. Xu. INQUERY does battle with TREC-6. In E. M. Voorhees and D. K. Harman, editors, *Proceedings of the Sixth Text REtrieval Conference (TREC-6)*, pages 169–206, Gaithersburg, MD, November 1997. National Institute of Standards and Technology (NIST) and Defense Advanced Research Projects Agency (DARPA), Department of Commerce, National Institute of Standards and Technology.

[2] L. A. Ballesteros and W. B. Croft. Phrasal translation and query expansion techniques for cross-language information retrieval. In N. J. Belkin, A. D. Narasimhalu, and P. Willett, editors, *Proceedings of the Twentieth Annual International ACM-SIGIR Conference on Research and Development in Information Retrieval*, pages 84–91, Philadelphia, PA, July 1997. ACM Press.

[3] L. A. Ballesteros and W. B. Croft. Resolving ambiguity for cross-language retrieval. In W. B. Croft, A. Moffat, C. J. van Rijsbergen, R. Wilkinson, and J. Zobel, editors, *Proceedings of the Twenty-First Annual International ACM-SIGIR Conference on Research and Development in Information Retrieval*, pages 64–71, Melbourne, Australia, August 1998. ACM Press.

[4] A. Berger and J. Lafferty. Information retrieval as statistical translation. In M. Hearst, F. Gey, and R. Tong, editors, *Proceedings of the Twenty-Second Annual International ACM-SIGIR Conference on Research and Development in Information Retrieval*, pages 222–229, Berkeley, CA, August 1999. ACM Press.

[5] P. F. Brown, J. Cocke, S. A. Della Pietra, V. J. Della Pietra, F. Jelinek, J. D. Lafferty, R. L. Mercer, and P. S. Roossin. A statistical approach to machine translation. *Computational Linguistics*, 16(2):79–85, 1990.

[6] W. B. Croft, D. J. Harper, D. H. Kraft, and J. Zobel, editors. *Proceedings of the Twenty-Fourth Annual International ACM-SIGIR Conference on Research and Development in Information Retrieval*, New Orleans, LA, September 2001. ACM Press.

[7] J. Gao, J.-Y. Nie, J. Zhang, E. Xun, Y. Su, M. Zhou, and C. Huang. TREC-9 CLIR experiments at

	Unigrams		Bigrams		Words		Combination	
Short Queries								
Monolingual baseline	0.2447		0.2375		0.2604		0.2874	
Monolingual Relevance Model	0.2404	-2%	0.2524	+6%	0.3072	+18%	0.3100	+8%
Probabilistic Translation Model	—		—		—		0.2549	-11%
Cross-lingual Relevance Model (dictionary)	0.2776	+13%	0.2684	+13%	0.2779	+7%	0.2807	-2%
Cross-lingual Relevance Model (parallel)	0.2258	-8%	0.2519	+6%	0.2493	-4%	0.2670	-7%
Long Queries								
Monolingual baseline	0.2750		0.3090		0.2837		0.3302	
Monolingual Relevance Model	0.2835	+3%	0.3414	+10%	0.3240	+14%	0.3767	+14%
Probabilistic Translation Model	—		—		—		0.2768	-16%
Cross-lingual Relevance Model (dictionary)	0.3002	+9%	0.3074	-1%	0.3178	+12%	0.3182	-4%

Table 3: Average Precision on the TREC9 cross-language retrieval task. Cross-lingual Relevance Models perform around 95% of the strong mono-lingual baseline

Precision	Monolingual	Mono R.M.		Translation Model		R.M. (dictionary)		R.M. (parallel)	
at 5 docs	0.2880	0.3360	+17%	0.2560	-11%	0.3200	+11%	0.3520	+22%
at 10 docs	0.2600	0.2880	+11%	0.2120	-19%	0.2320	-11%	0.2880	+11%
at 15 docs	0.2240	0.2427	+8%	0.1867	-17%	0.2080	-7%	0.2453	+10%
at 20 docs	0.2120	0.2220	+5%	0.1700	-20%	0.1960	-8%	0.2080	-2%
at 30 docs	0.1867	0.1907	+2%	0.1440	-23%	0.1693	-9%	0.1827	-2%

Table 4: Initial precision on the TREC9 CLIR task. Cross-lingual Relevance Models noticeably outperform the mono-lingual baselines.

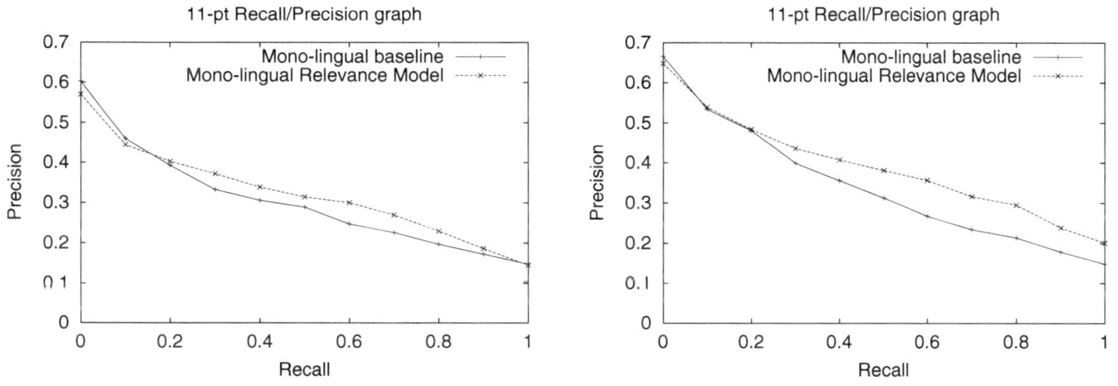

Figure 3: Mono-lingual results. Relevance Models provide a higher baseline for both short queries (left) and long queries (right).

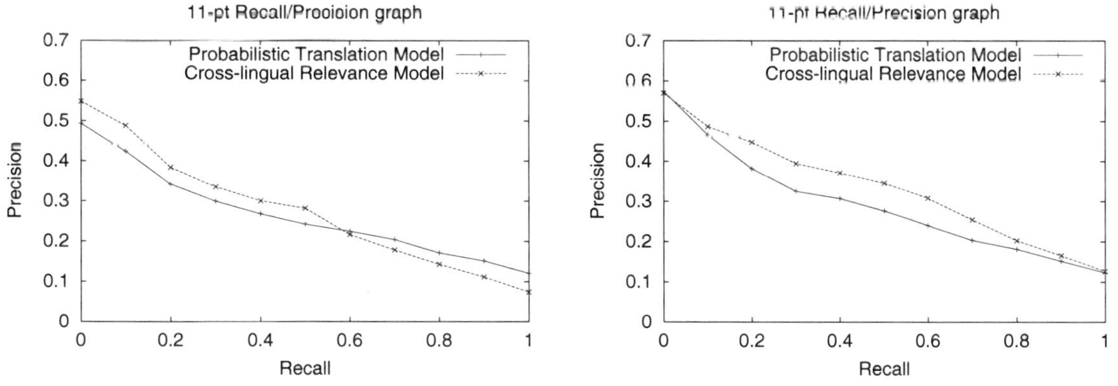

Figure 4: Cross-lingual Relevance Models outperform the Probabilistic Translation Model on both the short (left) and long (right) queries.

MSRCN. In Voorhees and Harman [17], pages 343–354.

[8] T. Gollins and M. Sanderson. Improving cross language information retrieval with triangulated translation. In Croft et al. [6], pages 90–95.

[9] D. Hiemstra and F. de Jong. Disambiguation strategies for cross-language information retrieval. In S. Abiteboul and A.-M. Vercoustre, editors, *Proceedings of the Third European Conference on Research and Advanced Technology for Digital Libaries, ECDL'99*, volume 1696 of *Lecture Notes in Computer Science*, pages 274–293. Springer-Verlag, Paris, September 1999.

[10] D. Hiemstra, F. de Jong, and W. Kraaij. A domain specific lexicon acquisition tool for cross-language information retrieval. In L. Devroye and C. Chrisment, editors, *Proceedings of the Fifth RIAO International Conference*, pages 255–270, Montréal, Canada, 1997. Centre de Hautes Études Internationales d'Informatique Documentaire (C.I.D).

[11] J. Lafferty and C. Zhai. Document language models, query models, and risk minimization for information retrieval. In Croft et al. [6], pages 111–119.

[12] V. Lavrenko and W. B. Croft. Relevance-based language models. In Croft et al. [6], pages 120–127.

[13] M. F. Porter. An algorithm for suffix stripping. *Program*, 14(3):130–137, July 1980.

[14] S. E. Robertson. The probability ranking principle in IR. *Journal of Documentation*, 33:294–304, 1977. Reprinted in [16].

[15] P. Sheridan and J. P. Ballerini. Experiments in multilingual information retrieval using the SPIDER system. In H.-P. Frei, D. Harman, P. Schäuble, and R. Wilkinson, editors, *Proceedings of the Nineteenth Annual International ACM-SIGIR Conference on Research and Development in Information Retrieval*, pages 58–64, Zurich, Switzerland, August 1996. ACM Press.

[16] K. Sparck Jones and P. Willett, editors. *Readings in information retrieval.* Multimedia Information and Systems. Morgan Kaufmann, San Francisco, CA, 1997.

[17] E. M. Voorhees and D. K. Harman, editors. *Proceedings of the Ninth Text REtrieval Conference (TREC-9)*, Gaithersburg, MD, November 2000. Department of Commerce, National Institute of Standards and Technology.

[18] J. Xu and R. Weischedel. TREC-9 cross-lingual retrieval at BBN. In Voorhees and Harman [17], pages 106–116.

[19] J. Xu, R. Weischedel, and C. Nguyen. Evaluating a probabilistic model for cross-lingual information retrieval. In Croft et al. [6], pages 105–110.

Resolving Query Translation Ambiguity using a Decaying Co-occurrence Model and Syntactic Dependence Relations

Jianfeng Gao*, Jian-Yun Nie**, Hongzhao He#, Weijun Chen##, Ming Zhou*

* Microsoft Research, Asia, Email: {jfgao, mingzhou, cnhuang}@microsoft.com

** Université de Montréal, Email: nie@iro.umontreal.ca

#Tianjin University, China.

##Tsinghua University, China.

ABSTRACT

Bilingual dictionaries have been commonly used for query translation in cross-language information retrieval (CLIR). However, we are faced with the problem of translation selection. Several recent studies suggested the utilization of term co-occurrences in this selection. This paper presents two extensions to improve them. First, we extend the basic co-occurrence model by adding a decaying factor that decreases the mutual information when the distance between the terms increases. Second, we incorporate a triple translation model, in which syntactic dependence relations (represented as triples) are integrated. Our evaluation on translation accuracy shows that translating triples as units is more precise than a word-by-word translation. Our CLIR experiments show that the addition of the decaying factor leads to substantial improvements of the basic co-occurrence model; and the triple translation model brings further improvements.

Categories and Subject Descriptors

H.3 [**Information Systems**]: Information Storage and Retrieval. F.1.2 [**Computation by Abstract Devices**]: Modes of Computation – *Probabilistic computation.* H.5.2 [**Information Interfaces and Presentation**]: User Interfaces – *Natural language*

General Terms: Algorithms, Measurement, Documentation, Performance, Design, Reliability, Experimentation, Languages, Theory.

Keywords: Query translation, CLIR, Statistical model, Parse, Co-occurrence

1. INTRODUCTION

Bilingual dictionaries have been commonly used for query translation in CLIR, but we are always faced with the problem of translation ambiguity, i.e. several translation words are provided for a source word by the dictionary, but only part of them are appropriate.

SIGIR'02, August 11-15, 2002, Tampere, Finland,

Recently, several studies [2, 4, 7, 11, 14, 19] have been proposed the use of co-occurrence information to deal with this problem. In those studies, usually a mutual information value between terms is estimated according to their co-occurrences within a predefined window. The translation word that has the highest mutual information score with the other translation words is selected. While these approaches have successfully improved the quality of query translation, there are still two main drawbacks. First, the standard calculation of mutual information does not take into account the distance between terms; whereas our intuition is that closer terms have stronger relationships. Second, the syntactic dependency between terms is not considered.

This paper presents two methods to improve the basic co-occurrence approaches. First, we incorporate a *decaying factor* that decreases the mutual information when the distance between the terms increases. Second, we present a statistical *triple* translation model, in which syntactic dependence relations (represented as triples) are integrated.

Our evaluation results show that the triple translation is more precise than the word-by-word translation with the co-occurrence model. The CLIR experiments on TREC collections show that the decaying co-occurrence method performs better than the basic co-occurrence method, and the triple translation model brings additional improvements.

The remainder of this paper is organized as follows: Section 2 provides a brief description on the related work. Sections 3 and 4 describe our co-occurrence approach and the triple translation model. Section 5 evaluates the proposed approaches. Section 6 presents our conclusion.

2. DEALING WITH TRANSLATION AMBIGUITY

To deal with the selection of the correct translation terms from a bilingual dictionary, several recent studies [2, 4, 7, 11, 14, 19] suggested the utilization of co-occurrence information. A term similarity is determined by the mutual information (or its variants) between terms. Then the most similar translation term among those in the dictionary is selected. While such a selection may lead to some improvements over a simple translation selection, we notice that in those studies, the co-occurrence of two terms within a predefined scope is treated in the same way, no matter how far they are from each other. This conception is against our intuition

This work was done while these authors were visiting Microsoft Research, Asia.

that the strength of the underlying relation is stronger when the distance between the two terms is shorter. Therefore, we will extend the previous methods by incorporating a decaying factor that decreases the mutual information when the distance between the terms increases. A similar idea has been applied successfully to statistical language modeling [5], showing improved performance of the cache language model. We expect similar improvements on CLIR, and this will be confirmed by our experiments.

While there is little research on using syntactic approaches for resolving translation ambiguity for CLIR, linguistic structures have been successfully exploited in other applications. For example, in [12], syntactic dependency was exploited for resolving word sense ambiguity. A term similarity measure based on triples was first proposed in [13]. [18] extended this measure to a cross-language term similarity term, and presented a statistical translation model for collocation translation. This model is adopted in this study for triple translations.

Another problem of simple dictionary approaches is the poor coverage of the dictionary. We demonstrate that the use of the triple translation model provides an interesting alternative solution to this problem.

In this paper, we focus the use of co-occurrence model and triple model for query translation. In our CLIR experiments, the query translation process may be summarized as follows:

(1) Triples are first identified in English (source language) queries using a dependency parser.
(2) The translation of the identified triples is determined using a triple translation model, which is trained on unrelated English and Chinese corpora.
(3) The remaining words in the query are translated as terms by the decaying co-occurrence model, which determine the best translation term among all those stored in the dictionary.

3. USING CO-OCCURRENCE INFORMATION FOR TRANSLATION SELECTION

3.1 Principle of the basic co-occurrence approach

A correct translation word is the one that fits well the context of the whole sentence. The original sentence (or query) reflects well the context of the sentence; but it would be difficult to find a way to directly compare a translation word with the original sentence, unless there is a similarity measure between words across languages. Another possible way is to consider that all the translation words selected for the other words of the source sentence form an alternative specification of the context. Then a good translation word is the one that has a high *cohesion* with the other translation words. The advantage of this alternative approach is that there is no need to have a cross-language word comparison. Only relationships between words of the same language are used. They can be obtained through their co-occurrences in a monolingual text corpus. This is the principle of co-occurrence approach to translation selection. It can also be expressed as follows: correct translations of query words tend to co-occur in the target language and incorrect translations do not [2]. A similar principle is also used in [14].

3.2 Decaying Co-occurrence Model

The basic co-occurrence approach uses mutual information (or its variants) as term similarity. Mutual information is defined as follows:

$$MI(x,y) = P(x,y) * \log(\frac{P(x,y)}{P(x) * P(y)}), \quad (1)$$

where

$$P(x,y) = \frac{C(x,y)}{\sum_{x',y'} C(x',y')}, \text{ and } P(x) = \frac{C(x)}{\sum_{x'} C(x')}.$$

Here $C(x, y)$ is the frequency of co-occurrences of terms x and y within predefined windows (e.g. sentences) in the collection, $C(x)$ is the number of occurrences of term x in the collection.

We observe that any co-occurrence within the windows is treated in the same way, no matter how far they are from each other. In reality, we find that closer words usually have stronger relationships, thus should be more similar. Therefore, we add a distance factor $D(x, y)$ in the mutual information calculation. This factor decreases exponentially when the distance between two terms x and y, increases, i.e.

$$D(x,y) = e^{-\alpha*(Dis(x,y)-1)}, \quad (2)$$

where α is the decay rate, which is determined empirically (see Section 3.3), and $Dis(x,y)$ is the average distance between x and y in the corpus.

Term similarity in the extended co-occurrence model consists of two components: (1) the mutual information $MI(x,y)$ as defined before, and (2) the decaying factor $D(x,y)$:

$$SIM(x,y) = MI(x,y) * D(x,y). \quad (3)$$

The cohesion between a term x and a set T of other terms is estimated as follows:

$$Cohesion(x,T) = \log(\sum_{y \in T} SIM(x,y)). \quad (4)$$

In query translation, each source word is translated by one target word. The internal cohesion of a set of target words is the sum of the cohesions of each target word with all the other target words. The set with the highest internal cohesion is selected as the query translation.

Finding an optimal set of translation words may be computationally very costly. Therefore, an approximate greedy algorithm has been proposed in [8] to select the best set. We use the same algorithm here.

3.3 Model Estimation and Evaluation in Monolingual IR

The decaying co-occurrence model is estimated on a collection of Chinese newspaper articles consisting of approximately 80 million characters. To investigate the effectiveness of the decaying model, we performed a preliminary test with query expansion in monolingual IR. For each query term, we expand it by an additional term that has the highest cohesion value with the other words of the original query. This expansion task is very similar to the translation selection in CLIR. Therefore, it gives a good indication on the possible impact on query translation.

A Chinese synonym dictionary is generated for query expansion from the LDC bilingual dictionaries[1] as follows: For each Chinese term *c*, and each of its English translation *e*, we consider all the Chinese translations *c'* of *e* as synonyms of *c*.

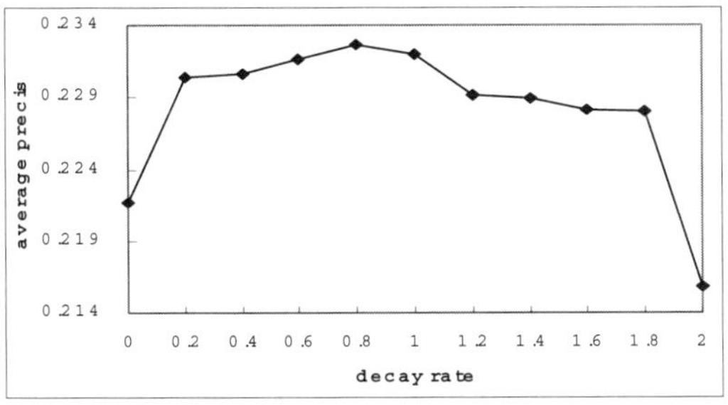

Figure 1: The impact of decaying factor on query expansion

Our experiments are carried out on the TREC-9 Chinese collection [16]. Figure 1 shows the retrieval results with query expansion while the decay rate varies. It can be seen that the decaying co-occurrence model performs generally better than the basic co-occurrence model (when decay rate = 0). With a decay rate of 0.8, we obtain the best performance of the average precision 23.3%, which is 5% better than the basic model. These experiments show that the decaying factor allows us to better distinguish strong and weak term relationships. As the problem of translation selection in CLIR is similar to this expansion task, we can expect a similar effect with the decaying factor. In our later experiments, the decay rate will be set to 0.8.

4. THE USE OF TRIPLES

The incorporation of triples is an attempt to take into account some syntactic dependences in translation selection. Our hypothesis is that strong syntactic dependences usually remain in the translations, and an ideal query translation should contain the same syntactic dependences as in the original query. Syntactic dependences also provide an additional criterion to the earlier cohesion measure: A good translation word should not only co-occur with other translation words, but also have the required syntactic dependence relations with them.

4.1 Principle

A triple represents a dependence relationship between two words, such as verb-object, subject-verb, and so on. We represent a triple as (*w,r,w'*), where *w* and *w'* are words and *r* is the dependence relation. It means that *w'* has an *r* relation with *w*. For example, (have, sub-verb, I) means that "I" is the subject of the verb "have". Figure 2 shows an English sentence and the triples that one can extract from it.

Sentence	I have a brown dog.
Triples	(have, sub-verb, I) (have, verb-obj, dog) (dog, adj-noun, brown) (dog, det-noun, a)

Figure 2: Examples of Dependence relations or triples

Among all the dependence relations, we only consider the following four that can be detected precisely using our parser: (1) sub-verb, (2) verb-object, (3) adjective-noun, and (4) adverb-verb[2].

It is our observation that there is a strong correspondence in dependence relations in the translation between English and Chinese, despite the great differences between the two languages. For example, a sub-verb relation in English (e.g. (have, sub-verb, I)) is usually translated into the same sub-verb relation in Chinese (e.g. (有, sub-verb, 我). This means, for an English triple $ETP = (w_e, r_e, w_e')$, the most likely Chinese translation should also be a triple $CTP = (w_c, r_c, w_c')$, where w_c and w_c' are the Chinese translations of the English terms w_e and w_e', respectively, and r_c is the Chinese counterpart of r_e.

4.2 Correspondence of Dependence Relations between English and Chinese

To test the assumption of strong correspondence of dependence relations between Chinese and English, we used a word-aligned bilingual corpus, which consists of 60,000 pairs of Chinese and English sentences. The corpus was first parsed using an English and Chinese parser– NLPWIN[3]. The four types of dependency relationship were extracted. We analyzed the correspondence on dependence relations between Chinese and English. The results are shown in Table 1. As we can see, more than 80% of dependence relations of sub-verb, adj-noun, and adv-verb have one-one mappings between English and Chinese, while the mapping rate of verb-object is approximately 65%.

Further analyses showed that the mapping errors of verb-object occur in the following situations: (1) one single English verb maps a Chinese triple (e.g. read → 读[read] v | 书[book] o), or (2) an English verb-prep-object sequence maps a Chinese verb-object sequence (e.g. change-to-currency → 用[use] v | 货 [currency] o). As the first case is not a triple translation, and will not affect the triple model, it is ignored. The second problem is quite common. In fact, the combination of verb-preposition in English is very often translated into a single verb in Chinese. If we consider such a combination in English as "verb", the mapping rate of verb-object is increased to more than 80% (see Table 1 – (*) case). This is the way we will use to map verb-object patterns between Chinese and English.

[1] http://morph.ldc.upenn.edu/Projects/Chinese/.

[2] Although noun-noun relation is also very important for IR and for appropriate translation of phrases, it is beyond the scope of this paper. Please see [8] for a detailed description of noun phrase detection and translation for CLIR.

[3] NLPWIN parser is developed at Microsoft Research. It construct a parse tree fro a sentence, then a logical form. Triple is one of the logical forms.

So, globally, the mapping rate is generally higher than 80%. We can conclude that there is indeed a very strong correspondence between Chinese and English in the four dependence relations considered.

Dependency	sub-verb	adj-noun	adv-verb	verb-obj	verb-obj (*)
Mapping Rate	81.2%	81.0%	80.9%	64.8%	80.7%

Table 1: Triple correspondence between Chinese and English

4.3 Triple Translation Model

Given an English triple $ETP = (w_e, r_e, w_e')$, and the set of its candidate translating Chinese triples CTP, the best Chinese triple $CTP^* = (w_c, r_c, w_c')$ is the one that maximizes the Equation below:

$$CTP^* = \arg\max_{CTP} P(CTP \mid ETP) \quad (5)$$
$$= \arg\max_{CTP} P(ETP \mid CTP) \times P(CTP),$$

where $P(ETP|CTP)$ is the translation probability, $P(CTP)$ is the *a priori* probability of words of the translated Chinese triple. $P(CTP)$ can be determined using maximum likelihood estimation (MLE) by

$$P(CTP) = \frac{|w_c, r_c, w_c'|}{|*,*,*|}, \quad (6)$$

where $|w,r,w'|$ is the frequency count of the triple (w,r,w'). The wildcard symbol * means that it can be any word/relation.

$P(ETP|CTP)$ cannot be estimated directly because there is no large triple-aligned corpus available (the one we used in Section 4.2. is too small). Therefore, we assume that the translations of the English terms w_e and w_e', and the English dependency relation r_e are independent, so $P(ETP|CTP)$ can be decomposed as follows:

$$P(ETP \mid CTP) = P(w_e, r_e, w_e' \mid w_c, r_c, w_c') \quad (7)$$
$$= P(w_e \mid w_c) \times P(w_e' \mid w_c') \times P(r_e \mid r_c).$$

Notice that $P(w_e|w_c)$ and $P(w_e'|w_c')$ are translation probabilities within triples. They are different from the unrestricted probabilities such as the ones in IBM models [3].

Between the same dependence relation r_c and r_e, $P(r_e|r_c)$ could be estimated from Table 1. However, we do not have the statistics for different r_c and r_e. As the correspondence between the same dependence relation across English and Chinese is strong, we simply assume $P(r_e|r_c) = 1$ for the corresponding r_c and r_e and $P(r_e|r_c) = 0$ for the other cases.

The remaining elements to be estimated are the within-triple word translation probabilities $P(w_e|w_c)$ and $P(w_e'|w_c')$. We further assume that they can be estimated by a similarity score (its estimation will be described later) between the words, i.e.

$$P(w_e|w_c) \propto Sim(w_e, w_c),$$

and $$P(w_e'|w_c') \propto Sim(w_e', w_c').$$

Then Equation (7) can be rewritten as:

$$P(ETP \mid CTP) \propto Score(ETP \mid CTP) \times P(r_e \mid r_c) \quad (8)$$
$$= Sim(w_e, w_c) \times Sim(w_e', w_c') \times P(r_e \mid r_c),$$

Now, the problem is the definition of $Sim(w_e, w_c)$[4]. This is done by extending the approach of [13] which estimates the similarity $Sim(w_1, w_2)$ for w_1 and w_2 in the same language. Let us first describe the approach of [13]. The basic idea is to consider all the dependence relations with a word w as forming its *dependence context*, denoted by $T(w)$. For example, in Figure 2, the dependence context of "dog" consists of three triples, i.e. *T("dog")*={(have, verb-obj, *), (*, adj-noun, brown), (*, det-noun, a)}. It is assumed that two words are likely to have similar meanings if their dependence contexts are identical. For the sake of simplicity, in what follows, we use (r,w') to denote either $(*,r,w')$ or $(w',r,*)$.

Using an information-theoretic definition, $Sim(w_1,w_2)$ is measured by the ratio between the amount of information needed to describe the commonality of w_1 and w_2 (denoted by $I(common(w_1,w_2))$) and the information needed to fully describe what w_1 and w_2 are (denoted by $I(describe(w_1,w_2))$):

$$Sim(w_1, w_2) = \frac{I(common(w_1, w_2))}{I(describe(w_1, w_2))} \quad (9)$$

Let $I(w,r,w')$ be the amount of information needed to describe a triple (w,r,w'), which is estimated by Equation (10)[5].

$$I(w,r,w') = \log \frac{P(w \mid r,w')}{P(w \mid r)}, \quad (10)$$

where

$$P(w \mid r,w') = \frac{|w,r,w'|}{|*,r,w'|}, \text{ and}$$

$$P(w \mid r) = \frac{|w,r,*|}{|*,r,*|}.$$

Then, assume that information can be additive, $I(common(w_1,w_2))$ is calculated as the sum of the information contained in common triples belonging to both dependence context sets $T(w_1)$ and $T(w_2)$:

$$\sum_{(r,w)\in T(w_1)\cap T(w_2)} (I(w_1,r,w) + I(w_2,r,w)) \quad (11)$$

Similarly, $I(describe(w_1,w_2))$ is calculated as the sum of the information contained in triples belonging to either dependency context sets $T(w_1)$ or $T(w_2)$:

$$\sum_{(r,w)\in T(w_1)} I(w_1,r,w) + \sum_{(r,w)\in T(w_2)} I(w_2,r,w) \quad (12)$$

Now, let us explain how Equation (9) is extended in [18] to the cross-language word similarity $Sim(w_e,w_c)$.

The basic idea is the same: two words are similar if they occur in similar dependence contexts. Simply, for an English dependence context (r_e,w'_e), a Chinese context (r_c,w'_c) is similar if r_c corresponds to r_e, and w'_c is a translation of w'_e stored in a bilingual dictionary. In this case, we call the Chinese dependence context a possible translation of the English dependence context.

The probability of such a translation may be estimated as $P(w'_c|w'_e)*P(r_c|r_e)$, where $P(w'_c|w'_e)$ is the translation probability from w'_e to w'_c. We assign an equal probability to all the w'_c

[4] The definition is a simplified version of that in [18].

[5] This formula is slightly changed from that used in [13].

stored in the bilingual dictionary for w'_e, i.e. $P(w'_c|w'_e) = 1/(\# \text{ of translation words for } w'_e)$ if w'_c is a dictionary translation of w'_e; otherwise, $P(w'_c|w'_e) = 0$. $P(r_c|r_e)$ is estimated as before.

So, the cross-language commonality between w_e and w_c $I(common(w_c,w_e))$ is modified from Equation (11) as follows:

$$\sum_{(r_c,w_c')\in T(w_c)} I(w_c,r_c,w_c')\times P(w_c'|w_e')\times P(r_c|r_e) + \sum_{(r_e,w_e')\in T(w_e)} I(w_e,r_e,w_e')\times P(w_e'|w_c')\times P(r_e|r_c) \qquad (13)$$

The descriptions of w_c and w_e are defined as before as follows:

$$I(describe(w_c)) = \sum_{(r,w)\in T(w_c)} I(w_c,r,w) \text{ and} \qquad (14)$$

$$I(describe(w_e)) = \sum_{(r,w)\in T(w_e)} I(w_e,r,w)$$

4.4 Model Training

One advantage of the triple translation model is that it can be trained on unrelated English and Chinese corpora. The triple model only requires the estimation of triple probabilities separately in the two languages, then through a bilingual dictionary and the assumption of strong correspondence of dependence relations, the whole triples in the two languages become related. There is a risk that unrelated triples in Chinese and English can be connected with this method. However, as the conditions that are used to make the connection are quite strong (i.e. possible words translations in the same triple structure), we believe that this risk, although exists, is not overwhelming. Our later experiments will show that the translation relations created among triples in this way bring significant benefits.

In our training, we used an English text corpus that contains articles published in the Wall Street Journal from 1987 to 1992, which amount to 750MB. The Chinese text corpus we used contains articles published in the People's Daily from 1980 to 1998. They amount to 1200MB. NLPWIN is used to extract triples in both corpora. Table 2 shows the number of different triples extracted.

As described in Section 4.3, for triple translation, two parameters have to be estimated: $P(CTP)$ and $Sim(w_e,w_c)$. They are respectively estimated according to Equations (6) and Equations (13) and (14).

Language	sub-verb	adj-noun	adv-verb	verb-object
Chinese	26,773,214	14,707,246	10,191,300	22,259,701
English	6,475,461	2,026,177	741,719	6,558,566

Table 2: Statistics of the extracted triples

5. EXPERIMENTS AND EXTENSION

In this section, we first present our experiments on the accuracy of triple translations, then the evaluations on CLIR.

5.1 The Evaluation of Triple Translations

5.1.1 Verb-object triple translation results

Verb-object triples seem to be the ones that represent the most serious translation ambiguity problem among the four main triple types. Therefore, we focus on this type of triple in our first experiments.

From the set of Chinese and English verb-object triples described in Section 4.4, 80% of them served as the training data. From the remaining 20% triples, several test sets are extracted, corresponding to different characteristics:

(1) **Test-set 1 (frequent verbs)**: This set contains 1000 triples with frequent verbs.

(2) **Test-set 2 (infrequent verbs)**: This set contains 275 triples with infrequent verbs.

(3) **Test-set 3 (frequent triples)**: This set contains frequent 1000 triples.

(4) **Test-set 4 (infrequent triples)**: This set contains 700 infrequent triples.

The translation performance is measured by accuracy, defined as (# of correct translated triples / # of triples in the test set).

The following three translation methods are compared:

(1) **Method A**: Each English word in a triple is translated by the most frequent translation word in the dictionary.

(2) **Method B**: The translation words are determined by the decaying co-occurrence model.

(3) **Method C**: The triple model is used.

The results are shown in Table 3. We can see that Method C achieves the highest performance in all four test sets. This shows that the most precise translation of a triple is obtained by using the triple model. These results also confirm that the risk of relating unrelated triples by using non-parallel corpora for training is small. We also notice that the translation accuracy varies very consistently among different test sets. This shows that the triple model performs well not only for frequent triples and verbs, but also for infrequent ones.

	Test-set 1	Test-set 2	Test-set 3	Test-set 4
Method A	42.4%	44.0%	54.1%	54.1%
Method B	55.0%	67.3%	62.3%	67.6%
Method C	74.2%	80.9%	73.3%	81.0%

Table 3: Verb-object triple translation results

We also observe that Method B is generally better than Method A. This determines the following preferred query translation strategy: When a triple is identified, it is translated by the triple model; the remaining words are translated by the co-occurrence model if covered by it; otherwise, the simple translation method is used.

5.1.2 Beyond the limit of the bilingual dictionary

Due to the limited coverage of the dictionary, a correct translation may not be stored in the dictionary. This naturally limit the coverage of triple translations. In order to generate more triple translations, the following two expansion methods are used to create new candidate translation triples:

(1) *Expansion by synonyms*: An English synonym dictionary is first generated from the bilingual dictionaries using the method described in Section 3.3. Translations of all the synonyms of the term w_e are added as the possible translations of w_e. This expansion corresponds to the method of pre- and post-translation expansion in [2].

(2) *Expansion by triples*: Given an English triple (w_e, r_e, w'_e), for each Chinese translation w_c of w_e stored in the dictionary, we select all Chinese words w'_c such that $I(w_c, r_c, w'_c)>0$ as the extended translations of w'_e; The $I(w_c, r_c, w'_c)>0$ condition means that (w_c, r_c, w'_c) is a significant triple (not a noise) in the corpus. The expansion on Chinese words is done similarly.

We now define a new word translation relation $s(w_c|w_e)$ between words in the expansion context. This relation is no longer a probability, but a generalized score. We use it to replace $P(w_c|w_e)$ in Equation (13). It is defined as follows. Let $|Tran1(w_e)|$, $|Trans2(w_e)|$ and $|Trans3(w_e)|$ be respectively the size of the translation set obtained by the non-expanded method and by the two expansion methods.

- For *unexpanded* method, each translation in $Tran1(w_e)$ will be assigned an equal score $1/|Tran1(w_e)|$ (this is the same as before).
- For *synonym expansion*, if a translation belongs to both $Tran1(w_e)$ and $Tran2(w_e)$, the score is $0.6/|Tran1(w_e)| + 0.4/|Tran2(w_e)|$; if it only belongs to $Tran1(w_e)$, then it is $0.6/|Tran1(w_e)|$; otherwise, it is 0.
- Similarly, for *triple model expansion*, if a translation belongs to both $Tran1(w_e)$ and $Tran3(w)_e$, the score is $0.6/|Tran1(w_e)| + 0.4 / |Tran3(w_e)|$; if it only belongs to $Tran1(w_e)$, then it is $0.6/|Tran1(w_e)|$; otherwise, it is 0.

The values of 0.6 and 0.4 are chosen empirically through experiments.

For example, in the triple expansion case, initially the dictionary does not contain "怀" (be pregnant [of a child]) as a translation of "bear". The triple model expansion will generate an additional translation "怀" (be pregnant [of a child]) for "bear" because "孩子" (child) and its translation "child" are frequent objects of these two verbs. That is s(怀 |bear) is relatively high. In addition, the triples (怀, verb-obj, 孩子) and (bear, verb-obj, child) are quite frequent in the corpora, so both I(怀, verb-obj, 孩子) and I(bear, verb-obj, child) are strong. So globally, the commonality between 怀" and "bear is high.

We performed comparison experiments on test-set 1, using Method C for triple translation. The results are shown in Table 4.

Method	Accuracy
No expansion	74.2%
Expansion by synonyms	69.8%
Expansion by triples	80.3%

Table 4: Results of translation expansion

	English triple	No expansion	Triple expansion
Positive examples	bear | child	忍 |孩子 (suffer from child)	怀|孩子 (bear child)
	break | silence	打 |沉 (smash silence)	打破|沉默 (break silence)
Negative examples	build | road	修 |公 (build road)	制 |办 (set up a method)
	make | sound	发 |声 (make sound)	发表|讲 (give a speech)

Figure 3: Example translations using triple model expansion

We found that synonym expansion does not bring any benefit because it introduces much noise along with some correct expansions. On the other hand, the triple model expansion achieves a substantial improvement. Its translations have a better coverage than the unexpanded method, and it also carries out a better expansion selection than the expansion by synonyms. Therefore, we integrate triple expansion in our triple translation method.

Unfortunately, it can also introduce wrong triples. Figure 3 shows some positive and negative examples. We found that the wrong expanded triple translations usually occur when the combinations of wrongly expanded translations are frequent ones in the corpus, thus cannot be filtered out using the triple translation model. The Chinese triples in the two negative examples of Figure 3 are very frequent ones. In these cases, even if the component words separately are strongly related to the original English words, their combination corresponds to a meaning different from the original one. Our current triple expansion is unable to deal with this problem.

5.2 CLIR Results

The two proposed query translation methods are tested on the TREC-9 Chinese corpus. This corpus contains articles published in Hong Kong Commercial Daily, Hong Kong Daily News, and Takungpao. They amount to 260MB. It also contains 25 English queries (with translated Chinese queries) evaluated by the NIST (National Institute of Standards and Technology). We use long queries in our experiments. Chinese texts are segmented into words using a dictionary containing 220,000 words. The bilingual lexical resources we used include three human compiled bilingual lexicons (including the LDC English-Chinese dictionary) and a bilingual lexicon generated from a parallel bilingual corpus automatically. The resulting combined dictionary contains 401,477 English entries, including 109,841 words, and 291,636 phrases. The use of the combined dictionary is motivated by previous studies [9, 17], which showed that larger lexicon resource improves CLIR performance significantly.

The Okapi system with BM2500 weighting [15] is used as the basic retrieval system. The main evaluation metric is interpolated 11-point average precision. Statistical t-test and query-by-query analysis are also employed. To decide whether the improvement by method *X* over method *Y* is significant, the t-test calculates a p-value based on the performance data of *X* and *Y*. The smaller the p-value, the more significant is the improvement. Usually, if the p-value is small enough (p-value<0.05), we can conclude that the improvement is statistically significant.

The following methods are compared to investigate the effectiveness of our models for query translation:

1. *Monolingual*: retrieval using the manually translated Chinese queries provided with the corpus.
2. *Simple translation*: retrieval using query translation obtained by taking the first translations from the bilingual dictionary.
3. *Best-sense translation*: retrieval using translation words selected manually from the dictionary, one translation per word. This method reflects the upper bound performance using the dictionary.

4. Our methods that incorporate the use of triple translation model and the decaying co-occurrence model.

Previous work [8, 15] showed that if multiple translations of a term were accepted in query translation, it is possible to obtain better performance of cross-language retrieval than that of monolingual retrieval, partly because of the query expansion effect. In order to separate the impact of query expansion from that of query translation, in our experiments, each English query term is translated by only one Chinese term[6].

The results of this series of experiments on query translation are shown in Table 5 and Figure 5. As shown in rows 4 and 5 of Table 5, both the co-occurrence model and the triple translation model bring substantial improvements over simple translation. The use of the decaying co-occurrence model results in a 48% improvement, which is statistically significant (p-value = 0.008).

#	Methods	Avg. P.	% Mono. IR
1	Monolingual	0.2862	
2	Simple translation	0.1613	56%
3	Best-sense translation	0.2730	95%
4	2 + co-occurrence model	0.2392	84%
5	2 + triple model	0.1908	67%
6	5 + co-occurrence model	0.2517	88%

Table 5: Retrieval effectiveness on TREC-9 corpus

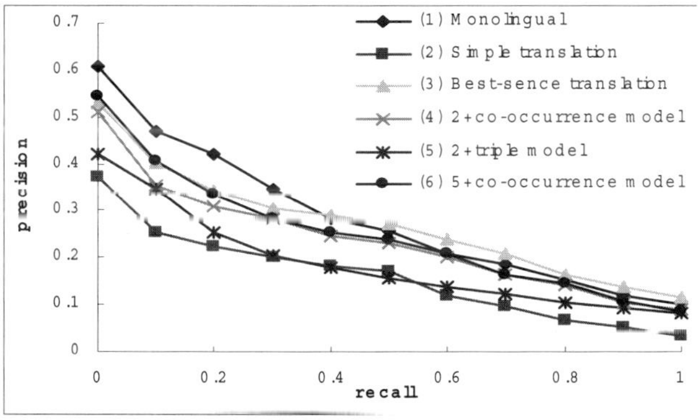

Figure 4: P-R curves (TREC-9 queries)

Row 6 corresponds to the preferred translation strategy. It shows that using both models in our query translation process, we achieve the best performance. It is better than using the co-occurrence model alone by 5%. This performance is partly due to the process of triple expansion.

We also observe that the combination of the triple model with the simple translation method (raw 5) leads to an effectiveness well below that with the co-occurrence model (raw 4). This is expectable because triples have a much lower coverage than co-occurrences. Therefore, in the combination of raw 5, only a few triples from 11 queries out of 25 have been translated by the triple model, while all the other words are translated by the first translation word in the dictionary. So this "counter-performance" is not surprising. Figure 5 shows a closer view on the 11 queries.

From the 11 queries, NLPWIN extracted 52 triples which appear at least 5 times in the corpus. The minimal occurrences of 5 is set due to the fact that many low frequency triples are in fact noise. The 52 triples include 12 verb-object triples, 8 sub-verb triples, and 32 adj-noun triples, and no adv-verb triples. As shown in Figure 5, for these queries, the triple translation has positive impact on the co-occurrence method for almost all the 11 queries, except for #61. In the case of query #61, only one translation word differs: (coal) consumption→消 (by the co-occurrence model), and consumption→消费 (by the triple model). Both translations are correct, but the first translation word is often used for industrial consumption (which is the case for this query); whereas the second is often used for consumption of particular consumers. For all the 11 queries, globally, the triple method makes a statistically significant improvement of 56% over simple translation (p-value = 0.015), and 10% over the decaying co-occurrence model (p-value = 0.02).

A further analysis shows that the triple translation model is able to assemble translation words correctly in a triple because the triples can capture the syntactic dependency between not only sequential words (i.e. phrases) but also non-sequential words in a sentence as the (originate, sub, computer-virus) triple in query #64 shown in Figure 6. All the translations in Figure 6 are correct.

We can compare some of examples of Figure 6 with those by the decaying co-occurrence model (Method 5). For Queries #63 and #64, the co-occurrence model gives some different but correct translations for the following words: develop→发展 originate→发源. However, the word "hacker" in Query #65 is wrongly translated as 耍 (joker), and "charge" as 保 (protect) by the co-occurrence method. For these cases, the triple translation method generates the correct translations. These examples show that the translations with triples can successfully correct some of the incorrect selections of translation words.

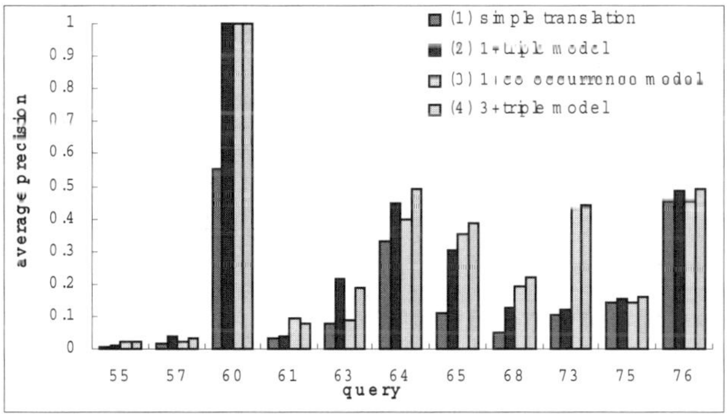

Figure 5: The queries containing triples

[6] This follows a suggestion by Douglas Oard.

[7] Usually, if p-value<0.05, one considers that the improvement is statistically significant.

Q#	Sentence, the extracted triples and translations
63	What new or renewable energy sources are being developed in China?
	(energy, adj-noun, renewable)→ 可 | 能 (energy, adj-noun, new)→ 新 | 能源 (develop, verb-obj, energy)→ 开 | 能源
64	Have any computer viruses been discovered to have originated in Asia?
	(discover, verb-obj, originate) →发新 | 起 (originate, sub-verb, computer-virus)→计 | 起源
65	Have any computer hackers been charged with crimes in Asia?
	(hacker, adj-noun, computer) →计算机 | 黑 (charge, verb-obj, hacker) →控 | 黑客

Figure 6: Some translations by the triple model

6. CONCLUSION

This paper proposed two statistical models for dealing with the problem of query translation ambiguity. We focused on the method that exploits linguistic dependency information represented as triples. The translations using triples showed three main benefits: a more precise translation; an extension of the coverage of the bilingual dictionary; and the possibility to train the model using unrelated bilingual corpora. Our experiments of CLIR showed that the triple translation has a positive impact on the query translation, and results in significant improvements of CLIR performance over the co-occurrence method. We also presented a revised version of the co-occurrence model. It differs from previous ones in that it includes a distance component that decays the mutual information between terms when the distance between them increases. Our experiments showed that the decaying co-occurrence model performs better than the standard co-occurrence model, and brings significant improvements over the simple dictionary approaches in CLIR.

An important problem we currently have with the triple translation is the robustness of the parser. A certain portion of incorrect triples are extracted, especially those with low frequencies. Many other triples cannot be extracted because the parser fails to parse the sentence completely. In order to increase the impact of triple translation, the robustness of the parser has to be improved. In fact, as we only need to extract triples, a partial parser may be more suitable. This alternative will be investigated in the future.

ACKNOWLEDGEMENTS

The authors would like to thank Ashley Chang, and Chang-Ning Huang for their suggestions and comments on a preliminary draft of this paper. Thanks also to four anonymous reviews for valuable and insightful comments.

REFERENCES

[1] Ballesteros, L., and Croft, W. B. (1997). Phrasal translation and query expansion techniques for cross-language information retrieval. In: *ACM SIGIR'97*. pp. 84-91.

[2] Ballesteros, L., and Croft, W. B. (1998). Resolving ambiguity for cross-language retrieval. In: *ACM SIGIR'98*. Melbourne, Australia., pp. 64-71

[3] Brown, P. F., Della Pietra, S. A., Della Pietra, V. J., and Mercer, R.L. (1993). The Mathematics of Statistical Machine Translation: Parameter Estimation. *Computational Linguistics*, 19(2): 263-311

[4] Bian, G.W. and Chen, H.H. (1998). Integrating query translation and document translation in a cross-language information retrieval system. *Machine Translation and Information Soup*, Lecture Notes in Computer Science, #1529, Spring-Verlag, pp. 250-265.

[5] Clarkson, P., and Robinson, A. (1997). Language model adaptation using mixtures and an exponentially decaying cache. In *Proceedings of ICASSP-97*, pp. 799--802.

[6] Davis, M. W., and Ogden, W. C. (1997). Free resources and advanced alignment for cross-language text retrieval. In: *TREC-6*, pp. 285-402.

[7] Fung, P., Liu, X., and Cheung, C. S. (1999). Mixed language query disambiguation. In *ACL-99*. The 37th Annual Meeting of the Association for Computational Linguistics, College Park, Maryland, USA, pp. 333-340.

[8] Gao, J., Nie, J. Y., Zhang, J., Xun, E., Zhou, M., and Huang, C. (2001) Improving query translation for CLIR using statistical Models. In: *ACM SIGIR'01,* New Orleans, Louisiana, pp. 96-104.

[9] Gao, J., Nie, J. Y., Zhang, J., Xun, E., Su, Y., Zhou, M., and Huang, C. (2000). TREC-9 CLIR experiments at MSRCN. In *TREC-9*, pp. 343-353..

[10] Hull, D. A., and Grefenstette, G. (1996). Querying across languages: a dictionary-based approach to multilingual information retrieval. In: *ACM SIGIR'96*. pp. 49-57.

[11] Jang, M.G., Myaeng, S. H., and Park S. Y. (1999). Using mutual information to resolve query translation ambiguities and query term weighting. In *ACL-99*. College Park, Maryland, pp. 223-229.

[12] Lin, D. (1997). Using syntactic dependency as local context to resolve word sense ambiguity. In *Proceedings of ACL/EACL-97*, Madrid, pp. 64-71.

[13] Lin, D. (1998). Automatic retrieval and clustering of similar words. In *COLING-ACL98,* Montreal, Canada, August, pp. 768-774.

[14] Peters, C., and Picchi, E. (1996). Cross language information retrieval: A system for comparable corpus querying. In *SIGIR'96 Workshop on Cross-linguistic Information Retrieval*, pp. 24--33.

[15] Robertson, S. E., and Walker, S. (2000). Microsoft Cambridge at TREC-9: Filtering track. In *TREC-9*, pp. 361-368.

[16] Voorhees, E., Harman, D. (2001). Overview of the ninth text retrieval conference (TREC-9). In *TREC-9* pp. 1-14.

[17] Xu, J., and Weischedel, R. (2000). TREC-9 cross-lingual retrieval at BBN. In *TREC-9*, pp. 106-116.

[18] Zhou, M., Ding, Y., and Huang, C. (2001). Improving translation selection with a new translation model trained by independent monolingual corpora. *Computational linguistics and Chinese Language Processing*. Vol. 6, No. 1, pp 1-26.

[19] Mandala, R., Tokunaga, T., and Tanaka, H. (1999). Combining multiple evidence from different types of thesaurus for query expansion. In: *ACM SIGIR'99*. pp 191-197.

Document Clustering with Cluster Refinement and Model Selection Capabilities

Xin Liu, Yihong Gong, Wei Xu
NEC USA, Inc.
C&C Research Laboratories
10080 North Wolfe Road
Cupertino, CA 95014, U.S.A.
{xliu,ygong,xw}@ccrl.sj.nec.com

Shenghuo Zhu
Computer Science Department
University of Rochester
P.O. Box 270226
Rochester, NY 14627, U.S.A.
zsh@cs.rochester.edu

ABSTRACT

In this paper, we propose a document clustering method that strives to achieve: (1) a high accuracy of document clustering, and (2) the capability of estimating the number of clusters in the document corpus (i.e. the model selection capability). To accurately cluster the given document corpus, we employ a richer feature set to represent each document, and use the Gaussian Mixture Model (GMM) together with the Expectation-Maximization (EM) algorithm to conduct an initial document clustering. From this initial result, we identify a set of discriminative features for each cluster, and refine the initially obtained document clusters by voting on the cluster label of each document using this discriminative feature set. This self-refinement process of discriminative feature identification and cluster label voting is iteratively applied until the convergence of document clusters. On the other hand, the model selection capability is achieved by introducing randomness in the cluster initialization stage, and then discovering a value C for the number of clusters N by which running the document clustering process for a fixed number of times yields sufficiently similar results. Performance evaluations exhibit clear superiority of the proposed method with its improved document clustering and model selection accuracies. The evaluations also demonstrate how each feature as well as the cluster refinement process contribute to the document clustering accuracy.

Categories and Subject Descriptors

H.3.3 [**Information Storage and Retrieval**]: Information Search and Retrieval—*Clustering, Information Filtering*

General Terms

Algorithms, Performance

Keywords

Document Clustering, Model Selection, Gaussian Mixtures Model, EM algorithm

1. INTRODUCTION

Traditional text search engines accomplish document retrieval by taking a query from the user, and then returning a set of documents matching the user's query. Nowadays, as the primary users of text search engines have shifted from librarian experts to ordinary people who do not have much knowledge about IR methods, and in light of the explosive growth of accessible text documents on the Internet, traditional IR techniques are becoming more and more insufficient for meeting diversified information retrieval needs, and for handling huge volumes of relevant text documents. The problems and limitations associated with traditional IR techniques reside in the following aspects. First, text retrieval results are sensitive to the keywords used by the user to form queries. To retrieve the documents of interest, the user must formulate the query using the keywords that appear in the documents. This is a difficult task, if not impossible, for ordinary people who are not familiar with the vocabulary of the data corpus. Second, as pointed out in [6], traditional text search engines cover only one end of the whole spectrum of information retrieval needs, which is a narrowly specified search for documents matching the user's query. They are not capable of meeting the information retrieval needs from the rest part of the spectrum in which the user has a rather broad or vague information need (e.g. what are the major international events in the year 2001), or has no well defined goals but want to learn more about general contents of the data corpus. Third, with an ever-increasing number of on-line text documents available on the Internet, it has become quite common that a keyword-based text search by a traditional search engine returns hundreds, or even thousands of hits, by which the user is often overwhelmed. As a consequence, access to the desired documents has become a more difficult and arduous task than ever before.

The above problems can be solved to certain degrees by clustering documents according to their topics and main contents. If the document clusters are appropriately created, each of which is assigned an informative label, then it is probable that the user can reach his/her documents of interest without having to worry about which keywords to choose to formulate a query. It is also obvious that information retrieval by browsing through a hierarchy of document clusters is more suitable for users who have a vague information need, or just want to discover general contents of the data corpus. Moreover, document clustering may also be useful as a complement to traditional text search engines when a keyword-based search returns too many documents. When the retrieved document set consists of multiple distinguishable topics/sub-topics, which is often true in most cases, organizing these documents by topics (clusters) certainly helps the user to identify the final set of the desired documents.

Document clustering methods can be mainly categorized into two types: document partitioning (flat clustering) and hierarchical clustering. Although both types of methods have been extensively investigated for several decades, accurately clustering documents without domain-dependent background information, nor predefined document categories or a given list of topics is still a challenging task. Document partitioning methods further face the difficulty of requiring prior knowledge of the number of clusters in the given data corpus. While hierarchical clustering methods avoided this problem by organizing the document corpus into a hierarchical tree structure, clusters in each layer, however, do not necessarily correspond to a meaningful grouping of the document corpus.

In this paper, we propose a document partitioning (flat clustering) method that strives to achieve: (1) a high accuracy of document clustering, and (2) the capability of estimating the number of clusters in the document corpus (i.e. the model selection capability). To accurately cluster the given document corpus, we employ a richer feature set to represent each document, and use the Gaussian Mixture Model (GMM) together with the Expectation-Maximization (EM) algorithm to conduct an initial document clustering. From this initial result, we identify a set of discriminative features for each cluster, and refine the initially obtained document clusters by voting on the cluster label of each document using this discriminative feature set. This self-refinement process of discriminative feature identification and cluster label voting is iteratively applied until the convergence of document clusters. On the other hand, the model selection capability is achieved by introducing randomness in the cluster initialization stage, and then discovering a value C for the number of clusters N by which running the document clustering process for a fixed number of times yields sufficiently similar results. Performance evaluations exhibit clear superiority of the proposed method with its improved document clustering and precise model selection accuracies. The evaluations also demonstrates how each feature as well as the cluster refinement process contribute to the document clustering accuracy.

2. RELATED WORK

Document clustering has been used as a means for improving document retrieval performances, and its potential of being an effective information access method in its own right has long been neglected [6]. Document clustering methods can be mainly categorized into two types: document partitioning and hierarchical clustering. Document partitioning methods decompose a collection of documents into a given number of disjoint clusters which are optimal in terms of some predefined criteria functions. Typical methods in this category include k-Means clustering [15], probabilistic clustering [12, 4], Gaussian Mixture Model (GMM), etc. A common characteristic of these methods is that they all require the user to provide the number of clusters comprising the data corpus. However, in real applications, this is a rather difficult prerequisite to satisfy when given a unknown document corpus without any prior knowledge about it.

There have been research efforts that strive to provide the model selection capability to the above methods. X-means proposed in [11] is an extension of K-means with an added functionality of estimating the number of clusters to generate. The Baysian Information Criterion (BIC) is employed to determine whether to split a cluster or not. The splitting is conducted when the information gain for splitting a cluster is greater than the gain for keeping that cluster.

On the other hand, hierarchical clustering methods cluster a document corpus into a hierarchical tree structure with one cluster at its root encompassing all the documents. The most commonly used method in this category is the hierarchical agglomerative clustering (HAC) [5, 14] which starts by placing each document into a distinct cluster. Pair-wise similarities between all the clusters are computed and the two closest clusters are then merged into a new cluster. This process of computing pair-wise similarities and merging the closest two clusters is repeated until all the documents are merged into one cluster. There are many variations of the HAC which mainly differ in the ways used to compute the similarity between clusters. Typical similarity computations include single-linkage, complete-linkage, group-average linkage, as well as other aggregate measures. The single-linkage, and the complete-linkage use the maximum, and the minimum distance between the two clusters, respectively, while the group-average uses the distance of the cluster centers, to define the similarity of the two clusters. There are also research studies that investigate different types of similarity metrics and their impacts on clustering accuracies [9].

In contrast to the HAC method and its variations, there are hierarchical clustering methods that use the annealed EM algorithm to extract hierarchical relations within the document corpus [10]. The key idea is the introduction of a temperature T, which is used as a control parameter that is initialized at a high value and successively lowered until the performance on the held-out data starts to decrease. Since annealing leads through a sequence of so-called phase transitions where clusters obtained in the previous iteration further split, it generates a hierarchical tree structure for the given document set. Unlike the HAC method, leaf nodes in this tree structure do not necessarily correspond to individual documents.

In recent years, document clustering techniques have been extended to incorporate the documents' time stamps for the topic detection and tracking tasks initiated by NIST. The CMU's topic detection system divides the chronologically ordered stream of news stories into non-overlapping and sequential buckets, clusters the stories within each bucket using the HAC algorithm, and then merges clusters among the buckets [17]. Additional shuffling and reclustering among stories in adjacent buckets are conducted, and have been proven effective, for improving the performances. The UMass's system is constructed based upon its INQUERY text search engine, using a combination of TD-IDF term weighting, single-pass clustering, and adaptive threshold finding [3]. The Dragon's system applies the unigram and bigram language models for event representation, and uses a k-means clustering method for document classification [16].

3. THE PROPOSED METHOD

The goals we set for the proposed document clustering method are: (1) a high document clustering accuracy, and (2) a high precision model selection capability. The proposed method is autonomous, unsupervised, and performs document clustering without the requirement of domain-dependent background information, nor predefined document categories or a given list of topics. It achieves a high document clustering accuracy in the following manner. First, a richer feature set is employed to represent each document. For document retrieval and clustering purposes, a document is typically represented by a term-frequency vector with its dimensions equal to the number of unique words in the corpus, and each of its components indicating how many times a particular word occurs in the document. However, our experimental study shows that document clustering based on term-frequency vectors often yields poor performances because not all the words in the documents are discriminative or characteristic words. An investigation of various data corpora also shows that documents belonging to the same topic/event usually share many name entities, such as names of people, organizations, locations, etc, and contain many similar word associations. For example, among the documents reporting the Clinton-Lewinsky scandal, "Clinton", "Lewinsky", "Ken Starr", "Linda Tripp", etc, are the common name entities, and "grand jury", "independent counsel", "supreme court" are the word pairs that most frequently appear. Based on these observations, we represent each document using a richer feature set that consists of frequencies of salient name identities, word-pairs, as well as all the unique terms. Using this feature set, we conduct initial document clustering based on the Gaussian Mixture Model (GMM) and the Expectation-Maximization (EM) algorithm. This clustering process generates a set of document clusters with a local maximum-likelihood.

To further improve the document clustering accuracy, we discover a group of discriminative features from the initial clustering result, and then refine the document clusters based on the majority vote using this discriminative feature set. A major deficiency of the above GMM+EM clustering method, as well as many other clustering methods in the literature, is that they treat all the features in a feature set equally, some of which are discriminative while others are not. In many document corpora, it is often the case that discriminative words (features) occur less frequently than non-discriminative words. When the feature vector of a document is dominated by non-discriminative features, clustering the document using the above methods may result in a misplacement of the document.

To determine whether a word is discriminative or not, we introduce a discriminative feature metric (DFM) which compares the word's occurrence frequency inside a cluster against that outside the cluster. If a word has the highest occurrence frequency inside cluster i and has a low occurrence frequency outside that cluster, this word is highly discriminative for cluster i. Using this DFM, we identify a set of discriminative features, each of which is associated with a particular cluster. This discriminative feature set is then used to vote on the cluster label of each document. Assume that the document d_j contains λ discriminative features, and that the largest number of the λ features are associated with cluster i, then document d_j is voted to belong to cluster i. By voting on the cluster labels for all the documents, we get a refined document clustering result. This process of determining discriminative features, and refining the clusters using the majority vote is repeated until the clustering result converges. Through this self-refinement process, the correctness of the whole cluster set is gradually improved, and eventually, documents in the corpus are accurately grouped according to their topics/main contents.

To achieve the model selection capability, we assume a value C for the number of clusters N comprising the data corpus, conduct the document clustering several times by randomly selecting C initial clusters, and observe the degree of disparity in the clustering results. Then we repeat these operations for different values of N, and select the value C_{min} of N that yields the minimum disparity in the clustering results. The basic idea here is that, if our guess on the number of clusters is correct, each repetition of the clustering process will produce similar sets of document clusters; otherwise, clustering result obtained from each repetition must be unstable, showing a large disparity.

The following subsections provide the detailed descriptions of main operations comprising the proposed document clustering method.

3.1 Feature Set

We use the following three kinds of features to represent each document d_i.

Term frequencies (TF): Let $\mathcal{W} = \{w_1, w_2, \ldots, w_\Gamma\}$ be the complete vocabulary set of the document corpus after the stop-words removal and words stemming operations. The term-frequency vector $\mathbf{t}_i$ of document d_i is defined as

$$\mathbf{t}_i = \{tf(w_1, d_i), tf(w_2, d_i), \ldots, tf(w_\Gamma, d_i)\} \quad (1)$$

where $tf(w_x, d_y)$ denotes the term frequency of word $w_x \in \mathcal{W}$ in document d_y.

Name entities (NE): which include names of people, organizations, locations, etc. We detect the name entities using a support vector machine-based classifier [13], and use the tagged Brown corpus [1] as training examples to train the classifier. Once the name entities are detected, we compute their occurrence frequencies within the document corpus, and discard those name entities which have very low occurrence values. Let $\mathcal{E} = \{e_1, e_2, \ldots, e_\Delta\}$ be the complete set of name entities whose occurrence values are above the predefined threshold T_e. The name-entity vector $\mathbf{e}_i$ of document d_i is defined as

$$\mathbf{e}_i = \{of(e_1, d_i), of(e_2, d_i), \ldots, of(e_\Delta, d_i)\} \quad (2)$$

where $of(e_x, d_y)$ denotes the occurrence frequency of name entity $e_x \in \mathcal{E}$ in document d_y.

Term pairs (TP): If the document corpus has a large vocabulary set, then the number of possible term associations will become unacceptably large. To make the feature set compact, we take only those term associations which have statistical significance for the document corpus. We use the χ^2 distribution metric $\phi(w_x, w_y)^2$ defined below [8] to measure the statistical significance for the association of terms w_x and w_y.

$$\phi(w_x, w_y)^2 = \frac{(ad - bc)^2}{(a+b)(a+c)(b+d)(c+d)} \tag{3}$$

where $a = freq(w_x, w_y)$, $b = freq(\overline{w_x}, w_y)$, $c = freq(w_x, \overline{w_y})$, and $d = freq(\overline{w_x}, \overline{w_y})$ denote the number of sentences in the whole document corpus that contain both w_x, w_y; w_y but no w_x; w_x but no w_y; and no w_x, w_y; respectively. Let $\mathcal{A}$ be the ordered set of term associations whose χ^2 distribution metric $\phi(w_x, w_y)^2$ are above the predefined threshold T_a: $\mathcal{A} = \{(w_x, w_y) | w_x \in \mathcal{W};\ w_y \in \mathcal{W};\ \phi(w_x, w_y) > T_a\}$. The term-pair vector $\mathbf{a}_i$ of document d_i is defined as

$$\mathbf{a}_i = \{count(w_x, w_y) | (w_x, w_y) \in \mathcal{A}\} \tag{4}$$

where $count(w_x, w_y)$ denotes the number of sentences in document d_i that contains both w_x and w_y.

With the above feature vectors $\mathbf{t}_i$, $\mathbf{e}_i$, and $\mathbf{a}_i$, the complete feature vector $\mathbf{d}_i$ for document d_i is formed as: $\mathbf{d}_i = \{\mathbf{t}_i, \mathbf{e}_i, \mathbf{a}_i\}$.

Text clustering tasks are well known for their high dimensionality. The document feature vector $\mathbf{d}_i$ created above has nearly one thousand dimensions. To reduce the possible over-fitting problem, we apply the singular value decomposition (SVD) to the whole set of document feature vectors $\mathcal{D} = \{\mathbf{d}_1, \mathbf{d}_2, \ldots, \mathbf{d}_N\}$, and select the twenty dimensions which have the largest singular values to form the clustering feature space. Using this reduced feature space, document clustering is conducted using the Gaussian mixture model together with the EM algorithm to obtain the preliminary clusters for the document corpus.

3.2 Gaussian Mixture Model

The Gaussian Mixture Model (GMM) for document clustering assumes that each document vector $\mathbf{d}$ is generated from a model Θ that consists of the known number of clusters c_i where $i = 1, 2, \ldots, k$.

$$P(\mathbf{d}|\Theta) = \sum_{i=1}^{k} P(c_i)P(\mathbf{d}|c_i) \tag{5}$$

Every cluster c_i is a m-dimensional Gaussian distribution which contributes to the document vector $\mathbf{d}$ independent of other clusters:

$$P(\mathbf{d}|c_i) = \frac{1}{(2\pi)^{m/2}|\Sigma_i|^{1/2}} \exp(-1/2(\mathbf{d} - \mu_i)^T \Sigma_i^{-1} (\mathbf{d} - \mu_i)) \tag{6}$$

With this GMM formulation, the clustering task becomes the problem of fitting the model Θ given a set of N document vectors $\mathcal{D}$. Model Θ is uniquely determined by the set of centroids μ_i's and covariance matrices Σ_i's. The Expectation-Maximization(EM) algorithm [7] is a well established algorithm that produces the maximum-likelihood solution of the model.

With the Gaussian components, the two steps in one iteration of the EM algorithm are as follows:

- *E-step* : re-estimates the expectations based on the previous iteration

$$P(c_i|\mathbf{d}_j) = \frac{P(c_i)^{old} P(\mathbf{d}_j|c_i)}{\sum_{i=1}^{k} P(c_i)^{old} P(\mathbf{d}_j|c_i)} \tag{7}$$

$$P(c_i)^{new} = \frac{1}{N} \sum_{j=1}^{N} P(c_i|\mathbf{d}_j) \tag{8}$$

- *M-step* : updates the model parameters to maximize the log-likelihood

$$\mu_i = \frac{\sum_{j=1}^{N} P(c_i|\mathbf{d}_j)\mathbf{d}_j}{\sum_{j=1}^{N} P(c_i|\mathbf{d}_j)} \tag{9}$$

$$\Sigma_i = \frac{\sum_{j=1}^{N} P(c_i|\mathbf{d}_j)(\mathbf{d}_j - \mu_i)(\mathbf{d}_j - \mu_i)^T}{\sum_{j=1}^{N} P(c_i|\mathbf{d}_j)} \tag{10}$$

In our implementation of the above GMM+EM algorithm, the initial set of centroids μ_i's are randomly chosen from a normal distribution with the mean $\mu_0 = \frac{1}{N}\sum_i \mathbf{d}_i$ and the covariance matrix $\Sigma_0 = \frac{1}{N}\sum_i (\mathbf{d}_i - \mu_0)(\mathbf{d}_i - \mu_0)^T$. The initial set of covariance matrices of Σ_i's are identically set to Σ_0. The log-likelihood that the data corpus is generated from the model Θ, $\mathcal{L}(\mathcal{D}|\Theta)$, is utilized as the termination condition for the iterative process. The EM iteration is terminated when $\mathcal{L}(\mathcal{D}|\Theta)$ comes to convergence.

The above approach to initializing centroids μ_i's and covariance matrices Σ_i's enables us to randomly pick up an initial set of clusters for each repetition of the document clustering process, and will play a significant role in achieving the model selection capability (see Section 3.4).

After the model Θ has been estimated, the cluster label l_i of each document $\mathbf{d}_i$ can be determined as $l_i = \arg\max_j p(\mathbf{d}_i|c_j)$.

3.3 Refining Clusters by Feature Voting

The above GMM+EM clustering method generates an initial set of clusters for the given document corpus. As described in Section 3, because the GMM+EM clustering method treats all the features equally, when the feature vector of a document is dominated by non-discriminative features, the document might be misplaced into a wrong cluster. To further improve the document clustering accuracy, we discover a group of discriminative features from the initial clustering result, and then iteratively refine the document clusters using this discriminative feature set.

To determine whether a feature f_i is discriminative or not, we define the following discriminative feature metric DFM(f_i),

$$\text{DFM}(f_i) = \log \frac{g_{in}(f_i)}{g_{out}(f_i)} \tag{11}$$

$$g_{in}(f_i) = \max(g(f_i, c_1), g(f_i, c_2), \ldots, g(f_i, c_k)) \tag{12}$$

$$g_{out}(f_i) = \frac{\sum_j g(f_i, c_j) - g_{in}(f_i)}{k - 1} \tag{13}$$

where $g(f_i, c_j)$ denotes the number of occurrences of feature f_i in cluster c_j, and k denotes the total number of document clusters. For the document clustering purpose, discriminative features are those that occur more frequently inside a particular cluster than outside that cluster, whereas non-discriminative features are those that have similar occurrence frequencies among all the clusters. What the metric DFM(f_i) reflects is exactly this disparity in occurrence frequencies of feature f_i among different clusters. In other words, the more discriminative the feature f_i, the larger value the metric $\text{DFM}(f_i)$ takes. In our real implementation, discriminative features are defined as those whose DFM values exceed the predefined threshold T_{df}.

When the discriminative feature f_i has the highest occurrence frequency in cluster c_x, we say that f_i is discriminative for c_x, and save the cluster label x for f_i (denoted as σ_i) for the later feature voting operation. By definition, σ_i can be expressed as:

$$\sigma_i = \arg\max_x \ g(f_i, c_x) \tag{14}$$

Once the set of discriminative features has been identified, we apply the following iterative voting scheme to refine the document clusters.

1. Obtain the initial set of document clusters $\mathcal{C} = \{c_1, c_2, \ldots, c_k\}$ using the GMM+EM method.

2. From the cluster set $\mathcal{C}$, identify the set of discriminative features $\mathcal{F} = \{f_1, f_2, \ldots, f_\Lambda\}$ along with their associate cluster labels $\mathcal{S} = \{\sigma_1, \sigma_2, \ldots, \sigma_\Lambda\}$.

3. For each document d_j in the whole document corpus, determine its cluster label l_j by the majority vote using the discriminative feature set.

   Assume that the document d_j contains a subset of discriminative features $\mathcal{F}^{(j)} = \{f_1^{(j)}, f_2^{(j)}, \ldots, f_\lambda^{(j)}\} \subseteq \mathcal{F}$, and that the cluster labels associated with this subset $\mathcal{F}^{(j)}$ are $\mathcal{S}^{(j)} = \{\sigma_1^{(j)}, \sigma_2^{(j)}, \ldots, \sigma_\lambda^{(j)}\}$. Then, the new cluster label for document d_j is determined as

   $$l_j^{new} = \arg\max_{\sigma_y \in \mathcal{S}^{(j)}} \ cnt(\sigma_y, \mathcal{S}^{(j)}) \tag{15}$$

   where $cnt(\sigma_y, \mathcal{S}^{(j)})$ denotes the number of times the label σ_y occurs in $\mathcal{S}^{(j)}$.

4. Compare the new document cluster set with $\mathcal{C}$. If the result converges, terminate the process; otherwise, set $\mathcal{C}$ to the new cluster set, and go to Step 2.

The above iterative voting process is a self-refinement process. It starts with an initial set of document clusters with a relatively low accuracy. From this initial clustering result, the process strives to find features that are discriminative for each cluster, and then refine the clusters by voting on the cluster label of each document using these discriminative features. Through this self-refinement process, the correctness of the whole cluster set is gradually improved, and eventually, documents in the corpus are accurately grouped according to their topics/main contents.

3.4 Model Selection

Our approach for realizing the model selection capability is based on the hypothesis that, if we search for solutions (i.e. correct document clusters) in an incorrect solution space (i.e. using an incorrect number of clusters), result obtained from each run of the document clustering will be quite randomized because the solution does not exist. Otherwise, results obtained from multiple runs must be very similar assuming that there is only one genuine solution in the solution space. Translating this into the model selection problem, it can be said that, if our guess on the number of clusters is correct, each run of the document clustering will produce similar sets of document clusters; otherwise, clustering result obtained from each run must be unstable, showing a large disparity.

To measure the similarity between the two sets of document clusters $\mathcal{C} = \{c_1, c_2, \ldots, c_k\}$ and $\mathcal{C}' = \{c_1', c_2', \ldots, c_k'\}$, we use the following mutual information metric $\text{MI}(\mathcal{C}, \mathcal{C}')$:

$$\text{MI}(\mathcal{C}, \mathcal{C}') = \sum_{c_i \in \mathcal{C}, c_j' \in \mathcal{C}'} p(c_i, c_j') \cdot \log_2 \frac{p(c_i, c_j')}{p(c_i) \cdot p(c_j')} \tag{16}$$

where $p(c_i)$, $p(c_j')$ denote the probabilities that a document arbitrarily selected from the corpus belongs to the clusters c_i and c_j', respectively, and $p(c_i, c_j')$ denotes the joint probability that this arbitrarily selected document belongs to the clusters c_i as well as c_j' at the same time. $\text{MI}(\mathcal{C}, \mathcal{C}')$ takes values between zero and $\max(\text{H}(\mathcal{C}), \text{H}(\mathcal{C}'))$, where $\text{H}(\mathcal{C})$ and $\text{H}(\mathcal{C}')$ are the entropies of $\mathcal{C}$ and $\mathcal{C}'$, respectively. It reaches the maximum $\max(\text{H}(\mathcal{C}), \text{H}(\mathcal{C}'))$ when the two sets of document clusters are identical, whereas it becomes zero when the two sets are completely independent. Another important character of $\text{MI}(\mathcal{C}, \mathcal{C}')$ is that, for each $c_i \in \mathcal{C}$, it does not need to find the corresponding counterpart in $\mathcal{C}'$, and the value keeps the same for all kinds of permutations. To simplify comparisons between different cluster set pairs, we use the following normalized metric $\widehat{\text{MI}}(\mathcal{C}, \mathcal{C}')$ which takes values between zero and one:

$$\widehat{\text{MI}}(\mathcal{C}, \mathcal{C}') = \frac{\text{MI}(\mathcal{C}, \mathcal{C}')}{\max(\text{H}(\mathcal{C}), \text{H}(\mathcal{C}'))} \tag{17}$$

The model selection algorithm is described as follows:

1. Get the user's input for the data range (R_l, R_h) within which to guess the possible number of document clusters.

2. Set $k = R_l$.

3. Cluster the document corpus into k clusters using the proposed method, and run the clustering process with the different cluster initializations for Q times.

4. Compute $\widehat{\text{MI}}$ between each pair of the results, and take the average on all the $\widehat{\text{MI}}$'s.

5. If $k < R_h$, $k = k + 1$, go to Step 3; otherwise, go to Step 6.

6. Select the k which yields the largest average $\widehat{\text{MI}}$.

4. EXPERIMENTAL EVALUATIONS

Our evaluation database is constructed using the NIST Topic Detection and Tracking (TDT2) corpus [2]. The TDT2 corpus is composed of documents from six news agencies, and contains 100 major news events reported in 1998. Each document in the corpus has a unique label that indicates which news event it belongs to. From this corpus, we have selected 15 news events reported by three news agencies including CNN, ABC, and VOA. Table 1 provides detailed statistics of our evaluation database.

4.1 Document Clustering Evaluation

The testing data used for evaluating the proposed document clustering method are formed by mixing documents from multiple topics arbitrarily selected from our evaluation database. At each run of the test, documents from a

Table 1: Selected topics from the TDT2 Corpus

Event ID	Event Subject	No. of Docs				Max sents /doc	Min sents /doc	Avg sents /doc
		ABC	CNN	VOA	Total			
01	Asian Economic Crisis	27	90	289	406	86	1	12
02	Monica Lewinsky Case	102	497	96	695	157	1	12
13	1998 Winter Olympics	21	81	108	210	47	1	11
15	Current Conflict with Iraq	77	438	345	860	73	1	12
18	Bombing AL Clinic	9	73	5	87	29	2	8
23	Violence in Algeria	1	1	60	62	42	1	9
32	Sgt. Gene McKinney	6	91	3	100	32	2	7
39	India Parliamentary Elections	1	1	29	31	45	2	15
44	National Tobacco Settlement	26	163	17	206	52	2	9
48	Jonesboro shooting	13	73	15	101	79	2	16
70	India, A Nuclear Power?	24	98	129	251	54	2	12
71	Israeli-Palestinian Talks (London)	5	62	48	115	33	2	9
76	Anti-Suharto Violence	13	55	114	182	44	1	11
77	Unabomber	9	66	6	81	37	2	10
86	GM Strike	14	83	24	121	37	2	8

selected number k of topics are mixed, and the mixed document set, along with the cluster number k, are provided to the clustering process. The result is evaluated by comparing the cluster label of each document with its label provided by the TDT2 corpus. Two metrics, the accuracy (AC) and the $\widehat{\text{MI}}$ defined by Equation (17), are used to measure the document clustering performance. Given a document d_i, let l_i and α_i be the cluster label and the label provided by the TDT2 corpus, respectively. The AC is defined as follows:

$$\text{AC} = \frac{\sum_{i=1}^{N} \delta(\alpha_i, \text{map}(l_i))}{N} \tag{18}$$

where N denotes the total number of documents in the test, $\delta(x, y)$ is the delta function that equals one if $x = y$ and equals zero otherwise, and $\text{map}(l_i)$ is the mapping function that maps each cluster label l_i to the equivalent label from the TDT2 corpus. Computing AC is time consuming because there are $k!$ possible corresponding relationships between k cluster labels l_i and TDT2 labels α_i, and we have to test all these $k!$ relationships to discover a genuine one. In contrast to AC, metric $\widehat{\text{MI}}$ is easy to compute because it does not require the knowledge of corresponding relationships, and provides a good alternative for measuring the document clustering accuracy.

Table 2 shows the results comprising 15 runs of the test. Labels in the first column denote how the corresponding test data are constructed. For example, label "ABC-01-02-15" means that the test data is composed of events 01, 02, and 15 reported by ABC, and "ABC+CNN-01-13-18-32-48-70-71-77-86" denotes that the test data is composed of events 01, 13, 18, 32, 48, 70, 71, 77 and 86 from both ABC and CNN. To understand how the three kinds of features as well as the cluster refinement process contribute to the document clustering accuracy, we also conducted document clustering using only the GMM+EM method under the following four different feature combinations: TF only, TF+NE, TF+TP, and TF+NE+TP. Note that the GMM+EM method using TF only is a close representation of traditional probabilistic document clustering methods [12, 4], and therefore, its performance can be used as a benchmark for measuring the improvements achieved by the proposed method.

Our finding can be summarized as follows: With the GMM+EM method itself, using TF, TF+NE, and TF+TP produce similar document clustering performances, while using all these three kinds of features generates the best performance. Regardless of the above feature combinations, results generated by using the GMM+EM in tandem with the cluster refinement process are always superior to the results generated by using the GMM+EM alone. Performance improvements made by the cluster refinement process become very obvious when the GMM+EM method generates poor clustering results. For example, for the test data "VOA-12-39-48-71" (row 11), the GMM+EM method using TF alone produces document clustering accuracy of 0.6939. Using all three kinds of features with the GMM+EM method increases the accuracy to 0.8061, a 16% improvement. Performing the cluster refinement process in tandem with the GMM+EM method further improves the accuracy to 0.9898, another 23% improvement.

4.2 Model Selection Evaluation

Performance evaluations for the model selection are conducted in a similar fashion to the document clustering evaluations. At each run of the test, documents from a selected number k of topics are mixed, and the mixed document set is provided to the model selection algorithm. This time, instead of providing the number k, the algorithm outputs its guess at the number of topics contained in the test data. Table 3 presents the results of 12 runs.

For comparisons, we also implemented the BIC-based model selection method [11] and evaluated its performances using the same test data. Evaluation results generated by the two methods are displayed side by side in Table 3. Clearly, the proposed method remarkably outperforms the BIC-based method: among the 12 runs of the test, the former made nine correct guesses while the latter made only four correct ones. The great performance gap comes from the different hypotheses adopted by the two methods. The BIC-based method is based on the naive hypothesis that a simpler model is a better model, and hence, it gives penalties to the choices of more complicated solutions. Obviously, this hypothesis may not be true for all real-world problems, especially for clustering document corpora with complicated internal structures. In contrast, our proposed method is

Table 2: Evaluation Results for Document Clustering

Test Data	GMM+EM								GMM+EM + Refinement	
	TF		TF+NE		TF+TP		TF+NE+TP			
	AC	$\widehat{MI}$	AC	MI	AC	$\widehat{MI}$	AC	$\widehat{MI}$	AC	$\widehat{MI}$
ABC-01-02-15	0.8571	0.6579	0.8132	0.5554	0.5055	0.3635	0.9011	0.7832	1.0000	1.0000
ABC-02-15-44	0.6829	0.4474	0.9122	0.6936	0.8195	0.6183	0.9659	0.8559	0.9902	0.9444
ABC-01-13-44-70	0.6531	0.6770	0.7653	0.6427	0.8673	0.7177	0.7449	0.6286	1.0000	1.0000
ABC-01-44-48-70	0.8111	0.7124	0.8444	0.7328	0.7111	0.6234	0.8000	0.6334	1.0000	1.0000
CNN-01-02-15	0.9688	0.8445	0.9707	0.8546	0.9678	0.8440	0.9795	0.8848	0.9756	0.9008
CNN-02-15-44	0.9791	0.8896	0.9827	0.9086	0.9791	0.8903	0.9927	0.9547	0.9964	0.9742
CNN-02-74-76	0.8931	0.3266	0.9946	0.9012	0.9909	0.8476	0.9982	0.9602	1.0000	1.0000
VOA-01-02-15	0.7292	0.5106	0.8646	0.6611	0.7812	0.5923	0.8438	0.6250	0.9896	0.9571
VOA-01-13-76	0.7396	0.4663	0.9479	0.8608	0.7500	0.4772	0.9479	0.8608	0.9583	0.8619
VOA-01-23-70-76	0.7422	0.5582	0.9219	0.8196	0.8359	0.6558	0.9297	0.8321	0.9453	0.8671
VOA-12-39-48-71	0.6939	0.5039	0.8673	0.7643	0.6429	0.4878	0.8061	0.8237	0.9898	0.9692
VOA-44-48-70-71-76-77-86	0.6459	0.6465	0.7535	0.7338	0.5751	0.6521	0.7734	0.7539	0.8527	0.7720
ABC+CNN-01-13-18-32-48-70-71-77-86	0.9420	0.8977	0.9716	0.9390	0.8343	0.8671	0.9633	0.9209	0.9704	0.9351
CNN+VOA-01-13-48-70-71-76-77-86	0.6985	0.6729	0.9339	0.8890	0.8939	0.8159	0.9431	0.9044	0.9262	0.8854
ABC+CNN+VOA-44-48-70-71-76-77-86	0.7454	0.7321	0.7721	0.8297	0.8871	0.8401	0.8768	0.9189	0.9938	0.9807

based on the hypothesis that searching for the solution in a wrong solution space yields randomized results, and therefore, it prefers solutions that are consistent and stable. The superior performance of the proposed method suggests that its underlying hypothesis provides a better description of real-world problems, especially for document clustering applications.

Table 3: Evaluation Results for Model Selection

Test Data	Proposed	BIC-based
ABC-01-03	○ 2	× 1
ABC-01-02-15	○ 3	× 2
ABC-02-48-70	× 2	× 2
ABC-44-70-01-13	○ 4	× 2
ABC-44-48-70-76	○ 4	× 3
CNN-01-02-15	× 4	× 26
CNN-01-02-13-15-18	○ 5	× 17
CNN-44-48-70-71-76-77	× 5	× 23
VOA-01-02-15	○ 3	○ 3
VOA-01-13-76	○ 3	○ 3
VOA-01-23-70-76	○ 4	○ 4
VOA-12-39-48-71	○ 4	○ 4

○, × indicate correct, wrong answers, respectively.

4.3 Discussions

There are analogies between our proposed document clustering method and the topic detection systems developed for the NIST's topic detection and tracking (TDT) project in that they are all aimed at detecting topics from the given data corpus and grouping the stories belonging to the same topics. However, the TDT project focuses on detecting and tracking topics from chronologically ordered stream of news stories, while our document clustering method works with more general data corpora which do not have chronological information. Because of this difference, temporal information is not explored by our proposed method. As for the performance measures, the TDT project emphasizes more on the accuracy of topic detections while gives no penalty to the inaccuracy of predicting the actual number of topics contained in the incoming data stream. More precisely, the TDT project evaluated each system by first finding the 25 system-defined clusters that best match the 25 manually defined events, and then counting the differences among the cluster/event pairs. In contrast, our document clustering method strives to achieve high accuracies for both clustering documents and predicting the number of document clusters, and performance evaluations have been conducted separately on these two matters. These differences of emphases have made it less meaningful to evaluate our clustering method using the TDT's performance metrics, and hence, we decide not to directly compare our method with the TDT's topic detection systems.

5. SUMMARIES

In this paper, we have proposed a document clustering method that achieves a high accuracy of document clustering and the model section capability. To accurately cluster the given document corpus, we employed a richer feature set to represent each document, and used the GMM Model together with EM algorithm to conduct the initial document clustering. From this initial result, we identified a set of discriminative features for each cluster, and used this feature set to refine the document clusters based on a majority voting scheme. The discriminative feature identification and cluster refinement operations were iteratively applied until the convergence of document clusters. On the other hand, the model selection capability has been achieved by guessing a value C for the number of clusters N, conducting the document clustering several times by randomly selecting C initial clusters, and observing the degree of disparity in the clustering results. The experimental evaluations not only showed the effectiveness of the proposed document clustering method, but also demonstrated how each feature as well as the cluster refinement process contribute to the document clustering accuracy.

6. REFERENCES

[1] Tagged brown corpus: http://www.hit.uib.no/icame/brown/bcm.html, 1979.

[2] Nist topic detection and tracking corpus: http://www.nist.gov/speech/tests/tdt/tdt98/index.htm, 1998.

[3] J. Allan, R. Papka, and V. Lavrenko. Online new event detection and tracking. In *Proceedings of the 21th ACM SIGIR Conference (SIGIR'98)*, 1998.

[4] L. Baker and A. McCallum. Distributional clustering of words for text classification. In *Proceedings of ACM SIGIR*, 1998.

[5] W. Croft. Clustering large files of documents using the single-link method. *Journal of the American Society of Information Science*, 28:341–344, 1977.

[6] D. R. Cutting, D. R. Karger, J. O. Pederson, and J. W. Tukey. Scatter/gather: A cluster-based approach to browsing large document collections. In *Proceedings of ACM/SIGIR*, 1992.

[7] R. O. Duda, P. E. Hart, and D. G. Stork. *Pattern Classification second edition.* Wiley, New York, 2000.

[8] W. A. Gale and K. W. Church. Identifying word correspondences in parallel texts. In *Proc. of the Speech and Natural Language Workshop*, page 152, Pacific Grove, CA, 1991.

[9] M. Goldszmidt and M. Sahami. A probabilistic approach to full-text document clustering. In *SRI Technical Report ITAD-433-MS-98-044*, 1997.

[10] T. Hofmann. The cluster-abstraction model: Unsupervised learning of topic hierarchies from text data. In *Proceedings of IJCAI-99*, 1999.

[11] D. Pelleg and A. Moore. X-means: Extending k-means with efficient estimation ofthe number of clusters. In *Proceedings of the Seventeenth International Conference on Machine Learning (ICML2000)*, June 2000.

[12] F. Pereira, N. Tishby, and L. Lee. Distributional clustering of english words. In *Proceedings of the Association for Computational Linguistics*, pages 183–190, 1993.

[13] J. Platt. J. platt. sequential minimal optimization: A fast algorithm for training support vector machines. technical report 98-14, microsoft research. http://www.research.microsoft.com/ jplatt/smo.html., 1998.

[14] P. Willett. Recent trends in hierarchical document clustering: a critical review. *nformaton Processing & Management*, 24(5):577–597, 1988.

[15] P. Willett. Document clustering using an inverted file approach. *Journal of Information Science*, 2:223–231, 1990.

[16] J. Yamron, I. Carp, L. Gillick, S. Lowe, and P. van Mulbregt. Topic tracking in a news stream. In *Proceedings of the DARPA Broadcast News Workshop*, Feb. 1999.

[17] Y. Yang, T. Pierce, and J. Carbonell. A study on retrospective and online event detection. In *Proceedings of the 21th ACM SIGIR Conference (SIGIR'98)*, 1998.

Document Clustering with Committees

Patrick Pantel and Dekang Lin
University of Alberta
Department of Computing Science
Edmonton, Alberta T6H 2E1 Canada
{ppantel, lindek}@cs.ualberta.ca

ABSTRACT

Document clustering is useful in many information retrieval tasks: document browsing, organization and viewing of retrieval results, generation of Yahoo-like hierarchies of documents, etc. The general goal of clustering is to group data elements such that the intra-group similarities are high and the inter-group similarities are low. We present a clustering algorithm called CBC (Clustering By Committee) that is shown to produce higher quality clusters in document clustering tasks as compared to several well known clustering algorithms. It initially discovers a set of tight clusters (high intra-group similarity), called committees, that are well scattered in the similarity space (low inter-group similarity). The union of the committees is but a subset of all elements. The algorithm proceeds by assigning elements to their most similar committee. Evaluating cluster quality has always been a difficult task. We present a new evaluation methodology that is based on the editing distance between output clusters and manually constructed classes (the answer key). This evaluation measure is more intuitive and easier to interpret than previous evaluation measures.

Categories and Subject Descriptors

H.3.3 [**Information Storage and Retrieval**]: Information Search and Retrieval---*Clustering*.

General Terms

Algorithms, Measurement, Experimentation.

Keywords

Document clustering, evaluation methodology, machine learning, document representation.

1. INTRODUCTION

Document clustering was initially proposed for improving the precision and recall of information retrieval systems [18]. Because clustering is often too slow for large corpora and has indifferent performance [8], document clustering has been used more recently in document browsing [3], to improve the organization and viewing of retrieval results [6], to accelerate nearest-neighbor search [1] and to generate Yahoo-like hierarchies [12].

Common characteristics of document clustering include:

- there is a large number of documents to be clustered;
- the number of output clusters may be large;
- each document has a large number of features; e.g., the features may include all the terms in the document; and
- the feature space, the union of the features of all documents, is even larger.

In this paper, we propose a clustering algorithm, CBC (Clustering By Committee), which produces higher quality clusters in document clustering tasks as compared to several well known clustering algorithms. Many clustering algorithms represent a cluster by the centroid of all of its members (e.g., K-means) [13] or by a representative element (e.g., K-medoids) [10]. When averaging over all elements in a cluster, the centroid of a cluster may be unduly influenced by elements that only marginally belong to the cluster or by elements that also belong to other clusters. To illustrate this point, consider the task of clustering words. We can use the contexts of words as features and group together the words that tend to appear in similar contexts. For instance, U.S. state names can be clustered this way because they tend to appear in the following contexts:

(List A)	___ appellate court	campaign in ___
	___ capital	governor of ___
	___ driver's license	illegal in ___
	___ outlaws sth.	primary in ___
	___'s sales tax	senator for ___

If we create a centroid of all the state names, the centroid will also contain features such as:

(List B)	___'s airport	archbishop of ___
	___'s business district	fly to ___
	___'s mayor	mayor of ___
	___'s subway	outskirts of ___

because some of the state names (like *New York* and *Washington*) are also names of cities.

SIGIR'02, August 11-15, 2002, Tampere, Finland.

Using a single representative from a cluster may be problematic too because each individual element has its own idiosyncrasies that may not be shared by other members of the cluster.

CBC constructs the centroid of a cluster by averaging the feature vectors of a subset of the cluster members. The subset is viewed as a committee that determines which other elements belong to the cluster. By carefully choosing committee members, the features of the centroid tend to be the more typical features of the target class. For example, our system chose the following committee members to compute the centroid of the state cluster: Illinois, Michigan, Minnesota, Iowa, Wisconsin, Indiana, Nebraska and Vermont. As a result, the centroid contains only features like those in List A.

Evaluating clustering results is a very difficult task. We introduce a new methodology that is based on the editing distance between clustering results and manually constructed classes (the answer key). We argue that it is easier to interpret the results of this evaluation measure than the results of previous measures.

The remainder of this paper is organized as follows. In the next section, we review related clustering algorithms that are commonly used in document clustering. Section 3 describes our representational model and in Section 4 we present the CBC algorithm. The evaluation methodology and experimental results are presented in Sections 5 and 6. In Section 7, we show an example application of CBC. Finally, we conclude with a discussion and future work.

2. RELATED WORK

Generally, clustering algorithms can be categorized as hierarchical and partitional. In hierarchical agglomerative algorithms, clusters are constructed by iteratively merging the most similar clusters. These algorithms differ in how they compute cluster similarity. In single-link clustering [16], the similarity between two clusters is the similarity between their most similar members while complete-link clustering [11] uses the similarity between their least similar members. Average-link clustering [5] computes this similarity as the average similarity between all pairs of elements across clusters. The complexity of these algorithms is $O(n^2\log n)$, where n is the number of elements to be clustered [7]. These algorithms are too inefficient for document clustering tasks that deal with large numbers of documents. In our experiments, one of the corpora we used is small enough (2745 documents) to allow us to compare CBC with these hierarchical algorithms.

Chameleon is a hierarchical algorithm that employs dynamic modeling to improve clustering quality [9]. When merging two clusters, one might consider the sum of the similarities between pairs of elements across the clusters (e.g. average-link clustering). A drawback of this approach is that the existence of a single pair of very similar elements might unduly cause the merger of two clusters. An alternative considers the number of pairs of elements whose similarity exceeds a certain threshold [4]. However, this may cause undesirable mergers when there are a large number of pairs whose similarities barely exceed the threshold. Chameleon clustering combines the two approaches.

Most often, document clustering employs K-means clustering since its complexity is linear in n, the number of elements to be clustered. K-means is a family of partitional clustering algorithms. The following steps outline the basic algorithm for generating a set of K clusters:

1. randomly select K elements as the initial centroids of the clusters;
2. assign each element to a cluster according to the centroid closest to it;
3. recompute the centroid of each cluster as the average of the cluster's elements;
4. repeat Steps 2-3 for T iterations or until the centroids do not change, where T is a predetermined constant.

K-means has complexity $O(K\times T\times n)$ and is efficient for many document clustering tasks. Because of the random selection of initial centroids, the resulting clusters vary in quality. Some sets of initial centroids lead to poor convergence rates or poor cluster quality.

Bisecting K-means [17], a variation of K-means, begins with a set containing one large cluster consisting of every element and iteratively picks the largest cluster in the set, splits it into two clusters and replaces it by the split clusters. Splitting a cluster consists of applying the basic K-means algorithm α times with K=2 and keeping the split that has the highest average element-centroid similarity.

Hybrid clustering algorithms combine hierarchical and partitional algorithms in an attempt to have the high quality of hierarchical algorithms with the efficiency of partitional algorithms. Buckshot [3] addresses the problem of randomly selecting initial centroids in K-means by combining it with average-link clustering. Cutting et al. claim its clusters are comparable in quality to hierarchical algorithms but with a lower complexity. Buckshot first applies average-link to a random sample of $\sqrt{n}$ elements to generate K clusters. It then uses the centroids of the clusters as the initial K centroids of K-means clustering. The complexity of Buckshot is $O(K\times T\times n + n\log n)$. The parameters K and T are usually considered to be small numbers. Since we are dealing with a large number of clusters, Buckshot and K-means become inefficient in practice. Furthermore, Buckshot is not always suitable. Suppose one wishes to cluster 100,000 documents into 1000 newsgroup topics. Buckshot could generate at most 316 initial centroids.

3. REPRESENTATION

CBC represents elements as feature vectors. The features of a document are the terms (usually stemmed words) that occur within it and the value of a feature is a statistic of the term. For example, the statistic can simply be the term's frequency, *tf*, within the document. In order to discount terms with low discriminating power, *tf* is usually combined with the term's inverse document frequency, *idf*, which is the inverse of the percentage of documents in which the term occurs. This measure is referred to as *tf-idf* [15]:

$$tf\text{-}idf = tf \times \log idf$$

We use the mutual information [2] between an element (document) and its features (terms).

In our algorithm, for each element e, we construct a **frequency count vector** $C(e) = (c_{e1}, c_{e2}, \ldots, c_{em})$, where m is the total number of features and c_{ef} is the frequency count of feature f occurring in element e. In document clustering, e is a document and c_{ef} is the term frequency of f in e. We construct a **mutual information vector** $MI(e) = (mi_{e1}, mi_{e2}, \ldots, mi_{em})$, where mi_{ef} is the mutual information between element e and feature f, which is defined as:

$$mi_{ef} = \log \frac{\frac{c_{ef}}{N}}{\frac{\sum_i c_{if}}{N} \times \frac{\sum_j c_{ej}}{N}}$$

where $N = \sum_i \sum_j c_{ij}$ is the total frequency count of all features of all elements.

We compute the similarity between two elements e_i and e_j using the *cosine coefficient* [15] of their mutual information vectors:

$$sim(e_i, e_j) = \frac{\sum_f mi_{e_i f} \times mi_{e_j f}}{\sqrt{\sum_f mi_{e_i f}^2 \times \sum_f mi_{e_j f}^2}}$$

4. ALGORITHM

CBC consists of three phases. In Phase I, we compute each element's top-k similar elements. In our experiments, we used k = 20. In Phase II, we construct a collection of tight clusters, where the elements of each cluster form a **committee**. The algorithm tries to form as many committees as possible on the condition that each newly formed committee is not very similar to any existing committee. If the condition is violated, the committee is simply discarded. In the final phase of the algorithm, each element is assigned to its most similar cluster.

4.1 Phase I: Find top-similar elements

Computing the complete similarity matrix between pairs of elements is obviously quadratic. However, one can dramatically reduce the running time by taking advantage of the fact that the feature vector is sparse. By indexing the features, one can retrieve the set of elements that have a given feature. To compute the top similar elements of an element e, we first sort the mutual information vector $MI(e)$ and then only consider a subset of the features with highest mutual information. Finally, we compute the pairwise similarity between e and the elements that share a feature from this subset. Since high mutual information features tend not to occur in many elements, we only need to compute a fraction of the possible pairwise combinations. With 18,828 elements, Phase I completes in 38 minutes. Using this heuristic, similar words that share only low mutual information features will be missed by our algorithm. However, in our experiments, this had no visible impact on cluster quality.

4.2 Phase II: Find committees

The second phase of the clustering algorithm recursively finds tight clusters scattered in the similarity space. In each recursive step, the algorithm finds a set of tight clusters, called committees, and identifies residue elements that are not covered by any committee. We say a committee **covers** an element if the element's similarity to the centroid of the committee exceeds some high similarity threshold. The algorithm then recursively attempts to find more committees among the residue elements. The output of the algorithm is the union of all committees found in each recursive step. The details of Phase II are presented in Figure 1.

Input: A list of elements E to be clustered, a similarity database S from Phase I, thresholds θ_1 and θ_2.

Step 1: For each element $e \in E$

- Cluster the top similar elements of e from S using average-link clustering.
- For each cluster discovered c compute the following score: $|c| \times$ avgsim(c), where $|c|$ is the number of elements in c and avgsim(c) is the average pairwise similarity between elements in c.
- Store the highest-scoring cluster in a list L.

Step 2: Sort the clusters in L in descending order of their scores.

Step 3: Let C be a list of committees, initially empty.

For each cluster $c \in L$ in sorted order

- Compute the centroid of c by averaging the frequency vectors of its elements and computing the mutual information vector of the centroid in the same way as we did for individual elements.
- If c's similarity to the centroid of each committee previously added to C is below a threshold θ_1, add c to C.

Step 4: If C is empty, we are done and return C.

Step 5: For each element $e \in E$

- If e's similarity to every committee in C is below threshold θ_2, add e to a list of residues R.

Step 6: If R is empty, we are done and return C.

Otherwise, return the union of C and the output of a recursive call to Phase II using the same input except replacing E with R.

Output: a list of committees.

Figure 1. Phase II of CBC.

In Step 1, the score reflects a preference for bigger and tighter clusters. Step 2 gives preference to higher quality clusters in Step 3, where a cluster is only kept if its similarity to all previously kept clusters is below a fixed threshold. In our experiments, we set $\theta_1 = 0.35$. Step 4 terminates the recursion if no committee is found in the previous step. The residue elements are identified in Step 5 and if no residues are found, the algorithm terminates; otherwise, we recursively apply the algorithm to the residue elements.

Each committee that is discovered in this phase defines one of the final output clusters of the algorithm.

4.3 Phase III: Assign elements to clusters

In Phase III, every element is assigned to the cluster containing the committee to which it is most similar. This phase resembles K-means in that every element is assigned to its closest centroid.

Unlike *K*-means, the number of clusters is not fixed and the centroids do not change (i.e. when an element is added to a cluster, it is not added to the committee of the cluster).

5. EVALUATION METHODOLOGY

Many cluster evaluation schemes have been proposed. They generally fall under two categories:

- comparing cluster outputs with manually generated answer keys (hereon referred to as **classes**); and
- embedding the clusters in an application (e.g. information retrieval) and using its evaluation measure.

One approach considers the average entropy of the clusters, which measures the purity of the clusters [17]. However, maximum purity is trivially achieved when each element forms its own cluster.

Given a partitioned set of n elements, there are $n \times (n - 1) / 2$ pairs of elements that are either in the same partition or not. The partition implies $n \times (n - 1) / 2$ decisions. Another way to evaluate clusters is to compute the percentage of the decisions that are in agreement between the clusters and the classes [19]. This measure sometimes gives unintuitive results. Suppose the answer key consists of 20 equally sized classes with 1000 elements in each. Treating each element as its own cluster gets a misleadingly high score of 95%.

The evaluation of document clustering algorithms in information retrieval often uses the embedded approach [6]. Suppose we cluster the documents returned by a search engine. Assuming the user is able to pick the most relevant cluster, the performance of the clustering algorithm can be measured by the average precision of the chosen cluster. Under this scheme, only the best cluster matters.

The entropy and pairwise decision schemes each measure a specific property of clusters. However, these properties are not directly related to application-level goals of clustering. The information retrieval scheme is goal-oriented, however it measures only the quality of the best cluster. We propose an evaluation methodology that strikes a balance between generality and goal-orientation.

Like the entropy and pairwise decision schemes, we assume that there is an answer key that defines how the elements are supposed to be clustered. Let C be a set of clusters and A be the answer key. We define the editing distance, *dist*(C, A), as the number of operations required to transform C into A. We allow three editing operations:

- merge two clusters;
- move an element from one cluster to another; and
- copy an element from one cluster to another.

Let B be the baseline clustering where each element is its own cluster. We define the quality of cluster C as follows:

$$1 - \frac{dist(C, A)}{dist(B, A)}$$

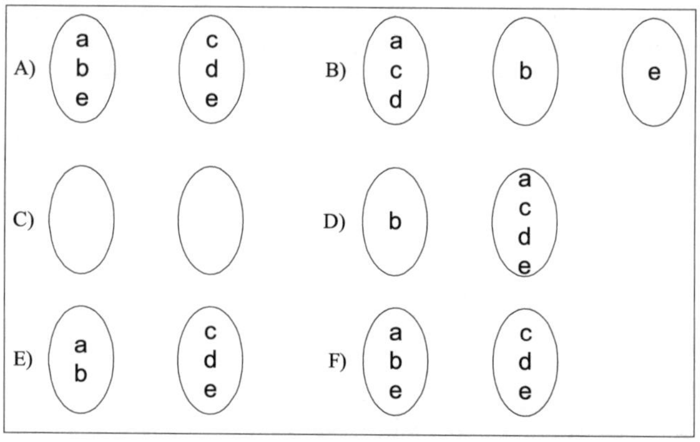

Figure 2. An example of applying the transformation rules to three clusters. A) The classes in the answer key; B) the clusters to be transformed; C) the sets used to reconstruct the classes (Rule 1); D) the sets after three merge operations (Step 2); E) the sets after one move operation (Step 3); F) the sets after one copy operation (Step 4).

This measure can be interpreted as the percentage of savings from using the clustering result to construct the answer key versus constructing it from scratch (i.e. the baseline).

We make the assumption that each element belongs to exactly one cluster. The transformation procedure is as follows:

1. Suppose there are m classes in the answer key. We start with a list of m empty sets, each of which is labeled with a class in the answer key.
2. For each cluster, merge it with the set whose class has the largest number of elements in the cluster (a tie is broken arbitrarily).
3. If an element is in a set whose class is not the same as one of the element's classes, move the element to a set where it belongs.
4. If an element belongs to more than one target class, copy the element to all sets corresponding to the target classes (except the one to which it already belongs).

dist(C, A) is the number of operations performed using the above transformation rules on C.

Figure 2 shows an example. In *D*) the cluster containing *e* could have been merged with either set (we arbitrarily chose the second). The total number of operations is 5.

6. EXPERIMENTAL RESULTS

In this section, we describe our test data and present an evaluation of our system. We compare CBC to the clustering algorithms presented in Section 2 and we provide a detailed analysis of *K*-means and Buckshot. We proceed by studying the effect of different clustering parameters on CBC.

Table 1. **The number of classes in each test data set and the number of elements in their largest and smallest classes.**

DATA SET	*TOTAL DOCS*	*TOTAL CLASSES*	*LARGEST CLASS*	*SMALLEST CLASS*
Reuters	2745	92	1045	1
20-news	18828	20	999	628

Table 2. Cluster quality (%) of several algorithms on the Reuters and 20-news data sets.

	REUTERS	*20-NEWS*
CBC	65.00	74.18
K-means	62.38	70.04
Buckshot	62.03	65.96
Bisecting *K*-means	60.80	58.52
Chameleon	58.67	n/a
Average-link	63.00	70.43
Complete-link	46.22	64.23
Single-link	31.53	5.30

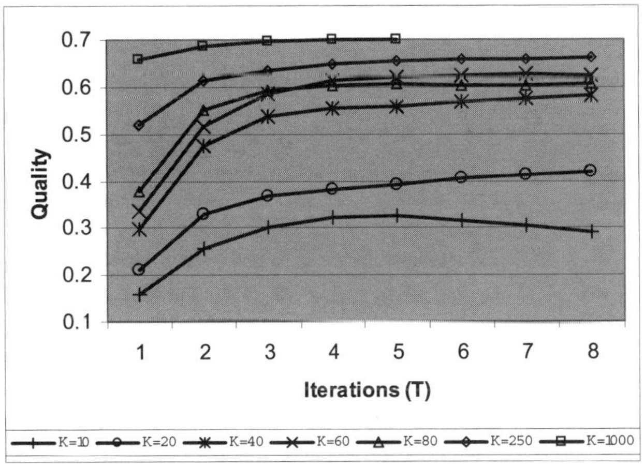

Figure 3. *K*-means cluster quality on the 20-news data set for different values of *K* plotted of over eight iterations.

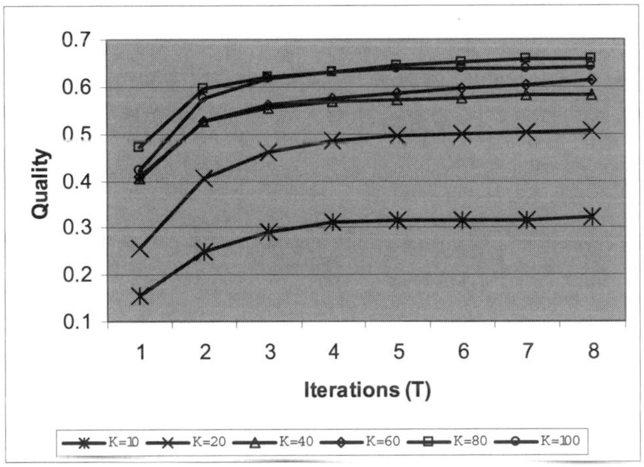

Figure 4. Buckshot cluster quality on the 20-news data set for different values of *K* plotted of over eight iterations.

6.1 Test Data

We conducted document-clustering experiments with two data sets: Reuters-21578 V1.2[1] and 20news-18828[2] (see Table 1). For the Reuters corpus, we selected documents that:

1. are assigned one or more topics;
2. have the attribute LEWISSPLIT="TEST", and
3. have <BODY> and </BODY> tags.

There are 2745 such documents. The 20news-18828 data set contains 18828 newsgroup articles partitioned (nearly) evenly across 20 different newsgroups.

6.2 Cluster Evaluation

We clustered the data sets using CBC and the clustering algorithms of Section 2 and applied the evaluation methodology from the previous section. Table 2 shows the results. The columns are our editing distance based evaluation measure. CBC outperforms *K*-means with *K*=1000 by 4.14%. On the 20-news data set, our implementation of Chameleon was unable to complete in reasonable time. For the 20-news corpus, CBC spends the vast majority of the time finding the top similar documents (38 minutes) and computing the similarity between documents and committee centroids (119 minutes). The rest of the computation, which includes clustering the top-20 similar documents for every one of the 18828 documents and sorting the clusters, took less than 5 minutes. We used a Pentium III 750MHz processor and 1GB of memory.

6.3 *K*-means and Buckshot

Figure 3 and Figure 4 show the cluster quality of different *K*'s on the 20-news data set plotted over eight iterations of the *K*-means and Buckshot algorithms respectively. The cluster quality for *K*-means clearly increases as *K* reaches 1000 although the increase in quality slows down between *K*=60 and *K*=1000.

Buckshot has similar performance to *K*-means on the Reuters corpus; however it performs much worse on the 20-news corpus. This is because *K*-means performs well on this data set when *K* is large (e.g. *K*=1000) whereas Buckshot cannot have *K* higher than $\sqrt{18828} = 137$. On the Reuters corpus, the best clusters for *K*-means were obtained with *K* = 50, and Buckshot can have *K* as large as $\sqrt{2745} = 52$. However, as *K* approaches 52, Buckshot degenerates to the *K*-means algorithm, which explains why Buckshot has similar performance to *K*-means. Figure 5 compares the cluster quality between *K*-means and Buckshot for different values of *K* on the 20-news data set.

[1] http://www.research.att.com/~lewis/reuters21578.html

[2] http://www.ai.mit.edu/people/jrennie/20_newsgroups/

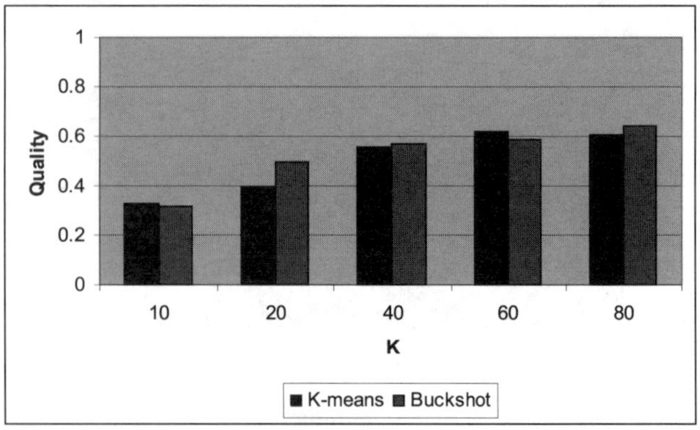

Figure 5. Comparison of cluster quality between *K*-means and Buckshot for different *K* on the 20-news data set.

Buckshot first applies average-link clustering to a random sample of $\sqrt{n}$ elements, where n is the number of elements to be clustered. The sample size counterbalances the quadratic running time of average-link to make Buckshot linear. We experimented with larger sample sizes to see if Buckshot performs better. For the 20-news data set, clustering 137 elements using average-link is very fast so we can afford to cluster a larger sample. Figure 6 illustrates the results for K=150 on the 20-news data set where F indicates the forced sample size and F=SQRT is the original Buckshot algorithm described in Section 2. Since $K > 137$, *F=SQRT* is just the *K*-means algorithm (we always sample at least K elements). Buckshot has better performance than *K*-means as long as the sample size is significantly bigger than K. All values of $F \geq 500$ converged after only two iterations while F=SQRT took four iterations to converge.

6.4 Clustering Parameters

We experimented with different clustering parameters. Below, we describe each parameter and their possible values:

1. **Vector Space Model** (described in Section 3):
   a) *MI* : the mutual-information model;
   b) *TF* : the term-frequency model;
   c) *TFIDF1* : the *tf-idf* model;
   d) *TFIDF2* : the *tf-idf* model using the following formula: $tf\text{-}idf = \sqrt{tf} \times log\ idf$.
2. **Stemming**:
   a) `S-` : terms are not stemmed;
   b) `S+` : terms are stemmed using Porter's stemmer [14].
3. **Stop Words**:
   a) `W-` : no stop words are used as features;
   b) `W+` : all terms are used.
4. **Filtering**:
   a) `F-` : no term filtering is performed;
   b) `F+` : terms with *MI*<0.5 are deleted.

When filtering is on, the feature vectors become smaller and the similarity computations become much faster.

We refer to an experiment using a string where the first position corresponds to the *Stemming* parameter, the second position corresponds to the *Stop Words* parameter and the third position corresponds to the *Filtering* parameter. For example, experiment `S+W-F+` means that terms are stemmed, stop words are ignored, and filtering is performed. The *Vector Space Model* parameter will always be explicitly given.

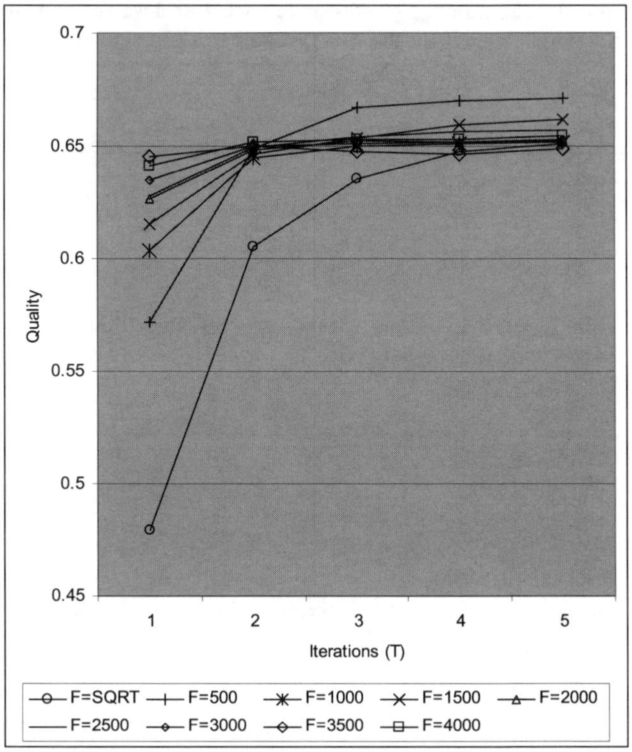

Figure 6. Buckshot cluster quality with *K*=150 for varying sample size (F) on the 20-news data set plotted over five iterations.

Figure 7 illustrates the quality of clusters generated by CBC on the Reuters corpus while varying the clustering parameters. Most document clustering systems use *TFIDF1* as their vector space model; however, the *MI* model outperforms each model including *TFIDF1*. Furthermore, varying the other parameters on the *MI* model makes no significant difference on cluster quality making *MI* more robust. *TF* performs the worse since terms with low discriminating power (e.g. *the*, *furthermore*) are not discounted. Although *TFIDF2* slightly outperforms *TFIDF1* (on experiment `S+W-F-`), it is clearly not as robust. Except for the *TF* model, stemming terms always produced better quality clusters.

7. EXAMPLE

We collected the titles and abstracts for the 46 papers presented at SIGIR-2001 and clustered them using CBC. For each paper, we used as part of its filename the session name in which it was presented at the conference and a number representing the order in which it appears in the proceedings. For example, Cat/017 refers to a paper that was presented in the *Categorization* session and that is the 17th paper in the proceedings. The results are shown in Table 3.

The features of many of the automatically generated clusters clearly correspond to SIGIR-2001 session topics (e.g. clusters 1,

Table 3. Output of CBC applied to the 46 papers presented at SIGIR-2001: the left column shows the clustered documents and the right column shows the top-7 features (stemmed terms) forming the cluster centroids.

#	*Cluster Elements*	*Top-7 Features* (stemmed)
1	Cat/017, Cat/019, Lrn/037	text, featur, learn, categor, classif, approach, svm
2	MS/035, Eval/011, MS/036, Sys/006, Cat/018	threshold, score, term, base, distribut, optim, scheme
3	LM/015, LM/041, LM/016, CL/012, CL/013, CL/014	model, languag, translat, expans, estim, improv, framework
4	US/029, US/028, US/027, Sys/008, Sum/024, Eval/009, Lrn/038	user, result, use, imag, system, search, index
5	Web/030, Sys/007, MS/033, Eval/010	search, engin, page, web, link, best
6	Sum/002, Lrn/039, LM/042	stori, new, event, time, process, applic, content
7	Sum/003, Sum/004, Sum/025, LM/043, Sum/001	summar, term, text, summari, weight, scheme, automat
8	Lrn/040, Sys/005	level, space, framework, vector, comput, recent
9	QA/046, QA/044, QA/045, MS/034	answer, question, perform, task, passag, larg, give
10	RM/021, RM/022, RM/023, RM/020	queri, languag, similar, data, framework, seri
11	Web/032, Sum/026, Web/031	link, algorithm, method, hyperlink, web, analyz, identifi

Cat=Categorization, CL=CrossLingual, Eval=Evaluation, LM=LanguageModels, Lrn=Learning, MS=MetaSearch, QA=QuestionAnswering, RM=RetrievalModels, Sum=Summarization, Sys=Systems, US=UserStudies, Web=Web

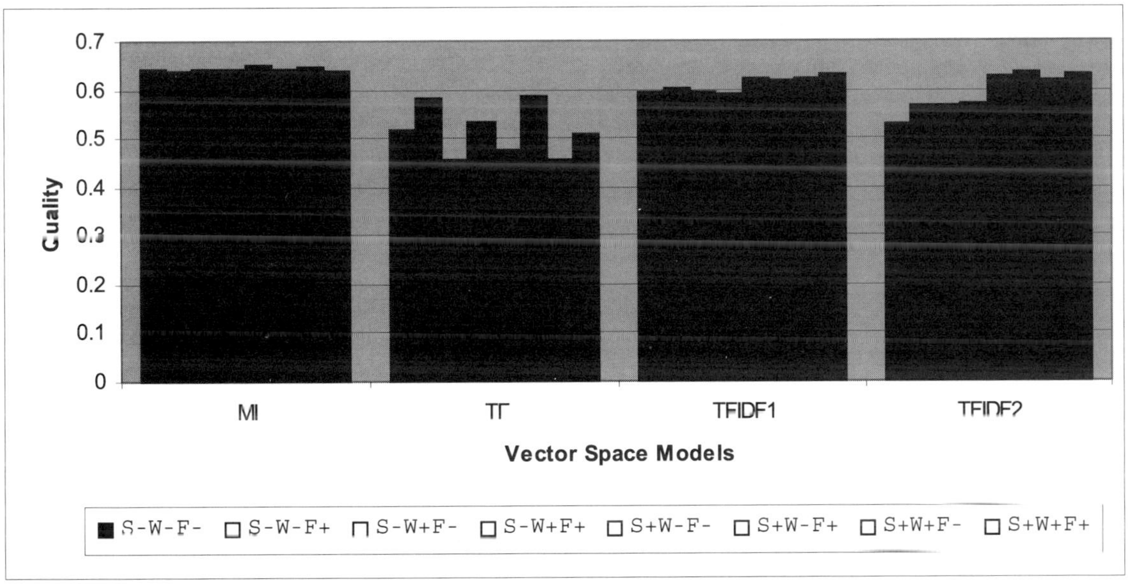

Figure 7. CBC evaluation of cluster quality when using different clustering parameters (Reuters corpus).

4, 7, 9, 10 and 11). Applying the evaluation methodology of Section 5 gives a score of 32.60%. This score is fairly low for the following reasons:

- Some documents could potentially belong to more than one session. For example, Lrn/037 was clustered in the categorization cluster #1 because it deals with learning and text categorization (it is titled "A meta-learning approach for text categorization"). Using the sessions as the answer key, Lrn/037 will be counted as incorrect.
- CBC generates clusters that do not correspond to any session topic. For example, all papers in Cluster #6 have news stories as their application domain and the papers in Cluster #5 all deal with search engines.

8. CONCLUSION

Document clustering is an important tool in information retrieval. We presented a clustering algorithm, CBC, which can handle a large number of documents, a large number of output clusters, and a large sparse feature space. It discovers clusters using well-scattered tight clusters called committees. In our experiments on document clustering, we showed that CBC outperforms several well-known hierarchical, partitional, and hybrid clustering algorithms in cluster quality. For example, in one experiment, CBC outperforms K-means by 4.14%.

Evaluating cluster quality has always been a difficult task. We presented a new evaluation methodology that is based on the editing distance between output clusters and manually constructed classes (the answer key). This evaluation measure is more intuitive and easier to interpret than previous evaluation measures.

CBC may be applied to other clustering tasks such as word clustering. Since many words have multiple senses, we can modify Phase III of CBC to allow an element to belong to multiple clusters. For an element e, we can find its most similar cluster and assign e to it. We can then remove those features from e that are shared by the centroid of the cluster. Then, we can recursively find e's next most similar cluster and repeat the feature removal. This process continues until e's similarity to its most similar cluster is below a threshold or when the total mutual information of all the residue features of e is below a fraction of the total mutual information of its original features. For a polysymous word, CBC can then potentially discover clusters that correspond to its senses. Preliminary experiments on clustering words using the TREC collection (3GB) and a proprietary collection (2GB) of grade school readings from Educational Testing Service gave the following automatically discovered word senses for the word *bass*:

```
(clarinet, saxophone, cello, trombone)
(Allied-Lyons, Grand Metropolitan, United Biscuits,
 Cadbury Schweppes)
(contralto, baritone, mezzo, soprano)
(Steinbach, Gallego, Felder, Uribe)
(halibut, mackerel, sea bass, whitefish)
(Kohlberg Kravis, Kohlberg, Bass Group, American
 Home)
```

and for the word *China*:

```
(Russia, China, Soviet Union, Japan)
(earthenware, pewter, terra cotta, porcelain)
```

The word senses are represented by four committee members of the cluster.

9. ACKNOWLEDGEMENTS

The authors wish to thank the reviewers for their helpful comments. This research was partly supported by Natural Sciences and Engineering Research Council of Canada grant OGP121338 and scholarship PGSB207797.

10. REFERENCES

[1] Buckley, C. and Lewit, A. F. 1985. Optimization of inverted vector searches. In *Proceedings of SIGIR-85*. pp. 97–110.

[2] Church, K. and Hanks, P. 1989. Word association norms, mutual information, and lexicography. In *Proceedings of ACL-89*. pp. 76–83. Vancouver, Canada.

[3] Cutting, D. R.; Karger, D.; Pedersen, J.; and Tukey, J. W. 1992. Scatter/Gather: A cluster-based approach to browsing large document collections. In *Proceedings of SIGIR-92*. pp. 318–329. Copenhagen, Denmark.

[4] Guha, S.; Rastogi, R.; and Kyuseok, S. 1999. ROCK: A robust clustering algorithm for categorical attributes. In *Proceedings of ICDE'99*. pp. 512–521. Sydney, Australia.

[5] Han, J. and Kamber, M. 2001. *Data Mining – Concepts and Techniques*. Morgan Kaufmann.

[6] Hearst, M. A. and Pedersen, J. O. 1996. Reexamining the cluster hypothesis: Scatter/Gather on retrieval results. In *Proceedings of SIGIR-96*. pp. 76–84. Zurich, Switzerland.

[7] Jain, A. K.; Murty, M. N.; and Flynn, P. J. 1999. Data Clustering: A Review. *ACM Computing Surveys* 31(3):264–323.

[8] Jardine, N. and van Rijsbergen, C. J. 1971. The use of hierarchical clustering in information retrieval. *Information Storage and Retreival*, 7:217–240.

[9] Karypis, G.; Han, E.-H.; and Kumar, V. 1999. Chameleon: A hierarchical clustering algorithm using dynamic modeling. *IEEE Computer: Special Issue on Data Analysis and Mining* 32(8):68–75.

[10] Kaufmann, L. and Rousseeuw, P. J. 1987. Clustering by means of medoids. In Dodge, Y. (Ed.) *Statistical Data Analysis based on the L1 Norm*. pp. 405–416. Elsevier/North Holland, Amsterdam.

[11] King, B. 1967. Step-wise clustering procedures. *Journal of the American Statistical Association*, 69:86–101.

[12] Koller, D. and Sahami, M. 1997. Hierarchically classifying documents using very few words. In Proceedings of ICML-97. pp. 170–176. Nashville, TN.

[13] McQueen, J. 1967. Some methods for classification and analysis of multivariate observations. In *Proceedings of 5th Berkeley Symposium on Mathematics, Statistics and Probability*, 1:281-298.

[14] Porter, M. F. 1980. An algorithm for suffix stripping. In *Proceedings of SIGIR-80*. pp. 318–327.

[15] Salton, G. and McGill, M. J. 1983. *Introduction to Modern Information Retrieval*. McGraw Hill.

[16] Sneath, P. H. A. and Sokal, R. R. 1973. *Numerical Taxonomy: The Principles and Practice of Numerical Classification*. Freeman. London, UK.

[17] Steinbach, M.; Karypis, G.; and Kumar, V. 2000. A comparison of document clustering techniques. *Technical Report #00-034*. Department of Computer Science and Engineering, University of Minnesota.

[18] van Rijsbergen, C. J. 1979. *Information Retrieval*, second edition. London: Buttersworth. Available at: *http://www*.dcs.gla.ac.uk/Keith/Preface.html

[19] Wagstaff, K. and Cardie, C. 2000. Clustering with instance-level constraints. In *Proceedings of ICML-2000*. pp. 1103–1110. Palo Alto, CA.

Probabilistic Combination of Text Classifiers Using Reliability Indicators: Models and Results

Paul N. Bennett
Computer Science Dept.
Carnegie Mellon University
Pittsburgh, PA 15213
pbennett+@cs.cmu.edu

Susan T. Dumais
Microsoft Research
One Microsoft Way
Redmond, WA 98052
sdumais@microsoft.com

Eric Horvitz
Microsoft Research
One Microsoft Way
Redmond, WA 98052
horvitz@microsoft.com

ABSTRACT

The intuition that different text classifiers behave in qualitatively different ways has long motivated attempts to build a better metaclassifier via some combination of classifiers. We introduce a probabilistic method for combining classifiers that considers the context-sensitive reliabilities of contributing classifiers. The method harnesses *reliability indicators*—variables that provide a valuable signal about the performance of classifiers in different situations. We provide background, present procedures for building metaclassifiers that take into consideration both reliability indicators and classifier outputs, and review a set of comparative studies undertaken to evaluate the methodology.

Categories and Subject Descriptors

H.3.3 [**Information Storage and Retrieval**]: Information Search and Retrieval; I.2.6 [**Artificial Intelligence**]: Learning; I.5.1 [**Pattern Recognition**]: Models

General Terms

Algorithms, Experimentation.

Keywords

Text classification, classifier combination, metaclassifiers, reliability indicators

1. INTRODUCTION

Researchers have long pursued the promise of harnessing multiple text classifiers to synthesize a more accurate classification procedure via some combination of the outputs of the contributing classifiers. The pursuit of classifier combination has been motivated by the intuition that, because different classifiers work in related but qualitatively different ways, an appropriate overlaying of classifiers might leverage the distinct strengths of each method.

Classifiers can be combined in different ways. In one approach, a text classifier is composed from multiple distinct classifiers via a procedure that attempts to select the best classifier to use in different situations. For example, we may work to identify the most accurate classifier in some setting, seeking to learn about accuracy over output scores or some combination of output scores and features considered in the text analysis. Other procedures for combining classifiers consider inputs generated by the contributing classifiers. For example, in a voting analysis, a combination function considers the final decisions made by each classifier as votes that influence an overall decision about document classification. In a finer-grained approach to combining multiple classifiers, the scores generated by the contributing classifiers are taken as inputs to the combination function. Whichever approach to combination employed, the creation of enhanced metaclassifiers from a set of text classifiers relies on developing an understanding of how different classifiers perform in different informational contexts.

We have pursued the development of probabilistic combination procedures that hinge on learning and harnessing the *context-sensitive* reliabilities of different classifiers. Rather than rely solely on output scores or on the set of domain-level features employed in text-classification, we introduce the use of *reliability-indicator* variables—a set of features that provide a low-dimensional abstraction on context for learning about reliability. We borrow the reliability-indicator methodology from work initially presented by Toyama and Horvitz [26] to the automated vision community. They introduced the reliability-indicator learning and inference framework and showed how the approach could be applied in vision to integrate several distinct scene analyses into an overall higher-accuracy composite visual analysis. We have found that the reliability-indicator methodology is useful in the text classification realm for providing context-sensitive signals about accuracy that can be used to weave together multiple classifiers in a coherent probabilistic manner to boost overall accuracy.

We will first review related work on the combination of text-classification procedures. Then we introduce the use of reliability indicators in text classification, and show how we employ these variables to learn about the context-sensitive reliabilities of naive Bayes, unigram, support vector machine (SVM), and decision-tree classifiers. We describe how we integrate the indicator variables with base-level features and scores output by classifiers to build meta-classifiers that show enhanced performance. We highlight our methodology and results by reviewing several sets of experiments. Finally, we summarize our contributions and discuss future directions.

2. RELATED WORK

The overlaying of multiple methodologies or representations has been employed in several areas of information retrieval. For example, past research in information retrieval has demonstrated that retrieval effectiveness can be improved by using multiple, distinct representations [2, 11, 22], or by using multiple queries or search strategies [3, 24]. In the arena of text classification, several researchers have achieved improvements in classification accuracy via the combination of different classifiers [9, 13, 18, 30]. Others have reported that combined classifiers work well compared to some particular approach [1] but have not reported results that compare the accuracy of the classifier with the accuracies of the individual contributing classifiers. Similarly, systems that seek to enhance classification performance by applying many instances of the same classifier, such as in boosting procedures [23, 28], have compared the overall performance of the final methodology to other systems rather than to the weaker component learners.

Much of the previous work on combining text classifiers has used relatively simple policies for selecting the best classifier or for combining the output of multiple classifiers. As some examples, Larkey and Croft [13] used weighted linear combinations of system ranks or scores; Hull et al. [9] used linear combinations of probabilities or log odds scores; Yang et al. [30] used a linear combination of normalized scores; and Li and Jain [18] used voting and classifier selection techniques. Lam and Lai [12] use category-averaged features to pick a (possibly different) classifier to use for each category.

As we shall highlight below, in contrast to prior research on classifier combination, our work centers on the use of a richer probabilistic combination of inputs, using combination functions learned with Bayesian and SVM learning methods. In this respect, our approach is similar to work by Ting and Witten [25] in stacked generalization, although they did not apply their approach to text problems. We also report baseline comparisons with voting and classifier-selection techniques.

Larkey and Croft [13] used rank-based measures of performance because they were interested in interactive systems in which a rank list of codes for each document would be displayed to users. Many other applications such as automatic routing or tagging require that binary class membership decisions be made for each document as it is processed. We focus on classifier combination to enhance such classification decisions. This goal appears to be more challenging than the use of classifiers for document ranking. As an example, Hull et al. [9] found that while combination techniques were able to improve document ranking, they did considerably less well at estimating probabilities.

3. PROBLEM APPROACH

Our work differs from earlier combination approaches for text classification by (1) the use of expressive probabilistic dependency models to combine lower-level classifiers, leveraging special signaling variables, we refer to as reliability indicators, and (2) a focus on measures of classification performance rather than the more common consideration of ranking.

3.1 Reliability Indicators

Previous approaches to classifier combination have typically limited the information considered at the metalevel to the output of the classifiers [25].

We address the challenge of learning about the reliability of different classifiers in different neighborhoods of the classification domain at hand by introducing variables referred to as *reliability indicators*. A reliability indicator is an evidential distinction with states that are linked probabilistically to regions of a classification problem where a classifier performs relatively strongly or poorly.

The reliability-indicator methodology was introduced by Toyama and Horvitz [26] and applied initially to the task of combining several different machine-vision analyses in a system for identifying the head and pose of computer users. The researchers found that different visual processing modalities had distinct context-sensitive reliabilities that depended on dynamically changing details of lighting, color, and the overall configuration of the visual scene. The authors introduced reliability indicators to capture properties of the vision analyses, and of the scenes being analyzed, that appeared to provide probabilistic indications of the reliability of the output of each of the modalities. To learn probabilistic models for combining the multiple modalities, data was collected about ground truth, the observed states of indicator variables, and the outputs from the concurrent vision analyses. The data was used to construct a Bayesian network model with the ability to appropriately integrate the outputs from each of the visual modalities in real time, providing an overall higher-accuracy composite visual analysis.

The value of the indicator-variable methodology in machine vision stimulated us to explore the analogous application of the approach for representing and learning about reliability-dependent classifier contexts. For the task of combining classifiers, we formulate and include sets of variables that hold promise as being related to the performance of the underlying classifiers. We consider the states of reliability indicators and the scores of classifiers directly, and, thus, bypass the need to make ad hoc modifications to the base classifiers. This allows the metaclassifier to harness the reliability variables if they contain useful discriminatory information, and, if they do not, to fall back to using the output of the base classifiers.

As an example, consider three types of documents where: (1) the words in the document are either uninformative or strongly associated with one class; (2) the words in the document are weakly associated with several disjoint classes; or (3) the words in the document are strongly associated with several disjoint classes. Classifiers (*e.g.*, a unigram model) will sometimes demonstrate different patterns of error on these different document types. We have pursued the formulation of reliability indicators that capture different association patterns among words in documents and the structure of classes under consideration. We seek indicator variables that would allow us to learn context-sensitive reliabilities of classifiers, conditioned on the observed states of the variable in different settings.

As a concrete example, Figure 1 shows a portion of the type of combination function we can capture with the reliability-indicator methodology. The nodes on different branches of a decision tree include the values output by base classifiers as well as the values of reliability indicators for the document being classified. The decision tree provides a probabilistic context-sensitive combination rule indicated by the particular relevant branching of values of classifier scores and indicator variables. In this case, the portion of the tree displayed shows a classifier-combination function that considers thresholds on scores provided by a base-level linear SVM (*OutputOfSmox*) classifier and a base-level unigram classifier (*OutputOfUnigram*), and then uses the context established by reliability-indicator variables (*UnigramVariance* and *%FavoringInClassAfterFS*) to make a final decision about a classification. The annotations in the figure show the threshold tests that are being performed, the number of examples in the training set that satisfied the test, and a graphical representation of the probability distribution at the leaves. The likelihood of class membership is indicated by the length of the rectangle at the leaves of the tree.

The variable *UnigramVariance* represents the variance of unigram weights for words present in the current document. The intuition is that the unigram classifier would be accurate when there is low variance in weights. The variable *%FavoringInClassAfterFS* is the percentage of words (after feature selection) that occur more often in documents within a target class than in other classes. Classifiers that weight positive and negative evidence differently should be distinguished by this variable. For the *Strive-D (norm)* classifier excerpt shown in Figure 1 we have further normalized the metafeatures to have zero mean and unit standard deviation so most values fall between -1 and 1 as a result.

The indicator variables used in our studies are an intuitive attempt at formulating states to represent influential contexts. We defined variables to represent a variety of contexts that showed promise as being predictive of accuracy—*e.g.*, the number of features present in a document before and after feature selection, the distribution of features across the positive vs. negative classes, and the mean and variance of classifier-specific weights.

Currently, our indicator variables roughly fall into of four types. Different indicator variables measure (1) the amount of information present in the original document, (2) the information lost or mismatch between the representation the classifier used and the original document, (3) the sensitivity of decision to evidence shift, and (4) some basic voting statistics. *DocumentLength* is an example of type 1. The performance of classifiers is sometimes correlated with document length, because longer documents give more information to use in making a classification. *DocumentLength* can also be informative since some classifiers will perform poorly over longer documents because they do not model length (*e.g.* they double count evidence and longer documents are more likely to deviate from a correct determination). *PercentRemoved* is an example of type 2. This represents the percent of features removed by feature selection. If most of the document was not represented by the feature set used in a classifier, then some classifiers may be unreliable. Others (*e.g.* decision trees that model missing attributes) may continue to be reliable. When the base classifiers are allowed to use different representations, then these features can play an even more important role. An example of type 3 is the *UnigramVariance* variable. Low variance means the decision of the classifier is unlikely to change with a small change in the document content; high variance increases the chances that the decision would change with only a small change in document content. Finally, *NumVotingForClass* or *PercentAgreement* are examples of the last type. These simple voting statistics improve the metaclassifier search space (since the metaclassifier is given the base classifier decisions as input as well). For a 2-class case the *PercentAgreement* variable may provide little extra information but for n-classes it can be used to determine if the base classifiers have fractured their votes among a small number of classes or across a wide array. We found all of these types to be useful in the final combination scheme, and the early analysis has not found that any one type dominates the combination models.

Reliability-indicator variables are qualitatively different than variables representing the output of classifiers because we do not assume that the reliability indicators have some threshold point that classifies the examples better than random, nor do we assume that classification confidence shows monotonicity trends as in classifiers. We currently do not exploit these underlying assumptions for the classifiers, but we hope to do so in the future. At a more practical level, the reliability indicators are usually much simpler than typical classification algorithms.

3.2 Strive: Metaclassifier with Reliability Indicators

We refer to our classifier combination learning and inference framework as *Strive* for **S**tacked **R**eliability **I**ndicator **V**ariable **E**nsemble. We select this name because the approach can be viewed as essentially extending the stacking framework by introducing reliability indicators at the metalevel. The Strive architecture is depicted in Figure 2.

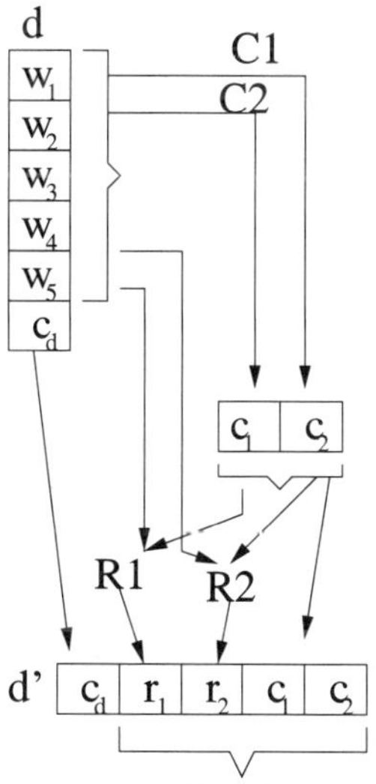

Figure 2: The basic architecture of Strive.

We map the original stacking learning problem to a new learning problem. Originally, we have some document, d, with words, $w_1, \ldots, w_n$ and class, c_d. Our classifiers, C_i, predict c_d from the words. We denote their predictions by c_i. Then, our set of reliability indicators, R_i, use the words and the classifier outputs to generate their values, r_i. We now have a new document, $d' =< r_1, \ldots, r_j, c_1, \ldots, c_k >$ with class c_d which we will give to the metaclassifier as the learning problem.

We require the outputs of the classifiers to train the metaclassifier. Thus, we perform cross-validation over the training data, and use the values obtained while an example serves as a validation item as the input to the metaclassifier.

3.3 BestSelect Classifier

When classifier combination is formulated as the process of *selecting* on a per-example basis the best base classifier, we can introduce a natural upper bound on combination. Such an upper bound can be useful as a benchmark in experiments with classifier combination procedures.

To classify a given document, if any of the classifiers correctly predict that document, the best combination would select any of the correct classifiers. Thus, such a classification combination errs only when all of the base classifiers are incorrect. We refer to this classifier as the BestSelect classifier. If all of the base classifiers are better than random, the BestSelect gives us a rough idea of the best we can do combining them in a selection framework.

We note that we are not using a pure selection approach, as our framework allows the possibility of choosing a class that none of the base classifiers predicted. In cases where the classifiers are not better than random (or are logically dependent), such an upper bound may be uninformative. If we simply seek an answer to the question, "How much of what we could optimistically expect to gain with this set of base classifiers have we gained?", then this loose bound provides a more pessimistic view of the results than is actually the case. Therefore, we evaluate the scores of the BestSelect classifier as a useful point of reference in our experiments.

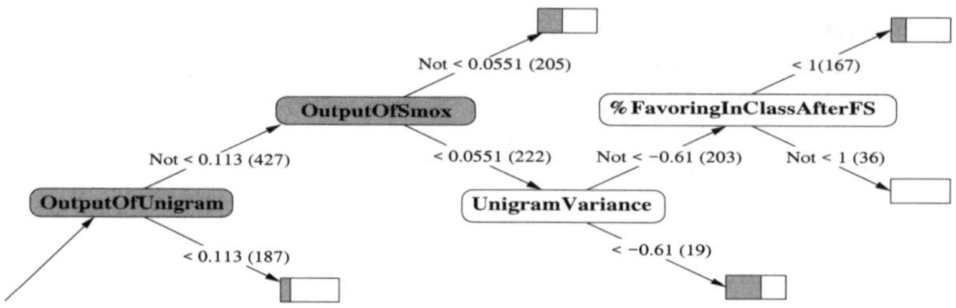

Figure 1: Portion of decision tree, learned by *Strive-D (norm)* for the *Travel & Vacations* class in the MSN Web Directory corpus, representing a combination policy at the metalevel that considers scores output by classifiers (dark nodes) and values of indicator variables (lighter nodes).

4. EXPERIMENTAL ANALYSIS

We engaged in a large number of experiments to test the value of probabilistic classifier combination with reliability indicator variables. We shall describe the corpora, methodology, and results.

4.1 Data

We examined several corpora, including the *MSN Web Directory*, *Reuters*, and *TREC-AP*.

4.1.1 MSN Web Directory

The MSN Web Directory is a large collection of heterogeneous web pages (from a May 1999 web snapshot) that have been hierarchically classified. We used the same train/test split of 50078/10024 documents as that reported in [6].

The MSN Web hierarchy is a 7-level hierarchy; we used all 13 of the top-level categories. The class proportions in the training set vary from 1.15% to 22.29%. In the testing set, they range from 1.14% to 21.54%. The classes are general subject categories such as *Health & Fitness* and *Travel & Vacation*. Human indexers assign the documents to zero or more categories.

For the experiments below, we used only the top 1000 words with highest mutual information for each class; approximately 195K words appear in at least 3 training documents.

4.1.2 Reuters

The Reuters 21578 corpus [15] contains Reuters news articles from 1987. For this data set, we used the ModApte standard train/ test split of 9603/3299 documents (8676 unused documents). The classes are economic subjects (*e.g.*, "acq" for acquisitions, "earn" for earnings, etc.) that human indexers decided applied to the document; a document may have multiple subjects. There are actually 135 classes in this domain (only 90 of which occur in the training and testing set); however, we only examined the 10 most frequent classes since small numbers of training examples makes estimating some performance measures unreliable due to high variance. Limiting to the 10 largest classes allows us to compare our results to previously published results [7, 10, 19, 20].

The class proportions in the training set vary from 1.88% to 29.96%. In the testing set, they range from 1.7% to 32.95%.

For the experiments below we used only the top 300 words with highest mutual information for each class; approximately 15K words appear in at least 3 training documents.

4.1.3 TREC-AP

The TREC-AP corpus is a collection of AP news stories from 1988 to 1990. We used the same train/test split of 142791/66992 documents that was used in [17]. As described in [16] (see also [14]), the categories are defined by keywords in a keyword field. The title and body fields are used in the experiments below. There are 20 categories total.

The frequencies of the 20 classes are the same as those reported in [17]. The class proportions in the training set vary from 0.06% to 2.03%. In the testing set, they range from 0.03% to 4.32%.

For the experiments described below, we use only the top 1000 words with the highest mutual information for each class; approximately 123K words appear in at least 3 training documents.

4.2 Classifiers

We employed several base-level classifiers and classifier combination methods in our comparative studies. We review the classifiers and combination methods here.

4.2.1 Base Classifiers

We worked to keep the representations for the base classifiers analyzed in our experiments nearly identical so as to isolate the benefits gained solely from the probabilistic combination of classifiers with reliability indicators. We would expect that varying the representations (*i.e.*, using different feature selection methods or document representations) would only improve the performance as this would likely decorrelate the performance of the base classifiers.

We selected four classifiers that have been used traditionally for text classification: decision trees, linear SVMs, naïve Bayes, and a unigram classifier.

For the decision-tree implementation, we employed the WinMine decision networks toolkit and refer to this as *Dnet* below [5]. Dnet builds decision trees using a Bayesian machine learning algorithm [4, 8]. While this toolkit is targeted primarily at building models that provide probability estimates, we found that Dnet models usually perform acceptably on error rate. However, we found that the performance of Dnet with regard to other measures is sometimes poor.

For linear SVMs, we use the *Smox* toolkit which is based on Platt's **S**equential **M**inimal **O**ptimization algorithm. After experimenting with a binary and a continuous model, we used a continuous model as it seemed to perform at approximately the same level.

The *naïve Bayes* classifier has also been referred to as a multivariate Bernoulli model. In using this classifier, we smoothed word and class probabilities using a Bayesian estimate (with the word prior) and a Laplace m-estimate, respectively.

The *unigram* classifier uses probability estimates from a unigram language model. This classifier has also been referred to as a multinomial naïve Bayes classifier. Probability estimates are smoothed in a similar fashion to smoothing in naïve Bayes classifier.

4.2.2 Basic Combination Methods

We performed experiments to explore a variety of combination methods. We considered several different combination procedures. The first combination method is based on selecting one classifier for each binary class problem, based on the one that performed best for a validation set. We refer to this method as the *Best By Class* method.

Another combination method is based on taking a majority vote of the base classifiers. This approach is perhaps the most popular combination methodology. When performing a majority vote, ties can be broken in a variety of ways (*e.g.*, breaking ties by always voting for *in class*). We experimented with several variants of this method, but we only present results here for the method which relies on breaking ties by voting with the *Best By Class* classifier because it nearly always outperformed the other majority vote methods. We refer to this method as *Majority BBC*.

4.2.3 Hierarchical Combination Methods

Stacking

Finally, we investigate several variants of the hierarchical models described earlier. As mentioned above, omitting the reliability-indicator variables is equivalent to stacking [25, 29]. We refer to these classifiers below as *Stack-X* where *X* is replaced by the first letter of the classifier that is performing the metaclassification. Therefore, *Stack-D* uses a decision tree as the metaclassifier, and *Stack-S* uses a linear SVM as the metaclassifier. It should be noted that *Stack-S* is also a weighted linear combination method since it is based on a linear SVM and uses only the classifier outputs.

It can be problematic to learn the weights for an SVM when the inputs have vastly different scales (in addition it may not be possible to pick good weights); therefore, we normalize the inputs to the metaclassifiers to zero mean and unit standard deviation. In order to perform consistent comparisons, we perform the same alteration for the metaclassifiers using Dnet. We also give for one of the Dnet variants the results without performing normalization; as would be expected the impact of normalization for decision-tree learners is relatively minimal (and has both positive and negative influences).

Strive

Similar to the notation described above, we add a letter to Strive to denote the metaclassifier being used. So, *Strive-D* is the Strive framework using Dnet as a metaclassifier. For comparison to the stacking methods, we evaluate *Strive-D* and *Strive-S*. Normalization is noted in the same way.

The experiments reported here use a total of 49 reliability indicators (including those specific examples given in Section 3.1). These variables were simply our initial pass at representing appropriate information. In the future, we intend to publish an analysis of which variables are most useful, in addition to extending the set of variables currently employed.

4.3 Performance Measures

To compare the performance of the classification methods we look at a set of standard performance measures. The F1 measure [27, 31] is the harmonic mean of precision and recall where $Precision = \frac{Correct\ Positives}{Predicted\ Positives}$ and $Recall = \frac{Correct\ Positives}{Actual\ Positives}$. We can often assess a cost function in classification settings that can be described as $C(FP, FN) = FP * P(FalsePos) + FN * P(FalseNeg)$ where FP is the cost of a false positive classification and FN is the cost of a false negative classification. The most commonly used function in the literature is the error rate which is $FP = FN = 1$. However, the importance of varying cost functions has been recognized by many researchers because applications rarely have equal costs for different types of errors [21]. In order to assess how sensitive performance is to the utility measure, we considered results for $C(10, 1)$ and $C(1, 10)$.

In addition, we computed and displayed a receiver operating characteristic (ROC) curve, which represents the performance of a classifier under any linear utility function [21]. We report results on the area under the ROC curve as an attempt to summarize[1] the linear utility space of functions.

For each performance measure, we can either macro-average or micro-average. Macro-averaging, which we present here, is computed separately for each class and then arithmetically averaged; this tends to weight rare classes more heavily. Micro-averaged values are computed directly from the binary decisions over all classes; this places more weight on the common classes. We evaluated the systems with both macro and micro averaging, but because of space limitations, we simply note that our analysis is consistent with the micro results and omit presentation of the full analysis.

4.4 Experimental Methodology

As the categories under consideration in the experiments are not mutually exclusive, the classification was done by training n binary classifiers, where n is the number of classes.

Decision thresholds for each classifier were set by optimizing them for each performance measure over the validation data; that is, a classifier could have different thresholds for each of the separate performance measures (and for each class). This ensures that the base classifiers are as competitive as possible across the various measures.

To generate the data for training the metaclassifier, (*i.e.*, reliability indicators, classifier outputs, and class labels), we used five-fold cross-validation on the training data from each of the corpora. The data set obtained through this process was then used to train the metaclassifiers. Finally, the resulting metaclassifiers were applied to the separate testing data described above.

4.5 Results

Tables 1, 2, and 3, present the performance results over the three corpora. In terms of the various performance measures, better performance is indicated by larger F1 or ROC area values or by smaller $C(FP, FN)$ values. The best performance (ignoring BestSelect) in each column is given in bold.

To determine statistical significance for the macro-averaged measures, a one-sided macro sign test and macro t-test was performed [31]. Differences with a p-level above 0.05 were not considered statistically significant.

We do not explicitly report significance results for the t-test comparisons; instead, our analysis follows the macro sign test which yielded more conservative comparisons (*i.e.*, the t-test primarily just increased the number of differences found to be significant in the tables).

The classifier combinations are annotated to indicate the results of a macro sign test. A † indicates the method significantly outperforms (at the 0.05 level) the best base classifier. In addition, on the variants of Stack and Strive, a ‡ indicates the method outperforms the basic combination methods. Results for the remaining sign test comparisons are omitted.

4.6 Discussion

First, we note that the base classifiers are competitive and consistent with the previously reported results over these corpora [6,

[1] We note that the area under the curve is not a precise summary of the linear utility space.

Method	Macro F1	Error	C(1,10)	C(10,1)	ROC Area
Dnet	0.5502	0.0583	0.3023	0.0771	0.8812
Smox	0.6705	0.0455	0.2239	0.0799	0.9125
Naïve Bayes	0.5527	0.0649	0.2853	0.0798	0.8915
Unigram	0.5982	0.0594	0.2589	0.0812	0.9003
Best By Class	0.6705	0.0455	0.2236	0.0783	N/A
Majority BBC	0.6668	0.0476	0.2173†	0.0761	N/A
Stack-D (norm)	0.6775	0.0446†‡	0.2118†	0.0784	0.9292†
Stack-S (norm)	0.6732	0.0450	0.2174†	0.0757	0.9210†
Strive-D	0.6877†‡	**0.0429**†‡	**0.1939**†‡	0.0742	0.9383†
Strive-D (norm)	0.6908†‡	0.0434	0.1949†‡	0.0742	**0.9398**†
Strive-S (norm)	**0.6948**†‡	0.0430†‡	0.2037†	**0.0712**	0.9114
Strive-D (norm, omit Smox)	0.6670	0.0464	0.2062†‡	0.0754	0.9361†
BestSelect	0.8365	0.0270	0.0905	0.0616	N/A

Table 1: Performance on MSN Web Directory Corpus

Method	Macro F1	Error	C(1,10)	C(10,1)	ROC
Dnet	0.7846	0.0242	0.0799	0.0537	0.9804
Smox	0.8480	0.0157	0.0580	0.0390	0.9815
Naïve Bayes	0.6574	0.0320	0.1423	0.0527	0.9703
Unigram	0.7645	0.0234	0.0713	0.0476	0.9877
Best By Class	0.8592	0.0153	0.0518	0.0409	N/A
Majority BBC	0.8524	0.0160	0.0448†	0.0446	N/A
Stack-D (norm)	0.8636†	0.0153	0.0449	0.0392	0.9893
Stack-S (norm)	0.8720†‡	0.0143†	0.0445†	0.0365	0.9930†
Strive-D	0.8547	0.0154	0.0472	0.0358	0.9903
Strive-D (norm)	0.8526	0.0157	0.0468	0.0359	0.9897
Strive-S (norm)	**0.8749**†	**0.0125**†‡	**0.0382**†	**0.0353**	**0.9939**
Strive-D (norm, omit Smox)	0.8433	0.0168	0.0484	0.0425	0.9900
BestSelect	0.9529	0.0050	0.0100	0.0202	N/A

Table 2: Performance on Reuters Corpus

7, 10, 14, 16, 19]. The results reported for Reuters are not directly comparable to those reported by Yang & Liu [31] as they report results over all 90 classes and do not give a breakdown for the 10 most frequent categories. Furthermore, the fact that the linear SVM Smox tends to be the best base classifier is consistent with the literature [7, 10, 31].

MSN Web Directory

Examining the results for the MSN Web Directory corpus in table 1 reveals several points. First, the basic combiners have only one significant win, C(1,10) for the Majority BBC approach. The results directly support the idea that a very good learner (Smox) tends to be brought down when combined via a majority vote scheme with weak learners; in addition, the win most likely results from the fact that the base learners (other than Smox) have a tendency to predict positive. When false negatives are weighed more heavily, the shift toward predicting positive helps reduce the number of false negatives.

Next, we see that Stacking posts several significant wins and appears to have some advantages over the base classifiers. However, the Stacking combination shows little significant improvement over the basic combination methods.

Strive-D and *Strive-S (norm)* show advantages that are robust across a variety of performance measures. Each shows a small (about 5% error reduction) but consistent improvement across a variety of performance measures. When viewed in terms of the approximate ceiling as established by the BestSelect model, the error reduction provided by the Strive combination methods is an even greater portion of the total possible reduction.

As can be inferred from the sign tests, these results are very consistent across classes. For example, on ROC area, *Strive-D* beats the base classifiers and basic combiners on 13/13 classes, and it beats the stacking methods on 12/13 classes. The notable exception is the performance of *Strive-S (norm)* on ROC area; graphical inspection of the ROC curves suggests this result is likely based on too much weight being placed on the strong classifier for a curve.

Often, there is a crossover in the ROC curve between two of the base classifiers further out on the false-positives axis. Most utility measures in practice correspond to the early part of the curve (this depends on the particular features of the given curve). Smox as a metaclassifier sometimes seems to lock onto the classifier that is strong in the early portion of the curve and loses out on the later part of the curve. Since this portion of the curve rarely matters, one could consider using an abbreviated version of curve area to assess systems.

In Figure 3, we can see that the two Strive variants dominate the

Method	Macro F1	Error	C(1,10)	C(10,1)	ROC
Dnet	0.6015	0.0065	0.0342	0.0079	0.9768
Smox	0.7335	0.0049	0.0294	0.0077	0.9691
Naïve Bayes	0.5676	0.0065	0.0455	0.0078	0.9755
Unigram	0.6001	0.0064	0.0347	0.0079	0.9819
Best By Class	0.7335	0.0049	0.0294	0.0077	N/A
Majority BBC	0.7145	0.0056	0.0292	0.0075	N/A
Stack-D (norm)	0.7357	0.0049	**0.0241**†‡	0.0086	0.9856
Stack-S (norm)	0.7351	0.0049	0.0288	**0.0075**	0.9656
Strive-D	0.7325	**0.0048**	0.0276	0.0078	0.9858
Strive-D (norm)	0.7280	0.0049	0.0271	0.0077	0.9855
Strive-S (norm)	**0.7431**	0.0048	0.0295	0.0076	0.9634
Strive-D (norm, omit Smox)	0.6938	0.0055	0.0313	0.0077	**0.9858**
BestSelect	0.8763	0.0034	0.0149	0.0062	N/A

Table 3: Performance on TREC-AP Corpus

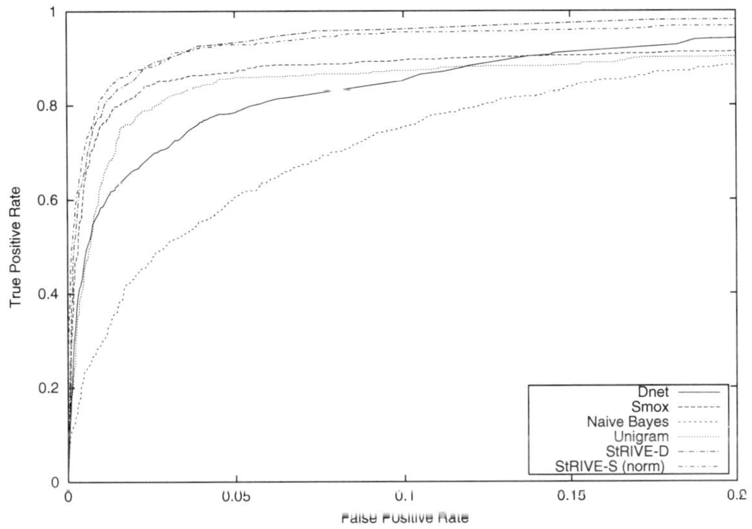

Figure 3: The ROC curve for the *Health & Fitness* class in the MSN Web Directory corpus

four base classifiers. In fact, *Strive-D* dominates (*i.e.*, its quality is greater than any other curve at every point) most of the MSN Web Directory corpus. We also can see (note the truncated scale) the base classifiers catching up with *Strive-S (norm)* on the right side of the curve. They, in fact, do surpass it. As a result, *Strive-D* is usually a more appropriate choice if the utility function penalizes false negatives significantly more heavily than false positives.

Referring back to Figure 1, we can understand why the decision tree is more appropriate for tracking crossovers in some cases. In this case, it is establishing a score region for Smox and a score region for Dnet where the reliability indicators give further information about how to classify an example.

Finally, we note that when we omit the base classifier Smox in *Strive-D (norm, omit Smox)*, the resulting combination improves by a large margin over the base methods; however, the resulting classifier generally still fails to beat Smox. This suggests that there are not enough indicator variables tied to Smox's behavior, or alternatively, that the other classifiers as a group behave like Smox, rather than classify in a complementary fashion.

Reuters and TREC-AP

The results for Reuters and TREC-AP in Tables 2 and 3 are consistent with the above analysis. We note that the level of improvement tends to be less pronounced for these corpora.

5. FUTURE WORK

We are excited about the opportunities for probabilistic combination of multiple classifiers with reliability indicators. We are pursuing several research directions. Foremost, we believe that a functional search that generates and tests a larger number of reliability indicators could provide valuable sets of informative reliability indicators.

In the experiments above, the classifiers were specifically held constant in order to distill the effect of indicator variables. In future studies, we will allow representations to vary to induce more variety among the base classifiers.

We are also interested in exploring the use of other classifiers as metaclassifiers. The metaclassifier should be a classifier that handles correlated input well (*e.g.*, use of maximum entropy) as classifiers performing better than random will be necessarily correlated.

6. SUMMARY AND CONCLUSIONS

We reviewed a methodology for building a metaclassifier for text documents that centers on combining multiple distinct classifiers with probabilistic learning and inference that leverages reliability-indicator variables. Reliability indicators provide information about the context-sensitive nature of classifier reliability. We reviewed several popular text classification methods, and described several combination schemes. We introduced the *Strive* methodology that uses reliability indicators in a hierarchical combination model and reviewed comparative studies comparing Strive with other combination mechanisms. The empirical evaluations support the conclusion that a simple majority vote in situations where one of the classifiers performs strongly can "water down" that classifier's performance. The experiments also show that stacking and *Strive* seem to provide robust combination schemes across a variety of performance measures.

Acknowledgments

We thank Max Chickering and Robert Rounthwaite for their special support of the WinMine toolkit, and John Platt for advice and code support for the linear SVM classifier.

7. REFERENCES

[1] K. Al-Kofahi, A. Tyrrell, A. Vacher, T. Travers, and P. Jackson. Combining multiple classifiers for text categorization. In *CIKM '01*, pages 97-104, 2001.

[2] B. T. Bartell, G. W. Cottrell, and R. K. Belew. Automatic combination of multiple ranked retrieval systems. In *SIGIR '94*, pages 173-181, 1994.

[3] N. Belkin, C. Cool, W. Croft, and J. Callan. The effect of multiple query representations on information retrieval system performance. In *SIGIR '93*, pages 339-346, 1993.

[4] D. Chickering, D. Heckerman, and C. Meek. A Bayesian approach to learning Bayesian networks with local structure. In *UAI '97*, pages 80-89, 1997.

[5] M. Corporation. WinMine Toolkit v1.0. http://research.microsoft.com/~dmax /WinMine/ContactInfo.html, 2001.

[6] S. T. Dumais and H. Chen. Hierarchical classification of web content. In *SIGIR '00*, pages 256-263, 2000.

[7] S. T. Dumais, J. Platt, D. Heckerman, and M. Sahami. Inductive learning algorithms and representations for text categorization. In *CIKM '98*, pages 148-155, 1998.

[8] D. Heckerman, D. Chickering, C. Meek, R. Rounthwaite, and C. Kadie. Dependency networks for inference, collaborative filtering, and data visualization. *Journal of Machine Learning Research*, 1:49-75, 2000.

[9] D. Hull, J. Pedersen, and H. Schuetze. Method combination for document filtering. In *SIGIR '96*, pages 279-287, 1996.

[10] T. Joachims. Text categorization with support vector machines: Learning with many relevant features. In *ECML '98*, pages 137-142, 1998.

[11] J. Katzer, M. McGill, J. Tessier, W. Frakes, and P. DasGupta. A study of the overlap among document representations. *Information Technology: Research and Development*, 1:261-274, 1982.

[12] W. Lam and K.-Y. Lai. A meta-learning approach for text categorization. In *SIGIR '01*, pages 303-309, 2001.

[13] L. S. Larkey and W. B. Croft. Combining classifiers in text categorization. In *SIGIR '96*, pages 289-297, 1996.

[14] D. D. Lewis. A sequential algorithm for training text classifiers: Corrigendum and additional data. *SIGIR Forum*, 29(2):13-19, Fall 1995.

[15] D. D. Lewis. Reuters-21578, distribution 1.0. http://www.daviddlewis.com/resources /testcollections/reuters21578, January 1997.

[16] D. D. Lewis and W. A. Gale. A sequential algorithm for training text classifiers. In *SIGIR '94*, pages 3-12, 1994.

[17] D. D. Lewis, R. E. Schapire, J. P. Callan, and R. Papka. Training algorithms for linear text classifiers. In *SIGIR '96*, pages 298-306, 1996.

[18] Y. Li and A. Jain. Classification of text documents. *The Computer Journal*, 41(8):537-546, 1998.

[19] A. McCallum and K. Nigam. A comparison of event models for naive bayes text classification. In *Working Notes of AAAI 1998, Workshop on Learning for Text Categorization*, pages 41-48, 1998.

[20] J. C. Platt. Probabilistic outputs for support vector machines and comparisons to regularized likelihood methods. In A. J. Smola, P. Bartlett, B. Scholkopf, and D. Schuurmans, editors, *Advances in Large Margin Classifiers*. MIT Press, 1999.

[21] F. Provost and T. Fawcett. Robust classification for imprecise environments. *Machine Learning*, 42:203-231, 2001.

[22] T. Rajashekar and W. Croft. Combining automatic and manual index representations in probabilistic retrieval. *Journal of the American Society for Information Science*, 6(4):272-283, 1995.

[23] R. E. Schapire and Y. Singer. BoosTexter: A boosting-based system for text categorization. *Machine Learning*, 39:135-168, 2000.

[24] J. Shaw and E. Fox. Combination of multiple searches. In D. K. Harman, editor, *TREC-3 Conference*, number 500-225 in NIST Special Publication, pages 105-108, 1995.

[25] K. Ting and I. Witten. Issues in stacked generalization. *Journal of Artificial Intelligence Research*, 10:271-289, 1999.

[26] K. Toyama and E. Horvitz. Bayesian modality fusion: Probabilistic integration of multiple vision algorithms for head tracking. In *ACCV 2000, Fourth Asian Conference on Computer Vision*, 2000.

[27] C. van Rijsbergen. *Information Retrieval*. Butterworths, London, 1979.

[28] S. Weiss, C. Apte, F. Damerau, D. Johnson, F. Oles, T. Goets, and T. Hampp. Maximizing text-mining performance. *IEEE Intelligent Systems*, 14(4), 1999.

[29] D. H. Wolpert. Stacked generalization. *Neural Networks*, 5:241-259, 1992.

[30] Y. Yang, T. Ault, and T. Pierce. Combining multiple learning strategies for effective cross validation. In *ICML '00*, pages 1167-1182, 2000.

[31] Y. Yang and X. Liu. A re-examination of text categorization methods. In *SIGIR '99*, pages 42-49, 1999.

Efficient Phrase Querying with an Auxiliary Index

Dirk Bahle Hugh E. Williams Justin Zobel
School of Computer Science and Information Technology
RMIT University, GPO Box 2476V
Melbourne, Australia, 3001.
{dbahle,hugh,jz}@cs.rmit.edu.au

ABSTRACT

Search engines need to evaluate queries extremely fast, a challenging task given the vast quantities of data being indexed. A significant proportion of the queries posed to search engines involve phrases. In this paper we consider how phrase queries can be efficiently supported with low disk overheads. Previous research has shown that phrase queries can be rapidly evaluated using nextword indexes, but these indexes are twice as large as conventional inverted files. We propose a combination of nextword indexes with inverted files as a solution to this problem. Our experiments show that combined use of an auxiliary nextword index and a conventional inverted file allow evaluation of phrase queries in half the time required to evaluate such queries with an inverted file alone, and the space overhead is only 10% of the size of the inverted file. Further time savings are available with only slight increases in disk requirements.

Categories and Subject Descriptors

H.3.4 [**Information Storage and Retrieval**]: Systems and Software evaluation—*(efficiency)*; E.2 [**Data**]: Storage Representations

General Terms

Algorithms, performance

Keywords

Indexing, query evaluation, phrase query evaluation, inverted index, nextword index, evaluation efficiency, index representation, stopping

1. INTRODUCTION

Search engines are used to find data in response to ad hoc queries. On the Web, most queries consist of simple lists of words. However, a significant fraction of the queries include phrases, where the user has indicated that some of the query terms must be adjacent, typically by enclosing them in quotation marks. Phrases have the advantage of being unambiguous concept markers and are therefore viewed as a valuable retrieval technique [5, 6, 7, 10]

In this paper, we explore new techniques for efficient evaluation of phrase queries.

A standard way to evaluate phrase queries is to use an inverted index, in which for each index term there is a list of postings, and each posting includes a document identifier, an in-document frequency, and a list of offsets. These offsets are the ordinal word positions at which the term occurs in the document. Given such a word-level inverted index and a phrase query, it is straightforward to combine the postings lists for the query terms to identify matching documents. This does not mean, however, that the process is fast. Even with an efficient representation of postings [16], the list for a common term can require several megabytes for each gigabyte of indexed text. Worse, heuristics such as frequency-ordering [13] or impact-ordering [1] are not of value, as the frequency of a word in a document does not determine its frequency of participation in a particular phrase.

A crude solution is to use stopping, as is done by some widely-used web search engines (the Google search engine, for example, neglects common words in queries), but this approach means that a small number of queries cannot be evaluated, while many more evaluate incorrectly [12]. Another solution is to index phrases directly, but the set of word pairs in a text collection is large and an index on such phrases difficult to manage.

In recent work, we proposed nextword indexes as a way of supporting phrase queries and phrase browsing [2, 3, 15]. In a nextword index, for each index term or *firstword* there is a list of the words or *nextwords* that follow that term, together with the documents and word positions at which the firstword and nextword occur as a pair. The disadvantage of a nextword index is its size, typically around half that of the indexed collection. Also, as described originally, nextword index processing is not particularly efficient, as the nextwords must be processed linearly and (compared to an standard inverted index) for rare firstwords the overhead of the additional layer of structure may outweigh the benefits.

In this paper we propose that phrase queries be evaluated through a combination of an inverted index on rare words and a form of nextword index on common words. We explore the properties of phrase queries and show experimentally that query evaluation time can be halved if just the three most common firstwords are supported through a nextword index. While phrase browsing is not possible with such an arrangement, the disk overheads of the partial nextword index are small and the benefits are substantial.

We have observed that many ordinary queries — those without quotation marks — nonetheless resolve successfully if processed as a phrase query, a phenomenon that search engine users are familiar with, as the most popular engines highly rank matches in which the query terms are adjacent. This suggests that phrase querying is a potential method for a fast "first cut" evaluation method, as it allows more rapid identification of documents in which the terms occur as a phrase.

2. PROPERTIES OF QUERIES

With large web search engines being used daily by millions of users, it has become straightforward to gather large numbers of queries and see how users are choosing to express their information needs. Some search engine companies have made extracts of their query logs freely available. In our research, we have made extensive use of query logs provided by Excite dating to 1997 and 1999, as well as more recent logs from other sources. These logs have similar properties (with regard to our purposes), and we report primarily on the Excite logs in this work. In the Excite log, after sanitizing to remove obscenity there are 1,583,922 queries (including duplicates). Of these, 132,276 or 8.3% are explicit phrase queries, that is, they include a sequence of two or more words enclosed in quotes. Amongst the rest of the queries—those without a phrase— about 5% contain a word that does not occur at all in the 21.9 gigabytes (Gb) of data we use. However, almost exactly 41% of the remaining non-phrase queries actually match a phrase in the 21.9 Gb dataset we use in our experiments.

A surprising proportion of the phrases include a common term. Amongst the explicit phrase queries, 11,103 or 8.4% include one of the three words that are commonest in our dataset, "the", "to", and "of". 14.4% of the phrase queries include one of the 20 commonest terms. In some of these queries the common word has a structural function only, as in `tower of london`, and can arguably be safely neglected during query evaluation. In other queries, however, common words play an important role, as in the movie title `end of days` or the band name `the who`, and evaluation of these queries is difficult with the common words removed, especially when both "the" and "who" happen to be common terms [12].

Taken together, these observations suggest that stopping of common words will have an unpredictable effect. Stopping may yield efficiency gains, but means that a significant number of queries cannot be correctly evaluated. We experimented with a set of 122,438 phrase queries that between them match 309×10^6 documents. Stopping of common words means that a query such as `tower of london` must be evaluated as `tower -- london`: the query evaluation engine knows that the two remaining query terms must appear with a single term between them. If the commonest three words are stopped, there are 390×10^6 total matches for all queries extracted from the log. However, these are distributed extremely unevenly amongst the queries: for some queries the great majority of matches are incorrect. The figure rises to 490×10^6 for the commonest 20 words, and 1693×10^6 for the commonest 254 words, while a significant number of queries, containing only stopped words, cannot be evaluated at all.

It can be argued that stopwords are often insignificant, and that even a document that is technically a mismatch—due to the wrong stopword being present—may be just as likely to be relevant as a document where the match is correct. However, it is worth emphasising that there are many queries in which stopwords do play an important role. The words "to" and "from" are often stopped, for example, but mismatches to the query `flights to london` are likely to be incorrect. Another instance is that the word "the" often forms part of a description, thus `the moon` should not match websites about a moon of Jupiter, Keith Moon, or a book publisher.

Amongst the phrase queries, the median number of words in a phrase is 2, and the average is almost 2.5. About 34% of the queries have three words or more, and 1.3% have six words or more. A few queries are much longer, such as titles: `the architect of desire beauty and danger in the stanford white family by suzannah lessard`.

Another point of interest is where in a phrase the common words occur. In English, the common words rarely terminate a phrase query. Only 0.4% of phrase queries with "the", "to", or "of" have these words at the end. Almost all of these queries are short: virtually no queries of four words or more terminate with one of the commonest terms. In the short queries ending in a common term, the other query terms are themselves usually common. We take advantage of these trends in the methods for phrase query evaluation proposed in this paper.

3. INVERTED INDEXES

Inverted indexes are the standard method for supporting queries on large text databases; there are no practical alternatives to inverted indexes that provide sufficiently fast ranked query evaluation. An inverted index is a two-level structure. The upper level is all the index terms for the collection. For text databases, the index terms are usually the words occurring in the text, and all words are included. The lower level is a set of postings lists, one per index term. Following the notation of Zobel and Moffat [17], each posting is a triple of the form:

$$\langle d, f_{d,t}, [o_1, \ldots, o_{f_{d,t}}] \rangle$$

where d is the identifier of a document containing term t, the frequency of t in d is $f_{d,t}$, and the o values are the positions in d at which t is observed. An example inverted file is shown in Figure 1. In this example, there is a vocabulary of five words, each of which has a postings list.

It is straightforward to use an inverted index to evaluate a phrase query. Consider the query `magdalene sue prentiss`. Of these terms, "magdalene" is the rarest, and its inverted list is fetched first. The postings are decoded and a temporary structure is created, recording which documents contain this word and the ordinal word positions in each document at which it occurs. The term "prentiss" is the next rarest, and is processed next. For each document identifier and word offset in the temporary structure created earlier, a posting is sought to see whether "prentiss" is in the document two words later. If the search fails, that word position is discarded from the temporary structure, as is the document identifier if no word positions for that document remain. As both the structure and the postings are sorted, this process is a linear merge. Then the postings list

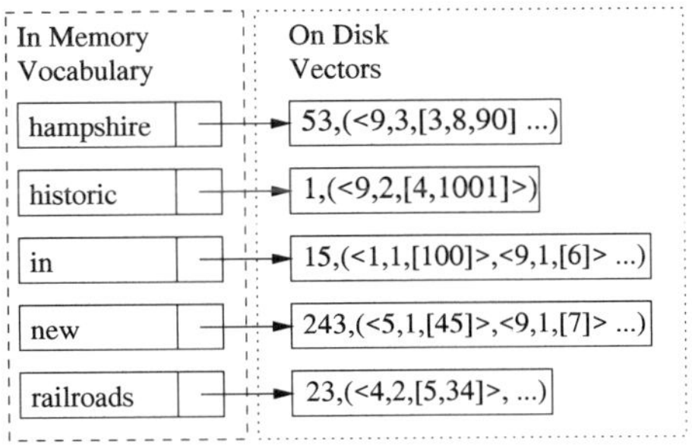

Figure 1: An inverted file for a collection with a vocabulary of five words.

for "sue" is fetched and decoded, and used to further delete entries from the temporary structure. The remaining entries are documents and word positions at which the phrase occurs.

Summarizing, phrase queries are evaluated as follows.

1. Sort the query terms from rarest to commonest, keeping note of their original position in the phrase.
2. Fetch the postings list for the first (rarest) query term. Decode this list into a temporary structure of document identifiers and word offset positions.
3. For each remaining query term, decode its postings list, merging it with the temporary data; this merge process discards from the temporary structure all document identifiers and word offsets that do not match any entry in the postings list.

In this query evaluation model, processing of the first query term establishes a superset of the possible locations of the complete phrase, which are maintained in a temporary structure; as the subsequent query terms are evaluated, this structure is pruned, never added to. It is thus essential to begin processing with the rarest query term, to avoid creation of an excessively large temporary structure (or of having to process the inverted lists in stages to stay within a memory limit).

A simple heuristic to address this problem is to directly merge the inverted lists rather than decode them in turn. On the one hand, merging has the disadvantage that techniques such as skipping [11] cannot be as easily used to reduce processing costs (although as we discuss later skipping does not necessarily yield significant benefits). On the other hand, merging of at least some of the inverted lists is probably the only viable option when all the query terms are moderately common.

Whether the lists are merged or processed in turn, the whole of each list needs to be fetched (unless query processing terminates early due to lack of matches). For ranked query processing it is possible to predict which postings in each inverted list are most likely to be of value, and move these to the front of the inverted list; techniques for such list modification include frequency-ordering [13] and impact-ordering [1]. With these techniques, only the first of the inverted lists need be fetched during evaluation of most queries, greatly reducing costs.

In contrast, for phrase querying it is not simple to predict which occurrences of the term will be in a query phrase, and thus such reordering is unlikely to be effective. Offsets only have to be decoded when there is a document match, but they still have to be retrieved.

Table 1: Size of inverted index (Mb) after stopping of common words.

Number of words stopped	Index size (Mb)
0	2350
3	2259
6	2195
10	2135
20	2089
254	1708

Other techniques do have the potential to reduce query evaluation time, in particular *skipping* [11], in which additional information is placed in inverted lists to reduce the decoding required in regions in the list that cannot contain postings that will match documents that have been identified as potential matches. On older machines, on which CPU cycles were relatively scarce, skipping could yield substantial gains. On current machines, however, disk access costs are the more important factor, and in other experiments we have observed that the increase in length of lists required by skipping outweighs the reduction in decoding time. We therefore do not use skipping in our experiments.

We have implemented a phrase query evaluator based on inverted lists, using compression techniques similar to those employed in MG [16] to reduce costs, and have used it to test the efficiency of phrase query evaluation. Our test data is 21.9 Gb of HTML containing about 8.3 Gb of text (drawn from the TREC large web track [9]).

Table 1 shows the size of the index with a range of levels of stopping. As can be seen, the three commonest words account for around 4% of the index size, and only small space savings are yielded by stopping. However, as Table 2 shows, the impact of stopping on query evaluation time is dramatic. Just removing the three commonest words reduces average time by about 60%, and by a factor of 3 for longer queries. For these longer queries, the savings continue to increase as more common words are stopped. It is the scale of these savings that make stopping attractive, despite the fact that they are at the cost of inaccurate query results.

Table 2: Times for phrase query evaluation (seconds) on an inverted index after stopping of common words. Results are shown for all queries; 2-word queries only; and 5-word queries only.

Number of words stopped	Overall time (sec)	2-word queries	5-word queries
0	1.56	0.49	6.41
3	0.66	0.30	1.94
6	0.45	0.29	1.07
10	0.40	0.28	0.81
20	0.37	0.28	0.70
254	0.18	0.16	0.26

4. NEXTWORD INDEXES

Inverted indexes allow evaluation of phrase queries, but faster evaluation is possible with phrase-oriented indexes. One possibility is to use a conventional inverted index in which the terms are word pairs. Another way to support phrase based query modes is to index and store phrases directly [8] or simply by using an inverted index and approximating phrases through a ranked query technique [5, 10]. Greater efficiency, with no additional in-memory space overheads, is possible with a special-purpose structure, the nextword index [15], where search structures are used to accelerate processing of word pairs. The nextword index takes the middle ground by indexing pairs of words and, therefore, is particularly good at resolving phrase queries containing two or more words. As noted above and observed elsewhere, the commonest number of words in a phrase is two [14].

A nextword index is a three-level structure. The highest level is of the distinct index terms in the collection, which we call *firstwords*. At the middle level, for each firstword there is a data structure (such as a front-coded list, or for fast access a structure such as a tree) of *nextwords*, which are the words observed to follow that firstword in the indexed text. For example, for the firstword "artificial", nextwords include "intelligence", "insemination", and "hip". At the lowest level, for each nextword there is a postings list of the positions at which that firstword-nextword pair occur.

An example nextword index is shown in Figure 2. In this example, there are two firstwords, "in" and "new". Some of the nextwords for "in" are "all", "new", and "the". For each firstword-nextword pair, there is a postings list. (A nextword index is of course a form of inverted index, but for consistency with other work we use "inverted index" solely to refer to a standard word-level inverted file.)

In nextword indexes, the postings lists are typically short, because most pairs only occur infrequently. For example, the postings list for the firstword-nextword pair "the"·"who" is orders of magnitude smaller than the postings lists for these words in an inverted file. It follows that phrase query evaluation can be extremely fast.

Nextword indexes also have the benefit of allowing phrase browsing or phrase querying [4, 15]; given a sequence of words, the index can be used to identify which words follow the sequence, thus providing an alternative mechanism for searching text collections. However, we do not consider phrase browsing further in this paper.

For phrase queries of more than two words, multiple postings lists must be fetched from the nextword index to resolve the query. Selection of which listings to fetch requires a little care. For example, with the query

```
boulder municipal employees credit union
```

the query can be resolved by fetching the postings lists for the firstword-nextword pairs "boulder"·"municipal", "employees"·"credit", and "credit"·"union". Alternatively, it would be possible to get the lists for "boulder"·"municipal", "municipal"·"employees", and "credit"·"union". Which is most efficient depends on which is shorter: the list for "employees"·"credit" or the list for for "municipal"·"employees".

Unfortunately, establishing which is shorter requires two disk accesses, to retrieve the nextwords for "employees" and "municipal". However, we have observed that the frequency of a firstword closely correlates to the lengths of its nextword lists.
Thus in the query

```
historic railroads in new hampshire
```

we can with confidence choose "railroads"·"in" in preference to "in"·"new", because "railroads" is much less common than "in". We have considered algorithms for choosing order of evaluation elsewhere [3]. An efficient algorithm for evaluating phrase queries with a nextword index is as follows.

1. If the number of query terms n is even, the query can consist of $n/2$ disjoint firstword-nextword pairs. If the number of query terms n is odd, $\lceil n/2 \rceil$ firstword-nextword pairs must be chosen. However, in both cases it is more efficient to choose more than the minimum number of pairs, if doing so avoids choice of a common word as a firstword.
2. The method we use is to choose all $n-1$ firstword-nextword pairs; then sort them by increasing firstword frequency; then discard from the list the pairs that are completely covered by preceding selections. This approach can lead to processing of more than $\lceil n/2 \rceil$ pairs, but experimentally was shown to reduces costs overall.
3. The selected word pairs are sorted by increasing frequency of the firstwords, then their postings lists are processed as for inverted file phrase query processing.

The nextword index for our Web collection is 4487 Mb in size, almost exactly twice that of an inverted file. For phrase queries, the savings in query evaluation time are dramatic. Average query evaluation time is reduced to 0.06 seconds, faster than inverted files by a factor of 25. For two-word queries, the time falls to 0.01 seconds, which is faster by a factor of 50. The time for 5-word queries is 0.32.

An interesting possibility suggested by these results is that—given space for a nextword index—all queries be evaluated as if they were phrases. We observed above that a significant fraction of all queries successfully evaluate, and indeed on browsing the query logs it is obvious that many of the queries without quotation marks are nonetheless intended to be phrases. Spink et al. [14] suggest that most two-word queries should be treated as a phrase query even if they were entered as a ranked query. Given that search engines return as highest matches the pages in which the

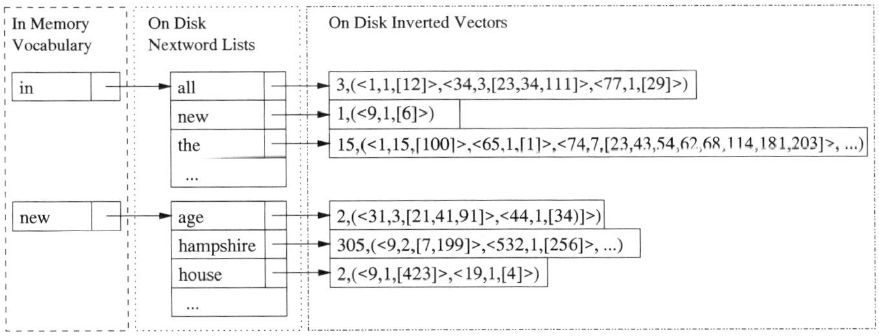

Figure 2: A nextword index with two firstwords.

query words appear in sequence, use of a nextword index provides a rapid mechanism for finding these pages.

Much of the speed improvement for phrase queries yielded by nextword indexes is for queries involving a non-rare word. Indeed, for queries of rare words there may be little gain, as query processing with nextword indexes involves more complex structures than does processing with inverted indexes. As the two approaches to phrase query processing appear, then, to have complementary advantages, it is attractive to try to combine their strengths.

5. COMBINED QUERY EVALUATION

We have observed above that inverted indexes are the least efficient for phrases involving common words, the case where nextword indexes yield the greatest speed advantage. We therefore propose that common words only be used as firstwords in a stripped-down nextword index, and that this new index be used where possible in evaluation of phrase queries. We call this a *top frequency* based scheme, since only the most frequent words are indexed in the nextword index. We have explored other schemes based on the frequency of words in the indexed collection, or based on the frequency of words in the query log. None of the investigated schemes offered a better space and time trade-off, so we report only results from the top frequency scheme.

An example of a top frequency combined index is shown in Figure 3. At the left there is a vocabulary of five words. Each word has an inverted list, together constituting a complete inverted file for these words. In addition, the common words "in" and "new" have a nextword index.

With a combined index, processing involves postings lists from both the inverted index and the nextword index. Consider again the query:

```
historic railroads in new hampshire
```

Neither "historic" nor "railroads" is a common word, so establishing that these terms occur in the phrase involves fetching their postings lists from the inverted index and processing in the usual way. However, "in" and "new" are both common. The posting list for the firstword-nextword pair "in"·"new" from the nextword index must be fetched and processed. Then there is a choice. On the one hand, the nextword index postings list for "new"·"hampshire" cannot be longer than the inverted index postings list for "hampshire" and in all likelihood is a great deal shorter. On the other hand, compared to the inverted index, an extra disk access is required to fetch a postings list from the nextword index. In our implementation, we process using the nextword index if possible, and resort to the inverted index only for terms that are not in an indexed firstword-nextword pair.

In summary, we use the following process:

1. Identify all pairs in the list in which the first term is an indexed firstword. Sort these terms, and prune the list as for standard evaluation of phrase queries via a nextword index.
2. For all terms not in a firstword-nextword pair, sort.
3. Process the postings lists in increasing order of firstword frequency, so that processing of nextword index lists and of inverted file lists is interleaved.

In this model, a common word need only be evaluated via its postings list in the inverted file if it occurs as the last word in a query, which in the Excite query log is a rare event.

We have tested other query resolution methods that involved term sorting based on nextword frequency (or NWF, the number of nextwords for a firstword), inverted document frequency (or IDF, the number of documents in which a word occurs), or both. We also experimented with resolving nextword entries of a given query always first, or always last. We found overall that these different resolution methods did not significantly vary in query speed and behaved almost identically to sorting by IDF only. We therefore sort inverted index terms and nextword terms based on IDF since we do not need to keep another statistical value per index term and sorting is straightforward.

6. EXPERIMENTAL RESULTS

All experiments were run on an Intel 700 MHz Pentium III-based server with 2 Gb of memory, running the Linux operating system under light load. In Table 3 we show sizes of nextword indexes in which only the commonest terms are allowed as firstwords. The table shows that a nextword index that contains only the three commonest terms consumes 254 Mb, that is, just over 10% of the space of the inverted index or around 1% of the size of the original HTML collection.

Query evaluation time with a combined index is shown in Table 4. (The "0" line is repeated from Table 2.) As can be seen, use of a nextword index allows evaluation of all phrase queries, and much more rapidly than was previously possible. Use of a partial nextword index of 1% of the HTML collection halves query evaluation time; a partial nextword

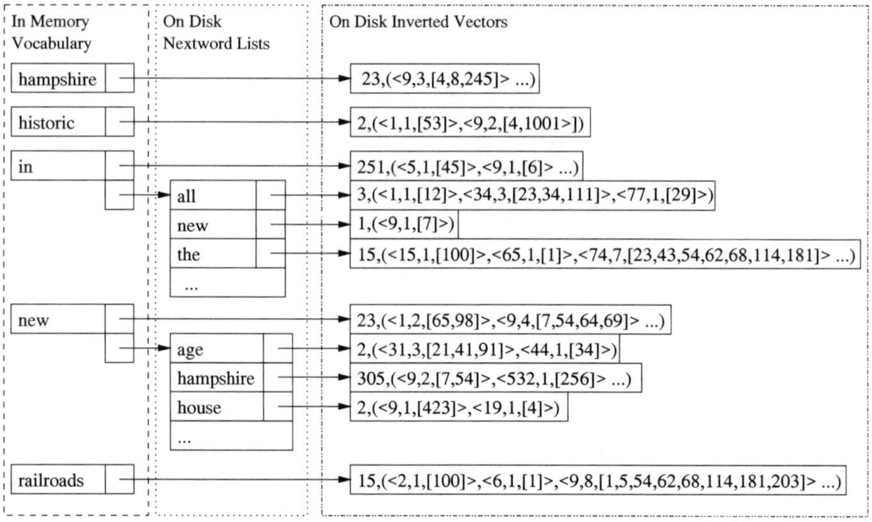

Figure 3: A combined inverted file and nextword index.

Table 3: Size of nextword index (Mb) containing only common firstwords.

Number of common words	Index size (Mb)
3	254
6	427
10	520
20	657
254	1366

index of less than 3% of the size of the collection cuts time to a third.

These are substantial savings at low cost. Phrase query processing time with a nextword index is only slightly greater than with a stopped inverted file, and no answers are lost.

Such combined processing can be integrated with other heuristics for phrase query evaluation. For example, a strategy that is likely to be successful in the context of a web search engine is to maintain indexes (perhaps for a limited time only) on phrases, or word pairs from phrases, that are commonly posed as queries. Amongst our 132,276 queries, 72,184 are distinct. The commonest phrase query (`thumbnail post`) occurs 205 times and involves no common words. The queries themselves contain 92,846 distinct word pairs; the commonest pair occurs 683 times. Indexing of common query pairs has the potential to yield significant further savings.

7. CONCLUSIONS

We have proposed that phrase queries on large text collections be supported by use of a small auxiliary index. In this approach, all words in the text are indexed via an inverted file; in addition, the commonest words are indexed via an auxiliary nextword index, which stores postings lists for firstword-nextword pairs. We have shown that the cost of evaluating phrase indexes can be cut by a factor of three, with an auxiliary index that is only 3% of the size of the indexed data.

Table 4: Times for phrase query evaluation (seconds) on a combined index, with different numbers of common words used in the nextword index. Results are shown for all queries; 2-word queries only; and 5-word queries only.

Number of common words	Overall time (sec)	2-word queries	5-word queries
0	1.56	0.49	6.41
3	0.76	0.31	2.99
6	0.57	0.31	2.28
10	0.53	0.30	2.10
20	0.50	0.30	1.98
254	0.46	0.27	1.83

These results show that there is no need to use stopping in phrases. Indeed, the statistics on the number of matches indicate that such stopping leads to significant error rates. While it can be argued that mistakes in matching due to stopping of common words are in many cases unimportant, there are numerous queries where the stopwords are significant; moreover, we have demonstrated that there is no reason to make such mistakes at all.

Our schemes have scope for improvement. In particular, choosing of pairs during query evaluation requires further exploration, and we are further investigating structures for representing nextword lists. However, our results show that evaluation of phrase queries can be dramatically accelerated with only a small additional index, and that stopping of phrases leads to errors and is not necessary for efficiency.

Acknowledgements

This research was supported by the Australian Research Council. We thank Amanda Spink, Doug Cutting, Jack Xu, and Excite Inc. for providing the query log.

8. REFERENCES

[1] V. N. Anh, O. Kretser, and A. Moffat. Vector-Space ranking with effective early termination. In W. B. Croft, D. J. Harper, D. H. Kraft, and J. Zobel, editors, *Proc. ACM-SIGIR International Conference on Research and Development in Information Retrieval*, pages 35–42, New York, Sept. 2001.

[2] D. Bahle, H.E. Williams, and J. Zobel. Compaction techniques for nextword indexes. In *Proc. 8th International Symposium on String Processing and Information Retrieval (SPIRE2001)*, pages 33–45, San Rafael, Chile, 2001.

[3] D. Bahle, H. E. Williams, and J. Zobel. Optimised phrase querying and browsing in text databases. In M. Oudshoorn, editor, *Proc. Australasian Computer Science Conference*, pages 11–19, Gold Coast, Australia, Jan. 2001.

[4] P. Bruza, R. McArthur, and S. Dennis. Interactive internet search: keyword, directory and query reformulation mechanisms compared. In N. J. Belkin, P. Ingwersen, and M.-K. Leong, editors, *Proc. ACM-SIGIR International Conference on Research and Development in Information Retrieval*, pages 280–287, Athens, 2000.

[5] C. L. Clarke, G. V. Cormack, and E. A. Tudhope. Relevance ranking for one- to three-term queries. In *Proc. of RIAO-97, 5th International Conference "Recherche d'Information Assistee par Ordinateur"*, pages 388–400, Montreal, CA, 1997.

[6] W. B. Croft, H. R. Turtle, and D. D. Lewis. The use of phrases and structured queries in information retrieval. In A. Bookstein, Y. Chiaramella, G. Salton, and V. V. Raghavan, editors, *Proc. ACM-SIGIR International Conference on Research and Development in Information Retrieval*, pages 32–45, Chicago, 1991.

[7] E. F. de Lima and J. O. Pedersen. Phrase recognition and expansion for short, precision-biased queries based on a query log. In *Proc. ACM-SIGIR International Conference on Research and Development in Information Retrieval*, pages 145–152, Berkeley, 1999.

[8] C. Gutwin, G. Paynter, I. Witten, C. NevillManning, and E. Frank. Improving browsing in digital libraries with keyphrase indexes. *Decision Support Systems*, 27(1/2):81–104, 1998.

[9] D. Hawking, N. Craswell, P. Thistlewaite, and D. Harman. Results and challenges in web search evaluation. In *Proc. of the Eighth International World-Wide Web Conference*, volume 31, pages 1321–1330, May 1999.

[10] D. D. Lewis and W. B. Croft. Term clustering of syntactic phrases. In J.-L. Vidick, editor, *Proc. ACM-SIGIR International Conference on Research and Development in Information Retrieval*, pages 385–404, 1990.

[11] A. Moffat and J. Zobel. Self-indexing inverted files for fast text retrieval. *ACM Transactions on Information Systems*, 14(4):349–379, 1996.

[12] G. W. Paynter, I. H. Witten, S. J. Cunningham, and G. Buchanan. Scalable browsing for large collections: A case study. In *Proc. of the 5th ACM International Conference on Digital Libraries*, pages 215–223, San Antonio, 2000.

[13] M. Persin, J. Zobel, and R. Sacks-Davis. Filtered document retrieval with frequency-sorted indexes. *Journal of the American Society for Information Science*, 47(10):749–764, 1996.

[14] A. Spink, D. Wolfram, B. J. Jansen, and T. Saracevic. Searching the web: The public and their queries. *Journal of the American Society for Information Science*, 52(3):226–234, 2001.

[15] H. Williams, J. Zobel, and P. Anderson. What's next? index structures for efficient phrase querying. In M. Orlowska, editor, *Proc. Australasian Database Conference*, pages 141–152, Auckland, New Zealand, 1999.

[16] I. H. Witten, A. Moffat, and T. C. Bell. *Managing Gigabytes: Compressing and Indexing Documents and Images*. Morgan Kaufmann, San Francisco, California, second edition, 1999.

[17] J. Zobel and A. Moffat. Exploring the similarity space. *SIGIR Forum*, 32(1):18–34, 1998.

Compression of Inverted Indexes For Fast Query Evaluation

Falk Scholer Hugh E. Williams John Yiannis Justin Zobel
School of Computer Science and Information Technology
RMIT University, GPO Box 2476V
Melbourne, Australia, 3001.
{fscholer,hugh,jyiannis,jz}@cs.rmit.edu.au

ABSTRACT

Compression reduces both the size of indexes and the time needed to evaluate queries. In this paper, we revisit the compression of inverted lists of document postings that store the position and frequency of indexed terms, considering two approaches to improving retrieval efficiency: better implementation and better choice of integer compression schemes. First, we propose several simple optimisations to well-known integer compression schemes, and show experimentally that these lead to significant reductions in time. Second, we explore the impact of choice of compression scheme on retrieval efficiency.

In experiments on large collections of data, we show two surprising results: use of simple byte-aligned codes halves the query evaluation time compared to the most compact Golomb-Rice bitwise compression schemes; and, even when an index fits entirely in memory, byte-aligned codes result in faster query evaluation than does an uncompressed index, emphasising that the cost of transferring data from memory to the CPU cache is less for an appropriately compressed index than for an uncompressed index. Moreover, byte-aligned schemes have only a modest space overhead: the most compact schemes result in indexes that are around 10% of the size of the collection, while a byte-aligned scheme is around 13%. We conclude that fast byte-aligned codes should be used to store integers in inverted lists.

Categories and Subject Descriptors

H.3.4 [**Information Storage and Retrieval**]: Systems and Software Performance evaluation (efficiency and effectiveness); E.4 [**Data**]: Coding and Information Theory Data compaction and compression

General Terms

Performance, Algorithms, Design

Keywords

Inverted indexes, retrieval efficiency, index compression, integer coding

1. INTRODUCTION

Search engines have demanding performance requirements. Users expect fast answers to queries, many queries must be processed per second, and the quantity of data that must be searched in response to each query is staggering. The demands continue to grow: the Google search engine, for example, indexed around one billion documents a year ago and now manages more than double that figure[1]. Moreover, the increasing availability and affordability of large storage devices suggests that the amount of data stored online will continue to grow.

Inverted indexes are used to evaluate queries in all practical search engines [14]. Compression of these indexes has three major benefits for performance. First, a compressed index requires less storage space. Second, compressed data makes better use of the available communication bandwidth; more information can be transfered per second than when the data is uncompressed. For fast decompression schemes, the total time cost of transfering compressed data and subsequently decompressing is potentially much less than the cost of transferring uncompressed data. Third, compression increases the likelihood that the part of the index required to evaluate a query is already cached in memory, thus entirely avoiding a disk access. Thus index compression can reduce costs in retrieval systems.

We have found that an uncompressed inverted index that stores the location of the indexed words in web documents typically consumes more than 30% of the space required to store the uncompressed collection of documents. (Web documents often include a great deal of information that is not indexed, such as HTML tags; in the TREC web data, which we use in our experiments, on average around half of each document is indexable text.) When the index is compressed, the index size is reduced to between 10%–15% of that required to store the uncompressed collection; this size includes document numbers, in-document frequencies, and word positions within documents. If the index is too large to fit entirely within main memory, then querying the uncompressed index is slower: as we show later, it is up to twice as slow as the fastest compressed scheme.

In this paper, we revisit compression schemes for the in-

[1]See `http://www.google.com/`

verted list component of inverted indexes. We also propose a new method for decoding lists. There have been a great many reports of experiments on compression of indexes with bitwise compression schemes [6, 8, 12, 14, 15], which use an integral number of bits to represent each integer, usually with no restriction on the alignment of the integers to byte or machine-word boundaries. We consider several aspects of these schemes: how to decode bitwise representations of integers efficiently; how to minimise the operations required for the most compact scheme, Golomb coding; and the relative performance of Elias gamma coding, Elias delta coding, Golomb coding, and Rice coding for storing indexes.

We question whether bitwise compression schemes are the best choice for storing lists of integers. As an alternative, we consider bytewise integer compression schemes, which require that each integer is stored in an integral number of blocks, where each block is eight bits. The length of each stored integer can therefore be measured in an exact number of bytes. An additional restriction is to require that these eight-bit blocks must align to machine-word or byte boundaries. We propose and experimentally investigate several variations of bytewise schemes.

We investigate the performance of different index compression schemes through experiments on large query sets and collections of Web documents. We report two surprising results.

- For a 20 gigabyte collection, where the index is several times larger than main memory, optimised bytewise schemes more than halve the average decoding time compared to the fastest bitwise approach.
- For a much smaller collection, where the index fits in main memory, a bytewise compressed index can still be processed faster than an uncompressed index.

These results show that effective use of communication bandwidths is important for not only disk-to-memory transfers but also memory-to-cache transfers. The only disadvantage of bytewise compressed indexes is that they are up to 30% larger than bitwise compressed indexes; the smallest bitwise index is around 10% of the uncompressed collection size, while the bytewise index is around 13%.

2. INVERTED INDEXES

An inverted index consists of two major components: the *vocabulary* of terms—for example the words—from the collection, and *inverted lists*, which are vectors that contain information about the occurrence of the terms [14].

In a basic implementation, for each term t there is an inverted list that contains *postings* $< f_{d,t}, d >$ where $f_{d,t}$ is the frequency f of term t in the ordinal document d. One posting is stored in the list for each document that contains the term t. Inverted lists of this form—along with additional statistics such as the document length l_d, and f_t, the number of documents that contain the term t—are sufficient to support ranked and Boolean query modes.

To support phrase querying or proximity querying, additional information must be kept in the inverted lists. Thus inverted list postings should be of the form

$$< f_{d,t}, d, [o_{0,d,t} \ldots o_{f_{d,t},d,t}] >$$

The additional information is the list of offsets o; one offset is stored for each of the $f_{d,t}$ occurrences of term t in document d. Postings in inverted lists are usually ordered by increasing d, and the offsets likewise ordered within the postings by increasing o. This has the benefit that differences between values—rather than the raw values—can be stored, improving the compressibility of the lists.

Other arrangements of the postings in lists are useful when lists are not necessarily completely processed in response to a query. For example, in frequency-sorted indexes [9, 10] postings are ordered by $f_{d,t}$, and in impact-ordered indexes the postings are ordered by quantised weights [1]. These approaches also rely on compression to help achieve efficiency gains, and the improvements to compression performance we describe in this paper are as applicable to these methods as they are to the simple index representations we use as a testbed for our compression methods.

Consider an example inverted list with offsets for the term "Matthew":

$$< 3, 7, [6, 51, 117] >< 1, 44, [12] >< 2, 117, [14, 1077] >$$

In this index, the terms are words, the offsets are word positions within the documents, and the lists are ordered by d. This inverted list states that the term "Matthew" occurs 3 times in document 7, at offsets 6, 51, and 117. It also occurs once in document 44 at offset 12, and twice in document 117, at offsets 14 and 1077.

Ranked queries can be answered using the inverted index as follows. First, the terms in the user's query are located in the inverted index vocabulary. Second, the corresponding inverted lists for each term are retrieved from disk, and then processed by decreasing f_t. Third, for each posting in each inverted list, an accumulator weight A_d is increased; the magnitude of the increase is dependent on the similarity measure used, and can consider the weight $w_{q,t}$ of term t in the query q, the weight $w_{d,t}$ of the term t in the document d, and other factors. Fourth, after processing part [1, 6] or all of the lists, the accumulator scores are partially sorted to identify the most similar documents. Last, for a typical search engine, document summaries of the top ten documents are generated or retrieved and shown to the user. The offsets stored in each inverted list posting are not used in ranked query processing.

Phrase queries require offsets and that a given sequence of words be contiguous in a matching document. For example, consider a combined ranked and phrase query:

"Matthew Richardson" Richmond

To evaluate such a query, the same first two steps as for ranked querying are applied. Then, instead of accumulating weights, it is necessary to construct a temporary inverted list for the phrase, by fetching the inverted list of each of the individual terms and combining them. If the inverted list for "Matthew" is as above and the inverted list for "Richardson" is

$$< 1, 7, [52] > < 2, 12, [1, 4] > < 1, 44, [83] >$$

then both words occur in document 7 and as an ordered pair. Only the word "Richardson" is in document 12, both words occur in document 44 but not as a pair, and only "Matthew" occurs in document 117. The list for "Matthew Richardson" is therefore

$$< 1, 7, [51] >$$

After this, the ranking process is continued from the third step, where the list for the term "Richmond" and the newly created list are used to adjust accumulator weights. Phrase queries can involve more than two words.

3. COMPRESSING INVERTED INDEXES

Special-purpose integer compression schemes offer both fast decoding and compact storage of inverted lists [13, 14]. In this section, we consider how inverted lists are compressed and stored on disk. We limit our discussions here to the special-purpose integer compression techniques that have previously been shown to be suitable for index compression, and focus on their use in increasing the speed of retrieval systems.

Without compression, the time cost of retrieving inverted lists is the sum of the time taken to seek for and then retrieve the inverted lists from disk into memory, and the time taken to transfer the lists from memory into the CPU cache before they are processed. The speed of access to compressed inverted lists is determined by two factors: first, the computational requirements for decoding the compressed data and, second, the time required to seek for and retrieve the compressed data from disk and to transfer it to the CPU cache before it is decoded. For a compression scheme to allow faster access to inverted lists, the total retrieval time and CPU processing costs should be less than the retrieval time of the uncompressed representation. However, a third factor makes compression attractive even if CPU processing costs exceed the saving in disk transfer time: compressing inverted lists increases the number of lists that can be cached in memory between queries, so that in the context of a stream of queries use of compression reduces the number of disk accesses. It is therefore important that a compression scheme be efficient in both decompression CPU costs and space requirements.

There are two general classes of compression scheme that are appropriate for storing inverted lists. Variable-bit or *bitwise* schemes store integers in an integral number of bits. Well-known bitwise schemes include Elias gamma and delta coding [3] and Golomb-Rice coding [4]. *Bytewise* schemes store an integer in an integral number of blocks, where a block is eight bits in size; we distinguish between blocks and bytes here, since there is no implied restriction that a block must align to a physical byte-boundary. A simple bytewise scheme is variable-byte coding [2, 13]; uncompressed integers are also stored in an integral number of blocks, but we do not define them as bytewise schemes since, on most architectures, an integer has a fixed-size representation of four bytes. In detail, these schemes are as follows.

Elias coding [3] is a non-parameterised bitwise method of coding integers. (Non-parameterised methods use static or fixed codes to store integers.) The Elias gamma code represents a positive integer k by $1 + \lfloor \log_2 k \rfloor$ stored as a unary code, followed by the binary representation of k without its most significant bit. Using Elias gamma coding, small integers are compactly represented; in particular, the integer 1 is represented as a single 1-bit. Gamma coding is relatively inefficient for storing integers larger than 15 [13].

Elias delta codes are suited to coding larger integers, but are inefficient for small values. For an integer k, a delta code stores the gamma code representation of $1 + \lfloor \log_2 k \rfloor$, and then the binary representation of k without its most significant bit.

Golomb-Rice bitwise coding [4] has been shown to offer more compact storage of integers and faster retrieval than the Elias codes [13]; indeed, it is bitwise optimal under the assumption that the set of documents with a given term is random. The codes are adapted to per-term likelihoods via a parameter that is used to determine the code emitted for an integer. In many cases, this parameter must be stored separately using, for example, an Elias code. For coding of inverted lists, a single parameter is used for all document numbers in a postings list, but each posting requires a parameter for its offsets. The parameters can be calculated as the lists are decoded using statistics stored in memory and in the lists, as we discuss later.

Coding of an integer k using Golomb codes with respect to a parameter b is as follows. The code that is emitted is in two parts: first, the unary code of a quotient q is emitted, where $q = \lfloor (k-1)/b \rfloor + 1$; second, a binary code is emitted for the remainder r, where $r = k - q \times b - 1$. The number of bits required to store the remainder r is either $\lceil \log_2 b \rceil$ or $\lfloor \log_2 b \rfloor$. To retrieve the remainder, the value of the "toggle point" $t = 1 \triangleleft ((\log_2 k)+1)) - b$ is required, where $\triangleleft$ indicates a left-shift operation. After retrieving $\lfloor \log_2 b \rfloor$ bits of the remainder r, the remainder is compared to t. If $r > t$, then one additional bit of the remainder must be retrieved. It is generally thought that caching calculated values of $\log_2 b$ is necessary for fast decoding, with a main-memory penalty of having to store the values. However, as we show later, when the standard log library function is replaced with a fast bit-shifting version, caching is unnecessary.

Rice coding is a variant of Golomb coding where the value of b is restricted to be a power of 2. The advantage of this restriction is that there is no "toggle point" calculation required, that is, the remainder is always stored in exactly $\lceil \log_2 b \rceil$ bits. The disadvantage of this scheme is that the choice of value for b is restricted and, therefore, the compression is slightly less effective than that of Golomb coding.

For compression of inverted lists, a value of b is required. Witten et al. [14] report that for cases where the probability of any particular integer value occurring is small—which is the usual case for document numbers d and offsets o—then b can be calculated as:

$$b = 0.69 \times \text{mean}(k)$$

For each inverted list, the mean value of document numbers d can be approximated as $k = N/f_t$ where N is the number of documents in the collection and f_t is the number of postings in the inverted list for term t [14]. This approach can also be extended to offsets: the mean value of offsets o for an inverted list posting can be approximated as $k = l_d/f_{d,t}$ where l_d is the length of document d and $f_{d,t}$ is the number of offsets of term t within that document. As the statistics N, f_t, and l are often available in memory, or in a simple auxiliary structure on disk, storage of b values is not required for decoding; approximate values of l can be stored in memory for compactness [7], but use of approximate values has little effect on compression effectiveness as it leads to only small relative errors in computation of b.

In bytewise coding an integer is stored in an integral number of eight-bit blocks. For variable-byte codes, seven bits in each block are used to store a binary representation of the integer k. The remaining bit is used to indicate whether the current block is the final block for k, or whether an additional block follows. Consider an example of an integer k

in the range of $2^7 = 128$ to $2^{14} = 16,384$. Two blocks are required to represent this integer: the first block contains the seven least-significant bits of the integer and the eighth bit is used to flag that another block follows; the second block contains the remaining most-significant bits and the eighth bit flags that no further blocks follow. We use the convention that the flag bit is set to 1 in the final block and 0 otherwise.

Compressing an inverted index, then, involves choosing compression schemes for the three kinds of data that are stored in a posting: a document number d, an in-document frequency $f_{d,t}$, and a sequence of offsets o. A standard choice is to use Golomb codes for document numbers, gamma codes for frequencies, and delta codes for offsets [14]. (We explore the properties of this choice later.) In this paper, we describe such a choice as a GolD-GamF-DelO index.

3.1 Fast Decoding

We experiment with compression of inverted lists of postings that contain frequencies $f_{d,t}$, documents numbers d, and offsets o. For fast decompression of these postings, there are two important considerations: first, the choice of compression scheme for each component of the posting; and, second, modifications to each compression scheme so that it is both fast and compatible with the schemes used for the other components. In this section, we outline the optimisations we use for fast decompression. Our code is publically available and distributed under the GNU public licence.[2]

Bitwise Compression

We have experimented with a range of variations of bitwise decompression schemes. Williams and Zobel [13] reported results for several efficient schemes, where vectors that contain compressed integers are retrieved from disk and subsequently decoded.[3] In their approach, vector decoding uses bitwise shift operations, bit masks, multiplication, subtraction, and function calls to retrieve sequences of bits that span byte boundaries. In our experiments on Intel Pentium-based servers running the Linux operating system, we have found that bitwise shift operations are usually faster than bit masks, and that the function calls are slow. By optimising our code to use bitwise shifts and to remove nested function calls, we have found that the overall time to decode vectors—regardless of the compression scheme used—is on average around 60% of that using the code of Williams and Zobel.

Other optimisations that are specific to Golomb-Rice coding are also of value. Golomb-Rice decoding requires that $\log_2 b$ is calculated to determine the number of remainder bits to be retrieved. It is practicable to explicitly cache values of $\log_2 b$ in a hash table as they are calculated, or to pre-calculate all likely-to-be-used values as the retrieval query engine is initialised. This saves recalculation of logarithms when a value of b is reused in later processing, with the penalty of additional memory requirements for storing the lookup table.

We measured the performance of Golomb coding with and without caching. Timings are average elapsed query evaluation cost to process index information for 25,000 queries on a 9.75 gigabyte (Gb) collection of Web data [5] using our prototype retrieval engine on a GolD-GamF-GolO index (that is, Golomb document numbers, gamma frequencies, Golomb offsets); we discuss collection statistics and experimental design further in Section 4. The cache lookup table size is unrestricted.

We found that, without caching of $\log_2 b$ values, the average query evaluation time is 0.961 seconds. Caching of $\log_2 b$ values as they are calculated during query processing roughly halves the average query evaluation time, to 0.494 seconds. Pre-calculating and storing the values offers almost no benefit over caching during query processing, reducing the time to 0.491 seconds; this reflects that only limited b values are required during query evaluation. Caching of toggle points yields 0.492 seconds. As toggle points are calculated using bitwise shifts, addition, and subtraction, this is further evidence that bitwise shifts are inexpensive on our hardware.

An alternative approach to managing log computations is to replace the standard library log function with a loop that determines $\lfloor \log_2 b \rfloor$ using bitwise shifts and equality tests; the logarithm value can be determined by locating the position of the most-significant 1-bit in b. We found that this led to slight additional improvements in the speed of decoding Golomb codes, outperforming explicit caching. All Golomb-Rice coding results reported in this paper are computed in this way.

Bytewise Compression

We have experimented with improvements to variable-byte coding. Unlike in bitwise coding, we have found that masking and shifting are equally as fast because of the large number of shifts required. We use shifts in our experiments.

Perhaps the most obvious way to increase the speed of variable-byte decoding is to align the eight-bit blocks to byte boundaries. Alignment with byte boundaries limits the decoding to only one option: the flag bit indicating if this is the last byte in the integer is always the most significant bit, and the remaining seven bits contain the value. Without byte alignment, additional conditional tests and operations are required to extract the flag bit, and the seven-bit value can span byte boundaries. We would expect that byte alignment would improve the speed of decoding variable-byte integers.

Figure 1 shows the effect of byte alignment of variable-byte integers. In this experiment, variable-byte coding is used to store the offsets o in each inverted list posting. The optimised Golomb coding scheme described in the previous section is used to code document numbers d and Elias gamma coding is used to store the frequencies $f_{d,t}$. We refer to this as a GolD-GamF-VbyO index.

The graph at the left of Figure 1 shows total index size as a percentage of the uncompressed collection being indexed. The first bar shows that, without byte alignment, the GolD-GamF-VbyO index requires almost 13% of the space required by the collection. The second bar shows that padding to byte alignment after storing the Gamma-coded $f_{d,t}$ values increases the space requirement to just over 13.5% of the collection size. We discuss the other schemes in this figure later in this section.

The graph at the right of Figure 1 shows elapsed query evaluation times using different index designs. Timings are

[2] The search engine used in these experiments and our integer compression code is available from `http://www.seg.rmit.edu.au/`

[3] The code used by Williams and Zobel in their experiments is available from `http://www.cs.rmit.edu.au/~hugh/software/`

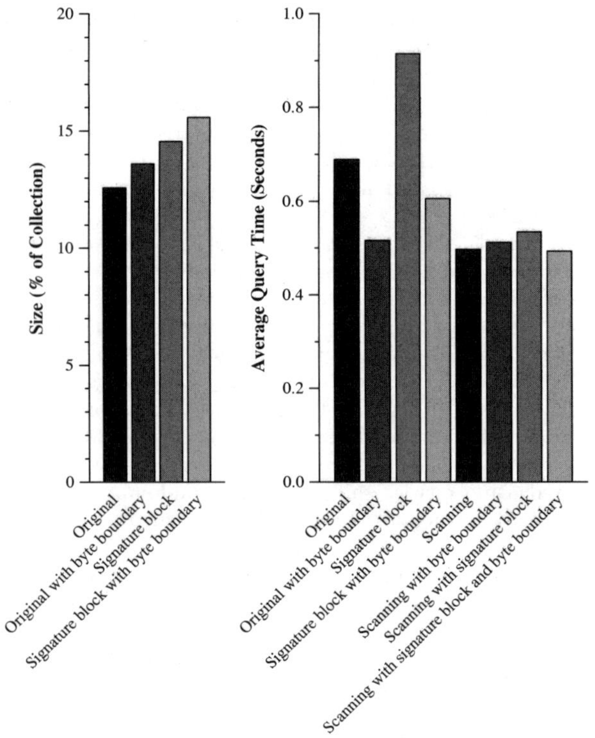

Figure 1: Variable-byte schemes for compressing offsets in inverted lists in a GolD-GamF-VbyO index. Four different compression schemes are shown and, for each, both original and scanning decoding are shown. Scanning decoding can be used when offsets are not needed for query resolution.

the average elapsed query evaluation cost to process the inverted lists for 25,000 queries on a 20 Gb collection of Web [5] data using our prototype retrieval engine. Queries are processed as conjunctive Boolean queries. The first bar shows that the average time is around 0.7 seconds for the GolD-GamF-VbyO index without byte alignment. The second bar shows that the effect of byte alignment is a 25% reduction in average query time. Therefore, despite the small additional space requirement, byte-alignment is beneficial when storing variable-byte integers.

A second optimisation to variable-byte coding is to consider the query mode when processing the index. For querying that does not use offsets—such as ranked and Boolean querying—decoding of the offsets in each posting is unnecessary. Rather, all that is required are the document numbers d and document frequencies $f_{d,t}$. An optimisation is therefore to only examine the flag bit of each block and to ignore the remaining seven bits that contain the value. The value of $f_{d,t}$ indicates the number of offsets o stored in the posting. By examining flag bits until $f_{d,t}$ 1-bits are processed, it is possible to bypass the offsets with minimal processing. We call this approach *scanning*.

Scanning can also be used in query modes that do require offset decoding. As we discussed earlier, phrase querying requires that all terms are present in a matching document. After processing the inverted list for the first term that is evaluated in a phrase query, a temporary inverted list of postings is created. This temporary list has a set D of documents that contain the first term. When processing the second term in the query, a second set of document numbers D' are processed. Offsets for the posting associated with document $d \in D'$ can be scanned, that is, passed over without decoding, if d is not a member of D. (At the same time, document numbers in D that are not in D' are discarded.)

We show the performance of scanning in Figure 1. The fifth and sixth bars show how scanning affects query evaluation time for variable-bytes that are either unaligned and aligned to byte boundaries in the GolD-GamF-VbyO index. Scanning removes the processing of seven-bit values. This reduces the cost of retrieving unaligned variable-bytes to less than that of the aligned variable-byte schemes; the small speed advantage is due to the retrieval of smaller lists in the unaligned version. Scanning has little effect on byte-aligned variable bytes, reflecting that the processing of seven-bit values using shift operations has a low cost. Overall, however, byte-alignment is preferred since the decoding cost of offsets is expensive in an unaligned scheme.

A third optimisation is an approach we call *signature blocks*, which are a variant of *skipping*. Skipping is the approach of storing additional integers in inverted lists that indicate how much data can be skipped without any processing [14]. Skipping has the disadvantage of an additional storage space requirement, but has been shown to offer substantial speed improvements [14]. A signature block is an eight-bit block that stores the flag bits of up to eight blocks that follow. For example, a signature block with the bit-string 11100101 represents that five integers are stored in the eight following eight-bit blocks: the string 111 represents that the first three blocks store one integer each; the string 001 represents that the fourth integer is stored over three blocks; and, the string 01 represents that the final integer is stored over two blocks. As all flag bits are stored in the signature block, the following blocks use all eight bits to store values, rather the seven-bit scheme in the standard variable-byte integer representation.

The primary use of signature blocks is skipping. To skip offsets, $f_{d,t}$ offset values must be retrieved but not processed. By counting the number of 1-bits in a signature block, the number of integers stored in the next eight blocks can be determined. If the value of $f_{d,t}$ exceeds this, then a second or subsequent signature block is processed until $f_{d,t}$ offsets have been skipped. The last signature block is, on average, half full. We have found that bitwise shifts are faster than a lookup table for processing of signature blocks.

The speed and space requirements are also shown in Figure 1. Not surprisingly, the signature block scheme requires more space than the previous variable-byte schemes. This space requirement is further increased if byte alignment of blocks is enforced. In terms of speed, the third and fourth bars in the right-hand histogram show that signature blocks are slower than the original variable-byte schemes when offsets are processed in the GolD-GamF-VbyO index. These results are not surprising: signature blocks are slow to process when they are unaligned, and the byte-aligned version is slow because processing costs are no less than the original variable-byte schemes and longer disk reads are required.

As shown by the seventh bar, when offsets are skipped the unaligned signature block scheme is slower than the original variable-byte scheme. The savings of skipping with signature blocks are negated by more complex processing when blocks are not byte-aligned. In contrast, the right-most bar shows that the byte-aligned signature block scheme with skipping is slightly faster on average than all other schemes. However, we conclude—given the compactness of the index and good overall performance—that the best all-round scheme is the original variable-byte scheme with byte alignment. Therefore, all variable-byte results reported in the Section 4 use the original byte-aligned variable-byte scheme with scanning.

Customised Compression

Combinations of bitwise and bytewise compression schemes are also possible. The aim of such approaches is to combine the fast decoding of bytewise schemes with the compact storage of bitwise schemes. For example, a simple and efficient custom scheme is to store a single bit that indicates which of two compression schemes is used, and then to store the integer using the designated compression scheme. We have experimented with several approaches for storing offsets. The simplest and most efficient approach we tested is as follows: when $f_{d,t} = 1$, we store a single bit indicating whether the following offset is stored as a bitwise Elias delta code or as a bytewise eight-bit binary representation. When storing values, we use Elias delta coding if the value is greater than 256 and the binary scheme otherwise. This scheme has the potential to reduce space because in the median posting $f_{d,t}$ is 1 and the average offset is around 200. Selective use of a fixed-width representation can save storage of the 6-bit prefix used to indicate magnitude in the corresponding delta code.

We report the results with this scheme, which we call *custom*, in the next section. This was the fastest custom scheme we tested. Other approaches we tried included switching between variable-byte and bitwise schemes, using the custom scheme when $f_{d,t}$ is either 1 or 2, and other simple variations. We omit results for these less successful approaches.

4. RESULTS

All experiments described in this paper are carried out on an Intel Pentium III based machine with 512 Mb of main-memory running the Linux operating system. Other processes and disk activity was minimised during timing experiments, that is, the machine was under light-load.

A theme throughout these experiments and greatly impacting on the results is the importance of caching. On a modern machine, caching takes place at two levels. One level is the caching of recently-accessed disk blocks in memory, a process that is managed by the operating system. When the size of the index significantly exceeds memory capacity, to make space to fetch a new inverted list, the blocks containing material that has not been accessed for a while must be discarded. One of the main benefits of compression is that a much greater volume of index information can be cached in memory. For this reason, we test our compression schemes with streams of 10,000 or 25,000 queries extracted from a query log [11], where the frequency distribution of query terms leads to beneficial use of caching. Again, queries are processed as conjunctive Boolean queries.

The other level at which caching takes place is the retention in the CPU cache of small blocks of data, typically of 128 bytes, recently accessed from memory. CPU caching

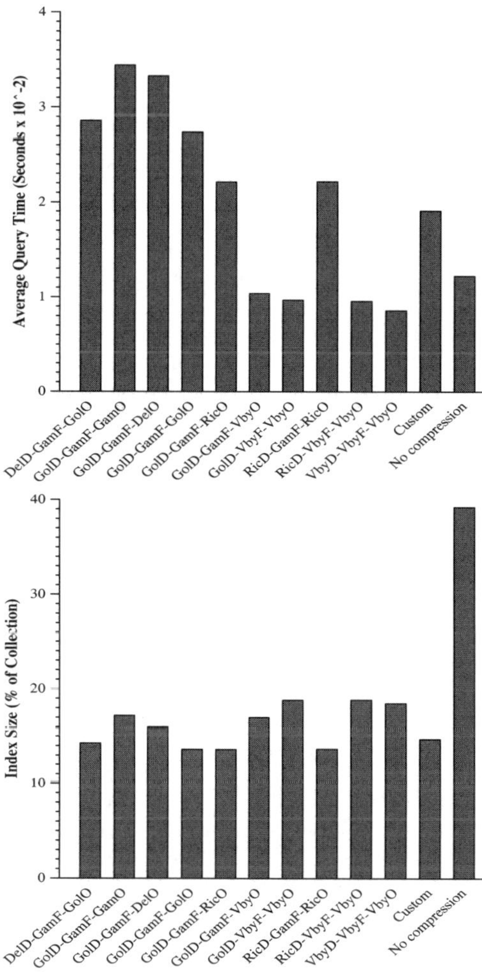

Figure 2: Performance of integer compression schemes for offsets in inverted lists, in an index with Golomb document numbers and gamma frequencies. In this experiment, the index fits in main memory. A 500 Mb collection is used, and results are averaged over 10,000 queries.

is managed in hardware. In current desktop computers, as many as 150 instruction cycles are required to fetch a single machine-word into the CPU. At a coarser level, compression of postings lists means that the number of fetches from memory to cache during decompression is halved.

Small collection

Figure 2 shows the relative performance of the integer compression schemes we have described for storing offsets, on a 500 Mb collection of 94,802 Web documents drawn from the TREC Web track data [5]; timing results are averaged over 10,000 queries drawn from an Excite search engine query log [11]. The index contains 703,518 terms.

These results show the effect of varying the coding scheme used for document numbers d, frequencies $f_{d,t}$, and offsets o. In all cases where both bitwise and variable-byte codes are used, the bitwise codes are padded to a byte boundary before a variable-byte code is emitted; thus, for example, in a GolD-GamF-VbyO index, there is padding between the gamma frequency and the sequence of variable-byte offsets. Not all code combinations are shown; for example, given that the speed advantage of using variable-byte document numbers is small, we have not reported results for index types such as VbyD-GamF-RicD, and due to the use of padding a choice such as VbyD-GamF-VbyD. Given the highly skew distribution of $f_{d,t}$ values, Golomb or Rice are not suitable coding methods, so these have not been tried.

In the "no compression" case, fixed-width fields are used to store postings. Document numbers are stored in 32 bits, frequencies in 16 bits, and offsets in 24 bits; these were the smallest multiples of bytes that would not overflow for reasonable assumptions about data properties.

The relative performance of Elias delta and gamma, Rice, and Golomb coding is as expected. The non-parameterised Elias coding schemes result in larger indexes than the parameterised Golomb-Rice schemes that, in turn, result in slower query evaluation. The average difference between offsets is greater than 15, making Elias delta coding more appropriate overall than gamma coding; the latter is both slower and less space-efficient.

On the lower graph in Figure 2, comparing the fourth and fifth columns and comparing the fifth and eighth columns, it can be seen that choice of Golomb or Rice codes for either offsets or document numbers has virtually no impact on index size. Comparing the fifth and eighth columns on the upper graph, the schemes yield similar decoding times for document numbers. However, Rice codes are markedly faster for decoding offsets, because no toggle point calculation is required. Among the bitwise schemes, we conclude that Rice coding should be used in preference to other schemes for coding document numbers and offsets.

The most surprising result is the effect of using the optimised byte-boundary variable-byte scheme for coding offsets. Despite the variable-byte index being 26% larger than the corresponding Rice-coded index, the overall query evaluation time is 62% less. Further speed gains are given by coding all values in variable-byte codes. Indeed, variable-byte decoding is faster even than processing uncompressed lists. This result is remarkable: the cost of transfering variable-byte coded lists from memory to the CPU cache and then decoding the lists is less than the cost of transferring uncompressed lists. To our knowledge, this is the first practical illustration that compression improves the efficiency of an in-memory retrieval system. We conclude from this that variable-byte coding should be used to store offsets to reduce both disk retrieval and memory retrieval costs.

In experiments with integers, Williams and Zobel found that variable-byte coding is faster than the bitwise schemes for storing large integers of the magnitude stored in inverted lists [13]. Our result confirms this observation for retrieval systems, while also showing that the effect extends to fast retrieval from memory and that improvements to variable-byte coding can considerably increase decoding speed.

The custom scheme uses both Elias delta and a binary bytewise scheme, reducing query evaluation to around 58% of the time for the Elias delta scheme. However, the custom scheme is almost twice as slow as the variable-byte scheme and, therefore, has little benefit in practice.

Large collection

Figure 3 shows the results of a larger experiment with an index that does not fit within the main-memory of our machine.

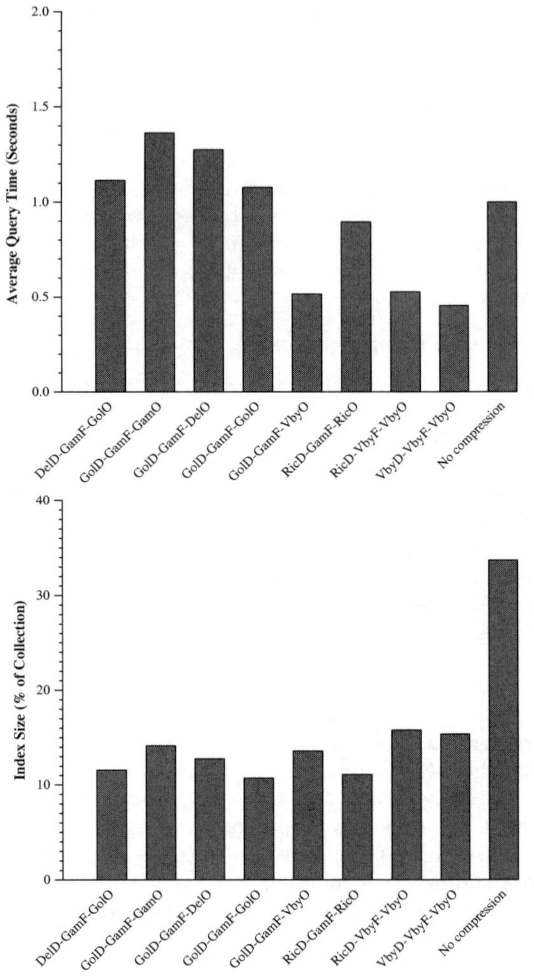

Figure 3: The performance of integer compression schemes for compressing offsets in inverted lists, with Golomb-coded document numbers and gamma-coded offsets. In this experiment, the index is several times larger than main memory. A 20 Gb collection is used, and results are averaged over 25,000 queries.

Exactly the same index types are tried as for the experiment above. A 20 Gb collection of 4,014,894 Web documents drawn from the TREC Web track data [5] is used and timing results are averaged over 25,000 Boolean queries drawn from an Excite search engine query log [11]. The index contains 9,574,703 terms. We include only selected schemes in our results.

We again note that we have not used heuristics to reduce query evaluation costs such as frequency-ordering or early termination. Indeed, we have not even used stopping; with stopwords removed, query times are greatly impoved. Our aim in this research is to measure the impact on index decoding time of different choices of compression method, not to establish new benchmarks for query evaluation time. Our improvements to compression techniques could, however, be used in conjunction with the other heuristics, in all likelihood further reducing query evaluation time compared to the best times reported previously.

The relative speeds of the bitwise Golomb, Elias delta, and variable-byte coded offset schemes are similar to that of our experiments with the 500 Mb collection. Again, variable-byte coding results in the fastest query evaluation. Perhaps unsurprisingly given the results described above, an uncompressed index that does not fit in main-memory is relatively much slower than the variable-byte scheme; the disk transfer costs are a larger fraction of the overall query cost when the index does not fit in memory, and less use can be made of the memory cache. Indexes with variable-byte offsets are twice as fast as indexes with Golomb, delta, or gamma offsets, and one-and-a-half times as fast as indexes with Rice offsets. VbyD-VbyF-VbyO indexes are twice as fast as any index type with non-variable-byte offsets.

In separate experiments we have observed that the gains demonstrated by compression continue to increase with collection size, as the proportion of the index that can be held in memory declines. Despite the loss in compression with variable-byte coding, indexes are still less than one-seventh of the size of the indexed data, and the efficiency gains are huge.

5. CONCLUSIONS

Compression of inverted lists can significantly improve the performance of retrieval systems. We have shown that an efficiently implemented variable-byte bytewise scheme results in query evaluation that is twice as fast as more compact bitwise schemes. Moreover, we have demonstrated that the cost of transferring data from memory to the CPU cache can also be reduced by compression: when an index fits in main memory, the transfer of compressed data from memory to the cache and subsequent decoding is less than that of transferring uncompressed data. Using byte-aligned coding, we have shown that queries can be run more than twice as fast as with bitwise codes, at a small loss of compression efficiency. These are dramatic gains.

Modern computer architectures create opportunities for compression to yield performance advantages. Once, the main benefits of compression were to save scarce disk space and computer-to-computer transmission costs. An equally important benefit now is to make use of the fact that the CPU is largely idle. Fetching a single byte from memory involves a delay of 12 to 150 CPU cycles; a fetch from disk involves a delay of 10,000,000 cycles. Compression can greatly reduce the number of such accesses, while CPU time that would otherwise be unused can be spent on decoding. With fast decoding, overall costs are much reduced, greatly increasing query evaluation speed. In current computers such architecture considerations are increasingly important to development of new algorithms for query processing. Poor caching has been a crucial shortcoming of existing algorithms investigated in this research.

There are several possible extensions to this work. We plan to investigate nibble-coding, a variant of variable-byte coding where two flag bits are used in each variable-byte block. It is likely that this approach may improve the performance of signature blocks. We will also experiment with phrase querying in practice and to explore the average query evaluation speed when partial scanning is possible.

6. REFERENCES

[1] V. Anh, O. de Kretser, and A. Moffat. Vector-Space ranking with effective early termination. In W. Croft, D. Harper, D. Kraft, and J. Zobel, editors, *Proc. ACM-SIGIR International Conference on Research and Development in Information Retrieval*, pages 35–42, New York, Sept. 2001.

[2] E. de Moura, G. Navarro, N. Ziviani, and R. Baeza-Yates. Fast and flexible word searching on compressed text. *ACM Transactions on Information Systems*, 18(2):113–139, 2000.

[3] P. Elias. Universal codeword sets and representations of the integers. *IEEE Transactions on Information Theory*, IT-21(2):194–203, Mar. 1975.

[4] S. Golomb. Run-length encodings. *IEEE Transactions on Information Theory*, IT–12(3):399–401, July 1966.

[5] D. Hawking, N. Creswell, and P. Thistlewaite. Overview of TREC-7 very large collection track. In E. Voorhees and D. Harman, editors, *Proc. Text Retrieval Conference (TREC)*, pages 91–104, Washington, 1999. National Institute of Standards and Technology Special Publication 500-242.

[6] A. Moffat and J. Zobel. Self-indexing inverted files for fast text retrieval. *ACM Transactions on Information Systems*, 14(4):349–379, Oct. 1996.

[7] A. Moffat, J. Zobel, and R. Sacks-Davis. Memory-efficient ranking. *Information Processing & Management*, 30(6):733–744, 1994.

[8] G. Navarro, E. de Moura, M. Neubert, N. Ziviani, and R. Baeza-Yates. Adding compression to block addressing inverted indexes. *Information Retrieval*, 3(1):49–77, 2000.

[9] M. Persin. Document filtering for fast ranking. In W. Croft and C. van Rijsbergen, editors, *Proc. ACM-SIGIR International Conference on Research and Development in Information Retrieval*, pages 339–348, Dublin, Ireland, 1994.

[10] M. Persin, J. Zobel, and R. Sacks-Davis. Filtered document retrieval with frequency-sorted indexes. *Journal of the American Society for Information Science*, 47(10):749–764, 1996.

[11] A. Spink, D. Wolfram, B. J. Jansen, and T. Saracevic. Searching the web: The public and their queries. *Journal of the American Society for Information Science*, 52(3):226–234, 2001.

[12] A. Vo and A. Moffat. Compressed inverted files with reduced decoding overheads. In R. Wilkinson, B. Croft, K. van Rijsbergen, A. Moffat, and J. Zobel, editors, *Proc. ACM-SIGIR International Conference on Research and Development in Information Retrieval*, pages 290–297, Melbourne, Australia, July 1998.

[13] H. Williams and J. Zobel. Compressing integers for fast file access. *Computer Journal*, 42(3):193–201, 1999.

[14] I. Witten, A. Moffat, and T. Bell. *Managing Gigabytes: Compressing and Indexing Documents and Images*. Morgan Kaufmann Publishers, Los Altos, CA 94022, USA, second edition, 1999.

[15] N. Ziviani, E. de Moura, G. Navarro, and R. Baeza-Yates. Compression: A key for next-generation text retrieval systems. *IEEE Computer*, 33(11):37–44, Nov. 2000.

Set-Based Model: A New Approach for Information Retrieval

Bruno Pôssas
Universidade Federal de Minas Gerais
30161-970 Belo Horizonte-MG, Brazil
bavep@dcc.ufmg.br

Nivio Ziviani
Universidade Federal de Minas Gerais
30161-970 Belo Horizonte-MG, Brazil
nivio@dcc.ufmg.br

Wagner Meira Jr.
Universidade Federal de Minas Gerais
30161-970 Belo Horizonte-MG, Brazil
meira@dcc.ufmg.br

Berthier Ribeiro-Neto
Universidade Federal de Minas Gerais
30161-970 Belo Horizonte-MG, Brazil
berthier@dcc.ufmg.br

ABSTRACT

The objective of this paper is to present a new technique for computing term weights for index terms, which leads to a new ranking mechanism, referred to as set-based model. The components in our model are no longer terms, but termsets. The novelty is that we compute term weights using a data mining technique called association rules, which is time efficient and yet yields nice improvements in retrieval effectiveness. The set-based model function for computing the similarity between a document and a query considers the termset frequency in the document and its scarcity in the document collection. Experimental results show that our model improves the average precision of the answer set for all three collections evaluated. For the TReC-3 collection, our set-based model led to a gain, relative to the standard vector space model, of 37% in average precision curves and of 57% in average precision for the top 10 documents. Like the vector space model, the set-based model has time complexity that is linear in the number of documents in the collection.

Categories and Subject Descriptors

H.3.3 [**Information Systems**]: Information Search and Retrieval—*Retrieval models*; H.2.8 [**Information Systems**]: Database Applications—*Data mining*; F.4.1 [**Mathematical Logic and Formal Languages**]: Mathematical Logic—*Set theory*

General Terms

Algorithms, Measurement, Performance, Experimentation

Keywords

Information retrieval models, closed association rule mining, weighting index term co-occurrences, data mining, set theory

1. INTRODUCTION

In the area of information retrieval, one popular model to locate answers that humans judge to be relevant is the vector space model. In the vector space model query terms and documents are represented as weighted vectors in a vector space, and the answers to a user query are the documents whose representative vectors have highest similarity to the query vector. The computation of similarities is based on weights assigned to the index terms that compose document and query vectors. Much of the success of the model is due to the long-term research efforts of Salton and his associates [18, 19].

The term weights can be calculated in many different ways and finding good term weights is a continuing challenge. The best known term weighting schemes use weights that are function of (i) the number of times an index term occurs in a document and (ii) the number of documents of the collection an index term occurs. Such term-weighting strategies are called $tf \times idf$ (term frequency times inverse document frequency) schemes [4, 22].

In this paper we propose a new model for computing index term weights, based on set theory, and for ranking documents. This model is referred to as *set-based model*. The set-based model uses a term weighting scheme based on association rules theory [1]. Association rules are interesting because they provide all the elements of the $tf \times idf$ scheme in an algorithmically efficient and parameterized approach. Also, they naturally provide for quantification of representative term co-occurrence patterns, something that is not present in the $tf \times idf$ scheme.

We evaluated and validated the set-based model through experimentation using three test collections. We compared our model against the vector space model and the generalized vector space model [24]. Our experimental results show that the set-based model yields higher retrieval performance, which is significantly superior for all the collections considered. For the TReC-3 collection [8], containing 3,225 megabytes of text and approximately 1 million documents, the set-based model yields average precision curves that are 37% higher than the vector space model. When only the first 10 answers are considered, this margin goes up to 57%. For the Wall Street Journal collection, containing 509 megabytes of text and 173,252 documents, the set-based model, in comparison with the generalized vector space model, is approximately 22% superior in average precision and approximately 16% superior in precision at the first 10 documents in the answer.

The set-based model is also competitive in terms of computing performance. Both the vector space and the set-based models are linear on the number of documents in the collection. The vector space model is $O(tN)$, where t is the size of the vocabulary collection and N is the number of documents in the collection. The set-based model is $O(cN)$, where c is the number of closed termsets, a value that is $O(2^{|q|})$, where $|q|$ is the number of terms in the query. These are worst case measures and the average measures for the constants involved are much smaller. For the TReC-3 collection, using the 151-200 range of topics, where average number of terms in the query is 22.43, the increase in the average response time for the set-based model over the vector space model is approximately 80%. These are relevant facts from both theoretical and practical points of view, considering that we introduced a new and more complex model for weighting index terms, which will often improve the quality of the results.

The remaining of the paper is organized as follows. In the next section we discuss some related work. Section 3 describes the method for computing co-occurrences among query terms based on a variant of association rules. The set-based model is presented in the Section 4. In section 5 we describe the reference collections and the experimental results comparing the vector-space model, the generalized vector-space model, and our model. Finally, we present some conclusions and future work in Section 6.

2. RELATED WORK

The vector space model was proposed by Salton [18, 15], and different weighting schemes were presented [19, 25, 16]. In the vector space model, index terms are assumed to be mutually independent. The independence assumption leads to a linear weighting function which, although not necessarily realistic, is ease to compute. Simple term weighting was used early on by Salton and Lesk [18]. Spark Jones introduced the *idf* factor [21], and Salton and Yang verified its effectiveness for improving retrieval [19].

Different approaches to account for co-occurrence among index terms during the information retrieval process have been proposed. Raghavan and Yu [13] use a statistical analysis of a set of queries in relation to relevant and non-relevant document sets to establish positive and negative correlations among index terms. The work by van Rijsbergen [14] constructs a probabilistic model incorporating dependence among index terms, and experimental results were later presented in a companion paper [9]. The extent to which two index terms depend on one another is derived from the distribution of co-occurrences in the whole collection or in the relevant and non-relevant sets, leading to a non linear weighting function. As shown in [17], the resulting formula for computing the dependency factors in [14, 9] does not seem computationally feasible, even for a relatively small number of index terms. The work in [6] presents a study of the necessity of term dependence in a query space for weighted based retrieval.

The work in [24, 23] presents an interesting approach to compute index term correlations based on automatic indexing schemes, defining a new information retrieval model called generalized vector space model. The work shows that index term vectors can be explicitly represented in a 2^t-dimensional vector space such that index term correlations can be incorporated into the vector space model in a straightforward manner. It represents index term vectors from a basic set of orthogonal vectors called min-terms, where each min-term represents a pattern of index term co-occurrence inside documents. The vector representing an index term k_i is obtained by adding all min-terms related to k_i. The model is not computationally feasible for moderately large collections because there are 2^t possible min-terms, where t is the number of terms in the collection vocabulary. Extensions of the generalized vector space model were used in [3, 11].

Our work differs from the above related works in the following aspects. First, determination of index term weights is derived directly from association rules theory, which naturally considers representative patterns of term co-occurrence. Second, experimental results show significant and consistent improvements in average precision curves in comparison to the standard vector space model and to the generalized vector space model. This improvement in average precision does not always occur in the generalized vector space model because exhaustive application of term co-occurrences to all documents in the collection might eventually hurt the overall effectiveness and performance. Third, the set-based model algorithm has computational costs that are linear on the number of documents in the collection. Thus, the implementation of our model is practical and efficient, with processing times close to the times to process the standard vector space model.

The work in [5] introduces a theoretical framework for the association rules mining based on a boolean model of information retrieval known as Boolean Retrieval Model. Our work differs from that presented in [5] in the following way. In our work we use association rules to define a new information retrieval model that provides not only the main term weights and assumptions of the $tf \times idf$ scheme, but also provides for quantification of term co-occurrence.

3. CLOSED TERMSETS

In this section we introduce the concept of closed termsets as a basis for computing term weights. Further, we analyze how closed termsets can be generated from a document inverted list and briefly analyze its computational costs.

3.1 Concepts

Let $T = \{k_1, k_2, ..., k_t\}$ be the vocabulary of a collection of documents D, that is, the set of t unique terms that may appear in a document from D. There is a total ordering among the vocabulary terms, which is based on the lexicographical order of terms, so that $k_i < k_{i+1}$, for $1 \leq i \leq t-1$. We define an n-termset s as an ordered set of n unique terms, such that $s \subseteq T$ and the order among terms follows the aforementioned total ordering. Let $S = \{s_1, s_2, ..., s_{2^t}\}$ be the vocabulary-set of a collection of documents D, that is, the set of 2^t unique termsets that may appear in a document from D. Each document j from D is characterized by a vector in the space of the termsets.

With each termset s_i, $1 \leq i \leq 2^t$, we associate an inverted list ls_i composed of identifiers of the documents containing that termset. We also define the frequency ds_i of a termset s_i as the number of occurrences of s_i in D, that is, the number of documents where $s_i \subseteq d_j$ and $d_j \in D$, $1 \leq j \leq N$. The frequency ds_i of a termset s_i is the length of its associated inverted list ($| ls_i |$).

Definition 1. A termset s_i is a frequent termset if its frequency ds_i is greater than or equal to a given threshold, which is known as *support* in the scope of association rules [1], and refered as minimal frequency in this work.

Definition 2. A closed termset cs_i is a frequent termset that is the largest termset among the termsets that are subsets of cs_i and occur in the same set of documents. That is, given a set $\mathcal{D} \subseteq D$ of documents and the set $\mathcal{S_D} \subseteq S$ of termsets that occur in all documents from $\mathcal{D}$ and only in these, a closed termset cs_i satisfies the property that $\nexists s_j \in \mathcal{S_D} | cs_j \subset s_j$.

Definition 3. A maximal termset ms_i is a frequent termset that is not a subset of any other frequent termset. That is, given the set $\mathcal{S}_{\mathcal{F}} \subseteq S$ of frequent termsets that occur in all documents from $\mathcal{D}$, a maximal termset ms_i satisfies the property that $\nexists s_j \in \mathcal{S}_{\mathcal{F}} | ms_i \subset s_j$.

For sake of information retrieval, closed termsets are interesting because they represent a reduction on the computational complexity and on the amount of data that has to be analyzed, without loosing information, since all termsets in a closure are represented by the respective closed termset.

It is proven that the set of maximal termsets associated with a document collection are the minimum amount of information necessary to derive all frequent termsets associated with a collection [26]. However, they do not embed the same amount of information that closed termsets do, since the occurrence pattern of each termset is discarded, making difficult its use for finding interesting term co-occurrences.

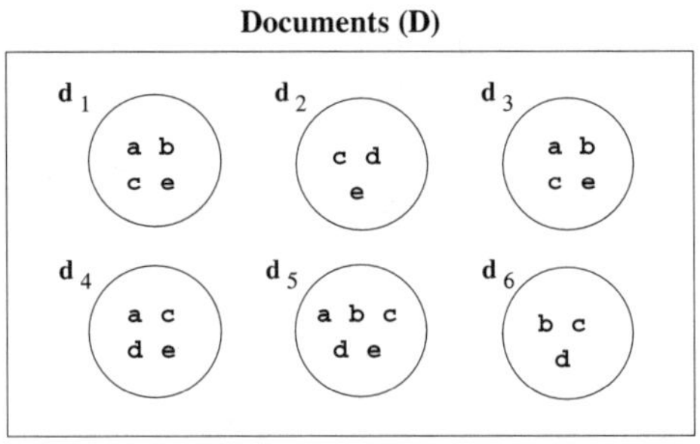

Figure 1: Sample document collection

Next we present a simple example to illustrate the concepts of frequent, closed and maximal termsets. Consider a vocabulary of five terms $T = \{a, b, c, d, e\}$, and a collection D of six documents d_j, $1 \leq j \leq 6$, that contain these terms, i.e., $D = \{(a, b, c, e), (c, d, e), (a, b, c, e), (a, c, d, e), (a, b, c, d, e), (b, c, d)\}$, as depicted in Figure 1. Table 1 shows all frequent and closed termsets for the sample document collection and their respective frequencies. The minimum frequency used for selecting the frequent termsets is equal to 50%, that is, a termset is frequent if it appears in at least three of the six documents. Notice that the number of frequent termsets, although potentially very large, is usually small in natural language texts. This number is a function of the minimum frequency and document collection characteristics. It is possible to vary the number of frequent termsets by changing the minimum frequency employed. Regarding the closed termsets, even in this small example, we can see that the number of closed termsets is significantly smaller than the number of frequent termsets. In our example, there are 20 frequent termsets and just 8 closed termsets, and 2 maximal termsets.

A major advantage of using closed termsets instead of frequent termsets is that they can be generated very efficiently, as proved in [26]. So far, there is just an upper bound on the number of frequent termsets, which is $O(nr2^l)$, where n is the number of documents in the collection, r is the number of maximal frequent termsets, and l is the length of the largest frequent termset. In practice, since the query processing is driven by the query, the largest frequent termset is bounded by the number of terms in the query. Since the number of closed termsets is at most equal to the number of frequent termsets, we may also use this bound as an upper limit of the number of closed termsets. As we show in Section 5, in practice the number of closed termsets is significantly smaller than

Table 1: Frequent, closed, and maximal termsets for the sample document collection

Frequency (ds)	Frequent Termsets	Closed Termsets	Maximal Termsets
100% (6)	c	c	
83% (5)	e,ce	ce	
67% (4)	a,ac,ae,ace	ace	
67% (4)	cd	cd	
67% (4)	b,bc	bc	
67% (4)	d,cd	cd	
50% (3)	ab,abc,abe be,bce,abce	acbe	abce
50% (3)	de,cde	cde	cde

the number of frequent termsets. For our example, the upper bound of the number of frequent termsets is $Onr2^l = 6 * 2 * 2^4 = 96$. However, its total number was 20, which is significantly smaller than its upper bound. Regarding the closed termsets, we can see that its number, 8, is smaller than the number of frequent termsets.

3.2 Algorithm Description

Determining closed termsets is a problem very similar to mining association rules and the algorithms employed for the latter are our starting point [1]. Our approach is based on an efficient algorithm for association rule mining, called CHARM [26], which has been adapted to handle terms and documents instead of items and transactions, respectively.

The algorithm for generating termsets is basically an incremental enumeration algorithm that employs a very powerful pruning strategy. More specifically, we start by verifying whether the frequency of 1-termsets is above a given threshold. This approach is based on the fact that, if a term is not frequent, none of the higher-order termsets that include it will be. These frequent 1-termsets will also be defined as closed. We then start grouping frequent termsets and verifying two criteria that are used to determine whether these new termsets are closed or not.

We determine $n+1$ termsets from n termsets, as follows. The process starts by determining all pairs of termsets (s_i, s_j), $1 \leq i, j \leq 2^t$, that have the same first $n-1$ terms. A new termset is determined by the union of these sets ($s_i \cup s_j$), creating an $n+1$ termset s_{new}. The list of documents where s_{new} appears can be easily determined by intersecting the lists of the two concatenated sets ($l_{new} = l_i \cap l_j$). After this, the first criterion that verifies whether the new termset is frequent, and was introduced by the original Apriori algorithm [2], is employed. An n-termset may be frequent only if all of its $n-1$-termsets are also frequent. For instance, we may enumerate the 4-termset ($\{$a b c e$\}$) based on the termsets $\{$a b c$\}$ and $\{$a b e$\}$ and we apply the frequency criterion by verifying whether the other 3-termsets of the new termset (in this case $\{$a b e$\}$ and $\{$b c e$\}$) are also frequent. Next, the inverted list associated with the new termset is generated and it is verified whether its length is above threshold.

The second criterion checks whether a frequent termset f being verified is closed. A termset f is defined as closed if there is no closed termset that is also a closure of f. In this case, all current closed termsets are tested for having f as its closure, being discarded if such condition holds. Otherwise, f is discarded, since its closure is already determined. In our sample collection, for example, the 1-termset $\{a\}$ is initially defined as closed. However, when we combine the 1-termsets $\{$a$\}$ and $\{$c$\}$ into $\{$a c$\}$, we discard $\{$a$\}$, since they occur in the same set of documents. The same happens when we enumerate {a c e} and find out that {a c} and {a c e} occur in the same documents, allowing us to discard {a c}.

In the next section we describe how we use closed termsets for retrieving documents efficiently.

4. SET-BASED MODEL

In our set-based model, a document is described by a set of closed termsets, extracted from the document itself. With each closed termset we associate a pair of weights representing (a) its importance in each document and (b) its importance in the whole document collection. In a similar way, a query is described by a set of closed termsets with a weight representing the importance of each closed termset in the query.

The algebraic representation of the set of closed termsets for both documents and queries correspond to vectors in a 2^t-dimensional Euclidean space, where t is equal to the number of unique index terms in the document collection. However, in practice, we use an efficient algorithm to obtain closed termsets which is based on association rules theory, thus reducing the number of closed termsets to a number that is linear on the number of documents in the collection (see Section 3 and Section 5.2).

4.1 Termset Weights

A successful ranking algorithm based on index terms weighting has to take into account the following three criteria. First, it has to consider the number of times that an index term occurs in a document. Second, emphasis must be given to scarce terms, and this can be accomplished by reducing term weights for terms that appear in many documents. Third, long documents with many terms will naturally be favored by the ranking process because they are likely to contain more of any given list of query terms, and usually a normalization factor is introduced to discount the contribution of long documents.

Term weights can be calculated in many different ways [19, 25, 16]. For the first two problems pointed out above, the best known term weighting schemes use weights that are function of (i) $tf_{i,j}$, the number of times that an index term i occurs in a document j and (ii) df_i, the number of documents that an index term i occurs in the whole document collection. Such term-weighting strategy is called $tf \times idf$ schemes. The expression for idf_i represents the importance of term i in the collection, it assigns a high weight to terms which are encountered in a small number of documents in the collection, supposing that rare terms have high discriminating value.

In the set-based model, the association rules scheme naturally provides for quantification of representative patterns of term co-occurrences, something that is not present in the $tf \times idf$ approach. To determine the weights associated with the closed termsets in a document or in a query, we also use the number of occurrences of a closed termset in a document, in a query, and in the whole collection. Formally, the weight of a closed termset i in a document j is defined as:

$$w_{i,j} = sf_{i,j} \times ids_i = sf_{i,j} \times \log \frac{N}{ds_i} \qquad (1)$$

where N is the number of documents in the collection, $sf_{i,j}$ is the number of occurrences of the closed termset i in document j (obtained from the index), and ids_i is the inverted frequency of occurrence of the closed termset in the collection. $sf_{i,j}$ generalizes $tf_{i,j}$ in the sense that it counts the number of times that the closed termset s_i appears in document j. The component ids_i also carries the same semantics of idf_i, but accounting for the cardinality of the closed termsets as follows. High-order closed termsets usually have low frequency, resulting in large inverted frequencies. Thus, this strategy assigns large weights to closed termsets that appear in small number of documents, that is, rare closed termsets result in greater weights.

4.2 Similarity Calculation

Since documents and queries are represented as vectors, we assign a similarity measure to every document containing any of the query closed termsets, defined as the normalized scalar product between the set of document vectors $\vec{d_j}$, $1 \le j \le N$, and the query vector $\vec{q}$. The similarity between a document d_j and a query q is defined as:

$$sim(q, d_j) = \frac{\vec{d_j} \bullet \vec{q}}{|\vec{d_j}| \times |\vec{q}|} = \frac{\sum_{s \in C_q} w_{s,j} \times w_{s,q}}{\sqrt{\sum_{i=1}^{t} w_{i,j}^2} \times \sqrt{\sum_{i=1}^{t} w_{i,q}^2}},$$

where $w_{s,j}$ is the weight associated with the closed termset s in document d_j, $w_{s,q}$ is the weight associated with the closed termset s in query q, C_q is the set of all closed termsets such that all $s \subseteq q$, $w_{i,j}$ is the weight of term i in document d_j, and $w_{i,q}$ is the weight of term i in query q. We observe that the normalization (i.e., the factors in the denominator) is done using the terms (instead of closed termsets) that compose the query and document vectors. This is important to reduce computational costs because computing the norm of a document d using closed termsets might be prohibitively costly. It solves the third problem pointed out in Section 4.1 because it accomplishes the effect of penalizing large documents, the major objective of normalization by document norms. Further, it allows efficient computation. Our experimental results corroborate the validity of adopting this alternative form of normalization.

4.3 Query Mechanisms

In this section we describe a simple algorithm for implementing a search mechanism based on the set-based model and the indexing information.

For large document collections, the cost to evaluate the similarity measure is potentially high, requiring the reading and processing of whole inverted lists for each query closed termset. This task may have a high cost since some query terms might occur in a large number of documents in the collection. One of the most effective techniques to compute an approximation of the similarity measure without modifying the final ranking is presented in [12]. It uses thresholds for early recognition of which documents are likely to be highly ranked to reduce costs. In the set-based model we employ a variant of this pruning scheme adapted to handle closed termsets instead of terms.

The steps performed by the set-based model to the calculation of the similarity metrics are equivalent to the standard vector space model. First we create the data structures that are used for calculating the document similarities among all closed termsets s_i of a document d. Then, for each query term, we retrieve its inverted list, and determine the first frequent termsets, i.e., the frequent termsets of size equal to 1, applying the minimal frequency threshold. The next step is the enumeration of all closed termsets based on the 1-termsets, as presented in Section 3.2. After enumerating all closed termsets, we employ the pruning scheme presented by Persin [12] to the evaluation of its inverted lists, allowing to discard closed termsets that will not influence the final ranking very early. After evaluating the closed termsets, we normalize the document similarities by dividing each document similarity by the respective document's norm. The final step is to select the k largest similarities and return the corresponding documents.

5. EXPERIMENTAL RESULTS

In this section we describe the experimental results for the evaluation of the set-based model (SBM) in terms of both effectiveness and computational efficiency. Our evaluation is based on a comparison to the standard vector space model (VSM) and to the generalized vector-space model (GVSM). We first present the experimental framework and the reference collections employed, and then discuss the retrieval performance and the computational efficiency of each model.

In our evaluation we use three reference collections, CFC [20], TReC-3 [8] and WSJ, respectively. The WSJ collection is a subcollection of TReC-3, and is used in our experiments because the full TReC-3 collection is too large for running the generalized vector space model. Table 2 presents the main features of these collections, which comprise not only the documents, but also a set of example queries and the relevant responses for each query, as selected by experts. We quantify the retrieval effectiveness of the various approaches through standard measures of average recall and precision. The computational efficiency is evaluated through the query response time, that is, the processing time to select and rank the documents for each query.

Table 2: Characteristics of the reference collections

Characteristics	Collection		
	CFC	WSJ	TReC-3
Number of Documents	1,240	173,252	1,078,166
Number of Distinct Terms	2,105	230,902	1,016,709
Number of Queries	100	300	300
Average Terms per Query	3.82	18.88	22.43
Average Relevants per Query	29.04	235.99	286.89
Size (MB)	1.9	509	3,225

The experiments were performed on a Linux-based PC with a Intel Pentium III 1.0 GHz processor and 1.5 GBytes RAM. Next we present the results obtained for the three collections, which are characterized in Table 2.

5.1 Retrieval Performance

We start our evaluation by verifying the precision-recall curves for each model when applied to each of the three collections. Each curve quantifies the precision as a function of the percentage of documents retrieved (recall). The GVSM could not be evaluated for the TReC-3 collection, because of the cost of the min-term building phase, which is exponential in the size of the vocabulary, making the computational cost of the associated experiments not feasible. The results presented for SBM are the best for a range of minimal frequencies from 1 to 30 documents (see Figure 5).

As we can see in Figures 2, 3, and 4, SBM yields better precision than both VSM and GVSM, regardless of the collection and of the recall level. Further, the gains increase with the size of the collection, because large collections allow computing a more representative set of closed termsets.

We confirm such observations by verifying the overall average precision achieved for each model in each collection, which is presented in Table 3. We also present, in the same table, the gains provided by SBM over the other two models in terms of overall precision. The gains ranged from 8.54% to 36.86%, increasing with the size of the collection and being consistently greater for the SBM. We should note that SBM provides significant gains over GVSM,

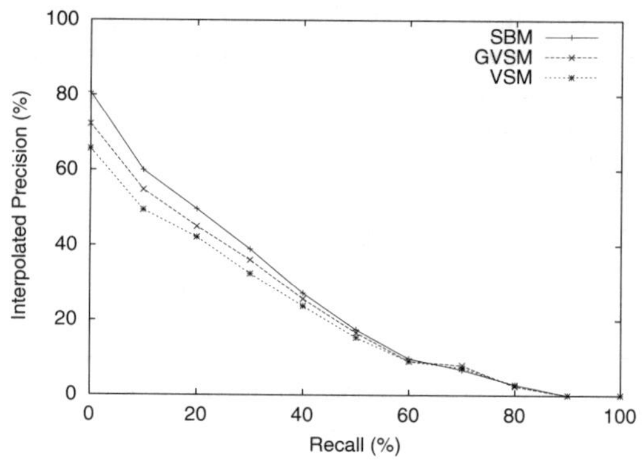

Figure 2: Recall-precision for CFC

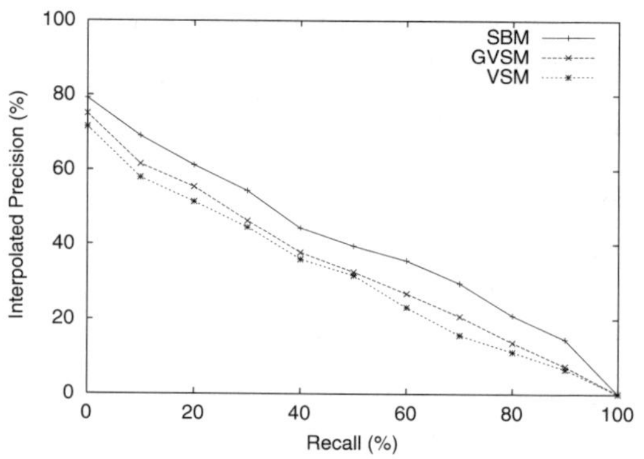

Figure 3: Recall-precision for WSJ

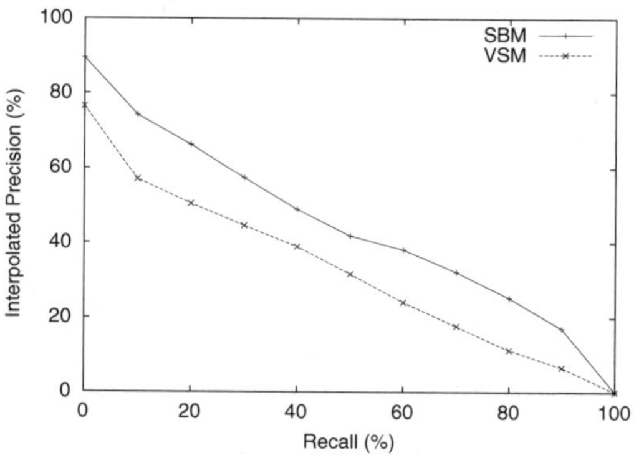

Figure 4: Recall-precision for TReC-3

although both exploit term co-occurrences. We believe that SBM outperforms GVSM because it considers just some interesting co-occurrence patterns that are uncovered by the closed termsets.

The set-based model provides even greater gains when we verify the average precision for the top 10 documents retrieved. This metric estimates the user "satisfaction" while using search engines, for instance. The results are presented in Table 4. We can see that the gains range from 15.62 to 56.80% and the highest gain is associated to the largest collection (TReC-3), showing that the SBM is specially powerful for handling large amounts of information. Again, although the gains over the GVSM are smaller, they are still very significative, showing that SBM not only improves the overall precision, but also ranks more relevant documents at the top.

Table 3: Average precision curves and gain provided by the SBM model

Collection	Average Precision (%)			SBM Gain(%)	
	VSM	*GVSM*	*SBM*	*VSM*	*GVSM*
CFC	22.42	24.47	26.56	18.47	8.54
WSJ	31.76	34.27	41.78	31.55	21.91
TReC-3	32.58	*	44.59	36.86	*

* The GVSM could not be evaluated for the TReC-3 collection due to the exponential cost of the min-term build phase

Table 4: Average precision curves for top 10 documents and gains provided by the SBM model

Collection	Average Precision at 10 (%)			SBM Gain(%)	
	VSM	*GVSM*	*SBM*	*VSM*	*GVSM*
CFC	10.97	12.93	16.02	46.03	23.90
WSJ	12.71	16.58	19.17	50.82	15.62
TReC-3	13.66	*	21.42	56.80	*

* The GVSM could not be evaluated for the TReC-3 collection due to the exponential cost of the min-term build phase

One of the key features of the set-based model is the possibility of controlling the minimal frequency threshold of a termset. It is interesting to note that the variation of the minimal frequency allows us to exploit the trade-off between precision and the number of termsets taken into consideration. We verified how variations in the minimal frequency threshold employed affect the precision achieved for the TReC-3 collection. We performed a set of SBM executions where the minimal frequency threshold is fixed for all queries and varies from 1 to 30 documents. The results are illustrated in Figure 5 and we show that the SBM precision is significantly affected by the minimal frequency employed. Initially, an increase in the minimal frequency results in better precision, achieving a maximum precision for minimal frequencies between 8 and 10 documents. When we increase the minimal frequency beyond 10, we observe that the precision decreases until it reaches almost 0. This behavior can be explained as follows. First, an increase in the minimal frequency causes irrelevant termsets to be discarded, resulting in a better precision. When the frequency gets above 10, then relevant termsets start to be discarded, leading to a reduction in terms of precision.

In summary, our set-based model (SBM) is the first information retrieval model that exploits term correlations effectively and provides significant gains in terms of precision, regardless of the size of the collection and of the size of the vocabulary. In the next section we discuss the computational costs associated with SBM.

5.2 Computational Efficiency

In this section we compare our model to the standard vector space model and the generalized vector space model regarding the query response time, in order to evaluate its feasibility in terms of computational costs. This is important because one major limitation of existing models that account for term correlations is their computational cost. Several of these models cannot be applied to large or even mid-size collections since their costs increase exponentially with the vocabulary size.

We start our evaluation by verifying the theoretical upper bounds

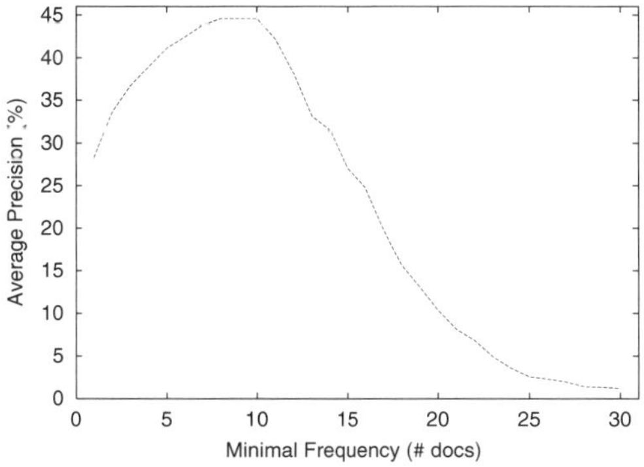

Figure 5: Impact of varying minimal frequency threshold on average precision for TReC-3

on the number of operations performed by VSM and SBM. The complexity of both models is linear with respect to the number of documents in the collection. Formally, the upper bound on the number of operations performed for satisfying a query in the vector space model is $O(|q| \times N)$, where $|q|$ is the number of terms in the query and N is the number of documents in the collection. The worst case scenario for the vector space model is a query comprising the whole vocabulary t ($|q| = t$), which results in a merge of all inverted lists in the collection. As discussed in Section 3, the complexity of the set-based model is $O(r2^l N)$, where r is the number of maximal termsets and l is the largest termset associated with the collection for a given minimal frequency.

The comparison between t and $r2^l$ allows quantifying the worst case cost increase of the SBM model, but the latter is dependent on the document collection and minimal frequency employed. We calculated r and l for each collection employing a 90% confidence interval and they are presented in Table 5. For the SBM model, the upper bound is $29.84 \times 2^{12.13} \times number - of - documents$ operations.

Table 5: Number of maximal termsets and largest frequent termset

Collection	r	l
CFC	3.38 ± 0.27	3.28 ± 0.56
WSJ	19.01 ± 1.15	11.89 ± 1.88
TReC-3	29.84 ± 1.99	12.13 ± 2.39

In fact, for SBM, we use the number of closed termsets, whose worst case is $r2^l$. We determined the average number of closed termsets and the average list sizes while using SBM and the results show that the average case scenario is much better than the worst case just presented, as we can see in Table 6. Considering the TReC-3 collection, the average number of closed termsets is 4,081.25, giving an average upper bound of 4,081.25 × 162.06 operations for the SBM model, where the number 162.06 is the average size of the inverted lists. The number 4,081.25 of closed termsets is approximately 2^l, where $l = 12.13$ from Table 5, Considering the TReC-3 collection, the average number of terms per query is 22.43, resulting in an average upper bound of 22.43 × 162.06 operations for the VSM model.

To validate our analysis, we compared the response time for the models and collections considered, which are summarized in Table 7. We also calculated the increase of the response time of GVSM and SBM when compared to VSM. We observe that SBM

Table 6: Average number of closed termsets and inverted list size

Collection	Closed Termsets	Inverted List Size
CFC	3.14	7.22
WSJ	3,217.28	140.10
TReC-3	4,081.25	162.06

results in a response time increase from 8.7 to 80.1% for the reference collections evaluated when compared to VSM. The results confirm the complexity analysis performed, indicating that the time for processing the lists dominates the processing costs for both VSM and SBM, and the SBM is comparable to VSM in terms of computational costs. As expected, the increase for GVSM is much greater, ranging from 243.5% to 469.9%.

Table 7: Average response time and response time increase

Collection	Average Response Time (s)			Increase(%)	
	VSM	*GVSM*	*SBM*	*GVSM*	*SBM*
CFC	0.0023	0.0056	0.0025	243.5	8.7
WSJ	0.4286	2.0143	0.6296	469.9	46.9
TReC-3	1.2732	*	2.2930	*	80.1

* The GVSM could not be evaluated for the TReC-3 collection due to the exponential cost of the min-term build phase

We identify two main reasons for the relatively small increase in execution time for SBM. First, there is a small number of query related termsets in the reference collections. As a consequence, the inverted lists associated tend to be small (as presented in Table 6) and are usually manipulated in main memory in our implementation of SBM. Second, we employ pruning techniques that discard irrelevant termsets early in the computation, as described in Section 4.2.

As mentioned, we may control the number of closed termsets, and thus the query processing time, by varying the minimal frequency threshold. We varied the minimal frequency used in SBM and measured the response time. Figure 6 shows the response time as a function of the minimal frequency employed, where we see that the increase in the minimal frequency causes significant reductions on the response time, at a possible penalty in average precision curves.

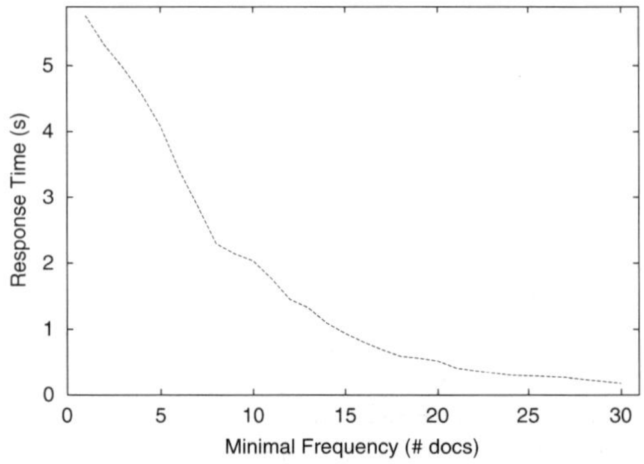

Figure 6: Impact of minimal frequency on response time for TReC-3

6. CONCLUSIONS

We presented a new approach to compute term weights, which is based on the theory of association rules. We showed that it is possible to significantly improve retrieval effectiveness, while keeping extra computational costs small. The computation of frequent termsets enumerated by an algorithm to generate association rules lead to a direct extension of the vector space model. The formal framework we adopted allowed naturally considering relevant patterns of term co-occurrence, with minimal changes to the standard vector space model formulation.

We evaluated and validated our proposed extension for the vector space model using three test collections. We showed through curves of recall versus precision that the new model presents results that are superior for all the collections considered and that the additional computational costs are acceptable. In fact, the computational costs measured allow the use of our set-based model with general large document collections.

Recent experimentation [10, 7] indicates that measurements involving the distance between term occurrences may provide good relevance assessments. For future work we will extend the set-based model to account for the proximity information about query terms in documents. We will also investigate the behavior of our model when applied to larger document collections and for collections formed by Web documents.

7. REFERENCES

[1] R. Agrawal, T. Imielinski, and A. Swami. Mining association rules between sets of items in large databases. In *Proceedings of the ACM SIGMOD International Conference Management of Data*, pages 207-216, Washington, D.C., May 1993.

[2] R. Agrawal and R. Srikant. Fast algorithms for mining association rules. In *The 20th International Conference on Very Large Data Bases*, pages 487-499, Santiago, Chile, September 1994.

[3] A. H. Alsaffar, J. S. Deogun, V. V. Raghavan, and H. Sever. Enhancing concept-based retrieval based on minimal term sets. In *Journal of Intelligent Information Systems*, volume 14(2-3), pages 155-173, 2000.

[4] R. Baeza-Yates and B. Ribeiro-Neto. *Modern Information Retrieval*. Addison Wesley, 1999.

[5] P. Bollmann-Sdorra, A. Hafez, and V. V. Raghavan. A theoretical framework for association mining based on the boolean retrieval model. In *Data Warehousing and Knowledge Discovery: Third International Conference*, pages 21-30, Munich, Germany, September 2001.

[6] P. Bollmann-Sdorra and V. V. Raghavan. On the necessity of term dependence in a query space for weighted retrieval. In *Journal of the American Society for Information Science*, volume 49(13), pages 1161-1168, November 1998.

[7] C. L. A. Clarke, G. V. Cormack, and F. J. Burkowski. Shortest substring ranking. In *In Fourth Text REtrieval Conference (TREC-4)*, pages 295-304, Gaithersburg, Maryland, USA, November 1995.

[8] D. Harman. Overview of the third text retrieval conference (trec 3). In *The Third Text Retrieval Conference*, 1993.

[9] D. J. Harper and C. J. V. Rijsbergen. An evaluation of feedback in document retrieval using co-occurrence data. In *Journal of Documentation*, volume 34, pages 189-216, 1978.

[10] D. Hawking and P. Thistlewaite. Proximity operators - so near and yet so far. In *In Fourth Text REtrieval Conference (TREC-4)*, pages 131-144, Gaithersburg, Maryland, USA, November 1995.

[11] M. Kim, A. H. Alsaffar, J. S. Deogun, and V. V. Raghavan. On modeling of concept based retrieval in generalized vector spaces. In *Proceedings International Symposium on Methods of Intelligent Systems*, pages 453-462, Charlote, N.C., USA, October 2000.

[12] M. Persin, J. Zobel, and R. Sacks-Davis. Filtered document retrieval with frequency-sorted indexes. In *Journal of the American Society of Information Science*, pages 749-764, 1996.

[13] V. V. Raghavan and C. T. Yu. Experiments on the determination of the relationships between terms. In *ACM Transactions on Databases Systems*, volume 4, pages 240-260, 1979.

[14] C. J. V. Rijsbergen. A theoretical basis for the use of co-occurrence data in information retrieval. In *Journal of Documentation*, volume 33, pages 106-119, 1977.

[15] G. Salton. *The SMART retrieval system - Experiments in automatic document processing*. Prentice Hall Inc., Englewood Cliffs, NJ, 1971.

[16] G. Salton and C. Buckley. Term-weighting approaches in automatic retrieval. In *Information Processing and Management*, volume 24(5), pages 513-523, 1988.

[17] G. Salton, C. Buckley, and C. T. Yu. An evaluation of term dependencies models in information retrieval. In *The 5th ACM-SIGIR Conference on Research and Development in Information Retrieval*, pages 151-173, 1982.

[18] G. Salton and M. E. Lesk. Computer evaluation of indexing and text processing. In *Journal of the ACM*, volume 15(1), pages 8-36, January 1968.

[19] G. Salton and C. S. Yang. On the specification of term values in automatic indexing. In *Journal of Documentation*, volume 29, pages 351-372, 1973.

[20] W. M. Shaw, J. B. Wood, R. E. Wood, and H. R. Tibbo. The cystic fibrosis database: Content and research opportunities. In *Library and Information Science Research*, volume 13), pages 347-366, 1991.

[21] J. K. Sparck. A statistical interpretation of term specificity and its application in retrieval. In *Journal of Documentation*, volume 28(1), pages 11-21, 1972.

[22] I. Witten, A. Moffat, and T. Bell. *Managing Gigabytes. Compressing and Indexing Documents and Images*. Morgan Kaufmann Publishers, 1999.

[23] S. K. M. Wong, W. Ziarko, V. V. Raghavan, and P. C. N. Wong. On modeling of information retrieval concepts in vector spaces. In *The ACM Transactions on Databases Systems*, volume 12(2), pages 299-321, June 1987.

[24] S. K. M. Wong, W. Ziarko, and P. C. N. Wong. Generalized vector space model in information retrieval. In *The 8th ACM-SIGIR Conference on Research and Development in Information Retrieval*, pages 18-25, New York, USA, 1985.

[25] C. T. Yu and G. Salton. Precision weighting - an effective automatic indexing method. In *Journal of the ACM*, volume 23(1), pages 76-88, January 1976.

[26] M. J. Zaki. Generating non-redundant association rules. In *6th ACM SIGKDD International Conference on Knowledge Discovery and Data Mining*, pages 34-43, Boston, MA, USA, August 2000.

Collaborative Filtering with Privacy via Factor Analysis

John Canny
Computer Science Division
University of California
Berkeley, CA 94720
jfc@cs.berkeley.edu

ABSTRACT

Collaborative filtering (CF) is valuable in e-commerce, and for direct recommendations for music, movies, news etc. But today's systems have several disadvantages, including privacy risks. As we move toward ubiquitous computing, there is a great potential for individuals to share all kinds of information about places and things to do, see and buy, but the privacy risks are severe. In this paper we describe a new method for collaborative filtering which protects the privacy of individual data. The method is based on a probabilistic factor analysis model. Privacy protection is provided by a peer-to-peer protocol which is described elsewhere, but outlined in this paper. The factor analysis approach handles missing data without requiring default values for them. We give several experiments that suggest that this is most accurate method for CF to date. The new algorithm has other advantages in speed and storage over previous algorithms. Finally, we suggest applications of the approach to other kinds of statistical analyses of survey or questionaire data.

Categories and Subject Descriptors

H.5.3 [**Information Storage and Retrieval**]: Information Search and Retrieval—*Information Filtering*; G.3 [**Probability and Statistics**]: Correlation and regression analysis; D.2.8 [**Management of Computing and Information Systems**]: Security and Protection

General Terms

Algorithms,Experimentation,Security,Human Factors

Keywords

Collaborative filtering, recommender systems, personalization, privacy, CSCW, surveys, sparse, missing data

1. INTRODUCTION

Collaborative filtering has important applications in e-commerce, in recreation (music, video, movie recommendations), and in information filtering in the office. Personalized purchase recommendations on a web site significantly increase the likelihood over a customer making a purchase, compared to unpersonalized suggestions. In future ubiquitous computing settings, users will routinely be able to record their own locations (via GPS on personal computing devices and phones), and their purchases (through digital wallets or through their credit card records). Through collaborative filtering, users could get recommendations about many of their everyday activities, including restaurants, bars, movies, and interesting sights to see and things to do in a neighborhood or city. But such applications are infeasible without strong protection of individual data privacy.

Most online vendors collect purchase records for their customers, and make reasonable efforts to keep the raw data private. However, there appear to be no studies of how easily recommender sites can be "mined" for customer preference information. With some simple techniques, we have found that several published schemes (especially correlation-based schemes) are extremely vulnerable. Furthermore, customer data is a valuable asset and it is routinely sold when companies have suffered bankruptcy. At this time this practice is supported by case law. In fact companies are required to disclose to customers that purchase records will likely be sold if the company suffers a bankruptcy.

A second problem with today's server-based systems is that they encourage monopolies. There are correlations between customer purchase choices across product domains. So companies that can acquire preference data for many users in one product domain have a considerable advantage when entering another. Even within one market, an established firm will have an advantage over a newer competitor, because the latter will have a smaller corpus of customer data to draw from, leading to less successful recommendations. From the customer's perspective, their purchase history is fragmented across many vendors reducing the quality of recommendations to them.

Finally, as collaborative filtering techniques become more widespread, they constitute an important part of the process of diffusion of innovations through society [18]. Diffusion in real societies relies on both *homophilous diffusion* where recommendations come from others like the inquirer, and *heterophilous* diffusion, where the inquirer explicitly seeks recommendations from individuals *not* like them (typically from experts or earlier adopters). Today's collaborative filtering systems support homophilous diffusion, but offer no plausible version of heterophily. One goal of our work is to support recommendations *from designated communities* including professionals, enthusiasts, members of particular interest groups etc. We wanted to design a system that would allow non-members of communities to gain recommendations from them, just as in natural heterophilous diffusion. This pushes two of our design criteria: (i) the protocol should protect the privacy of individuals in the community while allowing individuals both inside *and* outside the community to gain recommendations from it; (ii) a peer-to-peer design is very desirable to make it is as easy as possible for communities to construct electronic CF groups, even for communities with limited resources (e.g. ability to afford, configure and run a server).

Our work here builds on the recent paper [3] that introduced collaborative filtering with privacy. That paper describes a protocol for encrypting data and aggregating it and publishing the result. The aggregate can be downloaded by users who can use it to derive recommendations from their own preference data. The first contribution of the present paper is to introduce the privacy-preserving CF scheme to the SIGIR community and give a simplified description of the protocol. The second contribution is a new collaborative filtering scheme which preserves privacy and which appears to be the most accurate CF scheme developed so far. The third contribution is a set of experiments using the new method, characterizing its accuracy, speed and storage requirements.

This approach is applicable to traditional collaborative filtering applications, but also opens the door to many novel applications of CF in ubiquitous and everyday settings. Privacy protection should allow CF to be applied to log data that is too extensive or too sensitive to be sent to a server. In the next section, we describe the probabilistic model of user preferences, and how this model is used to generate new recommendations. Then we briefly explain how the model can be computed from encrypted data. Finally, we describe some experiments with the factor analysis model on CF datasets, including a common benchmark dataset. Our experiments support the claim that this is the most accurate collaborative filtering method to date, and that it has other advantages in speed and storage requirements.

2. PROBABILISTIC MODEL

In the most general setting, we want to construct probabilistic models of user behavior/preferences from observations of it. In this paper, we want to extrapolate user ratings from these observations for collaborative filtering. We chose a low-dimension linear model of user preferences after consideration of the most successful previous CF algorithms. The following design issues are important:

1. Among the most accurate CF methods to date are neighbor methods using Pearson correlation [2], [12], Singular Value Decomposition [19] and "Personality Diagnosis" [16]. SVD has an explicit linear model. Pearson correlation is known to be equivalent to linear fit. PD is harder to characterize, but if it is indeed "personality" diagnosis, it is known that linear models are good models for human personality traits [13]. Given that our goal is to extrapolate user ratings from a model, these precendents argue in favor of a *linear* model of user ratings.

2. CF data is extremely sparse. The EachMovie dataset described later, which contains only 3% of the possible ratings, is considered a "dense" dataset. Other datasets may have 0.1% or even 0.01% of the possible ratings. A good CF method should deal with missing data in a principled way (not by filling in missing values with defaults).

3. Signal and noise variances are comparable in typical CF applications (this is an empirical observation we have made during the experiments in section 5). So an explicit probabilistic model should be used, but not e.g. the simple least-squares fitting of SVD which effectively assumes that signal variance is infinite.

For these reasons we chose a linear factor analysis model. Factor analysis [8] is a probabilistic formulation of linear fit, which generalizes SVD and linear regression. In what follows, we will use upper case symbols (X, Y) to represent random variables, and lower case symbols (x, y) to represent *sets* of observations of those variables for all users. Let $Y = (Y_1, \dots, Y_n)$ be a random variable representing an abstract user's preferences for n items. Then Y_i is their preference for item i. An observation (lower case) y would be a particular set of ratings by all users, so e.g. y_{ij} would be user j's rating of movie number i, say $y_{ij} = 5$ on a scale of 0 to 10. Thus y is an $n \times m$ matrix whose rows are indexed by item, and whose columns are indexed by user.

Let $X = (X_1, \dots, X_k)$ be a random variable representing an abstract user's k canonical preferences, which is a kind of user profile. For instance, X_1 could be an individual's affinity for blockbuster movies. Other X_i's would affinities for other movie types. We do not need to know the meanings of the dimensions at any stage of the algorithm, and the model is automatically generated. The linear model for user preferences looks like this:

$$Y = \Lambda X + N \tag{1}$$

where Λ is a $n \times k$ matrix. $N = (N_1, \dots, N_n)$ is a random variable representing "noise" in user choices. The linear model we are looking for comprises Λ and the variances $\mathrm{VAR}(N_i)$ of the noise variables. X is automatically scaled so that it has unit variance, and therefore we dont need to find $\mathrm{VAR}(X)$. For simplicity, we assume all the $\mathrm{VAR}(N_i)$'s are the same, $\mathrm{VAR}(N_i) = \psi$. We also assume that X and N have gaussian probability distributions. If we could observe X and Y at the same time we would have a classical linear regression problem. We can't observe X, and instead we have a factor analysis problem.

There are several algorithms available for factor analysis. We chose to use an EM approach (Expectation Maximization) [6] for two reasons: firstly because it has a particularly simple recursive definition which can be combined with our privacy method, and secondly because it can be adapted to sparse data. When we solve the EM equations, we start by computing an approximation to Λ using linear regression. We do this because the regression equations are also compatible with our privacy scheme, and each regression iteration is faster than an EM iteration. The regression equations can be found in [14].

To initialize Λ *before* the linear regression begins, we fill it with random values from a gaussian distribution. Then we scale each of its columns to have a magnitude which matches the expected RMS noise for that CF domain (RMS noise is $\sqrt{< N^2 >}$ where $<>$ is expected value). The RMS noise for typical collaborative filtering domains is about 20% of the rating range. The scalar ψ should be initialized to the variance of the noise (the square of the RMS noise value).

2.1 EM Factor Analysis

We use an Expectation Maximization recurrence to solve the factor analysis model. The recurrence we use is known [8, 14] although the way we deal with sparseness (missing values) is new. We believe that careful treatment of sparseness is essential for good performance of CF algorithms, given the (usually) very high fraction of missing data. Most previous approaches have used defaults or inferred the missing values. This is simply incorrect from a statistical point of view. The available user ratings induce a probability distribution for each missing rating, which cannot be represented by any single value. For a detailed discussion of these issues we refer the reader to [9].

We start first with the dense situation, assuming that every user has rated every item. Once again y is the $n \times m$ matrix of ratings of n items by m users, and x is a $k \times m$ matrix which models the users' coordinates in preference space. The recurrence is

$$\begin{aligned} M &= (\psi I + \Lambda^T \Lambda)^{-1} \\ x &= M \Lambda^T y \\ \Lambda^{(p)} &= y x^T (x x^T + m \psi M)^{-1} \\ \psi^{(p)} &= (1/nm)\text{trace}(y y^T - \Lambda^{(p)} x y^T) \end{aligned}$$

where I is the $k \times k$ identity matrix, and M is a $k \times k$ intermediate matrix. The superscripted symbols $\Lambda^{(p)}$ and $\psi^{(p)}$ denote values after the iteration, unsuperscripted symbols are values before. This recurrence is based on a maximum likelihood model, and because of that it can be adapted to any sparse subset of the evidence y.

Our approach to dealing with sparseness is based on Gharamani and Jordan's paper [9]. The idea is to compute symbolic expected values for all the missing quantities *including quantities such as variances derived from missing ratings*, and to substitute them in the formulas so they are complete. Note that this is not equivalent to substituting only the expectations of missing ratings [9]. One must effectively work with the *distributions* of missing ratings, not just their expectations. We will not give the derivation here, and it turns out that substituting for quantities derived from missing ratings causes them to cancel later in the analysis. So the missing items disappear from the equations and are never needed. One can in fact derive the same set of equations by treating missing values as if they were never there, by deriving MAP (Maximum A-posteriori Probability) estimates for the linear model given only the known ratings.

2.1.1 *Sparse Formula*

First of all, we need to partition the formulas to data computable by each user. Let y_j be user j's vector of n ratings, and x_j be user j's estimated coordinates in preference space. Because user j hasn't rated every item, we need to introduce an $n \times n$ "trimming" matrix D_j. The matrix D_j is a diagonal matrix with 1 in positions (i, i) where i is an item that user j *has* rated, and D_j is zero everywhere else. The matrix D_j allows us to restrict the formulas for user j to the items they have rated. We use the notation $M|_j$ to denote the restriction of a matrix M in this way. Note that restriction does not change the dimensions of a matrix, and M and $M|_j$ are both $k \times k$ matrices. Then we have

$$\begin{aligned} \Lambda|_j &= D_j \Lambda \\ M|_j &= (\psi I + \Lambda^T D_j \Lambda)^{-1} \\ x_j &= M|_j \Lambda|_j^T y_j \end{aligned} \qquad (2)$$

All of these calculations can be done by user j, assuming they know Λ, which is public information. Notice that these equations are independent of missing data in y_j. This is because $\Lambda|_j^T = \Lambda^T D_j$, so when $\Lambda|_j^T$ is multiplied by y_j, elements of y_j in missing data positions are multiplied by zero.

The next expression comes from the maximization step of EM [8]

$$D_j \Lambda^{(p)} (x_j x_j^T + \psi M|_j) = D_j y_j x_j^T$$

which is a tricky equation to solve when summed over all users because $\Lambda^{(p)}$, the matrix we would like to solve for, is surrounded by non-constant factors. We will skip the details, but we can rewite the above as:

$$D_j \otimes (x_j x_j^T + \psi M|_j) \mathrm{L}(\Lambda^{(p)}) = \mathrm{L}(D_j y_j x_j^T)$$

where $\otimes$ is the kronecker product, and $\mathrm{L}(A)$ for a matrix A is the vector obtained by "stacking" columns of A one on top of another. These operations are available in many linear algebra packages (e.g. $\otimes$ is "kron" in Matlab and $\mathrm{L}(A)$ is $A(:)$). Once we have this form for the equations, we can add them up for all users and solve for $\Lambda^{(p)}$. The result is

$$\mathrm{L}(\Lambda^{(p)}) = \left(\sum_{j=1}^{m} \frac{1}{n_j} D_j \otimes (x_j x_j^T + \psi M|_j) \right)^{-1} \sum_{j=1}^{m} \frac{1}{n_j} \mathrm{L}(D_j y_j x_j^T) \qquad (3)$$

where n_j is the number of items that user j actually rated. The factors $(1/n_j)$ give appropriate weights to each user, and without them users who had voted for many items would overly influence the model.

Finally, we need to update ψ, which is slightly changed from before to

$$\psi^{(p)} = \frac{1}{m} \sum_{j=1}^{m} \frac{1}{n_j} (y_j^T D_j y_j - \text{trace}(\Lambda^{(p)} x_j y_j^T D_j)) \qquad (4)$$

Equations (2), (3) and (4) are the complete EM iteration for sparse factor analysis, which we will call EM-FA. In order to distribute the iteration among users, we decompose the sparse formula in the following way. Each user j computes

$$\begin{aligned} A_j &= \tfrac{1}{n_j} D_j \otimes (x_j x_j^T + \psi M|_j) \\ B_j &= \tfrac{1}{n_j} D_j y_j x_j^T \\ C_j &= \tfrac{1}{n_j} y_j^T D_j y_j \end{aligned} \qquad (5)$$

We leave it to the reader to confirm that these expressions are independent of any values in missing data positions of y_j. The user sends the results in encrypted form (see next section) to a totaler(s). The totaler(s) computes

$$\begin{aligned} \mathrm{L}(\Lambda^{(p)}) &= \left(\textstyle\sum_{j=1}^{m} A_j\right)^{-1} \textstyle\sum_{j=1}^{m} \mathrm{L}(B_j) \\ \psi^{(p)} &= \tfrac{1}{m} \textstyle\sum_{j=1}^{m} (C_j - \text{trace}(\Lambda^{(p)} B_j)) \end{aligned} \qquad (6)$$

where $L(A)$ is the matrix A written as a vector with its columns stacked one on top of another ($A(:)$ in Matlab).

The totaler(s) decrypts the results and sends them to all the clients. So the iterative procedure goes in rounds, with back-and-forth communication between clients and totalers using equations (2), (5) and (6). We call these the distributed EM-FA equations.

As suggested in the last section, our procedure is to initialize Λ and ψ, run a few (say 10) iterations of linear regression (which also easily distributes among clients) to move Λ nearer to the maximum likelihood value, and then to run iterations of EM-FA until convergence is obtained. In practice, the EM-FA procedure converges so reliably that we use a fixed number of iterations (15-25 typically) of EM-FA. From then on, we continue to run iterations periodically, which will keep the model fitted to the data as it changes.

2.2 Obtaining Recommendations

The result of the iteration above is a model Λ, ψ of the original dataset y. It can be used to predict a user's ratings from any subset of that user's ratings. Let y_j be user j's ratings. User j should download Λ, ψ and then locally compute x_j using equation (2). From x_j, user j should compute Λx_j which is a vector of ratings for all items. The ratings in this vector are the predictions for user j.

2.3 Removing Means

The factor analysis model assumes that the random variable Y has mean zero. In practice this isn't true. We can make it approximately true by subtracting an estimator of the mean for each user rating. If y is a training set, then the means should be subtracted before the model Λ, ψ is built from y. Then when recommendations are computed, we take the jth user's ratings y_j, subtract the means for all items and make the predictions for missing ratings using equation (2). The means should be added back to the missing ratings before they are used. There are two basic estimates for the mean of a given rating: the per-user mean, or the per-item mean. Either of these can be used. For datasets where the number of users is much larger than the number of items (as for Eachmovie or Jester), the per-item average will usually be more accurate. For other datasets, either estimator may work well, and it is best to experiment to see which is better. We implemented both methods.

3. PRESERVING PRIVACY

Having shown that we can reduce factor analysis to an iteration based on vector addition of per-user data A_j, B_j and C_j, we next sketch how to do vector addition with privacy. Putting both procedures together gives us factor analysis with privacy. The scheme we use for vector addition is the same as [3]. We will not repeat the derivation or mathematics here. We will give a high-level sketch of the method which we think should be useful for understanding the method. Among other things, it uses a social notion of trust that could well be the source of some interesting studies. We assume that a fraction α of users are honest. The value α must be at least 0.5 and preferably > 0.8. The goals of the protocol are that: The server should gain no information about an individual user's data y_j, and both user's data and totaler's calculations should be proved correct (no cheating). Our protocol achieves those goals [3].

The method uses a property of several common encryption schemes (RSA, Diffie-Hellman, ECC) called homomorphism. If $E(.)$ is an encryption function, and g is a multiplicative group element, we can define a function $H(m) = E(g^m)$. This function is a homomorphism, meaning that

$$H(m_1)H(m_2) = H(m_1 + m_2)$$

where multiplication is ring multiplication for RSA, or element-wise for DH or ECC. By induction, multiplying such encodings of several messages gives us the encoding of their sum. So by encoding numbers m_i and then multiplying the encodings, we can compute the encryption of a large sum without ever seeing the data. This seems to get us halfway there - we can add up encrypted items by just multiplying them. But how to decrypt the total?

The decryption scheme is somewhat more involved. It relies on key-sharing. The key needed to decrypt the total is not owned by anyone. It does not exist on any single machine. But it is "shared" among all the users. Like a jigsaw puzzle, if enough users put their shares together, we would see the whole key. There is some redundancy for practical reasons - we would not want to require all the users to contribute their shares in order to get back the key, or we could probably never get it back. Because the item that has been shared among the users is a decryption key, they can use it to create a share of the decryption of the total. To clarify this, everyone has a copy of the encrypted total $E(T)$. Each person can decrypt $E(T)$ with their share of the key, and the result turns out to be a share of the decryption of T. By putting these shares together, the users can compute T.

To summarize the outcome of the protocol: Each user starts with their own preference data, and knowledge of who their peers are in their community. By running the protocol, users exchange various encrypted messages. At the end of the protocol, every user has an *unencrypted* copy of the linear model Λ, ψ of the community's preferences. They can then use this to extrapolate their own ratings using equations as described in section 2.2. At no stage does unencypted information about a user's preferences leave their own machine. Users outside the community can request a copy of the model Λ, ψ from any community member, and derive recommendations for themselves as described in section 2.2.

There are some extra details to make sure that users and totalers (who compute the totals) are not cheating. We use a technique called zero-knowledge proofs (ZKPs) to require each user to prove that their hidden vote is valid (within the allowable range of ratings, so they cant excessively influence the total). And we use a sampling technique to check totalers' totals for accuracy. As well as making errors, totalers can compromise users' privacy by deliberately leaving out (or multiply adding) their data. The interested reader is refered to [3]. The protocols are simple and efficient, and although the numbers required are quite large (160 to 1024 bits) the bandwidth and computation demands are reasonable.

This protocol is designed to be robust with a fraction (say up to 0.2) of cheating totalers and users. It is also robust against a reasonable number of clients being offline (this parameter can be adjusted but 50% would be typical). It is a peer-to-peer application that doesnt require a server, although it does leverage some non-trivial peer services which are available now as prototypes (in systems like Groove or Oceanstore [15]) and which may become part of network infrastructure in the future. We would like any group of users to be able to create and maintain a collaborating affinity group that shares data internally and allows other groups to use it.

4. RELATED WORK

Two recent survey papers on collaborative filtering [2], [12], compared a number of algorithms for accuracy on available test data. Generally speaking, they found that neighbor weighting using Pearson correlation gave best accuracy among the algorithms considered at that time. Slight modifications to the Pearson method, like the significance weighting scheme from [12], can improve its performance by one or two percent. We implemented several of these extensions, but significance weighting was the only extension that reliably improved accuracy. We used it in our comparison experiments.

Since the surveys, there have been a few papers which gave comparable or better results than Pearson correlation on some datasets. The first uses SVD [19], which gives a linear least-squares fit to a dataset. SVD was used in our first paper [3] on CF with privacy. There are differences in the method of generating recommendations from the SVD however, and our scheme from [3] is based on a maximum likelihood model, and was more accurate than the scheme from [19] in experiments. The present work (sparse factor analysis) differs on both [3] and [19] by using the same probabilistic formulation to generate recommendations from a model, and to construct the model itself. It is always more accurate than either of the SVD schemes. Another recent paper uses a probabilistic method called "personality diagnosis" (PD) [16], and gives better accuracy than Pearson. As we will see in the next section, PD is more accurate than Pearson, but less accurate than sparse factor analysis on available data.

Recently, several researchers have combined collaborative and content-based recommenders. These algorithms use both user ratings and also metadata about the rated items, or possibly their content if that is appropriate. They are particularly useful in groups with few users, for items that have not been rated by many others, or in domains with extremely sparse ratings. In [1], the authors present a hybrid recommender. In [11], the authors use content-based agents to fill in missing ratings data. The paper [5] uses separate collaborative and content-based (metadata) recommenders and then combines the results with a weighted average. Popescul et al. [17] use a probabilistic aspect model to combine collaborative ratings with text content for the citeseer database. There is a simple extension to our method which supports meta-data which we have tried in a few experiments. It is described in a forthcoming paper [4].

Collaborative Filtering with low-dimensional linear models was apparently used in DEC's original Eachmovie recommender site. It is described in US patent number 6,078,740. Although the patent does not describe the algorithmic techniques, the system included a least-squares recurrence that worked directly on sparse data without added defaults [7].

5. EXPERIMENTS

To provide better comparability with earlier results, we re-implemented Pearson correlation which had been used in the two survey papers. We repeated published experiments on a well-known dataset. Then we compared Peason and our scheme on some new datasets to give a broader comparison. All the code for our algorithms, along with our implementations of Pearson as well as the SVD algorithm from [19], are available in MATLAB from the project website `www.cs.berkeley.edu/~jfc/'mender`.

5.1 Evaluation Metric

Several evaluation metrics for collaborative filtering have appeared in the literature. The most common is the MAE or Mean Absolute Error between predicted and actual ratings for a set of users. We used MAE exclusively in our experiments for several reasons. First of all, it is the most commonly used metric and allows us to compare our results with the largest set of previous works. Secondly, it correlates well with other metrics. In a recent paper by the Grouplens group [19] they noted that statistical metrics such as MAE, RMSE (Root Mean Squared Error) and Correlation "track each other closely". They also noted that MAE and the decision metric ROC "provide the same ordering of different experimental schemes". Thirdly, the differences in MAE between our scheme and others are quite large compared to earlier comparison papers. It seems unlikely that this disparity would be reversed under a different metric. Instead we concentrated on testing on a diversity of datasets to see how strong the disparity was across them.

5.2 Eachmovie Dataset

The EachMovie dataset was created by Compaq Equipment Corporation from a recommender site for movies that they ran. Eachmovie comprises ratings of 1628 movies by 72916 users. The ratings are on a scale of 0-5. The dataset has a density of approximately 3%, meaning that 97% of possible ratings are missing. Eachmovie was one of the datasets used in the recent survey by Breese [2]. Breese et al. tested several methods on the Eachmovie dataset, and used two different metrics, one of which was MAE. They found that that best performing algorithm on the EachMovie dataset under both metrics was a neighborhood scheme based on Pearson correlation.

Breese's experiments were done on a sample of 5000 users. Since our method involves a training phase, we created two disjoint sets y_T, y_P of 5000 users. We computed the model Λ, ψ on the first training set y_T using $k = 14$ and per-item averaging. Then we tested the model on the set y_P. We also ran our Pearson implementation on the y_P set, and obtained MAE ratings that matched Breese's within statistical error. We compared the EM-FA predictions with Breese's "Allbut1" case, which used all but one of a user's ratings to make a prediction, and compared the prediction with the remaining value. We felt this was the most realistic prediction case.

Because we tested against several datasets, we used a normalized value of MAE, or NMAE, as suggested by Goldberg [10]. The results appear in figure 1. The baseline predictor was are respectively the per-item average (average of a row of y). Per-item average is not personalized. Each movie's rating is the same for all users. These predictors provide a useful reality check for more sophisticated schemes. Also, many schemes, Breese's and ours included, make predictions *relative* to one of the baseline predictors. On the EachMovie dataset with 5000 items, we used per-item averaging. We tested per-user averaging on this dataset as well and it was 2% less accurate.

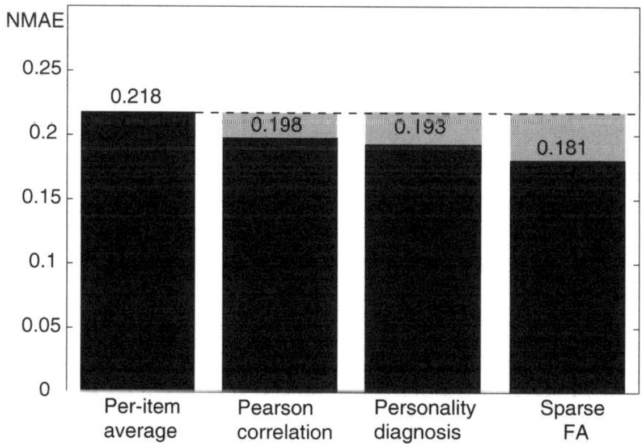

Fig 1. Results of sparse factor analysis ($k = 14$), Pearson correlation and Personality diagnosis against a baseline predictor for the EachMovie dataset. Lower bars indicate better performance. Lightly shaded regions show improvement over baseline.

Note that Pearson correlation, the most accurate reported scheme on Eachmovie from Breese's survey, achieves about a 9% improvement in MAE over non-personalized recommendations based on per-item average. Personality diagnosis achieves an 11% improvement over baseline. By contrast, sparse factor analysis achieves an 18% improvement over baseline, and a 9% improvement over Pearson correlation. It was a 10% improvement over simple SVD prediction. The predictions from sparse factor analysis improve if there is more training data. This will often be important because sparse FA is orders of magnitude faster than Pearson correlation or PD on large datasets. Therefore sparse FA can be often used on larger datasets than is practical with those methods. We tried training with 50,000 users, and the NMAE dropped a further 2.5% to 0.175. The standard deviations in all estimates are less than 0.25 %.

5.3 Jester Dataset

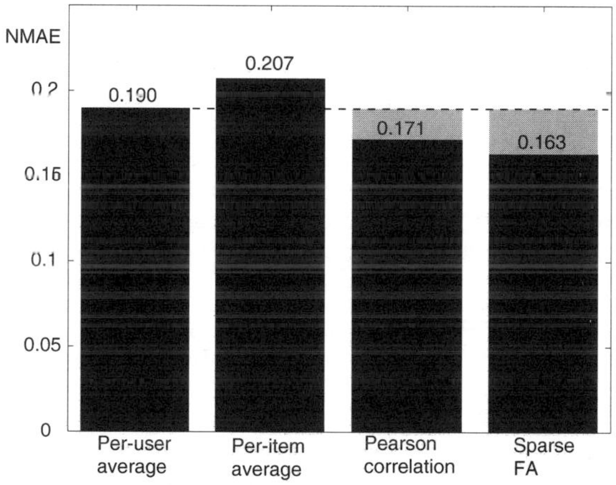

Fig 2. Results of sparse factor analysis ($k = 14$) and Pearson correlation on the Jester dataset. Lower bars indicate better performance, and the lightly shaded regions are improvement over baseline.

The Jester dataset comes from Ken Goldberg's joke recommendation website, Jester [10]. In Jester, users rate a core set of jokes, and then receive recommendations about others that they should like. The database has 100 jokes, and records of 17988 users. Some users end up reading and rating all the jokes, so Jester is much more dense than the other datasets we considered. Roughly 50% of all possible ratings are present. Jester has a rating scale from -10 to 10. Ratings are implemented with a slider, so Jester's scale is continuous. Perhaps because of the density, and/or because the continuous scale introduces less quantization error in ratings, Jester exhibits lower NMAE values than the other datasets we tested.

We split the data into training and test sets with approximately 9000 users in each. We computed a factor analysis model with $k = 14$ factors as before. The results are shown in figure 2. Notice that this time, the per-user average is a better baseline predictor than per-item average. This time Pearson correlation is a 10% improvement over the better of the two baseline predictors, while factor analysis is a 5% improvement over Pearson. Given that this data is not very sparse, we expected a lower improvement over Pearson. The best reported NMAE from among the methods described in [10] was 0.187, which is somewhat higher than Pearson on this dataset.

5.4 Clickthru Dataset

The last experiment used data from a large internet service provider. This dataset has anonymized web clickthru information from 15,000 users for 6 months. The basic dataset was a log file listing user ID number, URL accessed and the date and time. To limit the number of sites that might be considered, we truncated the URLs to 20 characters after the domain name. We also eliminated sites that had not been visited by at least 3 distinct users. The result was 210832 web sites. Our factor analysis model is most effective on datasets that have ratings of the items on some scale. So instead of a binary matrix indicating whether a user visited a site or not, we built an integer valued matrix y, where y_{ij} was the number of times that user j visited site i. The number of visits of a user to a site is an implicit rating of that site by the user. The implicit rating was clipped at 10, so the range of ratings for a site varied from 1 to 10 (0 represents no visit rather than a low rating). The dataset has about 2.2 million non-null entries, and is the most sparse dataset we used. It contains 0.07% of the possible ratings.

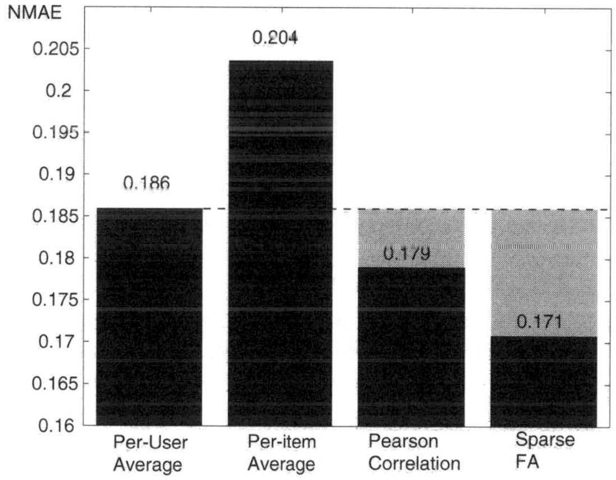

Fig 3. Results of sparse factor analysis ($k = 4$) and Pearson correlation on the web clickthru dataset. Lower bars indicate better performance, lightly shaded region is gain over baseline. Note that the Y-axis has been expanded.

The results are shown in figure 3. Both Pearson correlation and factor analysis methods used per-user mean as their baseline predictor, which is shown as a dotted line on the figure. For this example, factor analysis gives more than double the decrease in NMAE compared to Pearson. Note that the implicit rating (by frequency of visit) *does* behave like a rating, in the sense that there is a significant error reduction by using the predictive model. Sparse FA is able to give nearly a 10% improvement over baseline prediction on this dataset, which is the same improvement as Pearson over baseline on the two previous datasets, which were real user ratings.

5.5 Performance: Speed

The code for EM and Pearson correlation was written in Matlab. The complexity of one iteration of the sparse FA Matlab algorithm is $O(nmk^2)$, so it scales linearly with both n the number of items and m the number of users. If sparse matrix representations are used, the running time is $O(nm\rho k^2 + mk^3)$ where ρ is the fraction of possible ratings available. For the Eachmovie dataset with 5000 users and $k = 14$, the factor analysis training time was 11 minutes (20 iterations of the EM recurrence) on a PII-400 MHz machine with 256MB ram. Training with 50,000 users took a little under two hours. The time to predict all missing ratings for a user is $O(nk^2)$ and is independent of the number of users. Predictions for Eachmovie took 7 milliseconds (to generate approximately 1600 ratings for one user). For comparison, Breese reported a computing time to generate ratings for one user using Pearson correlation of about 300ms on a PII-266 MHz machine. Our Matlab implementation of Pearson correlation had similar performance to Breese's at 300ms per rec. With the same effort at optimization, our Matlab implementation of sparse factor analysis was about 50 times faster than our implementation of Pearson for generating ratings on a 5k dataset. It was 500 times faster on a 50k dataset. Of course, our method involves an additional training phase, while Pearson does not. Including model generation, the overall times to generate recommendations for everyone are comparable for SFA and Pearson with 5k users. But with 50k users, SFA is an order of magnitude faster, including model generation.

For the Jester dataset with 100 items, 9000 users and $k = 14$, time to construct the factor analysis model was 8 minutes. Generating all recommendations for one user took 7 milliseconds on the same hardware as the previous experiment. For the Clickthru dataset with 210832 items and 15000 users, we computed a factor analysis model with $k = 4$. The training time was 5 hours. Generating all recommendations for one user took 60 milliseconds.

5.6 Performance: Space

For the Eachmovie dataset with 5000 users and k=14, The model Λ was a dense array with 23072 elements compared with the original training array which had 234934 non-nulls. In other words, the model was a 10-fold compression of the original data. For Jester, which had a high density of available ratings, the model was a 300-fold compression.

The curve below shows how cross-validation NMAE varies with model size k and number of users m. To the left of the curve, it is clear that high k leads to large errors, implying that the model is over-fitting. As the number of users (and amount of non-null data) increases, the curves cross over, and with 50000 users, the model error decreases with k. However, it was difficult to detect a significant difference between $k = 14$ and $k = 20$, and we did not try larger values of k.

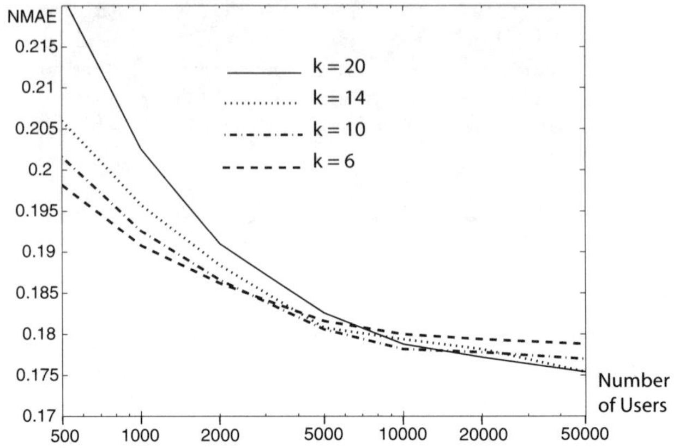

Fig 4. NMAE as a function of model dimension k and number of users m, for the Eachmovie dataset.

We can abstract the information above to the following heuristic to avoid over-fitting for typical collaborative filtering data:

Maximum Model Size The model dimension k should be chosen so that the total size of the model Λ is at most one tenth of the number of non-null elements in the original data. This criterion is equivalent to

$$10 \times k < \rho \times m$$

where m is the number of users as before, and ρ is the density (fraction of non-nulls) in the dataset.

A second test for overfitting is provided by our Matlab code mentioned earlier, which estimates ψ at both model creation and at prediction time. If these estimates differ significantly (say by more than 20%), the data has been overfit and k should be reduced.

The model size criterion implies that the factor analysis model is a substantial compression of the original dataset. Ten is the minimum compression ratio, twenty to thirty are desirable, and larger numbers will still give very accurate prediction. e.g. with 50000 users and $k = 14$, the model still gives very good accuracy from figure 4. In this case, the model is 100 times smaller than the original data.

6. DISCUSSION

Sparse factor analysis is an extremely promising approach to collaborative filtering. We ran it on three datasets of varying sparseness, including a well-studied reference dataset. In all cases, its accuracy improved significantly over other methods. The improvements increased with the sparseness of the dataset, as expected because sparse FA correctly handles sparseness. For memory-based methods such as Pearson correlation or personality diagnosis (PD), sparse FA is much faster per recommendation (50 times typical). It also and provides typical compression of the dataset of 10-100 times over memory-based methods. It is closest in speed and space requirements to singular value decomposition, but has a large accuracy advantage (about 10% on EachMovie data) over SVD. Sparse FA was implemented using a simple EM recurrence, so that it adapts easily to user datasets that are continually being updated. One or two iterations are enough to update the model after an update to the user data. It is the first CF algorithm to have an incremental implementation. Sparse FA supports computation on encrypted data, thereby protecting user privacy. Finally, the method is fully described by the recurrence equations (2), (3) and (4) and is easy to implement. It infers the statistical quantities it needs, and the only parameter to be set is the model dimension k, for which we gave some principles. The lack of other adjustable parameters or heuristics makes its performance easy to replicate. In our experience, its convergence is fast and reliable.

6.1 Limitations

The main limitation of this model is its suitability for binary recommendation problems, such as purchase records. For binary data such as "purchase/no purchase," there is no missing data, and the factor analysis model would not show as great an advantage over other schemes. It would still be applicable however, and should be more accurate than SVD or Pearson methods because of its full probabilistic model. How it compares with probabilistic models that *assume* binary data is another question.

We suggest that a better way to apply the model to e-commerce applications would be to extract some tacit rating info. For instance, if you own the site providing the commerce, you could record when a user views an item as well as when they purchase it. If they view and do not purchase, record a 0 for that item and user. If they do purchase, record a 1. In that way, you still acquire a (typically very) sparse matrix, and the factor analysis model would likely do much better than other models.

6.2 Extensions

One natural extension of the model is to location-based services. Using data recorded about user's positions and purchases using small mobile devices with GPS (phones or PDAs), we can offer recommendations about places to see, things to do etc. This application is described in a forthcoming paper [4]. The privacy protection that our method provides is extremely important in this application, because we expect users would be unwilling to expose their position data to a service provider without strong privacy guarantees.

Factor analysis and SVD are common data analysis techniques for surveys or performance studies. Our method can be easily adapted to that setting. Users run a client on their computer that gathers survey responses or logs user actions, and then forwards them in encrypted form to a server. The server can then compute a factor analysis which would hide individual responses. Such a scheme may enhance user response rate because users will be able to participate without worrying about loss of privacy.

7. REFERENCES

[1] C. Basu, H. Hirsh, and W. W. Cohen. Recommendation as classification: Using social and content-based information in recommendation. In *AAAI/IAAI*, pages 714–720, 1998.

[2] Breese, Heckermen, and Kadie. Empirical analysis of predictive algorithms for collaborative filtering. Technical report, Microsoft Research, October 1998.

[3] J. Canny. Collaborative filtering with privacy. In *IEEE Symposium on Security and Privacy*, pages 45–57, Oakland, CA, May 2002.

[4] J. Canny. Some techniques for privacy in ubicomp and context-aware applications. In *UBICOMP-2002*, Goteborg, Sweden, Sept. 2002. (submitted).

[5] M. Claypool, A. Gokhale, T. Miranda, P. Murnikov, D. Netes, and M. Sartin. Combining content-based and collaborative filters in an online newspaper. In *ACM SIGIR WS on Recommender Systems*, 1999.

[6] A. P. Dempster, N. M. Laird, and D. B. Rubin. Maximum likelihood from incomplete data via the em algorithm. *Journal of the Royal Statistical Society. Series B (Methodological)*, 39(1):1–38, 1977.

[7] J. DeTreville, 2002. personal communication.

[8] B. Frey. Turbo factor analysis. *Adv. Neural Information Processing*, 1999. (submitted).

[9] Z. Ghahramani and M. I. Jordan. Learning from incomplete data. Technical Report AIM-1509, MIT AI Lab, 1994.

[10] K. Goldberg, D. Gupta, M. Digiovanni, and H. Narita. Jester 2.0 : Evaluation of a new linear time collaborative filtering algorithm. In *ACM SIGIR*, August 1999. Poster Session and Demonstration.

[11] N. Good, J. B. Schafer, J. A. Konstan, A. Borchers, B. M. Sarwar, J. L. Herlocker, and J. Riedl. Combining collaborative filtering with personal agents for better recommendations. In *AAAI/IAAI*, pages 439–446, 1999.

[12] J. Herlocker, J. Konstan, A. Borchers, and J. Riedl. An algorithmic framework for performing collaborative filtering. In *Proc. ACM SIGIR*, 1999.

[13] O. P. John. The "big five" factor taxonomy: Dimensions of personality in the natural language and in questionnaires. In L. A. Pervin, editor, *Handbook of personality: Theory and research.* Guilford, NY, 1990.

[14] M. Jordan and C. Bishop. *An Introduction to Graphical Models.* MIT Press, 2002. In press.

[15] J. Kubiatowicz, D. Bindel, Y. Chen, S. Czerwinski, P. Eaton, D. Geels, R. Gummadi, S. Rhea, H. Weatherspoon, W. Weimer, C. Wells, and B. Zhao. Oceanstore: An architecture for global-scale persistent storage. In *ACM ASPLOS*, November 2000.

[16] D. Pennock and E. Horvitz. Collaborative filtering by personality diagnosis: A hybrid memory- and model based approach. In *IJCAI Workshop on Machine Learning for Information Filtering*, Stockholm, Sweden, August 1999.

[17] A. Popescul, L. Ungar, D. Pennock, and S. Lawrence. Probabilistic models for unified collaborative and content-based recommendation in sparse-data environments. In *17th Conference on Uncertainty in Artificial Intelligence*, Seattle, WA, August 2001.

[18] E. M. Rogers. *Diffusion of Innovations, Fourth Edition.* The Free Press, 1995.

[19] B. M. Sarwar, G. Karypis, J. A. Konstan, and J. Riedl. Application of dimensionality reduction in recommender system – a case study. In *ACM WebKDD 2000 Web Mining for E-Commerce Workshop*, 2000. Full length paper.

Inverted File Search Algorithms for Collaborative Filtering

Rickard Cöster
Stockholm University, DSV
Forum 100, SE-164 40 Kista, SWEDEN
rick@dsv.su.se

Martin Svensson
Swedish Institute of Computer Science
Box 1263, SE-164 29 Kista, SWEDEN
martins@sics.se

ABSTRACT

This paper explores the possibility of using a disk based inverted file structure for collaborative filtering. Our hypothesis is that this allows for faster calculation of predictions and also that early termination heuristics may be used to further speed up the filtering process and perhaps even improve the quality of the predictions. In an experiment on the EachMovie dataset this was tested. Our results indicate that searching the inverted file structure is many times faster than general in-memory vector search, even for very large profiles. The Continue termination heuristics produces the best ranked predictions in our experiments, and Quit is the top performer in terms of speed.

Categories and Subject Descriptors

H.3.3 [**Information Search and Retrieval**]: Information filtering; H.3.4 [**Systems and Software**]: Performance evaluation (efficiency and effectiveness)

General Terms

Algorithms, Performance

Keywords

Collaborative Filtering, Inverted Files, Performance

1. INTRODUCTION

The Internet is an ever-expanding repository of information that needs to be filtered and navigated. To meet this need collaborative filtering has emerged as a complementary method to traditional filtering methods such as content based filtering.

This paper explores the possibility to use an inverted file structure for collaborative filtering. Our hypothesis is that this structure allows for faster calculation of predictions and also that pruning strategies (Quit and Continue) from information retrieval can be used to further speed up the filtering process and perhaps even improve their quality.

SIGIR'02, August 11-15, 2002, Tampere, Finland.

We have two reasons for this. Firstly, matching user profiles in a collaborative filtering system can be very expensive. Secondly, if we are able to use a structure that allows us to access all user preferences stored directly from disk it is possible to maintain a much larger set of users and titles.

In order to evaluate this, we conducted a series of experiments on a large dataset. In these experiments, we compare inverted file search with in-memory vector search both in terms of prediction accuracy and neighbourhood formation time.

The rest of this paper is organised as follows. In section 2 we review collaborative filtering. In section 3 we express four common correlation algorithms in inverted form. The file organization we selected for implementing the inverted files is briefly described in section 4. In sections 5 and 6 we describe the experimental setup and our main results.

2. COLLABORATIVE FILTERING

The goal for a collaborative filtering system is to predict a user's preference regarding some set of titles: books, news articles, or perhaps radio channels. To do this, a collaborative filter use ratings from a database of users (either from all users or a subset of the users in the database). The filter can then be used in either of two ways: **(1)** users can explicitly ask what the system believes they would think about a certain title, or **(2)** users can ask the system to return a ranked list of titles the system thinks they like.

Collaborative filtering allows us to tackle three drawbacks found in traditional filtering methods:

- titles must be parsable, e.g. music and movies can not be searched for [13]
- it is difficult to achieve serendipity: content-based systems do not typically allow for discovery of information not sought for
- content based filtering disregards qualitative aspects such as genre [7].

Combined with regular content-based techniques collaborative filtering offers a powerful way of finding and filtering information.

As with content based filtering there are a number of problems that need to be resolved: **Bootstrapping**: Since collaborative filtering relies on the ability of matching user profiles, they will work poorly when little information has been collected [12]. **Concept drift**: Over time people and information change. What was interesting yesterday may be totally irrelevant today. Collaborative filtering systems tend to get "conservative" in the sense that once a user profile is built, it is difficult to change. **Scalability**: In systems with large number of users and titles, algorithms that scale up to that dimension are needed.

The heart of a collaborative filter, as indicated, lies in the ability to make fast and accurate predictions. Before we present how inverted files can be used as the basic structure for the collaborative filter algorithm, let us review the two dominant models for performing predictions.

2.1 Memory-based Prediction

Memory-based prediction uses a nearest-neighbour approach to find a subset of all users that have the most similar preference history as the active user [6]. When this neighbourhood is found, the similarity between the active user and a neighbour determines how much the neighbour influences the prediction for the active user. If the similarity is high, the neighbour has high influence on the final prediction. Thus, the final prediction is a weighted combination of the neighbours' preferences. Memory-based predictions have been used in systems such as GroupLens [8] and Ringo [13].

The advantage of the memory-based scheme over other methods is that its structure is dynamic and immediately reacts to changes in the user database. Every new rating added to the user database will be included in the neighbourhood search. The reason for this is of course that similarities between users are calculated "in memory" when needed. This property is also the potential drawback of the method. When user profiles are matched against each other every time a prediction is needed, the process can be extremely slow. This would not only take time, but also require a large amount of memory. In the general case this problem is solved by only keeping parts of the user database in memory and treat that as the set of users to draw the neighbourhood from(sampling), or to precompute the neighbourhoods.

2.2 Model-based Prediction

A common technique in machine learning to predict a value is to build a model of some input data and then run new data through that model to get a predicted output. This can also be applied to collaborative filtering. The user database is run through an algorithm that builds a model of that data in terms of the probability that a user would like a given title depending on what she has done in the past. For example, in a Bayesian network the titles would represent nodes where the state of each node would represent possible vote values [3]. Various other model-based techniques have been applied in collaborative filtering, e.g. Latent Semantic Indexing [11], Singular Value Decomposition [2] and Mixture Models [9].

In terms of predictive accuracy the model-based schemas perform as well as memory-based prediction [3]. On the other hand, the model-based prediction does not suffer from the performance and memory bottlenecks found in memory-based prediction. Once a good model has been found a predication takes a small amount of time and resources to calculate. The downside of the scheme is of course the inherent static structure of it. Once the model has been built it is difficult to update it without rebuilding it. In dynamic domains where users and votes are constantly changing the model could soon become inaccurate.

3. INVERTED SEARCH

The reason for using inverted files in information retrieval is the observation that a user query usually contains a small percentage of the total number of terms in the document collection. In collaborative filtering a user's votes (or profile) can be seen as a document, which in itself can be used as a query. However, there are some differences between a document and a profile. If the user, as in a movie recommender system, explicitly expresses the votes, the user's profile will certainly grow over time and perhaps contain several hundreds or even thousands of votes. In the case of implicit voting, the profile may grow even faster when, for example, each web page visit or news article read render a vote that is stored in the profile.

Since the user profiles are expected to grow over time, it may seem unlikely that inverted files are suited for collaborative filtering. We argue quite the opposite, for two main reasons: the first being that inverted file search is well researched and handles scalability very well. The second is that the inverted file structure makes it easy to employ heuristic stop conditions, so that it is not necessary to investigate all inverted lists in a neighbourhood search and thus further speed up execution.

The basic algorithm for inverted file search scans one inverted list at a time [15]. During this scan, accumulators are stored in main memory for holding partial sums of scores or weights. In our case, the partial sums will be the partial correlations or similarities between the active user and all other users. When all inverted lists are processed, the accumulators contain the complete sums. Usually there are one or more arrays of static weights, such as normalizing factors, which are combined with the accumulators to produce the final score for a user. The final score is calculated for all non-zero accumulators, and users with top scores are returned.

One of the most commonly used algorithms for calculating neighbours in memory-based predictions is Pearson correlation. Various extensions have been made to the basic correlation [3]. We will demonstrate, in sections 3.1 through 3.4, how these algorithms may be expressed in a form suitable for inverted retrieval.

3.1 Pearson Correlation

The Pearson correlation between users a and i is defined as

$$w(a,i) = \frac{\sum_j (v_{a,j} - \bar{v}_a)(v_{i,j} - \bar{v}_i)}{\sqrt{\sum_j (v_{a,j} - \bar{v}_a)^2 \sum_j (v_{i,j} - \bar{v}_i)^2}} \tag{1}$$

where v_a is the profile for user a, $v_{a,j}$ is that user's vote for title j and $\bar{v}_a$ is the mean value of the votes for user a. The index j runs over the intersecting titles in the two profiles, i.e. $j \in \{v_a \cap v_i\}$.

To apply inverted search to correlation, it is necessary to keep three different accumulator structures in memory: one for the sum in the nominator, and two for the sums in the denominator. Call these variables SAI, SAA and SII respectively. In addition, the mean values for each user must be easily accessible, and these are stored in the static array $MEANS$. Let N denote the number of users in the database. Algorithm 1 will then compute the top K neighbours to user a. The sorting at step 15 can e.g. be performed by min-heaps [15].

Algorithm 1 Inverted correlation neighbourhood search

Input is the user profile V_a, max number of neighbours K and array of means $MEANS$. Output is array of nearest neighbours.

Allocate accumulators SAI, SAA and SII of size N
Allocate array TOP of size K for nearest neighbours
for all $j \in v_a$ **do**
  locate inverted list L for title j
  for each user u and vote v in L **do**
    $SAI[u] = SAI[u] + (v_{a,j} - \bar{v}_a) * (v - MEANS[u])$
    $SAA[u] = SAA[u] + (v_{a,j} - \bar{v}_a)^2$
    $SII[u] = SII[u] + (v - MEANS[u])^2$
  end for
end for
for all $u \in SAI$, such that $SAI[u] \neq 0$ **do**
  $corr = SAI[u]/\sqrt{(SAA[u] * SII[u])}$
  if $corr > TOP[K-1]$ **then**
    add $(u, corr)$ to TOP
    restore TOP to sorted order
  end if
end for
return TOP

3.2 Inverse User Frequency

An extension to the basic Pearson correlation algorithm is inverse user frequency [3], which assigns lower weights to titles that have a larger number of votes. The assumption is that titles that are viewed by a large number of users are not as useful in capturing the similarity between two users as titles that have been viewed by fewer users. Inverse user frequency is similar to the inverse document frequency weighting [10] used in text retrieval.

The inverse user frequency for title j can be defined as $f_j = \log(N/n_j)$ where n_j is the number of users that have voted for title j. This weight is calculated for each title in the data set.

For the algorithm, we use the same notation as in [3]. The inverted search algorithm requires six accumulators for the different sums $\sum_j f_j$, $\sum_j f_j v_{a,j} v_{i,j}$, $\sum_j f_j v_{a,j}$, $\sum_j f_j v_{i,j}$, $\sum_j f_j v_{a,j}^2$ and $\sum_j f_j v_{i,j}^2$. Furthermore, the inverse frequencies should be kept in a static array IUF, which at index j holds the value $\log(N/n_j)$. The inner loop of the search algorithm is then similar to that of Algorithm 1.

3.3 Default Voting

Default voting is computed between two users a and i in the union of their votes. If both users have not voted for title j, a default vote d is used for the missing vote. The default vote is selected globally for the whole data set, as a neutral or slightly negative vote. Another parameter k estimates the number of titles two users have not seen or voted on but would agree on.

Let n be the number of titles that both user a and i have voted for. Default voting is then

$$w(a,i) = \frac{A_1 - B_1}{\sqrt{U_1 V_1}} \tag{2}$$

where

$$\begin{aligned}
A_1 &= (n+k)(\sum_j v_{a,j} v_{i,j} + kd^2) \\
B_1 &= (\sum_j v_{a,j} + kd)(\sum_j v_{i,j} + kd) \\
U_1 &= (n+k)(\sum_j v_{a,j}^2 + kd^2) - (\sum_j v_{a,j} + kd)^2) \\
V_1 &= (n+k)(\sum_j v_{i,j}^2 + kd^2) - (\sum_j v_{i,j} + kd)^2)
\end{aligned}$$

Recall that the inverted search finds the intersection of the votes of the active user and all other users. This leads to a slight complication when inverting default voting, since it is calculated in the union of the user's votes, i.e. now $j \in \{v_a \cup v_i\}$. To remedy this, we need to express the sum over union of titles in terms of the sum of the intersecting titles. The sum in A_1 can be written as

$$\begin{aligned}
\sum_j v_{a,j} v_{i,j} &= \sum_m v_{a,m} v_{i,m} + \\
&\quad + d(\sum_s v_{a,s} - \sum_m v_{a,m}) + \\
&\quad + d(\sum_t v_{i,t} - \sum_m v_{i,m})
\end{aligned} \tag{3}$$

where $j \in \{v_a \cup v_i\}$, $s \in \{v_a\}$, $t \in \{v_i\}$ and $m \in \{v_a \cap v_i\}$.

The idea is then to accumulate the sum over m during the search and have the sum over t in a static array. The sum over s (for the active user a) may be stored in the static array or calculated during the search.

The four remaining sums for equation 2 ($\sum_j v_{a,j}$, $\sum_j v_{i,j}$, $\sum_j v_{a,j}^2$ and $\sum_j v_{i,j}^2$) can be calculated using a similar argument. Consider e.g. the sum $\sum_j v_{a,j}$, which is equal to $\sum_s v_{a,s} + d(|v_i| - |v_a \cap v_i|)$. This may be calculated if we know $\sum_s v_{a,s}$ and $|v_i|$, and calculate $|v_a \cap v_i|$ during the search. This sum and the three remaining ones are symmetrical.

Altogether, three static arrays are needed to look up the values of $\sum_t v_{i,t}$, $\sum_t v_{i,t}^2$ and $|v_i|$. Four accumulators are needed, three for the partial sums over m ($\sum_m v_{a,m} v_{i,m}$, $\sum_m v_{a,m}$, $\sum_m v_{i,m}$) and one for the number of intersecting titles $|v_a \cap v_i|$. Again, the sums over s may be stored in the static arrays or calculated during the search. We chose the latter for our experiments.

3.4 Default Voting and Inverse User Frequency

The idea of weighting titles according to their inverse user frequency can also be applied to default voting. If we use the index variables j, s, t and m as in the previous section, then default voting with inverse user frequency can be expressed as

$$w(a,i) = \frac{A_2 - B_2}{\sqrt{U_2 V_2}} \tag{4}$$

where

$$A_2 = (n+k)(\sum_j f_j v_{a,j} v_{i,j} + kd^2)$$

$$B_2 = (\sum_j f_j v_{a,j} + kd)(\sum_j f_j v_{i,j} + kd)$$

$$U_2 = \sum_j f_j((n+k)(\sum_j f_j v_{a,j}^2 + kd^2) - (\sum_j f_j v_{a,j} + kd)^2)$$

$$V_2 = \sum_j f_j((n+k)(\sum_j f_j v_{i,j}^2 + kd^2) - (\sum_j f_j v_{i,j} + kd)^2)$$

The sum in A_2 can be rewritten as

$$\sum_j f_j v_{a,j} v_{i,j} = \sum_m f_m v_{a,m} v_{i,m} + +d(\sum_s f_s v_{a,s} - \sum_m f_m v_{a,m}) + +d(\sum_t f_t v_{i,t} - \sum_m f_m v_{i,m}) \quad (5)$$

The remaining sums to complete equation 4 are symmetrical to $\sum_j f_j v_{a,j} = \sum_s f_s v_{a,s} + d(\sum_t f_t - \sum_m f_m)$. Again, we require the sums over t to be kept in static arrays and accumulate the sums over m. The required arrays should contain at index i the values of $\sum_t f_t$, $\sum_t f_t v_{i,t}$, $\sum_t f_t v_{i,t}^2$ and $|v_i|$. Five accumulators are needed, where four are for the sums over m ($\sum_m f_m$, $\sum_m f_m v_{a,m} v_{i,m}$, $\sum_m f_m v_{a,m}$, $\sum_m f_m v_{i,m}$). The number of intersecting titles $|v_a \cap v_i|$ is also required, to calculate $n = |v_a \cup v_i|$.

3.5 Early Termination Heuristics

As we discussed in Section 3, user profiles can grow quite large, especially in the case of implicit voting. If there are ways that would allow us to only use parts of a user profile for prediction, it would further speed up execution time.

Several heuristic stop conditions for text retrieval have been devised [15]. Some of these take advantage of the properties of the similarity function. For example, if the document weights are normalized to unit length, then it is possible to bound the accumulator weights of the cosine function [4]. Other heuristics place stop conditions on the number of traversed inverted lists or, as in our case, stop conditions on the number of users that are retrieved during the scanning of the inverted lists.

Two strategies for this are well known: Quit and Continue [15]. In both methods, the query is sorted by decreasing weight and lists are then processed in this order until the stop condition is met. When the stop condition is reached, only those accumulators that are non-zero are considered. In the Quit strategy, no more lists are processed after this point and the accumulators are used as is. The other strategy is to continue processing lists but only to update those accumulators that are already non-zero. Thus, Continue will always calculate the total weight for users that have reached into non-zero accumulators, whereas Quit may not.

We have implemented both Quit and Continue for the four algorithms described in the previous sections. The titles were weighted according to inverse user frequency.

4. FILE ORGANIZATION

We chose a Prefix B^+-tree [5, 1] for storing our inverted index. The tree is divided into two separate files: one to store the index as minimal key separators (the index file) and one file to store the key/value pairs sorted (the value file). The key consists of a title id with the value containing either an inverted list or a pointer to a reference file that contains large inverted lists (lists larger than 256 bytes in size). The reference file was divided into 512 byte blocks and for each inverted list a pointer list was kept for tracking which blocks that list occupied.

4.1 Compression

To construct the index and the inverted lists, we used sort-based inversion [15]. The lists of run-lengths of user ids together with the vote were then compressed for each title, and stored in the reference file.

Four different compression algorithms were tried: Golomb, Elias delta, Elias gamma and variable byte coding. All these four methods are well described in the information retrieval literature [14, 15], so they will not be re-stated here. For the Golomb, Elias delta and Elias gamma codings, the vote was stored as a binary number of three bits. For variable byte coding, one byte was used.

We compressed the inverted lists for the first 60000 users that had voted for at least two titles, a total of 2805901 votes. The average number of bytes per pointer (user id, vote pair) was close to one on Golomb, Delta and Gamma coding (1.04, 1.10 and 1.11). Using variable byte coding the data was compressed to 2.05 bytes per pointer. The block file utilization was 93.7%, 93.5%, 93.2% and 96.2% respectively.

When running the experiments described in Section 5, we selected the simplest compression method, variable byte coding, since we wanted to see whether it was possible to use less complicated compression algorithms and still gain in performance by using inverted search.

4.2 Updating the Inverted Index

A collaborative filtering system will not serve its purpose if it is difficult to update it with new votes and users. In a memory-based model this is one of the greatest advantages over model-based approaches. How will the inverted file structure handle updates? The problem that needs to be solved is how to update the inverted lists.

There are two ways of handling updates, either incrementally or batch. If the index needs to be updated whenever new votes arrive, the inverted lists should be represented without the need of decompression in order to insert or delete votes. This approach has the drawback in that the list references will take up a larger amount of space. For batch updating changes would first be stored in a secondary index (i.e. in a stop-press file) and then, at some point in time, merged with the primary index.

The static arrays of weights must also be updated, and in most cases the weight depends only on local properties of the profile. It is more problematic to update the static arrays in default voting with inverse user frequency, since those values depend on global properties. If a frequency is changed for a title, all weights must be updated to reflect this change. The simplest solution is to search the inverted list for that title, and for each user in the list subtract the old value from its weight and add the new value.

5. EXPERIMENTS

To evaluate our hypothesis, we conducted a set of experiments. We measure the elapsed time to perform neighbourhood search and predictive accuracy.

We compare the inverted algorithms against in-memory vector searching. The user profiles are implemented as linked list, i.e. sparse vectors. Each object in the profile contains the title id and the vote, and each user profile is sorted on ascending title id. The different correlation algorithms were implemented as list intersection (sections 3.1 and 3.2) or list union (sections 3.3 and 3.4). The mean value was pre-computed for each profile.

5.1 Data Set and Experimental Setting

The largest available public dataset, EachMovie, was used for testing our algorithms. This set was also used in [3]. The dataset contains roughly 2.8 million explicit votes (0...5) for 61265 users on 1628 different movies. The experimental setting was then as follows:

- We cleaned the data so that if a user had duplicate votes for a title, we used the most recent.
- Users that had voted for less than 2 titles were removed, leaving a total of 60087 unique users.
- We evaluated the algorithms on the *AllBut1* protocol, meaning that for each user we held out a single vote that should be predicted on the basis of all the other votes in the profile.
- We selected the size of the training set to 55000 users and the test set to the remaining 5067 users.
- For each experiment, we ran 4 different implementations on the same data: inverted search, inverted search using Quit, inverted search using Continue and pure in-memory vector search, totalling 16 runs for an experiment. Each experiment was then performed 10 times.
- We limited the neighbourhood size to no more than 50, which has been found to be of reasonable size for movie data [6]. For Quit and Continue we set the threshold at 10000 users.

5.2 Metrics

To measure time we used two different metrics. The time for individual neighbourhood formations were plotted against the number of titles in the profile. The reason for this being that with larger profiles a neighbourhood takes longer time to calculate. In the case where there were many profiles of the same size, we used the mean time of profiles of that size. We compared the in-memory vector search with the inverse model using the basic Pearson correlation. Both these algorithms have an equal set of pre-calculated values: the inverse algorithm does not gain anything by performing pre-calculations.

We also measured mean neighbourhood formation time: how long on average the algorithm takes to form a neighbourhood.

For predictive accuracy, we use mean absolute error (MAE) for measuring single predictions. MAE calculates the absolute difference between the prediction and the actual vote, averaged over all predictions.

Table 1: Mean neighbourhood formation time

	CORR	IUF	DEF	DEFIUF
Algorithm				
VEC	664	727	1245	1420
INV	206	260	256	293
QUIT	54	52	55	63
CONT	256	308	251	271

For evaluating the ranked list we use the rank score (RS) measure developed in [3], where we used a half-life of 5. RS estimates the expected utility of a ranked list, which is taken to be the utility of a title times the probability that the user will view it. The utility of a title is in this case the difference between the vote and the default vote, and the probability than a user will view a title is an exponentially decreasing function of the position in the list.

6. RESULTS

In this section we describe the main results of applying inverted file search to collaborative filtering. We measure neighbourhood formation time in section 6.1 and predictive accuracy in section 6.2.

In Tables 1 through 3, the rows labelled INV and VEC give the results for the algorithm run on inverted search and in-memory vector search. In terms of accuracy, these two should produce the same result. The QUIT and CONT rows are the results of applying the early termination heuristics. The correlation algorithms are labelled CORR (Correlation), IUF (Inverse User Frequency), DEF (Default voting) and DEFIUF (Default voting with IUF).

6.1 Neighbourhood Formation Time

The mean time to compute neighbourhoods is shown in Table 1. The Quit method is the fastest, since only a few inverted lists are examined. The Continue method is sometimes a little slower than normal inverted search. We implemented the accumulators for Quit and Continue as dynamic structures (hash tables) and when the stop criterion is as high as 10000 users, this structure has less of an advantage over arrays.

Timing results for inverted search and vector search for the Pearson correlation for one of the runs are shown in Figure 1 and Figure 2. The x axis shows the size of the user profile and the y axis the average number of milliseconds to compute a neighbourhood for that profile size.

The improvement in mean neighbourhood formation time by using inverted search is very encouraging. We see not only that inverted search is much faster on neighbourhood formation when given small profiles (up to a few hundred titles), but also for the very largest.

In general, inverted search is many times faster than in-memory vector search, even when using such a simple compression algorithm as variable byte coding. Furthermore, all data in the inverted structure resides on disk. By caching parts of the index and the inverted lists, it is of course possible to further improve the neighbourhood formation time.

6.2 Predictive Accuracy

The mean absolute error and rank score for the *AllBut1* protocol is listed in Table 2 and Table 3.

The Quit method did not always find neighbours to all

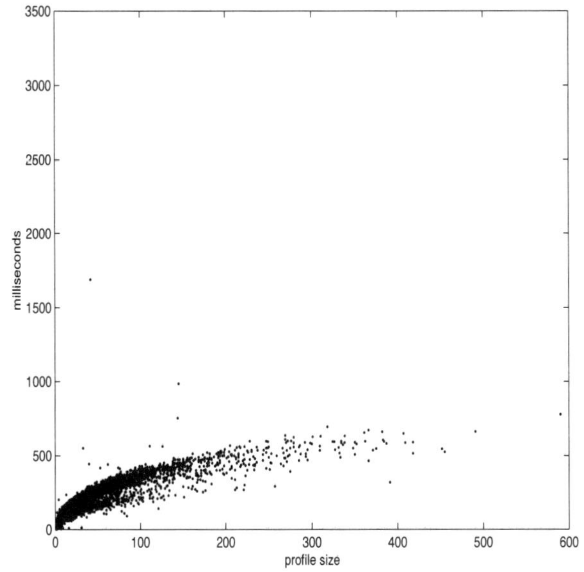

Figure 1: Inverted search time

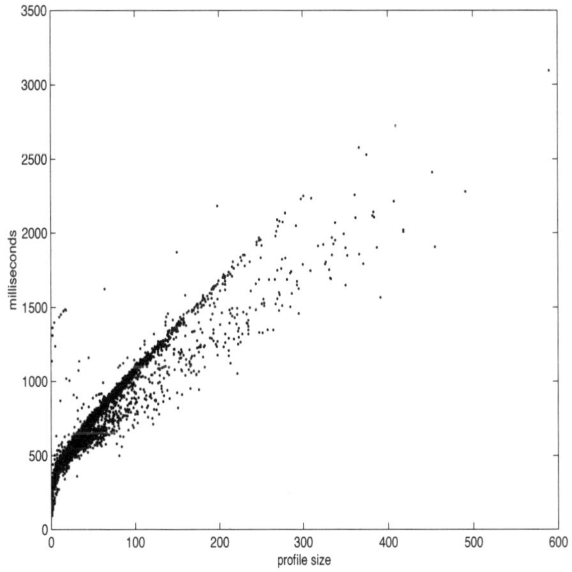

Figure 2: Vector search time

Table 2: Prediction results (MAE)

	CORR	IUF	DEF	DEFIUF
Algorithm				
VEC	1.08	1.07	1.03	1.05
INV	1.08	1.06	1.03	1.05
QUIT	1.03	1.02	1.04	1.03
CONT	1.06	1.05	1.00	1.03

Table 3: Prediction results (RS)

	CORR	IUF	DEF	DEFIUF
Algorithm				
VEC	7.37	13.13	24.42	18.04
INV	7.17	13.26	24.43	18.03
QUIT	17.94	16.37	21.61	18.14
CONT	10.65	11.40	27.50	20.78

users in the test set. On the CORR, IUF, DEF and DEFIUF it calculated neighbourhoods to 99%, 75%, 97% and 100% of the users, respectively. By contrast, the Continue strategy did find the same number of users as inverted search and vector, so the results among these variants are truly comparable.

The first interesting result is that the Continue strategy is the top performer in terms of rank score. Since we sorted the user profiles in descending weight order, this means that the shorter inverted lists (titles that have fewer votes) have high discriminating power, and that titles with a large number of votes actually corrupt the ranking.

We noted that Continue did not necessarily find exactly K neighbours, so another conclusion that we can draw is that this number should not be fixed, but dependent on which votes are in the user profile.

The second result is that the Quit method performs well on the users for which it could find correlations. We noted that in many cases only one inverted list was used by Quit. After all, if the size of the first list is greater than 10000, no more lists will be traversed. Furthermore, since Quit does not compute the true correlation (the accumulator sums are not complete), the effect of the pre-calculated values in the static arrays has yet to be analyzed. By varying the number of accumulators in Quit, and setting another threshold also on the number of inverted lists to traverse, we can find whether the method is useful.

In terms of mean absolute error, there is no large difference between any of the methods. Continue is still the top performer, and performs equally well or better than normal inverted search. Quit performs well compared to not using termination heuristics at all. This means that if we are interested in single predictions, we could do well by only taking into account a few titles from the profile.

We found that default voting was the most effective correlation method, both in terms of mean absolute error and rank score. This is a little surprising, since the top performer in a previous study [3] was default voting with inverse user frequency. One explanation for this could be that our training set was much larger than the one used in the previous study.

7. CONCLUSIONS

Collaborative filtering is a relatively new technique for information filtering. It has been successfully used in domains where the information content is not easily parsable and traditional information filtering techniques are difficult to apply. We believe that it is useful as a complement to traditional content based filtering techniques.

There are however a number of problems with collaborative filtering that needs to be resolved before it is truly useful. One important problem is that of scalability, i.e. how to manage a large number of users and titles. Our way of attacking this problem is to cast the collaborative filtering problem into an information retrieval setting.

Our hypothesis was that by the use of inverted files, we could speed up execution time and perhaps even improve the predictive performance with early termination heuristics.

In order to test this hypothesis, we selected four well-known algorithms for collaborative filtering and expressed these in a form suitable for inverted retrieval. We selected a large test set for evaluation, and found some interesting results:

- The inverted file search algorithms were generally many times faster than in-memory search, even when having an equal amount of pre-calculated values.
- The Continue termination heuristic was the top performing algorithm in terms of rank score, and about as fast as normal inverted search.
- The Quit termination heuristic was very fast compared to the other methods tested, and yielded good predictions as well. However, in one case the method did not find neighbours to the same number of users as the other methods, and has to be further investigated.

Research is needed on strategies for updating the inverted files, and we hope that this paper will lead to further discussions on the subject of using inverted files for collaborative filtering.

8. ACKNOWLEDGEMENTS

The authors would like to thank Jussi Karlgren, Preben Hansen and the anonymous reviewers for useful comments on the paper.

9. REFERENCES

[1] R. Bayer and K. Unterauer. Prefix B-trees. *ACM Trans. on Database Systems*, 2(1):11–26, March 1977.

[2] D. Billsus and M. J. Pazzani. Learning collaborative information filters. In *Proceedings of the Fifteenth International Conference on Machine Learning*, pages 46–54. Morgan Kaufmann, 1998.

[3] J. S. Breese, D. Heckerman, and C. Kadie. Empirical analysis of predictive algorithms for collaborative filtering. In *Proceedings of the Fourteenth Conference on Uncertainty in Artificial Intelligence*, Madison, WI, July 1998. Morgan Kaufman Publisher.

[4] C. Buckley and A. F. Lewit. Optimization of inverted vector searches. In *Proceedings of the eight annual international ACM SIGIR conference on Research and development in information retrieval*, 1985.

[5] M. J. Folk, B. Zoellick, and G. Riccardi. *File Structures: An Object-Oriented Approach with C++*. Addison-Wesley, 3rd edition, 1998.

[6] J. L. Herlocker, J. A. Konstan, A. Borchers, and J. Riedl. An algorithmic framework for performing collaborative filtering. In *Proceedings of the 22nd annual international ACM SIGIR conference on Research and development in information retrieval*, 1999.

[7] J. Karlgren. Stylistic experiments in information retrieval. In T. Strzalkowski, editor, *Natural Language Information Retrieval*. Kluwer, Dordrecht, 1999.

[8] J. A. Konstan, B. N. Miller, D. Maltz, J. L. Herlocker, L. R. Gordon, and J. Riedl. Grouplens: Applying collaborative filtering to usenet news. *Communications of the ACM*, 40(3):77–87, 1997.

[9] W. S. Lee. Collaborative learning and recommender systems. In *Proceedings of the Eighteenth International Conference on Machine Learning*. Morgan Kaufmann, 2001.

[10] G. Salton and M. McGill. *Introduction to Modern Information Retrieval*. McGraw-Hill, 1983.

[11] B. M. Sarwar, G. Karypis, J. A. Konstan, and J. Riedl. Application of dimensionality reduction in recommender system – a case study. In *ACM WebKDD 2000 Web Mining for E-Commerce Workshop*, 2000.

[12] B. M. Sarwar, J. A. Konstan, A. Borchers, J. L. Herlocker, B. N. Miller, and J. Riedl. Using filtering agents to improve prediction quality in the grouplens research collaborative filtering system. In *Proceedings of the 1998 Conference on Computer Supported Cooperative Work*, Nov 1998.

[13] U. Shardanand and P. Maes. Social information filtering: Algorithms for automating "word of mouth". In *Proceedings of ACM CHI'95 Conference on Human Factors in Computing Systems*, volume 1, 1995.

[14] H. E. Williams and J. Zobel. Compressing integers for fast file access. *The Computer Journal*, 42(3):193–201, 1999.

[15] I. H. Witten, A. Moffat, and T. C. Bell. *Managing Gigabytes: Compressing and Indexing Documents and Images*. Morgan Kaufmann Publishing, 2nd edition, 1999.

Methods and Metrics for Cold-Start Recommendations

Andrew I. Schein, Alexandrin Popescul, and Lyle H. Ungar

University of Pennsylvania
Dept. of Computer Science
200 South 33rd St.
Philadelphia, PA 19104-6389 U.S.A.

{ais,popescul,ungar}@gradient.cis.upenn.edu

David M. Pennock

NEC Research Institute
4 Independence Way
Princeton, NJ 08540
USA

dpennock@research.nj.nec.com

ABSTRACT

We have developed a method for recommending items that combines content and collaborative data under a single probabilistic framework. We benchmark our algorithm against a naïve Bayes classifier on the *cold-start* problem, where we wish to recommend items that no one in the community has yet rated. We systematically explore three testing methodologies using a publicly available data set, and explain how these methods apply to specific real-world applications. We advocate heuristic recommenders when benchmarking to give competent baseline performance. We introduce a new performance metric, the CROC curve, and demonstrate empirically that the various components of our testing strategy combine to obtain deeper understanding of the performance characteristics of recommender systems. Though the emphasis of our testing is on *cold-start* recommending, our methods for recommending and evaluation are general.

Categories and Subject Descriptors

H.1.m [**Information Systems**]: Models and Principals—*Miscellaneous*; I.2.6 [**Computing Methodologies**]: Artificial Intelligence—*Learning*; G.3 [**Mathematics of Computing**]: Probability And Statistics—*Contingency table analysis*

General Terms

Algorithms, Experimentation, Performance

Keywords

Recommender systems, collaborative filtering, content-based filtering, information retrieval, graphical models, performance evaluation

1. INTRODUCTION

Recommender systems suggest items of interest to users based on their explicit and implicit preferences, the preferences of other users, and user and item attributes. For example, a movie recommender might combine explicit ratings data (e.g., Bob rates *Shrek* a 7 out of 10), implicit data (e.g., Mary purchased *The Natural*), user demographic information (e.g., Mary is female), and movie content information (e.g., *Scream* is marketed as a horror movie) to make recommendations to specific users.

Pure *collaborative filtering* methods [3, 12, 15, 23, 30] base their recommendations on community preferences (e.g., user ratings and purchase histories), ignoring user and item attributes (e.g., demographics and product descriptions). On the other hand, pure *content-based filtering* or *information filtering* methods [17, 24] typically match query words or other user data with item attribute information, ignoring data from other users. Several hybrid algorithms combine both techniques [1, 4, 6, 8, 21, 29]. Though "content" usually refers to descriptive words associated with an item, we use the term more generally to refer to any form of item attribute information including, for example, the list of actors in a movie.

One difficult, though common, problem for a recommender system is the *cold-start* problem, where recommendations are required for items that no one (in our data set) has yet rated.[1] Pure collaborative filtering cannot help in a cold-start setting, since no user preference information is available to form any basis for recommendations. However, content information can help bridge the gap from existing items to new items, by inferring similarities among them. Thus we can make recommendations for new items that appear similar to other recommended items. In this paper, we evaluate the performance of two machine learning algorithms on cold start prediction. We present our own probabilistic model that combines content and collaborative information

[1]The phrase *cold start* has also been used to describe the situation when almost nothing is known about customer preferences [9] (e.g., a start-up company has no little or no purchase history). The problem of making recommendations for new users can also be thought of as a cold-start problem. We concentrate on the new-item problem, although the new-user problem is symmetric when we have access to user attribute (e.g., demographic) data. The new-user problem without attribute data essentially falls within the framework of pure information filtering or information retrieval [24].

by using expectation maximization (EM) learning to fit the model to the data. We perform benchmarking on movie ratings data and compare against a naïve Bayes method that has also been proposed for this task [16].

Some key questions in evaluating recommender systems on testbed data are: what to predict, how to grade performance and what baseline to compare with. We identify three useful components to predict on our data set, and show where past work has focussed. In deciding what metric to use in evaluating performance, we have borrowed heavily from the literature in addition to developing our own tool: the CROC curve. For baseline measures of performance we advocate the use of heuristic recommenders: algorithms that are trivial to implement yet give performance that is well above random. We find that heuristic recommenders do surprisingly well: in some cases outperforming more sophisticated methods. Our testing goal is to uncover the most informative characterization of performance for our method and the naïve Bayes algorithm.

2. BACKGROUND AND RELATED WORK

Early recommender systems were pure collaborative filters that computed pairwise similarities among users and recommended items according to a similarity-weighted average [22, 30]. Breese et al. [3] refer to this class of algorithms as *memory-based* algorithms. Subsequent authors employed a variety of techniques for collaborative filtering, including hard-clustering users into classes [3], simultaneously hard-clustering users and items [31], soft-clustering users and items [14, 21], singular value decomposition [26], inferring item-item similarities [27], probabilistic modeling [3, 6, 10, 20, 21, 29], machine learning [1, 2, 18], and list-ranking [5, 7, 19]. More recently, authors have turned toward designing hybrid recommender systems that combine both collaborative and content information in various ways [1, 4, 6, 8, 21, 29]. To date, most comparisons among algorithms have been empirical or qualitative in nature [11, 25], though some worst-case performance bounds have been derived [7, 18], some general principles advocated [7], and some fundamental limitations explicated [19]. Techniques suggested in evaluating recommender system performance include mean average error, receiver operator characteristic (ROC) curves, ranked list metrics [3, 11] and variants of precision/recall statistics [25].

In this work we extend the hybrid recommender system of Popescul et al. [21] to average content data in a model based fashion. In evaluating our method we introduce novel testing strategies and metrics that can discover fine-grain characterization of performance leading to actionable conclusions.

3. THE TWO-WAY ASPECT MODEL

In predicting an association between person p and movie m, we employ a latent class variable framework called the aspect model that has been designed for contingency table smoothing [13]. Figure 1 (a) shows a graphical model description of the aspect model for a person/movie contingency table and Table 1 explains our notation used in the graphical model as well as in other descriptions of the movie recommendation task.

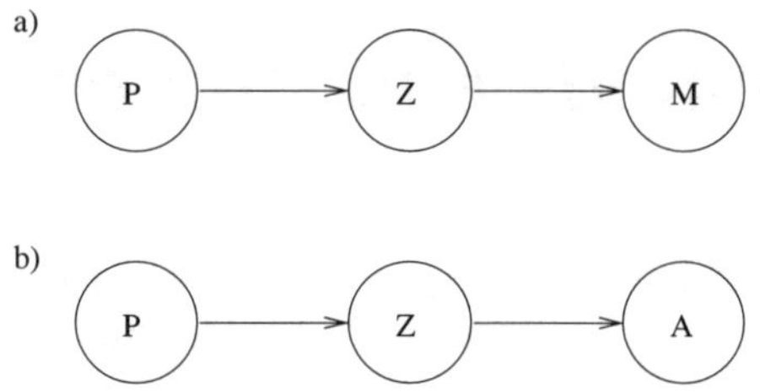

Figure 1: Graphical model of the person/movie aspect model (a) and the person/actor aspect model (b). These graphs can be interpreted precisely as belief networks.

Random Variable	Object	Interpretation
P	p	person
M	m	movie
A	a	actor
Z	z	latent class

Table 1: Notation used in our model descriptions.

3.1 Pure Collaborative Filtering Model

The aspect model of Figure 1 (a) encodes a probability distribution over each person/movie pair. Observations consist of tuples (p, m) recording that person p has seen/rated movie m. We store observations in a *count matrix* or *contingency table* with rows ranging over people and columns ranging over movies (or *vice versa*). Often our data may include multiple observations that are identical (e.g., Lyle saw *Memento* twice). With each observation we increment by one the count of the appropriate contingency table *cell* (or matrix entry). A naïve probability estimate for each cell is simply the observed frequency of events in that cell. However, notice that using this method of assigning probabilities, an empty cell implies that there is zero probability of the corresponding person seeing the corresponding movie, clearly an unrealistic inference.

An *aspect model* hypothesizes the existence of a hidden or *latent* cause z (e.g., an affinity for a particular style of movies) that motivates person p to watch movie m. According to the generative model semantics, person p chooses a latent class z, which in turn determines the movie m watched. The choice of movie m is assumed independent of p given knowledge of z. Since z is hidden, we sum over possible choices to define the distribution over (p, m):

$$\mathsf{P}(p, m) = \sum_z \mathsf{P}(p)\mathsf{P}(z|p)\mathsf{P}(m|z). \quad (1)$$

Parameters $\mathsf{P}(z|p)$ and $\mathsf{P}(m|z)$ correspond to the processes of p stochastically choosing a latent class z, and z stochastically choosing m. The $\mathsf{P}(p, m)$ values can be thought of as smoothed estimates of the probability distribution of the contingency table. The latent variables perform the smoothing in a manner that maximizes the model likelihood (by keeping estimates of $\mathsf{P}(p, m)$ close to the empirical distribution). The model also creates smoothed estimates for the values $\mathsf{P}(p)$ and $\mathsf{P}(m)$, both taking their interpretations from contingency table analysis. The parameters are calculated using the tempered EM algorithm as described in [13].

We choose the number of latent classes using performance on a partition of training data as the criterion. Recommendations to person p are made using: $\mathsf{P}(m|p) \propto \mathsf{P}(p,m)$. Our own source code for fitting the two way aspect model is available online [28]. We have found training to take only a few minutes using a Pentium II computer with 512 mb of RAM. Once trained, the method can generate a user's recommendations in a fraction of a second.

3.2 Adding Content Information

The recommender system described so far is a pure collaborative filtering algorithm developed by Hofmann and Puzicha [14]. We will not use the pure collaborative filtering aspect model since we wish to experiment on the cold start problem. The person/actor aspect model of Figure 1 (b) combines collaborative with content data in one model:

$$\mathsf{P}(p,a) = \sum_z \mathsf{P}(p)\mathsf{P}(z|p)\mathsf{P}(a|z). \qquad (2)$$

In using this model, we hope that casts of actors can act as surrogates for movies. We recommend movies to a user based on how similar the cast is to movies the user has already rated. We generate a dataset from the collaborative filtering model by taking the collaborative observations (p,m) and creating a set of observations (p,a_i) for each actor i in movie m. These newly formed observations are no-longer independent, breaking an assumption of the aspect model. We have found in our own experiments that the person/actor aspect model has strengths to offset potential disadvantages of broken independence assumptions (for an example, see [21]).

3.3 Folding In

Notice that the person/actor aspect model does not have a movie object in the event space. In order to recommend a movie, we must create a new movie object out of the set of actors that appear in that movie. This pseudo-movie is then placed in the latent space based on the content information. We use Hofmann's [13] *folding-in* algorithm (originally used to fold term-queries into a document-word aspect model). For example, suppose we have fit a person/actor model and want to fold-in a new movie. We create a new set of parameters $\mathsf{P}(z|m)$ and use the actors in the movie $\{(a,m)\}$ as evidence for placing the movie in latent space in a manner that maximizes the likelihood of the movie. All of the original parameters from (2) are held constant during the process. The exact EM algorithm operates as follows:

E-Step:

$$\mathsf{P}(z|a,m) \propto \mathsf{P}(a|z)\mathsf{P}(z|m)$$

M-Step:

$$\mathsf{P}(z|m) \propto \sum_a n(a,m)\mathsf{P}(z|a,m)$$

Recommendations are made using:

$$\mathsf{P}(p|m) = \sum_z \mathsf{P}(p|z)\mathsf{P}(z|m)$$

If we desire an estimated value of $\mathsf{P}(p,m)$, we will first need to estimate $\mathsf{P}(m)$. We are currently experimenting with Bayesian weighting of movie-queries that computes an average of $\mathsf{P}(a)$ for the various actors in the movie.

4. NAIVE BAYES RECOMMENDER

As an alternative to the aspect model, we use the bag-of-words naïve Bayes text classifier developed in [17] applied to person/actor data. For each person a separate naïve Bayes classifier is trained so that no collaborative information is used. Hence, this is a pure content-based method capable of cold-start recommendation. The model is trained using Laplace smoothing.

Ratings prediction is computed with the probability function:

$$\mathsf{P}(c_j|M) = \frac{\mathsf{P}(c_j)}{\mathsf{P}(M)} \prod_{i=1}^{|M|} \mathsf{P}(a_i|c_j) \qquad (3)$$

where the class c_j is a rating. Embedded in formula (3) is the belief that all movies in the data set are rated. In other words, the naïve Bayes generative model does not predict that an item will or won't be rated. We have tried to be consistent with the experiments of Melville et al. [16] who applied this classifier to a movie dataset similar to our own; we duplicate some of their testing strategies while adding our own.

5. TESTING METHODOLOGY

Our data primarily comes from the MovieLens data set assembled by the GroupLens project [11] consisting of actual ratings from a group of users. The core of this data set is a list of movie ratings grouped by person. Each person rates at least twenty movies. All MovieLens observations consist of a rating between 1 and 5 inclusive. In order to obtain actor and director information, we downloaded relevant pages from the Internet Movie Database (http://www.imdb.com). We speed up model fitting by considering only actors billed in the top ten and eliminating any actors who appear in only one movie.

In our experiments we randomly split the movies into a training set and a test set. In this manner we create a set of movies that have no observations in the training set. We test only using the 331 movies in the test set (out of 1682 total movies in the data set). There are 943 people we make recommendations for, with an average of 85 observations per person in the entire training set. There are 19,192 observed events for the test set movies out of a possible total of 312,133. 10,640 of the test set observations have rating of 4 or higher. All results reported below come from the same test set in order to facilitate comparison.

In testing various recommender systems on a static data set such as the MovieLens data, it is important to place test results in their proper context for those who may want to implement such systems. We have identified three modes of testing on our data set that correspond to different real-world applications. Statements about the performance of a recommender system should be based on what sort of recommendation task is simulated in testing. The differences in our testing modes are linked to the role of rating versus purchase data in the recommendation problem. We may wish to predict that a customer will purchase an item or that a customer will both purchase and like an item. A final task is to impute (guess) a customer's rating on an item that was purchased. These testing modes are elaborated below.

1. Implicit Rating Prediction

   Implicit rating prediction refers to prediction of data

such as purchase history; a purchase is not necessarily an indication of satisfaction, but a purchase is an indication of some implicit need or desire for an item. For MovieLens data we predict that a person has rated a movie, a task that is analogous to predicting a customer purchase. When evaluating performance, we do not consider the rating itself or events that occur in the training set (for domains where we don't recommend what a user already owns or has rated). implicit rating prediction is most appropriate for domains where explicit rating information is not available and we are satisfied to recommend products that the user is likely to purchase on their own. Past implicit evaluation work includes [21, 29]. We will refer to MovieLens observations stripped of a rating component as implicit rating data throughout this paper.

2. Rating Prediction

   In rating prediction we wish to predict both implicit rating and rating components of an observation simultaneously. In our MovieLens benchmarking we classify each person/movie pair that doesn't occur in the training observations into two groups:

   a) p_i rated $m_j \geq 4$.
   b) p_i did not rate $m_j \geq 4$.

   Condition b could imply that person i did not rate movie j at all.

3. Rating Imputation

   Rating imputation is prediction of ratings for items where we have implicit rating observations. In concrete terms, we ask "given that a person has seen movie x, how likely are they to rate it ≥ 4?" Our prior knowledge that the person has seen x means we have a implicit rating observation to this effect. Our goal is to guess the best rating. We implement rating imputation testing by taking held out observations from the MovieLens data and predicting ratings on this set.

   In real-world applications we may have data sets where implicit rating observations are available in large quantities, but the rating component is missing at random. Rating imputation measures success at filling in the missing values. Rating imputation has been used previously in [3, 11, 16] to evaluate recommender system performance.

6. EVALUATION METRICS

Before deploying an actual recommender system we would need to decide how often to recommend and to whom. For instance, in one application we may need to recommend k products to each customer in a database, where k is a number we may choose according to a desired false-positive rate. In other applications we may be permitted to recommend a greater number of products to customers who we understand better. In this section, we identify metrics that measure success in either mode of recommending and show in the results section how using both metrics on the same data uncovers fine grain recommender system characteristics.

Herlocker et al. [11] suggest using receiver operator characteristic (ROC) curves as one measure to evaluate recommender systems. We call the method of Herlocker et al. a global ROC (GROC) curve in order to distinguish it from the customer ROC (CROC) variation presented shortly. A ROC curve is a curve showing hit/miss rates for different classification thresholds. Currently, machine learning researchers use ROC curves to evaluate binary classification algorithms. We will employ ROC curves in this context (e.g., "our algorithm says a person *will* have rated a movie" is a predicted *positive* outcome). The area under a ROC curve is a performance measure with perfect performance indicated by area of one and random guessing indicated by area 0.5. ROC curves are nearly equivalent to precision/recall curves in the information retrieval community and lift curves of the marketing literature. The terms precision and recall are analogous to specificity and sensitivity respectively, where the latter terms are found on ROC curves. Sensitivity (or hit rate) is equal to the percentage of all positive values found above some threshold. 1 - Specificity (or miss rate) is equal to the fraction of all negative values found above some threshold. Miss rate and hit rate are plotted on the x and y axis respectively. Varying the threshold generates a series of points forming a *curve*. We will not actually connect the points of our plots to form the curve in order to make the figures more readable.

We use a global ROC (GROC) curve to measure performance when we are allowed to recommend more often to some users than others. GROC curves are constructed in the following manner:

1. Order the predictions $\textbf{pred}(p_i, m_j)$ in a list by magnitude, imposing an ordering: $(p, m)_k$.
2. Pick n, calculate hit/miss rates caused by predicting the top n $(p, m)_k$ by magnitude, and plot the point.

By selecting different n (e.g. incrementing n by a fixed amount) we draw a curve on the graph.

Customer ROC (CROC) curves measure performance of a recommender system when we are constrained to recommend the same number of items to each user. Unlike the GROC curve, the CROC curve is not a special case of the ROC curve, though it is constructed in an analogous manner:

1. For each person p_i, order the predictions $\textbf{pred}(p_i, m_j)$ in a list by magnitude imposing an ordering: $(m)_k$.
2. Pick n, calculate global hit/miss rates caused by recommending the top predicted n movies to each person and plot the point.

We vary n as in the GROC case.

In a GROC curve, the perfect recommender will generate a curve with area one, but for the CROC curve this is not the case. To see why, imagine using an omniscient recommender on a data set with three people: person a sees four movies, person b sees two movies, and person c sees six movies. When we recommend four movies to each person, we end up with two false-positives from person b, lowering the area of the curve. However, for any particular data set, we can plot the curve and calculate the area of the omniscient recommender in order to facilitate comparison.

Whether using GROC or CROC curves it is important to focus attention on the left hand side of the graph. This is the portion of the graph focusing on a low false positive rate. In most applications of recommender systems it is desirable to obtain the best possible performance in the low false positive region of the curve.

7. RESULTS

We test the person/actor aspect model against the naïve Bayes method of [17]. We conduct implicit rating and rating imputation since these two methods are most commonly used to evaluate the two recommender systems in the previous literature [16, 29]. Our preliminary experiments with naïve Bayes confirmed earlier observations [16] that naïve Bayes is sensitive to sparsity below 40 rated movies on this type of data (results not shown). In order to better duplicate the prior work in rating imputation [16] as well as present naïve Bayes in the best possible light, we perform rating imputation only for users who have rated 40 or more movies in the training set. We train the models separately according to precedent: the aspect model is trained on implicit rating data, while the naïve Bayes method is trained on the corresponding ratings data.

Implicit in the GROC and CROC curve is the performance of a random recommender: a 45 degree line with area 0.5 underneath. We feel that in many applications a superior baseline can be developed. For instance, we can recommend first to users that on average rate movies higher in order to obtain better-than-random rating imputation GROC performance. We call such recommendation algorithms *heuristic recommenders* since they use simple tricks to obtain above-random performance. Where possible we propose and include heuristic recommenders in the analysis.

7.1 Implicit Rating Testing

Figure 2 shows GROC and CROC plots comparing the person/actor aspect model, the naïve Bayes recommender and (for the GROC case) a heuristic recommender on the implicit rating prediction task. The heuristic recommender for the GROC plot is created by substituting the total number of movies seen by person i for the recommender output for pair: (p_i, m_j). In other words we list users by their relative activity in rating on the MovieLens site and recommend *all* movies to these users in that order. Note that the heuristic recommender performs nearly as well as the aspect model in the region of interest (the far left-hand side of the graph).

Figure 2 (b) shows CROC plots comparing the person/actor aspect and naïve Bayes methods on the implicit rating prediction task without a heuristic recommender. There is no obvious heuristic recommender to use here other than random recommendation due to the cold-start problem. Note that both machine learning methods perform noticeably better than the area 0.5 indicative of random prediction by both CROC and GROC metrics.

7.2 Rating Imputation Testing

Figure 3 shows GROC and CROC plots comparing the person/actor aspect model, the naïve Bayes recommender and (for the GROC case) a heuristic recommender on the rating imputation task. Here we predict that a user rates a movie 4 or higher. This technique of evaluation has been called ROC-4 [25]. The heuristic recommender is created by using the mean rating for each person i as the predicted rating for (p_i, m_j), for all m_j. Surprisingly, the mean rating method outperforms all other methods by GROC standards. As in the implicit rating prediction task, there is no obvious heuristic recommender to deploy in the CROC plot other than the implicit random recommender with area 0.5.

8. DISCUSSION

The aspect model performs better than the naïve Bayes method on the implicit rating prediction task, but the reverse is true on the rating imputation task. This is not surprising since the aspect model is trained solely on implicit rating data, and the naïve Bayes recommender is not designed for implicit rating prediction. Both methods need to be altered in order to optimize performance on the alternative test. Re-designing the aspect model training and test procedure for rating imputation and rating prediction will be a subject of future work. The current experiments test the degree to which implicit rating observations are sufficient for prediction in the rating imputation task by benchmarking the aspect model against naïve Bayes. In addition we test whether rating classification recommenders as embodied by the naïve Bayes method can predict implicit rating observations as well as our proposed aspect model.

Our empirical evaluation methods point out some interesting subtleties that occur in benchmarking recommender systems. On both GROC plots, some very simple methods are competitive with the more sophisticated aspect model and naïve Bayes methods. In the rating imputation case, the mean rating of a user is the single best predictor for rating imputation according to the GROC criteria. Likewise, the number of movies a person has rated is a very good method on the implicit rating prediction GROC plot. The use of intelligent *heuristic recommenders* like the ones described above are a key ingredient to interpreting the performance of a GROC curve. Past performance results using the MovieLens and similar datasets that employ the GROC curve including [11, 16, 29] should be evaluated with this observation in mind.

A natural question to ask is whether both the GROC and CROC curve are needed in evaluation. One hypothesis is that once a suitable heuristic recommender is chosen, relative performance on a GROC curve graph is sufficient to tell the whole story of recommender system performance characteristics. Our results show that this is not the case; in particular our empirical results demonstrate that GROC and CROC curves can often have no predictive power over each other: e.g., they often give conflicting measures. To see why, compare the relative performance of the user activity recommender and the aspect model recommender on the implicit rating prediction task (Figure 2). On the GROC plot, the two methods have nearly identical characteristics. If GROC and CROC metrics were necessarily correlated, we would expect similar behavior in the CROC graph for the implicit rating prediction task. Note that the CROC graph of the implicit rating prediction task does not include the user activity recommender because this method produces perfectly random performance (area 0.5) by CROC standards. In contrast, the aspect model performance has area 0.64: well above random. The GROC and CROC graphs together point out that the aspect model has nearly identical global (GROC) performance to the heuristic recommender while actually recommending to a more diverse group of people. A similar situation is visible in the rating imputation GROC and CROC plots.

Let's say we are deciding between the heuristic recommender and the aspect model for implicit rating prediction.

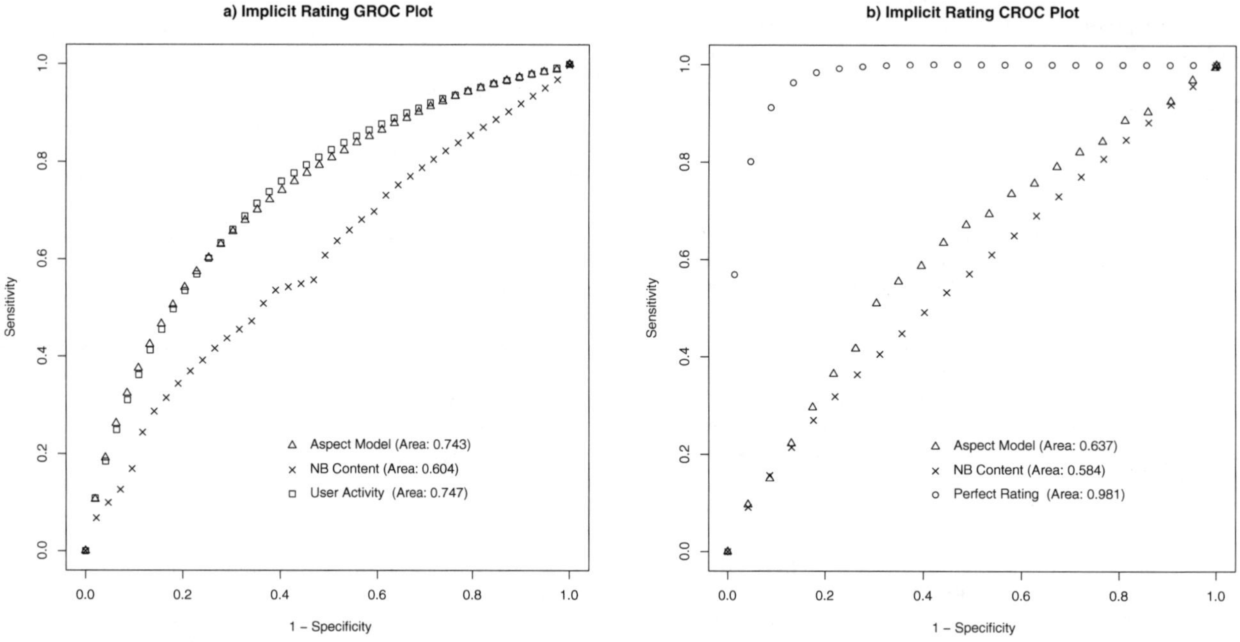

Figure 2: GROC (a) and CROC (b) plots comparing person/actor aspect model, naïve Bayes and a heuristic recommender on the implicit rating prediction task. To generate GROC plot points we increment the number of predictions by 7800. To generate CROC plot points we increment the number of movies predicted for each person by 15.

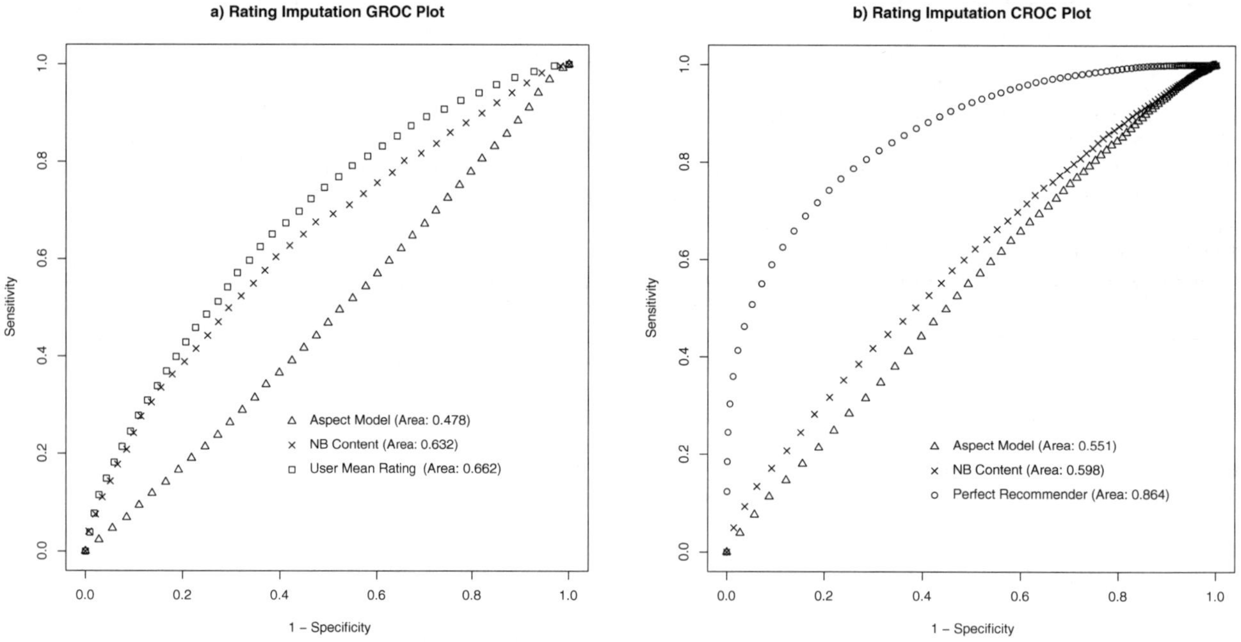

Figure 3: GROC (a) and CROC (b) plots comparing person/actor aspect model, naïve Bayes and a heuristic recommender on the rating imputation task. To generate GROC plot points we increment the number of predictions by 420. To generate CROC plot points we increment the number of movies predicted for each person by 1.

If greater customer coverage is a priority, then we will choose the aspect model based on its CROC plot, even though the two methods perform equivalently on the GROC plot. We will then return to the GROC plot to determine what decision threshold to use based on false positive rate (calculated from miss rate on a GROC plot).

9. CONCLUSIONS

We have proposed the aspect model latent variable method for cold-start recommending. Our aspect model combines both collaborative and content information in model fitting. The folding in algorithm allows us to make predictions for unrated items by using content data: averaging the set of content data (e.g. actors) that associate with an item (e.g. movie). Our method is tested against naïve Bayes and several heuristic recommenders on publicly available movie rating data. We have tested these methods on implicit rating and rating imputation tasks while evaluating performance under two different methods of recommending embodied by GROC and CROC curve metrics.

A surprising outcome of the empirical evaluation is the performance of so-called heuristic recommenders on the GROC curves. These methods are so effective that we feel that all future work using GROC curve plots should include appropriate heuristic predictors in order to give perspective on actual gain in performance caused by using sophisticated machine learning or other techniques. In many cases it is feasible to include heuristic recommenders for CROC curves as well. For instance we could use average rating of a movie in the training set as our rating prediction. However, when operating from a cold start we do not have this sort of information. Fortunately, GROC and CROC curves each have built-in baselines: the random recommender with area 0.5.

The combination of GROC/CROC testing and heuristic recommenders tells us when it makes sense to deploy the aspect model on the cold start task. On the implicit rating prediction task, we recommend the aspect model over the heuristic recommender for applications when it is important to recommend to as many users as possible. If real-world success is embodied exactly by the GROC curve, we feel that the heuristic recommender is up to the job and easiest to implement. On the rating imputation task, we draw the same conclusion regarding the effectiveness of naïve Bayes method over the corresponding heuristic recommender.

Our results demonstrate the value of using both GROC and CROC curves in evaluating recommender system performance. We can show when our aspect model recommender outperforms and underperforms alternatives and link testing performance to real-world problems. GROC and CROC curves each measure performance in a specific real world task. However, in situations where the evaluation goal is to characterize the performance of a recommender system generally, both GROC and CROC curves are needed since they are often conflicting measures of recommender system performance.

10. ACKNOWLEDGMENTS

Andrew Schein was supported by NIH Training Grant in Computational Genomics, T-32-HG00046. Alexandrin Popescul was supported in part by a grant from the NEC Research Institute.

11. REFERENCES

[1] C. Basu, H. Hirsh, and W. Cohen. Recommendation as classification: Using social and content-based information in recommendation. In *Proceedings of the Fifteenth National Conference on Artificial Intelligence*, pages 714–720, 1998.

[2] D. Billsus and M. J. Pazzani. Learning collaborative information filters. In *Proceedings of the Fifteenth International Conference on Machine Learning*, pages 46–54, 1998.

[3] J. S. Breese, D. Heckerman, and C. Kadie. Empirical analysis of predictive algorithms for collaborative filtering. In *Proceedings of the Fourteenth Conference on Uncertainty in Artificial Intelligence*, pages 43–52, 1998.

[4] M. Claypool, A. Gokhale, and T. Miranda. Combining content-based and collaborative filters in an online newspaper. In *Proceedings of the ACM SIGIR Workshop on Recommender Systems—Implementation and Evaluation*, 1999.

[5] W. W. Cohen, R. E. Schapire, and Y. Singer. Learning to order things. *Journal of Artificial Intelligence Research*, 10:243–270, 1999.

[6] M. K. Condliff, D. D. Lewis, D. Madigan, and C. Posse. Bayesian mixed-effect models for recommender systems. In *ACM SIGIR '99 Workshop on Recommender Systems: Algorithms and Evaluation*, 1999.

[7] Y. Freund, R. Iyer, R. E. Schapire, and Y. Singer. An efficient boosting algorithm for combining preferences. In *Proceedings of the Fifteenth International Conference on Machine Learning*, pages 170–178, 1998.

[8] N. Good, J. B. Schafer, J. A. Konstan, A. Borchers, B. M. Sarwar, J. L. Herlocker, and J. Riedl. Combining collaborative filtering with personal agents for better recommendations. In *Proceedings of the Sixteenth National Conference on Artificial Intelligence*, pages 439–446, 1999.

[9] H. Guo. Soap: Live recommendations through social agents. In *Fifth DELOS Workshop on Filtering and Collaborative Filtering, Budapest*, 1997.

[10] D. Heckerman, D. M. Chickering, C. Meek, R. Rounthwaite, and C. Kadie. Dependency networks for collaborative filtering and data visualization. In *Proceedings of the Sixteenth Conference on Uncertainty in Artificial Intelligence*, pages 264–273, 2000.

[11] J. L. Herlocker, J. A. Konstan, A. Borchers, and J. Riedl. An algorithmic framework for performing collaborative filtering. In *Proceedings of the Conference on Research and Development in Information Retrieval*, 1999.

[12] W. Hill, L. Stead, M. Rosenstein, and G. Furnas. Recommending and evaluating choices in a virtual community of use. In *Proceedings of the Conference on Human Factors in Computing Systems*, pages 194–201, 1995.

[13] T. Hofmann. Probabilistic latent semantic indexing. In *22nd Annual International ACM SIGIR Conference on Research and Development in Information Retrieval*, pages 50–57, 1999.

[14] T. Hofmann and J. Puzicha. Latent class models for collaborative filtering. In *Proceedings of the Sixteenth International Joint Conference on Artificial Intelligence*, pages 688–693, 1999.

[15] J. A. Konstan, B. N. Miller, D. Maltz, J. L. Herlocker, L. R. Gordon, and J. Riedl. GroupLens: Applying collaborative filtering to Usenet news. *Communications of the ACM*, 40(3):77–87, 1997.

[16] P. Melville, R. J. Mooney, and R. Nagarajan. Content-boosted collaborative filtering. In *Proceedings of the 2001 SIGIR Workshop on Recommender Systems*, 2001.

[17] R. J. Mooney and L. Roy. Content-based book recommending using learning for text categorization. In *Proceedings of the Fifth ACM Conference on Digital Libraries*, pages 195–204, 2000.

[18] A. Nakamura and N. Abe. Collaborative filtering using weighted majority prediction algorithms. In *Proceedings of the Fifteenth International Conference on Machine Learning*, pages 395–403, 1998.

[19] D. M. Pennock, E. Horvitz, and C. L. Giles. Social choice theory and recommender systems: Analysis of the axiomatic foundations of collaborative filtering. In *Proceedings of the Seventeenth National Conference on Artificial Intelligence*, pages 729–734, 2000.

[20] D. M. Pennock, E. Horvitz, S. Lawrence, and C. L. Giles. Collaborative filtering by personality diagnosis: A hybrid memory- and model-based approach. In *Proceedings of the Sixteenth Conference on Uncertainty in Artificial Intelligence*, pages 473–480, 2000.

[21] A. Popescul, L. H. Ungar, D. M. Pennock, and S. Lawrence. Probabilistic models for unified collaborative and content-based recommendation in sparse-data environments. In *Proceedings of the Seventeenth Conference on Uncertainty in Artificial Intelligence*, 2001.

[22] P. Resnick, N. Iacovou, M. Suchak, P. Bergstrom, and J. Riedl. GroupLens: An open architecture for collaborative filtering of netnews. In *Proceedings of the ACM Conference on Computer Supported Cooperative Work*, pages 175–186, 1994.

[23] P. Resnick and H. R. Varian. Recommender systems. *Communications of the ACM*, 40(3):56–58, 1997.

[24] G. Salton and M. McGill. *Introduction to Modern Information Retrieval.* McGraw Hill, 1983.

[25] B. M. Sarwar, G. Karypis, J. A. Konstan, and J. T. Riedl. Analysis of recommender algorithms for e-commerce. In *Proceedings of the 2nd ACM Conference on Electronic Commerce*, pages 158–167, 2000.

[26] B. M. Sarwar, G. Karypis, J. A. Konstan, and J. T. Riedl. Application of dimensionality reduction in recommender system—A case study. In *ACM WebKDD Web Mining for E-Commerce Workshop*, 2000.

[27] B. M. Sarwar, G. Karypis, J. A. Konstan, and J. T. Riedl. Item-based collaborative filtering recommendation algorithms. In *Proceedings of the Tenth International World Wide Web Conference*, pages 285–295, 2001.

[28] A. I. Schein, A. Popescul, and L. H. Ungar. PennAspect: A two-way aspect model implementation. Technical Report MS-CIS-01-25, Department of Computer and Information Science, The University of Pennsylvania, 2001.

[29] A. I. Schein, A. Popescul, L. H. Ungar, and D. M.Pennock. Generative models for cold-start recommendations. In *Proceedings of the 2001 SIGIR Workshop on Recommender Systems*, 2001.

[30] U. Shardanand and P. Maes. Social information filtering: Algorithms for automating 'word of mouth'. In *Proceedings of the Conference on Human Factors in Computing Systems*, pages 210–217, 1995.

[31] L. H. Ungar and D. P. Foster. Clustering methods for collaborative filtering. In *Workshop on Recommendation Systems at the Fifteenth National Conference on Artificial Intelligence*, 1998.

Term Selection for Searching Printed Arabic

Kareem Darwish
Electrical and Computer Engineering Dept.
University of Maryland, College Park
College Park, MD 20742
kareem@glue.umd.edu

Douglas W. Oard
College of Information Studies and UMIACS
University of Maryland, College Park
College Park, MD 20742
oard@glue.umd.edu

ABSTRACT

Since many Arabic documents are available only in print, automating retrieval from collections of scanned Arabic document images using Optical Character Recognition (OCR) is an interesting problem. Arabic combines rich morphology with a writing system that presents unique challenges to OCR systems. These factors must be considered when selecting terms for automatic indexing. In this paper, alternative choices of indexing terms are explored using both an existing electronic text collection and a newly developed collection built from images of actual printed Arabic documents. Character n-grams or lightly stemmed words were found to typically yield near-optimal retrieval effectiveness, and combining both types of terms resulted in robust performance across a broad range of conditions.

Categories and Subject Descriptors

H.3.3 [**Information Systems**]: # Information Search and Retrieval – *search process, selection process.*

General Terms: Algorithms, Design, Experimentation.

Keywords: OCR, Arabic, Information Retrieval, Term Selection.

1. INTRODUCTION

Since the advent of the printing press in the fifteenth century, the amount of printed text has grown to an overwhelming scale. Of course, a great deal of text is now generated in character-coded electronic formats (HTML, word processor files, etc.). But printed text remains important, in part because large collections of legacy documents exist only in printed form, and in part because printed text remains a ubiquitous distribution channel that can effectively deliver information without the technical infrastructure that is needed to deliver character-coded text. These factors are particularly important for Arabic, which is widely used in several countries where the installed computer infrastructure is quite limited. Furthermore, before the 1998 introduction of support for character-coded Arabic in the standard versions of Microsoft's Windows operating system, Arabic text on the World Wide Web was most often rendered as document images. Character coded Arabic is now becoming more common on the Web, but it is still not unusual to find Arabic documents that are available only as document images.

Printed documents can be browsed relatively easily in limited quantities, but effective access to the contents of large collections of printed documents requires some form of automation. Although we focus on the effect of term selection on supporting search, term selection has important consequences for other applications (e.g., text classification and information visualization) that also exploit a "bag-of-terms" document representation. Three basic approaches to searching printed documents are possible:

- Hire catalogers to examine each document and assign metadata that describes the content of the document. This is the approach used in library catalogs.
- Hire typists to read each document and rekey the material in a way that duplicates (or perhaps summarizes) the content of the document. This is the approach used by the U.S. Foreign Broadcast Information Service.
- Scan the document to produce a document image, then perform Optical Character Recognition (OCR) to obtain a representation (possibly containing errors) that approximates the content of the document.

We have chosen to focus on the third approach because it clearly offers the greatest potential for affordably scaling up to process very large collections. Widely available sheet feed scanners can scan thousands of pages per hour, and specialized hardware can be used to acquire document images in other situations (e.g., document cameras can be used with bound volumes). Arabic OCR poses a number of challenges, however. In Arabic text, letters are connected, letters change shape depending on their position in a word, special forms for letter combinations and word elongations are often used, many letters include dots, diacritic marks may optionally be present, and both dots and diacritics might be easily confused with dust and/or speckle that was introduced during the scanning process. Arabic morphology is rich and complex, and many researchers have found that indexing terms obtained using morphological analysis can yield better retrieval effectiveness than indexing the surface form of each word (c.f., [3]). Character recognition errors might therefore adversely impact retrieval effectiveness in two ways: (1) by altering terms in a way that would preclude accurate morphological analysis, and (2) by altering meaning-bearing terms in ways that would prevent accurate matching between query terms and the terms found in a document. Our goal in this paper is therefore to reexamine the question of term selection for Arabic information retrieval in the context of OCR-degraded text.

Although the Text Retrieval Conference (TREC) has recently produced a large test collection for experiments with retrieval from character-coded Arabic text, we are not aware of any similar resource for printed Arabic documents. We therefore developed a small test collection of Arabic document images for use in our experiments.

The remainder of the paper is organized as follows. In the next section, we describe previous research on the use of OCR for information retrieval and on retrieval of character-coded Arabic text. Section 3 then develops the experimental framework for comparing the effect of alternative indexing terms on retrieval effectiveness. Our Arabic document image test collection is introduced in Section 4, along with results of experiments to characterize the suitability of that collection for the evaluation of information retrieval effectiveness. In section 5, we explore the effect of OCR-degraded Arabic text on retrieval effectiveness. Finally, we conclude with some more general observations on the selection of index terms for Arabic information retrieval and suggest some future research directions.

2. BACKGROUND

The goal of OCR is to transform a document image into character-coded text. The usual process is to automatically segment the document image into character images in the proper reading order using image analysis heuristics, apply an automatic classifier to determine the character codes that are most likely to correspond to each character image [20], and then exploit sequential context (e.g., preceding and following characters and a list of possible words) to select the most likely character in each position. The character error rate can be influenced by reproduction quality (e.g., original documents are typically better than photocopies) [6], the resolution at which the document was scanned, and any mismatch between the instances on which the character image classifier was trained and the rendering of the characters in the printed document [5]. Arabic OCR presents several challenges, including:

- Connected characters, which change shape depending on their position in the word, make the isolation of individual character images challenging.
- Word elongations (kashida) and special forms for certain letter combinations (ligatures such as lam-alef (لا)) are often used in typed text [23], expanding the number of possibilities that the classifier must consider.
- 15 of the 28 Arabic letters include dots as an integral part of the character, and authors sometimes choose to additionally place diacritic marks on some letters. Dots and diacritic marks can easily be confused with speckle or dust, making detection of the correct character challenging.
- Due to the morphological complexity of Arabic, the number of legal words has been estimated to be 60 billion [1]. This limits the value of sequential context somewhat, since it would be impractical to store a complete vocabulary of that size.

There are a number of commercial Arabic OCR systems, with Sakhr's Automatic Reader and Shonut's Omni Page being perhaps the most widely used [15].

Retrieval of OCR degraded text documents has been reported for many languages, including English, French, Spanish, and Chinese [12, 22, 24], but we are not aware of prior work on Arabic. Three methods have been used to produce test collections for OCR-degraded text:

- Systematically altering character-coded text using a character-level confusion model that is trained on aligned pairs of character-coded and OCR-degraded texts. Large test collections can be efficiently produced using this technique by starting with an existing test collection for which topics and relevance judgments are already available. However, the degree of insight that can be obtained depends on the fidelity of the character confusion model, which might model some aspects of the process (e.g., character replacement) better than others (e.g., the effect of document skew during scanning). Harding, et al. used OCR errors that were simulated in this way to examine the effect of indexing character *n*-grams on retrieval from four English document collections (with 423 to 12,380 documents), finding that *n*-grams outperformed words [12].
- Typesetting character-coded text to produce a document image, optionally degrading the image to simulate speckle, page skew, bleed-through, varying illumination, and other factors [6, 14], and then performing OCR. Although the operations on large document images adds some time to the process, large test collections can still be constructed relatively efficiently because it is possible to start with a collection for which topics and relevance judgments already exist. Baird used this technique to show that that retrieval effectiveness falls dramatically with increases in the character recognition error rate [5].
- Scanning a collection of printed documents, performing OCR, and then manually creating appropriate topics and relevance judgments. The size of a test collection created in this way will be limited by the resources available for the relevance judgment process. However, this technique can accurately model many aspects that may be present in real applications (e.g., unfamiliar fonts, damaged pages, and handwritten annotations). Taghva, et al. experimented on a 204-document English document image collection using this technique. The average length of the documents was 38 pages. He observed no significant effect of degradation on retrieval [21]. Tseng and Oard experimented with different combinations of n-grams on a Chinese collection of 8,438 document images. The documents images were scanned from printed material. They observed that combinations of character 1-grams and character 2-grams performed best [24].

Arabic words are derived from a closed set of approximately 10,000 roots by attaching prefixes, suffixes and infixes. Often, vowel replacement and letter omission are required to construct words. Roots are mostly 3 letters, often 4 letters, and rarely 5 letters. Stems are derived from roots by inserting infixes only [9]. Several types of index terms have been studied, including word surface forms, clusters of words [25], and results of morphological processing, such as stems and morphological roots [3, 4, 13], and character *n*-grams of various lengths [10, 16]. The effects of normalizing alternative characters, removal of diacritics and stop-word removal have also been explored [8, 10, 26]. Because the earliest of these studies used very small test collections and more recent results are based on a single large test collection (from the 2001 Text Retrieval Conference), relatively few general conclusions can be drawn regarding the optimal choice of indexing terms for character-coded Arabic text. The preponderance of the evidence does, however, suggest that some form of morphological analysis and/or the use of character *n*-grams substantially outperforms use of word surface forms, and that some form of character normalization is helpful. In the next section, we explore these questions in greater detail.

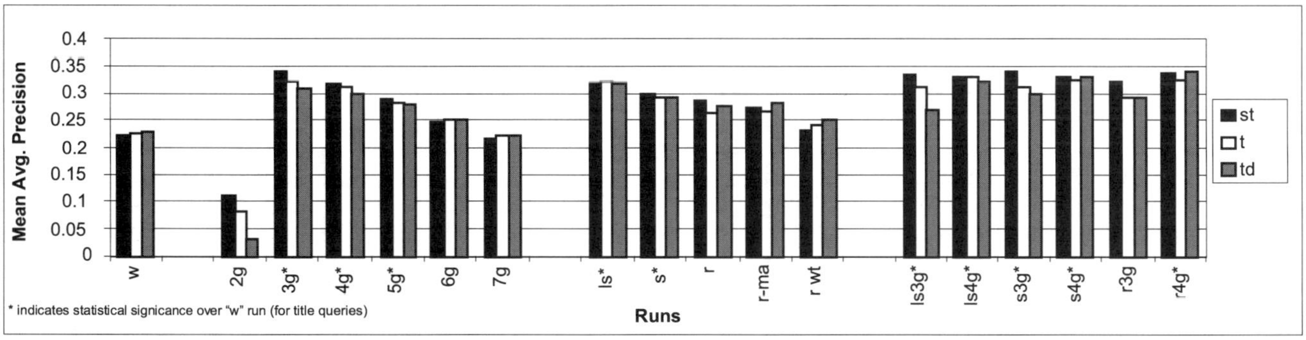

Figure 1: Runs on TREC collection with "short title" (st), "title" (t), and "title + description" (td) queries

3. INDEX TERMS FOR CHARACTER-CODED ARABIC

In this section we experimentally explore the effectiveness of information retrieval using different Arabic index terms on a large collection. We explored three categories of Arabic index terms: character *n*-grams, terms obtained through morphological analysis, and combinations of both. In the first category, we looked at within-word character *n*-grams, with values of *n* ranging between 2 and 7 characters. In the second category, we examined word surface forms, light stemming (in which common prefixes and suffixes were removed), aggressive stemming (in which all recognizable prefixes and suffixes were removed), and morphological roots (in which any infixes were also removed). To see the difference between the four approaches, consider the word "وكيتم " (wkrymthm). The derived terms "كرت " (krymt), "كريم" (krym), and "كم " (krm) are the lightly stemmed version of the word, the stem, and the root respectively.[1] Before forming the character *n*-grams and performing morphological analysis, all words were stripped of diacritics and variant forms of the letter alef (bare alef, alef-hamza, alef-madd, waw-hamza, and ya-hamza – ا، أ، آ، إ، ، ؤ) were all normalized to bare alef. Similarly, alef-maqsoura and ya (ى، ي) were normalized to ya.

We used the Linguistic Data Consortium (LDC) LDC2001T55 collection, which was used in the TREC 2001 cross-language track. For brevity, we refer to this as the TREC collection. The collection contains 383,872 articles from the Agence France Press (AFP) Arabic newswire. Twenty-five topics were developed cooperatively by the LDC and the National Institute of Standards and Technology (NIST), and relevance judgments were developed at LDC by manually judging a pool of documents obtained from combining the top 70 documents from 20 runs submitted by 10 teams to TREC's Cross Language track in 2001. The number of known relevant documents ranges from 6 to 556, with an average of 165 relevant documents per topic. This is larger than is typical for a TREC collection, and there is some indication that there may still be a substantial number of undiscovered relevant documents [11]. Nevertheless, this is presently the best available large Arabic information retrieval test collection.

The TREC topic descriptions each include a title field that briefly names the topic, a description field that usually consists of a single sentence description, and a narrative field that is intended to contain any information that would be needed by a human judge to accurately assess the relevance of a document [11]. We constructed three types of queries from the TREC topics:

a. the title and description fields (*td*). This is intended to model the sort of statement that a searcher might initially make when asking an intermediary such as a librarian for help with a search.
b. the title field only (*t*). The title field in recent TREC collections is typically designed as a model for Web queries, which typically contain only 2 or 3 words. However, the average length if the *t* queries is about 6 words.
c. a short version of the title field (*st*) in which words that were deemed by the first author not to be typical terms in a brief Web query were deleted. The average length of the *st* queries is 3.5 words.

We performed experiments for each query length with the following index terms:

- *w*: words.
- *2g, 3g, ... 7g*: character n-grams (2-7 gram).
- *ls*: lightly stemmed words, obtained by using pattern matching to remove common prefixes and suffixes.
- *s*: aggressively stemmed words, found using the Sebawai morphological analyzer.
- three ways of obtaining roots:
  - *r*: the top root found by the Sebawai morphological analyzer, which produces a ranked list of possible roots [9].
  - *r-ma*: the highest ranked root found by Sebawai that was also produced by ALPNET [7], if ALPNET produced an analysis; otherwise the top root found by Sebawai. For words that it can analyze, ALPNET produces an unranked set of possible roots that almost always contains the correct one, but it fails to produce an analysis more often than Sebawai.
  - *r-wt*: Sebawai's top 2 roots, weighted by their likelihood ratio.
- combinations of:
  - *ls3g*: lightly stemmed words and 3-grams.
  - *ls4g*: lightly stemmed words and 4-grams.
  - *s3g*: aggressively stemmed words and 3-grams.
  - *s4g*: aggressively stemmed words and 4-grams.
  - *r3g*: roots and 3-grams.
  - *r4g*: roots and 4-grams.

[1] The transliteration scheme used in the paper is define in [9]

Table 1: Comparing TREC runs using the *t*-test's p-value. A "bold" p-value indicates statistical significance.

3g	4g	5g	w	ls	s	r	ls3g	ls4g	s3g	s4g	r3g	r4g	
	.47	**.05**	**.00**	.87	.24	**.04**	.55	.58	.46	.84	.27	.87	**3g**
		.00	**.00**	.67	.56	.16	.98	.08	.94	**.02**	.61	.12	**4g**
			.02	**.06**	.78	.53	.30	**.00**	.36	**.00**	.78	**.00**	**5g**
				.00	**.05**	.19	**.01**	**.00**	**.01**	**.00**	.06	**.00**	**w**
					.18	**.02**	.71	.47	.65	.73	.39	.79	**ls**
						.02	.28	.22	.38	.28	.97	.29	**s**
							.02	.05	**.05**	.06	.25	.05	**r**
								.42	.81	.58	.30	.60	**ls3g**
									.38	.47	.24	.56	**ls4g**
										.51	.14	.52	**s3g**
											.32	.89	**s4g**
												.32	**r3g**
													r4g

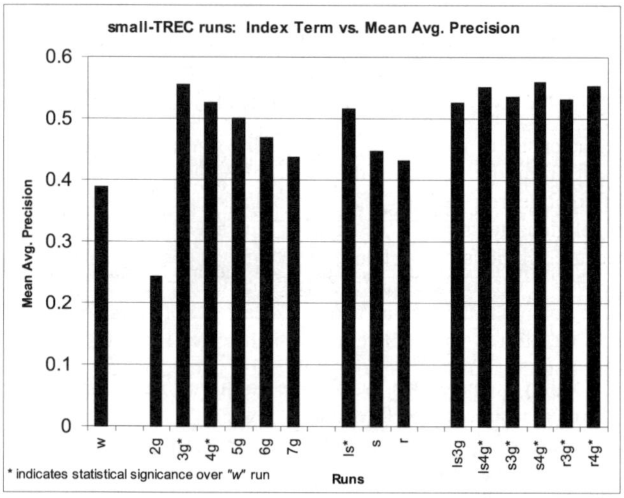

Figure 2: Runs on small-TREC collection

Table 2: Comparing small-TREC runs using the *t*-test's p-value.

3g	4g	5g	w	ls	s	r	ls3g	ls4g	s3g	s4g	r3g	r4g	
	.36	.09	**.00**	.29	**.04**	**.02**	.26	.93	.57	.91	.51	.98	**3g**
		.04	**.01**	.74	.09	.06	.98	.13	.72	.02	.87	.07	**4g**
			.02	.56	.27	.19	.39	**.00**	.27	**.00**	.43	***.01***	**5g**
				.00	.24	.39	**.00**	**.00**	**.00**	**.00**	**.01**	**.00**	**w**
					.10	.08	.73	.20	.55	.12	.71	.18	**ls**
						.27	**.05**	**.01**	**.02**	**.01**	**.03**	**.00**	**s**
							.03	**.01**	**.01**	**.01**	**.01**	**.00**	**r**
								.36	.43	.22	.81	.27	**ls3g**
									.49	.98	.41	.48	**ls4g**
										.40	.77	.46	**s3g**
											.39	.49	**s4g**
												.44	**r3g**
													r4g

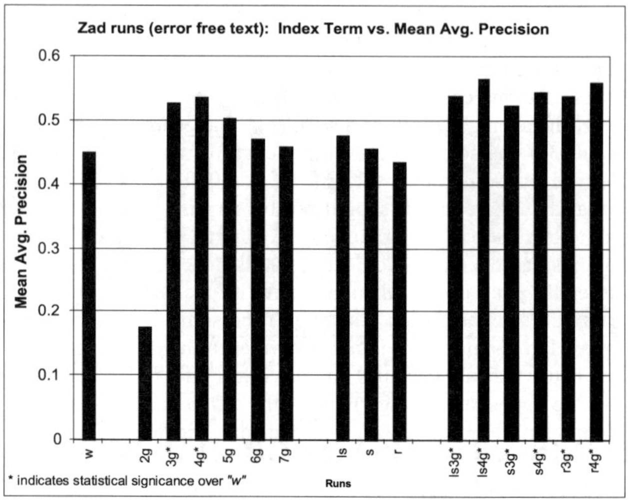

Figure 3: Runs on Zad collection

Table 3: Comparing Zad runs using the *t*-test's p-value.

3g	4g	5g	w	ls	s	r	ls3g	ls4g	s3g	s4g	r3g	r4g	
	.57	.34	**.03**	.09	**.04**	.07	.12	**.03**	.93	.15	.48	.06	**3g**
		.04	**.02**	.08	.08	.09	.85	**.03**	.69	.63	.93	.35	**4g**
			.08	.44	.29	.24	.16	**.01**	.45	.07	.23	**.03**	**5g**
				.52	.87	.76	**.02**	**.01**	**.04**	**.01**	**.02**	**.01**	**w**
					.58	.39	**.02**	**.01**	.11	**.02**	**.04**	**.01**	**ls**
						.47	**.02**	**.02**	**.02**	**.01**	**.01**	**.01**	**s**
							.04	**.03**	**.05**	**.03**	**.02**	**.01**	**r**
								.11	.35	.58	.95	.17	**ls3g**
									.23	.45	.32	.77	**ls4g**
										.21	.20	.06	**s3g**
											.71	.28	**s4g**
												.18	**r3g**
													r4g

We used a vector space information retrieval system with Okapi BM-25 term weights [18][2]. We chose to compare the effect of alternate indexing terms using mean uninterpolated average precision as our measure of retrieval effectiveness. We tested our results for statistical significance using a paired two-tailed *t*-test, claiming significance for *p* values at or below 0.05 (indicating—if the assumptions underlying the test were satisfied—that there would be no more than a 5% chance that the observed average precision values, paired by topic, were drawn from the same distribution). Sebawai, the light stemmer, and the IR system are freely distributable.

Figure 1 summarizes the results of these runs, and Table 1 presents the statistical significance test results for the *t* queries. These results indicate that if we were to pick a single index term, character 3-grams or 4-grams, or lightly or aggressively stemmed words would be good candidates. With few exceptions, all four

[2] IR engine, Sebawai and the Light Stemmer are available at www.glue.umd.edu/~kareem/research

types of terms statistically significantly outperformed words, roots, and character 5-grams, 6-grams and 7-grams on all three sets of queries. Any difference in effectiveness between the four types of terms could not be discerned using this test collection.

The average length of a stem (using aggressive stemming) is about 3.6 characters (the average length of an Arabic stem was derived by averaging the length of 250,000 stems produced by Sebawai). Therefore, it should not be surprising that 3 or 4 turn out to be the optimal *n*-gram length. Combining *n*-grams and with the results of morphological analysis in a single index was generally not harmful when compared to the use of either alone, although of course such a strategy necessarily results in a larger index. Interestingly, we found no evidence that longer queries do any better than shorter ones on this collection—in fact the trend is just the opposite (although none of the differences are statistically significant). For this reason, we focus on a single query type (title queries) in the remainder of our experiments.

Neither of the alternatives we tried for identifying roots outperformed Sebawai's top candidate, although neither difference is statistically significant for any query length. The fact that filtering Sebawai's candidates using ALPNET doesn't appear to help seems reasonable, since a prior study found that for words ALPNET could analyze, Sebewai's top candidate was right in 96% of the cases. The fact that weighting Sebawai's top two candidates did not help suggests that uncorrected likelihood values computed by Sebawai are not useful as probability estimates. For this reason, we present results only for Sebawai's first ranked roots (*r*) in the remainder of this paper. In some early work with small test collections [3, 13], roots had appeared to be a better choice than stems, but our experiments found just the opposite. One possible explanation for this is that earlier test collections contained at most a few hundred documents, and scaling up the size of the collection by several orders of magnitude might reward the choice of less ambiguous terms. An alternative explanation is that our morphological analysis might not be sufficiently accurate. In the earlier work, stems and roots had been obtained manually. For words that ALPNET fails to analyze (many of which are named entities), Sebawai often produces an incorrect analysis, ranking the correct root first in only [illegible]% of the cases [9].

4. CREATING AN ARABIC DOCUMENT IMAGE COLLECTION

In this section we explore the development of an information retrieval test collection that contains Arabic document images. Our goal is to construct a collection with the following characteristics:

1. It should be built from actual printed sources (the third approach identified in Section 2), so that we can be confident that the effects of printing and scanning on the Arabic character recognition process have been accurately modeled;
2. It should include include accurate character-coded text (which we call "clean" text) for each document, so that we can check what we have learned about term selection using the TREC collection; and
3. It should either be available without charge or licensable at a reasonable price, so that others can build on our work.

We built our collection from *Zad Al-Me'ad*, a printed book that is free of copyright restrictions and for which an electronic copy could be obtained without charge from Al-Areeb Electronic Publishers [3]. The book, written in the 14th century by a Muslim theologian, consists of 2,730 separate documents that address a variety of topics such as mannerisms, history, jurisprudence and medicine. The first author of this paper, a native speaker of Arabic, developed 25 topics and exhaustively searched the collection for relevant documents. The number of relevant documents per topic ranges from zero (for one topic) to 72, averaging 18. The average query length is 5.5 words. We refer to this collection as the Zad Collection.

We indexed and searched the clean (accurate character-coded) text in the Zad collection using the same range of character *n*-grams and terms obtained through morphological analysis as the TREC collection. Although the collection showed trends similar to those observed using title queries on the TREC collection, none of the differences were significantly significant. The failure to achieve statictical significance might be due to some obvious characteristic of the collection such as its size, or it might merely result from the fact that the two collections are drawn from different genres; perhaps affecting topic distinguishability (topics in religious texts might be diverse, but may frequently overlap because religious texts often have central underlying themes), or the way in which words are used (e.g., metaphorical usage may be more common in religious texts). To test the effect of collection size, we built a small collection (which we call small-TREC) by sampling documents from the full TREC collection in a manner that reflected the distribution of relevant documents in the Zad collection. We first randomly selected documents from the TREC collection to produce a 1% sample (a little over 2,900 documents). We then added relevant documents to approximate the distribution of relevant documents per topic in the Zad collection. The resulting small-TREC collection had 55,000 unique words, 4,200 unique roots, and an average document length of 186 words (compared to 62,000 unique words, 4,100 unique roots, and an average of 207 words per document for the Zad collection). We are not aware of any formal comparability measures for information retrieval test collections, but at least with respect to the parameters that we measured these two collections seem roughly comparable. Figure 2 and Table 2 show the results for the small-TREC collection using title queries. As with the full TREC collection, 3-grams, lightly stemmed words, and aggressively stemmed words typically outperformed words, roots, and 5-grams, with statistical significance in many cases. From this we conclude that our failure to obtain statistical significance on the Zad collection cannot be solely the result of collection size.

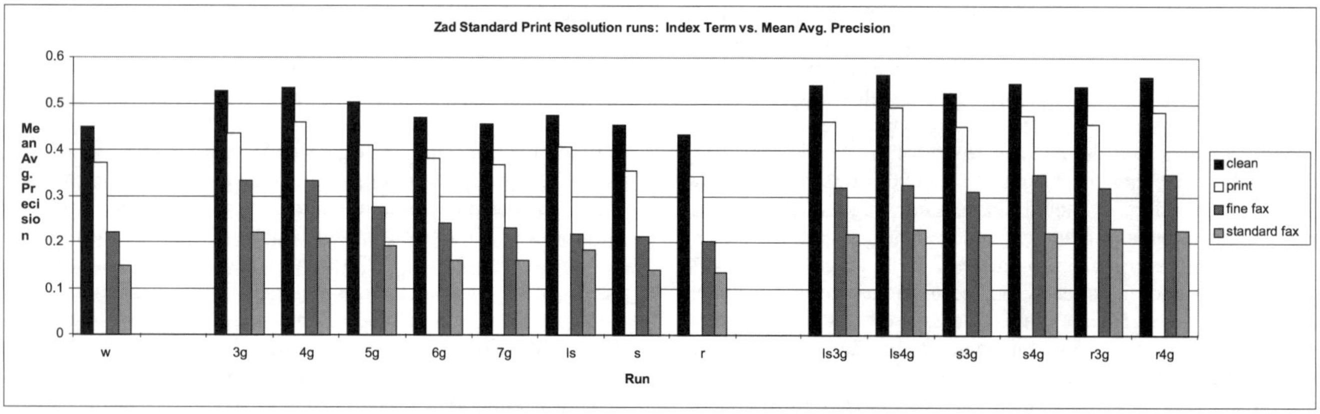

Figure 4: Runs on Zad at different degradation levels

Table 4: Comparing Zad--print resolution runs using the *t*-test's p-value.

3g	4g	5g	w	ls	s	r	ls3g	ls4g	s3g	s4g	r3g	r4g	
	.29	.30	**.05**	.32	**.03**	**.05**	.14	**.01**	.51	.07	.32	**.02**	**3g**
		.01	**.00**	.12	**.02**	**.04**	.85	**.01**	.78	.42	.93	.19	**4g**
			.06	.95	.24	.23	.06	**.00**	.22	**.02**	.15	**.01**	**5g**
				.34	.71	.54	**.02**	**.00**	**.01**	**.01**	**.01**	**.00**	**w**
					.11	.13	**.01**	**.00**	.12	**.02**	.08	**.01**	**ls**
						.58	**.00**	**.00**	**.00**	**.00**	**.00**	**.00**	**s**
							.01	**.01**	**.01**	**.01**	**.01**	**.00**	**r**
								.04	.44	.40	.71	.17	**ls3g**
									.26	.53	.36	.79	**ls4g**
										.18	.57	.06	**s3g**
											.41	.33	**s4g**
												.15	**r3g**
													r4g

Table 5: Comparing Zad—fine fax resolution--runs using the *t*-test's p-value.

3g	4g	5g	w	ls	s	r	ls3g	ls4g	s3g	s4g	r3g	r4g	
	.93	**.03**	**.00**	**.00**	**.00**	**.00**	.43	.58	.18	.22	.48	.38	**3g**
		.01	**.00**	**.00**	**.00**	**.00**	.57	.55	.42	.23	.57	.27	**4g**
			.00	.07	.08	**.04**	.15	**.05**	.20	**.01**	.09	**.00**	**5g**
				.94	.81	.54	**.01**	**.00**	**.01**	**.00**	**.00**	**.00**	**w**
					.81	.57	**.00**	**.00**	**.00**	**.00**	**.00**	**.00**	**ls**
						.45	**.00**	**.00**	**.00**	**.00**	**.00**	**.00**	**s**
							.00	**.00**	**.00**	**.00**	**.00**	**.00**	**r**
								.74	.71	.15	.95	.24	**ls3g**
									.57	.50	.89	.49	**ls4g**
										.05	.62	.10	**s3g**
											.15	.93	**s4g**
												.08	**r3g**
													r4g

One of the problems with the Zad collection is the existence of two topics with one relevant document and one topic with none[3]. Topics with no relevant documents certainly occur in real applications, but they cannot differentiate between systems. More importantly, uninterpolated average precision is subject to severe quantization effects when only a single relevant document is known (in this case, the value is always 1/rank, which can only take values of 1, 0.5, 0.33, 0.25, … etc.). We therefore decided to create new topics to replace these three problematic topics. The final set of 25 queries has an average length of 5.4 words and an average of 20 relevant documents per topic (with a minimum of 3 and a maximum of 72). Figure 3 and Table 3 show that after this change, statistical significance tests become informative. We now see combinations of *n*-grams and terms obtained though morphological analysis emerging as good choices, with the combination of 4-grams and lightly stemmed words producing results that are statistically significantly better than any single type of indexing term. From this we conclude that the modified Zad collection (which we henceforth refer to simply as the Zad collection) is a useful tool for exploring the effects of term selection on retrieval from scanned Arabic text.

[3] small-TREC had one topic with one relevant document and one topic with none.

5. RESULTS FOR RETRIEVAL OF OCR DEGRADED TEXT

In this section, we examine the effect of OCR on retrieval effectiveness. We scanned the 2,000 pages of the printed version of *Zad Al-Me'ad* using a Xerox Document Centre 460 Digital Copier, which is a high-volume copier and sheet feed scanner, in about two hours at 300x300 dpi (dots per inch) resolution. This corresponds to the resolution used commonly in older inkjet and laser printers, so we refer to this as "print" resolution. The images were then manually zoned into images of a single document (which might span multiple pages or parts of pages) to correspond exactly to the 2,730 documents in the character-coded clean copy of the collection. Two additional document image collections were then created using Corel PhotoPaint version 8.0 by resampling the zoned document images at both 203x196 and 203x98 dpi, which correspond to the fine and standard resolutions respectively of fax machines in the widely used "Group 3" standard. We then used Sakhr's Automatic Reader version 4.0 OCR engine [19] to convert the images into plain text. We computed the character error rate (insertions + deletions + substitutions) for the OCR degraded text with reference to the clean text using software from the University of Nevada at Las Vegas [17], obtaining 18.7%, 36.1%, and 42.4% for the print, fine fax, and standard fax resolutions respectively. Sakhr OCR engine is tuned for high resolution document images (corresponding to

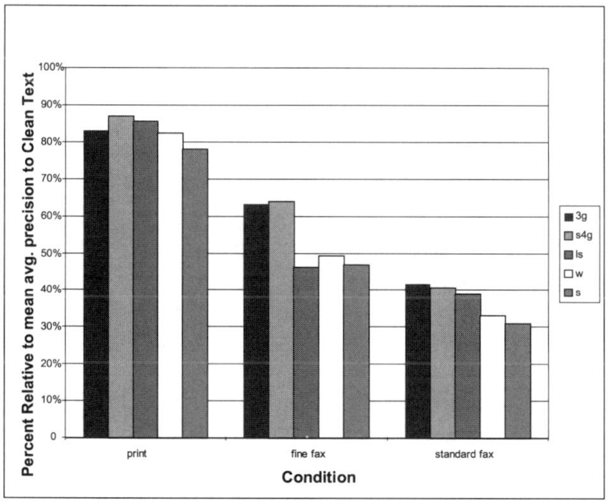

Figure 5: Condition vs. percent relative uniterpolated mean average precision to clean text

our print resolution), so the relatively high character error rate of the fine and standard fax resolution is understandable. Better results might be obtained if Sakhr's OCR engine was retrained on samples of the fine and standard fax resolutions prior to the recognition of the full collection (Sakhr's OCR software allows for manual retraining by the user).

Figure 4 compares the results of all the runs for all four version of the Zad collection (clean, print, fine fax, and standard fax versions), and Tables 4, 5, and 6 show the results of statistical significance testing for print, fine fax, and standard fax resolutions respectively. Higher character error rates clearly produced a substantial (and statistically significant) adverse effect on the retrieval effectiveness. Nonetheless, our system demonstrated the ability to reliably find some relevant documents with even the lowest resolution. This is consistent with results that have been obtained in other languages (c.f., [5]). Index terms that performed well for clean text continued to do so over the range of character error rates that we tested, with character 3-grams and 4-grams and all combinations of character n-grams with terms obtained using morphological analysis producing good results.

Table 6: Comparing Zad standard fax resolution--runs using the *t*-test's p-value.

3g	4g	5g	w	ls	s	r	ls3g	ls4g	s3g	s4g	r3g	r4g	
	.54	.21	.03	.33	.03	.03	.89	.70	.95	.91	.30	.63	**3g**
		.14	.00	.36	.06	.06	.65	.19	.60	.27	.27	.22	**4g**
			.01	.67	.11	.10	.24	.09	.19	.04	.08	.02	**5g**
				.44	.80	.66	.03	.01	.02	.00	.01	.00	**w**
					.33	.26	.21	.11	.33	.20	.24	.20	**ls**
						.43	.01	.03	.01	.01	.01	.01	**s**
							.01	.03	.02	.01	.02	.01	**r**
								.59	.92	.75	.44	.52	**ls3g**
									.40	.77	.68	.76	**ls4g**
										.85	.07	.44	**s3g**
											.51	.56	**s4g**
												.67	**r3g**
													r4g

Figure 5 shows some of the same results grouped by resolution, illustrating that *n*-grams produce a substantial (and statistically significant) advantage over any term obtained using morphological analysis for the fine fax resolution. With the increase of error level, retrieval effectiveness of indexing using words, stems, and roots deteriorated faster than indexing using 3-grams, 4-grams, or combinations of n-grams and terms obtained using morphological analysis. This effect may result from weaknesses in the Sebawai morphological analyzer, which was trained using clean text, resulting in failure to analyze words that have one or more misrecognized characters. Character *n*-grams are relatively robust as long as the character error rate is low enough to yield many correct sequences of contiguous, but ultimately n-gram performance decays as well. Similar results have been observed in other languages [12, 24]. Consistent with previous research [5], Figure 5 suggests that retrieval effectiveness deteriorates faster for higher error rates. Surprisingly, however, the three character error rate values that we obtained did not allow us to distinguish between 3-grams and 4-grams.

6. CONCLUSIONS AND FUTURE WORK

We have described the development of a test collection that can be used to evaluate alternative techniques for searching scanned Arabic text and a set of experiments that were designed to identify the effect of alternative indexing terms on retrieval effectiveness. From our experiments, we can conclude that character *n*-grams (specifically 3-grams and 4-grams) are well suited to Arabic document image retrieval applications, and that combining *n*-grams with terms obtained through some form of morphological analysis (particularly lightly stemmed words) can produce a robust system that is effective over a range of genres, collection sizes, and character error rates.

Searching printed Arabic is an important problem, in part because a great deal of Arabic text that is presently available only in printed form. We expect that our new Zad test collection will provide a useful basis for further work including:

- Improved morphological analysis. Because of the way it was trained, Sebawai does well on words that ALPNET can analyze, but poorly on most other words. Many of these problematic words are named entities, so we expect that substantial improvements could be made if named entities could be reliably detected and routed to an analysis system that is tuned to work well on such terms.
- Improved retrieval algorithms. Singhal has shown that for English byte length normalization is more robust to character recognition errors than the cosine normalization usually used in vector space retrieval systems [20], and Tseng and Oard have seen similar results for Chinese [24].
- Larger test collections. The development of good error models for Arabic OCR would make it possible to generate a large test collection directly from the TREC collection or from another collection of similar size. When this becomes possible, the insights that we have gained using the Zad collection can serve as a useful point of departure for further exploration of alternate indexing terms.
- Automatic layout analysis. In our experiments, individual documents within *Zad Al-Me'ad* were segmented manually, and no special processing was required to determine the appropriate reading order. Automatic layout analysis will,

however, be needed in many practical applications (e.g., searching printed newspapers).

- Image enhancement for low-resolution applications. Faxes, video captions, and scene text in video have significantly lower resolution than ordinary scanned documents, and video applications often also include unusual background characteristics. Image processing techniques such as mathematical morphology and multi-frame integration can be helpful in such cases.

Arabic is the eighth most widely spoken language in the world, and improved access to Arabic text could have profound implications for cross-cultural communication and economic development. At present, the dissemination of Arabic text is dominated by printed rather than character-coded electronic documents, which makes retrieval from document images a particularly salient task for Arabic. Both the morphology and the orthography of Arabic make this particularly challenging, but we believe that the results reported in this paper form a solid basis for future work on this important problem.

ACKNOWLDGEMENTS

The authors are grateful to Dr. Phillip Resnik, Mona Diab, Nizar Habash, and David Doermann for his valuable input. This work was supported in part by DARPA cooperative agreement N660010028910.

BIBLIOGRAPHY

1 Ahmed, Mohamed Attia. A Large-Scale Computational Processor of the Arabic Morphology, and Applications. Master's Thesis, Faculty of Engineering, Cairo University, Cairo, Egypt, 2000.

2 Al-Areeb Electronic Publishers, LLC. 16013 Malcolm Dr., Laurel, MD 20707, USA

3 Al-Kharashi, Ibrahim and Martha Evens. Comparing Words, Stems, and Roots as Index Terms in an Arabic Information Retrieval System. JASIS. 45 (8): 548-560, 1994.

4 Aljlayl, M., S. Beitzel, E. Jensen, A. Chowdhury, D. Holmes, M. Lee, D. Grossman, and O. Frieder. IIT at TREC-10. TREC-2001, 2001.

5 Baird, Henry. Document Image Defects Models and their Uses. Proceedings of the Second International Conference on Document Analysis and Recognition (ICDAR), 62-67, 1993.

6 Baird, Henry. State of the Art of Document Image Degradation Modeling. Proceedings of the 4th IAPR Workshop on Document Analysis Systems (DAS 2000), 2000.

7 Beesley, Kenneth. Arabic Finite-State Morphological Analysis and Generation. COLING-96, 1996.

8 Chen, Aitao and F. Gey. Translation Term Weighting and Combining Translation Resources in Cross-Language Retrieval TREC-2001, 2001.

9 Darwish, Kareem. Building a Shallow Morphological Analyzer in One Day. To appear in ACL 2002 Workshop on Computational Approaches to Semitic Languages, July 11, 2002.

10 Darwish, Kareem, D. Doermann, R. Jones, D. Oard, and M. Rautiainen. TREC-10 Experiments at Maryland: CLIR and Video. TREC-2001, 2001.

11 Gey, Fredric and D. Oard. The TREC-2001 Cross Language Retrieval Track: Searching Arabic using English, French, and Arabic Queries. TREC-2001, 2001.

12 Harding, S., W. Croft, and C. Weir. Probabilistic Retrieval of OCR Degraded Text Using N-Grams. European Conference on Digital Libraries, 1997

13 Hmeidi, Ismail, Ghassan Kanaan, and Martha Evens. Design and Implementation of Automatic Indexing for Information Retrieval with Arabic Documents. JASIS. 48 (10): 867-881, 1997.

14 Kanungo, Tapas. Document Degradation Models and Methodology for Degradation Model Validation. Ph.D. Thesis, Electrical Engineering Department, University of Washington, 1996.

15 Kanungo, Tapas, Gregory Marton, and Osama Bulbul. OmniPage vs. Sakhr: Paired Model Evaluation of Two Arabic OCR Products. Proceedings of SPIE Conference on Document Recognition and Retrieval (VI), Vol. 3651, San Jose, California, Jan. 27-28, 1999.

16 Mayfield, James, P. McNamee, C. Costello, C. Piatko, and A. Banerjee. JHU/APL at TREC 2001: Experiments in Filtering and in Arabic, Video, and Web Retrieval. TREC-2001, 2001.

17 Rice, S., Frank R. Jenkins, and Thomas A. Nartker. The fifth annual test of OCR accuracy. Technical Report 96-01Information Science Research Institute, University of Nevada, Las Vegas, April 1996.

18 Robertson, S. and K. S. Jones. Simple proven approaches to text retrieval. Tech. Rep. TR356, Cambridge University Computer Laboratory, 1997

19 Sakhr Technologies, Cairo, Egypt www.sakhr.com

20 Singhal, Amit, Gerard Salton, and Chris Buckley. Length Normalization in Degraded Text Collections. Proceedings of 5th Annual Symposium on Document Analysis and Information Retrieval, 149-162, April 15-17, 1996.

21 Taghva, Kazem, Julie Borasack, Allen Condit, and Jeff Gilbreth. Results and Implications of the Noisy Data Projects. Technical Report 94-01, Information Science Research Institute, University of Nevada, Las Vegas, 1994.

22 Taghva, Kazem, Julie Borasack, Allen Condit, and Padma Inaparthy. Querying Short OCR'd Documents. Technical Report 94-10, Information Science Research Institute 1995.

23 Trenkle, John, Andrew Gillies, Erik Erlandson, Steve Schlosser, and Stan Cavin. Advances in Arabic Text Recognition. Proceeding of Symposium on Document Image Understanding Technology, Columbia, Maryland, April 23-25, 2001.

24 Tseng, Yuen-Hsien and Douglas Oard. Document Image Retrieval Techniques for Chinese. Proceeding of Symposium on Document Image Understanding Technology, Columbia, Maryland, April 23-25, 2001.

25 Xu, Jinxi, A. Fraser, and R. Weischedel. TREC 2001 Cross-Lingual Retrieval at BBN. TREC-2001, 2001.

Empirical Studies in Strategies for Arabic Retrieval

Jinxi Xu
BBN Technologies
50 Moulton Street
Cambridge, MA 02138
jxu@bbn.com

Alexander Fraser
USC/ISI
4676 Admiralty Way
Marina del Rey, CA 90292
fraser@isi.edu

Ralph Weischedel
BBN Technologies
50 Moulton Street
Cambridge, MA 02138
weisched@bbn.com

ABSTRACT

This work evaluates a few search strategies for Arabic monolingual and cross-lingual retrieval, using the TREC Arabic corpus as the test-bed. The release by NIST in 2001 of an Arabic corpus of nearly 400k documents with both monolingual and cross-lingual queries and relevance judgments has been a new enabler for empirical studies. Experimental results show that spelling normalization and stemming can significantly improve Arabic monolingual retrieval. Character tri-grams from stems improved retrieval modestly on the test corpus, but the improvement is not statistically significant. To further improve retrieval, we propose a novel thesaurus-based technique. Different from existing approaches to thesaurus-based retrieval, ours formulates word synonyms as probabilistic term translations that can be automatically derived from a parallel corpus. Retrieval results show that the thesaurus can significantly improve Arabic monolingual retrieval. For cross-lingual retrieval (CLIR), we found that spelling normalization and stemming have little impact.

Categories and Subject Descriptors

H.3.1 [**Information Storage and Retrieval**]: Content Analysis and Indexing--*Dictionaries, Indexing methods, Linguistic processing, Thesauruses*; H.3.3 [**Information Storage and Retrieval**]. Information Search and Retrieval--*Relevance feedback, Retrieval models*

General Terms

Algorithms, Measurement, Performance, Experimentation

Keywords

Arabic retrieval, stemming, spelling normalization, thesaurus, n-grams, broken plurals, parallel corpora, cross-lingual retrieval

1 INTRODUCTION

Arabic is one of the most widely used languages in the world, yet there are relatively few studies on the retrieval of Arabic documents in the literature. Furthermore, the lack of a realistically large test corpus has been a problem in past studies on Arabic retrieval. This work will explore a few strategies for the retrieval of Arabic documents, using the recently available TREC Arabic corpus (Voorhees, 2001) for evaluation.

Arabic is a challenging language for information retrieval (IR) for a number of reasons. First, orthographic variations are prevalent in Arabic; certain combinations of characters can be written in different ways. For example, sometimes in glyphs combining HAMZA or MADDA with ALEF the HAMZA or MADDA is dropped, rendering it ambiguous as to whether the HAMZA or MADDA is present. Second, Arabic has a very complex morphology. Third, broken plurals are common. Broken plurals are somewhat like irregular English plurals except that they often do not resemble the singular form as closely as irregular plurals resemble the singular in English. Because broken plurals do not obey normal morphological rules, they are not handled by existing stemmers. Fourth, Arabic words are often ambiguous due to the tri-literal root system. In Arabic, a word is usually derived from a root, which usually contains three letters. In some derivations one or more of the root letters may be dropped, rendering many Arabic words highly ambiguous with one another. Fifth, short vowels are omitted in written Arabic. Sixth, synonyms are widespread, perhaps because variety in expression is appreciated as part of a good writing style by Arabic speakers (Noamany, 2001).

Those problems make exact keyword match inadequate for Arabic retrieval. We will explore a few search strategies to address the problems. Two techniques, spelling normalization and stemming, are well-known techniques for IR. Our experiments show that while these techniques can significantly improve retrieval, they are not adequate. The third technique, retrieval based on character n-grams, has been used by a few studies (Darwish et al, 2001; Mayfield et al, 2001; Kwok et al, 2001). We found that tri-grams from stems modestly improved retrieval on the test corpus, but the improvement is not statistically significant. To further improve Arabic retrieval, we propose a statistical thesaurus to deal with the large number of broken plurals and synonyms in Arabic. Our approach differs from existing techniques in that it is probabilistically motivated and employs a parallel corpus rather than a monolingual corpus for determining word associations. Experiments show that the thesaurus can significantly improve monolingual retrieval.

We also studied the effect of spelling normalization and Arabic stemming on cross-lingual retrieval, where English queries were used to retrieve Arabic documents. Interestingly, they had little impact on our CLIR experiments, as we had sufficient data to learn translations of each of the variants.

SIGIR '02, August 11-15, 2002, Tampere, Finland.

2 RETRIEVAL STRATEGIES

2.1 Spelling Normalization

Arabic orthography is highly variable. For instance, changing the letter YEH (ي) to ALEF MAKSURA (ى) at the end of a word is very common. (Not surprisingly, the shapes of the two letters are very similar.) Since variations of this kind usually result in an "invalid" word, in our experiments we detected such "errors" using a stemmer (the Buckwalter Stemmer, to be discussed later) and restored the correct word ending.

A more problematic type of spelling variation is that certain glyphs combining HAMZA or MADDA with ALEF (e.g. أ , إ and آ) are sometimes written as a plain ALEF (ا), possibly because of their similarity in appearance. Often, both the intended word and what is actually written are valid words. This is much like confusing "résumé" with "resume" in English. Since both the intended word and the written form are correct words, it is impossible to correct the spellings without the use of context. In our experiments, we converted every occurrence of these glyphs to a plain ALEF.

2.2 Arabic Stemming

Arabic has a complex morphology. Most Arabic words (except some proper nouns and words borrowed from other languages) are derived from a *root*. A root usually consists of three letters. We can view a word as derived by first applying a *pattern* to a root to generate a stem and then attaching prefixes and suffixes to the stem to generate the word (Khoja and Garside, 2001). For this reason, an Arabic stemmer can be either root-based or stem-based.

Experiments in this work used a stem-based stemmer, the Buckwalter Stemmer (Buckwalter, 2001), for two reasons. First, it is a simple algorithm and can be easily re-implemented in a way usable in our retrieval system. Second, judging from the published results in the TREC 2001 Proceedings (Voorhees, 2001), it is at par with other stemmers for retrieval purposes. The algorithm is table-driven, employing a number of tables that define all valid prefixes, stems, suffixes, and their valid combinations. Given an Arabic word w, the stemmer tries every segmentation of w into three sub-strings, $w=x+y+z$. If x is a valid prefix, y a valid stem and z a valid suffix, and if the combination is valid, then y is considered a stem. If several valid combinations are found, it returns all of the stems. We re-implemented the stemmer to make it faster and compatible with the UTF8 encoding. We also modified it so that if no valid combination of prefix-stem-suffix is found, the word itself is returned as the stem.

2.3 Character N-grams

Broken plurals, analogous to irregular nouns in English (e.g. "woman/women"), are very common in Arabic. There is no existing rule-based algorithm to reduce them to their singular forms, and it seems that it would be not be straight-forward to create such an algorithm. As such, broken plurals are not handled by current Arabic stemmers.

One technique to address this problem is to use character n-grams. Although broken plurals are not derived by attaching word affixes, many of the letters in broken plurals are the same as in the singular forms (though sometimes in a different order). If words are divided into character n-grams, some of the n-grams from the singular and plural forms will probably match. This technique can also handle words that have a stem but cannot be stemmed by a stemmer for various reasons. For example, the Buckwalter stemmer employs a list of valid stems to ensure the validity of the resulting stems. Although the list is quite large, it is still not complete. N-grams in this case provide a fallback where exact word match fails.

In this work, we have experimented with n-grams created from stems as well as n-grams from words. N-grams were created by applying a shifting window of n characters over a word or stem. If the word or stem has fewer than n characters, the whole word or stem was returned.

2.4 Deriving an Arabic Thesaurus from a Parallel Corpus

In all natural languages, synonyms present a challenge to IR. As discussed before, this problem is especially serious for Arabic. A common technique to address synonyms is to use a thesaurus. Here we discuss how to automatically derive an Arabic thesaurus from a parallel corpus, based on the intuition that synonyms in one language tend to be translated to the same words in the other language.

We treat synonyms as probabilistic translations between words. Our approach therefore attempts to estimate $p(b|a)$, the translation probability from one Arabic word a to another Arabic word b. We can imagine the user first translates a to some English word x and then translates x to b. Theoretically any English word could be the intermediate translation x. Therefore, $p(b|a)$ can be expressed as:

$$p_{thesaurus}(b \mid a) = \sum_{English\ words\ x} p(x \mid a) p(b \mid x)$$

To overcome the problem of data sparseness, the probability was smoothed using a mixture model:

$$p(b \mid a) = \beta\, p_{diag}(b \mid a) + (1-\beta)\, p_{thesaurus}(b \mid a)$$

where $p_{diag}(b|a)=1$ if $a=b$ and 0 otherwise. The smoothing parameter β controls how much confidence we have in the original word and how much confidence we have in the thesaurus.

In our experiments, the probability estimates $p(x|a)$ and $p(b|x)$ were estimated from a parallel corpus using GIZA++ (Och and Ney, 2000). GIZA++ is a freely available statistical machine translation toolkit whose theory was based on the statistical translation work pioneered by (Brown et al, 1993). GIZA++ implemented several models proposed by Brown for estimating term translation probabilities from sentence aligned parallel corpora; Model 1 was used in this work for its efficiency.

The parallel corpus used in our experiments was obtained from the United Nations (UN). The UN website (http://www.ods.un.org) publishes all UN official documents under a document repository, which is accessible by paying a monthly fee. We extracted around 38,000 document pairs from the UN archive, with over 50 million English words and a similar number of Arabic words. An algorithm developed in-house was used to align the corpus at the sentence level.

While thesaurus-based retrieval has been extensively studied over the decades (Spark Jones, 1971; Deerwester et al, 1990; Jing and Croft, 1994; Schütze and Pedersen, 1994), our approach is different from existing ones in two ways. Our approach extracts word associations from a parallel corpus, while existing techniques employed a monolingual corpus. We believe that a parallel corpus contains stronger semantic clues and therefore can result in more reliable word associations than a monolingual corpus. Second, word associations in our technique have a well-defined probabilistic interpretation. This enables a principled integration of the thesaurus model and a probabilistic retrieval model. An effective thesaurus-based technique must deal with the problem of word polysemy or ambiguity, which is particularly serious for Arabic retrieval. For words with multiple meanings, a probabilistic technique like ours can emphasize probable meanings with high probabilities and discount unlikely ones with low probabilities. This curbs the impact of spurious word associations on retrieval.

3 RETRIEVAL SYSTEM

Our retrieval system was based on the probabilistic generative model described in (Xu, Weischedel and Ngyuen, 2001). It ranks documents according to the probability that a query Q is generated from a document D:

$$p(Q|D) = \prod_{t_q \text{ in } Q} \left[\alpha\, p(t_q|GL) + (1-\alpha) \sum_{t_d \text{ in } D} p(t_d \mid D) p(t_q \mid t_d)\right]^{f(t_q, Q)}$$

where t_q's are query terms, t_d's are terms in the document, $p(t_q|t_d)$ is the translation probability from t_d to t_q and $f(t_q, Q)$ is the number of occurrences of t_q in Q. GL is a background corpus of the query language. The mixture weight α is fixed to 0.3. We estimate $p(t_q|GL)$ and $p(t_d|D)$ as:

$$p(t_q \mid GL) = \frac{\textit{frequency of } t_q \textit{ in } GL}{\textit{size of } GL}$$

$$p(t_d \mid D) = \frac{\textit{frequency of } t_d \textit{ in } D}{\textit{size of } D}$$

The retrieval model was originally proposed for CLIR. Since monolingual retrieval is a special case of CLIR, where the query terms and document terms happen to be of the same language (e.g. Arabic), the same retrieval system was also used for monolingual experiments. For simple monolingual IR, the lexicon used for term "translation" is an identity matrix, where $p(a|b)=1$ if $a=b$ and 0 otherwise. For thesaurus-based monolingual retrieval, the translation probabilities were calculated from the UN parallel corpus as discussed in the previous section.

For CLIR, translation probabilities were estimated from the same UN parallel corpus and were combined with a manual bilingual lexicon, the Buckwalter lexicon (Buckwalter, 2001), with around 86,000 Arabic-English word pairs. We assume that translation probabilities in the manual lexicon are uniformly distributed. That is, if an Arabic term has n English translations, each translation gets $1/n$ probability. The two lexical resources were combined using a mixture model with equal weights to produce a single probabilistic bilingual lexicon for term translation.

In our monolingual experiments, the background corpus GL is the TREC 2001 Arabic corpus. In our CLIR experiments, the background corpus consists of newspaper articles in TREC English disks 1-5.

4 EXPERIMENTAL SETUP

Our experiments were performed on the TREC 2001 Arabic corpus (Voorhees, 2001). That corpus has 383,872 Arabic documents from Agence France Presse (AFP) with 25 test topics. Each topic has three versions, Arabic, English and French. The Arabic topics were used in our monolingual experiments and the English topics in our CLIR experiments. Only the title and description fields of the topics were used in query formulation. Retrieval performance was measured using the TREC non-interpolated average precision (Voorhees, 2001).

In addition to average precision, standard t-test (Hull, 1993) was used to determine the statistical significance of the retrieval difference between two retrieval runs. A difference is considered to be statistically significant if the p_value is less than 0.05.

We used the Arabic stop word list compiled by Yaser Al-Onaizan (http://www.isi.edu/~yaser/arabic/arabic-stop-words.html). That list was augmented with a handful of manually selected high frequency words from the AFP corpus. In our experiments, English words were stemmed using the Porter stemmer (Porter, 1980).

5 BASELINE FOR ARABIC MONOLINGUAL RETRIEVAL

Experiments in this section will establish a baseline for Arabic monolingual retrieval. Since spelling normalization and stemming are well-studied IR techniques, they were employed in the baseline.

Ambiguities arise when the Buckwalter stemmer returns several stems for a word. We considered two alternatives, *sure-stem* and *all-stems*. With *sure-stem*, we only stemmed a word if it has exactly one possible stem. Otherwise, the word was left alone. Both the documents and the queries were processed in the same manner. With *all-stems*, we did not stem the words in the documents but instead probabilistically "translated" them to stems. The query words were stemmed though, by replacing each word by its possible stem(s). In the absence of training data, we assume that all possible stems are equally-probable. That is, if a word w has n possible stems s_1, s_2, ...s_n, then $p(s_i|w)=1/n$. The advantage of sure-stem is that it does not introduce additional ambiguity, while the advantage of all-stems is that it always finds a stem for a word when one exists.

To show the impact of spelling normalizations (see Section 2.1) and stemming, four retrieval runs were carried out:

1. There was no text processing except for the removal of the stop words from the documents and the queries.
2. Spelling normalization was used in addition to stop word removal
3. Sure-stem was used in addition to stop word removal and spelling normalization
4. All-stems was used in addition to stop word removal and spelling normalization

In 1-3, translation probability $p(t_q|t_d)=1$ if $t_q=t_d$ and 0 otherwise. That is, a term was only translated to itself.

Results in Table 1 show that spelling normalization produced a 22% relative improvement in retrieval performance. The improvement is statistically significant (p_value=0.017). This is not surprising because spelling variations are prevalent in the test corpus. Statistics from the test corpus indicate that about 80% of the words containing a glyph combining HAMZA or MADDA with ALEF also have a variant with just a plain ALEF in the corpus. A human assessment of a few hundred sentences indicates that if two words exist which are only different in that one has such a glyph and the other has a plain ALEF, most occurrences of the word with a plain ALEF would be written as the word containing the glyph under a strict writing standard.

Sure-stem stemming produced a remarkable 40% relative improvement in performance. The improvement is statistically significant (*p*_value=0.003). The impact of stemming on Arabic retrieval is far greater than the impact on English retrieval (Harman, 1991). The complex morphology of Arabic causes a high level of synonymy in its vocabulary. For example, the TREC Arabic corpus has over 500,000 unique unstemmed words. In comparison, an English corpus of comparable size (Wall Street Journal in TREC disks1&2) has about 200,000 unstemmed words. Many Arabic words can be conflated to the same stem. Statistics collected from the test corpus indicate that 1,300 stems have 50 or more unstemmed words, and 300 stems have over 100 unstemmed words. Given such data, it is understandable that stemming has such a big impact on retrieval.

There is little difference between the retrieval scores of sure-stem and all-stems. The difference is not statistically significant. Statistics show that 7% of words in the test corpus have two or more possible stems. The percentage is probably too small to have an impact on retrieval. We will use the sure-stem result as our monolingual baseline.

Table 1: Impact of spelling normalization and stemming on Arabic monolingual retrieval

Stop words removal	Normalization	Sure-stem	All-stems
0.1873	0.2291	0.3208	0.3131

6 IMPROVING ON THE MONOLINGUAL BASELINE

6.1 N-gram-based Retrieval

Two methods of creating n-grams were tried: from words and from stems. Retrieval scores in Table 2 show that stem-based n-grams are better than word-based n-grams for retrieval. The probable reason is that some of the word-based n-grams are prefixes or suffixes, which can cause false matches between documents and queries. The best results were obtained with trigrams, suggesting that bigrams carry too little contextual information while 4-grams and longer ones simply simulate word or stem-based retrieval.

Trigrams from stems produced the best result, with a 5% relative improvement over the baseline (from 0.3208 to 0.3365). However, the improvement is not statistically significant, meaning the benefit of using n-grams is not conclusive.

Table 2 : Retrieval results using n-grams

	Bigrams	Trigrams	4-grams
Words	0.1461	0.2990	0.2900
Stems	0.1655	0.3365	0.3165

6.2 Thesaurus-based Retrieval

Table 3 compares the retrieval performance of the statistical thesaurus described in section 2.4 with the baseline and the trigram results. The smoothing parameter β in the mixture model was set to 0.1 in the experiment. The relative improvement over the baseline is 18%. The improvement over trigrams is 13%. The improvements in both cases are statistically significant (*p*_value=0.006 and 0.031 respectively). The results clearly show that the thesaurus is a better technique than the use of n-grams for improving on the monolingual baseline. While it appears that both broken plurals and general synonyms have contributed to the improved retrieval, a breakdown of the two factors is not available because we do not have a human assessment on the word pairs in the thesaurus. This is left for future work.

Table 3 : Comparing baseline, trigrams and thesaurus for Arabic monolingual retrieval

Baseline	Trigrams	Thesaurus
0.3208	0.3365	0.3790

Figure 1 shows the retrieval performance as a function of the smoothing parameter β. As we discussed in Section 2.4, a larger β places more confidence in the original terms while a smaller β places more confidence in the translations learned from the parallel corpus. Retrieval performance peaks when β=0.1. Overall, retrieval performance is not sensitive to the choice of β: Any value between 0 and 0.4 works fine.

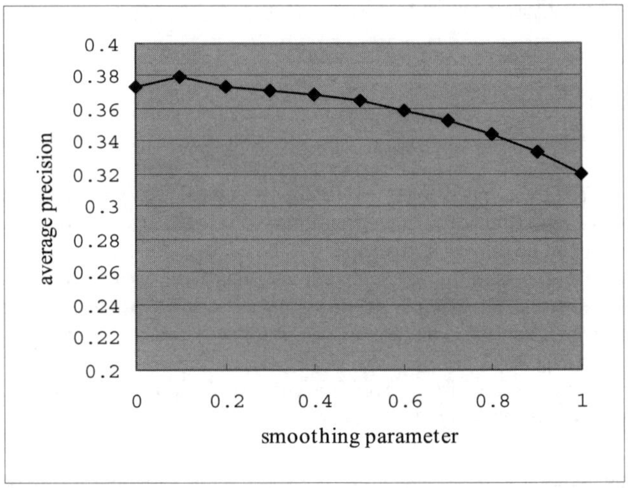

Figure 1: The effect of smoothing parameter β on thesaurus-based retrieval.

Using a thesaurus can be viewed as a query expansion technique. Another commonly used query expansion technique in IR is local feedback (Buckley et al, 1996). Local feedback selects terms from top retrieved documents and adds them to the initial query. The expanded queries usually significantly improve retrieval performance. One may wonder whether thesaurus and local feedback overlap, and whether using one eliminates the need for the other.

To address that concern, we compared two versions of local feedback. In one, the statistical thesaurus was used in both the initial retrieval and the final retrieval with the expanded queries.

In the other, the thesaurus was not used at all. In our experiments, local feedback selected 50 terms from 10 top retrieved documents based on their total *tf×idf* weight in the top documents. The expansion terms and the original query terms were re-weighted. In the probabilistic retrieval model used in this work, we interpret the weight of a query term to be the frequency of the term being generated in query generation. As described in Section 3, the frequency is used as an exponent in the retrieval function. With local feedback, the frequency of a term t in a query Q is calculated:

$$f(t,Q) = f_{old}(t,Q) + 0.4 \sum_{1 \le i \le 10} tfidf(t, D_i)$$

where D_i is a top retrieved document, $tfidf(t, D_i)$ is the *tf×idf* weight of term t in D_i, $f_{old}(t, Q)$ and $f(t, Q)$ are the old and new frequencies of t in the query. The *tf* and *idf* functions were based on the ones described in (Allan et al, 2000).

Results in Table 4 show that using local feedback and the thesaurus together is 15% better than local feedback alone. This is comparable to the 18% improvement produced by the thesaurus when local feedback was not used. The improvement is statistically significant (p_value=0.015). The results suggest that local feedback and the thesaurus are two different types of query expansion techniques.

Table 4: The impact of the thesaurus when used together with local feedback

Local feedback only	Local feedback + Thesaurus
0.4020	0.4630

7 CROSS-LINGUAL EXPERIMENTS

To explore the impact of spelling normalization and Arabic stemming on CLIR, we have compared three versions of bilingual lexicon creation for term translation. All three were formed from the UN parallel corpus and the Buckwalter lexicon using the same procedure described in Section 3. The only difference is that the Arabic terms are non-normalized words in the first lexicon, are non-normalized stems in the second, and are normalized stems in the third.

Results in Table 5 show that the differences between the three versions of lexicon are very small. The differences are not statistically significant. This is different from monolingual IR, where spelling normalization and stemming had a very big impact. The explanation is that the UN parallel corpus, with over 50 million words in each language, has enough data to enable GIZA++ to reliably learn the English translations for most Arabic words. It appears that the Buckwalter lexicon also lists the most common Arabic spelling variants. Therefore, the advantage of translating words by groups over translating them individually is very small. Besides, stemming and normalization invariably introduce ambiguity. Apparently, the small benefit of stemming and spelling normalization was canceled by the introduced ambiguity. Although their impact on CLIR performance is small, spelling normalization and stemming are still useful because they reduce the need for memory because there are fewer entries in the lexicon and they improve the retrieval speed by simplifying the score computation.

Table 5: The effect of spelling normalization and stemming of Arabic words on CLIR

Translation of non-normalized words	Translation of non-normalized stems	Translation of normalized stems
0.3447	0.3584	0.3604

One might wonder whether we can use the Arabic monolingual thesaurus to improve CLIR. The assumption is that the thesaurus would be useful for cases where we do not know how to translate a word but we do know how to translate its synonyms. We did not run such an experiment because it is computationally prohibitive, requiring multiplying three large matrices. But based on a similar argument to the one we just made, it is unlikely such an experiment would produce better retrieval results given that we already have enough resources for effective term translation.

8 RELATED WORK

A key enabling element for our work has been the release by NIST of a large Arabic corpus with relevance judgments for both monolingual and cross-lingual retrieval (Voorhees, 2001). Arabic stemming algorithms can be roughly classified as either stem-based or root-based. While stem-based algorithms such as the Buckwalter stemmer (Buckwalter, 2001) remove prefixes and suffixes from Arabic words, root-based algorithms (Beesley 1996; Khoja and Garside, 2001) further reduce stems to roots. A study reported better results using roots than stems on a very small test corpus (Abu-Salem et al, 1999). However, a later study on the TREC corpus showed that stem-based retrieval is more effective than root-based retrieval (Aljlayl et al, 2001). The idea of using n-grams for Arabic retrieval appeared in several studies (Darwish et al, 2001; Mayfield et al, 2001; Kwok et al, 2001).

The use of thesauri in IR has been extensively studied under a variety of names, such as keyword clustering (Spark Jones, 1971), co-ocurrence thesauri (Jing and Croft 1994; Schütze and Pedersen, 1994) and Latent Semantic Indexing (Deerwester et al, 1990). One difference from existing approaches is that our thesaurus was derived from a parallel corpus instead of a monolingual corpus. Another difference is that our thesaurus is probabilistically motivated. A similar idea was proposed by (Berger and Lafferty, 1999). But that work used artificially synthesized training data while ours used a parallel corpus. The use of parallel corpora for Cross-lingual IR has been well studied (Sheridan and Ballerini, 1996; Nie et al, 1999; J. McCarley, 1999). The use of probabilistic generative models for IR appeared in a number of studies (Ponte and Croft, 1998; Miller et al, 1999; Hiemstra and de Jong, 1999).

9 CONCLUSIONS AND FUTURE WORK

This work evaluated a number of search strategies for the retrieval of Arabic documents, using the TREC Arabic corpus as the test bed. For Arabic monolingual retrieval, spelling normalization significantly improved retrieval performance by 22%. Stemming is critical, improving retrieval performance by 40%. Two techniques were explored to further improve retrieval. Tri-grams from stems produced a modest improvement in retrieval, but the improvement is not statistically significant. In comparison, a sophisticated statistical thesaurus boosted retrieval performance by 18%. We also studied the impact of spelling normalization and stemming on Arabic CLIR. Retrieval results show that their impact on CLIR is very small.

There are a number of areas for future work. First, we would like to compare our stemming algorithms with other Arabic stemming algorithms. Second, we would like to compare our thesaurus-based technique with similar techniques such as Latent Semantic Indexing. Third, we would like to apply our thesaurus-based technique to other languages. For example, by simply swapping the roles of Arabic and English, we can induce an English thesaurus instead of an Arabic one from the UN parallel corpus. Fourth, we would like to classify the word pairs in our thesaurus and investigate which category (broken plurals or general synonyms) has the largest impact on retrieval. Fifth, we would like to validate our techniques on more test corpora when they are available. Such a validation is necessary since the problem of incomplete relevance judgments is potentially severe for the TREC 2001 Arabic corpus (Gey and Oard, 2001).

REFERENCES

[1] Abu-Salem, H., Al-Omari, M., and Evens, M. 1999. "Stemming Methodologies Over Individual Query Words for an Arabic Information Retrieval System". In *JASIS*, 50(6), May, 1999.

[2] Aljlayl, M., Beitzel, S., Jensen, E., Lee, M., Grossman, D., Frieder, O., Chowdhury, A. and Holmes, D. "IIT at TREC-10." In *TREC 2001 Proceedings*.

[3] Allan, J., Callan, J., Feng, F., and Malin, D. 2000. "INQUERY at TREC8." In *TREC8 Proceedings*, Special publication by NIST, 2000.

[4] Beesley, K. 1996. "Arabic Finite-State Morphological Analysis and Generation." *COLING*-96, 1996.

[5] Berger, A., and Lafferty, J. 1999. "Information retrieval as statistical translation." In *Proceedings of SIGIR,* 1999.

[6] Brown, P., Della Pietra, S., Della Pietra, V., Lafferty J., and Mercer., R. 1993. "The Mathematics of Statistical Machine Translation: Parameter Estimation". In *Computational Linguistics,* 19(2), 1993.

[7] Buckley, C., Singhal, A., Mitra M., and Salton, G. 1996. "New Retrieval Approaches using SMART". In *TREC 4 Proceedings*, NIST Special Publications.

[8] Buckwalter, T. 2001. Personal Communications.

[9] Darwish, K., Doermann, D., Jones, R., Oard D., and Rautiainen, M. "TREC-10 Experiments at Maryland: CLIR and Video." In *TREC* 2001 *Proceedings*.

[10] Deerwester, S., Dumais, S., Furnas, G., Landauer, T., Harshman, R. 1990. "Indexing by Latent Semantic Analysis." *JASIS*, 41, 391-407, 1990.

[11] Gey, F., and Oard, D. 2001. "The TREC-2001 Cross-Language Information Retrieval Track: Searching Arabic using English, French or Arabic Queries." In *TREC 2001 Proceedings*, to be published.

[12] Harman, D. 1991. "How effective is suffixing?" *JASIS*, 42:7-15, 1991.

[13] Hiemstra, D., and de Jong, F. 1999. "Disambiguation strategies for cross-language information retrieval." In *Proceedings of the third European Conference on Research and Advanced Technology for Digital Libraries*, pages 274-293, 1999.

[14] Hull, D. 1993. "Using statistical testing in the evaluation of retrieval experiments." In *Proceedings of SIGIR,* 1993, pages 329-328.

[15] Jing Y., and Croft, W. B. 1994. "An Association Thesaurus for Information Retrieval." In *Proceedings of RIAO,* 1994, pages 146-160.

[16] Khoja S., and Garside, R. 2001. "Stemming Arabic Text", Tech Report, Dept of CS, Lancaster Univ., U.K.

[17] Kwok, K., Grunfeld, L., Dinstl, N., Chan, M. 2001. "TREC 2001 Question Answering, Web, Cross-lingual Experiments using PIRCS." In *TREC 2001 Proceedings.*

[18] Mayfield, J., McNamee, P., Costello, C., Piatko, C., and Banerjee. A. 2001. "JHU/APL at TREC 2001: Experiments in Filtering and in Arabic, Video and Web retrieval." In *TREC 2001 Proceedings.*

[19] McCarley, J. 1999. "Should we translate the documents or the queries in cross-language information retrieval." In *Proceedings of ACL*, pages 208-214, June 1999.

[20] Miller, D., Leek, T., and Schwartz, R. 1999. "A Hidden Markov Model Information Retrieval System." In *Proceedings of SIGIR*, 1999.

[21] Nie, J., Simard, M., Isabella, P., Durand, R. 1999. "Cross-Language Information Retrieval based on Parallel Texts and Automatic Mining of Parallel Text from the Web." In *Proceedings of SIGIR*, 1999, pages 74-81.

[22] Noamany, M. 2001. Personal communications.

[23] Och, F., and Ney, H. 2000. "Improved Statistical Alignment Models." In *proceedings of ACL,* 2000.

[24] Ponte, J., and Croft, W. B. 1998. "A language modeling approach to information retrieval." In *Proceedings of SIGIR*, 1998, pages 275-281.

[25] Porter, M. 1980. "An algorithm for suffix stripping." *Program* 14, 3(1980), pages 130-137.

[26] Schütze, H., and Pedersen, J. 1994. "A Cooccurrence-based Thesaurus and Two Applications to Information Retrieval." In *Proceedings of RIAO*, 1994, pages 266-274.

[27] Sheridan, P., and Ballerini, J. 1996. "Experiments in Multilingual Information Retrieval using the SPIDER System." In *Proceedings of SIGIR*, 1996, pages 58-65.

[28] Spark Jones, K., 1971. *Automatic Keyword Classification for Information Retrieval.* Butterworth, London.

[29] Voorhees, E. 2001. *TREC 2001 Proceedings.* To be published by NIST.

[30] Xu, J,. Weischedel, R,. and Nguyen, C. 2001. "Evaluating A Probabilistic Model for Cross-lingual Information retrieval." In *Proceedings of SIGIR,* 2001, pages 105-110.

Improving Stemming for Arabic Information Retrieval: Light Stemming and Co-occurrence Analysis

Leah S. Larkey
Univ. of Massachusetts
Dept. of Computer Science
Amherst, MA 01003
larkey@cs.umass.edu

Lisa Ballesteros
Computer Science Dept.
Mt. Holyoke College
South Hadley, MA 01075
lballest@mtholyoke.edu

Margaret E. Connell
Univ. of Massachusetts
Dept. of Computer Science
Amherst, MA 01003
connell@cs.umass.edu

ABSTRACT
Arabic, a highly inflected language, requires good stemming for effective information retrieval, yet no standard approach to stemming has emerged. We developed several light stemmers based on heuristics and a statistical stemmer based on co-occurrence for Arabic retrieval. We compared the retrieval effectiveness of our stemmers and of a morphological analyzer on the TREC-2001 data. The best light stemmer was more effective for cross-language retrieval than a morphological stemmer which tried to find the root for each word. A repartitioning process consisting of vowel removal followed by clustering using co-occurrence analysis produced stem classes which were better than no stemming or very light stemming, but still inferior to good light stemming or morphological analysis.

Categories and Subject Descriptors
H.3.1 [**Information Storage and Retrieval**]: Content Analysis and Indexing – *Indexing methods, Linguistic processing;* H.3.3 [**Information Storage and Retrieval**]: Information Search and Retrieval – *Clustering.*

General Terms: Experimentation, Performance, Algorithms.

Keywords: Cross-language information retrieval, cross-lingual, stemming, Arabic.

1. INTRODUCTION
Stemming is one of many tools used in information retrieval to combat the vocabulary mismatch problem, in which query words do not match document words. Stemmers equate or *conflate* certain variant forms of the same word like (*paper, papers*) and (*fold, folds, folded, folding...*). In English and many other western European languages, stemming is primarily a process of suffix removal [32, 40]. Such stemmers do not conflate irregular forms such as (*goose, geese*) and (*swim, swam*). In this work, we use the term stemming to refer to any process which conflates related forms or groups forms into equivalence classes, including but not restricted to suffix stripping. Stemming has been shown to improve performance in information retrieval tasks, usually by a small amount [25] and is considered to aid recall more than precision [29].

Stemmers are generally tailored for each specific language. Their design requires some linguistic expertise in the language and an understanding of the needs of information retrieval. Stemmers have been developed for a wide range of languages including Malay [42], Latin [23], Indonesian [7], Swedish [11], Dutch [29], German [35], French [36], Slovene [39], and Turkish [15]. The effectiveness of stemming across languages is varied and influenced by many factors. A reasonable summary is that stemming doesn't hurt retrieval; it either makes little difference or it improves performance by a small amount. Stemming appears to improve effectiveness more for highly inflected languages [38, 39] and when queries and/or documents are short [30].

Statistical methods can provide a more language-independent approach to conflation. Related words can be grouped based on various string-similarity measures. Such approaches often involve n-grams. Equivalence classes can be formed from words that share word-initial letter n-grams or a threshold proportion of n-grams throughout the word, or by refining these classes with clustering techniques. This kind of statistical stemming has been shown to be effective for many languages, including English, Turkish, and Malay [15, 17, 18, 37].

Stem classes can also be built or refined using co-occurrence analysis, which Xu and Croft proposed as a promising language-independent approach to stemming [45]. They demonstrated an improvement in retrieval effectiveness for English and Spanish after clustering conventional and n-gram based stem classes. Initial n-gram based stem classes are probably not the right starting point for languages like Arabic in which suffixing is not the only inflectional process. (See the overview of Arabic language issues below). However, co-occurrence or other clustering techniques can be applied to Arabic without using n-grams.

In the research reported here, we developed several light stemmers for Arabic which remove a small number of prefixes and suffixes and a co-occurrence based statistical stemmer which creates large stem classes by vowel removal and then refines these classes using co-occurrence. We evaluate these and several other approaches to Arabic stemming.

2. THE ARABIC LANGUAGE AND ORTHOGRAPHY
Arabic information retrieval has a particularly acute need for effective normalization and stemming. Both orthography and morphology give rise to a huge amount of lexical variation. *Vocalized*

text includes diacritics for short vowels and other details, conveying a nearly phonetic representation of a word, but it is only found in special contexts. The newspaper articles that make up the TREC-2001 corpus are not vocalized. Nonvocalized orthography is more ambiguous, and can cause a mismatch with texts, dictionaries, or queries that are vocalized. Regional variations in spelling add to the vocabulary mismatch problem.

Other variability arises from the derivational and inflectional productiveness of Arabic. A given word can be found in huge number of different forms which should possibly be conflated for information retrieval. Many definite articles, conjunctions, particles and other prefixes can attach to the beginning of a word, and large numbers of suffixes can attach to the end. At a deeper level, most noun, adjective, and verb stems are derived from a few thousand roots by infixing, for example, creating words like *maktab* (office), *kitaab* (book), *kutub* (books), *kataba* (he wrote), and *naktubu* (we write), from the root *ktb* [44].

Thus, some of the most closely related forms such as singular and plural nouns are irregular, and are not related by simple affixing (prefixing and suffixing). This situation is seen in English for a tiny fraction of nouns and a small number of very frequent verbs like the examples in the first paragraph of this paper, but is very common in Arabic.

For information retrieval, this abundance of forms means a greater likelihood of mismatch between the form of a word in a query and the forms found in documents relevant to the query. Distributional analyses of Arabic newspaper text show more words occurring only once and more distinct words than English text samples of comparable size.[1] The token to type ratio (mean number of occurrences over all distinct words in the sample) is smaller for Arabic texts than for comparably sized English texts [22]. Stemming should therefore be very important for Arabic information retrieval.

3. PREVIOUS RESEARCH

3.1 Stemming in Arabic

All the factors described in the previous section make Arabic very difficult to stem. First, there is the choice between roots or stems as the desired level of analysis for information retrieval. Considerable research on stemming and morphological analysis is amassing for the Arabic language, but no standard IR-oriented algorithm has yet emerged.

Four different approaches to Arabic stemming can be identified – manually constructed dictionaries, algorithmic light stemmers which remove prefixes and suffixes, morphological analyses which attempt to find roots, and statistical stemmers, which group word variants using clustering techniques.

Manually constructed dictionaries of words with stemming information are in surprisingly wide use. Al-Kharashi and Evens worked with small text collections, for which they manually built dictionaries of roots and stems for each word to be indexed [4]. Tim Buckwalter [9] developed a set of lexicons of Arabic stems, prefixes, and suffixes, with truth tables indicating legal combinations. The BBN group used this table-based stemmer in TREC-2001 [46].

Light stemming refers to a process of stripping off a small set of prefixes and/or suffixes, without trying to deal with infixes, or recognize patterns and find roots. Light stemming is mentioned by some authors without details [3, 14]. No explicit lists of strippable prefixes and/or suffixes or algorithm had been published at the time we did this research. Although light stemming can correctly conflate many variants of words into large stem classes, it can fail to conflate other forms that should go together. For example, broken (irregular) plurals for nouns and adjectives do not get conflated with their singular forms, and past tense verbs do not get conflated with their present tense forms, because they retain some affixes and internal differences.

Several morphological analyzers have been developed for Arabic [2, 5, 6, 12, 27] but few have received a standard IR evaluation. Such analyzers find the root, or any number of possible roots for each word. In addition, some attempt a more complete grammatical analysis of the word [6]. A morphological analyzer developed by Kareem Darwish was used by some of the TREC participants in 2001 [12, 33]. We obtained a simple morphological analyzer from Khoja and Garside [27] for this research.

Published comparisons of stems vs. roots for information retrieval have claimed that roots are superior to stems, based on small, nonstandard test sets [1, 4]. Recent work at TREC found no consistent differences between roots and stems [12].

3.2 Statistical Approaches to Stemming

Statistical techniques have widely been applied to automatic morphological analysis in the field of computational linguistics [8, 13, 16, 20, 21, 24, 26, 28]. For example, Goldsmith finds the best set of frequently occurring stems and suffixes using an information theoretic measure [20]. Oard et al. consider the most frequently occurring word-final n-grams (1, 2, 3, and 4-grams) to be suffixes [37]. Although such systems can be used on many different languages, they cannot be expected to perform well on languages like Arabic in which suffixing is not the only inflectional process.

Mayfield et al. have developed a system which combines word-based and 6-gram based retrieval, which performs remarkably well for many languages [34] including Arabic [33].

Al-Fares and De Roeck [14] used clustering on Arabic words to find classes sharing the same root. Their clustering was based on morphological similarity, using a string similarity metric tailored to Arabic morphology, which was applied after removing "a small number of obvious affixes." They evaluated the technique by comparing the derived clusters to "correct" classes. They did not assess the performance in an information retrieval context.

Stemmers make two kinds of errors. Weak stemmers fail to conflate related forms that should be grouped together. Strong stemmers tend to form larger stem classes in which unrelated forms are erroneously conflated. Most stemmers fall between these two extremes and make both kinds of errors. Xu and Croft [45] employ a corpus analysis approach which is particularly suited to splitting up stem classes created by strong stemmers. The stem-classes are reclustered based on a co-occurrence measure, which is language independent in that it can be applied to any set of stem classes.

[1] We use the term *word* in simple sense of text segmented at white space or punctuation, without any morphological analysis.

Xu and Croft applied their technique to effectively stem English and Spanish and showed two important points. First, one can refine an already-good stemmer by co-occurrence analysis and improve average precision. Second, one can start with a strong crude stemmer like an n-gram stemmer and use co-occurrence analysis to yield stem classes that work as well as a sophisticated stemmer.

In this work we apply the technique to Arabic, which has a more complex morphology than Spanish or English. Our goal was to determine whether a simple and effective Arabic stemmer could be quickly developed without a considerable amount of linguistic knowledge. Details of this technique are given in Section 4.5.

4. OUR APPROACHES TO ARABIC STEMMING

In the present research we compare several different approaches: no stemming, light stemming, morphological analysis to find roots, and statistical stemming using co-occurrence analysis, on the TREC-2001 Arabic data.

4.1 Normalization

Before stemming, corpus and queries were normalized as follows:

- Convert to Windows Arabic encoding (CP1256)
- Remove punctuation
- Remove diacritics (primarily weak vowels). Some dictionary entries contained weak vowels. Removal made everything consistent.
- Remove non letters
- Replace آ , إ , and أ with ا
- Replace final ى with ي
- Replace final ة with ه

4.2 Light Stemmers

Although several researchers allude to light stemming, we found no publication explicitly listing which affixes should be removed. Our guiding principle was to try to remove strings which would be found as affixes far more often than they would be found as the beginning or end of an Arabic word without affixes. We also benefited from discussions with some colleagues at TREC-2001, particularly M. Aljlayl. We tried several versions of light stemming, all of which followed the same steps:

1. Remove و ("and") for light2, light3, and light8 if the remainder of the word is 3 or more characters long. Although it is important to remove و, it is also problematic, because many common Arabic words begin with this character, hence the stricter length criterion here than for the definite articles.
2. Remove any of the definite articles if this leaves 2 or more characters.
3. Go through the list of suffixes once in the (right to left) order indicated in Table 1, removing any that are found at the end of the word, if this leaves 2 or more characters.

The strings to be removed are listed in Table 1. The "prefixes" are actually definite articles and a conjunction. The light stemmers do not remove any strings that would be considered Arabic prefixes.

Table 1: Strings removed by light stemming

	Remove from front	Remove Suffixes
Light1	ال، وال، بال، ك، فل	none
Light2	ال، وال، بال، كال، فال، و	none
Light3	"	ه، ة
Light8	"	ها، ان، ات، ون، ين، يه، ية، ه، ة، ي

4.3 Morphological Analysis

For morphological analysis we used software developed by Khoja and Garside [27], which first peels away layers of prefixes and suffixes, then checks a list of patterns and roots to determine whether the remainder could be a known root with a known pattern applied. If so, it returns the root. Otherwise, it returns the original word, unmodified. This system also removes terms that are found on a list of 168 Arabic stop words. Unlike the Buckwalter approach, this scheme has no table restricting the patterns and affixes applicable to particular stems and roots. Preliminary work with the Khoja stemmer revealed problems with proper nouns, so our implementation included a list of country and major city names translated into Arabic, considered "unbreakable," and exempted from further stemming. We tested the morphological analyzer both with and without the unbreakables.

4.4 Simple Stemmers

Many of the variant patterns derived from a single Arabic root differ internally only in vowels (see the examples in section 2). Removing vowels collapses the light stem classes into a smaller number of larger classes, grouping many forms that belong together and many forms that do not. Simple stemming consisted of light stemming and removal of vowels ا ,و, ي, ء. (Short vowels were already removed during normalization). Our simple stemmers were intended to be strong, that is, to conflate too many forms, so that subsequent statistical analysis could find better classes by splitting.

We used three simple stemmers: *Simple* stems were derived by removing vowels from normalized words. *Simple2* applied light2 stemming, and then removal of vowels. *Simple8* applied light8 stemming, and then removal of vowels.

4.5 Co-occurrence Analysis

Co-occurrence analysis was used to refine the simple stemmers and the khoja stemmer, which were the strongest stemmers in the sense of creating the largest and overly-inclusive stem classes. We refer to the combined process of removing vowels and refinement with co-occurrence analysis as *repartitioning.*

Co-occurrence analysis is based on *em*, a variant of *EMIM* (expected mutual information) [43], which measures the proportion of word co-occurrences that are over and above what would be expected by chance. For two terms, *a* and *b*, *em* is defined as:

$$em(a,b) = \max(\frac{n_{ab} - En(a,b)}{n_a + n_b}, 0)$$

where n_{ab} is the number of times *a* and *b* co-occur in a text window of fixed size. n_a and n_b are the number of occurrences of *a* and *b* in the corpus. *En(a,b)*, the expected number of co-occurrences of a and b, is $kn_a n_b$, where k is a constant based upon the corpus and window size. k is estimated from a sample of 5000 randomly chosen word pairs:

$$k = \sum n_{ab} / \sum n_a n_b$$

In our experiments, $k = 4.85 \times 10^{-6}$. The Arabic documents are short (150 words on average), so we used document length as our window size.

To repartition a stem class, the *em* metric is calculated for all the pairs of words in the class. In a first pass, a connected component algorithm is used to connect term pairs if their *em* score exceeds a threshold, *emthresh*. When the size of a resulting cluster is greater than twelve, a second-pass optimization is performed via *approximate optimal partitioning* [45]. In this second pass all pair-wise *em* scores are used to calculate an overall fitness measure, *cohesion*, for the class. A greedy algorithm refines the class by keeping terms that maximize cohesion and removing terms that lower it. This is done by partitioning the class into singleton sets, then repeatedly forming the union of the two sets for which cohesion is greatest. The algorithm stops when no two classes have a positive cohesion or when all terms belong to one class. Cohesion for a pair of terms, a and b, is calculated as $em(a,b) - \delta$, where δ is a limit on the amount by which conflating the terms could hurt precision. Cohesion for a set is the sum of cohesions for all pairs of words in the set.

In Xu and Croft's work, *emthresh* = 0.01 and $\delta = 0.0075$ were found to work well for the range of collections to which they applied the technique. We varied the values of these parameters for Arabic and did not find better values.

5. MONOLINGUAL ARABIC STEMMING EXPERIMENTS

5.1 Experimental Method

The TREC-2001 Arabic corpus, also called the AFP_ARB corpus, consists of 383,872 newspaper articles in Arabic from *Agence France Presse*. This fills up almost a gigabyte in UTF-8 encoding as distributed by the Linguistic Data Consortium. There are 25 topics with relevance judgments, available in Arabic, French, and English, with *Title*, *Description*, and *Narrative* fields. Although this test collection is small and has some problems, it is the only standard Arabic test set available [19]. We used the Arabic titles and descriptions as queries in monolingual experiments, and the English titles and descriptions in cross-language experiments.

Corpus and queries were converted to CP1256 encoding and indexed using an in-house version of INQUERY [10]. Arabic strings were treated as a simple string of bytes, regardless of how they would be rendered on the screen. Text was broken up into words at any white space or punctuation characters, including Arabic punctuation. Words of one-byte length (in CP1256 encoding) were not indexed. The experiments reported here used INQUERY for retrieval.

For the normalized conditions and some stemming conditions, we stemmed all tokens before indexing, and stemmed the queries with the same stemmer for retrieval. The co-occurrence experiments employed *query-based stemming*, where all retrieval uses a normalized, unstemmed database. The query was expanded, replacing each query term with a #syn (synonym) operator enclosing all members of the query term's stem class. We verified for several baseline stemming conditions that we get identical results whether we stem queries and corpus, or use query-based-stemming.

Arabic queries were expanded using the technique of local context analysis, adding 50 terms from the top 10 documents, as described in detail in [31]. Expansion was performed in order to show the ultimate level of performance attainable using the stemmers in the context of our whole system.

5.2 Results

5.2.1 Comparison of Basic Stemmers

Figure 1 shows precision at 11 recall points for the primary stemmers tested. *Raw* means no normalization or stemming, *khoja* means the Khoja stemmer, and *khoja-u* refers to the Khoja stemmer with the addition of the *unbreakables* list of items exempted from stemming.

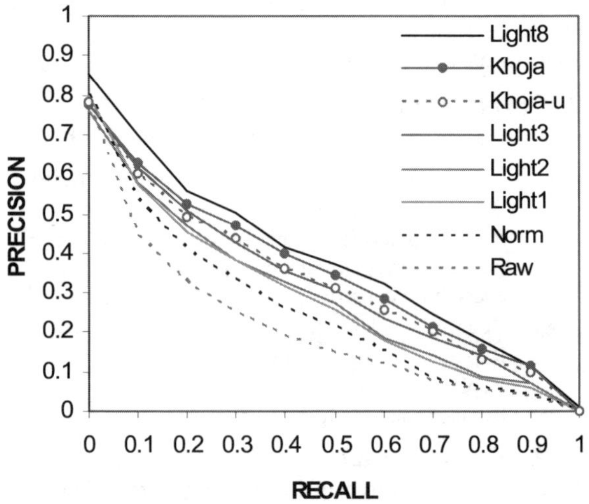

Figure 1: Monolingual 11 point precision for basic stemmers, unexpanded queries

Table 2: Monolingual average precision for basic stemmers, unexpanded

Stemmer	**raw**	**norm**	**light1**	**light2**	**light3**
Av. Precision	.194	.238	.273	.284	.317
Pct. Change		23.1	41.1	46.7	63.9

Stemmer	**raw**	**khoja-u**	**khoja**	**light8**
Av. Precision	.194	.313	.341	.376
Pct. Change		61.7	76.2	94.3

Table 2 shows uninterpolated average precision for the basic stemmers. For raw, normalized, and light stemming conditions performance is better with each successive increment in degree of stemming. Each of these increments is statistically significant.[2] Surprisingly, on this data set, the Khoja stemmer performed better without the unbreakable list of countries and cities. However, this difference is not statistically significant. Although the light8 stemmer looks better than Khoja these differences are also not significant. Because the Khoja stemmer removes stop words and the other stemmers do not, we consider stop word removal next.

5.2.2 Removing Stop Words

Table 3 shows the effect of removing stop words. For all four degrees of stemming: raw, norm, light2, and light8, removing stop words results in a small increase in average precision, which is statistically significant for light2 and light8, but not for raw and normalized conditions.

Table 3: Monolingual average precision for stemmers with and without removing stop words

Stemmer	raw	norm	light2	light8
Stop words in	.194	.238	.284	.376
Stop words removed	.196	.241	.291	.389
Pct.Change	1.3	1.1	2.4	3.6

The fairer comparison between the khoja stemmers and light8 after removing stop words (light8-s) is summarized in Table 4. The difference between light8-s and khoja-u (with unbreakables) is statistically significant, for both unexpanded and expanded queries. The difference between light8-s and khoja (without unbreakables) is not significant for unexpanded or expanded queries. In short, the best stemmers for monolingual information retrieval were light8-s, a light stemmer, and khoja, a morphological analyzer.

Table 4: Monolingual average precision with and without query expansion

Stemmer	raw	norm-s	khoja-u	khoja	light8-s
Unexp.	.194	.241	.313	.341	.389
Expanded	.271	.330	.360	.378	.427

5.2.3 Simple Stemming and Co-occurrence Analysis

The four sections of Table 5 show retrieval performance and stem class sizes for each of the four baseline stemmers (in boldface) that were subjected to repartitioning (*norm-s, light2-s, light8-s,* and *khoja*). For norm-s, light2-s, and light8-s, the corresponding simple stemmer performance is shown. The khoja stemmer already had very large stem classes, so simple stemming before clustering was unnecessary. Finally, for all four baselines, the clustered stemmer performance is shown. Relative to simple stemming, clustering by co-occurrence significantly improves retrieval effectiveness in all cases.

[2] All significance tests were conducted using the Wilcoxon test [41] with a criterion of p<.05 for significance.

Table 5: Average Precision for monolingual retrieval - baseline, simple, and clustered stemmers

	Average Precision	Query Words Class size		Non-singleton Class Size
		Average	Max	Average
norm-s	**.241**	**1**	**1**	-
simple	.245	34	237	34
simple-c	.268	2.0	11	2.5
light2-s	**.291**	**3.6**	**4**	**3.7**
simple2	.267	58	317	58
simple2-c	.316	3.4	15	4.5
light8-s	**.389**	**22**	**45**	**22**
simple8	.308	141	605	141
simple8-c	.390	5.4	26	7.1
khoja	**.341**	**262**	**929**	**265**
khoja-c	.347	5.6	30	7.0

Relative to the baseline stemmers norm-s and light2-s, repartitioning yields a net improvement. Simple-c (clustered simple stemmer) is significantly better than norm-s, and simple2-c (clustered simple2) is significantly better than light2-s. In other words, starting with no stemming or very light stemming (removing of definite articles and و from the beginnings of the words), then creating overly inclusive stem classes by removing vowels, and repartitioning the classes by co-occurrence analysis, results in a net improvement in stemming without a great deal of linguistic knowledge.

On the other hand, co-occurrence analysis did not improve the more sophisticated stemmers: *khoja-c* is not better than *khoja,* and *simple8-c* is not better than *light8-s*.

It may seem strange that co-occurrence analysis on the stronger baseline stemmers changed class sizes drastically but did not change performance very much. We took a closer look at light8-s stem classes to gain some understanding of this phenomenon. We found that although light8-s is our strongest light stemmer, it is still relatively weak in that it fails to conflate some forms that should be conflated. On the positive side, it rarely groups unrelated forms, and when it does, it groups variants of relatively few words e.g. 2 or 3, except for stop words where we see 5 or 6. The clusters for light8-s are fairly large (avg class size=22), and correctly so. Removing vowels (simple stemming) conflates many unrelated forms (avg class size=141); the co-occurrence clustering generally separates the unrelated forms back out. However, these repartitioned stem classes are much smaller than would be desired (mean class size=5) and contained only the highest frequency forms. This behavior was appropriate for the English and Spanish, for which this algorithm was developed, but not for Arabic. An algorithm that was not so biased against low frequency forms might have yielded a net improvement.

The example of stem classes for the word ي (*Arab* n. or adj.) in Table 6 is probably typical, given these numbers. The light8-s stem class contains 37 words, of which 26 are variants of the *Arab*. Nine words are variants of *chariot*. Two other words mean *earnest money*. Removing vowels (*simple8*) results in a stem class with 117 members (not shown) for the target word, which co-occurrence analysis (*simple8-c*) reduces to the 8 words shown. All of the variants of *chariot* and *earnest money* have gone away, but so have many good variants of *Arab*. This small new set includes one correct variant which was not in the original set of 36.

Ideally, the final stem class should include more of the original variants from light8-s and add more new variants if they appeared in simple8 and still keep the *chariot* and *earnest money* variants out. We are continuing to experiment with parameters and co-occurrence measures to see whether we can produce the larger classes appropriate to Arabic without bringing in too many unrelated forms.

Table 6: Example of stem classes under different stemmers

Stem class for ي under light8-s			
Variants of *Arab*		of *Chariot*	of *earnest money*
العربي	ين	ت	ن
العربي	ه	تها	العربون
العربيات	ب	والعربات	
العربيان	عربي	وعربات	
العربين	عربيات	العربات	
العربيه	عربيان	عربه	
العربيين	عربين	والعربه	
العربييه	عربيه	وعربه	
عرب	وعربي	العربه	
عربيين	والعربي		
عربييه	والعربيه		
والعرب	وعربيان		
وعرب	وعربيه		
Stem class under simple8-c			
All *Arab*			
العربي	عرب	عربيا	والعربي
العربيه	عربي	عربيه	العرب

5.3 Discussion

Although stemming is difficult in a language with complex morphology like Arabic, it is particularly important. For monolingual retrieval, we saw around 100% increase in average precision from raw retrieval to the best stemmer. The best stemmer in our experiments, light8-s was very simple and did not try to find roots or take into account most of Arabic morphology. It is probably not essential for the stemmer to yield the correct forms, whether stems or roots. It is sufficient for it to group most of the forms that belong together.

It was interesting that removing stop words had a significantly positive effect for stemmed Arabic, but not for unstemmed Arabic. This difference is probably due to the fact noted in section 5.2.3 that stem classes for stop words contain larger numbers of unrelated word variants than stem classes for other words.

6. CROSS-LANGUAGE ENGLISH-ARABIC EXPERIMENTS

For generality, the stemmers are compared on the cross-language retrieval task. The cross-language experiments reported here were carried out using the 25 English TREC-2001 queries and the same Arabic AFP_ARB corpus used for the monolingual experiments. Our approach is the common dictionary-based approach, in which each English query word is looked up in a bilingual dictionary. All the Arabic translations for that word are gathered inside an INQUERY #syn (synonym) operator. For an Arabic-English dictionary, we used a lexicon collected from several online English-Arabic and Arabic-English resources on the web, described more completely in [31]. Query expansion was carried out in conjunction with stemming. When English queries were expanded, 5 terms were added from the top 10 documents. When Arabic queries were expanded, 50 terms were added from the top 10 documents, as described [31].

Figure 2 shows precision on unexpanded queries for cross-language retrieval at 11 recall points for raw, norm-s (normalization and stop word removal), light8-s (light8 stemming with stop word removal), khoja-u (with unbreakables), and khoja stemmers. Table 7 shows uninterpolated average precision for unexpanded and expanded queries.

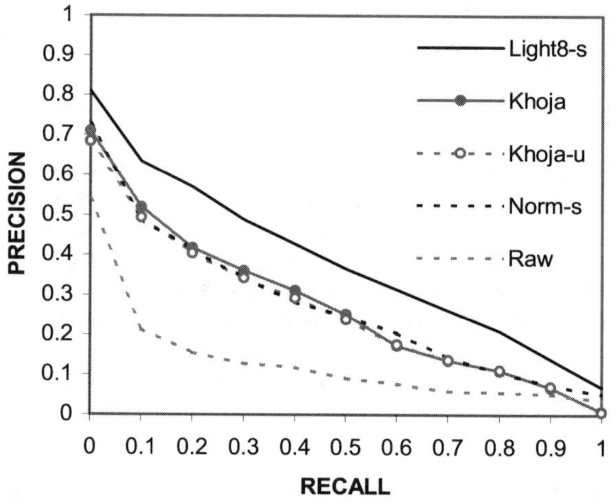

Figure 2: Cross-Language 11 point precision for unexpanded queries.

Table 7: Cross-language average precision different stemmers, unexpanded and expanded queries

Stemmer	**raw**	**norm-s**	**khoja-u**	**khoja**	**light8-s**
Av.Precision	.113	.262	.252	.260	.379
Pct. Change		133	123	130	236
With English Query expansion					
Av.Precision	.139	.306	.293	.308	.422
Pct. Change		120	111	121	204
With English and Arabic Query expansion					
Av.Precision	.163	.336	.316	.321	.436
Pct. Change		106	93	97	167

The results are somewhat different from the monolingual results. Raw retrieval without any normalization or stemming is far worse for cross-language retrieval than for monolingual retrieval. This is probably because many of the Arabic words occurred in vocalized form (with diacritics) in the online dictionary we used for cross-language retrieval. Without normalization these dictionary entries do not match their counterparts in the corpus. Other differences from the monolingual case are that here, the *light8-s* stemmer is significantly better than the root stemmer, *khoja*, which is no better than normalization for cross-language retrieval.

7. CONCLUSIONS

Stemming has a large effect on Arabic information retrieval, at least in part due to the highly inflected nature of the language. For monolingual retrieval we have demonstrated improvements of around 100% in average precision due to stemming and related processes, and an even larger effect for dictionary-based cross-language retrieval. This stemming effect is very large, compared to that found in many other stemming studies, but is consistent with the hypothesis of Popovič and Willett [39] and Pirkola [38] that stemming should be particularly effective for languages with more complex morphology.

It may seem contradictory that while we find a very large stemming effect for both mono- and cross-language Arabic retrieval, Xu et al. found stemming to make a difference only for monolingual Arabic, on the same TREC-2001 data [47]. We believe that the reason is that Xu et al. had a parallel corpus, so their bilingual lexicon contained all the variants of the Arabic words that were likely to occur in documents. Our bilingual lexicon was derived from an online dictionary, so it contained far fewer variants. Without stemming, the dictionary translations of query terms were unlikely to match the forms found in documents. In short, with sufficient parallel data, stemming may be unnecessary.

The best stemmer was a light stemmer that removed stop words, definite articles, and و ("and") from the beginning of words, and a small number of suffixes from the ends of words (*light8-s*). With query expansion, *light8-s* yielded results comparable to that of the top performers at TREC, monolingual and cross-language. We have not ruled out the possibility that a better morphological analyzer could work as well as or better than the light stemmer.

A repartitioning process consisting of vowel removal followed by clustering using co-occurrence analysis performed better than no stemming or very light stemming. However, stemmers produced this way were still inferior to the best light and morphological stemmers. Repartitioning one of these good hand-designed stemmers changes stem classes a great deal, but does not improve (or hurt) overall retrieval performance. We suspect that performance might be improved by modifying the clustering method to have less bias against low frequency variants.

8. ACKNOWLEDGMENTS

We would like to thank Shereen Khoja for providing her stemmer, Nicholas J. DuFresne for writing some of the stemming and dictionary code, Fang-fang Feng for helping with dictionary collection over the web, Mohamed Taha Mohamed, Mohamed Elgadi, and Nasreen Abdul-Jaleel for help with the Arabic language, Victor Lavrenko for the use of his vector and language modeling code. This work was supported in part by the Center for Intelligent Information Retrieval and in part by SPAWARSYSCEN-SD grant number N66001-99-1-8912. Any opinions, findings and conclusions or recommendations expressed in this material are the authors' and do not necessarily reflect those of the sponsor.

9. REFERENCES

[1] Abu-Salem, H., Al-Omari, M., and Evens, M. Stemming methodologies over individual query words for Arabic information retrieval. *JASIS*, 50 (6), pp. 524-529, 1999.

[2] Al-Fedaghi, S. S. and Al-Anzi, F. S. A new algorithm to generate Arabic root-pattern forms. In *Proceedings of the 1 th national computer conference.* King Fahd University of Petroleum & Minerals, Dhahran, Saudi Arabia, pp. 391-400, 1989.

[3] Aljlayl, M., Beitzel, S., Jensen, E., Chowdhury, A., Holmes, D., Lee, M., Grossman, D., and Frieder, O. IIT at TREC-10. In *TREC 2001*. Gaithersburg: NIST, 2001.

[4] Al-Kharashi, I. and Evens, M. W. Comparing words, stems, and roots as index terms in an Arabic information retrieval system. *JASIS*, 45 (8), pp. 548-560, 1994.

[5] Al-Shalabi, R. *Design and implementation of an Arabic morphological system to support natural language processing.* PhD thesis, Computer Science, Illinois Institute of Technology, Chicago, 1996.

[6] Beesley, K. R. Arabic finite-state morphological analysis and generation. In *COLING-96: Proceedings of the 16th international conference on computational linguistics*, vol. 1, pp. 89-94, 1996.

[7] Berlian, V., Vega, S. N., and Bressan, S. Indexing the Indonesian web: Language identification and miscellaneous issues. Presented at Tenth International World Wide Web Conference, Hong Kong, 2001.

[8] Brent, M. R. Speech segmentation and word discovery: A computational perspective. *Trends in Cognitive Science*, 3 (8), pp. 294-301, 1999.

[9] Buckwalter, T. *Qamus: Arabic lexicography.* http://members.aol.com/ArabicLexicons/

[10] Callan, J. P., Croft, W. B., and Broglio, J. TREC and TIPSTER experiments with INQUERY. *Information Processing and Management*, 31 (3), pp. 327-343, 1995.

[11] Carlberger, J., Dalianis, H., Hassel, M., and Knutsson, O. Improving precision in information retrieval for Swedish using stemming. In *Proceedings of NODALIDA '01 - 13th Nordic conference on computational linguistics*. Uppsala, Sweden, 2001.

[12] Darwish, K., Doermann, D., Jones, R., Oard, D., and Rautiainen, M. TREC-10 experiments at Maryland: CLIR and video. In *TREC 2001*. Gaithersburg: NIST, 2001.

[13] de Marcken, C. *Unsupervised language acquisition.* PhD thesis, MIT, Cambridge, 1995.

[14] De Roeck, A. N. and Al-Fares, W. A morphologically sensitive clustering algorithm for identifying Arabic roots. In *Proceedings ACL-2000*. Hong Kong, 2000.

[15] Ekmekcioglu, F. C., Lynch, M. F., and Willett, P. Stemming and n-gram matching for term conflation in Turkish texts. *Information Research News*, 7 (1), pp. 2-6, 1996.

[16] Flenner, G. Ein quantitatives Morphsegmentierungssytem fur Spanische Wortformen. In *Computatio linguae II*, U. Klenk, Ed. Stuttgart: Steiner Verlag, pp. 31-62, 1994.

[17] Frakes, W. B. Stemming algorithms. In *Information retrieval: Data structures and algorithms*, W. B. F. a. R. Baeza-Yates, Ed. Englewood Cliffs, NJ: Prentice Hall, chapter 8, 1992.

[18] Freund, E. and Willett, P. Online identification of word variants and arbitrary truncation searching using a string similarity measure. *Information Technology: Research and Development*, 1, pp. 177-187, 1982.

[19] Gey, F. C. and Oard, D. W. The TREC-2001 cross-language information retrieval track: Searching Arabic using English, French, or Arabic queries. In *TREC 2001*. Gaithersburg: NIST, 2002.

[20] Goldsmith, J. Unsupervised learning of the morphology of a natural language. *Computational Linguistics*, 27 (2), pp. 153-198, 2000.

[21] Goldsmith, J., Higgins, D., and Soglasnova, S. Automatic language-specific stemming in information retrieval. In *Cross-language information retrieval and evaluation: Proceedings of the CLEF 2000 workshop*, C. Peters, Ed.: Springer Verlag, pp. 273-283, 2001.

[22] Goweder, A. and De Roeck, A. Assessment of a significant Arabic corpus. Presented at the Arabic NLP Workshop at ACL/EACL 2001, Toulouse, France, 2001.

[23] Greengrass, M., Robertson, A. M., Robyn, S., and Willett, P. Processing morphological variants in searches of Latin text. *Information research news*, 6 (4), pp. 2-5, 1996.

[24] Hafer, M. A. and Weiss, S. F. Word segmentation by letter successor varieties. *Information Storage and Retrieval*, 10, pp. 371-385, 1974.

[25] Hull, D. A. Stemming algorithms - a case study for detailed evaluation. *JASIS*, 47 (1), pp. 70-84, 1996.

[26] Janssen, A. Segmentierung Franzosischer Wortformen in Morphe ohne Verwendung eines Lexikons. In *Computatio linguae*, U. Klenk, Ed. Stuttgart: Steiner Verlag, pp. 74-95, 1992.

[27] Khoja, S. and Garside, R. *Stemming Arabic text*. Computing Department, Lancaster University, Lancaster, 1999. http://www.comp.lancs.ac.uk/computing/users/khoja/stemmer.ps

[28] Klenk, U. Verfahren morphologischer Segmentierung und die Wortstruktur im Spanischen. In *Computatio linguae*, U. Klenk, Ed. Stuttgart: Steiner Verlag, 1992.

[29] Kraaij, W. and Pohlmann, R. Viewing stemming as recall enhancement. In *Proceedings of ACM SIGIR96*. pp. 40-48, 1996.

[30] Krovetz, R. Viewing morphology as an inference process. In *Proceedings of ACM SIGIR93*, pp. 191-203, 1993.

[31] Larkey, L. S. and Connell, M. E. Arabic information retrieval at UMass in TREC-10. In *TREC 2001*. Gaithersburg: NIST, 2001.

[32] Lovins, J. B. Development of a stemming algorithm. *Mechanical Translation and Computational Linguistics*, 11, pp. 22-31, 1968.

[33] Mayfield, J., McNamee, P., Costello, C., Piatko, C., and Banerjee, A. JHU/APL at TREC 2001: Experiments in filtering and in Arabic, video, and web retrieval. In *TREC 2001*. Gaithersburg: NIST, 2001.

[34] McNamee, P., Mayfield, J., and Piatko, C. A language-independent approach to European text retrieval. In *Cross-language information retrieval and evaluation: Proceedings of the CLEF 2000 workshop*, C. Peters, Ed.: Springer Verlag, pp. 129-139, 2000.

[35] Monz, C. and de Rijke, M. Shallow morphological analysis in monolingual information retrieval for German and Italian. In *Cross-language information retrieval and evaluation: Proceedings of the CLEF 2001 workshop*, C. Peters, Ed.: Springer Verlag, 2001.

[36] Moulinier, I., McCulloh, A., and Lund, E. West group at CLEF 2000: Non-English monolingual retrieval. In *Cross-language information retrieval and evaluation: Proceedings of the CLEF 2000 workshop*, C. Peters, Ed.: Springer Verlag, pp. 176-187, 2001.

[37] Oard, D. W., Levow, G.-A., and Cabezas, C. I. CLEF experiments at Maryland: Statistical stemming and backoff translation. In *Cross-language information retrieval and evaluation: Proceedings of the CLEF 2000 workshop*, C. Peters, Ed.: Springer Verlag, pp. 176-187, 2001.

[38] Pirkola, A. Morphological typology of languages for IR. *Journal of Documentation*, 57 (3), pp. 330-348, 2001.

[39] Popovic, M. and Willett, P. The effectiveness of stemming for natural-language access to Slovene textual data. *JASIS*, 43 (5), pp. 384-390, 1992.

[40] Porter, M. F. An algorithm for suffix stripping. *Program*, 14 (3), pp. 130-137, 1980.

[41] Siegel, S. *Nonparametric statistics for the behavioral sciences*. New York: McGraw-Hill, 1956.

[42] Tai, S. Y., Ong, C. S., and Abdullah, N. A. On designing an automated Malaysian stemmer for the Malay language. (poster). In *Proceedings of the fifth international workshop on information retrieval with Asian languages,* Hong Kong, pp. 207-208, 2000.

[43] van Rijsbergen, C. J. *Information retrieval*. London: Butterworths, 1979.

[44] Wightwick, J. and Gaafar, M. *Arabic verbs and essentials of grammar*. Chicago: Passport Books, 1998.

[45] Xu, J. and Croft, W. B. Corpus-based stemming using cooccurrence of word variants. *ACM Transactions on Information Systems*, 16 (1), pp. 61-81, 1998.

[46] Xu, J., Fraser, A., and Weischedel, R. TREC 2001 cross-lingual retrieval at BBN. In *TREC 2001*. Gaithersburg: NIST, 2001.

[47] Xu, J., Fraser, A., and Weischedel, R. Empirical studies in strategies for Arabic retrieval. In *Sigir 2002*. Tampere, Finland: ACM, 2002.

Automatic Query Refinement using Lexical Affinities with Maximal Information Gain

David Carmel, Eitan Farchi, Yael Petruschka, Aya Soffer
{carmel,farchi,petrus,ayas}@il.ibm.com

IBM Labs, Haifa University, Haifa 31905, ISRAEL

ABSTRACT

This work describes an automatic query refinement technique, which focuses on improving precision of the top ranked documents. The terms used for refinement are *lexical affinities* (LAs), pairs of closely related words which contain exactly one of the original query terms. Adding these terms to the query is equivalent to re-ranking search results, thus, precision is improved while recall is preserved. We describe a novel method that selects the most "informative" LAs for refinement, namely, those LAs that best separate relevant documents from irrelevant documents in the set of results. The *information gain* of candidate LAs is determined using unsupervised estimation that is based on the scoring function of the search engine. This method is thus fully automatic and its quality depends on the quality of the scoring function. Experiments we conducted with TREC data clearly show a significant improvement in the precision of the top ranked documents.

Categories and Subject Descriptors

H.3.3 [**Information Storage and Retrieval**]: Information Search and Retrieval

General Terms

Algorithms, Theory

Keywords

Automatic Query Refinement, Pseudo Relevance Feedback

1. INTRODUCTION

The goal of information retrieval systems is to identify documents from a given collection that best match the user's information needs. Existing search engines provide valuable assistance to users in locating relevant information, however, finding precise information is progressively becoming more difficult. This is especially true for large collections and for interactive systems where users tend to only look at the top k documents where k is small (e.g., 5-20 documents).

Automatic query refinement (AQR) has long been recognized as an effective technique to improve retrieval performance [3, 7, 19]. AQR techniques refine the user's query by adding terms which are considered to be related to the original query terms. The goal of the refinement is to cover additional aspects of the information need as specified by the query. The expansion terms can be selected from a thesaurus, a synonym table, or a semantic word network such as Wordnet [17]. Alternatively, AQR can be performed using pseudo relevance feedback techniques [19] which are based on the assumption that the top-ranked documents for a given query are indeed relevant. Traditional relevance feedback methods such as Rocchio refinement process [15] can then be used to effectively refine the query. In particular, a set of top-ranked documents is first retrieved using the original user query. The weight of the query terms is modified according to their frequency in this set. In addition, expansion terms are selected from this set, based on various selection criteria, and added to the query. The refined query is then submitted to the system, resulting in the final set of documents considered relevant to the original user query. Using this method with N, the number of top-documents used for expansion, ranging from 10 to 50, has been found to increase retrieval performance, by 6 to 13% on TREC corpora [12].

Recent studies have however shown that while AQR improves recall, it could harm precision, especially when applied to very large document collections [5]. Furthermore, traditional AQR techniques are not necessarily effective for improving the precision of the top results. Recall is generally improved by AQR since the expansion terms broaden the scope of the query. Specifically, all documents retrieved for the original query are also retrieved for the expanded query and new documents containing the expansion terms are added to the result set. Precision, however, may deteriorate if the expansion affects the order of results returned by the search engine, causing non-relevant documents to precede relevant ones. This phenomenon has been reported by Web track participants of the TREC 9 conference. Only one participant reported improvement in performance by automatic query expansion, while all other participants reported either a decline or no gain in terms of precision [5].

There are several reasons why the overall precision may diminish using AQR techniques:

- Expansion terms may cause a drift in the focus of the search topic. This can happen when terms are added to the query since they happen to meet the selection criteria but are not directly related to the information need specified by the user query. Consequently, documents that are relevant to the expanded query are not necessarily relevant to the original query. For example, Mitra et al. [12] analyze the TREC query "What is the economic impact of recycling tires?". Their AQR method expands the query with terms relevant to plastic recycling in general rather than specific to tire recycling. Thus, for this query, query expansion actually results in a significant loss of precision.

- AQR can additionally "punish" relevant documents that do not include the terms selected for expansion. As a result, a relevant document that does not contain some of the additional terms might be ranked lower than non-relevant documents which contain those terms. For example, consider the Web Track topic "Jennifer Aniston". Our AQR system, using Rocchio refinement process, added the terms ("actress", "movie", "player") to the original query terms. This expansion results in a loss of precision compared to the original query. The reason for this is a decrease in the score assigned to documents that include the original query terms but do not include the expansion terms. Additionally, documents dealing with movies and movie players (but not with Jennifer Aniston) were assigned a high score since they contain the expanded terms with high frequency. Consequently these irrelevant documents preceded relevant documents in the final result set.

- The documents that are used as a basis for selecting additional query terms (usually the top-ranked documents for the original query), may not be relevant to the original query. By expanding the query with terms extracted from the top results the system improves the rank of documents "similar" to the top results. However, for "difficult" queries, for which most of the top results are not relevant, AQR might fail. It turns out that AQR works best for "easy" queries. For difficult queries with non-precise top results it may not improve, and even harm precision.

In this paper we suggest a novel query refinement technique, which attempts to improve the precision rather than recall by overcoming the above obstacles. The main idea is that rather than expanding the query by adding additional terms, we should narrow the query by further qualifying query terms. In other words, the goal is to find expanded terms that sift up documents that were already deemed somewhat relevant to the original query but received a low score.

The basis for the method we suggest is *lexical affinities.* A lexical affinity (LA) represents the correlation of words co-occurring in a document, and is identified by looking at pairs of words found in close proximity to each other [10]. We consider LAs which contain exactly one of the original query terms. We show that adding such LAs to the query is equivalent to re-ranking search results, thus, precision might improve while recall is preserved.

The method used to select LAs for refinement is based on information theory. Specifically, we look for the most informative LAs, *i.e.,* the ones with the maximal information gain as defined in [16]. The LAs that best separate the relevant documents from the irrelevant ones in the set of results are selected for refinement. Since relevance information is clearly not available at the retrieval stage, our refinement process uses an unsupervised method which is fully automatic and can be applied without any manually labeled data. It estimates the relevance probability of a set of documents based on the relevance scores given by the search engine.

The remainder of the paper is organized as follows: In Section 2 we review AQR techniques in general and focus especially on work related to ours. Section 3 describes our refinement method which is based on information theory and provides the theoretical basis for this method. In Section 4 we show experimentally, using TREC data, the advantages of our AQR method. The experimental results clearly show that the AQR method proposed here significantly improves precision of the top results. Concluding remarks are given in Section 5.

2. RELATED WORK

Query expansion and pseudo relevance feedback have been studied quite extensively. The continuing desire to improve retrieval effectiveness has resulted in significant research in this area for quite some time. A good overview of AQR techniques by Gauch *et al.* appears in [4]. They divide the various AQR techniques according to the three main sources for candidate expansion terms:

1. Query specific terms identified by local analysis of top retrieved documents *e.g.* [19, 1, 14].

2. Corpus specific terms identified by global analysis of the whole corpus and the use of automatic thesaurus construction *e.g.* [3, 7, 19].

3. Language specific terms found in a generally available thesaurus *e.g.* [17].

These techniques are mostly focused on selecting terms for query refinement that will improve recall and precision. Our work, on the other hand, is focused on improving the precision of the top ranked results while preserving recall.

In [6], Hearst identifies the need to ensure high precision in the top-ranked documents retrieved by an interactive information access system. In order to provide better precision among the top-ranked documents, Hearst proposes to add manually formulated Boolean filters along with proximity constraints to the query. The work presented in [8] is also concerned with ways to improve the precision of the top-ranked documents. They use a two-stage document ranking method where at the second level, retrieved documents are re-ordered using a mutual information measure between query terms and document terms.

Mitra *et al.* [12] investigate ways to improve AQR process by increasing the precision of the top-ranked documents used for pseudo-relevance feedback. They add constraints to the original query in order to get stronger indications for document relevance. The new query is used to re-rank the initially retrieved documents and the refined set of top documents is used for expansion.

The use of phrases for query expansion appears in [7, 19, 9], all use the *INQUERY* information retrieval system. Jing and Croft [7] describe a system called *PhraseFinder* that identifies associations between phrases and query terms so that associated phrases can be used for improving retrieval performance via query expansion. In our work, the phrases (lexical affinities) used for query refinement are only those for which one of their terms is taken from the query. The phrases considered in [7] are the complementary phrases, *i.e.*, phrases including only query terms and phrases including no query terms.

The mutual information measure for re-ranking used by Kang *et al.* [8] considers phrases similar to LAs, *i.e.*, phrases that occur in a small window of terms around the query terms within the document.

In [2], Carpineto *et al.* present a selection method of terms for AQR which is based on information theory. They measure the difference between the probability distribution of a term in the set of (pseudo) relevant documents and its probability distribution in the whole corpus. Their method selects terms that maximize the divergence between the two probability distributions.

Our approach differs in two main aspects. First, our method uses unsupervised estimation of the relevance probability of a set of documents, based on document scores. Hence we consider range of relevancy of documents rather than binary (manually or automated) labeling. Second, in our method terms are judged according to their capabilities to differentiate between relevant and non-relevant documents in the result set. Specifically, we look for the terms that best split the result set into two subsets, one contains mostly relevant documents and the second contains mostly non-relevant documents. In the following section we describe our selection method in more detail.

3. AN AQR METHOD BASED ON INFORMATION THEORY

In this section we describe our AQR method which is based on the information gain obtained by adding lexical affinities to the query. Lexical affinities (LAs) represent the correlation between words co-occurring in a document, and are identified by looking at pairs of words found in close proximity to each other. Thus, an LA is a pair of distinct words (t_i, t_j). Previous work [10] explains how LAs, when used as indexing units, improve search precision by disambiguating terms. The same reference describes how LAs can be extracted from text by finding the most common pairs of words found close to each other in a window of small size.

Let $q = \{q_1 \dots q_k\}$ be the original query. Let D_q be the result set for query q (all documents associated with a positive score). Let L be a set of LAs, each one contains exactly one of the original query term,

$$L = \{(t_i, t_j)|\ t_i \subset q \text{ or } t_j \subset q, \text{ but not both}\}.$$

The set L can be extracted from the set of all LAs found in the collection, from a set of LAs extracted from the top-ranked documents in D_q, or from any other static thesaurus that provides LAs for a given term. // Our AQR method chooses the "best" LAs from L and adds them to the query. The selection method will be described in the following subsection. It is important to emphasize that if t_i belongs to the original query q and (t_i, t_j) is added to q, the term t_j is not added to the query. Thus, such an addition only affects the score of documents which contain the pair (t_i, t_j) while the score of documents containing only one of the pair terms, or none of them, is not affected[1].

Assume the original query contains the term t_i. By adding the LA (t_i, t_j) to the query all documents in D_q containing (t_i, t_j) will get a higher score while the score of all other documents will not change. Precision is expected to improve if the set of documents containing (t_i, t_j) includes more relevant documents than its complement, since many relevant documents will get a higher score which will improve their ranks. It might be the case that the set of documents not containing the added LA will include more relevant documents than its complement. In this case we should add the LA to the query with *negative* sign. Thus, by adding an "informative" LA to the query, *i.e.*, an LA that best differentiates relevant documents from non-relevant documents, precision is expected to improve. Figure 1 shows an illustration of the splitting process.

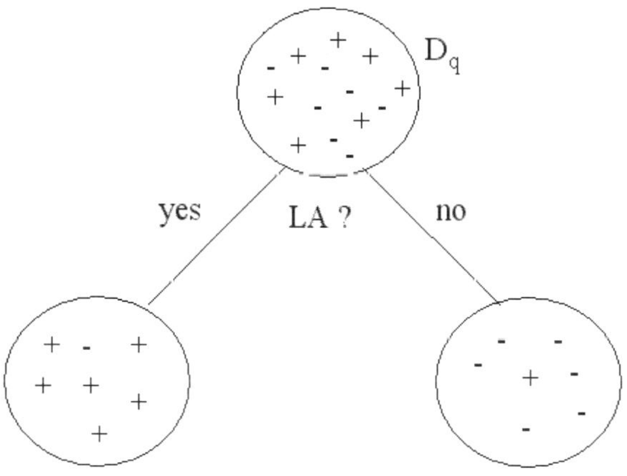

Figure 1: Splitting the result set by refining the query with LA. The '+' sign marks relevant documents while the '-' sign marks non-relevant documents.

Note that the refinement method does not change the score of any document not in D_q, thus the result set for the refined query remains the same. Consequently, recall is not affected by our refinement method, hence, the suggested AQR process is equivalent to re-ranking of the original result set according to the refined query. All disk accesses, required for the second retrieval stage performed by traditional two-stage AQR methods, are thus not necessary using our method.

We next describe the method used to select the best LAs for refinement.

3.1 Choosing the Best LAs for Refinement

As already defined, let D_q be the result set for query q, *i.e.*, the set of documents with positive score. We consider LAs that split the set D_q into two subsets, one set includes all documents containing the LA and one includes all document not containing it. An "informative" LA will be the one that successfully differentiates between relevant and non-relevant documents. Ideally, one subset will include all relevant documents while the second will include all the

[1]We assume an additive scoring function, *i.e.*, adding terms to the query increases the score of documents containing these terms and does not affect the score of other documents.

non-relevant documents. Thus we look for the most informative LA, *i.e.*, the one with the maximal *information gain* as defined in [16].

DEFINITION 3.1.: *The relevance probability of a set of documents D to a given query q, $p(D)$, is the probability of a document chosen randomly from D to be relevant to q. Let $R \subseteq D$ be the subset of relevant documents to q in D. Then $p(D) = |R|/|D|$.*

DEFINITION 3.2.: *The entropy of the set D, $H(D)$, is defined as*

$$H(D) = -p(D)\log(p(D)) - (1-p(D))\log(1-p(D)).$$

$H(D)$ commonly refers to the degree of disorder of the set.

DEFINITION 3.3.: *Given a document set D and a term l. Let D^+ be the subset of documents of D containing l and D^- its complement. The information gain of l, $IG(l)$, is defined by*

$$IG(l) = H(D) - \left[\frac{|D^+|}{|D|}H(D^+) + \frac{|D^-|}{|D|}H(D^-)\right]. \quad (1)$$

The first element describes the entropy of the set before splitting, the second describes the weighted average entropy of both subsets after splitting. The difference expresses the information gain achieved by the splitting process, *i.e.*, how much the entropy is reduced, or in other words how much order has been added to the set. For ideal splitting where all relevant documents belong to one of the subsets and all non-relevant documents belong to its complement, the entropy will be reduced to zero and IG is maximal.

The selection method is based on computing the IG for every LA in the set of candidate LAs and choosing the best LAs with maximal IG for query refinement. Alternatively we can compute the IG for all subsets of LAs of a given size and choose the subset with maximal IG for expansion.

The IG computation for a given LA depends on estimation of the relevance probability of subsets of documents to a given query. The following subsection describes how the relevance probability of a set of documents can be estimated.

3.2 Unsupervised Estimation of the Relevance Probability of a set of Documents to a Given Query

In order to choose the best lexical affinities we need to evaluate the relevance probability of a set of documents. This subsection describes an unsupervised method that estimates this probability.

The relevance probability of a set of documents can be estimated by supervised methods that are based on labeled training data. Given a subset of documents, labeled according to their relevance to the query, the relevance probability of the whole set can be estimated by simple sampling techniques. The problem is that it is hard to create a set of labeled documents since labeling is an expensive manual task.

Our method does not require any labeled training data. Rather, it uses the scoring function of the search engine used to rank the search results. The quality of our estimation depends on the quality of the scoring function. For a reasonable scoring function that correlates document scores with their relevance probability, our estimation can successfully replace labeled training data.

Given a set of n documents, $\{d_1 \ldots d_n\}$, and a query q. Let p_i be the probability that document d_i is relevant to query q. Later we will show how p_i can be induced from the document scores provided by the search engine. For each document d_i define an independent variable x_i representing the relevance of d_i. That is, x_i is set to 1 with probability p_i and to 0 with probability $(1-p_i)$. x_i is a binomial independent variable with expectation $E(x_i) = p_i$ and variance $Var(x_i) = p_i(1-p_i)$.

Let $X = \sum_{i=1}^{n} x_i$. X is a random variable that counts the number of relevant documents in the document set. The expectation of X is

$$E(X) = E\left(\sum_{i=1}^{n} x_i\right) = \sum_{i=1}^{n} E(x_i) = \sum_{i=1}^{n} p_i.$$

$E(X)$ estimates X, the number of relevant documents in the set.

Since $x_1 \ldots x_n$ are independent binomial variables, the distribution of X is normal and the variance of X is

$$Var(X) = \sum_{i=1}^{n} Var(x_i) = \sum_{i=1}^{n} p_i(1-p_i).$$

Given $\delta > 0$, the error of estimating X can be measured by applying the Chebyshev inequality:

$$Pr(|X - E(X)| > \delta) \le \frac{Var(X)}{\delta^2}.$$

Let $p(D) = \frac{X}{n}$ be the relevance probability of the set D. A straight forward estimation of $p(D)$ is

$$\hat{p}(D) = \frac{E(X)}{n} = \frac{\sum_{i=1}^{n}(p_i)}{n}.$$

Clearly, from Chebyshev inequality we can estimate the error of $\hat{p}(D)$.

$$Pr(|p(D) - \hat{p}(D)| > \frac{\delta}{n}) \le \frac{Var(X)}{\delta^2}.$$

As IG is a continuous function in $p(D)$, $p(D^+)$ and $p(D^-)$, we can estimate the error of IG which depends on the errors of these estimations. This can result in an improved term selection method but we leave this research direction for future work.

The above measure of $p(D)$ depends on our knowledge of the relevance probability of every document in the set to the query. These probabilities can be induced from the scoring function of the search engine. Scoring functions are usually designed for ranking purpose and not for probability estimation. For such scoring functions we need a tool that calibrates scores to probability values. Recently, some methods for modeling score distribution has been suggested [13, 11, 20] and can be applied for this purpose. In this work we use a simple straight forward approach.

Let s_{max} be the maximum score possible for a given query. We assume that the relevance probability of a document associated with such a score is 1. Let s_i be the score for document d_i. Thus, a natural approximation of the relevance probability of document d_i is $p_i = s_i/s_{max}$. This approximation guarantees that the probability assigned to each document preserves the order among documents (*if* $s_i >= s_j$ *then* $p_i >= p_j$), assigns relevance probability of 1 to documents with maximum score, and a zero probability to documents with zero score.

The maximum score for a given query, s_{max}, can be determined by computing a score of a virtual document identical to the query. This is based on the assumption that a document identical to the query must be relevant to the query.

The quality of our estimation mostly depends on the quality of the scoring function. For example, given a scoring function that associates a score of 1 to all relevant documents and 0 to all the rest, our estimation will succeed in measuring the true number of relevant documents in the set (with zero variance), while for a scoring function that associates a random score for all documents, our estimation is meaningless.

terms no.	P@1	P@5	P@10	P@15	P@20	MAP
0	0.533	0.346	0.264	0.233	0.213	0.252
1	0.533	0.351	0.282	0.241	0.219	0.270
2	**0.600**	**0.396**	**0.291**	**0.246**	**0.222**	**0.276**
3	**0.000**	**0.387**	**0.300**	**0.252**	**0.227**	**0.280**
4	0.556	0.373	0.282	0.239	0.216	0.275
5	0.556	0.347	0.256	0.236	0.213	0.271
6	0.533	0.338	0.256	0.233	0.209	0.265
7	0.533	0.347	0.251	0.227	0.209	0.266
8	0.533	0.347	0.258	0.225	0.210	0.266
9	0.533	0.333	0.260	0.222	0.208	0.263
10	0.533	0.333	0.262	0.225	0.207	0.261

Table 1: Precision as a function of the number of added terms.

4. EXPERIMENTAL RESULTS

In this section we report results from experiments we conducted to evaluate the influence of the suggested AQR method on search precision. We used the TREC collection [18] for our experiments and evaluated our methods on the ad hoc tasks for TREC-7, with topics 401-450. We experimented both with short queries and long queries. We used the topic title for short query construction, and the title concatenated with the topic description for long query construction. Original query terms extracted from the topic text include keywords and inner LAs (both terms belong to the query). We used precision at k ($P@k$) for $k = (1, 5, 10, 15, 20)$, and mean average precision (MAP) measures to measure search precision [18].

The refinement process for a given query is carried out as follows:

1. Retrieve the result set for the query (all documents with positive score)[2].
2. Extract the candidate LAs from the top-n documents (n was set to 10 in our experiments). A candidate LA is a pair of closely related terms which contains exactly one of the original query terms.
3. Compute the information gain for each candidate LA as defined by Equation 1.
4. Add the m LAs with maximal gains to the query.
5. Re-rank the result set using the refined query.

In the first experiment we tested how the number of terms added to the query in the refinement process affects the precision. Table 1 reports P@k and MAP for different values of m, the number of added terms. The first row (0 terms) shows the average result for the original 50 queries with no refinement. Row m shows the average results for the same queries, each expanded with the best m LAs.

Figure 2 graphically illustrates the improvement in precision for the refined queries relative to the original queries. From these results it is apparent that in general there is a significant improvement in precision when adding a small number of LAs (up to 4). Specifically $P@10$ improves by more than 10% when adding 2-3 LAs. Interestingly, adding more than 5 LAs to the original query decreases $P@k$, while still increasing the overall precision as measured by MAP. The reason for this phenomenon is that our selection process tests the gain of each candidate LA separately and does not consider the dependency between LAs. Ideally, the gain of each subset of candidates should be computed and the subset with maximal gain should be selected for refinement. This however is not computationally feasible in most cases.

Table 2 presents some of the queries and the LAs used for query refinement. Note that the refined LAs are shown in their stemmed form. It is interesting to notice that the term "subject" is part of several LAs selected for refinement. Such an LA is extracted due to the appearance of one of the query terms in the document title which is marked by the tag "subject". Our refinement method automatically deduces that the appearance of query terms in the document title is a good sign for relevancy.

The refined LAs for topic 450 demonstrate one of the weaknesses of AQR methods based on pseudo relevance feedback including the method presented here. Specifically, AQR can fail when handling "difficult" queries for which the system's scoring function is ineffective. This topic deals with King Hussein's contribution to the peace process in the middle east. However, the scoring function fails to place truly relevant documents high in the result list during the first phase of query processing. In fact it retrieves documents dealing with Saddam Hussein and consequently two of the three LAs selected as having the maximal gain are related to Sadam Hussein. Hence AQR, in this case, sifts up even more results dealing with Sadam Hussein and precision declines.

The second experiment tested how query length influences the effectiveness of our refinement method. We ran two tests, one using short queries (based on topic title only) and one using long queries (based on title plus description). In contrast to the previous experiment, the original queries include keywords only and do not include inner LAs extracted from the topic text.

For each test we computed the precision measures with and without refinement. The number of added terms for refinement was set to 3 for both tests. Table 3 reports the results for the original queries and the refined queries for both query types.

Figure 3 illustrates the change in precision for both query types. While refinement for short queries improves the $P@1$ measure by almost 20%, the improvement in precision for long queries is lower than 5%. It is clear that the refinement

[2]In huge collections such as TREC result sets may include hundred thousands documents. In practice, TREC evaluation procedures consider only the top-1000 documents as the result set. Similarly, from practical reasons, our method considers only the top-5000 documents as the result set for a query.

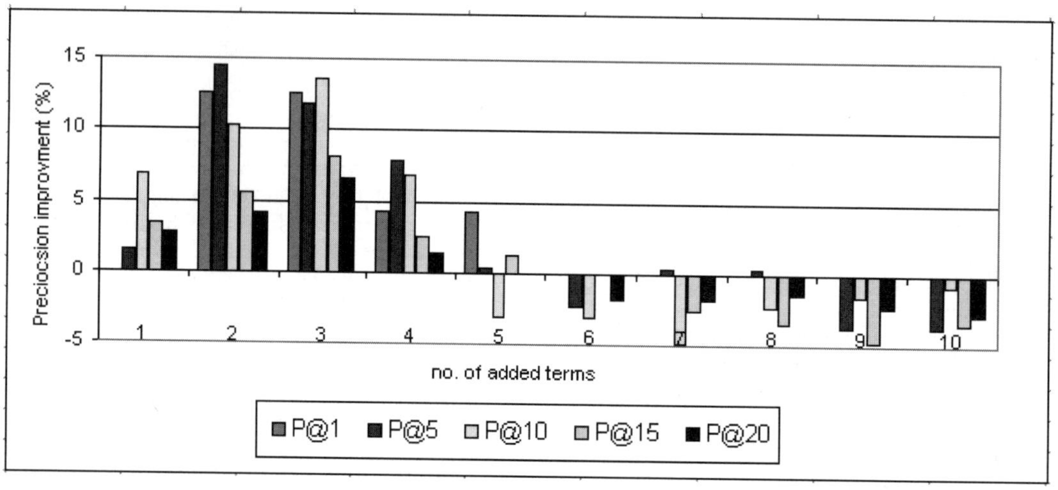

Figure 2: Change in precision as a function of number of added terms.

Query No.	query	P@10(orig)	P@10(refined)	added LAs
402	behavioral genetic	0.5	0.5	genetic*subject, genetic*research genetic*medic
406	parkinson's disease	0.3	0.4	parkinson*victim parkinson*symptom parkinson*patient
408	tropical storms	0.3	0.4	storm*subject, storm*type storm*weaken
412	airport security	0.7	0.8	airport*subject, airport*headline
416	drugs, golden triangle	0.1	0.1	drug*mule, golden*southeast
422	art, stolen, forged	0.5	0.7	art*theft, stolen*subject *stolen*work
434	estonia, economy	0.1	0.1	estonia*lithuania, estonia*republ estonia*latvia
438	tourism, increase	0.0	0.1	tourism*travel, tourism*unit tourism*year
440	child labor	0.6	0.7	labor*law, labor*violat child*violat
450	king hussein, peace	0.3	0.2	hussein*jordan, hussein*iraq hussein*saddam

Table 2: Some queries and LAs selected for refinement.

Query Type		P@1	P@5	P@10	P@15	P@20	MAP
Short	orig	0.467	0.32	0.256	0.24	0.216	0.256
	refined	0.556	0.340	0.271	0.250	0.218	0.272
Long	orig	0.467	0.338	0.273	0.244	0.215	0.258
	refined	0.489	0.350	0.278	0.246	0.210	0.263

Table 3: Precision as a function of query type.

process works much better for short queries. One of the reasons for this is that the results for the original long queries are more precise ($P@10 = 0.273$) than the results for the original short queries ($P@10 = 0.256$), hence improvement is much harder to achieve. Note however, that recently users tend to submit short queries to modern IR systems, thus it is crucial to improve the precision for this type of queries.

The third experiment compared our information theoretic LA selection process with other selection methods. We ran four tests with four different selection methods:

- Random – select m LAs randomly form the set of all candidate LAs.
- TfIdf – the gain of each candidate is computed by a traditional $tf \times idf$ formula. The gain is a multiplication of the term frequency (tf) of the candidate LA in the top-10 documents and the inverse document frequency (idf) in the whole collection.
- unsvIT – associates candidates with the information gain as defined in Section 3.
- svIT – associates candidates with information gain based on supervised labeled data. The relevance probability required for gain estimation is computed using the set of relevant documents provided for each topic by the TREC data. Given a document set of size n with $r \leq n$ relevant documents, the relevance probability of the set is determined by $p(D) = r/n$.

For this experiment the number of added terms was set to 3, and the number of top documents for candidate extraction was set to 10.

Figure 4 shows the change in precision of the refined queries compared to the precision of the original queries, using the

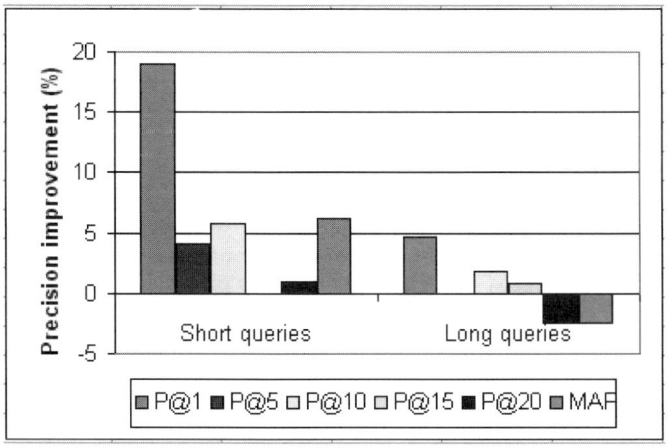

Figure 3: Change in precision for short and long queries.

four selection methods. The random selection completely fails and severely hurts precision. The unsupervised method improves precision by 6-15% and clearly outperforms the *tf* × *idf* method. The supervised method dramatically improves precision by 20-30%.

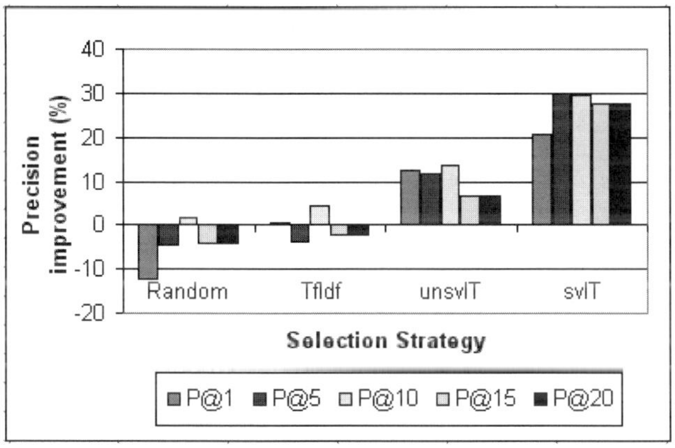

Figure 4: Change in precision for different selection methods.

Note that random selection is equivalent to invocation of the unsupervised selection method with a random scoring function. The supervised method is on the other hand equivalent to invocation of the unsupervised method with an ideal scoring function that associates a score of 1 to relevant documents and 0 to all others. Thus, these results can be treated as a lower bound and an upper bound on the achievable results using the unsupervised method. It clearly demonstrates the strong dependency of AQR on the quality of the scoring function.

5. CONCLUSIONS

In this paper we have described a query refinement technique, which focuses on improving precision of the top ranked documents. The candidate-terms used for the refinement are lexical affinities (LAs) which contain exactly one of the original query terms. Adding these terms to the query is equivalent to re-ranking search results, thus, precision is improved while recall is preserved. We describe a novel method to select the most "informative" LAs. Namely, those LAs that best separate relevant documents from the irrelevant documents in the set of results. The relevance probability of a set of documents to a specific query is determined using unsupervised estimation. This estimation is based on the scoring function of the given search engine rather than on labeled training data. Thus, our method is fully automatic and its quality depends on the quality of the scoring function.

The effectiveness of the suggested AQR method was evaluated using the TREC collection with the ad hoc-tasks of TREC-7. Our evaluation clearly shows a significant improvement in the precision of the top ranked documents compared to traditional $tf \times idf$ selection methods. When using a supervised relevance information (using TREC manual judgments), our method performs dramatically better.

Although our method significantly improves the precision of top ranked documents, it does not totally overcome the problem of "difficult" queries, *i.e.,* queries for which most of the top results are not relevant. The problem is that AQR methods based on pseudo-relevance feedback mistakenly assume that the top ranked results for such queries are relevant. Our method uses the top ranked documents only for extracting the candidate LAs, and then selects LAs for refinement by computing their information gain. Since difficult queries mislead the scoring function of the search engine to associate high scores to irrelevant documents, our computation of relevance probability is also faulty in this case.

In the future, we would like to find ways to overcome this problem and thus further improve top ranked precision of AQR based results. One possible direction is to improve our term selection method by considering the error estimation of the information gain. In addition, more sophisticated phrases should be considered for refinement. Another possible direction for improvement is to compute the information gain for subsets of LAs, and use the best subset (of any size) for the refinement.

6. REFERENCES

[1] C. Buckley, G. Salton, J. Allan, and A. Singhal. Automatic query expansion using SMART: TREC 3. In D. K. Harman, editor, *Proceedings of the Third Text REtrieval Conference (TREC-3).* National Institute of Standards and Technology. NIST, 1994.

[2] C. Carpineto, R. De Mori, G. Romano, and B. Bigi. An information-theoretic approach to automatic query expansion. *ACM Transactions on Information Systems,* 19(1):1–27, January 2001.

[3] C. Crouch and B. Yang. Experiments in automatic statistical thesaurus construction. In *Proceedings of the 15th Annual International ACM SIGIR Conference on Research and Development in Information Retrieval,* Copenhagen, Denmark, 1992.

[4] S. Gauch, J. Wang, and S. M. Rachakonda. A corpus analysis approach for automatic query expansion and its extension to multiple databases. *ACM Transactions on Information Systems,* 17(3):250–269, July 1999.

[5] D. Hawking. Overview of the TREC-9 Web Track. In E. M. Voorhees and D. K. Harman, editors, *Proceedings of the Ninth Text Retrieval Conference (TREC-9).* National Institute of Standards and Technology. NIST, 2000.

[6] M. A. Hearst. Improving full-text precision on short queries using simple constraints. In *Proceedings of the Symposium on Document analysis and Information Retrieval*, April 1996.

[7] Y. Jing and W. B. Croft. An association thesaurus for information retrieval. In *Proceedings of RIAO-94, 4th International Conference "Recherche d'Information Assistee par Ordinateur"*, pages 146–160, New York, NY, 1994.

[8] H. Kang and K. Choi. Two level document ranking using mutual information in natural language information rerieval. *Information Processing and Management*, 33(3):289–307, 1997.

[9] J. Kekalainen and K. Jarvelin. The impact of query structure and query expansion on retrieval performance. In *Proceedings of the 21st Annual International ACM SIGIR Conference on Research and Development in Information Retrieval*, Melbourne, Australia, 1998.

[10] Y. Maarek and F. Smadja. Full text indexing based on lexical relations: An application: Software libraries. In *Proceedings of the Twelfth International ACM SIGIR Conference on Research and Development in Information Retrieval*, pages 198–206, Cambridge, MA, June 1989.

[11] R. Manmatha, T. Rath, and F. Feng. Modeling score distributions for combining the outputs of search engines. In *Proceedings of the 24th Annual International ACM SIGIR Conference on Research and Development in Information Retrieval*, pages 267–275, New Orleans, LA., September 2001.

[12] M. Mitra, A. Singhal, and C. Buckley. Improving automatic query expansion. In *Proceedings of the 21st Annual International ACM SIGIR Conference on Research and Development in Information Retrieval*, Melbourne, Australia, 1998.

[13] S. Robertson and S. Walker. Microsoft Cambridge at TREC-9: Filtering track. In *Proceeding of Ninth Text REtrieval Conference (TREC-9). National Institute of Standards and Technology, Special Publication*, 2001.

[14] S. E. Robertson, S. Walker, S. Jones, M. M. Hancock-Beaulieu, and M. Gatford. Okapi at TREC-3. In D. K. Harman, editor, *Proceedings of the Third Text REtrieval Conference (TREC-3)*, pages 109–126. National Institute of Standards and Technology. NIST, 1994.

[15] J. J. Rocchio. Relevance feedback in information retrieval. In *The SMART Retrieval System: Experiments in Automatic Document Processing*, pages 313 – 323, Englewood Cliffs, NJ, 1971. Prentice-Hall Inc.

[16] C. E. Shannon and W. Weaver. *The Mathematical Theory of Communication.* The University of Illinois Press, Urbana, 1964.

[17] E. M. Voorhees. Query expansion using lexical semantic relations. In *Proceedings of the 13th Annual International ACM SIGIR Conference on Research and Development in Information Retrieval*, Dublin, Ireland, 1994.

[18] E. M. Voorhees and D. K. Harman. Overview of the Seventh Text REtrieval Conference (TREC-7). In *Proceedings of the Seventh Text REtrieval Conference (TREC-7).* National Institute of Standards and Technology, `http://trec.nist.gov/pubs.html`, 1999.

[19] J. Xu and W. B. Croft. Query expansion using local and global document analysis. In *Proceedings of the 19th Annual International ACM SIGIR Conference on Research and Development in Information Retrieval*, pages 4–11, New York, NY, 1996.

[20] Y. Zhang and J. Callan. Maximum likelihood estimation for filtering thresholds. In *Proceedings of the 24th Annual International ACM SIGIR Conference on Research and Development in Information Retrieval*, pages 294–301, New Orleans, LA., September 2001.

Web Question Answering: Is More Always Better?

Susan Dumais, Michele Banko, Eric Brill, Jimmy Lin, Andrew Ng
Microsoft Research
One Microsoft Way
Redmond, WA 98052 USA
{sdumais, mbanko, brill}@research.microsoft.com
jimmylin@ai.mit.edu; ang@cs.berkeley.edu

ABSTRACT

This paper describes a question answering system that is designed to capitalize on the tremendous amount of data that is now available online. Most question answering systems use a wide variety of linguistic resources. We focus instead on the redundancy available in large corpora as an important resource. We use this redundancy to simplify the query rewrites that we need to use, and to support answer mining from returned snippets. Our system performs quite well given the simplicity of the techniques being utilized. Experimental results show that question answering accuracy can be greatly improved by analyzing more and more matching passages. Simple passage ranking and n-gram extraction techniques work well in our system making it efficient to use with many backend retrieval engines.

Categories and Subject Descriptors

H.3.1. [**Content Analysis and Indexing**], H.3.3 [**Information Search and Retrieval**].

General Terms

Algorithms, Experimentation.

1. INTRODUCTION

Question answering has recently received attention from the information retrieval, information extraction, machine learning, and natural language processing communities [1][3][19][20] The goal of a question answering system is to retrieve 'answers' to questions rather than full documents or even best-matching passages as most information retrieval systems currently do. The TREC Question Answering Track which has motivated much of the recent work in the field focuses on fact-based, short-answer questions such as "*Who killed Abraham Lincoln?*" or "*How tall is Mount Everest?*". In this paper we focus on this kind of question answering task, although the techniques we propose are more broadly applicable.

The design of our question answering system is motivated by recent observations in natural language processing that, for many applications, significant improvements in accuracy can be attained simply by increasing the amount of data used for learning. Following the same guiding principle we take advantage of the tremendous data resource that the Web provides as the backbone of our question answering system. Many groups working on question answering have used a variety of linguistic resources - part-of-speech tagging, syntactic parsing, semantic relations, named entity extraction, dictionaries, WordNet, etc. (e.g., [2][8][11][12][13][15][16]).We chose instead to focus on the Web as gigantic data repository with tremendous redundancy that can be exploited for question answering. The Web, which is home to billions of pages of electronic text, is orders of magnitude larger than the TREC QA document collection, which consists of fewer than 1 million documents. This is a resource that can be usefully exploited for question answering. We view our approach as complimentary to more linguistic approaches, but have chosen to see how far we can get initially by focusing on data per se as a key resource available to drive our system design.

Automatic QA from a single, small information source is extremely challenging, since there is likely to be only one answer in the source to any user's question. Given a source, such as the TREC corpus, that contains only a relatively small number of formulations of answers to a query, we may be faced with the difficult task of mapping questions to answers by way of uncovering complex lexical, syntactic, or semantic relationships between question string and answer string. The need for anaphor resolution and synonymy, the presence of alternate syntactic formulations, and indirect answers all make answer finding a potentially challenging task. However, the greater the answer redundancy in the source data collection, the more likely it is that we can find an answer that occurs in a simple relation to the question. Therefore, the less likely it is that we will need to resort to solving the aforementioned difficulties facing natural language processing systems.

2. EXPLOITING REDUNDANCY FOR QA

We take advantage of the redundancy (multiple, differently phrased, answer occurrences) available when considering massive amounts of data in two key ways in our system.

Enables Simple Query Rewrites. The greater the number of information sources we can draw from, the easier the task of rewriting the question becomes, since the answer is more likely to be expressed in different manners. For example, consider the difficulty of gleaning an answer to the question "*Who killed Abraham Lincoln?*" from a source which contains only the text *"John Wilkes Booth altered history with a bullet. He will forever be known as the man who ended Abraham Lincoln's life,"*

SIGIR'02, August 11-15, 2002, Tampere, Finland.

versus a source that also contains the transparent answer string, *"John Wilkes Booth killed Abraham Lincoln."*

Facilitates Answer Mining. Even when no obvious answer strings can be found in the text, redundancy can improve the efficacy of question answering. For instance, consider the question: *"How many times did Bjorn Borg win Wimbledon?"* Assume the system is unable to find any obvious answer strings, but does find the following sentences containing "Bjorn Borg" and "Wimbledon", as well as a number:

(1) **Bjorn Borg** blah blah **Wimbledon** blah blah **5** blah

(2) **Wimbledon** blah blah blah **Bjorn Borg** blah **37** blah.

(3) blah **Bjorn Borg** blah blah **5** blah blah **Wimbledon**

(4) **5** blah blah **Wimbledon** blah blah **Bjorn Borg**.

By virtue of the fact that the most frequent number in these sentences is 5, we can posit that as the most likely answer.

3. RELATED WORK

Other researchers have recently looked to the web as a resource for question answering. The Mulder system described by Kwok et al. [14] is similar to our approach in several respects. For each question, Mulder submits multiple queries to a web search engine and analyzes the results. Mulder does sophisticated parsing of the query and the full-text of retrieved pages, which is far more complex and compute-intensive than our analysis. They also require global idf term weights for answer extraction and selection, which requires local storage of a database of term weights. They have done some interesting user studies of the Mulder interface, but they have not evaluated it with TREC queries nor have they looked at the importance of various system components.

Clarke et al. [9][10] investigated the importance of redundancy in their question answering system. In [9] they found that the best weighting of passages for question answering involves using both passage frequency (what they call redundancy) and a global idf term weight. They also found that analyzing more top-ranked passages was helpful in some cases and not in others. Their system builds a full-content index of a document collection, in this case TREC. In [10] they use web data to reinforce the scores of promising candidate answers by providing additional redundancy, with good success. Their implementation requires an auxiliary web corpus be available for full-text analysis and global term weighting. In our work, the web is the primary source of redundancy and we operate without a full-text index of documents or a database of global term weights.

Buchholz's Shapaqa NLP system [7] has been evaluated on both TREC and Web collections. Question answering accuracy was higher with the Web collection (although both runs were poor in absolute terms), but few details about the nature of the differences are provided.

These systems typically perform complex parsing and entity extraction for both queries and best matching web pages ([7][14]), which limits the number of web pages that they can analyze in detail. Other systems require term weighting for selecting or ranking the best-matching passages ([10][14]) and this requires auxiliary data structures. Our approach is distinguished from these in its simplicity (simple rewrites and string matching) and efficiency in the use of web resources (use of only summaries and simple ranking). We now describe how our system uses redundancy in detail and evaluate this systematically.

4. SYSTEM OVERVIEW

A flow diagram of our system is shown in Figure 1. The system consists of four main components.

Rewrite Query. Given a question, the system generates a number of rewrite strings, which are likely substrings of declarative answers to the question. To give a simple example, from the question *"When was Abraham Lincoln born?"* we know that a likely answer formulation takes the form "Abraham Lincoln was born on <DATE>". Therefore, we can look through the collection of documents, searching for such a pattern.

We first classify the question into one of seven categories, each of which is mapped to a particular set of rewrite rules. Rewrite rule sets range in size from one to five rewrite types. The output of the rewrite module is a set of 3-tuples of the form [`string, L/R/-, weight`], where "`string`" is the reformulated

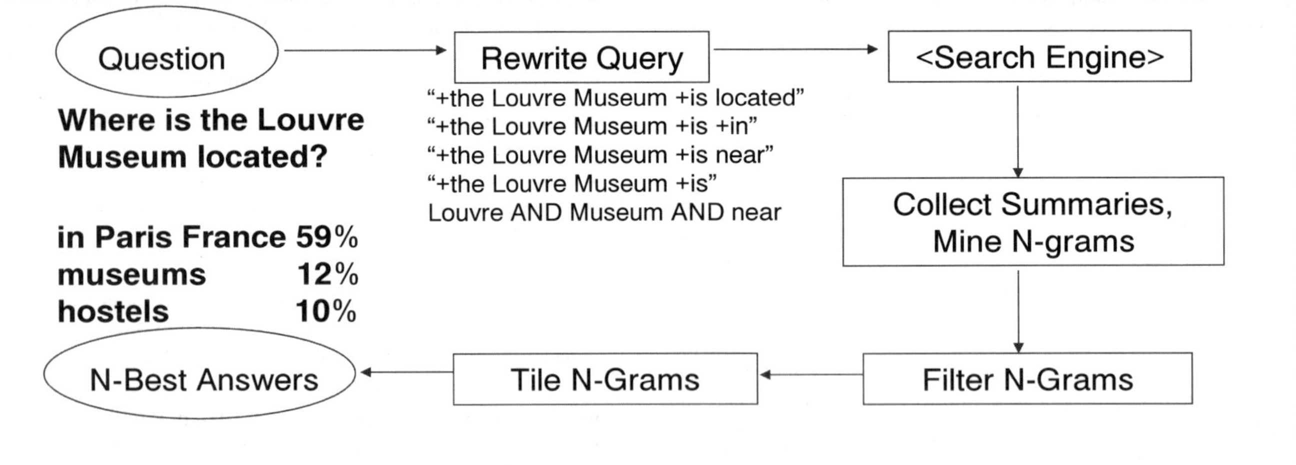

Figure 1. System Architecture

search query, "L/R/-" indicates the position in the text where we expect to find the answer with respect to the query string (to the left, right or anywhere) and "weight" reflects how much we prefer answers found with this particular query. The idea behind using a weight is that answers found using a high precision query (e.g., "Abraham Lincoln was born on") are more likely to be correct than those found using a lower precision query (e.g., "Abraham" AND "Lincoln" AND "born").

We do not use a parser or part-of-speech tagger for query reformulation, but do use a lexicon in order to determine the possible parts-of-speech of a word as well as its morphological variants. We created the rewrite rules and associated weights manually for the current system, although it may be possible to learn query-to-answer reformulations and weights (e.g. see Agichtein et al. [4]; Radev et al. [17]).

The rewrites generated by our system are simple string-based manipulations. For instance, some question types involve query rewrites with possible verb movement; the verb "*is*" in the question "*Where is the Louvre Museum located*?" should be moved in formulating the desired rewrite to "The Louvre Museum **is** located in". While we might be able to determine where to move a verb by analyzing the sentence syntactically, we took a much simpler approach. Given a query such as "Where is w_1 w_2 ... w_n", where each of the w_i is a word, we generate a rewrite for each possible position the verb could be moved to (e.g. "w_1 is w_2 ... w_n", "w_1 w_2 is ... w_n", etc). While such an approach results in many nonsensical rewrites (e.g. "The Louvre is Museum located in"), these very rarely result in the retrieval of bad pages, and the proper movement position is guaranteed to be found via exhaustive search. If we instead relied on a parser, we would require fewer query rewrites, but a misparse would result in the proper rewrite not being found.

For each query we also generate a final rewrite which is a backoff to a simple ANDing of the non-stop words in the query. We could backoff even further to ranking using a best-match retrieval system which doesn't require the presence of all terms and uses differential term weights, but we did not find that this was necessary when using the Web as a source of data. There are an average of 6.7 rewrites for the 500 TREC-9 queries used in the experiments described below.

As an example, the rewrites for the query "*Who created the character of Scrooge?*" are:

LEFT_5_"created +the character +of Scrooge"

RIGHT_5_"+the character +of Scrooge +was created +by"

AND_2 "created" AND "+the character" AND "+of Scrooge"

AND_1_"created" AND "character" AND "Scrooge"

To date we have used only simple string matching techniques. Soubbotin and Soubbotin [18] have used much richer regular expression matching to provide hints about likely answers, with very good success in TREC 2001, and we could certainly incorporate some of these ideas in our rewrites. Note that many of our rewrites require the matching of stop words like "in" and "the", in the above example. In our system stop words are important indicators of likely answers, and we do not ignore them as most ranked retrieval systems do, except in the final backoff AND rewrite.

The query rewrites are then formulated as search engine queries and sent to a search engine from which page summaries are collected and analyzed.

Mine N-Grams. From the page summaries returned by the search engine, n-grams are mined. For reasons of efficiency, we use only the returned summaries and not the full-text of the corresponding web page. The returned summaries contain the query terms, usually with a few words of surrounding context. In some cases, this surrounding context has truncated the answer string, which may negatively impact results. The summary text is then processed to retrieve only strings to the left or right of the query string, as specified in the rewrite triple.

1-, 2-, and 3-grams are extracted from the summaries. An N-gram is scored according the weight of the query rewrite that retrieved it. These scores are summed across the summaries that contain the n-gram (which is the opposite of the usual inverse document frequency component of document/passage ranking schemes). We do not count frequency of occurrence within a summary (the usual tf component in ranking schemes). Thus, the final score for an n-gram is based on the rewrite rules that generated it and the number of unique summaries in which it occurred. When searching for candidate answers, we enforce the constraint that at most one stopword is permitted to appear in any potential n-gram answers.

The top-ranked n-grams for the Scrooge query are:

Dickens 117
Christmas Carol 78
Charles Dickens 75
Disney 72
Carl Banks 54
A Christmas 41
uncle 31

Filter/Reweight N-Grams. Next, the n-grams are filtered and reweighted according to how well each candidate matches the expected answer-type, as specified by a handful of handwritten filters. The system uses filtering in the following manner. First, the query is analyzed and assigned one of seven question types, such as *who-question, what-question,* or *how-many-question.* Based on the query type that has been assigned, the system determines what collection of filters to apply to the set of potential answers found during n gram harvesting The answers are analyzed for features relevant to the filters, and then rescored according to the presence of such information.

A collection of approximately 15 filters were developed based on human knowledge about question types and the domain from which their answers can be drawn. These filters used surface string features, such as capitalization or the presence of digits, and consisted of handcrafted regular expression patterns.

After the system has determined which filters to apply to a pool of candidate answers, the selected filters are applied to each candidate string and used to adjust the score of the string. In most cases, filters are used to boost the score of a potential answer when it has been determined to possess the features relevant to the query type. In other cases, filters are used to remove strings from the candidate list altogether. This type of exclusion was only performed when the set of correct answers was determined to be a closed set (e.g. "Which continent....?") or definable by a set of closed properties (e.g. "How many...?").

Tile N-Grams. Finally, we applied an answer tiling algorithm, which both merges similar answers and assembles longer answers out of answer fragments. Tiling constructs longer n-grams from sequences of overlapping shorter n-grams. For example, "A B C" and "B C D" is tiled into "A B C D." The algorithm proceeds greedily from the top-scoring candidate - all subsequent candidates (up to a certain cutoff) are checked to see if they can be tiled with the current candidate answer. If so, the higher scoring candidate is replaced with the longer tiled n-gram, and the lower scoring candidate is removed. The algorithm stops only when no n-grams can be further tiled.

The top-ranked n-grams after tiling for the Scrooge query are:

Charles Dickens 117
A Christmas Carol 78
Walt Disney's uncle 72
Carl Banks 54
uncle 31

Our system works most efficiently and naturally with a backend retrieval system that returns best-matching passages or query-relevant document summaries. We can, of course, post-process the full text of matching documents to extract summaries for n-gram mining, but this is inefficient especially in Web applications where the full text of documents would have to be downloaded over the network at query time.

5. EXPERIMENTS

For our experimental evaluations we used the first 500 TREC-9 queries (201-700) [19]. For simplicity we ignored queries which are syntactic rewrites of earlier queries (701-893), although including them does not change the results in any substantive way. We used the patterns provided by NIST for automatic scoring. A few patterns were slightly modified to accommodate the fact that some of the answer strings returned using the Web were not available for judging in TREC-9. We did this in a very conservative manner allowing for more specific correct answers (e.g., Edward J. Smith vs. Edward Smith) but not more general ones (e.g., Smith vs. Edward Smith), and simple substitutions (e.g., 9 months vs. nine months). These changes influence the absolute scores somewhat but do not change relative performance, which is our focus here.

Many of the TREC queries are time sensitive - that is, the correct answer depends on when the question is asked. The TREC database covers a period of time more than 10 years ago; the Web is much more current. Because of this mismatch, many correct answers returned from the Web will be scored as incorrect using the TREC answer patterns. 10-20% of the TREC queries have temporal dependencies. E.g., *Who is the president of Bolivia? What is the exchange rate between England and the U. S.?* We did not modify the answer key to accommodate these time differences, because this is a subjective job and would make comparison with earlier TREC results impossible.

For the main Web retrieval experiments we used Google as a backend because it provides query-relevant summaries that make our n-gram mining techniques more efficient. Thus we have access to more than 2 billion web pages. For some experiments in TREC retrieval we use the standard QA collection consisting of news documents from Disks 1-5. The TREC collection has just under 1 million documents [19].

All runs are completely automatic, starting with queries and generating a ranked list of 5 candidate answers. Candidate answers are a maximum of 50 bytes long, and typically much shorter than that. We report the Mean Reciprocal Rank (MRR) of the first correct answer, the Number of Questions Correctly Answered (NumCorrect), and the Proportion of Questions Correctly Answered (PropCorrect). Correct answers at any rank are included in the number and proportion correct measures. Most correct answers are at the top of the list -- 70% of the correct answers occur in the first position and 90% in the first or second positions.

Using our system with default settings for query rewrite weights, number of summaries returned, etc. we obtain a MRR of 0.507 and answer 61% of the queries. The average answer length was 12 bytes, so the system is really returning short answers not passages. This is very good performance and would place us near the top of 50-byte runs for TREC-9. However, since we did not take part in TREC-9 it is impossible to compare our results precisely with those systems (e.g., we used TREC-9 for tuning our TREC-10 system increasing our score somewhat, but we return several correct answers that were not found in TREC-9 thus decreasing our score somewhat).

Redundancy is used in two key ways in our data-driven approach. First, the occurrence of multiple linguistic formulations of the same answers increases the chances of being able to find an answer that occurs within the context of a simple pattern match with the query. Second, answer redundancy facilitates the process of answer extraction by giving higher weight to answers that occur more often (i.e., in more different document summaries). We now evaluate the contributions of these experimentally.

5.1 Number of Snippets

We begin by examining the importance of redundancy in answer extraction. To do this we vary the number of summaries (snippets) that we get back from the search engine and use as input to the n-gram mining process. Our standard system uses 100 snippets. We varied the number of snippets from 1 to 1000. The results are shown in Figure 2.

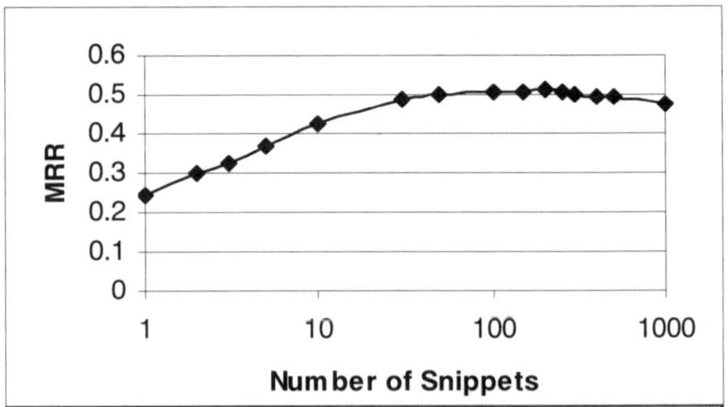

Figure 2. MRR as a function of number of snippets returned. TREC-9, queries 201-700.

Performance improves sharply as the number of snippets increases from 1 to 50 (0.243 MRR for 1 snippet, 0.370 MRR for 5, 0.423 MRR for 10, and 0.501 for 50), somewhat more slowly after that (peaking 0.514 MRR with 200 snippets), and then falling off somewhat after that as more snippets are included for n-gram analysis. Thus, over quite a wide range, the more snippets we consider in selecting and ranking n-grams the better. We believe that the slight drop at the high end is due to the increasing influence that the weaker rewrites have when many snippets are returned. The most restrictive rewrites return only a few matching documents. Increasing the number of snippets increases the number of the least restrictive matches (the AND matches), thus swamping the restrictive matches. In addition, frequent n-grams begin to dominate our rankings at this point.

An example of failures resulting from too many AND matches is Query 594: *What is the longest word in the English language?* For this query, there are 40 snippets matching the rewrite "is the longest word in the English language" with weight 5, 40 more snippets matching the rewrite "the longest word in the English language is" with the weight 5, and more than 100 snippets matching the backoff AND query ("longest" AND "word" AND "English" AND "language") with a weight of 1. When 100 snippets are used, the precise rewrites contribute almost as many snippets as the AND rewrite. In this case we find the correct answer, "pneumonoultramicroscopicsilicovolcanokoniosis", in the second rank. The first answer, "1909 letters long", which is incorrect, also matches many precise rewrites such as "the longest word in English is ## letters long", and we pick up on this. When 1000 snippets are used, the weaker AND rewrites dominate the matches. In this case, the correct answer falls to seventh on the list after "letters long", "one syllable", "is screeched", "facts", "stewardesses" and "dictionary", all of which occur commonly in results from the least restrictive AND rewrite. A very common AND match contains the phrase "the longest one-syllable word in the English language is screeched", and this accounts for two of our incorrect answers.

Using differential term weighting of answer terms, as many retrieval systems do, should help overcome this problem to some extent but we would like to avoid maintaining a database of global term weights. Alternatively we could refine our weight accumulation scheme to dampen the effects of many weakly restrictive matches by sub-linear accumulation, and we are currently exploring several alternatives for doing this.

Our main results on snippet redundancy are consistent with those reported by Clarke et al. [9], although they worked with the much smaller TREC collection. They examined a subset of the TREC-9 queries requiring a person's name as the answer. They varied the number of passages retrieved (which they call depth) from 25 to 100, and observed some improvements in MRR. When the passages they retrieved were small (250 or 500 bytes) they found improvement, but when the passages were larger (1000 or 2000 bytes) no improvements were observed. The snippets we used are shorter than 250 bytes, so the results are consistent. Clarke et al. [9] also explored a different notion of redundancy (which they refer to as c_i). c_i is the number of different passages that match an answer. Their best performance is achieved when both c_i and term weighting are used to rank passages. We too use the number of snippets that an n-gram occurs in. We do not, however, use global term weights, but have tried other techniques for weighting snippets as described below.

5.2 TREC vs. Web Databases

Another way to explore the importance of redundancy is to run our system directly on the TREC documents. As noted earlier, there are three orders of magnitude more documents on the Web than in the TREC QA collection. Consequently, there will be fewer alternative ways of saying the same thing and fewer matching documents available for mining the candidate n-grams. We suspect that this lack of redundancy will limit the success of our approach when applied directly on TREC documents.

While corpus size is an obvious and important difference between the TREC and Web collections there are other differences as well. For example, text analysis, ranking, and snippet extraction techniques will all vary somewhat in ways that we can not control. To better isolate the size factor, we also ran our system against another Web search engine.

For these experiments we used only the AND rewrites and looked at the first 100 snippets. We had to restrict ourselves to AND rewrites because some of the search engines we used do not support the inclusion of stop words in phrases, e.g., "*created +the character +of Scrooge*".

5.2.1 TREC Database

The TREC QA collection consists of just under 1 million documents. We expect much less redundancy here compared to the Web, and suspect that this will limit the success of our approach. An analysis of the TREC-9 query set (201-700) shows that no queries have 100 judged relevant documents. Only 10 of the 500 questions have 50 or more relevant documents, which the results in Figure 2 suggest are required for the good system performance. And a very large number of queries, 325, have fewer than 10 relevant documents.

We used an Okapi backend retrieval engine for the TREC collection. Since we used only Boolean AND rewrites, we did not take advantage of Okapi's best match ranking algorithm. However, most queries return fewer than 100 documents, so we wind up examining most of the matches anyway.

We developed two snippet extraction techniques to generate query-relevant summaries for use in n-gram mining. A *Contiguous* technique returned the smallest window containing all the query terms along with 10 words of context on either side. Windows that were greater than 500 words were ignored. This approach is similar to passage retrieval techniques albeit without differential term weighting. A *Non Contiguous* technique returned the union of two word matches along with 10 words of context on either side. Single words not previously covered are included as well. The search engine we used for the initial Web experiments returns both contiguous and non-contiguous snippets. Figure 3 shows the results of this experiment.

	AND Rewrites Only, Top 100		
	MRR	NumCorrect	PropCorrect
Web1	0.450	281	0.562
TREC, Contiguous Snippet	0.186	117	0.234
TREC, Non-Contiguous Snippet	0.187	128	0.256

Figure 3: Web vs. TREC as data source

Our baseline system using all rewrites and retrieving 100 snippets achieves 0.507 MRR (Figure 2). Using only the AND query rewrites results in worse performance for our baseline system with 0.450 MRR (Figure 3). More noticeable than this difference is the drop in performance of our system using TREC as a data source compared to using the much larger Web as a data source. MRR drops from 0.450 to 0.186 for contiguous snippets and 0.187 for non-contiguous snippets, and the proportion of questions answered correctly drops from 56% to 23% for contiguous snippets and 26% for non-contiguous snippets. It is worth noting that the TREC MRR scores would still place this system in the top half of the systems for the TREC-9 50-byte task, even though we tuned our system to work on much larger collections. However, we can do much better simply by using more data. The lack of redundancy in the TREC collection accounts for a large part of this drop off in performance. Clarke et al. [10] have also reported better performance using the Web directly for TREC 2001 questions.

We expect that the performance difference between TREC and the Web would increase further if all the query rewrites were used. This is because there are so few exact phrase matches in TREC relative to the Web, and the precise matches improve performance by 13% (0.507 vs. 0.450).

We believe that database size per se (and the associated redundancy) is the most important difference between the TREC and Web collections. As noted above, however, there are other differences between the systems such as text analysis, ranking, and snippet extraction techniques. While we can not control the text analysis and ranking components of Web search engines, we can use the same snippet extraction techniques. We can also use a different Web search engine to mitigate the effects of a specific text analysis and ranking algorithms.

5.2.2 Another Web Search Engine

For these experiments we used the MSNSearch search engine. At the time of our experiments, the summaries returned were independent of the query. So we retrieved the full text of the top 100 web pages and applied the two snippet extraction techniques described above to generate query-relevant summaries. As before, all runs are completely automatic, starting with queries, retrieving web pages, extracting snippets, and generating a ranked list of 5 candidate answers. The results of these experiments are shown in Figure 4. The original results are referred to as Web1 and the new results as Web2.

	AND Rewrites Only, Top 100		
	MRR	NumCorrect	PropCorrect
Web1	0.450	281	0.562
TREC, Contiguous Snippet	0.186	117	0.234
TREC, Non-Contiguous Snippet	0.187	128	0.256
Web2, Contiguous Snippet	0.355	227	0.454
Web2, Non-Contiguous Snippet	0.383	243	0.486

Figure 4: Web vs. TREC as data source

The Web2 results are somewhat worse than the Web1 results, but this is expected given that we developed our system using the Web1 backend, and did not do any tuning of our snippet extraction algorithms. In addition, we believe that the Web2 collection indexed somewhat less content than Web1 at the time of our experiments, which should decrease performance in and of itself. More importantly, the Web2 results are much better than the TREC results for both snippet extraction techniques, almost doubling MRR in both cases. Thus, we have shown that QA is more successful using another large Web collection compared to the small TREC collection. The consistency of this result across Web collections points to size and redundancy as the key factors.

5.2.3 Combining TREC and Web

Given that the system benefits from having a large text collection from which to search for potential answers, then we would expect that combining both the Web and TREC corpus would result in even greater accuracy. We ran two experiments to test this. Because there was no easy way to merge the two corpora, we instead combined the output of QA system built on each corpus. For these experiments we used the original Web1 system and our TREC system. We used only the AND query rewrites, looked at the Top1000 search results for each rewrite, and used a slightly different snippet extraction technique. For these parameter settings, the base TREC-based system had a MRR of .262, the Web-based system had a MRR of .416.

First, we ran an oracle experiment to assess the potential gain that could be attained by combining the output of the Web-based and TREC-based QA systems. We implemented a "switching oracle", which decides for each question whether to use the output from the Web-based QA system or the TREC-based QA system, based upon which system output had a higher ranking correct answer. The switching oracle had a MRR of .468, a 12.5% improvement over the Web-based system. Note that this oracle does not precisely give us an upper bound, as combining algorithms (such as that described below) could re-order the rankings of outputs.

Next, we implemented a combining algorithm that merged the outputs from the TREC-based and Web-based systems, by having both systems vote on answers, where the vote is the score assigned to a particular answer by the system. For voting, we defined string equivalence such that if a string X is a substring of Y, then a vote for X is also a vote for Y. The combined system achieved a MRR of .433 (a 4.1% improvement over the Web-based system) and answered 283 questions correctly.

5.3 Snippet Weighting

Until now, we have focused on the quantity of information available and less on its quality. Snippet weights are used in ranking n-grams. An n-gram weight is the sum of the weights for all snippets in which that n-gram appears.

Each of our query rewrites has a weight associated with it reflecting how much we prefer answers found with this particular query. The idea behind using a weight is that answers found using a high precision query (e.g., "Abraham Lincoln was born on") are more likely to be correct than those found using a lower precision query (e.g., "Abraham" AND "Lincoln" AND "born"). Our current system has 5 weights.

These rewrite weights are the only source of snippet weighting in our system. We explored how important these weight are and considered several other factors that could be used as additional sources of information for snippet weighting. Although we specify Boolean queries, the retrieval engine can provide a ranking, based on factors like link analyses, proximity of terms, location of terms in the document, etc. So, different weights can be assigned to matches at different positions in the ranked list. We also looked at the number of matching terms in the best fixed width window, and the widow size of the smallest matching passage as indicators of passage quality.

Rewrite Wts uses our heuristically determined rewrite weights as a measure the quality of a snippet. This is the current system default. *Equal Wts* gives equal weight to all snippets regardless of the rewrite rule that generated them. To the extent that more precise rewrites retrieve better answers, we will see a drop in performance when we make all weights equal. *Rank Wts* uses the rank of the snippet as a measure of its quality, *SnippetWt = (100-rank)/100*. *NMatch Wts* uses the number of matching terms in a fixed-width window as the measure of snippet quality. *Length Wts* uses a measure of the length of the snippet needed to encompass all query terms as the measure of snippet quality. We also look at combinations of these factors. For example, *Rewrite+Rank Wts* uses both rewrite weight and rank according to the following formula, *SnippetWt = RewriteScore + (100-rank)/100*. All of these measures are available from query-relevant summaries returned by the search engine and do not require analyzing the full text of the document. The results of these experiments are presented in Figure 4.

Weighting	MRR	NumCorrect	PropCorrect
Equal Wts	0.489	298	0.596
Rewrite Wts (Default)	0.507	307	0.614
Rank Wts	0.483	292	0.584
Rewrite + Rank Wts	0.508	302	0.604
NMatch Wts	0.506	301	0.602
Length Wts	0.506	302	0.604

Figure 5: Snippet Weighting

Our current default 5-level weighting scheme which reflects the specificity of the query rewrites does quite well. Equal weighting is somewhat worse, as we expected. Interestingly search engine rank is no better for weighting candidate n-grams than equal weighting. None of the other techniques we looked at surpasses the default weights in both MRR and PropCorrect. Our heuristic rewrite weights provide a simple and effective technique for snippet weighting, that can be used with any backend retrieval engine.

Most question answering systems use IR-based measures of passage quality, and do not typically evaluate the best measure of similarity for purposes of extracting answers. Clarke et al. [9] noted above is an exception. Soubbotin and Soubbotin [18] mention different weights for different regular expression matches, but they did not describe the mechanism in detail nor did they evaluate how useful it is. Harabagiu et al. [11] have a kind of backoff strategy for matching which is similar to weighting, but again we do not know of parametric evaluations of its importance in their overall system performance. The question of what kinds of passages can best support answer mining for question answering as opposed to document retrieval is an interesting one that we are pursuing.

6. DISCUSSION AND FUTURE DIRECTIONS

The design of our question answering system was motivated by the goal of exploiting the large amounts of text data that is available on the Web and elsewhere as a useful resource. While many question answering systems take advantage of linguistic resources, fewer depend primarily on data. Vast amounts of data provide several sources of redundancy that our system capitalizes on. Answer redundancy (i.e., multiple, differently phrased, answer occurrences) enables us to use only simple query rewrites for matching, and facilitates the extraction of candidate answers.

We evaluated the importance of redundancy in our system parametrically. First, we explored the relationship between the number of document snippets examined and question answering accuracy. Accuracy improves sharply as the number of snippets included for n-gram analysis increases from 1 to 50, somewhat more slowly after that peaking at 200 snippets, and then falls off somewhat after that. More is better up to a limit. We believe that we can increase this limit by improving our weight accumulation algorithm so that matches from the least precise rewrites do not dominate. Second, in smaller collections (like TREC), the accuracy of our system drops sharply, although it is still quite reasonable in absolute terms. Finally, snippet quality is less important to system performance than snippet quantity. We have a simple 5-level snippet weighting scheme based on the specificity of the query rewrite, and this appears to be sufficient. More complex weighting schemes that we explored were no more useful.

The performance of our system shows promise for approaches to question answering which makes use of very large text databases even with minimal natural language processing. Our system does not need to maintain its own index nor does it require global term weights, so it can work in conjunction with any backend retrieval engine. Finally, since our system does only simple query transformations and n-gram analysis, it is efficient and scalable.

One might think that our system has limited applicability, because it works best with large amounts of data. But, this isn't necessarily so. First, we actually perform reasonably well in the smaller TREC collection, and could perhaps tune system parameters to work even better in that environment. More interestingly, Brill et al. [6] described a projection technique that can be used to combine the wealth of data available on the Web with the reliability of data in smaller sources like TREC or an encyclopedia. The basic idea is to find candidate answers in a large and possibly noisy source, and then expand the query to include likely answers. The expanded queries can then be used on smaller but perhaps more reliable collections - either directly to find support for the answer in the smaller corpus, or indirectly as a new query which is issued and mined as we currently do. This approach appears to be quite promising. Our approach seems least applicable in applications that involve a small amount of proprietary data. In these cases, one might need to do much more sophisticated analyses to map user queries to the exact lexical form that occur in the text collection rather than depend on primarily on redundancy as we have done.

Although we have pushed the data-driven perspective, more sophisticated language analysis might help as well by providing more effective query rewrites or less noisy data for mining.

Most question answering systems contain aspects of both - we use some linguistic knowledge in our small query typology and answer filtering, and more sophisticated systems often use simple pattern matching for things like dates, zip codes, etc.

There are a number of open questions that we hope to explore. In the short term, we would like to look systematically at the contributions of other system components. Brill et al. [5] have started to explore individual components in more detail, with interesting results. In addition, it is likely that we have made several sub-optimal decisions in our initial implementation (e.g., omitting most stop words from answers, simple linear accumulation of scores over matching snippets) that we would like to improve. Most retrieval engines have been developed with the goal of finding topically relevant documents. Finding accurate answers may require somewhat different matching infrastructure. We are beginning to explore how best to generate snippets for use in answer mining. Finally, time is an interesting issue. We noted earlier how the correct answer to some queries changes over time. Time also has interesting implications for using redundancy. For example, it would take a while for a news or Web collection to correctly answer a question like "Who is the U. S. President?" just after an election.

An important goal of our work is to get system designers to treat data as a first class resource that is widely available and exploitable. We have made good initial progress, and there are several interesting issues remaining to explore.

7. REFERENCES

[1] AAAI Spring Symposium Series (2002). *Mining Answers from Text and Knowledge Bases.*

[2] S. Abney, M. Collins and A. Singhal (2000). Answer extraction. In *Proceedings of the 6th Applied Natural Language Processing Conference (ANLP 2000),* 296-301.

[3] ACL-EACL (2002). *Workshop on Open-domain Question Answering.*

[4] E. Agichtein, S. Lawrence and L. Gravano (2001). Learning search engine specific query transformations for question answering. In *Proceedings of the 10th World Wide Web Conference (WWW10),* 169-178.

[5] E. Brill, S. Dumais and M. Banko (2002). An analysis of the AskMSR question-answering system. In *Proceedings of 2002 Conference on Empirical Methods in Natural Language Processing (EMNLP 2002).*

[6] E. Brill, J. Lin, M. Banko, S. Dumais and A. Ng (2002). Data-intensive question answering. In *Proceedings of the Tenth Text REtrieval Conference (TREC 2001).*

[7] S. Buchholz (2002). Using grammatical relations, answer frequencies and the World Wide Web for TREC question answering. In *Proceedings of the Tenth Text REtrieval Conference (TREC 2001).*

[8] J. Chen, A. R. Diekema, M. D. Taffet, N. McCracken, N. E. Ozgencil, O. Yilmazel, E. D. Liddy (2002). Question answering: CNLP at the TREC-10 question answering track. In *Proceedings of the Tenth Text REtrieval Conference (TREC 2001).*

[9] C. Clarke, G. Cormack and T. Lyman (2001). Exploiting redundancy in question answering. In *Proceedings of the 24th Annual International ACM SIGIR Conference on Research and Development in Information Retrieval (SIGIR'2001),* 358-365.

[10] C. Clarke, G. Cormack and T. Lynam (2002). Web reinforced question answering. In *Proceedings of the Tenth Text REtrieval Conference (TREC 2001).*

[11] S. Harabagiu, D. Moldovan, M. Pasca, R. Mihalcea, M. Surdeanu, R. Bunescu, R. Girju, V. Rus and P. Morarescu (2001). FALCON: Boosting knowledge for question answering. In *Proceedings of the Ninth Text REtrieval Conference (TREC-9),* 479-488.

[12] E. Hovy, L. Gerber, U. Hermjakob, M. Junk and C. Lin (2001). Question answering in Webclopedia. In *Proceedings of the Ninth Text REtrieval Conference (TREC-9),* 655-664.

[13] E. Hovy, U. Hermjakob and C. Lin (2002). The use of external knowledge in factoid QA. In *Proceedings of the Tenth Text REtrieval Conference (TREC 2001).*

[14] C. Kwok, O. Etzioni and D. Weld (2001). Scaling question answering to the Web. In *Proceedings of the 10th World Wide Web Conference (WWW'10),* 150-161.

[15] M. A. Pasca and S. M. Harabagiu (2001). High performance question/answering. In *Proceedings of the 24th Annual International ACM SIGIR Conference on Research and Development in Information Retrieval (SIGIR'2001),* 366-374.

[16] J. Prager, E. Brown, A. Coden and D. Radev (2000). Question answering by predictive annotation. In *Proceedings of the 23rd Annual International ACM SIGIR Conference on Research and Development in Information Retrieval (SIGIR'2000),* 184-191.

[17] D. R. Radev, H. Qi, Z. Zheng, S. Blair-Goldensohn, Z. Zhang, W. Fan and J. Prager (2001). Mining the web for answers to natural language questions. In *Proceeding of the 2001* ACM *CIKM: Tenth International Conference on Information and Knowledge Management,* 143-150

[18] M. M. Soubbotin and S. M. Soubbotin (2002). Patterns and potential answer expressions as clues to the right answers. In *Proceedings of the Tenth Text REtrieval Conference (TREC 2001).*

[19] E. Voorhees and D. Harman, Eds. (2001). *Proceedings of the Ninth Text REtrieval Conference (TREC-9).* NIST Special Publication 500-249.

[20] E. Voorhees and D. Harman, Eds. (2002). *Proceedings of the Tenth Text REtrieval Conference (TREC 2001).).* NIST Special Publication 500-250.

Predicting Query Performance

Steve Cronen-Townsend
crotown@cs.umass.edu

Yun Zhou
yzhou@cs.umass.edu

W. Bruce Croft
croft@cs.umass.edu

Center for Intelligent Information Retrieval
Department of Computer Science
University of Massachusetts, Amherst, MA 01003

ABSTRACT

We develop a method for predicting query performance by computing the relative entropy between a query language model and the corresponding collection language model. The resulting *clarity score* measures the coherence of the language usage in documents whose models are likely to generate the query. We suggest that clarity scores measure the ambiguity of a query with respect to a collection of documents and show that they correlate positively with average precision in a variety of TREC test sets. Thus, the clarity score may be used to identify ineffective queries, on average, without relevance information. We develop an algorithm for automatically setting the clarity score threshold between predicted poorly-performing queries and acceptable queries and validate it using TREC data. In particular, we compare the automatic thresholds to optimum thresholds and also check how frequently results as good are achieved in sampling experiments that randomly assign queries to the two classes.

Categories and Subject Descriptors

H.3.3 [**Information Storage and Retrieval**]: Information Search and Retrieval—*Query formulation*

General Terms

Algorithms, Experimentation, Theory

Keywords

ambiguity, clarity, information theory, language models

1. INTRODUCTION

Dealing effectively with poorly-performing queries is a crucial issue in information retrieval systems. Even what a user believes to be well-formulated queries may, in fact, perform poorly depending on the nature of the collection. Since no user knows the full nuances of the documents in the collection they are searching, all queries are poorly formulated, to varying degrees.

For example, suppose a user interested in the competitors in the 1988-1989 soccer World Cup issues the query "World Cup" against the TREC AP88 collection of news articles. If those two words are the only evidence the system has about what the user means, it is simply impossible for the system to return the soccer articles consistently higher in the ranked list than the articles about World Cup chess tournaments. Articles about World Cup chess tournaments are predominant, in fact, in the chosen collection among the articles that use the query terms frequently. Despite the fact that the user might not have known that there was a World Cup in anything other than soccer, he or she would get a ranked list with chess articles predominating and with soccer articles interspersed sporadically throughout.

As highlighted in the above example, the degree of ambiguity of a query with respect to the collection of documents being searched is often closely related to query performance. Thus we seek to measure the degree of ambiguity of a query with respect to a collection of documents. Specifically, we measure the degree of dissimilarity between the language usage associated with the query and the generic language of the collection as a whole.

A query whose highly ranked documents are about a single topic (high coherence) has a model characterized by unusually large probabilities for a small number of topical terms. On the other hand, a query returning a mix of articles about different topics (low coherence) has a model that is smoother and more like the model of the collection as a whole. Hence the high-coherence query would get a high score (since its associated language is very different from the overall collection language), a while the low-coherence query would get a low score. Thus, this measure is closely related to the lack of ambiguity, and we call it the *clarity score*.

There is a strong correlation between the clarity score of a test query with respect to the appropriate test collection and the performance of that query. We believe this is due to the fact that a low-coherence retrieval is likely to contain many irrelevant documents in the top ranks and a high-coherence retrieval often contains many relevant documents in the top ranks. Hence it is possible to predict, to some degree, the performance of a query without relevance information. We show how to set the clarity score threshold optimally to predict whether a test query falls in to the upper or lower half of a set of test queries. Finally, we suggest a way to set the threshold without relevance information, making these techniques applicable to real systems.

2. COMPUTING CLARITY

Throughout this work we use a language modeling approach, similar to the approach first used in information retrieval by Ponte and Croft[16]. Language models, long used in speech recognition, capture statistical aspects of the generation of language[9]. In information retrieval they are often applied in a simple manner, modeling term occurrences at the document level with little or no regard to sequential effects. In the computations of this paper, a "language model" refers to a probability distribution over all single terms (morphologically-normalized words) and may be estimated based on a single document, or a query and collection of documents. Thinking about language models more generically, however, is often fruitful since simple language models can often be replaced by more sophisticated models in future work.

2.1 Definition

The first step in computing a clarity score is estimating a query language model. We have investigated both of the methods put forward by Lavrenko and Croft[13] for estimating such models[1]. Here we use Lavrenko and Croft's *Method 1.* In this approach one assumes, in effect, that the query terms and the terms in the documents are sampled identically and independently from the query model unigram distribution. This results in high probability estimates for terms that occur frequently in documents containing many query terms.

The query language model (unigram distribution over terms) is given by

$$P(w|Q) = \sum_{D \in R} P(w|D)P(D|Q), \tag{1}$$

where w is any term, Q the query, D is a document or the model estimated from the corresponding single document, and R is the set of documents that contain at least one query term.

As weights $P(D|Q)$ in Equation (1) we estimate the likelihood of an individual document model generating the query[19] as

$$P(Q|D) = \prod_{q \in Q} P(q|D), \tag{2}$$

and obtain $P(D|Q)$ by Bayesian inversion with uniform prior probabilities for documents in R and a zero prior for documents that contain no query terms.

We estimate $P(w|D)$ and $P(q|D)$ in (1) and (2) by relative frequencies of terms linearly smoothed[14] with collection frequencies as

$$P(w|D) = \lambda P_{ml}(w|D) + (1-\lambda)P_{coll}(w), \tag{3}$$

where $P_{ml}(w|D)$ is the relative frequency of term w in documents D, $P_{coll}(w)$ is the relative frequency of the term in the collection as a whole, and $\lambda = 0.6$ throughout this study. Figure 1 shows example query and collection language models.

The clarity score for the query is simply the relative entropy, or Kullback-Leibler divergence[4], between the query and collection language models (unigram distributions),

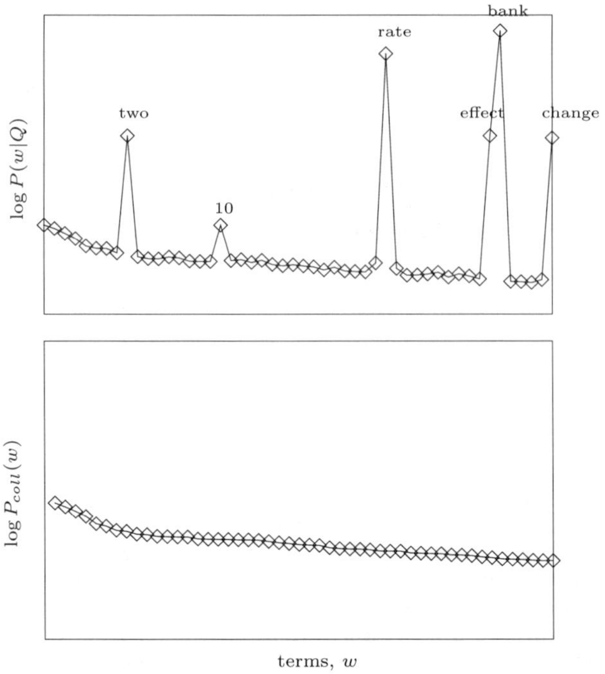

Figure 1: The query language model for query A, "Show me any predictions for changes in the prime lending rate and any changes made in the prime lending rates" in TREC disk 1 and the collection language model for that collection. The top 50 terms are plotted in order by their collection probabilities.

given by

$$\text{clarity score} = \sum_{w \in V} P(w|Q) \log_2 \frac{P(w|Q)}{P_{coll}(w)}, \tag{4}$$

where V is the entire vocabulary of the collection.

The efficiency of clarity score computation with Equation (4) is dominated by the estimation of the query language model by Equation (1), since the collection model can be precomputed at index-time. The query model is estimated most efficiently by sampling documents using standard techniques[10]. Throughout this paper we estimate query models by sampling until reaching a limit of 500 unique documents. Alternatively to (4), one can compute the divergence with the roles of the query language model and the collection language model reversed. The method shown in Equation 4 consistently performs slightly better in TREC evaluations of clarity score correlation with average precision (see section 4) and is used throughout this paper.

One can use Lavrenko and Croft's *Method 2* models as an alternative to Equation (1). The weaker independence assumptions employed in this method result in high probability estimates for terms that commonly co-occur in documents with individual query terms, but not necessarily many query terms at once. Except in AP88+89 tests, the *Method 1* models used in this section result in slightly better correlation between clarity score and average precision (see section 4) and are used unless otherwise noted.

[1]Lavrenko and Croft refer to these as *relevance models.*

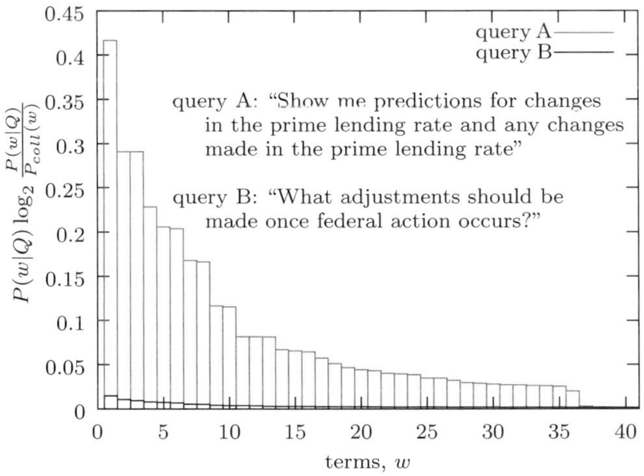

Figure 2: A clear versus a vague query in TREC disk 1 with the top 40 contributions plotted term-by-term. The top six contributions, in order, for query A are for the terms "bank", "hong", "kong", "rate", "lend" and "prime" while the top six for query B are "adjust", "federal", "action", "land", "occur" and "hyundai"

2.2 Examples

Consider two queries, A and B. A is "Show me any predictions for changes in the prime lending rate and any changes made in the prime lending rates" and B is "What adjustments should be made once federal action occurs?"

Figure 1 shows the language models used in computing the clarity score for query A, which is 2.85 bits. In terms of these figures, the clarity score is the top graph minus the bottom graph, times 2 to the power of the top graph and summed over terms. The difference between the two graphs makes a function with spikes at the most topical words and the final step of taking the expectation value of this quantity using the top distribution enhances the peaks further still. This procedure can also be interpreted as the number of bits wasted on average when one encodes term-occurrence events sampled from the query language model with a code optimally designed for the collection language model.

The best way to visualize the difference between clear and vague queries is to plot the clarity contributions on a term-by-term basis as in Figure 2. Here $P(w|Q) * \log(\frac{P(w|Q)}{P_{coll}(w)})$ is plotted for each of the top 40 contributing terms w, sorted in descending order of contribution. For example, the left-most gray bar in Figure 2 shows that the term "bank" made the biggest contribution (0.416) to the clarity score of the query A. This term is prominent in the query model (Equation (1)) because it occurs frequently in documents whose models are likely to generate the query. Note that "bank" does not, itself, occur in the query. This term makes a high contribution to the clarity score (Equation (4)) because its estimated probability is much higher in the query model than in the collection model. Visually, compare its value in the top graph of Figure 1 (the biggest spike) to the corresponding value directly below it on the collection model graph. Similarly, the small black bar in the leftmost position indicates that term "adjust" made the highest contribution to the clarity score of query B at 0.015. In this representation, the clarity score for a query is the total of all the heights of the corresponding bars, or the total area of the bars. The clarity score of query B is the total area of all the black bars (the tallest 40 of which are show in Figure 2) and is 0.37 as compared to the total of 2.85 for query A (grey bars). This representation makes the contrast evident between high and low clarity score queries.

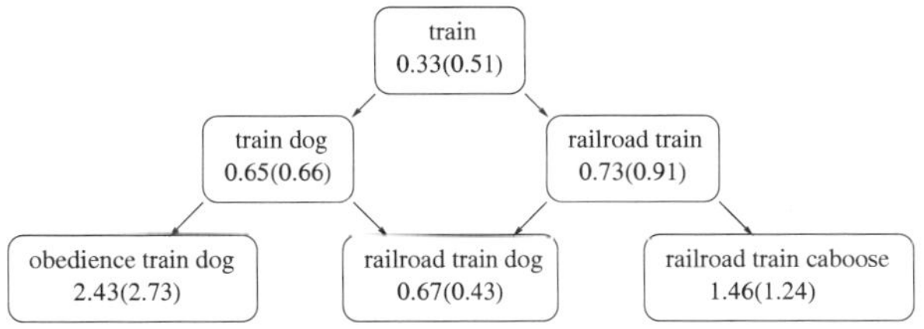

Figure 3: Clarity scores for some related queries against the TREC-7 collection. The scores are computed using Equation (4) and *Method 1* query models (Equation 1), with scores using *Method 2* models in parenthesis. Arrows indicate the addition of a query term.

3. CLARITY AND AMBIGUITY

Clarity scores were invented in an attempt to quantify the ambiguity of a query. Looking at the entropy of the query language model is a natural approach since entropy measures how strongly a distribution specifies certain values, in this case terms. Refining to the *relative* entropy of the model as compared to the collection model, allows the method to ignore large and fluctuating contributions due to generic terms.

The clarity scores for a series of related queries is shown in Figure 3. The left and right edges of this figure represent two distinct meanings starting with the term "train". The left side refers to training of dogs and the right side refers to railroad cars. The lowest central query "railroad train dog" is an ambiguous combination of the two meanings. With *Method 1* models this ambiguous query is far lower scoring than its more specific neighbors to the left and right but comparable to the two two-term queries up one level. Interestingly, though, with *Method 2* models (scores in parentheses in Figure 3) the score of this query is not only lower than the more specific three term queries, but is even lower than the score of the original one-term query "train." Clarity scores from *Method 2* models seems to "punish" more harshly the addition of a term that does not co-occur with the other query terms in documents in the collection. Clarity scores computed this way correlate less strongly with average precision in evaluations of the type we describe next. More detailed discussion of clarity scores as a measure of ambiguity appear in [6].

4. CLARITY AND AVERAGE PRECISION

4.1 TREC Ad Hoc Track Evaluations

To lay the groundwork for using clarity scores to predict the performance of a query, we measure the correlation between clarity scores and average precision scores for various TREC Ad Hoc Track test collections and queries. The re-

Collection	Queries	Num.	R	P-value
AP88+89	$101-200$	100	0.368	1.2×10^{-4}
TREC-4	$201-250$	50	0.490	3.0×10^{-4}
TREC-5	$251-300$	50	0.459	6.5×10^{-4}
TREC-7	$351-400$	50	0.577	2.7×10^{-5}
TREC-8	$401-450$	50	0.494	2.7×10^{-4}
TREC-7+8	$351-450$	100	0.536	4.8×10^{-8}

Table 1: The correlation of clarity scores with average precision in several TREC test collections. The queries are the titles of the TREC topics (usually a few words), except for TREC-4 where the description field is used due to a lack of titles, resulting in queries of 16.1 words, on average.

trieval is done with a simple multinomial language modeling approach[19][2].

Since the score distributions are unknown, an appropriate test is the Spearmann rank correlation test[8]. As a first step, each list of scores is replaced by the corresponding ranks (e.g. the lowest score is replaced with 1, the second lowest score with 2, et cetera, and the highest score is replaced with the number of queries). Then one computes what appears to be a correlation coefficient from elementary statistics between the two rankings. A score of 1 indicates perfect agreement in the rankings and a score of -1 indicates opposite rankings. This is a distribution-free statistic whose null distribution (the distribution if the two rankings are unassociated) is well-approximated by a normal for sample sizes as large as 50, our smallest sample size. Thus it is straightforward to estimate the p-values, or probabilities that results as extreme or more extreme occur by chance.

The results (Table 1) show a strong positive association between the clarity score of a query and the average precision of that query. The first row shows, for example, that with AP88 and AP89 TREC test collections combined and using the titles of the TREC topics numbered $101-200$ as queries (of which there 100), there is a rank correlation of 0.368 between clarity score and average precision. The corresponding p-value of 1.2×10^{-4} indicates the estimated probability that an apparent correlation as extreme, or more extreme, would occur by chance if clarity scores and average precision scores were actually unassociated.

Query length does not seem to effect the correlation results much since the rank correlation coefficient for TREC-4, where the average query length is 16.1, is similar to the other entries farther down the table, where the queries are a few words. The fact that the correlation persists at about the same level when TREC-7 and TREC-8 queries are combined into one set[3] results in a drastically lowered p-value, since such a correlation is much less likely to occur by chance with twice as many queries.

4.2 TREC Query Track Evaluations

We also show correlation results for the TREC-9 Query Track (see Table 2). In this evaluation, we check the correlation with precision among different queries for the same TREC topic. The queries, submitted by the 6 research groups that participated in the Query Track, include a variety of very short and one or two sentence queries[2]. There are 43 versions of queries for each of the 50 topics numbered $51-100$ for TREC disk 1, giving us 50 different values for the rank correlation coefficient. This evaluation is the most relevant our measure's ability to distinguish between user queries that are likely to work well and ones that are likely to perform poorly for the same information need.

[2]Standard TF.IDF retrieval gives similar correlation results.

[3]This is legitimate since the collections are the same.

Queries	Num.	R	P-value
aggregate	1804	0.39	2.2×10^{-61}
by topic	36.1 ± 3.7	0.247 ± 0.244	2.0×10^{-21}

Table 2: The correlation of clarity scores with average precision in the TREC Query track. "Aggregate" indicates all queries taken together while "topic ave." values are the averages over each of the 50 query track topics.

Once queries are stopped and stemmed[11] there are quite a few duplicates, resulting in 36.1 queries per topic, on average, and 1804 queries for the 50 topics in total. The Spearmann rank correlation coefficients and associated p-values are computed as explained previously. The p-value listed in the "by topic" results is the probability estimate for a result more extreme than the particular set of 50 rank correlation coefficients seen in that experiment.

It is interesting to note that, for a few individual topics, the rank correlation coefficient is actually negative. This is reflected in the entry showing $R = 0.247 \pm 0.244$ in Table 2. Examination of several of these poorly-correlating topics show that such topics have some high clarity queries that have low average precision, as well as some low clarity queries with high average precision.

For example, in topic 57, about the long term financial health of the company MCI, the queries "Future of MCI" and "MCI's profit" are low ranking in clarity but happen to have high ranking average precision (essentially, they place relevant documents near the top of the ranked list by luck) while there are some queries, like "Multiport Communications Interface" that are high ranking in clarity score but low ranking in average precision (this query actually receives a perfect zero in average precision). The query "Multiport Communications Interface" is in fact fairly specific and *should* get a reasonably high clarity score in the TREC disk 1 collection but clearly will not retrieve documents about the telecommunication company MCI. This query seems to have been generated by automatic (and mistaken) expansion of the acronym MCI. In this case and others like it, the failure of the clarity score ranking to predict the average precision ranking is clearly not a fault of our method; the query is essentially a high-clarity score query for a different information need. Since clarity scores are not computed with any reference to the underlying information need, clarity scores can not predict the poor performance of such off-topic queries or, indeed, any queries that specify a coherent set of documents that just happen to be about the wrong topic.

We believe that the slightly lower value of $R = 0.247$ (average) on a per-topic basis is the result of the presence of extremely low quality queries, such as the one mentioned in the previous paragraph. However, the persistence of the correlation over so many queries still results in an extremely

Collection	Queries	Num.	R	P-value
AP88+89	101 – 200	100	0.409	2.4×10^{-5}
TREC-4	201 – 250	50	0.298	0.019
TREC-5	251 – 300	50	0.289	0.022
TREC-7	351 – 400	50	0.467	5.4×10^{-4}
TREC-8	401 – 450	50	0.474	4.5×10^{-4}
TREC-7+8	351 – 450	100	0.449	4.0×10^{-6}

Table 3: The correlation of the average IDF of query terms with average precision in several TREC test collections. The queries are the titles of the TREC topics (usually a few words), except for TREC-4 where the description field is used, resulting in queries of 16.1 words, on average.

low p-value since such an apparent correlation is extremely unlikely to occur by chance over such a large data set.

5. ALTERNATIVE PREDICTORS

In order to better assess the significance of the clarity measure, we compare it to various other predictors of query performance. In particular, we evaluate the average and total term weights of query terms as predictors of performance using the methods of Kwok[12] and Wong[21], as well as the standard inverse document frequency measure given by

$$IDF(w) = \log_{10} \frac{\text{number of docs}}{\text{number of docs containing } w}. \quad (5)$$

The results for the average IDF of query terms are given in Table 3. Average Kwok score of query terms is less correlated with performance than average IDF and average Wong weight performs similarly to IDF. Using the sum of weights performs worse with all methods.

The results in Table 3 seem to show the average IDF of query terms as predicting the performance of queries to some degree, though not as well as clarity scores, in general (cf. Table 1). On TREC-7 plus 8, for example, the results with average IDF are about 83 times as likely to occur by chance as the correlations with clarity scores.

It is important, however, to look at the correlations of the term-weight-based predictors on the query track, the largest and most diverse test query set currently available. Table 4 shows the best performance, which is for the average IDF predictor.

All three term-weight-based methods show near random performance on the aggregate data. When looking at the correlations on a topic-by-topic basis the average IDF measure does much better than it does on the aggregate. The clarity results (Table 2, second row) are still about a million times less likely to occur by chance, however. The disparity between the aggregate and by-topic performance of average IDF of query terms as a performance predictor seems to indicate that it is particularly poor at comparing queries across topics.

In addition to the term-weight based predictors we consider the negative of the entropy of $P(D|Q)$ as a predictor of query performance. For this predictor we find no appreciable rank correlation with average precision, except at extremely high and low values of the entropy. This correlation makes sense, for example, since the highest values of this entropy indicate the most uniform distributions $P(D|Q)$ which never leads to a high average precision since documents are valued nearly evenly in such a case. Moreover, the overall lack of correlation in this case shows that our inclusion in clarity score computation of language statistics from the documents beyond just their likelihood of generating query terms is necessary for good prediction performance.

Queries	Num.	R	P-value
aggregate	1804	0.025	0.14
by topic	36.1 ± 3.7	0.220 ± 0.224	2.0×10^{-15}

Table 4: The correlation of the average IDF of query terms with average precision in the TREC Query track. "Aggregate" indicates all queries taken together while "topic ave." values are the averages over each of the 50 query track topics.

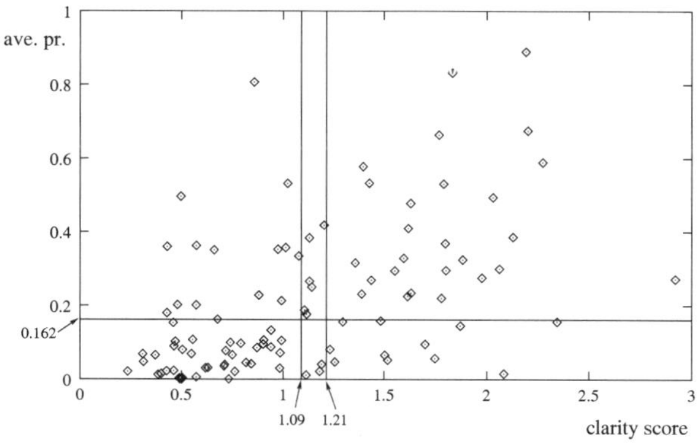

Figure 4: Average precision versus clarity score for the 100 title queries from the TREC-7 and TREC-8 adhoc tracks. The 0.162 threshold in average precision divides the estimated probability density in half (see Figure 5). The threshold of 1.09 in clarity score is the Bayes optimal level for classifying queries as high or low precision based on their clarity scores, based on the estimated probability densities(see Figure 6). The threshold of 1.21 is the automatic threshold set without relevance information at level where 80% of one-term queries have lower clarity scores (see Figure 7).

6. THRESHOLDING

We plan to use clarity scores to make a binary decision about each user query, namely, whether should it be singled out for special treatment on the basis of predicted poor performance, or not. We frame this task, in test collections, as classifying whether the query is likely to score better than a certain average precision threshold, or worse. We show how to set the optimal threshold in order to use clarity scores to make this classification. For the general case where no relevance information is available, we develop a heuristic for setting a clarity score threshold that is reasonable and performs nearly as well as the optimal method in various test collections.

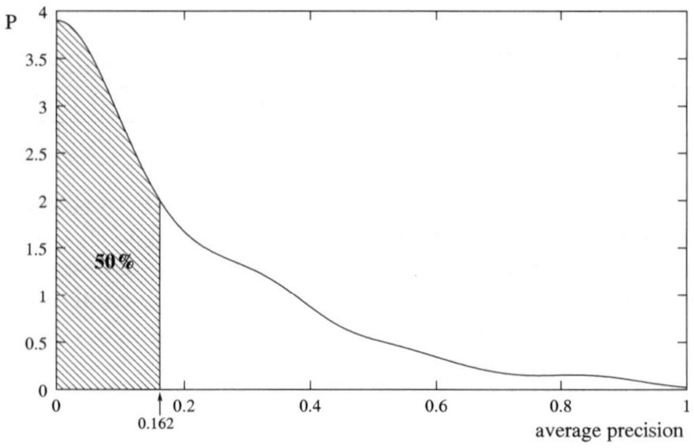

Figure 5: The kernel-estimated probability density for average precision based on the 100 title queries from the TREC-7 and TREC-8 adhoc tracks. The shaded area (average precision less than 0.162) is one half of the total area. So, based on the kernel estimated density for these queries, there is a 50% chance that a query is below this level and a 50% chance it is above this level in performance.

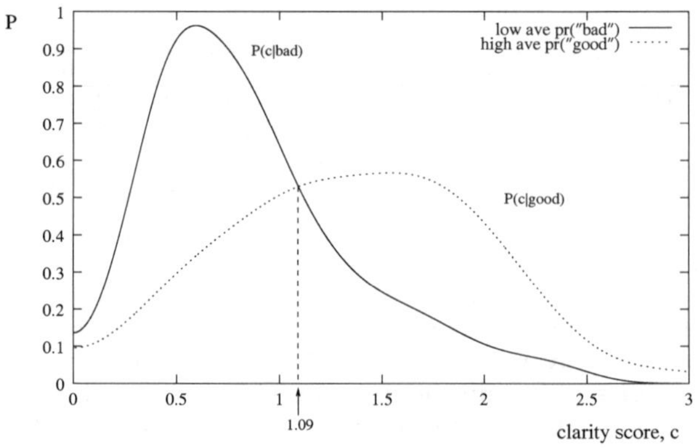

Figure 6: The class-conditional probability densities for the clarity scores of "bad" queries (below the 50% average precision threshold of 0.162) and "good" queries (above the same threshold) in the TREC-7 and TREC-8 adhoc tracks. P(bad) = P(good) = 0.5. The minimum Bayes error is obtained using the indicated decision boundary of 1.09 as a threshold to predict the whether queries fall in the high or low average precision classes.

6.1 Optimal Thresholding

When relevance information is available for the queries, we set the threshold for clarity scores optimally using standard Bayes decision theory[7]. The feasibility of this approach for the combined Ad Hoc Tracks of TREC-7 and TREC-8 is evident in Figure 4, where the strong positive association between clarity score and average precision can be seen.

We seek to divide the test queries into two classes, "good" (above a certain average precision threshold) and "bad" (below the same threshold). We set this threshold by performing kernel density estimation with automatic setting of the degree of smoothing[1]. Kernel density estimation is a smoothing technique that allows us to estimate the underlying probability density by summing gaussians centered at each observed data point. We require half of the estimated probability density to be below the threshold, as shown in Figure 5. That is to say, we pick the average precision threshold so the estimated probability of a good test query is 50%, and the probability of a bad test query is 50%. This is the horizontal line in Figure 4.

With the high and low average precision classes thus defined, we estimate the probability density functions for the clarity scores of queries as shown in Figure 6, again using kernel density estimation. Since the probability that a test query is in either class is 50%, the Bayes optimal decision boundary is simply where the two class-conditional distributions intersect. Put another way, we predict a query to be good if the estimated likelihood of its clarity score would be greater if it were known to be good than if it were known to be bad. This setting of the threshold is optimal in that it minimizes error rate, where the error of predicting a good query to be bad and the error of predicting a bad query to be good are scored equally. Optimal threshold settings for several collections are shown in Table 5, along with the automatically-set thresholds that we discuss next.

6.2 General Thresholding

In the general case there is no relevance information available for the queries. Our approach is to use the scale of possible clarity scores for the collection at hand to heuristically set the clarity score threshold.

To obtain information about the possible clarity scores for a given collection we sample single terms randomly from the vocabulary and evaluate their clarity scores as single term queries. We only consider terms that appear in at least 100 documents to avoid estimation problems in the query language models (we have observed that models estimated from too few documents result in clarity scores that are too high).

After estimating the probability density over single term queries with kernel density estimation, we set the threshold heuristically so that 80% of the probability density is below threshold (Figure 7). Simply put, a query is deemed "clear enough" if an estimated 80% or more of single term queries would have a lower clarity score. Since the automatic threshold can be computed when the collection is indexed, the decision takes no additional time once the clarity score of the query is computed.

Table 5 shows the results for several test collections. The bottom row, for example, represents the TREC-5 test collection and queries that are the titles of the topics numbered 251-300 (of which there are 50). Here the optimal threshold is 1.27 with a crudely-estimated p-value of 5.2×10^{-3} while the automatically set threshold (80%-rule) is 0.99 with a crudely-estimated p-value of 2.6×10^{-3}. The crudely estimated p-values are the relative frequencies of results as good or better in sampling experiments of 10^8 samples. In these sampling experiments queries are randomly assigned to the two classes with probabilities estimated from the observed number of test queries in the two classes.

The automatically set threshold performs nearly as well in the test collections as the optimal threshold (see Table 5). The clarity score thresholds for the TREC-4 and TREC-5 data, which were computed after the 80% rule was developed, do not agree as well as others, but the similarly low likelihood of classification results as good by chance in-

Collection	Queries	Number	Optimal	Automatic
AP88+89	101 – 200	100	$0.84(6 \times 10^{-4})$	$0.68(6.2 \times 10^{-5})$
TREC-7+8	351 – 450	100	$1.09(2 \times 10^{-5})$	$1.21(1.2 \times 10^{-5})$
Query(Aggregate)	51 – 100 *var.*	1804	0.96(0)	1.07(0)
TREC-4	201-250	50	$1.49(2.1 \times 10^{-3})$	$0.95(5.4 \times 10^{-3})$
TREC-5	251-300	50	$1.27(5.2 \times 10^{-3})$	$0.99(2.6 \times 10^{-3})$

Table 5: Bayes Optimal and automatic clarity thresholds for a few test collections. The values in parentheses are relative frequencies of classification results as good or better in 10^8 samples where the test queries are randomly assigned to the two classes. The assignment probabilities are estimated to be the observed relative frequencies of queries in the two classes in the set of test queries.

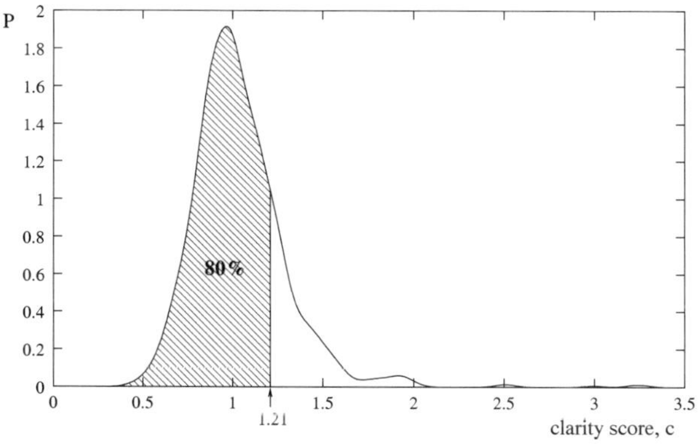

Figure 7: The kernel-estimated probability density for the clarity scores of queries whose single terms occur in at least 100 documents in the TREC-7 and TREC-8 adhoc collection. The shaded area is 80% of the total area under the curve, indicating an estimated 80% chance that an one-term query has a clarity score less than 1.21).

dicate that the automatic thresholds are still reasonable. We believe this variation is caused by the quality of the test queries, since queries of very low average precision (and average clarity scores) tend to push the optimal threshold higher, obtaining more correct classifications of these low-quality queries.

7. RELATED WORK

Prediction of query performance has long been of interest in information retrieval, though previous attempts have met with little success. This state of affairs is implicit in the emphasis on combination in information retrieval[5], for example, to combine the results from various versions of a query for the same information need. Without the ability to predict the performance of such multiple versions of a query, all one can do is combine their results equally. Several studies closely related to ours have been published recently, however.

In work on automatic query expansion, Carpineto, de Mori, Romano, and Bigi[3] use a weight very similar to the individual term contributions to the clarity score of a query (as shown in Figure 2, for example) to rank and weight terms within Rocchio query expansion. Also focussed on automatic query improvement, Pirkola and Jarvelin[15] examine individual term contributions to the retrieval effectiveness of queries and have some success at identifying the most important query term when there is no information as to the actual relevance of the documents to the query. In seeking to classify questions as easy or hard, Sullivan[20] models very long question text directly and compares questions in a sophisticated way to an existing set of questions whose effectiveness at retrieving relevant documents (when viewed as information retrieval-style queries) has been measured. The later two studies rely on relevance information to various degrees, though Pirkola and Jarvelin's work seeks to be free of this reliance.

Additionally, speculation has been made about using the dispersion of the top documents as a measure of query difficulty[18], and a nearly identical mathematical framework has been used to model selectional preferences in natural language[17].

8. FUTURE WORK

We plan to incorporate our methodology into a full information retrieval system. The planned system will compute the clarity score of a user query, before showing the user any results, and attempt to predict whether the query is going to be high- or low- performing. For a predicted high-performing query a normal ranked list will be presented to the user, but for a predicted low-performing query the retrieval results will be clustered by word usage and the user given a choice of seeing one of the cluster's members, or adding words to the query in an attempt to improve it. To return to the initial example, if the user issued the query "World Cup" against the AP88 collection, we would like the system to return representations of a clusters of documents related World Cup Soccer, World Cup Chess, perhaps several other topics, and a miscellaneous category. The user would be asked to choose a cluster that seems to correspond to their actual information need, or to add words to the query in an attempt to improve it.

As part of this system we have begun to investigate a novel language-model-based clustering method. The documents associated with a query (top-ranked documents, say) are modeled individually and each document defines a point in the space of all possible language models (i.e. the space of all unigram probability distributions, in our case). Kernel density estimation techniques are then applied to estimate the continuous probability density from which the documents are sampled. Alternatively, one can think of this as a smoothing technique. The coordinates of peaks in the estimated density represent cluster language models, which we loosely think of as topic language models, and the nearest peak to a given document point is that document's cluster. The degree of smoothing determines the granularity and the number of clusters found. With a high degree of smoothing, there is one cluster corresponding to the collection language model and lower amounts of smoothing result in greater numbers of clusters, with possible numbers of clusters determined by the data itself. To help deal with the high dimensionality of the problem in a sensible way, we plan to restrict the dimensions considered to be the probabilities of top-contributing terms to the query language model (i.e. For query B, the terms with the tallest bars in Figure 2).

We also plan to explore the use of clarity scores of various possible translations of a query to improve effectiveness in cross-lingual information retrieval and see possible applications of clarity score contributions (Figure 2) in selecting documents for retrieval and other core information retrieval technologies.

9. CONCLUSIONS

We have established that the query clarity score, as defined, correlates well with average precision in test collections, even for multiple versions of queries for the same information need. This indicates the possibility of predicting query performance using this measure. We have further grounded these results by comparing the clarity score correlations with the weaker correlations between the average IDF of query terms and performance. To facilitate appications, we have proposed a simple method of setting the threshold in clarity scores that does not require relevance information. We have validated this method by comparison with minimum Bayes error rate thresholds in a variety of test collections, in conjunction with sampling experiments that randomly classify documents. We believe that these strong results will open up interesting research pathways in information retrieval.

10. ACKNOWLEDGEMENTS

We thank Victor Lavrenko for advice on estimation of query models and probability densities. This work was supported in part by the Center for Intelligent Information Retrieval, in part by the National Science Foundation under grant number IIS-9907018, and in part by SPAWARSYSCEN-SD grant number N66001-99-1-8912, and in part by Advanced Research and Development Activity under contract number MDA904-01-C-0984. Any opinions, findings and conclusions or recommendations expressed in this material are the author's and do not necessarily reflect those of the sponsors.

11. REFERENCES

[1] A. Bowman and A. Azzilini. *Applied Smoothing Techniques for Data Analysis.* Oxford University Press, New York, 1997.

[2] C. Buckley. The trec-9 query track. In E. Voorhees and D. Harman, editors, *Proceedings of the Ninth Text REtrieval Conference(TREC-9)*, 2000. NIST Special Publication 500-249.

[3] C. Carpineto, R. de Mori, G. Romano, and B. Bigi. An information-theoretic approach to automatic query expansion. *ACM Transactions on Information Systems*, 19(1):1–27, 2001.

[4] T. M. Cover and J. A. Thomas. *Elements of Information Theory.* Wiley-Interscience, New York, 1991.

[5] W. B. Croft. Combining approaches in information retrieval. In W. B. Croft, editor, *Advances in Information Retrieval: Recent Research from the CIIR*, pages 1–36. Kluwer Academic Publishers, Boston, 2000.

[6] S. Cronen-Townsend and W. B. Croft. Quantifying query ambiguity. In *Proc. of Human Language Technology 2002*, pages 94–98, March 2002.

[7] R. O. Duda and P. E. Hart. *Pattern Classification and Scene Analysis.* John Wiley and Sons, New York, 1973.

[8] J. D. Gibbons and S. Chakraborty. *Nonparametric Statistical Inference, 3rd ed.* Marcel Dekker, New York, New York, 1992.

[9] F. Jelinek. *Statistical Models for Speech Recognition.* MIT Press, Cambridge, 1997.

[10] M. H. Kalos and P. A. Whitlock. *Monte Carlo Methods, Volume I: Basics.* Wiley-Interscience, New York, 1986.

[11] R. Krovetz. Viewing morpholgy as an inference process. In *Proc. of the 16th Annual ACM SIGIR Conference*, pages 191–202, June–July 1993.

[12] K. L. Kwok. A new method of weighting query terms for ad-hoc retrieval. In *Proc. of the 19th Annual ACM SIGIR Conference*, pages 187–195, 1996.

[13] V. Lavrenko and W. B. Croft. Relevance-based language models. In *Proc. of the 24th Annual ACM SIGIR Conference*, pages 120–127, September 2001.

[14] C. D. Manning and H. Schütze. *Foundations of Statistical Natural Language Processing.* MIT Press, Cambridge, Massachusetts, 1999.

[15] A. Pirkola and K. Jarvelin. Employing the resolution power of search keys. *Journal of the American Society for Information Science and Technology*, 52(7):575–583, 2001.

[16] J. Ponte and W. B. Croft. A language modeling approach to information retrieval. In *Proc. of the 21st Annual ACM SIGIR Conference*, pages 275–281, 1998.

[17] P. Resnik. Selectional constraints: An information-theoretic model and its computational realization. *Cognition*, 61:127–159, 1996.

[18] M. Rorvig. A new method of measurement for question difficulty. In *Proceedings of the 2000 Annual Meeting of the American Society for Information Science, Knowledge Innovations*, volume 37, pages 372–378, 2000.

[19] F. Song and W. B. Croft. A general language model for informatioon retrieval. In *Proceedings of the 22nd annual international ACM SIGIR conference*, pages 279–280, 1999.

[20] T. Sullivan. Locating question difficulty through explorations in question space. In *Proceedings of the 1st ACM/IEEE Joint Conference on Digital Libraries*, pages 251–252, 2001.

[21] S. K. M. Wong and Y. Y. Yao. An information-theoretic measure of term specificity. *Journal of the American Society for Information Science*, 43(1):54–61, 1992.

Using Part-of-speech Patterns to Reduce Query Ambiguity

James Allan and Hema Raghavan
Center for Intelligent Information Retrieval
Department of Computer Science
University of Massachusetts
Amherst, MA 01003
{allan,hema}@cs.umass.edu

ABSTRACT

Query ambiguity is a generally recognized problem, particularly in Web environments where queries are commonly only one or two words in length. In this study, we explore one technique that finds commonly occurring patterns of parts of speech near a one-word query and allows them to be transformed into clarification questions. We use a technique derived from statistical language modeling to show that the clarification queries will reduce ambiguity much of the time, and often quite substantially.

Categories and Subject Descriptors

H.3.1 [**Information Storage and Retrieval**]: Content Analysis and Indexing—*linguistic processing*; H.3.3 [**Information Storage and Retrieval**]: Information Search and Retrieval—*query formulation, search process*

Keywords

Clarity, part of speech, query ambiguity

1. INTRODUCTION

A generally acknowledged issue in information retrieval, particularly with Web search engines, is that users provide very short queries [15] that are sometimes very ambiguous. A classic example of this problem is the meaning of "Java" as a query: is the searcher's interest in coffee, a programming language, or tourism in Indonesia? There is quite a range of ways in which ambiguity can appear. In the "java" example, it is based on subject matter. A query could also be ambiguous because the user's underlying task is unclear (e.g., buy Java, use Java, introduction to Java), because the type of user is unknown (e.g., expert or novice), or because the style of querying is not clear (e.g., obtain facts, an overview, exhaustive coverage, or summary).

In this study, we investigate a particular technique for resolving ambiguity that is motivated by task-level ambiguity. How do the query words relate to other words in the text? What roles can they assume and which is the user interested in? For example, given a query "boat", the user might be interested in:

- things a boat does (floats, anchors, overturns)
- types of boats (whaling, fishing, red)
- ways to boat (quickly, safely)
- things to do with boats (drive them, paint them, sink them)

The intent is for the system to present a list of clarifying options to the searcher that can be selected if needed. Choosing one of those options focuses the query by including only those documents that use the query words in the right manner.

Ultimately, these ideas should be evaluated by field-testing a system that incorporates them. In this study we are laying the groundwork for such a system. Our focus is a novel evaluation to demonstrate that this approach generates useful clarifications of an ambiguous query. In the next section, we sketch some prior work toward coping with ambiguity. In Section 4 we discuss the approach that we use to find the clarifying options, the actual implementation is described in Section 3. We describe our evaluation technique in Section 5 and present results showing the value of this approach in Section 6. We conclude in Section 7 by describing where this work is headed.

2. RELATED WORK

There has been substantial work investigating issues surrounding word sense disambiguation [16], a type of query ambiguity that arises regularly in information retrieval. That type of ambiguity is often resolved implicitly when queries are long enough—the additional words provide sufficient context to clear up confusion—but is still a critical problem when queries are short [20]. Users of Web search engines generally provide short queries [15], and we are focusing on that situation in this study.

There is a range of information retrieval interface ideas that attempt to help the user deal with ambiguous queries. Sanderson, Lawrie, and Croft have been working on concept hierarchies that provide a hierarchical map of words and their relationships [19, 21, 11, 17]. A user can navigate the hierarchy to find the sense that is relevant. To date that research has not directly investigated whether the hierarchies help with disambiguation, looking instead at their ability to affect recall and precision.

SIGIR'02, August 11-15, 2002, Tampere, Finland.

Clustering the retrieved document set is another way to deal with ambiguity: ideally documents covering different senses of a word will be placed in different clusters. Much work has been done on clustering, either investigating the clustering directly [1, 2, 14] or exploring issues related to clustering and interactive search [13, 18, 23]. The Web service Northern Light[1] classifies returned documents into a set of labeled clusters, showing the clusters as well as the top ranked documents. All of these clustering techniques group documents by topic rather than by the way that the query word is used.

A limited number of studies have been done that directly evaluate the effectiveness of query reformulation when searching. It has been shown that query reformulation can improve the effectiveness of a query [5], though the focus was on the cognitive burden it places on the searcher.

This work was inspired by Tables 8 and 9 of a paper by Church et al. [7]. That work describes how statistical occurrence patterns of words in text can be used to find lexically interesting items. One of those is to look for verbs that occur near a particular word in an interesting way (measured by mutual information), allowing someone to find "what does a boat do?" or "what do you typically do with *food* and *water*?" We felt that if a query "boat" were used, then a possible clarification might be that question, and that documents containing the appropriate pattern (viz., boat as a subject and a verb "interestingly" near it) would be appropriate matches.

AltaVista[2] at one point provided a service called LiveTopics [22] that showed the inter-relationships between query terms and other terms in the corpus. This map was derived from the corpus (and human corrections) and provided another form of a "hyperindex" to allow the user to select words to improve a query.

The HiB system [4] allows the user to clarify (refine) the query by offering well-formed phrases in which the query appears. The user's query is mapped into a "hyperindex" by this approach, that shows relationships between words based on their occurrence in the titles of retrieved documents. The motivation for this work is similar to ours, but requires a much more elaborate infrastructure. They do not appear to have evaluated the value of the technique for query disambiguation. Grefenstette also suggests a system similar to ours [12], but also has no evaluation of its effectiveness.

Anick and Tipirneni [3] developed a query refinement technique based on calculating the lexical dispersion of words occurring in the top-ranked documents. Their work is similar to this study in that the candidates are identified by part-of-speech patterns at index time, but they use a substantially reduced set of patterns ("adjective? noun+"), they present patterns to the user on the assumption that the top ranked documents are a good source for them, and they are more focussed on query expansion than disambiguation (though the difference is often subtle). We believe that some aspects of their approach (e.g., using dispersion to find good candidates) may be valuable for our work, but we have not yet investigated those ideas.

3. EXPERIMENTAL SETUP

All experiments in this study were conducted using about 178,000 documents from the *trec5-fbis*, the FBIS subset of the fifth TREC volume. These are documents from FBIS dated 1994. We also used a second corpus, *tdt2*, which includes the English news stories from the TDT-2 collection, amounting to approximately 40,000 news stories from newswire and broadcast news sources. For stories from an audio source, the closed caption was used rather than speech recognition output.

Tag	*Part-Of-Speech*
NN	Common noun (singular)
NP	Proper noun
NNS	Common noun (plural)
VB	Verb (present tense)
VBN	Verb(Past participle)
VBD	Verb(Past tense)
JJ	Adjective
AT	Determiner
CC	Conjunction
IN	Preposition
CD	Number

Figure 1: Some of the common part of speech tags and their corresponding parts of speech in the Brown corpus.

Our indexing and retrieval was done using V3.2 of the CIIR's InQuery retrieval system [6]. This system incorporates fast and reasonably accurate part of speech tagging using JTAG [24]. JTAG uses the Brown tag-set (some tags of which are listed in Figure 1).

When documents were indexed, each word was indexed along with its part of speech. Proximity operators allow a particular part of speech to be selected for a word, as well as restrictions on which parts of speech occurred nearby. For example, `#1(boat VBD)` means the word "boat" immediately followed by the past participle of a verb (e.g., "boat sank"). The query `#0(boat NN)` means the word "boat" used *as* a noun rather than as another part of speech. The combined query,

```
#3( #0(boat NN) VBZ)
```

means "boat" as a noun followed within three words by the present third person singular form a verb (e.g., "boat sinks" or "boat quickly sinks"). This type of construction allows us to build up quite complex restrictions on query words and nearby parts of speech.

4. APPROACH

Given a corpus that has parts of speech indexed and that provides flexible query support such as that outlined above, we can attempt query disambiguation as follows. We (1) analyze the text to find patterns of parts of speech that occur frequently near the query word, (2) map the patterns to questions that reflect the patterns, (3) present the questions to the user as options to consider, and (4) re-run the retrieval based on the disambiguated question(s) the searcher selects.

In this section, we sketch how this approach works in a functional system. We show several examples that illustrate the value of this approach and suggest that it will be effective. In Section 5 we empirically evaluate the effectiveness of

[1]http://www.northernlight.com
[2]http://www.altavista.com

this approach toward reducing ambiguity. Our longer term goal is to implement these ideas in a fully functioning system to get user feedback.

4.1 Finding patterns

The patterns that we are looking for center around a single query word and incorporate a small number of words on either side. For example, given the query word *boat* we might look for the pattern "an adjective followed by the noun *boat*." In the trec5-fbis corpus, we would find adjectives such as *Haitian*, *fishing*, *wooden*, *speed*, and so on. If we find a sufficient number of occurrences of that pattern (regardless of how many different adjectives there are), we would note that "JJ boat:NN" is an interesting pattern ("JJ" is the part of speech code for an adjective, and "NN" denotes a singular noun).

Looking for all such patterns near a query word would be prohibitively expensive to carry out at search time. For that reason, we enhanced InQuery's indexing stage to extract all patterns centered around non-stopwords so that we could use it at run-time, and organized them by that keyword. To make this process slightly less expensive we used a 50% random sample of the corpus. For example, Figure 2 shows a sample of patterns and counts that appear in the 80,000 document subset of the trec5-fbis corpus.

We found by observation that any pattern that occurs more than 50 times in the corpus is "interesting" and ignored all others (a pattern might occur less than 50 times with particular query word, but many more than 50 times overall). Given the large number of patterns, making this decision in that way does not seem unreasonable, though it would ultimately be preferable to use a measure such as mutual information to select and keep the more interesting patterns [7].

4.2 Patterns to questions

The patterns are interesting, but they are not appropriate for displaying to a user. Instead, we convert them into questions that disambiguate the query. For example, here are some patterns and corresponding questions for the query word *party*:

JJ party:NN	varieties of a *party*
NP party:NP	names of a *party*
NN IN party:NN NNS	things done with a *party*
VB party:NN NN	things done to a *party*

For each pattern that has a corresponding question, we index the pattern by the query word and keep track of the number of times the pattern occurs

Given a user's single-word query, all patterns including that query word are obtained from the index, and the list of questions is constructed. Patterns that correspond to the same question are collapsed into a single question.

The questions are presented ranked in order of the most frequently occurring first. (The evaluation in Section 6 suggests that questions with many matches are not much less ambiguous than the original query, so it may be preferable to rank them by an approximation of ambiguity reduction.)

A partial list of patterns and corresponding questions is presented in Figure 3. Note that some language processing could be useful to handle variants of queries (e.g., to change "varieties of mouse" into "varieties of mice").

We wish to make it clear that the mapping from patterns

Pattern	Question
Q:noun VB	things that QQ does
Q:noun VBD	things that QQ did
Q:noun HV verb	things that QQ did
VBD Q:NN	things that happened to QQ
Q:VBN NN(S)	things that were QQ
Q:VBN TOIN AT noun	things one can QQ to
adv Q:verb	ways to be QQ
Q:VBG TO VB	things you could be QQ to do
adj Q:noun	varieties of QQ
Q:noun BER adj	varieties of QQ
Q:noun BER verb	things done to QQ
Q:noun BER noun	things that QQ are

Figure 3: Partial list of patterns recognized by the query clarification index component, along with the questions corresponding to those patterns. In the pattern, "Q:pos" means the query word occurring in that part of speech. The codes "noun," "verb," and "adj" are macros that indicate all varieties of nouns that the tagger identifies. In the Question column, QQ would be replaced by the query word.

to questions was created by hand. We found that a surprisingly small set of questions could accommodate most patterns, but it is most likely that some questions are absent. We are currently exploring better approaches for generating this mapping.

It is likely that the clarifying questions themselves may not be sufficient to help the user recognize the distinction. To help with that, we present the user which a list of several sample phrases that match the corresponding patterns. For example, for the query "*boat*", we might get (examples taken from our corpora):

> Are you interested in varieties of boats?
> *Haitian boat, makeshift boat, wooden boat, Cuban boat, big boat, ...*
> Are you interested in things a boat did?
> *boat followed, boat capsized, boat sank, boat hit, boat had, ...*
> Are you interested in things done with a boat?
> *rescue the boat, rock the boat, miss the boat, ...*

This sort of "keyword in context" list provides more information about the meaning of the clarification question, and does it in a corpus-specific way. That is, on a different corpus, the clarification questions chosen might not be the same, and the sample phrases including the query word would also be different.

4.3 Running the clarification question

When the user selects one of the query questions, the system then transforms it into an appropriate query and provides a new list of matching documents. The InQuery query is a logical "or" of all patterns that correspond to the selected query. For example, for the question "Are you interested in things done to a boat?", the following query could be generated

Instance	Count	Examples
JJ NN/NP IN		
JJ party:NP IN	2864	Democratic Party of, Communist Party of
JJ trade:NN IN	675	free trade with, foreign trade with
JJ tax:NN IN	175	new tax of, residential tax of
JJ war:NN IN	779	nuclear war in, psychological war to
VB NN/NNS NN		
VB tax:NN NN	114	improve tax collection, ensure tax fairness
VB president:NP NP	563	assassinate President Reina, meet President Husni
VB party:NN NN	149	strengthen party membership, promote party style
VB government:NN NNS	190	attend government sessions, include government officials
TO VB NN/NNS		
TO trade:VB NN	103	to trade protectionism, to trade fleece
TO finance:VB NN	110	to finance income, to finance pension
TO transport:VB NNS	36	to transport laborers, to transport weapons
TO address:VB NNS	32	to address rallies, to address imbalances
NNS/NN/NP NNS/NN/NP VB/VBD/VBG/VBZ		
NP citizens:NNS VBG	53	US citizens residing, African citizens living
NP ticket:NN VBZ	3	Samper-De la Calle ticket clears
NP clinton:NP VBD	647	Bill Clinton began, Bill Clinton met, President Clinton expressed
NP airlines:NP VBD	9	World Airlines said, Lufthansa Airlines opened

Figure 2: Some patterns that occur frequently in the trec5-fbis corpus, and selected instances of the patterns with a query word. The instances list the pattern with the query word inserted, the number of times that pattern occurs in the 80,000 document subset of the corpus, and then one or two examples of the pattern in the text.

```
#or( #1( #0(boat NN) BER verb )
     #1( #0(boat NN) NV BEN verb )
     #1( HVZ VBN #0(boat NN) )
     ... )
```

In practice, the patterns generally need to be relaxed slightly to find matches that are very close to the patterns. We have observed that allowing a few extra words improves the recall of useful documents, though we have not carried out a formal study of that effect. The above query is transformed into,

```
#or( #3( #0(boat NN) BER verb )
     #3( #0(boat NN) NV BEN verb )
     #3( HVZ VBN #0(boat NN) )
     ... )
```

5. EVALUATION

We are interested in whether the clarifying questions result in a more focused set of documents in response to the searcher's query. One way to measure that would be to ask someone to judge each set of returned documents to decide whether they were more or less focused than the original set. Such a process is time consuming and unwieldy.

Instead, we will use a measure of query clarity based on vocabulary distribution in both sets of retrieved documents [8, 9]. If one query has more "clarity" than another, it is less ambiguous, and perhaps more useful for retrieval.

5.1 Query clarity

Clarity is defined [8] as the Kullback-Liebler (KL) divergence between the collection and the query:

$$\text{clarity}(Q) \equiv \sum_{w \in V} P(w|Q) \log_2 \frac{P(w|Q)}{P(w)}$$

where V is the set of all terms in the collection (e.g., trec5-fbis or tdt2), Q represents the query, and $P(w)$ represents the probability of the word occurring in a document in the collection. To estimate the probability distribution of words given the query (the "query language model"), we use,

$$P(w|Q) \cong \sum_{d \in R} P(w|d)P(d|Q)$$

where R is the set of documents retrieved in response to the query, and $P(w|d) = \lambda P_{ML}(w|d) + (1 - \lambda)P(w)$, a linear combination of the corpus probability and the maximum likelihood estimate based on the document. We set $\lambda = 0.6$.

What the clarity measure does is compare the language model (probability distribution of words) of the corpus with the language model generated by a query. The way it is calculated means that if the distributions are identical, the clarity will be zero, and as they become more and more different, the value will rise. As a result, if the set of retrieved documents has roughly the same coverage as the entire corpus, the query that generated them will have a low clarity value—i.e., it is an ambiguous query.

It has also been shown that there is a strong correlation between clarity and the performance of the query as measured by average precision [10], so it is possible to predict, to some extent, the performance of a query on a collection without relevance information.

5.2 Using clarity

To determine whether the clarification questions are providing any focusing of the results, we compare the clarity of the original query word with that of the modified query. Each query Q_i has a set of clarifying questions $Q_{i,1}$ through

Q_{i,n_Q} where n_Q varies by query and indicates the number of questions whose patterns occurred more than 50 times in the corpus.

We compute the following measures to compare the effectiveness of the system.

- The number of times that the clarification question is clearer than the original query.

$$\sum_{j=1}^{n_Q} I(\text{clarity}(Q_{i,j}) > \text{clarity}(Q_i))$$

- The increase in clarity moving from the original query to the clarification question. If the number is negative or near zero, it means that the questions were not an improvement.

$$\sum_{j=1}^{n_Q} \text{clarity}(Q_{i,j}) - \text{clarity}(Q_i)$$

In addition, both measures are averaged across all clarification questions (per-question average, also called a pooled average), and weighted by the original queries (per-query average). The latter is important because n_Q can vary dramatically between queries and we do not want queries with few clarification possibilities to be overshadowed by the others.

6. RESULTS

To evaluate the disambiguation potential of this technique, we choose 50 one-word queries using a mix of several different ways:

- We used 25 common one word queries from web logs. This we found from multiple sources as follows: (1) words that were listed as being common single word queries using a Word Tracker[3] report that lists commonly used query terms mined from a large log of metasearch queries; (2) common one-word queries as reported by Google[4] and Metacrawler[5]. These words were all verified to occur within the trec5-fbis corpus.
- Since our database is a trec-5 collection, we analyzed the TREC-5 topics 251-300 that could be narrowed down to one word. We used 25 such queries. For example TREC topic 269 is "Foreign Trade," which we generalized to "trade".

We report below analysis of the clarity impact in the aggregate and then present detailed analysis of some of the query words.

6.1 Overall trends

Overall, the query clarity improves an average of 41% for TREC queries and 25% for Web queries (per-query average). The top of Figure 4 shows a breakdown of the improvement on a per-query basis for TREC queries and the bottom half shows the same for Web queries. Almost all queries have average improvements in clarity, and even when the average is negative, most of the clarification questions reduce ambiguity.

[3]http://www.wordtracker.com

[4]http://www.google.com/press/zeitgeist2001.html

[5]http://www.metaspy.com

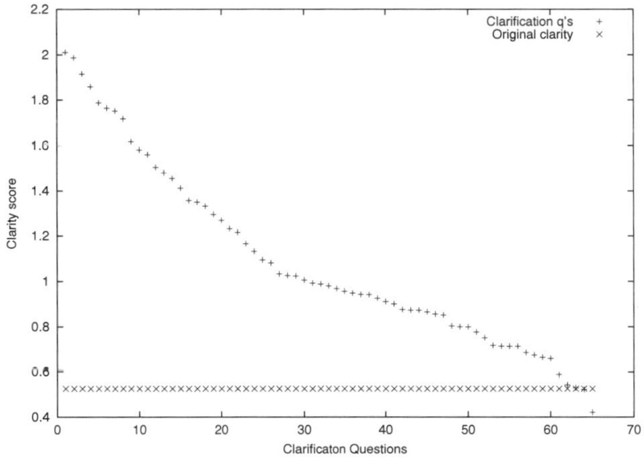

Figure 5: Graph shows the clarity values for the clarifying questions related to *tour*, the values shown in Figure 6. The values were sorted in order of clarity. The original clarity of *tour* is the solid horizontal line at 0.525

For example, for the original query word *defense* there were 85 patterns that occurred often enough to be recorded. The clarity of *defense* was 0.511 (not shown in the table). Of the 85 patterns, 71 of them (83.52%) showed an improvement in clarity, averaging 0.171 or 33% (the values ranged from -25% to 200%).

About 95% of the questions for the trec5 questions and 62% for the general web queries improved query clarity, strongly suggesting their value in reducing ambiguity. The reasonable similarity between the pooled and query-weighted averages suggests that the results are comparable across queries.

The percent improvement in clarity ranged from 347% to improve *mines* to *JJ mines:NNS NP* down to -51% trying to improve *heart* to *CD heart:NN CC* in the set of TREC questions. In the set of general Web queries this range is from 412% improving *apartment* to *AT apartment:NN VBN* to -62% for trying to improve *computer* to *NN computer:NN NNS*. It appears that the queries where ambiguity could be reduced the most were cases where the word could be either a noun or a verb (e.g., *tour, defense*) or where the word often appeared as a proper noun (e.g., *airline*).

If clarity numbers are calculated or approximated in advance, it would be possible to remove clarification questions that actually reduce clarity (i.e., increase ambiguity), making this technique even more useful.

6.2 Detailed analysis

The query word *tour* is not very common in the trec5-fbis corpus that we used: it occurs in 1668 out of the 178,000 stories. The word *tour* has a clarity value of 0.525. We show a partial breakdown of the results for *tour* clarification in Figure 6. The results are ordered by percent improvement in the original clarity value, ranging from a 283% improvement to a drop of almost 20%. Figure 5 shows a graph of the clarity values, with a straight line representing the original clarity of the query. It is clear that improvement is usually seen, and often quite large.

The pattern *JJ tourist:NN VBG* corresponds to phrases

TREC topic	Query word	Num. Quests	Number improved	Percent improved	Change in clarity	Percent improved
257	cigarette	15	5	33.33	-0.15	-9.69
282	crime	93	47	50.53	0.08	10.41
268	defense	85	71	83.52	0.17	33.47
288	diet	16	8	50.00	0.04	4.16
282,284	drug	95	78	82.10	0.18	23.05
255	environment	97	72	74.22	0.13	23.65
298	gun	80	32	40.00	-0.07	-6.13
275	health	82	46	56.09	0.07	7.73
254	heart	37	15	40.54	-0.03	-2.85
289	hospital	70	59	84.28	0.31	27.67
294	husbandry	16	15	93.75	0.51	86.22
279	magnetic	29	25	86.20	0.52	55.14
293	military	91	58	63.73	0.09	18.63
277	mines	51	50	98.03	0.67	129.65
258	security	88	67	76.13	0.13	26.91
252	smuggling	64	50	78.12	0.40	54.96
271	solar	29	25	86.20	0.31	35.51
285	submarine	64	63	98.43	0.57	90.30
287	surveillance	30	28	93.33	0.70	102.57
291	tax	97	42	43.29	-0.01	-1.48
269,283	trade	94	64	68.08	0.07	14.81
300	traffic	87	69	79.31	0.22	26.89
276	uniform	44	40	90.90	0.53	64.63
265	violence	73	53	72.60	0.20	22.60
292	welfare	46	33	71.73	0.32	51.80
Per-question averages		1165	1118	95.96	0.24	35.68
Per-query averages		46	45	97.8	0.27	40.96
	airlines	36	19	52.77	0.05	4.15
	apartment	45	30	66.66	0.18	17.27
	attorney	29	20	68.96	0.24	21.80
	author	92	32	34.78	-0.04	-5.14
	biotech	24	24	100.00	0.55	76.012
	birthday	16	12	75.00	0.26	22.95
	cheap	44	40	90.90	0.48	64.65
	computer	75	11	14.66	-0.34	-24.50
	divorce	13	3	23.08	-0.22	-14.73
	employment	92	76	82.60	0.23	44.91
	fish	72	58	80.55	0.34	43.16
	free	96	66	68.75	0.17	26.56
	homes	23	2	8.69	-0.70	-34.10
	house	83	65	78.31	0.27	37.66
	international	94	82.00	87.23	0.29	74.17
	investing	29	22	75.86	0.29	49.72
	job	78	34	43.58	0.04	5.064
	loan	82	36	43.90	0.02	2.59
	marijuana	37	37	100.00	0.53	54.64
	master	38	21	55.26	0.13	13.60
	software	50	16	32.00	-0.18	-15.19
	tour	65	63	96.92	0.59	113.60
	travel	67	31	46.26	0.02	1.63
	vacation	23	19	82.60	0.22	23.02
	vietnam	45	20	44.44	-0.09	-9.12
Per-question averages		1351	842	62.32	0.14	23.76
Per-query averages		54	33	61.10	0.14	25.43

Figure 4: Summary evaluation of change in clarity broken down by query and overall for TREC queries (top) and general Web queries (bottom).

Pattern	Count	Clarity	Percent Improvement
np tourists:nns cc	12	2.01	283.1
nn toured:vbd at	20	1.98	278.5
jj tour:nn np	34	1.91	264.8
np tourist:np np	23	1.85	253.9
np tourist:nn nn	24	1.78	240.4
cc tourism:nn np	27	1.76	236.0
jj tourists:nns cc	22	1.75	233.6
cc tourism:nn nn	39	1.71	227.2
jj tour:nn wdt	24	1.61	208.1
jj tour:nn in	188	1.56	197.1
nn tourism:nn nns	15	1.50	186.4
cd tourist:nn nns	14	1.48	181.9
at tour:nn nn	35	1.45	177.1
nn tourism:in nn	14	1.41	169.0
in tour:at nn	33	1.35	158.6
jj tours:nns in	13	1.35	157.2
cc tourism:nn at	21	1.33	153.8
in tourism:nn at	15	1.29	147.0
...			
...			
cc tourist:nn nns	40	0.52	0.8
jj tourists:nns vbg	19	0.52	-0.6
np tour:nn in	54	0.42	-19.7

Figure 6: Breakdown of changes in clarity for the patterns recorded for the query *tour*. The original clarity of that query was 0.525

Pattern	Count	Clarity	Percent Improvement
in defense:np bez	27	2.01	302.3
np defense:np in	56	1.98	297.4
punc defense:np np	147	1.91	283.1
at defense:nn cc	64	1.85	271.6
at defense:np in	109	1.78	257.5
in defense:np rb	32	0.99	98.5
in defense:nn at	49	0.98	96.1
nns defense:nn np	39	0.96	93.8
in defense:np cc	192	0.95	91.4
np defense:np np	3978	0.94	89.7
in defense:nn nns	272	0.94	88.5
nn defense:np np	137	0.94	88.3
nn defense:cc nn	59	0.90	80.2
at defense:nn nn	1470	0.87	75.2
in defense:np nn	47	0.87	74.7
np defense:np nn	46	0.86	73.2
cc defense:np np	265	0.85	71.2
nn defense:np	31	0.85	70.3
nn defense:in nn	84	0.80	60.8
...			
...			
toin defense:np np	55	0.52	4.4
in defense:nn in	373	0.42	-15.7

Figure 7: Breakdown of changes in clarity for the patterns recorded for the query *defense*. The original clarity of that query was 0.511

such as "typical tourist visiting" and does not provide much focusing of the query. On the other hand, the pattern *NP tourist:NP NP* represents phrases such as "National Tourist Board" and the documents in which such phrases are present focus more on information, announcements, etc., for tourists, providing a fairly tight set of retrieved documents.

Figure 7 shows a similar effect for the query word *defense*, the word with a high improvement of clarity in the TREC query set. Note that *defense* also occurs about as often as *tour*: 1199 times in trec5-fbis. The clearest clarification in this case is "IN defense:NP BEZ " which corresponds to "[Department/Ministry] of Defense is" and occurs 27 times. The clarification "CD defense:NN CC" corresponding to phrases such as "[team will use] a 52 defense and" which although it occurs an equal number of times, does not show as great an improvement in clarity. In the first case almost all documents are military related, whereas *defense* as a common noun could appear in any context—viz. defense, sports, law, etc. There is no apparent relation between the number of occurrences of a pattern and clarity.

7. CONCLUSION AND FUTURE WORK

We have shown a method for extracting patterns of word usage from a corpus and for using those patterns to help the user clarity an ambiguous query. The patterns represent sequences of parts of speech that occur around the query word often enough in the corpus that they are likely to be meaningful. Frequent patterns are mapped to human-generated clarification questions that the user may choose from. Note that we envision this as an optional side-bar to the return of query results—there seems little value in requiring the searcher to clarify the question if his or her desired document is already in the top ranks.

Once the user has selected a clarification question, we can re-issue the query based on the part of speech patterns, though slightly relaxed to increase recall. A list of sample patterns is generally helpful for the user interpreting the question.

We used a statistical measure called query clarity [8] to demonstrate that the clarification questions generally provide a much more focused set of documents.

We are working on extending these ideas to build a better set of clarification questions for the patterns and to determine ways for automatically constructing such questions (because it is tedious to do so by hand). In Figure 3 it is apparent that certain clarification questions have multiple patterns associated with them. We are studying methods by which these patterns for a given question can be learned using training data. We are also building a system that implements these ideas to field test an interface to find out what works best in live settings.

Acknowledgments

The original motivation for this work arose out of conversations with W. Bruce Croft. We are grateful to Ted Allen and Hema Krishnan for some preliminary work they did suggesting that this technique could succeed. We also thank Victor Lavrenko, Steve Cronen-Townsend, Margie Connell, and Steve Harding for their help making software work.

This material is based on work supported in part by the Center for Information Retrieval, in part by NSF grant numbers IIS-9907018 and IIS-9907331, and in part by Advanced Research and Development Activity under contract number MDA904-01-C-0984. Any opinions, findings and conclusions or recommendations expressed in this material are the authors' and do not necessarily reflect those of the sponsors.

8. REFERENCES

[1] A.Leuski. Evaluating document clustering for interactive information retrieval. In *Proceedings of the ACM CIKM 2001 Tenth International Conference on Information and Knowledge Management*, pages 33–40, 2001.

[2] A.Leuski. *Interactive Information Organization: Techniques and Evaluation.* PhD thesis, University of Massachusetts, Amherst, 2001.

[3] Peter G. Anick and Suresh Tipirneni. The paraphrase search assistant: Terminological feedback for iterative information seeking. In *Proceedings of the ACM Conference on Research in Information Retrieval (SIGIR)*, pages 153–159, 1999.

[4] P.D. Bruza and S. Dennis. Query-reformulation on the internet: empirical data and the hyperindex search engine. In *Proceedings of the RIAO Conference: Intelligent Text and Image Handling*, pages 488–499, Montreal, Canada, 1997.

[5] Peter Bruza, Robert McArthur, and Simon Dennis. Interactive internet search: Keyword, directory and query reformulation mechanisms compared. In *Proceedings of the ACM Conference on Research in Information Retrieval (SIGIR)*, pages 280–287, 2000.

[6] James P. Callan, W. Bruce Croft, and Stephen M. Harding. The INQUERY retrieval system. In *Proceedings of DEXA-92, 3rd International Conference on Database and Expert Systems Applications*, pages 78–83, 1992.

[7] K.W. Church, W.Gale, P.Hanks, and D.Hindle. Using statistics in lexical analysis. In *Lexical Acquisition: Exploiting On-Line Resources to Build a Lexicon*, pages 115–164, 1991.

[8] W.B. Croft, S. Cronen Townsend, and V.Lavrenko. Relevance feedback and personalization: A language modeling perspective. In *Proceedings of the DELOS-NSF Worshop on Personalization and Recommender Systems in Digital Libraries*, pages 49–54, 2001.

[9] Steve Cronen-Townsend and W. Bruce Croft. Quantifying query ambiguity. In *Proceedings of the Conference on Human Language Technology (HLT 2002)*, pages 94–98, 2002.

[10] Steve Cronen-Townsend, Yun Zhou, and W. Bruce Croft. Predicting query performance. In *Proceedings of the ACM Conference on Research in Information Retrieval (SIGIR)*, 2002.

[11] D.Lawrie, W.B. Croft, and A.Rosenberg. Finding topic words for hierarchical summarization. In *Proceedings of the ACM Conference on Research in Information Retrieval (SIGIR)*, pages 349–357, 2001.

[12] G.Grefenstette. SQLET: Short query linguistic expansion techniques: Palliating one or two-word queries by providing intermediate structure to WWW pages. In *Proceedings of RIAO '97. (1997)*, 1997.

[13] Marti Hearst and Jan Pedersen. Reexamining the cluster hypothesis: Scatter/gather on retrieval results. In *Proceedings of the ACM Conference on Research in Information Retrieval (SIGIR)*, pages 76–84, 1996.

[14] J.Allan, A.Leuski, R. Swan, and D.Byrd. Evaluating combinations of ranked lists and visualizations of inter-document similarity. In *Information Processing and Management (IPM), vol. 37*, pages 435–458, 2000.

[15] K.Franzen and J.Karlgren. Verbosity and interface design. Technical Report T2000:04, Swedish Institute of Computer Science (SICS), 2000. Also available at http://citeseer.nj.nec.com/313985.html.

[16] R. Krovetz. *Word Sense Disambiguation for Large Text Databases.* PhD thesis, University of Massachusetts, Amherst, 1995.

[17] Dawn Lawrie and W.B. Croft. Discovering and comparing topic hierarchies. In *Proceedings of RIAO 2000 Conference*, pages 314–330, 2000.

[18] Anton Leuski and James Allan. Lighthouse: Showing the way to relevant information. In *Proceedings of the IEEE Symposium on Information Visualization 2000 (InfoVis 2000)*, pages 125–130, 2000.

[19] M.Sanderson and D.Lawrie. Building, testing, and applying concept hierarchies. In W. Bruce Croft, editor, *Advances in Information Retrieval: Recent Research from the CIIR, W. Bruce Croft, ed., Kluwer Academic Publishers*, chapter 9, pages 235–266. Kluwer Academic Press, 2000.

[20] Mark Sanderson. Word sense disambiguation and information retrieval. In *Proceedings of the ACM Conference on Research in Information Retrieval (SIGIR)*, pages 142–151, 1994.

[21] Mark Sanderson and W. Bruce Croft. Deriving concept hierarchies from text. In *Proceedings of the ACM Conference on Research in Information Retrieval (SIGIR)*, pages 206–213, 1999.

[22] Richard Seltzer. Taking "snapshots" with livetopics: Watch out for mirages, 1997. http://www.samizdat.com/cobb/oct97.html.

[23] Russell C. Swan and James Allan. Aspect windows, 3-d visualizations, and indirect comparisons of information retrieval systems. In *Proceedings of the ACM Conference on Research in Information Retrieval (SIGIR)*, pages 173–181, 1998.

[24] J. Xu, J. Broglio, and W.B. Croft. The design and implementation of a part of speech tagger for english. Technical Report IR-52, University of Massachusetts, Amherst, Center for Intelligent Information Retrieval, 1994.

Keynote Address

Is Natural Language an Inconvenience or an Opportunity for IR?

Kimmo Koskenniemi
University of Helsinki

Natural language (NL) has evolved to facilitate human communication. It enables the speaker to make the listener's mind wander among her experiences and mental associations roughly according to the intentions of the speaker. The speaker and the listener usually share experiences and expectations, and they use mostly the same units and rules of a shared NL. Written language functions similarly, but in a less interactive way, with fewer possibilities for feedback.

Both the symbols of NL (i.e. words or morphemes), and their arrangements are meaningful. Not with universal and precise meanings, but similar enough among different speakers and accurate enough for the communication mostly to succeed.

NLs are mostly very large systems. Hundreds of thousands of words and infinitely many possible utterances. Even inflection alone might produce huge numbers of forms, e.g. more than ten thousand distinct forms out of every Finnish verb entry.

NL processing (for IR or any other purpose) must cope with phenomena like (1) inflection and compounding, (2) synonymy, (3) polysemy, (4) ambiguity, (5) anaphora and (6) head-modifier relations among words and phrases.

Language technology can neutralize much of the effect of these 'inconveniences' inherent with NL, but what kinds of advantages could NL have?

- Redundant use of synonymous expressions can effectively identify new concepts.
- Multilingual parallel documents may help in identifying their exact content.
- NLs typically carry connotations, i.e. what is implied but not explicitly said (e.g. attitudes, politeness).
- Vague associations are easy to express in NL, but not always in formal systems (e.g. "a few years ago there was an article about the rival of Yeltsin - I don't remember his name but - he then went over to some region in Siberia - but what did the guy promise?")
- Jokes and humor belong to NLs, not to formal systems.

Are there any alternatives for NL? Not really, because any artificial and more precise formalisms fail to adapt to new concepts and they do not easily allow restructuring of previous ideas.

One challenge for language technology is to find better solutions for the above 'inconveniences' in order to provide various IR, document classification, indexing and summarizing methods with more accurate and adequate input data. With more accurate input some of the more demanding tasks of IR can perhaps be solved.

AAMAS'02, July 15-19, 2002, Bologna, Italy.
ACM 1-58113-480-0/02/0007.

The Effect of Topic Set Size on Retrieval Experiment Error

Ellen M. Voorhees
National Institute of Standards and Technology
Gaithersburg, MD 20899
ellen.voorhees@nist.gov

Chris Buckley
Sabir Research Inc.
Gaithersburg, MD 20878
chrisb@sabir.com

ABSTRACT

Retrieval mechanisms are frequently compared by computing the respective average scores for some effectiveness metric across a common set of information needs or topics, with researchers concluding one method is superior based on those averages. Since comparative retrieval system behavior is known to be highly variable across topics, good experimental design requires that a "sufficient" number of topics be used in the test. This paper uses TREC results to empirically derive error rates based on the number of topics used in a test and the observed difference in the average scores. The error rates quantify the likelihood that a different set of topics of the same size would lead to a different conclusion. We directly compute error rates for topic sets up to size 25, and extrapolate those rates for larger topic set sizes. The error rates found are larger than anticipated, indicating researchers need to take care when concluding one method is better than another, especially if few topics are used.

Categories and Subject Descriptors

H.3.4 [**Information Storage and Retrieval**]: Systems and Software—*performance evaluation*

General Terms

Experimentation, Measurement

Keywords

Test collections, measurement error

1. INTRODUCTION

Much of the experimental work in information retrieval is based on the Cranfield paradigm of using test collections in laboratory tests to compare the effectiveness of different retrieval mechanisms. The Cranfield paradigm was introduced by Cleverdon and his colleagues in the Cranfield 2 experiments [3], and has been refined and extended through the collective experience of IR experimenters [6]. A test collection consists of a set of documents, a set of topics, and a set of relevance judgments. A topic is a description of the information being sought, while the relevance judgments specify the documents that should be retrieved in response to each topic. A test collection defines the common task that allows the effectiveness of different retrieval mechanisms to be directly compared.

In earlier work, we list three features of acceptable experimental design within the Cranfield paradigm: a sufficient number of topics, a reasonable effectiveness measure, and a large enough difference between two effectiveness scores before concluding that two retrieval runs are different [2]. We showed how these different features interact with one another so that a particular experimental design can trade one off another. For example, an experiment that uses a less stable effectiveness measure can use a larger number of topics, or require a larger difference between evaluation scores, to maintain a given level of confidence in the results of the experiment. Each of these aspects is a required part of good experimental design because comparative retrieval system performance is known to vary greatly across different topics. An analysis of variance model fitted to the TREC-3 results demonstrated that the topic and system effects, as well as the interaction between topic and system, were all highly significant, with the topic effect the largest [1]. In other words, retrieval effectiveness depends on which question is asked, which retrieval mechanism is used, and how the retrieval mechanism deals with the question type. On average, the question asked has a bigger effect on effectiveness than the retrieval mechanism used, though different mechanisms work relatively better on different question types. Larger numbers of topics, more stable effectiveness measures, and greater differences among scores all increase the reliability of concluding one mechanism is better than another in the face of this variability.

Unfortunately, including arbitrarily large numbers of topics in a retrieval experiment is not practical. Even if a large source of topics is available, each topic requires relevance judgments, which are costly to produce. Experienced researchers have made suggestions regarding how many topics are sufficient, though little quantitative evidence exists to support these suggestions. In their report regarding requirements for an ideal test collection [8], Sparck Jones and van Rijsbergen demonstrate the range of topics (or requests) thought necessary:

> ...concerning requests, under 75 are of little use, 250 are usually acceptable, and 1,000 are sometimes needed.

SIGIR'02, August 11-15, 2002, Tampere, Finland.

Due to the costs involved, the TREC program committee has used 25 topics as a minimum, with 50 topics as the the preferred default [10]. Experiments using the TREC-6 results showed that system rankings based on results from five or ten topics were relatively unstable, while rankings based on 25 topics were much more stable [11].

This paper uses the results from the past eight TRECs to empirically derive a relationship between the number of topics used in a retrieval experiment, the observed difference in evaluation scores produced by the two retrieval mechanisms, and the confidence that can be placed in the conclusion that one mechanism is better than the other. In particular, we directly compute error rates as a function of topic set size and difference in retrieval scores for topic set sizes up to 25 using TREC results, and then extrapolate the error rates to topic set sizes up to 50. The extrapolated error rate curve when using mean average precision (MAP) as the effectiveness measure shows that on average an absolute difference of 0.05 in retrieval scores is necessary to obtain an error rate no larger than 5 %. Since the best reported performance on the TREC collections is a MAP of approximately 0.30, this corresponds to a percentage difference of approximately 15 %, a larger difference in scores than is generally used to conclude a difference is meaningful. We also compute error rates for individual TREC collections, and suggest that the error rate for a collection be reported as a characteristic of a collection once it is created. Such a characteristic should help researchers interpret the results of experiments using the collection.

The paper is organized is follows. The next section defines the basic procedure for computing error rates and describes the archive of TREC results used in the calculations. The following section describes the extrapolation procedure and discusses the implications of the error rates at larger topic set sizes. Section 4 repeats the computations for individual TREC collections. The following two sections look at small changes to the basic procedure. In Section 5 we compute error rates using only pairs of runs such that each run in the pair was submitted to TREC by the same group. These error rates are slightly smaller than the error rates computed for arbitrary runs, and may be more applicable for single-system experiments. In Section 6 we look at the effect of using precision after ten documents are retrieved rather than mean average precision as the effectiveness measure. The final section summarizes the results.

2. COMPUTING ERROR RATES

Our goal is to compute the probability that the decision that one retrieval mechanism is better than another would change if tested with a different set of topics. A decision is made by computing the average score for some effectiveness measure over a set of topics for each of the two mechanisms, and concluding that the mechanism with the better average score is the better mechanism. We can estimate the likelihood of a changed decision or "swap" by comparing two mechanisms many different times using different topic sets and counting how many times the decisions differ. By repeating the process using many different pairs of mechanisms, we compute an estimate of the probability of a swap for the comparison of two arbitrary retrieval mechanisms. The probability of a swap defines an error rate in that it specifies how likely it is that the outcome of one experiment leads to the wrong conclusion.

In this section, we calculate error rate as a function of the observed difference between two retrieval runs for different topic set sizes. We use the archive of TREC retrieval runs as the source of the large sample of retrieval results required to produce reliable estimates. The TREC data is described in the next subsection, which is followed by a description of the procedure used to calculate the error rate.

2.1 The TREC Archive

TREC is a workshop series designed to foster research in text retrieval by providing the infrastructure needed for large-scale evaluation of retrieval systems [10]. There have been ten TRECs so far; in each TREC, participants submit their retrieval results for a common retrieval task. The TREC archive contains all of the retrieval runs for each TREC from TREC-2 to the present (see `http://trec.nist.gov/results.html`). A retrieval run is a list of up to 1000 documents per topic, ordered by similarity to the topic. For this paper, we used the "Category A" ad hoc results from TRECs 3–8 plus the web track results from TREC-9 and TREC 2001 (TREC-10). Each of these retrieval runs contains 50 topics, except for the TREC-4 runs that contain only 49 topics.

The topic statements used in TREC have varied over the years, but usually contain a very short *title* field (2-3 words), a one sentence *description* field, and a *narrative* field that describes how documents will be judged for relevance. Participants may derive query statements from the topics manually or automatically, perhaps using only part of the topic statement. While the query construction method used affects retrieval performance, no distinctions among runs were made for these experiments. That is, the only information stored about a run was the TREC to which it was submitted (and thus the test collection it used) and its effectiveness scores for each topic.

TREC is a workshop targeted at testing research prototypes. As such, each year there are runs produced by systems that aren't fully working by the TREC deadlines. The vast majority of the documents retrieved by these runs are not relevant, and thus their effectiveness is very poor. To prevent these uninteresting runs from having an effect on our calculations, only the top 75 % of the runs (as measured by mean average precision averaged over all the topics in the test collection) from each TREC are used in the experiments. The 75 % cut-off is arbitrary, but is sufficient to insure that no very poor run is included in the calculations. Once the low-performing runs were removed, there was a total of 484 runs across the eight TRECs, with TREC-4 having the fewest runs at 25, and TREC-8 the greatest number of runs at 97.

2.2 Basic Procedure

The core of the procedure to compute the error rate is comparing the effectiveness of a pair of retrieval runs on two disjoint topic sets of equal size to see if both topic sets agree as to which of the runs is better. Since the TREC collections have 50 topics, we can compute the error rate for topic set sizes up to 25 (24 for TREC-4 runs).

We use mean average precision (MAP) as the effectiveness measure in the comparisons. The average precision score for a single topic is the mean over all relevant documents of the precision obtained after each relevant document is retrieved, where precision at rank r is the number of relevant documents retrieved by rank r divided by r and the precision for an unretrieved relevant document is defined to be 0. The MAP score over a set of topics is the mean of the average precision scores of the individual topics. Mean average precision is one of the main measures used in TREC, and has been shown to be a stable effectiveness measure [2]. MAP is bounded between 0 and 1 inclusive, where higher scores indicate better performance. When calculating the error rate, the difference between two runs' MAP scores is categorized into one of 21 bins based on the size of the difference. The first bin contains runs with a difference of less than 0.01 (including no difference at all). The next bin contains runs whose difference is at least 0.01 but less than 0.02. The limits for the remaining bins increase by increments of 0.01, with the last bin containing all runs with a difference of at least 0.2.

The requirement that the topic sets be disjoint ensures that the comparisons are made on independent samples of topic space. That is, we assume a universe of all possible topics, and an (unknown) probability distribution of the MAP scores for each of the two runs. We also assume that the set of topics included in a TREC collection is a random sample of the universe of topics. A random selection from the TREC topic set gives a random, paired selection from each of the runs' MAP distributions. We take one random sample as a base case, and a different random sample (the disjoint sets) as the test case to see if the retrieval results agree.

The procedure for computing the error rate is shown in Figure 1. Each topic set size is treated as a separate experiment (the outer loop). Within the experiment, we count the number of times we see a swap for all pairs of runs in all TRECs, using the bins to segregate the counts by the size of the difference in the scores, and performing 50 trials for each run pair. The ratio of the number of swaps to the total number of cases that land in the bin is the error rate for that bin.

We perform 50 different trials using different combinations of topics in the two topic sets for each pair of runs to increase the sample size. While the two topic sets used within any one trial are disjoint, and thus independent samples, the topic sets across trials are drawn from the same 50 TREC topics and thus overlap. Because the topic sets among the different trials overlap, there may be correlations among the trials that could bias the estimates of the error rates as compared to what would be obtained with an equal number of samples drawn from a larger number of initial topics. We ran several of our experiments with no repeated trials; we obtained basically the same values with and without repetition, though the 50-trial curves were much smoother. Without repetition, there were as few as 66 samples for some combinations of bin and topic set size. With 50 trials, the smallest combination contained 3470 samples. We present only the curves with repeated trials in this paper.

The results of the error rate computations are shown in Figure 2. The figure plots the error rate against topic set size for each of the 21 bins representing the size of the difference between MAP scores. As expected, all but one of the curves show the error rate decreasing as the topic set size increases. The exception is the bin representing differences in MAP scores of less than 0.01 that remains mostly flat at just under a 50 % error rate. A 0.01 difference in retrieval scores is clearly within the noise of current retrieval experiments.

```
foreach topic set size z from 1...25 {
  set counters for all bins to 0
  foreach TREC t from 3...10 {
    foreach pair of runs X,Y from TREC t {
      foreach trial from 1...50
        select two disjoint sets of topics A,B of size z
          from the TREC t topic set
        d_A = MAP(X,A) − MAP(Y,A)
        d_B = MAP(X,B) − MAP(Y,B)
        increment counter of bin for d_A
        if d_A d_B < 0 {
          increment swap counter of bin for d
        }
      } } }

  foreach bin b {
    error-rate of b = swap counter / counter
  }
}
```

Figure 1: Algorithm for calculating error rates from TREC data. MAP(X,A) stands for the mean average precision score for run X on topic set A. Bins represent ranges of differences in scores.

As a way of gauging the importance of an experimental result, Sparck Jones proposed that differences in scores of 0.05 were noticeable and differences of 0.1 were material [7]. These differences are represented in Figure 2 as the dashed line with a solid circle marker (labeled $> .05$) and the dotted line with a solid circle marker (labeled $> .1$), respectively. For topic set sizes of 25, the error rate for a difference between .05 and .06 is approximately 13 %. That is, if we know nothing about systems A and B except their MAP scores which differ by 0.05, and if we repeat the experiment on 100 different sets of 25 topics, then on average we can expect 13 out of those 100 sets to favor one system while the remaining 87 to favor the other. The error rate for a difference between 0.10 and 0.11 is down to 3 %.

The differences in MAP scores used in this paper are absolute differences, while much of the IR literature reports percentage differences (see Keen [4] for a discussion of which to present). An absolute difference of 0.10 is a substantial difference, especially when the best runs on a test collection have MAP scores of approximately 0.30, as is the case for the TREC collections. The percentage difference between a run with a 0.30 MAP score and a run with a 0.10 absolute difference is at least 33 %.

3. EXTRAPOLATING TO LARGER TOPIC SET SIZES

Using the TREC data we can directly compute estimates of the error rates only for topic set sizes from 1 to 25. To get an estimate for the error rates for larger topic sets, we must extrapolate the curves from Figure 2. Extrapolation is fraught with peril: Mark Twain used it to demonstrate that the Mississippi river will be only 2 miles long in 500 years [9]. Nonetheless, sets of 25 topics are known to be fairly small. With all the appropriate caveats, we present an extrapolation to topic set sizes up to 50 topics.

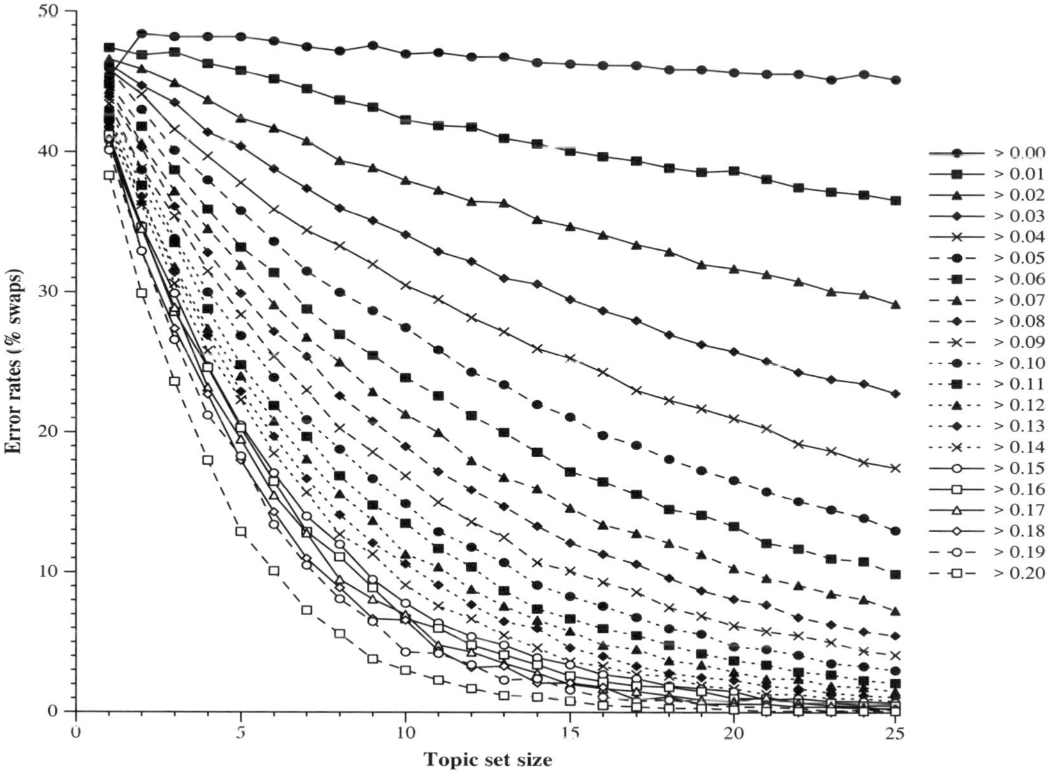

Figure 2: Error rate by topic set size averaged over all TRECs. The legend for each curve indicates the size of the difference in MAP scores was at least the given value and was less than the next curve's value.

We used the FUDGIT package of gnuplot [5] to perform the extrapolation. FUDGIT fits only curves, not surfaces, so we fit one bin at a time. The model we use, after trying a number of possibilities, is the simple equation

$$\text{ErrorRate} = A_1 e^{-A_2 S}$$

where S is the topic set size, and A_1 and A_2 are the parameters to be estimated. (We were not able to derive this model from statistical principles, though that may indeed be possible.) We used only topic set sizes 5–25 to fit the curves since very small topic set sizes are both uninteresting and problematic. We also did not fit differences of less than 0.01 (bin 0), or all differences greater then 0.2 (bin 20) since this last bin is not a range of differences as in the other bins

The simple model fits the data well. Table 1 gives the parameter values, parameter standard deviations (σ), and χ^2 values for each of the 19 curves. The χ^2 values, representing the quality of the fit, are uniformly low for all curves.

Figure 3 plots the equations given by Table 1, extrapolated to topic set sizes up to 50 topics. The extrapolated error rates for 50 topics are definitely smaller than the observed error rates for 25 topics, but are still large. To have an error rate of 5 % when using 50 topics, there needs to be a difference of approximately 0.051 between two systems. This agrees well with the Sparck Jones' noticeable difference, but is still a much larger relative percentage difference than is treated as important in many published papers. Researchers may need to do a deeper analysis of the differences between systems, rather than just compare MAP scores, before drawing conclusions.

Table 1: Parameters used to fit a model to the error rate curves. Each bin represents a range of differences in MAP scores and is one curve. The χ^2 value gives the quality of the fit. A_1 and A_2 are the parameters to be estimated, both their values and standard deviations (σ) are given.

		A_1		A_2	
bin	χ^2	value	σ	value	σ
1	2.18	47.76	0.66	0.01	0.001
2	1.54	46.12	0.71	0.02	0.001
3	2.16	45.65	0.79	0.03	0.001
4	0.95	45.32	0.88	0.04	0.001
5	1.45	45.25	1.00	0.05	0.002
6	1.79	44.62	1.12	0.06	0.002
7	1.93	45.27	1.28	0.07	0.002
8	1.04	45.91	1.47	0.09	0.003
9	1.58	46.20	1.69	0.10	0.004
10	1.05	47.12	1.97	0.12	0.004
11	0.90	47.18	2.26	0.13	0.005
12	0.51	48.76	2.63	0.14	0.006
13	0.45	50.08	3.05	0.16	0.007
14	0.64	52.95	3.66	0.17	0.009
15	0.70	51.58	4.08	0.19	0.010
16	1.09	55.11	4.82	0.20	0.012
17	1.27	57.56	5.60	0.22	0.014
18	1.92	55.52	6.12	0.23	0.016
19	1.74	63.50	7.87	0.25	0.018

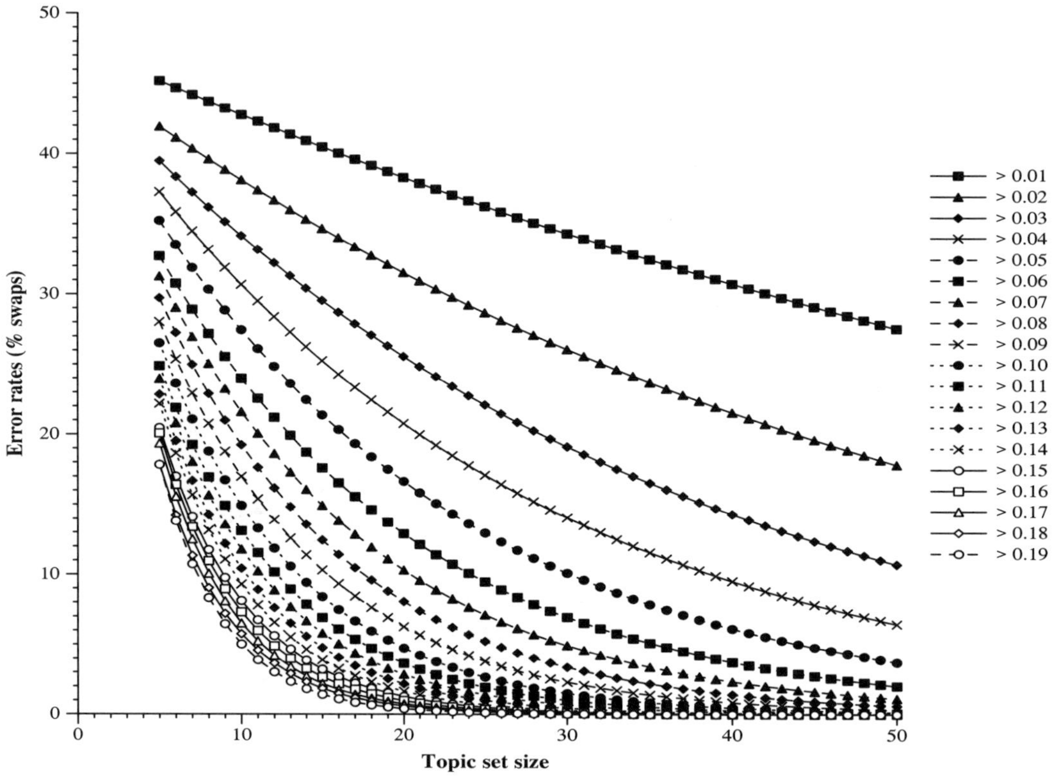

Figure 3: Error rates extrapolated to topic set sizes up to 50 topics.

Extrapolating out to 100 topics gives a 5 % error rate with a difference of about 0.03. Of course, this figure needs to be viewed with some skepticism given the extent of the extrapolation, but it should give at least a ballpark idea of what would happen.

4. CHARACTERIZING TEST COLLECTIONS

The error rates plotted in Figure 2 are grand averages over pairs of runs in all TRECs. By restricting the procedure to an individual TREC collection, we can perform a post hoc analysis of the test collection itself. We plotted the error rates when computed only over pairs of runs from a given TREC, and found the same general shape of the curves as in the overall plot for each TREC. There is more variability in the individual TREC plots since there are fewer samples for each bin and topic set size combination. (Almost all combinations have at least 100 samples, though one combination for TREC-4 has only 68 samples.) As examples, the plots for TREC-3 and TREC-6 are shown in Figure 4.

The values of the curves for corresponding bins do vary noticeably from TREC to TREC. To quantify this difference, as well as to provide information for reinterpreting existing TREC results as to what constitutes an important difference, we repeat the extrapolation in the previous section for each TREC. These extrapolations are not as sound as in the overall case since they are based on data that is more variable, but error rates for topic set size 25 match well. The second column of Table 2 gives the absolute difference required in MAP scores to have only a 5 % error rate when using topic sets of size 50 for each TREC.

Table 2: Difference in MAP scores required to have a 5 % error rate using topic sets of size 50 for individual TREC collections ("Abs. Diff."). Error rates are extrapolated and interpolated. Also given are the top MAP score obtained by an automatic run for that TREC ("Top MAP") and the percentage difference the 5 % error rate absolute difference represents with respect to the top score ("% Diff.").

	Abs. Diff.	Top MAP	% Diff.
TREC-3	0.041	.401	10.2
TREC-4	0.055	.294	18.7
TREC-5	0.061	.247	24.7
TREC-6	0.072	.288	25.0
TREC-7	0.044	.303	14.5
TREC-8	0.043	.330	13.0
TREC-9	0.054	.280	19.3
TREC 2001	0.053	.283	18.7

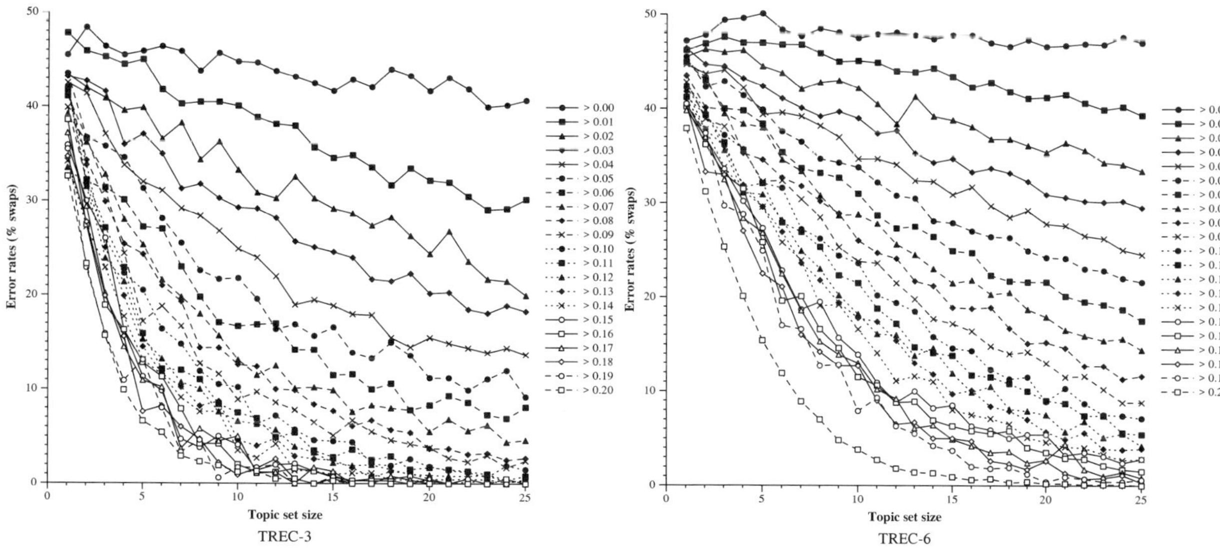

Figure 4: Error rates computed over individual TREC collections. Plots for TREC-3 and TREC-6 are shown.

The absolute difference required for a 5 % error rate fluctuates in a relatively narrow band from 0.041 (TREC-3) to 0.072 (TREC-6). These two endpoints agree with researchers' perception of the difficulty of the task that year. TREC-3 is regarded as an easy task; the topics were deliberately made shorter and more difficult in the following years. TREC-6 is regarded as a difficult task; many groups reported that techniques that had worked well in previous TRECs did not perform well for TREC-6. Note, however, that the percentage difference of the top scoring run required to match the absolute difference for a 5 % error rate ranges much more broadly. The final two columns in Table 2 give the top score by an automatic run in the given TREC and the percentage difference the figure in the first column represents with respect to that score. For the TREC-6 collection, you would need a relative difference of 25 % over the top run to have 95 % confidence that the difference was true.

Repeating the error rate computation on future collections built using the TREC methodology may provide a way of calibrating the difficulty of the collection. Such a characteristic would be a valuable tool for interpreting what differences between systems really mean for a given collection.

5. OPENING THE BLACK BOX

One of the goals for determining the error rate is to give researchers a finer context for deciding when observed differences in retrieval scores are meaningful. So far, we have computed error rates assuming that each run was a black box for which only the values of the effectiveness scores are known. This is appropriate when trying to compare operational systems that are not under a researcher's control and comparing current results to previously published work. Error rates may be smaller, though, for the common case of a researcher comparing variants of a single system. In this case, much of the processing is the same for each of the system variants, so the variance of the results is frequently smaller than for arbitrary runs.

We computed error rates using the same procedure as in Figure 1, except instead of comparing all pairs of runs we compared only pairs of runs such that each run in the pair was submitted to TREC by the same group (this was approximated by matching common prefixes of the run names). For this experiment, we included all runs submitted to each TREC, not just the top 75 % of runs used in the other experiments. While runs submitted to TREC by the same group are not necessarily variants of a common system, very frequently they are, so the comparisons should approximate same-system error rates. The computed error rates are shown in the graph on the right-hand side of Figure 5; the graph on the left-hand side of the figure is the same graph as in Figure 2, repeated here to make comparisons across the graphs easier.

The single-group curves have slightly lower error rates at very small topic set sizes, and somewhat steeper slopes, so there is a larger difference in the error rates for larger topic set sizes, especially for smaller differences between runs. (The curves in the single-group graph are clearly less smooth than the other curves, but that is simply because the single-group curves are based on many fewer comparisons.) While the error rate for small topic set sizes is slightly smaller for single-system comparisons, it is still very large (greater than 30 %), so the change is not important in practice. For sets of 25 topics, the size of the difference required before reaching a 5 % or 10 % error rate is reduced. A 10 % error rate is reached for differences of at least 0.04 for same-group comparisons, as compared with differences of at least 0.06 for arbitrary run comparisons. For a 5 % error rate, the same-group comparisons require a difference of at least 0.07, and the arbitrary-run comparisons a difference of 0.09. Runs produced by variants of the same system are likely to produce fairly small differences in average performance, so this reduction in error rate may be useful in practice.

6. PRECISION AT 10 DOCUMENTS

All of the above experiments are done using mean average precision as the effectiveness measure. Since different evaluation measures have different inherent stability [2], the error rates computed here will differ for different measures. In this section we repeat the error rate calculations using precision after 10 documents are retrieved, P(10), instead of

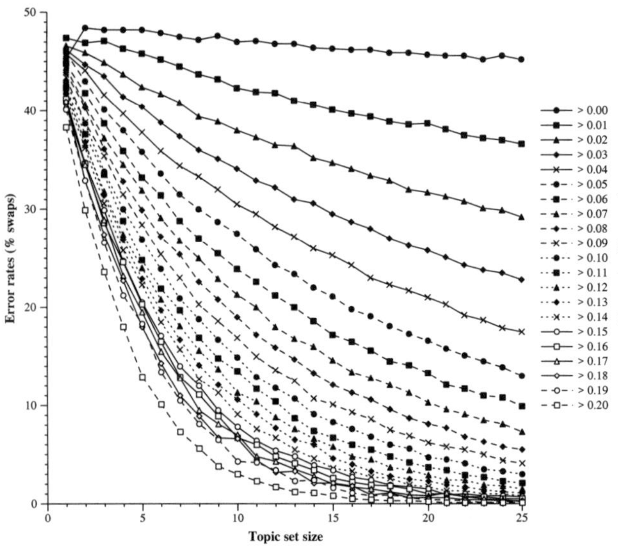

a) Error rates using all pairs of runs

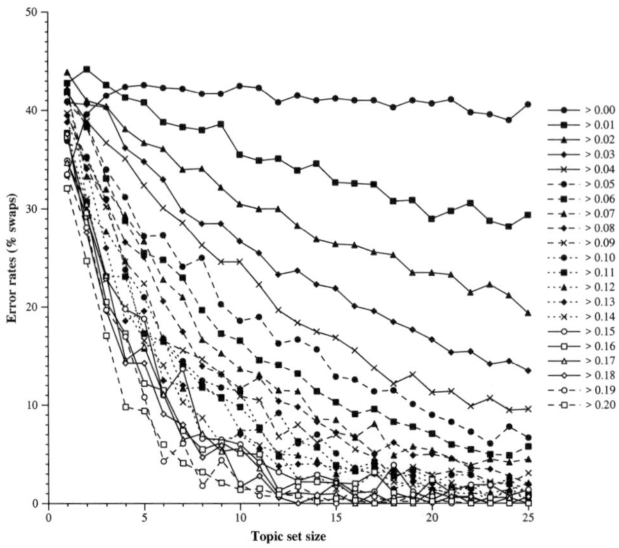

b) Error rates using intragroup pairs of runs

Figure 5: Comparison of error rates when computed using all run pairs (graph a) versus pairs of runs from the same group (graph b). Graph a) is the same graph as in Figure 2, repeated here for convenience.

Table 3: Difference in P(10) scores required to have a 5 % error rate using topic sets of size 50 for individual TREC collections. Error rates are extrapolated and interpolated.

	Required Difference
TREC-3	0.076
TREC-4	0.122
TREC-5	0.094
TREC-6	0.110
TREC-7	0.095
TREC-8	0.109
TREC-9	0.078
TREC 2001	0.085
Overall	0.094

MAP as the effectiveness measure. Table 3 gives the equivalent values as reported in Table 2 when using P(10). That is, Table 3 gives the absolute differences required in P(10) scores to have no more than a 5 % error rate for each TREC using extrapolated curves and topic sets of size 50.

The results are much the same, except the variability of P(10) is greater, and the error rates themselves are larger. The χ^2 values during curve fitting are two to three times higher in general. While the absolute differences are substantially higher than with MAP, the relative differences are about the same since P(10) scores are generally greater than MAP scores. For example, the 0.076 absolute difference required for a 5 % error rate for TREC-3 is approximately a 9 % relative percentage difference of the top TREC-3 P(10) scores. For TREC-6, the 0.110 difference is approximately a 25 % relative percentage difference. The relationship between error rates and the inherent stability of different measures requires further study.

7. LIMITATIONS AND FUTURE WORK

The experiments described here are all descriptive examinations of past experiments. The fact that we achieve very similar results on eight different test collections is good evidence that our results may be valid in other environments, but we should be cautious until we understand the factors affecting our results better.

In addition to our previously mentioned assumptions about randomness of topic sets, we are also making the assumption that our retrieval runs are random representatives of the retrieval run space we are interested in. For most of these experiments we used all available runs, but these runs actually belong to a number of different non-random categories which may affect the results (e.g., manual vs. automatic, short topics vs. long topics, query expansion vs. no expansion, same base retrieval system vs. different system). In the future we need to explore the effects of these categories, especially those categories which are expected to increase or decrease the topic variability of a system. In particular, it could be very interesting to examine the difference between using short topics and long topics.

8. CONCLUSION

Comparing two information retrieval mechanisms is the core of much information retrieval research. Given this, surprisingly little attention has been devoted to analyzing what the differences in evaluation scores of two mechanisms mean in practice. This paper examines the large number of retrieval results from eight years of TREC tasks to empirically determine how meaningful an observed difference can be expected to be. We do this by splitting a single experiment comparing two systems on 50 topics into two separate experiments using 25 or fewer topics. We then count the number of times that these two experiments disagree as to which system is better, conditioned on the size of the difference of the scores.

We expect that as the difference in retrieval scores increases, the likelihood that a second run will contradict the first decreases. Indeed, we found a strong, consistent relationship among contradiction (or error) rate, the size of the difference in scores, and the number of topics used. A smooth exponential curve of the form

$$\text{ErrorRate} = A_1 e^{-A_2 S}$$

nicely fits each plot of error rate versus score difference for a given topic set size. Using this curve to extrapolate to topic sets of size 50, we find that absolute differences of approximately 0.05 are required to fall below a 5 % error rate. A 0.05 absolute difference in mean average precision scores corresponds to approximately a 15 % relative percentage difference with respect to the top TREC results, which is a larger difference than has generally been used within TREC experiments to signify meaningful differences. The 0.05 figure does correspond nicely with Sparck Jones' recommendation [7]. The larger differences required to be confident in a conclusion suggests researchers need to do a deeper analysis of how systems differ, rather than just compare MAP scores, before drawing conclusions.

The error rate computations can be applied to individual collections that are built using the TREC methodology. Each collection will have a characteristic score difference that is required to reach the 5 % error rate limit. By publishing the error rate as a feature of the collection after it is created, researchers will have a finer context for judging the importance of retrieval results on that collection.

9. REFERENCES

[1] D. Banks, P. Over, and N.-F. Zhang. Blind men and elephants: Six approaches to TREC data. *Information Retrieval*, 1:7–34, 1999.

[2] C. Buckley and E. M. Voorhees. Evaluating evaluation measure stability. In N. Belkin, P. Ingwersen, and M. Leong, editors, *Proceedings of the 23rd Annual International ACM SIGIR Conference on Research and Development in Information Retrieval*, pages 33–40, 2000.

[3] C. W. Cleverdon, J. Mills, and E. M. Keen. Factors determining the performance of indexing systems. Two volumes, Cranfield, England, 1968.

[4] E. M. Keen. Presenting results of experimental retrieval comparisons. *Information Processing and Management*, 28(4):491–502, 1992.

[5] M.-D. Lacasse. FUDGIT A multi-purpose data-processing and fitting program user's manual version 2.31. Technical report, Center for the Physics of Materials and Department of Physics, Montreal, Canada, April 1993.

[6] G. Salton. The state of retrieval system evaluation. *Information Processing and Management*, 28(4):441–449, 1992.

[7] K. Sparck Jones. Automatic indexing. *Journal of Documentation*, 30:393–432, 1974.

[8] K. Sparck Jones and C. van Rijsbergen. Information retrieval test collections. *Journal of Documentation*, 32(1):59–75, 1976.

[9] M. Twain. Life on the Mississippi, 1883. Reprinted at `http://www.lhup.edu/~dsimanek/twain.htm`.

[10] E. M. Voorhees. Special issue: The sixth Text REtrieval Conference (TREC-6). *Information Processing and Management*, 36(1), January 2000.

[11] E. M. Voorhees. Variations in relevance judgments and the measurement of retrieval effectiveness. *Information Processing and Management*, 36:697–716, 2000.

Liberal Relevance Criteria of TREC – Counting on Negligible Documents?

Eero Sormunen
University of Tampere
FIN 33014 University of Tampere
Finland
+358-3-2156972
Eero.Sormunen@uta.fi

ABSTRACT

Most test collections (like TREC and CLEF) for experimental research in information retrieval apply binary relevance assessments. This paper introduces a four-point relevance scale and reports the findings of a project in which TREC-7 and TREC-8 document pools on 38 topics were reassessed. The goal of the reassessment was to build a subcollection of TREC for experiments on highly relevant documents and to learn about the assessment process as well as the characteristics of a multigraded relevance corpus.

Relevance criteria were defined so that a distinction was made between documents rich in topical information (relevant and highly relevant documents) and poor in topical information (marginally relevant documents). It turned out that about 50% of documents assessed as relevant were regarded as marginal. The characteristics of the relevance corpus and lessons learned from the reassessment project are discussed. The need to develop more elaborated relevance assessment schemes is emphasized.

Categories and Subject Descriptors

H.3.3 Information Search and Retrieval

General Terms: Experimentation

Keywords: Test collections, TREC, Relevance Assessments, Graded relevance, Experiment

1. INTRODUCTION

Relevance judgments are of critical importance to an information retrieval test collection. In TREC, for example, the pooling method was developed to guarantee that the list of documents assessed for relevance is as comprehensive as possible [13, 14]. The effects of variations in relevance assessments on the measured retrieval effectiveness have also been studied [10]. On the other hand, the notion of relevance has been operationalized in a very simple way. A binary scale has been used to classify documents either topically relevant or topically irrelevant. Relevance criteria have been quite liberal. The guidelines of TREC state:

> *"Only binary judgments ("relevant" or "not relevant") are made, and a document is judged relevant if any piece of it is relevant (regardless of how small the piece is in relation to the rest of the document)."* [9]

The use of binary assessments has been criticized for the lack of realism. For example, studies on Web searching have raised the need for improving the capability of IR systems to find highly relevant documents at the expense of marginally relevant ones [3]. Järvelin and Kekäläinen [5] and Voorhees [11] suggested that IR systems effective in finding highly relevant documents might suffer of binary and liberal relevance criteria. In the most recent TREC Web tracks, a three-point relevance scale has been used: *irrelevant*, *relevant* and *highly relevant* [4]. Other TREC collections have held to binary assessments.

The notion *degree of relevance* brings into play the potential usefulness of documents for a reader trying to learn about a topic. This includes an assumption that the reader has already at least an intuitive idea about the topic. This assumption is fair since we expect that the person is able to formulate a query about the topic.

For example, if the topic is *What are the applications of robotics in the world today* (TREC topic 392) we may assume that the user has a general intuition what robots are (some kind of automatic machinery) and that robots may be used for different types of applications. A document that tells that some Company X develops robot-based applications, but does not specify them, is topically relevant but does not help the user to learn about the topic. The document gave only a pointer to an external source of information (Company X).

The above example emphasizes the need to define more explicitly the criteria used in topical relevance assessments especially when the degree of relevance is considered. Earlier research has not defined clearly the criteria for multigraded relevance. The borderline between irrelevant, marginally relevant and useful documents is especially interesting.

This paper reports a project (at the University of Tampere) in which a set of 38 topics from TREC-7 and TREC-8 was exposed to graded relevance assessments. The main goal of the project was to create a subcollection where the capability of IR systems to focus on highly relevant documents could be studied. We also wanted to analyze and characterize the pools of relevant

SIGIR'02, August 11-15, 2002, Tampere, Finland.

documents. The third goal was to learn more about the process and the outcome of graded relevance assessments.

Section 2 gives a general description of the reassessment project. Section 3 presents the basic characteristics of the graded relevance corpus, and its major differences compared to TREC. Section 4 sums up the main findings and presents conclusions.

2. DATA AND METHODS

We accepted the basic topicality assumption on which relevance assessments in the TREC collection are based. We just expanded relevance criteria to cover the degree of relevance. We attempted to follow the procedures of TREC as strictly as possible. However, some obvious differences between processes should be kept in mind when comparing results:

- TREC assessors create the topics, define relevance criteria, and compose topic descriptions by themselves. Our assessors used written topic descriptions as they had been documented by the TREC assessors.
- Our document pools contained the same relevant documents but only about 5% of irrelevant documents processed by TREC assessors.
- TREC assessors read documents on screen and could enter any keywords they liked to be highlighted in texts. We used documents printed on paper without highlighting.

We could use the original TREC assessments as a reference for the present work (but of course this information was not available for our assessors).

2.1 The subset of topics and documents

The topics and, especially, the way of representing the topics have varied during the history of TREC. We were encouraged to use topics from TREC-6 to TREC-8 because various reasons justified the avoidance of topics from earlier TRECs [Personal communications, Donna Harman, April 10, 2001]. For technical reasons we selected the topics 351-450 of TREC-7 and TREC-8 for further consideration.

We could not afford assessing the documents from the pools of one hundred topics, and therefore selected a subset of topics applying the following criteria:

- The number of documents assessed relevant by TREC should be more than 30 per topic. The lower limit was an attempt to keep the number of highly relevant documents adequate for testing. If the number of highly relevant documents is small, performance measures tend to become unstable making comparisons unreliable [11].
- The upper limit for the number of documents per topic was set to keep the cost of assessment reasonable. The sum of relevant documents and a 5% sample of irrelevant documents from the TREC pool should not exceed 200. (For the first 8 topics assessed, the criterion for the upper bound was slightly different, and the sample size of irrelevant documents was 10%.)
- All topics that were expected to require good background knowledge of American or British life and culture (e.g. administration or justice) were excluded. Similarly, any topic with which all assessors felt uncertain was excluded.

Some 40 topics were selected for the project but the assessment process could be completed for 38 topics, only. The pool contained 5737 documents of which 2772 had been assessed relevant in TREC. The 5% sample of irrelevant documents was selected by using the end digits of document identifiers as a sampling criterion.

2.2 Relevance criteria

Assessors were guided to base their work on simple assumptions about the user. The relevance should be judged considering a user needing general or specific information about a topic (for example, an author writing a review on the topic). Other aspects than topicality and the degree of topical relevance (the extent to which the text discusses the topic) should be overlooked.

The relevance of documents was assessed on a four-point scale developed originally for a Finnish test collection at the University of Tampere [7]:

(0) The document does not contain any information about the topic.

(1) The document only points to the topic. It does not contain more or other information than the topic description. Typical extent: one sentence or fact.

(2) The document contains more information than the topic description but the presentation is not exhaustive. In case of a multi-faceted topic, only some of the sub-themes or viewpoints are covered. Typical extent: one text paragraph, 2-3 sentences or facts.

(3) The document discusses the themes of the topic exhaustively. In case of a multi-faceted topic, all or most sub-themes or viewpoints are covered. Typical extent: several text paragraphs, at least 4 sentences or facts.

The basic threshold for accepting a document relevant was the same as in TREC. The criteria for *marginally relevant* items (level 1) embody so low degree of relevance that the document hardly contributes the user although it contains a piece of text mentioning the topic. Documents graded *relevant* (level 2) are expected to gain some new information to the user already having a general intuition about the topic. *Highly relevant* (level 3) documents are expected to help the user to take a good command of the topic.

Most experimenters [e.g. 1, 6, 2] as well as the TREC Web track [4] applying graded relevance scales have not made a distinction between relevant but useless (level 1) and relevant and restrictedly useful (level 2) documents. If we take a stringent standpoint, the IR system should reject marginally relevant documents although they may contain the same words and phrases as more relevant documents.

2.3 Recruitment of assessors

Native speakers of English were not available for the project but, fortunately, fluent readers of English texts could be recruited. The group of six Master's students of information studies - two of them already having a Master's degree in another subject – was selected. All assessors had learned the basics of English at school (typically 2-4 hours per week for a period of ten or eleven years), passed the English courses at the University, and trained their reading proficiency in literature exams. In addition, individual assessors had remarkable but different experiences in practicing

English: formal university studies in English or English literature, studies abroad, a long-lasting hobby of reading fiction in English, etc.

Our aim was to guarantee that the proficiency of assessors in English would not become an issue of concern in the project. As it turned out later, the specific fields of expertise needed in interpreting the themes of documents – not the language - were a problem in some topics. However, this is not a problem specific to our project. All assessors working with documents of varying themes feel uncomfortable with some documents of unfamiliar subjects.

We did not test the proficiency of assessors in English or their general or special traits formally. We knew their backgrounds and success in Master's studies. We focused on organizing and controlling the assessment work itself. We also used TREC relevance data as a reference to identify potential problems.

2.4 Assessment procedure

The assessors were given written guidelines and a short introduction to the goals and tasks of the project. Next, all assessors judged a small set of documents from two topics (from TREC-6). Resulting judgments were compared and the problems observed were discussed in a meeting to clarify the details of assessment practices. Also later, regular meetings were organized for the group to discuss the problems at hand and to refine working practices through the project lasting a period of six months.

The documents shorter than one hundred pages were printed on paper for assessments. Longer documents were judged on screen. The relevance values were put down on the top of printed documents and the passages of documents that contained relevant information were also marked up.

The assessors were asked to make written notes of all interpretations they made on the description of the topic or on relevance criteria applied. They were also asked to document any problems or contradictions faced in topic descriptions. We emphasized that the assessor should clarify and fix their relevance criteria by first scanning some 20-30 documents to get a general touch on the topic and on the content of documents in hand. The assessors were advised to mark problematic documents by a question mark for a collective consideration later, if necessary.

The practices of assessment were created by three assessors during the first phase of the project. At this phase, two assessors worked on each topic to produce parallel assessments. We could use parallel data to control the quality of work and to develop working practices. Soon we realized that the project was advancing too slowly and we could not afford duplicate assessments. Three new assessors we recruited and trained. During the second phase, each topic was treated by one assessor, only. As a result, we have two parallel assessments for eight topics and single assessments for 30 topics.

2.5 Follow-up

Our goal was not only to produce a corpus of graded relevance for the selected topics of TREC but also to learn about the process itself. Our basic principle was that the group of assessors is the major intellectual resource in this project, and that we focus on collecting data on their experiences. To avoid any disturbance affecting relevance assessments we did not observe the actual behavior of subjects and did not ask them to document their inference in individual assessments. The only extra task for non-problematic documents was to roughly mark up the passages of text that contained relevant information.

Later, the new relevance corpus was compared to the original relevance assessments of TREC to identify all documents where assessments diverged. The assessors were given a sample of documents where they had rated a document irrelevant although it had been rated relevant in TREC, and vice versa relevant or highly relevant although irrelevant in TREC. They were asked to analyze each document once more and reconsider if they (a) remain firm in the original assessment, (b) accept TREC assessment as the right one, or (c) change the original assessment but do not accept that of TREC. In all cases, the assessor was asked for reasons on which the decision was based.

The analysis of documents where assessments diverged was part of a larger effort to collect data about assessor experiences. For each topic an assessor had worked on, s/he was given a bundle of documents including a copy of the topic description page on which they had made their own notes, a couple of sample documents assessed relevant (to recollect the assessment process), two pairs of highly and marginally relevant documents (to explain topic related arguments how marginally and highly relevant documents differ), and the set of documents where assessments had diverged from TREC (as described above). The bundle of documents contained also a questionnaire focusing on the characteristics of the topic and the set of documents assessed.

The assessors analyzed the bundle of documents and answered the questionnaires at their own pace. After the material had been returned and analyzed, the assessors were invited to a personal interview to clarify unclear or incomplete answers in the previous data collection phase, and to discuss their experiences. The results from the post-interview are not discussed here.

Table 1. Distribution of documents across relevance levels earlier assessed relevant or irrelevant in TREC and reassessed in the UTA project (38 topics, # = number of documents).

Levels of	TREC rel		TREC irrel		Total			UTA rel	
relevance	#	%	#	%	#	%	#/topic	#	%
Rel=3	353	13 %	11	0 %	364	6 %	10	364	16 %
Rel=2	724	26 %	40	1 %	764	13 %	20	764	34 %
Rel=1	1004	36 %	134	5 %	1138	20 %	30	1138	50 %
Rel=0	691	25 %	2780	94 %	3471	61 %	91		
Total	2772	100 %	2965	100 %	5737	100 %	151	2266	100 %

3. RESULTS

The basic data on assessed documents are presented in Table 1. The total number of documents assessed was 5737 of which 2772 (48%) had been assessed relevant and 2965 (52%) irrelevant in TREC. In the reassessment, 61% of documents were found irrelevant, 20% marginally relevant, 13% relevant, and only 6% highly relevant.

On the average, 60 more or less relevant documents are available per topic of which 10 were highly relevant, 20 relevant and 30 marginally relevant. About 50% of documents assessed relevant were considered marginal, one third relevant, and only 16% highly relevant (Table 1, the last column).

Table 1 (the first column) shows that 691 documents rated relevant in TREC were rated irrelevant in our reassessments (25% of relevant in TREC). We call this deviation as *type A inconsistency*. In addition, 1004 documents relevant in TREC (36%) were considered as marginally relevant by our assessors. The figures suggest that the degree of relevance seems to be quite low in over 60% of documents assessed relevant in TREC. However, before making conclusions we need to analyze further inconsistently assessed documents and the arguments on which our assessors based their decisions. Some relevant documents were either missed or assessed differently.

Another result was that our assessors found some relevant documents that had not been identified, or considered as relevant by the TREC assessors. We call this deviation as *type B inconsistency*. The number of relevant and highly relevant documents missed or judged irrelevant by TREC was very small (about 1% of all assessed irrelevant in TREC). However, our evidence on the missed relevant documents is weak since our sampling method for irrelevant documents was not directed to hunt the missed ones. This problem has been discussed and experimented by Zobel [14].

Table 2. The effect of asking assessors to reassess type A inconsistently judged documents (a sample of 69 out of 691 documents).

Relevance	1st time	2nd time	
level	#	#	%
Rel=3		0	0 %
Rel=2		4	6 %
Rel=1		21	30 %
Rel=0	69	44	64 %
Total	69	69	100 %

Table 3. The effect of asking assessors to reassess type B inconsistently judged documents (all relevant or highly relevant documents).

Relevance	1st time	2nd time	
level	#	#	%
Rel=3	6	5	11 %
Rel=2	41	30	62 %
Rel=1		2	4 %
Rel=0		10	22 %
Total	47	47	100 %

3.1 Type A inconsistency

A sample of 69 documents (about 10%) regarded as relevant in TREC but rated as irrelevant in our assessments (type A inconsistency) was sent to the assessors for post-analysis. The sample was created using the following criteria: 1) If at least one inconsistently assessed document was available for a topic, it should be included. 2) No more than three documents were selected per topic. 3) All documents should be from different sub-collections if possible. 4) All documents longer than 5 pages were excluded.

The aim of criteria 1-3 was to guarantee that the sample was representative in terms of topics, assessors, and document types. The fourth criterion was used not to overload and demotivate our assessors at a critical stage of data collection.

The results of the second assessment are presented in Table 2. The assessors did not change their ratings for two thirds of documents (64%), accepted 30% as marginally relevant, and 6% as relevant. None of the documents reassessed were judged highly relevant. This finding suggests that we can trust that our assessors were quite reliable in identifying highly relevant documents at least if we believe on their criteria and arguments in the second assessment.

Based on 4 unrecognized relevant (rel=2) documents from the sample we may estimate that about 40 relevant (rel=2) documents out of the 691 documents judged relevant by TREC assessors may have been missed by our assessors. This is about 0.6% of all documents assessed and would add, on average, one extra relevant document per topic to the relevance corpus. Adding estimated misses would increase the share of rel=2 documents slightly from 26% to 28% (the third column in Table 1).

The share of missed marginally relevant documents is quite high in the sample (30%). We may estimate that about 210 marginally relevant documents were regarded as irrelevant by our assessors. This finding suggests that the share of marginally relevant documents is even higher (about 44% instead of 36%) than expressed in Table 1. On the other hand, the number of irrelevant documents would decrease from 691 to some 440 documents, and the share from 25% to 16%, respectively.

Above figures suggest that our assessors were less effective in identifying marginally relevant documents than their TREC colleagues. This difference is probably associated with differences in the assessment practices. Our assessors read printed documents while their TREC colleagues scanned documents on screen by a browser highlighting topic related keywords. Documents where the topic is mentioned in one sentence only are easily missed in traditional scanning of text on paper.

To sum up, the set of 691 documents judged irrelevant by our assessors (type A inconsistency) is estimated to consist of 1) missed relevant and 2) differently judged documents:

- Highly relevant documents were recognized reliably.
- About 6% of relevant, and 30% of marginally relevant were missed.
- About 64% of documents were judged differently.

We will analyze the last group and reasons for different judgments in Section 3.3.

3.2 Type B inconsistency

A set of 185 documents that had been assessed irrelevant in TREC but relevant (at levels 1-3) by our assessors (type B inconsistency,

Column 4 in Table 1). Of these, 47 were rated relevant or highly relevant and we asked our assessors to reassessed them. Marginally relevant documents were excluded since we considered their role less important. Table 3 presents the results of the second assessment. It turned out that our assessors accepted TREC relevance ratings at least partially (rel=0 or 1) for 12 documents (26%) but defended their original judgment for 35 documents (74%).

The rate of missing relevant or highly relevant documents by TREC was about 0.6% of all documents in the sample. Practically, there was no difference in the rate of missing relevant and highly relevant documents between TREC and our assessors.

3.3 Why documents were assessed differently?

Documents where assessments differed between TREC and us were not evenly distributed over the 38 topics. 90% of documents which our assessors had rated irrelevant contrary to TREC came from 16 topics. 90% of relevant and highly relevant documents rated irrelevant by the TREC assessors were related to 9 topics. This is not a surprise since the clarity of relevance criteria varied from topic to topic as the analysis of assessor experiences revealed.

The assessors were asked to judge the clarity of descriptions for each topic they had evaluated (4-point scale: 1. very ambiguous ... 4. clear), and their general confidence on decisions concerning each topic (scale: 1. lower than typical, 2. typical, 3. higher than typical). We were interested to see if assessor perceived clarity and confidence was associated with the variation of consistency with TREC assessments.

The topics were sorted in order of descending number of documents assessed irrelevant although regarded as relevant in TREC (type A inconsistency). The sorted list of topics was divided into quartiles containing 9, 10, 10, and 9 topics. The averages for perceived topic clarity and confidence of decisions were calculated for each quartile of topics. The upper quartile of topics yielded 67%, the second 29%, and the third 3% of type A inconsistent documents.

Table 4. Topic ambiguity and confidence of decisions in topic groups organized in the descending order of inconsistency instances (Type A: TREC relevant -> irrelevant; Type B: TREC irrelevant -> relevant or highly relevant).

		Clarity 1...4		Confidence 1...3	
Topics	n	Type A	Type B	Type A	Type B
I Quartile	9	2,3	2,3	1,9	1,9
II Quartile	10	2,9	2,6	2,0	2,3
III Quartile	10	2,8	2,7	2,2	1,9
IV Quartile	9	2,8	3,2	2,3	2,4

Similar grouping of topics was made on basis of documents assessed relevant or highly relevant although irrelevant in TREC (type B inconsistency). However, the low number of type B documents (only 39) limits the reliability of this comparison.

For type A inconsistency, the average perceived clarity of topics was clearly lower for the first quartile of topics (2.3) than for topics in other quartiles (2.8-2.9). Similarly, the average confidence of decisions tended to be low for this quartile of topics (1.9 vs. 2.0-2.3). In type B inconsistency, trends were similar but the figures were not so steady because of the smaller number of topics where type B inconsistency occurred.

The figures suggest that the consistency of assessments is difficult to achieve if the assessors feel topic descriptions ambiguous. This is also associated with the confidence of decisions. In the personal interviews, assessors complained that for many topics the description (including the title) and the narrative presented contradicting relevance criteria or otherwise did not give a solid basis for relevance assessments. Our assessors had to specify relevance criteria by themselves to guarantee consistent treatment of documents. However, new criteria were probably not always in line with the intentions of original assessors.

3.4 Economics of graded assessments

Judging document relevant is a quite straightforward process if liberal criteria are applied. The assessor only needs to identify one sentence or a text paragraph where the topic is discussed. In graded assessments, some extra work is required to specify the degree of relevance for documents found relevant. If the relevance of a document cannot be identified easily, the treatment of documents is the same in binary and graded assessments. The assessor is expected to verify the irrelevance by reading the whole document.

In all, the total time needed to assess slightly more than 7000 documents (parallel assessments included) required approximately 78 full workweeks (about 36 hours each). This figure includes training, meetings; printing of documents, data entry, vacations, etc. but excludes the work done by supervisors.

The average number of 73 documents was processed per week and per person during the first phase of the project. The speed rose up to 105 documents per week in the second phase. During the second phase, the practices were already fixed and more time could be allocated for actual assessments.

Individual differences in effectiveness were notable and having enough practice in assessments seemed to increase output. During the second phase, one of the experienced assessors reached an average rate of 220 assessed documents per week (about 6 documents per hour) but none of the newcomers could exceed 130 documents per week. The figures suggest that pre-testing of assessors is worth considering in major assessment projects.

4. CONCLUSIONS AND DISCUSSION

4.1 Binary and graded assessments

One major contribution of this study is based on the distinction between documents only pointing to the topic (rel=1, marginal) and those really containing some potentially useful information (rel=2, relevant). About 50% of the documents assessed as relevant were marginal. The other half of documents contained potentially useful information to the user. Only 16% of the relevant documents were highly relevant.

The share of documents rated as irrelevant or marginal in the TREC relevance corpus was even higher (about 60%). The figure is biased by the differences in the assessment processes between us, and TREC. Voorhees [12] found in a parallel test that secondary assessors working on the basis of written topic descriptions tend to reject a notable share of documents that the author of a TREC topic (primary assessor) regards as relevant. On the other hand, Voorhees [12] observed that secondary assessors found very few new, relevant documents. Our data was in line with this finding (6%).

Anyhow, the results show that the relevance threshold is quite low in TREC. This is quite natural if we consider the themes of discussions in the past: the concern about missed relevant documents [14] together with liberal relevance criteria and binary scaling [9, 13]. Binary relevance has been a convenient approach in test collections since it makes performance calculations simple, keeps the cost of assessments low, and maximizes the number of relevant documents per topic guaranteeing the stability of measures.

This is all good, but we have to ask: are we able to conduct experiments that we consider as meaningful? Without a doubt, TREC is an indispensable tool for studying retrieval systems aimed at high-recall searching. However, we definitely need test collections for IR systems aimed to retrieve highly relevant documents effectively from large databases (e.g. Web indexes). This requires that we build test collections that provide more differentiated relevance data.

4.2 Assessment costs and procedures

Can we afford the higher cost of graded relevance assessments? Our project was not optimized in terms of costs and the volume of throughput. The productivity of assessments can be substantially increased by using appropriate browsing tools, developing the routines, and recruiting the most effective assessors. Obviously, the costs are higher for graded assessments than for binary assessments. However, one might imagine that the assessment cost when using our 4-point scale does not differ much from the cost when using the 3-point scale of the Web Track. This comparison suggests that if the costs are manageable in the Web Track, they can be afforded when using the 4-point scale.

In TREC, browsers highlighting topic related keywords in the document help one locate a text of interest. The use of this tool could be improved by developing the procedure of how and how exhaustively keywords are composed. Relevant and highly relevant documents contain a larger variety and number of topic related terms, [see 8]. It is likely that they can be identified quite reliably if the highlighting procedure is designed well.

In a test collection based on graded relevance assessments, it is a minor issue if a small share of marginally relevant documents is missed. This fact raises the question: could the pooling techniques be developed to decrease the total number of documents assessed?

The easiest way to resolve the need for test collections providing a multigraded relevance corpus is to reassess the pools of selected TREC topics. It is not likely that TREC could afford multigraded relevance assessments instead of binary ones as an annual routine. The costs of reassessment can be limited, because most (if not all) of the irrelevant documents can be ignored.

4.3 Performance measures

The number of highly relevant documents per topic tends to be small. As Voorhees [11] pointed out, results based on small document sets may be unstable. Thus, she recommended the use of the Discounted Cumulative Gain (DCG) method proposed by Järvelin and Kekäläinen [5] to combine and weight the evidence from different levels of relevance. The advantage of the 4-point relevance scale is that relevant and useful (rel=2) and relevant but potentially useless (rel=1) documents can be weighted differently. The problem of small sets can be reduced, if the difference of weights between highly relevant (rel=3) and relevant (rel=2) is kept modest to increase the stability of measures. On the other hand, marginally relevant documents may be given a very low, if any, weight. Another method to increase stability is to have more topics [8].

The three-point relevance scale launched in the Web Track of TREC is only a small step forward since the distinction between topically relevant but potentially useless (rel=1) and topically relevant and potentially useful (rel=2) has not been made. The three-point scale gives fewer choices in the use of weights.

4.4 Problems and future research

The ultimate test for the usefulness of graded relevance scales is: does it matter in practice if we use graded relevance instead of binary relevance? This could be done by using old TREC data to investigate the effect of graded relevance scales on measured performance differences. If the results are clearly different when graded relevance is used, the extra effort required and resources consumed may be justified. Voorhees [11] did a test of this kind to find out the potential benefits of the Discounted Cumulative Gain (DCG) method.

The use of old TREC data is necessary only if we want to verify a hypothesis that the findings in the past TREC experiments were biased by the liberal relevance assessments. We expect that liberal binary assessments are ok for experiments focusing on high recall searching. Our main point is that we need multigraded relevance data to study retrieval phenomena associated with the degree of relevance.

The set of 38 topics is small for retrospective analysis, and even that set is divided among TREC-7 and TREC-8. We found more reasonable to design new experiments in which research questions deal with retrieving highly relevant documents. This experiment is in progress. The relevance corpus will become available to the TREC community after the data has been checked in course of the experiment.

Apart from actual tests, more research is needed to develop graded relevance scales. For example, the benefits of using a 4 point scale instead of a 3-point scale together with a higher basic threshold, is an open question. If we do not require that all marginally relevant documents need to be found and pooled, the goals and practices of relevance assessment processes have to be reconsidered.

Our project applied an empirical approach to emphasize the methodological challenge of developing relevance assessments in test collections. This was a modest but determined step towards realism in relevance assessments as the degree of relevance was taken into account. The next natural step could be to develop relevance schemes than can be used to handle overlaps between document contents. Any static characteristic of a document is a potential search criterion and also a potential target for relevance assessments in test collections.

5. ACKNOWLEDGMENTS

The author is very grateful to Professors Jaana Kekäläinen and Kal Järvelin for their effort in the project. We all thank Donna Harman for her encouraging advice. I am also very grateful to the group of referees for their constructive criticism and comments.

Otto Auranen, Jussi Koivisto, Marko Panttila, Mira Roine, Reetta Saine and Mikael Vakkari made an enormous assessment work and were actively developing the procedure of assessment.

The members of the FIRE group have also helped to improve the manuscript. Especially, the author thanks the visiting colleagues in FIRE, Diane Sonnenwald and Per Ahlgren, for their valuable comments.

6. REFERENCES

[1] Blair, D.C. and Maron, M.E. An evaluation of retrieval effectiveness for a full-text document retrieval system. Commun. ACM 28, 3, 289-299.

[2] Burgin, R. Variations on relevance judgments and the evaluation of retrieval performance. Information Processing & Management 28, 5, 619-627,

[3] Gordon, M. and Pathak, P. Finding information on the world wide web: The retrieval effectiveness of search engines. Information Processing and Management, 35, 2, 141 – 180.

[4] Hawking, D. Overview of the TREC-9 Web Track. http://trec.nist.gov/pubs/trec9/papers/web9.pdf [Cited 2 January 2002].

[5] Järvelin, K. & Kekäläinen, J. IR evaluation methods for highly relevant documents. In: Belkin, N.J., Ingwersen, P. and Leong, M.-K. (eds.) Proceedings of the 23rd Annual International ACM SIGIR Conference on Research and Development in Information Retrieval. ACM Press, New York 2000, 41-48.

[6] Saracevic, T., Kantor. P. et al. A study of information seeking and retrieving. I Background and methodology. Journal of the American Society for Information Science 39, 3, 161-176.

[7] Sormunen, E. A method for measuring wide range performance of Boolean queries in full-text databases. Doctoral Thesis. University of Tampere. Acta Electronica Universitatis Tamperensis 34, URL: http://acta.uta.fi/teos.phtml?3786, Tampere 2000.

[8] Sormunen, E., Kekäläinen, J., Koivisto, J. & Järvelin, K. Document text characteristics affect the ranking of the most relevant documents by expanded structured queries. Journal of Documentation 57, 3, 358-374.

[9] TREC homepage, Data – English relevance judgements. Available at: http://trec.nist.gov/data/reljudge_eng.html [Cited 31 December 2001].

[10] Voorhees, E. Variations in relevance judgments and the measurement of retrieval effectiveness. In: Croft, W.B. et al. (eds.), Proceedings of the 21st Annual International ACM SIGIR Conference on Research and Development in Information Retrieval (Melbourne, August 1998). ACM Press, New York., 315-323.

[11] Voorhees, E. Evaluation by highly relevant documents. In: Croft, W.B. et al. (eds.). Proceedings of the 24th Annual International ACM SIGIR Conference on Research and Development in Information Retrieval (New Orleans, September 2001). ACM Press, New York, 74-82.

[12] Voorhees, E. Variations in relevance judgments and the measurement of retrieval effectiveness. Information Processing & Management 36, (2000), 697-716.

[13] Voorhees, E. & Harman, D. Overview of the Seventh Text Retrieval Conference (TREC-7). 1999. http://trec.nist.gov/pubs/trec7/papers/overview_7.pdf.gz [Cited 2 January 2002].

[14] Zobel, J. How reliable are the results of large-scale information retrieval experiments? In: Croft, W.B. et al. (eds.), Proceedings of the 21st Annual International ACM SIGIR Conference on Research and Development in Information Retrieval (Melbourne, August 1998). ACM Press, New York.

Robust Temporal and Spectral Modeling for Query By Melody

Shai Shalev-Shwartz
Hebrew University
Jerusalem, Israel
shais@cs.huji.ac.il

Shlomo Dubnov
Ben-Gurion University
Be'er-Sheva,Israel
dubnov@bgumail.bgu.ac.il

Nir Friedman
Hebrew University
Jerusalem, Israel
nir@cs.huji.ac.il

Yoram Singer
The Hebrew University
Jerusalem, Israel
singer@cs.huji.ac.il

ABSTRACT

Query by melody is the problem of retrieving musical performances from melodies. Retrieval of real performances is complicated due to the large number of variations in performing a melody and the presence of colored accompaniment noise. We describe a simple yet effective probabilistic model for this task. We describe a generative model that is rich enough to capture the spectral and temporal variations of musical performances and allows for tractable melody retrieval. While most of previous studies on music retrieval from melodies were performed with either symbolic (e.g. MIDI) data or with *monophonic* (single instrument) performances, we performed experiments in retrieving live and studio recordings of operas that contain a leading vocalist and rich instrumental accompaniment. Our results show that the probabilistic approach we propose is effective and can be scaled to massive datasets.

Categories and Subject Descriptors

H.2.4 [**Database Management**]: Systems—*Multimedia databases, query processing*; H.3.3 [**Information storage and retrieval**]. Information Search and Retrieval—*Query formulation, Retrieval models*; I.5.4 [**Pattern Recognition**]: Applications—*Signal processing.*

General Terms

Algorithms, Experimentation.

Keywords

Music Information Retrieval, Query by Melody, Graphical Models, Spectral Modeling.

1. INTRODUCTION

A natural way for searching a musical audio database for a song is to look for a short audio segment containing a melody from the song. Most of the existing systems are based on textual information, such as the title of the song and the name of the composer. However, people often do not remember the name of the composer and the song's title but can easily recall fragments from the soloist's melody.

The task of *query by melody* attempts to automate the music retrieval task. It was first discussed in the context of query by humming [11, 13, 14]. These works focus on converting hummed melodies into symbolic MIDI format (MIDI is an acronym for Musical Instrument Digital Interface. It is a symbolic format for representing music). Once the query is converted into a symbolic format the challenge is to search for musical performances that approximately match the query. Most of the research so far has been conducted with music stored in MIDI format [12] or in *monophonic* (i.e. single vocal or instrument) recordings (see for instance [9, 7] and the references therein). In this paper, we suggest a method for query by melody where the query is posed in symbolic form as a monophonic melody and the database consists of real polyphonic recordings.

When dealing with real polyphonic recordings we need to address several complicating factors. Ideally melodies can be represented as sequences of notes, each is a pair of frequency and temporal duration. In real recordings two major sources of difficulty arise. The first is the high variability of the actual durations of notes. A melody can be performed faster or slower than the one dictated by the musical score. This type of variation is often referred to as tempo variability. Furthermore, the tempo can vary within a single performance. For instance, a performance can start with a slow tempo which gradually increases. The second complicating factor is the high variability of the spectrum due to many factors such as differences in tone colors (timbre) of different singers/instruments, the intentional variation by the leading vocalists (e.g. vibrato and dynamics) and by "spectral masking" of the leading vocal by the accompanying vocals and orchestra.

We propose to tackle these difficulties by using a generative probabilistic approach that models the temporal and spectral variations. We associate each note with a hidden tempo variable. The tempo variables capture the temporal variations in the durations of notes. To enable efficient computation, the hidden tempo sequence is modeled as a first order Markov process. In addition, we also describe a simple probabilistic spectral distribution model that is robust to the masking noise of the accompanying instruments and

SIGIR'02, August 11-15, 2002, Tampere, Finland.

singers. This spectral distribution model is a variant of the harmonic likelihood model for pitch detection [16]. Combining the temporal and spectral probabilistic components, we obtain a joint model which can be thought of as a dynamic Bayesian network [8]. This representation enables efficient alignment and retrieval using dynamic programming.

This probabilistic approach is related to several recent works that employ Hidden Markov Models (HMM) for music processing. Raphael [15] uses melody information (pitches and durations of notes) in building an HMM for a score following application. A similar approach is taken by Durey and Clements [9] who use the pitch information of notes for building HMMs for melody retrieval. However, both approaches were designed for and evaluated on monophonic music databases. Most work on polyphonic music processing addressed tasks such as music segmentation into textures [6], polyphonic pitch tracking [18], and genre classification [17, 10]. We believe that the approach we describe in this paper is a step toward an effective retrieval procedure for massive musical datasets.

2. PROBLEM SETTING

In our setting, we are given a melody and our task is to retrieve musical performances containing the requested melody and to find its location within the retrieved performances. A melody is a sequence of notes where each note is a pair of a pitch value and a duration value. Our goal is to retrieve melodies from audio signals representing real performances.

Formally, let $\mathcal{R}_+$ denote the positive real numbers. Let $f_l, f_h \in \mathcal{R}_+$ be frequency values (in Hz) and let $[f_l, f_h]$ be a *diapason*. A *diapason* of a singer (or an instrument) is the range of pitch frequencies that are in use by the singer (or by the instrument). For instance, a tenor singer typically employs a *diapason* of $[110Hz, 530Hz]$. Let Λ denote the set of all possible frequencies of notes. In the well-tempered Western music tuning system, $\Lambda = \{f_{ref} \cdot 2^{s/12} | s \in \mathcal{Z}\}$, where $f_{ref} = 440Hz$. Let $\Gamma = [f_{low}, f_{high}] \cap \Lambda$ denote all the possible pitches of notes in the *diapason*. A melody is described formally by a sequence of pitches, $\boldsymbol{p} \in \Gamma^k$, and a sequence of durations, $\boldsymbol{d} \in {\mathcal{R}_+}^k$, in a predefined time units (e.g. seconds or samples).

A performance of a melody is a discrete time sampled audio signal, $\boldsymbol{o} = o_1, ..., o_T$. A performance is formally entirely defined given the melody: play or sing using pitch p_1 for the first d_1 seconds, then play or sing pitch p_2 for the next d_2 seconds, and so on and so forth. In reality, a melody does not impose a rigid framework. The actual frequency content of a given note varies with the type of instrument that is played and by the performer. Examples for such variations are the vibrato and timbre effects. The accompaniment also greatly influences the spectral distribution. While playing a note using pitch p, we are likely to see a local concentration of energy close to multiples of the frequency p in the power spectrum of the signal. However, there may be other spectral regions with high levels of energy. We will address this problem later on in this section. Another source of variation is local scaling of the durations of notes as instructed by the melody. The performer typically uses a tempo that scales the duration and moves from one tempo to another, thus using a different time scale to play the notes. Therefore, we also need to model the variation in the tempo which we describe now.

Rallentando	1.2 1.2 1.25 1.3 1.3
Accelerando	0.7 0.65 0.6 0.5 0.5

Table 1: Examples of scaling factor sequences: In the first sequence the scaling factors are gradually increasing and thus the tempo is decreasing ("Rallentando"). In the second example the scaling factors are decreasing and the tempo is increasing ("Accelerando").

A tempo sequence is a sequence of scaling factors, $\boldsymbol{m} \in {\mathcal{R}_+}^k$. The actual duration of note i, denoted $\widetilde{d}_i$ is d_i scaled by m_i, $\widetilde{d}_i = d_i m_i$. Seemingly, allowing different scaling factors for the different notes adds a degree of freedom that makes the melody duration values redundant. However, a typical tempo sequence does not change rapidly and thus reflects most of the information of the original durations (up to a scaling factor). Table 1 shows two examples of tempo sequences. A pitch–duration–tempo triplet $(\boldsymbol{p}, \boldsymbol{d}, \boldsymbol{m})$ generates an actual pitch–duration pair $(\boldsymbol{p}, \widetilde{\boldsymbol{d}})$.

In order to describe the generation of the actual performance audio signal $\boldsymbol{o}$ from $(\boldsymbol{p}, \widetilde{\boldsymbol{d}})$ we introduce one more variable, $\boldsymbol{s} \in {\mathcal{R}_+}^k$ where s_i is the starting time (sample number) of note i in the performance. We define $s_i = 1 + \sum_{j=1}^{i-1} \widetilde{d}_j$ for $i = 1, \ldots, k+1$. Notes generate consecutive blocks of signal samples. Let $\bar{o}_i = (o_{s_i}, ..., o_{s_{i+1}-1})$ be the block of samples generated by note i.

The power spectrum of $\bar{o}_i$ varies significantly from performance to performance, according to various factors such as the spectral envelope of the soloist and pitches of accompaniment instruments. Since our goal is to locate and retrieve a melody from a dataset that may contain thousands of performances, we resort to a very simple spectral model and do not explicitly model these variables. We use an approximation to the likelihood of a block spectrum given its pitch.

3. FROM MELODY TO SIGNAL: A GENERATIVE MODEL

To pose the problem in a probabilistic framework, we need to describe the likelihood of a performance given the melody, $P(\boldsymbol{o}|\boldsymbol{p}, \boldsymbol{d})$. We cast the tempo sequence $\boldsymbol{m}$ as a hidden random variable, thus the likelihood can be written as,

$$P(\boldsymbol{o}|\boldsymbol{p}, \boldsymbol{d}) = \sum_{\boldsymbol{m}} P(\boldsymbol{o}, \boldsymbol{m}|\boldsymbol{p}, \boldsymbol{d}) \ . \qquad (1)$$

For simplicity, we assume that the tempo sequence does not depend on the melody. While this assumption, naturally, does not always hold, we found empirically that these types of correlations can be ignored in short pieces of performances. With this assumption and the identity $\widetilde{\boldsymbol{d}} = \boldsymbol{dm}$,

Equ. (1) can be rewritten as,

$$P(\boldsymbol{o}|\boldsymbol{p},\boldsymbol{d}) = \sum_{\boldsymbol{m}} P(\boldsymbol{m}|\boldsymbol{p},\boldsymbol{d})P(\boldsymbol{o}|\boldsymbol{p},\boldsymbol{d},\boldsymbol{m}) = \sum_{\boldsymbol{m}} P(\boldsymbol{m})P(\boldsymbol{o}|\boldsymbol{p},\boldsymbol{d},\boldsymbol{m}) = \sum_{\boldsymbol{m}} P(\boldsymbol{m})P(\boldsymbol{o}|\boldsymbol{p},\tilde{\boldsymbol{d}}) \ .$$

We now need to specify the prior distribution over the tempo, $P(\boldsymbol{m})$, and the posterior distribution of the signal given the pitches and the actual durations of the notes $P(\boldsymbol{o}|\boldsymbol{p},\tilde{\boldsymbol{d}})$.

3.1 Tempo modeling

We chose to model the tempo sequence as a first order Markov process. As we see in the sequel this choice on one hand allows an efficient alignment and retrieval, and on the other hand, was found empirically to be rich enough. Therefore, the likelihood of $\boldsymbol{m}$ is given by,

$$P(\boldsymbol{m}) = P(m_1)\prod_{i=2}^{k} P(m_i|m_{i-1}) \ .$$

We use the log-normal distribution to model the conditional probability $P(m_i|m_{i-1})$, that is $\log_2(m_i) \sim \mathcal{N}(\log_2(m_{i-1}),\rho)$, where ρ is a scaling parameter of the variance. The prior distribution of the first scaling factor $P(m_1)$ is also assumed to be log-normal around zero with variance ρ, $\log_2(m_i) \sim \mathcal{N}(0,\rho)$. In our experiments, the parameter ρ was determined manually according to musical knowledge. This parameter can also be learned from MIDI files.

3.2 Spectral Distribution Model

In this section we describe our spectral distribution model. There exist quite a few models for the spectral distribution of singing voices and harmonic instruments. However, most of these models are rather general. These models typically assume that the musical signal is contaminated with white noise whose energy is statistically independent of the signal. See for instance [16] and the references therein. In contrast, we assume that there is a leading instrument, or soloist, that is accompanied by an orchestra or a chorus. The energy of the accompaniment is typically highly correlated with the energy of the soloist. Put another way, the dynamics of the accompaniment matches the dynamics of the soloist. For instance, when the soloist sings pianissimo the chorus follows her with pianissimo voices. We therefore developed a simple model whose parameters can be efficiently estimated that copes with the correlation in energy between the leading soloist and the accompaniment. In Fig. 1 we show the spectrum of one frame of a performance signal from our database. The harmonics are designated by dashed lines. It is clear from the figure that there is a large concentration of energy at the designated harmonics. The residual energy, outside the harmonics, is certainly non-negligible but is clearly lower than the energy of the harmonics. Thus, our assumptions, although simplistic, seem to capture to a large extent the characteristics of the spectrum of singing with accompaniment.

Using the definition of a block $\bar{o}_i$ from Sec. 2, the likelihood of the signal given the sequences of pitches and durations can be decomposed into a product of likelihood values

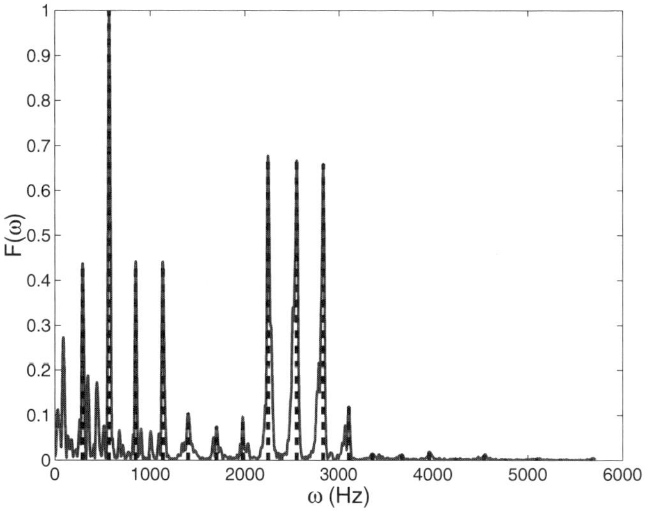

Figure 1: The spectrum of a single frame along with an impulse train designating the harmonics of the soloist.

of the individual blocks,

$$P(\boldsymbol{o}|\tilde{\boldsymbol{d}},\boldsymbol{p}) = \prod_{i=1}^{k} P(\bar{o}_i|p_i) \ .$$

Therefore, the core of our modeling approach is a probabilistic model for the spectral distribution of a whole block given the underlying pitch frequency of the soloist. Our starting point is similar to the model presented in [16]. We assume that a note with pitch p_i attains high energy at frequencies which are multiples of p_i, namely at $p_i h$ for integer h. These frequencies are often referred to as harmonics. Since our signal is band limited, we only need to consider a finite set of harmonics h, $h \in \{1,2,...,H\}$. For practical purposes we set H to be 20 which enables a fast parameter estimation procedure. Let $F(\omega)$ denote the observed energy of the block $\bar{o}_i$ at frequency ω. Let $S(\omega)$ denote the energy of the soloist at frequency ω. The harmonic model assumes that $S(\cdot)$ is bursts of energy centered at the harmonics of the pitch frequency, $p_i h$, and we model it as a weighted sum of delta functions,

$$S(\omega) = \sum_{h=1}^{H} A(h)\delta(p_i h - \omega) \ , \tag{2}$$

where $A(h)$ is the volume gain for the harmonic whose index is h. The residual of the spectrum at frequency ω is denoted $N(\omega)$ and is equal to $N(\omega) = F(\omega) - S(\omega)$. We now describe a probabilistic model that leads to the following log-likelihood score,

$$\log P(\bar{o}_i|p_i) \propto \log \frac{\|S\|^2}{\|N\|^2} \ , \tag{3}$$

where $\|\cdot\|$ denotes the ℓ_2-norm.

To derive the above equation we assume that the spectrum of the ith block, F, is comprised of two components. The first component is the energy of the soloist, $S(\omega)$ as defined in Equ. (2). The second component is a general masking noise that encompasses the signal's energy due to the accompaniment and affects the entire spectrum. We denote the noise energy at frequency ω as $\eta(\omega)$. The energy of the spectrum at frequency ω is therefore modeled as,

$$F(\omega) = \sum_{h=1}^{H} A(h)\left(\eta(\omega) + \delta(p_i h - \omega)\right) \ . \quad (4)$$

We now impose another simplifying assumption by setting the noise η to be a multivariate normal random variable and further assuming that the noise values at each frequency ω are statistically independent with equal variance. Thus, the noise density function is

$$f(\eta|v) = \frac{1}{(2\pi v)^{L/2}} e^{-\frac{\|\eta\|^2}{2v}} \quad (5)$$

where v is the variance and L is the number of spectral points computed by the discrete Fourier transform. (We chose $L = 2^{15}$ to get a good spectral resolution.) Taking the log of the above density function we get,

$$\log f(\eta|v) = -\frac{L}{2}\log(2\pi v) - \frac{\|\eta\|^2}{2v} \ . \quad (6)$$

The gain values $A(h)$ are free parameters which we need to estimate from the spectrum. Assuming that the noise level is relatively small compared to the bursts of energy at the harmonics of the pitch frequency, we set the value of $A(h)$ to be $F(p_i h)$. We also do not know the noise variance v. For this free parameter we use the simple maximum likelihood (ML) estimate which can be easily found as follows. The maximum likelihood estimate of v is found by taking the derivative of $\log f(\eta|v)$ with respect to v,

$$\frac{\partial \log f(\eta|v)}{\partial v} = -\frac{L}{2}\frac{2\pi}{2\pi v} + \frac{\|\eta\|^2}{2v^2} = 0 \quad \Rightarrow v^* = \frac{\|\eta\|^2}{L} \ .$$

Rearranging Equ. (4), the noise value at frequency ω, $\eta(\omega)$, can be written as,

$$\eta(\omega) = \frac{F(\omega) - \sum_{h=1}^{H} A(h)\delta(p_i h - \omega)}{\sum_{h=1}^{H} A(h)} \ .$$

By using above equation for $\eta(\omega)$ along with values set for $A(h)$ and the maximum likelihood estimate v^* in Equ. (6) we get,

$$\begin{aligned}\log f(\eta|v*) &= -\frac{L}{2}(\log(2\pi) + \log(\|\eta\|^2) - \log(L) - 1) \\ &= c + \frac{L}{2}\log\left(\frac{\|S\|^2}{\|N\|^2}\right) \ . \quad (8)\end{aligned}$$

Since the stochastic ingredient of our spectral model is the accompanying noise, the noise likelihood above also constitute the likelihood of the spectrum.

To summarize, we now overview our approach for retrieval. We are given a melody $(\boldsymbol{p}, \boldsymbol{d})$ and we want to find an audio signal $\boldsymbol{o}$ which represents a performance of this melody. Using our probabilistic framework, we cast the problem as the problem of finding a signal portion $\boldsymbol{o}$ whose likelihood given the melody, $P(\boldsymbol{o}|\boldsymbol{p}, \boldsymbol{d})$, is high. Our search strategy is as follows. We find the best alignment of the signal to the melody as we describe in the next section. The score of the alignment procedure we devise is also our means for retrieval. We then rank the segments of signals in accordance with their likelihood scores and return the segments achieving high likelihoods scores.

1. **Initialization**

$$\forall_{1 \le t \le T}, \gamma(0, t, 1) = 1$$

2. **Recursion**

$$\gamma(i, t, \xi) = \max_{\xi' \in M} \gamma(i-1, t', \xi') P(\xi|\xi') P(o_{t'+1}, \ldots, o_t|p_i)$$

where $t' = t - d_i\xi$.

3. **Termination**

$$P^* = \max_{1 \le t \le T,\ \xi \in M} \gamma(k, t, \xi)$$

Figure 2: The alignment algorithm.

4. ALIGNMENT AND RETRIEVAL

Alignment of a melody to a signal is performed by finding the best assignment of a tempo sequence. Formally, we are looking for the scaling factors $\boldsymbol{m}^*$ that attain the highest likelihood score, $\boldsymbol{m}^* = \arg\max_{\boldsymbol{m}} P(\boldsymbol{o}, \boldsymbol{m}|\boldsymbol{d}, \boldsymbol{p})$. Although the number of possible sequences of scaling factors $\boldsymbol{m}$ grows exponentially with the sequence length, the problem of finding $\boldsymbol{m}^*$ can be efficiently solved using dynamic programming, as we now describe.

Let $\boldsymbol{m}^i = (m_1, ..., m_i)$ denote the scaling factors of the first i notes of a melody. Let $\boldsymbol{o}^t = (o_1, ..., o_t)$ denote the first t samples of a signal. Let M be a discrete set of possible scaling factor values. For $\xi \in M$, let $M_{i,t,\xi}$ be a set of all possible sequences of i scaling factors, $\boldsymbol{m}^i$, such that $m_i = \xi$ is the scaling factor of note i and $t = \sum_{j=1}^{i} m_j d_j$ is the actual ending time of note i. Let $\gamma(i, t, \xi)$ be the joint likelihood of $\boldsymbol{o}^t$ and $\boldsymbol{m}^i \in M_{i,t,\xi}$

$$\gamma(i, t, \xi) = \max_{\boldsymbol{m}^i \in M_{i,t,\xi}} P(\boldsymbol{o}^t, \boldsymbol{m}^i|\boldsymbol{p}, \boldsymbol{d})$$

The pseudo code for computing $\gamma(i, t, \xi)$ recursively is shown in Fig. 2.

The most likely sequence of scaling factors $\boldsymbol{m}^*$ is obtained from the algorithm by saving the intermediate values that maximize each expression in the recursion step. The complexity of the algorithm is $O(kT|M|^2 D)$, where k is the number of notes, T is the number of samples in the digital signal, $|M|$ is the number of all possible tempo values and D is the maximal duration of a note. Using a pre-computation of the likelihood values we can reduce the time complexity by a factor of D and thus the run time of the algorithm reduces to $O(kT|M|^2)$. It is important to clarify that the pre-computation does not completely determine a single pitch value for a frame. It calculates the probability of the frame given each possible pitch in the diapason.

As mentioned above, our primary goal is to retrieve the segments of signals representing the melody given by the query. Theoretically, we need to assign a segment $\boldsymbol{o}$ its likelihood score, $P(\boldsymbol{o}|\boldsymbol{p},\boldsymbol{d}) = \sum_{\boldsymbol{m}} P(\boldsymbol{m}|\boldsymbol{p},\boldsymbol{d})$. However, this marginal probability is rather expensive to compute. We thus approximate this probability with the joint probability of the signal and most likely sequence of scaling factors, $P(\boldsymbol{o},\boldsymbol{m}^*|\boldsymbol{p},\boldsymbol{d})$. That is, we use the likelihood score of the alignment procedure as a retrieval score.

5. EXPERIMENTAL RESULTS

To evaluate our algorithm we collected 50 different melodies from famous opera arias, and queried these melodies in a database of real recordings. The recordings consist of 832 performances of opera arias performed by more then 40 different tenor singers with full orchestral accompaniment. Each performance is one minute. The data was extracted from seven audio CDs [2, 3, 5, 1, 4], and saved in *wav* format. Most of the performances (about 90 percent) are digital recordings (DDD/ADD). Yet, some performances are digital remastering of old analog recordings (AAD). This introduced additional complexity to the retrieval task due to varying level of noise.

The melodies for the experiments were extracted from MIDI files. About half of the MIDI files were downloaded from the Internet [1] and the rest of the MIDI files were performed on a MIDI keyboard and saved as MIDI files.

We compared three different tempo-based approaches for retrieval. The first method simply uses the original durations given in the query without any scaling. We refer to this simplistic approach as the *Fixed Tempo* (FT) model. The second approach uses a single scaling factor for all the durations of a given melody. However, this scaling factor is determined independently for each signal so as to maximize the signals likelihood. We refer to this model as the *Locally Fixed Tempo* (LFT) model. The third retrieval method is our variable tempo model that we introduced in this paper. We therefore refer to this method as the *Variable Tempo* (VT) model. By taking a prefix subset of each melody used in a query we evaluated three different lengths of melodies: 5 seconds, 15 seconds, and 25 seconds.

To assess the quality of the spectral distribution model described in Sec. 3.2, we implemented the spectral distribution model described in [16]. This model assumes that the harmonics of the signal are contaminated with noise whose mean energy is independent of the energy of the harmonics. We refer to our model as the *Harmonics with Scaled Noise* (HSN) model and to the model from [16] as the *Harmonics with Independent Noise* (HIN) model.

To evaluate the performances of the methods we used three evaluation measures: *one-error*, *coverage* and *average precision*. To explain these measures we introduce the following notation. Let N be the number of performances in our database and let M be the number of melodies that we search for. (As mentioned above, in our experiments $N = 832$ and $M = 50$.) For a melody index i we denote by Y_i the set of the performances containing melody i. The probabilistic modeling we discussed in this paper induces a natural ordering over the performances for each melody. Let $R_i(j)$ denote the ranking of the performance indexed j with respect to melody i. Based on the above definitions we now give the formal definitions of the performance measures we used for evaluation.

One-Error. The one-error measures how many times the top-ranked performance did *not* contain the melody posed in the query. Thus, if the goal of our system is to return a single performance that contains the melody, the one-error measures how many times the retrieved performance did not contain the melody. Formally, the definition of the one-error is,

$$\text{OErr} = \frac{1}{M}\sum_{i=1}^{M}[\![\arg\min_j R_i(j) \notin Y_i]\!] \ .$$

where $[\![\pi]\!] = 1$ if predicate π holds and 0 otherwise.

Coverage. While the one-error evaluates the performance of a system with respect to the top-ranked performance, the goal of the coverage measure is to assess the performance of the system for all of the possible performances of a melody. Informally, Coverage measures the number of excess (non-relevant) performances we need to scan until we retrieve all the relevant performances. Formally, Coverage is defined as,

$$\text{Cov} = \frac{1}{M}\sum_{i=1}^{M}(\max_{j\in Y_i} R_i(j) - |Y_i|) \ .$$

Average Precision. The above measures do not suffice in evaluating the performances of retrieval systems as one can achieve good (low) coverage but suffer high one-error rates, and vice versa. In order to assess the ranking performance as a whole we use the frequently used average precision measure. Formally, the average precision is defined as,

$$\text{AvgP} = \frac{1}{M}\sum_{i=1}^{M}\frac{1}{|Y_i|}\sum_{j\subset Y_i}\frac{|\{j' \in Y_i | R_i(j') \le R_i(j)\}|}{R_i(j)} \ .$$

In addition we also use precision versus recall graphs to illustrate the overall performances of the different approaches discussed in the paper. A precision-recall graph shows the level of precision for different recall values. The graphs presented in this paper are non-interpolated, that is, they were calculated based on the precision and recall values achieved at integer positions of the ranked lists.

In Table 2 we report results with respect to the performance measures described for the FT, LFT, and VT models. For each tempo model we conducted the experiments with the two spectral distribution models HIN and HSN. It is clear from the table that the *Variable Tempo* model with the *Harmonics with Scaled Noise* spectral distribution outperforms the rest of the models and achieves superior results. Moreover, the performance of the *Variable Tempo* model consistently improves as the duration of the queries increases. In contrast, the *Fixed Tempo* does not exhibit any improvement as the duration of the queries increases and the *Locally Fixed Tempo* shows only a moderate improvement when using fifteen second long queries instead of five second long queries and it does not improve as the duration grows to twenty five seconds. A reasonable explanation for these phenomena is that the amount of variability in a very short query is naturally limited and thus the leverage

[1] http://www.aria-database.com,
http://www.musicscore.freeserve.co.uk,
http://www.classicalmidi.gothere.uk.com

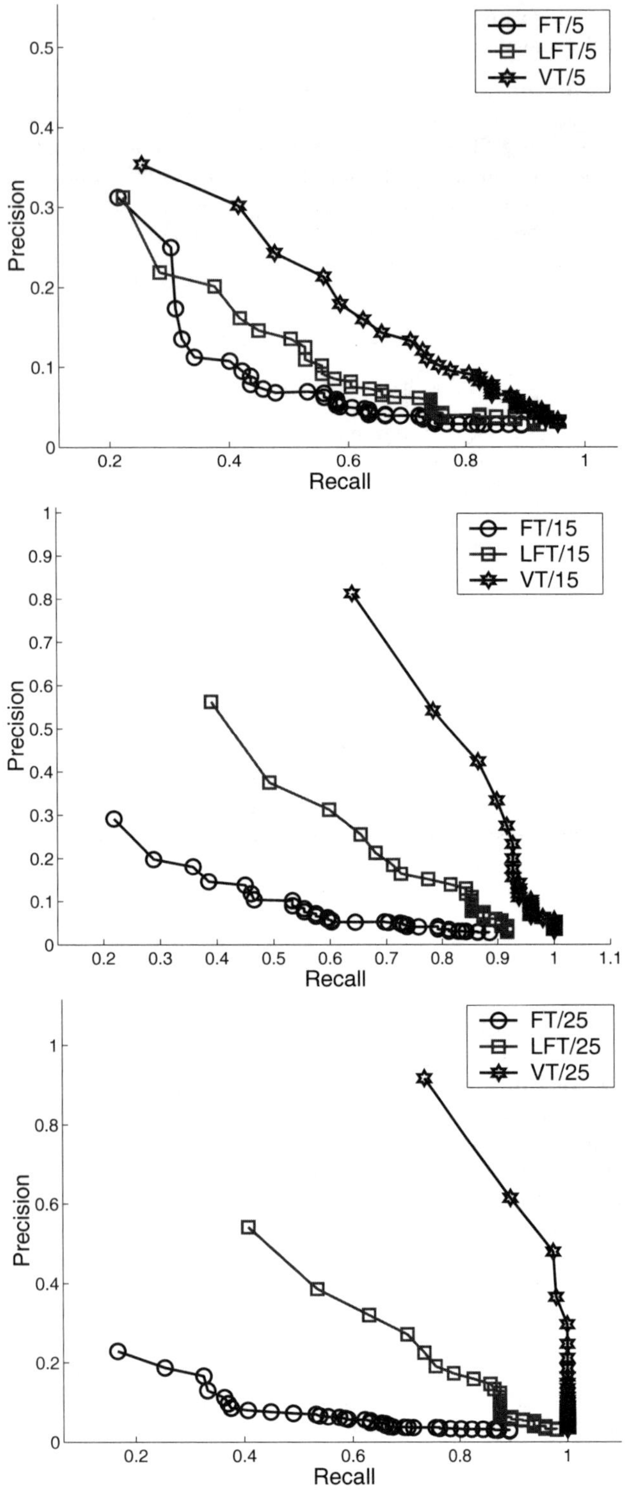

Figure 3: Precision-recall curves comparing the performance of three tempo models for queries consisting of five seconds (top), fifteen second (middle), and twenty five seconds (bottom).

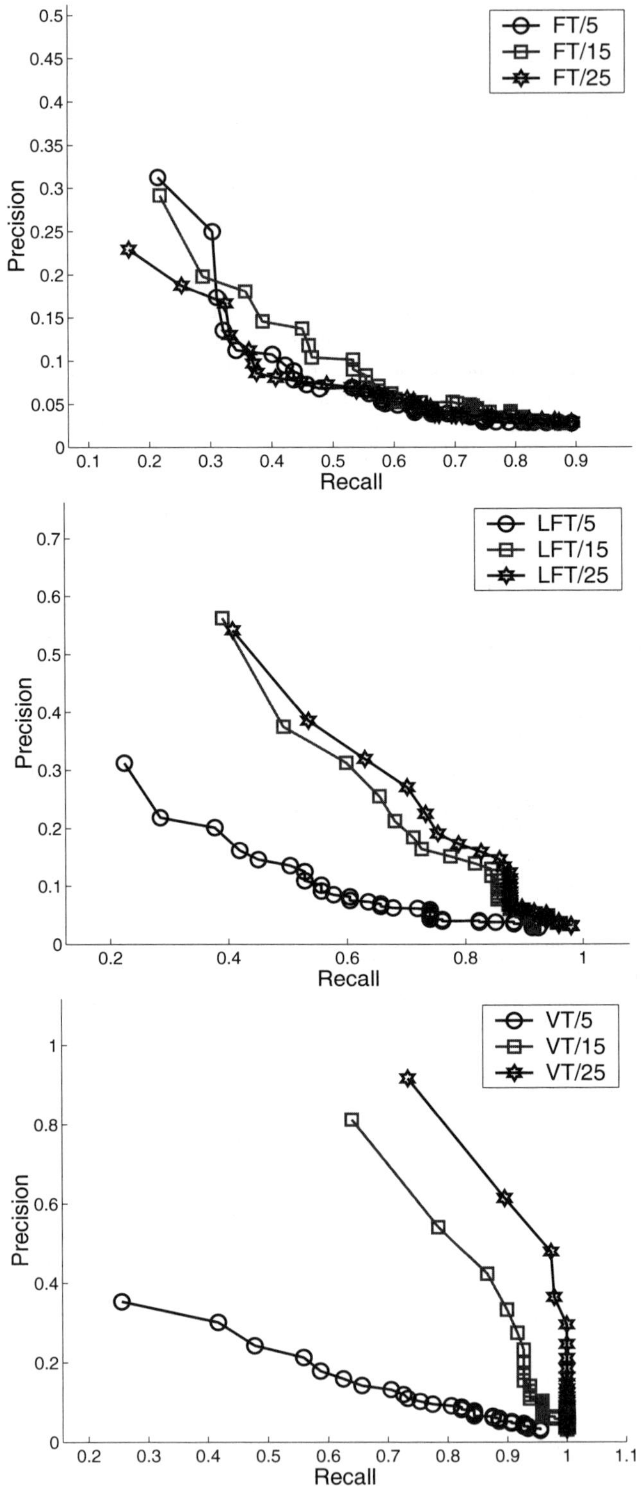

Figure 4: Precision-recall curves comparing the performance of each of the tempo models for three different query lengths.

			Spectral Distribution Model					
			HSN			HIN		
			AvgP	Cov	Oerr	AvgP	Cov	Oerr
Melody length (sec.)	25	VT	**0.95**	**0.21**	**0.08**	0.92	0.40	0.10
		LFT	0.66	5.90	0.46	0.63	5.98	0.48
		FT	0.34	20.69	0.77	0.33	22.46	0.79
	15	VT	**0.86**	**1.75**	**0.19**	0.83	3.02	0.19
		LFT	0.66	8.10	0.44	0.66	8.15	0.42
		FT	0.38	19.83	0.71	0.36	19.08	0.73
	5	VT	**0.51**	**10.67**	**0.65**	0.46	11.83	0.69
		LFT	0.43	17.33	0.69	0.37	17.94	0.75
		FT	0.38	22.96	0.69	0.35	21.67	0.75

Table 2: Retrieval results

gained by accurate tempo modeling which takes into account the variability in tempo is rather small. Thus, as the query duration grows the power of the variable tempo model is better exploited. The *Locally Fixed Tempo* can capture the average tempo of a performance but clearly fails to capture changes in the tempo. Since the chance of a tempo change grows with the duration of the query the average tempo stops from being a good approximation and we do not see further improvement in the retrieval quality.

In Fig 3 we give precision-recall graphs that compare the three tempo models. Each graph compares FT, LFT and VT for different query durations. The VT model clearly outperforms both the FT and LFT models. The longer the query the wider the gap in performance. In Fig 4 we compare the precision-recall graphs for each model as a function of the query duration. Each graph shows the precision-recall curves for 5, 15, and 25 seconds queries. We again see that only the VT model consistently improves with the increase in the query duration. Using a globally fixed tempo (FT) is clearly inadequate as it results in very poor performance – precision is never higher than 0.35 even for low level of recall. The performance of the LFT model is more reasonable. A precision of about 0.5 can be achieved for a recall value of 0.5. However, the full power of our approach is utilized only when we use the VT model. We achieve an average precision of 0.92 with a recall of 0.75. It seems that with the VT model we reach an overall performance that can serve as the basis for large scale music retrieval systems.

Lastly, as a final sanity check of the conjecture of the robustness of the VT model we used the VT and LFT model with three long melody queries (one minute) and applied the retrieval and alignment process. We then let a professional musician listen to the segmentation and browse the segmented spectogram. An example of a spectogram with a segmentation of the VT model is given in Fig 5. The example is of a performance where the energy of accompaniment is higher than the energy of the leading tenor. Nonetheless, a listening experiment verified that our system was able to properly segment and align the melody posed by the query. Although these perceptual listening tests are subjective, the experiments indicated that the VT model also provides an accurate alignment and segmentation.

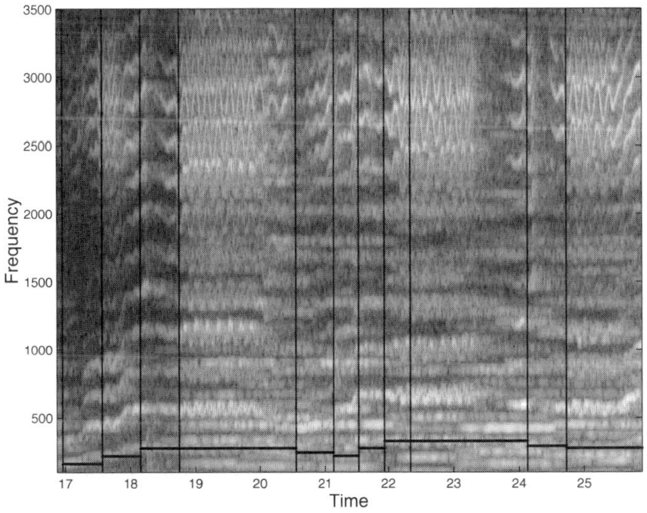

Figure 5: An illustration of the alignment and segmentation of the VT model. The pitches of the notes in the melody are overlayed in solid lines.

6. DISCUSSION

In this paper we presented a robust probabilistic model for query by melody. The proposed approach is simple to implement and was found to work well on polyphony-rich recordings with various types of accompaniments. The probabilistic model that we developed focuses on two main sources of variability. The first is variations in the actual durations of notes in real recordings (tempo variability) and the second is the variability of the spectrum mainly due to the "spectral masking" of the leading vocal by the accompanying vocals and orchestra. In this work we assumed that the pitch information in a query is accurate and only the duration can be altered in the performance. This assumption is reasonable if the queries are posed using a symbolic input mechanism such as a MIDI keyboard. However, an easier and more convenient mechanism is to hum or whistle a melody. This task is often called "query by humming". In addition to the tempo variability and spectral masking, a query by humming system also needs to take into account imperfections in the pitch of the hummed melody. Indeed, much of the work on query by humming have been devoted to music retrieval using noisy pitch information. The majority of the work on query by humming though have focused on search of noisy queries in symbolic databases. Since the main thrust of this research is searches in real polyphonic recordings, it complements the research on query by humming and can supplement numerous systems that search in symbolic databases. We plan to extend our algorithm so it can be combined with a front end for hummed queries. In addition, we have started conducting research on supervised methods for musical genre classification. We believe that by combining highly accurate genre classification with a robust retrieval and alignment we will be able to provide an effective tool for searching and browsing for both professionals and amateurs.

Acknowledgments

We would like to thank Moria Koffman for her help in creating the queries used in the experiments and Leo Kontorovitch for useful comments on the manuscript.

7. REFERENCES

[1] Arien. famous tenor arias. Decca 450 005-2.

[2] Best of opera. Disky 701812.

[3] Les 40 tenors. EMI 5720072 (Two CDs).

[4] Luciano pavarotti. nessun dorma, arias and duets. Decca 467 462-2.

[5] The young domingo. BMG 63527 (Two CDs).

[6] J. Aucouturier and S. M. Segmentation of musical signals using hidden markov models. *Audio Engineering Society*, May 2001.

[7] R. Dannenberg. An on-line algorithm for real-time accompaniment. *Proc. Int'l Computer Music Conference*, 1984.

[8] T. Dean and K. Kanazawa. A model for reasoning about persistent and causation. *Computational Intelligence*, 5(3):142–150, 1989.

[9] A. S. Durey and M. A. Clements. Melody spotting using hidden Markov models. In *Proceedings of the International Symposium on Music Information Retrieval*, pages 109–117, Bloomington, IN, October 2001.

[10] J. Foote. An overview of audio information retrieval. *Multimedia Systems*, 7(1):2–10, 1999.

[11] A. Ghias, J. Logan, D. Chamberlin, and B. C. Smith. Query by humming: Musical information retrieval in an audio database. In *ACM Multimedia*, pages 231–236, 1995.

[12] K. Lemstrom and J. Tarhio. Searching monophonic patterns within polyphonic sources. In *Proc. Content-Based Multimedia Information Access (RIAO'2000)*, pages 1261–1279, April 2000.

[13] R. McNab, L. Smith, D. Bainbridge, and I. Witten. The new zealand digital library melody index, 1997.

[14] M. Mongeau and D. Sankoff. Comparison of musical sequences. *Computers and the Humanities, 24:161– 175*, 1990.

[15] C. Raphael. Automatic segmentation of acoustic musical signals using hidden markov models. *IEEE transactions on Pattern Analysis and Machine Intelligence*, 21(4), Apr. 1999.

[16] J. Tabrikian, S. Dubnov, and Y. Dickalov. Speech enhancement by harmonic modeling via map pitch tracking. *ICASSP2002, Orlando, Florida*, 2002.

[17] G. Tzanetakis and P. Cook. Audio information retrieval (air) tools. In *Proc. International Symposium on Music Information Retrieval*, 2000.

[18] P. Walmsley, S. Godsill, and P. Rayner. Polyphonic pitch tracking using joint bayesian estimation of multiple frame parameters. In *Proc. 1999 Ieee Workshop on Applications of Signal Processing to Audio and Acoustics*, Oct. 1999.

Video Retrieval using an MPEG-7 Based Inference Network

Andrew Graves
Department of Computer Science
Queen Mary, University of London
London, England, E1 4NS
andrew@dcs.qmul.ac.uk

Mounia Lalmas
Department of Computer Science
Queen Mary, University of London
London, England, E1 4NS
mounia@dcs.qmul.ac.uk

ABSTRACT

This work proposes a model for video retrieval based upon the inference network model. The document network is constructed using video metadata encoded using MPEG-7 and captures information pertaining to the structural aspects (video breakdown into shots and scenes), conceptual aspects (video, scene and shot content) and contextual aspects (context information about the position of conceptual content within the document). The retrieval process a) exploits the distribution of evidence among the shots to perform ranking of different levels of granularity, b) addresses the idea that evidence may be inherited during evaluation, and c) exploits the contextual information to perform constrained queries.

Keywords

Structured Video Retrieval, MPEG-7, Inference network, Combination of evidence

Categories and Subject Descriptors

H.3.3 [**Information Storage and Retrieval**]: Information Search and Retrieval—*Retrieval models*; H.3.7 [**Information Storage and Retrieval**]: Digital Libraries—*Standards*

General Terms

Theory, Management

1. INTRODUCTION

Recent years have witnessed a large increase in the usage and generation of digital video information. As a consequence, there is a need for advanced video storage, transmission, indexing and retrieval techniques. The goal of video retrieval systems is to find video data upon demand, but not necessarily to understand it. An initial step in video processing systems is to ascertain the shots and scenes in the video by performing shot-boundary-detection and scene-change-detection. This is an active research area whereby a video is decomposed into its constituent shots (syntactic boundaries) and scenes (semantic boundaries) [17].

The common video retrieval method has been to adopt a query-by-example content-based approach, whereby the video data is quantified according to the detectable features (such as colour, texture or motion) and compared against a submitted query clip (or keyframe) to form a similarity metric, which is then used to perform ranking. The effectiveness of this approach is limited owing to the semantic gap [5] that exists between the user and the system. Whereas the user has an inherent information need expressed in semantics, or high-level concepts, the system operates according to the low-level features. Either the user has to make the semantic-content translation or has to find a suitable video clip (or keyframe) to represent the query. Adopting this approach also makes the assumption that semantically similar video-clips have a small distance between them in feature space which is not always the case.

Clearly there is the need to adopt a semantic based approach, whereby the content-semantic translation is done by the system and the query is expressed in semantic keywords. Such as system would involve the automatic extraction of semantics (or automatic generation of video annotation) [13], the storage of these semantics in some suitable arbitrary metadata format, and finally, performing keyword based retrieval based upon the metadata [9].

MPEG-7, formally called "*Multimedia Content Description Interface*", is a new standard that aims at describing the content of multimedia data by attaching metadata to multimedia content. MPEG-7 specifies a standard set of description tools, which can be used to describe various types of multimedia information. In this paper, we are concerned with the development of access methods for searching video data using MPEG-7 annotation. Our aim is not to derive the MPEG-7 annotation that shall be associated with a video stream, but to develop a model that exploits the characteristics of MPEG-7 for the effective retrieval of video data.

We use the inference network as a basis for the model because the inference network is able to represent the distributed multitude of evidence abundant in MPEG-7, in particular structural, conceptual, and contextual aspects. The video structure (ie: video breakdown into scenes and shots) is extensively dealt with in MPEG-7 and allows us to produce a ranking for each structural element. The concepts within the video are extracted from certain MPEG-7 elements known to contain concepts (eg: using the terms within the video <Abstract> element). The information regarding the document-content relationship in MPEG-7 (eg: the position of the concept within the document metadata) is considered to provide context. Such contextual information can be exploited to perform constrained queries (eg: retrieve documents with a certain concept within a certain context).

The rest of the paper is structured as follows: Section 2 introduces the background material of MPEG-7 and inference network; Section 3 introduces our model for MPEG-7 based retrieval; Sec-

SIGIR'02, August 11-15, 2002, Tampere, Finland.

tion 4 presents an example network showing how the probabilities are estimated; Section 5 presents an illustration of video retrieval; and Section 6 presents some concluding remarks.

2. BACKGROUND

We consider video indexing and retrieval systems to consist of two modules: the video analysis module (or *indexer*); and the video retrieval module. The video analysis module processes the video to extract low-level and high-level information, both of which can then be stored in an MPEG-7 file. In this work we are concerned with exploiting high-level MPEG-7 annotation, as well as the video structure, for performing retrieval using the inference network model.

2.1 Structured Document Retrieval

We consider a video document to be a structured document as illustrated in figure 1. The video consists of scenes which themselves consist of shots. This structure can be ascertained using video processing techniques such as shot-boundary-detection and scene-boundary-detection.

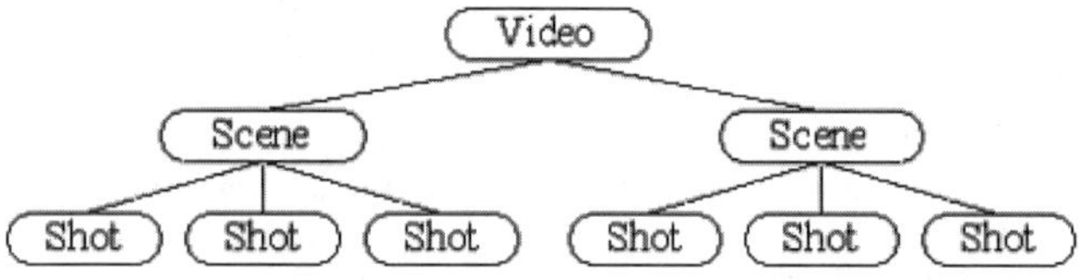

Figure 1: The structural nature of video

We aim to build a retrieval system that is capable of ranking different levels of granularity [7] (ie: video, scene and shot in the result ranking), as the individual scenes and shots may be more relevant to the query than the entire video. We consider the evidence pertaining to a video object as being contained within the scenes, and a similar dissemination of scene evidence occurs among the shots. To perform retrieval the question of evidence aggregation must be answered.

In previous work [16], we aimed to provide the best entry points into a hierarchical structure, given the aggregated evidence in the individual objects. In the model presented in this paper, we perform an estimation of document relevance for each retrievable element in turn where the distributed evidence is considered. The result is a ranked list consisting of the various document component types

2.2 MPEG-7

MPEG-7 is a standard derived by the Moving Pictures Expert Group [11]. It has the ability to describe the low-level features, high-level semantics and structural aspects of any multimedia file. The standard is both extensive and extendible and is becoming increasingly popular [6, 15, 14] as the metadata format of choice for building practical multimedia information systems.

MPEG-7 consists of the following three main components, the relationship between which is shown in figure 2.

- Description Definition Language (DDL), based on the XML Scheme language.

- Descriptors (D), representing the individual items of information.

- Description Schemes (DS), modelling the organisation of the Descriptors.

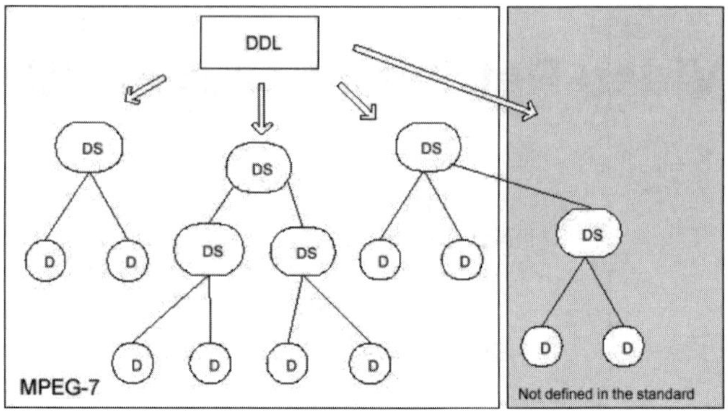

Figure 2: The main MPEG-7 components

We are concerned with the representation of the structural aspects (ie: video, scene and shots) and the high-level semantics (or concepts). The structural breakdown of a video can be described using the <Segment> and <SegmentDecomposition> DSs. The concepts associated to the video, scene and shot elements are then described in various Descriptors including the <TextAnnotation> Descriptor, an example of which is given below.

```
<TextAnnotation>
   <FreeTextAnnotation>
      Basil attempts to mend the
      car without success
   </FreeTextAnnotation>
   <StructuredAnnotation>
      <Who>Basil</Who>
      <WhatObject>Car</WhatObject>
      <WhatAction>Mend</WhatAction>
      <Where>Carpark</Where>
   </StructuredAnnotation>
</TextAnnotation>
```

The above excerpt contains high-level semantics that could be associated with either the video or one of the scenes or shots. It is important to note the unusual behaviour of evidence within this structure: if this information were associated with the video, then it also applies to the scenes and shots (a form of *evidence inheritance*); if this information were associated with a scene or shot, then it inherently applies to the video as the video contains the scene or shot.

2.3 Inference Network Model

To model the evidence contained within the MPEG-7 documents, and specifically, the structural and unusual conceptual characteristic of evidence inheritance, we adopt the Inference Network model for IR as developed by Turtle [18]. The Inference Network (IN) model has ability to perform a ranking given many sources of evidence by performing a combination of evidence. The IN model is basically a Bayesian Network used to model documents, the document contents, and the query. The IN consists of two sub-networks: the Document Network (DN) produced during indexing and then static during retrieval; the Query Network (QN) produced from the query text during retrieval.

The DN represents the document collection and consists of nodes for each document (called document nodes) and nodes for each concept with the collection (document concept nodes). The document nodes represent the retrievable units within the network, that is, those items we wish to see in the resultant ranking. A causal link (represented as $\longrightarrow$) between document node and the document concept node indicates that the document content is represented by the

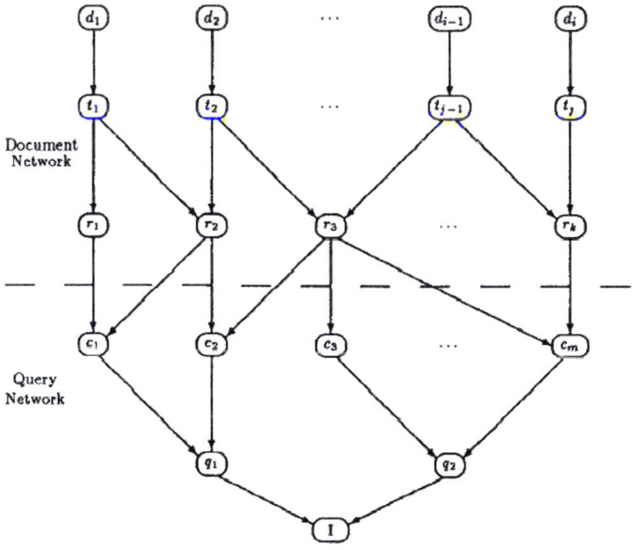

Figure 3: An Inference Network

concept. Each link contains a conditional probability, or weight, to indicate the strength of the relationship. The evaluation of a node is done using the value of the parent nodes and the conditional probabilities.

The QN represents the submitted query and consists of a framework of nodes that represent the required concepts (query concept nodes) and the operators (query operator nodes), connected in an inverted tree structure. The QN is constructed with a final leaf node I that represents the user Information Need. The framework permits statistical operators and statistical approximations of the Boolean operators, a number of which are given in Table 1 (as in the INQUERY implementation [2]).

#and	AND the terms
#or	OR the terms
#not	Negate the term (incoming belief)
#sum	Sum of the incoming beliefs
#wsum	Weighted sum of the incoming beliefs
#max	Maximum of the incoming beliefs

Table 1: Operators supported by the IN model

Two further processes are done to perform retrieval: the attachment process, where by the QN is attached to the DN to form the complete IN and is done where concepts in both networks are the same; the evaluation process, whereby the complete IN is evaluated for each document node to form the probability of the relevance to the query. The evaluation is initialised by setting the output of one document node to 1 and all the other document nodes to 0. This is done for each document node in turn and the network is evaluated (see [19] for exact detail and examples on how nodes are evaluated). The probability of document relevence is taken from the final node I and is used to produce the ranking.

3. MODEL

The basis for our model is the Inference Network (IN) model as it has the ability to model the structural, conceptual and contextual aspects available in MPEG-7. This framework has been successfully used before [12] to perform retrieval of SGML documents by modelling the structure and contents. This section discusses our Document and Query sub-networks; the modifications to the attachment and evaluation processes; and how the probabilities within the network are estimated.

3.1 Document Network

The DN captures the structural elements of the documents, the concepts found in the collection, and the relationships (and strengths) between each document and concept.

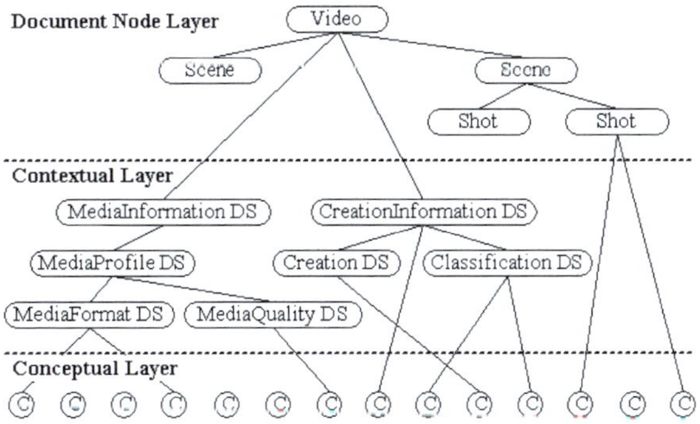

Figure 4: The three-layered Document Network

It consists of three layers as follows:

- The document node layer, which contains nodes that represent the retrievable units in the collection.
- The contextual layer, which contains nodes that represent the contextual information about the document→concept links.
- The conceptual layer, which contains nodes that represent all the concepts in the collection.

In the document node layer we have a hierarchical structure of document nodes to represent the structure of the video as represented in the MPEG-7 file. Each video is thus represented by a Video node, each of which can contain Scene nodes to represent scenes, each of which can contain Shot nodes to represent the shots. This structure can be extracted from the MPEG-7 structural components [11]. The Video→Scene and Scene→Shot links represents the decomposition of the Video into smaller parts, and the conditional probabilities on these links indicate the importance of the child element with respect to the parent (ie: how much a particular Scene contributes to the content of the Video).

The conceptual layer contains concept nodes that represent the identified concepts within the document collection. Concepts are identified during an extraction process where each document is parsed and concepts recognised (as in INQUERY). The presence of a concept within a document is represented as a relationship (direct or indirect) between the document node and the concept node. In reality, such a link exists for every document→concept relationship and the non-presence of a concept is indicated with a conditional probability of 0.5 (as thus, during evaluation, the value of the parent will not influence the value of the child). Our methods for estimating these conditional probabilities are discussed in section 3.5.

The contextual layer contains context nodes. The layer attempts to exploit the rich structure that is available within the MPEG-7 documents, namely the location of the concept within DS hierarchy.

This structural information can be used for both:

- Enabling a more precise estimation of how much a concept represents a document considering the context (eg: contexts may be of variable quality as some may be a better indicator of content than others). Concept nodes are included in the DN for all of the MPEG-7 elements we wish to monitor, resulting in Document→Context(s)→Concept relationships;
- Enable the identification of concepts that occur only within a particular context (eg: the query concerns the "bbc" concept that occurs only within the "Creation DS" context). This is exploited in our query network using a constrained concept.

3.2 Query Network

Our QN consists of the standard query concept nodes and query operator nodes as previously described. The operators supported are those in Table 1, which operate in the same manner as in INQUERY. Our QN also includes query context nodes, which are associated to a query concept node to form a constraint. The constraints specify the desired context of the concept within the expected matching documents (eg: we wish the "bbc" concept to occur under the "Creation DS" context). Our constraints are of two types, normal or complex.

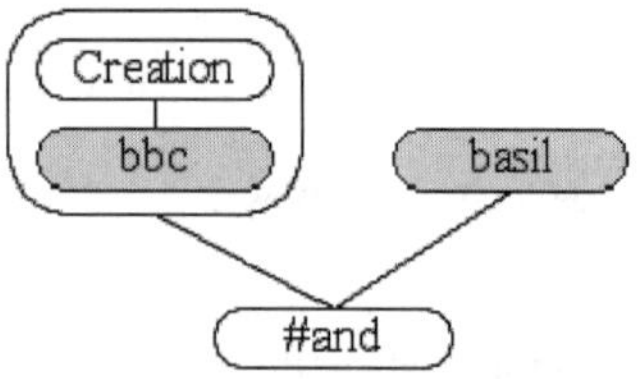

Figure 5: A normal constraint

The QN in figure 5 contains two query concept nodes (these are grey), a single query operator node (begins with #) and a query constraint node. The query constraint node is attached to the "bbc" concept node to form a normal constraint. This is denoted diagrammatically by enclosing the query concept node with the query constraint node. This query structure specifies that the query concept node "bbc" should only be attached to document concept nodes "bbc" which satisfy the constraint, that is, those nodes which occur under the context "Creation".

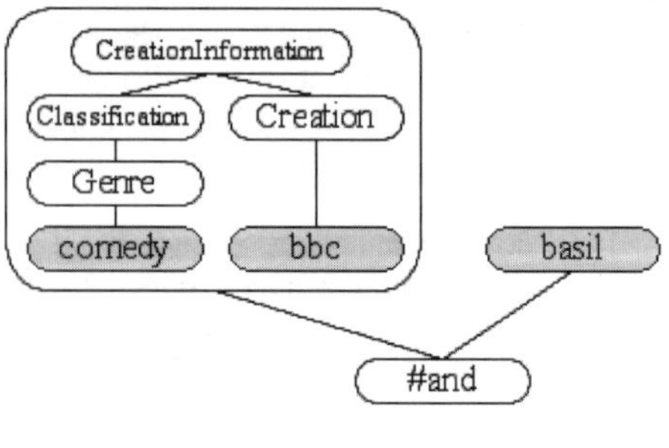

Figure 6: A complex constraint

The QN in figure 6 shows an example of a complex constraint. In this case, a structure is specified in the query that we wish to occur in the matching documents. The structure shown consists of two concepts and their relationship via a number of contexts. The query therefore demands those documents that match this subquery structure. The constraints are considered in the attachment process described in section 3.3.

In addition therefore to the standard INQUERY query text, we propose two new keywords that allow the construction of normal and complex constraints: #constraint for placing a normal constraint upon a concept; and #tree for creating a complex constraint. Two examples are given below which represent the QNs shown in figures 5 and 6.

```
#and(#constraint(Creation, "BBC") "Basil")

#and(#tree(CreationInformation,
      #constraint(Classification/Genre,"Comedy")
      #constraint(Creation,"BBC") "Basil")
```

3.3 Attachment

The attachment process is performed during retrieval once the QN has been built and requires attaching to the DN. The result of the process is a number of DN→QN links where the concepts are considered to be the same, and where any specified constraints are matched. This link contains a weight, or conditional probability, that we can use to indicate the strength of the attachment (ie: how close the concepts and constraints matched).

The attachment process performs the following tasks:

1. Create candidate attachments (DN→QN links) by comparing the concepts in the QN against the concepts in the DN. In our implementation we compare the text of the QN concept nodes against the text of the DN concept nodes and create a link when it is the same. At this point we could consider miss-spellings, localisation, thesauri and stemming [1] in order to intelligently group similar concepts. We call this *conceptual fusion.*

2. Create attachments according to the constraints.

   (a) For unconstrained candidate attachments we create a firm attachment (the same for every document node).

   (b) For constrained candidate attachments we analyse the constraints. This is performed individually for every document node as only nodes that occur under the document node are considered to be part of the candidate DN structure. We calculate the *Edit Distance* (ED) [20] between the candidate DN structure and the QN concept constraint by counting the number of insertions, deletions and amendments that would be necessary to transform the former into the latter. This results in an ED metric for each constrained query (normal or complex) for each document node. This metric measures the closeness of fit.

3. For each document node we then create document specific attachments from the candidate attachments either using a threshold or a weighted link method. In the former we create the attachment using a weight of 1 (the conditional probability on the DN→QN link) if the ED is below a specified threshold. In the latter we create the attachment and use the ED to form the weight using the formula:

```
P(QN node | DN node) = 1 / (ED + 1)
```

The conditional probability represents the strength in the belief in the attachment considering how closely the structures fit (as ED tends to 0 the weight tends towards 1). At this point, we can also use the information about the conceptual fusion process (use of thesauri, localisation, etc) in calculating the conditional probability on the DN→QN link. One advantage of using the weighted link method is that it produces a larger results list.

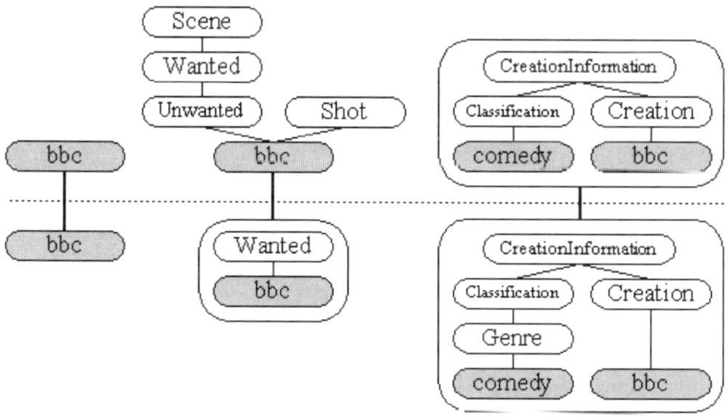

Figure 7: (a)(b)(c) Three examples of attachment

The result of the attachment process is a set of firm attachments and a set document specific attachments for each document node. This is known as the *complete network*. Figure 7 demonstrates three examples of attachment where the structures above the dotted line are in the DN and those below are in the QN. These examples are described below.

a) Shows an example of an unconstrained query concept and a matching document concept node, so a firm attachment is created with P(QN|DN) = 1.

b) Shows an example of a normally constrained query concept. The "Creation" document node satisfies the "Wanted" constraint with an ED = 1 if we delete the "Unwanted" node. We then create a document specific attachment. Using the threshold method we create the attachment with P(QN|DN) = 0 or 1 according to whether the ED is below the threshold. Using the weighted link method we create the attachment with P(QN|DN) = 1 / (1+1) = 0.5.

c) Shows an example of a complex constraint. The DN candidate structure shown satisfies the constraint as the root context node "CreationInformation" and the two concept nodes "comedy" and "bbc" all occur.

3.4 Evaluation

The evaluation process is performed for each document node using the complete network. The network is evaluated for each document node using the document specific attachments for that document. The result of the network evaluation is taken from the information need node in the QN. In addition to the standard method of complete IN evaluation [18, 19, 2], we consider two methods that exploit the structure within the DN:

- Link Inheritance (LI), is the situation when a child node can inherit context nodes from the parent nodes.
- Path Cropping (PC), is the situation where a parental contribution to a DN concept node is cropped (removed) as it does not satisfy the constraint on the attached QN query concept node.

LI is illustrated in figure 8. The Video node has two child document nodes that indicate the structure, the Scene and Shot nodes. The Video node also contains a context "Creation" (which can contain links to concept nodes). The idea of link inheritance is that this context also applies to the children of the Video node, the Scene and Shot nodes. For example, the context may contain concept nodes that describe when the video was created, information that is applicable to the scenes and shots within the video. The child document nodes therefore inherit the Video→Creation link from their parent during evaluation.

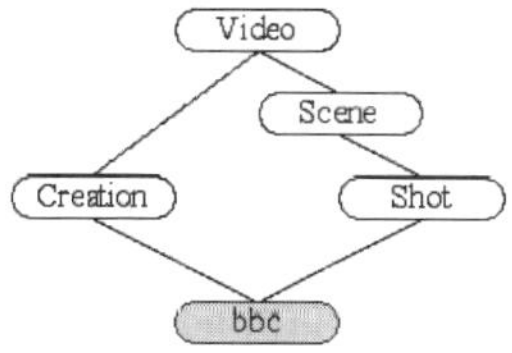

Figure 8: Link Inheritance

Although the inherited context is applicable to the child nodes, it becomes less influential as the number of generations between the child and the context increases. In our example, the "Creation" context is mostly applicable to the Video node, then the Scene node, and least applicable to the Shot node. To capture this fact, we degrade the conditional probability on the inherited Video→Creation link. We refer to this as Link Inheritance with Degradation (LID). The size of degradation is calculated according to size of the generation gap (the node distance between the real parent of the context and the node inheriting the context). The degradation could also consider the frame duration ratio.

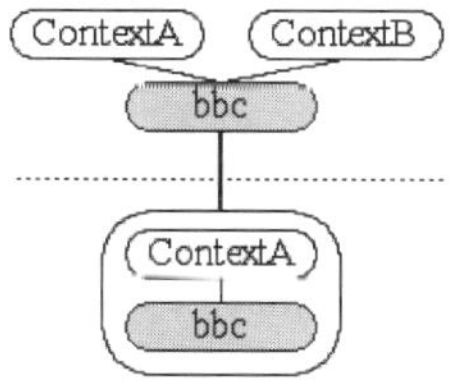

Figure 9: Path Cropping

PC is illustrated in figure 9. The figure shows a document concept node "bbc" with two parental contexts, attached successfully to a normally constrained query concept node. During the evaluation of the document concept node, we can choose to ignore the parental influence "ContextB" as this particular concept is not specified within the constraint. That is, the influence of this parent is not of interest to the query and hence is cropped; the document context node in the figure is evaluated as though it has only one parent.

3.5 Probability Estimation

The final part of our model is concerned with specifying how the conditional probabilities (or weights) between the nodes are estimated. A high conditional probability between two nodes would indicate that they are closely coupled and the child value should closely reflect the value of the parent. The weights need only be estimated for the DN as the QN uses a fixed behaviour according to the operators.

Two types of conditional probability need to be estimated:

- Context→Context. Between a parental context and a child context. Two subtypes:
  - Structural (eg: Video→Scene)
  - Contextual (eg: Video→CreationInformation)
- Context→Concept. Between a context and the concepts that are associated with it.

The structural probabilities are estimated using *duration ratio* information (duration-of-parent/duration-of-child), as each document node has a frame duration encoded in MPEG-7. The contextual probabilities are estimated using *context sibling information* using (1/total-number-of-siblings). Alternatively, we could consider the context size, frequency, or perceived quality of the child context in this estimation [8].

We estimate the Context→Concept probability according to two factors: the statistical properties of the concept (eg: term frequency, inverse document frequency [1]); and information about how the concept was extracted.

```
Weight  = tf(t,d) * idf(t)
Pweight = 0.5 + (0.5 * weight)
```

The statistical properties of the concept provide information about the quality of the term as a discriminating factor and information about how much a document (or context in our case) is represented by the term. We use the above Weight formula to calculate the conditional probability from the term statistics. We use the above Pweight formula [19] throughout the network in order to ensure that the weight is above 0.5 and therefore a positive influence on the result.

```
<StructuredAnnotation>
   <Who>Basil,Sybil,Andre</Who>
</StructuredAnnotation>
```

The MPEG-7 file itself can provide clues about the quality of a term which we can analyse during the extraction process. In the above example MPEG-7 excerpt, three concepts (Basil, Sybil and Andre) are contained within a single MPEG-7 Descriptor using a comma delimiter. Each concept is therefore not as representative as a single concept as it has two descriptor siblings. We use this information to refine the probabilities using (1/total-number-of-siblings).

4. EXAMPLE NETWORK

This section describes an example of how the probabilities within the document network are estimated. The resultant example network is used later in section 5.

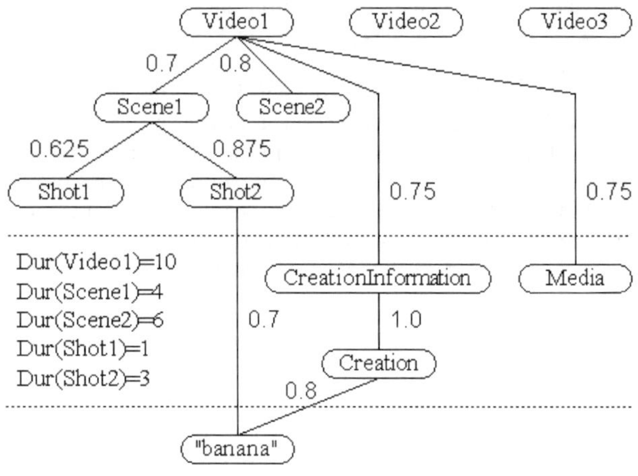

Figure 10: An Example DN

The example DN shown in figure 10 contains 3 Videos, 2 Scenes and 2 Shots, and also two occurrences of the concept "banana" within two different contexts:

```
Video1->CreationInformation->Creation->Concept
Video1->Scene1->Shot2->Concept.
```

Given the structure in figure 10, where Dur(Element) states the duration of the document node, the structural Context→Context probabilities are estimated as follows: (using the duration ratio and Pweight formula)

```
P(Scene1|Video1) Duration ratio = 4/10 = 0.4
   PWeight = 0.5 + (0.5 * 0.4) = 0.7
P(Scene2|Video1) Duration ratio = 6/10 = 0.6
   PWeight = 0.5 + (0.5 * 0.6) = 0.8
P(Shot1|Scene1) Duration ratio = 1/4 = 0.25
   PWeight = 0.5 + (0.5 * 0.25) = 0.625
P(Shot2|Scene1) Duration ratio = 3/4 = 0.75
   PWeight = 0.5 + (0.5 * 0.75) = 0.875
```

The contextual Context→Context probabilities are estimated as follows: (using the total-number-of-siblings and Pweight formula)

```
P(CreationInformation|Video1) and P(Media|Video1)
   Total number of siblings = 2
   Sibling weight = 1 / 2 = 0.5
   PWeight = 0.5 + (0.5 * 0.5) = 0.75
P(Creation|CreationInformation)
   Total number of siblings = 1
   Sibling weight = 1 / 1 = 1.0
   PWeight = 0.5 + (0.5 * 1.0) = 1.0
```

In our model the Context→Concept probabilities are estimated using term statistics. However, in our example DN we have too few terms to perform this calculation so we have assigned the values:

```
P(banana|Creation) = 0.8
P(banana|Shot2) = 0.7
```

The probability estimation is conducted during the indexing phase resulting in the DN shown in figure 10. The DN consists of a number of nodes and probabilistic links between them. All of conditional probabilities are positive (ie: >0.5, owing to the Pweight formula), meaning that those units that influence the parents of the "banana" concept (ie: Creation and Shot2) will be ranked higher.

5. ILLUSTRATION

To illustrate our approach, we implemented our model with two major modules: the extraction module; the evaluation module. The extraction module builds the DN from the MPEG-7 files, using the structural aspects when building the document node layer and other select MPEG-7 DSs and Descriptors for building the contextual and conceptual layers. At this point the conditional probabilities are also estimated. The evaluation module performs the query processing and evaluation according to the system parameters.

We conducted two experiments on the system which illustrate the working of the model. In particular we wish to examine whether the model can produce a good ranking; whether different levels of granularity can be retrieved; and whether the novel elements (constrained queries, link inheritance, path cropping) influence the results.

```
#constraint(CreationInformation,"banana")
```

The first experiment uses the example DN described in section 4 and the above query. The query states that we wish to retrieve elements (document nodes) containing the concept "banana" that adhere to the constraint "CreationInformation". Note that the constraint will only be enforced on tests where the functionality is enabled.

0.3640 Video1	0.4550 Shot2	0.3850 Shot2
0.2450 Shot2	0.4225 Scene1	0.3738 Scene1
0.2275 Scene1	0.3640 Video1	0.3640 Video1
0.1050 Shot1	0.1950 Shot1	0.1725 Scene2
0.1050 Scene2	0.1950 Scene2	0.1650 Shot1
0.1050 Video2	0.1050 Video2	0.1050 Video2
0.1050 Video3	0.1050 Video3	0.1050 Video3

Table 2: The results of tests 1, 2 and 3

Test 1 was performed with no parameters (no link inheritance, no constraints, no path cropping). Test 2 was performed with LI only. Test 3 was performed with LID only. The results shown in table 2 are thought to show promise.

With no parameters, Video1 is ranked 1st as this has influence over both parental influences of the concept (the first path is via Video1→CreationInformation→Creation→Concept, second path is via Shot2→Concept). Shot2 is ranked 2nd as this is the closest to the concept on the second path. The other elements are ranked according to the second path influence as only Video1 influences the first path. Note that if Shot2=0 and Creation=0 then no evidence exists for the concept, however, due to the uncertain probabilistic nature of the network the result is 0.1050.

With the introduction of LI in Test 2, the child nodes of Video1 now inherit first path and thus are ranked higher. Shot2, Scene1 and Video1 are now ranked 1st, 2nd and 3rd, according to the amount of influence they exert on the second path. Shot1 and Scene2 are ranked lower as these have no influence on the second path, but are ranked above Video2 and Video3 as these have no influence on either path. This in particular was thought to be a good result.

In Test 3 LID produces a similar result but is thought to be more satisfactory. Scene2 is now ranked above Shot1 because the degradation is larger according to the number of generations. Shot1 is two generations from Video1 whereas Scene2 is only one generation.

We then performed tests with the constraints enabled. The Video1 node is the only document node that satisfies the constraint with an ED of 1 (as there is one extra node "Creation"). Using the threshold method with threshold = 3 the Video1 obtains the same probability as in Test 1 as the document specific attachment is used. All the other document nodes score 0. With threshold = 0 the score is 0 for the Video1. These results proved that the constraint was being enforced. Using the weighted link method we found that the score was slightly lower. When we introduced PC we found that the score was slightly higher as the concept node is only calculated with a single parent and the uncertainty introduced from the second parent is removed.

The second experiment uses a DN generated from a small MPEG-7 collection consisting of: two comedy clips [3, 4] and one drama clip [10]; each approximately 10 minutes long. We performed shot detection of 329 shots. Scenes were then created manually by grouping the semantically similar shots together. Finally annotation was manually added:

- <Abstract> using the official video box abstract.
- <StructuredAnnotation> for each scene specifying exactly the characters, the location and additional facts.
- <FreeTextAnnotation> for each video, scene and shot, written to describe the action.
- <FreeTextAnnotation> for each shot containing all of the speech that occurs.

Figure 11: Example Keyframes

Although automatic generation of video metadata is desirable for many applications, manual annotations are still very much in use. The model described in this paper can be applied to MPEG-7 metadata whether created automatically or manually. It must be noted that the quality of the retrieval is dependent upon the quality of the annotations.

The MPEG-7 files in the collection were then parsed to form the DN. The DN is stored as XML an example of which is given below:

```
<Video id="GourmetNight"\>
   <Scene id="TheMajorComplains"\>
      <Concept weight="0.5106"\>mushroom</Concept>
      <Concept weight="0.5211">mushrooms</Concept>
      <Shot id="Shot_68"/>
      <Shot id="Shot_69">
         <Concept weight="0.5211">mushrooms
         </Concept>
      </Shot>
      <Shot id="Shot_70"/>
   </Scene>
</Video>
```

We then conducted four tests using the queries:

```
Q1) #or("mushroom" "mushrooms")
Q2) #or("chips" #and("salad" "cream"))
Q3) #constraint(Classification "comedy")
Q4) #or("bedroom" "room" "rooms")
```

We enabled LID, constraints and PC. The results for the four queries were as expected. Q1 produced a ranking of Scene, Video, Shot which replicates the findings from the first experiment. Q2 also ranked highly the scenes and shots that contained the evidence. Q3 produced a ranking for the two comedy videos but not the drama video which was the expected result considering the constraint. Q4 was used for generating recall/precision metrics using a subjective assessment of the most relevant documents. The average was 69.25 however the results were not significant owing to a) the small size of the test collection, and b) the lack of independent queries and relevance assessments. However, these initial results demonstrate the potential of the model working with an MPEG-7 collection.

6. CONCLUDING REMARKS

In this work we have adopted a metadata-based approach to video retrieval. We propose the use of MPEG-7 files to encode the content and to hold the video structure. MPEG-7 provides a rich set of tools for this purpose. We consider the MPEG-7 Description Scheme structure to contain additional knowledge about the document-content relationship (we call this context).

We presented a model based upon the Inference Network model that preserves and uses the structural, conceptual and contextual aspects of MPEG-7. We use the structural aspects to allow the retrieval of different levels of granularity where the evidence for a higher-level unit is contained within its children (eg: the evidence for a scene is contained in the shots). We use the duration ratio between structural units to estimate the conditional probabilities between them. We extract document concepts from the conceptual aspects of MPEG-7 and use term statistics and extraction information to estimate the probabilities. We use the contextual aspects to decompose the documents into smaller contexts and to allow constrained queries. In addition, we perform evidence inheritance during the evaluation process.

The quality of the results when performing a metadata-based approach is based upon the quality of the metadata itself. Presently this is low and thus the experimental results presented in this paper are not conclusive. However, the initial results presented indicate that the metadata-based approach is well founded. Our next steps are to establish a larger more consistent MPEG-7 collection and to consider further how the inheritance of evidence should effect the retrieval process. This can be done in conjunction with TREC when an MPEG-7 collection becomes available.

7. ACKNOWLEDGEMENTS

We wish to acknowledge the MPEG-7 generation tool provided by Laboratoires d'Electronique Philips. The first author was funded by the EPSRC.

8. REFERENCES

[1] R. Baeza-Yates and N. Ribeiro-Neto. *Modern Information Retrieval.* Addison Wesley, Essex, England, 1999.

[2] J.P. Callen, W.B. Croft, and S.M. Harding. The inquery retrieval system. In *3rd International Conference on Database and Expert Systems Applications*, pages 78–83, 1992.

[3] J. Cleese and C. Booth. Fawlty towers: Gourmet night. BBC ©, 1975.

[4] J. Cleese and C. Booth. Fawlty towers: Communication problems. BBC ©, 1979.

[5] C. Colombo, A. Del Bimbo, and P. Pala. Semantics in visual information retrieval. *IEEE Multimedia*, 6(3):38–53, July-September 1999.

[6] N. Fatemi and O. Abou Khaled. Indexing and retrieval of tv news programs based on mpeg-7. In *IEEE International Conference on Consumer Electronics*, Los Angeles, California, USA, June 2001.

[7] N. Fuhr and K. Großjohann. Xirql: A query language for information retrieval in xml documents. In *24th ACM-SIGIR Conference on Research and Development in Information Retrieval*, pages 172–180, New Orleans, Louisiana, USA, 2001.

[8] A. Graves. Video indexing and retrieval using an mpeg-7 based inference network. Master's thesis, Queen Mary, University of London, 2001.

[9] J. Hunter and R. Iannella. The application of metadata standards to video indexing. In *Second European Conference on Research and Advanced Technology for Digital Libraries*, Crete, Greece, September 1998.

[10] J. Ivory. A room with a view. Merchant Ivory Productions ©, 1996.

[11] ISO MPEG-7. Text of iso/iec cd 15938-2 information technology - multimedia content description interface - part 5 multimedia description schemes, iso/iec jtc 1/sc 29/wg, March 2001.

[12] S. Myaeng, D.H. Jang, M.S. Kim, and Z.C. Zhoo. A flexible model for retrieval of sgml documents. In *21st ACM-SIGIR Conference on Research and Development in Information Retrieval*, pages 138–145, Melbourne, Australia, 1998.

[13] M.R. Naphade and T.S. Huang. A probabilistic framework for semantic video indexing, filtering, and retrieval. *IEEE Multimedia*, 3(1):141–151, March 2001.

[14] A. Pearmain, M. Lalmas, E. Moutogianni, D. Papworth, P. Healey, and T. Rölleke. Using mpeg7 at the consumer terminal in broadcasting. In *EURASIP (European Association for Signal, Speech and Image Processing) Journal on Applied Signal Processing*, volume 4, pages 354–361, April 2002.

[15] W. Putz. The use of mpeg-7 metadata in a broadcast application. In *Media Future*, Florence, Italy, May 2001.

[16] T. Rölleke, M. Lalmas, G. Kazai, I. Ruthven, and S. Quicker. The accessibility dimension for structured document retrieval. In *24th European Colloquium on Information Retrieval Research*, Glasgow, Scotland, March 2002.

[17] A. Smeaton. Indexing, browsing and searching of digital video and digital audio information. In *European Summer School in Information Retrieval*, pages 93–110, Varenna, Lago di Como, Italy, 2000.

[18] H.R. Turtle. *Inference Networks for Document Retrieval.* PhD thesis, University of Massachusetts, 1990.

[19] H.R. Turtle and W.B. Croft. Efficient probabilistic inference for text retrieval. In *RIAO 3*, pages 644–661, 1991.

[20] J.T.L. Wang, K. Zhang, and C. Chang. Identifying approximately common substructures in trees based on a restricted edit distance. *Information Sciences*, 121(3-4):367–386, December 1999.

Posters

Using Self-Supervised Word Segmentation in Chinese Information Retrieval 349
F. Peng, X. Huang, D. Schuurmans, N. Cercone (University of Waterloo), S. E. Robertson (Microsoft Research and City University)

Automatic Classification in Product Catalogs 351
B. Wolin (Commerce One Laboratories)

PageRank, HITS and a Unified Framework for Link Analysis 353
C. Ding, X. He, P. Husbands (Lawrence Berkeley National Laboratory), H. Zha (Pennslyvania State University), H. D. Simon (Lawrence Berkeley National Laboratory)

Task Orientation in Question Answering 355
V. Murdock, W. B. Croft (University of Massachusetts)

Experiments in High-Dimensional Text Categorization 357
F. J. Damerau, T. Zhang, S. M. Weiss, N. Indurkhya (IBM T.J. Watson Research Center)

The Relationship Betweem ASK and Relevance Criteria 359
X.-J. Yuan, N. J. Belkin, J.-Y. Kim (Rutgers University)

ICA and SOM in Text Document Analysis 361
E. Bingham, J. Kuusisto, K. Lagus (Helsinki University of Technology)

Improving Hierarchical Text Classification Using Unlabeled Data 363
V. Boyapati (Whizbang! Laboratories-Research)

Do Thumbnail Previews Help Users Make Better Relevance Decisions about Web Search Results? 365
S. Dziadosz, R. Chandrasekar (Microsoft Corporation)

Amilcare: Adaptive Information Extraction for Document Annotation 367
F. Ciravegna, A. Dingli, Y. Wilks, D. Petrelli (University of Sheffield)

The Impact of Corpus Size on Question Answering Performance 369
C. L. A. Clarke, G. V. Cormack, M. Laszlo, T. R. Lynam, E. L. Terra (University of Waterloo)

Effective Collection Metasearch in a Hierarchical Environment: Global vs. Localized Retrieval Performance 371
J. G. Conrad (TLR Research & Development), C. Yang (Oracle Corporation), J. S. Claussen (West Group)

Experimenting with Graphical User Interfaces for Structured Document Retrieval 373
F. Crestani (University of Strathclyde), P. de la Fuente, J. Vegas (Universidad de Valladolid)

The Web Retrieval Task and its Evaluation in the Third NTCIR Workshop 375
K. Eguchi, K. Oyama, E. Ishida, K. Kuriyama, N. Kando (National Institute of Informatics)

How Many Bits are Needed to Store Term Frequencies? 377
M. Franz, J. S. McCarley (IBM T.J. Watson Research Center)

Non-Linear Reading for a Structured Web Indexation 379
M. Géry (MRIM Group)

Document Normalization Revisited 381
A. Chowdhury (America Online), M. C. McCabe (U.S. Government), D. Grossman, O. Frieder (Illinois Institute of Technology)

User-Centered Interface Design for Cross-Language Information Retrieval 383
P. Hansen (Swedish Institute of Computer Science), D. Petrelli (University of Sheffield), J. Karlgren (Swedish Institute of Computer Science), M. Beaulieu, M. Sanderson (University of Sheffield)

Implementation of Relevance Feedback for Content-based Music Retrieval Based on User Preferences 385
K. Hoashi (KDDI R&D Laboratories, Inc.), E. Zeitler (Uppsala University), N. Inoue (KDDI R&D Laboratories, Inc.)

Spatial Information Retrieval and Geographical Ontologies—An Overview of the SPIRIT Project 387
C. B. Jones (Cardiff University), R. Purves (University of Zurich), A. Ruas (IGN Paris), M. Sanderson (University of Sheffield), M. Sester (University of Hannover), M. van Kreveld (Utrecht University), R. Weibel (University of Zurich)

A Visualisation Tool for Topic Tracking Analysis and Development 389
G. J. F. Jones, S. M. Gabb (University of Exeter)

A New Method of Parameter Estimation for Multinomial Naive Bayes Text Classifiers 391
S.-B. Kim, H.-C. Rim (Korea University), H.-S. Lim (Chonan University)

Study of Category Score Algorithms for k-NN Classifier 393
H. Kou (University of Versailles), G. Gardarin (e-XMLMedia)

Higher Precision for Two-Word Queries 395
K. L. Kwok (Queens College, CUNY)

The Boomerang Effect: Retrieving Scientific Documents via the Network of References and Citations 397
B. Larsen, P. Ingwersen (Royal School of Library and Information Science)

A Logistic Regression Approach to Distributed IR 399
R. R. Larson (University of California, Berkeley)

Automatic Metadata Generation & Evaluation 401
E. D. Liddy, E. Allen, S. Harwell, S. Corieri, O. Yilmazel, N. E. Ozgencil, A. Diekema, N. McCracken, J. Silverstein (Syracuse University), S. Sutton (University of Washington)

A Critical Examination of TDT's Cost Function 403
R. Manmatha, A. Feng, J. Allan (University of Massachusetts)

Converting On-Line Bilingual Dictionaries from Human-Readable to Machine-Readable Form 405
J. Mayfield, P. McNamee (The Johns Hopkins University Applied Physics Laboratory)

Modeling (In)Variability of Human Judgments for Text Summarization 407
T. Nomoto (National Institute of Japanese Literature), Y. Matsumoto (Nara Institute of Science and Technology)

Content-based Music Indexing and Organization 409
A. Rauber (Vienna University of Technology), E. Pampalk (Austrian Research Institute for Artificial Intelligence), D. Merkl (Vienna University of Technology)

Relative and Absolute Term Selection Criteria: A Comparative Study for English and Japanese IR 411
T. Sakai (Toshiba Corporate R & D Center), S. E. Robertson (Microsoft Research Ltd. and City University)

Experiments on Data Fusion Using Headline Information 413
X. M. Shou, M. Sanderson (University of Sheffield)

Building Thematic Lexical Resources by Term Categorization 415
A. Lavelli, B. Magnini (ITC-irst),
F. Sebastiani (Istituto di Elaborazione dell'Informazione)

Topic Structure Modeling 417
D. A. Evans, J. G. Shanahan, V. Sheftel (Clairvoyance Corporation)

Language Model for IR Using Collection Information .. 419
R. Jin, L. Si, A. G. Hauptmann, J. Callan (Carnegie Mellon University)

Automatic Evaluation of World Wide Web Search Services 421
A. Chowdhury (America Online Inc.), I. Soboroff (National Institute of Standards and Technology)

Does WT10g Look Like the Web? 423
I. Soboroff (National Institute of Standards and Technology)

Biterm Language Models for Document Retrieval 425
M. Srikanth, R. Srihari (State University of New York at Buffalo)

Selecting Indexing Strings using Adaptation 427
Y. Takeda, K. Umemura (Toyohashi University of Technology)

Error Correction in a Chinese OCR Test Collection 429
Y.-H. Tseng (Fu Jen Catholic University)

User Interface Effects in Past Batch Versus User Experiments 431
A. Turpin (Curtin University of Technology),
W. Hersh (Oregon Health & Sciences University)

K-tree/forest: Efficient Indexes for Boolean Queries 433
R. M. Verma, S. Behl (University of Houston)

Example-Based Phrase Translation in Chinese-English CLIR 435
B. Wang, X. Cheng, S. Bai (Chinese Academy of Sciences)

Probabilistic Multimedia Retrieval 437
T. Westerveld (University of Twente)

Chinese Keyword Extraction Based on Max-duplicated Strings of the Documents 439
W. Yang, X. Li (Tsinghua University)

A Hierarchical Approach: Query Large Music Database by Acoustic Input 441
Y. Feng, Y. Zhuang, Y. Pan (Zhejiang University)

Correlating Multilingual Documents via Bipartite Graph Modeling 443
H. Zha, X. Ji (The Pennsylvania State University)

Using Self-Supervised Word Segmentation in Chinese Information Retrieval

Fuchun Peng[1] Xiangji Huang[1] Dale Schuurmans[1] Nick Cercone[1] Stephen E. Robertson[2]
[1]School of Computer Science, University of Waterloo, Waterloo, Canada
{f3peng, jhuang, dale, ncercone}@uwaterloo.ca
[2]Microsoft Research, Cambridge, U.K. and City University, London, U.K.
ser@microsoft.com

ABSTRACT

We propose a self-supervised word-segmentation technique for Chinese information retrieval. This method combines the advantages of traditional dictionary based approaches with character based approaches, while overcoming many of their shortcomings. Experiments on TREC data show comparable performance to both the dictionary based and the character based approaches. However, our method is language independent and unsupervised, which provides a promising avenue for constructing accurate multilingual information retrieval systems that are flexible and adaptive.

Categories and Subject Descriptors

I.2 [**Computing Methodologies**]: artificial intelligence

General Terms

Experimentation

Keywords

Self supervised word segmentation, Chinese IR

1. INTRODUCTION

Tokenization is the first step in Chinese information retrieval, where traditionally two approaches have been taken: dictionary based and character based [2, 3]. In the dictionary based approach, one pre-defines a lexicon containing a large number of Chinese words and then uses heuristic methods such as maximum matching to segment Chinese sentences. In the character based approach, sentences are tokenized simply by taking each character to be a basic unit. Both of these approaches have advantages and disadvantages. The dictionary based approach has the advantage of requiring a smaller inverted index file, hence achieving faster retrieval times while allowing additional linguistic information to be incorporated into the retrieval system (e.g. synonyms). The main disadvantage of the dictionary based approach however is that it requires a large pre-defined lexicon, which normally must be constructed by hand with significant amount of labor and time. In the character based approach, the most prominent advantage is that it does not require a pre-defined lexicon. Each character is simply considered as a basic unit. However, the disadvantages are that the character based approach requires a huge index file, resulting in slower retrieval speed, and creates difficulty in incorporating any additional linguistic information.

In this paper, we propose using an EM based segmentation technique for Chinese information retrieval, self-supervised segmentation [4], which has many of the advantages of the character based and dictionary based approaches, while overcoming many of the shortcomings of both methods.

SIGIR'02, August 11-15, 2002, Tampere, Finland.
ACM 1-58113-561-0/02/0008.

2. SELF-SUPERVISED SEGMENTATION

In a general word segmentation task where there are no identifying markers between words, one could effectively exploit *known* words to guide the segmentation of unknown words. For example, if the word "*computer*" is already known then upon seeing the text "*computerscience*" it is natural to segment "*science*" as a possible new word. To exploit this observation, we develop an EM based word discovery method that is a variant of standard EM training, but avoids getting trapped in local maxima by keeping two lexicons: a *core* lexicon which contains words that are judged to be trustworthy, and a *candidate* lexicon which contains all other candidate words that are not in the core lexicon.

Assume we have a sequence of characters $C = c_1c_2...c_T$ that we wish to segment into chunks $S = s_1s_2...s_M$, where T is the number of characters in the sequence and M is the number of words in the segmentation. Here chunks s_i will be chosen from the core lexicon $V_1 = \{s_i, i = 1, ..., |V_1|\}$ or the candidate lexicon $V_2 = \{s_j, j = 1, ..., |V_2|\}$. If we already have the probability distributions $\theta = \{\theta_i|\theta_i = p(s_i), i = 1, ..., |V_1|\}$ defined over the core lexicon and $\phi = \{\phi_j|\phi_j = p(s_j), j = 1, ..., |V_2|\}$ over the candidate lexicon, then we can recover the most likely segmentation of the sequence $C = c_1c_2...c_T$ into chunks $S = s_1s_2...s_M$ as follows. First, for any given segmentation S of C, we can calculate the joint likelihood of S and C by

$$prob(S, C|\theta, \phi) = \prod_{i=1}^{M_1} \frac{p(s_i)}{2} \prod_{j=1}^{M_2} \frac{p(s_j)}{2} = \frac{1}{2^M} \prod_{k=1}^{M} p(s_k)$$

where M_1 is the number of chunks occurring in the core lexicon, M_2 is the number of chunks occurring in the candidate lexicon, and s_k can come from either lexicon. (Note that each chunk s_k must come from exactly one of the core or candidate lexicons.) Our task is to find the segmentation S^* that achieves the maximum likelihood:

$$S^* = \underset{S}{argmax}\{prob(S, C|\theta, \phi)\} \tag{1}$$

Given a probability distribution defined by θ and ϕ over the lexicon, the Viterbi algorithm can be used to efficiently compute the best segmentation S of character string C. Estimation of the probabilities can be done by the EM algorithm. The parameter re-estimation formulas are as follows.

$$\theta_i^{k+1} = \frac{\sum_S \#(s_i, S) \times prob(S, C|\theta^k, \phi^k)}{\sum_{s_i} \sum_S \#(s_i, S) \times prob(S, C|\theta^k, \phi^k)} \tag{2}$$

$$\phi_j^{k+1} = \frac{\sum_S \#(s_j, S) \times prob(S, C|\theta^k, \phi^k)}{\sum_{s_j} \sum_S \#(s_j, S) \times prob(S, C|\theta^k, \phi^k)} \tag{3}$$

where $\#(s_i, S)$ is the number of times s_i occurring the segmentation S.

The two lexicons are constructed automatically as follows. Let us define C_1, C_2 as the training corpus and the validation corpus respectively, and let V_1 and $V2$ be the core candidate lexicons respectively. Initially, V_1 is set to be empty and V_2 is initialized to contain all candidate "words" that are generated from the training corpus by enumerating contiguous character strings of lengths 1 to L for some predefined maximum length L. In a first pass, starting from the uniform distribution, EM is used to increase the likelihood of the training corpus C_1. When the training process stabilizes, the M words with highest probability are selected from V_2 and moved to V_1, after which all the probabilities are rescaled so that V_1 and V_2 each contain half the total probability mass. EM is then run again. The rationale for shifting half of the probability mass to V_1 is that this increases the influence of core words in determining segmentations and allows them to act as more effective guides in processing the training sequence. We call this procedure of successively moving the top M words to V_1 *forward selection*. Forward selection is repeated until the segmentation performance of Viterbi on the validation corpus C_2 leads to a decrease in F-measure (which means we must have included some erroneous words in the core lexicon). After forward selection terminates, M is decremented and we carry out a process of *backward deletion*, where the M words with the lowest probability in V_1 are moved back to V_2, and EM training is successively repeated until F-measure again decreases on the validation corpus C_2 (which means we must have deleted some correct core words). The two procedures of forward selection and backward deletion are alternated, decrementing M at each alternation, until $M \leq 0$;

3. EXPERIMENTAL RESULTS

We evaluate the IR performance of the *self-supervised* segmentation algorithm with the Okapi system [1, 2] on TREC data sets. Performance measures include *Average Precision*: average precision over all 11 recall points (0.0, 0.1, 0.2,..., 1.0) and *R Precision*: precision after the number of documents retrieved is equal to the number of known relevant documents for a query.

Our segmenter is trained on a 90M collection of data containing one year of *People's Daily* news service stories, and uses 2000 random sentences from the segmented Chinese Treebank as the validation set. Our segmentation accuracy is around 70-74% on the Chinese Treebank.

We compare the IR performance of our method against two standard tokenization methods. The first method uses a hand built dictionary of words, compound words, and phrases to index the texts. We refer to this method as the dictionary-based approach. The dictionary we use in the experiments contains 69,353 Chinese words and phrases. The second method we compare to is a character based approach where documents are indexed by the single Chinese characters that appear in the text. We show the experimental results of the three methods on TREC data sets in the following table. We set the dictionary based method as the baseline.

Results comparison on TREC-5 data set			
	character	dictionary	EM-based
Average precision	0.3795	0.3468	0.3661
Avg. pre. improvement	9.43%	baseline	5.57%
R-Precision	0.3963	0.3863	0.4027
R-Precision improvement	2.59%	baseline	4.25%

Results comparison on TREC-6 data set			
	character	dictionary	EM-based
Average precision	0.5348	0.5044	0.4970
Avg. pre. improvement	6.03%	baseline	-1.47%
R-Precision	0.5404	0.5055	0.5001
R-Precision improvement	6.90%	baseline	-1.07%

On TREC-5 data, we find the EM based segmentation gives a 5.57% improvement in average accuracy over the dictionary based method, but it does a little worse than the character based method. In terms of R-precision, the EM based method yields better performance than both the character based and dictionary based methods. On TREC-6 data, the EM based method yields slightly worse results than both the dictionary based and the character based methods.

In terms of retrieval time, the EM based methods are at the same level as the dictionary based methods, which are about three times faster than the character based approach.

4. CONCLUSIONS

Although our EM based segmentation method does not yield completely accurate segmentations by itself, it nevertheless performs well as a basis for Chinese IR. We achieve retrieval performance that this comparable (and sometimes even better) than the manual dictionary based and the expensive character based methods. Our results demonstrate the machine learning techniques can be successfully applied to Chinese IR to build an adaptable system.

5. REFERENCES

[1] M. Beaulieu, M. Gatford, X. Huang, S. Robertson, S. Walker, and P. Williams. Okapi at TREC-5. In *D.K.Harman (ed): Proceedings of TREC-5*, pages 143-166, 1997

[2] X. Huang and S. Roberton. A Probabilistic Approach to Chinese Information Retrieval: Theory and Experiments. In *Proceedings of the BCS-IRSG 2000.*

[3] J. Nie and F. Ren. Chinese information retrieval: using characters or words? In *Information Processing and Management*, 35:443-462, 1999.

[4] F. Peng and D. Schuurmans. Self-supervised Chinese Word Segmentation. In *Proceedings of IDA-01*, 2001.

Automatic Classification in Product Catalogs

Ben Wolin
Commerce One Labs
19191 Vallco Parkway
Cupertino, CA 95014 USA
bwolin@acm.org

ABSTRACT

In this paper, we present the AutoCat system for product classification. AutoCat uses a vector space model, modified to consider product attributes unavailable in traditional document classification. We present key features of our user interface, developed to assist users with evaluating and editing the output of the classification algorithm. Finally, we present observations about the use of this technology in the field.

Categories and Subject Descriptors

H.3.1 [**Information Storage and Retrieval**]: Content Analysis and Indexing.

General Terms

Algorithms, Experimentation, Human Factors

Keywords

Text classification, categorization, product classification.

1. THE CLASSIFICATION PROBLEM

Classification of product catalogs into a common taxonomy is frequently requirement of trading communities to support browsing, data syndication, category specific schema extensions and catalog interoperability. Service bureaus performing classification for a fee are expensive (as much as $0.25 USD per line item), have long turnarounds, and are frequently inaccurate.

The solution we present is agnostic about the target taxonomy, requiring only that it can be represented as an acyclic directed graph with unique node identifiers. The results we present are based on the UNSPSC [7] taxonomy, version 4.0. We focused on a subset of the taxonomy containing 272 categories related to computer hardware, network products, peripherals and software.

2. DESCRIPTION OF DATA

Product definitions differ between data sources, but typically contain the following features: Short Description, Long Description, Manufacturer Name, Supplier Name, Unit Price. The quality of product descriptions varies widely from terse and jargonistic to lengthy marketing prose. The results described in this paper were obtained using 206,301 parts from 8 suppliers, which are considered to be high quality. The data is still somewhat noisy due to differing interpretations of the taxonomy as well as outright categorization errors.

SIGIR '02, August 11-15, 2002, Tampere, Finland
ACM 1-58113-561-0/02/0008

3. TRAINING METHODOLOGY

AutoCat uses an approach similar to traditional IR systems [4], operating on a sparse matrix containing term references indexed to a list of categories in which the term has been observed. Our approach is also similar to the classic bag-of-words [2][5] approach. The key difference is that instead of representing individual documents or products as sparse, high-dimensional vectors, products are grouped into category vectors.

As each product in the training set is evaluated, terms and phrases are added to the appropriate category vector for the product being considered. Phrases are generated from pairs of consecutive non-stop words in the short description.

Terms are tagged [3] based on their feature source to permit differential weighting during categorization. The intuitive inspiration for this is the belief that the short description is likely to have less extraneous information than the long description and should therefore be weighted higher. A stochastic gradient descent algorithm [1] was used to optimize the feature weights.

Due to the variable length of category vectors, we use a typical normalized [2][6] *tf idf* term weighting formula:

$$\omega_{ik} = \frac{(\log(f_{ik}) + 1.0) * \log(N / n_k)}{\sqrt{\sum_{k=1}^{t} [(\log(f_{ik}) + 1.0) * \log(N / n_k)]^2}}$$

Where w_{ik} is the weight of term k in category i, N is the number of distinct categories, f_{ik} is the frequency of term k in category i, and n_k is the number of categories with term k. The *idf* term in the numerator, $log(N / n_k)$, decreases as the term appears in more categories. The denominator provides length normalization so terms appearing in categories with significantly more training data are not given disproportionally high weights.

Additional post processing is done to exclude terms that do not appear an arbitrary minimum number of times. Test runs were performed using 3 and 5 for the minimum term count per category threshold.

4. CATEGORIZATION METHODOLOGY

As unknown products are considered, terms from each product feature are represented as sparse, high dimensional vectors. Closeness with candidate categories is measured by the cosine of the feature vector and the category vector:

$$\mathrm{Sim}(F,C) = \sum_{i=1}^{t} f_i c_i$$

Where F is the feature vector, C is the category vector, t is the set of feature terms, f_i is the weight of term i in feature F, and c_i is the weight of term i in category C. These are combined to form a matrix A, containing a row for each category and a column for each feature source. Each cell A_{ij} represents the relative confidence of feature j in category i. The matrix A is multiplied by a feature weight vector x to generate a solution vector b. The element with the maximal value in b is proposed as the final candidate classification.

$$Ax = b$$

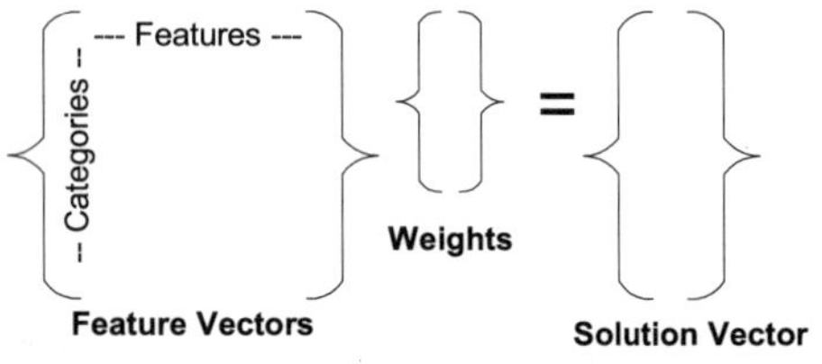

4.1 Numeric Attributes

One significant difference between product classification and traditional document classification is the availability of numeric attributes. We assume that pricing is reasonably efficient and that product prices should therefore have some classification utility when compared with mean category prices.

We implemented an algorithm to adjust the confidence downward by multiplying against the probability of inclusion based on a Z statistic about the mean category price. This confidence interval approach provided limited value due to the extremely broad distribution of prices. The standard deviation exceeded the mean price in 82.5% of categories.

This implied price inefficiency appears to be the result of overly broad category definitions as well as the bundling of multiple products. While the data model [8] allows for unit prices to be set for specific quantity ranges, the minimum order quantity is commonly buried in the free text

5. USER INTERFACE FEATURES

The AutoCat user interface is designed to facilitate viewing and manipulation of large data sets as quickly as possible. When viewing a set of products after a categorization run, results are initially presented in reverse confidence order. This tends to bring miscategorized products to the top of the list.

When the user decides a product is incorrectly categorized, the categorization engine is invoked as part of the editing process to generate a list of alternate choices. The alternate choices presented are the 10 highest scoring categories. The correct category appears in the top ten lists for 88.1% of the incorrectly classified product instances. The time required for the user to find the correct category in a short list is considerably less than the time required to locate the correct category in a tree view containing over 10,000 categories.

6. RESULTS

Accuracy is measured by agreement between the maximal output element in the solution vector and the category value stored for the product in the database. Using training matrices built with minimum term filtering at 3 and 5, the observed test accuracies were .795 and .773 respectively.

7. OBSERVATIONS FROM FIELD USE

AutoCat has been in use at an internal content production facility at Commerce One since 1999. User feedback has been largely positive. For domain areas with sufficient training data, users claim to get upwards of 90% accuracy.

Field users developed a process to simulate a more hierarchical solution by partitioning training data by vertical market. Since AutoCat does not allow categorization results to be limited to subsets of the taxonomy, users would switch to an appropriate training matrix based on a priori knowledge about the supplier's domain. This technique reduces the amount of completely spurious errors significantly.

8. CONCLUSION

The research described here explores the use of a vector space model for product categorization. Vector space models have been proven to be effective for text categorization, but not widely explored for use in product categorization. Attempts to extend the vector space model with pricing information appear to have promise, but will require normalization of unit of measure.

9. ACKNOWLEDGMENTS

Thanks to Bob Glushko and Marti Hearst for their coaching and guidance during AutoCat's design and development. This research was partly funded by the National Institute of Standards and Technology, under the Advanced Technology Program (Cooperative Agreement Number 70NANB7H3048).

10. REFERENCES

[1] Bishop, c. 1995. Neural Networks for Pattern Recognition. New York, Oxford University Press, Chapter 2

[2] Buckley, C.; Allan, J.; and Salton, G. 1994. Automatic Routing and Ad-hoc Retrieval Using SMART: TREC 2. In D.K. Harmon, editor, *Proceedings of the Second Text REtrieval Conference (TREC-2)*. NIST Special Publication 500-215. p.45-56

[3] Creecy, R.; Masand, B.; Smith, S.; Waltz, D. 1992. Trading MIPS and Memory for Knowledge Engineering. *Communications of the ACM* Volume 35 Issue 8: p. 48-64.

[4] Frakes, W. B; Baeza-Yates, R. 1992. *Information Retrieval: Data Structures and Algorithms*. Englewood Cliffs, NJ, USA, Prentice Hall.

[5] Salton, G.; Wong A.; and Yang C. 1975. A vector space model for automatic indexing. *Communications of the ACM* 18(11):613-620

[6] Salton, G.; Buckley, C. 1987. Term Weighting Approaches in Automatic Text Retrieval. Technical Report: 87-881 *Department of Computer Science.* Cornell University, Ithaca, NY, USA.

[7] UNSPSC – Universal Standard Products and Services Classification schema. http://www.unspsc.org

[8] xCBL 3.5 - Product Price Definition. http://www.xcbl.org/xcbl35/SOX/schemas/ProductPrice.html #ProductPrice

PageRank, HITS and a Unified Framework for Link Analysis*

Chris Ding[a], Xiaofeng He[a], Parry Husbands[a], Hongyuan Zha[b], Horst D. Simon[a]
[a]Lawrence Berkeley National Laboratory, Berkeley, CA 94720, USA
[b]Pennsylvania State University, University Park, PA 16802, USA
{chqding,xhe,pjrhusbands,hdsimon}@lbl.gov, zha@cse.psu.edu

ABSTRACT

Two popular link-based webpage ranking algorithms are (i) PageRank[1] and (ii) HITS (Hypertext Induced Topic Selection)[3]. HITS makes the crucial distinction of *hubs* and *authorities* and computes them in a mutually reinforcing way. PageRank considers the hyperlink *weight normalization* and the equilibrium distribution of *random surfers* as the citation score. We generalize and combine these key concepts into a unified framework, in which we prove that rankings produced by PageRank and HITS are both highly correlated with the ranking by in-degree and out-degree.

Categories and Subject Descriptors

H.3.3 [**Information Systems**]: Information Search and Retrieval

General Terms

Algorithms, Experimentation

1. HITS ALGORITHM

In the HITS algorithm[3], each webpage i has both a hub score y_i and an authority score x_i. The intuition is that a good *authority* is pointed to by many good *hubs* (this defines the $\mathcal{I}^{op}$ operation) and a good *hub* points to many good *authorities* (this defines the $\mathcal{O}^{op}$ operation). This mutually reinforcing relationship can be represented as the following general operations,

$$\mathbf{x} = \mathcal{I}^{op}(\mathbf{y}), \quad \mathbf{y} = \mathcal{O}^{op}(\mathbf{x}). \tag{1}$$

Here vectors $\mathbf{x} = (x_1, \cdots, x_n)^T$ and $\mathbf{y} = (y_1, \cdots, y_n)^T$ contain the authority score and hub score of each webpage, respectively. $\mathcal{I}^{op}$ and $\mathcal{O}^{op}$ can be written as

$$\mathcal{I}^{op}(\cdot) = L^T, \quad \mathcal{O}^{op}(\cdot) = L. \tag{2}$$

L is the adjacency matrix of the web graph. Final scores are obtained at convergence through the iterations,

$$\begin{aligned} \mathbf{x}^{(t+1)} &= \mathcal{I}^{op}(\mathcal{O}^{op}(\mathbf{x}^{(t)}) = L^T L \mathbf{x}^{(t)} \\ \mathbf{y}^{(t+1)} &= \mathcal{O}^{op}(\mathcal{I}^{op}(\mathbf{y}^{(t)}) = L L^T \mathbf{y}^{(t)} \end{aligned} \tag{3}$$

*LBNL-50007. Nov. 2001. The full paper is available online: `www.nersc.gov/~cding/papers/#web`.

SIGIR'02, August 11-15, 2002, Tampere, Finland.
ACM 1-58113-561-0/02/0008.

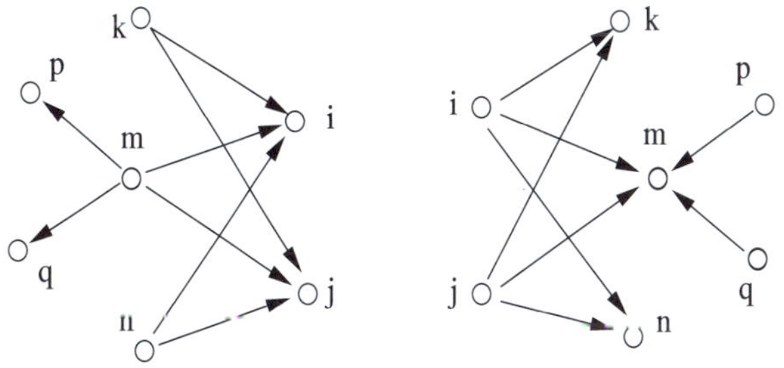

Figure 1: Importance of hyperlink weight normalization. Left: webpages i, j are co-cited by webpages k, m, n. However, since webpage m also cites other webpages p, q, the co-citation of i, j by m is not as significant as the co-citation by either k or n. This fact can be compensated by normalizing the weights on the out-bound links of a webpage; now the co-citation by m is only 2/4=50% as important as the co-citation by either k or n.
Right: webpages i, j co-reference webpages k, n, m. However, since webpage m is also referenced by other webpages p, q, the co-reference of i, j to m is not as significant as the co-reference to either k or n. This fact can be compensated by normalizing the weights on the in-bound links of a webpage.

where $\mathbf{x}^{(t)}, \mathbf{y}^{(t)}$ denote scores at the t-th iteration.

Co-citation and co-reference

We emphasize the role of co-citation and co-reference(Fig.1). Since $L^T L$ determines the authority ranking, we call $L^T L$ the *authority matrix*. We prove that $L^T L = D_{in} + C$, where D_{in} is the diagonal matrix containing in-degrees of all nodes, and C is the co-citation matrix. This shows the close relationship between authority and co-citation.

Since LL^T determines the hub scores, we call LL^T the *hub matrix*. We prove that $LL^T = D_{out} + R$, where D_{out} is the diagonal matrix containing out-degrees of all nodes, and R is the co-reference matrix. This shows the close relationship between hubs and co-references.

Assuming the web graph is a fixed degree sequence random graph, HITS results in average case can be solved in closed form [2], which proves that authority ranking by HITS is *identical* to the ranking by in-degrees. Similarly, hub ranking in HITS is identical to the ranking by out-degrees.

Scheme	$\mathcal{I}^{op}$	$\mathcal{O}^{op}$
HITS	L^T	L
PageRank	$L^T D_{out}^{-1}$	LD_{in}^{-1}
Auth-Rank	$L^T D_{out}^{-1}$	L
Hub-Rank	L^T	LD_{in}^{-1}
Sym-Rank	$D_{in}^{-1/2} L^T D_{out}^{-1/2}$	$D_{out}^{-1/2} L D_{in}^{-1/2}$

Table 1: $\mathcal{I}^{op}$ and $\mathcal{O}^{op}$ operations for HITS, PageRank, Auth-Rank, Hub-Rank, and Sym-Rank.

2. PAGERANK

The key feature of PageRank is the hyperlink weight normalization, as shown in Fig.1 from the perspective of co-citation and co-reference. We may state this as *Internet Democracy*: each website (webpage) has a total of one vote. Another key feature is that PageRank adopts a web surfing model based on a Markov process in determining the scores:

$$\mathbf{x} = \mathcal{I}^{op}(\mathbf{x}),\ \mathcal{I}^{op}(\cdot) = L^T D_{out}^{-1}.$$

The equilibrium distribution of random surfers on webpages is a measure of a webpage's "importance", is the authority score in PageRank.

Hubs in PageRank

We generalize the weight normalization idea to in-bound hyperlinks. One reason is illustrated in Fig.1. Co-reference to a webpage with a large in-degree is not as significant as co-reference to a webpage with a small in-degree. For example, the fact that we all make reference to a highly referenced site such as *New York Times* says little about whether we are similar. But if two persons make reference to Knuth's *The Art of Computer Programming*, it is likely that both persons are interested in computer algorithms.

We propose to define hub in PageRank using the same random surfer model as in definition of authority. The hub scores are obtained through

$$\mathbf{y} = \mathcal{O}^{op}(\mathbf{y}),\ \mathcal{O}^{op}(\cdot) = LD_{in}^{-1} \tag{4}$$

3. A UNIFIED FRAMEWORK

The most important feature of HITS is the mutual reinforcement between hubs and authorities, while the most important feature of PageRank is the hyperlink weight normalization. These features are summarized in Table 1. They can be generalized and combined. We also clarify and formalize *weight propagation* and *random surfing* as two different but related method to compute ranking scores. All these form a unified framework for link analysis.

In this framework, one can easily design new ranking algorithms. We study three new ranking algorithms: the Auth-Rank, the Hub-Rank and the Sym-Rank. Their $\mathcal{I}^{op}, \mathcal{O}^{op}$ operations are defined in Table 1. All these three rankings combine both features of HITS and PageRank, thus they are expected to be somewhere between the rankings produced by HITS and PageRank. The most important results are: all three rankings can be solved in closed-form. The authority rankings of Auth-Rank and Sym-Rank are identical to the ranking by indegrees. The hub rankings of Hub-Rank and Sym-Rank are identical to the ranking by outdegrees. We therefore conclude that even though PageRank and HITS use different methods to compute the link-based ranking, their final rankings will correlate highly with rankings by indegree or outdegree. HITS ranking and PageRank ranking are very similar, too.

Experiment 1. This dateset was supplied by the Internet Archive and was extracted from a crawl performed over 1998-1999. It has 4,906,214 websites and represents a site-level graph of the Web. Rankings are shown below.

Authority Ranking

Hits	InDgr	Page	URL
1	4	6	www.yahoo.com
2	3	3	www.geocities.com
3	1	1	www.microsoft.com
4	6	5	members.aol.com
5	2	2	home.netscape.com
6	10	12	www.excite.com
7	11	15	www.lycos.com
8	9	9	members.tripod.com
9	15	11	ourworld.compuserve.com
10	5	7	www.netscape.com
11	20	25	www.cnn.com
12	28	22	www.webcom.com
13	33	20	sunsite.unc.edu
14	7	4	www.adobe.com
15	35	24	www.teleport.com
16	17	26	www.altavista.digital.com
17	25	16	www.w3.org
18	19	28	www.infoseek.com
19	18	19	www.angelfire.com
20	21	34	www.hotbot.com

Experiment 2. This dataset is about the topic *Running* which contains a total of 13152 webpages. This is a sub-category of a larger category *Fitness* from the Open Directory Project (*www.dmoz.org*). Rankings are shown below.

Authority Ranking

Hits	InDgr	Page	URL
1	2	1	www.runnersworld.com/
2	5	5	sunsite.unc.edu/drears/running/
3	4	2	www.usatf.org/
4	1	3	www.coolrunning.com/
5	6	6	www.clark.net/pub/pribut/spsport
6	8	9	www.runningnetwork.com/
7	9	8	www.iaaf.org/
8	14	20	www.sirius.ca/running.html
9	12	12	www.wimsey.com/~dblaikie/
10	15	17	www.kicksports.com/
11	7	7	www.nyrrc.org/
12	18	14	www.usaldr.org/
13	20	32	www.halhigdon.com/
14	25	30	www.ontherun.com/
15	10	89	www.runningroom.com/
16	23	31	www.webrunner.com/webrun/running
17	22	23	www.doitsports.com/
18	21	79	www.arfa.org/
19	19	16	www.adidas.com/
20	11	13	www.uta.fi/~csmipe/sport/

In both datasets, HITS ranking and PageRank ranking are highly correlated with indegree ranking.

4. REFERENCES

[1] S. Brin and L. Page. The anatomy of a large-scale hypertextual web search engine. *Proc. of 7th WWW Conferece*, 1998.

[2] C. Ding, H. Zha, X. He, P. Husbands, and H. Simon. Analysis of hubs and authorities on the web. *Lawrence Berkeley Nat'l Lab Tech Report* 47847, May 2001.

[3] J. M. Kleinberg. Authoritative sources in a hyperlinked environment. *J. ACM*, 48:604–632, 1999.

Task Orientation in Question Answering

Vanessa Murdock
Center for Intelligent Information Retrieval
Computer Science Department
University of Massachusetts
Amherst, MA 01003
vanessa@cs.umass.edu

W. Bruce Croft
Center for Intelligent Information Retrieval
Computer Science Department
University of Massachusetts
Amherst, MA 01003
croft@cs.umass.edu

Categories and Subject Descriptors

H.3.4 [Information Storage and Retrieval]: Systems and Software - *Performance evaluation*

General Terms

Measurement and Performance

Keywords

Query Classification, Task-Orientation

1. INTRODUCTION

Information retrieval techniques treat questions democratically: all questions, regardless of their grammar or orientation, are processed by the same rules and manipulated in similar ways. In about 12% of the questions in our data users ask about a process. Treating a request for how to do something as a request for information about a topic disregards an important subtlety in the question. We use the knowledge that a question asks about a process, rather than a fact, to develop categories of information need implied by the questions to aid in retrieval. We focus on questions because by their nature questions carry more information.

A well-known technique for improving retrieval is query expansion. A variety of query expansion and disambiguation techniques have been studied [1] [2] [3] [5], and although none distinguish between fact-orientation and task-orientation, several do distinguish categories of information need not explicit in the queries.

Understanding that the user has already made their information need clear by using a question rather than a keyword query, we utilized information encoded in the fact or task orientation to infer the type of information need. We found a measurable difference between task- and fact-oriented questions, and preliminary results indicate that treating fact- and task oriented questions differently improves retrieval.

2. FACT AND TASK QUESTIONS

Our corpus of 4100 questions came from the query logs of the search engine, Govbot [1]. About 4 in every 1000 queries to Govbot were well-formed questions, with an average length of 8 words, and a total vocabulary of 3700 unique words pertaining to government. Variation in the grammatical structure of the sentence was reduced because every question began with a question word (who, what, where, when, why, how).

To get an initial estimate of the number of fact-oriented and task-oriented questions in our corpus, we developed rules based on the question words. We divided the 4100 questions into a fact-oriented set and a task-oriented set. According to these rules, 700 of the questions were task-oriented, and 3400 were fact-oriented. We did not filter out ambiguous questions; they were included in either the fact-oriented set or the task-oriented set depending on their question words.

In order to analyze the question structure in more depth, we constructed parse trees of the questions using a statistical parser, SIFT, from BBN [4]. From our set of 700 task-oriented questions, 630 contained the same distinctive parse of the verb phrase. Of our 3400 fact-oriented questions, only 490 contained that specific internal structure.

This suggests fact-oriented questions and task-oriented questions are distinct. It also suggests that task-oriented questions relate the verb to the noun phrase more directly than fact-oriented questions. Traditional information retrieval techniques do not give the verb any special consideration. The verb is frequently stemmed into a noun, or removed as a stop-word, altering the relationship between the verb and the noun phrase.

3. CLASSIFYING QUESTIONS USING LANGUAGE MODELS

There are many approaches to classification. Because we are interested in applications of language modeling in information retrieval, we built a classifier using language models, with perplexity as our metric.

Examining each question by hand, we created a training corpus of 580 task-oriented questions, and a test corpus of 60 task-oriented questions. We created two training corpora of 720 and 2930 fact-oriented questions, and a test corpus of 80 fact-oriented questions. For the sake of the accuracy of the language model, we eliminated questions that were ambiguous because they could not be answered with a fact or a process, such as those asking for opinions.

Table 1 shows the percentage of questions correctly classified by a variety of techniques. Trigram models performed the best, in terms of classification accuracy. Increasing the

[1] Govbot was a search engine for .gov and .mil domains, in operation from 1995 to 2001 at the Center for Intelligent Information Retrieval, at the University of Massachusetts.

SIGIR'02, August 11-15, 2002, Tampere, Finland.
ACM 1-58113-561-0/02/0008.

Technique	Accuracy	
	task	fact
unigram model	75%	59%
bigram model	88%	70%
trigram model	88%	74%
4-gram model	88%	73%
Increasing training set size	93%	73%
using VB-NP for task questions	28%	89%
fitting the perplexity curve	95%	75%
parse trees	77%	87%
rule-based approach	81%	99%

Table 1: Percent of questions correctly classified using a variety of classification techniques.

training-set size of the fact-oriented model from 720 questions to 2930 questions produced an improvement in accuracy of 5% for task-oriented questions.

Questions may use the same vocabulary but have a different orientation, as in "How do I apply for a passport" and "How long does it take to apply for a passport." The similarity in the vocabulary makes it nearly impossible for a language-model based classifier to distinguish between them. To reduce the similarity between the two training corpora, we reduced the task-oriented training set to its verb-noun phrase component. The fact-oriented training set could not be reduced because it doesn't share this construction. We trained a language model on the verb-noun phrase pairs from the task-oriented training set, and used a trigram model trained on 720 fact-oriented questions. The fact oriented questions showed an improvement of 15%.

Each of these classifiers assumes, by choosing the strictly lower perplexity score, that the threshold dividing the two classes is the line at which the perplexity scores of the two models is the same, i.e. the line $y = x$. But the threshold between the two classes may be a curve, or it may be a line with a different slope. To improve upon the simple trigram model we combined the best classifier for the task-oriented questions, and the best classifier for fact-oriented questions. The curve that best incorporates both classifiers is:

$$0.1 * [(0.95C_1)^3 + (0.05C_2)^3]^{1/3}$$

where C_1 is the classifier most accurate for task questions and C_2 is the classifier most accurate for fact questions. Using this classifier, we were able to correctly classify 95% of the task questions, and 75% of the fact questions.

From the parse trees, we know that the task questions have a more regular syntactic structure, whereas the fact questions have much more structural variation. In addition there were more than five times as many fact questions as task questions, introducing more uncertainty in those language models. For these reasons, the classification of fact questions is much less reliable than task questions. Choosing training sets with less linguistic variety, increasing the size of the task-oriented training set, or incorporating syntactic information into the language model may improve the accuracy of the classification.

Looking only for the verb-noun phrase structure we correctly classified 87% of fact questions, and 77% of task questions. Using only the first three words of the questions we had 99% accuracy in fact-oriented questions and 81% accuracy in task-oriented questions. This isn't surprising considering that we devised the rules by looking at a subset of the training set, and the questions in the corpus were selected from the query logs with criteria very similar to the rules in our classifier. In other words, the high accuracy of the rule-based approach reflects over-fitting the data.

That said, there is a strong correlation between the first three words of the sentence and the orientation of the sentence. There is a strong relationship between the syntactic structure of the questions and their orientation. There is a high degree of similarity between questions of one orientation, as suggested by the language model classification. This gives us three pieces of strong evidence that there is a measurable and significant difference between the two types of questions, a difference we can exploit to improve retrieval.

4. CONCLUSION

We have shown that we can classify questions as fact- or task-oriented in three ways: based on the question words, using their grammatical structure, and by training language models. Knowing that the information need implied by the question is different depending on its orientation allows us to develop techniques specific to each genre of question.

A manual analysis of ten questions suggested certain genres of document (specifically forms and FAQs) were almost always relevant to task-oriented questions. We are currently examining whether query expansion by adding genre-specific terms will improve retrieval for task-oriented questions. Since the syntactic difference between the two question types is consistent, we are also looking at whether preserving the relationship between verb and noun phrase, or weighting the verb in the query, improves retrieval.

Acknowledgments

This work was supported in part by the Center for Intelligent Information Retrieval and in part by NSF grant #IIS-9907018, and in part by Advanced Research and Development Activity under contract number MDA904-01-C-0984. Any opinions, findings and conclusions or recommendations expressed in this material are the authors' and do not necessarily reflect those of the sponsor.

5. REFERENCES

[1] A. Berger, R. Caruana, D. Cohn, D. Freitag, and V. Mittal. Bridging the lexical chasm: Statistical approaches to answer-finding. In *Proceedings of the 23rd Annual Conference on Research and Development in Information Retrieval (ACM SIGIR)*, pages 192–199, 2000.

[2] C. Buckley, G. Salton, J. Allan, and A. Singhal. Automatic query expansion using SMART : TREC 3. In D. K. Harmon, editor, *NIST Special Publication 500-225: The Third Text Retrieval conference (TREC 3)*, pages 69–80, 1995.

[3] E. J. Glover, S. Lawrence, M. D. Gordon, W. P. Birmingham, and C. L. Giles. Web search your way. *Communications of the ACM*, 44(12):97–102, December 2001.

[4] S. Miller, M. Crystal, H. Fox, L. Ramshaw, R. Schwartz, R. Stone, R. Weischedel, and the Annotation Group. Algorithms that learn to extract information–BBN: Description of the SIFT system as used for MUC-7. In *Proceedings of the Seventh Message Understanding Conference (MUC-7)*, 1998.

[5] J. Xu and B. Croft. Query expansion using local and global document analysis. In *Proceedings of the 19th Annual Conference on Research and Development in Information Retrieval (ACM SIGIR)*, pages 4–11, 1996.

Experiments in High-Dimensional Text Categorization

Fred J. Damerau, Tong Zhang, Sholom M. Weiss and Nitin Indurkhya
IBM T.J. Watson Research Center
P.O. Box 218, Yorktown Heights, NY 10598, USA
damerau@us.ibm.com, tongz@us.ibm.com, sholom@us.ibm.com, nitin@data-miner.com

ABSTRACT

We present results for automated text categorization of the Reuters-810000 collection of news stories. Our experiments use the entire one-year collection of 810,000 stories and the entire subject index. We divide the data into monthly groups and provide an initial benchmark of text categorization performance on the complete collection. Experimental results show that efficient sparse-feature implementations of linear methods and decision trees, using a global unstemmed dictionary, can readily handle applications of this size. Predictive performance is approximately as strong as the best results for the much smaller older Reuters collections. Detailed results are provided over time periods. It is shown that a smaller time horizon does not diminish predictive quality, implying reduced demands for retraining when sample size is large.

Categories and Subject Descriptors

H.3.1 [**Information Storage and Retrieval**]: Content Analysis and Indexing

General Terms

Experimentation

1. INTRODUCTION

Automated text categorization methods have gradually improved over time, to the point where they can often rival human performance. One major contributor to progress in the field has been the availability of standard benchmarks that allow researchers to evaluate performance relative to prior work, e.g., the Reuters-21578 collection of 21,578 stories from the year 1987. A new, far larger collection of Reuters newswires is now publicly available[2]. In this paper, we make use of this data set to establish a new benchmark for evaluating text categorization performance in a high dimensional space. A more complete discussion of our experiments and results is found in [1]. The new Reuters-810000 collection was examined in restricted form during the 2001 TREC Filtering Track, where only the first 26,150 cases were used for training. Here we use all months except the last for training, and all original topics are considered.

The availability of a very large collection of texts with classification codes from Reuters has made possible the exploration of some open questions in the construction of classification models. One of these questions is how rapidly a classification model decays, i.e., a classification model trained with documents from t_1 to t_2 has a certain accuracy at time t_3, but presumably will have a lower accuracy at time t_n, decreasing with increasing n.

2. CORPUS DETAILS

The new Reuters corpus consists of some 810 thousand stories covering the Reuters newswire over a year, August 20, 1996 to August 19, 1997. Uncompressed, it is about 2.5 gigabytes. Each story has a certain amount of associated metadata, such as creation date, publication date, source, etc. Included in the metadata are three codes: region codes, topic codes and industry codes. We focus here on the topic codes.

3. CLASSIFICATION METHODS

In our applied work for text categorization, we ordinarily use one of two models, a decision tree or a linear classifier. The decision tree classifier has the advantage that the tree can be reduced to a set of more or less understandable classification rules, which allow a classification model to be manually adjusted if desired. The linear model is, however, generally more accurate. Brief descriptions of our algorithms and implementations follow; details can be found in the references.

4. EXPERIMENTS

We partitioned the documents into 12 groups, each corresponding to all stories appearing during a month.[1]. A key concept that we wished to explore was the rate of decay of a classification model over time. We used the 12th month as our test data, and trained classification models based on each of the 11 preceding months, the previous two months, the previous three months, the previous six months and the preceding 11 months, i.e., all the available training

[1]A month for our Reuters data commences on the 20th calendar day and continues through the 19th day of the following month.

SIGIR'02, August 11-15, 2002, Tampere, Finland.

Num of features	Classifier type	Training Data (Months)														
		1	2	3	4	5	6	7	8	9	10	11	10:11	9:11	6:11	1:11
1K	tree	71.9	72.2	72.5	72.5	71.9	73.0	72.7	73.4	74.2	74.3	74.9	76.6	77.5	78.5	79.2
	linear	80.9	81.0	81.1	81.2	80.2	80.6	80.4	81.2	81.8	81.8	82.4	82.6	82.7	82.5	82.5
5K	tree	73.8	73.8	74.5	74.4	73.9	75.0	74.5	75.3	76.0	76.0	76.5	78.1	78.9	79.8	80.6
	linear	83.9	83.9	84.0	84.1	83.2	83.6	83.4	84.1	84.8	84.9	85.2	85.5	85.7	85.6	85.6
20K	tree	73.8	74.0	74.7	74.6	73.9	75.1	74.6	75.4	76.2	76.3	76.6	78.3	79.1	79.9	80.8
	linear	84.2	84.4	84.3	84.5	83.6	84.0	83.7	84.5	85.1	85.2	85.6	85.9	86.0	86.0	86.0
365K (Titles)	tree	75.0	75.2	75.6	75.9	75.1	76.3	75.9	76.6	77.1	77.0	77.7	79.1	79.9	80.9	81.6
	linear	84.8	84.9	84.9	85.1	84.1	84.5	84.2	85.0	85.7	85.7	86.0	86.3	86.5	86.4	86.5

Table 1: F-measure micro-average over all categories by feature set size for decision tree and linear classifier

data. Our methods can exploit very large feature sets. In the case of text classification, a feature is a word and the feature value is some measure of the frequency of that word. The feature sets ranged from all possible tokens, to tokens not including numbers, to tokens which had been stemmed by an inflectional stemmer. Token set sizes ranged from almost 400,000 to 10,000 to 1000. We ran a few preliminary experiments with 150 features, but the results were not satisfactory and we did not do a full experiment with the small feature set. Results from these experiments are shown in the tables which follow.

Common performance measures for text categorization are: (1) precision: the proportion of classifications that are right with respect to the total of those proposed, (2) recall: the proportion of classifications that are correct with respect to the true classification, (3) F-measure(F): the harmonic mean of precision and recall:

$$F = 2 * (recall * precision)/(recall + precision) \quad (1)$$

In this paper we report only the F-measure of equation 1. Complete tables showing recall and precision for each experiment are available from the authors.

5. RESULTS AND DISCUSSION

Consider first the results micro-averaged over all categories using using titles and stemming by feature set size, Table 1. Let's first focus on the results for 365K features, the complete set of unstemmed, non-numerical words. In all cases, the linear method is substantially better than the decision tree for all models. (As we will see below, for some of the infrequently occurring categories, the decision tree is better, but the results are still not very good. We will look in detail at one of the rarer categories, religion-GREL.) Returning to the micro average and looking at the models generated by the linear method from month 1 through the full collection of months 1-11, we can see that the F-measure is increasing, but it is not monotonically increasing. Moreover, the model built on month 1 is less than two points lower than the model built on the whole collection for the linear model. The decision tree model is substantially worse, about 5 points lower for month 1 than for the entire collection. The implications of this in an operational environment are significant and comforting. At least for this kind of data, frequent model updating does not appear to be necessary, if the original linear model was built on sufficient data. The situation for decision tree models is not as encouraging. In this case, using more historical data provides a clear improvement over using only one of the preceding months. Whether the transparency of a rule based system merits the use of significantly more training training data depends on the application.

Looking further at Table 1, we see that for the linear method there is a clear gain in going from 1000 features to 5000 features, but beyond that the gains are much smaller. Because our methods are relatively insensitive to feature set size, we will continue to focus discussion on the the results with 365,000 features. The decision tree classifier, however, does not improve greatly when going from 1000 features to 365,000 features, showing a trend to overfit in a very large, noisy feature space.

The Reuters-810000 collection is nearly 40 times larger than the previous collection. The earlier version served as a source of benchmarks in text categorization. Using sparse-feature methods, we readily processed this huge collection of labeled news stories. Results are competitive with the best results for the smaller collections. Our results provide an initial benchmark for future comparisons and improvements. Whether these results apply outside the newswire domain will require further experimentation on other labeled document collections.

The larger collection of documents increases dimensions in many directions, including a much larger feature or word space, and an increased sample size for most topics. Operating in this much larger feature space, we found that the simplest methods were effective. For example, we did not have to do any special processing to create a dictionary; rather we just gather all words in all training documents. For our sparse-data machine-learning methods, the increase in the number of words is of minor consequence. Word lookup is by hash table, and only a small percentage of words occur in any document. For this application, words with numerical content had no additional predictive value. For other applications, such as those containing specialized part numbers, they may be of critical importance.

It is clear that the amount and recency of training data needed to build a classification model for newswire texts is dependent on the model. A linear model is much less sensitive to the recency effect and requires less training data, as well as being more accurate overall as compared to a decision tree. In the case of less frequent categories, however, a decision tree can be more accurate. We made no attempt to train differently for any category. It may very well be the case that results will improve when training procedures are modified to take into account highly skewed populations for rare topics.

6. REFERENCES

[1] F. J. Damerau, T. Zhang, S. M. Weiss, and N. Indurkhya Experiments in High-Dimensional Text Categorization *IBM Research Report RC22330*, 2002.

[2] See web site for details. *http://about.reuters.com/researchandstandards/corpus/available.htm.*

The Relationship Between ASK and Relevance Criteria

Xiao-Jun Yuan Nicholas J. Belkin Ja-Young Kim
Rutgers University, SCILS
4 Huntington Street, New Brunswick, NJ 08901-1071, USA
+1 732 932 7500
xjyuan@scils.rutgers.edu nick@belkin.rutgers.edu jaykim@scils.rutgers.edu

1. INTRODUCTION

Throughout the past decade, there have been many studies of human relevance judgment behavior, with particular reference to the criteria that people use to evaluate the relevance or usefulness of documents [1] [2] [7] [8]. There have also been attempts to understand under what circumstances particular criteria might be preferentially used. Most of the latter studies have, as their underlying independent variable, some concept related to the person's "information need" or "information problem", for instance, the person's stage in the information seeking process [10]. But none that we know of has attempted to operationalize the information problem and to relate that to the use of relevance criteria. We present results of a preliminary investigation of the relationship of one representation of information problem, the Anomalous State of Knowledge (ASK) [3] of users of an Information Retrieval Service (IRS), to their judgments of the usefulness of documents with respect to their information problems. Our goal is to be able to: a) characterize and distinguish between different types of information problems, so that b) we can predict which types of relevance criteria may be most significant for each type (or state) of problem.

Categories & Subject Descriptors: H.3.3 [Information Storage and Retrieval]: Information Search and Retrieval - search process, query formulation.

General Terms: Human Factors.

Keywords: Relevance judgments, relevance criteria, anomalous state of knowledge

2. ASKs

Belkin [3] proposed that why people engage in information seeing behavior could be explained as their finding themselves in a state of knowledge that is inadequate or *anomalous* with respect to the achievement of some goal. He further suggested that one could represent such an *ASK* as an associative structure of concepts and their relationships; that is, as a graph or network. Subsequently, Belkin, Oddy & Brooks [5], suggested a classification of ASKs based on several characteristics of the graphs, the most significant of which was their connectivity. By connectivity, they meant the proportion of actual links between nodes, to the total possible number of links in the graph. They identified five classes of ASKs, which were meant to reflect how well-formed and understood was the ASK by the user. A well-formed ASK has high connectivity, and reflects an information problem such as that faced by an expert writing a literature review. An ill-formed ASK has low connectivity, and reflects an information problem such as that faced by a student who is attempting to identify a thesis topic.

[7] and [4] investigated the relationships between ASK structures and equivalent document structures, to establish retrieval rules sensitive to different ASK structures. In the course of these investigations, they collected 35 narrative oral "problem statements" from users of an operational IRS, which were converted into associative ASK structures, and four-point "usefulness" judgments for up to 15 documents read by each user. The users were asked to indicate *why* they made each judgment. We use these data, from 28 of the subjects, for whom we have a total of 158 judgments, as the basis for our study. We are primarily interested in the "why", in order to understand what criteria the users, as represented by their ASK structures, were applying.

3. METHOD

[9] identified 8 classes of relevance criteria that seem to be common to all such studies. We used these criteria (Table 1) as the basis for content-analytic coding of each of the explanations.

Table 1. Relevance criteria categories (after [1])

Criteria	Examples
1. Topicality	About my topic
2. Novelty	Unique or the only source me; Familiar
3. Currency	Up-to-date information
4. Quality of Info.	Well-written; Credible; Understandable;
5. Presentation	Presentation of information; Comprehensive
6. Source Aspects	Prominent; I know the author or source
7. Info. Aspects	Describes treatment or techniques; Examples
8. Appeal.	I like it; Interesting; Enjoyable

To relate criteria to ASK type, we used just the connectivity of the ASK graphs, but at several levels of association strength, as suggested by [4]. They identified 4 levels of connectivity, according to the 4 levels of strength of association between nodes that they used in their analysis. Level 4 connectivity is overall connectivity without regard to association strength; level 1 connectivity is the connectivity when only the highest level of association strength is considered. On the basis of [5], we categorized the ASKs into 5 classes, at each of the four levels, using the SPSS function Frequencies in descriptive statistics.

4. RESULTS

Our coding results of relevance criteria further confirm the results of Barry and Schamber's [1] study, with a few new examples (Table 1). The most, second and the least frequently used

SIGIR'02, August 11-15, 2002, Tampere, Finland.
ACM 1-58113-561-0/02/0008.

relevance criteria are respectively *topicality*, *information aspects* and *currency*. The other criteria display nearly equal frequencies.

After equally dividing ASKs into 5 classes, Pearson Chi-Square test results shows that the relationships between relevance criteria and overall connectivity at level 3 (p=.011) and level 4 (p=.029) are statistically significant. But more important is the pattern of different criteria and classes of ASK, shown in Table 2, where 1 means the least and 5 the most connected ASK classes, as computed at level 4 connectivity. Here we can see that there are definitely different patterns of use of criteria according to the type of ASK. Type 5, for instance, uses information aspects most frequently, with other criteria used roughly equally, while Type 3 is strongly skewed toward both topicality and novelty. Type 1 uses quality relatively more often than do the other Types, and currency is most important to Type 2. Presentation appears more important to Types 1 and 2 than to the others.

Table 2. Distribution of criteria by ASK Type at level 4, frequency of use = n **and percent of criteria used by Type =** (n)

	ASK Types				
Criteria	**1**	**2**	**3**	**4**	**5**
Topic	16 (25)	8 (16)	21 (54)	28 (30)	5 (14)
Novel	5 (08)	4 (08)	1 (26)	12 (13)	3 (09)
Current		5 (10)		3 (03)	1 (03)
Quality	10 (16)	4 (08)	3 (08)	3 (03)	4 (11)
Present.	9 (14)	7 (14)	2 (05)	8 (09)	3 (09)
Source	5 (08)	5 (10)	4 (10)	10 (11)	5 (14)
Inform.	11 (17)	12 (24)	5 (13)	21 (22)	8 (23)
Appeal.	7 (11)	5 (10)	3 (08)	9 (10)	6 (17)
Totals	63	50	39	94	35

5. DISCUSSION AND CONCLUSIONS

Our study confirms the idea [1] that there exists a core set of relevance criteria that applies to a wide variety of information use and information problem types. Although topicality is the most frequently used relevance criterion in this study, currency is the not one of the most important relevance criteria as suggested by [2]. Instead, it is the least frequently used relevance criterion. This may be attributed to the different data sources of these two studies. The users in our study were quite diverse in terms of their topics of interest, but were similar in that they all came to use an academic IRS. More important, we were able to identify differences in the use of relevance criteria according to a purely formal classification of ASK types. This is, as far as we know, the first time that a direct representation of a person's information "need" or problem has been shown to be related to the relevance criteria which that person would bring to bear when evaluating documents. Although the number of subjects in the study was small, and we do not at the moment have convincing explanations of these relationships, we find these preliminary results highly suggestive, and worthy of being followed up by more detailed investigation.

A limitation of our study was the use of one primary judge of the relevance criteria from usefulness judgments. However, there are definite safeguards peculiar in this study—the standard of judgment stays consistent from the beginning to the end and it would be relatively simple and reliable to compare our judgments with others in future work.

6. REFERENCES

[1] Barry, C. & Schamber, L. (1998). Users' criteria for relevance evaluation: A cross-situational comparison. Information Processing and Management, 34 (2/3), 219-236.

[2] Bateman, J. (1999). Modeling the importance of end-user relevance criteria. Proceedings of the 62nd ASIS Annual Meeting, 36, 396-406.

[3] Belkin, N.J. (1980). Anomalous states of knowledge as a basis for information retrieval. Canadian Journal of Information Science, 5, 133-143.

[4] Belkin, N.J. & Kwasnik, B. (1986). Using structural representations of anomalous states of knowledge for choosing document retrieval strategies. Proceedings of 1986 ACM Conference on Research and Development in Information Retrieval, Pisa, Italy, 11-22.

[5] Belkin, N.J., Oddy, R.N., & Brooks, H.M. (1982). ASK for information retrieval, Part II. Results of a design study. Journal of Documentation, 38 (2), 145-167.

[6] Cool, C., Belkin, N.J., Frieder, O. & Kantor, P. (1993) Characteristics of texts affecting relevance judgments. In M.E. Williams, ed. *Proceedings of the Fourteenth National Online Meeting*. Medford, NJ, Learned Information, Inc: 77-83

[7] Hapeshi, K. & Belkin, N.J. (1985). Developing and evaluating a automatic on-line information retrieval system based on user problem statements. Proceedings of RIAO '85, Grenoble, France, I.M.A.G., 681-698.

[8] Schamber, L., Eisenberg, M, & Nilan, M. (1990). A re-examination of relevance: Toward a dynamic, situational definition. Information Processing and Management, 26, 775-776.

[9] Schamber, L. & Bateman, J. (1996). User criteria in relevance evaluation: Toward development of a measurement scale. Proceedings of the 59th ASIS Annual Meeting, 33, 218-225.

[10] Spink, A. & Saracevic, T. (1997). Interactive information retrieval: Sources and effectiveness of search terms during mediated online searching. Journal of the American Society for Information Science, 48(8), 741-761

ICA and SOM in Text Document Analysis

Ella Bingham, Jukka Kuusisto and Krista Lagus
Neural Networks Research Centre, Helsinki University of Technology, Finland
ella@iki.fi, jukka.kuusisto@hut.fi, krista.lagus@hut.fi

ABSTRACT

In this study we show experimental results on using Independent Component Analysis (ICA) and the Self-Organizing Map (SOM) in document analysis. Our documents are segments of spoken dialogues carried out over the telephone in a customer service, transcribed into text. The task is to analyze the topics of the discussions, and to group the discussions into meaningful subsets. The quality of the grouping is studied by comparing to a manual topical classification of the documents.

Categories and Subject Descriptors

I.2.7 [**Artificial Intelligence**]: Natural Language Processing—*Text analysis*; I.5.4 [**Pattern Recognition**]: Applications—*Text processing*

General Terms

Algorithms, Experimentation

1. INTRODUCTION AND METHODS

The automatic analysis of textual documents and their topics is one of the challenges of modern information processing systems. One of the applications of this analysis is information retrieval. Given a set of documents, the task is to find out what a document is about, and which documents share similarities.

The methods used in this study are the Self-Organizing Map (SOM) and Independent component analysis (ICA). Both are completely unsupervised methods: when grouping a set of documents into subsets, no labeled training data is needed to aid in forming the groups.

ICA [2, 5] is a method for presenting a set of multivariate observations as a (linear) combination of unknown latent variables that are statistically independent. ICA was originally developed for signal processing purposes, but lately it has been found out that it is a suitable method for analyzing text documents, too, if documents are presented using the vector space model. The latent variables are in this case the document topics, and these can be regarded as probability distributions on the universe of terms. First approaches of finding the latent topics of a set of documents using ICA were presented in [6, 11].

It has been shown that the SOM [9] can be used to automatically organize very large document collections onto document maps [10]. On the ordered two-dimensional map, documents that are similar in content are found near each other. Using the SOM in text retrieval is described in [12].

SIGIR'02, August 11-15, 2002, Tampere, Finland.
ACM 1-58113-561-0/02/0008.

2. DATA

The data used in the experiments were Finnish dialogues, recorded from the customer service phone line of Helsinki City Transport. The data was manually transcribed into text and base forms of the words were found automatically — in a morphologically rich language such as Finnish, this task is not straightforward. The data was provided by the Interact project [7]. In total, 57 dialogues were collected. A number of topic categories were selected so that they comprehensively encompass the subjects occurring in the data. The dialogues were manually tagged and segmented, so that each segment belongs to a topic category and forms a separate document. The total number of such documents was 195. The topic categories are 'timetables' (45 documents), 'beginnings' (57), 'tickets' (18), 'endings' (55) and 'out of domain' (20).

Characteristic of the transcribed data is that it is extremely colloquial: Both the customer and the customer servant use a lot of expletive words, such as 'nii' ('so', 'yea') and 'tota' ('hum', 'er', 'like'), often the words appear in reduced or otherwise non-standard forms, the word order does not always follow grammatical rules and quite frequently there is considerable overlap between the dialogue turns.

3. EXPERIMENTS AND DISCUSSION

The documents were encoded as vectors using the methods described in [10]. In short, the encoding was as follows. Stopwords (function words etc.) and words that appeared fewer than 2 times were removed. The remaining 1894 words were weighted using their entropy over manual document classes (cf. [10]). The documents were then encoded using the vector space model by Salton [14].

Furthermore, sparse random projection of the word vectors was applied to reduce the dimensionality of the vectors [10, 8]: for each word, 5 random dimensions out of a 500-dimensional vector were set to one, the rest being zeros. A document vector was then calculated as the sum of the vectors of its words, weighted by the word weights.

Results on ICA. We considered both the original 1894-dimensional data and 500-dimensional random projected data, as described above. The use of random projection as a means of speeding up computation in the context of ICA of text documents has not been reported elsewhere, up to our knowledge.

As a preprocessing step, the dimensionality of the term by document matrix was reduced using Latent Semantic Indexing [3] from the original high dimensionality (1894 or 500) to 10 or 15, which were the numbers of estimated topics.

Table 1: Classification accuracies and CPU times of ICA and SOM.

Method	Classification accuracy of topic categories, %					Total	CPU time, seconds
	timetables	beginnings	tickets	endings	out of domain	accuracy, %	(ICA in Matlab, SOM in C)
ICA 10	93.3	100	94.4	98.2	0	87.2	8.04
ICA RP 10	84.4	99.5	94.4	96.4	0	84.5	7.12
ICA 15	87.0	100	62.2	97.4	48.00	87.4	18.37
ICA RP 15	67.2	99.7	81.9	93.2	53.0	83.9	11.41
SOM RP	93.3	100	77.8	100	60.0	92.3	7.10

The FastICA algorithm[1] [4] was used to estimate the latent topics. As an output of the algorithm we get projection directions into which the data must be projected to reveal the latent variables (topics). The projections now tell the topic activities in documents; i.e. how good an example an observed document is of the topic.

Each estimated latent topic variable is mapped to the manual document category whose documents have the highest sum of topic activities in the latent variable. Also, each document is classified to that latent variable in which the document has highest topic activity. If the document is classified to a latent variable representing a different category than where the document was manually grouped, we consider the document misclassified. The total classification accuracy is the percentage of correct classifications.

The numbers of estimated topics (10 and 15) were found by trial and error. A smaller number than 10 lead to smaller classification accuracy; but as we see in Table 1, estimating 15 topics did not increase the accuracy but only required more computing power.

Results on the SOM. In our experiment, a SOM of $6 \times 4 = 24$ units was organized. Each document was placed into its best-matching map unit. Next, each map unit was assigned a topic by a majority vote of the documents in that unit. When the minority documents were counted as errors, the accuracy was 92.3% on the whole data set.

A size of 6×4 was chosen in order to have a non-square map grid where the proportion between number of documents and number of map units is roughly 1/10.

Comparison of results and discussion. A summary of the results and CPU times is presented in Table 1. The ICA results are averages over 20 runs, as different initializations may cause fluctuations. 10 or 15 latent ICA topics were estimated, and the data was either used in its original or random projected (RP) form; SOM only used random-projected data. The CPU times are not fully comparable as SOM uses C code and FastICA is realized in Matlab, and the implementations are somewhat different.

Both methods successfully classified large topic categories, especially 'beginnings' and 'endings'. In these categories, the documents are quite similar within the category, which may help the classification. The category 'out of domain' is hard to classify especially on ICA as there are only a few documents, and they do not form a statistically meaningful and coherent entity.

The estimated topic groups can be analyzed by their keywords. In the contexts of ICA and SOM, these are found as described in [1] and [13], respectively. The keywords (not listed here due to space limitations) nicely correspond to the true topic categories.

As a conclusion, ICA and SOM perform quite similarly in document analysis of a small dialogue data. A larger corpus with more categories would perhaps be needed to distinguish between the methods.

[1] `http://www.cis.hut.fi/projects/ica/fastica/`

4. REFERENCES

[1] E. Bingham. Topic identification in dynamical text by extracting minimum complexity time components. In *Proc. ICA2001*, pages 546–551, 2001.

[2] P. Comon. Independent component analysis — a new concept? *Signal Processing*, 36:287–314, 1994.

[3] S. Deerwester, S. T. Dumais, G. W. Furnas, T. K. Landauer, and R. Harshman. Indexing by latent semantic analysis. *Journal of the American Society for Information Science*, 41(6):391–407, 1990.

[4] A. Hyvärinen. Fast and robust fixed-point algorithms for independent component analysis. *IEEE Tr. on Neural Networks*, 10(3):626–634, May 1999.

[5] A. Hyvärinen, J. Karhunen, and E. Oja. *Independent component analysis.* Wiley Interscience, 2001.

[6] C. L. Isbell and P. Viola. Restucturing sparse high dimensional data for effective retrieval. In *Adv. in Neural Inf. Proc. Systems 11*, pages 480–486, 1998.

[7] K. Jokinen. Sigdial — the USIX Interact project: Adaptivity in dialogue systems. *Elsnews*, 10(2):10, Summer 2001.

[8] S. Kaski. Dimensionality reduction by random mapping: Fast similarity computation for clustering. In *Proc. IJCNN'98*, volume 1, pages 413–418. 1998.

[9] T. Kohonen. *Self-Organizing Maps*, volume 30 of *Springer Series in Information Sciences.* Springer, Berlin, 1995.

[10] T. Kohonen, S. Kaski, K. Lagus, J. Salojärvi, V. Paatero, and A. Saarela. Organization of a massive document collection. *IEEE Tr. on Neural Networks*, 11(3):574–585, May 2000.

[11] T. Kolenda, L. K. Hansen, and S. Sigurdsson. Independent components in text. In M. Girolami, editor, *Advances in Independent Component Analysis*, chapter 13, pages 235–256. Springer-Verlag, 2000.

[12] K. Lagus. Text retrieval using self-organized document maps. *Neural Processing Letters*, 15(1):21–29, 2002.

[13] K. Lagus and S. Kaski. Keyword selection method for characterizing text document maps. In *Proc. ICANN99*, volume 1, pages 371–376, 1999.

[14] G. Salton and M. McGill. *Introduction to modern information retrieval.* McGraw-Hill, New York, 1983.

Improving Hierarchical Text Classification Using Unlabeled Data

Vijay Boyapati
Whizbang! Labs – Research
vijayboyapati@yahoo.com

Categories & Subject Descriptors: H.3.3

General Terms: Algorithms

1. INTRODUCTION

Large text classification tasks are often organized hierarchically to minimize the cognitive effort required to manage them. Recent research has focused on how to best use the extra information provided by the hierarchical organization of these tasks to build more accurate automatic text classifiers [1,2]. Common among many of these research efforts is an approach to building hierarchical text classifiers by first subdividing the task into a number of smaller classification tasks – one per decision point in the hierarchy – then building a separate classifier for each of the smaller tasks. An overall classification is made by greedily following the most probable classification decisions down the hierarchy from the Root class. This "pachinko machine" approach is illustrated in figure 1.

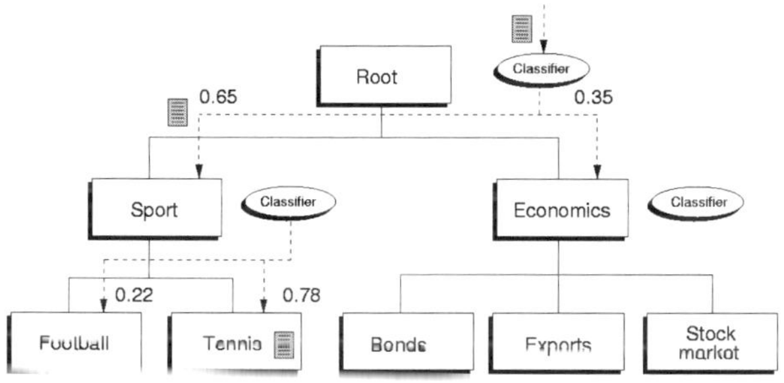

Figure 1

Most research into building hierarchical text classifiers has used machine learning to construct the classifiers that are placed at each decision point in the hierarchy (e.g., [1,2]). That is, for each decision point in the hierarchy, training examples are provided for each class and a machine learning algorithm is used to build a model of the examples provided. While this approach has provided good results, it ignores the fact that it is usually very expensive to gather training examples. The problem is exacerbated for large hierarchical classification tasks where training examples need to be gathered for each smaller task. It would be beneficial to minimize the number of training examples needed to build accurate classifiers at each decision point in the hierarchy. Recent research has shown that it is possible to reduce the number of training examples needed to build accurate classifiers by using unlabeled documents and the EM algorithm [3]. However, this research focused on using the EM algorithm for non-hierarchical classification tasks. In this report we show a novel way to incorporate the EM algorithm within a hierarchical classification setting to minimize the number of labeled examples required to build an accurate hierarchical classifier.

SIGIR'02, August 11-15, 2002, Tampere, Finland.
ACM 1-58113-561-0/02/0008.

This paper is organized as follows: First the EM algorithm is described. This is followed by a description of a new hierarchical form of the EM algorithm. Finally, results comparing this algorithm to baseline algorithms are given on a hierarchical document collection consisting of 17,000 newsgroup postings.

2. Expectation Maximization (EM)

EM is an iterative algorithm used for maximum likelihood parameter estimation in problems with incomplete data [6]. The EM algorithm can be used to improve the accuracy of a text classifier by exploiting the extra information present in unlabeled documents. In particular, unlabeled documents provide information about the joint probability distribution over words within documents. Given a set of labeled training documents T, and a set of unlabeled documents U, the form of the EM algorithm used by Nigam et al., for non-hierarchical text classification is given below:

- Train an initial classifier K using the training set T
- Loop while K's parameters have changed:
  - Use K to assign probabilistic labels to documents in U to create a pseudo-labeled set U'.
  - Retrain K on the union of T and U'

The underlying training algorithm used by Nigam et al., was the multinomial form of the Naïve Bayes algorithm [5,7]. Naïve Bayes is a probabilistic algorithm that assumes a generative model of the data and makes the simplifying assumption that words are generated independently of each other given a class.

3. Hierarchical EM

Probably the most obvious way to incorporate unlabeled data into the training process of a hierarchical pachinko machine would be to use the EM algorithm and the entire unlabeled set U while training the classifiers at each decision point in the hierarchy. However, Boyapati provides an argument and empirical evidence showing that this is not the best strategy [4]. For decision points near the bottom of the hierarchy, most of the unlabeled collection will not belong to any class at that decision point and will simply add noise to the EM algorithm. To address the problems raised by Boyapati, a top-down form of the EM algorithm is introduced which progressively filters unlabeled documents down the hierarchy. The algorithm is described below:

- Set the unlabeled collection of the top-most classifier to U
- For n = 0 to Depth - 1 do:
  - For each classifier K at depth n do:
    - Use EM with K's unlabelled collection U_K to improve K's parameter estimates (as described in section 2).
    - Using the improved classifier K, classify documents in U_K into K's set of classes.

- Using the classification provided by K, separate U_K into unlabelled collections that are passed to each of K's child classifiers to be used in the next iteration.

An illustration of the algorithm is given in the following figure.

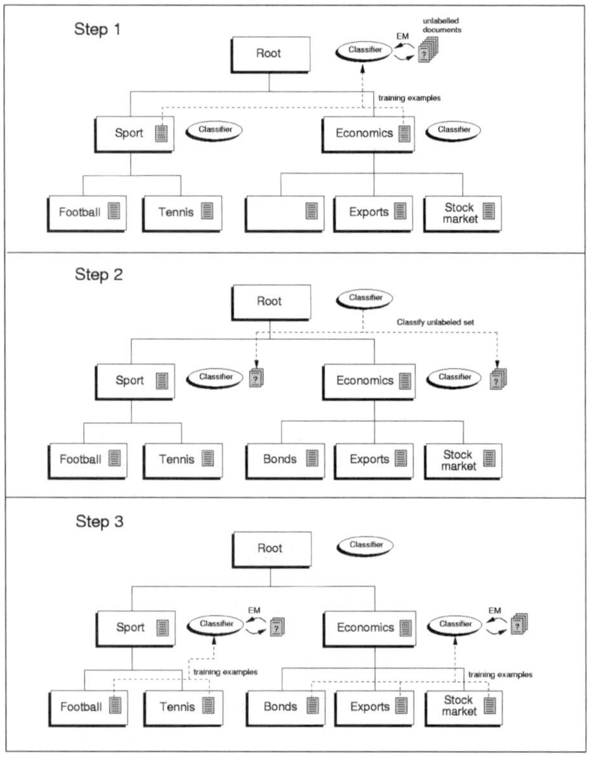

Figure 2

The main benefit of this algorithm is that it uses EM to boost the performance of parent classifiers, which are then used to separate the unlabeled collection appropriately for use with the EM algorithm in the child classifiers below.

4. RESULTS

The HEM algorithm described in the previous section was applied to a collection of 17,000 newsgroup articles taken from the 20 Newsgroup dataset [8]. The set of classes in the dataset were organized hierarchically using the hierarchy implicit in the naming of the newsgroups. E.g., with the newsgroup `comp.sys.ibm`, `comp` would be the parent class of `sys`, which would be the parent class of `ibm`. The HEM algorithm was compared to a baseline Naïve Bayes algorithm (NB) and the EM algorithm applied to Naïve Bayes (EM). In both cases, the hierarchical relationship between classes was ignored in training, since neither algorithm can make use of the hierarchy. The document collection was randomly divided into a test set containing 5000 documents and an unlabeled set containing 8000 documents. The remaining pool of documents were used to create training sets of varying size to measure the improvement provided by HEM for varying amounts of training examples provided. The experiments were repeated 30 times for each split and the averaged results of these experiments are shown in figure 3. The error bars in the figure, representing the standard error of the averaged values, show that the results are statistically significant. The results show that when there is a dearth of training data, the HEM algorithm significantly outperforms EM and Naïve Bayes by exploiting both the unlabelled documents and the hierarchical relationship between classes. It also shows that when there is ample training data, there is little benefit in using HEM and it can in fact hurt performance.

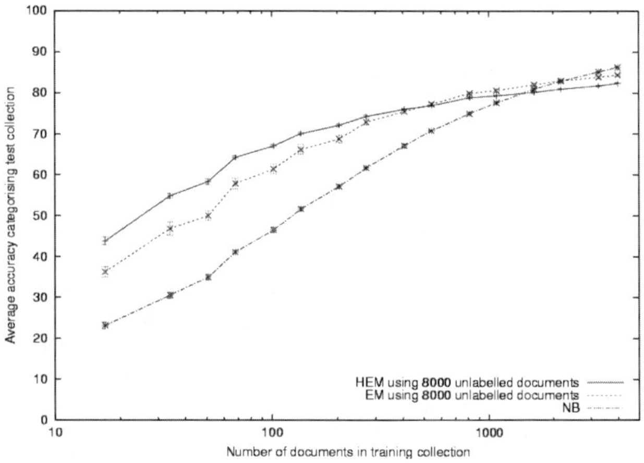

Figure 3

5. ACKNOWLEDGMENTS

Thanks to Peter Bailey, Jonathan Baxter Kamal Nigam and Tom Mitchell for providing advice and encouragement. Thanks to my colleagues at Whizbang! Labs for providing the most enriching environment a young researcher could hope for.

6. REFERENCES

[1] Koller, D., and Sahami, M. Hierarchically Classifying Documents Using Very Few Words. In Proceedings of ICML '97, 170—178.

[2] Ruiz, M. E., and Srinivasan., P. Hierarchical Neural Networks for Text Categorization. Proceedings of SIGIR '99, 281—282.

[3] Nigam K., McCallum A., Thrun S., and Mitchell T. Learning to Classify Text from Labeled and Unlabeled Documents. In Proceedings *of AAAI '98*, 792—799.

[4] Boyapati V. Towards a Comprehensive Topic Hierarchy for News. Honours Thesis, 2000.

[5] McCallum A., and Nigam K. A Comparison of Event Models for Naive Bayes Text Classification. In AAAI/ICML '98 Workshop of Learning for Text Categorization. 41—48.

[6] Dempster, A. P., Laird, N. M., and Rubin, D. B. Maximum likelihood from incomplete data via the EM algorithm. Journal of the Royal Statistical Society. (B 39):1—38.

[7] Lewis D. Naive (Bayes) at Forty: The Independence Assumption in Information Retrieval. In ECML '98. 4—15.

[8] Lang K. Newsweeder: Learning to filter net news. In Proceedings of ICML '95. 331—339.

Do Thumbnail Previews Help Users Make Better Relevance Decisions about Web Search Results?

Susan Dziadosz
Microsoft Corporation
One Microsoft Way, Redmond, WA 98052
+1 (425) 703 8697
sudzi@microsoft.com

Raman Chandrasekar
Microsoft Corporation
One Microsoft Way, Redmond, WA 98052
+1 (425) 705 2883
ramanc@microsoft.com

ABSTRACT

We describe an empirical evaluation of the utility of thumbnail previews in web search results. Results pages were constructed to show text-only summaries, thumbnail previews only, or the combination of text summaries and thumbnail previews. We found that in the combination case, users were able to make more accurate decisions about the potential relevance of results than in either of the other versions, with hardly any increase in speed of processing the page as a whole.

Categories and Subject Descriptors

H.3.3 [**Information Search and Retrieval**]: Search Process.
H.1.2 [**User/Machine Systems**]: Human Factors

General Terms: Design, Experimentation, Human Factors

Keywords: Web search, search engine, thumbnails

1. WEB INFORMATION SEEKING

The interaction between an end-user and any text-based information retrieval system can be described in three basic steps. *Query Formulation*: the user translates the information need into words s/he thinks the system will understand, and types them into a box. *Relevance Prediction*: the user inspects the search results page and guesses which items will lead to the desired information. *Relevance Evaluation*: the user attempts to locate the desired information in the documents s/he predicted would be helpful. Users flow freely among these stages.

Our interest in this paper is in supporting the user's decision-making process in the *relevance prediction* step. Ideally, a search engine should make it easy for users to accurately discriminate between irrelevant and relevant documents by inspection. We investigated how thumbnail previews support this process.

2. UTILITY OF THUMBNAILS

Previous work [1, 2] has shown that thumbnail previews can be valuable when users are trying to find something they have already seen. Searching the web, though, usually involves encountering items that the user has not seen before. Web search engines typically present the user with document surrogates such as page titles, summaries, URLs, category information, or snippets of text from the destination webpage.

In [3], it was shown that for certain types of web search tasks, textually-enhanced thumbnails assisted users in finding their target information more quickly than text-alone or plain thumbnails. The textual enhancements included highlighting and increasing the fonts of page headings and showing where the various query keywords appeared in the document. However, creating such thumbnails enhanced with query information is computationally costly, and not practical for a real-time web search service. Instead, plain thumbnails (a miniature version of the whole page) can be created offline and presented with traditional text-based document summaries.

Our hypothesis was that the text + thumbnails combination would help users make better decisions than text alone, and that both these would be more helpful than thumbnails alone. We set up a study to test this.

3. THE STUDY

3.1 Participants & Types of Results Pages

35 participants who were experienced with web searching were selected for this study. As shown in Figure 1, three variations of the results pages of the popular web search engine MSN Search were manually constructed for these participants – text-only, thumbnails-only and text plus thumbnails combination – for each of six queries. Each results page contained fifteen search results.

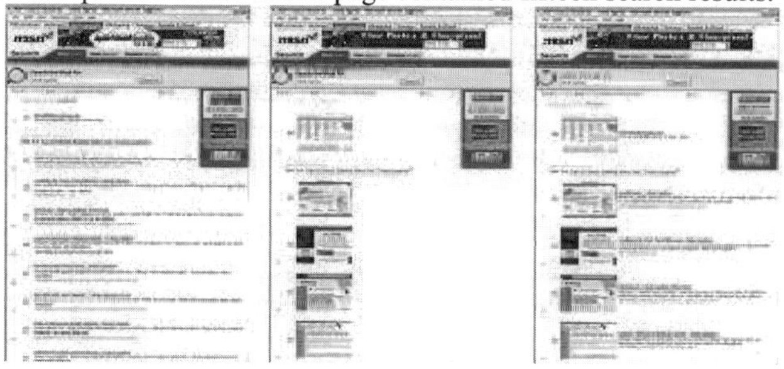

Figure 1. Three types of results pages (text-only, thumbnails only, text+thumbnails)

The text-only version was identical to the search engine's results page interface as of September 2001; it showed titles, summaries and URLs for each document. The thumbnails-only version replaced the titles, summaries and URLs with a 25% (160 x 120 pixel) representation of the exact destination document. We did not attempt to control web page design elements of the destination

SIGIR'02, August 11-15, 2002, Tampere, Finland.
ACM 1-58113-561-0/02/0008.

documents. The combination version showed the same thumbnail used in the thumbnails-only condition, with the document titles, summaries and URLs to the right of the thumbnail.

3.2 Procedure

The three conditions were presented to the participants in blocks of two queries each, with the presentation order counterbalanced across participants. They were given an information-seeking scenario for each query and asked to keep it in mind while evaluating the search results. For example, "You need to know how to remove carpenter ants from your home", or "You want to read reviews of snowboarding gear for an upcoming purchase".

For each query's result page, the participant performed two tasks. The first task was to identify all of the results they believed were likely to be relevant using only the information available on the results page. Participants voted either *relevant* or *not relevant* for each result. The second task was to visit each of the fifteen websites, examine it briefly, and decide whether it was relevant or not relevant. We recorded each of their "votes" and the time it took them to make their decisions.

We define a *correct decision* occurs when a participant's prediction about a search result was confirmed after s/he visited the site to evaluate it. An *incorrect decision* occurs when the participant's prediction about a site does not match her/his evaluation of it upon visiting it.

4. FINDINGS

Consistent with our expectation, the participants made more accurate decisions with the combination of text and thumbnails than with text-only or thumbnails-only.

4.1 User performance

The participants evaluated 30 websites in each of 3 conditions, for a total of 1050 evaluations per condition.

Table 1. Correct vs. Incorrect decisions

	TEXT	THUMBS	COMBO
Correct decisions	761	706	781
Incorrect decisions	289	344	269

Table 1 shows the breakdown of participant decisions in each condition. Participants made 20 more correct decisions with the combination condition than in the text-only condition and 75 more than in the thumbnail-only condition. Participants made 55 fewer incorrect decisions with the text-only condition than the thumbnails-only condition. Where do the gains in accuracy come from? Table 2 breaks down correct and incorrect decisions into Correct Picks and Rejects, and Incorrect Picks and Rejects. For example, an Incorrect Pick is when the user predicts relevance, and later finds it irrelevant; and a Correct Reject is when the user predicts irrelevance, and finds the page to be irrelevant.

Table 2. Detailed Breakup of User Decisions

	TEXT	THUMBS	COMBO
Correct Picks	281	317	319
Correct Rejects	480	389	462
Incorrect Picks	154	166	181
Incorrect Rejects	135	178	88

The main advantage of the text + thumbnails combination is in the reduction of Incorrect Rejects – in this condition, participants incorrectly rejected 47 fewer relevant documents than in the text condition, and 90 fewer than in thumbnails alone. The participants also identified more Correct Picks in the combination case, than in the text-only case (319 vs. 281); the tradeoff is an increase in the number of Incorrect Picks.

Interestingly, the presence of thumbnails caused the participants to be much less conservative in their predictions. Thumbnails give the appearance of relevance to more documents than text summaries alone. Look at the sum Correct Picks + Incorrect Picks (the number of "Relevant" predictions) for the three conditions: 435, 483, and 500 respectively. So, when thumbnails were present these participants "gave the benefit of the doubt" to many more results than in the text-only case.

The absence of text caused the participants to be less generous in their evaluations of the websites themselves. The number of relevant documents (sum of Correct Picks and Incorrect Rejects) should ideally be consistent for the three conditions, but is not (the totals are 416, 495 and 406, for the three columns). Thus, in the Thumbs-only case, users tended to judge more sites relevant.

4.2 Mental processing time

The average time it took participants to make predictions about a page of results was 84.8 seconds in the thumbnail-only condition, 92.9 seconds in the text-only condition, and 95.9 seconds in the combination condition. This confirms previous findings [3] that the average reader skims images more rapidly than text. While thumbnails-only proved to be the fastest condition, the presence of thumbnails in the combination condition did not seem to unduly slow users' decision making.

5. DISCUSSION

The study suggests that thumbnails used along with text summaries help in reducing errors in predicting relevance, at little cost in processing time. However, if the user does not recognize the site from previous encounters or does not know what particular types of websites to expect for the topic, thumbnails alone might hinder more than help them, and we plan to study this. We are planning another study with user-supplied queries, and a method of obtaining a user-independent gold standard for relevant sites, so as to remove biases due to users being unwilling to mark sites irrelevant that they had earlier presumed relevant.

6. ACKNOWLEDGMENTS

The authors thank David Snelling and Thomas White for helping create and conduct the study and Bill Bliss for his encouragement.

7. REFERENCES

1. Czerwinski, M., van Dantzich, M., Robertson, G., and Hoffman, H. The Contribution of Thumbnail Image, Mouse-over Text and Spatial Location Memory to Web Page Retrieval in 3D. Proc. INTERACT '99, 1999, 163-170.
2. Kaasten, S. and Greenberg, S. Integrating Back, History and Bookmarks in Web Browsers. In Proceedings of CHI'01, ACM Press, 379-380.
3. Woodruff, A., Faulring, A., Rosenholtz, R., Morrison, J., and Pirolli, P. Using Thumbnails to Search the Web. In Proceedings of CHI'01, ACM Press, 198-205.

Amilcare: Adaptive Information Extraction for Document Annotation

Fabio Ciravegna, Alexiei Dingli and Yorick Wilks
Department of Computer Science,
University of Sheffield,
Regent Court, 211 Portobello Street,
S1 4DP, Sheffield, UK +44-114-2221814
{fabio|alexiei|Yorick}@dcs.shef.ac.uk

Daniela Petrelli
Department of Information Studies,
University of Sheffield,
Regent Court, 211 Portobello Street,
S1 4DP, Sheffield, UK, +44-114-2222683
D.Petrelli@sheffield.ac.uk

Categories & Subject Descriptors: I.2.7 [Artificial Intelligence]: **Natural Language Processing – *text analysis.***

General Terms: Management, Performance, Design, Experimentation, Human Factors, Theory

1. AMILCARE

The traditional process of document annotation for knowledge identification and extraction in Knowledge Management (KM) is complex and time consuming, as it requires manual annotation by domain experts. In the typical scenario a domain expert:(1) builds an ontology describing the application domain: (2) annotates a number of texts in order to identify instances of elements (i.e., concepts and relations) in the texts. There is a strong interest in Text Mining technologies (and in particular in Human Language-based Technologies), for reducing the burden of text annotation for KM [1]. In this paper we show how Information Extraction from texts (IE) can provide support for document enrichment and make the text annotation process more effective and efficient. The main challenge to be addressed by IE researchers in this framework is portability of IE systems to new applications with no knowledge of HLT. As a matter of fact, in terms of IE each annotation task (e.g. tagging texts about failures in cars in order to identify faults and involved car parts) requires to port the IE system to a new application domain. IE is just one of the many technologies required by complex KM environments: wide use of IE tools will come only when the definition of such application domain will not require any specific IE skill apart from notions of KM. Moreover there is the need to port across different text types without major recoding of system resources, as documents in KM can range from free texts (technical reports, newspaper-like texts) to structured marked up texts (e.g. highly structured XML/HTML documents) and even a mixture of them [2].

Amilcare is a tool for adaptive IE for supporting active annotation of documents for KM. Its design addresses the portability requirement above: to be adapted to new applications the system just requires the ability of annotating documents. Once adapted, the system can be used either for unsupervised annotation or as a support for human annotation. Amilcare is based on $(LP)^2$, a supervised learning algorithm for IE [3]. Adaptation starts with the definition of a tagset for annotation possibly organized as an ontology where tags are associated to concepts and relations. This is consistent with the current practice in KM, where ontologies are used for describing application domains. Then users have to manually annotate a corpus for training the learner. Amilcare provides an easy-to-use interface for corpus annotation where different colors are associated to different tags. Annotations are inserted by first selecting a tag from the ontology and then identifying the text area to annotate with the mouse. Differently from similar annotation tools [4, 5], Amilcare actively helps in annotating the training corpus. While users annotate texts, Amilcare learns how to reproduce the inserted annotation by running in the background its learner. Moreover the induced rules are silently applied to each new text and their results are compared with the user annotation. When its rules reach a (user-defined) level of accuracy, Amilcare presents each new text with a proposed preliminary annotation derived by the rule application. In this case users have just to revise the proposed annotation by correcting mistakes and adding missing annotations. User corrections are inputted back to the learner for retraining. This technique focuses the slow and expensive user activity on uncovered cases, avoiding requiring annotating cases where a satisfying effectiveness is already reached. Moreover validating extracted information is a much simpler task than tagging bare texts (and also less error prone), speeding up the process considerably. At the end of the corpus annotation process, the system is trained and the application can be delivered.

SIGIR'02, August 11-15, 2002, Tampere, Finland.
ACM 1-58113-561-0/02/0008.

1.1 Users, Applications and Skills

The only knowledge required for building new applications is the ability to annotate documents, i.e. no knowledge of IE is necessary. Actually, Amilcare is designed to accommodate the needs of different user types. While naïve users can build new applications without delving into the complexity of HLT, IE experts are provided with a number of facilities for tuning the final application. Induced rules can be inspected, monitored and edited to obtain some additional accuracy, if needed. The interface also allows balancing precision (P) and recall (R). The system is run on an annotated unseen corpus and users are presented with statistics on accuracy, together with details on correct matches and mistakes. Retuning the P&R balance does not generally require major retraining. Facilities for inspecting the effect of different P&R balances are provided.

1.2 Adapting to text types

While most of the IE literature has focused on IE from free newspaper-like texts, KM applications, with their composite web-based scenarios, require portability across text types (see above). Linguistically-based methodologies used for free texts (e.g. [6]) can be difficult to apply or even ineffective on highly structured marked up documents. They are not able to cope with the extra-linguistic structures (e.g. tags, document formatting) used to convey information in such documents. On the other hand, wrapper-like algorithms designed for highly structured documents are largely ineffective on unstructured texts given their inability to overcome

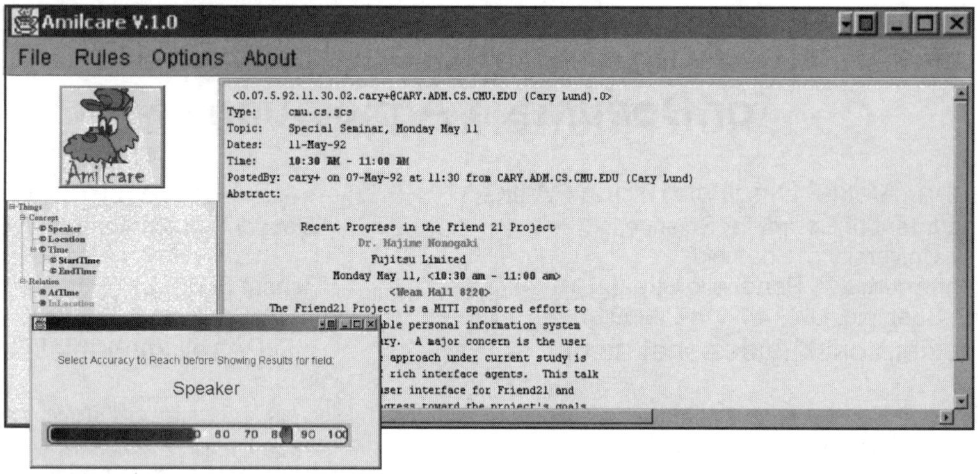

Figure 1: The tagging Interface: left is the tagset, right the text. Note the dialog box for tailoring active learning.

data sparseness due to linguistic variation [3]. Amilcare is based on Lazy-NLP, a methodology that attempts to fill the gap between linguistic and wrapper-like approaches [3]. A Lazy-NLP learner learns the best (most reliable) level of linguistic analysis useful (or effective) for a specific IE task by mixing linguistic and shallow strategies. The learner starts inducing wrapper-like rules that make no use of linguistic information. Then it progressively adds linguistic information to its rules, stopping when the use of NLP information becomes unreliable or ineffective. The measure of reliability here is not linguistic correctness (immeasurable by incompetent users), but effectiveness in extracting information using linguistic information as opposed to using shallower approaches. Lazy NLP-based learners learn which is the best strategy for each information/context separately. For example they may decide that using parsing is the best strategy for recognizing speakers in seminar announcements, but not to spot seminar locations. This is quite effective on documents with mixed genres, a common situation in web documents [2].

1.3 Adapting Generic Resources

Even if Lazy-NLP learners use generic NLP modules and resources not to be modified for specific application needs, Amilcare provides a way of retuning some types of generic IE resources. For example Named Entity Recognizers (NERs) can become quite ineffective if used to analyze reports of trials from the 19th century because location names had different styles at the time, or because a number of first names for people have now disappeared. In this case it is either possible to let the learning algorithm decide how and when the NER is reliable (in a pure Lazy-NLP perspective), or it is possible to use Amilcare to learn how to patch the NER's results. Even naïve users can accomplish this by using the same interface provided for annotating corpora. In this case the generic resource is used to provide the initial preliminary tagging of texts to be corrected by users. User corrections are inputted back to Amilcare that learns how to reproduce such correction, i.e. how to cover missing cases and to shift misplaced tags. We are currently modifying the (LP)^2 algorithm so to remove spurious annotations.

2. CONCLUSION

Amilcare is a tool for adaptive IE designed for KM purposes that requires no IE skills for porting to new applications. It is able to cope with different texts types without requiring major recoding of resources. It easily integrates with the usual manual document annotation process. Initially it appears as one of the usual KM annotation tools. When its rules become reliable it automatically starts helping in the annotation process. At some point the user can decide either to leave Amilcare to continue the annotation process (unsupervised annotation) or to continue to manually annotate the documents letting Amilcare suggesting a draft annotation (supervised annotation). Either way the result is a more efficient and effective process. Amilcare uses cutting edge IE technology: the (LP)^2 algorithm obtains excellent results in scientific experiments and was also used to build a number of real world applications [3]. Concerning suitability for KM purposes: on the one hand Amilcare has been successfully integrated in the AKT2 architecture and is used to build experimental applications within the AKT project (www.aktors.org). On the other hand Amilcare's learning kernel has been integrated in two tools for Knowledge Management: Mnm (the Open University) and Ontomat, (University of Karlsruhe).

3. REFERENCES

[1] M. Maybury (ed.): Proc. of the 2001 EACL/ACL Workshop on Human Language Technology and Knowledge Management, at the at the 39th meeting of the ACL, July 6-11, 2001, Toulouse, France

[2] F. Ciravegna: "Challenges in Information Extraction from Text for Knowledge Management", *IEEE Intelligent Systems and Their Applications*, November 2001.

[3] F. Ciravegna: "Adaptive Information Extraction from Text by Rule Induction and Generalisation" in *Proc. of 17th International Joint Conference on Artificial Intelligence (IJCAI)*, Seattle, August 2001."

[4] D. Day, J. Aberdeen, L. Hirschman, R. Kozierok, P. Robinson and M. Vilain *Mixed-initiative development of language processing systems*. In Proc. of the Fifth Conference on Applied Natural Language Processing, Washington, 1997.

[5] H. Cunningham, D. Maynard, V. Tablan, C. Ursu, K. Bontcheva: "Developing Language Processing Components with GATE", www.gate.ac.uk

[6] 7th Message Understanding Conference Proc., www.itl.nist.gov/iaui/894.02/related_projects/muc/

The Impact of Corpus Size on Question Answering Performance

C. L. A. Clarke G. V. Cormack M. Laszlo T. R. Lynam E. L. Terra

Department of Computer Science, University of Waterloo, Canada
mt@plg.uwaterloo.ca

ABSTRACT

Using our question answering system, questions from the TREC 2001 evaluation were executed over a series of Web data collections, with the sizes of the collections increasing from 25 gigabytes up to nearly a terabyte.

Categories and Subject Descriptors

H.3.4 [**Information Systems**]: Information Storage and Retrieval—*Systems and Software*

General Terms

Measurement, Performance, Experimentation

Keywords

Question answering

1. QUESTION ANSWERING

The goal of an open-domain question answering (QA) system is to provide concise answers to short, factual questions. Questions might range from those eliciting straightforward facts, such as names or dates, to those requiring brief explanations. Examples of the former include "What is the speed of light?" and "Who won the world series in 1993?". Examples of the latter include "Who is Harry Houdini?" and "Why is the sky blue?". Often, the answers are drawn from a target corpus consisting of documents created for other purposes, such newspaper articles and Web pages.

Since 1999 a QA track has been part of the annual TREC evaluation of information retrieval systems conducted by the U.S. National Institute of Standards and Technology (NIST) [8]. In TREC 2001, the main QA task used a set of 500 questions and a 3GB target corpus [7]. Each system was requested to return five ranked responses to each question, where each response could have a maximum length of 50 bytes. A response was judged correct only if an answer was contained in the 50 bytes.

The main evaluation measure for the task was *mean reciprocal rank* (MRR). To compute an MRR, each question is assigned a score that is the inverse of the rank of the first response that is judged correct. If no response contains an answer, the question is assigned a score of zero. The scores of the individual questions are then averaged to produce an MRR value for the question set as a whole.

Our QA system was one of the better-performing systems in both the 2000 and 2001 TREC QA experiments [3]. The system takes a simple statistical approach to QA [2]. A lightweight parser first performs question analysis and generates a query and a set of question-specific selection rules. The query is used by a passage retrieval component to locate short text fragments within the target corpus that are related to the topic of the question. The passages and the selection rules are then passed to an answer selection component that identifies 50-byte text snippets within the retrieved passages that are likely to include the answer.

A new feature of our system for TREC 2001 was the use of Web data for candidate reinforcement during answer selection [3]. In the experiment reported here, we continue this work, using Web data as the target corpus and examining the impact of target corpus size on system performance.

SIGIR'02, August 11-15, 2002, Tampere, Finland.
ACM 1-58113-561-0/02/0008.

2. EXPERIMENT

A terabyte of HTML, crawled from the general Web in mid-2001, forms the basis for the experiment. Starting with a seed set of URLs representing the home pages of 2392 universities and other educational organizations, pages were gathered in breadth-first order with one exception. If a breadth-first ordering would place an excessive load on a single host, defined as more than 0.2% of total crawler activity over a time period of approximately one hour, URLs associated with that host were removed and requeued until the anticipated load dropped to an acceptable level. Pages at a given depth from the seed set were crawled in random order. During the crawl, duplicate pages were detected and eliminated, and do not form part of the final collection. A breadth-first ordering is known to produce high-quality pages [6], and we expected the crawl to contain the answer to many simple factual questions.

To generate responses, we used an archived version of our QA system as it existed at the time our TREC 2001 experimental runs were generated. Thus, the system has not been trained or influenced by the TREC 2001 questions. For the experiments reported here, the Web reinforcement component was disabled.

The TREC 2001 questions were executed over a range of target corpus sizes, representing from 3% to 100% of the available Web collection. During the experiment a small portion of the full terabyte collection was off-line, and the experiment was run over an actual Web collection consisting of 960GB of HTML.

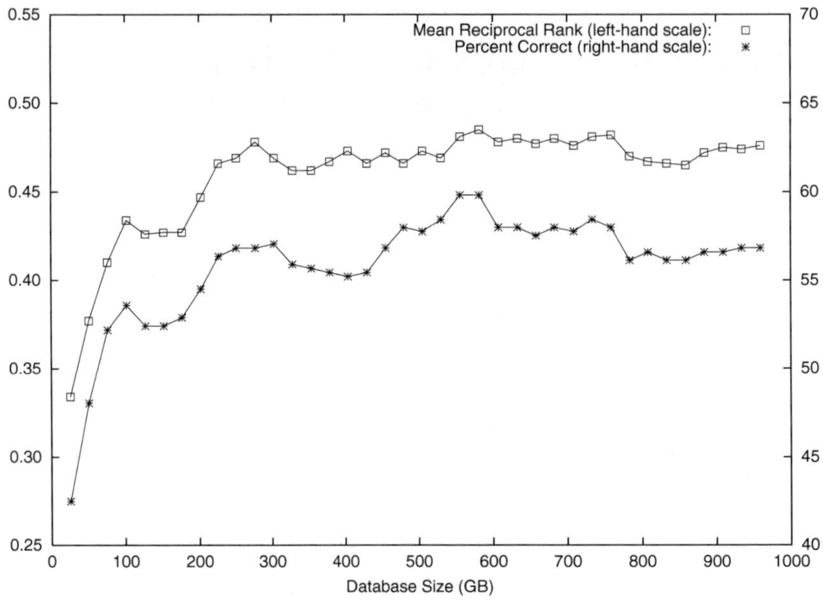

Figure 1: The Impact of Corpus Size on Question Answering Performance

Responses are judged using an automatic evaluation script created by Ken Litkowski of CL Research, which is similar to earlier scripts created by Ellen Voorhees for the 1999 and 2000 TREC questions [8]. The script executes a series of question-specific regular expressions over the responses returned for each question. Whenever a match occurs, the response is marked as correct. The script contains patterns for only 433 of the original 500 TREC 2001 questions. Most of the remaining questions either did not have an answer in the TREC 2001 target corpus or were discarded by NIST due to typos and similar errors. The 67 missing questions are not considered in our calculation of MRR.

The results are presented in Figure 1. The figure reports both the MRR and the percentage of questions with a correct answer among the top five responses. For comparison, the same system and questions executed over the official 3GB TREC 2001 QA corpus and evaluated with the automatic script gave a MRR of 0.408.

3. DISCUSSION

We expected performance to improve with corpus size. While performance does improve up to 400-500GB, it then appears to reach an asymptote and actually declines slightly after that. Experience with traditional IR systems indicates that system performance is directly related to corpus size [4] and we have observed a similar relationship in QA systems with corpora in the range 10-100GB [2]. Further work is needed to determine if the observed asymtote represents a real effect, or if it is an artifact of our system or of the evaluation methodology.

An examination of the answers returned by the system suggests a possible weakness in the evaluation methodology. Generally, automatic evaluation by a script is not as accurate as manual evaluation by a human judge. Automatic scripts err both by marking responses as correct when the surrounding context does not support the answer and by missing correct answers that do not match the expected syntactic form. In this case, the script may be "overfitted" to the syntactic forms that appear in the TREC corpus. Certainly many correct answers are missed.

Other groups have used Web data to support open-domain question answering, generally by depending on a commerical search engine to supply the target corpus and information retrieval facilities [1, 5]. While this approach can produce practical systems, it does not allow the information retrieval strategies for question answering to be studied in detail.

4. REFERENCES

[1] E. Brill, J. Lin, M. Banko, S. Dumais, and A. Ng. Data-intensive question answering. In *2001 Text REtrieval Conference*, 2001.

[2] C. L. A. Clarke, G. V. Cormack, and T. R. Lynam. Exploiting redundancy in question answering. In *24th ACM SIGIR Conference*, pages 358–365, 2001.

[3] C. L. A. Clarke, G. V. Cormack, T. R. Lynam, C. M. Li, and G. L. McLearn. Web reinforced question answering. In *2001 Text REtrieval Conference*, 2001.

[4] G. V. Cormack, O. Lhotak, and C. R. Palmer. Estimating precision by random sampling. In *22rd ACM SIGIR Conference*, pages 273–274, 1999.

[5] C. C. T. Kwok, O. Etzioni, and D. S. Weld. Scaling question answering to the Web. In *Tenth International World Wide Web Conference*, pages 150–161, 2001.

[6] M. Najork and J. L Wiener. Breadth-first search crawling yields high-quality pages. In *10th International World Wide Web Conference*, pages 114–118, 2001.

[7] E. M. Voorhees. Overview of the TREC 2001 Question Answering Track. In *2001 Text REtrieval Conference*, 2001.

[8] E. M. Voorhees and D. Tice. Building a question answering test collection. In *23rd ACM SIGIR Conference*, pages 200–207, 2000.

Effective Collection Metasearch in a Hierarchical Environment: Global vs. Localized Retrieval Performance

Jack G. Conrad
TLR Research & Development
Thomson Legal & Regulatory
St. Paul, MN 55123 USA
Jack.Conrad@WestGroup.com

Changwen Yang
Oracle Corporation
500 Oracle Parkway
Redwd Shores, CA 94065
Changwen.Yang@Oracle.com

Joanne S. Claussen
Technology Product Dev.
West Group
Eagan, MN 55123 USA
Joanne.Claussen@WestGroup.com

ABSTRACT

We compare standard global IR searching with user-centric localized techniques to address the *database selection problem*. We conduct a series of experiments to compare the retrieval effectiveness of three separate search modes applied to a hierarchically structured data environment of textual database representations. The data environment is represented as a tree-like directory containing over 15,000 unique databases and over 100,000 total leaf nodes. Our search modes consist of varying degrees of *browse and search*, from a global search at the root node to a refined search at a sub-node using dynamically-calculated inverse document frequencies (*idfs*) to score candidate databases for probable relevance. Our findings indicate that a browse and search approach that relies upon localized searching from sub-nodes is capable of producing the most effective results.

Categories and Subject Descriptors

H.3.3 [**Information Storage and Retrieval**]: Information Search and Retrieval—*search process,selection process*

General Terms

Performance, Experimentation, Human Factors

1. INTRODUCTION

The continued growth of online databases has made the work of finding the most relevant collections increasingly difficult. Until recently, the ability to execute a 'search' in a database directory as well as 'drill down' into its hierarchical structure have largely been regarded as separate activities. If either approach does not provide desired results, large numbers of users exit online systems with unmet information needs. *Yahoo!* and the *Open Directory Project* are exceptions that permit integrated browse and search. Research has begun to explore categorization and retrieval in such environments [4]. We hypothesized that if users could first browse to a potentially relevant sub-node in a large directory, results from a search in the sub-directory would be more precise than results from a search in the entire directory. To test the effectiveness of browse plus search functionality, we designed and conducted a series of experiments on three search modes. Using the same set of real user queries, these search modes included: (1) a global search of the directory from the root node, (2) a localized search of the relevant sub-directories using global idfs, and (3) a localized search of the relevant sub-directories using the appropriate dynamically-calculated local idfs.

SIGIR'02, August 11-15, 2002, Tampere, Finland.
ACM 1-58113-561-0/02/0008.

2. OPERATIONAL ENVIRONMENT

The *Westlaw* system actually provides both a dedicated (single database search) and integrated (multiple database search) environment, while delivering merged document result lists. Park found that users ultimately desire more control over their searches where databases are concerned [2]. We wanted to pursue this issue of flexibility in alternative ways. To expand upon integrated versus dedicated database search capability and notions of simplicity plus control, we wanted to investigate another type of hybrid system, one which offers users effective browse *and* search functionality. We first wanted to inspect whether results from suitably restricted searching (following a user's navigation into a hierarchically arranged directory structure) would be measurably better than those from a simple global search at the root level. Secondly, we wanted to determine whether restricted search using standard collection-wide idf values or using localized idf values (defined by the sub-collection being searched) provided better performance. In both of these investigations, we wanted to determine whether higher precision could be achieved without a substantial loss of recall.

2.1 Data

West Group's data repository now contains over 5 million published case law opinions from virtually every state and federal jurisdiction. In the past decade, however, the amount of *non-legal* data available on Westnews, Westlaw's news-based data, has been growing at nearly exponential rates and now consists of millions more documents. *The Westlaw Directory* organizes over 15,000 unique databases in a tree-like structure and lists roughly 100,000 databases at its leaf nodes (with an average of 20,000 documents per database). In some regions, the Directory is 12 or more levels deep, but it averages 4-6 levels. Overall, it represents several terabytes of data. Available for use in this project are database profiles consisting of metadata documents containing the titles, topical coverage, and additional significant content associated with each database. Profile lengths vary from tens of core terms to several thousand characteristic tokens, depending on a database-related set of criteria.

#	User Queries	#	User Queries
1.	Labor Relations	5.	Compensation Planning
2.	State Legis. News	6.	Board of Immigration
3.	Voting Rights	7.	Food & Drug Admin.
4.	Admin. Materials Relating to Specific Occupations		

Table 1: ***Sample Queries***

2.2 Queries

We began with a set of 50 real user queries from an existing database selection system's query logs. We examined the granularity of the queries and determined that roughly 60% of them focused on mid-level nodes of the Directory.[1] This task was performed by a legal domain expert with a background in library science. The average query length was over three terms before stop words were removed and slightly under three terms after (Table 1).

3. SYSTEM ENVIRONMENT

Our system harnessed the WIN search engine[2], a cousin to the INQUERY engine developed at UMass–Amherst. INQUERY's and WIN's algorithms for ranking documents have been previously reported [1, 3], although we modified WIN's scoring formula for our last search mode which incorporated the use of dynamically calculated sub-directory specific local idf values (computed only when necessary for the user-selected sub-directory). WIN was run against all or a portion of the Westlaw Directory data (i.e., the database profiles described in section 2.1 and subsequently judged for relevance by the domain expert). Below is the $tf \cdot idf$ expr. used.

$$p_{bel}(w_i|d_j) = d_b + (1-d_b)\cdot tf_b \cdot idf_b, \qquad where$$

$$tf_b = d_t + (1-d_t)\cdot \frac{\log(tf_i+0.5)}{\log(tf_{max}+1.0)} \quad and \quad \underline{idf_b} = \frac{\log(\frac{N+0.5}{n})}{\log(N+1.0)}$$

d_b is the minimum belief component and d_t is the minimum term frequency component when term w_i is present in a database profile document, d_j. The value tf_{max} is the frequency of the most frequently occurring term in the corpus. n represents the number of database profile documents in which the query term w_i appears while N is the total number of database profile 'documents.'

4. EXPERIMENTS

We ran the set of resultant queries in three search modes: (1) global search of the entire data hierarchy using global idfs; (2) local search of the relevant sub-directories using global idfs; (3) local search of the relevant sub-directories using the appropriate dynamically calculated local idfs; where the $\underline{idf_b}$ parameter (above) was modified depending on the currently defined scope of the profile set, either global or local.

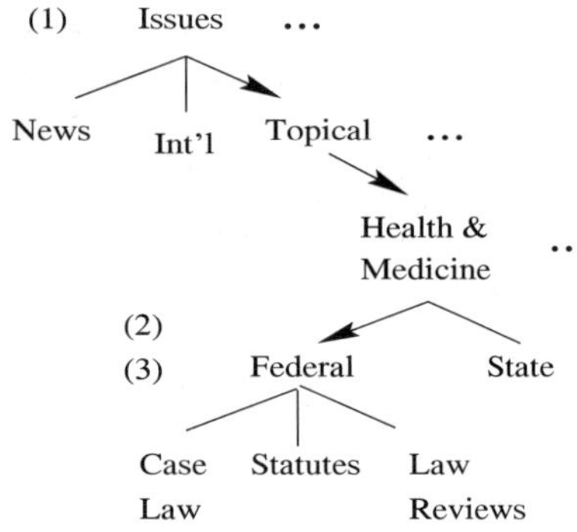

Figure 1. *Sample Search / Browse Scenario*

The "relevant sub-directories" were determined by a domain expert assigned to the project. They were selected as the first sub-directory or sub-directories under which a user could expect to find the initial relevant materials [e.g., (2) and (3) in Figure 1]. Emphasis was placed on precision at 20 and recall at 20 databases returned, since there is evidence that users generally do not examine candidate databases beyond this initial set.

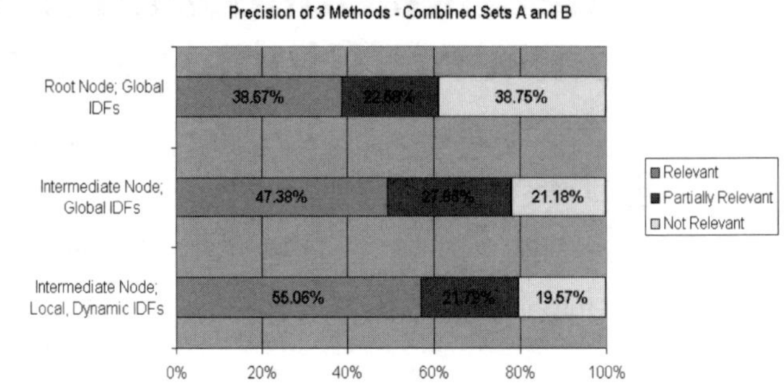

Figure 2. *Search Mode Results (Precision)*[1]

5. RESULTS

Our experimental findings suggest that browse+refined search can improve precision in relation to conventional global searches in environments where the data is organized in a hierarchical fashion such as in the Westlaw Directory. We further determined that restricted searches using localized idfs defined by the applicable sub-branches perform better than restricted searches using the more easily obtainable global idfs (Figure 2, with improvements of as much as 40%) with little evidence of a meaningful loss in recall (Figure 3, with losses averaging around 15%).

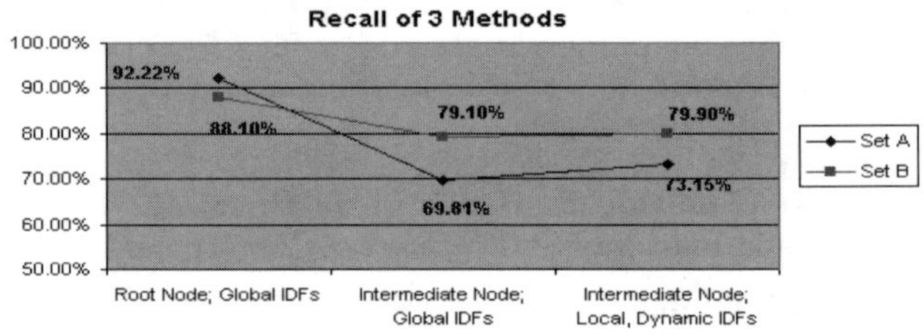

Figure 3. *Search Mode Results (Recall)*[1]

6. CONCLUSIONS

Professional users would apply a narrower concept of *on point* relevance to their queries than those used for our judgments, given their contextual understanding of their information need. Thus the recall obtained for the restricted search modes likely represents a lower bound on this performance. As a result of these alternative, user-centric search modes, energy previously spent on time-consuming source selection searches can be more productively spent on actual document retrieval and analysis. Moreover, an effective browse+search paradigm provides users the ability to exert more control over their searches.

7. REFERENCES

[1] J. Allan, J. Callan, W. B. Croft, L. Ballesteros, D. Byrd, R. Swann, and J. Xu. INQUERY does battle with TREC-6. In *Proc. of TREC-6*, pages 169–206, Nov. 1997.

[2] S. Park. Usability, user preferences, effectiveness, and user behaviors when searching individual and integrated full-text databases: Implications for digital libraries. *JASIS*, 51(5):456–468, March 2000.

[3] P. Thompson, H. Turtle, B. Yang, and J. Flood. TREC-3 ad hoc experiments using the WIN system. In *Proc. of TREC-3*, pages 211–217. NIST, Nov. 1995.

[4] W. Wang, W. Meng, and C. Yu. Concept hierarchy based text database categorization in a metasearch engine environment. In *Proc. of WISE '00*, June 2000.

[1]This activity resulted in two query subsets, one for tax and employment queries (Set A), the other for general queries (Set B).

[2]WIN stands for Westlaw is Natural.

Experimenting with Graphical User Interfaces for Structured Document Retrieval

Fabio Crestani
Dept. Computer and Information Sciences
University of Strathclyde
Glasgow, Scotland, UK
f.crestani@cis.strath.ac.uk

Pablo de la Fuente
Dpto. Informática
Universidad de Valladolid
Valladolid
Spain
pfuente@infor.uva.es

Jesús Vegas
Dpto. Informática
Universidad de Valladolid
Valladolid
Spain
jvegas@infor.uva.es

Categories and Subject Descriptors

H.3.3 [**Information Storage and Retrieval**]: Information Search and Retrieval; H.5.2 [**Information Interfaces and Presentation**]: User Interfaces

General Terms

Design, Human Factors, Documentation, Performance

1. MOTIVATIONS

Standard Information Retrieval (IR) deals with documents as they were atomic entities, indexing and retrieving them as single objects. However, modern IR needs to be able to deal with more elaborate document representations, like for example *structured* documents, that is documents that are organised around a well defined structure. The increasingly popular SGML, HTML, or XML are formalisms that enable to represent and describe such documents. These new standards in structured document representation compel IR to design and implement models and tools to index and retrieve documents according to the given document structure. This means that documents should no longer be considered as atomic entities, but as aggregates of interrelated objects that need to be indexed, retrieved, and presented both as a whole and separately, in relation to the their structure and the user's needs.

Given the complexity of the IR task, interactivity has been widely recognised as a very effective way of improving information access performance. A good user interface enables the IR process to be highly interactive. In structured document retrieval, the need for a good interface between user and system becomes even more pressing. Structured documents are often long and complex and it has been observed that a certain form of disorientation occurs in situations where the user does not understand why certain documents appear in the retrieved list. This user disorientation makes the task of query reformulation much harder, since the user has first to understand the response of the system and then to decide if any of the retrieved document is a good enough representation of the information need to provide the system with precise relevance feedback. This added difficulties obviously increase the cognitive load of the user and decrease the quality of the interaction with the system.

An approach to this problem consists in providing the IR system with a graphical user interface (GUI) with *explanatory* and *selective feedback* capabilities. In other words, the system should be able to explain the user why a particular document has been estimated as relevant and where the clues of this estimated relevance lie. In addition, the user should be able to select for relevance feedback only those parts of the document that are relevant to the information need and not the entire document, has it is done in standard IR. Being able to focus on the parts of the document that makes it appear relevant, without losing the view of the relationships between these parts and the whole document reduces the user's cognitive load and the interaction is enhanced in quality and effectiveness.

2. GRAPHICAL USER INTERFACES FOR STRUCTURED DOCUMENT RETRIEVAL

We are currently experimenting with a number of GUIs for structured document retrieval. The first GUI we have developed has the following characteristics:

- it enables the modelling of hierarchically structured documents, that is of the most common type of long structured documents;
- it allows the user to forget about structural elements, if the user wishes so, but still informs the user of the use the system makes of the structure;
- it allows the user to chose the structural elements the system should consider as most important;
- it allows the user to provide inclusive or selective relevance feedback by indicating or not which structural part of the document should be considered most relevant;
- it provides the user with a view of the overall search interaction with the system, giving the user a sense of where the search is going to and enabling the user to go back to any past stage of the search process.

SIGIR'02, August 11-15, 2002, Tampere, Finland.
ACM 1-58113-561-0/02/0008.

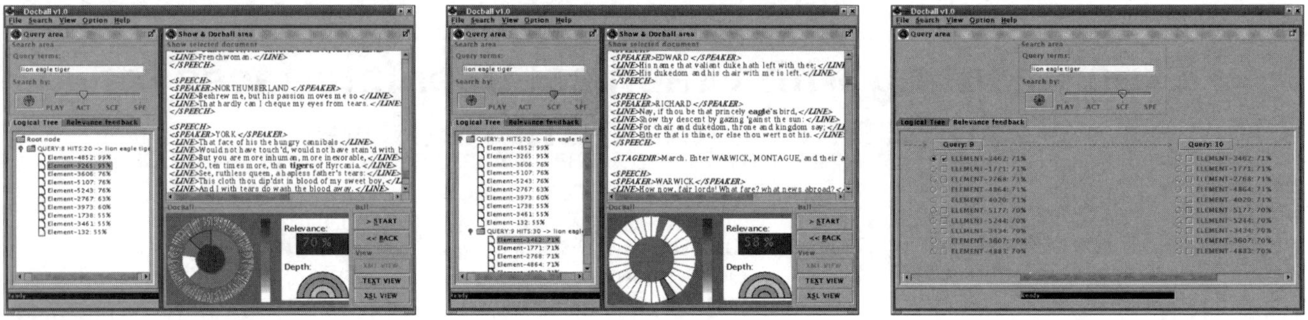

Figure 1: From left to right: visualisation of query results at the "act" structural level, visualisation of query results at the "scene" structural level, and query history and relevance feedback at the "scene" structural level.

In [1] we presented in detail the design and the visual elements of the GUI.

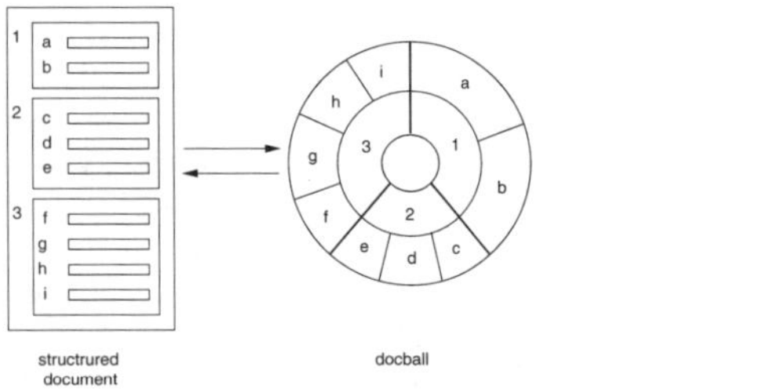

Figure 2: Visualisation of a structured document.

Figure 1 shows an example of the GUI. At the core of the GUI is the representation of a single structured document. A document is represented using an iconic representation called *docball*. An example of a docball with a corresponding hierarchically structured document is depicted in Figure 2. Using a docball it is possible to represent the different structural elements of the document: the whole document (the inner circle), or its sections and subsections (elements of the outer circles), down to the smallest elements that the system designer decides to represent (the outermost circle). The docball also represents the way structural elements of the document are hierarchically included one into another and enables the user to select any element with the touch of the mouse.

The GUI has a query area, in which the user can write the text of the query and select the structural level of interest. Just below the query area is the query history area, where the results of each query is presented. There is also a document display area, that shows the text of the document and the docball representation of the document. The specific structural element selected in the query history area is displayed and also highlighted in the docball. The docball shows in different colours the parts of the document that are relevant and by moving the mouse on top of any structural element in the docball the text of that element is displayed and so is its relevance estimate value. Visualised documents can be displayed in XML, text, or XSL format using the view buttons.

The user can ask that hits for the same query be displayed ranked in relation to others structural level. This new interaction becomes part of the query history and the user can always go back to the previous retrieved list. The user can expand the window with the query history and provide relevance feedback on any retrieved element, as can be seen in the last picture in Figure 1. Pressing the search button activates the relevance feedback at that structural level, and elements similar to the ones indicated as relevant by the user are retrieved and displayed in a new retrieved list.

3. CURRENT AND FUTURE WORK

The work presented in this paper is part of wider work aimed at the design, implementation, and evaluation of a complete system for structured document retrieval. However, at this stage, our work is mainly directed toward the design, implementation, and evaluation of the GUI. In order to evaluated the GUI effectively, we carried out a *formative design-evaluation* using a task-oriented methodology. At this stage we used a rather simplistic retrieval engine that will not be presented here for space limitations (see [1]). The task-oriented evaluation involved 10 users and a document collection comprising the XML version of 4 Shakespeare plays. The collection contained 37 acts, divided in 162 scenes and 5300 speeches. The results of this first evaluation can not be presented here for space limitations. It suffices to say that users appreciated the docball metaphor. They had no difficulties in drawing a docball for any specific structured document presented to them or in deriving a document structure given a docball. In addition, 8 out of 10 users had no difficulties in accomplishing all the tasks requested in the evaluation and found that the GUI improves their effectiveness in the search and browsing of results. Nevertheless, the evaluation suggested that there are still a number of directions to explore to improve the usability of the GUI. We are currently working on them, targeting a much larger collection of more highly structured documents.

In parallel, we are also currently working on a more complex retrieval engine. The design of the engine will follow an *aggregation-based approach* to the estimation of the relevance of the document, using a formal framework to combine the relevance evidence of different structural elements.

4. REFERENCES

[1] J. Vegas, P. de la Fuente, and F. Crestani. A graphical user interface for structured document retrieval. In *Proceedings BCS-IRSG European Colloquium in Information Retrieval Research*, pages 268–283, Glasgow, UK, March 2002.

The Web Retrieval Task and its Evaluation in the Third NTCIR Workshop

Koji Eguchi Keizo Oyama Emi Ishida Kazuko Kuriyama Noriko Kando
National Institute of Informatics
2-1-2 Hitotsubashi, Chiyoda-ku, Tokyo 101-8430, Japan
{eguchi,oyama,emi,kuriyama,kando}@nii.ac.jp

ABSTRACT

This paper gives an overview of the evaluation method used for the Web Retrieval Task in the Third NTCIR Workshop, which is currently in progress. In the Web Retrieval Task, we try to assess the retrieval effectiveness of each Web search engine system using a common data set, and attempt to build a re-usable test collection suitable for evaluating Web search engine systems. With these objectives, we have built 100-gigabyte and 10-gigabyte document sets, mainly gathered from the '.jp' domain. Relevance judgment is performed on the retrieved documents, which are written in Japanese or English.

Categories and Subject Descriptors

H.3.3 [**Information Systems**]: Information Search and Retrieval

General Terms

Experimentation, Human Factors, Performance, Reliability

Keywords

evaluation method, test collection, Web information retrieval

1. INTRODUCTION

This paper describes the evaluation method for the Web Retrieval Task in the Third NTCIR Workshop (hereafter 'NTCIR Web Task')[1], which is currently in progress. The objective of the NTCIR Web Task is 'to research the retrieval of Web documents that have a structure with tags and links, and that are written in Japanese or English'. The task design and the evaluation method are considered from the viewpoint of features of Web retrieval. Thirteen teams are currently participating in the NTCIR Web Task. The dry run has been completed, and the formal run is currently in progress.

2. DOCUMENT SET

Past TREC Web Tracks[2] have used data sets extracted from 'the Internet Archive'[3] as document sets. They assessed the relevance only on information given in English. In the NTCIR Web Task, we have prepared two document sets, mainly gathered from the '.jp' domain: one is over 100 gigabytes and the other is a selection of 10 gigabytes. Almost all the documents seem to be written in Japanese or English. Participants are only allowed to use the original document sets inside the National Institute of Informatics (NII), because the data sets are too large to handle easily and there are some restrictions on the delivery of the original data. Participants use the computer resources in the 'Open-Lab' located at NII to perform data processing, e.g., indexing of the original document data, and then take the resulting data and perform experiments on them in their own laboratories.

SIGIR'02, August 11-15, 2002, Tampere, Finland.
ACM 1-58113-561-0/02/0008.

3. THE TOPICS

The topic format is basically inherited from past NTCIRs[4], except for the definitions of ⟨TITLE⟩, ⟨RDOC⟩, and ⟨USER⟩, and the format of ⟨NARR⟩. The usable fields and mandatory fields vary according to the tasks described in **5**. Each field is flanked by a pair of tags having the following meaning:

- ⟨NUM⟩ indicates the topic identification number.
- ⟨TITLE⟩ gives 1-3 terms that the topic creator considers are similar to query terms used in real Web search engines. When specifying them, the topic creator is instructed in advance not to be excessively conscious of individual features of search engine systems. The topic creator selects one of the following three search strategies, which are suitable for obtaining the necessary information using search engines, and, according to the selected strategy, he or she specifies 1-3 terms for input to search engine systems. The terms in ⟨TITLE⟩ are listed in their order of importance for searching. The title has the attribute of 'CASE', which indicates the types of search strategies, as follows:

  (a) All of the terms have the same or strongly related meanings.

  (b) All of the terms have different meanings that correspond to different semantic categories.

  (c) Only two of the terms have the same meaning, or strongly related meanings, and they are specified by the attribute of 'RELAT' in ⟨TITLE⟩.

  For example, participants using a Boolean search may use the AND operator for strategy (a), the OR operator for strategy (b), and combinations of the AND and OR operators for strategy (c).
- ⟨DESC⟩ ('description') represents the most fundamental description of the user's information needs in a single sentence.
- ⟨NARR⟩ ('narrative') describes in a number of paragraphs the background or retrieval purposes, term definitions, and relevance judgment criteria, and these are flanked on either side by ⟨BACK⟩, ⟨TERM⟩, and ⟨RELE⟩, respectively, in ⟨NARR⟩. Items may be omitted.
- ⟨CONC⟩ ('concepts') gives the synonyms, related terms, or broader terms that are defined by the topic creator.

- ⟨RDOC⟩ ('given relevant documents') gives the document identification numbers of three relevant documents, which are used for 'Similarity Retrieval' as described in **5.1**. To describe ⟨RDOC⟩, the assessor selects the three most relevant documents from the highly-ranked documents retrieved by an organizer's search system.
- ⟨USER⟩ ('user attributes') gives the attributes of the topic creator, e.g., social position, gender, and search experience.

All of the topics are written in Japanese. A topic example translated into English is shown in **Figure 1**. We used

> ⟨TOPIC⟩
> ⟨NUM⟩0004⟨/NUM⟩
> ⟨TITLE CASE="c" RELAT="2-3"⟩computer virus, preventive, countermeasure⟨/TITLE⟩
> ⟨DESC⟩I want to find sentences that explain preventives or countermeasures against computer viruses.⟨/DESC⟩
> ⟨NARR⟩⟨BACK⟩Because the use of the Internet has spread explosively, computer viruses have become a serious problem in our daily lives. I want to know what kind of preventives are required, and what kind of countermeasures I should take when my computer becomes infected.⟨/BACK⟩ ⟨RELE⟩Relevant documents must provide some information on preventives or countermeasures against computer viruses. Documents that describe only the victim's reports or the types of computer viruses are regarded as not relevant. Pages that provide some information on a particular virus are regarded as partially relevant.⟨/RELE⟩⟨/NARR⟩
> ⟨CONC⟩computer virus, worm, information security, illegal access, preventive, countermeasure, infection⟨/CONC⟩
> ⟨RDOC⟩NW003214039, NW013338047, NW013315769
> ⟨/RDOC⟩
> ⟨USER⟩1st year of Master Course, Male, 5 years of search experience⟨/USER⟩
> ⟨/TOPIC⟩

Figure 1: An English translation of a topic example

seven topics for the dry run. For the formal run, we delivered 140 topics to the participants. Although the topics were created without using any search systems, the 140 topics were selected before delivering topics, by investigating the search results of an organizers' search system to discard inappropriate topics. We also performed 'shallow pooling', which cut off and merged the top-ranked 20 documents of each run submitted by the participant. We will discard 40 topics and use the remaining 100 topics for the final evaluation by assessing the relevance of each document included in the 'shallow pool'. The 'Target Retrieval Task' in the formal run will be performed using all 100 topics. However, the 'Survey Retrieval Task' will be done using only 50 of the 100 topics.

4. RELEVANCE JUDGMENTS

In one case an 'information unit' on the Web should be hyper-linked pages, while in another case it should be an individual page or a passage included on a page. In the NTCIR Web Task, usually the assessor who created the topic judges the relevance of each element in the document pool, which is composed of the top-ranked search results from each participant's search engine system. When the assessor judges the relevance of a page, we allow him or her to browse the out-linked pages on condition that they are included in the document pool, assuming that most of the relevant documents are included in the document pool. Here, the 'out-lined pages' means the pages linked from a certen page. Although pages included in the document data set are described in various languages, the assessor judges the relevance only on information given in Japanese or English, although we do not discard documents described in other languages from the document data set.

5. TASK DESCRIPTION

The Web Retrieval Task is composed of the following tasks for the two document sets of 100 gigabytes and 10 gigabytes.

5.1 Survey Retrieval Task

'Survey Retrieval' is divided into the two following tasks: retrieval using topic sentences and terms (hereafter 'Topic Retrieval'), and that using certain specified relevant documents (hereafter 'Similarity Retrieval'). The Topic Retrieval Task is similar to traditional ad hoc retrieval of scientific documents or newspapers, and ensures the reusability of the test collection. The participants in the Topic Retrieval Task must submit run results using the respective ⟨TITLE⟩ and ⟨DESC⟩, and may optionally use the other topic fields. In the Similarity Retrieval Task, we specify the mandatory and optional runs as follows:

mandatory: The first term in ⟨RDOC⟩ must be used. ⟨TITLE⟩ may be used. The second and third terms in ⟨RDOC⟩ may not be used.

optional: The first term in ⟨RDOC⟩ must be used. ⟨TITLE⟩ may be used. The second and third terms in ⟨RDOC⟩ may be used.

5.2 Target Retrieval Task

'Target Retrieval' attempts to evaluate the effectiveness of the retrieval in a case where the user requires just one answer or only a few answers, where precision should be emphasized. The runs will be evaluated using the 10 top-ranked documents retrieved for each topic. The mandatory runs are the same as for the Topic Retrieval Task. Several evaluation measures will be applied.

5.3 Optional Tasks

The participants can freely submit proposals relating to their own research interests, using the document set used in the above tasks. The results will be presented as a paper/poster in the workshop meeting. The proposals can be adopted as tasks and investigated in detail, if they involve several participants. The tasks that have been adopted are 'Search Results Classification' and 'Speech-Driven Retrieval'[1].

6. CONCLUSIONS

We described an overview of the evaluation and design used for the Web Retrieval Task in the Third NTCIR Workshop, which is currently in progress. In the Web Retrieval Task, we have built 100-gigabyte and 10-gigabyte document sets, mainly gathered from the '.jp' domain. Participants use the computer resources in the 'Open-Lab' located at NII to perform data processing using the original document data. The topics are designed to resemble Web retrieval tasks. Relevance judgments will be performed on the retrieved documents written in Japanese or English, partly by considering the effects of linked pages.

7. REFERENCES

[1] ⟨http://research.nii.ac.jp/ntcir/workshop/web/⟩.

[2] D. Hawking. Overview of the TREC-9 Web Track. In *Proc. of TREC-9*, pages 87–102, 2000.

[3] ⟨http://www.archive.org/⟩.

[4] ⟨http://research.nii.ac.jp/ntcir/⟩.

How Many Bits are Needed to Store Term Frequencies?

Martin Franz, J. Scott McCarley
IBM T.J. Watson Research Center
P.O. Box 218, Yorktown Heights, NY 10598
{franzm, jsmc}@us.ibm.com

1. CATEGORIES & SUBJECT DESCRIPTORS

H. Information Systems, H.3 Information Storage and Retrieval, H.3.2 Information Storage, *File Organization*

2. GENERAL TERMS

Algorithms

3. ABSTRACT

Search algorithms in most current text retrieval systems use index data structures extracted from the original text documents. In this paper we focus on reducing the size of the indices by reducing the amount of space dedicated to store term frequencies. In experiments using TREC Ad Hoc [2, 3] corpora and query sets, we show that it is possible to store the term frequency in only two bits without decreasing retrieval performance.

4. INTRODUCTION

With the amount of text data to be searched by information retrieval systems constantly growing, it is increasingly important to efficiently represent the data structures used by search algorithms. Most current IR systems convert the original text documents into index structures containing information about frequencies of terms (words and phrases) in the individual documents. The index structures are typically organized in two ways. An *inverted index* stores for each term a list of documents containing the term, together with the number of occurrences (term frequency, or tf) of each term in the document. A *direct index* contains for each document a list of terms with their frequencies in the document. Many information retrieval algorithms use a multiple-pass strategy: in the first pass, the database is searched using the original query, then the query is expanded by adding terms found frequently in documents scored high in the first pass; the search is then repeated using the expanded query. Such approach typically requires both the inverted index, used in the scoring phases, and the direct index, used by the query expansion algorithm.

Current methods of compressing index files, as summarized in [5, 1], focus on reducing the space required in the index files to store the document or term identifiers; less emphasis has been placed on the storage of the associated term frequencies, which can be significant when the document and term identifiers are compressed efficiently. Most applications use either 8 or 16 bits of storage per term and document to store the actual number of occurrences of a term in a document, allowing the application to store term frequencies up to 255 or 65535, respectively. Here, we focus on reducing the space used to store the term frequencies by *binning* the term frequencies.

SIGIR'02, August 11-15, 2002, Tampere, Finland.
ACM 1-58113-561-0/02/0008.

5. BINNING

A simple example of binning is to divide the space of term frequency values into two intervals, namely $tf \leq 2$ and $tf > 2$. We compress the index by storing only a label indicating in which interval each term frequency value belongs, rather than the full term frequency. The number of bins is typically significantly fewer than the number of distinct term frequency values. More generally, we choose the endpoints of the intervals so that each bin contains roughly the same number of *events*, where an event is defined as a term occurring in a document with certain frequency. The actual term frequencies used by scoring algorithms are replaced by the average of the term frequencies of the events assigned to the corresponding bin.

We used three approaches to constructing the bins. In "static" binning, the bin boundaries are the same for all the indexed terms. In "word-dependent" binning, we create a separate set of bins for each term, depending on its distribution of document frequencies. Finally in "warped" binning, we modified the values of term frequencies representing a bin in scoring so that they reflect the way the term frequencies are applied in the scoring formula. For the Okapi formula [4], the term frequency assigned to a bin was computed as the average of "warped" term frequencies $tf_{warped} = tf/(2.0 + tf)$.

6. RESULTS

We tested these algorithms with the test collections used in the TREC-7 and TREC-8 Ad Hoc tasks [2, 3]. This database consists of 528155 documents, representing 1904 megabytes of data from various news sources. As part ot the TREC Ad Hoc task, the database is annotated with respect to two sets of 50 queries. We used very short "title" and medium length "description" versions of the queries. We used a two-pass retrieval strategy. The first pass is based on the Okapi formula the [4]. The second pass uses the Okapi formula on queries expanded by the Local Context Analysis algorithm [6].

average precision	TREC-7		TREC-8	
baseline	0.2382		0.2700	
	2 bins	4 bins	2 bins	4 bins
static	0.2286	0.2359	0.2714	0.2697
w. dependent	0.2311	0.2383	0.2737	0.2715
warped	0.2395	0.2383	0.2733	0.2729

Table 1: Comparing binning methods (see text), average precision, TREC-7, TREC-8, pass 2.

In Figs. (1, 2) we plot retrieval performance, measured by precision at 20 documents, as a function of numer of bins. We compare against a baseline in which the term frequency is fully represented, i.e. not binned. Table 1 compares average precision measured over the top 1000 documents, obtained using different binning methods.

We observe the following trends:

- Binning with four or more word-dependent bins shows no measurable performance degradation as compared to the baseline. For most of the conditions, reducing the number of bins to two does not cause the performance to change by as much as a single relevant document in the top twenty documents retrieved.
- Significant performance degradation occurs when the term frequencies are compressed to one bin (boolean.) Conversely, almost all of the benefit of retaining the term frequency is obtained with only one additional bit (2 bins.)
- The word-dependent binning strategy outperforms the word-independent binning strategy by a small margin under most conditions.
- Using "warped" term frequencies to represent the bins brings a modest gain in average precision.

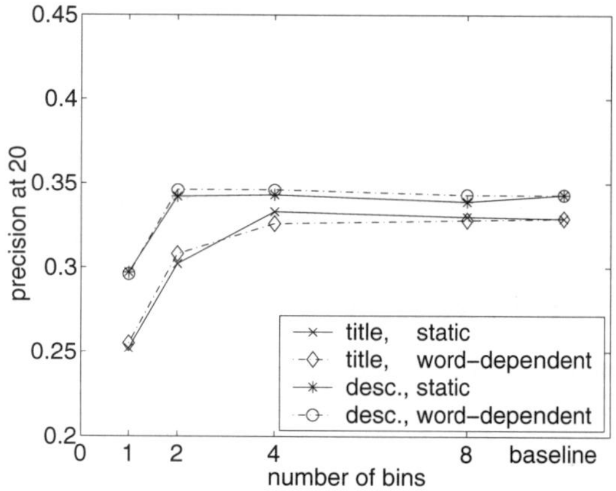

Figure 1: Comparing precision at 20 documents for changing number of bins with unbinned baseline (far right) on TREC-7, pass 1.

7. CONCLUSION

We observe that by binning the document's term frequency values, it it possible to reduce the number of bits

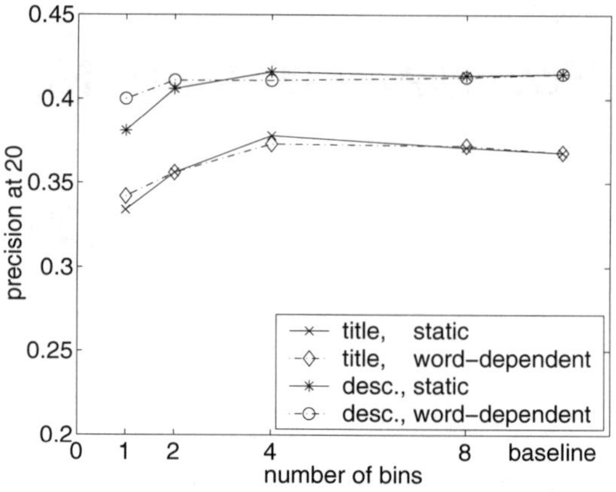

Figure 2: Comparing precision at 20 documents for changing number of bins with unbinned baseline (far right) on TREC-7, pass 2.

used to store the individual frequency values to two without any retrieval performance degradation and to one bit with performance degradation negligible for many practical purposes. Using the proposed method reduces significantly the memory space required to store index structures, of which the frequency values represent a sizable portion.

8. ACKNOWLEDGEMENTS

This work was partially supported by the Defense Advanced Research Projects Agency and monitored by SPAWAR under contract No. N66001-99-2-8916. The views and findings contained in this material are those of the authors and do not necessarily reflect the position of policy of the Government and no official endorsement should be inferred.

9. REFERENCES

[1] R. Baeza-Yates and B. Ribiero-Neto. *Modern Information Retrieval.* ACM Press, 1999.

[2] D.Harman and E.Voorhees. Overview of the Seventh Text REtrieval Conference (TREC-7). In *Proceedings of the Seventh Text REtrieval Conference (TREC-7), NIST Special Publication 500-242*, pages 1–23, 1999.

[3] D.Harman and E.Voorhees. Overview of the Eighth Text REtrieval Conference (TREC-8). In *Proceedings of the Eighth Text REtrieval Conference (TREC-8), NIST Special Publication 500-246*, pages 1–23, 2000.

[4] S. Robertson, S. Walker, S. Jones, M. Hancock-Beaulieu, and M. Gatford. Okapi at TREC-3. In *Proceedings of the Third Text REtrieval Conference (TREC-3), NIST Special Publication 500-226*, pages 109–126, 1995.

[5] I. H. Witten, A. Moffat, and T. C. Bell. *Managing Gigabytes: Compressing and Indexing Documents and Images.* Van Nostrand Reinhold, New York, 1994.

[6] J. Xu and W. B. Croft. Query Expansion Using Local and Global Document Analysis. In *Proceedings of the 19th Annual International ACM SIGIR Conference on Research and Development in Information Retrieval*, pages 4–11, 1996.

Non-Linear Reading for a Structured Web Indexation

Mathias Géry CLIPS-IMAG Laboratory
MRIM Group (Modeling and Multimedia Information Retrieval)
B.P. 53, 38041 Grenoble Cedex 9, France
Mathias.Gery@imag.fr

ABSTRACT

The growth of the Web has posed new challenges for Information Retrieval (IR). Most of the current systems are based on traditional models, which have been developed for atomic and independents documents and are not adapted to the Web. A promising research orientation consists of studying the impact of the Web structure on indexing. The HyperDocument model presented in this article is based on essential aspects of information comprehension: content, composition and linear/non-linear reading.

Categories and Subject Descriptors

H.3.3 [**Information Search and Retrieval**]: Retrieval models

General Terms

Algorithms

Keywords

Hypertext, Web structure, HyperDocument, reading path

1. INTRODUCTION

The Web is a huge and heterogeneous information space: retrieving relevant information in this context looks like *Finding the Needle in the Haystack*. Well-known search engines like Google allow finding pages using criteria mainly related to the textual content. In [7], 20 Web search engines have shown a low results quality, the best of them reaching the average precision of the "median TREC system". These systems are based mainly on classical IR models, as proposed by Salton 30 years ago [10]: documents are considered as being atomic and independent, as their physical HTML page aspect. However, the Web is structured, and its structure is an essential constituent of information description. Several works have showed that it is possible to extract a hierarchical structure describing Web sites [5], while other deal with macroscopic structure [2]. An index should represent the semantic content of documents, including the structure.

SIGIR'02, August 11-15, 2002, Tampere, Finland.
ACM 1-58113-561-0/02/0008.

2. STRUCTURED IR ON THE WEB

Data modeling approaches allow querying a database using content and structure [9]. *Information propagation* approaches consider links: Chiaramella propagates terms from sub-parts of a document to the top [4], and Google propagates terms from context (anchors) to a given page [1]. *Macroscopic distillation* approaches propagate popularity: Kleinberg calculates two "prestige scores" at query time (*Hubs and Authorities*[1] [8]), and Brin calculates another "prestige score" at indexing time (*PageRank* [1]).

Most of these systems are based on a Web model simplified to a directed graph with HTML pages as nodes and hyperlinks as edges. Very few methods try to analyze what do these links really mean, and how to use them for IR. Gurrin proposes to distinguish functional and structural links [6], and Chakrabarti proposes a fine-grained model representing pages as trees, and an associated fine-grained distillation algorithm giving better results than macroscopic [3].

3. WEB MODELING AND INDEXING

A Web site is based on a *hierarchical structure* (composition), and a *reading structure* allowing a non-linear reading (reading relation). We consider these relations, especially their impact on Web information building and comprehension while reading.

3.1 Web non-linear reading

The Web is composed of Structured Documents SD_i, usually read in a linear way: firstly the introduction, then the first section, etc, until the conclusion. On the other hand, the Web is also a Hypertext, and the author of a Web site defines reading paths: on each node, the reader chooses between one or more possibilities to navigate. Thus, a textual fragment will not always be understood similarly, depending on the previous reading fragments. Each reader and each reading can lead to a new comprehension and build a new significance. The Web as hypertext should be indexed considering several reading paths. So, a SD_i composed of n fragments d_1, d_2, ..., d_n corresponds also to a *non-linear reading* of a *HyperDocument* HD_i composed of d_i as nodes and reading relations as edges.

[1] "A good Hub points to many good Authorities, and a good Authority is pointed to by many good Hubs."

3.2 Structured Documents, HyperDocuments

We propose a $\mathcal{HD}$ model integrating composition and reading relations that considers the two points of view: a Web site is a SD_i or a HD_i. We use the Vector Space Model (VSM) [10] and a classical weighting function to index atomic contents d_i with a vector $\vec{d_i}$.

3.2.1 *Composition: Structured Documents* (SD_i)

Our document model is based on a hierarchical structure with various granularity levels, with the underlying problem of composition. SD_i indexation considers semantic content of each non-leaf node as an aggregation of its children's contents, and is made recursively using children's indexes. Thus, indexes are propagated from the leaves to the root, building a vector $\vec{sd_i}$. This indexation process corresponds to a *linear reading* of a *Structured Document* SD_i.

3.2.2 *Reading path: HyperDocuments* (HD_i)

A Web site is also represented by a HD_i, which is modeled as a directed graph with atomic contents as nodes and reading relations as edges. A potential reading of a HD_i is represented by a set of *reading paths*. Thus, the semantic extraction of a HD_i builds a vector $\vec{path_j}$ for each reading path. The *reading algorithm* integrates the *reading context*, making the following hypotheses:

Hypothesis 1: reading context: the reading of a d_i depends on the previous $d_1, d_2, ...d_{i-1}$ that were read.

Hypothesis 2: accumulation: the beginning of the reading path is more important, considering that it is reused afterward as reading context. It benefits from an accumulation effect.

Hypothesis 3: a semantic breakdown shows a narrative discontinuity and implies a loss of reading context.

We use a vector of reading context $\vec{accu}$ and a coefficient of semantic breakdown α_{break} between the source and the destination node, expressing the narrative discontinuity during the reading. The same HD_i can be read following two different reading paths, which may give two different indexes.

4. STRUCTURED IRS (SIRS)

It is not possible to build a SIRS above an existing Web search engine. Thus, we have developed a complete SIRS based on a VSM-based IRS kernel. A spider[2] crawls the Web, collecting up to 3 millions pages/day. We have developed a set of tools to analyze, index and query the collected corpora. An HTML analyzer, processing up to 25 Gb per day, aims to extract normalized Web corpora (text, links, meta-data, etc), eliminating mirrors, extracting the lexicon and various statistics, etc. The different link types are considered, using a link typing module [5] that allows indexing reading paths. Our index size grow by a factor of 2 to 6 compared to a classical VSM. For example, the index of a Web corpus containing 65'000 pages (1.5 Gb HTML) grows from 280 Mb to 1.1 Gb.

Finally, a querying module allows retrieving *reading paths*. It uses the SD_i indexes ($\vec{sd_i}$) to filter the best HD_i, and the HD_i indexes ($\vec{path_j}$) to retrieve the best reading path for each relevant HD_i (a path that allows navigating among most relevant pages, avoiding the non-relevant pages).

[2]CLIPS-Index : http://clips-index.imag.fr

5. CONCLUSION

Our $\mathcal{HD}$ model is based on content, composition and non-linear reading. It integrates Web structure, and the indexation process depends on the structure. A HyperDocument is represented by its contents (atomic content + hierarchical structure) and its set of reading paths (atomic content + reading structure). The context (information space referencing HD_i and accessible by browsing from HD_i) is also considered, although if not presented here. Our system is able to retrieve information according to granularity (from a paragraph to a Web site), that allows retrieving SD_i which would not have been retrieved otherwise because of their fragmentation in several HTML pages. Our system is also able to find the best reading path among the existing paths, that allows retrieving a sub-set of pages of HD_i which would not have been retrieved as a SD_i. Indeed, a reading path can link few pages of a SD_i mixed with hundreds of non-relevant pages. Also, reading paths can help the user with the "navigation problem", avoiding the user's disorientation.

The first step of our SRIS project is completed: we have developed its framework, from spider to end-user interface, that allows querying a few thousands of pages. Several components need to be improved to allow indexing and querying millions of pages. The next important step is the evaluation of our system: classical test collections are not adapted to the Web IR evaluation. The major inconvenience is related to the judgment atomicity, considering only documents content without taking structure into account. Our model integrates relations and allows finding reading paths: what is a "reading path relevance" in this context?

6. REFERENCES

[1] S. Brin and L. Page. The anatomy of a large-scale Hypertextual Web Search Engine. In *World Wide Web Conference*, Brisbane, Australia, 1998.

[2] A. Broder, R. Kumar, F. Maghoul, P. Raghavan, S. Rajagopalan, R. Stata, A. Tomkins, and J. Wiener. Graph structure in the Web. In *World Wide Web Conference*, Amsterdam, Netherlands, 2000.

[3] S. Chakrabarti. Integrating the Document Object Model with Hyperlinks for Enhanced Topic Distillation and Information Extraction. In *World Wide Web Conference*, Hong-Kong, China, 2001.

[4] Y. Chiaramella, P .Mulhem, and F. Fourel. A Model for Multimedia Information Retrieval. Technical Report Fermi ESPRIT BRA 8134, University of Glasgow, 1996.

[5] M. Géry and J.-P. Chevallet. Toward a structured Information Retrieval System on the Web: Automatic structure extraction of Web pages. In *Workshop on Web Dynamics*, London, 2001.

[6] C. Gurrin and A. F. Smeaton. A connectivity analysis approach to increasing precision in retrieval from hyperlinked documents. In *Text REtrieval Conference*, Gaithersburg, United States, 1999.

[7] D. Hawking, N. Craswell, P. Bailey, and K. Griffiths. Measuring search engine quality. *Journal of Information Retrieval*, 4:33–59, 2001.

[8] J. M. Kleinberg. Authoritative sources in a hyperlinked environnement. *Journal of the ACM*, 46:604–632, 1999.

[9] A. Mendelzon, G. A. Mihaila, and T. Milo. Querying the World Wide Web. *Journal of Digital Libraries*, 1:68–88, 1997.

[10] G. Salton and M. J. McGill. *Introduction to Modern Information Retrieval*. McGraw-Hill, 1983.

Document Normalization Revisited

Abdur Chowdhury
America Online
Reston, Virginia
chowdhury@ir.iit.edu

M. Catherine McCabe
U.S. Government
Washington D.C.
mcatherm@comcast.net

David Grossman, Ophir Frieder
Illinois Institute of Technology
Chicago, IL 60616
{dagr, ophir} @ ir.iit.edu

Abstract
Cosine Pivoted Document Length Normalization has reached a point of stability where many researchers indiscriminately apply a specific value of 0.2 regardless of the collection. Our efforts, however, demonstrate that applying this specific value without tuning for the document collection degrades average precision by as much as 20%.

Categories & Subject Descriptors: H.3.3
Information Search and Retrieval

General Terms: Algorithms, Measurement

Keywords: Information Retrieval, Text Search, Similarity Measure, Relevance Measure, TREC

1. Introduction
The cosine measure normalizes document length so that long documents are not favored simply because they have more terms. Later work empirically showed that, for the TREC collection, longer documents actually have a higher probability of being relevant [1]. One interesting claim from this study was:

> ...the slope value is very stable, i.e., the changes in retrieval effectiveness with minor deviations in slope (from the optimal slope value) are very small for all the collections. A constant slope value of 0.20 was effective across collections...

We show that the slope should be recalibrated for fundamentally different document collections. We recomputed the normalization for the web track and obtained a 16% improvement in our baseline run. The resulting effectiveness from this sole modification was an average precision higher than any other group who submitted results to the TREC-10 web track.

2. Calibrating the Slope for Ad Hoc Task
Using pivoted document normalization, we tested slope values from 0.01 to 0.9 and measured the average precision for each value. This was done for the TREC 6-7-8 adhoc tasks (the shaded area in Table 1) that use the TREC disks four and five and the TREC-9 and TREC-10 tasks that use the WT10G collection. For queries over disks four and five, the slope values below 0.4 are indistinguishable. That is, there is only about a 5% difference between the best slope value and the worst (See Table 1). However, for the TREC-9 and TREC-10 tasks, the slope makes a significant difference – up to 36%. For the TREC-9 and TREC-10 tasks, a slope of 0.05 results in the best average precision of 0.2057 and 0.1737, respectively.

Table 1: Effect of Slope on Average Precision

Slope	TREC 10	TREC 9	TREC 8	TREC 7	TREC 6
0.01	0.1951	0.1706	0.2290	0.1696	0.2312
0.05	**0.2057**	**0.1737**	0.2370	0.1724	0.24
0.1	0.1944	0.1660	0.2386	0.1728	0.2425
0.2	0.1706	0.1507	0.2303	0.1683	0.2432
0.3	0.1519	0.1353	0.2246	0.1631	0.2326
0.4	0.1297	0.1204	0.2172	0.1562	0.2241
0.5	0.1090	0.1073	0.2059	0.1480	0.2162
0.6	0.0890	0.0969	0.1902	0.1366	0.2017
0.7	0.0657	0.0849	0.1717	0.1206	0.1783
0.8	0.0444	0.0669	0.1500	0.0978	0.1518
0.9	0.0215	0.0335	0.1114	0.0688	0.1204

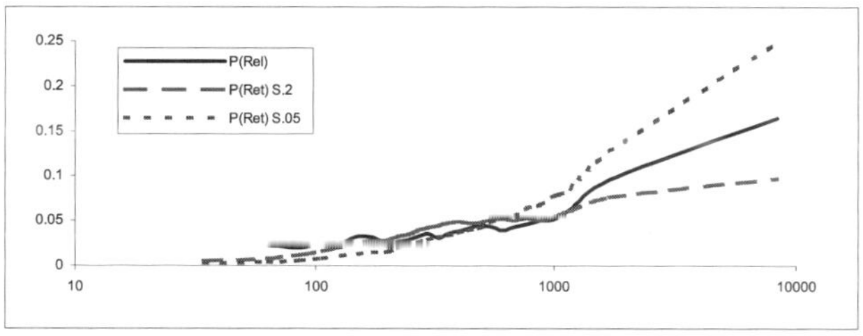

Figure 1: TREC 8

To determine why the variance in slope has a varying degree of impact for different collections, we examine the probability of relevance and the probability of retrieval given different document lengths. As described in [1], we partitioned the document collection into bins of equal size and computed the probability of retrieval and the probability of relevance for each bin. The bin median document size is given on the *x-axis*. These measures are plotted in Figure 1 and Figure 2 using a slope of 0.20 and 0.05, respectively. The slope value is designed so that the retrieval curve will track the relevance curve. For the TREC-8 task (similarly also for the TREC-6 and TREC-7 tasks), both slope values of 0.2 and 0.05 track very closely to the probability of relevance line. This explains the relatively small difference in average precision for the TREC disks four and five.

Turning to Figure 2, with document collection WT10G, we see that both slope values track the relevant curve reasonably well for small document sizes while both diverge for large documents (over 5,400 terms). To identify the cause of a significant difference in average precision found for these two slopes, we then examine the results for only the top 100 documents retrieved.

In Figure 3, we illustrate the results. Here, we can see that the slope value of 0.05 tracks the relevant curve much more closely for large documents. This implies that the cause of a difference in average precision was simply masked in Figure 2 by some low ranking documents that were still retrieved. Further verifying this hypothesis, we examine Figure 4, which shows probabilities for retrieval at only ten documents. Again, we see that the probability of retrieval much more closely tracks the probability of relevance for a slope of 0.05 then a slope of 0.2.

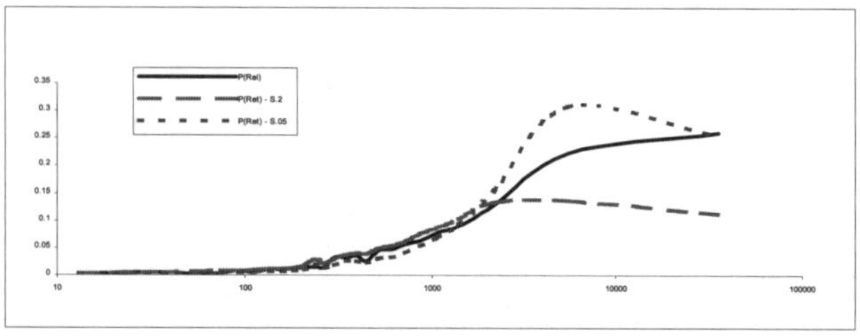

Figure 2: TREC 10 - Top 1000 Retrieved

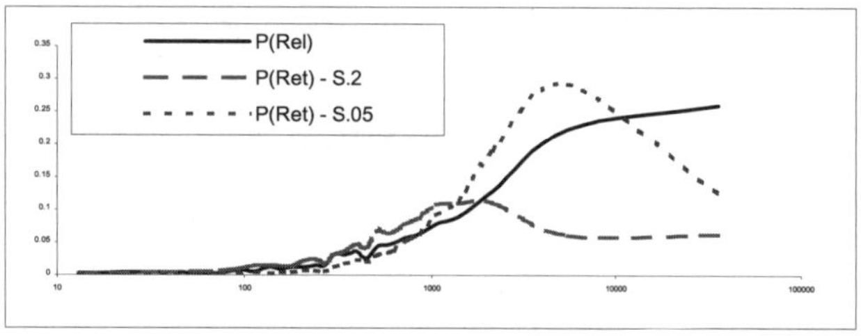

Figure 3: TREC 10 - Top 100 Retrieved

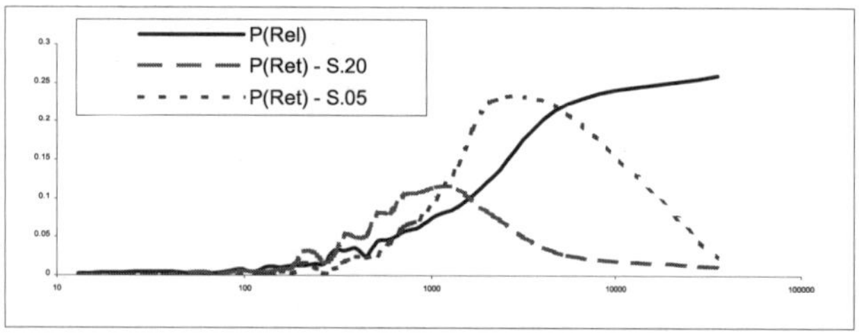

Figure 4: TREC 10 - Top 10 Retrieved

3. Recomputing Probabilistic Normalization

The probabilistic retrieval model also relies on an adjustment for document length [3]. The *b* value of the BM25 strategy is used in a manner quite similar to the slope with sloped cosine. We calibrated the optimal value for *b* across collections and across tasks. We found that, as with the slope, it is critical to adjust the *b* value when significantly changing the document collections as well as when dramatically changing the retrieval task. We find that a slope of 0.25 is 22% better than the values published at 0.75.

Table 2. Average Precision for various BM25 b-values

		Average Precision				
	b	***T10***	***T9***	***T8***	***T7***	***T6***
	0.1	0.208	0.1694	0.2276	0.1711	0.2346
Optimal	**0.25**	**0.213**	**0.1711**	0.2338	0.1734	0.241
	0.5	0.2023	0.1614	0.2327	0.1709	0.2428
Published	**0.75**	0.1786	0.1419	0.2243	0.1662	0.2374
	0.9	0.152	0.1274	0.2166	0.1574	0.2279

4. Conclusion

We have shown that there is a clear need to calibrate, for a specific document collection, the document length component of pivoted document length normalization and the BM25 probabilistic model. We incorporated the new slope value into our TREC-10 system, which uses additional techniques such relevance feedback. Our results improved significantly, yielding an average precision of 0.241 with BM25 and 0.231 with cosine normalization. This performance exceeds the best submission of TREC-10 that had an average precision of .2226.

5. References

[1] Singhal, A., C. Buckley, and M. Mitra, "Pivoted Document Length Normalization," ACM SIGIR 96.

[2] S.E. Robertson, S. Walker, M. Beaulieu, "Okapi at TREC-7: automatic ad hoc, filtering, VLC and interactive," TREC 7, page 253, 1996.

User-Centered Interface Design for Cross-Language Information Retrieval

Preben Hansen[1], Daniela Petrelli[2], Jussi Karlgren[1], Micheline Beaulieu[2], Mark Sanderson[2]

[1] Swedish Institute of Computer Science, Box 1263, SE-164 29 Kista, Sweden, +46 8 633 15 00
{preben,jussi} @sics.se

[2] University of Sheffield, 211 Portobello Street, Sheffield – S1 4DP – UK, +44 (0) 114 22 683
{d.petrelli,m.beaulieu,m.sanderson}@shef.ac.uk

ABSTRACT

This paper reports on the user-centered design methodology and techniques used for the elicitation of user requirements and how these requirements informed the first phase of the user interface design for a Cross-Language Information Retrieval System. We describe a set of factors involved in analysis of the data collected and, finally discuss the implications for user interface design based on the findings.

Categories and Subject Descriptors

H.3.3 [Information Search and Retrieval]; H.5.2 [User Interfaces]; I.2.7 [Natural Language Processing]

General Terms: Design, Human Factors, Languages.

Keywords: Cross-language information retrieval, user studies, interface design, requirement specification.

1. INTRODUCTION

Building tools to access multi-lingual collections of documents poses all the problems of tool design familiar from mono-lingual information access systems but adds several new issues. Cross language information retrieval systems allow users to retrieve documents written in one language using a query written in another (4): in general, people are able to read several more languages than they are able to formulate queries in. However, assessing the worth of documents in a foreign language is more complex than in one's first language – and building a system to present results in several languages is a complex design issue.

Retrieval effectiveness of cross-language systems has been studied through the application of established test collection approaches, (e.g. TREC and CLEF (1)) but comparatively few studies have addressed the specifics of how to design hospitable interfaces for information access in a multilingual environment.

A cross-lingual interface should provide the user with integrated support for all those information access tasks in the search process that are changed through the introduction of multiple languages: e.g. query formulation and reformulation, relevance assessment, document selection, obtaining a collection overview (3).

SIGIR'02, August 11-15, 2002, Tampere, Finland.
ACM 1-58113-561-0/02/0008.

The goal of this field study was to observe current practice on how real cross-language tasks are accomplished through monolingual tools in order to understand what is needed to fully support multi-language information handling tasks.

2. USER-CENTERED DESIGN

Designing with a user-centered approach requires that the user be involved from the very beginning. It is important to integrate user's expertise and knowledge and to understand what people are doing, how, when, and why. There are varied sets of techniques that may be applied for this purpose (2). Generally, elaborating on the outcome of the knowledge acquisition phase, designers define a first version of the system using techniques like task analysis or scenarios of use. Promising solutions can then be tested with users. This formative evaluation verifies choices and indicates design revisions. The design cycle ends when a satisfying solution is reached and implemented. The prototype generated at this stage should be close to the final system and is tested in a summative evaluation to detect minor problems.

We realized the first part of this user-centered design cycle following the steps below:

1. *Preliminary requirements specification*: informal initial definition of user needs together with experts.
2. *Scenarios and preliminary design phase*: based on the results from the previous stage, ***proposed scenarios*** are created.
3. *Formative evaluation*: the proposed scenarios are used to design a ***mock-up user interface***, for user judgment.
4. *Detailed requirements specification*: direct observation of users in real work situations performing real tasks in real environments for detailed information gathering.
5. *Main design phase*: integration of outcome from the previous step resulting in a revision of the first mock-ups.

2.1 CLIR User-Interface Proposal

The initial interface layout was based on proposed scenarios (2 above) formulated by designers taking into account advices coming from representatives of the user's and consisted of 6 individual panes: a *system set-up* pane; a *query formulation and translation* pane; a *result overview pane* of the retrieved set; a ranked list in a *result presentation* pane for relevance judgment; a *multi-document inspection* pane which provides a concurrent display of several documents; and finally, a *search working area* pane for keeping track of searches, query strings and terms and documents.

2.2 The Field Study

Two sites were involved: Alma Media, Finland, and BBC Monitoring, UK. A total of 10 subjects participated representing 4 different user categories: a business analyst, a journalist, 3 librarians, and 5 translators. In order to obtain a rich picture about users and tasks, we applied a combination of qualitative and quantitative data collection techniques.

The study was set-up with the purpose of collecting information on a) *Potential users*: characteristics, needs and desires, opinions; b) *Different tasks*: goals, workflows, current practices; and c) *Environments of use*: desktop or remote access, collaboration in information seeking. The field study focused on four data collection activities of users searching for cross-lingual information:

1. Real time user-task observation and interview through direct observation in their actual work environment;
2. "Informal tests" viewing the interaction with a CLIR system available on the Web (ARCTOS) and machine-translated web pages (Google). This collection of user feedback revealed further details about user characteristics and the way they perform search tasks;
3. Quantitative data were collected through questionnaires in order to sample a larger population;
4. End-user participatory design sessions were undertaken in order to evaluate and discuss the interface mock-ups and design choices.

With one minor exception, all the field study sessions were video recorded. The video evidence provided a valuable support for data analysis, but direct observation by the researchers and first hand interpretation recorded in real time together with note taking proved to be very valuable.

2.3 Data Analysis Approach

All data collection sessions were analyzed according to the following list of factors: *Goals* (the user's information seeking objective); Tasks (a set of actions done for a purpose); *Acts* (a single atomic action or move); *Community context* (e.g. interaction between people); *Procedures* (responses to certain situations); *Design implications* (user suggested improvements); and *Opinions* (user expressed opinions or preferences).

Exploiting the videos generated lists of factual observations, which were organized following the sequence of the observed users' tasks ("task-flows") and translated into task scenarios, which provided a detailed description of each of the user profiles, goals, information task performance, and environment as well as individual requirements. Together with the observation notes, the scenarios served to identify key factors for system design. The following list of user requirements related to CLIR was derived:

1. Search multiple languages at the same time
2. Change query language in same search session
3. Support multilingual queries
4. Support queries with compound names and phrases
5. Use lexical and morphological tools, such as synonym lists
6. Combine Boolean and ranked retrieval
7. Filter results by language, genre, date, or other features
8. Create user-specific dictionaries and term lists

2.4 Implication For System Design

The user requirements list above can be divided with respect to the influence over different software module(s) of the system: a) the user interface (points 2, 7, 8 above); b) generic mechanism of information retrieval (4, 5, and 6), and c) specific for the cross-language task (1 and 3). The strongest impact of the user field study was on the user interface. One important finding related to the amount of control a user required over the *translation process*. They were primarily concerned with the actual search outcome and user control only became an issue when subjects encountered problems in getting satisfactory results. Another major result that called for redesign was related to the *ranked list*. Users expected the result of their search to be presented in a ranked order. Consequently, a graphical overview of the results was set aside in the first design stage. The *presentation of information* for each item in the ranked list was also subject for revision.

3. CONCLUSIONS

By observing current practices with monolingual search engines, we were able to make an advance in assessing what support users would require in a cross-language information retrieval search. The findings led to the redesign of a number of different components of the user interface: in several cases sufficient evidence was gathered to suggest a sound solution. The redesigned interface will be implemented in the near future and will undergo further iteration of the design-evaluation cycle.

4. ACKNOWLEDGEMENTS

This work has been done in Clarity, a EU founded project. Partners participating are: Alma Media, Finland; BBC Monitoring, UK; Swedish Institute of Computer Science, Sweden; University of Sheffield, UK, and University of Tampere, Finland.

5. REFERENCES

[1] Braschler, M., Peters, C. and Schäuble, P. Cross language information retrieval (CLIR) track overview. In: Voorhees, E.M. and Harman, D. K. (eds,). *(TREC-8).* Gaithersburg, MD: National Institute of Standards and Technology, 2000, pp. 25-33.

[2] Hackos, J. T. and Redish, J. C., User and task analysis for interface design.Wiley, 1998.

[3] Ogden, W. C. and Davis, M.W. Improving cross-language text retrieval with human interactions, Proceedings of the Hawaii International Conference on System Science – HICSS-33, 2000

[4] Pirkola, A. The effects of query structure and dictionary setups in dictionary-based cross-lingual information retrieval. In: Proceedings of the ACM SIGIR 1998, Melbourne: Australia, August 1998, 55-64

Implementation of Relevance Feedback for Content-based Music Retrieval Based on User Prefences

Keiichiro Hoashi
KDDI R&D Laboratories, Inc.
2-1-15 Ohara Kamifukuoka
Saitama 356-8502 Japan
hoashi@kddilabs.jp

Erik Zeitler
Uppsala University
Signals & Systems, Box 528
SE-751 20 Uppsala Sweden
erik.zeitler@ieee.org

Naomi Inoue
KDDI R&D Laboratories, Inc.
2-1-15 Ohara Kamifukuoka
Saitama 356-8502 Japan
inoue@kddilabs.jp

Categories and Subject Descriptors

H.3.3 [**Information Systems**]: Information Storage and Retrieval—*relevance feedback*

General Terms

Algorithms, Experimentation.

1. INTRODUCTION

The main task of conventional music retrieval systems is to retrieve a music data, which matches the request of a user. The importance of such systems is expected to increase due to the rapid spread of digital music data formats such as MP3. However, conventional systems can only be used to search a particular song from a database. In this research, we investigate the performance of a conventional music retrieval method to retrieve songs based on the user's musical preferences. Furthermore, we propose the application of relevance feedback techniques to improve the music retrieval performance. Through evaluation experiments, we prove the effectiveness of our method.

2. TREE-STRUCTURED VECTOR QUANTIZATION

Foote has developed a tree-structured vector quantization algorithm (TreeQ)[2] for audio data, and has conducted music retrieval and categorization experiments based on this method. The approach of the TreeQ method is to train a vector quantizer (VQ) instead of modelling the sound data directly. Each audio datum in the training data set, which is a collection of audio data associated with a class such as artist or genre, is first parameterized into a spectral representation, by calculating mel-frequency cepstral coefficients (MFCC)[1]. Next, a learning algorithm constructs a quantization tree that attempts to put samples from different training classes into different bins (leaves). A histogram of an audio file can be generated by looking at the relative frequencies of samples in each quantization bin. The relative frequency can be considered as the probability of a data sample to end up in a certain leaf. If the resulting histograms are considered as vectors, typical vector similarity measures such as cosine similarity can be applied to calculate the similarity between any incoming audio data and category vectors. This method has been used for music and audio retrieval experiments. In Reference [2], experiments were conducted to to categorize music data based on musical genre.

SIGIR'02 August 11-15, 2002, Tampere, Finland.
ACM 1-58113-561-0/02/0008.

3. PROBLEMS

If a sufficient amount of music preferences of a user is collected and used as training data for the TreeQ method, this approach can be applied to construct a system which retrieves music data based on user preferences. However, it is not realistic to expect a potential user of a music retrieval system to provide preferences of hundreds of songs prior to using the system.

Furthermore, the acoustical differences between songs which a user likes or dislikes is expected to be more ambiguous than the difference between songs of different genres, or between songs composed by different artists. Therefore, when the TreeQ method is applied on a small set of user preference data, the performance of the system is expected to be highly dependent on the selection of the songs within the training data set.

4. IMPLEMENTATION OF RELEVANCE FEEDBACK

Due to previously described problems, it is unlikely that a music retrieval system based on existing methods will achieve satisfactory performance. Therefore, in order to improve retrieval performance, we propose the implementation of relevance feedback. The outline of this method is illustrated in Figure 1.

In our proposed method, relevance feedback is applied to refine category vectors generated by the TreeQ method. This is accomplished by inputting relevant data through the VQ tree, and accumulating the results on the original category vector. The refined vector is used to retrieve a new list of music data. The approach taken here is similar to Rocchio's algorithm[4], where weights of terms occurring in relevant documents are accumulated to the initial query.

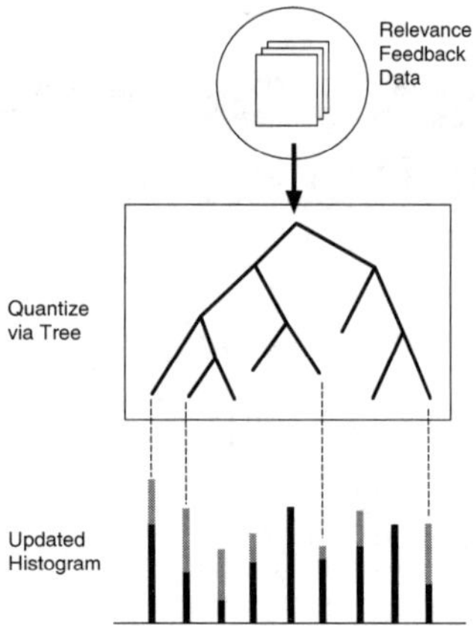

Figure 1: Outline of relevance feedback method

5. EXPERIMENTS

We conducted experiments to evaluate the effectiveness of relevance feedback for music retrieval. For our experiments, we collected user ratings of songs in a music data collection which consists of 107 popular songs composed by various artists. For each song in the collection, a rating ranging from 1 to 5 (Bad:1 $\sim$ Good:5) was given by experiment subjects. The rated data was then classified into 3 categories according to the subject ratings: the category of "good" songs (C_g), "bad" songs (C_b), and "fair" songs (C_f). Categories C_g, C_b, and C_f consist of songs rated (4 or 5), (1 or 2), and 3, respectively.

N songs were randomly extracted from each category, and used as training data for the TreeQ method. As a result of training, a vector which expresses each category is obtained. Vectors for test music data can also be obtained by inputting the data through the VQ tree. By calculating vector similarity between $\vec{C_g}$ and a test data $\vec{K}$, each song in the test data set can be ranked by similarity to category C_g ($Sim(\vec{C_g}, \vec{K})$), assuming that higher similarity to category C_g expresses higher probability that the subject will like the regarded song. Another scoring measure can be defined by the formula: $Sim(\vec{C_g}, \vec{K}) - Sim(\vec{C_b}, \vec{K})$, where the difference between the similarity of each test song and categories C_g and C_b is calculated. These two scoring measures are referred to as Sim (similarity) and $DiffSim$ (difference of similarity), respectively.

For relevance feedback, the top M-ranked relevant songs, i.e., songs which are included in C_g are extracted. The extracted songs are used to refine $\vec{C_g}$ by the method described in the previous section. $\vec{C_b}$ can also be refined by extracting the top M-ranked non-relevant songs (songs which are included in C_b) from the ranked list.

6. RESULTS

For evaluation of experiment results, the average precision is calculated based on each ranked list obtained per experiment. Results obtained based on the refined vectors are compared to the results prior to relevance feedback, which are referred to as the "baseline" results.

Due to the randomness of training data, the average precision of baseline results have a wide variance. Therefore, baseline experiments were conducted 10 times for each N,

Table 1: Improvement rate (%) of avg precision (*Sim*)

	Amount of training data (N)				
M	1	3	5	7	9
1	14.78	2.29	4.37	0.84	1.71
3	27.72	14.45	19.00	14.84	12.46
5	36.55	22.54	31.91	28.10	22.84
7	41.20	32.19	43.69	39.48	34.78

Table 2: Improvement rate (%) of avg precision (*DiffSim*)

	Amount of training data (N)				
M	1	3	5	7	9
1	27.68	5.88	10.22	2.52	4.74
3	40.94	19.70	23.80	17.20	27.50
5	52.15	32.14	34.08	27.99	40.59
7	62.89	43.45	43.76	36.45	52.89

and relevance feedback experiments were conducted based on each baseline run. Furthermore, the mean improvement rate of average precision for all experiments per parameter set of M and N was calculated for performance evaluation, since average precision after relevance feedback is highly dependent on the regarded baseline results. Tables 1 and 2 show the mean improvement rate of average precision for scoring methods *Sim* and *DiffSim*, respectively.

As clear from these results, implementation of relevance feedback has constantly improved average precision. Relevance feedback was especially effective in cases where the amount of training data was low. It is also apparent that *DiffSim* has overperformed compared to *Sim*, which shows that relevance feedback of non-relevant information was also effective.

7. CONCLUSION

In order to improve the performance of content-based music retrieval based on user preferences, we proposed the implementation of relevance feedback. Experiments conducted on user preference data showed that the proposed method improved overall retrieval performance. We plan to increase the number of songs in the music collection and conduct similar experiments in the near future.

Acknowledgments

This research used the TreeQ package[3] developed by Jonathan T. Foote.

8. REFERENCES

[1] David, Mermelstein: "Comparison of parametric representations for monosyllabic word recognition in continuously spoken sentences", IEEE Trans. Acoustic, Speech, Singal Proc., ASSP-28(4), 1980.

[2] Foote: "Content-based retrieval of music and audio", Proceedings of SPIE, Vol 3229, pp 138-147, 1997.

[3] Foote: "The TreeQ Package", `ftp://svr-ftp.eng.cam.ac.uk/pub/comp.speech/tools/treeq1.3.tar.gz`

[4] Rocchio: "Relevance Feedback in Information Retrieval", in "The SMART Retrieval System – Experiments in Automatic Document Processing", Prentice Hall Inc., pp 313-323, 1971.

Spatial Information Retrieval and Geographical Ontologies An Overview of the SPIRIT Project

Christopher B. Jones
Cardiff University, Department of Computer Science, Cardiff, UK, +44 29 2087 4796 {c.b.jones@cs.cf.ac.uk}

R. Purves[1], A. Ruas[2], M. Sanderson[3], M. Sester[4], M. van Kreveld[5], R. Weibel[1]
[1]University of Zurich, [2]IGN Paris, [3]University of Sheffield, [4]University of Hannover, [5]Utrecht University

Categories & Subject Descriptors: add here

General Terms: add here

1. INTRODUCTION

A large proportion of the resources available on the world-wide web refer to information that may be regarded as geographically located. Thus most activities and enterprises take place in one or more places on the Earth's surface and there is a wealth of survey data, images, maps and reports that relate to specific places or regions. Despite the prevalence of geographical context, existing web search facilities are poorly adapted to help people find information that relates to a particular location. When the name of a place is typed into a typical search engine, web pages that include that name in their text will be retrieved, but it is likely that many resources that are also associated with the place may not be retrieved. Thus resources relating to places that are inside the specified place may not be found, nor may be places that are nearby or that are equivalent but referred to by another name. Specification of geographical context frequently requires the use of spatial relationships concerning distance or containment for example, yet such terminology cannot be understood by existing search engines. Here we provide a brief survey of existing facilities for geographical information retrieval on the web, before describing a set of tools and techniques that are being developed in the project SPIRIT : Spatially-Aware Information Retrieval on the Internet (funded by European Commission Framework V Project IST-2001-35047).

1.1 Current Support for Geographical Information Access on the Web

The Northern Light GeoSearch tool from Vicinity (http://www.northernlight.com/geosearch.html) includes a facility for geographical information retrieval. It allows the user to enter part or all of an address, along with a category of interest and a search radius. It finds other places within the specified radius, with the aid of a digital map. A similar facility is found on www.somewherenear.com. Retrieval facilities to find resources associated with a specific place or post code (or zip code) are to be found in association with yellow pages services and some digital map web sites.

A major shortcoming of these approaches is that they cannot recognise alternative names for the same place, whether they be modern and historical variants, informal names or names of contained places. Furthermore their user interfaces are limited in the options they offer to specify and refine a search and to visualise the results, reflecting their lack of knowledge of the semantics of geographical terminology and the associated spatial structures. There have been several recent initiatives to develop location-specific referencing of internet domain names.

Buyukokkten [1] associated IP addresses with telephone area codes of the associated network administrators, and hence, via zip code databases, to place names and geographical coordinates. The approach facilitates the analysis of the geographical distribution of web sites, but is limited in retrieving web pages on the basis of subject matter and geography, since it cannot be assumed that the content of a web page is related to the place where it was created.

The Stanford Research Institute proposed a top level domain based on geographical referencing (.geo). The domain name refers to a strict hierarchy of quadrilateral cells defined by latitude and longitude. Existing domain names would be able to register themselves with a *.geo* domain server which would store, for a set of cells, all registered web sites that relate to each of the given cells. Effective geographical search would depend upon the ability to map from the user's specification of geographical location to the relevant cells. Thus the approach still leaves the requirement for a semantic level of retrieval tools to exploit it.

An experimental system for geographical navigation of the web has been described by [2]. Techniques are proposed for extraction of the geographical context of a web page, based on the occurrence of text addresses and post codes, place names and telephone numbers. This information is transformed to one of a limited set of point-referenced map locations. Geographic search is initiated by the user asking to find web sites that refer to places in the vicinity of a currently displayed web site. The geographical user interface does not allow user specification of place names.

2. TECHNIQUES FOR SPATIALLY-AWARE INFORMATION RETRIEVAL

The SPIRIT project addresses shortcomings of existing facilities such as those described by developing:

- ontologies that model geographical terminology;
- query expansion and relevance ranking procedures based on the geographical ontologies;
- machine learning techniques for the extraction of geographical context from web documents and for generating metadata providing spatial context;
- a multi-modal user interface providing textual input and interactive map feedback of the context of retrieved documents;
- spatial indices for web collections.

SIGIR'02, August 11-15, 2002, Tampere, Finland.
ACM 1-58113-561-0/02/0008.

These facilities are to be tested and evaluated with a 1Tb web collection that will be stored and indexed within a parallel architecture.

2.1 Geographical and conceptual ontologies

The geographical ontology within SPIRIT models both the vocabulary and the spatial structure of places for purposes of information retrieval. The approach facilitates the retrieval of resources that employ alternative and spatially-related place names to that in the query. This will result in accessing not just those resources with an exact locational match to the terms of the query, but also those that relate to places that are similar or nearby in location to the query. The search facilities will furthermore recognise different versions of place names as well as historical alternatives. The potential of building geographical models that combine qualitative and quantitative spatial information for purposes of information retrieval has been recognised in literature on gazetteers and geographical thesauri [3] [4] [[5], but has yet to be proven. This project extends the concepts of gazetteers and thesauri to include a richer set of qualitative and quantitative spatial properties that can be exploited for information retrieval.

In the field of IR, automatic query expansion to add terms to the user's query has received much attention. Although techniques using statistically derived associations have proven useful [6], methods using thesauri with synonyms have shown less success [7]. This has been due to ambiguity of the query terms and its propagation to synonyms that may be unrelated to the user's interests. In geographical terminology, ambiguities are relatively easily resolved and there is good reason to believe that, with very simple user dialog, effective term expansion can be achieved.

2.2 Geographical relevance ranking

The geographical ontology maintains qualitative and quantitative information that can be used to create geographical similarity measures and document ranking techniques using methods analogous to [5]. In the fields of image recognition and general pattern matching, geometric similarity measures have been a topic of study for many years [9]. In parallel, semantic similarity measures have been developed in the field of information retrieval, e.g. [9]. We draw upon both of these strands to develop novel similarity measures, combining geometric, qualitative spatial, and non-spatial information that will be evaluated with large web data collections.

2.3 A multi-modal user interface for geographical information retrieval

Multi-modal interfaces are known to be an effective way to interact with geographical information, yet no research has been conducted in this area for geographical information retrieval. SPIRIT users will be able to describe geographical location textually with terminology for place names, spatial relationships and information descriptors. The ontologies will help to disambiguate the query and to reflect its geographical extent textually and on a map, revealing the system's interpretation of imprecise qualitative spatial terms relating to direction and proximity. Alternatively the user will be able to mark the required extent of search on the map. This could include selecting displayed place names, drawing regions of interest, and using displayed map features to delineate the region of interest. The level of detail of the map will adapt to the user's interests and will reflect the hierarchical structures of geographic space encoded in the ontology.

2.4 Geographical metadata enrichment

Intelligent use of information on the internet depends upon it being accessible to mobile agents and search engines. This depends in turn upon essential aspects of the content of the documents being abstracted and made available in the form of semantic annotations. The process of annotation however requires methods of extracting the information.

In the context of spatial data annotation, progress has been made in the production of metadata *encoding* methods that describe the location and quality of the data sets [10]. The process of annotation is however typically manual. Here we develop techniques for *automatic extraction* and metadata encoding of information from digital map datasets, exploiting techniques from computational geometry, image interpretation and spatial data mining. We will also develop geographical metadata extraction techniques for unstructured web documents, employing a machine learning approach, using training datasets of documents that have already been accurately tagged on the basis of key words such as place names, addresses, telephone numbers and postcodes.

3. REFERENCES

[1] Buyukokkten, O., et al. Exploiting geographical location information of web pages. in WebDB'99 (with ACM SIGMOD'99), 1999, 91-96.

[2] McCurley, K.S. Geospatial mapping and navigation on the web. in WWW10, 2001 http://www10.org/cdrom/papers/278/

[3] Harpring, P., Proper words in proper places: The Thesaurus of Geographic Names. MDA Information, 1997, 2(3): 5-12.

[4] Hill, L.L., J. Frew, and Q. Zheng, Geographic Names. The implementation of a gazetteer in a georeferenced digital library. Digital Library, 1999, 5(1): www.dlib.org/dlib/january99/hill/01hill.html.

[5] Jones, C.B., H. Alani, and D. Tudhope Geographical information retrieval with ontologies of place, in Spatial Information Theory, LNCS 2205, 2001 322-35.

[6] Xu J and W.B.Croft Query Expansion Using Local and Global Document Analysis.ACM SIGIR 1996 4-11.

[7] Voorhees, E.M. Query expansion using lexical-semantic relations. in ACM SIGIR 1994: 61-70.

[8] Veltkamp, R.C. and M. Hagedoorn State-of-the-art in shape matching, in Principles of Visual Information Retrieval, M. Lew, Editor, 2001, Springer, 87-119.

[9] Sintichakis, M. and P. Constantopoulos. A method for monolingual thesauri merging. in ACM SIGIR 1997, 129-138.

[10] WMS, OpenGIS® Web Map Server Interfaces Implementation Specification, 2001, http://www.opengis.org/techno/specs.htm.

A Visualisation Tool for Topic Tracking Analysis and Development

Gareth J. F. Jones
Department of Computer Science
University of Exeter, Exeter EX4 4PT, U.K.
G.J.F.Jones@exeter.ac.uk

Steven M. Gabb
Department of Computer Science
University of Exeter, Exeter EX4 4PT, U.K.
S.M.Gabb@exeter.ac.uk

ABSTRACT

Topic Detection and Tracking (TDT) research explores the development of algorithms to detect novel events and track their development over time for online reports. Development of these methods requires careful evaluation and analysis. Traditional reductive methods of evaluation only represent some of the available information of algorithm behaviour. We describe a visualisation tool for topic tracking which makes it easy to analysis and compare the temporal behaviour of tracking algorithms.

Categories and Subject Descriptors

H.3.3 [**Information Storage and Retrieval**]: Information Search and Retrieval

General Terms

Algorithms, Design, Experimentation

Keywords

topic tracking, visualisation, analysis, development

1. INTRODUCTION

The rapid increase in easily available online reports relating to issues such as news, commercial, and specialist interests has led to research into the development of methods for locating and delivering personalised digests of stories. A key component of these systems is the algorithms used to detect stories of interest to a user and track them as they develop. The Topic Detection and Tracking (TDT) evaluation [1] provides a standard set of news documents with a number of topics to be tracked and a list of relevant documents for each topic. In our own work we are interested in the development of systems for the generation of personalised newspapers. In our research we have found that performance measures from the TDT evaluation to be of limited usefulness in comparative analysis of algorithms. In order address this problem we have developed a novel interactive visualisation tool for analysis of topic tracking behaviour. This paper outlines our topic tracking research, but focuses on describing the features of our visualisation tool.

2. ALGORITHM DEVELOPMENT TASK

Our initial development collection was gathered over a period of one month in November 2000. The choice of sources was motivated as follows. The target group for our personalised newspaper system is the British general public. We wished to investigate tracking from diverse sources within the British media and other English language reports from around the world. With regard to the latter sources, we were interested in whether regional topics could be correctly identified as related or unrelated to the British sources, and similarly whether unrelated British sources were classed as belonging with regional international stories.

Eight sources were used in total as follows: *The Guardian*, *The Times* (British broadsheet newspapers), *The Daily Mirror* (British tabloid), *BBC on-line* (British internet news source), and *Washington Post*, *The Japan Times*, *The Australian Arabic News* (international online newspapers). Eight test topics taken from this period and their relevant stories from the collection were identified reflecting international and local news stories, e.g. U.S. election vote re-counts, Japanese Prime Minister, U.K. floods.

3. TOPIC TRACKING ALGORITHMS

Research in TDT is exploring a variety of tracking algorithms, for example [4]. In our current investigation we are examining the use of the Okapi term weighting and query expansion techniques [3], although any other algorithms can easily be integrated into our visualisation system. Our strategy is as follows. Documents are processed to convert them to a standard markup format, stop words are removed and Porter stemming applied. Terms are then weighted for each day using all documents available up to this date. For each topic, documents are scored by matching them with the topic statement. If the matching score is above a given threshold the document is marked as relevant. Topic statements are modified over time to reflect changes in the topic. Terms appearing in documents marked by the system as relevant are ranked using the Robertson selection value [3] and the top ranking 15 terms selected as the revised topic statement. In order to account for regional topics, a counter is maintained of the number of times a relevant story is sourced for each region. The threshold value for this region is then modified for subsequent stories. In addition we incorporate a "topic inactivity factor" which increases the threshold each day after the last relevant story has been found.

4. TOPIC-TRACKING VISUALISATION

The standard performance measures usually used in topic tracking research are *recall*, *precision*, *miss rate*, *false alarm rate* and *DET (detection error trade-off* [4]. The latter shows the trade-off in story misses and false alarms for a

SIGIR'02, August 11-15, 2002, Tampere, Finland.
ACM 1-58113-561-0/02/0008.

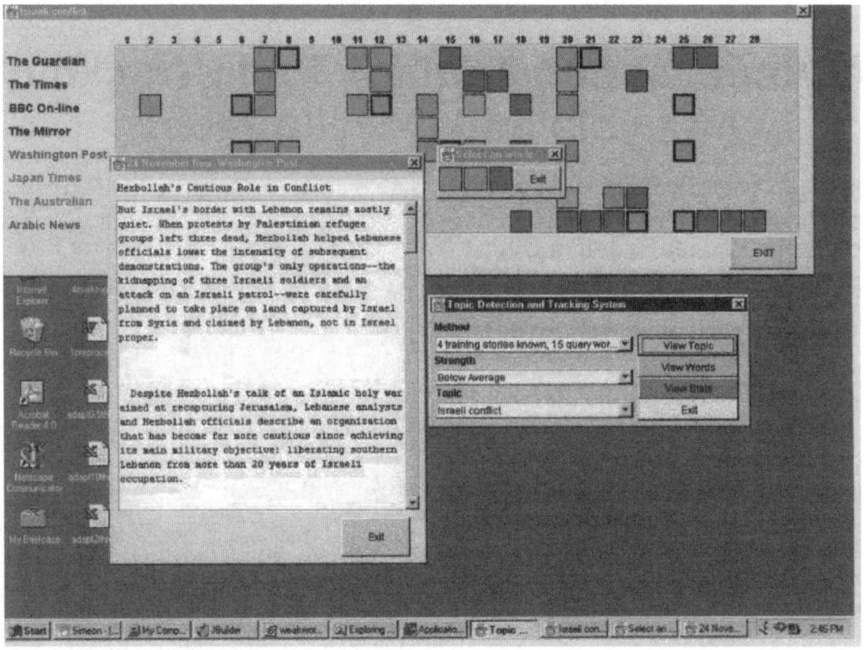

Figure 1: Topic tracking visualisation tool.

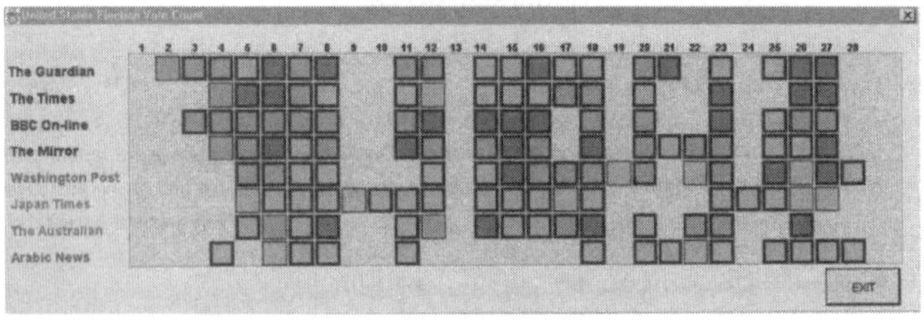

Figure 2: Topic tracking frame.

Figure 3: Accessing multiple stories from single source on one day.

tracking scheme and is usually represented graphically. These measures all give valuable information about behaviour of topic tracking schemes, but it is difficult to interpret the contrasting behaviour of different schemes.

In order to address this problem in our work, we developed an interactive graphical visualisation tool for use in algorithm development. Visualisation is a very powerful way of representing large amounts of information for rapid interpretation, see for example the *Tilebars* tool showing structured query-document matching and document structure [2].

Our tool consists of several components. The main topic frame is shown in Figure 2. The eight news sources are shown on the left hand side. For a given topic hits, misses and false alarms for each new set of stories are illustrated graphically by the colour coded boxes in each column. On topic stories are shown green, misses red, and false alarms blue. Sources for more than one story is associated with a topic for a given day are indicated by a black border. The colouring of this box is prioritised as: hit, miss, false alarm. Clicking on this box brings up another box showing the individual stories and their result, shown in Figure 3. The topic frame is integrated into the complete system shown in Figure 1. The system enables individual stories to be viewed to explore their classification. The composition of the topic statement at each point can also be viewed. The system enables easy selection of system parameters settings with interactive graphical display of the results (which can be pre-computed), as well as the standard tracking measures discussed above.

A simple example of using the system is as follows. It was observed that a low initial threshold setting produced low overall recall for the test set. We found this result surprising, but analysis of the topic tracking frame easily showed a high number of false alarms for early stories (caused by the low threshold) resulted in significant drift in the topic definition leading to very low numbers of accurate hits as more stories are encountered. Changing to a threshold which adapts over time as more evidence for the topic is gathered was then observed to give much more consistent behaviour over time.

5. REFERENCES

[1] J. G. Fiscus *et al.*, NIST's 1998 Topic Detection and Tracking Evaluation (TDT2). In *Proceedings of the DAPRA Broadcast News Transcription and Understanding Workshop*, pages 19-26, 1999.

[2] M. A. Hearst, TileBars: Visualisation of Term Distribution Information in Full Text Information Access. In *Proceedings of ACM SIGCHI*, pages 59-66, 1995

[3] S. E. Robertson *et al.*, Okapi at TREC-3. In *Proceedings of the Third Text REtrieval Conference (TREC-3)*, pages 109-126, 1995.

[4] Y. Yang *et al.*, Improving text categorization methods for event tracking. In *Proceedings of ACM SIGIR*, pages 65-72, Athens, 2000.

A New Method of Parameter Estimation for Multinomial Naive Bayes Text Classifiers

Sang-Bum Kim
Korea University,
SEOUL, 136-701, KOREA
sbkim@nlp.korea.ac.kr

Hae-Chang Rim
Korea University,
SEOUL, 136-701, KOREA
rim@nlp.korea.ac.kr

Heui-Seok Lim
Chonan University
ChungChong-NamDo,
330-180, KOREA
limhs@infocom.chonan.ac.kr

ABSTRACT

Multinomial naive Bayes classifiers have been widely used for the probabilistic text classification. However, their parameter estimation method sometimes generates inappropriate probabilities. In this paper, we propose a topic document model approach for naive Bayes text classification, where their parameters are estimated with an expectation from the training documents. Experiments are conducted on Reuters 21578 and 20 Newsgroup collection, and our proposed approach obtained a significant improvement in performace over the conventional approach.

Categories and Subject Descriptors

H.3.3 [**Information Systems**]: Information Search and Retrieval—*Information Filtering*

General Terms

Experimentation

1. INTRODUCTION

Naive Bayes text classifiers have been widely used because of its simplicity. Among the various versions of classifiers, multinomial naive Bayes text classifier[1] is mostly used. This classifier has adopted a *topic unigram language model approach* to estimate the term probabilities given a class as follows[1]:

$$P(w_k|c_j) = \frac{\#\ w_k \text{ in the documents belonging to } c_j}{\#\ \text{tokens in the documents belonging to } c_j} \quad (1)$$

Unfortunately, this method can cause inappropriate estimation as shown in Figure 1. In this example, w1, w2, and w3 have the same probability given a class c with the topic unigram language model approach, and it is because that this model doesn't consider the document boundaries. The main claim of this paper is that the term occurrences in the short

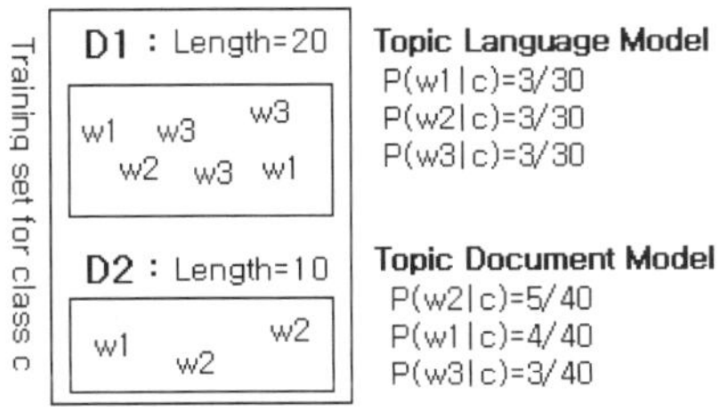

Figure 1: Example of parameter estimation methods

documents should be more emphasized than those in the long documents. Intuitively, the short documents usually have fewer unnecessary terms and probably consist of more essential terms to represent a concept of a topic. Based on this observation, we propose an alternative approach: *topic document model approach* where the term probabilities given a class are estimated by considering the document boundaries.

2. TOPIC DOCUMENT MODEL APPROACH

In the topic unigram language model, the parameter $P(w_k|c_j)$ indicates the probability that the term w_k occurs next in the stream of words about a topic c_j. This kind of *language model* framework leaves no room for considering document boundaries in the training collection to estimate the model parameters. For this reason, we are forced to use a new alternative model: *topic document model*. This model is specified with a unigram distribution in a document about a specific topic. Thus, the parameters of our model are defined by the probabilities for the occurrences of terms in a document whose topic is c_j, and this probability is determined by the expectation value from the training documents as follows:

$$\begin{aligned} & P(w_k \in d_i | Topic(d_i) = c_j) \\ = & \sum_{x=1}^{|\mathcal{D}|} P(w_k \in d_x) P(d_x|c_j) \\ = & \frac{1}{N_{c_j}} \sum_{x=1}^{|\mathcal{D}|} P(w_k \in d_x, Topic(d_x) = c_j) \end{aligned} \quad (2)$$

where $\mathcal{D}$ and N_{c_j} stand for a set of training documents and the number of documents belonging to c_j, respectively.

In the equation (2), each training document is equally treated by assuming that a document prior given a class,

SIGIR'02, August 11-15, 2002, Tampere, Finland.
ACM 1-58113-561-0/02/0008.

Table 1: Performances of TLM and TDM

(a) BEP Performances on Reuters21578

	TLM	TDM	Δ%
10 cat.	0.8822	**0.8833**	+1.25%
90 cat.	0.7576	**0.8121**	+7.9%

(b) Accuracies on 20 Newsgroup Collections

	TLM	TDM	Δ%
Avg.	0.8431	**0.9016**	+6.94%

$P(d_x|c_j)$, is uniform, and consequently the term probabilities from each training document are averaged. A similar static was used by [2] for a different purpose. The most important difference between our estimation and the traditional one is that the term occurrences in the short training documents have more influence on the parameters than those in the long training documents. As shown in Figure 1, our approach assigns the higher probability to the term w2 given a class c than the term w1 or w3. If we assume that $P(d_x|c_j)$ is not uniform but defined as the number of tokens in d_x over the number of tokens in every document belonging to c_j, then the result turns out to be same as the equation (1). Accordingly, it is clear that the traditional method violates a generally accepted assumption that all the training documents have the same prior given a class.

Now, $P(w_k \in d_x)$ in the equation (2) can be estimated as follows:

$$P(w_k \in d_x) = \frac{\theta + TF_{kx}}{\theta \cdot |V| + \text{length}(d_x)} \quad (3)$$

where TF_{kx}, $|V|$ and length(d_x) mean the term frequency of w_k in d_x, vocabulary size, and the number of tokens in d_x, respectively. For the efficiency issues, we substitute average document length for length(d_x) for the missing terms in our experiments. To avoid the zero or one probability, additive smoothing is used with θ, which is empirically set as 0.0001.

3. EXPERIMENTAL RESULTS

In order to compare the performaces of multinomial naive Bayes text classifiers with *topic unigram language model approach*(TLM) and our *topic document model approach*(TDM), we have conducted experiments on the two standard benchmark collections: Reuters21578 and 20 Newsgroups. We removed the stopwords and conducted stemming, but do not use any feature selection techniques. "ModApte" split was used to separate into the train set and the test set. For 20 Newsgroups, we have used 2/3 of the collection for training and 1/3 for testing. Break even point(BEP) and its micro-averaged values are used to evaluate the performances on Reuters21578. For the experiments on 20 Newsgroups collection, the classifiers are evaluated by using the accuracy measure.

Table 1(a) shows micro-averaged BEP performances on Reuters 21578 collection for 10 major categories and all 90 categories. In this experiment, we obtain 7.9% performance improvement for the 90 categories, but there is no significant performance improvement for the 10 categories. TDM works very well especially in the categories with small number of training documents. Figure 2 shows the BEP performaces for the rare categories in Reuters21578.[1] This result is quite meaningful since naive Bayes has been reported as a poor-performing classifier especially in the rare categories compared to the other learning algorithms[3]. Table 1(b) shows the experimental result on the 20 Newsgroup collection. The baseline performance 0.8431 is similar to the other reported performances[1], and there is 6.94% improvement of the accuracy. Figure 3 shows the performances according to the number of training examples. In this experiment, TDM achieves the top-performance of the traditional approach when only about 3,000 training documents are used.

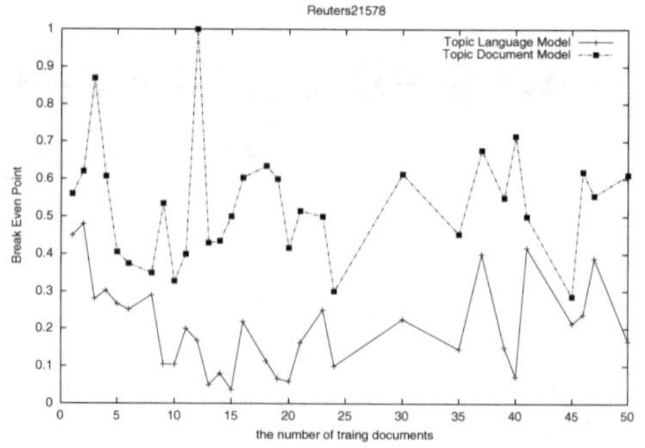

Figure 2: Performaces for the rare categories in Reuters21578

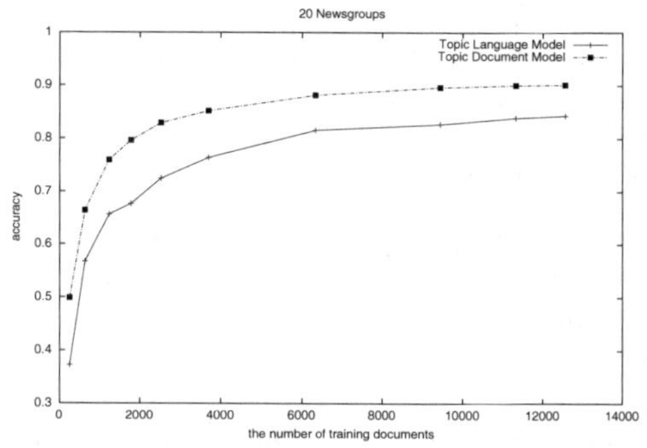

Figure 3: Performaces according to the number of training examples in 20 Newsgroups

4. CONCLUSION AND FUTURE WORK

We have proposed a topic document model approach, where a term probability given a class is estimated by averaging the occurrence probabilities in each training document belonging to that class. Experimental results show that our approach significantly outperforms the traditional topic unigram language model approach. For the future work, we will try to further formalize our framework and extend our model to the probabilisitic IR model.

5. REFERENCES

[1] A. K. McCallum and K. Nigam. A comparison of event models for naive bayes text classification. In *Proceedings of AAAI-98 Workshop on Learning for Text Categorization*, pages 137–142, 1998.

[2] J. M. Ponte and W. B. Croft. A language modeling approach to information retrieval. In *Proceedings of SIGIR-98*, pages 275–281, 1998.

[3] Y. Yang and X. Liu. A re-examination of text categorization methods. In *Proceedings of SIGIR-99*, pages 42–49, 1999.

[1]For the categories with the same number of training documents, performance is averaged.

Study of Category Score Algorithms for k-NN Classifier

Huaizhong KOU
PRiSM Laboratory , University of Versailles
45, AV Etats-Unis
78035 Versailles, France
+33 (0)1 39 25 43 15
Huaizhong.Kou@prism.uvsq.fr

Georges Gardarin
e-XMLMedia
31 Avenue du Général LECLERC
92340 BOURG LA REINE, France
+33 (0)1 45 36 41 20
Georges.Gardarin@e-XMLMedia.fr

Abstract

We analyzes category score algorithms for k-NN classifier found in the literature, including majority voting algorithm (**MVA**), simple sum algorithm (**SSA**). **MVA** and **SSA** are two mainly used algorithms to estimate score for candidate categories in k-NN classifier systems. Based on the hypothesis that utilization of internal relation between documents and categories could improve system performance, two new weighting score models: concept-based weighting (**CBW**) score model and term independence-based weighting (**IBW**) score model are proposed. Our experimental results confirm our hypothesis and show that in the term of precision average **IBW** and **CBW** are better than the other score models, while **SSA** is higher than **MVA**. According to macro-average F1 **CBW** performs best. Rocchio-based algorithm (**RBA**) always performs worst.

Categories & Subject Descriptors: Document And Text Processing

General Terms: Algorithm

Keywords k-NN, document categorization, category score

1. Introduction

Document categorization is a useful component of various language processing applications. Many algorithms have been widely investigated for document categorization, including for example support vector machine algorithm (**SVM**) [1], k-nearest neighbor (**k-NN**) algorithm [4],naïve Bayes algorithm[3], etc. Among them **k-NN** is one of the top-performing classifiers[1][4]. According to **k-NN**, given a new document to be categorized, the system ranks its nearest neighbors among all training documents by calculating document similarity. The category score will be calculated for each candidate category by using the similarity of nearest neighbor documents to the new document. Then one or more categories can be assigned to the new document by a suitable thresholding strategy[5].

The calculation approaches to category score have important impact on **k-NN** classifier. Majority voting algorithm and similarity summing algorithm are commonly used for category score calculation. But these two algorithms do not take into account the different contribution of neighbor documents to category score. One refinement to k-NN is to weight contribution of each of k neighbors giving greater to closer neighbors.

SIGIR'02, August 11-15, 2002, Tampere, Finland.
ACM 1-58113-561-0/02/0008.

2. Category Score Algorithms

2.1 Majority Voting Algorithm (MVA)

For each candidate category c_i majority voting algorithm (MVA) takes the number of positive documents in D_k as its category score, and is defined by (2.1).

$$Score.MVA(c_k, d) = \sum_{d' \in D_k} \delta(c_k, d') \qquad (2.1)$$

and $\delta(c_k, d') = 1 \quad if\ d' \in c_k ; 0\ if\ d' \notin c_k$

where D_k consists of k nearest neighbor training documents.

2.2 Simple Sum Algorithm (*SSA*)

Given a category, it takes the simple sum of similarity between a new document and the positive documents in the nearest neighbors as category score. A lot of researchers have adapted this algorithm. The computation formula is defined by (2.2).

$$Score.SSA(c, d) = \sum_{d' \in D'_c} simil(d, d') \qquad (2.2)$$

Where $D'_k = \{d' | d' \in D_k \wedge d' \in c\}$ consists of the positive neighbor documents of category c. In contrast to the MVA, SSA makes use of the values of similarity between new document and positive documents in D_k.

3. Weighting Category Score Algorithms

Neither **MVA** nor **SSA** weight the different contribution of neighbor instances to category. The similarity between neighbor instance and new instance are directly used. They will produce wrong assignments for multiple-categories. Now we present two algorithms of category score calculation. The idea is of taking into account different roles that individual sample instance document plays in each category when calculating category score.

Hypothesis: utilization of internal relations between documents and categories can improve categorization performance.

Definition: **affinity** between a document d and a category c is a measure of the level of membership that the document belongs to the category, noted as $Aff(d, c)$.

3.1 Independence-based Weighting Score Model

Based on a well-known naïve Bayes independence assumption, the conditional probability of presence can be simply calculated for every category[1]. We take such conditional probability as affinity between training document and category:

$$Aff(d, c) = P(c|d) \qquad (3.1)$$

$P(c|d)$ can reflect the affinity between a training document and a category. Given a training document d and a category c, the category score can be calculated by the following score model called as independence-based weighting(***IBW***) model (3.2).

$$Score.IBW(c_k,d) = \sum_{d' \in D_k} simil(d,d') \bullet Aff(d',c_k) \qquad (3.2)$$

$Aff(d',c_k)$ is introduced in (3.2) to weight the contribution of training document to category score.

3.2 Concept-based Weighting Score Model

Some observations have shown that centroid vector of category can reflect the category theme and summarize the characteristics of the category [2]. So, centroid vectors can represent categories at the level of concepts. Due to these observations, centroid is also called concept vector of category. The similarity between training document and centroid of category can measure the membership of document to category. It is reasonable to consider the value of cosine similarity between document vector d and concept vector v_c of category c as affinity (3.3).

$$Aff(d,c) = simil(d,v_c) \qquad (3.3)$$

With the formula (3,3), a concept-based weighting (***CBW***) model of category score calculation can be defined by (3.4):

$$Score.CBW(c_k,d) = \sum_{d' \in D_k} simil(d,d') \bullet Aff(d',c_k) \qquad (3.4)$$

4. Experiments and Analysis

We use Reuter-21578 collections as experiment benchmark. ApteMod split strategy is taken. The category score algorithms **MVA**, **SSA**, **IBW** and **CBW** are tested by using **k-NN** with the value of k as 10,20,30,40,50,60,70 respectively, and RCut thresholding strategy is used with its value 1 . Due to the limit of space, only part of results is presented here.

According to the average of macro-average F1,the experimental results show that **CBW** outperforms the other 3 score, **SSA** achieves the same performs as **CBW** at 40, 50, 60 and 70. **MVA** is less than **IBW** and **SSA**. For the small k value (10, 20, 30) **IBW** is higher than **SSA** while it is lower than **SSA** for the big k value (40,50, 50, 70).

Figure below displays average precision of score models over middle recall range and high recall range respectively. The up part shows that **IBW** and **CBW** outperform the others and **MVA** performs worst over middle recall range [0.3,0.7]. This confirms our hypothesis: the performance of **k-NN** can be improved by integrating affinity information between training document and category into calculation of category score. The score models can be ranked as $IBW > CBW \geq SSA > MVA$.

The down part shows the performances of score models over high recall range [0.7,1]. Both **SSA** and **MVA** outperforms the other models and the former behaves relatively better than the later. **IBW** is comparable to them for k=20,30,40 and 50, but **CBW** is lower than **IBW**, **SSA** and **MVA** in most cases (k=20,30,40,50 and 60). Overall the following results have been achieved:

(a) **IBW** is better than other score models. One explanation to this is utilization of internal relations between documents and categories in **IBW** models. This furthermore proves our hypothesis made in **Section 3**. (b) **CBW** and **SSA** and **MVA** are complementary: **CBW** is higher than other two ones over low recall level and is lower than them over high recall level. (c)**SSA** is slightly superior to **MVA**. It is understandable because more internal information between document and category is used in **SSA** model than **MVW**.

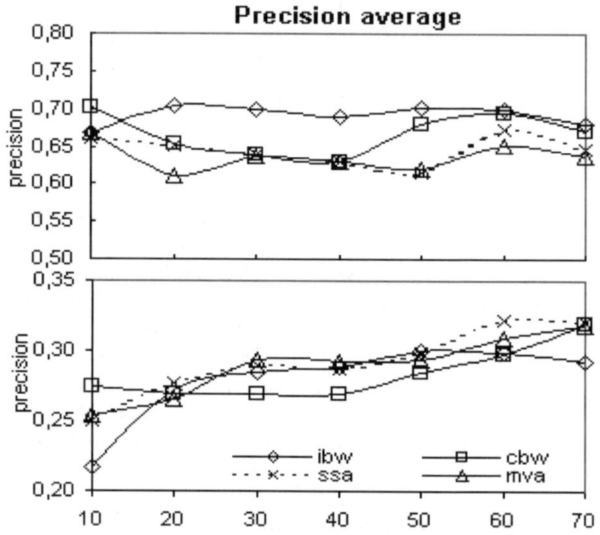

5. Concluding Remarks

This paper discussed existing calculation models (**SSA**, **MVA**) of category score used in **k-NN** classifiers and analyzed their advantages and disadvantages. We believe that subtle utilization of internal relation between documents and categories for calculating category score can profit performance of **k-NN** classifier. Then two affinity-based weighting algorithms (**CBW** and **IBW**) are proposed. The empirical results confirm that subtle utilization of internal relation between documents and categories for calculating category score can benefit performance of **k-NN** classifier. In the term of precision average **IBW** and **CBW** are better than the other score models, while **SSA** is higher than **MVA**. According to macro-average F1 **CBW** performs best.

6. References

[1] Joachims, T. Text categorization with support vector machines: Learning with many relevant features. In proceedings of ECML,1998.

[2] George K. and Eui-Hong H. Concept Indexing: A fast Dimensionality Reduction Algorithm with Applications to Document Retrieval & Categorization, Technical Report TR-00-0016, University of Minnesota, 2000

[3] Lewis, D. D. & Ringuette, M. Comparison of two learning algorithms for text categorization. The 3rd Annual Symposium on Document Analysis and Information Retrieval (SDAIR'94).

[4] Yang, Y. & Liu, X. A re-examination of text categorization methods, ACM SIGR,42-49,1999.

[5] Yang, Y.(2001). A study on thresholding strategies for text categorization, ACM SIGIR, pp.137-145,2001.

Higher Precision for Two-Word Queries

K. L. Kwok
C. S. Dept., Queens College, CUNY,
Flushing, NY 11367
Tel: +1 718 997 3482
kwok@ir.cs.qc.edu

ABSTRACT

Queries have specific properties, and may need individualized methods and parameters to optimize retrieval. Length is one property. We look at how two-word queries may attain higher precision by re-ranking using word co-occurrence evidence in retrieved documents. Co-occurrence within document context is not sufficient, but window context including sentence context evidence can provide precision improvements at low recall region of 4 to 10% using initial retrieval results, and positively affects pseudo-relevance feedback.

Categories and Subject Descriptors

H.3.3 [**Information Storage and Retrieval**]: Information Search and Retrieval.

General Terms: Experimentation.

Keywords: Term co-occurrence; re-ranking of retrieval list.

1. INTRODUCTION

2-word queries (after stop-word removal) present a unique opportunity to study how word co-occurrence may influence retrieval effectiveness. In such a query, the two words can form a phrase (such as noun-noun) that has more specific meaning than the single words alone. This phrase is either in the order presented, or the reverse if a preposition (e.g. 'of') exists between them. If they do not form a phrase, we assume they form a list and that both words are important because the query is so short. In contrast, 1-word queries present no opportunity to use relationships between words. 3 (or more)-word queries lead to ambiguity as to which 2-word combinations are more meaningful (in addition to the 3-word construct). 2-word queries often have low effectiveness (usual with short queries) unless the words are very specific. We study how co-occurrence of the two query words may be used to re-rank the retrieval based on single stems to achieve higher precision. Higher precision at 10 to 30 documents retrieved could also be important for pseudo-relevance feedback (PRF). Previous studies of re-ranking [1,2] normally consider a query set of all types, and use a single technique without discrimination. We believe each query may have its own specific properties, especially ultra-short ones, and a more individualized approach using varied techniques or parameters for different query types may be a better strategy. One property is length, and we start with query length of two.

SIGIR'02, August 11-15, 2002, Tampere, Finland.
ACM 1-58113-561-0/02/0008.

2. METHODOLOGY

The different ways in which query words appear in documents may provide evidence of relevance. [3,4] employed such occurrence patterns for all query types to do primary ranking of documents. Here, we use these patterns to re-rank the top n documents of retrieval based on single stems. One common co-occurrence factor to study is the context unit in which query terms occur: document, sentence, or a window within sentence. For document context (coordinate matching) we followed [1] to re-rank all 2-word matching before single word matching, and retain the original RSV's (retrieval status value) to resolve ties. One may also use sentence context to provide tighter control of the matching to avoid erroneous evidence. In coordinate matching, binary count was used. Original retrievals were performed using Porter's stemming. In [1], it has also been reported that for re-ranking with un-stemmed words provide better evidence than stemmed words.

For window co-occurrence, we include more detailed considerations such as: 1) weight modification for re-ranking; 2) matching order and window size w; 3) number of co-occurrence matches in a document; and 4) hardness of improvement. Previous works in phrase retrieval have tried to define the weight of a phrase match [5], which is then added to the normal RSV due to single stems. We made the assumption that the original single stem RSV already provides an overall measure of the relevance of a document. Additional co-occurrence matches serve to improve this measure by a proportion. Thus, the new RSV for ranking becomes: RSV' = $(1+\alpha)$ * RSV, (with $0<=\alpha<1$). We limit matching patterns to exact phrase with highest α=w0, and ordered or unordered matching within window size w<5 with α=w0/(w+0.5). For w>=5 up to a sentence, α=w0/5.5. For each sentence only one tightest match is counted. For each document, repeat tightest matches are counted. We differentiate one from many by giving a repeat factor r>1 to the latter. Our RSV' then becomes r*(1+w0/(w+0.5)), w=0..5. Experimentation with various schemes show that this weight formula is simple and gives reasonable performance.

3. EXPERIMENTS & DISCUSSIONS

We studied 25 2-word queries from TREC-8 and 20 from TREC-7. An initial retrieval that does not employ adjacent 2-word phrases for representation, collection enrichment or other special techniques is used as basis (displayed as Col. 2 in Table 1). Standard TREC evaluation measures as labeled on the rows are used, emphasizing on precision at 10, 20, 30 documents retrieved since we do re-ranking. Cols. 3 & 4 show coordinate matching re-ranking of initial results with and without stemming. Cols. 5 & 6 are re-ranking results using our window weighting formula.

Contrary to [1], stemming or no-stemming does not lead to much difference. However, coordinate matching re-ranking is less effective than that based on our window formula. This is because these queries have only two words, and retrieved documents are often ordered by coordinate matching already during 1st stage retrieval. Window co-occurrence imposes tighter relevance evidence, and results improve when sentence context are also included. This window re-ranking method gives low recall precision (the mean of p@10, 20 and 30) improvements of about 4% for TREC-8 and 9-10% for TREC-7. This result does not involve 2-stage PRF, but can be useful in time-critical retrievals (such as in high volume web environment) where 2-stage retrieval may be too costly compared to re-ranking the top 200 documents of an initial retrieval.

We next look at how this improved initial retrieval may affect pseudo-relevance feedback. A fixed number of 40 terms were used for query expansion, but a varying number of top documents: 10, 20 and 30 were used. The original PRF results are displayed in Columns 7-9, and those involving co-occurrence re-ranking of 1st stage are shown in Columns 10-12. One may notice the original PRF (without re-ranking) for TREC-8 was not much better than the 1-stage retrieval until '30doc'. On the other hand, PRF retrieval after co-occurrence re-ranking provides more stable, better performance throughout. Re-ranking also considers the 'hardness of improvement' factor, i.e. several initial retrievals already have over 40% of their top 50 documents containing the exact query phrase, and these have their re-ranking proportion further reduced. Using the "30doc" column as example, co-occurrence re-ranking improves 2nd stage retrieval by about 8% for both TREC-8 and 7. Some of the tested queries are originally three-word, but reduced to two after high frequency thresholding. However, co-occurrence weighting made use of them in pairs. If the third words were not considered, the effectiveness would be reduced to 3% to 4%.

4. CONCLUSION

2-word queries provide the least complicated environment to study co-occurrence effects on retrieval. It is shown that it can improve retrieval of single stems by re-ranking using a simple inverse distance formula for window matching. Studying these queries may give hints on how to do better weighting for longer queries. This is a first step in our approach to use more individualized processes to optimize retrieval for different query types.

5. ACKNOWLEDGMENTS

This work was partially sponsored by the Space and Naval Warfare Systems Center San Diego, under Grant No. N66001-00-1-8912.

6. REFERENCES

[1] Crouch, C.J., Crouch, D.B., Chen, Q. & Holtz, S.J. Improving the retrieval effectiveness of very short queries. Info. Process. & Mngmt. 38(1) 2002, 1-36.

[2] Kwok, K.L. Improving English and Chinese ad-hoc retrieval: a Tipster Text Phrase 3 project report. Information Retrieval, 3(4) 2000, 313-338.

[3] Hawking, D. & Thistlewaite, P. Proximity operators – so near and yet so far. In: The Fourth Text Retrieval Conference (TREC-4). NIST SP 500-236, pp.131-144. GPO:D.C. 1996.

[4] Clarke, C.L.A, Cormack, G.V. & Burkowski, F.J. Shortest substring ranking (Multitext experiments for TREC-4). In: The Fourth Text Retrieval Conference (TREC-4). NIST SP 500-236, pp.295-304. GPO: Washington, D.C. 1966.

[5] Fagan, J.L. The effectiveness of a nonsyntactic approach to automatic phrase indexing for document retrieval. JASIS 40, 1989, 115-132.

Table 1: Effect of Co-Occurrence Evidence on Performance of 2-Word Queries

Col. 1	2	3	4	5	6	7	8	9	10	11	12
Trec8	**Initial**	**<------**	**Rerank**	**Stge-1**	**-------->**	**<-------**	**PRF**	**------->**	**<------**	**PRF**	**------->**
	Stge-1	**coord**	**coord**	**windw**	**windw**	**<-------**	**original**	**------->**	**<after**	**Stge-1**	**Rerank>**
		stem	**nostem**	**stem**	**nostem**	**10doc**	**20doc**	**30doc**	**10doc**	**20doc**	**30doc**
MAP	.2552	.2514	.2519	.2577	.2595	.2461	.2553	.2693	.2512	.2720	.2835
p@10	**.4640**	.4560	.4480	.4720	**.4640**	.4560	.4800	**.4840**	.4760	**.5480**	.5200
p@20	**.3940**	.3740	.3780	.4120	**.4060**	.3880	.3980	**.4420**	.4320	**.4580**	.4580
p@30	**.3453**	.3520	.3467	.3693	**.3760**	.3587	.3533	**.3760**	.3840	**.4013**	.3920
Trec7											
MAP	.2026	.2129	.2167	.2099	.2124	.2662	.2680	.2541	.2759	.2766	.2674
p@10	**.4400**	.4250	.4400	.4700	**.4700**	.4700	.5100	**.4900**	.5200	**.5150**	.4950
p@20	**.3650**	.3650	.3875	.4075	**.4075**	.3975	.4450	**.4250**	.4250	**.4625**	.4500
p@30	**.3200**	.3183	.3350	.3517	**.3600**	.3650	.3867	**.3667**	.3750	**.4083**	.3950

The Boomerang Effect: Retrieving Scientific Documents via the Network of References and Citations

Birger Larsen and Peter Ingwersen
Department of Information Studies, Royal School of Library and Information Science
Birketinget 6, DK-2300 Copenhagen S, Denmark
{blar,pi}@db.dk

Categories & Subject Descriptors: H.3.3. Information Search and Retrieval; H.3.7. Digital Libraries.

General Terms: Algorithms; Performance; Experimentation.

Keywords: Boomerang Effect; Citation Search Strategies; Citations; Cognitive Overlap; Information Retrieval; Links; Polyrepresentation; Structured Documents.

1. INTRODUCTION

In Information Retrieval (IR) research interest has increased in extending the traditional bag-of-words approach to accommodate other features of documents than text words and exploit, for example, the document structure [e.g., 1] and links in and between documents [e.g., 5] to improve retrieval performance.

The theory of polyrepresentation [2, 3] provides a theoretical background for how to exploit such features. In summary, the theory hypothesises that *overlaps* between different cognitive representations of both users' information needs as well as documents can be exploited for reducing the uncertainties inherent in IR, and thereby improve the performance of IR systems. Two or more different cognitive representations pointing at the same documents is regarded as multi-evidence of those documents being relevant, and suggests to apply a principle of 'intentional redundancy' [2] with the purpose of reducing the uncertainties by placing emphasis on overlaps between representations. Better results are expected when cognitively unlike representations are used, e.g., the document title (made by the author) vs. intellectually assigned descriptors from indexers.

Based on the theory of polyrepresentation we propose the so-called Boomerang effect as a method for retrieving scientific documents, with representations generated from 1) the structure of these documents as composed by the author(s) (i.e. title, abstract, introduction, methodology, (sub)sections, conclusion etc.), and 2) links, citations, intellectually assigned descriptors, etc. generated by other cognitive agents. A special matching function is used where bibliographic references *from* documents and citations *to* documents are used as index terms for matching documents with the query, resulting in an expansion of the initially retrieved set. The bibliometric aspects of the Boomerang effect were introduced in [4] along with detailed results from a pre-experiment testing the approach. In this paper we present the Boomerang effect from an IR perspective along with the main results from the pre-experiment, and develop the method from a purely Boolean approach to a best match approach.

2. THE BOOMERANG EFFECT

The theory of polyrepresentation from IR is extended with methods from bibliometrics and scientometrics to generate the Boomerang effect. Studies from the operational online IR community have shown that using citation search strategies can yield high performance [e.g., 6], but these strategies typically require a user to select intellectually one or more seed documents at least a few years old that are relevant for the information need, and may have been cited subsequently – a situation not readily applicable to most IR research settings. The purpose of the Boomerang effect is to exploit the potentially high performance offered by incorporating link or citation information, and at the same time allow for queries formulated in natural language.

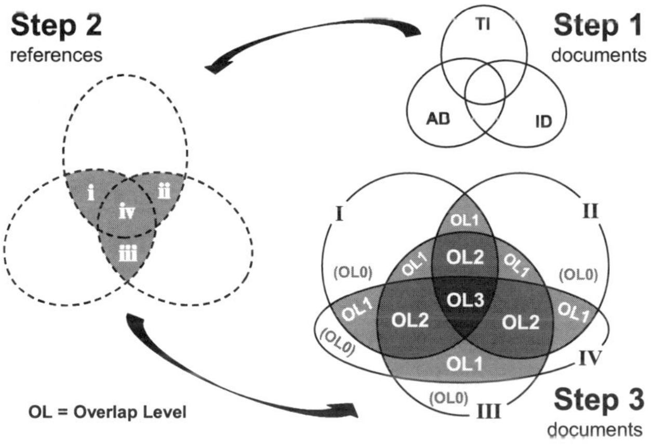

Figure 1: Example of the Boomerang effect with 3 representations. At step 3, 4 sets of documents (I-IV) citing the references contained in the overlaps at step 2 (i-iv) are retrieved, using the references as query terms. (Modified from [4])

In short, several sets of documents are retrieved using natural language queries in different cognitive representations (Fig. 1, step 1). From the retrieved sets of documents the references are extracted into a *pool* for each set, and distinct overlaps between these pools of references are identified (overlaps i-iv in Fig. 1, step 2). Following the theory of polyrepresentation and the principle of intentional redundancy only the references in the overlaps are used in the following, where, for each overlap, the set of documents that cite the references in the overlaps at step 2 are retrieved (Fig. 1, step 3). Finally, the overlaps between these citing documents at step 3 are identified and used to order the documents in an overlap structure. The result of the Boomerang effect is the documents retrieved in step 3, and the overlap structure generated in step 3, where the documents are partially ordered in a number of overlap levels (OL). The hypothesis in the Boomerang effect is that the computed precision at OL3 will be greater than at OL2, which will be greater than at OL1 etc. The number of possible OLs in step 3 is determined by the number of sets in step 1 and the number of non-empty overlaps in step 2. Note that additional documents not present in step

SIGIR'02, August 11-15, 2002, Tampere, Finland.
ACM 1-58113-561-0/02/0008.

1 may be retrieved in step 3, because they (co-)cite the same references.

3. PRE-EXPERIMENT

Three work tasks describing an information need were constructed in co-operation with a researcher at a hospital, who subsequently assessed the relevance of the retrieved documents. A query for each work task was constructed manually and submitted to four document representations (Title, abstract, identifiers and free-text) in Science Citation Index® (SCI), which resulted in an average of 88 documents per work task. The Boomerang effect was executed as detailed above, and returned 476 documents from SCI on average per work task at OL1-4, expanding the initially retrieved set considerably. A document in step 1 will also be retrieved in step 3 if at least one of its references is contained in an overlap at step 2 – 91% of the documents were retrieved in both steps in the pre-experiment. Due to the large number of documents retrieved not all could be assessed, and two samples were drawn: Table 1 shows the precision calculated for 135 documents from step 1 also retrieved in step 3 (A), and for 143 *additional* documents retrieved by the Boomerang effect (B). It can be seen at each OL that precision is greater than or equal to the OL below. This holds for both samples, as well as for each individual work task (not shown).

Table 1. Precision calculated on overlap levels (OL) for sample A: 135 documents from step 1 also retrieved in step 3, and for sample B: 143 *additional* documents retrieved in step 3. The figures cover all three work tasks (Modified from [4])

	Sample A		**Sample B**	
	# documents	Precision	# documents	Precision
OL4	1	100,0 %	1	100,0 %
OL3	5	100,0 %	10	80,0 %
OL2	28	92,9 %	23	56,5 %
OL1	59	72,9 %	68	39,7 %
OL0	42	66,7 %	41	17,1 %
	135	76,3 %	143	39,2 %

4. BEST MATCH BOOMERANG EFFECT

The Boomerang effect can, as demonstrated above, retrieve documents that are potentially relevant, partially ordered in a number of levels. However, it does not rank the documents *within* a given OL because it uses a strictly Boolean approach. Below a best match Boomerang effect is proposed.

In the Boomerang effect the bibliographical references extracted from the documents in step 1 (See Fig. 1) are in essence used as *index terms*, and may as such be weighted. The frequency of occurrence of a reference in a pool in step 2 can be normalised by the total number of references in that pool. As only references occurring in the *overlaps* in step 2 are considered each reference will occur in at least two pools and may therefore have several weights assigned. In accordance with the theory of polyrepresentation, that emphasises the importance of multi- evidence, these can be *added* into one, final weight for every reference in the overlaps in step 2. In Table 2 a matrix is shown, which maps the occurrences of five references ($i_{1\text{-}5}$) in three pools ($p_{1\text{-}3}$) as an example. Note that i_5 is not assigned any weight as it occurs in one pool only. The references with associated weights can be used as weighted query terms in step 3 in an IR model that allows this, e.g., the vector space model. The result will be a list of documents with at least one of these references, ranked by how many and how heavily weighted references they contain. Using this approach the rigidity of the Boolean sets from the pre-experiment has been broken down, and a single, continuous rank can be created by the Boomerang effect that may be compared to the performance of other best match systems.

[1] We use the boomerang as an analogy because of the loop made back in time and past research, returning to yield (ideally) high precision (See Fig. 1).

Table 2. Example of the calculation of weights for references in the overlaps at step 2, based on the occurrence of references ($i_{1\text{-}5}$) in the reference pools ($p_{1\text{-}3}$).

	Frequency of occurrence of references in each pool						*References weighted by the total number of references in each pool*				
	i_1	i_2	i_3	i_4	i_5	$\sum_{i=1}^{5} fr_i$	i_1	i_2	i_3	i_4	i_5
p_1	2	1	1	0	0	4	$2/4$	$1/4$	$1/4$	0	–
p_2	1	2	0	1	0	4	$1/4$	$2/4$	0	$1/4$	–
p_3	2	1	2	1	1	7	$2/7$	$1/7$	$2/7$	$1/7$	–
	Final weights for i_{1-5}:						**1,04**	**0,89**	**0,54**	**0,39**	–

5. CONCLUSION AND FUTURE WORK

The potential of the Boomerang effect for yielding high precision and expanding the initial set has been indicated with data from a Boolean pre-experiment. A best match Boomerang effect is proposed with focus on weighting references based on their frequency of occurrence. Further work is presently being done on implementing and testing the best match approach with a high number of cognitive representations generated from a corpus of 12,000 scientific full text articles in XML (The INEX collection – http://qmir.dcs.qmw.ac.uk/inex).

6. ACKNOWLEDGMENTS

The authors wish to acknowledge the Danish branch of Dialog for generous access to their files, the helpful comments and support from the researchers at the Department for Information Studies at Tampere University, Finland, as well as the constructive comments from the three anonymous reviewers. The research reported in this paper is carried out as part of the TAPIR (Text Access Potentials for interactive Information Retrieval) research project at the Royal School of Library and Information Science.

7. REFERENCES

[1] Chiaramella, Y. (2001): Information retrieval and structured documents. In: *Lectures on Information Retrieval: ESSIR 2000.* Berlin: Springer, p. 286-309. (LNCS; 1980).

[2] Ingwersen, P. (1994): Polyrepresentation of information needs and semantic entities: elements of a cognitive theory for information retrieval interaction. In: *Proceedings of SIGIR 1994,* p. 101-110.

[3] Ingwersen, P. (1996): Cognitive perspectives of information-retrieval interaction - elements of a cognitive IR theory. *Journal of Documentation*, 52(1), p. 3-50.

[4] Larsen, B. (2002): Exploiting citation overlaps for Information Retrieval - generating a boomerang effect from the network of scientific papers. *Scientometrics*, 54(2), p. 155-178.

[5] Lee Giles, C., Bollacker, K. D. and Lawrence, S. (1998): CiteSeer: An automatic citation indexing system. In: *Proceedings of Digital Libraries 1998*, p. 89-98.

[6] Pao, M. L. (1993): Term and citation retrieval - a field-study. *Information Processing & Management*, 29(1), p. 95-112.

A Logistic Regression Approach to Distributed IR

Ray R. Larson
School of Information Management and Systems
University of California, Berkeley
Berkeley, California, USA, 94720-4600
ray@sherlock.berkeley.edu

ABSTRACT

This poster session examines a probabilistic approach to distributed information retrieval using a Logistic Regression algorithm for estimation of collection relevance. The algorithm is compared to other methods for distributed search using test collections developed for distributed search evaluation.

Categories and Subject Descriptors

H.3.3 [**Information Search and Retrieval**]: Search process; H.3.7 [**Digital Libraries**]: Systems issues

General Terms

Algorithms, Performance

Keywords

Distributed Information Retrieval

1. INTRODUCTION

This poster will present some recent effectiveness results for the application of Logistic Regression to the problem of distributed Information Retrieval (IR). This approach, and the rationale for its use, is described in this extended abstract of the work. During the poster session new experiments and evaluation currently underway will be described. In this proposal we briefly describe the problem, our approach and how this approach compares to some other well-known methods for distributed search using test collections developed for distributed search evaluation[5, 4, 8].

As increasing numbers of sites around the world make their databases available through protocols such as OAI or Z39.50 the problem arises of determining, for any given query, which of these databases are likely to contain information of interest to a world-wide population of potential users. This is the central problem of distributed IR and has been an area of active research interest for many years. Some of the best known work has been that of Gravano, et al. [6] on GlOSS and Callan's [1] application of inference networks to distributed IR (CORI). French and Powell, along with a number of collaborators [5, 4, 8], enabled comparative evaluation of distributed IR by defining test collections derived from TREC data, where the TREC databases are divided into sub-collections representing virtual distributed collections. In addition they defined a number of measures for evaluation of the performance of distributed IR[5] used in this paper to compare previously published results on collection selection with a probabilistic model based on logistic regression.

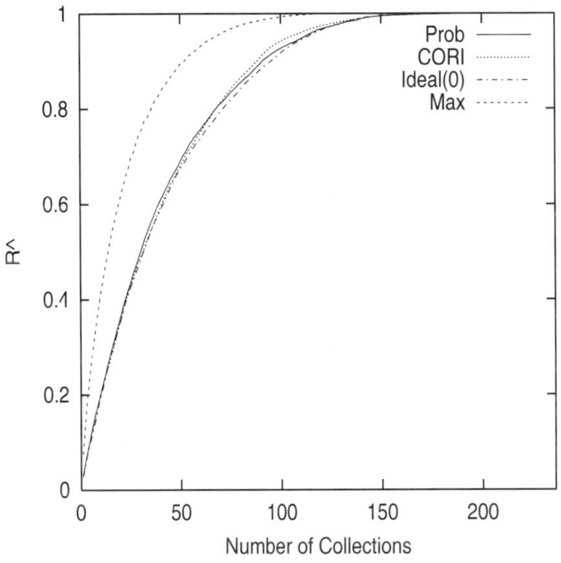

Figure 1: Title Query Performance

2. THE APPROACH

The algorithms developed for this research are based on the *logistical regression* method developed by researchers at U.C. Berkeley and tested in TREC evaluations [3, 2]. Since the "collection documents" used for this evaluation represent collections of documents and not individual documents, a number of differences from the usual logistic regression measures were used. In addition, analysis showed that different forms of the TREC queries (short titles only, longer queries including the concepts fields and the very long title, concepts, description and narrative) behaved quite differently in searching the distributed collection, so three different regression equations were derived and applied automatically based on the length of the query. In this paper only the "title" and "long" (title and concepts) queries are discussed, since they best approximate actual queries.

In the logistic regression model of IR, the estimated probability of relevance for a particular query and a particular collection (or collection document) $P(R \mid Q, C)$, is calculated and collections are ranked in order of decreasing values of that probability. In the current system this is calculated as the "log odds" of relevance $\log O(R \mid Q, C)$, Logistic regression provides estimates for a set of coefficients, c_i, associated with a set of S statistics, X_i, derived from the query and database of collection documents, such that:

$$\log O(R \mid Q, C) \approx c_0 \sum_{i=1}^{S} c_i X_i \tag{1}$$

where c_0 is the intercept term of the regression. For the set of M terms that occur in both a particular query and a given collection document. This formula is similar to that used in TREC 3[2]. The statistics used in this study were:

$X_1 = \frac{1}{M}\sum_{j=1}^{M} logQAF_{t_j}$. This is the log of the absolute frequency of occurrence for term t_j in the query averaged over the M terms in common between the query and the document.

$X_2 = \sqrt{QL}$. This is square root of the query length (i.e., the number of terms in the query disregarding stopwords).

$X_3 = \frac{1}{M}\sum_{j=1}^{M} logCAF_{t_j}$. This is is the log of the absolute frequency of occurrence for term t_j in the collection averaged over the M common terms.

$X_4 = \sqrt{\frac{CL}{10}}$. This is square root of the collection size.

$X_5 = \frac{1}{M}\sum_{j=1}^{M} logICF_{t_j}$. This is is the log of the *inverse collection frequency*(ICF) averaged over the M common terms. ICF is calculated as the total number of collections divided by the number that contain term t_j

$X_6 = logM$. The log of the number of terms in common between the collection document and the query.

For short (title only) queries, for example, the equation used in ranking was:

$$\begin{aligned}\log O(R \mid Q, C) &= -3.70 + (1.269 * X_1) + (-0.310 * X_2) \\ &+ (0.679 * X_3) + K \\ &+ (0.223 * X_5) + (2.01 * X_6);\end{aligned}$$

(K is a constant because query term frequency is always 1 in short queries).

3. EVALUATION

We used collections formed by dividing the documents on TIPSTER disks 1, 2, and 3 into 236 sets based on source and month[5]. Collection relevance information was based on whether *any* documents in the collection were relevant according to the relevance judgements for TREC queries 51-150. The relevance information was used both for estimating the logistic regression coefficients (using a sample of the data) and for the evaluation (with full data).

Figure 1 summarizes some preliminary results of the evaluation. The X axis is the number of collections in the ranking and the Y axis, $\hat{R}$, is a Recall analog that measures the proportion of the total possible relevant documents that have been accumulated in the top N databases, averaged across all of the queries. The Max line is the optimal results based where the collections are ranked in order of the number of relevance documents they contain. Ideal(0) is an implementation of the GlOSS "Ideal" algorithm and CORI is an implementation of Callan's Inference net approach (described in [8]. The Prob line is the logistic regression method described above. For title queries (Figure 1) the described method performs slightly better than the CORI algorithm for up to about 100 collections, where CORI exceeds it. Both CORI and the logistic regression method outperform the Ideal(0) implementation.

We are continuing to examine probabilistic distributed IR using logistic regression. Further work is underway to refine the model and to apply it to actual systems in the U.K. using collection harvesting techniques described in [7]. This ongoing work will be described at the poster session.

4. ACKNOWLEDGMENTS

The author would like to thank James French and Allison Powell for kindly suppling the CORI and Ideal(0) results used in the evaluation for this paper. They were derived from versions of the algorithms as described in Allison Powell's dissertation[8]. This work was supported by the National Science Foundation and the Joint Information Systems Committee (U.K.) under *International Digital Libraries Program* award #IIS-9975164.

5. REFERENCES

[1] J. Callan. Distributed information retrieval. In W. B. Croft, editor, *Advances in Information Retrieval: Recent research from the Center for Intelligent Information Retrieval*, chapter 5, pages 127–150. Kluwer, Boston, 2000.

[2] W. S. Cooper, F. C. Gey, and A. Chen. Full text retrieval based on a probabilistic equation with coefficients fitted by logistic regression. In D. K. Harman, editor, *The Second Text Retrieval Conference (TREC-2)*, pages 57–66, Gaithersburg, MD, 1994. NIST.

[3] W. S. Cooper, F. C. Gey, and D. P. Dabney. Probabilistic retrieval based on staged logistic regression. In *SIGIR '92*, pages 198–210, New York, 1992. ACM.

[4] J. C. French, A. L. Powell, J. P. Callan, C. L. Viles, T. Emmitt, K. J. Prey, and Y. Mou. Comparing the performance of database selection algorithms. In *SIGIR '99*, pages 238–245, 1999.

[5] J. C. French, A. L. Powell, C. L. Viles, T. Emmitt, and K. J. Prey. Evaluating database selection techniques: A testbed and experiment. In *SIGIR '98*, pages 121–129, 1998.

[6] L. Gravano, H. García-Molina, and A. Tomasic. GlOSS: text-source discovery over the Internet. *ACM Transactions on Database Systems*, 24(2):229–264, 1999.

[7] R. R. Larson. Distributed resource discovery: Using Z39.50 to build cross-domain information servers. In *JCDL '01*, pages 52–53. ACM, 2001.

[8] A. L. Powell. *Database Selection in Distributed Information Retrieval: A Study of Multi-Collection Information Retrieval.* PhD thesis, University of Virginia, Virginia, 2001.

Automatic Metadata Generation & Evaluation

Elizabeth D. Liddy, Eileen Allen, Sarah Harwell, Susan Corieri, Ozgur Yilmazel, N. Ercan Ozgencil, Anne Diekema, Nancy McCracken
Center for NLP,
School of Information Studies,
Syracuse University, 315.443.5484
liddy@syr.edu

Joanne Silverstein
Information Institute,
Syracuse University,
Syracuse, NY
315.443.3640
jlsilver@syr.edu

Stuart Sutton
Information School,
University of Washington,
Seattle, WA
208.685.6618
sasutton@u.washington.edu

ABSTRACT
The poster reports on a project in which we are investigating methods for breaking the human metadata-generation bottleneck that plagues Digital Libraries. The research question is whether metadata elements and values can be automatically generated from the content of educational resources, and correctly assigned to mathematics and science educational materials. Natural Language Processing and Machine Learning techniques were implemented to automatically generate metadata for learning resources provided by the Gateway for Education (GEM), a service that offers web access to a wide range of educational materials. In a user study, education professionals evaluated the metadata assigned to learning resources by either automatic tagging or manual assignment. Results show minimal difference in the eyes of the evaluators between automatically generated metadata and manually assigned metadata

Categories & Subject Descriptors: Natural Language Processing; Text analysis.

General Terms: Experimentation

Keywords: NLP, metadata generation

1. Problem
There are currently numerous digital library projects underway worldwide. These projects are building collections of electronic resources and providing access to them for information seekers. The goals of our research project are to: 1) develop and evaluate a technology that automatically '*indexes*' (via metadata) the electronic resources being submitted to the library, and: 2) produce metadata records that will enable users to retrieve relevant resources. The '*indexing*' semantically interprets the resources' content using advanced NLP technologies that have proven their value in other information access technologies, and assigns the appropriate metadata to each resource. The metadata will be utilized both to access the collection in response to queries from teachers, students, and parents, and to provide a summary-like description of the retrieved resources for preview by the user.

Within the digital library community, the use of metadata has been fairly widely accepted as the solution for making electronic resources accessible to users. However, most metadata efforts to-date have focused mainly on defining appropriate metadata schemas, or element sets, and adopting standards to insure interoperability. Coming from the domain of automatic document processing and access, we attempted to go one step further by automatically assigning and then evaluating the values of an accepted metadata schema to electronic resources.

The long-term goals of our project are to: 1) increase the **speed** with which educational resources are made available via a digital library; 2) increase the **number** of educational resources that can be made available electronically, and; 3) provide improved **access** to a digital library via richer metadata values and more complete and consistent metadata records.

2. Methodology
To accomplish these goals, we: 1) selected a metadata schema which has broad approval from the digital library community; 2) chose the collection to work on for development and testing; 3) adapted our information extraction software to the task of identifying and extracting values for the metadata schema; 4) automatically metadata-tagged a sample of documents from the collection; 5) assigned documents to subjects that had either manual or automatic metadata records to educational professionals for their evaluation, and; 6) reviewed and analyzed the results of the human evaluation.

The task of automatically assigning metadata values to educational resources requires software that can ingest electronic documents, evaluate the citation and content of each document, and then assign values to as many of the 23 of the Dublin Core + Educational Extension metadata elements as warranted by the resource. We adapted the NLP-based Information Extraction (IE) software we have developed for other applications by applying the sub-language development methodology we have used successfully in past projects. The software utilizes various linguistic features of this particular genre - features that can be interpreted to determine what metadata element and value should be automatically assigned by the system. We applied the sublanguage analysis framework to the development of rules that identify and extract the features of the educational materials needed as metadata elements and their values. These rules were then implemented in an internally developed rule language.

Next, we conducted a user study in which automatic-ally metatagged documents and documents tagged by experts at

SIGIR'02, August 11-15, 2002, Tampere, Finland.
ACM 1-58113-561-0/02/0008.

GEM were provided to teaching professionals. The hypothesis of the study was that automatic metatagging could perform as well as manual metatagging. While it is expected that the efficiency of automatic metatagging will substantially increase the amount of science and mathematics materials made accessible on the web, it is essential that the quality of access provided by manual tagging be maintained. While awaiting the implementation of the communal digital library in order to conduct a full retrieval experiment, this qualitative study provides insight into how professionals evaluate the metadata representation of the teaching resources, whether automatically or manually assigned.

A random set of lesson plans were drawn from the GEM collection. Twenty-six education students, teachers, professionals and others associated with the educational field examined 15 records each for a total of 390 records (195 CNLP & 195 GEM) and assigned scores on a scale of one to five (with five being the most best). In 'Expectation', the subjects looked at the metadata first and then the lesson plan to see if the lesson plan matched the expectations generated by the metadata. In the 'Satisfaction' condition, subjects looked at the lesson plan first and then judged the metadata based on the information in the lesson plan.

3. Results

Preliminary analysis of the numeric scores shows relative close scores if comparing the automatic (3.55) to the manual (3.81) when the resource is reviewed before the metadata record for the 'Satisfaction' condition, and if comparing the automatic (3.76) to the manual (4.03) when the metadata record is reviewed before viewing the resource for the 'Expectation' condition. The results suggest that there is minimal difference in the eyes of these twenty-six subjects between manual and automatically assigned metadata.

As the first testing of automatic metadata generation known to us, the results are indeed promising. The significance of these preliminary results suggesting that the metadata generation bottleneck may in fact be unblocked by the utilization of NLP for producing metadata profiles should not be understated. Today, many, many resources are in electronic format, ready to be added to digital libraries, but their addition to the digital library is held up by the time and human resources currently required to produce their metadata records. With increased availability of the automatic metadata generation we've created in our MetaExtract system, resources can soon be added to digital libraries at a rate that will make these digital libraries richer and more useful.

4. Future Work

While these preliminary results are promising, we plan to conduct further experimental evaluations. Some of these will be further qualitative analyses by subject experts who would be likely users of a digital library in this domain.

In addition, we will conduct quantitative evaluations following the standard Information Retrieval experimental paradigm, where both precision and recall will be determined based on automatically produced metadata as compared to manually produced metadata in response to users' real world queries.

5. Acknowledgements

The research reported herein is supported by funding from NSF's National Science Digital Library Program for Science, Math, Engineering, and Technology.

A Critical Examination of TDT's Cost Function *

R. Manmatha, Ao Feng and James Allan
Center for Intelligent Information Retrieval
Department of Computer Science
University of Massachusetts
Amherst, MA 01003
{manmatha,aofeng,allan}@cs.umass.edu

ABSTRACT

Topic Detection and Tracking (TDT) tasks are evaluated using a cost function. The standard TDT cost function assumes a constant probability of relevance $P(\text{rel})$ across all topics. In practice, $P(\text{rel})$ varies widely across topics. We argue using both theoretical and experimental evidence that the cost function should be modified to account for the varying $P(\text{rel})$.

Categories and Subject Descriptors

H.3.3 [**Information Search And Retrieval**]: Information Filtering

Keywords

Modeling score distributions, Topic Detection and Tracking, threshold, normalization

1. INTRODUCTION

Tasks in Topic Detection and Tracking (TDT) are evaluated based on miss and false alarm rates. One generally employed evaluation device is the Detection Error Tradeoff (DET) curve [4], a graph that shows how miss and false alarm vary inversely. The official measure, however, is a cost function defined as a linear combination of the two error rates. It is that cost function that is used to tune system parameters on training data and that is the basis for deciding which system "wins" an evaluation task.

Fiscus and Doddington [2] provide an excellent review of the TDT community's motivations in coming up with that cost function. To compensate for the fact that the number of off-topic stories is far greater than the number of on-topic stories, and that the difference varies across topics, the cost also includes a factor which depends on the prior probability of finding an on-topic story. We denote that value $P(\text{rel})$, the probability of relevance (it is also referred to as $P(\text{target})$; we use the more IR-related form). The TDT cost function assumes that this probability is constant across topics.

Experiments make it clear that the number of on-topic stories - hence $P(\text{rel})$ - varies over different topics. In TDT, the cost function is often used to set thresholds. We show that assuming $P(\text{rel})$ constant leads to the undesirable theoretical result that the optimal threshold in probability space varies with the topic. We also show theoretically that by allowing $P(\text{rel})$ to vary by topic, one can obtain a constant optimal threshold in the probability space. This suggests that the standard TDT cost function should be modified to account for the varying $P(\text{rel})$.

1.1 Standard TDT Cost Function

The TDT cost function is defined as as a linear combination of $P(\text{miss})$, the probability of a miss, and $P(\text{fa})$, the probability of a false alarm [2]:

$$C_{\text{det}} = C_{\text{miss}} P(\text{miss}) P(\text{rel}) + C_{\text{fa}} P(\text{fa})(1 - P(\text{rel})) \quad (1)$$

where C_{miss} and C_{fa} are the costs of missed detection and false alarm respectively, and $P(\text{rel})$ is the prior probability of finding a relevant story. Fiscus and Doddington [2] argue that in TDT misses should be penalized much more heavily than false alarms, so $C_{\text{miss}} = 1$ and $C_{\text{fa}} = 0.1$. A constant value for $P(\text{rel})$ is used over all topics. Anecdotal information from TDT participants indicates that this value was chosen using training data to be 0.02. The standard TDT cost function used for all evaluations in TDT is therefore, $C_{\text{det}} = 0.02P(\text{miss}) + 0.098P(\text{fa})$. We can now look at the implications of having a constant $P(\text{rel})$.

Consider the scores produced by a TDT system for each document. Let the distribution of scores of off topic (non relevant) documents be given by $p(x|\text{nrel})$ and let the distribution of scores of on-target (relevant) documents be given by $p(x|\text{rel})$. Experimental modeling shows that the distribution of scores of on-target documents may be approximated using a Gaussian and the distribution of scores of off-topic documents may be approximated using an exponential. This is similar to the model for the score distributions of search engines [3]. For our discussion here, we do not need to assume a form for these densities and can let the densities $p(x|\text{rel})$ and $p(x|\text{nrel})$ be arbitrary. We will assume for our discussion that we have perfect knowledge of these densities.

We can compute $P(\text{miss})$ and $P(\text{fa})$ using these densities. The system decides that documents with scores above a certain threshold θ are relevant. Then $P(\text{miss})$ is given by the area under $p(x|\text{rel})$ bounded by θ on the right (see [1] for a similar expression in the filtering case), and $P(\text{fa})$ is similarly found:

$$P(\text{miss}) = \int_{-\infty}^{\theta} p(x|\text{rel})dx \text{ and } P(\text{fa}) = \int_{\theta}^{+\infty} p(x|\text{nrel})dx \quad (2)$$

*This material is based on work supported in part by the Center for Intelligent Information Retrieval and in part by SPAWARSYSCEN-SD grant number N66001-99-1-8912 Any opinions, findings and conclusions or recommendations expressed in this material are the author(s) and do not necessarily reflect those of the sponsor(s).

SIGIR'02, August 11-15, 2002, Tampere, Finland.
ACM 1-58113-561-0/02/0008.

The optimal threshold is found by substituting the expressions for $P(\text{miss})$ and $P(\text{fa})$ in the expression for the cost function and minimizing the cost function by setting $\frac{dC_{\text{det}}}{d\theta} = 0$. This gives:

$$p(\theta|\text{rel}) = 4.9p(\theta|\text{nrel}) \quad (3)$$

One can compute the posterior probability of relevance given the scores $P(rel|x)$ from the above densities. Using Bayes rule gives:

$$P(rel|x) = \frac{p(x|\text{rel})P(\text{rel})}{P(\text{rel})p(x|\text{rel}) + P(\text{nrel})p(x|\text{nrel})} \quad (4)$$

The threshold in the posterior probability space may be computed by using the relationship between $p(x|\text{rel})$ and $p(x|\text{nrel})$ at the optimal threshold from equation 3 giving:

$$\begin{aligned} P(rel|\theta) &= \frac{p(\theta|\text{rel})P(\text{rel})}{p(\theta|rel}P(\text{rel}) + \frac{p(\theta|\text{rel})(1 - P(\text{rel}))}{4.9} \\ &= \frac{1}{1 + \frac{1}{4.9}(\frac{1}{P(\text{rel})} - 1)} \quad (5) \end{aligned}$$

This expression is true for any arbitrary form of $p(x|\text{rel})$ and $p(x|\text{nrel})$. The threshold varies with $P(\text{rel})$ (and hence with the topic) as a consequence of assuming that $P(\text{rel})$ is constant for the cost function. That is, even if we had perfect knowledge of the non-relevant and relevant distributions, the optimum threshold at the posterior probability (equation 5) is not constant across topics but depends on $P(\text{rel})$. The problem lies in the assumption of $P(\text{rel})$ being constant. It is desirable in TDT to have a cost function which has a constant threshold across topics. Currently, this is artificially forced upon systems during evaluation.

2. A NEW COST FUNCTION FOR TDT

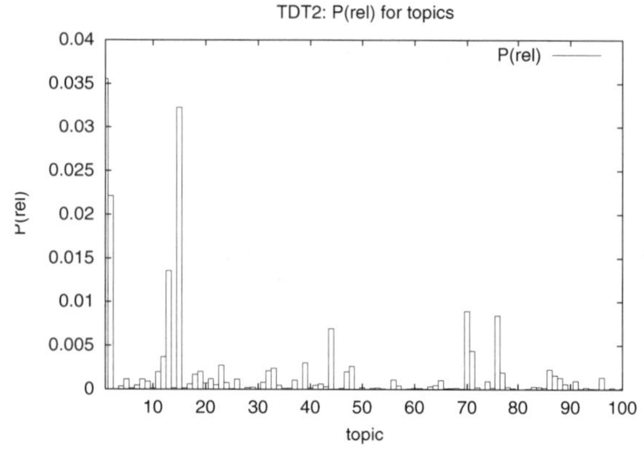

Figure 1: Probability of relevance for different topics in the TDT-2 corpus. Computed using actual relevance judgements.

The TDT cost function assumes a constant value of $P(\text{rel})$ across different topics to obtain the standard TDT cost function described above. Figure 1 shows a histogram of $P(\text{rel})$ for all topics in the TDT-2 corpus. There is a considerable variation in $P(\text{rel})$ depending on the topic. Further, the average $P(\text{rel})$ across all stories is 0.002 which is different from the number assumed in the standard TDT cost function (0.02). Assuming that they used a different training corpus to select a value, this indicates that even the averages vary with the corpus and cannot be assumed constant.

Is there any way to achieve a constant threshold for all topics at least for the ideal case? This is, after all, one of the goals of TDT. By going back to first principles we can derive a new cost function which will have a constant threshold. Specifically, we look at the original form of the cost function in equation 1. Assume that $P(\text{rel})$ is not constant. As before we can use equation 2 to write $P(\text{miss})$ and $P(\text{fa})$ in terms of $p(x|\text{rel})$, $p(x|\text{nrel})$ and the threshold θ. Minimizing this cost function at the optimal threshold gives:

$$p(\theta|\text{rel}) = \frac{C_{\text{fa}}(1 - P(\text{rel}))}{C_{\text{miss}}P(\text{rel})}p(\theta|\text{nrel}) \quad (6)$$

In terms of posterior probabilities the threshold is given by:

$$\begin{aligned} P(rel|\theta) &= \frac{p(\theta|\text{rel})P(\text{rel})}{p(\theta|\text{rel})P(\text{rel}) + p(\theta|\text{nrel})P(\text{nrel})} \quad (7) \\ &= \frac{1}{1 + \frac{C_{\text{miss}}}{C_{\text{fa}}}} \quad (8) \end{aligned}$$

where we use the expression of $p(\theta|\text{nrel})$ from equation 6.

Given a set of costs C_{miss} and C_{fa}, this new cost function has a constant threshold for all topics. This is an intuitively satisfying result which argues that if one takes into account the fact that $P(\text{rel})$ varies with the topic (which is what happens in reality) then a constant threshold can be obtained. For the specific case of $C_{\text{miss}} = 1$ and $C_{\text{fa}} = 0.1$ the threshold is:

$$P(rel|\theta) = \frac{1}{1 + \frac{C_{\text{miss}}}{C_{\text{fa}}}} = \frac{1}{1 + 10} = \frac{1}{11} \quad (9)$$

We don't expect that systems will need to know $P(\text{rel})$. The cost function is primarily an evaluation tool and for evaluation purposes $P(\text{rel})$ is known. Even otherwise, there are approaches (see [3]) which would allow systems to estimate $P(\text{rel})$.

3. CONCLUSIONS

The TDT evaluation program assumes a constant for the probability that a story is on topic. Although that assumption was known to be incorrect, it is used in the evaluation's official cost function. As a result, systems are torn between providing a threshold that yields consistent results across topics or one that yields a minimum cost function. We feel that a TDT system would do better to attempt both of those at the same time. There are interesting problems with using this cost function in the context of a DET curve, the other official TDT measure. We are investigating those issues.

4. REFERENCES

[1] A. Arampatzis and A. van Hameren. The score-distributional threshold optimization for adaptive binary classification tasks. In *the Proc. of the 24th ACM SIGIR conf.*, pages 285-293, Sept 2001.

[2] J. Fiscus and G. R. Doddington. Topic detection and tracking evaluation overview. In J. Allan, editor, *Topic Detection and Tracking: Event-based Information Organization*, pages 17-31. Kluwer Academic Publishers, 2002.

[3] R. Manmatha, T. Rath, and F. Feng. Modeling score distributions for combining the outputs of search engines. In *the Proc. of the 24th ACM SIGIR conf. on Research and Developement in Information Retrieval*, pages 267-275, Sept 2001.

[4] A. Martin, T. K. G. Doddington, M. Ordowski, and M. Przybocki. The DET curve in assessment of detection task performance. In *Proceedings of EuroSpeech'97*, volume 4, pages 1895-1898, 1997.

Converting On-Line Bilingual Dictionaries from Human-Readable to Machine-Readable Form

James Mayfield and Paul McNamee
The Johns Hopkins University Applied Physics Laboratory
11100 Johns Hopkins Road, Laurel MD 20723-6099 USA
+1 240-228-6944
{mayfield,mcnamee}@jhuapl.edu

ABSTRACT

We describe a language called ABET that allows rapid conversion of on-line human-readable bilingual dictionaries to machine-readable form.

Categories & Subject Descriptors: H.3.3 Information Search and Retrieval, H.3.7 Digital Libraries.

General Terms: Languages

Keywords: Bidicts, bilingual dictionaries, cross-language information retrieval, scripting languages, information extraction.

1. INTRODUCTION

A key resource for many approaches to cross-language information retrieval (CLIR) is a bilingual dictionary (bidict). Unfortunately, like other cross-language resources, machine-readable on-line bidicts that are suitable for use in CLIR are scarce. However, the availability of on-line cross-language dictionaries in human readable format (such as PDF versions of printed dictionaries, or HTML wordlists) is broader. It makes sense then to examine how human-readable dictionaries might be converted to machine-readable form, such as might be useful for CLIR or machine translation (MT).

Such dictionary conversion is tedious work. Each dictionary has its own format. Often, because machine readability is not a primary goal of dictionary authors, the format is inconsistent throughout the document. Extraction of the text form of the human-readable dictionary from its native document type (*e.g.,* PDF) prior to conversion can introduce further noise that makes identification of the source language words or their target language translations difficult. Yet there are certain key processes that are the same across most extraction tasks. We have developed a language called the *APL Bidict Extraction Tool* (ABET) that automates these common processes, while providing for simple descriptions of document-specific formatting. Using ABET, it is possible to quickly convert a human-readable on-line dictionary to machine-readable form, without getting bogged down in the mechanistic details of the conversion. ABET is easy to learn, and lends the full power of Perl pattern matching to the scriptwriter.

More heavily automated approaches include pattern and wrapper induction [3], maximum entropy [1] and HMMs [2]. Such approaches are most useful when many documents use the same format, and when more general document models are needed.

2. The ABET Language

Because bidicts are essentially tabular data, the ABET document model holds that every bidict or bidict component of interest comprises an (optional) header, followed by a list of one or more entries. For example, a typical bidict might contain some introductory text (which can likely be ignored), followed by a sequence of dictionary entries. The model is recursive, so that the individual components can also be expressed as header plus list. For example, each dictionary entry might comprise a source language word, followed by one or more comma-separated translations. Figure 1 shows a sample of such a dictionary,[1] mapping Turkmen to English, produced by the U. S. Peace Corps. This document model significantly simplifies extraction patterns (scripts) for data that conform to the model, and makes ABET easier to use than tools designed for more general models.

agyrmak to hurt	**akylly** smart, clever
agyrtmak to hurt, cause pain	**akylsyz** stupid
agyry 1. ill 2. troubles	**akylsyzlyk** stupidity
agyz beklemek to fast	**akym** stream, flow
agyz mouth	**akytmak** to pour
agyzzyryk horse's bit	**al** pink
	ala multi-colored (2 colors)

Figure 1. Sample Turkmen/English human-readable (PDF) dictionary

```
{ PRE_KILL => [\&strip_ascii_nulls],
 CROP => "\nA\n(.*?)\nA\n",
 FIND => "\n([^\n]{3,})",
 POST_KILL => [\&kill_parens,\&kill_brackets],
 NO_TRIM => "TRUE",
 PARSE => {
 HEADER_FIND => "(.*?)\s{2,}([^:]*)",
 SPLIT => "\s*[;,]\s*|\s*[\dIV]\.\s*",
 POST_KILL => [\&kill_leading_abbrevs],
 FN => sub {
  my ($text,$dict,$context,$offsets) = @_;
  add($dict,'en',$text,'tk',$context->[0]);
  }
 }
}
```

Figure 2. Sample ABET script for extracting Turkmen/English dictionary

The ABET language structures the extraction process around this simple document model. An ABET script is a brace-delimited block containing a set of key/value pairs whose keys are drawn from a fixed set of action keywords. Figure 2 depicts a sample ABET script, which successfully extracts a machine-readable bidict from the Turkmen/English dictionary of Figure 1. (Readers familiar with Perl will realize that an ABET script is simply a Perl hash; however, very little knowledge of Perl beyond pattern matching is required to use ABET.)

SIGIR'02, August 11-15, 2002, Tampere, Finland.
ACM 1-58113-561-0/02/0008.

1 <http://www.chaihana.com/lang.html>

At each level, extraction processing comprises four steps: text preprocessing; header and body identification; text postprocessing; and recursive header and body parsing, or entry into output dictionary. First, preprocessing of the entire text under consideration is performed. Preprocessing commands are **CROP** to delete surrounding extraneous material, **PRE_KILL** to perform an arbitrary transformation on the entire text before parsing (called **KILL** because the most common operation is to delete text, *e.g.*, parenthesized expressions, extraneous characters, *etc.*), and **PRE_MACROS** to expand macro lists, such as replacing the HTML entity **<** with <. The top level of our example in Figure 2 uses **PRE_KILL** to delete ASCII null characters from the input, and **CROP** to delete extraneous surrounding text.

Second, an optional header, and a list of entries are identified. Three main ABET commands are available: **HEADER_FIND** to identify a pattern that selects the header entry; **FIND** to identify a pattern that selects the list items; and **SPLIT** to identify a pattern that detects the text *between* list items (which is sometimes easier than matching the items themselves). In addition, **HEADER_POS**, **START_POS** and **END_POS** may be used to select the indices of the header, and of the first and last legitimate list items, within the list of items created by **FIND** or **SPLIT**. In this case, matching the entries themselves is easier than matching the text between entries, so the `FIND` command is used.

The third phase, text postprocessing, includes the commands **POST_KILL** and **POST_MACROS**, which are used like **PRE_KILL** and **PRE_MACROS**, but are applied to individual list items after they are identified; **NO_TRIM**, which suppresses removal of whitespace from the ends of identified list items; and **KEEP_EMPTIES**, which retains list items that contain no text (and which may be useful *e.g.* to keep two lists in synch with one another). In the example, parenthesized and bracketed expressions are deleted using the **POST_KILL** command, and whitespace removal is suppressed with **NO_TRIM**.

The final processing phase is either to recursively parse each item, or to invoke a function on each item (typically one that adds an entry to the output dictionary). Commands include **HEADER_PARSE** and **PARSE**, to recursively parse the header entry and list items, respectively, using a different ABET script; **HEADER_FN** and **FN**, to apply an arbitrary function to the header or list items respectively; and **LIST_FN**, to apply a function to the list as a whole, rather than item-by-item. The most commonly used function simply adds an entry to the output dictionary. One of the arguments to various functions is the (now parsed) surrounding context. This can, for example, provide the function with the text of a column header indicating the language of the current entry. In our example, **PARSE** is used to recursively parse each line of the dictionary. **PARSE** takes as its argument another ABET script. This latter script recognizes the Turkmen word or phrase using **HEADER_FIND**, identifies the English words and phrases (or more accurately, the characters that separate them) using **SPLIT**, and adds each resulting pairing to the output dictionary with **FN**. In addition to the extraction commands described, various debugging commands and switches are available to assist the user write effective extraction scripts. ABET also comes with a library of commonly used transformations, *e.g.*, **kill_parens** to remove parenthesized expressions.

Table 1. Dictionaries built using ABET

Lang	#Words	Lang	#Words	Lang	#Words
Afrikaans	6499	Gaelic	1218	Portuguese	31575
Albanian	1319	German	94901	Romanian	2305
Bulgarian	2156	Greek	8647	Russian	31983
Catalan	1142	Hungarian	63940	Slovak	1221
Chinese	1488	Icelandic	2134	Spanish	25028
Danish	5371	Indonesian	23376	Swahili	1031
Dutch	15591	Italian	18461	Swedish	25372
Finnish	3063	Japanese	50404	Tagalog	1438
French	23332	Latin	10033	Turkish	2495
Frisian	4727	Norwegian	6655	Turkmen	8928

3. DISCUSSION

Over the past year, we have collected over 50MB of on-line, human-readable bidicts amenable to harvesting by ABET. These bidicts appear as HTML, PDF, and a host of nonstandard, undocumented flat file formats. The longest ABET extraction script to date is a mere twenty-four lines, which we attribute to the fact that the ABET document model matches the data so well. The results of our extraction are shown in Table 1, which indicates for each language the number of English words for which at least one translation has been extracted; many are languages that have no commercial MT available, and no E.U. or U.N. coverage.

ABET is difficult to evaluate empirically, because it is a programming language rather than a utility. For example, extraction accuracy is a property of a particular ABET program, not of the ABET language. Our subjective evaluation is that ABET allows the scriptwriter to quickly capture the structure of a source, and to identify and correct common errors in the data; this rapid turnaround induces us to use ABET whenever we locate a new on-line bidict.

ABET is important for four reasons:

1. **Lexical coverage is critical.** There is a growing consensus in the CLIR community that lexical coverage is the most important factor in CLIR performance. Thus, tools that increase lexical coverage are desirable.
2. **Resources are scarce.** Machine-readable bidicts, parallel corpora, and MT systems are all rare. ABET broadens this set of resources to include human-readable on-line bidicts.
3. **Extraction is tedious.** ABET automates a significant portion of the extraction process, and allows the user to decompose extraction into simple pattern-matching steps.
4. **Data are restricted.** ABET allows resource sharing without risking copyright infringement—the tool itself is shared, but the data are not. Individual sites may then apply the tool to those resources to which they have access.

Future work includes updating the system to handle Unicode (once Unicode support is integrated into Perl) and integrating text extraction from formats such as PDF. ABET is publicly available at `<http://www.csee.umbc.edu/~mayfield/ABET/>`.

4. References

[1] Borthwick, A., Sterling, J., Agichtein, E. and Grishman, R. 'Exploiting diverse knowledge sources via maximum entropy in named entity recognition.' *Sixth COLING-ACL Workshop on Very Large Corpora.* 1998.

[2] Freitag, D. and McCallum, A. 'Information extraction with HMMs and shrinkage.' *AAAI-99 Workshop on Machine Learning for Information Extraction.* 1999.

[3] Muslea, Ion. 'Extraction patterns for information extraction tasks: A survey.' *AAAI-99 Workshop on Machine Learning for Information Extraction.* 1999.

Modeling (In)Variability of Human Judgments for Text Summarization

Tadashi Nomoto
National Institute of Japanese Literature
1-16-10,Yutaka Shinagawa
Tokyo, 142-8585, Japan
nomoto@acm.org

Yuji Matsumoto
Nara Institute of Science and Technology
8916-5 Takayama Ikoma
Nara,630-0101, Japan
matsu@is.aist-nara.ac.jp

ABSTRACT

The paper proposes and empirically motivates an integration of supervised learning with unsupervised learning to deal with human biases in summarization. In particular, we explore the use of probabilistic decision tree within the clustering framework to account for the variation as well as regularity in human created summaries.

1. INTRODUCTION

In our recent study [1], we observed that an unsupervised method based on clustering sometimes better approximates human created extracts than a supervised approach. That appears somewhat contradictory given that a supervised approach should be able to exploit information about whether or not to include a given sentence in an extract, whereas an unsupervised approach blindly chooses sentences according to some selection scheme. A question is, why this should be the case.

The reason, we speculate, may have to do with the variation among judges in selecting sentences for a summary. Prior work on summarization informs us that judgments on extraction can vary widely among humans. Curiously, however, there is also a finding in [1] that a supervised system performs much better on data for which there is high agreement among humans than an unsupervised system, suggesting that there are indeed some regularities to be found and exploited to the system's advantage. So we might conclude that there are two, apparently conflicting aspects to human judgments on sentence extraction.

In the paper, we will explore an integration of supervised and unsupervised paradigms as a potential approach to accounting for the (in)variability of human judgments. More specifically, we will be concerned with extending the summarization framework in [1] by embedding a probabilistic decision tree within the clustering framework. The idea is to call upon clustering to deal with the variability and decision tree to deal with the invariability or significant biases.

SIGIR'02, August 11-15, 2002, Tampere, Finland.
ACM 1-58113-561-0/02/0008.

2. METHOD

We basically follow our previous work [1] in building a generic summarizer which we call the diversity based summarizer (DBS). DBS is a two step summarizer which first brings up clustering to identify diverse topical areas in text and then refers to a tfidf ranking model to choose the best sentence from each topic area identified. In the present paper, we take a step further by extending DBS to incorporate supervised learning, in particular probabilistic decision tree (ProbDT). ProbDT works like a regular decision tree except that instead of generating a class label for a given instance, it generates the probability that it belongs to a particular class. The modification allows us to directly exploit human supplied information on which sentence to extract for a summary, which would not be possible with the clustering/tfidf-based-ranking framework. ProbDT also allows a ranking of sentences, which one would need to deal with variable length summarization.

Combining ProbDT and DBS can be done quite straightforwardly by replacing the tfidf based ranking part with ProbDT. Thus instead of picking up a sentence with the highest tfdif score, DBS/ProbDT strives to find a sentences with the highest score for $P(Select \mid \vec{u}, \mathrm{DT})$, the probability that a given sentence u is selected as one to be included in a summary, using a decision tree DT. A specific value of the probability is found by using the following equation:

$$P(Select \mid \vec{u}, \mathrm{DT}) = \alpha\left(\frac{\text{the number of ``Select'' sentences at } t(\vec{u})}{\text{the total number of sentences at } t(\vec{u})}\right).$$

$\vec{u}$ is a vector representation of sentence u. $t(\vec{u})$ denotes a leaf node in DT assigned to $\vec{u}$, and α some smoothing function.

Moreover, it would be interesting to examine whether performance of DBS coupled with ProbDT depends on a choice of decision tree algorithm. To see this, we consider three decision tree algorithms of different flavors: C4.5, MDL-DT, and SSDT. MDL-DT is like C4.5 except that it makes use of an optimized pruning based on Minimum Description Length Principle (MDL) in place of reduced error pruning used in C4.5. Another approach called SSDT aims at discovering recurring patterns in highly biased data, where a target class accounts for a tiny fraction of the whole data [2]. Note that the issue of biased data distribution is particularly relevant for summarization, as a set of sentences to be identified as summary-worthy usually account for a very small portion of the data.

Attributes for the decision trees include location, length

Table 1: Performance on JFD-1995 at varying compression rates. 'V' indicates that the relevant classifier is coupled with clustering.

cmpr. rate	C4.5*	C4.5*/V	MDL-DT*	MDL-DT*/V	SSDT*	SSDT*/V	Z	DBS(Z/V)
0.2	0.371	**0.459**	0.353	**0.418**	0.437	**0.454**	0.231	**0.429**
0.3	0.478	**0.507**	0.453	**0.491**	**0.527**	0.517	0.340	**0.491**
0.4	0.549	**0.554**	0.535	**0.545**	**0.605**	0.553	0.435	**0.529**
0.5	**0.614**	0.600	0.585	**0.593**	**0.639**	0.606	0.510	**0.582**

Table 2: Performance on synthetic data generated from the DUC-2001 corpus.

cmpr. rate	C4.5*	C4.5*/V	MDL-DT*	MDL-DT*/V	SSDT*	SSDT*/V	Z	DBS(Z/V)
0.2	**0.503**	0.263	0.215	**0.238**	**0.385**	0.232	0.093	**0.240**
0.3	**0.501**	0.295	0.262	**0.289**	**0.402**	0.274	0.110	**0.289**
0.4	**0.491**	0.354	0.297	**0.310**	**0.416**	0.305	0.127	**0.322**
0.5	**0.491**	0.335	**0.342**	0.338	**0.426**	0.318	0.150	**0.334**

and (tfidf) weight of a sentence.[1] Classes include 'Select' for those to be included in a summary and 'Don't Select' for those not. As a naming convention, we superscript a classifier's name with an asterisk to mean a probabilistic version of the associated classifier. Thus a probabilistic version of C4.5 is referred to as 'C4.5*.'

3. TEST DATA

We asked 112 Japanese subjects (students at graduate and undergraduate level) to extract 10% sentences in a text which they consider most important in making a summary. The number of sentences to extract varied from two to four, depending on the length of a text. We used 75 texts from three different categories (25 for each category); column, editorial and news report. Texts were selected randomly from articles that appeared in a Japanese financial daily *Nihon Keizai Shimbun* published in 1995. We assigned about 7 subjects to each article for the extraction task. The agreement among subjects turned out to be modest, scored 0.25 on the kappa scale, indicating the considerable variability in subjects' decisions. We assigned sentences with one or more votes to 'Select' class and those without to 'Don't Select' class. Of the total of 1424 sentences in the data, 707 were assigned to 'Select' and the remaining 717 were assigned to 'Don't Select.' Let us call the data set supplemented with human judgments 'JFD-1995.'

Another set of test data was *artificially* created from the DUC-2001 corpus (www-nlpir.nist.gov/projects/duc).[2] In contract to JFD-1995, which carries sentence by sentence judgments on extraction, the corpus comes with *abstracts*, along with the source texts. The problem is of course, an abstract often involves thorough restatements of its sources in the text so that it is no longer possible to identify sentences the abstract is actually based on. As a way out of the problem, we artificially assigned a 'Select' label to three sentences (in the source text) lexically most similar to each sentence in the abstract. The data set contained the total of 3775 sentences, of which 704 instances were labeled as 'Select' and the remaining cases were labeled as 'Don't Select.' We note one important difference from the Japanese corpus: while several people were involved in creating abstracts, each abstract was created by one judge.

[1] We define the tfidf weight of a sentence as the sum of tfidf's of terms it contains.

[2] The corpus consists of new wire articles from several sources such as Wall Street Journal, Associated Press, San Jose Mercury News, etc .

4. RESULTS AND DISCUSSION

Table 1 and 2 summarize results for the JFD-1995 and DUC-2001 data, respectively.[3] All the figures are in F-measure, i.e., $F = \frac{2*P*R}{P+R}$, and determined by 10-fold cross-validation, where one divides test data in 10 blocks, allocates nine for training and the remaining one for testing and averages scores over 10 folds. In either table, 'Z' refers to a baseline summarizer based on the tfidf based ranking model, which simply selects sentences whose sum of tfidf's for terms they contain ranks highest. Either table compares performance of C4.5*, MDL-DT*, and SSDT* against their performance when combined with clustering. Furthermore, we note that DBS is in fact Z/V, i.e, Z coupled with clustering.

Results in Table 1 and 2 strike one as rather 'similar' for the most part, even though they come from sources in different languages and domains: in either JFD-1995 or DUC-2001, clustering appears to boost performance of a summarizer whose ranking model is weak, e.g., Z, MDL-DT*; on the other hand, for a summarizer with a strong ranking model such as SSDT* and also C4.5* (for DUC-2001), clustering tends to hurt its performance. The fact that clustering is generally ineffective in DUC-2001 compared to JFD-1995 may imply that there are significant regularities to be exploited by supervised ranking models such as C4.5* and SSDT*, perhaps because each abstract in DUC-2001 is created singlehandedly.

It is curious to note that MDL-DT* is not performing as well as C4.5* and SSDT* in either corpus. The reason has to do with the property of MDL-DT* that it produces as small a tree as possible, covering the entire data space with a few regions. This could cause problems since points (sentences) would be assigned to the same probability even when they are separated far apart in the same region.

5. REFERENCES

[1] T. Nomoto and Y. Matsumoto. An experimental comparison of supervised and unsupervised approaches to text summarization. In *Proceedings of 2001 IEEE International Conference on Data Mining*, pages 630–632, San Jose, 2001. IEEE Computer Society.

[2] H. Wang and P. Yu. SSDT: A scalable subspace-splitting classifier for biased data. In *Proceedings of 2001 IEEE International Conference on Data Mining*, pages 542–549, San Jose, December 2001. IEEE Computer Society.

[3] Note that compressing a text by α% means picking up α% of sentences in the text.

Content-based Music Indexing and Organization

Andreas Rauber*
Dept. of Software Technology
Vienna Univ of Technology
A-1040 Vienna, Austria
andi@ifs.tuwien.ac.at

Elias Pampalk
Austrian Research Institute for
Artificial Intelligence
A-1010 Vienna, Austria
elias@ai.univie.ac.at

Dieter Merkl
Dept. of Software Technology
Vienna Univ of Technology
A-1040 Vienna, Austria
dieter@ifs.tuwien.ac.at

ABSTRACT

While electronic music archives are gaining popularity, access to and navigation within these archives is usually limited to text-based queries or manually predefined genre category browsing. We present a system that automatically organizes a music collection according to the perceived sound similarity resembling genres or styles of music. Audio signals are processed according to psychoacoustic models to obtain a time-invariant representation of its characteristics. Subsequent clustering provides an intuitive interface where similar pieces of music are grouped together on a map display.

Categories and Subject Descriptors

H.5.5 [**Information systems**]: Sound and Music Computing; H.3.1 [**Information Systems**]: Information Storage and Retrieval—*content analysis and indexing*

General Terms

Algorithms

Keywords

Music Retrieval, Genre, Rhythm, Psychoacoustic Models, Clustering, Self-Organizing Map, Neural Networks

1. INTRODUCTION

With the advent of electronic music archives the need for searching these archives becomes eminent. Several methods of locating a piece of music can be distinguished, which can be characterized as (1) title search, (2) melody search, and (3) genre-based search. When a specific piece of music is to be located, of which title and/or interpret are known, conventional database search will suffice. Content-based searching, i.e. looking for a specific tune, melody, or musical theme, requires the analysis of audio data. Acoustic queries are usually transformed into symbolic melody representations, which are matched against a database of scores relying e.g. on the MIDI format. Research in this direction is reported in [1, 3, 5].

However, a third form, taking a more exploratory approach to music location, can be discerned, where a specific kind or style of music is looked for, rather than a specific title or melody. With this concept, new interprets and unknown groups can be discovered, an important feature for highly dynamic music archives. It might be interesting to note that most conventional music archives and shops are primarily organized by genre as well, with only subsequent alphabetical or label-based ordering. Most electronic music archives currently are organized along some sort of genre hierarchy, some of which, due to their sheer size of up to several hundred categories, and subjectivity, are hard to comprehend. Initial work on automatically classifying music into a small genre hierarchy based on surface and rhythm features has been reported in [9], while style-based organization relying on frequency snapshots is reported in [7].

In our approach we organize music automatically according to its perceived sound similarity. To achieve this, we rely on the audio data, as it is available from MP3 or audio CD files, rather than on the MIDI format containing information on how to produce sounds. The acoustical wave signal is preprocessed in order to obtain a time-invariant representation capturing the perceived characteristics of music following psychoacoustic models. Subsequently, the *Self-Organizing Map (SOM)* [4], a popular unsupervised neural network is used to cluster the pieces of music, resulting in a map, where similar pieces of music are grouped together, providing an interface for exploratory analysis of music archives.

2. FEATURE EXTRACTION

To obtain an organization of music according to perceived sound similarity, we need a time-invariant representation of music that is robust to variations which are insignificant to our hearing sensation. Digital sound is usually represented in the form of a *Pulse-Code-Modulated (PCM)* signal, providing a discrete representation of a continuous acoustical wave, sampled at usually 44.1 kHz at 16 bit amplitude levels. By reducing two available stereo channels to one mono channel and down-sampling to 11 kHz, the data volume is significantly reduced while incurring only hardly noticeable differences on low-cost audio speakers. Furthermore, only a subset of 6-seconds sequences of each piece of music is used for further indexing, this duration being by far sufficient for human beings to recognize sound and style similarity. Specifically, lead-in and fade-out sequences are ignored.

The raw audio data is further decomposed into frequency ranges using a discrete Fourier transform using Hanning Windows to counter ringing or side-lobe effects, resulting in 129 frequency values (at 43Hz intervals) every 12 ms. The inner ear can be regarded as a complex system of a series of band-pass filters with an asymmetrical shape of frequency response, the centers and widths of which have been determined by psychoacoustic experiments [10], resulting in the so-called *critical bands*, also referred to by their unit *bark*. The bark value of

*Part of this work was done while the author was an ERCIM Research Fellow at IEI, Consiglio Nazionale delle Ricerche (CNR), Pisa, Italy.

SIGIR'02 August 11-15, 2002, Tampere, Finland.
ACM 1-58113-561-0/02/0008.

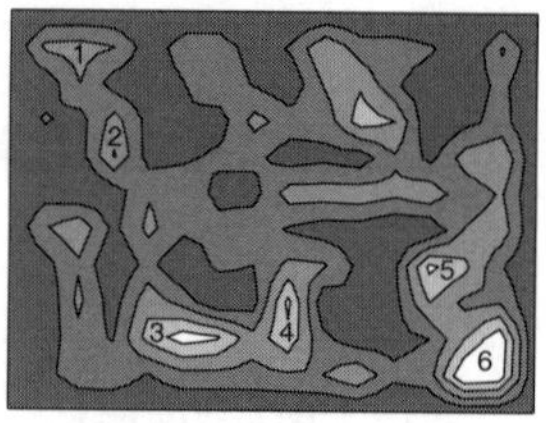

Figure 1: SOM of music collection

the frequency spectra is calculated by summing up the values of the power spectrum between the limits of the respective critical band, resulting in 20 critical-band values. To account for *masking effects*, i.e. the masking of simultaneous or subsequent sounds by a given sound, which can last for up to 200ms and has significant impacts on our hearing sensation, a *spreading function* [8] is applied. The spread critical-band values are transformed into the logarithmic *decibel* scale, describing the sound pressure level in relation to the hearing threshold. Yet, the relationship between the dB-based sound pressure levels and our hearing sensation is not linear, but rather depends on the frequency of a tone, requiring the calculation of *loudness levels*, referred to as *phon*, using the equal-loudness contour matrix. Finally, from the loudness levels, the specific loudness sensation per critical band, referred to as *sone*, is calculated, resulting in a representation of audio signal following closely the perceived characteristics.

Some further processing steps are required to obtain a time-invariant representation of the signal in order to facilitate comparison of sound characteristics, as currently two identical pieces of music would yield significantly different representations if shifted only by a slight fraction of time. To obtain a time-invariant representation, reoccurring patterns in the individual critical bands, resembling rhythm, are extracted by transforming the individual frequency spectra back into the time domain using again a discrete Fourier transform, resulting in amplitude modulations of the loudness in individual critical bands. These amplitude modulations have different effects on our sensation depending on their frequency, the most significant of which, referred to as *fluctuation strength* [2], is most intense at 4Hz and decreasing towards 15Hz, where it is followed by the sensation of *roughness*, and then by the sensation of *three separately audible tones* at around 150Hz. We thus weight the modulation amplitudes according to the fluctuation strength sensation, resulting in a time-invariant, comparable representation of the rhythmic patterns in the individual critical bands. To emphasize the differences between strongly reoccurring beats at fixed intervals and pieces with less beat emphasis, but stronger tempo variations, a final gradient filter is applied, to obtain the *modified fluctuation strength (MFS)* representation, further used for data signal comparison.

3. A SOM OF MUSIC

For organizing the pieces of music in an intuitive manner, the vector representations were clustered using the *Self-Organizing Map* (*SOM*) [4], a popular unsupervised neural network providing a topology-preserving mapping from a high-dimensional feature space onto a two-dimensional output space. Data are organized on the *SOM* such that similar data items are located close to each other. Using visualization methods for the *SOM*, such as Smoothened Data Histograms (SDH) [6], clusters of different genres are visualized as peaks on the map display.

We present results from analyzing a collection of 359 pieces of music, representing about 23 hours of music from a variety of genres. Extensive experiments analyzed different modes of organizing both (1) the individual 6-second-sequences, as well as (2) whole pieces of music on a *SOM*. With the former setting, a rather fine-grained representation of the various characteristics of music can be obtained, allowing, for example, the detection of pieces of music changing between two different genres, or having significantly differing verse and chorus parts. For the latter set of experiments, the individual 6-second-sequence representation were combined to form one single feature vector for each piece of music. Their median proved to be a simple, yet sufficiently detailed method to capture the various differences, and to provide an intuitive clustering of music.

Figure 1 represents the SDH-visualization of a 10×10 *SOM* organizing the 359 pieces of music. A number of clusters is clearly visible from the resulting SDH representation, such as, e.g., the cluster labeled with "1" representing music with very strong beats. In particular, several songs of the group *Bomfunk MCs* are located there, but also songs by *Eiffel 65* or *Jennifer Lopez*. Cluster 2 represents music mainly by the rock band *Red Hot Chili Peppers*. Cluster 3 represents more aggressive music by bands such as *Limp Bizkit*, *Papa Roach*, *Korn*. Cluster 4 represents slightly less aggressive music by groups such as *Guano Apes* and *K's Choice*. Cluster 5 represents concert music and classical music used for films, e.g., the well known *Star Wars* theme. Cluster 6 represents peaceful, classical pieces e.g. by *Beethoven* or *Mozart*.

4. CONCLUSIONS

We have demonstrated a system capable of organizing music according to their genres facilitating intuitive browsing and exploration of unknown music collections. Raw audio data is preprocessed according to psychoacoustic models to obtain a time-invariant representation reflecting the human hearing sensation of its content. The resulting data is clustered on a *SOM*, such that pieces of music that are perceived similarly are located close to each other.

5. REFERENCES

[1] D. Bainbridge et al.. Towards a digital library of popular music. In *Proc ACM Conf on Digital Libraries (ACMDL'99)*, 1999. ACM.

[2] H. Fast. Fluctuation strength and temporal masking patterns of amplitude-modulated broad-band noise. *Hearing Research*, 8:59–69, 1982.

[3] A. Ghias et al. Query by humming: Musical information retrieval in an audio database. In *Proc ACM Int'l Conf on Multimedia*, 1995. ACM.

[4] T. Kohonen. *Self-organizing maps*. Springer-Verlag, Berlin, 1995.

[5] N. Kosugi, et al.. A practical query-by-humming system for a large music database. In *Proc ACM Int'l Conf on Multimedia*, 2000. ACM.

[6] E. Pampalk, A. Rauber, and D. Merkl. Using smoothed data histograms for cluster visualization in self-organizing maps. In *Proc Int'l Conf on Neural Networks (ICANN)*, 2002. Springer.

[7] A. Rauber and M. Frühwirth. Automatically analyzing and organizing music archives. In *Proc Europ Conf on Research and Advanced Technology for Digital Libraries*, 2001. Springer.

[8] M. Schröder, B. Atal, and J. Hall. Optimizing digital speech coders by exploiting masking properties of the human ear. *J. of the Acoustical Society of America*, 66:1647–1652, 1979.

[9] G. Zanetakis, G. Essl, and P. Cook. Automatic musical genre classification of audio signals. In *Proc Int'l Symp on Music Information Retrieval*, 2001.

[10] E. Zwicker and H. Fastl. *Psychoacoustics, Facts and Models*. Springer, Berlin, 1999.

Relative and Absolute Term Selection Criteria: A Comparative Study for English and Japanese IR

Tetsuya Sakai
Knowledge Media Laboratory
Toshiba Corporate R&D Center, Japan

Stephen E. Robertson
Microsoft Research Ltd, Cambridge, UK *and*
Department of Information Science
City University, London, UK

1. INTRODUCTION

Pseudo-relevance feedback (PRF) is an unreliable method, as it does not use any *true* relevance information. Typically, it extracts candidate expansion terms from the top R documents initially retrieved, sorts them using a *term selection criterion*, and adds the top T terms to the initial query. In [9], we explored *flexbile PRF* for selecting appropriate R and/or T for each request to enhance the reliability of PRF. Although this did not show any substantial gain over traditional PRF, the results suggested that the *top 10 average document scores in the initial ranked output* and the *number of initial search terms* may be useful clues for predicting R and/or T. Since then, we tackled a simpler problem, of deciding whether PRF should be applied or not: using the above two statistics as predictors, we applied *quadratic discriminant analysis* to separate requests that PRF cannot improve from others. However, as the requests could not be discriminated accurately, we realised that even this "binary decision" version of the flexible PRF problem is challenging.

Thus this paper explores an alternative way of improving the reliability of PRF, namely, to enhance the term selection criterion itself. We refine an existing criterion based on *regression analysis*, and compare various criteria using English and Japanese test collections of respectable size.

2. RELATIVE CRITERIA & REGRESSION

In the Okapi/BM25 framework, the *offer weight* is often used as the term selection criterion, based on the arguments in [1]. It is given by $rw * r$, where r is the number of known (pseudo) relevant documents containing the term, and rw is the *relevance weight* [5]. The offer weight is a *relative* criterion, i.e. it is designed for *ranking* terms. Since it is based only on the presence/absence of the term in each document, incorporating the *term frequency* (tf) information seems attractive. However, this was not successful in [5]. We reexamine this approach in our comparative experiments by including $rw{*}rtf$ as a candidate criterion, where rtf is the total number of occurrences of the term in the pseudo-relevant document set. With Okapi, we also consider $rw * ctf$, where ctf is the same as rtf except that each tf is calibrated for each document using the Okapi parameters k_1 and b [5]. A similar approach was adopted in [3], but it was not clear whether such a method is superior to the traditional offer weight.

We also tried to refine the offer weight using regression analysis. Our regression experiments, which used the "TREC6-8" test collection (which consists of TREC Topics 301-450 and documents from Disks 4 and 5) [8], consisted of the following steps: (1) For each topic, extract candidate expansion terms from the *truly* relevant documents; (2) For each candidate term, obtain basic statistics such as r and n (the number of documents containing the term). (3) For each candidate term, construct a query that consists of the initial terms *plus* this term, and search the database; Calculate the *gain in average precision* obtained by adding this term. (4) Apply regression analysis, with the gain in average precision as the target, and the basic statistics and the offer weight as the predictors. The above experiments aimed at discovering good term selection criteria for *true* relevance feedback: similar experiments were conducted for the PRF case as well.

Our regression experiments for the *true* relevance case suggested that the offer weight over-emphasises r: regressing the gain in average precision against $rw * r$ and r gave a siginificant negative r effect. Furthermore, the data suggested that $rw * \sqrt{r}$ and $rw * \log r$ are better predictors than $rw * r$. On the other hand, we were disheartened by our results for the *pseudo*-relevance case: none of our predictors explained the gain in average precision well, suggesting that the offer weight is far from optimal for PRF. However, if the PRF problem can be decomposed into (a) Finding a good pseudo-relevant document set; and (b) Selecting good terms from the above, then "discounting" r as shown above could still be of some use for PRF, provided that Subproblem (a) is handled well. We therefore include $rw * \sqrt{r}$ and $rw * \log r$ as candidate criteria in our comparative experiments. We consider similar variants for $rw * rtf$ and $rw * ctf$ as well.

3. ABSOLUTE CRITERIA

When using the *relative* criteria described above, it makes sense to take the top T terms as expansion terms for each query. However, it is possible to use *absolute* term selection criteria instead. In such a case, the values are usually comparable across queries, and therefore a fixed *threshold* can be used to determine which terms should be included. We consider two absolute term selection criteria for PRF:

SIGIR'02, August 11-15, 2002, Tampere, Finland.
ACM 1-58113-561-0/02/0008.

Robertson's "absolute criterion" [6, 8] and the Chi-square, both of which are based on statistical significance tests. (Hearst *et al.* [1] used the Chi-square with a fixed value of T rather than a threshhold: however, in our preliminary experiements, neither using the Chi-square with T nor using the offer weight with a threshold had any significant impact on performance.) Like the offer weight, both the absolute criterion and the Chi-square are based on the two-way contingency table, and do not rely on term frequency.

4. COMPARATIVE EXPERIMENTS

In our English IR experiments, we used the Okapi Basic Search System [5] and the TREC6-8 test collection. 75 "odd" topics were used for training, and 75 "even" topics were used for testing [8]. In our Japanese IR experiments, we used the Toshiba KIDS retrieval System [7] and the IREX-IR test collection [11] which provides 6 training topics and 30 test topics, and we regarded both A-relevant and B-relevant documents as relevant.

All queries were generated from the DESCRIPTION fields only. The number of pseudo-relevant documents were fixed to $R = 10$ and $R = 30$, and all expansion terms were downweighted (compared to initial terms) as in [8]. In the training phase, T was optimised for the traditional offer weight, and the same value was used for the other relative criteria. The threshold for the absolute criterion (c) and that for the Chi-square (c') were also optimised, but at most 100 expansion terms were added to each query [8].

Table 1(A)-(B) summarise the mean average precision results for the test requests. Based on the sign test at $\alpha = 0.05$, statistically significant differences with the "No PRF" run and those with the traditional offer weight run are indicated by $\star$ and $*$, respectively.

5. CONCLUSIONS

The main findings from our experiments are:

- Although the differences are very small, $rw * \log r$ is at least as effective as $rw * r$ in (A)-(D), and the difference is statistically significant in (B). Moreover, $rw * \sqrt{r}$ outperforms $rw * r$ on average for Japanese IR ((C) and (D)). Thus it seems worthwhile to consider discounting r appropriately for given data. Recent Japanese IR experiments at NTCIR-3 confirm this as well [10].

- As in [5], the advantage of incorporating *tf* into the term selection criterion is not clear: while (A) appears to suggest a small positive effect, $rw * rtf$ is significantly worse than $rw * r$ for Japanese IR. The advantage of calibration (i.e. using *ctf*) for Okapi is not clear either.

- As in [8], relative criteria generally do at least as well as the absolute ones.

Combining different expansion runs as in [2] did not give any improvements in our experiments. Since there is no single outstanding criterion for PRF, the best strategy available at present is to carefully select a good criterion from several candidates during the training phase. As for future work, we would like to tackle Subproblem (a) mentioned in Section 2, along with other flexible PRF problems, in order to make PRF as close to true relevance feedback as possible.

Table 1: PRF Results for English and Japanese IR.

(A)	$rw * \sqrt{rtf}$	$(T = 30)$	0.2529		
TREC6-8	$rw * \log rtf$	$(T = 30)$	0.2529		
(English	$rw * ctf$	$(T = 30)$	0.2516		
IR with	$rw * rtf$	$(T = 30)$	0.2514		
Okapi)	$rw * \log ctf$	$(T = 30)$	0.2511		
$R = 10$	$rw * \sqrt{ctf}$	$(T = 30)$	0.2509		
	$rw * \log r$	$(T = 30)$	0.2501		
	$rw * r$	$(T = 30)$	**0.2500**		-
	$rw * \sqrt{r}$	$(T = 30)$	0.2498		
	Absolute Criterion	$(c = 0)$	0.2464		
	Chi-Square	$(c' = 400)$	0.2436		
	No PRF	-	**0.2251**	-	
(B)	$rw * \log ctf$	$(T = 50)$	0.2352		
TREC6-8	$rw * \log r$	$(T = 50)$	0.2348		$*$
(English	$rw * \log rtf$	$(T = 50)$	0.2341		
IR with	$rw * r$	$(T = 50)$	**0.2338**		-
Okapi)	$rw * ctf$	$(T = 50)$	0.2330		
$R = 30$	$rw * \sqrt{rtf}$	$(T = 50)$	0.2327		
	$rw * rtf$	$(T = 50)$	0.2312		
	$rw * \sqrt{ctf}$	$(T = 50)$	0.2309		
	$rw * \sqrt{r}$	$(T = 50)$	0.2297		
	Chi-Square	$(c' = 0)$	0.2262		
	Absolute Criterion	$(c = 0)$	0.2256		
	No PRF	-	**0.2251**	-	
(C)	Chi-Square	$(c' = 400)$	0.5189	$\star$	
IREX-IR	$rw * \sqrt{r}$	$(T = 10)$	0.5152	$\star$	
(Japanese	$rw * \log r$	$(T = 10)$	0.5129	$\star$	
IR with	Absolute Criterion	$(c = 5)$	0.5124	$\star$	
KIDS)	$rw * \sqrt{rtf}$	$(T = 10)$	0.5122	$\star$	
$R = 10$	$rw * r$	$(T = 10)$	**0.5116**		-
	$rw * \log rtf$	$(T = 10)$	0.5083		
	$rw * rtf$	$(T = 10)$	0.5038		$*$
	No PRF	-	**0.4650**	-	
(D)	$rw * \sqrt{r}$	$(T = 10)$	0.4926		
IREX-IR	$rw * \log r$	$(T = 10)$	0.4916		
(Japanese	$rw * \sqrt{rtf}$	$(T = 10)$	0.4904		
IR with	$rw * r$	$(T = 10)$	**0.4896**		-
KIDS)	$rw * \log rtf$	$(T = 10)$	0.4859		
$R = 30$	Absolute Criterion	$(c = 10)$	0.4854		
	Chi-Square	$(c' = 300)$	0.4841		
	$rw * rtf$	$(T = 10)$	0.4805		$*$
	No PRF	-	**0.4650**	-	

6. REFERENCES

[1] Hearst, M. *et al.*: Xerox Site Report: Four TREC-4 Tracks, *TREC-4 Proceedings* (1996).

[2] Lee, J. H.: Combining the Evidence of Different Relevance Feedback Methods for Information Retrieval, *Information Processing and Management*, Vol. 34, No. 6, pp. 681–691 (1998).

[3] Ogawa, Y. *et al.*: Structuring and Expanding Queries in the Probabilistic Model, *TREC-8 Proceedings* (2000).

[4] Robertson, S. E.: On Term Selection for Query Expansion, *Journal of Documentation* 46, pp. 359–364 (1990).

[5] Robertson, S. E. *et al.*: Okapi at TREC-3, *TREC-3 Proceedings* (1995).

[6] Robertson, S. E. and Walker, S.: Okapi/Keenbow at TREC-8, *TREC-8 Proceedings* (2000).

[7] Sakai, T. *et al.*: Cross-Language Information Retrieval for NTCIR at Toshiba, *NTCIR-1 Proceedings*, pp. 137–144 (1999). `http://research.nii.ac.jp/~ntcadm/workshop/OnlineProceedings/017-IR-Sakai.pdf`

[8] Sakai, T., Robertson, S. E. and Walker, S.: Flexible Pseudo-Relevance Feedback via Direct Mapping and Categorization of Search Requests, *BCS-IRSG ECIR 2001 Proceedings*, pp. 3–14 (2001).

[9] Sakai, T. and Robertson, S.E.: Flexible Pseudo-Relevance Feedback Using Optimization Tables, *ACM SIGIR 2001 Proceedings*, pp. 396-397 (2001).

[10] Sakai, T. *et al.*: Toshiba KIDS at NTCIR-3: Japanese and English-Japanese IR, *NTCIR-3 Proceedings, to appear* (2002).

[11] Sekine, S. and Isahara, H.: IREX: IR and IE Evaluation Project in Japanese, *LREC 2000 Proceedings* (2000).

Experiments on Data Fusion Using Headline Information

Xiao Mang Shou
Department of Information Studies
University of Sheffield
Western Bank, Sheffield, S10 2TN, UK
+44 (0)114-2222677
x.m.shou@sheffield.ac.uk

Mark Sanderson
Department of Information Studies
University of Sheffield
Western Bank, Sheffield, S10 2TN, UK
+44 (0)114-2222648
m.sanderson@sheffield.ac.uk

ABSTRACT
This poster describes initial work exploring a relatively unexamined area of data fusion: fusing the results of retrieval systems whose collections have no overlap between them. Many of the effective meta-search/data fusion strategies gain much of their success from exploiting document overlap across the source systems being merged. When the intersection of the collections is the empty set, the strategies generally degrade to a simpler form. In order to address such situations, two strategies were examined: re-ranking of merged results using a locally run search on the text fragments returned by the source search engines; and re-ranking based on cross document similarity, again using text fragments presented in the retrieved list. Results, from experiments, which go beyond previous work, indicate that both strategies improve fusion effectiveness.

Categories & Subject Descriptors: H3.3 Information Storage and Retrieval

General Terms: Performance, Experimentation

1. INTRODUCTION
Data fusion is the merging of ranked document lists from *source search engines* into a unified list. Several merge methods have been proposed, each relying on different conditions or forms of information being returned by search engines. Lee described CombMNZ, which multiplied the sum of the scores returned by each search engine by the number of engines with non-zero scores [3]. Aslam & Montague [1] proposed a Borda-fuse voting model where documents were considered to have been 'voted' for by the search engines that retrieved them. The votes a document received determined its fused rank position. Manmatha et al [4] reported a double distribution fit model, which was almost as effective as CombMNZ, despite ignoring document overlap. However, the method was only tested on source ranks of 1,000 documents containing a good number of relevant documents. The method's effectiveness on more common situations of short rankings with few relevant documents remains to be demonstrated. The three strategies rely on collection overlap and/or score information being returned by search engines. Overlap is expected when fusing different retrieval strategies, and is common for meta-search engines on the Web, but when merging the results returned by a set of dispirit digital libraries, overlap is much less likely. In addition, source search engines rarely return a similarity score when presenting a retrieved set.

Taking an approach that does not require such conditions, Lawrence & Giles performed a *local search* on a collection formed by downloading all documents retrieved by the source search engines [2]. Despite working well, full text downloading is slow and on some digital libraries may incur cost. Addressing this problem, Tsikrika & Lalmas [6] reported on a local search method using only title & summary text as well as source rank position when fusing[1]. Tested on 10 queries, the method was found to be as effective as Lawrence and Giles's 'full text' local search, a somewhat striking result.

For our experiments, we chose to test methods that do not rely on overlap or document score information being present as it is our contention that such a situation is common, and is relatively unexplored. Our methods test the success of Tsikrika & Lalmas's local search [6] on a much wider range of queries, combinations of retrieval systems, and sizes of text returned including much shorter texts such as document title only. In addition, we examined a novel approach inspired by CombMNZ and Borda-fuse: approximating document overlap by measuring the similarity of documents across the source rankings to be merged. As with the overlap-based methods, which ranked higher documents that were duplicates of each other, our *cross rank* approach, places documents higher in the fused ranking if they are similar to each other.

The rest of this short paper describes our fusion methods in more detail and means by which we tested them. Results are presented next, before concluding.

2. SEARCH METHODS
Local search: Here, the document titles returned by the source search engines were formed into a new collection and a search (based on BM25 weighting) was performed locally with the resulting single ranking being evaluated for effectiveness. To establish an upper bound on our experimental results, local search on full document text [2] was also conducted.

Lower bounds – random and round robin: To establish a lower bound on performance, the effectiveness of a *round robin* technique was measured: ranking the fused documents based solely on their rank position from source search engines. An additional lower bound based on randomly sorting the fused ranking was also measured.

Cross Rank Similarity Comparison: Here, we examined how similar a document was to other retrieved documents. If there were more documents similar to a specific document, then it was ranked higher. Cross rank similarity comparison was computed by summing the (BM25-based) similarity score of a source document headline with the headlines of the other source documents. The

[1] It is our understanding that a similar idea was reported at a SIGIR workshop some years ago, though not published.

SIGIR'02, August 11-15, 2002, Tampere, Finland.
ACM 1-58113-561-0/02/0008.

similarity scores were normalised and documents were fused into a single ranking sorted by their normalised score.

3. TEST DATA SET

The target of our experiments on data fusion tried to simulate a realistic situation where each source engine searched a different non-overlapping document collection. For our experiments, we decided to examine fusing the top 20 documents returned by 4 non-overlapping search engines. Our fusion models worked on ranking the 80 resultant documents. As with other fusion work (e.g. [1], [3], [5]), TREC data was used in our experiment. We examined sets of 4 rankings chosen from the 21 systems that submitted runs to the short topic category-A adhoc part of TREC-5. In order to test fusion of non-overlapping collections, the rankings for each source system was filtered so that each only returned documents from a ¼ of the TREC collection. We additionally restricted our collection to the newspapers/wires of TREC-5 alone: FT, WSJ, and AP. Those files were interleaved and split into 4 sub collections so that the words were evenly distributed across the collections. The average length of the headlines in collection was 12 words. Four search engines associated with the 4 sub collections were selected from the 21 available. Based on each source search engine's *mean average precision* (MAP) calculated by TREC, they were ranked from 1 to 21. Different combinations of search engines were chosen in order to observe the methods in a range of fusion situations. Fifty queries (Topic 251-300 from trec-5) were used in our experiments.

4. EXPERIMENT RESULTS

The results of our experiments are listed in Table 1, presenting MAP, rows are sorted by round robin score. From the table, it can be seen that cross rank works slightly better than round robin, which is encouraging since it ignored source rank position and was based on inter-headline similarity alone. Local search on headlines was markedly better than the other two regardless of the systems being fused. The upper bound of local full text search was the best by far; quite a different result from Tsikrika & Lalmas who reported local searching on the different amounts of source text resulting in similar effectiveness. We note that in their work, local search only improved on round robin by 10% where here, improvement was 159%. We speculate that the known success of BM25 ranking used in our system may be the reason. Tsikrika & Lalmas used an alternative ranking method.

Other than the presented results, various other fusion models were tried such as cross rank comparison using different lengths of a document's opening section (i.e. 40, 50, 60, 80, 100 words), computing cross rank similarity across smaller document sets, mixture of cross rank and local headline search, mixture of cross rank and round robin method, etc. In general, the more text used, the better fusion became. The performance of the mixture of cross rank and local headline search was in between applying these two models alone. Therefore, under these conditions, local search on retrieved headlines was found to be the most cost effective and efficient method.

5. CONCLUSION

We have presented 2 methods of data fusion that make minimal assumptions of the source systems being searched. Despite ignoring score information and document overlap and using only the minimal text returned in a ranked list, an effective means of merging has been produced. This is, however, preliminary work and we plan to extend our study examining further means of merging cross rank and local search. Also, we will explore improvements on the cross rank similarity calculation and local search ranking method: both computed *inverse document frequency* (IDF) scores of terms from the local 80-document collections, estimating IDF from a larger collection maybe beneficial.

Search Engine rank	Rndm Sort	Round Robin	Cross Rank	Local Hdln	Local Full Text
1,3,4,5 (best)	0.1518	0.2025	0.1747	0.2337	0.4149
1,8,15,21	0.1353	0.1857	0.1691	0.2224	0.3997
4,9,14,17	0.1702	0.1829	0.1866	0.2325	0.4020
1,3,5,21	0.1364	0.1708	0.1769	0.2464	0.3960
11,12,13,14	0.1297	0.1634	0.1629	0.2216	0.4317
2,3,18,19	0.1596	0.1594	0.1788	0.2197	0.4305
1,19,20,21	0.1252	0.1337	0.1714	0.2299	0.4525
18,19,20,21 (worst)	0.1109	0.1025	0.1179	0.2326	0.4501[2]
Average	**0.1399**	**0.1626**	**0.1673**	**0.2299**	**0.4222**
% change	-14%	0.0%	+2%	+41%	+159%

Table 1: Mean average precision for different fusion methods and different search engines

6. REFERENCES

[1] Javed A, Aslam and Mark Montague; Models for Metasearch; Proceedings of the 24th Annual International ACM SIGIR Conference on Research and Development in Information Retrieval (SIGIR'01), New Orleans, Louisiana, USA, pp 276-284

[2] Steve Lawrence and C. Lee Giles; Context and page Analysis for Improved Web Search; IEEE Internet Computing, Volume 2, Number 4, pp 38-46, 1998

[3] Joon Ho Lee; Analyses of Multiple Evidence Combination; Proceedings of the 20th Annual International ACM SIGIR Conference on Research and Development in Information Retrieval (SIGIR'97), Philadelphia, Pennsylvania, UAS, July 1997, pp 267-275

[4] R. Manmatha, T. Rath and F. Feng; Modelling Score Distributions for Combining the Outputs of search Engines; Proceedings of the 24th Annual International ACM SIGIR Conference on Research and Development in Information Retrieval (SIGIR'01), New Orleans, Louisiana, USA, pp 267-275

[5] Jacques Savoy, Anne Le Calvé and Dana Vrajitoru; report on the TREC-5 Experiment: Data Fusion and Collection Fusion; Proceedings of the TREC'5, NIST Publication 500-238, Gaithersburg (MD), November 1997, pp 489-502

[6] Theodora Tsikrika and Mounia Lalmas; Merging Techniques for Performing Data Fusion on the Web; Proceedings of ACM CIKM'01 conference, November 5-10, 2001, Atlanta, Georgia, USA, pp 127-134

[2] The high MAP when fusing worse source rankings is due to fewer relevant source documents being retrieved.

Building Thematic Lexical Resources by Term Categorization

Alberto Lavelli & Bernardo Magnini
ITC-irst
Via Sommarive, 18 – Località Povo
38050 Trento, Italy
E-mail: {lavelli,magnini}@itc.it

Fabrizio Sebastiani
Istituto di Elaborazione dell'Informazione
Consiglio Nazionale delle Ricerche
56124 Pisa, Italy
E-mail: fabrizio@iei.pi.cnr.it

ABSTRACT

We discuss the automatic generation of *thematic lexicons* by means of *term categorization*, a novel task employing techniques from information retrieval (IR) and machine learning (ML). Specifically, we view the generation of such lexicons as an iterative process of learning previously unknown associations between terms and *themes* (i.e. disciplines, or fields of activity). The process is iterative, in that it generates, for each c_i in a set $C = \{c_1, \ldots, c_m\}$ of themes, a sequence $L_0^i \subseteq L_1^i \subseteq \ldots \subseteq L_n^i$ of lexicons, bootstrapping from an initial lexicon L_0^i and a set of text corpora $\Theta = \{\theta_0, \ldots, \theta_{n-1}\}$ given as input. The method is inspired by *text categorization*, the discipline concerned with labelling natural language texts with labels from a predefined set of themes, or categories. However, while text categorization deals with documents represented as vectors in a space of terms, term categorization deals (dually) with terms represented as vectors in a space of documents, and labels terms (instead of documents) with themes. As a learning device we adopt *boosting*, since (a) it has demonstrated state-of-the-art effectiveness in a variety of text categorization applications, and (b) it naturally allows for a form of "data cleaning", thereby making the process of generating a thematic lexicon an iteration of generate-and-test steps.

1. TERM CATEGORIZATION

The generation of *thematic lexicons* (i.e. lexicons consisting of specialized terms, all pertaining to a given theme or discipline) is a task of increased applicative interest, since such lexicons are important in a variety of tasks pertaining to natural language processing and information access. Unfortunately, the generation of thematic lexicons is expensive, since it requires the intervention of specialized manpower, i.e. lexicographers and domain experts working together. There is thus a need of cheaper and faster methods for answering application needs than manual lexicon generation.

We propose a methodology for the or automatic generation of thematic lexicons by *term categorization*, a novel task that employs a combination of techniques from information retrieval (IR) and machine learning (ML). We view the generation of such lexicons as an iterative process of learning previously unknown associations between terms and *themes* (i.e. disciplines, or fields of activity, or domains). The process is iterative, in that it generates, for each c_i in a set $C = \{c_1, \ldots, c_m\}$ of predefined themes, a sequence $L_0^i \subseteq L_1^i \subseteq \ldots \subseteq L_n^i$ of lexicons, bootstrapping from a lexicon L_0^i given as input. Associations between terms and themes are learnt from a sequence $\Theta = \{\theta_0, \ldots, \theta_{n-1}\}$ of sets of documents (hereafter called *corpora*); this allows to enlarge the lexicon as new corpora from which to learn become available. At iteration y, the process builds the lexicons $L_{y+1} = \{L_{y+1}^1, \ldots, L_{y+1}^m\}$ for all the themes $C = \{c_1, \ldots, c_m\}$ in parallel, from the same corpus θ_y.

The method we propose is inspired by *text categorization* [5], the activity of automatically building, by means of machine learning techniques, *automatic text classifiers*, i.e. programs capable of labelling natural language texts with (zero, one, or several) thematic categories from a predefined set $C = \{c_1, \ldots, c_m\}$.

While the purpose of text categorization is that of classifying documents represented as vectors in a space of terms, the purpose of term categorization is (dually) that of classifying terms represented as vectors in a space of documents. In our task, terms are thus items that may belong, and must thus be assigned, to (zero, one, or several) themes belonging to a predefined set. In other words, starting from a set Γ_y^i of preclassified terms, a new set of terms Γ_{y+1}^i is classified, and the terms in Γ_{y+1}^i which are deemed to belong to c_i are added to L_y^i to yield L_{y+1}^i. The set Γ_y^i is composed of lexicon L_y^i, acting as the set of "positive examples", plus a set of terms known not to belong to c_i, acting as the set of "negative examples". For input to the learning device and to the term classifiers that it will eventually build, we use "bag of documents" representations for terms, dual to the "bag of terms" representations commonly used in text categorization.

The novelty of this *supervised* approach to the generation of thematic lexicons is that there is basically no requirement on the corpora $\Theta = \{\theta_0, \ldots, \theta_{n-1}\}$ to be employed in the process. This differs from the classic *unsupervised* approach (see e.g. [1]), in which in order to generate a thematic lexicon for topic c_i, a corpus of documents *labelled by* c_i is needed. This may be problematic, since labelled data are sometimes hard to obtain, and labelling them requires expert manpower. In our approach, the only requirement on θ_y is that at least some of the terms in each of the lexicons in $L_y = \{L_y^1, \ldots, L_y^m\}$ should occur in it (if none among the terms in a lexicon L_y^j occurs in θ_y, then no new term is added to L_y^j in iteration y).

SIGIR'02, August 11-15, 2002, Tampere, Finland.
ACM 1-58113-561-0/02/0008.

# of docs	# of training terms	# of test terms	# of labels per term	min # of docs per term	Precision micro	Recall micro	F_1 micro	Precision macro	Recall macro	F_1 macro
2,689	4,424	2,212	1.96	1	0.542029	0.043408	0.080378	0.584540	0.038108	0.071551
2,689	1,685	842	2.36	5	0.512903	0.079580	0.137782	0.487520	0.078677	0.135489
2,689	1,060	530	2.55	10	0.517544	0.086131	0.147685	0.560876	0.084176	0.146383
16,003	7,975	3,987	1.76	1	0.720165	0.049631	0.092863	0.701141	0.038971	0.073837
16,003	4,132	2,066	2.02	5	0.733491	0.075121	0.136284	0.738505	0.065472	0.120281
16,003	2,970	1,485	2.15	10	0.740260	0.091405	0.162718	0.758044	0.078162	0.141712
67,953	11,313	5,477	1.66	1	0.704251	0.043090	0.081211	0.692819	0.034241	0.065256
67,953	6,829	3,414	1.83	5	0.666667	0.040816	0.076923	0.728300	0.050903	0.095155
67,953	5,335	2,668	1.92	10	0.712406	0.076830	0.138701	0.706678	0.056913	0.105342
67,953	4,521	2,261	1.99	15	0.742574	0.086445	0.154863	0.731530	0.064038	0.117766
67,953	3,317	1,659	2.10	30	0.745455	0.098439	0.173913	**0.785371**	0.075573	0.137878
67,953	2,330	1,166	2.25	60	**0.760417**	**0.117789**	**0.203982**	0.755136	**0.086809**	**0.155718**

Table 1: Preliminary results obtained on the automated lexicon generation task. The three blocks of lines correspond to using one day (08.11.1996), one week (08.11.1996 to 14.11.1996), and one month (01.11.1996 to 30.11.1996) of Reuters Corpus Volume 1 newswires, respectively.

As the learning device we adopt AdaBoost.MH^{KR} [6], a more efficient and more effective variant of AdaBoost.MH^{R} [3]. Both algorithms are an implementation of *boosting*, a method for supervised learning which has proven one of the best performers in text categorization applications so far. Boosting is based on the idea of relying on the collective judgment of a committee of classifiers that are trained sequentially; in training the k-th classifier special emphasis is placed on the correct categorization of the training examples which have proven harder (i.e. have been misclassified more frequently) for the previously trained classifiers.

2. EXPERIMENTS

We are currently experimenting this methodology by using WordNet Domains(42) [2] as the lexical resource. WordNet Domains(42) is an extension of WordNet in which each word has been labelled with one or more from a set of 42 themes (such as e.g. Zoology, Medicine, Sport) commonly used in dictionaries. Each thematic lexicon (i.e. the set of the words labelled by the same theme) is partitioned into a training and a test set, so that the purpose of the experiment is to check the ability of the algorithm to extract the terms of the test set from the texts. As the evaluation measure, we are using (both micro- and macro-averaged) F_1. As the texts from which to extract the terms, we are using a sequence $\Theta = \{\theta_0, \ldots, \theta_{n-1}\}$ of subsets of the Reuters Corpus Volume 1(see `http://groups.yahoo.com/group/ReutersCorpora/`). Only the text of the documents is used, and the Reuters categories labelling the documents are not used. We lemmatize the documents and annotate the lemmas with part-of-speech tags using the TreeTagger package [4].

Table 1 reports some results from preliminary experiments involving a single iteration of the process and committees of 500 decision classifiers. Only training and test terms occurring in at least x documents were considered (see Column 5); the experiments reported in the same block of lines differ for the choice of the x parameter.

The first conclusion we can draw from them is that F_1 values are still low; a lot of work is still needed in tuning this approach in order to obtain significant categorization performance. The low values of F_1 are mostly the result of low recall values, while precision tends to be much higher, often well above the .70 mark.

The second conclusion is that results show a constant and definite improvement when higher values of x are used, despite the fact that higher levels of x mean (see Column 4) a higher number of labels per term, i.e. more polysemy. This is not surprising, since when a term occurs e.g. in one document only, this means that only one entry in the vector that represents the term is non-null (i.e. significant). This is in sharp contrast with text categorization, in which the number of non-null entries in the vector representing a document equals the number of distinct terms contained in the document, and is usually at least in the hundreds. This alone might suffice to justify the difference in performance between term categorization and text categorization.

3. REFERENCES

[1] H. Chen, B. R. Schatz, T. D. Ng, J. Martinez, A. Kirchoff, and C. Lin. A parallel computing approach to creating engineering concept spaces for semantic retrieval: the Illinois Digital Library Initiative project. *IEEE Transactions on Pattern Analysis and Machine Intelligence*, 18(8):771–782, 1996.

[2] B. Magnini and G. Cavaglià. Integrating subject field codes into WordNet. In *Proceedings of LREC-2000, 2nd International Conference on Language Resources and Evaluation*, pages 1413–1418, Athens, GR, 2000.

[3] R. E. Schapire and Y. Singer. BoosTexter: a boosting-based system for text categorization. *Machine Learning*, 39(2/3):135–168, 2000.

[4] H. Schmid. Probabilistic part-of-speech tagging using decision trees. In *Proceedings of the International Conference on New Methods in Language Processing*, pages 44–49, Manchester, UK, 1994.

[5] F. Sebastiani. Machine learning in automated text categorization. *ACM Computing Surveys*, 34(1):1–47, 2002.

[6] F. Sebastiani, A. Sperduti, and N. Valdambrini. An improved boosting algorithm and its application to automated text categorization. In *Proceedings of CIKM-00, 9th ACM International Conference on Information and Knowledge Management*, pages 78–85, McLean, US, 2000. ACM Press, New York, US.

Topic Structure Modeling

David A. Evans
Clairvoyance Corporation
5001 Baum Blvd., Suite 700
Pittsburgh PA 15213-1854, USA
+1-412-621-0570
dae@clairvoyancecorp.com

James G. Shanahan
Clairvoyance Corporation
5001 Baum Blvd., Suite 700
Pittsburgh PA 15213-1854, USA
+1-412-621-0570
jimi@clairvoyancecorp.com

Victor Sheftel
Clairvoyance Corporation
5001 Baum Blvd., Suite 700
Pittsburgh PA 15213-1854, USA
+1-412-621-0570
v.sheftel@clairvoyancecorp.com

ABSTRACT

In this paper, we present a method based on document probes to quantify and diagnose topic structure, distinguishing topics as monolithic, structured, or diffuse. The method also yields a structure analysis that can be used directly to optimize filter (classifier) creation. Preliminary results illustrate the predictive value of the approach on TREC/Reuters-96 topics.

Categories and Subject Descriptors

I.2.7: ARTIFICIAL INTELLIGENCE, Natural Language Processing, Text analysis. **H.3.3**: Information Systems, INFORMATION STORAGE AND RETRIEVAL, Information Search and Retrieval, Retrieval models. **H.3.1**: Information Systems, INFORMATION STORAGE AND RETRIEVAL, Content Analysis and Indexing, Indexing methods.

General Terms

Algorithms, Measurement, Experimentation, Languages.

Keywords

Topic Structure, Topic Modeling, Clustering, Probes.

1. INTRODUCTION

User information needs, typically expressed in terms of a short description or a set of example documents, tend to vary from very focused, such as "find me information about product *XYZ*," to very broad, such as "keep me posted on *world politics*." Traditionally, both types of information needs have been modeled using single or monolithic filters [1][2]. These approaches provide good levels of performance on focused topics, but generally yield poor performance for broad ones [3]. If one could diagnose topic structure, one could apply different query or filtering strategies to optimize performance, such as the use of committees (e.g., cascades) of filters [3].

One general approach to topic analysis has been suggested by Cronen-Townsend and Croft that exploits the difference in the language model of the query (or topic) and the language model of the corpus to provide a measure of topic ambiguity [4]. The "clarity" score they develop may help predict performance, but it does not directly distinguish query types or lead to specific strategies for improving performance.

SIGIR'02, August 11-15, 2002, Tampere, Finland.
ACM 1-58113-561-0/02/0008.

In fact, we have found it useful to distinguish three types of topics: monolithic, structured, and diffuse. A **monolithic topic (MT)** is a topic that is well focused. Any subset of positive examples of such a topic will generally show a high degree of similarity to any other subset. An example might be a topic on "approaches to adaptive filtering." A **structured topic (ST)**, in contrast, may contain several threads or sub-topics of information, each of which is relatively monolithic. In such cases, one subset of positive examples might not show similarity to another subset, but there may be one or more specific subsets in which the documents they contain show a high degree of similarity to one another. An example might be a topic such as "recent developments in biomedicine," where we might find documents on many special (sub-)topics (e.g., cancer, AIDS, cloning, etc.). A **diffuse topic (DT)**, finally, is either inherently vague or overly general and shows little underlying structure. Any one document from a sample of positive examples may bear no similarity to any other. An example of such a topic might be "management practices," under which one might expect to find a great variety of "management" described—ranging from controlling assembly lines to organizing marketing campaigns—and many kinds of "practices"—from instituting frequent inventory controls to behavioral modification.

2. QUANTIFYING TOPIC STRUCTURE

Document clustering can be used to some degree to diagnose topic structure. One can cluster a sample of positive documents into groups, for example, by pruning the cluster branches when they reach join similarities of 0.01 or less. The number of resulting groups and the stability of those groups when the cluster tree is re-factored by increasing or decreasing the join similarity score provide important clues as to how a topic is structured. One large stable group (say, consisting of 60–70% of the documents) suggests an MT. Several stable groups (say, 3, each containing 20–30% of the documents), suggest an ST. And the absence of large or stable groups suggests a DT.

Such a clustering approach to topic structure discovery, however, is computationally expensive when dealing with large numbers of documents (say, over 1,000), especially as we have to repeat the process many times under different clustering conditions to assess stability.

An alternative method for calculating the specificity of topic structure is based on using random document probes. Probes or queries are constructed using a small sample of similar documents (typically two or three) taken from the positive examples for a topic. Subsequently, each probe is used as a query over the entire set of positive examples, resulting in a ranked list of documents. The probing process continues until a significant sample of documents has been used as probe seeds. An Average Probe Score (APS) is calculated as follows:

$$APS = \frac{\sum_{i=1}^{|Probes|} \sum_{j=1|NS(Doc_j,Probe_i)>0.1}^{|Topic|} NS(Doc_j, Probe_i)}{|Probes|}$$

where Doc_j denotes a positive document for a topic, $|Topic|$ denotes the number of positive examples for a topic, $Probe_i$ denotes a query probe constructed from a small number (two or three) of randomly selected positive example documents for a topic, $|Probes|$ denotes the number of query probes, $NS(Doc_j, Probe_i)$ denotes the degree of similarity between the document Doc_i and the query probe $Probe_i$ normalized by the score of the first-ranked document returned by this query probe. Note that documents with a normalized similarity score of less than 0.1 are not considered. The APS measure can be regarded intuitively as being proportional to the average number of high scoring documents that various random probes return. The more monolithic a topic is, the more documents of high similarity a probe returns; the more diffuse, the fewer documents—and their scores will be generally lower.

3. MODELING TOPIC STRUCTURE

Once the probing process is completed, each document can be characterized by a new set of features, viz., the probes under which it was retrieved. The value of each probe feature will be the normalized similarity score between that probe and the document. Using such an abstract document representation, we can cluster the documents based on probe-features. The documents in such clusters can be ranked by their cumulative probe scores, providing an interesting measure of "importance" relative to their cohort in the cluster. More relevantly, the resulting clusters can be used directly to construct component filters that model the topic.

4. RESULTS AND DISCUSSION

A valuable measure that the process provides is the degree (and rate) of convergence on topic coverage. (Cf. Figure 1.) The observation in MT cases (such as Reuters-96 [3] Topic 10) is that, where there are many similar documents, each probe will touch many other documents above the threshold score (e.g., 0.1 NS); after a few probes, virtually all the documents in the sample set will have been touched. In ST cases (such as Reuters-96 Topics 5, 8), the first probes will touch fewer documents, but after several probes, the total number of documents touched (at least once) will grow and eventually approach the total in the set. Finally, in DT cases (such as Reuters-96 Topics 1, 11, 19), we expect no probe to touch many documents; even after many probes the total touched will not approach the total number of documents in the set.

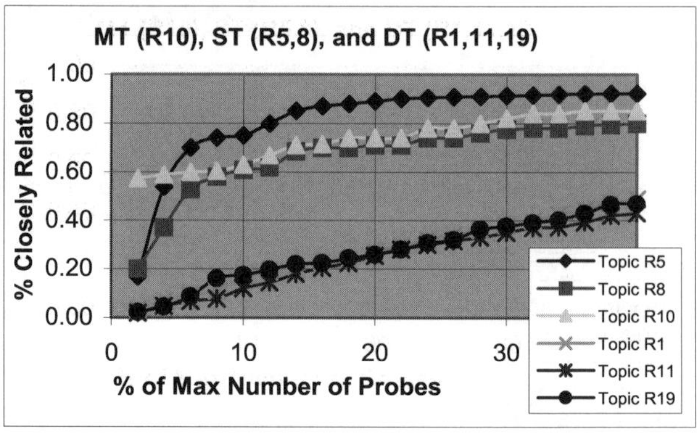

Figure 1. Convergence on Coverage by Repeated Probes

As a preliminary test of APS to predict filter (classifier) performance, we compared the APS for all Reuters-96 topics having more than 20 example documents to the best performing monolithic filters we constructed for the topics, as shown in Figure 2. The regression line shows a strong prediction value.

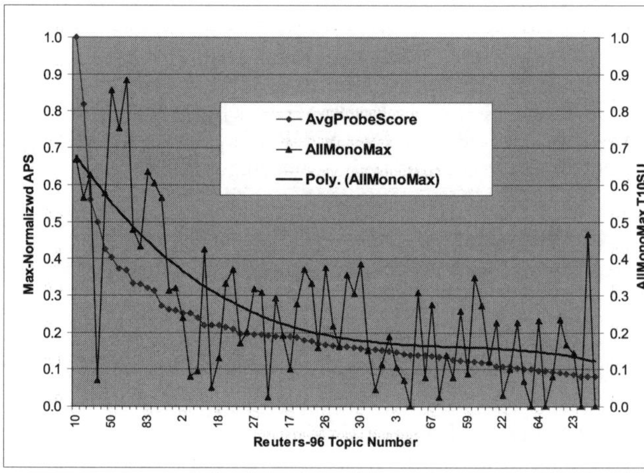

Figure 2. Prediction of Filter Performance x APS

5. REFERENCES

[1] Zhai C., Jansen P., Stoica E., Grot N., Evans D.A., "Threshold Calibration in CLARIT Adaptive Filtering". *Seventh Text Retrieval Conference (TREC-7)*, 1999, 149–156.

[2] Zhai C., Jansen P., Roma N., Stoica E., Evans D.A., "Optimization in CLARIT TREC-8 Adaptive Filtering." *Eighth Text Retrieval Conference (TREC-8)*, 2000, 253–258.

[3] Evans D.A., Shanahan J., Tong X., Roma N., Stoica E., Sheftel V., Montgomery J., Bennett J., Fujita S., Grefenstette G., "Topic-Specific Optimization and Structuring." *Tenth Text Retrieval Conference (TREC-10)*, to appear, 2002.

[4] Cronen-Townsend, S., and Croft, W.B., "Quantifying Query Ambiguity." *Proceeding of HTL*, 2002, 94–98.

Language Model for IR Using Collection Information

Rong Jin
School of Computer Science
Carnegie Mellon University
Pittsburgh, PA 15213
rong+@cs.cmu.edu

Luo Si
School of Computer Science
Carnegie Mellon University
Pittsburgh, PA 15213
lsi@cs.cmu.edu

Alex G. Hauptmann
School of Computer Science
Carnegie Mellon University
Pittsburgh, PA 15213
alex+@cs.cmu.edu

Jamie Callan
School of Computer Science
Carnegie Mellon University
Pittsburgh, PA 15213
callan+@cs.cmu.edu

ABSTRACT

Information retrieval using meta data can be traced back to the early age of IR where documents are represented by the controlled vocabulary. In this paper, we explore the usage of meta-data information under the framework of language model. We present a new language model that is able to take advantage of the category information for documents to improve the retrieval accuracy. We compare the new language model with the traditional language model over the TREC4 dataset where the collection information for documents is obtained using the k-means clustering method. The new language model outperforms the traditional language model, which verifies our statement.

Categories & Subject Descriptors:

H.3.3 **[Information Search and Retrieval]:** Language Model Uses Collection Information

General Terms: Algorithms

Keywords: Language Modeling, Collection Information

1. INTRODUCTION

In traditional information retrieval, a document is usually assumed to be a sequence of words, which is essentially the only evidence to be used by the retrieval system to judge. However, in the web environment, documents contain many useful meta-data such as topic information in XML format. Therefore, it becomes an interesting question as how to take advantage of the meta-data of documents to improve the retrieval accuracy.

Information retrieval using meta data can be traced back to the early age of IR where documents are represented by the controlled vocabulary. Previous works on the combination of full texts with the controlled vocabulary are mainly done within the framework of vector space model [1]. In this paper, we extend the similar study to the framework of language model. The meta-data examined in this study is the category labels for documents and the problem that we address here is how to adapt language models to make use of the category labels for documents. The basic idea underlying the new language model that we propose is to combine the evidence of the words together with category labels to help predict whether a document is relevant to the query. The documents within a category that is relevant to a query will have a better chance to be relevant than those in a category that is surely irrelevant to the query. The crucial problem with the new language model is how to compute the relevance of a category to a query and then use the computed relevance information for categories to help determine the relevance information for documents.

2. MODEL DESCRIPTION

The traditional language model defines the similarity between a document and a query as the probability $P(Q|D)$, i.e. the probability of generating query Q given the observation of the document D [2]. When category labels of documents are available, it would be appropriate to define the document-query similarity as the probability $P(Q|D,C_D)$, where C_D stands for the unique category label for the document D.

As the confidence on the relevance of a document to a query depends on both the words in that document and the document label, we expand the probability $P(Q|D,C_D)$ as

$$P(Q \mid D, C_D) = \frac{P(Q \mid D)P(C_D \mid Q, D)}{P(C_D \mid D)} \tag{1}$$

where probability $P(Q|D,C_D)$ is decomposed into a product of two parts, with the first part $P(Q|D)$ relying only on the document D and the second part $P(C_D|Q,D)/P(C_D|D)$ depending on both collection C_D and document D. To remove the influence of document D from the second part, we can further expand probability $P(Q|D,C_D)$ as a linear combination of predictions from document D and query Q, i.e.

$$P(C_D \mid Q, D) = \alpha P(C_D \mid Q) + (1-\alpha)P(C_D \mid D) \tag{2}$$

where α is the parameter weighting the relative importance between the evidence Q and evidence D. By substituting Equation (2) for $P(C_D|Q,D)$ in Equation (1), we have the expression for $P(Q|D,C_D)$ i.e.

$$P(Q \mid D, C_D) = (1-\alpha)P(Q \mid D)\left(\frac{\alpha}{(1-\alpha)P(C_D \mid D)}P(C_D \mid Q) + 1\right) \tag{3}$$

Furthermore, by assuming that the assignment of document D to collection C_D is usually correct, we can have $P(C_D|D)$ approximated as a constant p which is close to 1. Then, Equation (3) can be simplified as

$$P(Q \mid D, C_D) \propto P(Q \mid D)(\beta P(C_D \mid Q) + 1) \tag{4}$$

where constant β is defined as $\frac{\alpha}{(1-\alpha)p}$ and constant term $(1-\alpha)$ is ignored in Equation (4). As seen from Equation (4), probability $P(Q|D,C_D)$ is influenced by the document information through the term $P(Q|D)$ and the collection label information through the term $\beta P(C_D|Q)+1$.

To accomplish the computation in Equation (4), we need to compute both probability $P(C_D|Q)$ and $P(Q|D)$. For term $P(C_D|Q)$, we can simply apply Bayesian rule, which results in

$$P(C_i \mid Q) = \frac{P(Q \mid C_i)P(C_i)}{\sum_i P(Q \mid C_i)P(C_i)} \tag{5}$$

The probability $P(Q|C)$ in above equation, i.e. how likely the collection C is able to answer the query Q, can be computed by looking at the averaged likelihood for the documents in collection C to be relevant to the query Q, or

SIGIR '02, August 11-15, 2002, Tampere, Finland.
ACM 1-58113-561-0/02/0008.

$$P(Q \mid C) \approx \sum_{D' \in C} P(Q, D' \mid C) = \sum_{D' \in C} P(Q \mid D', C) P(D' \mid C)$$
$$\approx \frac{1}{|C|} \sum_{D' \in C} P(Q \mid D', C) \quad (6)$$

As indicted by Equation (6), the similarity between a collection and a query is measured by the document-query similarity averaged over all the documents of that collection. Finally, term $P(Q|D)$ can be computed using the traditional language model [2], which can be expressed as

$$P(Q \mid D) = \prod_{qw \in Q} (\lambda P(qw \mid D) + (1 - \lambda) P(qw \mid GE)) \quad (7)$$

where λ is a smoothing constant.

3. EXPERIMENTS

To evaluate the effectiveness of the new language model, we conduct a contrastive experiment by comparing the new language model with the traditional language model. Since we don't have a collection with both manually assigned category labels and human relevance judgments for documents, we use the TREC4 collection as the test bed where the category labels are automatically computed using k-means clustering method [3]. There are altogether 100 different categories. Of course, the automatically generated category labels for documents are not of high qualities and therefore may have negative impact on the retrieval performance of the new language model.

The exact formula for the traditional language model is shown in Equation (2), which is also used to compute the $P(Q|D)$ in the new language model. The smoothing constant λ is set to 0.5 for both language models.

Since the weight β reflects the importance of query words in determining the document-query similarity, and in most case, query words provide much more information than the document labels, β here is set to 19 empirically.

Table 1: Average precision and precisions at different recall points for both traditional language model and the new language model over TREC4 dataset

Precision@Recall	Tradition LM	New LM
0%	0.6794	0.7013
10%	0.4097	0.4270
20%	0.3366	0.3568
30%	0.2669	0.2803
40%	0.1999	0.2161
50%	0.1659	0.1688
60%	0.1130	0.1173
70%	0.0662	0.0627
80%	0.0227	0.0304
90%	0.0028	0.0027
100%	0.0004	0.0008
Avg. Precision	0.1825	0.1911

Table 1 lists the average precision and precisions at different recall points for both the traditional language model and the new language model. As seen from Table 1, the new language model outperforms the traditional language model in terms of both average precision and precision at most recall points except the precision at 90% recall. The quality of the categories labels used in the experiments is not very high as we only use pseudo labels generated by k-means algorithms. It can be imagined that the performance will be further improved if we can incorporate high quality labels such as those generated by domain experts.

Notice that the difference between this work and the work on combining full-text and controlled vocabulary indexing is that, for the later problem, the retrieval accuracy is improved by the extra matches of query words with the manually assigned keywords, while in our work the improvement is obtained by using the estimated matching probabilities of collections with respect to the query.

4. CONCLUSIONS & FUTURE WORK

In this paper, we proposed a new language model for information retrieval that is able to make use of the document labels. In the experiment with TREC4 data, where the category labels for documents are simulated using k-means clustering method, the new language model outperforms the traditional language model. Therefore, we conclude that the new language model is a very promising method for exploring category information to improve the retrieve performance.

One problem left in the new framework is the parameter β, which was set to be 19 empirically. How to adjust this parameter automatically is a question for future work. In principle, the proposed method can be extended to incorporate other meta information. However, the problem of how to set the parameters such as lambdas needs to be explored in the future study. Furthermore, since we only explore the linear combination as the way of combining evidences in this work, more studies need to be carried out on different combination methods.

5. ACKNOWLEDGES

We thank ChengXiang Zhai for valuable discussions related to this work. This material is based on work supported by NSF grants EIA-9983253, IIS-0118767, and DUE-0085834, NSF Cooperative Agreement IRI-9817496, and Advanced Research and Development Activity (ARDA) contract MDA908-00-C-0037. Any opinions, findings, conclusions or recommendations expressed in this material are the authors', and do not necessarily reflect those of the sponsor.

6. REFERENCES

[1] T.B. Rajashekar and W.B. Croft. Combining Automatic and Manual Index Representations in Probabilistic Retrieval. Journal of American Society for Information Science, 1993

[2] J. Lafferty, C. Zhai. Document Language Models, Query Models and Risk Minimization for Information Retrieval. In Proc. of the 24th Annual Int'l ACM SIGIR Conference on Research and Development in Information Retrieval, 2001.

[3] J. Xu and W.B. Croft. Cluster-based language models for distributed retrieval. In Proc. of the 22nd Annual Int'l ACM SIGIR Conference on Research and Development in Information Retrieval, 1999.

Automatic Evaluation of World Wide Web Search Services

Abdur Chowdhury
America Online Inc.
cabdur@aol.com

Ian Soboroff
National Institute of Standards and Technology
ian.soboroff@nist.gov

ABSTRACT

Users of the World-Wide Web are not only confronted by an immense overabundance of information, but also by a plethora of tools for searching for the web pages that suit their information needs. Web search engines differ widely in interface, features, coverage of the web, ranking methods, delivery of advertising, and more. In this paper, we present a method for comparing search engines automatically based on how they rank known item search results. Because the engines perform their search on overlapping (but different) subsets of the web collected at different points in time, evaluation of search engines poses significant challenges to the traditional information retrieval methodology. Our method uses known item searching; comparing the relative ranks of the items in the search engines' rankings. Our approach automatically constructs known item queries using query log analysis and automatically constructs the result via analysis of editor comments from the ODP (Open Directory Project). Additionally, we present our comparison on five (Lycos, Netscape, Fast, Google, HotBot) well-known search services and find that some services perform known item searches better than others, but the majority are statistically equivalent.

Categories & Subject Descriptors: H.3.4 [Information Storage and Retrieval]: Systems and Software -- Performance evaluation; H.3.5 [Information Storage and Retrieval]: Online Information Services -- Web-based services

General Terms: Experimentation, Performance.

Keywords: IR Evaluation, Automatic Mean Reciprocal Ranking.

1. INTRODUCTION

Web search evaluation poses a considerable number of challenges to traditional IR evaluation methods. First, the collection is constantly changing, i.e. any evaluation is not reproducible in the future. Since the collection is so large, it is not possible to manually judge enough queries to a sufficient result depth to be able to measure recall in any reasonable way. Other researchers have also enumerated these fundamental challenges of web evaluations, however they have focused on the ad-hoc search task [1]. While other researchers have examined the effectiveness of various search services, their primary evaluation technique has been some precision variant evaluation of informational queries [3, 4]. Singhal et al. evaluated the search tasks of web users and proposed that navigational queries were more significant to web search than traditional TREC ad-hoc information gathering [2]. In addition, Singhal compared the effectiveness of TREC systems for navigation queries in comparison to web search engines and concluded that the search services were performing known item search better than traditional ad-hoc approaches. Navigational queries were examined in the TREC 2001 web track so a standard corpus could be created with relevance judgments and reproducible results [5]. Most recently, Spink classified the types of data that people are looking for but did not examine the effectiveness of their searching [8].

Given the dynamic nature of the web, the difficulty of creating a large representative test collection and the resources needed for traditional evaluation methodologies, we present a technique that is able to automatically compare search services at regular, short intervals. Since our technique uses a large number of search queries that are automatically assessed, the problems of having to devote large numbers of assessors to determine the effectiveness of the various systems is removed. In addition, since this is an automatic task it can be repeated giving general rankings of effectiveness. In the next section, we present our evaluation method and results from the known item search task.

2. EVALUATION METHOD

Our method for evaluating search engine rankings is as follows and is based on a proposal by Chris Buckley made on the TREC Web Track mailing list [6]. We construct a large number of query-document pairs. Queries are mined from search service query logs and documents are mined from the Open Directory Project (ODP). We then issue the queries to the search engines, collect the results, and find the rank at which the engine returns the document we have paired with that query. We score each ranked list using the reciprocal rank of the target document. The overall score for a search engine is the mean reciprocal rank over all query-document pairs.

For this method to be useful, the query-document pairs need to be both reasonable and unbiased. Since we do not require that the document be the most relevant for a query (this might be difficult to determine, although it is commonly the goal in known item searching), it could be the case that the best search engine for that query is the one that ranks the document *lower* than the others. However, if the documents are reasonably good matches to the query, then in the aggregate, the better engines will be those that rank the documents higher.

If the documents are biased such that they favor some particular search engine, then the results will not be reliable. For example, if we chose as a query's target document the web page retrieved at rank 1 by Google, then it would not be fair to include Google, or metasearch engines which use Google, in the comparison. One method to avoid engine bias might be to manually construct a query according to a random web page. The problem with that is that the queries are then biased and may not be representative of user needs.

SIGIR'02, August 11-15, 2002, Tampere, Finland.
ACM 1-58113-561-0/02/0008.

2.1 Query-document Pairs

To construct the query-document pairs, we began with a 12M-entry log of queries submitted to AOL Search. We eliminated the very small fraction of queries which used special query operators such as '+' and quoted phrases. The log was from taken from a single server over several days. Each server is presented user queries in a round robin fashion, thus each server log is a sub-set sample of the larger set of queries.

We drew our target documents from the Open Directory Project, also known as the ODP. Each page in the ODP is compiled by a human editor, and consists of a list of titles for web pages linked from that directory page, each accompanied by a short description. The browser formatting is similar to Yahoo!, but the data itself (which can be freely downloaded) is stored in RDF format [7]. A directory entry title does not necessarily correspond to the title of the web page pointed to, since the directory page is composed by a human editor. Since it is freely available, the Open Directory is used by several search engines in different ways, but rarely as the prime search collection.

We indexed the entry titles and links in the ODP, excluding the Adult, World, Netscape, and Kids & Teens sub-trees. We then matched each query in the query log to an exact directory entry title in the ODP. For example, we matched the query "alpha technologies" to the ODP entry titled "Alpha Technologies", which points to the web site http://www.alphafittings.com/. Most queries in the log did not match any title in the ODP. This matching process resulted in nearly 41,000 query-document pairs.

We then constructed three random samples of 500, 1000, and 2000 pairs respectively. The pairs in the samples were constrained such that:

1. The query is between one and four words long
2. The document URL is longer than just a hostname (i.e., there is at least one path component)
3. The query does not appear verbatim in the URL

The last two constraints were intended to avoid a query like "foo bar" matched trivially to http://www.foobar.com/. The process of constructing the query-document pairs described above is completely automated from a query log and the Open Directory resource.

2.2 Search Engine Results

Each engine was queried for the respective query sets, 500, 1000, and 2000. The MRR was calculated for each engine for each set and Table 1 gives the details of those query sets. Using our original query log of 12 million as a population size, and limiting sampling error to 3%, a sample size of 756 pairs would be needed for a 90% confidence interval. For a 95% confidence interval a sample size of 1067 and for 99% a query sample size of 1843 would be needed.

Since our sample size of 2000 exceeds our sample size needed for a 99% confidence interval we examine those results in more detail. With 2000 samples, our sampling error is 2.2% thus showing that E1 and E3 are equivalent with about a 1% difference in MRR. E3 and E4 are only about 2.5% different. Thus, three of the five engines are within 3.8% difference or equivalent given the sampling error. Further E4 and E5 are 14% different putting E5 as clearly the lowest performing service for known item search. E2 does 55% better than the next best search service and 91% better than the worst showing that for known item searching it is clearly out-performing the other services.

Table 1 Mean Reciprocal Ranking of Search Services

	500		1000		2000	
	MRR	Found	MRR	Found	MRR	Found
E1	26.69%	200	24.94%	356	22.70%	673
E2	38.39%	254	36.53%	484	35.68%	972
E3	26.23%	201	24.63%	347	22.96%	676
E4	22.11%	171	24.01%	335	21.66%	627
E5	18.82%	128	18.65%	250	18.63%	497

3. CONCLUSION

We presented an automatic navigational task evaluation approach that finds the effectiveness of various web search services automatically. Our approach builds upon the idea that web searches have a navigational intent and providing an automatic way to evaluate effectiveness can guide both research and commercial solutions to better effectiveness for end users. Additionally we show that while most engines are roughly the same in terms of effectiveness, there is a considerable gap between the best and worse in terms of MRR.

4. REFERENCES

[1] D. Hawking, N. Craswell, P. Thistlewaite, and D. Harman. "Results and challenges in web search evaluation. ", in Proc. Eighth Int'l World Wide Web Conf., pages 243-252, May 1999.

[2] Amit Singhal and Marcin Kaszkiel, "A case study in web search using TREC algorithms", in Proc Tenth Int'l World Wide Web Conf., pages 708-716, 2001.

[3] M. Gordon and P. Pathak, "Finding information on the world wide web: the retrieval effectiveness of search engines", IP&M, 25(2):141-180, 1999.

[4] Leighton, H. Vernon and Jaideep Srivastava. "First 20 Precision among World Wide Web Search Services (Search Engines)," JASIS 50 (July 19, 1999): 870-881.

[5] D. Hawking, TREC Web Track Guidelines, 2001, http://www.ted.cmis.csiro.au/TRECWeb/guidelines_2001.html

[6] Chris Buckley, TREC Web Track mailing list, 2001.

[7] Open Directory Project, http://www.dmoz.org

[8] Spink, A., Jansen, B.J., Wolfram, D. & Saracevic, T. (2002). From E-sex to e-commerce: Web search changes. IEEE Computer, 35 (3) 107-109.

Does WT10g Look Like the Web?

Ian Soboroff
National Institute of Standards and Technology
Gaithersburg, MD
ian.soboroff@nist.gov

ABSTRACT

We measure the WT10g test collection, used in the TREC-9 and TREC 2001 Web Tracks, with common measures used in the web topology community, in order to see if WT10g "looks like" the web. This is not an idle question; characteristics of the web, such as power law relationships, diameter, and connected components have all been observed within the scope of general web crawls, constructed by blindly following links. In contrast, WT10g was carved out from a larger crawl specifically to be a web search test collection within the reach of university researchers. Does such a collection retain the properties of the larger web? In the case of WT10g, yes.

Categories & Subject Descriptors: H.3.m [Information Storage and Retrieval]: Miscellaneous – Test Collections

General Terms: Experimentation, Measurement

Keywords: web test collections, TREC

1. INTRODUCTION

A critical requirement of a retrieval test collection is that it match the task. When the collection in question is a web collection, the issue expands to cover not only the content of the pages, but the broader hypertext structure of the collection as a whole. Since it is impossible to conduct repeatable retrieval experiments as we understand them on the "live web", several static web test collections have been built and used by the retrieval community in the past few years.

Bailey et al. [1] describe the construction of WT10g, the Web Track test collection used for TREC-9 and TREC 2001. This collection is about 10GB in size, and contains 1.69 million web pages. Their goal was to create a testbed for "realistic and reproducible" experiments on web documents with traditional, distributed and hyperlink-based retrieval algorithms. They began with VLC2, a 100GB subset of a 1997 crawl by the Internet Archive. From this they selected documents using a process designed to maximize inter-server connectivity, retain as many pages as possible from each server represented, incorporate documents likely to be relevant to a wide variety of queries, and exhibit a realistic distribution of server sizes. This process is described in detail in [1]. They measured the properties of the resulting collection according to mean in- and out-links per server, fraction of connected servers in the collection, and server "relevance", measured using a large query set.

SIGIR'02, August 11-15, 2002, Tampere, Finland.
ACM 1-58113-561-0/02/0008.

One question that they did not answer was, does WT10g look like the World Wide Web? To answer that, we first need to understand more about what the web looks like. Singhal and Kaszkiel [4] looked at average in- and out- links, within and across hosts, between the smaller WT2g corpus and their own large crawl. They concluded that linkage in WT2g was inadequate for web experiments. However, the mean is a poor statistic to describe the power-law distributions of links on the web; average linkage is dominated by the many pages with few links and gives little insight into the topology.

Broder et al. [2] analyzed two large web crawls of about 200M pages each done by Altavista in 1999, and compared their structure to two important earlier studies. They looked at the distributions of in-links and out-links in their crawls, illustrating that these distributions obey power laws with exponents close to those observed in other studies. Further, using breadth-first traversals from a large sample of starting points they sketched out the high-level structure of the web in what has become the well-known "bow-tie model". These characteristics seem to hold for the web in general, however, Pennock et al. [3] found that category-specific subsets of the web can deviate strongly from power law scaling

In order to show that WT10g indeed does resemble the web in many important ways, we measured the collection's link graph using the yardsticks of Broder et al. We show that while WT10g is small, structurally it does resemble larger web crawls that have been studied. This is an important result, because a primary criticism of web test collections is that they are inherently too small to be realistic testbeds of the web. These metrics can also be used to tune the construction methods of future test collections.

2. POWER-LAW DISTRIBUTIONS

Broder et al. found that the distributions of links in their crawls followed a power-law, that is, that the probability that a node has (in- or out-) degree d is proportional to $1/x^d$ for some $d > 1$. The exponents in their crawls was 2.1 for in-degree, and 2.72 for out-degree. Figure 1 shows the degree distributions in WT10g. These graphs are very similar to those found by Broder et al. In particular, notice the linear shape in the log-log plot, the messy tails for those few pages of very high degree, and that out-links diverge from the fitted curve at very low degree. The power-law exponents are 2.03 for in-degree, and 2.49 for out-degree. We are missing some spikes that they found and attributed to a spammer.

Power laws of hyperlink degree have been found in nearly

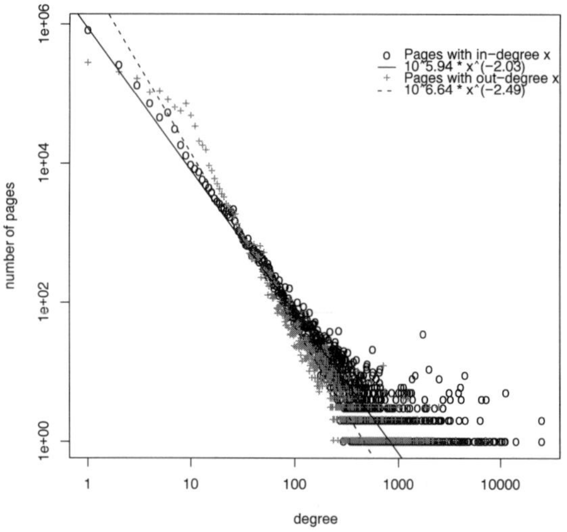

Figure 1: In- and out-degree distributions in WT10g.

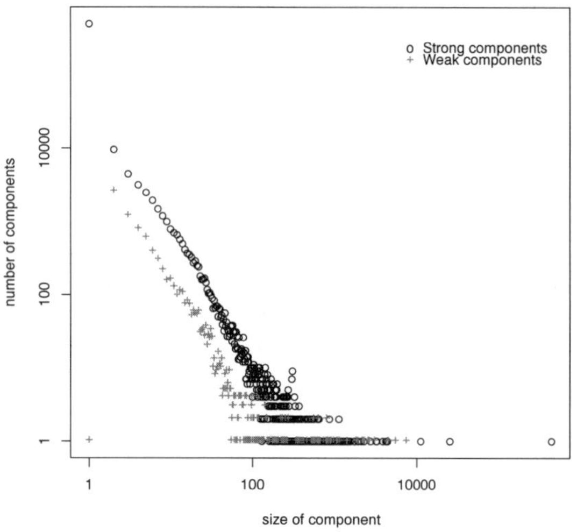

Figure 2: Distributions of strongly and weakly connected components in WT10g.

every study of a web crawl, through a wide variety of crawl sizes. In contrast, WT10g is a subset of a web crawl carefully chosen to incorporate whole servers and highlight inter-site links, but without regard to the overall link distribution.

3. CONNECTED COMPONENTS

Broder et al. also examined strongly- and weakly-connected components of the link graphs of their crawls. A strongly connected component (or, "strong component") of a graph G is a subgraph G' such that every node in G' is reachable from every other node in G' by following forward links through the graph. A weak component is the equivalent structure in an undirected graph; in our web graphs, this means taking the union of in-links and out-links into consideration when finding connected components. Figure 2 shows the distributions of strong and weak components in WT10g.

These graphs also follow a power law (exponents 1.79 for SCCs, 1.37 for WCCs) similar to the distributions found in the Altavista crawls. Our largest weak component contains 91% of the pages in WT10g, the same fraction as in the Altavista crawls. The largest strong component encompasses 29.4% of all the pages in the collection, compared to 28% in the Altavista crawls. The similarity in largest component coverage is striking, but the smaller exponents in the WT10g distributions indicate a more gradual falling-off of component sizes. This probably reflects the tendency of WT10g to favor entire servers while at the same time having many fewer pages overall than the Altavista crawls.

4. EXPLORING WITH BFS

The third and most interesting component of Broder's study was designed to probe the dichotomy in coverage between the largest weak and strong components: if 91% of the collection is connected by undirected links, but only 29.4% by browseable links, what happened to all the other pages? If nothing else, it means that understanding the web to have uniformly small diameter is inaccurate; obviously, some pages are only reachable from certain places in the web, and a large fraction are all reachable from each other within a short distance. To explore this phenomenon, they conducted breadth-first searches backward and forward from random starting nodes, noting the depth of each traversal. We did the same for 500 random starting points.

Our findings again mirror those from the Altavista crawls. The traversal depths are sharply bimodal: either they would stop after reaching a small set of pages (often, fewer than 100), or they would balloon to a huge node set (roughly 740,500 following in-links, 926,500 for out-links). For about 30% of the start nodes, both directions would balloon; 30% would balloon following in-links only, and 10% following out-links. Following Broder's analysis, we find a bow-tie in WT10g with an IN set leading into the large SCC of 270,059 pages, an OUT set of pages reachable from the SCC of 456,059 pages, and 261,828 TENDRILS pages. WT10g's OUT set is larger than IN, compared to the Altavista crawls, where the sets were of roughly equal size. We hypothesize that the strategy in WT10g of selecting by server in order of size is biased somewhat toward SCC+OUT pages.

5. REFERENCES

[1] Peter Bailey, Nick Craswell, and David Hawking. Engineering a multi-purpose test collection for web retrieval experiments. *Information Processing and Management*, to appear.

[2] Andrei Broder, Ravi Kumar, Farzin Maghoul, Prabhakar Raghavan, Sridhar Rajagopalan, Raymie Stata, Andrew Tomkins, and Janet Wiener. Graph structure on the web. In *Proceedings of the 9th International WWW Conference*, pages 309–320, Amsterdam, The Netherlands, May 2000.

[3] David M. Pennock, Gary W. Flake, Steve Lawrence, Eric J. Glover, and C. Lee Giles. Winners don't take all: Characterizing the competition for links on the web. *Proceedings of the National Academy of Sciences*, 99(8):5207–5211, April 2002.

[4] Amit Singhal and Marcin Kaszkiel. A case study in web searching using TREC algorithms. In *Proceedings of the 10th International World Wide Web Conferenece*, pages 708–716, Hong Kong, May 2001.

Biterm Language Models for Document Retrieval

Munirathnam Srikanth
State University of New York at Buffalo
Buffalo, NY, 14228
srikanth@cedar.buffalo.edu

Rohini Srihari
State University of New York at Buffalo
Buffalo, NY, 14228
rohini@cedar.buffalo.edu

Categories and Subject Descriptors

H.3.3 [**Information storage and retrieval**]: Information search and retrieval—*Retrieval models*; H.3.3 [**Information storage and retrieval**]: Systems and software—*Performance evaluation*

General Terms

Algorithms, Experimentation, Theory

Keywords

Language models, Information retrieval, N-Grams, Biterms

1 Introduction

Statistical Language Models(LM) have been used in many natural language processing tasks including speech recognition and machine translation [5, 2]. Recently language models have been explored as a framework for information retrieval [9, 4, 7, 1, 6]. The basic idea is to view each document to have its own language model and model querying as a generative process. Documents are ranked based on the probability of their language model generating the given query. Since documents are fixed entities in information retrieval, language models for documents suffer from sparse data problem. Smoothed unigram models have been used to demonstrate better performance of language models against vector space or probabilistic retrieval models for document retrieval.

Song and Croft [10] proposed a general language model that combined bigram language models with Good-Turing estimate and corpus-based smoothing of unigram probabilities. Improved performance was observed with combined bigram language models. The language models explored for information retrieval mimic those used for speech recognition. Specifically, in the bigram model a document d represented as word sequence $w_1, w_2, \cdots, w_n$ is modeled as

$$P(w_1, w_2, \cdots, w_n) = P(w_1)P(w_2|w_1)\cdots P(w_n|w_{n-1}) \quad (1)$$

Here the order of terms is important. A combined bigram model is an interpolation model with back-off to unigram probabilities.

$$P(w_i|w_{i-1}) = \lambda_1 \; P_2(w_i|w_{i-1}) + (1-\lambda_1) \; P_1(w_i) \quad (2)$$

where λ_1 is bigram weighting factor. In practice, the bigram probability P_2 is approximated to the ratio of the occurrence counts of (w_{i-1}, w_i) to that of w_{i-1} in document d.

$$P_2(w_i|w_{i-1}, d) \approx \frac{C(w_{i-1}, w_i|d)}{C(w_{i-1}|d)} \quad (3)$$

2 Language models designed for IR

Unlike language modeling for speech recognition, the language models for information retrieval need only to record co-occurrence of features or words. For a query of *information retrieval*, a back-off bigram model will give more weight to document containing *information retrieval* than a document containing *retrieval of information*. To this end, *Biterm Language Models* are introduced. Biterm language models are similar to bigram language models except that the constraint of order in terms is relaxed. A document containing *information retrieval* and a document containing *retrieval of information* will be assigned the same probability of generating the query using biterm language models.

To distinguish unordered word-pairs from order word-pairs or *bigrams* in statistical language modeling terminology, we refer to the former as *biterms*. Unordered word-pairs have been explored as document features for document retrieval [8] in vector space models as well as text categorization [3] applications.

The biterm probabilities can be approximated using the frequency of occurrence of terms. Three approximation methods are suggested here. In the first case, biterm probability of $\{w_{i-1}, w_i\}$ is viewed as an average of bigram probabilities (P_{bg}) of the ordered pairs – (w_{i-1}, w_i) and (w_i, w_{i-1}).

$$\begin{aligned} P_{BT1}(w_{i-1}, w_i|d) \;\; &\approx \;\; \frac{1}{2}[P_{bg}(w_{i-1}, w_i|d) \\ &\quad + P_{bg}(w_i, w_{i-1}|d)] \end{aligned} \quad (4)$$

The second approximation is based on computing biterm probabilities from the term frequency in documents. It is similar to the bigram probability in (3). The biterm probability of term pair $\{w_{i-1}, w_i\}$ is computed as the ratio of the number of occurrences of the term pair $\{w_{i-1}, w_i\}$ to that of the occurrence count of the term w_{i-1} in document d.

$$P_{BT2}(w_i|w_{i-1}, d) \;\; \approx \;\; \frac{C(w_{i-1}, w_i|d) + C(w_i, w_{i-1}|d)}{C(w_{i-1}|d)} \quad (5)$$

In P_{BT2} the denominator depends on the occurrence count of w_{i-1}. To make the approximation truly independent of the term order, it can be set to the ratio of the frequency

SIGIR'02, August 11-15, 2002, Tampere, Finland.
ACM 1-58113-561-0/02/0008.

of the term-pair to the minimum of the frequencies of terms w_{i-1} and w_i.

$$P_{BT3}(w_i|w_{i-1},d) \approx \frac{C(w_{i-1},w_i|d)+C(w_i,w_{i-1}|d)}{min\{C(w_{i-1}|d),C(w_i|d)\}} \quad (6)$$

P_{BT2} and P_{BT3} are *ad-hoc* approximations for biterm probabilities.

The sparse data problem in representing documents using language models is handled by smoothing biterm probabilities using unigram probabilities. The unigram probability $P(w_i|d)$ of a term in a document is in turn smoothed using its corpus probability $P(w_i|C)$. Thus the biterm and unigram probabilities are computed by

$$P(w_i|w_{i-1},d) = \alpha_1 P_{BT}(w_i|w_{i-1},d) + (1-\alpha_1)P(w_i|d) \quad (7)$$

$$P(w_i|d) = \alpha_2 P_1(w_i|d) + (1-\alpha_2)P(w_i|C) \quad (8)$$

where α_1 and α_2 are constants.

The weights for biterm and document models can be learned from a training corpus [7]. However, we conducted our experiments using fixed model weights.

3 Experiments and Results

We implemented different retrieval systems and performed experiments on the Wall Street Journal (WSJ) subset of TREC4 test collection. The WSJ collection has 74,520 documents with around 250MB of data. TREC4 topic queries were used in the evaluation. SMLE(40) is a unigram language model that combines a document model with corpus model through linear interpolation of term probabilities with the weighting factor of 40% set to the document model. BG(40+10) is a bigram language model which combines bigram document model and smoothed unigram language model. The weighting parameter between document and corpus models in the unigram model is set to 40% and the weighting parameter for bigram document model set to 10%.

Biterm retrieval systems were implemented with different approximations for biterm probabilities. The interpolation parameters were set at 40% for document model over corpus model and 10% for biterm models over unigram models. BT1(40+10) uses average of bigram probabilities as given by (4). BT2(40+10) is the biterm language model using the *ad-hoc* probability given by (5) and BT3(40+10) corresponds to the biterm probability in (6). For comparison, the language model suggested by Ponte and Croft [9] was implemented (referred as PCLM).

Table 1 shows the comparison of non-interpolated average precision between different retrieval systems on the WSJ data set.

Method	AveP	%Change	%Change	%Change
SMLE(40)	0.2023	-	-	-
PCLM	0.2070	2.32	-	-
BG(40+10)	0.2229	10.18	7.68	-
BT1(40+10)	0.2176	7.56	5.12	-2.38
BT2(40+10)	0.2247	11.07	8.55	0.81
BT3(40+10)	0.2272	12.31	9.76	1.93

Table 1: Experimental results on the WSJ data set

Based on our experiments on a WSJ data set, the performance of different biterm approximations is around the bigram language models. With fixed model weights, the *ad-hoc* approximations of biterm probabilities in biterm language model perform better than bigram language models. The reduction in average precision for BT1 in comparison to BG can be attributed to the averaging of probabilities reducing the effect of term pairs. The *ad-hoc* approximation P_{BT2} for biterms improves slightly over bigram language model since it ignores the order of term-occurrence while computing the frequency of term-pair occurrence.

If w_{i-1} occurs more often than w_i in the term pair $\{w_{i-1}, w_i\}$ in a document, the effect of the co-occurrence of term-pair to the biterm probability is reduced. Choosing the minimum of the term occurrence count for the denominator as in BT3 has improved performance than bigram language model. All approximations of biterm probabilities perform better than Ponte and Croft language model (PCLM) and smoothed unigram language model (SMLE(40)).

4 Conclusion

We present a novel method for generating language models for documents for information retrieval tasks. It is our belief that the assumptions for deriving language models for information retrieval are different from those for speech recognition or machine translation. Biterm language models capture term co-occurrence better than bigram models. Different approximations for biterm probabilities have been shown to provide better average precision than bigram language model. We have used *ad-hoc* approximations for biterm probabilities. We plan to explore better models to represent biterms. While constant weighting parameters were used in our experiments, the performance can be improved by learning and optimizing the combination weights.

REFERENCES

[1] A. Berger and J. D. Lafferty. Information retrieval as statistical translation. In *Proceedings of SIGIR'99*, pages 222–229, 1999.

[2] P. F. Brown, J. Cocke, S. D. Pietra, V. J. D. Pietra, F. Jelinek, J. D. Lafferty, R. L. Mercer, and P. S. Roossin. A statistical approach to machine translation. *Computational Linguistics*, 16(2):79–85, 1990.

[3] M. F. Caropreso, S. Matwin, and F. Sebastiani. Statistical phrases in automated text categorization. Technical Report IEI-B4-07-2000, Istituto di Elaborazione dell'Informazione, Pisa, IT, 2000.

[4] D. Hiemstra. A linguistically motivated probabilistic model of information retrieval. In *European Conference on Digital Libraries*, pages 569–584, 1998.

[5] F. Jelinek. *Statistical Methods for Speech Recognition.* The MIT Press, Cambridge, Massachusetts, 1998.

[6] J. Lafferty and C. Zhai. Document language models, query models, and risk minimization for information retrieval. In *Proceedings of SIGIR'01*, pages 111–119, 2001.

[7] D. R. H. Miller, T. Leek, and R. M. Schwartz. A hidden markov model information retrieval system. In *Proceedings of SIGIR'99*, pages 214–221, 1999.

[8] M. Mitra, C. Buckley, A. Singhal, and C. Cardie. An analysis of statistical and syntactic phrases. In *Proceedings of RIAO-97, 5th International Conference "Recherche d'Information Assistee par Ordinateur"*, pages 200–214, Montreal, CA, 1997.

[9] J. M. Ponte and W. B. Croft. A language modeling approach to information retrieval. In *Proceedings of SIGIR'98*, pages 275–281. ACM, New York, 1998.

[10] F. Song and W. B. Croft. A general language model for information retrieval. In *Proceedings of SIGIR'99*, pages 279–280, 1999.

Selecting Indexing Strings using Adaptation

Yoshiyuki Takeda Kyoji Umemura
Toyohashi University of Technology Dept. of Information and Computer Sciences
1-1, Tempaku, Toyohashi, Aichi 441-8580, Japan
+81-532-44-6762
take@ss.ics.tut.ac.jp, umemura@ics.tut.ac.jp

ABSTRACT
It is not easy to tokenize agglutinative languages like Japanese and Chinese into words. Many IR systems start with a dictionary-based morphology program like ChaSen [4]. Unfortunately, dictionaries cannot cover all possible words; unknown words such as proper nouns are important for IR. This paper proposes a statistical dictionary-free method for selecting index strings based on recent work on adaptive language modeling.

Categories & Subject Descriptors
H.3 Information Storage and Retrieval

General Terms
Algorithms

Keywords
agglutinative language, word segmentation, adaptation.

1. INTRODUCTION
Term selection is important for IR. Stop words need to be removed. For agglutinative languages such as Japanese and Chinese, it is challenging to find words because there is no white space in the orthography. It is common practice to use dictionary-based morphology programs such as ChaSen [4], but depending on a dictionary in this way introduces the unknown word problem. Unknown words such as proper nouns, acronyms and technical terms are important for IR. Dictionaries are also expensive.

Term weighting is closely related to term selection. What is a term, and whether it receives a non-negligible weight, depends on the collection. The term "security" is more important in some collections (newspapers) than others (security alerts).

This paper proposes a statistical dictionary-free method for term selection, based on recent work on adaptive language modeling. The method addresses the two issues mentioned above: (a) unknown words and (b) different choices for different collections.

2. ADAPTATION RATIO
Adaptive language models have been used to distinguish English content words from function words [1]. Content words have a large adaptation ratio, df_2/df_1, where df_k is a generalization of document frequency. df_k is the number of documents that contain a term k or more times. The adaptation ratio is an estimate of the probability of repetition (probability of two or more instances of a term in a document, given that there was one).

This paper will show that the adaptation ratio is also useful for term selection in Japanese and Chinese. Good keywords have larger ratios than meaningless substrings, as illustrated in Figure 1 and 2. All experiments reported here are based on two standard test collections of abstracts and newspapers in Japanese and Chinese: (a) Ntcirl/2 and (b) Chinese Information Retrieval Benchmark 1.0 (CIRB010) [2]. Following standard notational practices, N denotes the size of collection (in documents).

3. TERM SELECTION
The method for selecting terms consists of two steps. First, sentences are divided into candidates. Each candidate is assigned a score by equation (1). Finally, these scores are combined to produce an output segmentation using equation (2).

$$\mathrm{score}(w_i) = \begin{cases} \log df_2/df_1 & \cdots\ df_2 \geq 3, df_1/N \leq 0.5 \\ \log 0.5 & \cdots\ df_2 \geq 3, df_1/N > 0.5 \\ -\infty & \cdots\ df_2 < 3 \end{cases} \tag{1}$$

$$words = \mathrm{argmax}_W \left(\sum\nolimits_{W=\{w_1,w_2,\cdots,w_n\}} \mathrm{score}(w_i) \right) \tag{2}$$

The notation w_i denotes a candidate word. W denotes a sequence of candidate words. Candidate words must satisfy the conditions in equation (3).

$$conditions = \{0.1 < df_2/df_1, 0.00005 < df/N < 0.1, l > 1\} \tag{3}$$

The thresholds in these three equations were determined empirically based on data such as Figure 1.

4. IMPROVEMENTS
Table 2 compares the performance of the proposed term selection method (SIS) with two baseline term selection methods: (a) ALL, all character bigrams, and (b) CHA, a well-established dictionary-based word segmentation system ChaSen [4]. Two retrieval engines are shown in Table 2: (a) a well-established standard, $TF \cdot IDF$ (TFIDF) and (b) a more recent proposal, Empirical Term Weighting (ETW) [3]. The conditions, strict and loose, are borrowed from the NTCIR1 workshop. The main point of Table 2 is the relatively high performance of SIS compared to the baselines. In addition, as a side note, we observe that ETW consistently outperforms the TFIDF baseline.

Table 3 breaks down the results in Table 2 in terms of events which we call WIN. A query is called WIN if the average precision of method is higher for the query than others. Each cell in Table 3 is a number between 0 and 83, since there are 83 queries. The data in Table 3 is used to test the hypothesis that performance is less than ideal (less than 50%). Equation (4) tests this hypothesis, assuming a binomial distribution, where m is the number of WINs and n is the number of trials.

SIGIR'02, August 11-15, 2002, Tampere, Finland.
ACM 1-58113-561-0/02/0008.

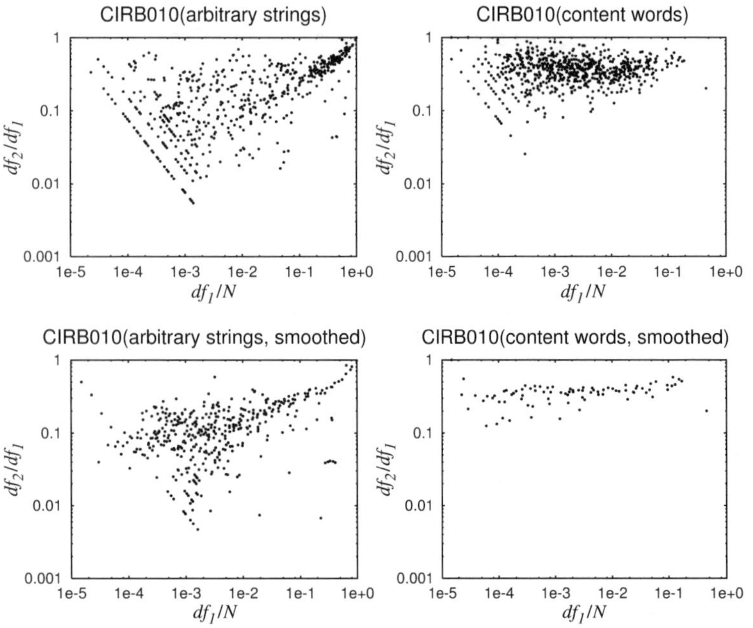

Figure 1. The adaptation ratio df_2/df_1 is larger for content words than meaningless substrings of Chinese characters. The bottom two panels are smoothed versions of the top two panels.

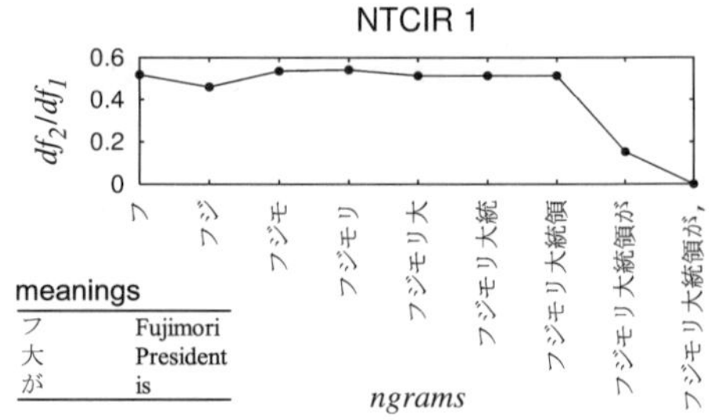

Figure 2. The adaptation ratio df_2/df_1 drops rapidly on the first character after the word boundary.

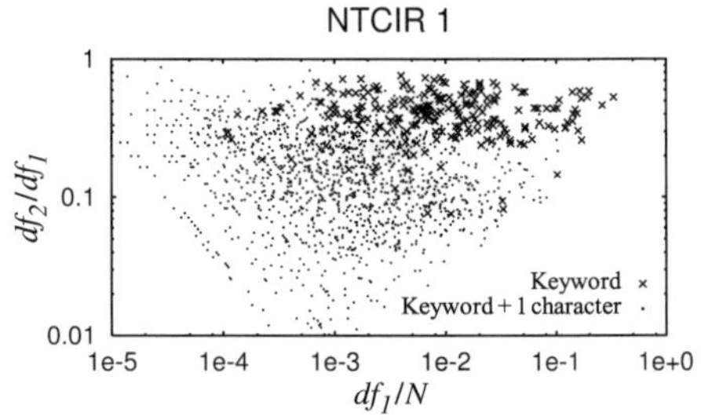

Figure 3. The adaptation ratio df_2/df_1 is larger for a content word than the string which consists of the content word and one character.

Table 1. Example of a query and selected indexing strings

query	日
selected	**日本語文** / の / **語り受け解析** / 手法について
meanings	About the **dependency-analysis** technique of a **Japanese sentence**

Table 2. Proposed method (SIS) outperforms both baselines (ALL & CHA) in terms of 11pt. average precision.

	strict			loose		
	ALL	CHA	SIS	ALL	CHA	SIS
TFIDF	0.2294	0.1928	0.2705	0.2356	0.2028	0.2830
ETW	0.2644	0.2110	0.2913	0.2723	0.2195	0.2999

Table 3. A number of WINs

	strict				loose			
	SIS	ALL	SIS	CHA	SIS	ALL	SIS	CHA
TFIDF	59	24	50	33	62	21	51	32
ETW	50	33	50	33	52	31	51	32

$$P(X \geq m) = 0.5\int_0^{0.5} \sum_m^n C_m^n p^m (1-p)^{n-m} dp \leq \sum_m^n C_m^n (0.5)^n \quad (4)$$

In the worst case scenario in which m equals 50, the value computed by equation (4) is 3.92×10^{-2}, which is lower than the significance level of 0.05. This infers that the hypothesis introduced above should be rejected. From another standpoint, the SIS has features for information retrieval systems. Therefore, we conclude that the proposed method can significantly improve the information retrieval performance level.

5. CONCLUSION

We proposed a dictionary-free statistical term selection method based on ideas borrowed from the adaptive language modeling literature. Adaptive language models are used in speech recognition to model the fact that words are very likely to be repeated, a fact that runs counter to standard bag-of-words models. The proposed method uses the adaptation ratio df_2/df_1, where df_k is a generalization of document frequency. The adaptation ratio is an estimate of the probability of repetition. It was previously reported that content words in English have larger adaptation ratios than function words. This paper found that content words in Japanese and Chinese have larger ratios than arbitrary substrings of Japanese and Chinese characters.

The proposed term selection method makes use of this observation in the scoring of candidate terms. The proposed term selection method finds the sequence of candidates with the largest adaptation ratio scores. Retrieval experiments demonstrated that the proposed term selection method outperforms two baseline conditions: (a) bigrams, and (b) ChaSen [4], a dictionary-based method. The proposed method is based on collection statistics, and is therefore better positioned to cope with the unknown word problem than dictionary-based methods. It is also ideally suited to take advantage of the fact that the choice of terms depends on the collection.

6. REFERENCES

[1] Kenneth W. Church (2000), Empirical Estimates of Adaptation: The chance of Two Noriegas is closer to $p/2$ than p^2, *Coling*, pp. 173--179.

[2] NTCIR Project, http://research.nii.ac.jp/ntcir/

[3] Kyoji Umemura and Kenneth W. Church (2000), Empirical Term Weighting and Expansion Frequency, *Workshop SIGDAT*, pp. 117--123.

[4] Yuji Matsumoto, Akira Kitauchi, Tatsuo Yamashita, Yoshitaka Hirano, Osamu Imaichi, and Tomoaki Imamura (1997), Japanese Morphological analysis System ChaSen Manual, NAIST Technical Report NAIST-IS-TR97007, http://cactus.aist-nara.ac.jp/lab/nlt/chasen.html

Error Correction in a Chinese OCR Test Collection

Yuen-Hsien Tseng
Dept. of Library & Information Science,
Fu Jen Catholic University
Taipei, Taiwan, R.O.C. 242

tseng@blue.lins.fju.edu.tw

ABSTRACT
This article proposes a technique for correcting Chinese OCR errors to support retrieval of scanned documents. The technique uses a completely automatic technique (no manually constructed lexicons or confusion resources) to identify both keywords and confusable terms. Improved retrieval effectiveness on a single term query experiment is demonstrated.

Categories and Subject Descriptors
H.3.3 [**INFORMATION STORAGE AND RETRIEVAL**]: Information Search and Retrieval – *clustering*; I.7.5 [**DOCUMENT AND TEXT PROCESSING**]: Document Capture –*Optical character recognition (OCR)*;

General Terms
Algorithms, Documentation, Performance, Languages.

Keywords
Error correction, term clustering, Chinese, confusing pair.

1. INTRODUCTION
Optical Character Recognition (OCR) systems provide a low-cost approach to access retrospective printed documents. However, even the best OCR systems may inevitably produce recognition errors. The techniques that could prevent retrieval effectiveness from being severely degraded by such errors are in great demand.

One might use various retrieval techniques such as n-gram indexing to alleviate the problem of OCR errors [1]. A complementary approach would be to correct the errors before or during the search process. Although OCR systems often have incorporated a word correction process in the final recognition stage, retrieval systems always build a collection-specific word index that might further help correct more possible errors.

Taghva et al had proposed an error-correction method for English [2]. The method first divides index words into *centroids* and *misspellings* based on a dictionary. The misspellings are then clustered around centroids based on similarity measured by approximate string matching. Finally, words in multiple clusters are resolved by their centroids' term frequencies or by a confusion table having information about the errors likely to be made during the OCR process. Comparing to no error correction, the automatic method was able to reduce percentage of missed documents from 2.4% to 1.3% using a Boolean search system.

SIGIR '02, August 11-15, 2002, Tampere, Finland.
ACM 1-58113-561-0/02/0008.

2. CHINESE OCR ERROR CORRECTION
For languages like Chinese, automatic error correction seems much more difficult. Because there is no delimiter between written Chinese words, identifying a correct word automatically is itself a problem, let alone identifying words with characters in error. But if the same error repeats, which often occurs in real-world OCR processes, one can use such information to extract words and their corrupted counterparts as well. Terms like these can then be clustered for correction. Figure 1 shows the proposed algorithm to correct OCR errors for Chinese text.

Step 1:
- Extract maximally repeated patterns as terms from each document, using the algorithm described in [3].

Step 2:
- Collect only those terms with 3 characters or more.
- For each pair of such terms of the same length, compare their constituent characters.
- If two terms only differ in one character, these 2 terms are clustered together with the term having higher document frequency considered as the correct term and the other the erroneous one.
- The two characters that differentiate these 2 terms are reported as a confusing pair and its occurrence is accumulated.

Step 3:
- The confusing pairs are sorted according to their occurrences in descending order.

Figure 1. The OCR error correction algorithm.

By observing that keywords or key-phrases often repeat in texts, an algorithm was proposed to extract maximally repeated strings as keywords without using any human-maintained resources such as dictionaries or corpora [3]. By maximally, it means that either the repeated strings are the longest or have highest term frequency. Surely there are illegal terms that might be extracted as well. But after some simple stop word filtering, the algorithm can achieve more than 84% word accuracy.

In Step 1 one may alternatively use a dictionary to match the document strings to find clean words. Meanwhile approximate string matching can be applied to identify possible corrupted terms. However, the set of Chinese words is open-ended. In a recent experiment [4], 33% keywords extracted by Tseng's algorithm from Chinese news articles are unregistered in a dictionary of 123,226 words. Therefore, although the use of dictionaries may improve word correction capability, we do not use this vocabulary knowledge in this work to see how well we can achieve using only automatic methods.

Next step is to identify correct terms and their corresponding erroneous ones. In printed Chinese documents, each character takes up almost the same width and length. Thus deletion or insertion errors likely to happen in English OCR texts are almost impossible in Chinese OCR texts. This allows us to compare only those words of the same length to identify the source of errors. Since very short words differing in one character may still be two individual correct words, we compare only those words with 3 characters or more to find one-character error patterns.

Once a confusion character pair is found, we may use a confusion table like that in Taghva's work to determine whether it is a real OCR error or an incorrect pair. We have thus asked the OCR software company from whose software our texts were converted to provide us a confusion table. The table has 4720 confusion pairs. But our experiments showed that many confusion pairs that are not in the table are found by our algorithm, showing that many recognition errors are far beyond the correction capability of the OCR software. Thus we do not rely on the provided confusion table. Instead, we use a simple heuristic rule to determine whether a term is correct or not: the one that has higher document frequency is considered as correct, the other is not.

3. EXPERIMENT

The above algorithm was applied to a Chinese OCR test collection. The collection consists of 8,438 scanned clippings collected from newspaper articles between 1950 and 1976 from China, Taiwan and Hong Kong in a mix of traditional and simplified Chinese. A commercial OCR system was used to produce digital texts, with an estimated character accuracy of 69%. Exhaustive relevance assessment was performed by 3 judges over the entire collection for 30 Chinese query topics (in a format similar to the TREC topics) collected from various journal articles published at about the same time as the news stories.

Since incorrect terms due to OCR errors lead to vocabulary mismatch and in turn may finally lead to document miss during document retrieval, the recall capability of single-term queries is evaluated in a Boolean retrieval environment. To prepare the query terms, we segmented the texts from all the fields of the 30 queries using the "correct" (higher frequency) term in each of the term pairs obtained from the algorithm. This collects 20 single-term queries. Since the source of these queries comes from the test collection's query topics, the choice of the single-term queries should reflect no bias in our testing.

Figure 2 shows two query terms and other information. Column 1 (separated by semicolon) lists the queries: "Sino-Japanese Relations" and "Liberating Taiwan". Column 2 is their document frequencies. Column 3 lists all those terms that differ in only one character with the query terms. Column 4 is these terms' document frequencies. Column 5 and 6 lists the corresponding confusion pairs. Column 7 lists the number of times that the confusion pair occurs in all term pairs. Column 8 is the number of documents that contain the erroneous term but not the query term. Column 9 is the sum of column 8 for the same query term. This sum shows the possible number of documents that the query term will miss if it is used in a Boolean search environment.

In Figure 2, the term associated with the first query in row 1 means "Sino-Russian Relations". The term in row 2 is "Sino-Czech Relations". These two terms are incorrectly clustered. The term in row 3 is correctly clustered with the query term. (Despite its confusing character pair occurs only once in all term pairs.) The first query term retrieve 5 documents. If the 3 corresponding terms are used as queries, more 6 documents return, although only 1 of them is the desired (contributed by the term in row 3). Similarly, the second query retrieves 138 documents, while its erroneous counterparts (in the third column from row 4 to12) together retrieve other 76 desired documents. In total, the 20 single-term queries retrieve 3283 documents. Their counterparts retrieve 572 extra desired documents and 164 undesired ones. This amounts to an improvement in gross micro-average recall by 572/(572+3238)=15.01% and a reduction in micro-average precision by 164/(164+572+3238)= 4.13%. Compared to no error correction at all, these results are encouraging.

1.	中日关系	5	中苏关系	3	日	苏	7	3	6
2.	中日关系	5	中捷关系	2	日	捷	3	2	6
3.	中日关系	5	中日关东	2	系	东	1	1	6
4.	解放台湾	138	解放台湛	6	湾	湛	3	6	76
5.	解放台湾	138	解放台沿	5	湾	沿	2	5	76
6.	解放台湾	138	解放台泻	1	湾	泻	2	1	76
7.	解放台湾	138	解放台海	9	湾	海	2	9	76
8.	解放台湾	138	解放台褐	1	湾	褐	1	1	76
9.	解放台湾	138	解放台渴	28	湾	渴	4	27	76
10.	解放台湾	138	解放台溜	24	湾	溜	3	24	76
11.	解放台湾	138	解放台门	2	湾	门	2	2	76
12.	解放台湾	138	解放台沁	2	湾	沁	1	1	76

Figure 2. Two query terms and their corresponding term pairs.

4. CONCLUSIONS

A fully automatic error correction method is proposed for use in Chinese OCR text retrieval. A direct application of this technique would be term suggestion in an interactive retrieval environment. Another application is to strengthen the recognition capability of OCR techniques. The proposed method does not rely on any human-maintained resources. Thus it can be readily applied to other collections of various domains without efforts. This also means that the effectiveness of the automatic approach can likely be further improved if domain-specific vocabulary knowledge is used. Future work will explore this direction to automatically reduce false drops due to incorrect clustering.

5. ACKNOWLEDGMENTS

This work is support in part by NSC 90-2413-H-030-004-.

6. REFERENCES

[1] Yuen-Hsien Tseng, "Automatic Cataloguing and Searching for Retrospective Data by Use of OCR Text", JASIST, Vol. 52, No. 5, 2001, pp. 378-390.

[2] K. Taghva, J. Borsack, A. Condit, S. Erva, "The Effects of Noisy Data on Text Retrieval," JASIS, Vo.45. No. 1, 1994, pp.50-58.

[3] Yuen-Hsien Tseng, "Content-Based Retrieval for Music Collections," Proceedings of ACM SIGIR '99, Aug. 15-19, Berkeley, U.S.A., 1999, pp.176-182.

[4] Yuen-Hsien Tseng, "Automatic Thesaurus Generation for Chinese Documents", to appear in JASIST, 2003.

User Interface Effects in Past Batch Versus User Experiments

Andrew Turpin
Curtin University of Technology
Perth, Australia
andrew@cs.curtin.edu.au

William Hersh
Oregon Health & Sciences University
Portland, OR USA
hersh@ohsu.edu

Categories and Subject Descriptors

H.3.4 [**Information Search and Retrieval**]: performance evaluation

General Terms

Algorithms, Performance

1. INTRODUCTION

In the last two SIGIR conferences we presented evidence that users perform equally well with search engines running a basic Cosine weighting scheme, or a state-of-the-art Okapi based ranking system [2, 3]. However, the Okapi based system clearly outperforms the basic system on the standard precision and recall measures that are commonly used to compare IR systems in forums such as TREC [1] and SIGIR. These observations call into question the appropriateness of relying on measurements of the performance of IR systems obtained in a batch setting using the Cranfield style methodology.

In both of our experiments the Okapi based system found more relevant documents than the basic system, and ranked them higher in the list of results presented to the users. Users of the Okapi based systems, however, ignored the "extra" relevant documents, hence on average users of either system performed equally on any given query.

It is not clear why the users tended to ignore the extra relevant documents that were presented with the Okapi based systems. One possible reason is that our user interface discouraged users from selecting these documents. The interface was a web-browser style window broken into three panes. The top pane allowed entry of the query and contained a "Search" button which, once clicked, would cause a list of 50 document titles as returned by the underlying search engine to be presented in the bottom-left pane. The users could click on these document titles and have the full document displayed in the bottom-right pane.

Initial user judgments, therefore, were made on the document title as it appeared in the document collection. Presumably if a title was obscure or seemingly unrelated to the user's information need, they would not even open the full text of the document. If a title seemed to be on-topic, then the users proceeded to browse the full text of the document. Often these document titles do not reflect information that is contained in the document that is relevant to the query.

It is reasonable to suspect, therefore, that many of the relevant documents that were presented to users were overlooked because their titles did not appear relevant to the user's information need. This poster aims to prove or disprove the following two conjectures:

Conjecture 1–Obscurity. The Okapi based systems in both experiments were more likely than the baseline system to have relevant documents with irrelevant titles high in the ranked list of documents returned to the user.

Conjecture 2–Distraction. The Okapi based systems in both experiments were more likely than the baseline system to have irrelevant documents with relevant titles high in the ranked list of documents returned to the user.

If either conjecture holds, then the poor performance of the Okapi based systems can be (partially at least) attributed to the user interface employed in the experiments. Either the extra relevant documents were hidden behind obscure titles (Conjecture 1), and so users never examined the full document text for relevant information; or relevant documents were hidden amongst irrelevant documents with relevant titles (Conjecture 2), and so the user spent time reading the full text of irrelevant documents.

2. JUDGING TITLES

In order to gauge the effect of title relevance on the performance of the users, our first step was to get a set of document titles judged for relevance against the topics used in the experiments. To limit the judging task to something manageable, we had judged all titles that occurred in one of the top 10 ranking positions for all queries issued related to each topic. Each title was judged for relevance by two people: a graduate level student and a postdoctoral fellow, both with searching experience. For each title the judges were instructed to make the decision: "Would you read a document with this title in order to find an answer to the query? Do not spend more than a few seconds on each title."

Table 1 shows the number of titles for each topic (6 topics in the TREC-8 experiment and 8 topics in the TREC-9

SIGIR'02, August 11-15, 2002, Tampere, Finland.
ACM 1-58113-561-0/02/0008.

Table 1: Level of agreement between judges

Topic	Number of titles	Disagree	Agree Relevant	Agree irrelevant
TREC-8				
408i	208	11%	28%	61%
414i	133	25%	29%	46%
428i	228	18%	4%	78%
431i	78	15%	22%	63%
438i	194	16%	18%	66%
446i	358	13%	16%	71%
Total	1199			
TREC-9				
1i	102	21%	16%	64%
2i	292	5%	2%	93%
3i	130	12%	4%	85%
4i	85	25%	40%	35%
5i	114	11%	2%	87%
6i	42	7%	17%	76%
7i	74	16%	5%	79%
8i	281	13%	3%	84%
Total	1120			

experiment) and the level of agreement between the judges. As may be expected, the level of disagreement was high in some cases, reflecting the difficulty of making a definitive judgment of relevance on only a few words in a document title. Accordingly, we defined a document title to be relevant to a topic if at least one of the judges stated that it was relevant.

Table 2: Proportion of top 10 documents returned to users with misleading titles

	Relevant documents with irrelevant titles		Irrelevant documents with relevant titles	
	Baseline	Okapi	Baseline	Okapi
TREC-8				
408i	19%	19%	33%	27%
414i	11%	17%	52%	57%
428i	36%	35%	26%	15%
431i	17%	13%	10%	50%
438i	9%	0%	17%	37%
446i	17%	11%	22%	22%
mean	18%	16%	27%	35%
p-value		0.341		0.350
TREC-9				
1i	60%	67%	30%	40%
2i	0%	60%	6%	9%
3i	80%	90%	16%	25%
4i	0%	17%	63%	48%
5i	50%	50%	8%	16%
6i	50%	33%	33%	25%
7i	50%	69%	17%	30%
8i	—	—	16%	11%
mean	46%	51%	25%	26%
p-value		0.175		0.473

3. DOCUMENT RELEVANCE VERSUS TITLE RELEVANCE

Table 2 shows the proportion of relevant documents that were found to have irrelevant titles according to our definition in the previous section, and the proportion of irrelevant documents that have relevant titles for each topic-system pair. Table 3 shows the absolute numbers of relevant and irrelevant documents that were used to calculate these proportions. In this case document relevance was as determined by the NIST assessors as part of the TREC project. For Experiment 1 a document was relevant if it contained at least one instance. To support Conjecture 1–that Okapi returned more relevant documents with irrelevant titles–we would expect a significant difference between columns 2 and 3 of Table 2. A paired t-test shows there is no such difference for either experiment, with the p-values reported in the table. Similarly, if Conjecture 2 holds we would expect a significant difference between columns 4 and 5 of the table, but again a paired t-test reveals no difference.

Table 3: Number of relevant and irrelevant documents returned in one of the top 10 positions for any user query

	Number of relevant documents		Number of irrelevant documents	
	Baseline	Okapi	Baseline	Okapi
TREC-8				
408i	27	47	73	98
414i	9	12	44	95
428i	11	17	101	118
431i	18	23	48	2
438i	11	25	120	51
446i	30	27	199	142
TREC-9				
1i	5	6	61	47
2i	1	5	168	149
3i	5	10	77	61
4i	14	23	35	27
5i	4	6	73	43
6i	2	3	21	32
7i	6	16	48	27
8i	0	9	142	150

4. USER'S CHOICES

Looking at all the top 10 documents returned to the users in the previous section found no support for either of our conjectures. An alternate approach is to examine the actual relevant documents that users did not select in the top 10 for further examination, rather than all relevant documents returned in the top 10. In this case we can look at the number of relevant documents in the top 10 "missed" by a user in any particular query for each topic-system pair. Similarly we can examine the number of irrelevant documents "opened" by the users that have relevant titles. When this analysis is performed, we again see no statistical difference between either system (see poster for details).

5. CONCLUSION

There is no statistically significant evidence to support either conjecture. We conclude, therefore, that our user interface that presented titles to the users did not bias performance towards one of the systems in either of our previous experiments.

6. REFERENCES

[1] D. Harman. Overview of the Second Text Retrieval Conference (TREC-2). Info Proc & Man, 1995.

[2] W. Hersh, et al. Do batch and user evaluations give the same results. SIGIR2000, Athens, Greece.

[3] A. Turpin and W. Hersh. Why batch and user evaluations do not give the same results. SIGIR2001, New Orleans.

K-tree/forest: Efficient Indexes for Boolean Queries*

Rakesh M. Verma
Computer Science Department
University of Houston, Houston, Texas 77204
(713)743-3348/Fax:(713)743-3335
rmverma@cs.uh.edu

Sanjiv Behl
Computer Science Department
University of Houston, Houston, Texas 77204
(713)218-9420
sanbehl@yahoo.com

ABSTRACT

In Information Retrieval it is well-known that the complexity of processing boolean queries depends on the size of the intermediate results, which could be huge (and are typically on disk) even though the size of the final result may be quite small. In the case of inverted files the most time consuming operation is the merging or intersection of the list of occurrences [1]. We propose, the Keyword tree (K-tree) and forest, efficient structures to handle boolean queries in keyword-based information retrieval. Extensive simulations show that K-tree is orders-of-magnitude faster (i.e., far fewer I/O's) for boolean queries than the usual approach of merging the lists of occurrences and incurs only a small overhead for single keyword queries. The K-tree can be efficiently parallelized as well. The construction cost of K-tree is comparable to the cost of building inverted files.

Categories and Subject Descriptors

H.3.1 [Content Analysis and Indexing]: Indexing methods; H.3.3 [Information Search and Retrieval]: Search Process

General Terms

Algorithms, Performance, Experimentation

Keywords

Keyword tree, keyword-based retrieval, indexing, parallelization

1. INTRODUCTION

Boolean queries are frequent in information retrieval. However, not much effort seems to have been spent on developing efficient solutions to handle boolean queries. The usual approach to handle a simple boolean query such as: Alice and Bob, is to find the list of "documents" containing Alice and the corresponding list for Bob and then merge the two lists to calculate the final result. The intermediate results can be quite big in general (and are typically on disk) and the final result can be quite small in comparison, so that a lot of I/O (and CPU) overhead is involved in generating a small result. In this paper we propose efficient indexing structures, the Keyword tree and forest (K-tree/forest), to efficiently handle boolean queries. Extensive simulations show that K-tree is orders-of-magnitude faster for boolean queries than the usual approach of merging the lists of occurrences and is quite competitive with popular indexing structures for single keyword queries such as inverted files. The K-tree can be efficiently parallelized as well. The construction cost of K-tree is linear in the size of the collection just as for building inverted files/lists. The inverted file could be replaced by the K-tree since the K-tree is competitive for single keyword queries.

*Research supported in part by NSF grant CCR-9732186

SIGIR'02, August 11-15, 2002, Tampere, Finland.
ACM 1-58113-561-0/02/0008.

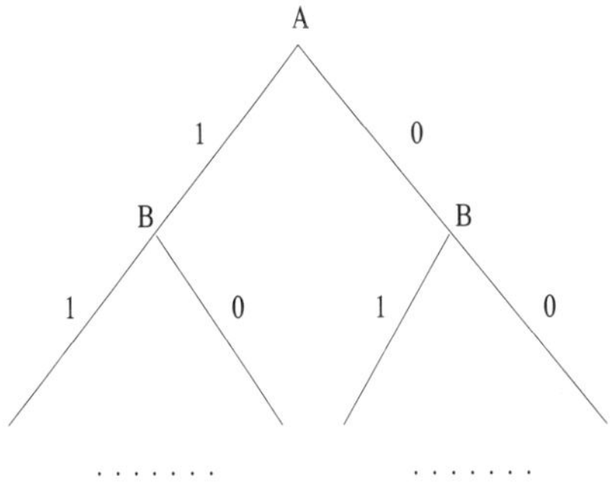

Figure 1. K-tree (Top two levels shown)

2. KEYWORD TREE

For convenience, we present the K-tree assuming that the entire set of keywords is known beforehand. Later, we outline an incremental construction procedure for the K-tree/forest. A total ordering is imposed on the keywords arbitrarily (e.g., lexicographic). Given a total ordering on the keywords, a K-tree is an ordered rooted binary tree where each internal node is labeled by a keyword, each leaf has a pointer to a list of documents (or document id's), and the two outgoing edges of a node labeled by keyword k are labeled by 1 or 0 representing that k is present or absent respectively in the documents accessible from the subtree rooted at this node. Moreover, the node labels for every path of the K-tree must respect the given ordering and each keyword appears exactly once on each path. For example, if keyword A is smaller than keyword B in the ordering, then a node labeled A cannot appear after a node labeled B on any path from the root (see Figure 1 for an illustration of the K-tree).

With the K-tree a boolean query A but B is processed by starting a traversal from the root with the rule that at nodes labeled A we just follow the 1-edge, at nodes labeled B we just follow the 0-edge, and at nodes labeled $k \notin \{A, B\}$ we follow both edges. This gives us a collection of lists from the leaves reached by the traversal, which is the final result without any further processing required. Note that the longer the boolean query (i.e. more keywords) specified by the user, the lesser the K-tree traversal required and also the fewer the lists retrieved.

3. EXPERIMENTS

To study the utility of the K-tree we implemented it using an array of pointers, where the bit pattern of the array index corresponds to the edge labels from the root to leaves. For example, the array index 5 has the bit pattern 101 representing the documents that contain the first and third keywords but not the second in the keyword ordering. We assume for now that the K-tree fits in main memory so no disk I/O's are required and that the lists (postings files) are on the disk. More on this assumption later. For comparison, we implemented inverted files with a binary search tree structure for the dictionary with each node labeled by a keyword and pointing to the postings file for that keyword. Again the dictionary was assumed to be in main memory and the postings files on disk.

We randomly chose more than 10 documents containing more than 100,000 words each and one document containing more than a million words, that were further subdivided into pages of 100 words each. The pages were stored in buckets of size 5 each. The number of keywords was varied from 10 to 19.

Results were obtained for both single-keyword queries, and boolean and/but queries involving two keywords. Each keyword was used for single-keyword queries and every possible pair of keywords was used for boolean queries, and the results were averaged. For the BST-based inverted files, the boolean query I/O time is equal to the sum of the I/O times for the individual keywords.

For lack of space, we omit the results for the 10 smaller documents, which are consistent with the results shown. Average number of I/O's are shown for the million word document and single keyword queries in Table 1, and boolean queries in Table 2.

BST-based inverted file	31.2632
K-tree (parallel)	25.3684
K-tree (sequential)	37.0526
K-tree (sequential no frag.)	31.2632

Table 1: Avg. I/Os for Single Keyword Query

BST-based inverted file	62.5263
K-tree (parallel)	0.578947
K-tree (sequential)	0.77193
K-tree (sequential no frag.)	0.614035

Table 2: Avg. I/Os for 2-Keyword Boolean Queries

4. DISCUSSION

As seen from the results, the K-tree significantly outperforms the BST-based inverted files for boolean queries and is quite competitive for single keyword queries. Experiments show that the fragmentation, i.e., wastage of buckets due to a list (postings file for a single keyword) being subdivided into several sub-lists in the K-tree, for both types of queries is quite small (fragmentation was between 6 and 9 bucket accesses for bucket sizes ranging from 5 to 1000 for single-keyword queries). Observe also that the average output size in buckets (I/O time) for boolean queries with just 2 keywords is already quite small.

However, the drawback of K-tree is that for a collection indexed on K keywords the size of the K-tree is 2^K, which is too big to fit in main memory for $K > 25$ and also an overkill since users almost never specify all the available keywords in a single query. Hence, we do not propose to build a single K-tree for the entire set of keywords, but a forest of K-tree's for a reasonable number of keywords between 2 and 20, say l. The forest corresponds to the C_l^K many size l subsets of K keywords. Each K-tree requires only an array of size 2^l. l is chosen to be such that $C_l^K \times 2^l \leq M$, where M represents the memory available. Currently $l = 2$ is feasible for up to 100,000 keywords, which is approximately 1/3 of the words in the English dictionary. $l = 3$ is feasible for up to 10,000 keywords. These small values of l are justifiable since a study of user queries in search engines on the Web found that most queries contain up to 4 or 5 keywords [2]. For an efficient K-forest, the leaves should contain lists of document id's only. K can be reduced by standard techniques such as stemming/stop word elimination, etc. Thus, the total space required is polynomial in K, which is smaller than the size of the collection. However, now the queries with more than l keywords will require merging of the lists obtained from the K-tree forest (binary merging technique can be used for efficiency). So there is a tradeoff between the space required by the K-tree structure and the I/O time for queries.

The K-tree is also efficiently parallelizable since the array locations corresponding to the don't-care keywords (the ones not in the query - for which both edges must be taken in the K-tree) can be accessed in parallel. Thus, the access cost for the K-tree structure is sped-up by the number of processors available yielding almost perfect parallelism. For the parallel case, the I/O time is equal to the length of the longest list divided by the bucketsize assuming each list is on a separate disk.

We now eliminate the assumption about the keywords being known in advance. The ordering on the keywords can be constructed incrementally as they are inserted into a global trie structure for all the documents (see [1]), and each document (or its id) can be appended into the K-tree (or forest) lists using the current set of keywords found in the document. As new keywords are identified, the forest itself grows. Once the entire document has been scanned we know the keywords it does not contain and the processing for this document can be completed, i.e. appending it or its id into the remaining lists.

5. REFERENCES

[1] R. Baeza-Yates and B. Ribeiro-Neto. Modern Information Retrieval. Addison-Wesley, 1999.

[2] Bruce Croft. The future of web search. In Invited Keynote Address at the 25th Australasian Computer Science Conference, Melbourne, Australia, 2002.

Example-Based Phrase Translation in Chinese-English CLIR

Bin Wang Xueqi Cheng and Shuo Bai
Institute of Computing Technology, Chinese Academy of Sciences
No. 6, Kexueyuan South Road, Zhongguanchun
Beijing 100080 China
+86 010 62587953
{Wangbin,cxq,bai}@ict.ac.cn

ABSTRACT

This paper proposes an example-based phrase translation method in a Chinese to English cross-language information retrieval (CLIR) system. The method can generate much more accurate query translations than dictionary-based and common MT-based methods, and then improves the retrieval performance of our CLIR system.

Categories and Subject Descriptors

H.3.3 [**Information Storage and Retrieval**]: Information Search and Retrieval – *query formulation.*

General Terms

Design, Experimentation.

Keywords

CLIR, Example-Based, Phrase Translation.

1. INTRODUCTION

CLIR is to retrieve documents in one language (target language) providing queries in another language (source language). Most present CLIR methods fall into three categories: dictionary-based, MT-based and corpus-based methods[1]. Although different resources or techniques are used, all these methods try to generate the best target queries.

Example-based method is one of the main approaches used in machine translation (MT) field. In EBMT, old translated pairs are aligned and stored in the example base (EB), and when translating a new object, the most similar example in the EB will be selected to generate the translation. Compared with the other methods used in MT, example-based method can generate much better translation results for the objects that have most similar examples in the EB. However, the similarity between sentences is very difficult to define and compute; this greatly degrades the usability of the method. On the contrary, the similarity computation between phrases seems simpler. As we know, in real world, IR queries are often one to three words long and most of them are phrases. Therefore, when translating these queries, we use example-based method that may generate accurate translations.

SIGIR'02, August 11-15, 2002, Tampere, Finland.
ACM 1-58113-561-0/02/0008. …$5.00.

2. ALIGNMENT

In order to be used in later translation, all translated phrases are aligned at the word level at first[2].

Supposing the Chinese phrase C is $C_1C_2...C_m$, the corresponding English phrase E is $E_1E_2...E_n$, where each C_i ($1 \leqslant i \leqslant m$) or E_j ($1 \leqslant j \leqslant n$) is a word. Four methods are combined[2] to align a Chinese word with an English word. Other alignment modes such as 1-*t*, *s*-*t*, s-0, 0-*t* ($s,t>1$)are also considered in our system.

(1) Alignment based on dictionary

For each word in Chinese or English phrase, if one of its translations in the C-E or E-C dictionary appears in the other phrase, the word and its translation can be aligned with each other.

(2) Alignment based on location information

In alignment based on dictionary, one word may have more than one alignment word. This kind of ambiguities can be solved via location(word order) information. The candidate alignment word that has smallest *LocDist* will be selected as the alignment result. *LocDist* between location *i* in source phrase and location *j* in target phrase is defined as:

$$LocDist(i,j)=min(|Slope_L-1|,|Slope_R-1|)$$

Where $Slope_L=(j-j_L)/(i-i_L)$, $Slope_R=(j-j_R)/(i-i_R)$, (i_L,j_L) is the closest reliable alignment on the left of *i*, and (i_R,j_R) is the closest reliable alignment on the right of *i*.

(3) Alignment based on semantic distance

Because of the limited coverage of bilingual dictionaries, we try to align words based on their semantic similarity. In our system, a Chinese thesaurus named *CILIN*[3] and an English-Chinese dictionary is used to define the semantic distance between Chinese and English words. *CILIN's* categories can be represented as a hierarchical tree as follows:

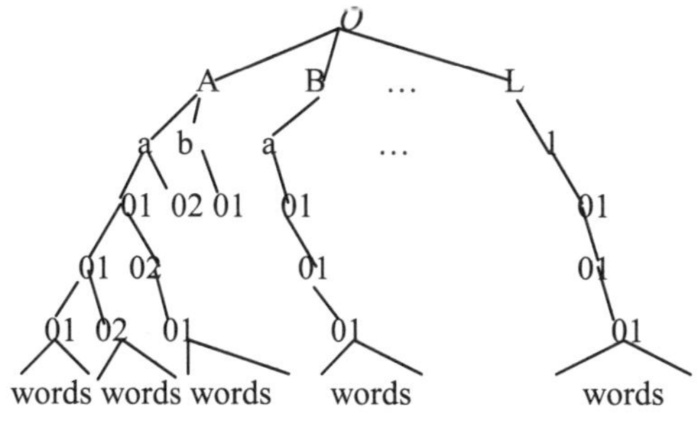

Figure 1. *CILIN's* categories and codes.

The semantic distance between two Chinese words can be defined as the reciprocal of the shortest path length between the two words within the above tree. And the semantic distance between a Chinese word and an English word is defined as the minimal distance between the Chinese word and all the Chinese translation words of the English word in the English-Chinese dictionary.

(4) Alignment based on co-occurrence frequency

The word pair co-occurrence frequency information can be also used to align words throughout the example base collection. A word pair with high co-occurrence frequency can be marked as an alignment.

The above alignment also makes a useful statistics-based bilingual dictionary for later use.

3. QUERY TRANSLATION

To find the most similar example to the input Chinese query phase in the EB can be also regarded as an IR process. So some IR techniques are used here.

3.1 Inverted Index

Inverted file data structure is used here to store the example base. Each example can be represented by its words. The word order and word count information within a phrase are also recorded in the posting files. For instance, the phrase "模式识别" should be represent as "模式 1 2" and "识别 2 2" in the corresponding posting files. To speed up the retrieval process, the index file is organized using a hashing function.

3.2 Phrase Matching

When a new phrase is submitted to the example base, the most similar phrase will be selected to generate the translation.

First, the words and word counts in the new phrase are used to picked out those candidate phrases, then the similarity between the new phrase and each candidate phrase is computed as follows:

$$dis(C', C) = \prod_{i=1}^{m} dis(C_i', C_i)$$

Where $dis(C_i', C_i)$ is the semantic distance between C_i' and C that can be computed as in section 2. Our goal is to get the C that minimizes the above distance. At the same time, the minimal distance must be lower than a preset threshold θ.

Sometimes, the new phrase may be longer than all the phrases in the example base, or we cannot find a suitable phrase whose similarity is above θ. Then we can segment the phrase into smaller chunks to use the above formula recursively. The semantics of the last word within a phrase is used to represent the semantics of the whole phrase.

3.3 Phrase Translation

In EBMT, the translation process is very simple. Each translation pair can be viewed as a translation template and the target phrase can be used to generate the translation result through a few words substituting some words. For example, the phrase "文本检索"can be translated into "text retrieval" via translation pair "情报[1] 检索[2]/information retrieval". What we should do is to pick out the best translation of "文本" in the C-E dictionary and put it in the corresponding location of the target phrase. While translating, part-of-speech information should also be considered.

4. EXPERIMENTAL RESULTS

In our experiments, we have about 700,000 phrase pairs that are mostly science and technology terms, most of them are collected from different on-line dictionaries or bilingual corpora. About 69% of them are two-word or three-word phrases. At first, we segment all the Chinese phrases into words, and then we align them with corresponding English phrases. Necessary manual work is also done to correct the misaligned results.

100 multi-word Chinese query phrases are selected from a WEB IR log file. 77 of them are 2-word phrases, 15 are 3-word phrases, and the others are more than 3 words long.

Besides the above phrase translation method, we also use another two methods in our Chinese-English CLIR system: CEMT-based method and dictionary-based method. In CEMT-based method, we use a CEMT system named *TransEasy*[4] to translate the queries into English. In dictionary-based method, we use the statistics-based dictionary to map the queries into English via dictionary lookup.

Out of the 100 queries, our method generates 78 completely correct translation results($\theta = 0.01$), while the num for CEMT-based method and dictionary-based method are respectively 47 and 53. 14 translation results using our method are partially correct and the others cannot be translated because of the unknown words. These results confirm our expectation.

5. CONCLUSIONS

Most IR queries are quite short, i.e., they are most words or phrases. Therefore the main task in CLIR is not translating sentences but translating phrases. Example-based method can provide very good translation results but the similarity computation between sentences is quite complex. Based on the above consideration, we apply example-based query phrase translation in our Chinese-English CLIR system, and the experiments achieve good results.

In our near future, we will apply a chunk recognizer to process more than one phrase long queries and we may cluster all the examples to reduce the phrase search time.

6. REFERENCES

[1] Yiming Yang, Jaime G. Carbonell, Ralf D. Brown, Robert E. Frederking,. Translingual Information Retrieval : Learning from Bilingual Corpora. AI Journal special issue: Best of IJCAI-97.

[2] Bin Wang, Qun Liu, Xiang Zhang, Word Alignment on Chinese-English Bilingual Corpora, in Proceedings of JSCL-99 (Beijing, November 1999), 123-128.

[3] Mei, Jia-Ju, Yi-Ming Zhu, Yun-Qi Gao, Hong-Xiang Yin, Tongyici CiLin (Chinese Synonym Forest), Shanghai Press of Lexicon and Books, 1983 (In Chinese).

[4] Qun Liu, ShiWen Yu, *TransEasy*: A Chinese-English MT system Based on Hybrid Approach, in Proceedings of AMTA'98 (Langhorne, PA. USA, October 1998), 514-517

Probabilistic Multimedia Retrieval

Thijs Westerveld
TKI, Dept. of Computer Science, University of Twente
PO Box 217, 7500 AE Enschede, The Netherlands
westerve@cs.utwente.nl

ABSTRACT

We present a framework in which probabilistic models for textual and visual information retrieval can be integrated seamlessly. The framework facilitates searching for imagery using textual descriptions and visual examples simultaneously. The underlying Language Models for text and Gaussian Mixture Models for images have proven successful in various retrieval tasks.

Categories and Subject Descriptors

H.3.3 [**Information Storage and Retrieval**]: Information Search and Retrieval

General Terms

Design

Keywords

Multimedia Retrieval, Mixture Models, Language Models

1. INTRODUCTION

Basically, two ways of specifying a visual information need exist: *textual*, using words to describe the images or video's one is after, or *visual*, presenting an example of what one's looking for (either as a sketch or as a similar image). In parallel, there exist two techniques for disclosing collections of visual material: by indexing collateral texts (e.g. captions, subtitles or manual annotations) using standard text retrieval techniques, or by extracting visual features from the documents and measuring visual similarity between them using the query by example paradigm. Rarely, the two approaches are combined. Of course, systems that offer *both* search modalities exist and textual search *is* often used to solve the page zero problem (how to find a first set of images to start browsing from?), but few have truly integrated the different modalities to allow for search on textual and visual features simultaneously (for a noteable exception cf. [7, 1]). This document presents a probabilistic model in which visual and textual indexing are integrated seamlessly.

2. PROBABILISTIC RETRIEVAL MODEL

In a probabilistic retrieval setting, the goal is to find the document D^* with highest probability given a query Q:

$$D^* = \text{argmax}_i\ P(D_i|Q) = \text{argmax}_i\ \frac{P(Q|D_i)P(D_i)}{P(Q)} \quad (1)$$

Usually, (1) is used as a scoring function and a ranked list is returned rather than the one most probable document.

SIGIR'02, August 11-15, 2002, Tampere, Finland.
ACM 1-58113-561-0/02/0008.

If we assume that all documents have equal prior probability, (1) reduces to the maximum likelihood criterion, which is approximated by the minimum KL-divergence between query model and document model: $D^* = \text{argmin}_i\ KL[P_q(\mathbf{x})||P_i(\mathbf{x})]$.

$$KL[P_q(\mathbf{x})||P_i(\mathbf{x})] = \int P(\mathbf{x}|D_q) log \frac{P(\mathbf{x}|D_q)}{P(\mathbf{x}|D_i)} d\mathbf{x}$$

$$= \int P(\mathbf{x}|D_q) log P(\mathbf{x}|D_q) d\mathbf{x} - \int P(\mathbf{x}|D_q) log P(\mathbf{x}|D_i) d\mathbf{x},$$

where $\mathbf{x}$ are feature vectors describing the documents.

The first integral is independent of D_i and can be ignored, thus

$$D^* = \text{argmax}_i \int P(\mathbf{x}|D_q) log P(\mathbf{x}|D_i) d\mathbf{x} \quad (2)$$

Now suppose query and document models generate a mixture of textual features $\mathbf{x}_t$ and visual features $\mathbf{x}_v$

$$P(\mathbf{x}|D_i)) = P(\mathbf{x}_t|D_i)P(t) + P(\mathbf{x}_v|D_i)P(v)^1.$$

We can then integrate over these different featuresets sepearately and arrive at the following ranking formula for multimodal retrieval [8].

$$D^* = \text{argmax}_i\ [P(t) \int_{\mathbf{x}_t} P(\mathbf{x}_t|D_q) log P(\mathbf{x}_t|D_i) d\mathbf{x}_t + P(v) \int_{\mathbf{x}_v} P(\mathbf{x}_v|D_q) log P(\mathbf{x}_v|D_i) d\mathbf{x}_v] \quad (3)$$

2.1 Text Model

To describe the probability distributions of the textual terms, we take a language modelling approach to information retrieval [3]. Such a model operates on discrete signals (i.e. words), thus we can replace the integral from (3) by a sum. Moreover, the query model D_q is usually nothing more than the empirical distribution of the query[2], therefore we only need to sum over the words in the query. The document model is usually taken to be a mixture of foreground ($P(x_{t,j}|D_i)$) and background ($P(x_{t,j})$) probabilities for the query terms $x_{t,j}$, interpolated using mixing parameter λ (cf. section 3.1). If our textual query consists of N terms $\mathbf{x}_t = (x_{t,1}, x_{t,2}, \ldots, x_{t,N})$ then the textual part of our ranking formula is the following.

$$D_t^* = \text{argmax}_i \frac{1}{N} \sum_{j=1}^{N} log[\lambda P(x_{t,j}|D_i) + (1-\lambda)P(x_{t,j})] \quad (4)$$

[1] $P(t)$ and $P(v)$ are the prior probabilities of drawing respectively textual or visual features from a document; assumed uniform accross documents.

[2] For alternative query models cf. [4]

2.2 Image Model

We use a Gaussian Mixture Model for describing both query and document densities (cf [6]).

$$P(\mathbf{x}_v|D_i) = \sum_{c=1}^{C} P(\omega_{i,c})\, \mathcal{G}(\mathbf{x}_v, \mu_{i,c}, \mathbf{\Sigma}_{i,c}),$$

where C is the number of components in the mixture model, $\omega_{i,c}$ is component c of document model D_i and $\mathcal{G}(\mathbf{x}, \mu, \mathbf{\Sigma})$ is the Gaussian density with mean vector μ and co-variance matrix $\mathbf{\Sigma}$:

$$\mathcal{G}(\mathbf{x}, \mu, \mathbf{\Sigma}) = \frac{1}{\sqrt{(2\pi)^n|\mathbf{\Sigma}|}} e^{-\frac{1}{2}\|\mathbf{x}-\mu\|_{\mathbf{\Sigma}}}, \quad (5)$$

$$\text{where } |\mathbf{x}-\mu\|_{\mathbf{\Sigma}} = (\mathbf{x}-\mu)^T\mathbf{\Sigma}^{-1}(\mathbf{x}-\mu)$$

and n is the length of the feature vector $\mathbf{x}$.

There is no closed-form solution for the Kullback-Leibler divergence for a mixture of Gaussian densities. However, Vasconcelos [6] derives an approximation, the asymptotic likelihood approximation (ALA).

$$- KL[P_q(\mathbf{x}_v)||P_i(\mathbf{x}_v)] \propto \int_{\mathbf{x}_v} P(\mathbf{x}_v|D_q)\, logP(\mathbf{x}_v|D_i) d\mathbf{x}_v$$

$$\approx ALA[P_q(\mathbf{x}_v)||P_i(\mathbf{x}_v)] = \sum_c P(\omega_{q,c}) \cdot \{\ log\ P(\omega_{i,\alpha(c)}) +$$

$$+\, log\ \mathcal{G}(\mu_{q,c}, \mu_{i,\alpha(c)}, \mathbf{\Sigma}_{i,\alpha(c)}) - \frac{1}{2} trace[\mathbf{\Sigma}_{i,\alpha(c)}^{-1}\mathbf{\Sigma}_{q,c}]\ \}, \quad (6)$$

$$\alpha(c) = k \Leftrightarrow \|\mu_{q,c} - \mu_{i,k}\|_{\mathbf{\Sigma}_{i,k}} < \|\mu_{q,c} - \mu_{i,l}\|_{\mathbf{\Sigma}_{i,l}} \forall l \neq k$$

Subscripts indicate documents and components (e.g. $\mu_{i,c}$ is the mean for component c of document i). The main assumption behind the ALA is that the Gaussians for the components within an image model have small overlap. In a high dimensional feature space, this assumption is valid. Our visual ranking formula is

$$D_v^* = \text{argmax}_i ALA[P_q(\mathbf{x}_v)||P_i(\mathbf{x}_v)] \quad (7)$$

3. PARAMETER ESTIMATION

This section shows how we calculate the parameters to be used in the model outlined in the previous section.

3.1 Text Parameters

The features in the textual part of our model are simply the words themselves. For the textual part of our retrieval function (4), we only need to estimate foreground ($P(x_{t,j}|D_i)$) and background ($P(x_{t,j})$) probabilities. Both measures are estimated in the standard way, by taking the term frequency and document frequency respectively [3]. The optimal value for the mixing parameter λ can be estimated by evaluating retrieval performance for a range of different values on a test collection.

3.2 Image Parameters

For the visual part of our retrieval function (6), (7) we have to estimate mixture models to describe the documents (images) in our collection. The idea behind the mixture modelling approach is that each sample from an image (i.e. each block of say 8 x 8 pixels) is drawn from one of C classes. However, we don't know in advance which block is drawn from which class and we don't know what the classes are. We use the Expectation Maximisation (EM) algorithm [2] to find descriptions (models) of the classes.

Following Vasconcelos [6], we cut an image into blocks of 8 by 8 pixels. On these blocks we perform the Discrete Cosine Transform (DCT), which is used in the JPEG compression standard. We use the first 10 DCT-coefficients from each colour channel[3]. We also take the position of the image block into account. These feature vectors are used to find the parameters (μ_c, $\mathbf{\Sigma}_c$ and $P(\omega_c)$) for the components $\{c_1 \ldots c_C\}$ of the mixture model of the image under consideration using the EM algorithm. This is done in the following way. First we assign each image block to a random class. Then for each class we compute the prior, the mean and the covariance, based on the feature vectors of the samples assigned to that class[4] (maximisation step). Then we re-estimate the class assignments, i.e. for each sample we compute the most probable class from which it was drawn (expectation step). We iterate between expectation and maximisation steps until the algorithm converges. Then we have descriptions of the C different classes in a particular image. It turns out that in practise, at this point the Gaussians for the different components in an image are pretty well separated (i.e. each sample is assigned mainly to one component), thus we can use the asymptotic likelihood assumption (eq. 6) for ranking images.

4. CONCLUSION

We presented a framework in which probabilistic models for textual and visual retrieval are integrated seamlessly. Both models have proven successful individually at various tasks [3, 6]. The combined model has not been tested extensively yet, however, preliminary experiments have been conducted in the context of TREC's video track [5, 8]. The probabilistic nature of the framework allows for easy extension to a more heavily integrated setting in which we can naturally go from one modality (text) to the other (image). Future work will investigate cross modal (blind) relevance feedback and other ways to cross the boundaries between different modalities.

5. REFERENCES

[1] K. Barnard and D. Forsyth. Learning the semantics of words and pictures. In *International Conference on Computer Vision*, volume 2, pages 408–415, 2001.

[2] A. Dempster, N. Laird, and D. Rubin. Maximum likelihood from incomplete data via the em algorithm. *Journal of the Royal Statistical Society, series B*, 39(1):1–38, 1977.

[3] D. Hiemstra. *Using language models for information retrieval.* PhD thesis, Centre for Telematics and Information Technology, University of Twente, 2001.

[4] J. Lafferty and C. Zhai. Document language models, query models, and risk minimization for information retrieval. In *Proc. of the 24rd Annual International Conference on Research and Development in Information Retrieval (SIGIR 2001)*, 2001.

[5] The Lowlands team. Lazy users and automatic video retrieval tools in (the) lowlands. In *The 10th Text Retrieval Conference (TREC-2001)*, 2002.

[6] N. Vasconcelos. *Bayesian Models for Visual Information Retrieval.* PhD thesis, Massachusetts Institut of Technology, 2000.

[7] T. Westerveld. Image retrieval: Content versus context. In *Proceedings of RIAO 2000*, volume 1, pages 276–284, Paris, 2000.

[8] T. Westerveld, A. P. de Vries, D. Hiemstra, F. M. G. de Jong, and A. van Ballegooij. Retrieval experiments with multimodal video. *EURASIP Journal on Applied Signal Processing, special issue on Unstructured Information Management from Multimedia Data Sources*, 2003, to appear.

[3] We usually work in the YCbCr colour space.

[4] In practice a sample does not always belong entirely to one class. In fact we compute means, covariance and priors on the weighed feature vectors. The feature vectors are weighed by their proportion of belonging to the class under consideration

Chinese Keyword Extraction Based on Max-duplicated Strings of the Documents

Wenfeng Yang
Electronic Engineering Department
Tsinghua University, P.R.China
yangwenfeng97@mails.tsinghua.edu.cn

Xing Li
Electronic Engineering Department
Tsinghua University, P.R.China
xing@cernet.edu.cn

ABSTRACT

The corpus analysis methods in Chinese keyword extraction look on the corpus as a single sample of language stochastic process. But the distributions of keywords in the whole corpus and in each document are very different from each other. The extraction based on global statistical information only can get significant keywords in the whole corpus. Max-duplicated strings contain the local significant keywords in each document. In this paper, we designed an efficient algorithm to extract the max-duplicated strings by building PAT-tree for the document, so that the keywords can be picked out from the max-duplicated strings by their SIG values in the corpus.

Categories & Subject Descriptors: H.3.1 [Information Storage and Retrieval]: Content Analysis and Indexing – Dictionaries

General Terms: Algorithms

Keywords: MDS, Chinese keyword extraction, PAT tree

1. INTRODUCTION

With the fast development of the Internet, the number of electronic documents in Chinese becomes enormous. There are increasing needs to retrieve, filter and mine Chinese text through world-wide information networks. Unfortunately, Chinese text is different from English text in that there is no explicit word boundary. The techniques developed for English text processing can not be directly applied to Chinese text processing. Chinese text is made up of ideographic characters, and a word can comprise one, two or more such characters, without explicit indication where one word ends and another begins. The words out of the vocabulary, such as names, locations and translated terms, are difficult to be detected in Chinese text. Automatic keyword extraction is a critical problem in Chinese language processing.

Sproat and Shih [1] developed a purely statistical keyword extraction method that utilizes the mutual information between two characters in the corpus: $I(x,y) = \log p(x,y) - \log p(x) - \log p(y)$. The character pairs with the largest mutual information are assumed to be keywords. The limitation of this method is that it can only deal with keywords of 2 statistical units. In order to extract the keywords of arbitrary length, Chien [2] designed a PAT-tree-based method. The PAT tree can provide indices to all possible streams of characters in the corpus. All of the required statistical parameter can be extracted directly from the PAT tree. All the keyword extraction methods based on the global statistical analysis of the whole collection are easy to be impacted by the frequency fluctuation of keywords with the same substrings. For example, the famous name "曹雪芹" occurs 350 times in our 600M corpus, the total frequency of the other name beginning with "曹雪" is only 41 times. The global statistical method can not efficiently extract these unsignificant keywords, such as "曹雪华", "曹雪涛". In this paper, we present a keyword extraction method based on string frequency analysis in documents. Firstly, we designed a modified PAT-tree building algorithm to get the local significant strings in each document, then use the distributions of these strings in the corpus to select the eligible keywords.

SIGIR'02, August 11-15, 2002, Tampere, Finland.
ACM 1-58113-561-0/02/0008.

2. KEYWORD EXTRACTION

2.1 Word Segmentation

The training corpus used in our experiments consisted of news articles from People Daily and some other electronic novels. The data-set consisted of approx. 277,000 documents. Word segmentation is a necessary step to bring language knowledge into statistical approaches and can make the max-duplicated strings more meaningful. Forward and backward maximal matching algorithms are used in word segmentation. On the purpose of keyword extraction, there are no needs to deal with the ambiguities of word segmentation. The single characters in the ambiguous parts of the documents are treated as one-character words.

2.2 Max-duplicated String

Let S stand for the string whose beginning and ending are word boundaries in a segmented document, $f(S)$ is the frequency of the string S, $|S|$ is the length of string S, and $S \subset S'$ means that the string S' has a sub-string S. Then max-duplicated string is the string S, whose $f(S)>1$ and the frequencies $f(S')$ of all the strings S' containing the string S is smaller than $f(S)$.

2.3 Modified PAT-tree Building Algorithm

PAT tree is an efficient data structure successfully used in information retrieval. It was developed by Gonnet[3] from Morrison's PATRICIA algorithm. Since Chinese documents are segmented by words and punctuation marks, the semi-infinite strings can be generated at word level. For example, The string "自然语言处理" are segmented by the words "自然", "语言" and "处理". The semi-infinite strings generated for the string at word level are:

"自然语言处理 000…"
"语言处理 0000000…"
"处理 00000000000…"

A semi-infinite string is recorded by one path from the root to the leaf in the PAT tree. All the semi-infinite strings with the same prefix have the same path from the root to an internal node. In the process of building a PAT tree for one document, all the strings with $f(S) > 1$ can be detected. In order to keep the suffix relation of the semi-infinite strings for one sentence, the semi-infinite strings must be inserted to the PAT tree by their original orders in the sentence. If one duplicated string S_1 is found by inserting one semi-infinite string, the next duplicated string S_2 found by next semi-infinite string should be carefully checked. There are three cases:

(1) $S_2 \subset S_1$ and $f(S_2)=f(S_1)$, then S_2 is not a max-duplicated string.
(2) $S_2 \subset S_1$ and $f(S_2)>f(S_1)$, then S_2 is a max-duplicated string.
(3) $S_2 \not\subset S_1$, then S_2 is a max-duplicated string.

2.4 Filtering Max-duplicated Strings

Noises are unavoidable in the keyword extraction. Some max-duplicated strings are produced by high frequency keywords randomly attaching function words, such as "的", "以" and "用". The frequencies of those max-duplicated strings are much lower than its central keywords'. We define the stability of a max-duplicated string as *stab(S)*:

$$stab(S) = f(S) * |S|$$

Similar to word segmentation, we then segment the document once again by these max-duplicated strings. In the ambiguous segmentations of the document, only the max-duplicated string with the largest stability can be chosen as a suitable segmentation. After the document is segmented, those max-duplicated strings not being selected in any segmentation should be filtered out.

2.5 SIG Parameter and Selecting Keywords

The distributions of max-duplicated strings in the corpus represent its specialization. If one max-duplicated string occurs in several documents with high frequency, then the max-duplicated string has high specialization and is a good keyword candidate. By our hypothesis, the typical distributions of keyword and extraction noise are shown in Figure 1. Because the extraction noise has a high document frequency and its frequency in single document is low, its distribution curve is smooth. On the contrary, the keyword has a sharper distribution curve.

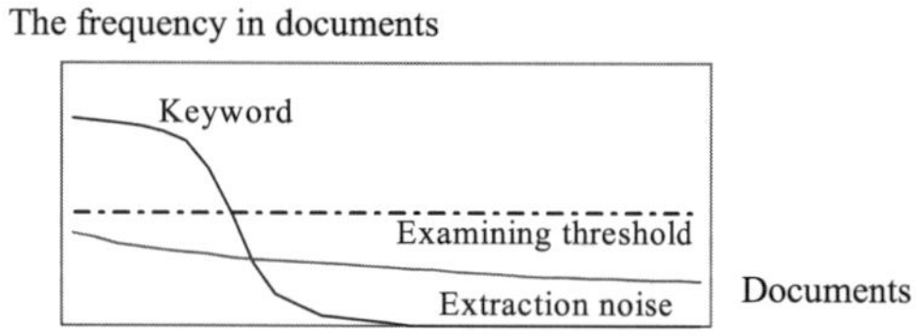

Figure 1: The distribution curves of keyword and noise

TOTAL(S) is the total frequency of the string S in the corpus and stands for the whole area under the distribution curve. If the value of the examining threshold is n, then the $FREQ_n(S)$ is the total frequency of the string S which occurs at least n times in one document and stands for the area under the distribution curve but above the threshold line. The significance of the string in corpus can be evaluated by the *SIG* parameter:

$$SIG_n(S) = FREQ_n(S) / TOTAL(S)$$

Since the max-duplicated string at least occurs 2 times in documents, the default of examining threshold is 2. After the SIG values of all the max-duplicated strings calculated, we can sort these max-duplicated strings by their SIG value. The strings with high SIG values are good keywords and those with low SIG values are assumed as extraction noises.

3. RESULTS

The size of the data-set used in our experiment is about 600M. In order to examine the effects of the word segmentation, we firstly tried keyword extraction without word segmentation and max-duplicated string filtering. We got 20,449,484 max-duplicated strings. The precision of keyword extraction is about 50.7%. After having segmented the documents by one 50,000-word dictionary, we got 17,247,407 max-duplicated strings and the precision is improved to 59.3%. The language knowledge in the dictionary is very helpful to keyword extraction.

Secondly, we filtered the 17,247,407 max-duplicated strings using the max-duplicated string filtering algorithm. We got 6,233,217 stable max-duplicated strings. The precision is up to 76.4%. Max-duplicated string filtering can greatly improve the precision of the extraction.

In the 6,233,217 max-duplicated strings there are about 430,000 unique strings. After removing the strings whose frequencies are less than 30, we got 200,199 keyword candidates and 30,153 of them are in the dictionary. We sorted the 170,046 candidates out of the dictionary by their SIG value from up to down and get a sorted candidate list. The precision of keyword extraction is proportional to candidates' SIG values (Figure 2). The candidates with the largest SIG value have the precision near to 100%. But at the end of the list, the candidates with small SIG values are almost extraction noises. Using the SIG value, we can easily select the good keywords from these candidates.

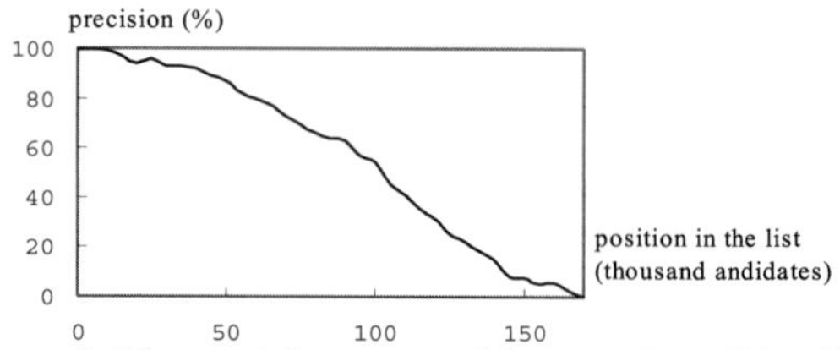

Figure 2: The precision curve of the sorted candidate list

4. CONCLUSION

We present a statistical approach to extract the keywords on base of the max-duplicated strings of the documents in the corpus. The results show that the word segmentation and max-duplicated string filtering algorithm are very helpful to the extraction and the SIG parameter provides a way to control the quality of the keywords.

5. REFERENCES

[1] R.Sproat, C.Shih. A statistical method for finding word boundaries in Chinese text. Computer Processing of Chinese and Oritental languages, Vol.4, 336-351, 1990

[2] Lee-Feng Chien, PAT-tree-based Keyword Extraction for Chinese Information Retrieval, ACM SIGIR'97, 50-59.

[3] Gaston H.Gonnet, Ricardo A.Baeza-yates and Tim Sinder, New Indices for Text: Pat Tree and Pat Arrays, Information Retrieval Data Structure & algorithm, Prentice Hall, pp.66-82, 1992

A Hierarchical Approach: Query Large Music Database by Acoustic Input

Yazhong Feng Yueting Zhuang Yunhe Pan

Department of Computer Science, Zhejiang University, Hangzhou 310027, China

Categories & Subject Descriptors: H.3.3 Retrieval models, H.3.7 Systems issues

General Terms: Algorithms, Design

Keywords: music information retrieval, recurrent neural network,correlation degree

1. INTRODUCTION

Digital music download activity is becoming the dominant traffic stream on internet, research on content-based music retrieval tool is increasing. Our goal is to develop efficient music content search engine which accepts multi-modal inputs, such as score, text, speech, and humming, query by score and query by text such as music metadata or lyrics are traditional music retrieval methods, query by speech is a query by text application in nature, except that the speech to text interface is employed, query by humming (QBH) is the most natural way to query music by its content. A rich range of researchers are contributing to content-based music retrieval, [1] introduced a "Query by Humming" system, [2] developed a system to query music in digital library via acoustic input, [3] retrievals music by text retrieval, [4] retrievals music by beat information, [5] made index on music database by recurrent neural network. With regard to melody representation, only pitch information is used in [1], [6] represents melody by a triple <T P B>, [7] uses another triple (pitch contour, pitch interval, duration) to represent melody. We implement a music retrieval system on a large music database, which contains MIDI music, it accepts acoustic input, indices are made on music database via the weights of recurrent neural network, and retrieval results are ranked by self-designed correlation degree.

2. MUSIC REPRESENTATION

To retrieval music by acoustic input, we represent both human humming and music in database by <P B>, P is pitch contour, B is beat information. We know that the most impressed part of music is its melody, pitch and rhythm are important components of melody, pitch determines which note is played by instruments or sung by people, to eliminate transcription or memory errors, we use pitch contour for pitch information, rhythm is the beat movement, we represent rhythm by beat in this paper. The reason why we use only pitch contour and beat information to represent melody is as followings: when humming, people tend to use his or her own tempo, which is sometime different from original music, so we do not use tempo information such as T in <T P B> of [6], most people can not keep right pitch interval and duration when they hum, so, unlike [7], we use only pitch contour for pitch information. Autocorrelation or cepstrum is used to track pitch from acoustic input, beat information is derived from acoustic input by method suggested in [9].

SIGIR'02, August 11-15, 2002, Tampere, Finland.
ACM 1-58113-561-0/02/0008.

3. HEURISTIC RULES

To make music retrieval more robust, music perception knowledge should be embedded into signal processing tools to perform pitch tracking of humming, after analyzing our music database which has about 1200 pieces of MIDI music, we deduce the following heuristic rules to aid signal processing in music retrieval:

- Five-level pitch contour is more robust than three-level contour in music matching.

Based on our music database, the statistic result is almost the same as [4][6], the melodic intervals of most adjacent MIDI notes are in the range of [-2 2].

The five-level contour (-2 –1 0 1 2) is defined as following:

$$Contour_5 = \begin{cases} -2, when N_{i+1} - N_i < -2 \\ -1, when -2 \le N_{i+1} - N_i < 0 \\ 0, when N_{i+1} = N_i \\ 1, when 0 < N_{i+1} - N_i \le 2 \\ 2, when 2 < N_{i+1} - N_i \end{cases}$$

N_i is the ith MIDI note.

- Frequency of human humming or singing is in the range of [80Hz, 800Hz]. When performing pitch tracking, if the fundamental frequency of a frame is not in above range, this frame is not a note candidate.
- The melody variation of humming or singing is not very severe. If the fundamental frequency of a frame is bigger than that of each two frames on its left and right, this frame is not a note candidate.
- The experimental knowledge [4] that most music is self-similar supports the use of recurrent neural network to remember melody and make index.

4. SYSTEM COMPONENTS

Our system has three components: signal processing of humming input, music database and matching strategy.

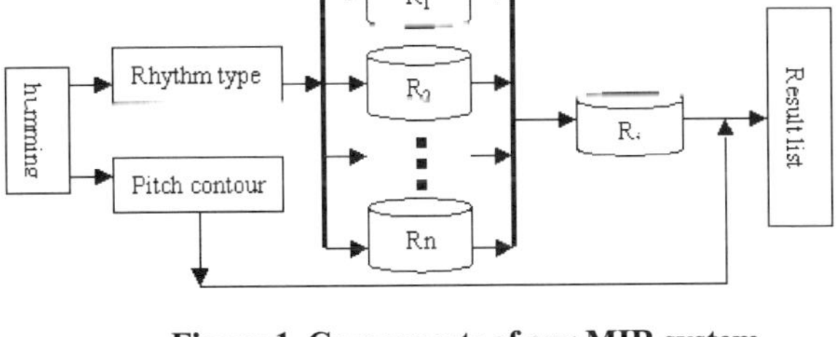

Figure 1. Components of our MIR system.

Pitch-tracker translates humming into Five-level pitch contour, rhythm detector calculate time signature from humming. Music database is separated into regions according to rhythm type, such as

T=(2/4, 3/4, 5/4, 6/4, 7/4, 6/8). Let M be a music database, $n = |T|$, then $M = \bigcup_{i=1}^{n} R_i$.

4.1 Pitch Tracker

Although pitch tracking on polyphonic music is not very successful, tracking pitch from acoustic humming input is straightforward and reliable; usually autocorrelation or cepstrum is employed to track pitch.

4.2 Rhythm Detector

Our rhythm detector is the same as [8], MFCC (Mel-Frequency Cepstral Coefficients) feature vector v is extracted from humming audio, and the element of similarity matrix S is calculated by

$$s(i,j) = \frac{v_i \bullet v_j}{\|v_i\|\|v_j\|}. \quad \textbf{(Eq. 1)}$$

Beat spectrum (Eq.2) reveals that the beat information of humming input is b:

$$B(k,l) = \sum_{i,j} S(i,j)S(i+k, j+l) \quad \textbf{(Eq. 2)}$$

4.3 Music Database Regions

Beat information b is used to locate the region in which to match humming with music, let $i = \arg(\min(|b - T|))$, then R_i is the selected region.

4.4 Indices on Music Database

Melody contour for each music is trained by a recurrent neural network [5], its weight matrix acts as the index of this piece of music in the database. Because of the same structure of neural network, index size for every piece of music is same and the indices on the whole music database increase linearly to the database size.

4.5 Retrieval by Correlation Degree

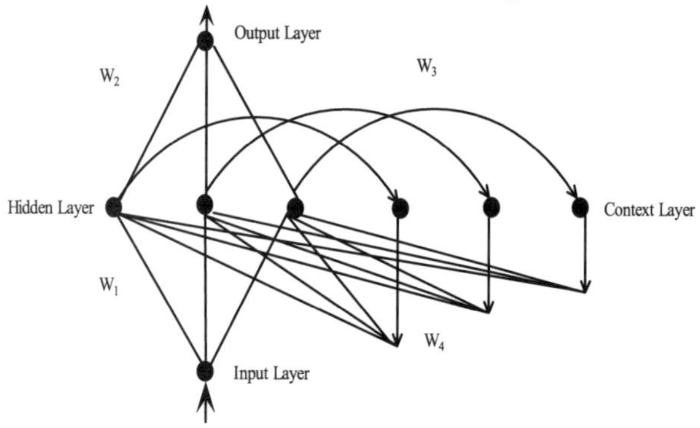

Figure 2. Structure of recurrent neural network used for memorizing music.

Let P be pitch contour of humming, then the retrieval result is $\arg(\max(P \aleph R_i))$. Let $R_i = \{m_{ij}\}$, where m_{ij} be the jth piece of music in region R_i, $Net(m_{ij})$ is the recurrent neural network that remembers music m_{ij}, $P * Net(m_{ij})$ is the network output when input is P, define $\gamma(P, P * Net(m_{ij}))$ to be the correlation degree of P with $P * Net(m_{ij})$, then

$$P \aleph R_i = \{\gamma(P, P * Net(m_{ij}))\}, j = |R_i| \quad \textbf{(Eq. 3)}$$

5. Experimental Result

Experiment on the database that has 1200 pieces of MIDI music shows the following result:

Resolution	Successful Rate
Top3	68%
Top10	89%

It is much more difficult to extract melody from polyphonic music in raw audio format such as WAV or AU, otherwise different approach that matches singing which is characteristic of songs may be promising. We are now exploring a technique to retrieval popular songs directly by singing with lyrics, the basic idea is to extract singing from stereo music recordings by independent component analysis (ICA) [10], then we perform matching on melody contour derived from singing. We hope this will contribute a bit to multi-modal model of music information retrieval system.

6. REFERENCES

[1] Ghias, A. Logan, J. Chamberlin, D. and Smith, B. "Query by humming," in ACM Multimedia, 1995.

[2] McNab, R. Smith, L. Witten, I. Henderson, C. and Cunningham, S. "Towards the digital music library: Tune retrieval from acoustic input," in Digital Libraries 1996.

[3] Downie, J. S. "Music retrieval as text retrieval: Simple yet effective," in Proceedings of SIGIR '99 Conference, 297-298.

[4] Kosugi, N. et al. "A practical query-by-humming system for a large music database," in ACM Multimedia 2000, Los Angeles, CA, November, 2000.

[5] Feng, Y. Z. Zhuang, Y. T. and Pan, Y. H. "Query similar music by correlation degree," in IEEE PCM2001, 885-890.

[6] Kim, Y. Chai, W. Garcia, R. and Vercoe, B. "Analysis of a contour-based representation for melody," in ISMIR2000, Oct. 2000.

[7] Lu, L. You, H. Zhang, H. J. "A new approach to query by humming in music retrieval," in ICME2001, Tokyo, August 2001.

[8] Foote, J. and Uchihashi, S. "The Beat Spectrum: A New Approach to Rhythm Analysis," in ICME2001, IEEE, Tokyo, August 2001.

[9] Wei Cai, "Melody Retrieval on the Web," Master's thesis, MIT, September 2001.

[10] Lewicki, M. S. "Efficient coding of natural sounds," Nature Neuroscience, Vol. 5, No. 4, pp 356 - 363, April 2002.

Correlating Multilingual Documents via Bipartite Graph Modeling

Hongyuan Zha Xiang Ji
Department of Computer Science and Engineering
The Pennsylvania State University
University Park, PA
zha@cse.psu.edu, xji@cse.psu.edu

ABSTRACT

There is enormous amount of multilingual documents from various sources and possibly from different countries describing a single event or a set of related events. It is desirable to construct text mining methods that can compare and highlight similarities and differences of those multilingual documents. We discuss our ongoing research that seeks to model a pair of multilingual documents as a weighted bipartite graph with the edge weights computed by means of machine translation. We use spectral method to identify dense subgraphs of the weighted bipartite graph which can be considered as corresponding to sentences that correlate well in textual contents. We illustrate our approach using English and German texts.

Categories and Subject Descriptors

H.3.3 [**Information Systems**]: Information Search and Retrieval—*Clustering*; H.4.m [**Information Systems**]: Miscellaneous—*Text Summarization*; G.1.3 [**Numerical Analysis**]: Numerical Linear Algebra—*Singular value decomposition*; G.2.2 [**Discrete Mathematics**]: Graph Theory—*Graph algorithms*

General Terms

Algorithms, Experimentation, Theory

Keywords

translingual text summarization, bipartite graph, graph partitioning, singular value decomposition

1. INTRODUCTION

As pointed out in [2], English is only a small fraction of the total textual information available; a great deal of vital information exists only in, or appears sooner in, other languages. We discuss text analysis methods that seek to compare and highlight similarities and differences of multilingual documents providing the first step towards translingual summarization. Previous research in translingual summarization emphasizes developing language-neutral methods so that a summarizer producing summaries for one language can be rapidly adapted to work in other languages. We focus on methods for extracting and correlating textual contents against sources in various languages and then making the essential information available in English.

SIGIR'02, August 11-15, 2002, Tampere, Finland.
ACM 1-58113-561-0/02/0008.

2. THE METHOD

In the context of analyzing a pair of documents in two different languages, we first construct a *cross-similarity* bipartite graph as follows: we extract the set of sentences $A = \{a_1, \ldots, a_m\}$ and $B = \{b_1, \ldots, b_n\}$ from the two documents in questions. (In our experiments we used English and German texts.) The key data structure we use to represent the pair of documents is a weighted bipartite graph $G(A, B, W)$ with the sentences in A and B as the vertices of the graph, and W is the adjacency matrix representing the edge weights. To compute the pair-wise similarity between a sentence in A and a sentence in B: we first use machine translation to translate the German text into English. We then compare an English sentence in A and the English translation of a German sentence in B. For our experiments, we use the dot-product of a pair of sentence vectors as the measurement of sentence similarity. Since we are only interested in sentence similarity computation, we can tolerate certain degradation in machine translation quite well. One may also resort to phrase translation for sentence similarity computation, although some of the translations will likely to be out of context. We denote $W = [w_{ij}]$ the m-by-n weight matrix with w_{ij} measuring the similarity between sentence i in A and sentence j in B. We now discuss several approaches to extracting desirable structures from this cross-similarity weighted bipartite graph.

First we seek to extract a dense subgraph from the bipartite graph consisting of sentences that are similar and well correlated with each other in content. To this end, we compute the largest singular value triplet $\{u, \sigma, v\}$ of W, i.e,

$$Wv = \sigma u, \quad W^T u = \sigma v,$$

where W^T stands for the matrix transpose of W, u and v are the left and right singular vectors of W corresponding to the largest singular value σ. Since W is nonnegative, it is guaranteed that both u and v have *nonnegative* compo-

English text	German text
Defense Secretary Donald Rumsfeld warned the United States faces even more deadly terror attacks than it has already suffered, as investigators pored over documents found in Afghanistan that suggest that the U.S. Capitol, Seattle's Space Needle and a portion of Los Angeles were being targeted.	Als Beispiele nannte Rumsfeld am Donnerstag (Ortszeit) so genannte Cyber-Attacken, das heit, die Lahmlegung von Computern durch Viren, Angriffe auf Militärstützpunkte im Ausland und den Beschuss amerikanischer Städte mit ballistischen Raketen.
He said that the country is vulnerable to a broad range of terrorism, from attacks on computer systems to biological war fare to missile attacks on U.S. cities.	US-Verteidigungsminister Donald Rumsfeld hat gewarnt, die USA müssten sich auf mögliche überraschungsangriffe vorbereiten, die noch weitaus verheerender sein könnten als die Anschläge vom 11. 8 September.
Moments before Rumsfeld began his speech, FBI Director Robert Mueller said there may be terrorist "sleeper cells" in the United States waiting to strike, and the nation needs to remain on high alert.	Der Chef des Bundeskriminalamts FBI, Robert Mueller, äußerte die Vermutung, dass sich in den USA mehrere Schläfer der Terroristen-Organisation El Kaida befinden könnten.

Table 1: Shared topics extracted from English/German texts

nents. We then reorder the sentences in A and B according to their corresponding component values in u and v, respectively to obtain a permuted weighted matrix $\hat{W}$. To estimate the number of sentences to include in the dense subgraph, for $\hat{W} = [\hat{W}_{s,t}]_{s,t=1}^2$ we compute for $i = 1, \ldots, m$ and $j = 1, \ldots, n$, the following quantity

$$J_{ij} = h(\hat{W}_{11})/n(\hat{W}_{11}) + h(\hat{W}_{22})/n(\hat{W}_{22}),$$

where $\hat{W}_{11}$ is i-by-j, and $h(\cdot)$ is the sum of all the elements of a matrix and $n(\cdot)$ is the square root of the product of the row and column dimensions of a matrix. We then choose i^* and j^* such that

$$J_{i^*j^*} = \max\{\ J_{ij} \mid i = 1, \ldots, m, j = 1, \ldots, n\}.$$

The i^* sentences from A corresponding to the first i^* rows of $\hat{W}$ and the j^* sentences from B corresponding to the first j^* columns of $\hat{W}$ are extracted and displayed as portions of documents A and B that correlate with each other the most.

The above approach usually extracts a dominant topic that is shared by the two documents in question. In order to extract other less dominant shared topics, we can apply the bi-clustering algorithm [3] to the weighted bipartite graph $G(A, B, W)$ to obtain several clusters each containing sentences from the two documents: each cluster corresponds to a shared topic, and bi-clustering provides a map or correspondence linking similar topics from each document. Within each shared topic, we can apply the above approach to extract the corresponding sentences.

3. PRELIMINARY RESULTS

We illustrate our approach using two news articles, one in English and one in German with urls

```
http://story.news.yahoo.com/news?tmpl=story&u=/abc/
      20020131/ts_abc/strike_main
http://de.news.yahoo.com/020201/3/2mf2p.html
```

and titles *Rumsfeld Warns of Future Threats* and *USA planen keine neuen Antiterror-Militraktionen.* The first part of Table 1 lists the first top two sentences from each document for the dense subgraph extracted from the weighted bipartite graph. Although the German text is mainly about US not taking immediate military actions against some nations, it has a section on potential threats to USA which matches the major theme of the English text well. We also apply the bi-clustering approach to the above example, besides the the first shared topic found above, we found another shared topic dealing with operations of the FBI and CIA, we list the corresponding top one sentence in the second part of Table 1. The two approaches we proposed identify shared topics represented as sentence extracts from multilingual documents that are similar in content. To find potential differences or inconsistencies, one possibility is to review each cluster in the context of the main themes of the two documents (represented by summaries of the documents). For the above example, even though both documents discuss terrorist threats to USA, the German text discuss it with the emphasis of USA not planning military actions in the near future.

4. FUTURE WORK

In this paper we proposed methods for extracting the shared topics of multilingual documents. Our preliminary experiment indicates our method can effectively generate similarities and differences of multilingual documents. We are collecting news articles in English, German and Chinese for conducting more extensive experiments. Future directions for research include simultaneously handling documents in more than two different languages and multiple documents in each language.

Acknowledgement. The research was supported in part by NSF grant CCR-9901986. The authors thank the referees for many constructive comments and suggestions.

5. REFERENCES

[1] Systran: Information and Translation Technologies. http://www.systransoft.com/

[2] Translingual Information Detection, Extraction and Summarization. http://www.darpa.mil/ito/research/tides/

[3] Hongyuan Zha, Xiaofeng He, Chris Ding, Ming Gu and Horst Simon. Bipartite Graph Partitioning and Data Clustering. *Proceedings of ACM CIKM 2001, the Tenth International Conference on Information and Knowledge Management*, 25-32, 2001.

Demonstrations

A System Using Implicit Feedback and Top Ranking Sentences to Help Users Find Relevant Web Documents 446
R. W. White, J. M. Jose (University of Glasgow),
I. Ruthven (University of Strathclyde)

Indexing, Searching, and Retrieving of Recorded Live Presentations with the AOF (Authoring on the Fly) Search Engine 447
W. Hürst (Universität Freiburg)

UTACLIR -- General Query Translation Framework for Several Language Pairs 448
H. Keskustalo, T. Hedlund, E. Airio (University of Tampere)

HyREX: Hyper-media Retrieval Engine for XML 449
N. Fuhr, N. Gövert, K. Groβjohann (University of Dortmund)

Query Performance Analyser — a Web-Based Tool for IR Research and Instruction 450
E. Sormunen, S. Hokkanen, P. Kangaslampi, P. Pyy, B. Sepponen
(University of Tampere)

Adaptive Information Extraction for Document Annotation in Amilcare 451
F. Ciravegna, A. Dingli, Y. Wilks, D. Petrelli (University of Sheffield)

ExWrap: Semi-Automatic Wrapper Generation by Example 452
B. Schmitt, M. Christoffel, J. Schneider (University of Karlsruhe)

Souvenir: Flexible Note-Taking Tool to Pinpoint and Share media Highlights 453
A. Spoerri (Rutgers University)

Hierarchical Approach to Term Suggestion Device 454
H. Joho, M. Sanderson, M. Beaulieu (University of Sheffield)

Translingual Vocabulary Mappings for Multilingual Information Access 455
F. C. Gey, A. Chen, M. Buckland, R. Larson
(University of California, Berkeley)

GS Textplorer — Adaptive Framework for Information Retrieval 456
J. Honkela, V. H. Tuulos (Gurusoft, Inc.)

CuTeX: A System for Extracting Data from Text Tables 457
H. Davulcu, S. Mukherjee, A. Seth,
I. V. Ramakrishnan (SUNY Stony Brook)

YellowPager: A Tool for Ontology-based Mining of Service Directories from Web Sources 458
P. Choudhari, H. Davulcu, A. Joglekar, A. More, S. Mukherjee, S. Patil,
I. V. Ramakrishnan (SUNY Stony Brook)

A System Using Implicit Feedback and Top Ranking Sentences to Help Users Find Relevant Web Documents

Ryen W. White
Department of Computing Science
University of Glasgow
Glasgow. G12 8QQ
whiter@dcs.gla.ac.uk

Joemon M. Jose
Department of Computing Science
University of Glasgow
Glasgow. G12 8QQ
jj@dcs.gla.ac.uk

Ian Ruthven
Department of Computer and Information Sciences
University of Strathclyde
Glasgow. G1 1XH
ir@cis.strath.ac.uk

ABSTRACT
We present a web search interface designed to encourage users to interact more fully with the results of a web search. Wrapping around a major commercial search engine, the system combines three main features; real-time query-biased web document summarisation, the presentation of sentences highly relevant to the searcher's query, and evidence captured from searcher interaction with the retrieval results.

Categories and Subject Descriptors: H.3.3 [Information Search and Retrieval]: - search process, relevance feedback.

General Terms: Design, Human Factors

Keywords: WWW, sentence extraction, implicit feedback

1. INTRODUCTION
For many web users, assessing document relevance based on typical web search result lists can be problematic. The abstracts provided may give an insufficient clue about page content and searchers are forced to visit each page to assess its relevance.

These users are also often reluctant to browse beyond the first page of results, meaning they may miss out on relevant documents. Instead they prefer to reformulate and resubmit their query, a process both computationally and cognitively expensive. In such web search situations, there is also a tendency to exhibit a limited interaction with the retrieved document set.

When using *relevance feedback* systems, users may be unwilling to view individual documents and relay their personal relevance assessments to the search system (usually via checkboxes).

Our system seeks to address each of these concerns, and in what follows we will outline its design.

2. DESCRIPTION
Our system (Figure 1) is an interface for a web search engine result list, in this case AltaVista [1]. The query submitted is passed to the underlying search engine, the result list is parsed and threads are dispatched to each document in this list (up to a maximum of thirty at any one time). In a similar way to [1] the system then creates a query-biased summary of each of these thirty documents in parallel. The summaries are created in real-time and the entire process takes around 7 seconds. On the mouseover of a document title – the only thing shown in the result list – a small window 'pops-up' containing the summary.

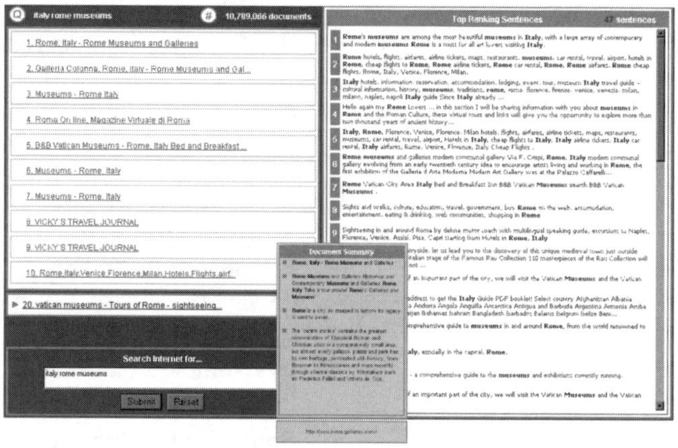

Figure 1. Interface with document summary pop-up.

Despite some thirty documents being summarised, only ten document titles are shown at any time to the user. We use a list of whole sentences that highly match the searcher's query, taken from *all* summarised documents. These *top ranking sentences* provide access to potentially relevant pages outwith the top ten. We create this list by splitting the top thirty documents into component sentences and rank these sentences according to the words and the query words they contain. The intention is to encourage searchers to make assessments on page content, rather than the more usual titles and abstracts representations.

We also endeavour to *predict* what users find relevant. Working under the assumption that users will view relevant document summaries for longer than irrelevant summaries we base our implicit feedback model around viewing time. Each time the system believes the searcher has identified a useful summary, important terms are taken from all assumed relevant summaries, combined with the query terms, and used to re-rank the top ranking sentences list. We are relating the searcher's search *actions* with the information displayed in the interface.

During this demonstration we will work with the live Internet and give those interested an opportunity to use their choice of query.

[1] http://www.altavista.com

SIGIR'02, August 11-15, 2002, Tampere, Finland.
ACM 1-58113-561-0/02/0008.

3. REFERENCES
[1] R.W. White, J. M. Jose and I. Ruthven. *A task-oriented study on the influencing effects of query-biased summarisation in web searching*. Information Processing and Management. 2002. *in press*

Indexing, Searching, and Retrieving of Recorded Live Presentations with the AOF (Authoring on the Fly) Search Engine

Wolfgang Hürst
Institut für Informatik, Universität Freiburg,
Georges-Köhler-Allee, D-79110 Freiburg, Germany
huerst@informatik.uni-freiburg.de

ABSTRACT
The tremendous amount of data resulting from the regular usage of tools for automatic presentation recording demand for elaborate search functionality. A detailed analysis of the according multimedia documents is required to allow search at a very detailed level. Unfortunately, the produced data differs significantly from traditional documents. In this demo, we discuss the problems appearing in the presentation retrieval scenario and introduce *aofSE,* a search engine to study and illustrate these problems as well as to develop and present according solutions and new approaches for this task.

Categories and Subject Descriptors
H.3.7 [**Information Storage and Retrieval**]: Digital Libraries – *collection, system issues, user issues.*

General Terms: Algorithms, Design, Reliability, Experimentation, Human Factors.

Keywords: E-Learning, Presentation Recording, Multimedia Retrieval.

1. PRESENTATION RECORDING
Many research systems for automatic presentation recording were developed within the last few years (see [1] or [2] for an overview). Meanwhile, commercial systems and (partly free) add-ons to common presentation software exist, as well. The result of regular usage of presentation recording in the classroom is a tremendous amount of data. The according documents, each of which contains one recorded presentation, form a large knowledge data base that can be used, for example, for permanent education, to deepen the understanding of a particular topic, to look up a specific problem, and so on. Hence, there is a strong need for information retrieval techniques in this area. Unfortunately, most systems for automatic presentation recording offer only very limited indexing and searching functionality.

2. PRESENTATION RETRIEVAL
New retrieval approaches have to be found to index and search recorded presentations. One reason for this is that we are dealing with multimedia documents, that do not only consist of text (on the slides) but other media as well, such as audio and video (voice and image of the lecturer, respectively). In addition, there are specific characteristics regarding the data that have to be considered when developing a search engine for this particular task. For example, the text on the slides usually contains only keywords instead of continuous, redundant sentences, making common ranking approaches that are based on term distribution unsuitable in this context. The audio recordings can differ significantly from regular speech signals, for example, because of higher background noises. Another problem is that sometimes words are used in different languages even during one presentation (a problem appearing especially in none English computer science lectures because of the strong dominance of the English language in this specific field). Because of all these problems (and many more), common approaches for information retrieval have to be adapted when used to retrieve recorded presentations and new solutions have to be introduced. To identify and study these problems as well as to introduce new techniques to solve them we used a large document collection that was created with the AOF (Authoring on-the-Fly) system [2]. AOF is a system for automatic presentation recording used by a large number of institutions on a regular basis. This demo illustrates *aofSE* [3], a search engine we developed to test and evaluate our approaches. We show how automatic presentation recording as well as automatic indexing is done with the system. The demonstration of the search functionality illustrates characteristic problems in this task as well as the solutions we propose, e.g., the introduction of a different ranking approach. In addition, we demonstrate what functionality is offered by the system to navigate and browse the according documents and how this can support a user who is searching for information.

3. ACKNOWLEDGMENTS
This research was funded by the *German Research Foundation* (DFG) as part of the research initiative V3D2 (*"Distributed Processing and Delivery of Digital Documents"*).

4. REFERENCES
[1] Brusilowsky, P. (2000) Electronic Lectures and Presentations in Web-Based Education. In Syllabus Magazine, Vol 13/5.

[2] Müller, R., and Ottmann, T. (2000) The "Authoring on the Fly" System for Automated Recording and Replay of (Tele)presentations. In ACM/Springer Multimedia Systems Journal, Vol 8/3.

[3] The aofSE Web Site:
http://ad.informatik.uni-freiburg.de/aofSE

SIGIR'02, August 11-15, 2002, Tampere, Finland.
ACM 1-58113-561-0/02/0008.

UTACLIR – General Query Translation Framework for Several Language Pairs

Heikki Keskustalo
Department of Information Studies
University of Tampere
Finland
+358 50 378 3066
heikki.keskustalo@uta.fi

Turid Hedlund
Department of Information Studies
University of Tampere
Finland
+358 50 056 2933
hedlund@shh.fi

Eija Airio
Department of Information Studies
University of Tampere
Finland
+358 3 215 6182
eija.airio@uta.fi

1. SYSTEM DESCRIPTION

The UTACLIR query translation process was first designed for the CLEF 2000 campaign [2], followed by an improved version for the CLEF 2001 [3]. The present implementation constitutes a completely revised version of the software. The process input is a structured or unstructured source language query together with codes expressing the source and target languages. The output is the translated target query. The solution is based on building a tree data structure consisting of three levels: (1) the original source keys, (2) the processed source keys, and (3) the translated and processed target keys. Key processing is based on key type [2][3]. The following six key types are recognized in case of non-compound source languages. In case the source key is recognized by morphological software: (i) keys producing only such basic forms which all are stop words, (ii) keys producing at least one translatable basic form, (iii) keys producing no translatable basic forms. In case the source key is not recognised: (iv) the key itself is a stop word, (v) the key is translatable, (vi) the key is untranslatable. For compound languages, a 7th key type is added: (vii) untranslatable but splittable source key. In the target query formation we support key normalization, synonym structuring of translation equivalents, and phrase-based structuring of target phrases [5]. For untranslatable keys, fuzzy matching techniques [4] are utilized to select keys from the database index. The system operates on Solaris workstation. It is programmed in C and consists of a library archive containing general and resource specific functions. General functions are called to implement the translation service. Resource specific functions (e.g. interfaces to local dictionaries) and general functions (e.g. new ways to structure the target query) can be added by writing functions satisfying function prototype definitions given by the general system framework. Morphological analysis and word translation are performed by utilizing the library archives of morphological software TWOL (4 languages) and GlobalDix dictionary (over 300 language pairs). Present approach has already been put to practice as part of European Union funded CLARITY project [6]. Future development includes developing effective transitive query translation methods [1].

Categories & Subject Descriptors: H.3.3. INFORMATION STORAGE AND RETRIEVAL

General Terms: Design, Experimentation, Languages

Keywords: Query translation, CLIR, cross-lingual information retrieval, dictionary based retrieval

SIGIR'02, August 11-15, 2002, Tampere, Finland.
ACM 1-58113-561-0/02/0008.

2. ACKNOWLEDGEMENTS

ENGTWOL (Morphological Transducer Lexicon Description of English): Copyright © 1989-1992 Atro Voutilainen and Juha Heikkilä. FINTWOL (Morphological Description of Finnish): Copyright © Kimmo Koskenniemi and Lingsoft Oy. 1983-1993. GERTWOL (Morphological Transducer Lexicon Description of German): Copyright © 1997 Kimmo Koskenniemi and Lingsoft, Inc. GlobalDix and MOT Dictionary software was used for automatic word-by-word translations. Copyright © 1998-2002 Kielikone Oy, Finland. SWETWOL (Morphological Transducer Lexicon Description of Swedish): Copyright © 1998 Fred Karlsson and Lingsoft, Inc. TWOL-R (Run-Time Two-Level Program): Copyright © Kimmo Koskenniemi and Lingsoft Oy. 1983-1992.

3. REFERENCES

[1] Gollins T. and Sanderson M. (2001) Improving Cross Language Information Retrieval with Triangulated Translation. In *SIGIR '01* (New Orleans, USA, 2001), ACM Press, 90-95.

[2] Hedlund T, Keskustalo H, Pirkola A, Sepponen M & Järvelin K, 2001. Bilingual tests with Swedish, Finnish and German queries: dealing with morphology, compound words and query structure. In *CLEF 2000* (Lisbon, Portugal, 2001), Springer, 210-223.

[3] Hedlund T, Keskustalo H, Pirkola A, Airio E & Järvelin K, 2002. UTACLIR@CLEF 2001 – Effects of Compound Splitting and N-gram Techniques. *To appear in CLEF 2001 Workshop proceedings.*

[4] Pirkola A., Keskustalo H., Leppänen E., Känsälä, A-P., Järvelin K., 2002. Targeted s-gram matching: a novel n-gram matching technique for cross- and monolingual word form variants. *Information Research*, 7 (2) [Available at http://InformationR.net/ir/7-2/paper126.html].

[5] Pirkola A, Hedlund T, Keskustalo H & Järvelin K, 2001. Dictionary-Based Cross-Language Information Retrieval: Problems, Methods, and Research Findings. *Information Retrieval,* 4(3/4), pp. 209-230.

[6] Project description of Clarity. [Available at: http://clarity.shef.ac.uk/].

HyREX: Hyper-media Retrieval Engine for XML

Norbert Fuhr Norbert Gövert Kai Großjohann

University of Dortmund, Germany
http://ls6-www.cs.uni-dortmund.de/ir/projects/hyrex/

1. INTRODUCTION

While XML query languages as proposed by the W3C are targeting towards database-oriented applications and thus do not consider the needs of IR, we developed the query language XIRQL (*X*ML *IR* *Q*uery *L*anguage) which takes into account the intrinsic imprecision and vagueness of IR. We present HyREX, the *Hy*per-media *R*etrieval *E*ngine for *X*ML, which implements XIRQL. On the user interface side (HyGate), we present innovative concepts for the presentation of structured retrieval results.

2. XIRQL

The query language XIRQL [1] extends the XPath part of the query language XQuery (proposed standard of the W3C) by the following features:

Weighting and ranking: While XQuery supports Boolean retrieval only, XIRQL allows for weighting document terms as well as query terms. Thus, retrieval results are presented to users as a ranking.

Relevance-oriented search: Traditional IR queries specify only the requested content, but pose no restrictions on the structure of the result. In the case of structured (XML) documents, the IR system should be able to retrieve the most relevant parts of a documents by choosing the most specific element(s) that satisfy the query.

Data types and vague predicates: Since XML allows for a fine-grained markup of elements, there should be the possibility to use special search predicates for different elements of various data types (e. g. person names, dates, names of geographic regions). For each data type, the system must provide appropriate search predicates, most of which should be vague (e. g. phonetic similarity of names, approximate matching of dates, closeness of geographic locations).

Structural relativism: Query languages for XML allow for conditions with respect to the structure of the documents to be retrieved. In order to support uncertainty and vagueness for this type of conditions, appropriate methods ignore the difference between elements and attributes, exploit hierarchies over element names defined in an ontology, and allow for searching for elements of a specific data type (e. g. search for all elements containing person names).

SIGIR'02, August 11-15, 2002, Tampere, Finland.
ACM 1-58113-561-0/02/0008.

3. HYREX

The XIRQL language is implemented within the HyREX system. Its system architecture is similar to that of database management systems. Thus, there is a clear separation between the logical and the physical level. At the logical level, XIRQL queries are transformed into a path algebra. A path describes the sequence of document nodes leading from the root of an XML document to a specific element. The path algebra contains operators for manipulating sets of paths that describe intermediate results in query processing.

The connection between the logical and the physical level is formed by the vague predicates, which take a value and/or structure condition as arguments and return a list of paths as result. In order to perform efficient retrieval, appropriate index structures are available at the physical level.

HyREX is Open Source software. It is designed as an extensible IR architecture. The whole system is written in Perl (with time-critical parts in C). For specific applications, new data types can be added to the system, possibly together with new index structures. The current version allows for efficient retrieval of XML collections up to the gigabyte range.

4. HYGATE

HyGate forms the user interface (UI) to HyREX. The development of an UI to an XML IR engine poses a number of new challenges. For query formulation, we present an approach based on the concept of *query by example*; as *example*, either the DTD, the logical structure or the final layout of a specific document can be used. Visualization of retrieval results has to cope with two problems: There may be multiple matches in a single document, and even one match may contain other matches. Here variants of tile bars and tree maps are presented as a visualization of retrieval results.

5. REFERENCES

[1] N. Fuhr and K. Großjohann. XIRQL: A query language for information retrieval in XML documents. In *Proceedings of the 24th SIGIR Conference*, pages 172–180, New York, 2001. ACM.

Query Performance Analyser — a Web-based tool for IR research and instruction

Eero Sormunen, Sakari Hokkanen, Petteri Kangaslampi, Petri Pyy, and Bemmu Sepponen
University of Tampere
FIN 33014 University of Tampere
Finland
+358-3-2156972
{lieeso, sh61446, petteri.kangaslampi, lipepy, lomise}@uta.fi

The Interactive Query Performance Analyser (QPA) for information retrieval systems is a Web-based tool for analysing and comparing the performance of individual queries. On top of a standard test collection, it gives an instant visualisation of the performance achieved in a given search topic by any user-generated query. In addition to experimental IR research, QPA can be used in user training to demonstrate the characteristics of and compare differences between IR systems and searching strategies.

The first prototype (versions 3.0 and 3.5) of the Query Performance Analyser was developed at the Department of Information Studies, University of Tampere, to serve as a tool for rapid query performance analysis, comparison and visualisation [4,5]. Later, it has been applied to interactive optimisation of queries [2,3]. The analyser has served also in learning environments for IR [1].

The demonstration is based on the newest version of the Query Performance Analyser (v. 5.1). It is interfaced to a traditional Boolean IR system (TRIP) and a probabilistic IR system (Inquery) providing access to the TREC collection and two Finnish test collections. Version 5.1 supports multigraded relevance scales, new types of performance visualisations, and query conversions based on mono- and multi-lingual dictionaries.

The motivation in developing the analyser is to emphasise the necessity of analysing the behaviour of individual queries. Information retrieval experiments usually measure the average effectiveness of IR methods developed. The analysis of individual queries is neglected although test results may contain individual test topics where general findings do not hold. For the real user of an IR system, the study of variation in results is even more important than averages.

Categories and Subject Descriptors
H.3.3 Information Search and Retrieval

General Terms
Experimentation

Keywords
Queries, Performance, Analysis, Interactive searching

References
[1] Halttunen, K. & Sormunen, E. (2000). Learning information retrieval through an educational game. Is gaming sufficient for learning? Education for Information 18(4): 289-311.

[2] SORMUNEN, E. (2000). A Method for measuring Wide Range Performance of Boolean Queries in Full-Text Databases. Doctoral Thesis. Tampere: University of Tampere. Acta Electronica Universitatis Tamperensis, ISBN: 951-44-4732-8, URL: http://acta.uta.fi/teos.phtml?3786

[3] Sormunen, E. (2002). A Retrospective Evaluation Method for Exact-Match and Best-Match Queries Applying an Interactive Query Performance Analyser. Accepted to the 24th BCS-IRSG European Colloquium on IR Research March 25-27, 2002, Glasgow, Scotland, UK.

[4] Sormunen, E., Laaksonen, J., Keskustalo, H., Kekäläinen, J., Kemppainen, H., Laitinen, H., Pirkola, A., Järvelin, K. (1998). The IR Game - A Tool for Rapid Query Analysis in Cross-Language IR Experiments. PRICAI '98 Workshop on Cross Language Issues in Artificial Intelligence. Singapore, Nov 22-24, 1998, p. 22-32.

[5] Sormunen, E., Halttunen, K., & Keskustalo, H. (2002). Query Performance Analyser - a tool for bridging information retrieval research and instruction. Submitted to Information Retrieval (September 28th, 2001).

SIGIR'02, August 11-15, 2002, Tampere, Finland.
ACM 1-58113-561-0/02/0008.

Adaptive Information Extraction for Document Annotation in Amilcare

Fabio Ciravegna, Alexiei Dingli and Yorick Wilks
Department of Computer Science,
University of Sheffield,
Regent Court, 211 Portobello Street,
S1 4DP, Sheffield, UK +44-114-2221814
{fabio|alexiei|Yorick}@dcs.shef.ac.uk

Daniela Petrelli
Department of Information Studies,
University of Sheffield,
Regent Court, 211 Portobello Street,
S1 4DP, Sheffield, UK, +44-114-2222683
D.Petrelli@ sheffield.ac.uk

Categories & Subject Descriptors: I.2.7 [Artificial Intelligence]: **Natural Language Processing** – ***text analysis.***

General Terms: Management, Performance, Design, Experimentation, Human Factors, Theory

Amilcare is a tool for Adaptive Information Extraction (IE) designed for supporting active annotation of documents for the Semantic Web (SW). It can be used either for unsupervised document annotation or as a support for human annotation. Amilcare is portable to new applications/domains without any knowledge of IE, as it just requires users to annotate a small training corpus with the information to be extracted. It is based on $(LP)^2$, a supervised learning strategy for IE able to cope with different texts types, from newspaper-like texts, to rigidly formatted Web pages and even a mixture of them[1][5].

Adaptation starts with the definition of a tag set for annotation, possibly organized as an ontology. Then users have to manually annotate a small training corpus. Amilcare provides a default mouse-based interface called Melita, where annotations are inserted by first selecting a tag from the ontology and then identifying the text area to annotate with the mouse. Differently from similar annotation tools [4, 5], Melita actively supports training corpus annotation. While users annotate texts, Amilcare runs in the background learning how to reproduce the inserted annotation. Induced rules are silently applied to new texts and their results are compared with the user annotation. When its rules reach a (user-defined) level of accuracy, Melita presents new texts with a preliminary annotation derived by the rule application. In this case users have just to correct mistakes and add missing annotations. User corrections are inputted back to the learner for retraining. This technique focuses the slow and expensive user activity on uncovered cases, avoiding requiring annotating cases where a satisfying effectiveness is already reached. Moreover validating extracted information is a much simpler task than tagging bare texts (and also less error prone), speeding up the process considerably. At the end of the corpus annotation process, the system is trained and the application can be delivered. MnM [6] and Ontomat annotizer [7] are two annotation tools adopting Amilcare's learner.

In this demo we simulate the annotation of a small corpus and we show how and when Amilcare is able to support users in the annotation process, focusing on the way the user can control the tool's proactivity and intrusivity. We will also quantify such support with data derived from a number of experiments on corpora. We will focus on training corpus size and correctness of suggestions when the corpus is increased.

1. REFERENCES

[1] F. Ciravegna: "Adaptive Information Extraction from Text by Rule Induction and Generalisation" in *Proceedings of 17th IJCAI*, Seattle, August 2001.

[2] F. Ciravegna (2001): "Challenges in Information Extraction from Text for Knowledge Management", *IEEE Intelligent Systems and Their Applications* 16(6) 88-90.

[3] F. Ciravegna (2001c): "$(LP)^2$, an Adaptive Algorithm for Information Extraction from Web-related Texts" in *Proc. of the IJCAI-2001 Workshop on Adaptive Text Extraction and Mining*, Seattle

[4] D. Day, J. Aberdeen, L. Hirschman, R. Kozierok, P. Robinson and M. Vilain *Mixed-initiative development of language processing systems*. In Proc. of the Fifth Conference on ANLP, Washington, 1997.

[5] H. Cunningham, D. Maynard, V. Tablan, C. Ursu, K. Bontcheva: "Developing Language Processing Components with GATE", www.gate.ac.uk

[6] J.B. Domingue, M. Lanzoni, E. Motta, M. Vargas-Vera and F. Ciravegna: "MnM: Ontology driven semi-automatic or automatic support for semantic markup", submitted paper.

[7] S. Handschuh, S. Staab and F. Ciravegna. "S-CREAM - Semi-automatic CREAtion of Metadata", submitted paper.

SIGIR'02, August 11-15, 2002, Tampere, Finland.
ACM 1-58113-561-0/02/0008.

ExWrap: Semi-Automatic Wrapper Generation by Example

Bethina Schmitt Michael Christoffel Jürgen Schneider
Institute for Program Structures and Data Organization (IPD), University of Karlsruhe
Am Fasanengarten 5
D-76128 Karlsruhe
{ schmitt, christof, schneidj } @ ipd.uka.de

1. MOTIVATION

Within the WWW there are lots of different information retrieval services like search engines, news archives, product catalogs, or literature services. In order to support the user, meta search systems provide great benefits and synergies: For instance, a user query can be evaluated on a larger set of documents and by applying duplicate detection meta search systems can both improve the quality of the results and reveal different purchase options for the same document or product. Within the UniCats project [1] we develop a meta search system based on digital library services like bookstores, library OPACs, or archives of research papers.

Meta systems need a wrapping component that provides mappings between the different query and result formats of the underlying retrieval systems and the internal query and result representation. So, wrappers overcome syntactical and semantical heterogeneity. Actually, generating and maintaining wrappers is quite laborious and time-consuming, especially when they rely on the public web interfaces of the services. Thus, the challenge is to develop a mechanism for a fast wrapper generation and to design this process of generation as simple as possible because not only programmers but also librarians or even users should be able to generate wrappers in order to create useful meta search systems.

Categories & Subject Descriptors: H.3.7 Digital Libraries, H.3.5 Online Information Services

General Terms: Design, Human Factors

Keywords: wrapper generation, semi-automatic, programming by example, web interfaces, literature services

2. IDEA AND DESIGN OF EXWRAP

The ExWrap toolkit meets these challenges by a "Wrapping by Example" approach: A user conducts a sample search within the retrieval service that he wants to generate a wrapper for. And while formulating his search terms and browsing through the results the user marks the pieces of information that the wrapper should extract automatically later on.

Within the demonstration, we present our ExWrap toolkit [3] and show how to generate a wrapper for a typical online bookstore like Amazon – fairly quick and without the need of any expert knowledge. To issue the sample query, ExWrap supports navigation through HTML pages until the user has reached the page with the initial search form. ExWrap automatically extracts all available parameters and values, so the user can easily insert his search terms. Afterwards, the user can study the results (see Figure 1). ExWrap offers three kinds of views: a DOM-tree representation of the HTML code, a text-only view, and a typical browser view (①-③). The user can mark and name the interesting pieces of information, e.g. title, author, year, price, time of delivery, ISBN, summary, … Therefore, the user can navigate through the different levels of result pages. In Figure 1 (④) the user has already specified three attributes on the first level (root) and two attributes on the second level (details). Right now, he is going to define an ISBN attribute on the detail level.

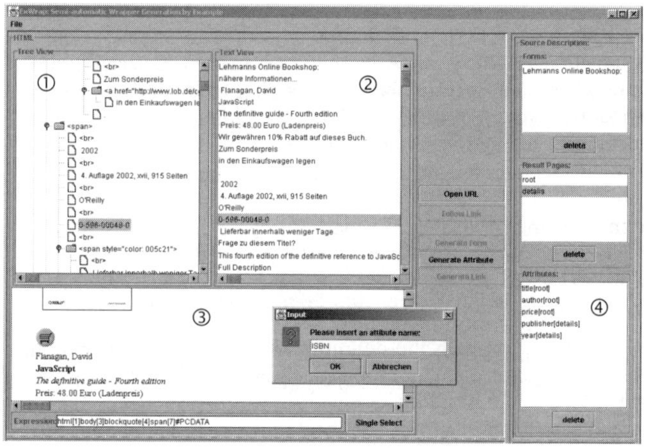

Figure 1. Semi-Automatic Wrapper Generation with the ExWrap Toolkit for a Typical Online Bookstore

Actually, the result of this sample search is not a wrapper program or any java code but a specific source description file for the queried retrieval service, which is stored in XML format. Our UniCats wrapper [2] is designed as a combination of a "generic" wrapper component together with a source description file which contains the specific properties of the retrieval service.

For further information about our wrappers, wrapper generation or other parts of the UniCats architecture, please visit our project homepage at http://www.unicats.de.

3. REFERENCES

[1] Christoffel, M., Nimis, J., Pulkowski, S., Schmitt, B., Lockemann, P., 2000. An Infrastructure for an Electronic Market of Scientific Literature. In: Proc. of the 4th IEEE Intl. Baltic Workshop on DB&IS, Vilnius, 155-166.

[2] Pulkowski, S., 2000. Intelligent Wrapping of Information Sources: Getting Ready for the Electronic Market. In: Proc. of the 10th VALA Conference, Melbourne, 113-124.

[3] Christoffel, M., Schmitt, B., Schneider, J., 2002. Semi-automatic Wrapper Generation and Adaption: Living with Heterogeneity in a Market Environment. In: Proc. of the 4th ICEIS, Ciudad Real, 65-72.

SIGIR'02, August 11-15, 2002, Tampere, Finland.
ACM 1-58113-561-0/02/0008.

Souvenir:
Flexible note-taking tool to pinpoint and share media highlights

Anselm Spoerri
School of Communication, Information & Library Studies
Rutgers University
4 Huntington Street, New Brunswick, NJ 08901, USA
aspoerri@scils.rutgers.edu

ABSTRACT
Digital media audio/video can be difficult to search and share in a personal way. **Souvenir** is a software system that offers users a flexible and comprehensive way to use their handwritten or text notes to retrieve and share specific media moments. Users can take notes on a variety of devices, such as the paper-based CrossPad, the Palm Pilot and standard keyboard devices. Souvenir segments handwritten notes into an effective media index without the need for handwriting recognition. Users can use their notes to create hyperlinks to random-access media stored in a digital library. Souvenir also has web publishing and email capabilities to enable anyone to access or email media moments directly from a web page. Souvenir annotations capture information that can not be easily inferred by automatic media indexing tools.

Unstructured Handwritten Notes: Handwriting is ideal for taking quick notes. However, handwritten notes are "unstructured" and text notes are highly structured. Hence, handwritten notes need to be structured to enable both digital ink and text in the same Souvenir document and to be an effective query index for digital media. Furthermore, people need to be able to interact with digital ink at a level of organization that is easy and familiar.

Media-enabled Notes: Souvenir time stamps the user's note-taking activity so that these time stamps can be used to synchronize the notes with the timeline of a media recording to enable pinpoint media playback.

Segmentation of Handwritten Notes: Souvenir organizes digital ink into segments by exploiting spatial and temporal characteristics of how people write without having to recognize their handwriting. Souvenir employs a "segment-oriented" framework to support: (a) both handwritten and text notes as well as (b) the playback of multiple media recordings in the same document, (c) to enable users to interact with digital ink at a higher-level of organization than instead of having to manage many individual strokes, and (d) to create hyperlinks to random-access media wherever it is stored. Users can easily edit the detected ink segments by merging or splitting them.

Text Annotation of Digital Ink: Handwritten notes are often hard to read and therefore difficult to share with others. In Souvenir, users can easily annotate an ink segment, where the text is displayed directly below it.

Media Synchronization: Souvenir can automatically synchronize notes and media if (a) the audio/video is recorded on the same device used for taking notes, or (b) the media playback occurs in the Souvenir Media Player. In all other cases, users simply need to identify a specific media moment to be linked

SIGIR'02, August 11-15, 2002, Tampere, Finland.
ACM 1-58113-561-0/02/0008.

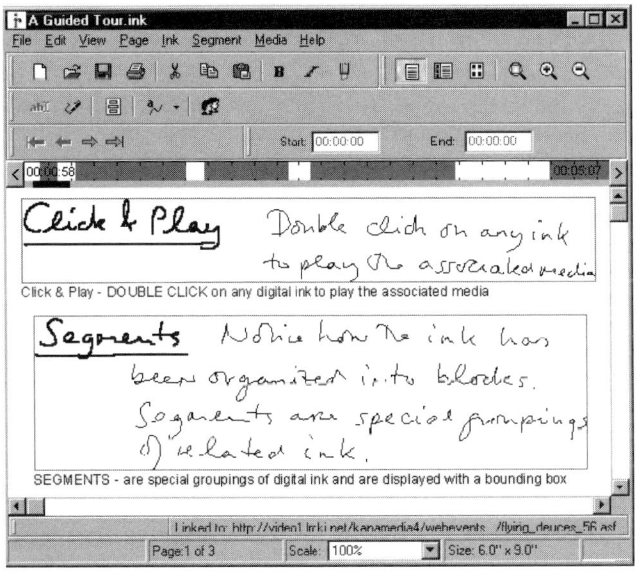

Figure 1: *Souvenir Desktop* displays media-enabled ink and text.

with a specific note. After that, Souvenir does the rest. Double clicking on the digital ink or text will play the associated media.

Text View of Notes: Souvenir has been designed so that users can use their text editing skills to organize and refine their initial, quick notes to create a full report to be shared with others. They can edit and rearrange their text notes as well as "copy & paste" notes from other Souvenir documents that reference different media files. The Souvenir Desktop contains a media timeline that enables users to fine-tune the relationship between their notes and the associated media.

Web Publishing & Email Sharing: Users can publish their Souvenir documents as a set of web pages so that others can access or share via email specific media moments directly from a web page. The media owners do not lose control over their content, because users are only creating and sharing pointers to specific media moments instead of actually copying the content.

Discussion: Souvenir has been downloaded by quite a few people. Informal tests of Souvenir's digital ink segmentation algorithm are encouraging. Souvenir makes it easy for anybody to bookmark specific moments in streaming media hosted on the Internet. However, some media sites make it difficult to identify the URLs of their media content to prevent "deep linking."

ACKNOWLEDGMENTS
Souvenir was developed while the author was at i-Recall Inc. Special thanks to Nathaniel Polish, Daniel Magill and Oliver Daniel for their invaluable development help.

Hierarchical Approach to Term Suggestion Device

Hideo Joho
Department of Information Studies
University of Sheffield
Western Bank, Sheffield, S10 2TN
+44 (0)114 222 2675
h.joho@sheffield.ac.uk

Mark Sanderson
Department of Information Studies
University of Sheffield
Western Bank, Sheffield, S10 2TN
+44 (0)114 222 2648
m.sanderson@sheffield.ac.uk

Micheline Beaulieu
Department of Information Studies
University of Sheffield
Western Bank, Sheffield, S10 2TN
+44 (0)114 222 2640
m.beaulieu@sheffield.ac.uk

ABSTRACT

Our demonstration shows the hierarchy system working on a locally run search engine. Hierarchies are dynamically generated from the retrieved documents, and visualised on the menus. When a user selects a term from the hierarchy, the documents linked to the term are listed, and the term is then added to the initial query to rerun a search. Through the demonstration we illustrate how hierarchical presentation of expansion terms is achieved, and how our approach supports users to articulate their information needs using the hierarchy.

Categories & Subject Descriptors: H.5.2 User Interfaces

General Terms: Design

Keywords: Concept hierarchies, interactive query expansion.

1. DESCRIPTION

Traditionally term suggestion devices in Interactive Query Expansion (IQE) have been designed to present candidate expansion terms in a form of list, regardless the underlying ranking techniques. While such a list has been the dominant form of presentation, it seems less effective to provide users with the contexts from which the terms are derived.

To explore an alternative approach to support IQE, we have been investigating methods of presenting expansion terms in a hierarchical form: automatically and dynamically derived from a set of retrieved documents; terms (concepts) are organised based on term specificity, with allowing links to contextually related terms (e.g. Yahoo Directory). It is anticipated that such a hierarchy will provide users with an overview of documents, and can be useful to allow users to articulate their information need.

In our demonstration, we use a technique called "subsumption hierarchy" [1] to construct a concept hierarchy. The subsumption hierarchy uses the co-occurrence information to identify a pair of terms that are related, and measures term specificity using document frequency. Although this is a simple technique, it is encouraging that the technique takes account into term specificity in constructing hierarchies. A user test has shown a positive reaction of the hierarchy in the expansion task [2].

Our live demonstration shows the hierarchy system working on a locally run search engine. Hierarchies are dynamically generated from the retrieved documents, and visualised on the menus (see Figure 1: the number in brackets beside terms indicates the number of documents linked to the terms). When a user selects a term from the hierarchy, the documents linked to the term are listed, and the term is then added to the initial query to rerun a search. Through the demonstration we illustrate how hierarchical presentation of expansion terms is achieved, and how our approach will support users to articulate their information needs using the hierarchy. We also briefly discuss possible ways to improve the current system.

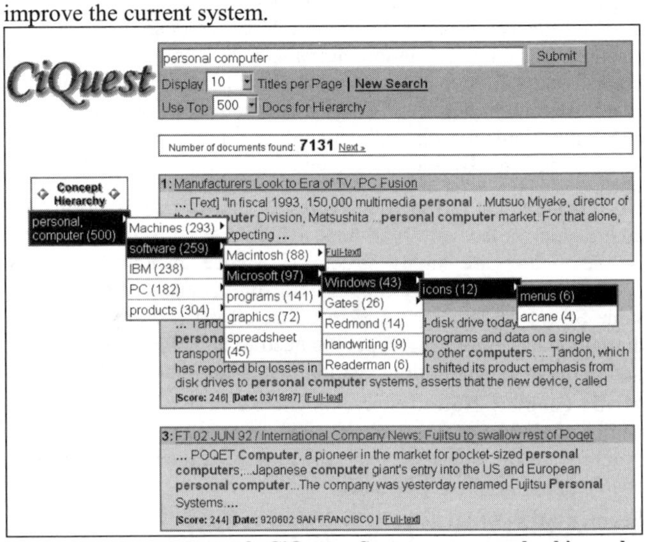

Figure 1. Screenshot of CiQuest System: a sample hierarchy generated from the top 500 documents retrieved in response to a query "personal computer". The maximum number of terms at each level was truncated to five for this screenshot.

2. ACKNOWLEGEMENT

This work was carried out as a part of the CiQuest project, which is funded by the Library and Information Commission (now *re*:source, the Council for Museums, Archives and Libraries). Any opinions, findings, and conclusions described here are the authors and do not necessarily reflect those of the sponsor.

3. REFERENCES

[1] Sanderson, M. and Croft, B. Deriving Concept Hierarchies from Text. In: *Proceedings of the 22nd Annual International ACM SIGIR Conference on Research and Development in Information Retrieval*, 206-213, Berkeley, CA, 1999, ACM.

[2] Joho, H., Coverson, C., Sanderson, M. and Beaulieu, M. Hierarchical Presentation of Expansion Terms. In: *Proceedings of the 17th ACM Symposium on Applied Computing (SAC'2002)*, 645-649, Madrid, Spain, 2002, ACM.

SIGIR '02, August 11-15, 2002, Tampere, Finland.
ACM 1-58113-561-0/02/0008.

Translingual Vocabulary Mappings for Multilingual Information Access *

Fredric C. Gey
UC Data Archive & Technical Assistance
University of California
Berkeley, CA 94720
gey@ucdata.berkeley.edu

Aitao Chen Michael Buckland Ray Larson
School of Information Management and Systems
University of California
Berkeley, CA 94720
(aitao,buckland,ray)@sims.berkeley.edu

Categories and Subject Descriptors

H.3.1 [**Information Storage and Retrieval**]: Content Analysis – *Dictionaries, Linguistic Processing, Thesauruses*; H.3.3 [**Information Storage and Retrieval**]: Information Search and Retrieval– *Query Formulation, Retrieval Models*

General Terms

Algorithms

Keywords

Cross-Languge Information Retrieval, Multilingual Information Access

1. DEMONSTRATION DESCRIPTION

This demonstration presents a completely new resource to support the multilingual information requirements of cross-language information retrieval and statistical machine translation. The resource can create both customized bilingual dictionaries and multilingual query mappings from a source language to many target languages. The resource coverage is broad (over 100 written languages can potentially be supported) and is truly multilingual as opposed to bilingual pairings. Our current prototype software maps between ten languages (English, Arabic, Chinese, French, German, Italian, Japanese, Portuguese, Russian, Spanish) but extensions to additional languages are straightforward.

Our search for this new source of multilingual resources derives from a background of library research. The world's great research university libraries have book content which spans the world's languages. Through the offices of the University of California Digital Library, we obtained a private copy of the University of California Book Catalog with 10,091,737 records, of which 4,626,793 were non-English. We utilized our entry vocabulary index technology (described in [1]) to create maximum likelihood mappings from Library of Congress Subject Headings (LCSH) to words found in book titles in the following nine languages: Arabic, Chinese, French, German, Italian, Japanese, Portuguese, Russian and Spanish. There are 106 additional languages with at least 500 catalog records. Unlike web pages, a significant presence of the Latin language is present. Moreover, a number of Eastern European languages are represented, as well as four of the major Indian subcontinent languages (Hindi, Urdu, Bengali and Tamil).

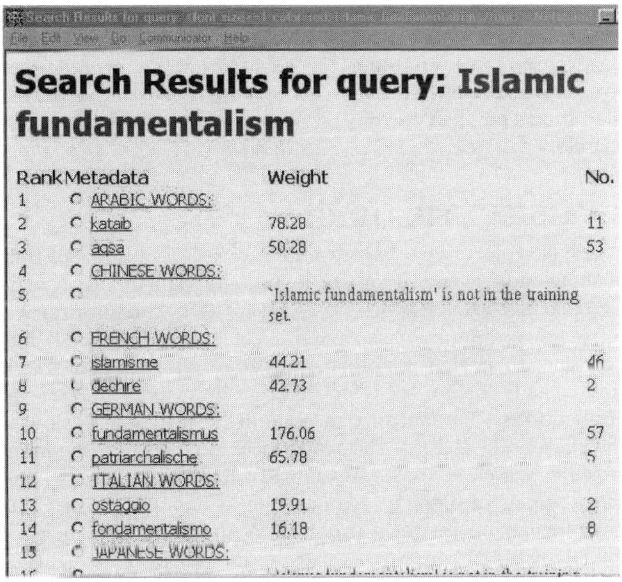

Figure 1: Mapping Subject Heading "Islamic Fundamentalism" to several languages

Figure 1 shows an example mapping from the LCSH term "Islamic Fundamentalism" to the highest ranked three words in in these languages (the message "not in the training set" means that for there were no books on that subject in that language). Our prototype translingual vocabulary resource can be found at *http://otlet.sims.berkeley.edu/mulevm2.html*

2. REFERENCES

[1] F. Gey, M. Buckland, A. Chen, and R. Larson. Entry Vocabulary – A Technology to Enhance Digital Object Search. In *Proceedings of the First Internation Conference on Human Language Technology*, pages 91–95, March 2001.

SIGIR'02, August 11-15, 2002, Tampere, Finland.
ACM 1-58113-561-0/02/0008.

GS Textplorer - Adaptive Framework for Information Retrieval

Jukka Honkela
Gurusoft, Inc.
Munkkiniemen puistotie 25
FIN-00330 Helsinki, Finland
jukka.honkela@gurusoft.fi

Ville H. Tuulos
Gurusoft, Inc.
Munkkiniemen puistotie 25
FIN-00330 Helsinki, Finland
ville.tuulos@gurusoft.fi

1. BACKGROUND: WEBSOM METHOD

The WEBSOM is a method developed originally at Helsinki University of Technology for analyzing and visualizing large document collections [1, 4].

In the WEBSOM method, the self-organizing map algorithm [3] is used to automatically organize collections of documents on a map to enable easy exploration and search of the collection. Map regions that are close to each other contain similar documents. The main objectives in developing the WEBSOM method has been to offer a method for exploring text collections that is different from the query-result approach, enabling the user to get an overall view to the document collection. Moreover, there are no principled limits on the type of text material that the method can handle.

2. GS TEXTPLORER

GS Textplorer enables automatic creation of maps of tens of thousands, even millions of documents. Motivation for the GS Textplorer framework raises from the visual information retrieval paradigm, based on the WEBSOM method. The aim was to design a robust and adaptable system which could easily be tailored for different information retrieval applications. Instead of one monolithic implementation of the chosen algorithms, the system was divided in three main modules which could be assembled separately. A set of *opcodes* which implement various operations and algorithms for information retrieval problems act as building blocks of the Document Processor. Correspondingly the Visualization Engine allows rather free combinations of different encapsulated visualization and user interaction schemes.

3. VERSATILE SYSTEM ARCHITECTURE

The main features of GS Textplorer include modular architecture separating map creation and map use through a client-server solution, visualization of keyword search results on the map, and associative search of similar documents (query-by-example).

The modular system architecture of GS Textplorer with open application programming interfaces enables efficient system integration. The system provides a common framework that makes it possible to combine various text analysis, document mapping and visualization algorithms and methods using XML-based configuration specifications, yet in an efficient and scalable manner. The current visualization options include e.g. cluster coloring [2], document density visualization, and visualization of associated numerical information.

GS Textplorer has already proven to be useful in application areas such as customer feedback analysis, competence analysis, intranet document management, and analysis of hybrid data containg both numerical and textual content.

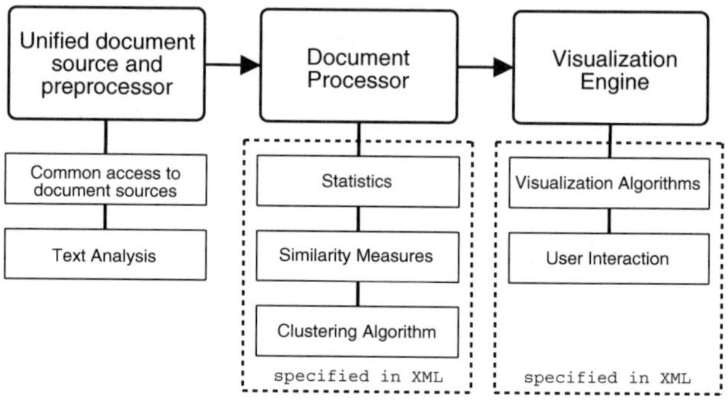

Figure 1: Basic architecture of GS Textplorer.

SIGIR'02, August 11-15, 2002, Tampere, Finland.
ACM 1-58113-561-0/02/0008.

4. REFERENCES

[1] S. Kaski, T. Honkela, K. Lagus, and T. Kohonen. WEBSOM—self-organizing maps of document collections. *Neurocomputing*, 21:101–117, 1998.

[2] S. Kaski, J. Venna, and T. Kohonen. Coloring that reveals high-dimensional structures in data. In T. G. et al., editor, *Proc. of ICONIP'99*, volume II, pages 729–734. IEEE, Piscataway, NJ, 1999.

[3] T. Kohonen. *Self-Organizing Maps*. Springer, Berlin, 2001.

[4] T. Kohonen, S. Kaski, K. Lagus, J. Salojärvi, J. Honkela, V. Paatero, and A. Saarela. Self-organization of a massive document collection. *IEEE Transactions on Neural Networks*, 11:574–585, 2000.

CuTeX: A System for Extracting Data from Text Tables *

Hasan Davulcu, Saikat Mukherjee, Arvind Seth, I.V. Ramakrishnan

Dept. of Computer Science
SUNY Stony Brook
Stony Brook, NY 11794, USA
{davulcu,saikat,arvind,ram}@cs.sunysb.edu

A wealth of information relevant for e-commerce often appears in text form. This includes specification and performance data sheets of products, financial statements, product offerings etc. Typically these types of product and financial data are published in tabular form. The only separators between items in the table are white spaces and line separators. We will refer to such tables as *text tables*. Due to the lack of structure in such tables, the information present is not readily queriable using traditional database query languages like SQL. One way to make it amenable to standard database querying techniques is to extract the data items in the tables and create a database out of the extracted data. But extraction from text tables poses difficulties due to the irregularity of the data in the columns.

Existing techniques like [1] and [3] are based on finding fixed separators between successive columns. However, it is not always possible to find fixed separators. Even if fixed separators exist they may not unambiguously separate columns that have multiword items. Another set of techniques are based on regular expressions. The problems here are: (i) they are difficult to construct and (ii) they depend on lexical similarity between column items.

Note that, by visual inspection a casual observer can correctly associate every item in a text table to its corresponding column. This is because all the items belonging to a column appear "clustered" more closely to each other than to items in different columns. Whereas such clusters can be clearly discerned by a human observer, making them machine recognizable is the key to robust automated extraction of data items from text-based tables. Clustering enables us to make associations between items in a column based not merely on examining items in adjacent rows but across all the rows in the table.

We have designed and implemented the *CuteX* system for extracting data from irregular text tables. The input is a file containing only text tables. The output produced by *CuteX* is an association between every items in a column. Note that *CuteX* does not do table detection in text. The innovative aspect of *CuteX* is its clustering-based algorithm that drives the extraction process. In *CuteX* each line is broken down into a set of tokens. Each token is a contiguous sequence of non white-space characters. The center of any token in a cluster is closer to the center of some other token in the same cluster. Inter-cluster gaps are gaps between the extremal tokens in the clusters. Starting with an initial set of clusters, adjacent clusters are merged into bigger clusters based on the inter-cluster gaps. The algorithm terminates when no more clusters can be merged. We have formalized the notion of a correct extraction and developed a syntactic characterization of tables on which this algorithm will always produce a correct extraction. Details appear in [2]. An unique aspect of the algorithm is its robustness in the presence of misalignments.

Precision of extraction can be improved by supplying the minimum separation between columns as a parameter. Such a separator is estimated by sampling a few input tables. The clustering algorithm does not merge adjacent clusters if the gap between them is larger than this parameter value. Note though that the minimum column gap cannot be used as a fixed separator since doing so amounts to doing localized determination, making it brittle to misalignments

CuteX is implemented in Java and is approximately about 3000 lines of code. The system automatically partitions the set of input text tables into directories containing correct and incorrect extractions. At the end of an extraction, the user can examine the directory containing incorrectly extracted tables, sample a few of them, identify if it was caused by an erroneous estimate of the minimum column gap, readjust the configuration parameter and start a new extraction on all these tables. Successive iterations can generate a higher extraction yield.

The primary focus of the demonstration will be on illustrating the robustness and the iterative process of improving the extraction yield of the clustering algorithm.

*This work was supported by industry and university grant - NSF IIS0072927

SIGIR'02, August 11-15, 2002, Tampere, Finland.
ACM 1-58113-561-0/02/0008.

1. REFERENCES

[1] Brad Adelberg. Nodose - a tool for semi-automatically extracting semi-structured data from text documents. In *ACM SIGMOD*, 1998.

[2] Hasan Davulcu, Saikat Mukherjee, and I.V. Ramakrishnan. A clustering technique for mining data from text tables. In *SIAM ICDM*, 2002.

[3] Pallavi Pyreddy and W. Bruce Croft. Tintin: A system for retrieval in text tables. In *ACM DL*, 1997.

YellowPager: A Tool for Ontology-based Mining of Service Directories from Web Sources *

Prashant Choudhari Hasan Davulcu Abhishek Joglekar
Akshay More Saikat Mukherjee Supriya Patil
I.V. Ramakrishnan
Dept. of Computer Science
SUNY Stony Brook
Stony Brook, NY 11794, USA
{cprashan,davulcu,abhishek,amore,saikat,supriya,ram}@cs.sunysb.edu

The web has established itself as the dominant medium for doing electronic commerce. Realizing that its global reach provides significant market and business opportunities, service providers, both large and small are advertising their services on the web. A number of them operate their own web sites promoting their services at length while others are merely listed in a referral site. Aggregating all of the providers into a queriable service directory makes it easy for customers to locate the one most suited for his/her needs.

YellowPager is a tool for creating service directories by mining web sources. Service directories created by *YellowPager* have several merits compared to those generated by existing practices, which typically require participation by service providers (e.g. Verizon's SuperYellowPages.com). Firstly, the information content will be rich. Secondly since the process is automated and repeatable the content can always be kept current. Finally the same process can be readily adapted to different domains.

YellowPager builds service directories by mining the web through a combination of keyword-based search engines,web agents, text classifiers and novel extraction algorithms.The extraction is driven by a services ontology consisting of a taxonomy of service concepts and their associated attributes (such as names and addresses) and type descriptions for the attributes. In addition the ontology also associates an extractor function with each attribute. Applying the function to a web page will identify all the occurrences of the attribute in that page.

YellowPager's mining algorithm consists of a training step followed by classification and extraction steps. In the training step a classifier is trained to identify web pages relevant to the service of interest. The classification step proceeds by doing a search for the particular service of interest using a keyword based web search engine and retrieves all the matching web pages. From these pages the relevant ones are identified using the classifier. The final step is extraction of attribute values, associated with the service, from these pages. Each web page is parsed into a DOM tree and the extractor functions are applied. All of the attributes corresponding to a service provider are then correctly aggregated. This can pose difficulties especially in the presence of multiple service providers in a page. Using a novel concept of scoring and conflict resolution to prevent erroneous associations of attributes with service provider entities in the page, the algorithm aggregates all the attribute occurrences correctly. The extractor function may not be complete in the sense that it cannot always identify all the attributes in a page. By exploiting the regularity of the sequence in which attributes occurr in referral pages, the mining algorithm automatically learns generalized patterns to locate attributes that the extractor function misses. The distinguishing aspects of *YellowPager*'s extraction algorithm are: (i) it is unsupervised, and (ii) the attribute values in the pages are extracted independent of any page-specific relationships that may exist among the markup tags.

YellowPager has been used by a large pet food producer to build a directory of veterinarian service providers in the United States. The resulting database was found to be much larger and richer than that found in Vetquest, Vetworld, and the Super Yellow pages.

YellowPager is implemented in JAVA and is interfaced to Rainbow, a library utility in C that is used for classification. The tool will demonstrate the creation of a service directory for any service domain by mining web sources.

*This work was supported by industry and university grant – NSF IIS0072927

SIGIR'02, August 11-15, 2002, Tampere, Finland.
ACM 1-58113-561-0/02/0008.

Author Index

Airio, E. 448
Allan, J. 89
Allan, J. 307
Allan, J. 403
Allen, E. 401
Amini, M.-R. 105
Anh, V. N. 3
Bahle, D. 215
Bai, S. 435
Ballesteros, L. 275
Banko, M. 291
Beaulieu, M. 383
Beaulieu, M. 454
Behl, S. 433
Belkin, N. J. 359
Bennett, P. N. 207
Bertoldi, N. 167
Bingham, E. 361
Boyapati, V. 363
Brill, E. 291
Buckland, M. 455
Buckley, C. 316
Callan, J. 19
Callan, J. 81
Callan, J. 419
Canny, J. 238
Carmel, D. 283
Cercone, N. 349
Chai, K. M. A. 97
Chandrasekar, R. 365
Chen, A. 455
Chen, M. 65
Chen, W. 183
Cheng, X. 435
Chieu, H. L. 97
Choquette, M. 175
Choudhari, P. 458
Chowdhury, A. 381
Chowdhury, A. 421
Christoffel, M. 452
Ciravegna, F. 367
Ciravegna, F. 451
Clarke, C. L. A. 369
Claussen, J. S. 371
Connell, M. E. 275
Conrad, J. G. 371
Corieri, S. 401
Cormack, G. V. 369
Cöster, R. 246
Crammer, K. 151
Crestani, F. 373
Croft, W. B. 175
Croft, W. B. 299
Croft, W. B. 355
Cronen-Townsend, S. 299
Damerau, F. J. 357
Darwish, K. 261
Davulcu, H. 457
Davulcu, H. 458
de la Fuente, P. 373
Diekema, A. 401
Ding, C. 353
Dingli, A. 367
Dingli, A. 451
Dubnov, S. 331
Dumais, S. 291
Dumais, S. T. 207
Dziadosz, S. 365
Eguchi, K. 375
Evans, D. A. 417
Farchi, E. 283
Federico, M. 167
Feng, A. 403
Feng, Y. 441
Franz, M. 377
Fraser, A. 269
Frieder, O. 381
Friedman, N. 129
Friedman, N. 331
Fuhr, N. 449
Gabb, S. M. 389
Gallinari, P. 105
Gao, J. 183
Gardarin, G. 393
Géry, M. 379
Gey, F. C. 455
Giles, C. L. 11
Gong, Y. 191
Gövert, N. 449
Graves, A. 339
Grossman, D. 381
Großjohann, K. 449
Hansen, P. 383
Hardy, H. 121
Harwell, S. 401
Hauptmann, A. G. 42
Hauptmann, A. G. 419
He, H. 183
He, X. 353
Hedlund, T. 448
Hersh, W. 431
Hiemstra, D. 27
Hiemstra, D. 35
Hoashi, K. 385
Hokkanen, S. 450
Honkela, J. 456

Horvitz, E. 207
Huang, X. 349
Hürst, W. 447
Husbands, P. 353
Indurkhya, N. 357
Ingwersen, P. 397
Inoue, N. 385
Ishida, E. 375
Ji, X. 443
Jin, R. 42
Jin, R. 419
Joglekar, A. 458
Joho, H. 454
Jones, C. B. 387
Jones, G. J. F. 389
Jose, J. M. 57
Jose, J. M. 446
Kando, N. 375
Kangaslampi, P. 450
Karlgren, J. 383
Kawatani, T. 137
Keskustalo, H. 448
Kim, J.-Y. 359
Kim, S.-B. 391
Koskenniemi, K. 315
Kou, H. 393
Kraaij, W. 27
Krovetz, R. 11
Kuriyama, K. 375
Kuusisto, J. 361
Kwok, K. L. 395
Lafferty, J. 49
Lagus, K. 361
Lalmas, M. 339
LaPaugh, A. S. 65
Larkey, L. S. 275
Larsen, B. 397
Larson, R. 455
Larson, R. R. 399
Laszlo, M. 369
Lavelli, A. 415
Lavrenko, V. 175
Lee, Y.-B. 145
Leuski, A. 89
Li, X. 439
Liddy, E. D. 401
Lim, H.-S. 391
Lin, D. 199
Lin, J. 291
Liu, X. 191
Lynam, T. R. 369
Magnini, B. 415
Manmatha, R. 403
Matsumoto, Y. 407
Mayfield, J. 159
Mayfield, J. 405
McCabe, M. C. 381
McCarley, J. S. 377
McCracken, N. 401
McNamee, P. 159
McNamee, P. 405
Meira, Jr., W. 230
Merkl, D. 409
Minka, T. 81
Moffat, A. 3
More, A. 458
Mukherjee, S. 457
Mukherjee, S. 458
Murdock, V. 355
Myaeng, S. H. 145
Ng, A. 291
Ng, H. T. 97
Nie, J.-Y. 183
Nomoto, T. 407
Oard, D. W. 261
Oyama, K. 375
Ozgencil, N. E. 401
Pampalk, E. 409
Pan, Y. 441
Pantel, P. 199
Park, S.-T. 11
Patil, S. 458
Peng, F. 349
Pennock, D. M. 11
Pennock, D. M. 253
Petrelli, D. 367
Petrelli, D. 383
Petrelli, D. 451
Petruschka, Y. 283
Popescul, A. 253
Pôssas, B. 230
Purves, R. 387
Pyy, P. 450
Raghavan, H. 307
Ramakrishnan, I. V. 457
Ramakrishnan, I. V. 458
Rauber, A. 409
Ribeiro-Neto, B. 230
Rim, H.-C. 391
Robertson, S. E. 349
Robertson, S. E. 411
Ruas, A. 387
Ruthven, I. 57
Ruthven, I. 446
Sakai, T. 411
Sanderson, M. 383
Sanderson, M. 387
Sanderson, M. 413
Sanderson, M. 454
Schein, A. I. 253

Schmitt, B. 452
Schneider, J. 452
Scholer, F. 222
Schuurmans, D. 349
Sebastiani, F. 415
Sepponen, B. 450
Sester, M. 387
Seth, A. 457
Shalev-Shwartz, S. 331
Shanahan, J. G. 417
Sheftel, V. 417
Shimizu, N. 121
Shou, X. M. 413
Si, L. 19
Si, L. 419
Silverstein, J. 401
Simon, H. D. 353
Singer, Y. 151
Singer, Y. 331
Singh, J. P. 65
Slonim, N. 129
Smith, D. A. 73
Soboroff, I. 421
Soboroff, I. 423
Soffer, A. 283
Sormunen, E. 324
Sormunen, E. 450
Spoerri, A. 453
Srihari, R. 425
Srikanth, M. 425
Strzalkowski, T. 121
Sutton, S. 401
Svensson, M. 246
Takeda, Y. 427
Terra, E. L. 369
Ting, L. 121
Tishby, N. 129
Tseng, Y.-H. 429
Turpin, A. 431
Tuulos, V. H. 456
Umemura, K. 427
Ungar, L. H. 253
van Kreveld, M. 387
Vegas, J. 373
Verma, R. M. 433
Voorhees, E. M. 316
Wang, B. 435
Weibel, R. 387
Weischedel, R. 269
Weiss, S. M. 357
Westerveld, T. 27
Westerveld, T. 437
White, R. W. 57
White, R. W. 446
Wilks, Y. 367
Wilks, Y. 451
Williams, H. E. 215
Williams, H. E. 222
Wise, G. B. 121
Wolin, B. 351
Xu, J. 269
Xu, W. 191
Yang, C. 371
Yang, W. 439
Yiannis, J. 222
Yilmazel, O. 401
Yuan, X.-J. 359
Zeitler, E. 385
Zha, H. 113
Zha, H. 353
Zha, H. 443
Zhai, C. 42
Zhai, C. 49
Zhang, T. 357
Zhang, X. 121
Zhang, Y. 81
Zhou, M. 183
Zhou, Y. 299
Zhu, S. 191
Zhuang, Y. 441
Ziviani, N. 230
Zobel, J. 215
Zobel, J. 222

NOTES